LUKE

VOLUME 4

THE PREACHER'S OUTLINE & SERMON BIBLE®

LUKE

VOLUME 4

THE PREACHER'S OUTLINE & SERMON BIBLE®

NEW TESTAMENT

NEW INTERNATIONAL VERSION

Leadership Ministries Worldwide
PO Box 21310
Chattanooga, TN 37424-0310

THE PREACHER'S OUTLINE & SERMON BIBLE®
NEW INTERNATIONAL VERSION

The Preacher's Outline & Sermon Bible® is written for God's people to use in their preparation for preaching and teaching. The purpose of the copyright is to prevent the reproduction, misuse, and abuse of the material.

May our Lord bless us all as we preach, teach, and write for Him, fulfilling His great commission to make disciples of all nations.

Previous Editions of **The Preacher's Outline & Sermon Bible®**,
King James Version,
Copyright © 1991, 1996
by Alpha-Omega Ministries, Inc.

Please address all requests for information or permission to:
LEADERSHIP MINISTRIES WORLDWIDE
PO Box 21310
Chattanooga TN 37424-0310
Ph.# (423) 855-2181 FAX (423) 855-8616
E-Mail outlinebible@compuserve.com
http://www.outlinebible.org

Library of Congress Catalog Card Number: 98-067967
International Standard Book Number: 1-57407-078-9

Printed in the United States of America

Publisher &
Distributer

DEDICATED:

To all the men and women of the world
who preach and teach the Gospel of our
Lord Jesus Christ
and
To the Mercy and Grace of God.

- Demonstrated to us in Christ Jesus our Lord.

"In him we have redemption through his blood, the forgiveness of sins, in accordance with the riches of God's grace." (Eph. 1:7 NIV)

- Out of the mercy and grace of God His Word has flowed. Let every person know that God will have mercy upon him, forgiving and using him to fulfill His glorious plan of salvation.

"For God so loved the world, that he gave his one and only Son, that whosoever believes in him shall not perish, but have eternal life. For God did not send his Son into the world to condemn the world, but to save the world through him." (Jn 3:16-17 NIV)

"This is good and pleases God our Saviour; who wants all men to be saved and to come to the knowledge of the truth." (I Tim. 2:3-4 NIV)

&

The Preacher's Outline and Study Bible®
is written for God's people to use
in their study and teaching of God's Holy Word.

9/98

OUTLINE BIBLE RESOURCES

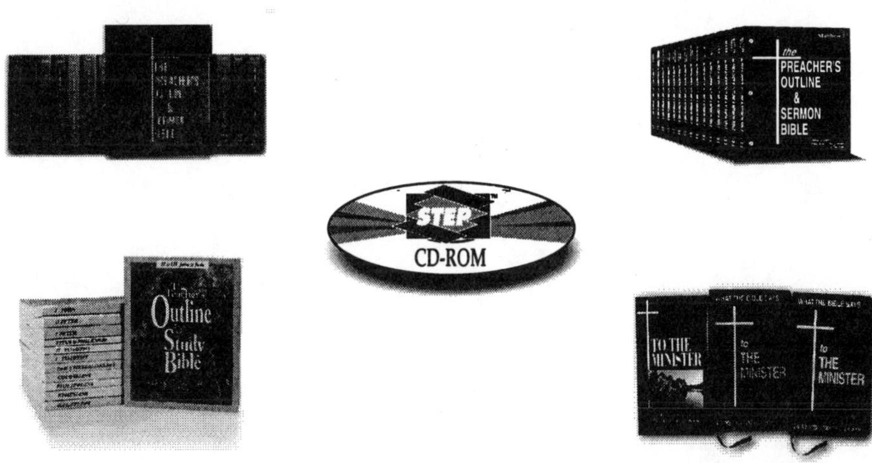

This material, like similar works, has come from imperfect man and is thus susceptible to human error. We are nevertheless grateful to God for both calling us and empowering us through His Holy Spirit to undertake this task. Because of His goodness and grace **The Preacher's Outline & Sermon Bible®** - New Testament is complete in 14 volumes, and the Old Testament volumes release periodically. **The Minister's Handbook** is available and *OUTLINE* Bible materials are releasing electonically on **POSB-CD** and our **Web site**.

God has given the strength and stamina to bring us this far. Our confidence is that, as we keep our eyes on Him and grounded in the undeniable truths of the Word, we will continue working through the Old Testament volumes and the second series known as **The Teacher's Outline & Study Bible.** The future includes helpful ***Outline Bible*** books and **Handbook** materials for God's dear servants.

To everyone everywhere who preaches and teaches the Word, we offer this material firstly to Him in whose name we labor and serve, and for whose glory it has been produced.

Our daily prayer is that each volume will lead thousands, millions, yes even billions, into a better understanding of the Holy Scriptures and a fuller knowledge of Jesus Christ the incarnate Word, of whom the Scriptures so faithfully testify.

As you have purchased this volume, you will be pleased to know that a small portion of the price you have paid has gone to underwrite and provide similar volumes in other languages (Russian, Korean, Spanish and others yet to come) — To a preacher, pastor, lay leader, or Bible student somewhere around the world, who will present God's message with clarity, authority, and understanding beyond their own. *Amen.*

For information and prices, kindly contact your *OUTLINE* Bible bookseller or:

LEADERSHIP MINISTRIES WORLDWIDE

P.O. Box 21310, 515 Airport Road, Suite 107
Chattanooga, TN 37424-0310
(423) 855-2181 FAX (423) 855-8616
E-Mail - outlinebible@compuserve.com
www.outlinebible.org — *FREE* download materials

9/98

PUBLISHER & DISTRIBUTOR OF OUTLINE BIBLE MATERIALS

Currently Available Materials, with New Volumes Releasing Regularly

- **THE PREACHER'S OUTLINE & SERMON BIBLE® — DELUXE EDITION**
  3-Ring, looseleaf binder

  Volume 1 .... **St. Matthew I** (chapters 1-15)
  Volume 2 .... **St. Matthew II** (chapters 16-28)
  Volume 3 .... **St. Mark**
  Volume 4 .... **St. Luke**
  Volume 5 .... **St. John**
  Volume 6 .... **Acts**
  Volume 7 .... **Romans**
  Volume 8 .... **1, 2 Corinthians** (1 volume)
  Volume 9 .... **Galatians, Ephesians, Philippians, Colossians** (1 volume)
  Volume 10 .... **1,2 Thessalonians, 1,2 Timothy, Titus, Philemon** (1 volume)
  Volume 11 .... **Hebrews -James** (1 volume)
  Volume 12 .... **1,2 Peter, 1,2,3 John, Jude** (1 volume)
  Volume 13 .... **Revelation**
  Volume 14 .... **Master Outline & Subject Index**
  FULL SET — 14 Volumes

- **THE PREACHER'S OUTLINE & SERMON BIBLE® — OLD TESTAMENT**

  Volume 1 .... **Genesis I** (chapters 1-11)
  Volume 2 .... **Genesis II** (chapters 12-50)
  Volume 3 .... **Exodus I** (chapters 1-18)
  Volume 4 .... **Exodus II** (chapters 19-40)
  Volume 5 .... **Leviticus**
  New volumes release periodically

- **THE PREACHER'S OUTLINE & SERMON BIBLE® — SOFTBOUND EDITION**
  Identical content as Deluxe above. Lightweight, compact, and affordable for overseas & traveling
- **THE PREACHER'S OUTLINE & SERMON BIBLE® — 3 VOL HARDCOVER w/CD**
- **THE PREACHER'S OUTLINE & SERMON BIBLE® — NIV SOFTBOUND EDITION**
- **The Minister's Personal Handbook - What the Bible Says...to the Minister**
  12 Chapters - 127 Subjects - 400 Verses *OUTLINED* - Paperback, Leatherette, 3-ring
- **THE TEACHER'S OUTLINE & STUDY BIBLE™ • New Testament Books •**
  Complete 45 minute lessons - 4 months of studies/book; 200± pages - Student Journal Guides
- **OUTLINE Bible Studies series: 10 Commandments - The Tabernacle**
- **Practical Word Studies: New Testament - 2,000 Key Words Made Easy**
- **CD-ROM: Preacher, Teacher, and Handbook- (Windows/STEP) - WORD*Search***
- **Translations of Preacher, Teacher, and Minister's Handbook: Limited Quantities**
  Russian — Spanish — Korean *Future: French, Portuguese, Hindi, Chinese*
  — Contact us for Specific Language Availability and Prices —

For quantity orders and information, please contact either:

LEADERSHIP MINISTRIES WORLDWIDE ***Your OUTLINE Bible Bookseller***
PO Box 21310
Chattanooga, TN 37424-0310
(423) 855-2181 (9am - 5pm Eastern) • FAX (423) 855-8616 (24 hours)
E•Mail - outlinebible@compuserve.com.

→ FREE Download Sample Pages — www.outlinebible.org

• ***Equipping God's Servants Worldwide with OUTLINE Bible Materials*** •
LMW is a nonprofit, international, nondenominational mission agency 9/98

ACKNOWLEDGMENTS

Every child of God is precious to the Lord and deeply loved. And every child as a servant of the Lord touches the lives of those who come in contact with him or his ministry. The writing ministry of the following servants have touched this work, and we are grateful that God brought their writings our way. We hereby acknowledge their ministry to us, being fully aware that there are so many others down through the years whose writings have touched our lives and who deserve mention, but the weaknesses of our minds have caused them to fade from memory. May our wonderful Lord continue to bless the ministry of these dear servants, and the ministry of us all as we diligently labor to reach the world for Christ and to meet the desperate needs of those who suffer so much.

THE GREEK SOURCES

1. Expositor's Greek Testament, Edited by W. Robertson Nicoll. Grand Rapids, MI: Eerdmans Publishing Co., 1970

2. Robertson, A.T. Word Pictures in the New Testament. Nashville, TN: Broadman Press, 1930.

3. Thayer, Joseph Henry. Greek-English Lexicon of the New Testament. New York: American Book Co, No date listed.

4. Vincent, Marvin R. Word Studies in the New Testament. Grand Rapids, MI: Eerdmans Publishing Co., 1969.

5. Vine, W.E. Expository Dictionary of New Testament Words. Old Tappan, NJ: Fleming H. Revell Co. No date listed.

6. Wuest, Kenneth S. Word Studies in the Greek New Testament. Grand Rapids, MI: Eerdmans Publishing Co., 1966.

THE REFERENCE WORKS

7. Cruden's Complete Concordance of the Old & New Testament. Philadelphia, PA: The John C. Winston Co., 1930.

8. Josephus' Complete Works. Grand Rapids, MI: Kregel Publications, 1981.

9. Lockyer, Herbert. Series of Books, including his Books on All the Men, Women, Miracles, and Parables of the Bible. Grand Rapids, MI: Zondervan Publishing House, 1958-1967.

10. -Nave's Topical Bible. Nashville, TN: The Southwestern Co., No date listed.

11. The Amplified New Testament. (Scripture Quotations are from the Amplified New Testament, Copyright 1954, 1958, 1987 by the Lockman Foundation. Used by permission.)

12. The Four Translation New Testament (Including King James, New American Standard, Williams - New Testament In the Language of the People, Beck - New Testament In the Language of Today.) Minneapolis, MN: World Wide Publications.

13. The New Compact Bible Dictionary, Edited by T. Alton Bryant. Grand Rapids, MI: Zondervan Publishing House, 1967.

14. The New Thompson Chain Reference Bible. Indianapolis, IN: B.B. Kirkbride Bible Co., 1964,

THE COMMENTARIES

15. Barclay, William. Daily Study Bible Series. Philadelphia, PA: Westminster Press, Began in 1953.

16. Bruce, F.F. The Epistle to the Ephesians. Westwood, NJ: Fleming H. Revell Co., 1968.

17. Bruce, F.F. Epistle to the Hebrews. Grand Rapids, MI: Eerdmans Publishing Co., 1964.

18. Bruce, F.F. The Epistles of John. Old Tappan, NJ: Fleming H. Revell Co., 1970.

19. Criswell, W.A. Expository Sermons on Revelation. Grand Rapids, MI: Zondervan Publishing House, 1962-66.

20. Greene, Oliver. The Epistles of John. Greenville, SC: The Gospel Hour, Inc., 1966.

21. Greene, Oliver. The Epistles of Paul the Apostle to the Hebrews. Greenville, SC: The Gospel Hour, Inc., 1965.

22. Greene, Oliver. The Epistles of Paul the Apostle to Timothy & Titus. Greenville, SC: The Gospel Hour, Inc., 1964.

23. Greene, Oliver. The Revelation Verse by Verse Study. Greenville, SC: The Gospel Hour, Inc., 1963.

24. Henry, Matthew. Commentary on the Whole Bible. Old Tappan, NJ: Fleming H. Revell Co.

25. Hodge, Charles. Exposition on Romans & on Corinthians. Grand Rapids, MI: Eerdmans Publishing Co., 1972-1973.

26. Ladd, George Eldon. A Commentary On the Revelation of John. Grand Rapids, MI: Eerdmans Publishing Co., 1972-1973.

27. Leupold, H.C. Exposition of Daniel. Grand Rapids, MI: Baker Book House, 1969.

28. Morris, Leon. The Gospel According to John. Grand Rapids, MI: Eerdmans Publishing Co., 1971.

29. Newell, William R. Hebrews, Verse by Verse. Chicago, IL: Moody Press, 1947.

30. Strauss, Lehman. Devotional Studies in Galatians & Ephesians. Neptune, NJ: Loizeaux Brothers, 1957.

31. Strauss, Lehman. Devotional Studies in Philippians. Neptune, NJ: Loizeaux Brothers, 1959.

32. Strauss, Lehman. James, Your Brother. Neptune, NJ: Loizeaux Brothers, 1956.

33. Strauss, Lehman. The Book of the Revelation. Neptune, NJ: Loizeaux Brothers, 1964.

34. The New Testament & Wycliffe Bible Commentary, Edited by Charles F. Pfeiffer & Everett F. Harrison. New York: The Iverson Associates, 1971. Produced for Moody Monthly. Chicago Moody Press, 1962.

35. The Pulpit Commentary, Edited by H.D.M. Spence & Joseph S. Exell. Grand Rapids, MI: Eerdmans Publishing Co., 1950.

36. Thomas, W.H. Griffith. Hebrews, A Devotional Commentary. Grand Rapids, MI: Eerdmans Publishing Co., 1970.

37. Thomas, W.H. Griffith. Outline Studies in the Acts of the Apostles. Grand Rapids, MI: Eerdmans Publishing Co., 1956.

38. Thomas, W.H. Griffith. St. Paul's Epistle to the Romans. Grand Rapids, MI: Eerdmans Publishing Co., 1946.

39. Thomas, W.H. Griffith. Studies in Colossians & Philemon. Grand Rapids, MI: Baker Book House, 1973.

40. Tyndale New Testament Commentaries. Grand Rapids, MI: Eerdmans Publishing Co., Began in 1958.

41. Walker, Thomas. Acts of the Apostles. Chicago, IL: Moody Press, 1965.

42. Walvoord, John. The Thessalonian Epistles. Grand Rapids, MI: Zondervan Publishing House, 1973.

MISCELLANEOUS ABBREVIATIONS

&	=	And
Arg.	=	Argument
Bckgrd.	=	Background
Bc.	=	Because
Circ.	=	Circumstance
Concl.	=	Conclusion
Cp.	=	Compare
Ct.	=	Contrast
Dif.	=	Different
e.g.	=	For example
Et.	=	Eternal
Govt.	=	Government
Id.	=	Identity or Identification
Illust.	=	Illustration
K.	=	Kingdom, K. of God, K. of Heaven, etc.
No.	=	Number
N.T.	=	New Testament
O.T.	=	Old Testament
Pt.	=	Point
Quest.	=	Question
Rel.	=	Religion
Resp.	=	Responsibility
Rev.	=	Revelation
Rgt.	=	Righteousness
Thru	=	Through
V.	=	Verse
Vs.	=	Verses
Vs.	=	Versus

"*Woe to me if I do not preach the gospel!*"

(I Cor. 9:16 NIV)

LUKE

INTRODUCTION

AUTHOR: Luke (1:3). Luke is also the author of Acts.

The early church fathers held Luke to be the author of both the Gospel of Luke and Acts: Irenaeus (about A.D. 130-200); Clement of Alexandria (about A.D. 150-215); Origen (about A.D. 185-254); and Tertullian (about A.D. 160-200). (See *The Pulpit Commentary*, Vol.16. Grand Rapids, MI: Eerdmans, 1950, p.1f, for an excellent discussion on the introductory material on Luke.)

A study of both books bears evidence that Luke is the author. The writer was evidently a physician. Greek medical terms are used. An analysis of the Gospel and Acts together shows the same style and language. There is also a clear understanding of the Roman and Greek world of the first century. The content of the two books shows a strong unity. There is a stress upon the resurrection, the Holy Spirit, the person of Christ, and the ministry to the Gentiles.

There is also enormous evidence that the writer of Acts was an acquaintance of Paul. This is clearly seen in the "we" section of Acts. In three sections of Acts, there is a remarkable switch from "they" and "he" to "we." The "we" sections give a first-hand account (Acts 16:10-17; 20:5-21:18; 27:1-28:16).

1. Luke is first seen with Paul at Troas. He switches from using "he" and "they" to "we." Luke joined Paul on his journey to Philippi and evidently remained in Philippi until Paul returned from Jerusalem (Acts 16:10).

2. Luke later went to Jerusalem with Paul when Paul was arrested (Acts 20:5-21:15).

3. Luke is seen with Paul again while Paul was a prisoner in Caesarea. He also accompanied Paul the prisoner to Rome (Acts 27:1-28:15).

4. Paul calls Luke "our dear friend Luke, the doctor" (Col.4:14; Phile.24).

5. Luke is the last one to remain with Paul in his imprisonment (2 Tim.2:11).

DATE: uncertain. Probably A.D. 58-62.

The author ends Acts abruptly with Paul's two-year imprisonment at Rome, so the writing would have been done some time after Jesus' ascension, just prior to the end of Acts. Another factor is that Luke says nothing about the Fall of Jerusalem. The fall of the city was prophesied by Jesus, and it actually took place in A.D. 70; therefore, the writing took place before A.D. 70. Considering these two factors, Luke must have written the Gospel sometime between A.D. 58-62.

TO WHOM WRITTEN: to "tmost excellent Theophilus," a Gentile convert (Lk.1:3; Acts 1:1). The words "most excellent" indicate that he was a high official in the Roman government. The book of Acts is also addressed to him personally. (See note, <u>Theophilus</u>--Acts 1:1 for more discussion.)

PURPOSE: to set forth an eyewitness account of Jesus, the Son of Man, the Savior of the world.

Luke wished Theophilus to know the certainty of those things which he had believed. Thus Luke sets out to write an orderly and accurate account of the whole life of Jesus (Lk.1:1-4).

SPECIAL FEATURES:

1. Luke is "The Gospel for Man" or "The Gospel for Gentiles." Luke shows that God is interested in all men everywhere, not just in the Jews (Lk.2:14, 32; 3:38; 4:25-27; 7:2-10; 9:51-54; 10:30-37; 13:29; 17:16; 24:47).

2. Luke is "The Gospel of Individuals." Luke shows that Jesus was deeply interested in individuals. He tells of Zechariah and Elizabeth, the parents of John the Baptist (Lk.1:5-25, 39-45; 67-79); of Mary and Martha (Lk.10:38-42); of Zacchaeus (Lk.19:2-10); of Cleopas and his companion (Lk.24:18); and of the woman who anointed Jesus' feet in the home of Simon the Pharisee (Lk.7:36f). The parables in Luke also tend to stress individuals, whereas in Matthew they stress the Kingdom.

3. Luke is "The Gospel of Salvation." Luke uses the words "salvation" and "Savior" or their various forms many more times than any of the other Gospel writers.

4. Luke is "The Gospel of the Outcasts and Sinners." Luke tells of the feast Matthew held for tax collectors and sinners (Lk.5:30); of the woman anointing Jesus' feet with her tears and wiping them with her hair (Lk.7:36-50); of tax collectors and sinners drawing near to hear Jesus teach (Lk.15:1). He alone tells of the Prodigal Son (Lk.15:11-32); of the Pharisee and tax collector (Lk.18:9-14); of Zacchaeus, the tax collecting "sinner" (Lk.19:1-10). Many of his parables center around the outcasts (Lk.7:41f; 12:13-21; 16:1-12, 19-31; 18:1-8, 9-14).

5. Luke is "The Gospel of the Poor." Luke tells of the shepherds who were of a poor class (Lk.2:8f); of Mary, who made the purification offering of the poor (Lk.2:24; cp. Lev.12:8). He says that Jesus came to preach the Gospel to the poor (Lk.4:18-6:20), and the poor have the Gospel preached to them (Lk.7:22).

6. Luke is "The Gospel of Women." Luke's world was a world that treated women only as things, as little more than chattel property, knowing nothing of women's rights. But Luke gives them a special place. He shows how God honored Elizabeth, Mary, and Anna (Lk.1:5f; 2:25f). He tells about the widow of Nain (Lk.7:11-18); the sinful woman who anointed Jesus' feet (Lk.7:36-50); and the three women who were healed of evil spirits including Mary Magdalene, Joanna, and Susanna (Lk.8:2-3). He writes about the sisters Mary and Martha (Lk.10:38-42); the bent-over lady (Lk.13:11-13); the widow who gave all to God (Lk.21:1-4); and the women who lined the road and wept as Jesus sagged under the weight and burden of the cross (Lk.23:27-31). He also includes women in some of his parables (Lk.15:8-10; 18:1-8).

7. Luke is "The Gospel of Children." The birth of Jesus and John the Baptist are given in detail (Lk.1-2). Luke's point is to show that God was at work even in the infant stages of the Savior. Luke alone gives the story of Jesus' boyhood (Lk.2:41-52). He alone emphasizes Jesus' ministry to the "only son" and "only daughter" of a desperate parent (Lk.7:12; 8:42; 9:38).

8. Luke is "The Gospel of Prayer" or "The Gospel of Devotion." Prayer is often emphasized.

a. There are the prayers of Jesus: at His baptism (Lk.3:21); in the wilderness (Lk.5:16); before choosing the disciples (Lk.6:12); immediately prior to predicting His death (Lk.9:18); at the transfiguration (Lk.9:28f); when the seventy returned (Lk.10:17-24, esp. 21-22); before giving the Lord's Prayer (Lk.11:1); for Peter (Lk.22:32); in the Garden of Gethsemane (Lk.22:39-46); for His enemies (Lk.23:34); and on the cross (Lk.23:46). Most of these are recorded by Luke alone. They show Jesus' facing every crisis of life by prayer.

b. There are the parables of Jesus that deal with prayer: the friend at midnight (Lk.11:5-8); the unjust judge (Lk.18:1-8); the Pharisee and Publican (Lk.18:9-14).

c. There are the exhortations and warnings about prayer (Lk.6:28; 11:2; 10:47; 22:40, 46).

9. Luke is "The Gospel of Praise." He uses the phrase "praising God" more than all the rest of the New Testament combined.

a. Some of the great Christian hymns are taken from Luke. The "Ava Maria" from the words of the angel to Mary (Lk.1:28-33); "The Magnificat" from Mary's song (Lk.1:46-55); "The Benedictus" from Zacharias (Lk.1:68-79); the "Gloria in Excelsis" from the song of the heavenly angels (Lk.2:13-14); and "The Nunc Dimittis" from the rejoicing of Simeon (Lk.2:29-32).

b. People are seen praising God when helped (Lk.2:20; 5:25-26; 7:16; 13:13; 17:15; 18:43).

c. The words "joy" and "rejoicing" are used time and time again (for example Lk.1:14, 44, 47; 10:21).

d. There are references to laughter (Lk.6:21) and merriment (Lk.15:23, 32) and to joy (Lk.15:6, 9; 19:6).

e. The Gospel ends with joy (Lk.24:52) even as it began with joy (Lk.1:14).

10. Luke is "The Gospel of Christ's Passion." This is seen in three significant emphases.

a. There are the many references to His death. Moses and Elijah discuss Jesus' death at His transfiguration (Lk.9:31). Luke says the time for Jesus to be received up has arrived (Lk.9:51); therefore, Jesus sets His face to go up to Jerusalem (Lk.9:51). Jesus refers to His death as a baptism and stresses a constraint to accomplish it (Lk.12:50). Jesus sends a message to Herod that after His ministry He will finish His course on the third day (Lk.13:32). He then continues to speak of perishing in Jerusalem (Lk.13:33-35). And Jesus foretells His passion in a statement that is unique to Luke (Lk.17:25).

b. There is the long space given over to the passion narrative.

c. There are the times that Scripture is said to be fulfilled by Jesus death (Lk.9:22; 13:33; 17:25; 18:31; 20:17; 22:37; 24:7, 26f, 44, 46).

11. Luke is "The Gospel of the Holy Spirit."

a. The persons involved in the preparation for the Savior's coming are said to be Spirit filled and Spirit led: John the Baptist (Lk.1:15); Elizabeth and Zechariah (Lk.1:41, 67); and Simeon (Lk.2:25-27).

b. The Holy Spirit is said to be active in the life and ministry of Jesus. Mary was told that the Holy Spirit would come upon her (Lk.1:35). John the Baptist predicted Jesus would be baptized with the Holy Spirit and fire (Lk.3:16). The Holy Spirit came upon Jesus after His baptism "in bodilyform, like a dove" (Lk.3:22). The Holy Spirit filled and led Him into the wilderness to be tempted by the devil (Lk.4:1). Jesus returned from His temptations to begin His ministry in Galilee "in the power of the Spirit" (Lk.4:14). While preaching, He claimed "the Spirit of the Lord is on me" (Lk.4:18). He rejoiced in the Spirit when the seventy returned and gave a good report (Lk.10:21); He told His disciples that the Father would give the Spirit to those who asked (Lk.11:13). He said that blasphemy against the Holy Spirit is an unforgivable sin (Lk.12:10). He told His disciples that the Holy Spirit would tell them what to say in emergencies (Lk.12:12).

He closed His ministry by assuring His disciples, "I am going to send you what my father has promised...." (Lk.24:49).

OUTLINE OF LUKE

THE PREACHER'S OUTLINE & SERMON BIBLE® is *unique*. It differs from all other Study Bibles & Sermon Resource Materials in that every Passage and Subject is outlined right beside the Scripture. When you choose any *Subject* below and turn to the reference, you have not only the Scripture, but you discover the Scripture and Subject *already outlined for you—verse by verse*.

For a quick example, choose one of the subjects below and turn to the Scripture, and you will find this marvelous help for faster, easier, and more accurate use.

In addition, every point of the Scripture and Subject is *fully developed in a Commentary with supporting Scripture* at the bottom of the page. Again, this arrangement makes sermon preparation much easier and faster.

Note something else: The Subjects of John's Gospel have titles that are both Biblical and *practical*. The practical titles sometimes have more appeal to people. This *benefit* is clearly seen for use on billboards, bulletins, church newsletters, etc.

A suggestion: For the quickest overview of John, first read *all the major titles* (I, II, III, etc.), then come back and read the subtitles.

OUTLINE OF LUKE

R. Jesus and the Women Who Supported Him, 8:1-3
S. Jesus Teaches the Sure Fate of the Word: How People Receive the Word, 8:4-15
(Matthew 13:1-23; Mark 4:1-20)
T. Jesus Teaches Three Fundamental Principles of Life, 8:16-18
(Matthew 5:15-16; 10:26-27; 13:12; Mark 4:21-23; cp. Luke 11:33-36)
U. Jesus Teaches the Basis of True Kinship, 8:19-21
(Matthew 12:46-50; Mark 3:31-35)
V. Jesus Calms a Storm: Jesus' Deity and Sovereignty, 8:22-25
(Matthew 8:23-27; Mark 4:35-41)
W. Jesus Casts Out Demons in Gadara: Power to Free Men from Evil Spirits, 8:26-39
(Matthew 8:28-34; Mark 5:1-20)
X. Jesus Raises Jairus' Daughter and Heals a Woman: The Reward of True Faith, 8:40-56
(Matthew 9:18-26; Mark 5:21-43)
Y. Jesus Commissions His Disciples, 9:1-9
(Matthew 9:35-10:42; Mark 6:7-13)
Z. Jesus Teaches How to Minister, 9:10-17
(Matthew 14:15-21; Mark 6:30-44; John 6:1-14)

IV. THE SON OF MAN'S INTENSIVE PREPARATION OF HIS DISCIPLES FOR JERUSALEM AND DEATH, 9:18-50

A. The First Prediction of Death: Who Jesus Really Is, 9:18-22
(Matthew 16:13-23; Mark 8:27-33)
B. The Terms of Discipleship, 9:23-27
(Matthew 16:24-28; Mark 8:34-9:1)
C. The Events of the Transfiguration: A Glimpse into Glory, 9:28-36
(Matthew 17:1-13; Mark 9:2-13)
D. The Second Prediction of Death: A Rebuke of the Present Generation, 9:37-45
(Matthew 17:14-23; Mark 9:14-32)
E. The Way of Greatness: Humility, 9:46-50
(Matthew 18:1-4; Mark 9:33-41)

V. THE SON OF MAN'S GREAT JOURNEY TO JERUSALEM (STAGE I): HIS MISSION AND PUBLIC CHALLENGE, 9:51-13:21

A. The Son of Man's Mission: Jesus' Mission Misunderstood, 9:51-56
B. The Great Cost of Discipleship, 9:57-62
(Matthew 8:18-22)
C. The Seventy Sent Forth: Great Purpose, 10:1-16
(cp. Matthew 10)
D. The Seventy Return (Part I): Great Power, 10:17-20
E. The Seventy Return (Part II): Great Privileges, 10:21-24
(Matthew 11:25-27)
F. The Parable of the Good Samaritan: The Two Supreme Questions of Life, 10:25-37
(cp. Matthew 22:34-40; Mark 12:28-34)
G. The One Thing Needed: To Sit at Jesus' Feet, 10:38-42
H. The Great Subject of Prayer, 11:1-13
(cp. Matthew 6:5-15; cp. Mark 11:20-26)
I. The Proof that Jesus is the Messiah, 11:14-28
(Matthew 12:22-30; Mark 3:22-30)
J. The Great Proof that Jesus is the Messiah: The Resurrection, 11:29-36
(Matthew 5:14-16; 12:38-42; Mark 4:21-22; cp. Luke 8:16)
K. The Severe Charges Against Religionists, 11:37-54
(cp. Matthew 23:13-36)
L. The Things Men Should Fear, 12:1-12
M. The Parable of the Rich Fool: The Man of Wealth and What He Should Fear, 12:13-21
N. The Genuine Believer: Worry Not About Necessities, 12:22-34
(Matthew 6:25-34)
O. The Parable of the Faithful and Unfaithful Steward: A Strong Warning—Be Prepared, 12:35-48
(Matthew 24:37-25:30)
P. The Three Gross Misconceptions of Man, 12:49-59
Q. The Truth About Suffering and Sin: The Great Need for All to Repent, 13:1-9
(cp. Matthew 21:18-21; Mark 11:12-14, 20-26; Isaiah 5:1-7)
R. People vs. Religion: Which is More Important? 13:10-17
S. The Parables of the Mustard Seed and Leaven: The Kingdom of God, 13:18-21
(Matthew 13:31-33; Mark 4:30-32)

VI. THE SON OF MAN'S GREAT JOURNEY TO JERUSALEM (STAGE II): HIS TEACHING AND PUBLIC CONFLICT, 13:22-17:10

A. The Saved Discussed, 13:22-30
B. The Tragic Rejection of Jesus, 13:31-35
(Matthew 23:37-39; cp. Luke 19:41-44)
C. The Religionists and Their Error, 14:1-6
(cp. Matthew 12:9-13)
D. The Importance of Humility, 14:7-14
E. The Parable of the Great Supper: The Invitation and Man's Excuses, 14:15-24
(cp. Matthew 22:1-14)
F. The Cost of Discipleship, 14:25-35
(cp. Matthew 5:13; cp. Matthew 10:37-39; Mark 9:50)
G. The Parable of the Lost Sheep: The Lost Sinner Out in the World, 15:1-7
(cp. Matthew 18:11-14)
H. The Parable of the Lost Coin: The Lost Sinner Within the Home, 15:8-10
I. The Parable of the Prodigal Son: The Wayward Son, 15:11-24
J. The Parable of the Elder Son: The Self-Righteous Religionist, 15:25-32
K. The Parable of the Unjust Steward: Man and Money, 16:1-13
L. The Misunderstanding About Wealth and God's Kingdom, 16:14-18
M. The Rich Man and Lazarus: The Self-Indulgent vs. the Man of Faith, 16:19-31
N. The Christian Disciple and Four Laws, 17:1-10
(cp. Matthew 18:6; 17:20)

VII. THE SON OF MAN'S GREAT JOURNEY TO JERUSALEM (STAGE III): HIS LESSONS AND WARNINGS, 17:11-19:27

A. The Lesson on Need and Gratitude, 17:11-19
B. The Coming Day of God's Kingdom and Jesus' Return, 17:20-37
(cp. Matthew 24; Mark 13)
C. The Parable of the Unjust Judge: The Secret of Prayer—Persistence, 18:1-8
D. The Parable of the Pharisee and the Publican: The Spirit Needed for Prayer, 18:9-14
E. The Little Children and Jesus, 18:15-17
(Matthew 19:13-15; Mark 10:13-16)
F. The Rich Young Ruler: The Cost of Eternal Life, 18:18-30
(Matthew 19:16-30; Mark 10:17-31)
G. The Prediction of the Cross, 18:31-34
(Matthew 20:17-19; Mark 10:32-34)
H. The Healing of Blind Bartimaeus: Steps to Getting Help from God, 18:35-43
(cp. Matthew 20:29-34; Mark 10:46-52)
I. The Conversion of Zaccheus: The Meaning of Conversion, 19:1-10
J. The Parable of the Pounds: Every Man is Being Tested, 19:11-27

VIII. THE SON OF MAN'S DRAMATIC ENTRANCE INTO JERUSALEM: HIS CLAIM AND CONFLICT, 19:28-21:4

A. The Triumphal Entry: Jesus' Claim to be King, 19:28-40
(Matthew 21:1-11; Mark 11:1-11; John 12:12-19)
B. The Dramatic Prediction: Judgment Upon Jerusalem, 19:41-44
(cp. Matthew 23:37-39; Luke 13:34-35)
C. The Cleansing of the Temple: The Righteous Anger of Jesus, 19:45-48
(Matthew 21:12-16; Mark 11:15-19; cp. John 2:13-16)
D. The Question of Authority: Who is Jesus? 20:1-8
(Matthew 21:23-27; Mark 11:27-33)
E. The Parable of the Wicked Husbandmen: The Overview of World History, 20:9-18
(Matthew 21:33-46; Mark 12:1-12; cp. Isaiah 5:1-7)
F. The Question of Government and Religion: Which is Supreme? 20:19-26
(Matthew 22:15-22; Mark 12:13-17)
G. The Question of the Resurrection: The Two Worlds (Earth and Heaven) Differ, 20:27-38
(Matthew 22:23-33; Mark 12:18-27)
H. The Question of David's Son: Two Misunderstandings Corrected, 20:39-47
(Matthew 22:41-46; 23:6-7, 14; Mark 12:35-40)
I. The Widow's Mite: The Question of Giving, 21:1-4
(Mark 12:41-44).

IX. THE SON OF MAN'S PROPHETIC SIGNS: HIS PREDICTION CONCERNING THE FATE OF JERUSALEM AND THE WORLD, 21:5-38
(Matthew 24-25, Mark 13)

A. The Predicted Signs of the Present Age, 21:5-11
(Matthew 24:1-14; Mark 13:1-13)
B. The Tragic Sign Prior to the End: Persecution, 21:12-19
(Matthew 24:9-10, 13; Mark 13:9, 11-12)
C. The Destruction of Jerusalem, 21:20-24
(Matthew 24:15-28; Mark 13:14-23)
D. The Coming of Jesus, the Son of Man, 21:25-28
(Matthew 24:29-31; Mark 13:24-27)
E. The Parable of the Fig Tree: The Signs are Clearly Seen, 21:29-33
(Matthew 24:32-35; Mark 13:28-34)
F. The Warning: Watch and Pray for the Day of Jesus' Return, 21:34-36
(Matthew 24:42-44; Mark 13:35-37)
G. The Daily Ministry of Jesus, 21:37-38

X. THE SON OF MAN'S LAST SUPPER: HIS TRAITOR, INSTRUCTIONS, AND WARNINGS, 22:1-38

A. The Plot Against Jesus, 22:1-6
(Matthew 26:14-16; Mark 14:1-2, 10-11)
B. The Lord's Supper, 22:7-23
(Matthew 26:17-30; Mark 14:12-25; John 13)
C. The Dispute Over Greatness, 22:24-30
(Matthew 20:20-28; Mark 10:35-45)
D. The Denial of Peter Foretold: The Great Warning of Satan's Attack, 22:31-38
(Matthew 26:31-35; Mark 14:27-31; John 13:36-38)

XI. THE SON OF MAN'S SUFFERINGS: HIS AGONY, TRIALS, AND CRUCIFIXION, 22:39-23:56

A. Jesus' Great Agony: Bearing Unbelievable Weight, 22:39-46
(Matthew 26:36-46; Mark 14:32-42; John 18:1; cp. Hebrews 5:7-8; 12:3-4)
B. Jesus' Arrest: Terrible Sins Against Jesus, 22:47-53
(Matthew 26:47-56; Mark 14:43-52; John 18:3-11)
C. Peter's Denial: The Great Tragedy of Denial, 22:54-62
(Matthew 26:57, 69-75; Mark 14:53-54; 66-72; John 18:15-18, 25-27)
D. Jesus Tried Before the Sanhedrin Court: The Phenomenal Claims of Jesus, 22:63-71
(Matthew 26:57-68; 27:1; Mark 14:53-65; 15:1; John 18:12-14, 19-24)
E. Jesus' First Trial Before Pilate and Herod: The Shirking of Duty and Personal Concern, 23:1-12
(Matthew 27:11-14; Mark 15:1-5; John 18:28-38)
F. Jesus' Second Trial Before Pilate: The Tragedy of a Compromising Man, 23:13-25
(Matthew 27:15-25; Mark 15:6-15; John 18:39-19:16)
G. Jesus' Crucifixion and Its Events, 23:26-49
(Matthew 27:26-56; Mark 15:16-41; John 19:16-37)
H. Jesus' Burial: A Secret Disciple Stirred to Step Forth, 23:50-56
(Matthew 27:57-61; Mark 15:42-47; John 19:38-42)

XII. THE SON OF MAN'S GLORY: HIS RESURRECTION AND ASCENSION, 24:1-53

A. Jesus' Empty Tomb: Its Discovery, 24:1-12 (cp. Matthew 28:1-15; Mark 16:1-11; John 20:1-18)
B. Jesus' Appearance to Two Believers on the Road to Emmaus: An Immortal Journey, 24:13-35 (Mark 16:12-13)
C. Jesus' Appearance to the Disciples: The Great Statements of the Christian Faith, 24:36-49 (Mark 16:14; John 20:19-23; 20:26-21:25)
D. Jesus' Last Appearance: The Ascension, 24:50-53 (Mark 16:19-20; Acts 1:9-11)

LUKE

Outline	Chapter	Scripture	Outline
	CHAPTER 1 **I. THE ANNOUNCEMENT OF THE COMING OF JESUS, THE SON OF MAN, 1:1-2:52** **A. Luke's Gospel Account: The Truth of the Word, 1:1-4**		
1 The gospel is a record of historical events	Many have undertaken to draw up an account of the things that have been fulfilled	among us,	
		2 Just as they were handed down to us by those who from the first were eyewitnesses and servants of the word.	**2 The gospel is a record of eyewitnesses & servants of the Word**
		3 Therefore, since I myself have carefully investigated everything from the beginning, it seemed good also to me to write an orderly account for you, most excellent Theophilus,	**3 The gospel is a record of a man who was led to write**
		4 So that you may know the certainty of the things you have been taught.	**4 The gospel is a record to establish the truth**

DIVISION I

THE ANNOUNCEMENT OF THE COMING OF JESUS, THE SON OF MAN, 1:1-2:52

A. Luke's Gospel Account: The Truth of the Word, 1:1-4

(1:1-4) **Introduction**: the Gospel of Luke is a written proclamation of the truth about Jesus Christ. This is the thrust of this first passage in Luke's gospel. Luke is writing to declare the glorious news that the Son of Man, God's Son, has come to earth to seek and to save all who are lost. Luke's gospel is an accurate, orderly account of the truth about Jesus Christ. Note: this introduction of Luke is the very form used by the historians of his day. This points strongly to the fact that Luke intended it to be circulated among churches and believers.

1. The gospel is a record of historical events (v.1).
2. The gospel is a record of eyewitnesses and servants of the Word (v.2).
3. The gospel is a record of a man who was led to write (v.3).
4. The gospel is a record to establish the truth (v.4).

1 (1:1) **Scripture—Gospel**: Luke's gospel is a record of historical events. Note several facts.

1. "Many...have undertaken to draw up" the events of Christ's life. Many had written about the life and work of Christ, but they were not as *complete* nor as *orderly* as Luke wished to record (cp. v.3). A quick comparison of the first two chapters of Luke with Mark and Matthew will show this. Luke includes many more events than the other two Synoptic Gospels, and the Gospel of John had not yet been written. The fact that *many* had written a record on the life of Christ is strong evidence that the events are true.

2. The events or things of Christ's life were "things that have been fulfilled." The words for "things that have been fulfilled" (plerophoreo, peplero phoremenon) also mean things that were believed. The things were actually performed or had run their full course (cp. 2 Tim.4:5). Luke is saying that the *things of Christ* were not only believed, but they were also accomplished or fulfilled among the believers of that day. The *things* (events, matters) of Christ actually took place; they were purposeful; they were destined to be accomplished and fulfilled.

The point is this: the things of Christ are a record of historical events, things that actually happened and that actually fulfilled the purpose of God. Therefore, the things "have been fulfilled among us [believers]." What are the *things* accomplished and believed? Both the things of the New Testament and of the Old Testament. The whole Bible is a record of "the things."

> **"For God so loved the world that he gave his one and only Son, that whoever believes in him shall not perish but have eternal life. (John 3:16)**
>
> **For the Son of Man came to seek and to save what was lost." (Luke 19:10)**
>
> **Since the children have flesh and blood, he too shared in their humanity so that by his death he might destroy him who holds the power of death—that is, the devil—and free those who all their lives were held in slavery by their fear of death. For surely it is not angels he helps, but Abraham's descendants. For this reason he had to be made like his brothers in every way, in order that he might become a merciful and faithful high priest in service to God, and that he might make atonement for the sins of the people. Because he himself suffered when he was tempted, he is able to help those who are being tempted. (Heb 2:14-18)**
>
> **[Christ Jesus] who, being in very nature God, did not consider equality with God something to be grasped, but made himself nothing, taking the very nature of a servant, being made in human likeness. And being found in appearance as a man, he humbled himself and became obedient to death— even death on a cross! Therefore God exalted him to the highest place and gave him the name that is above every name, that at the name of Jesus every knee should bow, in heaven and on earth and under the earth, and every tongue confess that Jesus Christ is Lord, to the glory of God the Father. (Phil 2:6-11)**
>
> **He himself bore our sins in his body on the tree, so that we might die to sins and**

live for righteousness; by his wounds you have been healed. (1 Pet 2:24)

For he has rescued us from the dominion of darkness and brought us into the kingdom of the Son he loves, in whom we have redemption, the forgiveness of sins. He is the image of the invisible God, the firstborn over all creation. For by him all things were created: things in heaven and on earth, visible and invisible, whether thrones or powers or rulers or authorities; all things were created by him and for him. He is before all things, and in him all things hold together. And he is the head of the body, the church; he is the beginning and the firstborn from among the dead, so that in everything he might have the supremacy. For God was pleased to have all his fullness dwell in him, and through him to reconcile to himself all things, whether things on earth or things in heaven, by making peace through his blood, shed on the cross. (Col 1:13-20)

For in Christ all the fullness of the Deity lives in bodily form, and you have been given fullness in Christ, who is the head over every power and authority. (Col 2.9-10)

Therefore, if anyone is in Christ, he is a new creation; the old has gone, the new has come! (2 Cor 5:17)

Thought 1. The early believers had no difficulty whatsoever believing the *things* of Christ.
1) The *things* were *fulfilled among us*.
2) Many were writing an account of the events.

Thought 2. The "many" who wrote about the life of Jesus are not known by name. They are the silent and humble heroes of God, never known by the world, but well-known by God. Some of their writings served as a *source* for Luke (v.3). Note two things.
1) Their ministry of writing was used greatly by God. Some of what they wrote was either included in the Gospel of Luke or at least stirred thoughts in Luke's mind to record an event.
2) God's silent, quiet, and humble servants are always used by Him just as much as the ones out in the forefront. Their ministry is just as important, if not more so. Some that are last will most definitely be first.

Indeed there are those who are last who will be first, and first who will be last." (Luke 13:30; cp. Mat 19:30; 20:16; Mark 10:31)

2 (1:2) **Servants—The Word, Proof of**: Luke's gospel is both a record of *eyewitnesses* and a record of *servants of the Word*. Luke himself was not an eyewitness of the day-to-day life of Christ. If he ever saw Christ personally, there is no mention of it. However, Luke was a constant and very dear companion of Paul (see Introduction—Luke; note—Acts 16:10). He also had contact with other apostles. What Luke says is that the sources of his writing were eyewitnesses of Christ and servants of the Word of Christ. The apostles, of course, would be his prime sources. In addition, there were other disciples who followed Jesus either continuously or occasionally. Note these simple facts.

1. The servants of the Word were eyewitnesses of both *The Word* (Christ Himself) and of the Word of Christ (His teaching, doctrine, and instructions).
2. The servants of the Word were eyewitnesses "from the first," eyewitnesses of every event and word of Christ, eyewitnesses of His life day by day.
3. The servants of the Word heard as well as saw Christ; some heard and saw Him day by day. Therefore, Luke's gospel is a true record of both the acts and words of Christ.
4. The servants of the gospel set out immediately to *minister* the Word to others. The word was of critical importance to them. They gave their lives to the ministry of the Word.
5. The servants of the gospel did not create the Word (message) themselves. They were not ministering their own ideas and thoughts; they were ministering "The Word of God."
6. The servants of the Word have given us a written gospel that is an eyewitness account. It agrees exactly with what was seen, heard, and proclaimed by Christ and preached to the people of His day and to the world since then.

That which was from the beginning, which we have heard, which we have seen with our eyes, which we have looked at and our hands have touched—this we proclaim concerning the Word of life. The life appeared; we have seen it and testify to it, and we proclaim to you the eternal life, which was with the Father and has appeared to us. We proclaim to you what we have seen and heard, so that you also may have fellowship with us. And our fellowship is with the Father and with his Son, Jesus Christ. We write this to make our joy complete. (1 John 1:1-4)

3 (1:3) **Gospel—Scripture**: Luke's gospel is the record of a man who was led to write. Four facts point out just how strongly Luke felt led to record the life of Christ.

1. Luke carefully investigated everything. The word "investigated" means to study, to follow up, to search out diligently, to investigate, to trace accurately, to become acquainted with. Luke says that having been acquainted with and having investigated everything, he was determined to record the facts himself.
2. Luke says he had carefully investigated everything "from the beginning." The word "beginning" (anothen) can and often does mean *from above*. Some understand Luke to be saying that he had investigated the things *from above*. Several things point to this translation.
   a. If Luke meant *from the first or beginning,* why did he not use the same word (arches) which he used in verse 2? It seems to be much more accurate to say he chooses a different word, (anothen), because he is saying something different, *from above*.
   b. The prophets are said to have proclaimed things *from above*. They are said to "Concerning this salvation, the prophets, who spoke of the grace that was to come to you, searched intently and with the greatest care, trying to find out the time and circumstances to which the Spirit of Christ in them was pointing when he predicted the sufferings of Christ and the glories that would follow. It was revealed to them that they were not serving

themselves but you, when they spoke of the things that have now been told you by those who have preached the gospel to you by the Holy Spirit sent from heaven. Even angels long to look into these things" (1 Pt.1:10-12). Scripture also says, "For prophecy never had its origin in the will of man, but men spoke from God as they were carried along by the Holy Spirit" (2 Pt.1:21).

c. Luke is certainly recording *all things from above*, investigating and searching diligently to write what "the Spirit of Christ in them was pointing" (1 Pt.1:11). He is certainly speaking as a holy man of God "carried along by the Holy Spirit" (2 Pt.1:21). He is certainly proclaiming the gospel of the Lord Jesus Christ, the good news of Him who came from above.

3. Luke says he is writing things in "an orderly account" (kathexes). Luke is the only writer in the New Testament to use this word. He uses it in the gospel only once and in Acts twice (Acts 11:4; 18:23). The question is, what does Luke mean by *orderly*? Consecutive or chronological arrangement? Logical arrangement? Subject arrangement? Inspired or Spirit-led arrangement? The meaning is not clear. Perhaps he is saying that he is writing a full account of the life of Christ and that his account is a *better arrangement*, that is, it has more order and is better arranged than those in existence.

4. Luke is writing to a man named "Theophilus." Who was he? We are not told. But note two facts.

a. He was called "most excellent Theophilus." "Most excellent" (kratistos) is a title of rank and honor. The same title is used of Felix and Festus (Acts 23:26; 24:3; 26:25).

b. He was a person who desired or needed to know about Jesus Christ. He was probably a convert for whom Luke deeply cared. Some feel he was a man investigating the validity of Christianity. Theophilus is the immediate reason Luke *felt led* to write. (See note, Theophilus—Acts 1:1 for more discussion.)

Thought 1. Note two critical points.

1) A person must be *prepared* to serve Christ. A person must study, investigate, search out, become acquainted with the truth of Christ.

Do your best to present yourself to God as one approved, a workman who does not need to be ashamed and who correctly handles the word of truth. (2 Tim 2:15)

2) A person must be led to serve Christ, no matter the task. He must be led by the Spirit of Christ.

Because those who are led by the Spirit of God are sons of God. (Rom 8:14)

You did not choose me, but I chose you and appointed you to go and bear fruit—fruit that will last. Then the Father will give you whatever you ask in my name. (John 15:16)

Thought 2. We can have great confidence in the truth and accuracy of the written record of Christ.

All Scripture is God-breathed and is useful for teaching, rebuking, correcting and training in righteousness, (2 Tim 3:16)

Thought 3. Note a tremendous challenge to us. Luke cared so much for one man that he dedicated himself to writing not a long letter, but a whole book in order to instruct the man. Imagine the dedication and the days and months required! All for one person (initially)!

"Suppose one of you has a hundred sheep and loses one of them. Does he not leave the ninety-nine in the open country and go after the lost sheep until he finds it? (Luke 15:4)

4 (1:4) **Gospel—Truth**: Luke's gospel is a record to establish the truth. Luke's purpose is clearly stated: "So that you may know the certainty of the things you have been taught."

1. The man (Theophilus) *had already heard.*
2. The man *needed to know* the absolute truth of those things.

Thought 1. Luke's account of Christ is the absolute truth. We can "know the certainty of the things."

Thought 2. Hearing the things of Christ, even being instructed in them is not enough. We are to study and learn, to know the absolute certainty of them.

For prophecy never had its origin in the will of man, but men spoke from God as they were carried along by the Holy Spirit. (2 Pet 1:21; cp. Mark 13:31; Luke 21:33)

Now the Bereans were of more noble character than the Thessalonians, for they received the message with great eagerness and examined the Scriptures every day to see if what Paul said was true. (Acts 17:11)

1 The parents of John the Baptist
- a. They lived in the time of Herod
- b. The father was a priest & the mother was of a priestly family

2 They were parents who were righteous

3 They were parents with human problems
- a. They had no child
- b. They were elderly

4 They were parents who worshipped

5 They were parents who prayed & led others to pray

6 They were parents greatly favored by God
- a. Their worship & prayers were favored by a visit from an angel
- b. Their prayers were answered: They received the promise of a son
- c. Their son was to be great

B. Zechariah and Elizabeth, The Parents of John the Baptist: Godly Parents, 1:5-25

5 In the time of Herod king
of Judea there was a priest
named Zechariah, who be-
longed to the priestly division
of Abijah; his wife Elizabeth
was also a descendant of
Aaron.
6 Both of them were upright
in the sight of God, observing
all the Lord's commandments
and regulations blamelessly.
7 But they had no children,
because Elizabeth was barren; and they were both well
along in years.
8 Once when Zechariah's
division was on duty and he
was serving as priest before
God,
9 He was chosen by lot, according to the custom of the
priesthood, to go into the
temple of the Lord and burn
incense.
10 And when the time for the
burning of incense came, all
the assembled worshipers
were praying outside.
11 Then an angel of the Lord
appeared to him, standing at
the right side of the altar of
incense.
12 When Zechariah saw him,
he was startled and was
gripped with fear.
13 But the angel said to him:
"Do not be afraid, Zechariah;
your prayer has been heard.
Your wife Elizabeth will bear
you a son, and you are to give
him the name John.
14 He will be a joy and delight to you, and many will
rejoice because of his birth,
15 For he will be great in the
sight of the Lord. He is never
to take wine or other fer-
mented drink, and he will be
filled with the Holy Spirit
even from birth.
16 Many of the people of Israel will he bring back to the
Lord their God.
17 And he will go on before
the Lord, in the spirit and
power of Elijah, to turn the
hearts of the fathers to their
children and the disobedient
to the wisdom of the righteous—to make ready a peo-
ple prepared for the Lord."
18 Zechariah asked the angel, "How can I be sure of
this? I am an old man and my
wife is well along in years."
19 The angel answered, "I
am Gabriel. I stand in the
presence of God, and I have
been sent to speak to you and
to tell you this good news.
20 And now you will be silent and not able to speak
until the day this happens,
because you did not believe
my words, which will come
true at their proper time."
21 Meanwhile, the people
were waiting for Zechariah
and wondering why he stayed
so long in the temple.
22 When he came out, he
could not speak to them.
They realized he had seen a
vision in the temple, for he
kept making signs to them but
remained unable to speak.
23 When his time of service
was completed, he returned
home.
24 After this his wife Elizabeth became pregnant and for
five months remained in se-
clusion.
25 "The Lord has done this
for me," she said. "In these
days he has shown his favor
and taken away my disgrace
among the people."

- d. Their son was to be a prophet
- e. Their son was to be the forerunner of the Messiah

7 They were parents who found it difficult to believe the humanly impossible[DS1]

8 They were parents who had to be disciplined by God

9 They were parents who saw God fulfill His promise

DIVISION I

THE ANNOUNCEMENT OF THE COMING OF JESUS, THE SON OF MAN, 1:1-2:52

B. Zechariah and Elizabeth, The Parents of John the Baptist: Godly Parents, 1:5-25

(1:5-25) **Introduction**: every generation needs the example of godly parents. The parents of John the Baptist were godly, dynamic examples of what parents should be. They were human, showing some weaknesses, but they were striking examples for all.

1. The parents of John the Baptist (v.5).
2. They were parents who were righteous (v.6).
3. They were parents with human problems (v.7).
4. They were parents who worshipped (v.8-9).
5. They were parents who prayed and led others to pray (v.10).
6. They were parents greatly favored by God (v.11-17).
7. They were parents who found it difficult to believe the humanly impossible (v.18-19).
8. They were parents who had to be disciplined by God (v.20-22).
9. They were parents who saw God fulfill His promise (v.23-25).

1 (1:5) **John the Baptist, Family of**: the parents of John the Baptist. Note three facts.

1. The baby John was promised to his parents during the reign of Herod the Great, right at the very end of his reign (B.C.37-4) (See DEEPER STUDY # 3—Mt.2:3-4.)
2. John's father was Zechariah.
   a. His name means *Remembered of Jehovah.*
   b. He was from the country, a mountainous or hilly section.
   c. He was of "the priestly division of Abijah." This simply means a division of the priests. Remember that all the male descendants of Aaron were priests. There were over twenty thousand at this time and only one temple, so they had to be divided into groups (1 Chron.24:1-6). Zechariah served in the eighth group or division (1 Chron.24:10). There were twenty-four groups, and each group served in the temple for one week, twice a year.
3. John's mother was Elizabeth.
   a. Her name means *One whose oath is to God.*
   b. She was the daughter of a priest.
   c. She was a pure woman, a virgin at her marriage. A priest was required to marry a virgin (Lev.21:14).

2 (1:6) **Righteousness—Family**: they were parents who were righteous. Note four facts.

1. They "were *both* upright." They were joined together and committed to each other, and they lived for God and for each other as husband and wife.

2. They were "upright *in the sight of God.*" Together they came before God seeking Him, that is, seeking to please Him and to live as He said.

3. They were "observing *all* the Lord's commandments and regulations." They controlled their thoughts, minds, tongues, and behavior, diligently seeking to please the Lord in all they did.

4. They were blameless. This, of course, does not mean they were perfect. It means they were faithful, living in such a way that no one could charge them with open sin. They offended no one; they lived honestly before both God and men.

3 (1:7) **Family—Parents**: they were parents with human problems. Being righteous did not free them from problems. They had to face the problems of this world just as all persons do. But there was a difference: they were upright in the sight of God. Therefore, they had the presence of God to help them through the problems. They had two serious problems.

1. They were childless. This was a terrible calamity to the people of that day. Children were considered a blessing from God, a great heritage of the Lord. In fact, a Jew whose wife could not bear children was thought to be cut off from God. He was expected to divorce his wife, remarry, and bear children. Therefore, being childless was a critical problem to Zechariah and Elizabeth, a problem that weighed ever so heavily upon their hearts and never left their minds. They felt disfavored and displeasing to God.

2. They were elderly. All the problems that come with age either faced them or stood before them as a threat.

> **That you may be sons of your Father in heaven. He causes his sun to rise on the evil and the good, and sends rain on the righteous and the unrighteous. (Mat 5:45)**
>
> **No temptation [trial] has seized you except what is common to man. And God is faithful; he will not let you be tempted beyond what you can bear. But when you are tempted, he will also provide a way out so that you can stand up under it. (1 Cor 10:13)**
>
> **Scorn has broken my heart and has left me helpless; I looked for sympathy, but there was none, for comforters, but I found none. (Psa 69:20)**

4 (1:8-9) **Parents—Worship**: they were parents who worshipped. Zechariah was faithful to his priesthood. He had been chosen and ordained by God to be a priest, and he was faithful to that call. He was faithful and steadfast in his duties despite the lack of blessings from God, that is, being childless. Remember that bearing a son in that day and time was considered one of the greatest blessings and signs of God's approval. Not having a son was thought to be an indication of God's disapproval.

What happened was this. In the temple's daily worship, incense was burned upon the altar by a priest before the morning sacrifice and after the evening sacrifice. The offering of incense symbolized that the sacrifices were being offered up to God in the sweetest and most prayerful of spirits. The aroma of the incense was just like prayer; it enveloped the sacrifice and carried it before the very throne of God.

The priests considered the burning of incense to be the highest privilege of the priestly functions. However, because of the large number of priests, some never had the opportunity to offer it up to God. Just who received this privilege was determined by drawing lots. On this particular day, Zechariah experienced one of the greatest days of his life. The lot fell upon him. He was the chosen priest to offer the incense.

The point is this: Zechariah was faithful to God's call. He had been chosen and ordained by God to be a priest, and he had accepted and given his life to that call. He was faithful in his worship despite his *problems and lack of blessings* from God (being childless).

> **Blessed is the man who perseveres under trial, because when he has stood the test, he will receive the crown of life that God has promised to those who love him. (James 1:12)**
>
> **As you know, we consider blessed those who have persevered. You have heard of Job's perseverance and have seen what the Lord finally brought about. The Lord is full of compassion and mercy. (James 5:11)**

5 (1:10) **Father—Prayer**: they were parents who prayed. Zechariah was praying while he offered the incense up to God, and he had led the people to pray while he sought the Lord in their behalf (cp. v.13). He had led them to be a praying people. They were to be as involved in the prayer and worship as he was. (What a lesson for congregations!)

> **"Again, I tell you that if two of you on earth agree about anything you ask for, it will be done for you by my Father in heaven. (Mat 18:19)**
>
> **Look to the LORD and his strength; seek his face always. (1 Chr 16:11)**

He will call upon me, and I will answer him; I will be with him in trouble, I will deliver him and honor him. (Psa 91:15)

6 (1:11-17) **Parents—Blessings**: they were parents greatly favored by God. God is bound to bless and highly favor any parent...

- who is righteous or upright
- who worships
- who prays
- who leads others to worship and pray

God favored Zechariah and Elizabeth in five ways.

1. Their need was met by God in a very personal way. God sent an angel to Zechariah. Note the angel appeared on the right side of the altar of incense, the very place of prayer. It was while he was praying, in the act of obedience, that God met his need in this special way.

2. Their prayers were answered. Note the exact words of the Scripture: "Your prayer has been heard." What prayer?

⇒ Was Zechariah pouring his heart out about being childless, despite his age?

⇒ Was Zechariah praying for the redemption of Israel, for the coming of the Messiah?

Scripture does not say. But *both* prayers were now being answered. Elizabeth was to bear a son, and the Messiah was to be born. Their son was to be named John which means *the grace of Jehovah.*

3. Their son was to be great.

a. He would cause his parents to rejoice because of his *life*. He was to be everything that parents could want in a child. He would not shame them, but he would bring joy to their hearts.

b. He would cause many to rejoice because of his *contribution* to society. He would bring joy to all their friends, and he would bring joy to the nation as a whole. Many would joy in such a commitment and contribution as his.

c. He would be great in the sight of God Himself, great because of his *faithfulness* (obedience). He would be like one of the great prophets of old.

d. He would live a *disciplined* and *controlled* life, abstaining from wine and strong drink and from the very appearance of evil.

e. He would be filled with the *Holy Spirit* from the very first, a vessel chosen by God for a very special service, *fitted* in a very special way.

Thought 1. Note the five traits that made John great. How desperately believers need the same traits in their own lives.

Therefore, I urge you, brothers, in view of God's mercy, to offer your bodies as living sacrifices, holy and pleasing to God—this is your spiritual act of worship. Do not conform any longer to the pattern of this world, but be transformed by the renewing of your mind. Then you will be able to test and approve what God's will is—his good, pleasing and perfect will. (Rom 12:1-2)

I thank Christ Jesus our Lord, who has given me strength, that he considered me faithful, appointing me to his service. (1 Tim 1:12)

Thought 2. The point to see about Zechariah and Elizabeth is that God did hear their prayer and bless them richly. He favored them because they were faithful to Him.

If you remain in me and my words remain in you, ask whatever you wish, and it will be given you. (John 15:7)

And receive from him anything we ask, because we obey his commands and do what pleases him. (1 John 3:22)

4. Their son was to be a prophet, turning many to the Lord God.

5. Their son was to be the forerunner of the promised Messiah. His ministry was to be like that of Elijah, the greatest of the prophets (Mal.4:5; cp. Mt.17:10).

7 (1:18-19) **Parents—Promises—Faith, Weakness of**: they were parents who found it difficult to believe the humanly impossible. Note two things.

1. Zechariah just could not believe the message and the promise of God. He had been praying, but apparently he had not thought God would answer, certainly not by doing the impossible—by overruling the laws of nature. Note that Zechariah's question was the question of unbelief. He asked the very same question asked by Abraham (Gen.15:8), but Zechariah asked the question in a spirit of unbelief. He informed the angel that he and Elizabeth were too old to have children.

2. The very Word and promise of God should have been enough to convince Zechariah, but he was weak in faith. He had to ask for additional assurance. He asked for a sign—a sign other than *God's Word and promise* (see DEEPER STUDY # 1, Gabriel—Lk.1:19).

DEEPER STUDY # 1

(1:19) **Gabriel**: means the *man of God* or the *hero of God* or the *mighty one of God.* Note that Gabriel said two things about himself...

1. He is the one who actually stands in the presence of God.

2. He is the one who brings good news to men.

⇒ He shared the restoration of Israel with Daniel (Dan.8:16; 9:21f).

⇒ He shared the birth of the forerunner with Zechariah (Lk.1:13f).

⇒ He shared the birth of the Messiah with Mary (Lk.1:26f).

8 (1:20-22) **Distrust—Unbelief—Discipline of God**: they were parents who had to be disciplined by God. Zechariah had failed to believe God; therefore, he had to be disciplined and taught to grow in trust more and more.

1. Zechariah had asked for a sign. He had let his tongue speak instead of his heart. Therefore, God gave him a sign—the sign of stopping his tongue during the nine months before John was born.

2. Zechariah had failed to receive the Word of God. Therefore, God took away his ability to share the Word to men.

3. Zechariah had spoken words of distrust and unbelief; therefore, God saved him from speaking any more words of distrust and unbelief.

Thought 1. Every true child of God knows the discipline of God's hand. His discipline differs with each of us, but each of us can recognize His discipline nevertheless (see outline and notes—Heb.12:5-13).

And you have forgotten that word of encouragement that addresses you as sons: "My son, do not make light of the Lord's discipline, and do not lose heart when he rebukes you, because the Lord disciplines those he loves, and he punishes everyone he accepts as a son." (Heb 12:5-6)

Those whom I love I rebuke and discipline. So be earnest, and repent. (Rev 3:19)

Know then in your heart that as a man disciplines his son, so the LORD your God disciplines you. (Deu 8:5)

Blessed is the man you discipline, O LORD, the man you teach from your law; (Psa 94:12)

My son, do not despise the Lord's discipline and do not resent his rebuke, because the LORD disciplines those he loves, as a father the son he delights in. (Prov 3:11-12)

Correct me, LORD, but only with justice— not in your anger, lest you reduce me to nothing. (Jer 10:24)

Thought 2. God will not allow man to disbelieve and distrust forever. The day is coming when he will stop all disbelief and distrust just as He did with Zechariah.

Note that Zechariah tarried in the temple much longer than usual. The people became restless, wondering what had happened. When he came out, he was supposed to lead the people in a benediction, but he was unable to speak. All he could do was motion with his hand. Note a significant lesson: the people could tell Zechariah had been in the presence of God. They thought he had seen a vision. Despite Zechariah's unbelief, he had still lived a faithful life before God; therefore, God still met him and gave His promise to Zechariah and Elizabeth.

Thought 1. What hope for us all, even when our faith is weak!

9 (1:23-25) **Promises—Seeking God**: they were parents who saw God fulfill His promise. But note: these parents did two things that reveal why God was able to bless them.

1. They were responsible. Zechariah was sick; he had lost his voice completely. Yet he fulfilled his duties despite being disciplined with the infirmity. He did what he could, responsibly and faithfully. What an example!

2. They withdrew into the presence of God. After Zechariah completed his duties, he and his dear wife returned home. Of course, Zechariah would stick close to home, walking in meditation and prayer because of his experience and being unable to talk with others. But note especially Elizabeth's behavior. She hid herself for five months. Why? For the same reason any of us would withdraw after being visited by such an angelic being with so great a message. She needed time alone with God to absorb all that was happening and to prepare herself for the rearing of one who was destined to be so greatly used by God.

Note how the thought that she was hiding her pregnancy from the public is inaccurate. She hid herself only for the first five months of her pregnancy. She became public after the five months (cp. v.39-40, 57).

Thought 1. Note a crucial point. The call to special service necessitates a period of preparation, especially the preparation of oneself in the presence of God. Time alone with God for meditation and prayer over God's call is essential.

'Even now,' declares the LORD, 'return to me with all your heart, with fasting and weeping and mourning.' Rend your heart and not your garments. Return to the LORD your God, for he is gracious and compassionate, slow to anger and abounding in love, and he relents from sending calamity. (Joel 2:12-13)

Let us draw near to God with a sincere heart in full assurance of faith, having our hearts sprinkled to cleanse us from a guilty conscience and having our bodies washed with pure water. (Heb 10:22)

Come near to God and he will come near to you. Wash your hands, you sinners, and purify your hearts, you double-minded. (James 4:8)

Is any one of you in trouble? He should pray. Is anyone happy? Let him sing songs of praise. (James 5:13)

The LORD is close to the broken-hearted and saves those who are crushed in spirit. (Psa 34:18)

Have mercy on me, O God, have mercy on me, for in you my soul takes refuge. I will take refuge in the shadow of your wings until the disaster has passed. (Psa 57:1)

	C. Mary, the Mother of Jesus: Submission to God's Will, 1:26-38 (cp. Mt.1:18-25)
1 **The angel Gabriel** a. Was sent from God b. Was sent to the most obscure place	26 In the sixth month, God sent the angel Gabriel to Nazareth, a town in Galilee,
2 **Mary was pure, a virgin**[DS1]	27 To a virgin pledged to be married to a man named Joseph, a descendant of David. The virgin's name was Mary.
3 **Mary was highly favored by God**	28 The angel went to her and said, "Greetings, you who are highly favored! The Lord is with you."
4 **Mary was very human** a. Greatly troubled	29 Mary was greatly troubled at his words and wondered what kind of greeting this might be.
b. Fearful	30 But the angel said to her, "Do not be afraid, Mary, you have found favor with God.
5 **Mary was told she was to bear the Messiah** a. His name: Jesus[DS2]	31 You will be with child and give birth to a son, and you are to give him the name Jesus.
b. His great person 1) Son of the Most High 2) Son of David[DS3]	32 He will be great and will be called the Son of the Most High. The Lord God will give him the throne of his father David,
c. His eternal kingdom	33 And he will reign over the house of Jacob forever; his kingdom will never end."
6 **Mary was expected to believe the miraculous** a. Her perplexity	34 "How will this be," Mary asked the angel, "since I am a virgin?"
b. Her conception: By the Holy Spirit & the power of God c. Her child: The Son of God	35 The angel answered, "The Holy Spirit will come upon you, and the power of the Most High will overshadow you. So the holy one to be born will be called the Son of God.
7 **Mary was encouraged to believe: "For nothing is impossible with God"** a. God's other miracle	36 Even Elizabeth your relative is going to have a child in her old age, and she who was said to be barren is in her sixth month.
b. God's great power	37 For nothing is impossible with God."
8 **Mary was submissive**	38 "I am the Lord's servant," Mary answered. "May it be to me as you have said." Then the angel left her.

DIVISION I

THE ANNOUNCEMENT OF THE COMING OF JESUS, THE SON OF MAN, 1:1-2:52

C. Mary, the Mother of Jesus: Submission to God's Will, 1:26-38

(1:26-38) **Introduction**: little information is given about Mary in the Bible. However, what is said is striking and sets before us a tremendous example of *submissiveness to God's will*. Submissiveness to God is an absolute essential for every believer.

1. The angel Gabriel (v.26).
2. Mary was pure, a virgin (v.27).
3. Mary was highly favored by God (v.28).
4. Mary was very human (v.29-30).
5. Mary was told she was to bear the Messiah (v.31-33).
6. Mary was expected to believe the miraculous (v.34-35).
7. Mary was encouraged to believe: "For nothing is impossible with God" (v.36-37).
8. Mary was submissive (v.38).

1 (1:26) **Nazareth—Gabriel**: the angel Gabriel was sent from God. This was Gabriel's second mission surrounding the birth of Jesus (see DEEPER STUDY # 1—Lk.1:19). Note the time is given. It was six months after Elizabeth's conception that Gabriel was sent to an obscure village, Nazareth of Galilee. Galilee bordered Gentile or heathen nations; therefore, it was sometimes called Galilee of the Gentiles. Nazareth was a despised city, considered inferior by the rest of Israel. The people were a conquered people especially despised by the Romans. The city and its citizens were the object of deep prejudice by Jews and Romans alike (cp. Jn.1:46). (See DEEPER STUDY # 4, Nazareth—Mt.2:23; 13:53-58.)

Thought 1. God is no respecter of persons or places. He sends a message to Nazareth as readily as He does to Jerusalem (cp. Lk.1:5-25), to a believer in Nazareth (Mary) as quickly as he does to a believer in Jerusalem (Zechariah).

Thought 2. A place, whether city or nation, is not judged by its institutions and advantages, but by the righteous people within its borders (cp. Gen.18:23f).

2 (1:27) **Jesus Christ, Birth—Mary—Betrothed—Espoused—Purity**: Mary was pure, a virgin. She had never been touched by a man, not immorally. This is unmistakably and clearly stated. She confirmed the fact herself (cp. v.34).

1. The argument that the Hebrew word "alma" means a young woman who could have a questionable character is weak (Is.7:14). When a Hebrew spoke of a young woman (alma) he meant virgin. This is clear when the word *alma* is studied. The word is used six times in the Bible, always referring to a young woman with pure character.

⇒ Rebekah, the young woman, was certainly a virgin (Gen.24:43). The whole context verifies the point.

⇒ Miriam, the young sister of Moses, was also pointed to as a virgin by the context (Ex.2:8).

⇒ Young women of pure character were those who were worthy to participate in the worship of God (Ps.68:25).

⇒ The young women who were worthy of Solomon's love were not of impure character (Song of Sol.1:3).
⇒ There were young women who were compared with queens and concubines (Song of Sol.6:8).
⇒ The maiden (young woman) of Proverbs was contrasted with the adulterous woman (Pr.30:19-20).

In view of the heavy weight of this argument, the logical translation of *alma* is virgin. Of course, the virgin birth does not rest on this argument. However, we need to realize that unbelief snatches at every little gnat, trying its best to add every thing it can to disprove the divinity of Christ.

Thought 1. Man desperately needs to turn from his unbelief and to trust Christ with all his heart. There is little time left for any of us.

"For God so loved the world that he gave his one and only Son, that whoever believes in him shall not perish but have eternal life. (John 3:16)

Just as man is destined to die once, and after that to face judgment, (Heb 9:27)

2. Mary was espoused to Joseph. Being espoused was something like an engagement, except it was more binding. It lasted one year. Two matters are important in discussing Mary's virginity.

a. In the espousal period sexual contact was adultery and resulted in stoning.
b. The espousal was so serious a matter that if it were broken a divorce had to be secured.

3. Mary and Joseph were both godly, so godly that God could choose them to be the parents of His Son. It was impossible that God would have chosen an immoral man and woman to bear and rear His Son, not when He had the power to control the events.

Thought 1. There are two striking lessons in the purity of Mary.

1) God expects both women and men to be sexually pure, untouched by a man or woman until they are married.
2) God is looking for pure women and men to use in the ministry of the gospel and in meeting the desperate needs of the world.

It is God's will that you should be sanctified: that you should avoid sexual immorality; that each of you should learn to control his own body in a way that is holy and honorable, For God did not call us to be impure, but to live a holy life. (1 Th 4:3-4, 7)

Now for the matters you wrote about: It is good for a man not to marry. But since there is so much immorality, each man should have his own wife, and each woman her own husband. (1 Cor 7:1-2)

But among you there must not be even a hint of sexual immorality, or of any kind of impurity, or of greed, because these are improper for God's holy people. (Eph 5:3)

Do not be hasty in the laying on of hands, and do not share in the sins of others. Keep yourself pure. (1 Tim 5:22)

Likewise, teach the older women to be reverent in the way they live, not to be slanderers or addicted to much wine, but to teach what is good. Then they can train the younger women to love their husbands and children, to be self-controlled and pure, to be busy at home, to be kind, and to be subject to their husbands, so that no one will malign the word of God. (Titus 2:3-5)

"You have heard that it was said, 'Do not commit adultery.' But I tell you that anyone who looks at a woman lustfully has already committed adultery with her in his heart. (Mat 5:27-28)

These are those who did not defile themselves with women, for they kept themselves pure. They follow the Lamb wherever he goes. They were purchased from among men and offered as firstfruits to God and the Lamb. (Rev 14:4)

Who may ascend the hill of the LORD? Who may stand in his holy place? He who has clean hands and a pure heart, who does not lift up his soul to an idol or swear by what is false. (Psa 24:3-4)

DEEPER STUDY # 1

(1:27) **Jesus Christ, Virgin Birth**: in looking at the virgin birth of Christ, man needs to think deeply and honestly. Both are necessary: man must be honest, and he must engage in concentrated thought. One question needs to be asked. Why would God's Son have to enter the world through a virgin? Or more simply put, why was Christ born of a virgin? Why was a virgin birth necessary? (Note: Mary confirmed that she was a virgin, v.34.)

1. The birth of God's Son required a miracle. He could not be born through the natural process as other men are. If He had been born as other men, His very birth would indicate that He was no more than mere man. Very simply, any person who enters the world through a man and a woman is a mere man or a mere woman. He or she can be nothing more. But this is not so with Christ. Christ already existed. Therefore, if God willed to send His Son into the world, He would have to choose another way. All Christ needed was a body. As He Himself said to God the Father: "A body you prepared for me" (Heb.10:5).

2. The birth of God's Son required a combined act on God's part and on woman's part. If God's Son was to become a man and identify with men, He had to come through the process of conception through a woman. Why? Because man can only come through the woman. Therefore, if God willed to send His Son into the world as a man, He would have to perform a miracle, causing Mary to conceive by an act of His divine power.

Thought 1. A question needs to be asked. Why is it so hard to believe that God can cause Mary to miraculously conceive? Why is it so hard to believe that God exists and that "For God so loved the world that he gave his one and only Son, that whoever believes in him shall not perish, but have eternal life" (Jn.3:16)?

Thought 2. Just imagine what science can do in the fertilization of female eggs today. Is God not able to do so much more? How foolish our unbelief causes us to act. The problem is not God, but our faith: "For nothing is impossible with God" (Lk.1:37; 18:27. Cp. Heb.11:6, which is a warning to all.)

3. The birth of God's Son required a miraculous nature—both a divine nature and a human nature.

⇒ He had to be born of a woman to partake of human nature. (Cp. Heb.2:14-18.)

⇒ He had to be born by a miraculous act of God so as not to partake of man's corruption. This was critical if we are to escape corruption and live forever. Think about it. Our faith must be in an incorruptible Savior if we are to be covered by His incorruption. God had to identify with us by becoming one with us and by conquering our depraved and doomed nature. (See DEEPER STUDY # 3, Jesus Christ, Birth—Mt.1:16 for more discussion.)

4. The birth of God's Son required the birth of a perfect nature. Why? Because a perfect life needed to be lived. Righteousness, that is, perfection, needed to be secured. An Ideal Life (that is, a perfect, righteous life) had to be lived so that it could stand for and cover all men in perfection and in righteousness. Honest thought confesses that no man has been or is perfect. Man comes short. His *coming short* of God's glory is tragically pictured in the ultimate fate of life: death.

But God acted. God did everything to secure righteousness and perfection for man. He took every step and performed every act necessary to *save His people* from their sins and from death. He did it from beginning to end, from birth to exaltation. God sent His Son into the world, not through a man and a woman but through a miraculous act of His own upon the virgin Mary. Jesus Christ was thereby the God-Man. This says at least four things. (See notes—Ro.5:1; DEEPER STUDY # 2—8:3 for more discussion.)

a. As God-Man, Christ was able to consummate both the human and divine. He had the capacity and innate power not to sin (see DEEPER STUDY # 3—Mt.1:16). Therefore His Godly nature empowered Him to live righteously, never doing wrong and always choosing and doing right (Heb.5:8; 2 Cor.5:21). By living a sinless life, Christ was able to secure righteousness, the Ideal Righteousness, that will cover and stand for all men.

b. As God-Man, Christ was also able to bear the sins and the judgment of sin for all men. When He died, He died as the Perfect and Ideal Man. Therefore, His death is able to cover and stand for all men.

c. As God-Man, Christ was able to arise from the dead. Note the phenomenal words: "regarding his Son, who as to his human nature was a descendant of David, and who through the Spirit of holiness was declared with power to be the Son of God by his resurrection from the dead: Jesus Christ our Lord" (Ro.1:3-4). He lived a perfect and holy life by which He became the Perfect and Ideal Man; therefore, His resurrection covers and stands for every man.

d. As God-Man, Christ was exalted to sit at the right hand of the Father—to live eternally in the heavenly dimension of being, in God's very own presence. As the Perfect and Ideal Man, His exaltation into the heavenly or spiritual dimension is able to blaze the path into heaven for every man. He is the forerunner into heaven for every man (Heb.6:20). His exaltation as the Ideal Man covers and stands for the exaltation of every man.

5. The birth of God's Son required the creative Word of God. God created the world by simply speaking the Word. God always creates by the power of His Word and the power of His Word alone. Therefore, when God chose...

- to create a body for His Son, He created that body by simply speaking the Word (Heb.10:5).
- to send His Son into the world, He sent His Son by simply speaking the Word.

It is the same with the new birth or the re-creation of man's spirit. It is by the Word of God, God's simply speaking the Word, that man is born again. The act of the spiritual birth, of the re-creation, is not seen, felt, or touched. Nothing physical happens, but the re-creation does occur. *It occurs by the Word of God* (cp. 1 Pt.1:23).

6. The birth of God's Son required the virgin birth because Christ is the *one and only* Son of God. He possesses all the nature and fulness of God Himself (Ph.2:6-7; Col.2:9). Therefore, His birth had to be different. He had to enter the world differently from others, for He is different by the very nature of His being. He had to enter the world in such a way as to proclaim His divine nature, yet in such a way that would allow Him to partake of human nature. This is critically important. His birth had to involve both the act of mankind and of God Himself. Why? Because the Son of God had to be proclaimed to be the Son of God.

⇒ There is no salvation apart from His *being* the Son of God.

⇒ There is no salvation apart from His being *proclaimed* to be the Son of God.

Man can be saved only if the Son of God *is*, only if He exists, and only if He is *proclaimed.* The Son of God must *exist*, and we must *hear* of Him if we are to be saved. He and His message are both essential. His virgin birth proclaims Him to be the *only begotten* Son of God, the only Son sent into the world by the direct and miraculous intervention of God.

7. The birth of God's Son required a second Adam, a second man...

- born just like the first Adam, by the Word of God using natural substance.
- born to become what the first Adam failed to become: the Representative Man, the Ideal Man, the Pattern, the Perfect One in whom all men could find their Representative, their Ideal, their Pattern, their Perfection.
- born to be what Adam failed to be: the Man who always chose to love and obey God in all things, thereby passing on the nature of the ideal righteousness and perfection that can stand for and cover all men.
- born to become what the first Adam failed to pass on to man: the Way to God, the Truth of God, and the Life of God which all men can trust and follow (Jn.14:6).
- born to offer what the first Adam failed to pass on to man: the nature of righteousness and life, both life abundant and life eternal (cp. Ro.5:15-19; Jn.10:10).

8. The birth of God's Son required an espoused state, and not a single or married state. Why?

⇒ Because a single woman would cause far more questioning and heap far more contempt upon Christ and His followers.

⇒ Because a married woman would not be a virgin and God's Son had to be born of a virgin as indicated by the points above.

The espoused state provided the ideal marital relationship for God to use in sending His Son into the world (see note 2—Lk.1:27). The fact that Jewish society was using the espoused relationship as a preparation for marriage shows how God was preparing the world for the coming of His Son. (See DEEPER STUDY # 1, Fulness of Time—Gal.4:4.)

But when the time had fully come, God sent his Son, born of a woman, born under law, (Gal 4:4)

3 (1:28) **Grace—God, Call of—Favored by God**: Mary was highly favored by God. Three simple, yet meaningful, things were said to Mary.

1. She was to be highly favored by God. Note the angel did not immediately tell Mary how she was to be favored by God, that she was God's choice to bear and to be the mother of the Messiah. That came later in the conversation. The angel had to give her time to adjust to the shock of his spectacular appearance. For right now, he simply announced that she was to be highly favored by God—*a unique privilege.*

Thought 1. Just think! God does *favor* us: He saves us, gifts us, uses us. We are favored by the God of the universe—a phenomenal privilege and an awesome responsibility to make ourselves available to receive His favors.

2. The Lord was also with Mary. She did not walk through life alone. God was with her. Mary's life had pleased God to the point that He could favor her and be with her. She allowed God to walk with her and look after her life, so God was able to be with her. This means that God...

- *had been* with her (past)
- *was* with her (present)
- *would be* with her (future)

No matter where Mary had to walk or what she had to do, God promised to be with her.

4 (1:29-30) **Humility**: Mary was very human. She was both troubled and stricken with fear. The fear was understandable, for an angelic being from God stood before her. He stood in all the dazzling splendor that is necessary to reveal that he was truly from God. The fact that Mary was *greatly troubled* needs to be briefly considered.

1. Mary was "greatly troubled at his words," at what the angel told her. It was the message that caused her to be troubled, the fact that...

- she was highly favored
- the Lord was with her
- she was blessed among women

Thought 1. Since Christ has come, every person can now...

- be highly favored by God
- have the Lord's presence
- be blessed among all others

2. Mary was troubled because she did not understand how God could so greatly favor a person like herself. She never expected to be greatly favored by Him. This was deep humility. Mary was not a proud, self-centered, flighty, or frivolous young lady who was conscious of herself or felt that she merited and deserved the attention of others. She was a young lady who loved God and had determined to live a pure and responsible life. Apparently, from her response throughout this passage, she had a sweet spirit that was full of softness, warmth, and tenderness, and was responsive and willing, subjective and giving, thoughtful and kind. However, Mary never dreamed she was anyone special. Therefore, when she heard that God was to favor her and use her in a very special way, she was troubled. How could she, so ordinary and humble, do anything special for God? What a striking example Mary was!

But he gives us more grace. That is why Scripture says: "God opposes the proud but gives grace to the humble." (James 4:6)

Has not my hand made all these things, and so they came into being?" declares the LORD. "This is the one I esteem: he who is humble and contrite in spirit, and trembles at my word. (Isa 66:2)

Though the LORD is on high, he looks upon the lowly, but the proud he knows from afar. (Psa 138:6)

5 (1:31-33) **Jesus Christ, Deity**: Mary was told by the angel how she was to be favored by God. She was to bear and be the mother of the Messiah. Note three startling and profound things about Mary's Son.

1. *His name.* Mary was actually told what she was to name the Messiah: Jesus (see DEEPER STUDY # 2, Jesus—Lk.1:31).

2. *His great person.*

a. He was to be called the Son of the Most High. The Highest, of course, is God. Therefore, Jesus is the Son of God, that is, of the very nature of God. He is "God over all, forever praised! Amen" (Ro.9:5).

b. He was to be the Son of David and was to receive the throne of David. He was of the line of David. This indicates that Mary was a descendant of David; therefore, Christ Himself would become a descendant of David (see DEEPER STUDY # 3—Lk.1:32-33).

3. *His eternal kingdom.* Jesus was to teach that His kingdom would not be of this earth, for nothing on this earth lasts (Jn.19:36). Therefore, the kingdom was to be spiritual, by which it would be eternal (see DEEPER STUDY # 3—Mt.19:23-24).

DEEPER STUDY # 2

(1:31) **Jesus** (iesous): Savior; He will save. The Hebrew form is *Joshua* (yasha), meaning Jehovah is salvation or He is the Savior. The idea is that of deliverance, of being saved from some terrible disaster that leads to perishing (cp. Jn.3:16). (Cp. Lk.9:23; Ro.8:3; Gal.1:4; Heb.2:14-18; 7:25.)

DEEPER STUDY # 3

(1:32-33) **Jesus Christ, Names—Titles, Son of David**: Christ is the Son of David, a descendant of David. Note two things.

1. Christ is to reign upon the throne of David. But it will not be the people who will give Him the throne. They will not allow Him to rule over them. The throne will be given to Him by God. God will be the One to place Him upon the throne and give Him the rule over the people (see note—Mt.1:1).

2. The promise of ruling over the house of Jacob and of possessing a kingdom forever apparently has both a literal and a spiritual meaning, both a temporal and eternal

meaning (see DEEPER STUDY # 3—Mt.19:23-24; note—Lk.3:24-31; DEEPER STUDY # 3—Jn.1:45; DEEPER STUDY # 4—1:49; note—Ro.11:1-36, esp. 11:25-36).

6 (1:34-35) **Jesus Christ, Birth; Deity; Son of God—Faith**: Mary was expected to believe the miraculous, but she was puzzled. She was not doubting or distrusting the message. She was not asking for some sign or proof like Zechariah (v.18). She was simply asking for more information. She was single and had never known a man sexually. How could she possibly bear a child without knowing a man? Note exactly what is said about her conception.

1. "The Holy Spirit will *come upon you*." The thought *is not after* the manner of men, but *after the manner* of God's Spirit. What is the manner or operation of God's Spirit? God's Spirit sets apart and activates, creates and re-creates by *the Word of God*. God's Spirit simply speaks and it is done (see DEEPER STUDY # 1, pt.5—Lk.1:27). There is no such idea as a *crude mating* between the Holy Spirit and Mary. God's Spirit simply speaks and it is done, no matter what is to be done. (How foolish are the *crude thoughts* and unbelief of men!)

2. "The power of the Most High [God] will overshadow you." God Himself was going to look after the whole matter. The child's conception and growth during pregnancy and His birth and life were under the shadow and wing of Almighty God. It was God's power that saw to the whole operation, not the presence or power of an angel or of a man or of any other creature.

3. The child born of Mary would *be holy*, "the Son of God." Note the most critical point: who "the Son of God" is.

⇒ He is "the holy One" born by the power and the Word and the will of God through the virgin Mary.

⇒ He is "the holy One" whom "God sent his Son, born of a woman" by His power, Word, and will (Gal.4:4).

Thought 1. Believers are to believe the miraculous.

> **He replied, "Because you have so little faith. I tell you the truth, if you have faith as small as a mustard seed, you can say to this mountain, 'Move from here to there' and it will move. Nothing will be impossible for you." (Mat 17:20)**
>
> **"'If you can'?" said Jesus. "Everything is possible for him who believes." (Mark 9:23)**
>
> **Commit your way to the LORD; trust in him and he will do this: (Psa 37:5)**
>
> **Trust in the LORD with all your heart and lean not on your own understanding; (Prov 3:5)**

7 (1:36-37) **Faith—God, Power of**: Mary was encouraged to believe that "nothing is impossible with God." God encouraged Mary with two *impossible* facts.

1. The news that her sister Elizabeth, who was beyond child-bearing age, had conceived a son in her old age and was now six months pregnant. The fact that God could take her sister in her old age and cause her to conceive demonstrated God's power. Visiting Elizabeth would encourage Mary.

2. With men much is impossible. To say that all things are possible with men is far from the truth. When Mary heard and meditated upon the simple statement that "all things are possible with God," she was bound to be encouraged. The statement was simple and striking. It could be easily remembered and understood.

Thought 1. God expects us to believe Him and His power, regardless of circumstances and our feelings of insignificance.

> **Jesus looked at them and said, "With man this is impossible, but with God all things are possible." (Mat 19:26)**
>
> **"I know that you can do all things; no plan of yours can be thwarted. (Job 42:2)**
>
> **Our God is in heaven; he does whatever pleases him. (Psa 115:3)**

8 (1:38) **Surrender**: Mary was submissive. Her response was immediate and brief, only one short sentence, yet it was striking and meaningful.

1. The word "servant" (doule) means slave-girl. Mary was saying that she was a bond-slave, willing to sell herself out completely to God. She would possess herself no longer but would give herself completely to God.

2. God's Word was her will. She surrendered totally to obey God. She would serve as He willed, being completely obedient and fulfilling His purpose entirely. She would act and do exactly what God had said ."

Imagine what Mary was saying, the enormous depth of her trust and dedication to God.

1. There was the idea of being an unwed mother (Lk.1:26f; Mt.1:18). Who of that day would ever believe Mary's story? Required was a willingness to be available to God regardless of the price.

2. There was Joseph's discovery of her pregnancy (Mt.1:19). The shock of broken trust and of personal embarrassment were more than a person could be expected to bear (Mt.1:20). Required was a willingness on Joseph's part to forget self completely.

3. There was the threat of being condemned to death because of adultery (Dt.22:23f). She had to face the possibility of being stoned because she would appear to be immoral (cp. Jn.8:5).

Thought 1. Surrender to God is an absolute essential both for salvation and service.

> **For whoever does the will of my Father in heaven is my brother and sister and mother." (Mat 12:50)**
>
> **In the same way, any of you who does not give up everything he has cannot be my disciple. (Luke 14:33)**
>
> **The world and its desires pass away, but the man who does the will of God lives forever. (1 John 2:17)**
>
> **I desire to do your will, O my God; your law is within my heart." (Psa 40:8)**
>
> **Teach me to do your will, for you are my God; may your good Spirit lead me on level ground. (Psa 143:10)**
>
> **My son, give me your heart and let your eyes keep to my ways, (Prov 23:26)**

	D. Elizabeth's Supernatural Proclamation: A Very Unusual Testimony, 1:39-45	42 In a loud voice she exclaimed: "Blessed are you among women, and blessed is the child you will bear!	with the Spirit 4) Spoke loudly **2 She proclaimed a uniqueness about Mary & her child**
1 Mary visited Elizabeth a. Went in a hurry b. Went to the town of Juda c. Entered Elizabeth's home & greeted her	39 At that time Mary got ready and hurried to a town in the hill country of Judea, 40 Where she entered Zechariah's home and greeted Elizabeth.	43 But why am I so favored, that the mother of my Lord should come to me? 44 As soon as the sound of your greeting reached my ears, the baby in my womb leaped for joy.	**3 She proclaimed that Mary's child was her Lord** a. The great confession b. The clear sign
d. Was welcomed by Elizabeth's supernatural proclamation 1) Heard Mary's greeting 2) Felt the baby leap 3) Was instantly filled	41 When Elizabeth heard Mary's greeting, the baby leaped in her womb, and Elizabeth was filled with the Holy Spirit.	45 Blessed is she who has believed that what the Lord has said to her will be accomplished!"	**4 She proclaimed that Mary's faith would receive the promise**

DIVISION I

THE ANNOUNCEMENT OF THE COMING OF JESUS, THE SON OF MAN, 1:1-2:52

D. Elizabeth's Supernatural Proclamation: A Very Unusual Testimony, 1:39-45

(1:39-45) **Introduction**: whatever confession was borne about the Baby conceived in Mary was of critical importance. Why? Because the baby was...

- Jesus (v.31).
- The Son of the Most High (v.32).
- The Son of David (v.32).
- The Ruler over the house of Jacob forever (v.33).
- The Ruler whose kingdom will never end (v.33).
- The One born of the Holy Spirit (v.35).
- The Son of God Himself (v.35).

In this passage God sees to it that a supernatural confession is proclaimed, a crucial confession that needs to be studied in depth. Note that this is the very first testimony ever given by human lips about Jesus.

1. Mary visited Elizabeth (v.39-42).
2. Elizabeth proclaimed a uniqueness about Mary and her child (v.42).
3. Elizabeth proclaimed the child to be her Lord (v.43-44).
4. Elizabeth proclaimed that Mary's faith would receive the promise (v.45).

1 (1:39-42) **Encouragement—Comfort—Trials**: Mary visited Elizabeth, and her visit was memorable. She hurried (spoudes). The word means speed, diligence, care, earnestness, zeal. The idea is that Mary went with purpose and earnestness. She was not going on a casual, friendly visit. She had a very specific reason for going, a meaningful purpose. She was going so that she and Elizabeth could encourage and share with each other. They both had similar situations. God had acted upon both their bodies, performing a miracle for both. Elizabeth's womb was made alive for the son of Zechariah to be conceived, and Mary's womb had conceived as a virgin. Mary in particular could be encouraged, for Elizabeth was already six months pregnant. The six months' pregnancy was visible evidence that God had already acted upon her miraculously. It should be noted that Mary knew about Elizabeth's miraculous conception, but Elizabeth did not know about Mary's conception. Zechariah and Elizabeth lived in Juda. The town is unknown today, but most commentators think it was the same as Hebron. Hebron is said to be in the hill country of Juda and to belong to the priests (Josh. 21:10-11).

Mary entered Elizabeth's home and greeted her. It was at the *very moment* of Mary's greeting that Elizabeth's supernatural greeting began. Mary greeted Elizabeth, and three unusual things immediately happened.

1. The baby leaped in Elizabeth's womb. The baby had leaped or kicked before, but this leap was different from all the others. It was a sign to Elizabeth that the Baby within Mary was someone very, very special, someone who was about to be revealed to her under the filling (influence) of the Holy Spirit.

2. Elizabeth was instantly "filled with the Holy Spirit," and a very special spirit of prophecy was given her. The Holy Spirit seized her and led her to greet Mary as the mother of the Messiah, the coming Lord. Note: Elizabeth was living an obedient life before God. This was the reason God was able to use her and the Holy Spirit was able to infill her with His presence.

3. Elizabeth spoke in a loud voice. She was full of joy and exaltation for the Messiah, full of unusual emotions. She was under the influence and impulse of the Spirit of God. She was being guided to proclaim that the Baby of Mary was "the Lord" (v.43, 45).

2 (1:42) **Jesus Christ, Honored—Mary, Blessed—Humility—Envy**: Elizabeth proclaimed a uniqueness about Mary and her child. Note three things.

1. The very first act toward Christ was a *proclamation of praise*. Elizabeth was the *first* person to know about the birth of Christ other than Mary, and God saw to it that her first act was to honor His Son. God would have His Son to be honored on earth even as He is honored in heaven.

> **Through Jesus, therefore, let us continually offer to God a sacrifice of praise—the fruit of lips that confess his name. (Heb 13:15)**
>
> **But you are a chosen people, a royal priesthood, a holy nation, a people belonging to God, that you may declare the praises of him who called you out of darkness into his wonderful light. (1 Pet 2:9)**

2. Mary was blessed, but she was blessed because of the child she was to bear: the child was blessed.

3. Elizabeth demonstrated a very sweet and humble spirit, a meekness and love that were so desperately needed by so many. She was older, and by being the wife of a priest, she was recognized by the world as being of a higher social class and more honorable. Yet Mary, poor and unrecognized by the world, had been chosen by God to serve in a more special way. Elizabeth showed no envy or jealousy, no hurt or withdrawal. Contrariwise, she rejoiced over Mary's call.

> **Do nothing out of selfish ambition or vain conceit, but in humility consider others better than yourselves. Each of you should look not only to your own interests, but also to the interests of others. (Phil 2:3-4)**

3 (1:43-44) **Confession—Jesus Christ, Deity**: Elizabeth proclaimed the child to be her Lord.

1. Note the great confession of Elizabeth. Elizabeth called Mary's Baby, "my Lord." In a moment of quickening power, the Holy Spirit revealed that the Baby was not only the promised Messiah, but He was the Son of the Most High, of God Himself (Lk.1:32, 35). There was no question that Elizabeth was using the term "Lord" in its highest sense. She was under the power of the Holy Spirit; therefore, she was confessing the truth under the influence of God. The truth was that the coming Child of Mary was the Messiah, the Son of the living God. She was also contrasting her son with the Son of Mary. Her own son was to be great, but the Son of Mary was greater. He was *her Lord*, the Lord God Himself, the Son of the Most High.

2. Note the clear sign given to Elizabeth. The sign was unmistakable. Upon hearing the greeting of Mary as she entered the door, Elizabeth's heart leaped for joy and the baby in her womb leaped much more than usual. In Elizabeth's words, "The baby in my womb leaped *for joy* [exultation]." God caused the baby to leap (the word is strong, indicating a struggling leap) as a sign of great joy in the presence of One so great that Elizabeth would call Him "my Lord."

Thought 1. Elizabeth's confession of her Lord was a very personal thing. She apparently never shared it with John. John did not know Jesus was the Messiah until Jesus' baptism (Jn.1:31-34). John had to discover and confess Christ for himself. So do we all. It is a *personal* decision.

> **"Whoever acknowledges me before men, I will also acknowledge him before my Father in heaven. (Mat 10:32)**
>
> **"But what about you?" he asked. "Who do you say I am?" Simon Peter answered, "You are the Christ, the Son of the living God." Jesus replied, "Blessed are you, Simon son of Jonah, for this was not revealed to you by man, but by my Father in heaven. (Mat 16:15-17)**
>
> **If anyone acknowledges that Jesus is the Son of God, God lives in him and he in God. (1 John 4:15)**

Thought 2. Elizabeth's confession was bound to encourage Mary.

1) *God sees to it that we are encouraged* when we need encouragement. Mary needed assurance, so God took her where she could be assured. But note: she obeyed God. She went where God led her. It was while she was obeying that God was able to encourage her.

> **And even the very hairs of your head are all numbered. So don't be afraid; you are worth more than many sparrows. (Mat 10:30-31)**
>
> **For I am the LORD, your God, who takes hold of your right hand and says to you, Do not fear; I will help you. (Isa 41:13)**
>
> **But now, this is what the LORD says— he who created you, O Jacob, he who formed you, O Israel: "Fear not, for I have redeemed you; I have summoned you by name; you are mine. (Isa 43:1)**

2) Elizabeth willingly humbled herself to help Mary. She was older and held a higher position as the wife of a priest, yet she denied and surrendered herself to push Mary and her child forward.

> **In everything I did, I showed you that by this kind of hard work we must help the weak, remembering the words the Lord Jesus himself said: 'It is more blessed to give than to receive.'" (Acts 20:35)**
>
> **Rejoice with those who rejoice; mourn with those who mourn. (Rom 12:15)**
>
> **We who are strong ought to bear with the failings of the weak and not to please ourselves. (Rom 15:1)**
>
> **Carry each other's burdens, and in this way you will fulfill the law of Christ. (Gal 6:2)**

4 (1:45) **Faith—Promise**: Elizabeth proclaimed that Mary's faith would receive the promise. Note two significanct points.

1. There are two reasons why Mary has been blessed by believers of every generation.

a. Mary believed the Word of God sent to her (Lk.1:38). Contrast her belief with Zechariah's unbelief (Lk.1:20).

b. Mary was related to Christ in a very, very special way.

Thought 1. The same two facts are essential for us if we wish to be blessed by God.

1) We must believe the Word of God sent to us.

> **He replied, "Blessed rather are those who hear the word of God and obey it." (Luke 11:28)**
>
> **Jesus replied, "If anyone loves me, he will obey my teaching. My Father will love him, and we will come to him and make our home with him. (John 14:23)**
>
> **If you remain in me and my words remain in you, ask whatever you wish,**

and it will be given you. (John 15:7)

And we also thank God continually because, when you received the word of God, which you heard from us, you accepted it not as the word of men, but as it actually is, the word of God, which is at work in you who believe. (1 Th 2:13)

If anyone is ashamed of me and my words in this adulterous and sinful generation, the Son of Man will be ashamed of him when he comes in his Father's glory with the holy angels." (Mark 8:38)

2) We must become related to Christ by adoption. We must become the adopted children of God.

But when the time had fully come, God sent his Son, born of a woman, born under law, to redeem those under law, that we might receive the full rights of sons. Because you are sons, God sent the Spirit of his Son into our hearts, the Spirit who calls out, *"Abba,* Father." (Gal 4:4-6)

2. The result of Mary's believing the Word of God was that she was to see the performance of God's promises, the things told her from the Lord.

Through these he has given us his very great and precious promises, so that through them you may participate in the divine nature and escape the corruption in the world caused by evil desires. (2 Pet 1:4)

Know therefore that the LORD your God is God; he is the faithful God, keeping his covenant of love to a thousand generations of those who love him and keep his commands. (Deu 7:9)

He remembers his covenant forever, the word he commanded, for a thousand generations, (Psa 105:8)

Outline	Scripture	Scripture (cont.)	Outline (cont.)
	E. Mary's Magnificent Song About God: God's Glorious Mercy & Deliverance, 1:46-56	51 He has performed mighty deeds with his arm; he has scattered those who are proud in their inmost thoughts.	**4 God had reversed the order of things on earth** a. Had scattered the proud
		52 He has brought down rulers from their thrones but has lifted up the humble.	b. Had dethroned the mighty & exalted the humble
1 God was the subject of her song	46 And Mary said: "My soul glorifies the Lord		
2 God was her Savior	47 And my spirit rejoices in God my Savior,	53 He has filled the hungry with good things but has sent the rich away empty.	c. Had filled the hungry & emptied the rich
a. Had considered her low estate b. Causes her to be remembered	48 For he has been mindful of the humble state of his servant. From now on all generations will call me blessed,	54 He has helped his servant Israel, remembering to be merciful	**5 God had helped His people** a. Remembered His mercy
3 God was to be proclaimed a. His power b. His holiness	49 For the Mighty One has done great things for me—holy is his name.	55 To Abraham and his descendants forever, even as he said to our fathers."	b. Remembered promise to send the Messiah
c. His mercy	50 His mercy extends to those who fear him, from generation to generation.	56 Mary stayed with Elizabeth for about three months and then returned home.	**6 Conclusion: Mary visited Elizabeth for about three months**

DIVISION I

THE ANNOUNCEMENT OF THE COMING OF JESUS, THE SON OF MAN, 1:1-2:52

E. Mary's Magnificent Song About God: God's Glorious Mercy and Deliverance, 1:46-56

(1:46-56) **Introduction**: Mary's song is known as the *Magnificat*. It has some similarity to the Song of Hannah (1 Sam.2:1-10). However, there is a striking difference between the two songs. Hannah proclaimed a triumph over her enemies; Mary proclaimed God and His glorious mercy to man. Mary was proclaiming the salvation of God, a salvation wrought through the promised Messiah, her Savior. She predicted that the Savior would be welcomed by those who reverenced Him (v.50); but He would be rejected by the proud, the powerful, and the rich (v.51-53).

1. God was the subject of her song (v.46).
2. God was her Savior (v.47-48).
3. God was to be proclaimed (v.49-50).
4. God had reversed the order of things on earth (v.51-53).
5. God had helped His people (v.54-55).
6. Conclusion: Mary visited Elizabeth for about three months (v.56).

1 (1:46) **Praise of God**: God was the subject of Mary's song. Mary was not singing about herself; she was not praising herself. She was not thinking about things which she might accomplish. She said very definitely, "My soul glorifies the Lord." The Lord was the subject of her song, the subject of her praise and rejoicing. Note two things.

1. Mary was bound to be tired and exhausted. She had just arrived from a long trip and had not even had time to sit down. As soon as she walked in the door, Elizabeth began her proclamation of praise under the inspiration of the Holy Spirit. Mary's song followed right on the heels of Elizabeth's song. Mary forgot her tiredness, for her faith was being confirmed. She now knew that the angel who had come to her was not a figment of her imagination, not an illusion, not a false vision, not some dreamy state of mind (v.28). He was real; and his message that she, as a virgin, would bear the Son of God was true. Her faith was reassured and confirmed.

Thought 1. God assures and confirms the faith of us all. We believe and trust, and as the need arises, God steps in to confirm the reality of what we believe.

Know therefore that the LORD your God is God; he is the faithful God, keeping his covenant of love to a thousand generations of those who love him and keep his commands. (Deu 7:9)

Thought 2. The one thing that can overcome tiredness and exhaustion is an experience with God. More than anything else, the experience of *genuine* prayer and seeking God will cause a person to forget tiredness of body. How desperately we need to seek God!

"Come to me, all you who are weary and burdened, and I will give you rest. (Mat 11:28)

2. The word "glorify" (megalunei) means to declare the greatness of. The idea is habitual; that is, it was the habit of Mary's soul to glorify the Lord. She kept on glorifying Him.

Thought 1. Mary was greatly blessed by God, yet she did not slip into the sin of pride, nor did she think that she was a favorite of God. The more we are blessed by God, the more dangerous the sin of pride becomes. We must learn to live praising God more and more. The more He blesses us, the more we must learn to praise Him.

But you are a chosen people, a royal priesthood, a holy nation, a people belonging to God, that you may declare the praises of him who called you out of darkness into his wonderful light. (1 Pet 2:9)

Sing praises to the LORD, enthroned in Zion; proclaim among the nations what he has done. (Psa 9:11)

Enter his gates with thanksgiving and his courts with praise; give thanks to him and praise his name. (Psa 100:4)

2 (1:47-48) **Humility**: God was Mary's Savior. Mary said three significant things.

1. God saw her need for a Savior. Mary recognized her need, that she was a sinner and needed a Savior just like everyone else. And, more importantly, she made a *personal confession*: "God is *my* Savior." She was proclaiming that God saw her need and saved her.

2. God saw her low estate. Mary recognized where she had come from, just how lowly a person she was. In the eyes of the world, she was a *nobody: poor, obscure, unknown, insignificant,* of *little purpose* and *meaning* in life. The very expression "the humble state of his servant" suggests that Mary was even considered the least within her own household.

> **Thought 1.** God usually chooses the least person to more clearly demonstrate His mercy and power (cp. Gideon, Judg.6:15; Leah, Gen.29:31; believers, 1 Cor.1:26-29).
>
> **Thought 2.** We must all know where we have come from, just how far down we were when God saved us (Ro.3:23).
>
> **But God demonstrates his own love for us in this: While we were still sinners, Christ died for us. (Rom 5:8)**
>
> **Here is a trustworthy saying that deserves full acceptance: Christ Jesus came into the world to save sinners—of whom I am the worst. (1 Tim 1:15)**
>
> **For Christ died for sins once for all, the righteous for the unrighteous, to bring you to God. He was put to death in the body but made alive by the Spirit, (1 Pet 3:18)**
>
> **Thought 3.** No matter how *low*, how *nothing* we may be, God cares and will reach down and out to us. He will take us by the hand, lift us up, and give us purpose, meaning, and significance. God will make us somebody and use us, giving us a full and meaningful life (Jn.10:10).
>
> **Humble yourselves before the Lord, and he will lift you up. (James 4:10)**
>
> **For this is what the high and lofty One says— he who lives forever, whose name is holy: "I live in a high and holy place, but also with him who is contrite and lowly in spirit, to revive the spirit of the lowly and to revive the heart of the contrite. (Isa 57:15)**

3. God will cause her to be remembered. All believers will highly esteem her and her great dedication to God. But note what Christ said:

> **As Jesus was saying these things, a woman in the crowd called out, "Blessed is the mother who gave you birth and nursed you." He replied, "Blessed rather are those who hear the word of God and obey it." (Luke 11:27-28)**

3 (1:49-50) **God, Attributes**: God was to be proclaimed. Mary proclaimed three of the glorious attributes of God.

1. Mary proclaimed God's power. Two things in particular were in her mind, two phenomenal things.

a. The promised Messiah was *now* to be born. The hope of the world was now to be fulfilled after so many generations of waiting. God's power was now to be demonstrated in a way never before witnessed.

b. The promised Messiah was to be born of a virgin. It was to be an event and a method never before witnessed. A miracle was to be performed! The enormous power of God was to be demonstrated *even in the birth of the Messiah*! As Mary testified, "the Mighty One has done great things for me."

> **When he came near the place where the road goes down the Mount of Olives, the whole crowd of disciples began joyfully to praise God in loud voices for all the miracles they had seen: (Luke 19:37)**
>
> **O Lord, open my lips, and my mouth will declare your praise. (Psa 51:15)**
>
> **Let them sacrifice thank offerings and tell of his works with songs of joy. (Psa 107:22)**

2. Mary proclaimed God's holiness: "holy is his name"; that is, God is to be set apart as different from all others (see note and DEEPER STUDY # 1—1 Pt.1:15-16). His very nature, His very being is different. God is both pure being and pure in being, both perfect being and perfect in being. God is holy in name and holy in being, set apart and different from all others.

> **"Who among the gods is like you, O LORD? Who is like you— majestic in holiness, awesome in glory, working wonders? (Exo 15:11)**
>
> **Exalt the LORD our God and worship at his holy mountain, for the LORD our God is holy. (Psa 99:9)**

3. Mary proclaimed God's mercy. There were at least two thoughts in Mary's mind.

a. God's glorious mercy to her. He had proven to be her personal Savior (see note—Lk.1:47-48).

> **Because of the Lord's great love we are not consumed, for his compassions never fail. They are new every morning; great is your faithfulness. (Lam 3:22-23)**
>
> **Who is a God like you, who pardons sin and forgives the transgression of the remnant of his inheritance? You do not stay angry forever but delight to show mercy. (Micah 7:18)**

b. God's glorious mercy in finally sending the Messiah (Savior) to those who feared (reverenced) Him. Note that Mary saw God's mercy passing down from generation to generation.

> **Giving thanks to the Father, who has qualified you to share in the inheritance of the saints in the kingdom of light. For he has rescued us from the**

dominion of darkness and brought us into the kingdom of the Son he loves, (Col 1:12-13)

Give thanks in all circumstances, for this is God's will for you in Christ Jesus. (1 Th 5:18)

Through Jesus, therefore, let us continually offer to God a sacrifice of praise—the fruit of lips that confess his name. (Heb 13:15)

But from everlasting to everlasting the Lord's love is with those who fear him, and his righteousness with their children's children— (Psa 103:17)

For great is your love, higher than the heavens; your faithfulness reaches to the skies. (Psa 108:4)

4 (1:51-53) **God, Sovereignty—Power**: God had reversed the order of things on earth. Mary proclaimed what the results of the Messiah's coming were to be. There were to be three results, and all three are given in the Greek aorist tense; that is, they are proclaimed as having already happened. Mary saw into the future, and standing there in the future, she proclaimed what the Messiah's coming had already done.

What Mary saw was that the Lord had reversed the order of things on earth. And note: He had done it with "His arm," that is, not by love but by power.

1. The Lord had scattered the proud. The proud are prideful in their thoughts, in "their inmost thoughts." They think themselves better...

- by looks
- by person
- by position
- by wealth
- by ability
- by heritage
- by achievement
- by possessions

Mary predicted that at the end of time, the Lord will have scattered all such pride. The proud will have been scattered "their inmost thoughts."

2. The Lord had dethroned the mighty and exalted the humble. The mighty are those who sit in positions of power, authority, and influence over others. The picture concerns those who take their power and...

- seek their own ends
- fail to serve
- deprive others
- push others down
- abuse others
- enslave others
- bypass others
- misuse others

Mary predicted that at the end of time, the Lord will have dethroned the mighty and exalted them of low degree (see notes—Mt.19:28).

3. The Lord had filled the hungry and emptied the rich. Those who were rich only in this world's goods are seen stripped of all their earthly goods and sent away empty. And those who had nothing of this world, but who put their trust in God, are seen as having received all good things (see note—Eph.1:3 for discussion).

5 (1:54-55) **God, the Savior; Love of**: God had helped His people. Two specific helps were proclaimed.

1. God had remembered His mercy. The people (Israel) desperately needed God's mercy and God's deliverance. They were enslaved by the Romans; therefore, they were frantic in their search for deliverance, so frantic many were turning to false messiahs and other answers to escape their plight. Some were even finding their security in the Roman state and in humanistic answers instead of God. If a people ever needed God to remember His mercy, it was then. Mary proclaimed that the Lord had remembered His mercy.

2. God had remembered His promise of the Messiah. He had promised the Messiah to the fathers of Israel, to Abraham and to Abraham's seed. And note: the promise had now been fulfilled. God had sent the Messiah, the Savior of the world. (See DEEPER STUDY # 1, Abraham—Jn.4:22; DEEPER STUDY # 1—Ro.4:1-25 for more discussion.)

The promises were spoken to Abraham and to his seed. The Scripture does not say "and to seeds," meaning many people, but "and to your seed," meaning one person, who is Christ. (Gal 3:16)

Jesus said to them, "If God were your Father, you would love me, for I came from God and now am here. I have not come on my own; but he sent me. (John 8:42)

The Jews gathered around him, saying, "How long will you keep us in suspense? If you are the Christ, tell us plainly." Jesus answered, "I did tell you, but you do not believe. The miracles I do in my Father's name speak for me, but you do not believe because you are not my sheep. My sheep listen to my voice; I know them, and they follow me. I give them eternal life, and they shall never perish; no one can snatch them out of my hand. My Father, who has given them to me, is greater than all ; no one can snatch them out of my Father's hand. (John 10:24-29)

6 (1:56) **The Conclusion**: Mary remained with Elizabeth for about three months, the very time that was needed to make sure she was pregnant. She needed the encouragement of Elizabeth until the fact had actually happened and was proven. Note the simple childlikeness of Mary, her need for the support and encouragement of her older sister who was probably more spiritually mature.

We who are strong ought to bear with the failings of the weak and not to please ourselves. (Rom 15:1)

Carry each other's burdens, and in this way you will fulfill the law of Christ. (Gal 6:2)

1 The child's birth a. Sealed God's power b. Sealed God's mercy c. Caused all to rejoice **2 The child's name sealed a prophetic witness** a. The child was circumcised: Given up to God b. The name was disputed	**F. John's Birth and Naming: An Event for All Generations, 1:57-66** 57 When it was time for Elizabeth to have her baby, she gave birth to a son. 58 Her neighbors and relatives heard that the Lord had shown her great mercy, and they shared her joy. 59 On the eighth day they came to circumcise the child, and they were going to name him after his father Zechariah, 60 But his mother spoke up and said, "No! He is to be called John." 61 They said to her, "There is no one among your relatives who has that name."	62 Then they made signs to his father, to find out what he would like to name the child. 63 He asked for a writing tablet, and to everyone's astonishment he wrote, "His name is John." 64 Immediately his mouth was opened and his tongue was loosed, and he began to speak, praising God. 65 The neighbors were all filled with awe, and throughout the hill country of Judea people were talking about all these things. 66 Everyone who heard this wondered about it, asking, "What then is this child going to be?" For the Lord's hand was with him.	c. The father confirmed the name John **3 The child's birth caused several important results** a. The father was miraculously healed and praised God b. The people were awe-stricken c. The events were spread abroad d. The sense of destiny surrounded the child

DIVISION I

THE ANNOUNCEMENT OF THE COMING OF JESUS, THE SON OF MAN, 1:1-2:52

F. John's Birth and Naming: An Event for All Generations, 1:57-66

(1:57-66) **Introduction**: the birth of a child is a significant event for every parent. But the birth of John was a significant event for every generation, an event that says much to every man.

1. The child's birth (v.57-58).
   a. Sealed God's power.
   b. Sealed God's mercy
   c. Caused all to rejoice.
2. The child's name sealed a prophetic witness (v.59-63).
3. The child's birth caused several important results (v.64-66).

1 (1:57-58) **God, Mercy of—Mercy**: the child's birth sealed God's power and mercy.

1. The child's birth sealed God's power. Note these facts.

⇒ Elizabeth had conceived when she was old, beyond child-bearing years (Lk.1:18, 36).
⇒ Zechariah had been visited by the angel of God and told exactly what would happen (Lk.1:11f).

The fact that the child was born just as God had said is evidence of God's glorious power. God was able to control natural events and to send forth the forerunner of the Messiah *exactly* as He had promised.

> **For nothing is impossible with God." (Luke 1:37)**
> **Jesus looked at them and said, "With man this is impossible, but with God all things are possible." (Mat 19:26)**
> **"I know that you can do all things; no plan of yours can be thwarted. (Job 42:2)**
> **Our God is in heaven; he does whatever pleases him. (Psa 115:3)**

2. The child's birth sealed God's mercy, showed that God was merciful in two ways.

a. The fact that John was born as a *baby of promise* demonstrated that God has mercy upon people, even upon an insignificant woman with a desperate need (see note—Lk.1:7).

> **The LORD is compassionate and gracious, slow to anger, abounding in love. (Psa 103:8; cp. v.1-8 for a description of God's mercy)**
> **But from everlasting to everlasting the Lord's love is with those who fear him, and his righteousness with their children's children— (Psa 103:17)**
> **Praise the LORD. Give thanks to the LORD, for he is good; his love endures forever. (Psa 106:1)**

b. The fact that God used John in His plan of salvation demonstrated God's mercy. John was to be greatly involved with the Messiah. God allowed him the glorious privilege. Such a high privilege and call clearly demonstrated God's glorious mercy.

Thought 1. The very same privilege is given to us. God wants to use everyone of us in His plan of salvation, both to be saved and to bear witness of His salvation.

> **This is good, and pleases God our Savior, who wants all men to be saved and to come to a knowledge of the truth. For there is one God and one mediator between God and men, the man Christ Jesus, (1 Tim 2:3-5)**

3. The child's birth caused all to rejoice. God's mercy upon a person's life was bound to make some rejoice.

Elizabeth's neighbors and cousins rejoiced with her and all believers rejoice since her. God has had mercy upon the world, and John's birth was one of the significant proofs of His mercy. God sent the forerunner to proclaim the coming of the promised Messiah. The fact that John was born as Scripture predicted and as Zechariah witnessed is proof of God's mercy. God did exactly as He had said. He sent the forerunner to prepare the way for the coming Savior of the world.

2 (1:59-63) **Prophecy, Fulfilled—Obedience**: the child's name sealed a prophetic witness. What happened is interesting. All Jewish males were circumcised on the eighth day after birth (see DEEPER STUDY # 1—Ph.3:3; cp. Gen.17:12; Lev.12:3). Circumcision was the Jewish ceremony where the child was offered up or dedicated to God. Circumcision was the rite or sign that the child was to be a follower of God, a true Jew. It was also the day on which the child was officially named.

Some of the neighbors and relatives wanted the child to be named after the father, Zechariah. However, Elizabeth objected, knowing that the angel had told Zechariah to name the child John. The relatives took the matter to Zechariah, asking him to write the name out for all to see. They, of course, were expecting Zechariah to be pleased with their suggestion that the child be called after him. But Zechariah shocked them. He confirmed that the child was to be named John. He dared not doubt and disobey God again. He was under the discipline of God for having disobeyed Him before.

The point is that the name John sealed the prophetic witness. The angel had told Zechariah what to name the child. His name was to be John, and Zechariah had borne witness to the angel's visit and promise, even to the angel revealing that the child was to be named John. John was the *prophetic name* given by God's messenger. Zechariah obeyed God and bore testimony to the prophecy; thus, Zechariah sealed the prophetic witness by confirming the name John.

> **Thought 1.** The very fact that the child was named John adds proof to the whole event's being true, as having really happened.
>
> **Thought 2.** The prophetic witness is true. Zechariah confirmed it by naming the child John.
>
> > **But these [signs] are written that you may believe that Jesus is the Christ, the Son of God, and that by believing you may have life in his name. (John 20:31)**
>
> **Thought 3.** Note that the obedience of Zechariah removed the discipline of God for his sin. Zechariah named the child John despite all the pressure from friends and the practice of the day to name the first son after the father. God had *told* Zechariah what to do in naming the child, and when he obeyed, the discipline of God was removed from his life.

3 (1:64-66) **John the Baptist, Birth**: the child's birth caused several important results.

1. The father was miraculously healed; consequently, he began to praise God. The restraint upon Zechariah's tongue was removed. Note: he had been shut up with his own thoughts, deaf and dumb for nine months. God healed him, opened his ears and loosed his tongue and he began to do exactly what he should do: praise God. Note that his last spoken words had been words of questioning, distrust, and unbelief (Lk.1:18).
2. The people were awe-stricken. The word "awe" (phobos) means reverence. It means a reverential awe, a reverential fear of God. The people stood in reverence before the events, awe-stricken over what was happening and wondering what else was going to happen. God was working. His hand was evident.
3. The events were spread abroad. God's hand upon the child was the subject of the countryside. (Note. It *should* have been the subject of all. God's movement should always be at the very center of men's conversations.)
4. The sense of destiny surrounded the child. Note that the people kept the things in their hearts and "wondered" about them. They did not forget what they were hearing. There was something unusual about the message surrounding the child. Expectations were running high, and many were holding the things in their memory waiting for the child to grow, to see what would happen.

> **Thought 1.** All four results should take place in our lives. We should be praising God; we should be awe-stricken at the events; we should spread the events abroad; we should see the destiny surrounding John. We have the privilege of knowing just who John was, the forerunner of the Messiah Himself.
>
> > **Since you call on a Father who judges each man's work impartially, *live your lives as strangers here in reverent fear.* For you know that it was not with perishable things such as silver or gold that you were redeemed from the empty way of life handed down to you from your forefathers, but with the precious blood of Christ, a lamb without blemish or defect. He was chosen before the creation of the world, but was revealed in these last times for your sake. (1 Pet 1:17-20)**
> >
> > **He provided redemption for his people; he ordained his covenant forever— holy and awesome is his name. The fear of the LORD is the beginning of wisdom; all who follow his precepts have good understanding. To him belongs eternal praise. (Psa 111:9-10)**
> >
> > **In the council of the holy ones God is greatly feared; he is more awesome than all who surround him. (Psa 89:7)**

	G. Zechariah's Inspired	of our enemies, and to enable	God without fear
	Prophecy: God's Savior	us to serve him without fear	
	& His Forerunner,	75 In holiness and right-	2) Enables us to live
	1:67-80	eousness before him all our	righteously & to serve
		days.	God forever
1 Zechariah was filled with	67 His father Zechariah was	76 And you, my child, will	**3 Part 2: God's forerunner,**
the Holy Spirit	filled with the Holy Spirit	be called a prophet of the	**John the Baptist**
	and prophesied:	Most High; for you will go	a. To be called the prophet
2 Part 1: God's SaviorDS1	68 "Praise be to the Lord, the	on before the Lord to prepare	of the Most High
a. The One through	God of Israel, because he has	the way for him,	b. To prepare Lord's way
whom God visited &	come and has redeemed his	77 To give his people the	c. To proclaim salvation:
redeemed His people	people.	knowledge of salvation	Forgiveness of sins
b. The mighty Savior:	69 He has raised up a horn of	through the forgiveness of	
Of David's house	salvation for us in the house	their sins,	
c. The One prophesied	of his servant David	78 Because of the tender	d. To proclaim the rise of
1) The time: Since the	70 (As he said through his	mercy of our God, by which	the heavenly Son
world began	holy prophets of long ago),	the rising sun will come to us	1) Through God's mercy
2) The prediction: He	71 Salvation from our ene-	from heaven	
will save us from	mies and from the hand of all	79 To shine on those living	2) To give light
our enemies	who hate us—	in darkness and in the shadow	
d. The One who fulfilled	72 To show mercy to our	of death, to guide our feet	
the promised mercy &	fathers and to remember his	into the path of peace."	
covenant, the oath	holy covenant,	80 And the child grew and	**4 Conclusion: John's child-**
made to Abraham	73 The oath he swore to our	became strong in spirit; and	**hood fulfills the prophecy**
	father Abraham:	he lived in the desert until he	
1) Enables us to serve	74 To rescue us from the hand	appeared publicly to Israel.	

DIVISION I

THE ANNOUNCEMENT OF THE COMING OF JESUS, THE SON OF MAN, 1:1-2:52

G. Zechariah's Inspired Prophecy: God's Savior and His Forerunner, 1:67-80

(1:67-80) **Introduction**: Zechariah's song is known as the Benedictus to many worshippers. Benedictus is the opening word of the song in the Latin translation. It is sometimes recited in worship services. Note that it is a prophecy (v.67) about the coming Messiah (v.68-75) and His forerunner, John the Baptist (v.76-80). The person and ministry of both are predicted and proclaimed.

1. Zechariah was filled with the Holy Spirit (v.67).
2. Part 1: God's Savior (v.68-75).
3. Part 2: God's forerunner, John the Baptist (v.76-79).
4. Conclusion: John's childhood fulfills the prophecy (v.80).

1 (1:67) **Holy Spirit**: Zechariah was filled with the Holy Spirit. Once Zechariah obeyed God, God removed His discipline and healed him of his deafness and dumbness (v.62, 64). Immediately thereafter, God filled Zechariah with the Holy Spirit. The infilling with God's Spirit indicated two things.

1. Zechariah was forgiven his sin of unbelief. It was his questioning of God, that is, his distrust and unbelief, that had caused his deafness and dumbness (Lk.1:20-22). As soon as Zechariah demonstrated faith in God's promise, he was healed and was forgiven his sin (cp. v.64-66).

2. Zechariah's being filled with the Holy Spirit is a picture of what happens to us. We believe and obey God, then God immediately forgives our sins and fills us with His Spirit.

> **Peter replied, "Repent and be baptized, every one of you, in the name of Jesus Christ for the forgiveness of your sins. And you will receive the gift of the Holy Spirit. (Acts 2:38)**

2 (1:68-75) **Jesus Christ, Son of David—Covenant, Abrahamic—Salvation—Righteousness**: the first part of Zechariah's prophetic song concerned God's Savior. Four things were predicted about the Messiah. Note that Zechariah was standing in the future and looking back. The verbs are in the past tense. He was predicting how someone could stand in the future and proclaim *what the Messiah had done*.

1. The Messiah was the One through whom God has come and redeemed His people. It was God Himself who visited the earth in the Person of the Messiah. He had not neglected nor left the world alone. In the past God had been actively involved in the world's affairs. He had sent His Word and His messengers to the world, but now God was becoming *personally* involved in the world. He was visiting the world Himself.

Note the purpose for His visit. He came to redeem His people, to save and rescue them from sin and death and separation from God. It cost Him; He had to pay the enormous price of redemption—a life for a life (see note, Redemption—Eph.1:7).

2. The Messiah was the mighty Savior of David's house. The phrase "horn of salvation" is a reference to Christ. The word "horn" throughout the Old Testament was a symbol of strength, power, and might. The Messiah is called the "horn" or the "mighty One of salvation" (v.69) because He alone possesses the might, the strength, and the power to save.

But note where the horn or the Messiah was raised up: "in the house of His servant David." David was raised up by God to deliver and to rule over His people Israel. But Christ was raised up to deliver and to rule over God's people. There is one huge difference. Christ was sent to deliver and to rule over everyone, and His deliverance and rule were to be forever. The Messiah was the horn promised to David, the One who fulfilled the prophecies made concerning David (see note—Mt.1:1).

> **"Here I will make a horn grow for David and set up a lamp for my anointed one. (Psa 132:17; cp. Psa 89:24, 29)**

3. The Messiah was the One prophesied. The idea is that God was working out His plan for the world. He was on the throne bringing to pass all that He had promised.

a. The Messiah had been foretold since the world began. He was *the Seed of the woman* who was to break the serpent's head (Gen.3:15). He was the Seed promised to Abraham and his heirs (Gen.12:1-4. See DEEPER STUDY # 1—Ro.4:1-25.)

b. The prediction of the Messiah dealt with salvation. The Messiah was to save believers from their enemies and from all who hated them. Carnal men (the Jews, the fleshly, the worldly-minded) think of salvation as material and physical deliverance; but God never meant salvation to last only for a few short years, the years of a man's life. He cares much more for man than that. By salvation God means spiritual and eternal salvation, a deliverance and life that will never end. He is interested in saving men from the enemies that wage an endless war against the spirit and enslave men both now and eternally: the enemies of sin, death, and condemnation.

4. The Messiah was the One who fulfilled the promised mercy and covenant, the oath made to Abraham. God had promised Abraham both mercy and the covenant of faith. God promised Abraham that if he would get up and leave his old country to follow Him, then Abraham would receive both the mercy of God and the covenant of faith. The covenant was based upon "the promised seed," Christ Himself. Thus Zechariah, under the inspiration of the Holy Spirit, was proclaiming the Messiah to be the fulfillment of the promised mercy and covenant to Abraham. The Messiah was *the promised mercy and Seed to Abraham* (see DEEPER STUDY # 1, Abraham—Ro.4:1-25 for detailed discussion. Cp. Dt.6:9, 12-13; 1 Ki.8:23; Neh.1:5; 9:32.)

⇒ The Messiah brings the mercy of God to man (the mercy promised to Abraham and his seed): the Messiah delivers man out of the hands of his enemies (cp. v.71, 74).

⇒ The Messiah establishes the covenant of faith with man (the covenant promised to Abraham and his seed): the Messiah saves all who believe the promises of God just as Abraham believed (cp. Ro.4:1-25).

> **Yet he [Abraham] did not waver through unbelief regarding the promise of God, but was strengthened in his faith and gave glory to God, being fully persuaded that God had power to do what he had promised. This is why "it was credited to him as righteousness." The words "it was credited to him" were written not for him alone, but also for us, to whom God will credit righteousness—for us who believe in him who raised Jesus our Lord from the dead. He was delivered over to death for our sins and was raised to life for our justification. (Rom 4:20-25)**

Now note: God has mercy and delivers man through faith for two very specific purposes.

1. The first purpose is that men might serve Him without fear. God does not want men living in fear, fearing the future and the *imaginary gods and demons* of this world. He does not want men's fearing the pain of death and the coming judgment of hell. God wants men to have peace of mind and heart, to feel secure and to know meaning and purpose throughout all of life.

> **Since the children have flesh and blood, he too shared in their humanity so that by his death he might destroy him who holds the power of death—that is, the devil—and free those who all their lives were held in slavery by their fear of death. (Heb 2:14-15)**
>
> **Surely God is my salvation; I will trust and not be afraid. The LORD, the LORD, is my strength and my song; he has become my salvation." (Isa 12:2)**

2. The second purpose is that men might live righteously and serve God *forever*.

> **But when the kindness and love of God our Savior appeared, he saved us, not because of righteous things we had done, but because of his mercy. He saved us through the washing of rebirth and renewal by the Holy Spirit, whom he poured out on us generously through Jesus Christ our Savior, so that, having been justified by his grace, we might become heirs having the hope of eternal life. (Titus 3:4-7)**
>
> **God made him who had no sin to be sin for us, so that in him we might become the righteousness of God. (2 Cor 5:21)**
>
> **And to put on the new self, created to be like God in true righteousness and holiness. (Eph 4:24)**
>
> **Filled with the fruit of righteousness that comes through Jesus Christ—to the glory and praise of God. (Phil 1:11)**
>
> **Come back to your senses as you ought, and stop sinning; for there are some who are ignorant of God—I say this to your shame. (1 Cor 15:34)**
>
> **Sow for yourselves righteousness, reap the fruit of unfailing love, and break up your unplowed ground; for it is time to seek the LORD, until he comes and showers righteousness on you. (Hosea 10:12)**

DEEPER STUDY # 1

(1:68) **Israel**: Zechariah addressed God as "the Lord, the God of Israel." Why did he limit God to Israel? Why did he not address God as *the Lord God of the earth*? There are several reasons (see DEEPER STUDY # 1, Israel—Jn.4:22).

1. Israel was the chosen people of God, the people chosen to love, obey, and worship Him supremely.

2. As the *chosen* people of God, Israel had been given (entrusted with) both the Word and promises of God to a lost and dying world.

3. As the *recipient* of God's Word and promises, Israel was to be given the Messiah, His salvation and redemption.

4. As the *people* of salvation and redemption, Israel was given the task to make God known, to be the missionary force to reach a lost and dying world.

Zechariah was thinking of God's promise to Israel, of the glorious fact that the promise of the Messiah was now being fulfilled. He knew nothing of Israel's rejection of the Messiah, of God's turning to the Gentiles, of the birth of a new people (the church). Therefore, he did the natural thing: he praised the Lord God of Israel.

3 (1:76-79) **John the Baptist—Jesus Christ, Purpose**: the second part of Zechariah's prophecy concerned John the Baptist. Four things were also predicted about John.

1. John was to be the prophet of the Most High. Note several facts.
   a. There had been no prophet in Israel for some four hundred years. John was to be the first since Malachi.
   b. Christ was called "the *Most High,* which is a title for God. Thus the deity, the very Incarnation of God in Christ, was being proclaimed. He is "God over all, forever praised" (Ro.9:5).
   c. John was called the prophet of the Most High, of Christ, or of God Himself.
2. John was to prepare the Lord's way. He was to be the forerunner of the Messiah, the one who was to prepare the people for the coming of the Lord (cp. Lk.3:3-6).
3. John was to proclaim salvation, even the forgiveness of sins. Note that salvation comes by the forgiveness of sin. Salvation is conditional. One's sins must be forgiven before he can be saved (Eph.1:7). John's purpose was to call men to salvation, to be forgiven of their sins.
4. John was to proclaim the heavenly Son's rise. Note that Christ, the Messiah, is called "the Sun of righteousness" (Mal.4:2; 2 Pt.1:19; Rev.22:16). He is the "rising sun," the morning light, the rising sun who has "come to us." John was to proclaim the rise of the Messiah, and in particular two things about His rise.
   a. The Messiah was being sent through the tender mercy of God.

> **"For God so loved the world that he gave his one and only Son, that whoever believes in him shall not perish but have eternal life. For God did not send his Son into the world to condemn the world, but to save the world through him. (John 3:16-17)**
>
> **But because of his great love for us, God, who is rich in mercy, made us alive with Christ even when we were dead in transgressions—it is by grace you have been saved. (Eph 2:4-5)**

   b. The Messiah was being sent to give light…
   - to those who sit in darkness

> **A light for revelation to the Gentiles and for glory to your people Israel." (Luke 2:32)**
>
> **In him was life, and that life was the light of men. The true light that gives light to every man was coming into the world. (John 1:4, 9)**
>
> **This is the verdict: Light has come into the world, but men loved darkness instead of light because their deeds were evil. Everyone who does evil hates the light, and will not come into the light for fear that his deeds will be exposed. But whoever lives by the truth comes into the light, so that it may be seen plainly that what he has done has been done through God." (John 3:19-21)**
>
> **When Jesus spoke again to the people, he said, "I am the light of the world. Whoever follows me will never walk in darkness, but will have the light of life." (John 8:12)**
>
> **I have come into the world as a light, so that no one who believes in me should stay in darkness. (John 12:46)**

   - to those who are in the shadow of death

> **"I tell you the truth, whoever hears my word and believes him who sent me has eternal life and will not be condemned; he has crossed over from death to life. (John 5:24)**
>
> **Since the children have flesh and blood, he too shared in their humanity so that by his death he might destroy him who holds the power of death—that is, the devil—and free those who all their lives were held in slavery by their fear of death. (Heb 2:14-15)**

   - to guide our feet into the way of peace

> **Jesus answered, "I am the way and the truth and the life. No one comes to the Father except through me. (John 14:6)**
>
> **Peace I leave with you; my peace I give you. I do not give to you as the world gives. Do not let your hearts be troubled and do not be afraid. (John 14:27)**
>
> **"I have told you these things, so that in me you may have peace. In this world you will have trouble. But take heart! I have overcome the world." (John 16:33)**

4 (1:80) **John the Baptist—Growth, Spiritual**: John's childhood is described only in this single verse. Nothing else is known. He grew as a normal boy physically, but three things are said about him that differ from the normal child.

1. He advanced far beyond other boys spiritually. He grew and became strong in spirit. He was a boy of strong heart and commitment, of strong will and decisiveness, of strong conscience and conviction, of strong drive and initiative. He was God's servant, a young man who was committed to follow, obey, and serve God.
2. He was reared in a different environment than most boys—in the desert. The desert was an obscure place, a place of quietness, far from the worldliness of the cities and masses of men. The desert was made for meditation and thought, for seeking God.
3. He stayed at his desert home until God called him to launch his ministry to Israel. This points to a life of obedience both to parents and to God.

Thought 1. The crying need of the hour is for believers to grow in the Lord Jesus Christ—to grow strong in the spirit.

Then we will no longer be infants, tossed back and forth by the waves, and blown here and there by every wind of teaching and by the cunning and craftiness of men in their deceitful scheming. Instead, speaking the truth in love, we will in all things grow up into him who is the Head, that is, Christ. (Eph 4:14-15)

But grow in the grace and knowledge of our Lord and Savior Jesus Christ. To him be glory both now and forever! Amen. (2 Pet 3:18)

"Now I commit you to God and to the word of his grace, which can build you up and give you an inheritance among all those who are sanctified. (Acts 20:32)

1 The miraculous taxation
  a. An event of the world used by God to fulfill His plan
  b. An event that forced Joseph to Bethlehem
    1) From Galilee
    2) Out of Nazareth
    3) Into Judaea
    4) To the city of David, Bethlehem
  c. An event that led to the fulfillment of Scripture despite man's plans

2 The shocking place of birth

3 The unbelievable appearance of a real angel to shepherds
  a. His appearance: Shone in the glory of the Lord
  b. His message: Reassured—good news
    1) A proclamation: The Messiah's birth[DS1,2]
    2) A charge: Visit the child
    3) A sign: The location & dress

CHAPTER 2

H. Jesus' Birth: Its Unusual Events, 2:1-24
(Mt.1:18-25; 2:1; cp. Jn.1:14)

In those days Caesar Augustus issued a decree that a census should be taken of the
entire Roman world.
2 (This was the first census
that took place while Quir-
inius was governor of Syria.)
3 And everyone went to his
own town to register.
4 So Joseph also went up
from the town of Nazareth
in Galilee to Judea, to
Bethlehem the town of
David, because he belonged
to the house and line of
David.
5 He went there to register
with Mary, who was pledged
to be married to him and was
expecting a child.
6 While they were there, the
time came for the baby to be
born,
7 And she gave birth to her
firstborn, a son. She wrapped
him in cloths and placed him
in a manger, because there
was no room for them in the
inn.
8 And there were shepherds
living out in the fields
nearby, keeping watch over
their flocks at night.
9 An angel of the Lord appeared to them, and the glory
of the Lord shone around
them, and they were terrified.
10 But the angel said to
them, "Do not be afraid. I
bring you good news of great
joy that will be for all the
people.
11 Today in the town of
David a Savior has been born
to you; he is Christ the Lord.
12 This will be a sign to you:
You will find a baby wrapped
in cloths and lying in a manger."
13 Suddenly a great com-
pany of the heavenly host appeared with the angel, praising God and saying,
14 "Glory to God in the
highest, and on earth peace to
men on whom his favor
rests."
15 When the angels had left
them and gone into heaven,
the shepherds said to one another, "Let's go to Bethlehem
and see this thing that has
happened, which the Lord has
told us about."
16 So they hurried off and
found Mary and Joseph, and
the baby, who was lying in
the manger.
17 When they had seen him,
they spread the word con-
cerning what had been told
them about this child,
18 And all who heard it were
amazed at what the shepherds
said to them.
19 But Mary treasured up all
these things and pondered
them in her heart.
20 The shepherds returned,
glorifying and praising God
for all the things they had
heard and seen, which were
just as they had been told.
21 On the eighth day, when it
was time to circumcise him,
he was named Jesus, the
name the angel had given
him before he had been conceived.
22 When the time of their
purification according to the
Law of Moses had been
completed, Joseph and Mary
took him to Jerusalem to present him to the Lord
23 (As it is written in the
Law of the Lord, "Every
firstborn male is to be consecrated to the Lord"),
24 And to offer a sacrifice in
keeping with what is said in
the Law of the Lord: "a pair
of doves or two young pi-
geons."

4 The spectacular appearance of the heavenly host

5 The excited shepherds seeking evidence
  a. They immediately decided to visit
  b. They rushed to see
  c. They excitedly shared the message
  d. They caused a stir

6 The awe-stricken, pondering mother

7 The common, non-religious shepherds worshipping God

8 The unusual naming of the child: Named by God Himself

9 The unexpected observance of the legal ceremonies
  a. Circumcision[DS3]
  b. Purification after childbirth
  c. Dedication to the Lord

10 The deliberate choice of God to have a poor family bear His Son

DIVISION I

THE ANNOUNCEMENT OF THE COMING OF JESUS, THE SON OF MAN, 1:1-2:52

H. Jesus' Birth: Its Unusual Events, 2:1-24

(2:1-24) **Introduction**: the prophecy given by Jacob back in Genesis was now being fulfilled.

> **The scepter will not depart from Judah, nor the ruler's staff from between his feet, until he [the Messiah] comes to whom it belongs and the obedience of the nations is his. (Gen 49:10)**

1. Note how the scepter of rule had departed from Judea. Judea was under the rule of Rome with Caesar Augustus reigning as emporer. Cyrenius was governor of Syria, and Judea was included in the province of Syria.

Herod was now the *King of Judea*. A usurper, a foreign, alien power, now ruled over Judea.

⇒ Judea was no longer ruled by one of its own princes; it was ruled by an Idumean prince, a descendant of Esau, Herod the Great.
⇒ The promised land was no longer in the hands of Israel; it was in the hands of a heathen power.
⇒ The prince (ruler) was no longer appointed by God; he was empowered by Rome.
⇒ The temple was no longer cared for by the prince of God; it was (misused) under the authority of a usurper.
⇒ The priests of God were no longer the ministers of God; they were the servants of the secular world.

2. Note how clearly and how dramatically the prophecy was fulfilled: the scepter had most definitely departed from Judea, and *now* it was time for Shiloh to come. And He would come. God destined His coming in the counsel and foreknowledge of His will.

The prophecy of *Shiloh's coming* was fulfilled in Jesus Christ. Jesus Christ was Shiloh who was to come (Gen.49:10). His coming into the world was surrounded by the most unusual events.

1. The miraculous taxation (v.1-6).
2. The shocking place of birth (v.7).
3. The unbelievable appearance of a real angel to shepherds (v.8-12).
4. The spectacular appearance of the heavenly host (v.13-14).
5. The excited shepherds seeking evidence (v.15-18).
6. The awe-stricken, pondering mother (v.19).
7. The common, non-religious shepherds worshipping God (v.20).
8. The unusual naming of the child: named by God Himself (v.21).
9. The unexpected observance of the legal ceremonies (v.22-23).
10. The deliberate choice of God to have a poor family bear His Son (v.24).

1 (2:1-6) **Jesus Christ, Birth—Bethlehem—God, Providence**: there was the miraculous taxation. Three things should be noted.

1. The taxation was used by God to fulfill His plan for the birth of the Messiah. It had been prophesied that the Messiah was to be born in Bethlehem, and Scripture had to be fulfilled. Joseph and Mary lived in Galilee, and Mary was now great with child. How was God going to make sure that the child was born in Bethlehem? The taxation happened just at the right time and in the right way; that is, everyone had to return to the city of his birth to pay his taxes. God was miraculously controlling the events of the world, working all things out for good so that He might fulfill His promise to send the Savior into the world.

2. The taxation forced Joseph to Bethlehem. Everyone had to return to the city of his birth. Note the great detail given in describing the journey to Bethlehem. The point is that Bethlehem was the prophesied city of the Messiah's birth (Mic.5:2). The Scribes understood it (Mt.2:5-6) and so did the common people (Jn.7:42). The taxation was certainly an event wrought in the plan of God to fulfill Scripture.

3. The taxation led to the fulfillment of Scripture, despite man's plans. Mary was about to deliver; she was "expecting a child" (v.5). Apparently, Joseph and Mary had planned for the child to be delivered in Nazareth; but God overruled. He either caused or used the taxation and saw to it that Joseph and Mary were forced to Bethlehem.

Now in summary, why was all this necessary? Why did Jesus have to be born in Bethlehem?

a. The Messiah was the prophesied Son of David (see notes—Lk.3:24-31; Mt.1:1; DEEPER STUDY # 3—Jn.1:45; DEEPER STUDY # 4—1:49 for discussion).
b. David had been born in Bethlehem; therefore, it was necessary for the Son of David to be born there.
c. Scripture foretold that the Messiah would be born in Bethlehem (Mic.5:2).

2 (2:7) **Jesus Christ, Birth**: there was the shocking place of birth. Jesus was not born in comfortable surroundings. Shockingly, He was born in a stable and laid in a manger or feeding trough. The birth is covered in one simple verse, yet much can be gleaned from it.

1. Jesus was born in a smelly stable. He was neglected and turned away by men from the very beginning. There was no room in the inn and Mary was about to deliver. If someone had cared, room could have been made for her.

2. Jesus was born in poverty. If Joseph had possessed the money, he could have bought a room.

3. Jesus was born in obscurity and loneliness. The birth took place away from people, all alone. Note that Mary herself wrapped the child in clothes and laid Him in a manger.

4. Jesus was born in humiliation. He did not enter the world...

- in a hospital,
- in a comfortable home,
- in the home of a friend or relative,
- under a doctor's care,
- under the stars of heaven, nor even out in the open,
- but in a smelly stable, the lowest imaginable place for a birth.

5. Jesus was born into a corruptible world full of sin and selfishness, greed and unkindness. This is seen in that...

- the world (represented in the innkeeper) was so wrapped up in its affairs that it could not help a woman bearing a child.
- no one would make room for Mary in the inn. Money and personal comfort were more important to all who had become aware of the situation.

Thought 1. Note how so many missed the first coming of Christ. How many will miss the second coming of Christ?

"Be careful, or your hearts will be weighed down with dissipation, drunkenness and the anxieties of life, and that day will close on you unexpectedly like a trap. (Luke 21:34)

It teaches us to say "No" to ungodliness and worldly passions, and to live self-controlled, upright and godly lives in this present age, while we wait for the blessed hope—the glorious appearing of our great God and Savior, Jesus Christ, (Titus 2:12-13)

3 (2:8-12) **Shepherds**: there was the unbelievable appearance of a real angel to shepherds. In the eyes of many, an angel would never appear to a shepherd. Shepherds would seldom be found praising and worshipping God; as a result they were looked upon as anything but worshippers. Their reputation was lowly at best, and religious people snubbed and ignored them. They were despised because they were unable to attend services and to keep the ceremonial laws of washing and cleansing. Their flocks just kept them too busy. What a beautiful foretaste of the salvation to come: God gave the first message of His Son to common shepherds, those looked upon as sinners.

1. The angel's appearance was that of splendor and glory. This was the shekinah glory (see note—Mt.17:5-8).

2. The angel's message was one of reassurance and good news. He proclaimed the Messiah's birth and charged the shepherds to visit the child. He gave them a sign: they will find a baby wrapped in clothes and lying in a manger.

Thought 1. The Savior was coming to call sinners to repentance; therefore, the first announcement of His coming was given to sinners.

> **Jesus answered them, "It is not the healthy who need a doctor, but the sick. I have not come to call the righteous, but sinners to repentance." (Luke 5:31-32)**
>
> **Brothers, think of what you were when you were called. Not many of you were wise by human standards; not many were influential; not many were of noble birth. But God chose the foolish things of the world to shame the wise; God chose the weak things of the world to shame the strong. He chose the lowly things of this world and the despised things—and the things that are not—to nullify the things that are, so that no one may boast before him. (1 Cor 1:26-29)**

DEEPER STUDY # 1
(2:11) **Jesus—Savior**: see DEEPER STUDY # 2—Lk.1:31; note—2:21.

DEEPER STUDY # 2
(2:11) **Christ—Messiah**: see DEEPER STUDY # 2—Mt.1:18; note—Lk.2:21.

4 (2:13-14) **Angels**: there was the spectacular appearance of the heavenly host. The word "host" means an army of angels, "ten thousand times ten thousand" (Dan.7:10; cp. Ps.68:17). God either gave the shepherds a special sight into the spiritual world and dimension or caused the spiritual dimension to appear to physical sight. Note: the angels did two things.

1. They cried out for glory to be lifted up to God...
   - who is the highest possible Being.
   - who dwells in the highest realm of being possible, in heaven itself.

2. They cried out for peace, for good will toward men. By peace is meant the peace of reconciliation, the good will between God and man. The alienation and separation, struggle and divisiveness, restlessness and fear caused by sin needed to be solved. The heavenly host was praising God that the alienation and separation were now being solved in the birth of the "Savior...he is Christ the Lord" (v.11).

> **And through him to reconcile to himself all things, whether things on earth or things in heaven, by making peace through his blood, shed on the cross. (Col 1:20)**

5 (2:15-18) **Shepherds**: there were the excited shepherds' seeking evidence. Note their excitement.

1. They decided immediately to visit. "They [the shepherds] said to one another, 'let's go'...."

2. They *rushed* to see for themselves. There is a sense of extreme urgency in these words. They acted with haste, rushed, hurried. They felt an urgency to act and to act now. They wasted no time. Note: they found the baby just as the angel had said.

3. They shared the message. They first experienced seeing the child themselves, then they shared their experience wherever they went. They were the first to bear witness to the Savior of the world.

4. They caused a stir among the people. Note that nothing is said about these hearers' seeking out the child. They only wondered about what they heard; they never responded and never moved to find Him for themselves.

6 (2:19) **Mary—Humility—Trust**: there was the awe-stricken, pondering mother. This is a beautiful picture of a humble, trusting heart. Mary had been told that her child was of God, truly of God. Above all others she knew that the Messiah, the very Son of God, had now come. She had been through so much: pregnant, yet unmarried; the possibility of being found out and of rumors heaped upon rumors; the discussions with Joseph and with her parents; the long trip from Nazareth; the exhaustion of giving birth without help in a smelly stable; the visit of some rough-hewn shepherds with an amazing story of the heavenly host's proclaiming the praises of God. Mary was tired, as weary and exhausted as a person could be. So much had happened, and she was at the very center of it all. No one could even begin to know the thoughts that had filled her mind for nine months, nor could anyone know the feelings and emotions of the experience. The wonder, the amazement, the astounding reality was too much to talk about. All she could do was continue in the humble sweetness that had so characterized her over the past months. She merely bowed once again in *humble adoration* to God and *quietly entrusted* all these things into God's keeping. She said nothing, only pondered in her heart what was happening.

7 (2:20) **Shepherds**: there were the common, non-religious shepherds worshipping God.

1. The shepherds had spread the message, but note a shocking fact. The shepherds alone are seen praising God. No one else is seen seeking or praising the Savior.

2. The shepherds were praising God for what they had *heard* and *seen.* God had spoken to them and they had received the message. They obeyed God's instructions to seek out the Messiah; therefore, they had been privileged to see the Messiah. They had reason to praise God. (How many hear and see, yet never respond and never praise God?)

> **For I know the plans I have for you," declares the LORD, "plans to prosper you and not to harm you, plans to give you hope and a future. Then you will call upon me and come**

and pray to me, and I will listen to you. You will seek me and find me when you seek me with all your heart. (Jer 29:11-13)

8 (2:21) **Jesus Christ, Name**: there was the unusual naming of the child. The child was named by God Himself.

1. The child Jesus was named by God before He was conceived in the womb (Lk.1:31).
2. The name Jesus (iesous) means Savior or He will save. The Hebrew form of the name is Joshua which means *Jehovah is salvation.*

This is good, and pleases God our Savior, who wants all men to be saved and to come to a knowledge of the truth. For there is one God and one mediator between God and men, the man Christ Jesus, who gave himself as a ransom for all men—the testimony given in its proper time. (1 Tim 2:3-6)

But when the kindness and love of God our Savior appeared, he saved us, not because of righteous things we had done, but because of his mercy. He saved us through the washing of rebirth and renewal by the Holy Spirit, whom he poured out on us generously through Jesus Christ our Savior, so that, having been justified by his grace, we might become heirs having the hope of eternal life. (Titus 3:4-7)

9 (2:22-23) **Jesus Christ, Fulfills Law**: there was the unexpected observance of the legal ceremonies. There were three legal ceremonies which Jesus underwent.

1. There was the ceremony of circumcision (see DEEPER STUDY # 1—Ph.3:3).
2. There was the ceremony of purification. This was a ceremony Mary had to go through. After the birth of a boy child, a woman was considered unclean for forty days (eighty for a girl child). She could work around the home and engage in normal activities, but she could not take part in religious ceremonies. She was religiously, that is, ceremonially, unclean. After a woman's forty or eighty days were up, she was to make an offering in the temple (Lev.12:1-8).
3. There was the ceremony of dedication to the Lord (v.23; cp. Ex.13:2, 12, 15; Lev.27:6; Num.18:15-16). A male child was presented (dedicated) in the temple when the family was close to Jerusalem.

Why would Jesus, the Son of God, be subjected to the legal observances of the law? He was not a stranger to the covenants of God (circumcision). He had created the covenants Himself. He was not lacking in commitment (the Dedication Ceremony). He was God Himself, the One to whom all babies were dedicated, yet He was subjected to all the legal requirements. Why? Very simply...

But when the time had fully come, God sent his Son, born of a woman, born under law, to redeem those under law, that we might receive the full rights of sons. (Gal 4:4-5)

For this reason he had to be made like his brothers in every way, in order that he might become a merciful and faithful high priest in service to God, and that he might make atonement for the sins of the people. Because he himself suffered when he was tempted, he is able to help those who are being tempted. (Heb 2:17-18)

"Do not think that I have come to abolish the Law or the Prophets; I have not come to abolish them but to fulfill them. (Mat 5:17 see note—Mat 5:17-18)

DEEPER STUDY # 3
(2:22) **Circumcision**: see DEEPER STUDY # 1—Ph.3:3.

10 (2:24) **Offering of Poor**: there was the deliberate choice of God to have a poor family bear His Son. Note that Mary offered two pigeons. This was the offering of the poor. Rich people were required to offer a lamb and a pigeon. Therefore, God chose a poor family to rear His only Son in an ordinary home without any luxuries.

Thought 1. No matter what we have to bear in life, Christ has already borne it—even poverty (see note 3—Lk.2:40 for discussion). He knows the suffering we undergo; therefore, He is able to strengthen and carry us through the suffering.

For we do not have a high priest who is unable to sympathize with our weaknesses, but we have one who has been tempted in every way, just as we are—yet was without sin. Let us then approach the throne of grace with confidence, so that we may receive mercy and find grace to help us in our time of need. (Heb 4:15-16)

Outline	Scripture	Scripture	Outline
1 Simeon, a man who walked close to God a. A man who was righteous & devout b. A man who looked for the Messiah c. A man who was led by the Holy Spirit d. A man who was given an unusual promise e. A man who saw & held the Messiah **2 The child was God's salvation**	**I. Simeon's Prophecy: Jesus' Life and Fate Foretold, 2:25-35** 25 Now there was a man in Jerusalem called Simeon, who was righteous and de- vout. He was waiting for the consolation of Israel, and the Holy Spirit was upon him. 26 It had been revealed to him by the Holy Spirit that he would not die before he had seen the Lord's Christ. 27 Moved by the Spirit, he went into the temple courts. When the parents brought in the child Jesus to do for him what the custom of the Law required, 28 Simeon took him in his arms and praised God, say- ing:	29 "Sovereign Lord, as you have promised, you now dismiss your servant in peace. 30 For my eyes have seen your salvation, 31 Which you have prepared in the sight of all people, 32 A light for revelation to the Gentiles and for glory to your people Israel." 33 The child's father and mother marveled at what was said about him. 34 Then Simeon blessed them and said to Mary, his mother: "This child is des- tined to cause the falling and rising of many in Israel, and to be a sign that will be spo- ken against, 35 So that the thoughts of many hearts will be revealed. And a sword will pierce your own soul too."	a. The source of peace b. The One appointed to be God's salvation c. The One prepared for all people d. The light to unbelievers e. The glory to believers f. The parents marvelled at the predictions **3 The child was cause the rise and fall of many** **4 The child's fate was sealed** a. His fate: To be opposed & put to death b. His purpose: To reveal the inner thoughts of man's heart

DIVISION I

THE ANNOUNCEMENT OF THE COMING OF JESUS, THE SON OF MAN, 1:1-2:52

I. Simeon's Prophecy: Jesus' Life and Fate Foretold, 2:25-35

(2:25-35) **Introduction**: it was time for the child to be dedicated and offered up for God's keeping and care. The parents took the child to the temple, and someplace in the temple, they came across a man named Simeon. Just who Simeon was is not known. Some think he was a priest, but Scripture does not say. All we know is what is recorded here. He was a man who loved God very much, so much that God was able to use him in a most magnificent way. He used Simeon to proclaim one of the greatest messages of all time: the events and fate of the child Messiah's life.

1. Simeon, a man who walked close to God (v.25-27).
2. The child was God's salvation (v.28-33).
3. The child was to cause the rise and fall of many (v.34).
4. The child's fate was sealed (v.34-35).

1 (2:25-27) **Simeon—Dedication**: Simeon was a man who walked closely with God. He walked so closely that God was able to use him in a most magnificent way to encourage Joseph and Mary. Five things are said about him personally.

1. Simeon was a righteous and devout man. The word "righteous" (dikaios) means well-behaved, living as one should live. Simeon was a man who treated other people as he should: justly.

The word "devout" (eulabes) means cautious and careful in relation to God. It means reverence for God, being pious. Simeon was very careful in his relation toward God.

2. Simeon was a man who looked for the coming of the Messiah (see DEEPER STUDY # 2—Mt.1:18). This is what is meant by "the consolation of Israel." Faithful believers among the Jews felt that Israel could find consolation only in the Messiah. They longed and ached with all hope and patience for His coming. Joseph of Arimathaea was another example of one who "was waiting for the kingdom of God" (Mk.15:43).

Thought 1. The world can find consolation only in the coming of Christ.

> **For the grace of God that brings salvation has appeared to all men. It teaches us to say "No" to ungodliness and worldly passions, and to live self-controlled, upright and godly lives in this present age, while we wait for the blessed hope—the glorious appearing of our great God and Savior, Jesus Christ, who gave himself for us to redeem us from all wickedness and to purify for himself a people that are his very own, eager to do what is good. (Titus 2:11-14)**

Thought 2. Believers must long for the Messiah, ache with all hope and patience for His return (cp. 2 Pt.3:3-18).

3. Simeon was a man led by the Holy Spirit. The idea seems to be that the Spirit was upon him continually. In most instances throughout the Old Testament the Spirit only came upon men for special service. It is not said that the Spirit abode upon them continually; however, the Spirit does seem to have rested upon Simeon continually. This shows just how closely Simeon was living to God. He must have been a very, very special man, a man who held God ever so dear to his heart and whom God held ever so close to His heart.

4. Simeon was a man who was given an unusual promise. Apparently, Simeon was constantly studying the Scriptures, in particular searching the prophecies concerning the coming salvation of the Messiah (1 Pt.1:10). At some point, the Holy Spirit revealed to him that he would not die until he had seen the Messiah. Just think how closely Simeon must have lived to God! He was unquestionably a very special person to God.

5. Simeon was a man who saw and held the Messiah. Note that Simeon was again led by the Spirit; he was led into the temple. This was the day for which he had longed and ached, the day he was to see and embrace the Messiah. A first-born son was always taken to the temple to be dedicated to the Lord. Immediately, Simeon saw that this child was different from all the others; he recognized the child as the Christ-child. He took the child up into his arms and proclaimed Him to be the long-awaited Messiah.

Thought 1. The point to note about Simeon is his closeness to God. He was a man who stands as a dynamic example of *strong dedication.* Because of his *strong dedication*, God was able to bless Simeon beyond imagination.

Love the LORD, all his saints! The LORD preserves the faithful, but the proud he pays back in full. (Psa 31:23)

Though you have not seen him, you love him; and even though you do not see him now, you believe in him and are filled with an inexpressible and glorious joy, (1 Pet 1:8)

Keep yourselves in God's love as you wait for the mercy of our Lord Jesus Christ to bring you to eternal life. (Jude 1:21)

I know your deeds, your love and faith, your service and perseverance, and that you are now doing more than you did at first. (Rev 2:19)

2 (2:28-33) **Salvation—Jesus Christ, Life and Fate**: the child was God's salvation. Once Simeon had embraced the Messiah, he broke out into song. The song is called the *Nunc Dimittis*, again being known by the opening words of the song in the Latin. Note several points.

1. The child was God's salvation; He was to be the source of peace for the world. Simeon had "seen and embraced" the Messiah, God's salvation. Therefore, he was now ready to die in peace. Note that He believed and trusted God—all of God's promises. He praised God for fulfilling His Word "as you have promised." It was because of God's faithfulness that he was ready to die. He knew that he would live on "with his fathers" forever. (See note—Jn.14:27.)

Peace I leave with you; my peace I give you. I do not give to you as the world gives. Do not let your hearts be troubled and do not be afraid. (John 14:27)

"I have told you these things, so that in me you may have peace. In this world you will have trouble. But take heart! I have overcome the world." (John 16:33)

2. The child was the One appointed to be God's salvation. He was appointed and prepared in "by God's set purpose and foreknowledge" (Acts 2:23). Note also this was the confession of Simeon. He confessed that the child was God's salvation.

Thought 1. Everyone must confess that the child Jesus is God's salvation, through whom God saves the world.

"Whoever acknowledges me before men, I will also acknowledge him before my Father in heaven. (Mat 10:32)

If anyone acknowledges that Jesus is the Son of God, God lives in him and he in God. (1 John 4:15)

3. The child, God's salvation, was prepared for all people. Simeon saw that God's salvation was not for any one people or nation or group. The Messiah had come to save all men. Anyone could now be saved, no matter who he was or what he had done. Prejudice and favoritism were unknown to God. He was not willing that any should perish.

I am not ashamed of the gospel, because it is the power of God for the salvation of everyone who believes: first for the Jew, then for the Gentile. (Rom 1:16)

The Lord is not slow in keeping his promise, as some understand slowness. He is patient with you, not wanting anyone to perish, but everyone to come to repentance. (2 Pet 3:9)

4. The child, God's salvation, was to be a light to the Gentiles, to the unbelievers of the world. The child came to be the Light of the world. This simply means that He came to be the Revelation of God, to reveal the way, the truth, and the life to men (see note, pt.4—Lk.1:76-79).

Jesus answered, "I am the way and the truth and the life. No one comes to the Father except through me. (John 14:6)

When Jesus spoke again to the people, he said, "I am the light of the world. Whoever follows me will never walk in darkness, but will have the light of life." (John 8:12)

5. The child, God's salvation, was to be the glory of Israel, of true believers. The Messiah was to be the glory of all Israelites (Jews) who truly believed. In fact, He was to be the glory of all who believed, no matter what nationality. The reason is clearly given by Scripture.

a. The believer is justified, made righteous.

But in the LORD all the descendants of Israel will be found righteous and will exult. (Isa 45:25)

b. The believer is saved to live with God eternally.

"Although you have been forsaken and hated, with no one traveling through, I will make you the everlasting pride and the joy of all generations. No longer will violence be heard in your land, nor ruin or destruction within your borders, but you will call your walls Salvation and your gates Praise. The sun will no more be your light by day, nor will the brightness of the moon shine on you, for the LORD will be your everlasting light, and your God will be your glory. (Isa 60:15, 18-19)

6. The parents marvelled at the predictions. The predictions would amaze anyone, but they were given for an additional reason. Joseph and Mary needed to be assured and encouraged. Their need was only natural. Imagine what they had been through and were yet to go through because of the child (see note—Lk.2:7; 2:40; DEEPER STUDY # 1—Mt.1:18-25). God saw to it that they were strengthened in this experience.

3 (2:34) **Jesus Christ, Person; Work—Decision**: the child was to cause the rise and fall of many. The child was to be what the Scripture calls the *stone of stumbling* and the *chief cornerstone*.

Many would stumble and fall over Him. They would not notice, look, study, prefer, choose, believe, or trust Him and the salvation He was to bring. They would simply choose another way other than God. Therefore, they would stumble and fall over Him just as they would stumble over a stone lying in their path.

Many would rise because of Him. They would take notice, choose, and believe Him and the salvation He was to bring. Therefore, He would become their foundation, their cornerstone.

> **Thought 1.** Decisively, Jesus Christ causes every man to make a choice. A man either rejects the Messiah, God's salvation, and falls (eternally); or he accepts and he rises (eternally). (See DEEPER STUDY # 7, Jesus Christ, the Stone—Mt.21:42; DEEPER STUDY # 9—21:44 for more discussion.)
>
> **The LORD Almighty is the one you are to regard as holy, he is the one you are to fear, he is the one you are to dread, and he will be a sanctuary; but for both houses of Israel he will be a stone that causes men to stumble and a rock that makes them fall. And for the people of Jerusalem he will be a trap and a snare. Many of them will stumble; they will fall and be broken, they will be snared and captured." (Isa 8:13-15)**
>
> **Now to you who believe, this stone is precious. But to those who do not believe, "The stone the builders rejected has become the capstone," and, "A stone that causes men to stumble and a rock that makes them fall." They stumble because they disobey the message—which is also what they were destined for. (1 Pet 2:7-8)**

4 (2:34-35) **Jesus Christ, Death—Humanism**: the child's fate was sealed. The child was to be opposed and eventually killed. He was the "sign that will be spoken against."

> **Thought 1.** Christ was a sign of both God's love and judgment. It is this that causes men to react. Men want a god that brings only enough law and morality to give order to society. They want a god that allows them to live as they desire, not a God who demands total self-denial and obedience (see note and DEEPER STUDY # 1—Lk.9:23). *They want a god of indulging love, not of sacrificial love; a god of license, not of demanding love.* Therefore, when Christ is set before men as the Messiah of self-denying love and obedience, they react. Why? Because if they disobey Him and fail to live sacrificial lives, they bring judgment upon themselves.
>
> **Thought 2.** Within every society, Christ and His genuine followers are *spoken against* with varying degrees of reaction and persecution. The *speaking against* ranges all the way from simply ignoring believers to killing them (martyrdom). There is...
>
> - ignoring
> - ridiculing
> - abusing
> - hating
> - imprisoning
> - murdering
> - persecuting
> - slandering

Note the words spoken to Mary, "And a sword will pierce through your own soul too." This is a reference to the sorrow she was to experience at the cross, seeing her Son, the only begotten Son of God, rejected and killed by men (cp. Jn.19:25-27).

Note also, the purpose for the child's death: to reveal the inner thoughts of man's heart.

> **Thought 1.** Man either sees the love of God and surrenders to the saving grace of God, or else he looks upon the cross as a repulsive sight and rejects the saving grace of God. He either sees Christ's dying for his sins and receives the forgiveness of God offered by the cross, or else he recoils from the thought of sin within himself and turns from the forgiveness of the cross (see note, pts.2-4—Mt.16:21-23).
>
> **For the message of the cross is foolishness to those who are perishing, but to us who are being saved it is the power of God. (1 Cor 1:18)**
>
> **Or do you show contempt for the riches of his kindness, tolerance and patience, not realizing that God's kindness leads you toward repentance? (Rom 2:4)**
>
> **Therefore, as tongues of fire lick up straw and as dry grass sinks down in the flames, so their roots will decay and their flowers blow away like dust; for they have rejected the law of the LORD Almighty and spurned the word of the Holy One of Israel. (Isa 5:24)**
>
> **To whom can I speak and give warning? Who will listen to me? Their ears are closed so they cannot hear. The word of the LORD is offensive to them; they find no pleasure in it. (Jer 6:10)**
>
> **The wise will be put to shame; they will be dismayed and trapped. Since they have rejected the word of the LORD, what kind of wisdom do they have? (Jer 8:9)**
>
> **They made their hearts as hard as flint and would not listen to the law or to the words that the LORD Almighty had sent by his Spirit through the earlier prophets. So the LORD Almighty was very angry. (Zec 7:12)**

	J. Anna's Praise: The Child Jesus is Praised by a Prophetess, 2:36-38	37 And then was a widow until she was eighty-four. She never left the temple but worshiped night and day, fasting and praying.	**4 She never ceased to worship—night & day**
1 She was a prophetess **2 She never lost hope over many, many years** **3 She never grew bitter in the face of sorrow**	36 There was also a prophetess, Anna, the daughter of Phanuel, of the tribe of Asher. She was very old; she had lived with her husband seven years after her marriage,	38 Coming up to them at that very moment, she gave thanks to God and spoke about the child to all who were looking forward to the redemption of Jerusalem.	**5 She knew the child instantly & gave thanks** **6 She shared the message with all believers**

DIVISION I

THE ANNOUNCEMENT OF THE COMING OF JESUS, THE SON OF MAN, 1:1-2:52

J. Anna's Praise: The Child Jesus is Praised by a Prophetess, 2:36-38

(2:36-38) **Introduction**: nothing is known about Anna except what is given here. She was the daughter of Phanuel. Apparently, her father's name had been taken from the place Phanuel, the place where Jacob wrestled with God face to face (Gen.32:24-30). Anna's name means *gracious*. She seems to have been a person of enormous devotion, one who lived as though face to face with God, ever receiving His grace and sharing His grace with others. She knew she had descended from the tribe of Aser.

A man, Simeon, had just borne witness that the child Jesus' was the *Salvation of God*. Now a woman, Anna, bore the very same witness. Both men and women acknowledged the child to be the Messiah, the Salvation of God. Both men and women of every generation are urged to hope in Him for salvation. Jesus is our hope.

1. She was a prophetess (v.36).
2. She never lost hope over many, many years (v.36).
3. She never grew bitter in the face of sorrow (v.36).
4. She never ceased to worship—night and day (v.37).
5. She knew the child instantly and gave thanks (v.38).
6. She shared the message with all believers (v.38).

1 (2:36) **Prophetess**: Anna was a prophetess. This was most unusual. There had not been a prophet in Israel for some three hundred years, yet God is seen as having raised up a prophet, and a woman at that. Women leaders were very rare in that day. She was apparently a very special person, one who loved God and hoped in God with all her being (cp. v.37). She was evidently on a spiritual par with other saintly women used by God throughout Scripture such as Miriam, Hannah, and Deborah. As a prophetess, she was constantly studying the Word of God that she might be approved of God and proclaim the unsearchable riches of His grace (cp. 2 Tim.2:15; 4:2). The point is, Anna's hope was in God; therefore, God blessed her greatly. God will always bless the person who hopes in Him.

Be strong and take heart, all you who hope in the LORD. (Psa 31:24)

But the eyes of the LORD are on those who fear him, on those whose hope is in his unfailing love, (Psa 33:18)

"But now, Lord, what do I look for? My hope is in you. (Psa 39:7)

Why are you downcast, O my soul? Why so disturbed within me? Put your hope in God, for I will yet praise him, my Savior and my God. (Psa 42:11)

For you have been my hope, O Sovereign LORD, my confidence since my youth. (Psa 71:5)

"But blessed is the man who trusts in the LORD, whose confidence is in him. (Jer 17:7)

2 (2:36) **Steadfastness—Perseverance**: Anna never lost hope over many, many years. She was about eighty-four years old (v.37), but she still believed and still looked for the Messiah. She still looked for the salvation that God was to send to the world. She never forsook her belief, but held fast, *enduring to the end.*

Because of the increase of wickedness, the love of most will grow cold, but he who stands firm to the end will be saved. (Mat 24:12-13)

"As the Father has loved me, so have I loved you. Now remain in my love. (John 15:9)

Let us not become weary in doing good, for at the proper time we will reap a harvest if we do not give up. (Gal 6:9)

As you know, we consider blessed those who have persevered. You have heard of Job's perseverance and have seen what the Lord finally brought about. The Lord is full of compassion and mercy. (James 5:11)

I am coming soon. Hold on to what you have, so that no one will take your crown. (Rev 3:11)

3 (2:36) **Dedication—Sorrow—Widow**: Anna never grew bitter in the face of sorrow. She had been married at an early age and had lived with her husband only seven years when he died. She remained a widow, but not out of bitterness or disappointment. She never remarried because of conviction—the conviction that her life belonged to God. Before her husband died, she had been committed to her husband; and from what is recorded in this passage, she was bound to have been an ideal wife. When her husband died, she apparently understood this to be a sign that God wanted her life totally committed to Him. Therefore, she dedicated herself to serving Him and Him alone for the remainder of her life. She placed her hope in God and in God alone.

> **Now to the unmarried and the widows I say: It is good for them to stay unmarried, as I am. (1 Cor 7:8)**
>
> **What I mean, brothers, is that the time is short. From now on those who have wives should live as if they had none; those who mourn, as if they did not; those who are happy, as if they were not; those who buy something, as if it were not theirs to keep; those who use the things of the world, as if not engrossed in them. For this world in its present form is passing away. I would like you to be free from concern. An unmarried man is concerned about the Lord's affairs—how he can please the Lord. But a married man is concerned about the affairs of this world—how he can please his wife—and his interests are divided. An unmarried woman or virgin is concerned about the Lord's affairs: Her aim is to be devoted to the Lord in both body and spirit. But a married woman is concerned about the affairs of this world—how she can please her husband. I am saying this for your own good, not to restrict you, but that you may live in a right way in undivided devotion to the Lord. (1 Cor 7:29-35)**

Note in particular the words, "that you may live in a right way in undivided devotion [without distraction] to the Lord."

4 (2:37) **Devotion—Worship**: Anna never ceased to worship, night or day. This is a phenomenal statement: she never left the temple, but "worshiped night and day, fasting and praying." This either means that she had been given some kind of *room* at the temple or else she was at worship every day never missing a service (cp. Lk.24:53). Anna was a godly woman, a woman to whom God meant everything. She was totally devoted to God, sold out to Him completely, hoping in Him and in Him alone. Note two things.

1. The fastings and prayers indicate that she was extremely disciplined, possessing the consistency in devotions that so many lack.
2. She fasted and prayed night and day despite being elderly, eighty-four years old. She did not give herself to the flesh as she grew old: overeating, oversleeping, immoral gratification, or meaningless activities that waste time. She devoted herself to serving and hoping in God, praying and bearing witness as His servant.

> **Look to the LORD and his strength; seek his face always. (1 Chr 16:11)**
>
> **Then Jesus told his disciples a parable to show them that they should always pray and not give up. (Luke 18:1 cp. Eph 6:18; 1 Thes 5:17)**
>
> **But in your hearts set apart Christ as Lord. Always be prepared to give an answer to everyone who asks you to give the reason for the hope that you have. But do this with gentleness and respect, (1 Pet 3:15)**
>
> **"You are my witnesses," declares the LORD, "and my servant whom I have chosen, so that you may know and believe me and understand that I am he. Before me no god was formed, nor will there be one after me. (Isa 43:10)**

5 (2:38) **Jesus Christ, Savior—Redemption**: Anna knew the child instantly and gave thanks. She was the Lord's servant, so the Lord guided her life step by step. He took care of her, looking after her welfare. She belonged to God so much that God could guide her every step. He saw to it that her path crossed the path of the child Messiah. He fulfilled her hope. Note she came in at the very moment that Jesus was in the temple, and she immediately began giving thanks to God for the Christ-child. What is the message of her thanksgiving? *Redemption.* Redemption is that for which she praised God. The child was the Messiah who was to redeem all people (see note, pts. 1, 2, 3—Lk.2:28-33. See note—Eph.1:7.) Note that she prophesied and proclaimed the same message as Simeon: the child Jesus is the glorious hope of man's redemption.

> **He provided redemption for his people; he ordained his covenant forever— holy and awesome is his name. (Psa 111:9)**
>
> **O Israel, put your hope in the LORD, for with the LORD is unfailing love and with him is full redemption. (Psa 130:7)**
>
> **But now, this is what the LORD says—he who created you, O Jacob, he who formed you, O Israel: "Fear not, for I have redeemed you; I have summoned you by name; you are mine. (Isa 43:1)**
>
> **And are justified freely by his grace through the redemption that came by Christ Jesus. (Rom 3:24)**
>
> **It is because of him that you are in Christ Jesus, who has become for us wisdom from God—that is, our righteousness, holiness and redemption. (1 Cor 1:30)**
>
> **Christ redeemed us from the curse of the law by becoming a curse for us, for it is written: "Cursed is everyone who is hung on a tree." (Gal 3:13)**
>
> **In him we have redemption through his blood, the forgiveness of sins, in accordance with the riches of God's grace (Eph 1:7; cp. Col 1:14)**
>
> **Who gave himself for us to redeem us from all wickedness and to purify for himself a people that are his very own, eager to do what is good. (Titus 2:14)**
>
> **He did not enter by means of the blood of goats and calves; but he entered the Most Holy Place once for all by his own blood, having obtained eternal redemption. (Heb 9:12)**
>
> **For you know that it was not with perishable things such as silver or gold that you were redeemed from the empty way of life handed down to you from your forefathers, (1 Pet 1:18)**
>
> **And they sang a new song: "You are worthy to take the scroll and to open its seals, because you were slain, and with your blood you purchased men for God**

from every tribe and language and people and nation. (Rev 5:9)

6 (2:38) **Witnessing**: Anna shared the message with all believers. She knew of others who were looking for the Messiah's coming, so she shared the glorious news with them (see DEEPER STUDY # 2—Mt.1:18). She had seen the child-Messiah, the salvation of God, the glorious hope of all men.

Let the redeemed of the LORD say this— those he redeemed from the hand of the foe, (Psa 107:2)

And the things you have heard me say in the presence of many witnesses entrust to reliable men who will also be qualified to teach others. (2 Tim 2:2)

Therefore go and make disciples of all nations, baptizing them in the name of the Father and of the Son and of the Holy Spirit, and teaching them to obey everything I have commanded you. And surely I am with you always, to the very end of the age." (Mat 28:19-20)

	K. Jesus' Growth as a Child, 2:39-40
1 He was led by His parents to fulfill all the law **2 He was reared in Nazareth**[DS1]	39 When Joseph and Mary had done everything required by the Law of the Lord, they returned to Galilee to their own town of Nazareth.
3 He grew as a child: Physically, spiritually, & mentally **4 He possessed God's grace**	40 And the child grew and became strong; he was filled with wisdom, and the grace of God was upon him.

DIVISION I

THE ANNOUNCEMENT OF THE COMING OF JESUS, THE SON OF MAN, 1:1-2:52

K. Jesus' Growth as a Child, 2:39-40

(2:39-40) **Introduction**: Jesus' growth as a child is simply stated. What is said is meaningful and applicable to the life of all thoughtful readers.

1. He was led by His parents to fulfill all the law (v.39).
2. He was reared in Nazareth (v.39).
3. He grew as a child: physically, spiritually, and mentally (v.40).
4. He possessed God's grace (v.40).

1 (2:39) **Jesus Christ, Fulfilled Law**: Jesus was led by His parents to fulfill all the law. Note two significant facts.

1. God had sent His Son into the world to fulfill the law, not to destroy it. By keeping all the law, Jesus would be perfectly righteous and become the *Ideal Man*, the Man who would be the *Pattern* for all men to follow.

Another way to say the same thing is that God has given us a perfect life to follow, not just written letters and words. By fulfilling the law and by never failing in a single point, Jesus became the Perfect Man, the Ideal Life which men are to imitate. Men are now to look to Jesus and follow Him instead of following the law. Jesus has fulfilled the law; therefore, He embraces and includes all the law *and more* in His life (see notes—Mt.5:17-18; DEEPER STUDY # 2—Ro.8:3).

2. In order to fulfill the law, Jesus had to keep the law and every observance of it. He had to "fulfill all righteousness" (Mt.3:15). Now note: by keeping all of the law, Jesus was symbolically predicting what He was to do for sinful man. He was going to secure righteousness and perfection by fulfilling the law, and thereby He was to become the Ideal Man. As the Ideal Man, whatever He did would cover any man who followed Him. The man who followed Jesus would be covered by His righteousness (perfection), His death, His resurrection, and His ascension. The man who truly trusted Jesus Christ to cover him with His righteousness would be covered by His righteousness.

It is for these reasons that God led Mary and Joseph to fulfill all the law for the child Messiah (also see notes—Lk.2:22-23; DEEPER STUDY # 3—Mt.8:20 for more discussion).

> **Jesus replied, "Let it be so now; it is proper for us to do this to fulfill all righteousness." Then John consented. (Mat 3:15)**
> **"Do not think that I have come to abolish the Law or the Prophets; I have not come to abolish them but to fulfill them. (Mat 5:17)**
> **For what the law was powerless to do in that it was weakened by the sinful nature, God did by sending his own Son in the likeness of sinful man to be a sin offering. And so he condemned sin in sinful man, (Rom 8:3)**
> **For since death came through a man, the resurrection of the dead comes also through a man. (1 Cor 15:21)**

2 (2:39) **Jesus Christ, Childhood—Nazareth**: Jesus was reared in Nazareth.

1. Luke simply says that after Jesus' dedication in the temple, His parents returned to Nazareth. There is no mention of Matthew's account...

- of their return to Bethlehem where the wise men visited them (Mt.2:1-12).
- of their flight into Egypt (Mt.2:13-15).
- of Herod's slaughter of the children (Mt.2:16-18).
- of the threat of Archaleus (Mt.2:19-22).

2. Nazareth was an ideal place for the child Messiah to be brought up (see DEEPER STUDY # 1, Nazareth—Lk.2:39 for discussion). However, Nazareth was an obscure place, despised and reproached by other people (cp. Jn.1:46). It was a humiliating place to be reared. Therefore, as with Jesus' birth in a stable, which was the lowest of places, He continued to identify with people in the most severe circumstances. He, too, knew what it was to be born and brought up in a despicable place. From the very first, He *made Himself nothing* (Ph.2:7).

> **But made himself nothing, taking the very nature of a servant, being made in human likeness. (Phil 2:7)**
> **For you know the grace of our Lord Jesus Christ, that though he was rich, yet for your sakes he became poor, so that you through his poverty might become rich. (2 Cor 8:9)**
> **For even Christ did not please himself but, as it is written: "The insults of those who insult you have fallen on me." (Rom 15:3)**

DEEPER STUDY # 1

(2:39) **Nazareth**: the hometown of Joseph and Mary and of Jesus Himself during His childhood and early manhood. There were at least two advantages to Jesus' being brought up in Nazareth.

1. It was a quiet town, small and infamous, ready-made for a close community and for neighborliness and quiet contemplation.

2. It was also a town in touch with the modern life and world events of that day. Two of the major roads in the ancient world passed within eyesight of the hills surrounding the city: the road stretching between the great cities of the North and South (from Rome to Africa), and the road stretching between the great cities of the East and West. Jesus can be imagined sitting and standing on the hills observing (perhaps even meeting) some of the travellers and caravans using the major routes as they crisscrossed the world. He had opportunity to observe and study the nature and dealings of all kinds of men and nationalities as they used the major routes. How often His heart must have ached and wept as a child over a world lost and needing to be found.

3 (2:40) **Jesus Christ, Childhood—Humiliation**: Jesus grew as a child—physically, spiritually, and mentally.

1. The idea is that Jesus grew as a normal child. But note the added words: *"became strong"* [ekrataiouto] in spirit (a vigorous growth). He did not just grow in wisdom, He was *"filled* with wisdom" (pleroumenon sophiai). Simply stated, Jesus grew perfectly at every stage of life.

⇒ He grew physically as well as the human body could grow (perfectly well and healthy).

⇒ He "became strong," as strong as a child could grow.

⇒ He was "filled with wisdom," as much as a child could be filled.

No other child had ever been or ever will be perfect in growth at the various stages of childhood, but the Christ-child was. He grew as well as a child can grow: *filled* perfectly with all the qualities that fill a child.

2. Why did Christ come into the world as a child and not as a full-grown man? The first man, Adam, stood at the head of the human race as the natural representative of man, and he had been created as a full-grown man. Why not Jesus Christ, the second Adam? He, too, was sent into the world to stand at the head of the human race as the spiritual representative of man. Going through the stages of growth as a baby, then as a child, and then as a teenager is a humbling experience. Why did God subject His Son to such humiliation? There are at least two reasons.

a. Christ needed to set a striking example for every person, no matter the age, even for children. In *humility*, He went through the experience of a helpless babe, then a dependent child, and then an independent and responsible man. The very fact that the Son of God stooped so low is shocking to any thoughtful person. It sets a striking example of *humility and lowliness of mind* for every man.

> **Do nothing out of selfish ambition or vain conceit, but in humility consider others better than yourselves. Each of you should look not only to your own interests, but also to the interests of others. Your attitude should be the same as that of Christ Jesus: Who, being in very nature God, did not consider equality with God something to be grasped, but made himself nothing, taking the very nature of a servant, being made in human likeness. And being found in appearance as a man, he humbled himself and became obedient to death— even death on a cross! (Phil 2:3-8)**

b. Christ needed to demonstrate a striking truth to all men: no person can enter heaven unless they first become as a little child. There was no better way to demonstrate the lesson than for the Son of God Himself to go through the humbling experience of becoming a child before becoming a man.

> **And he said: "I tell you the truth, unless you change and become like little children, you will never enter the kingdom of heaven. Therefore, whoever humbles himself like this child is the greatest in the kingdom of heaven. (Mat 18:3-4)**

c. Christ needed to experience every situation, condition, and trial of man in order to become the *Perfect Sympathizer or Savior*. For this reason, He experienced the most humiliating experiences possible. He experienced...

- being born to an unwed mother (Mt.1:18-19).
- being born in a stable, the worst of conditions (Lk.2:7).
- being born to poor parents (Lk.2:24).
- having his life threatened as a baby (Mt.2:13f).
- being the cause of unimaginable sorrow (Mt.2:16f).
- having to be moved and shifted as a baby (Mt.2:13f).
- being reared in a despicable place, Nazareth (Lk.2:39).
- having His father die during His youth (see note, pt.3—Mt.13:53-58).
- having to support His mother and brothers and sisters (see note, pt.3—Mt.13:53-58).
- having no home, not even a place to lay His head (Mt.8:20; Lk.9:58).
- being hated and opposed by religionists (Mk.14:1-2).
- being charged with insanity (Mk.3:21).
- being charged with demon possession (Mk.3:22).
- being opposed by His own family (Mk.3:31-32).
- being rejected, hated, and opposed by listeners (Mt.13:53-58; Lk.4:28-29).
- being betrayed by a close friend (Mk.14:10-11, 18).
- being left alone, rejected, and forsaken by all of His friends (Mk.14:50).
- being tried before the high court of the land on the charge of treason (Jn.18:33).
- being executed by crucifixion, the worst possible death (Jn.19:16f).

Note that each of these experiences reaches the depth of humiliation. Christ stooped to the lowest point of human experience in every condition in order to become the *Per-*

Note that each of these experiences reaches the depth of humiliation. Christ stooped to the lowest point of human experience in every condition in order to become the *Perfect Sympathizer* (Savior). He can now identify with and feel for any person's circumstances.

> **For surely it is not angels he helps, but Abraham's descendants. For this reason he had to be made like his brothers in every way, in order that he might become a merciful and faithful high priest in service to God, and that he might make atonement for the sins of the people. Because he himself suffered when he was tempted, he is able to help those who are being tempted. (Heb 2:16-18)**
>
> **For we do not have a high priest who is unable to sympathize with our weaknesses, but we have one who has been tempted in every way, just as we are—yet was without sin. Let us then approach the throne of grace with confidence, so that we may receive mercy and find grace to help us in our time of need. (Heb 4:15-16)**

4 (2:40) **Jesus Christ, Childhood—Fulness of God's Grace**: Jesus possessed God's grace (charis theou). The idea is that God's grace rested upon Jesus in *full measure*, without any lack or shortcoming whatsoever.

Jesus was choosing to grow perfectly, coming short in nothing. Therefore, God showered Him with His grace, His favor. God favored Him by looking after and taking care of Him perfectly.

> **For the one whom God has sent speaks the words of God, for God gives the Spirit without limit. (John 3:34)**
>
> **It is because of him that you are in Christ Jesus, who has become for us wisdom from God—that is, our righteousness, holiness and redemption. (1 Cor 1:30)**

Outline	Scripture	Scripture	Outline
	L. Jesus as a Young Boy in the Temple: Jesus' First Recognition of Messiahship, 2:41-52	sitting among the teachers, listening to them and asking them questions.	a. He listened to teachers b. He asked questions
1 His faithfulness in worship was noteworthy a. Parents' faithfulness b. Parents taught Him c. Jesus' special year: Became a man at age twelve	41 Every year his parents went to Jerusalem for the Feast of the Passover. 42 When he was twelve years old, they went up to the Feast, according to the custom.	47 Everyone who heard him was amazed at his understanding and his answers. 48 When his parents saw him, they were astonished. His mother said to him, "Son, why have you treated us like this? Your father and I have been anxiously searching for you."	**4 His mission was misunderstood by His parents**
2 His social development was normal a. His parents left to return home b. Jesus was missing from the caravan c. His parents thought He was with others, playing and socializing	43 After the Feast was over, while his parents were returning home, the boy Jesus stayed behind in Jerusalem, but they were unaware of it. 44 Thinking he was in their company, they traveled on for a day. Then they began looking for him among their relatives and friends.	49 "Why were you searching for me?" he asked. "Didn't you know I had to be in my Father's house?" 50 But they did not understand what he was saying to them. 51 Then he went down to Nazareth with them and was obedient to them. But his mother treasured all these things in her heart.	**5 His first known recognition of Messiahship was at an early age** **6 His obedience to His parents was striking**
d. His parents returned to find Him **3 His knowledge was surprising**	45 When they did not find him, they went back to Jerusalem to look for him. 46 After three days they found him in the temple courts,	52 And Jesus grew in wisdom and stature, and in favor with God and men.	**7 His growth was in favor with both God and man**[DS1]

DIVISION I

THE ANNOUNCEMENT OF THE COMING OF JESUS, THE SON OF MAN, 1:1-2:52

L. Jesus as a Young Boy in the Temple: Jesus' First Recognition of Messiahship, 2:41-52

(2:41-52) **Introduction**: this is an extremely important and interesting passage. It is the only passage that covers Jesus' childhood. It is important, for it gives us the first *known* time that Jesus claimed to be the Messiah. The lessons found within the passage are inexhaustable.

1. His faithfulness in worship was noteworthy (v.41-42).
2. His social development was normal (v.43-45).
3. His knowledge was surprising (v.46-47).
4. His mission was misunderstood by His parents (v.48).
5. His first known recognition of Messiahship was at an early age (v.49-50).
6. His obedience to His parents was striking (v.51).
7. His growth was in favor with both God and man (v.52).

1 (2:41-42) **Worship—Jesus Christ, Childhood**: Jesus' faithfulness in worship as a young boy was noteworthy. Note several things.

1. Jesus' parents were faithful in their worship. This fact is specifically stated. It was their *custom* to keep the feast of the Passover every year. All male Jews who lived within twenty miles of Jerusalem were required by law to attend the temple three times a year: at the Passover, Pentecost, and the Feast of Tabernacles (Ex.23:14-17). Women were exempt from the law, but they could attend if they wished. Note what Mary chose to do: every year His "parents went to Jerusalem." They were both faithful in their worship by choice, not by restraint.

2. Jesus' parents led and taught Him to be faithful in worship. It is not specifically said that Jesus went to Jerusalem with His parents every year, but the implication is that He did. Note the words, "Every year his parents went...for the... Passover." It was the custom for "all who were able to understand" to be present if at all possible (Neh.8:2).

Also note His knowledge and ability to discuss issues with religious authorities (v.46-47). This indicates that His parents continually taught Jesus, seeing to it that He was in the synagogue worshipping and learning at every opportunity. God had placed the child Jesus into their hands as a *bundle of trust*. The child belonged to God. He had only entrusted the child's keeping into their hands to see that He was looked after and taught. It was their responsibility to see that He grew physically, mentally, and spiritually and to see that He became all He could become. The parents were faithful to their duty.

> **Thought 1.** What an example for all parents. Children are but a *bundle of trust* placed into our hands by God. They belong to God, not us. Therefore, we are to train up a child in the way he should go (Pr.22:6).

3. This was a very special year for Jesus. He had just turned twelve years old. When a Jewish boy reached thirteen years of age, he became a *son of the law* which meant that he was now considered a man and was expected to keep all the law. It was suggested that a boy be brought to the Passover Feast a year or two early so that he might become familiar with the Temple and the Feasts. When the eleven- and twelve-year old initiates arrived, they were naturally given a great deal of attention and special instruction (v.46-47).

Thought 1. Note two critical points.
1) Every child should be taught from the very first about God and worship, about the world and a person's responsibility in it.
2) Every child, when he comes of age, should be charged with becoming a "son of the law," a man *before God*, being responsible and making his contribution to the world—*all in the name of the Lord.*

> **Impress them on your children. Talk about them when you sit at home and when you walk along the road, when you lie down and when you get up. (Deu 6:7)**
>
> **Train a child in the way he should go, and when he is old he will not turn from it. (Prov 22:6)**
>
> **Come, my children, listen to me; I will teach you the fear of the LORD. (Psa 34:11)**

2 (2:43-45) **Jesus Christ, Childhood**: Jesus' social development was normal. This is gleaned from what happened in these verses. The parents had finished their worship obligations and were returning home to Nazareth. Jesus had remained behind, but they did not know it. They thought He was off playing and socializing with some of the other families and children in the caravan. The caravans were large and the roads were packed with thousands of pilgrims leaving the Feast. We can glean from this that Jesus was sociable and fit right in with people. The very fact that His parents would think He was off socializing with others points to a normal social development. Note: they were so sure that He was socializing that they did not bother to look for Him until nightfall (v.44). When they did not find Him among their relatives and friends, they returned to Jerusalem to search for Him.

Thought 1. A child's social development is important. A child is to be helped and encouraged, led and directed to play with others. However, he must also be taught how to play and how to associate with others. He must be taught to be...

- patient
- giving
- joyful
- loving
- kind
- helpful
- peaceful
- loyal
- caring
- disciplined

...not bragging, revengeful, arrogant, jealous, selfish, or easily provoked.

3 (2:46-47) **Jesus Christ, Knowledge of**: Jesus' knowledge was surprising. It took His parents three days to find Him. When they found Him, He was in the temple, in the very precinct or room where classes and discussion took place among the doctors of theology and religion. It was a prominent place, and it was a custom to hold open classes and discussions so that the public could listen and learn. The stress of Luke at this point is the surprising knowledge of Jesus. His knowledge and understanding were phenomenal.

1. Jesus was found "sitting among the teachers." There were some very prominent *Doctors of Religion* in that day, men who were very capable theologically. There was...

- Gamaliel, the great teacher of Paul or Saul of Tarsus.
- Hillel, one of the most revered liberal teachers with a large school of followers (see DEEPER STUDY # 1—Mt.19:1-12).
- Shammai, one of the most revered conservative teachers who also had a school of followers (see DEEPER STUDY # 1—Mt.19:1-12).
- Jonathan, who paraphrased the sacred books.
- Simeon, who was to later succeed Hillel.
- Nicodemus, who was so revered by his peers that he was sent to interview Jesus alone.

Some of these scholars were probably engaged in the discussion with Jesus, for news of the young boy and his phenomenal understanding must have swept through the halls of the temple, arousing the curiosity of the *teachers* or *Doctors*. Remember, Jesus had been in the temple for at least three days. The point to note is how Jesus was making use of the opportunity He had. He was in Jerusalem exposed to these eminent scholars for only a few days, so He grasped the opportunity to learn and perhaps teach all He could.

2. Jesus was found thirsting for knowledge and understanding. Note exactly what is said.

a. He was "*listening to them*" (akouonta) what the teachers said. He listened closely, attentively, with rapt attention. He was "quick to listen" (Jas.1:19).
b. He was "asking them questions" (eperotonta). He wanted answers, more understanding. He thirsted for truth and sought it.
c. He answered (apokrisesin) their questions.

Note that His questions and answers revealed phenomenal knowledge and understanding, so much so that everyone was astonished, even the teachers or doctors. The word amazed (existanto de) means that all were astonished, overwhelmed, bewildered, and wondered at His understanding.

> **I have more insight than all my teachers, for I meditate on your statutes. I have more understanding than the elders, for I obey your precepts. (Psa 119:99-100)**

Thought 1. This is a striking lesson for both children and adults.
1) Every opportunity to learn the truth should be grasped.
2) We should *thirst* for knowledge and understanding.

> **To the Jews who had believed him, Jesus said, "If you hold to my teaching, you are really my disciples. Then you will know the truth, and the truth will set you free." (John 8:31-32)**
>
> **For this very reason, make every effort to add to your faith goodness; and to goodness, knowledge; (2 Pet 1:5)**
>
> **But let him who boasts boast about this: that he understands and knows me, that I am the LORD, who exercises kindness, justice and righteousness on earth, for in these I delight," declares the LORD. (Jer 9:24)**
>
> **And if you call out for insight and cry aloud for understanding, (Prov 2:3)**
>
> **Blessed is the man who finds wisdom, the man who gains understand-**

ing, (Prov 3:13)
Get wisdom, get understanding; do not forget my words or swerve from them. (Prov 4:5)
The discerning heart seeks knowledge, but the mouth of a fool feeds on folly. (Prov 15:14)
Buy the truth and do not sell it; get wisdom, discipline and understanding. (Prov 23:23)
Let us acknowledge the LORD; let us press on to acknowledge him. As surely as the sun rises, he will appear; he will come to us like the winter rains, like the spring rains that water the earth." (Hosea 6:3)

4 (2:48) **Jesus Christ, Mission—Forgetfulness**: Jesus' mission was misunderstood by His parents. This is seen in Mary's words to Jesus. She was rebuking Jesus rather sternly. In her disturbance and sorrow, she forgot who He was. It is not that she was not to teach and discipline or direct Him; she was. But He was now a young man by law, and He was where He should be, in His Father's house.

Thought 1. There is warning here. Too often disturbance and sorrow cause us to *forget who Jesus is*. We allow circumstances to cloud our minds, to disturb us and bring sorrow into our lives. And we soon *forget Jesus*, His understanding of the situation and His business of ministering to our needs.

Only be careful, and watch yourselves closely so that you do not forget the things your eyes have seen or let them slip from your heart as long as you live. Teach them to your children and to their children after them. (Deu 4:9)

5 (2:49-50) **Messiahship**: Jesus' first known recognition of Messiahship was at an early age. This is a very significant point. This is the first time that Jesus claimed to be the Son of God. Note two points.

1. He called God His Father. Joseph was standing there, so Jesus was gentle in the way He worded His statement, but He was clear and definite in referring to God as His Father. Just *when* He knew He was the Messiah, the Son of God, is not known; and frankly, all suggestions are pure speculation. But this fact is known. At age twelve, He was conscious of a *unique relationship with God*, a relationship unlike other children: God was His Father, and He was the Son of God, the *unique Son* in the sense that He was the One and Only *who came from* the Father (cp. Jn.1:14). This is seen even more clearly when Jesus' answer is studied.

2. Jesus was saying to His mother that His Father (God) had been looking after Him. He had been in His Father's house, doing what His Father wanted Him to do; therefore, He was under His Father's care and watchful eye. There was no need for her, His mother, to be worrying.

Thought 1. Every man needs to *place himself under* God's care and watchful eye. A decision to follow Christ as Lord causes God to adopt a person as a child of His and places a person under the Father's care.

3. Jesus was saying that He had work to do for His Father (God) even if that work was not understood. He could not go home with them until He had finished His Father's work. He first had to do what His Father willed.

Jesus said to them, "My Father is always at his work to this very day, and I, too, am working." (John 5:17)
As long as it is day, we must do the work of him who sent me. Night is coming, when no one can work. (John 9:4)
Jesus answered, "I did tell you, but you do not believe. The miracles I do in my Father's name speak for me, (John 10:25)
I have brought you glory on earth by completing the work you gave me to do. (John 17:4)

Thought 1. Christ is the Son of God, His One and Only Son, the only begotten Son of the Father (Jn.3:16f).

Thought 2. Every person is to serve God first, even if the work is not understood. And it is often not understood. We must be faithful to God and His call even if we are misunderstood and opposed.

Remember your Creator in the days of your youth, before the days of trouble come and the years approach when you will say, "I find no pleasure in them"— (Eccl 12:1)

Thought 3. Sometimes our families are the strongest opposition confronting our decision and work for God (cp. Mt.10:37).

6 (2:51) **Children—Family—Obedience**: Jesus' obedience to His parents was striking. This is both a beautiful and striking picture. Jesus was *subject* to His parents; He obeyed them. As the Son of God, He set the perfect example of what a child should be to His parents. He obeyed His parents despite the fact...

- that Joseph was not His true father
- that He was stronger in spirit
- that He was filled with wisdom
- that God was His Father

Children, obey your parents in the Lord, for this is right. "Honor your father and mother"—which is the first commandment with a promise—"that it may go well with you and that you may enjoy long life on the earth." (Eph 6:1-3; cp. Col 3:20)
But if a widow has children or grandchildren, these should learn first of all to put their religion into practice by caring for their own family and so repaying their parents and grandparents, for this is pleasing to God. (1 Tim 5:4)
Even a child is known by his actions, by whether his conduct is pure and right. (Prov 20:11)
Listen to your father, who gave you life, and do not despise your mother when she is old. (Prov 23:22)

Note that Mary again kept all these things in her heart. In humble faith she said nothing, not talking with relatives or neighbors nor boasting in her Son and His uniqueness. She was quiet, humbly waiting upon God to use Jesus as He so willed. In due time she knew that God would reveal Him and His salvation to the world.

7 (2:52) **Jesus Christ, Childhood**: Jesus' growth was in favor with both God and man.

1. Mentally, Jesus was "filled with wisdom" (v.40). He learned from teachers and from personal study and thought just as all children learned. Yet He differed from other children in that He learned perfectly, coming short in nothing.

> **Thought 1.** Note how few children follow the example of Jesus. Few really seek to learn. Most just take what is assigned and do the minimum that is required. Few pursue real excellence.

2. Physically, He grew in an orderly fashion just as all other children grow.

> **Thought 1.** Some children do not develop physically, not like they should. Some are incapable due to deformity or abnormality. However, there are other children who fail to develop as they should because they do not get the physical exercise necessary to develop. They sit around instead of being outside playing and working.

3. Spiritually, He "grew strong [in spirit]" (v.40) and "in favor with God" (v.52). He looked to God in perfect obedience, and God nurtured Him in His perfect favor.

> **Thought 1.** Note how few children follow the example of Jesus. Few children really grow spiritually. Few are willing to buck the crowd, accepting the challenge of Jesus and standing up for Him.

4. Socially, He grew in favor with men. He was friendly, loving, caring, helpful, unselfish, pure, honest, and humble. He was welcomed by the other families in His community.

> **Thought 1.** Note that some children do not follow Jesus' example in developing socially. Some children are not welcomed by other families.

DEEPER STUDY # 1

(2:52) **Grew—Increased** (proekorten): means to grow steadily, to keep advancing. The picture is that of Jesus' cutting His way through the advancing years just as a pioneer cuts through the wilderness to reach his destination.

CHAPTER 3

II. THE SON OF MAN'S APPEARANCE, 3:1-4:15

A. The Forerunner, John the Baptist: The Pivotal Point of History, 3:1-6
(Mt.3:1-6; Mk.1:2-6; Jn.1:19-28)

In the fifteenth year of the
reign of Tiberius Caesar—
when Pontius Pilate was governor of Judea, Herod tetrarch
of Galilee, his brother Philip
tetrarch of Iturea and Tra-
conitis, and Lysanias tetrarch
of Abilene—
2 During the high priesthood
of Annas and Caiaphas, the
word of God came to John
son of Zechariah in the desert.
3 He went into all the country around the Jordan,
preaching a baptism of repentance for the forgiveness of
sins.
4 As is written in the book of
the words of Isaiah the
prophet: "A voice of one
calling in the desert, 'Prepare
the way for the Lord, make
straight paths for him.
5 Every valley shall be filled
in, every mountain and hill
made low. The crooked roads
shall become straight, the
rough ways smooth.
6 And all mankind will see
God's salvation.'"

1 He was a man who launched the most pivotal point of history

2 He was a man called out of the wilderness

3 He was a man who preached repentance & forgiveness of sin

4 He was a man who cried out apocalyptically: Prepare, make the paths of God straight
- a. Humbled shall be exalted
- b. Proud shall be made low
- c. Crooked shall be straightened out
- d. Rough shall be smoothed
- e. God's salvation shall be seen

DIVISION II

THE SON OF MAN'S APPEARANCE, 3:1-4:15

A. The Forerunner, John the Baptist: The Pivotal Point of History, 3:1-6

(3:1-6) **Introduction—History, Pivotal Point of**: the coming of Jesus Christ was the pivotal point of human history. When He came to earth, earth saw the Son of God Himself (1 Jn.1:1-3). His impact upon the world can never be overstated. He changed the world so much that men measure their years by Him. Some may dispute His significance, but they are wrong. And their misjudgment will be confronted some day in the future. When? When Christ returns. Scripture declares that He is going to return to earth. He is going to return as a Judge, not as a Savior—the Judge who will prove that He is the King of kings and Lord of lords, the God of very God, the Messiah. He is going to prove that He is the Salvation of God Almighty.

A Person of such magnitude, the Person whose coming was to be the pivotal point of history, needed a forerunner. He needed someone who could run ahead of Him and arouse the people to prepare for His coming. That forerunner was John the Baptist, a man who is an example to us all.

1. He was a man who launched the most pivotal point of history (v.1).
2. He was a man called out of the wilderness (v.2).
3. He was a man who preached repentance and forgiveness of sin (v.3).
4. He was a man who cried out apocalyptically: prepare, make God's paths straight (v.4-6).

1 (3:1) **History, Pivotal Point—Jesus Christ—Fullness of Time**: John was a man who launched the most pivotal point of history—the coming of Christ. Some may dispute that the coming of Christ is the most significant event in history, but Scripture proclaims that God will someday reveal the fact to all. Luke points to the fact by dating the coming of Christ with significant events and historical rulers. The very first event was God's call of John. Therefore, the beginning of the greatest period in all history began with the call of John, the Lord's forerunner. Note several facts.

1. Tiberius Caesar was in the fifteenth year of his reign when God called John. Tiberius was the second Roman Emporer, beginning his reign in A.D. 14. Therefore, the emergence of John took place between A.D. 28-29.

2. Pontius Pilate was governor of Judea. He was both the civil ruler and a military commander. The situation had grown so bad in Judea that Rome had to remove Archelaus from civil control and move in a military commander. Therefore, Judea was ruled directly by Roman authority at this time. Pilate held office from A.D. 26-36.

3. Herod Antipas was tetrarch of Galilee and Perea. Tetrarch simply means a ruler over a fourth part. Herod Antipas was the son of Herod the Great. He inherited his territory at his father's death and ruled from B.C. 4 to A.D. 39. Note that he was the ruler over Galilee where Jesus spent most of His time ministering. (See DEEPER STUDY # 1,2, Herod—Mt.14:1-14 for more discussion.)

4. Philip was tetrarch of Ituraea and Trachonitis. He was a reputable leader, known as a fair and just ruler. Caesarea Philippi was built and named after him. Caesarea was where Peter made his great confession.

5. Lysanius was tetrarch of Abilene. Nothing of importance is known about him.

6. Annas and Caiaphas were High Priests. This statement throws a revealing light upon the high priesthood of Jesus' day. It shows just how political and corrupt the high priesthood had become. There was never to be more than one priest at any given time, for the priesthood was supposed to be for life and was supposed to be hereditary. But with the coming of Roman rule, the High Priest became a political power base. Rome used the position to secure power over Jewish life. They offered and gave the position to men who were cooperative and willing to let the people follow Roman rule. For example, between B.C. 37-A.D. 26 twenty-eight different men were installed and removed as High Priests.

The point Luke is making is just this: the High Priest's office had become corrupted, and religious positions had become politically motivated. Annas, who had served as High Priest between A.D. 7-14, was still the power behind the throne. Caiaphas was officially the High Priest in Rome's eyes, but Annas was still the one to whom most

Jewish leaders looked. This is actually seen during the trials of Jesus. Jesus was taken first to Annas, despite the fact that he was not the official High Priest (Jn.18:13).

> **Who gave himself for our sins to rescue us from the present evil age, according to the will of our God and Father, (Gal 1:4)**
> **"The time has come," he said. "The kingdom of God is near. Repent and believe the good news!" (Mark 1:15)**

2 (3:2) **Minister, Call of—God, Call of—Institutional Religion**: John was a man called out of the wilderness. Note three points.

1. God's call came to John in the wilderness, in an obscure place. The place where John was reared was so slightly populated that it was known as a wilderness. The area consisted of only six small towns or villages scattered far apart. God found him in the most obscure place.

> **Thought 1.** The place where a person is does not matter; a person's heart is what matters. If a person's heart is right toward God, God will call him no matter where he is. No one is hidden from God, no matter how obscure his residence is. The Word of God is not limited; it reaches even to the wilderness.

2. God's call was a very personal matter. Note: John never revealed how God spoke to him. Did God call him through a vision, through the appearance of an angel, through an audible voice, or through an inner sense? We do not know. John kept the matter in his heart; it was just too intimate, too meaningful an experience. And his heart was genuine and pure. He was not willing to lower his intimacy with God by talking about it and boasting in it, that is, by acting super-spiritual.

3. God's call was for John to serve God rather than to serve institutional religion. John was somewhere around thirty years of age, the age when he was to become a full-fledged priest by descent. Remember, his father Zechariah was a priest, and the priesthood was by descent. He was supposed to have been in training for some five years, and when he reached age thirty he was to begin serving in the temple. But God's call to John was to a different ministry, a ministry that fitted into God's plans much more than institutional religion.

> **Thought 1.** It is God who calls a man, not institutional religion. A man's first loyalty is to God, not to institution-al religion.
>
> **Thought 2.** God moves outside *institutional religion* as well as within institutional religion (cp. Simeon, probably a priest, and Anna, a prophetess within the temple). Note two things.
> 1) *Institutional religionists* often frown and oppose those ministering *outside* the institution. They feel threatened, as though the *outside minister* is against them. Sometimes they are right; the outsider is sometimes against them. But if the outside minister is truly ministering, there should be support and encouragement. However, too often co-operation is not given. The institutional religionist too often fears the loss of authority, position, and security; therefore, he opposes the *outside minister*. Such motives are corrupt and need to be corrected. Ministers, both within and without institutional religion, need to be about God's call and business. They should not be wasting time by struggling against each other. Time is too short, and God's call comes to men both within and without institutional religion. Each needs to support the other in God's calling.
> 2) A man must do and serve God as God calls and wills.

> **You did not choose me, but I chose you and appointed you to go and bear fruit—fruit that will last. Then the Father will give you whatever you ask in my name. (John 15:16)**
> **All this is from God, who reconciled us to himself through Christ and gave us the ministry of reconciliation: We are therefore Christ's ambassadors, as though God were making his appeal through us. We implore you on Christ's behalf: Be reconciled to God. (2 Cor 5:18, 20)**
> **I became a servant of this gospel by the gift of God's grace given me through the working of his power. (Eph 3:7)**
> **I thank Christ Jesus our Lord, who has given me strength, that he considered me faithful, appointing me to his service. (1 Tim 1:12)**
> **And of this gospel I was appointed a herald and an apostle and a teacher. (2 Tim 1:11)**

3 (3:3) **Repentance—Forgiveness—Baptism**: John was a man who preached repentance and forgiveness of sins. Note the exact wording: he preached "a baptism of repentance for the forgiveness of sins." This simply means that if a man wished to be forgiven his sins, he repented. He turned from his sins, and changed his life; then he was baptized. Baptism was the sign to his neighbors and the world that he was changing his life (repenting) because he wanted God to forgive his sins. The order is this:

⇒ A man wanted God to forgive his sins.
⇒ The man therefore made a decision to repent, to turn from his sinful ways, and to change his life (see note and DEEPER STUDY # 1, Repentance—Acts 17:29-30).
⇒ The man was immediately baptized.

Now note. It was baptism that proclaimed to everyone that the man wanted forgiveness and was turning from his sins (repenting). Baptism was the act, the sign, that said to the world that the man was thereafter going to live a changed life so that God would forgive his sins.

Two simple facts are being stated.

1. Forgiveness of sins is conditional. A man must repent to be forgiven, and if he truly repents, he is baptized. Baptism is part of the act of repentance!

2. Baptism is the immediate witness and sign that a man is repenting and changing his life. If a man is truly sincere in seeking forgiveness, he is baptized and does change his life, turning away from sin and turning to God (see DEEPER STUDY # 2—Mt.3:11; notes—Mk.1:3-5; Jn.1:24-26 for more detailed discussion on John's baptism).

> **Peter replied, "Repent and be baptized, every one of you, in the name of Jesus Christ for the forgiveness of your sins.**

And you will receive the gift of the Holy Spirit. (Acts 2:38)

"I baptize you with water for repentance. But after me will come one who is more powerful than I, whose sandals I am not fit to carry. He will baptize you with the Holy Spirit and with fire. (Mat 3:11)

I tell you, no! But unless you repent, you too will all perish. (Luke 13:3)

Repent, then, and turn to God, so that your sins may be wiped out, that times of refreshing may come from the Lord, (Acts 3:19)

Rid yourselves of all the offenses you have committed, and get a new heart and a new spirit. Why will you die, O house of Israel? (Ezek 18:31)

'Even now,' declares the LORD, 'return to me with all your heart, with fasting and weeping and mourning.' (Joel 2:12)

4 (3:4-6) **Prepare**: John was a man who cried out apocalyptically: "Prepare the way for the Lord, make straight paths for Him" (see DEEPER STUDY # 3, Roads—Mk.1:3). John warned the people and he quoted Isaiah 40:3-5 as his authority. He took the points Isaiah had made and proclaimed them to the people.

1. Prepare, for the humbled shall be exalted. Every valley (the humble believers of the earth) shall be filled, that is, received, enriched, raised up, and exalted.

2. Prepare, for the proud shall be made low—cut down, leveled down. Every mountain and hill shall be made low. The mountains and hills would be the great and the less great, the self-sufficient and the self-confident, the prideful and the boastful, the conceited and the arrogant. They shall lose everything they have and be brought low. They shall be made as the dust of the earth if they do not repent.

3. Prepare, for the crooked roads shall be straightened. The crooked thief and businessman, the crooked husband and wife, the crooked student and professor—all the crooked sinners of the earth who are bent out of shape—all who repent shall be made straight by the Messiah.

4. Prepare, for the rough ways shall be made smooth. All the rough ways of the earth—the ways of hopelessness, helplessness, loneliness, emptiness, insecurity, guilt, shame, sin, death, false religion, and empty worship—all shall be made smooth. The way to life and peace shall be planed, made level, and easy to reach.

5. God's salvation shall be seen by all mankind. Not only the Jews, but all people shall see the Messiah, God's salvation to the world. When the way is prepared, the Savior will appear.

John's preaching aroused thousands. It woke them and stirred them to prepare and to look for the Messiah. Apparently, it was the multitude who listened to John who eventually became the followers of Christ. It was also the same multitude who created the excitement needed to spread the news of the Messiah's coming.

Prepare to meet your God, O Israel." (Amos 4:12)

Sow for yourselves righteousness, reap the fruit of unfailing love, and break up your unplowed ground; for it is time to seek the LORD, until he comes and showers righteousness on you. (Hosea 10:12)

'Even now,' declares the LORD, 'return to me with all your heart, with fasting and weeping and mourning.' Rend your heart and not your garments. Return to the LORD your God, for he is gracious and compassionate, slow to anger and abounding in love, and he relents from sending calamity. (Joel 2:12-13)

In a large house there are articles not only of gold and silver, but also of wood and clay; some are for noble purposes and some for ignoble. If a man cleanses himself from the latter, he will be an instrument for noble purposes, made holy, useful to the Master and prepared to do any good work. (2 Tim 2:20-21)

So you also must be ready, because the Son of Man will come at an hour when you do not expect him. (Mat 24:44)

"Therefore keep watch because you do not know when the owner of the house will come back—whether in the evening, or at midnight, or when the rooster crows, or at dawn. (Mark 13:35)

Outline	Scripture	Scripture	Outline
	B. The Plain Message of John the Baptist: A Message for All Ages, 3:7-20 (Mt.3:7-12; Mk.1:7-8)	14 Then some soldiers asked him, "And what should we do?" He replied, "Don't extort money and don't accuse people falsely—be content with your pay."	c. The soldiers: Were to love and care enough to provide security & service to the nation
1 He preached condemnation	7 John said to the crowds coming out to be baptized by him, "You brood of vipers! Who warned you to flee from the coming wrath?	15 The people were waiting expectantly and were all wondering in their hearts if John might possibly be the Christ.	**6 He preached the Messiah's coming**
2 He preached repentance	8 Produce fruit in keeping with repentance. And do not	16 John answered them all, "I baptize you with water.	a. The Messiah's person
3 He preached against pride	begin to say to yourselves, 'We have Abraham as our father.' For I tell you that out of these stones God can raise up children for Abraham.	But one more powerful than I will come, the thongs of whose sandals I am not worthy to untie. He will baptize you with the Holy Spirit and with fire.	b. The Messiah's baptism[DS1]
4 He preached judgment	9 The ax is already at the root of the trees, and every tree that does not produce good fruit will be cut down and thrown into the fire."	17 His winnowing fork is in his hand to clear his threshing floor and to gather the wheat into his barn, but he will burn	c. The Messiah's judgment[DS2]
5 He preached social justice	10 "What should we do then?" the crowd asked.	up the chaff with unquenchable fire."	
a. The people: Were to love & care enough to share their material possessions	11 John answered, "The man with two tunics should share with him who has none, and the one who has food should do the same."	18 And with many other words John exhorted the people and preached the good news to them.	**7 He preached many other things**
b. The tax collectors: Were to love and care enough to stop exerting their authority & cheating people	12 Tax collectors also came to be baptized. "Teacher," they asked, "what should we do?"	19 But when John rebuked Herod the tetrarch because of Herodias, his brother's wife, and all the other evil things he had done,	**8 He preached against sin in high places** a. He preached against the governor's sin
	13 "Don't collect any more than you are required to," he told them.	20 Herod added this to them all: He locked John up in prison.	b. The result: He was arrested

DIVISION II

THE SON OF MAN'S APPEARANCE, 3:1-4:15

B. The Plain Message of John the Baptist: A Message for All Ages, 3:7-20

(3:7-20) **Introduction**: the message of John the Baptist was powerful, a message for all ages.

1. He preached condemnation (v.7).
2. He preached repentance (v.8).
3. He preached against pride (v.8).
4. He preached judgment (v.9).
5. He preached social justice (v.10-14).
6. He preached the Messiah's coming (v.15-17).
7. He preached many other things (v.18).
8. He preached against sin in high places (v.19-20).

1 (3:7) **Condemnation—Preaching**: John preached condemnation. Note two things.

1. He preached the truth about men, what they *were* and *had become*. They were "vipers," poisonous. They had allowed themselves to be poisoned and were now poisonous to others. They were sick and doomed, and they were biting others, making them sick and dooming them.

2. He preached the wrath to come (cp. v.8, 17).

> **Whoever believes in the Son has eternal life, but whoever rejects the Son will not see life, for God's wrath remains on him." (John 3:36)**
>
> **For of this you can be sure: No immoral, impure or greedy person—such a man is an idolater—has any inheritance in the kingdom of Christ and of God. Let no one deceive you with empty words, for because of such things God's wrath comes on those who are disobedient. (Eph 5:5-6)**
>
> **Kiss the Son, lest he be angry and you be destroyed in your way, for his wrath can flare up in a moment. Blessed are all who take refuge in him. (Psa 2:12)**

2 (3:8) **Repentance**: John preached repentance. Note that a man must first repent, then bear fruit. And the fruit must be worthy (deserving), consistent with repentance—fruit that shows a changed heart and a turning away from sin. (See notes—Lk.3:3; note and DEEPER STUDY # 1—Acts 17:29-30).

> **I tell you, no! But unless you repent, you too will all perish. (Luke 13:3)**
>
> **Rid yourselves of all the offenses you have committed, and get a new heart and a new spirit. Why will you die, O house of Is-**

rael? (Ezek 18:31)

And we pray this in order that you may live a life worthy of the Lord and may please him in every way: bearing fruit in every good work, growing in the knowledge of God, (Col 1:10)

3 (3:8) **Pride—Preaching—Self-righteousness**: John preached against pride (see note—Ro.12:16. Cp. 1 Cor.4:10; 5:6.) Many of the people believed they were acceptable to God simply because they were Jews, that is, because they were children of Abraham and of godly forefathers. Many felt acceptable to God because they had undergone a religious ritual, that of circumcision. They felt the righteousness of their fathers had saved them. How they lived mattered little. They were saved because they were *special*—special enough to be acceptable to God (see DEEPER STUDY # 1—Ro.4:1-25).

Thought 1. Most people are prideful. They feel they are special enough to be acceptable to God, that God would never reject them. They feel acceptable because they...

- have godly parents
- have been baptized
- are not too bad
- are good enough
- are blessed with so much
- are somewhat religious
- are members of a church
- are regular worshippers

To some who were confident of their own righteousness and looked down on everybody else, Jesus told this parable: (Luke 18:9)

The way of a fool seems right to him, but a wise man listens to advice. (Prov 12:15)

All a man's ways seem innocent to him, but motives are weighed by the LORD. (Prov 16:2; cp. Prov 21:2)

Many a man claims to have unfailing love, but a faithful man who can find? (Prov 20:6)

Those who are pure in their own eyes and yet are not cleansed of their filth; (Prov 30:12)

You say, 'I am innocent; he is not angry with me.' But I will pass judgment on you because you say, 'I have not sinned.' (Jer 2:35)

4 (3:9) **Judgment—Preaching**: John preached judgment. Note several things.

1. God is the Divine Woodman who cuts down the trees.
2. The axe is already lying at the roots of the trees.
3. The trees are *not yet* cut down, but all men are warned.
4. There are many trees: some lofty (the proud), some stately (leaders), some diseased, some bearing good fruit, some bearing bad fruit, and some bearing no fruit at all.
5. All trees that do not bear good fruit will be cut down and cast into the fire (see DEEPER STUDY # 4—Lk.16:24; DEEPER STUDY # 2—Mt.5:22).

But land that produces thorns and thistles is worthless and is in danger of being cursed. In the end it will be burned. (Heb 6:8)

But now a righteousness from God, apart from law, has been made known, to which the Law and the Prophets testify. This righteousness from God comes through faith in Jesus Christ to all who believe. There is no difference, for all have sinned and fall short of the glory of God, (Rom 3:21-23)

For it is time for judgment to begin with the family of God; and if it begins with us, what will the outcome be for those who do not obey the gospel of God? And, "If it is hard for the righteous to be saved, what will become of the ungodly and the sinner?" (1 Pet 4:17-18)

But the cowardly, the unbelieving, the vile, the murderers, the sexually immoral, those who practice magic arts, the idolaters and all liars—their place will be in the fiery lake of burning sulfur. This is the second death." (Rev 21:8)

5 (3:10-14) **Justice—Preaching—Fruit—Repentance—Life, Changed**: John preached social justice. John stirred people. The people wanted to know how repentance would affect their lives, just what a changed life would mean. What kind of fruit should they bear? John answered in the most practical terms.

1. The average citizen was to love and care enough to share his material goods with those who were in need. John mentioned clothing and food, the basic necessities of life. But note: the giving was to be sacrificial. The *giver* was to give all but one coat and half a meal. The giver was to love and care so much that he would be gripped with mercy and unselfishness. He would give what he had. Such fruit would be evidence of repentance, of a life truly changed, of a man who was truly seeking God to forgive his sins (see note—Lk.3:3).

2. The despised tax collectors were to love and care enough to stop exerting their authority and cheating people. Tax collectors in Jesus' day were literally despised because they represented the Roman government and levied more taxes than necessary, pocketing the excess. A tax collector who wanted God to forgive his sins had to change his life, becoming a man of justice and equitableness. He had to love and care for others enough to treat them fairly and respectfully and justly.

3. The soldiers were to be respectful and loving, truthful and honest, contented and responsible. Note the three specific charges to soldiers.

   a. They were not to extort money. The word "extort" (diaseisete) means to shake violently, agitate, terrify. The thought is that some extorted money by terrifying people. Roman soldiers were, of course, posted to protect the interests of Rome. It was common for soldiers to allow illegal things to go on for a bribe.
   b. They were to accuse no man falsely. If a man did not pay a bribe, he was often falsely accused by the soldier.
   c. They were to be content with their pay or wages. Dissatisfaction and grumbling over their pay or wages was a common complaint of soldiers.

A soldier was to change his life completely: to respect and love people, be truthful and honest, contented and responsible.

Note that John's message demanded a changed life. What then were the fruits that demonstrated one was truly repenting and seeking forgiveness of sins? Very practically, "*the fruits of righteousness*" (cp. v.8).

> **And this is my prayer: that your love may abound more and more in knowledge and depth of insight, so that you may be able to discern what is best and may be pure and blameless until the day of Christ, filled with the fruit of righteousness that comes through Jesus Christ—to the glory and praise of God. (Phil 1:9-11)**
>
> **But the fruit of the Spirit is love, joy, peace, patience, kindness, goodness, faithfulness, gentleness and self-control. Against such things there is no law. (Gal 5:22-23)**
>
> **(For the fruit of the light consists in all goodness, righteousness and truth) (Eph 5:9)**
>
> **But the wisdom that comes from heaven is first of all pure; then peace-loving, considerate, submissive, full of mercy and good fruit, impartial and sincere. (James 3:17)**

6 (3:15-17) **Jesus Christ, Messiah—Preaching**: John preached the Messiah's coming. He stressed three points in particular.

1. The Messiah's person. The Messiah was more "worthy" and "more powerful" than he.
   a. More worthy: John was not worth the rank of a slave before Christ. Slaves were the ones who loosed the sandals and washed the feet of guests. He was as *nothing* before the Lord. What an attitude of humility!
   b. More powerful: Jesus was mightier in both person (as above) and work (baptism and judgment, v. 16-17).
2. The Messiah's baptism (see DEEPER STUDY # 1—Lk.3:16 for discussion).
3. The Messiah's judgment. Note these points.
   a. The winnowing fork (pluon) is the Messiah's power to pick up both the wheat and the chaff.
   b. The "threshing floor" is the earth which will be purged or cleansed of all chaff.
   c. The "wheat" represents believers who truly repent and bring forth fruit. They will be gathered into His barn (His kingdom or the new heavens and earth).
   d. The "chaff" represents those who only profess, who are counterfeit wheat. They lie on the floor (the earth) with the wheat, but they are not wheat. They shall be burned with "unquenchable fire." (See note—Lk.3:17 for discussion.)

DEEPER STUDY # 1

(3:16) **Baptism**: the word "baptism" (baptizein) means to dip, to immerse, to submerge, to place into. John's baptism was with water, but Jesus' baptism was "with [en] the Holy Spirit and with fire."

1. John's baptism was both a preparation and a symbol of the spiritual baptism that Jesus was to bring. John's water baptism meant two things.

First, it symbolized cleansing from all sin. A person was being prepared for the cleansing that Christ would provide.

Second, it symbolized separation or dedication. A person was setting his life apart to God in a renewed spirit of dedication. He was committing himself to the Christ about whom John was preaching.

2. Jesus' spiritual baptism is a double baptism. Only one preposition is used for "the Spirit and fire," the preposition "with" or "in."

First, Jesus baptizes the person *with the Spirit*. He dips, immerses, and places the person in the Spirit. A person may be carnal and materialistic, but once he has been baptized into the Spirit by Christ, he becomes spiritually minded (Ro.8:5-7). The Jews had longed and looked for the day when the Spirit would come. The prophets had predicted His coming time and again; therefore, the people knew exactly what John was predicting (cp. Ezk.36:26-27; 37:14; 39:29; Is.44:3; Joel 2:28). Note: John's baptism was called "the baptism of repentance"; that is, the person who repented was baptized. There could be no question; it was understood. If one repented and actually turned to the Lord, he was baptized.

Second, Jesus baptized the person *with fire*. Fire has several functions that graphically symbolize the work of Christ. It illuminates, warms, melts, burns, and utterly destroys. The difference between baptism with water and fire is the difference between an outward work and an inward work. Water only cleanses the outside; fire purifies within, that is, the heart. Jesus Christ separates a person from his former life and purifies him within by the fire of His Holy Spirit. It should be noted that in John's mind the "baptism of fire" meant that the Messiah was to destroy the enemies of Israel. It was "the messianic fire of judgment" that was to come from the throne of David (see DEEPER STUDY # 2—Mt.1:18; notes—11:1-6; 11:2-3; DEEPER STUDY # 1—11:5; DEEPER STUDY # 2—11:6; note—Lk.7:21-23).

DEEPER STUDY # 2

(3:17) **Unquenchable Fire** (puri asbesto): this literally reads "with unquenchable fire." It is fire that cannot be quenched, snuffed out, extinguished. The idea is that the fire is everlasting, burning on and on and never ending (see DEEPER STUDY # 3—Mt.25:41).

7 (3:18) **Preaching**: John preached many other things. Note the word "exhorted" (parakalon). It means to admonish, urge, beseech, entreat. John pierced the ears and the hearts of the people; he pressed and pressed upon the people their need to prepare for the coming of the Lord.

> **In a large house there are articles not only of gold and silver, but also of wood and clay; some are for noble purposes and some for ignoble. If a man cleanses himself from the latter, he will be an instrument for noble purposes, made holy, useful to the Master and prepared to do any good work. (2 Tim 2:20-21)**
>
> **'Even now,' declares the LORD, 'return to me with all your heart, with fasting and weeping and mourning.' Rend your heart and not your garments. Return to the LORD your God, for he is gracious and compassionate, slow to anger and**

abounding in love, and he relents from sending calamity. (Joel 2:12-13)

8 (3:19-20) **Preaching—Sin, Preaching Against**: John preached against sin in high places. He rebuked the ruler Herod for his evil life and carnal excess, for his terrible sin of adultery. (See DEEPER STUDY # 1—Mt.14:1-14.)

Then the Spirit of God came upon Zechariah son of Jehoiada the priest. He stood before the people and said, "This is what God says: 'Why do you disobey the Lord's commands? You will not prosper. Because you have forsaken the LORD, he has forsaken you.'" (2 Chr 24:20)

The acts of the sinful nature are obvious: sexual immorality, impurity and debauchery; idolatry and witchcraft; hatred, discord, jealousy, fits of rage, selfish ambition, dissensions, factions and envy; drunkenness, orgies, and the like. I warn you, as I did before, that those who live like this will not inherit the kingdom of God. (Gal 5:19-21)

Enoch, the seventh from Adam, prophesied about these men: "See, the Lord is coming with thousands upon thousands of his holy ones to judge everyone, and to convict all the ungodly of all the ungodly acts they have done in the ungodly way, and of all the harsh words ungodly sinners have spoken against him." (Jude 1:14-15)

	C. The Baptism of Jesus: Obedience and God's Approval, 3:21-22 (Mt.3:13-17; Mk.1:9-11; Jn.1:29-34)
1 Jesus' obedience a. Obedient along with the people b. Obedient in prayer **2 God's signs of approval** a. The heavens were opened b. The Spirit descended c. The voice of God spoke	21 When all the people were being baptized, Jesus was baptized too. And as he was praying, heaven was opened 22 And the Holy Spirit descended on him in bodily form like a dove. And a voice came from heaven: "You are my Son, whom I love; with you I am well pleased."

DIVISION II

THE SON OF MAN'S APPEARANCE, 3:1-4:15

C. The Baptism of Jesus: Obedience and God's Approval, 3:21-22

(3:21-22) **Introduction—Baptism**: baptism is both obeying God and securing God's approval. This is why Jesus was baptized, and it is why we are to be baptized.

1. Jesus' obedience (v.21).
2. God's signs of approval (v.22).

1 (3:21) **Baptism—Obedience—Prayer**: baptism is an act of obedience to God. Jesus was obeying God in being baptized. This is seen in two acts.

1. Jesus obeyed God by being baptized with the people. Note the words, "When all the people were being baptized." Some scholars say Jesus was baptized *after* all the people were baptized; others *while* they were being baptized. It does not matter which is factual. The point is this: Jesus was right in the midst of the people, *obeying* God with them. He was doing exactly what God wanted, identifying with the people.

One thing sets these people apart from the rest of the public. They heard John's message and responded, doing exactly what God wanted. They were obeying God's call, doing what was right, obeying righteousness. Now again, note that Jesus was baptized "when all the people were being baptized," right along with them. He was doing at least two things. (see outline and notes—Mt.3:13; 3:15; Mk.1:9-11 for more discussion).

a. He was demonstrating that He, the Son of God, was *fulfilling all righteousness* (see note—Mt.5:17-18). He, too, was being obedient to God, *fulfilling every law* of God for man.
b. He was demonstrating His humiliation, that He was Man, fully Man. As Man He was required to live obediently to God just as other men were. There was one difference, however; Jesus lived a sinless life, and by such He became the Perfect and Ideal Man, the Pattern for all men (see DEEPER STUDY # 3—Mt.8:20).

Thought 1. Every man should respond to the gospel of God; that is, he should seek God to forgive his sins, repent, and be baptized. This is God's will for every man. Every man should obey God and fulfill all righteous-ness. Baptism is an act of obedience; it is obeying God right along with other believers.

> **Then Jesus came from Galilee to the Jordan to be baptized by John. But John tried to deter him, saying, "I need to be baptized by you, and do you come to me?" Jesus replied, "Let it be so now; it is proper for us to do this to fulfill all righteousness." Then John consented. (Mat 3:13-15)**
>
> **Whoever believes and is baptized will be saved, but whoever does not believe will be condemned. (Mark 16:16)**
>
> **Jesus answered, "I tell you the truth, no one can enter the kingdom of God unless he is born of water and the Spirit. (John 3:5)**

Thought 2. No man is above any other man, not in the eyes of God. God's own Son had to obey Him; He had to be baptized as a *sign of obedience* to God. We, too, have to be baptized if we are truly repenting and seeking God to forgive our sins. We are not above God's will and His instructions to "repent and be baptized" (Acts 2:38).

> **Peter replied, "Repent and be baptized, every one of you, in the name of Jesus Christ for the forgiveness of your sins. And you will receive the gift of the Holy Spirit. (Acts 2:38)**
>
> **Therefore go and make disciples of all nations, baptizing them in the name of the Father and of the Son and of the Holy Spirit, (Mat 28:19)**
>
> **And now what are you waiting for? Get up, be baptized and wash your sins away, calling on his name.' (Acts 22:16)**

2. Jesus obeyed God in prayer. While Jesus was being baptized, He was praying. His mind and thoughts were upon God. He was in fellowship and communion with God. This is as it should be. Why would a person's mind be elsewhere while he is being baptized if he is sincere?

⇒ Baptism is an *outward* sign of God's working *within* the heart of a person. The *inward working* and *inward grace of God is sought by prayer*. Thus, *true* baptism is the first act whereby a man shows that he is in communion with God.

⇒ Baptism, the most significant act of discipleship, will be followed by a changed life. A changed life demonstrates that a person is repenting and seeking God to forgive his sins. Therefore, while a person is being baptized, he is in a spirit of prayer seeking God's grace and favor as he walks out into an alien and wicked world.

⇒ Baptism launches the new life of the believer. Baptism is to be the first act of the repenting believer, the first confession to the public that a person is going to change his life and live for God. (See DEEPER STUDY # 1, Baptism—Acts 2:38 for more discussion.) *Baptism is the first public confession of a person's inward prayer of confession to God.* Thus baptism, the outward public confession to man, should follow right upon the heels of the inward private confession to God. The spirit of prayer that started it all should be the same spirit of prayer that finishes it all. The prayer that confessed to God privately should continue right on through to the prayer that confesses to the public at large. In fact, from the very moment of the inward prayer of a person's confession to God, the heart should continue in a spirit of prayer right on through life. The believer's very spirit should be a spirit of continued prayer. Such was Jesus' obedience in prayer. Such is to be our obedience in prayer. An unbroken communion with God in prayer is the ache of God for us.

> **They should always pray and not give up. (Luke 18:1)**
> **Faithful in prayer. (Rom 12:12)**
> **And pray in the Spirit on all occasions with all kinds of prayers and requests. With this in mind, be alert and always keep on praying for all the saints. (Eph 6:18)**
> **Do not be anxious about anything, but in everything, by prayer and petition, with thanksgiving, present your requests to God. (Phil 4:6)**
> **We always thank God, the Father of our Lord Jesus Christ, when we pray for you, (Col 1:3)**
> **Devote yourselves to prayer, being watchful and thankful. (Col 4:2)**
> **Night and day we pray most earnestly that we may see you again and supply what is lacking in your faith. (1 Th 3:10)**
> **Pray continually; (1 Th 5:17)**
> **The prayer of a righteous man is powerful and effective. (James 5:16)**
> **The end of all things is near. Therefore be clear minded and self-controlled so that you can pray. (1 Pet 4:7)**

2 (3:22) **Baptism**: baptism secures God's approval. When a person is baptized, God is very pleased, for the person is *obeying* and *following* in the steps of Jesus. Jesus' baptism pleased God. God showed His approval in three ways.

1. The heavens were opened (v.21). This was probably for two purposes.
   a. To give Jesus a very special sight and sense of God's glory and presence. The Lord's baptism was the launch of His ministry to men. He needed a very special glimpse and sense of God's glory and presence. He needed the stamp of God's approval and power (cp. Acts 7:56; Ezk.1:1).
   b. To reveal to John and perhaps to the others standing there (if the opening of heaven were isible to all) that Jesus was truly the Lamb of God who takes away the sin of the world (Jn.1:29).

2. The Holy Spirit descended upon Jesus "in a bodily form like a dove." The dove was a sacred bird to the Jews. It was a symbol of peace and gentleness, of purity and innocence, but even more significant it was often identified with the Spirit of God. When the dove descended upon Jesus, it symbolized the Spirit of God Himself descending upon Jesus. He was descending upon Jesus to identify Jesus as the Messiah and to endue Jesus with the power of God (see outline and notes—Mk.1:9-10). John went out of his way to stress that the Spirit's descent upon Jesus was unique: He abode (Jn.1:32) and He remained upon Jesus (Jn.1:33). The Holy Spirit entered the life of Jesus once for all, permanently and powerfully, in His full manifestation and unlimited power.

3. The voice of God was heard (see note—Mt.3:16-17).

Thought 1. When we genuinely obey God and are baptized, God is pleased. We also secure His approval in the same three ways.

1) God opens heaven up to us and gives us a very special sense of His presence, a sense of His approval, a sense that we are pleasing Him immensely.

> **Praise be to the God and Father of our Lord Jesus Christ, who has blessed us in the heavenly realms with every spiritual blessing in Christ. (Eph 1:3)**
> **But because of his great love for us, God, who is rich in mercy, made us alive with Christ even when we were dead in transgressions—it is by grace you have been saved. And God raised us up with Christ and seated us with him in the heavenly realms in Christ Jesus, (Eph 2:4-6)**

2) God manifests and reveals His Spirit to us in a very special sense. We are obeying Him, and significant moments of obedience bring special manifestations of the Spirit (see note—Jn.14:21).

> **Whoever has my commands and obeys them, he is the one who loves me. He who loves me will be loved by my Father, and I too will love him and show myself to him." (John 14:21)**
> **However, as it is written: "No eye has seen, no ear has heard, no mind has conceived what God has prepared for those who love him"—but God has revealed it to us by his Spirit. The Spirit searches all things, even the deep things of God. (1 Cor 2:9-10)**
> **In him we have redemption through his blood, the forgiveness of sins, in accordance with the riches of God's grace that he lavished on us with all wisdom and understanding. And he made known to us the mystery of his will according to his good pleasure, which he purposed in Christ, to be put**

> **into effect when the times will have reached their fulfillment—to bring all things in heaven and on earth together under one head, even Christ. (Eph 1:7-10)**
>
> **The mystery that has been kept hidden for ages and generations, but is now disclosed to the saints. To them God has chosen to make known among the Gentiles the glorious riches of this mystery, which is *Christ in you, the hope of glory*. (Col 1:26-27)**

3) God's Word is heard. The fact that we are baptized is a sign that we have heard His command to be baptized, and because we are obeying Him, He continues to speak to us day by day as we seek His will in the Bible and prayer.

> **Here I am! I stand at the door and knock. If anyone hears my voice and opens the door, I will come in and eat with him, and he with me. (Rev 3:20)**
>
> **We proclaim to you what we have seen and heard, so that you also may have fellowship with us. And our fellowship is with the Father and with his Son, Jesus Christ. (1 John 1:3)**

D. The Genealogy of Jesus: The Roots of the Messiah,[DS1] **3:23-38**
(Mt.1:1-17)

1 Jesus was about thirty years of age

23 Now Jesus himself was
about thirty years old when
he began his ministry. He
was the son, so it was
thought, of Joseph, the son of
Heli,

2 Davidic heir: To be the Messianic King (v.24-31)

24 The son of Matthat, the
son of Levi, the son of Melki,
the son of Jannai, the son of
Joseph,
25 The son of Mattathias, the
son of Amos, the son of Na-
hum, the son of Esli, the son
of Naggai,
26 The son of Maath, the son
of Mattathias, the son of Se-
mein, the son of Josech, the
son of Joda,
27 The son of Joanan, the
son of Rhesa, the son of
Zerubbabel, the son of Sheal-
tiel, the son of Neri,
28 The son of Melki, the son
of Addi, the son of Cosam,
the son of Elmadam, the son
of Er,
29 The son of Joshua, the son
of Eliezer, the son of Jorim,
the son of Matthat, the son of
Levi,
30 The son of Simeon, the
son of Judah, the son of Joseph, the son of Jonam, the
son of Eliakim,
31 The son of Melea, the son
of Menna, the son of Mat-
tatha, the son of Nathan, the
son of David,

3 Adamic heir: To be Messianic High Priest (v.32-38)

32 The son of Jesse, the son
of Obed, the son of Boaz, the
son of Salmon, the son of
Nahshon,
33 The son of Amminadab,
thet son of Ram, the son of
Hezron, the son of Perez, the
son of Judah,
34 The son of Jacob, the son
of Isaac, the son of Abraham,
the son of Terah, the son of
Nahor,
35 The son of Serug, the son
of Reu, the son of Peleg, the
son of Eber, the son of
Shelah,
36 The son of Cainan, the
son of Arphaxad, the son of
Shem, the son of Noah, the
son of Lamech,
37 The son of Methuselah,
the son of Enoch, the son of
Jared, the son of Mahalalel,
the son of Kenan,

4 Godly heir: To be Messianic Prophet of God

38 The son of Enosh, the son
of Seth, the son of Adam, the
son of God.

DIVISION II

THE SON OF MAN'S APPEARANCE, 3:1-4:15

D. The Genealogy of Jesus: The Roots of the Messiah, 3:23-38

(3:23-38) **Introduction**: Jesus was now ready to begin His ministry. But did He have the *right*? What proof was there that He was the Messiah, the Son of God? In this passage Luke makes a phenomenal point. He says that even the roots of Jesus, His genealogy, prove He is the Messiah. His roots give Him the right to claim Messiahship, to claim that He is the Savior, the Son of God.

1. Jesus was about thirty years of age (v.23).
2. He was Davidic heir: He was to be the Messianic King (v.24-31).
3. He was Adamic heir: He was to be the Messianic High Priest (v.32-38).
4. He was Godly heir: He was to be the Messianic Prophet of God (v.38).

DEEPER STUDY # 1

(3:23-38) **Jesus, Genealogy**: there are two significant facts here. First, Luke follows Mary's line (genealogy), the line of Jesus' mother. Second, he traces Mary's line all the way back to Adam. What he does is show that God's Son actually became a man. Jesus was the promised Messiah. Luke is writing to Gentiles who placed great emphasis on a transcendental God, a God way out in space someplace who was thought to be far removed from the day-to-day affairs of men. Luke had to show that Jesus was man, fully human. He was a man born of a woman, full of emotions and feelings and personal day-to-day experiences just like all other men.

Matthew's genealogy is different (Mt.1:1). Matthew was writing primarily to Jews who placed great emphasis on pure lineage. An impure lineage deprived a Jew of his nationality, of his right to be called a Jew; and tragically, this meant that he lost his right to be called a child of God. To combat this problem, Matthew traces Jospeh's line all the way back through King David and Abraham, the founding father of Israel. He does this to show that Jesus had the legal right to the throne of David and to the promises made to Abraham. This is not to say that Jesus was the actual physical son of Joseph, but rather as the Son of God, Jesus was sent into the family of Joseph. By such He became the legal heir of Joseph (see DEEPER STUDY # 3—Mt.1:16; DEEPER STUDY # 2—Jn.8:23). This meant two things. First, Jesus was legally of the pure line of the Jewish nation. He fulfilled the Old Testament prophecies that said the Messiah would be born of the Jewish nation. Second, as a Jew and as the Son of God, Jesus had the legal right to claim Messiahship. He had the legal right to the throne of David and to the promises made to Abraham (see DEEPER STUDY # 1—Jn.4:22; DEEPER STUDY # 1—Ro.4:1-25. Cp. Gen.12:1-3.)

1 (3:23) **Jesus Christ, Age of**: Jesus was about thirty years of age when He launched His ministry. Why did He wait until He was thirty before beginning His ministry?

1. Thirty was the age when the Levites began their work (Num.4:47).
2. Thirty was also the age when a Scribe was allowed to begin his teaching ministry.
3. Thirty was the age whan a man was thought to reach full development and maturity.

Now, note a crucial point. Jesus needed to live thirty years as other men lived, learning and maturing in the day-to-day routine of life and responsibility (cp. Heb.5:8). Why?

1. Jesus needed to prove faithful, to secure righteousness right down where men live, right in the day-to-day duties...

- of work (He was a carpenter by trade).
- of family (He became the head of the house when Joseph died).
- of physical growth (He grew and matured as all men do, day by day).
- of mental growth (He studied and learned as all men do).
- of spiritual growth (He sought God as all men should).

Although he was a son, he learned obedience from what he suffered (Heb 5:8)

2. Jesus needed to show (demonstrate, paint the picture of) how men should live in the routine of day-to-day living.

3. Jesus needed to learn from the day-to-day experiences of life (as Man)—learn so that He could teach men from experience exactly how they should live.

4. Jesus needed to learn from day-to-day experiences so He could better help and succor men throughout their lives. By ploughing through the experiences of life, He could better help men plough through their day-to-day experiences (see note—Lk.2:40 for detailed discussion).

2 (3:24-31) **Jesus Christ, Davidic Heir—King**: Jesus was the Davidic heir—He was qualified to be the Messianic King. God had given to David and His seed (the Messiah) the promise of eternal government (2 Sam.7:12; Ps.39:3f; 132:11).

The Jews believed these promises of God. Therefore Jesus, "who is called Christ" (Mt.1:16), was the promised Son of Abraham, the promised Son of David (Mt.1:1).

Note how often Jesus was called the son of David. (Cp. Mt.12:23; 15:22; 20:30-31; 21:9, 15; Acts 2:29-36; Ro.1:3; 2 Tim.2:8; Rev.22:16.) It was the common title and popular concept of the Messiah. Generation after generation of Jews looked for the promised deliverer of Israel. The people expected Him to be a great general who would deliver and restore the nation to its greatness. In fact, they expected Him to make the nation the center of universal rule. He would, under God, conquer the world and center the glory and majesty of God Himself in Jerusalem. And from His throne, the throne of David, He would execute "the Messianic fire of judgment" upon the nations and peoples of the world (see DEEPER STUDY # 2—Mt.1:18; DEEPER STUDY # 3—3:11; notes—11:1-6; 11:2-3; DEEPER STUDY # 1—11:5; DEEPER STUDY # 2—11:6; Lk.7:21-23. Referring to these notes will show what the Jewish concept of the Messiah was.) If Luke can prove that Jesus' roots (genealogy) go all the way back to David and Adam, then he will have shown how seriously one must take the claims of Jesus to be the Messiah (see DEEPER STUDY # 2—Mt.1:18).

1. The Messianic King was prophesied.

He is the one who will build a house for my Name, and I will establish the throne of his kingdom forever. (2 Sam 7:13)

You have delivered me from the attacks of the people; you have made me the head of nations; people I did not know are subject to me. (Psa 18:43)

He will rule from sea to sea and from the River to the ends of the earth. All kings will bow down to him and all nations will serve him. (Psa 72:8, 11)

You said, "I have made a covenant with my chosen one, I have sworn to David my servant, 'I will establish your line forever and make your throne firm through all generations.'" Selah (Psa 89:3-4)

Once you spoke in a vision, to your faithful people you said: "I have bestowed strength on a warrior; I have exalted a young man from among the people. I have found David my servant; with my sacred oil I have anointed him. My hand will sustain him; surely my arm will strengthen him. I will crush his foes before him and strike down his adversaries. (Psa 89:19-21, 23)

I will also appoint him my firstborn, the most exalted of the kings of the earth. I will establish his line forever, his throne as long as the heavens endure. that his line will continue forever and his throne endure before me like the sun; it will be established forever like the moon, the faithful witness in the sky." Selah (Psa 89:27, 29, 36-37)

Of David. A psalm. The LORD says to my Lord: "Sit at my right hand until I make your enemies a footstool for your feet." The LORD will extend your mighty scepter from Zion; you will rule in the midst of your enemies. (Psa 110:1-2)

The LORD swore an oath to David, a sure oath that he will not revoke: "One of your own descendants I will place on your throne—"Here I will make a horn grow for David and set up a lamp for my anointed one. I will clothe his enemies with shame, but the crown on his head will be resplendent." (Psa 132:11, 17-18)

He will judge between the nations and will settle disputes for many peoples. They will beat their swords into plowshares and their spears into pruning hooks. Nation will not take up sword against nation, nor will they train for war anymore. (Isa 2:4)

In the year that King Uzziah died, I saw the Lord seated on a throne, high and exalted, and the train of his robe filled the temple. (Isa 6:1)

For to us a child is born, to us a son is given, and the government will be on his shoulders. And he will be called Wonderful Counselor, Mighty God, Everlasting Father, Prince of Peace. Of the increase of his government and peace there will be no end. He will reign on David's throne and over his kingdom, establishing and upholding it with justice and righteousness from that time on

and forever. The zeal of the LORD Almighty will accomplish this. (Isa 9:6-7)

A shoot will come up from the stump of Jesse; from his roots a Branch will bear fruit. (Isa 11:1)

In that day the Root of Jesse will stand as a banner for the peoples; the nations will rally to him, and his place of rest will be glorious. (Isa 11:10)

See, a king will reign in righteousness. (Isa 32:1)

Your eyes will see the king in his beauty. (Isa 33:17)

See, the Sovereign LORD comes with power, and his arm rules for him. See, his reward is with him, and his recompense accompanies him. (Isa 40:10)

How beautiful on the mountains are the feet of those who bring good news, who proclaim peace, who bring good tidings, who proclaim salvation, who say to Zion, "Your God reigns!" (Isa 52:7)

See, my servant will act wisely ; he will be raised and lifted up and highly exalted. (Isa 52:13)

"The days are coming," declares the LORD, "when I will raise up to David a righteous Branch, a King who will reign wisely and do what is just and right in the land. In his days Judah will be saved and Israel will live in safety. This is the name by which he will be called: The LORD Our Righteousness. (Jer 23:5-6)

Instead, they will serve the LORD their God and David their king, whom I will raise up for them. (Jer 30:9)

For this is what the LORD says: 'David will never fail to have a man to sit on the throne of the house of Israel, (Jer 33:17)

This is what the Sovereign LORD says: Take off the turban, remove the crown. It will not be as it was: The lowly will be exalted and the exalted will be brought low. A ruin! A ruin! I will make it a ruin! It will not be restored until he comes to whom it rightfully belongs; to him I will give it.' (Ezek 21:26-27)

"'My servant David will be king over them, and they will all have one shepherd. They will follow my laws and be careful to keep my decrees. They will live in the land I gave to my servant Jacob, the land where your fathers lived. They and their children and their children's children will live there forever, and David my servant will be their prince forever. (Ezek 37:24-25)

Then the iron, the clay, the bronze, the silver and the gold were broken to pieces at the same time and became like chaff on a threshing floor in the summer. The wind swept them away without leaving a trace. But the rock that struck the statue became a huge mountain and filled the whole earth. (Dan 2:35)

"In the time of those kings, the God of heaven will set up a kingdom that will never be destroyed, nor will it be left to another people. It will crush all those kingdoms and bring them to an end, but it will itself endure forever. (Dan 2:44)

"In my vision at night I looked, and there before me was one like a son of man, coming with the clouds of heaven. He approached the Ancient of Days and was led into his presence. He was given authority, glory and sovereign power; all peoples, nations and men of every language worshiped him. His dominion is an everlasting dominion that will not pass away, and his kingdom is one that will never be destroyed. (Dan 7:13-14)

"Know and understand this: From the issuing of the decree to restore and rebuild Jerusalem until the Anointed One, the ruler, comes, there will be seven 'sevens,' and sixty-two 'sevens.' It will be rebuilt with streets and a trench, but in times of trouble. (Dan 9:25)

Afterward the Israelites will return and seek the LORD their God and David their king. They will come trembling to the LORD and to his blessings in the last days. (Hosea 3:5)

The LORD will roar from Zion and thunder from Jerusalem; the earth and the sky will tremble. But the LORD will be a refuge for his people, a stronghold for the people of Israel. 'Then you will know that I, the LORD your God, dwell in Zion, my holy hill. Jerusalem will be holy; never again will foreigners invade her. (Joel 3:16-17)

"But you, Bethlehem Ephrathah, though you are small among the clans of Judah, out of you will come for me one who will be ruler over Israel, whose origins are from of old, from ancient times." He will stand and shepherd his flock in the strength of the LORD, in the majesty of the name of the LORD his God. And they will live securely, for then his greatness will reach to the ends of the earth. (Micah 5:2, 4)

"In that day I will restore David's fallen tent. I will repair its broken places, restore its ruins, and build it as it used to be, (Amos 9:11)

He will judge between many peoples and will settle disputes for strong nations far and wide. They will beat their swords into plowshares and their spears into pruning hooks. Nation will not take up sword against nation, nor will they train for war anymore. (Micah 4:3)

The LORD has taken away your punishment, he has turned back your enemy. The LORD, the King of Israel, is with you; never again will you fear any harm. (Zep 3:15)

Tell him this is what the LORD Almighty says: 'Here is the man whose name is the Branch, and he will branch out from his place and build the temple of the LORD. It is he who will build the temple of the LORD, and he will be clothed with majesty and will sit and rule on his throne. And he will be a priest on his throne. And there will be harmony between the two.' (Zec 6:12-13)

Rejoice greatly, O Daughter of Zion! Shout, Daughter of Jerusalem! See, your king comes to you, righteous and having salvation, gentle and riding on a donkey, on a colt, the foal of a donkey. I will take away the chariots from Ephraim and the war-horses from Jerusalem, and the battle bow will be broken. He will proclaim peace to the nations. His rule will extend from sea to sea and from the River to the ends of the earth. (Zec 9:9-10)

(Also see some Topical Bible or Reference Work: God and Jesus Christ, Kingdom of.)

2. Jesus Christ was the Messianic King.

And asked, "Where is the one who has been born king of the Jews? We saw his star in the east and have come to worship him." "'But you, Bethlehem, in the land of Judah, are by no means least among the rulers of Judah; for out of you will come a ruler who will be the shepherd of my people Israel.'" (Mat 2:2, 6)

The Son of Man will send out his angels, and they will weed out of his kingdom everything that causes sin and all who do evil. (Mat 13:41)

"When the Son of Man comes in his glory, and all the angels with him, he will sit on his throne in heavenly glory. (Mat 25:31)

Meanwhile Jesus stood before the governor, and the governor asked him, "Are you the king of the Jews?" "Yes, it is as you say," Jesus replied. (Mat 27:11)

Then Jesus came to them and said, "All authority in heaven and on earth has been given to me. (Mat 28:18)

He will be great and will be called the Son of the Most High. The Lord God will give him the throne of his father David, and he will reign over the house of Jacob forever; his kingdom will never end." (Luke 1:32-33)

Then Nathanael declared, "Rabbi, you are the Son of God; you are the King of Israel." (John 1:49)

Jesus said, "My kingdom is not of this world. If it were, my servants would fight to prevent my arrest by the Jews. But now my kingdom is from another place." "You are a king, then!" said Pilate. Jesus answered, "You are right in saying I am a king. In fact, for this reason I was born, and for this I came into the world, to testify to the truth. Everyone on the side of truth listens to me." (John 18:36-37)

Pilate had a notice prepared and fastened to the cross. It read: JESUS OF NAZARETH, THE KING OF THE JEWS. (John 19:19)

God exalted him to his own right hand as Prince and Savior that he might give repentance and forgiveness of sins to Israel. (Acts 5:31)

For this very reason, Christ died and returned to life so that he might be the Lord of both the dead and the living. (Rom 14:9)

But each in his own turn: Christ, the firstfruits; then, when he comes, those who belong to him. Then the end will come, when he hands over the kingdom to God the Father after he has destroyed all dominion, authority and power. For he must reign until he has put all his enemies under his feet. The last enemy to be destroyed is death. (1 Cor 15:23-26)

Which he exerted in Christ when he raised him from the dead and seated him at his right hand in the heavenly realms, far above all rule and authority, power and dominion, and every title that can be given, not only in the present age but also in the one to come. And God placed all things under his feet and appointed him to be head over everything for the church, (Eph 1:20-22)

Therefore God exalted him to the highest place and gave him the name that is above every name, that at the name of Jesus every knee should bow, in heaven and on earth and under the earth, and every tongue confess that Jesus Christ is Lord, to the glory of God the Father. (Phil 2:9-11)

Which God will bring about in his own time—God, the blessed and only Ruler, the King of kings and Lord of lords, who alone is immortal and who lives in unapproachable light, whom no one has seen or can see. To him be honor and might forever. Amen. (1 Tim 6:15-16)

But when this priest had offered for all time one sacrifice for sins, he sat down at the right hand of God. Since that time he waits for his enemies to be made his footstool, (Heb 10:12-13)

Who has gone into heaven and is at God's right hand—with angels, authorities and powers in submission to him. (1 Pet 3:22)

And from Jesus Christ, who is the faithful witness, the firstborn from the dead, and the ruler of the kings of the earth. To him who loves us and has freed us from our sins by his blood, and has made us to be a kingdom and priests to serve his God and Father—to him be glory and power for ever and ever! Amen. Look, he is coming with the clouds, and every eye will see him, even those who pierced him; and all the peoples of the earth will mourn because of him. So shall it be! Amen. (Rev 1:5-7)

"To the angel of the church in Philadelphia write: These are the words of him who is holy and true, who holds the key of David. What he opens no one can shut, and what he shuts no one can open. (Rev 3:7)

To him who overcomes, I will give the right to sit with me on my throne, just as I overcame and sat down with my Father on his throne. (Rev 3:21)

I looked, and there before me was a white horse! Its rider held a bow, and he was given a crown, and he rode out as a conqueror bent on conquest. (Rev 6:2)

Then the kings of the earth, the princes, the generals, the rich, the mighty, and every slave and every free man hid in caves and among the rocks of the mountains. They called to the mountains and the rocks, "Fall on us and hide us from the face of him who sits on the throne and from the wrath of the Lamb! For the great day of their wrath has come, and who can stand?" (Rev 6:15-17)

The seventh angel sounded his trumpet, and there were loud voices in heaven, which said: "The kingdom of the world has become the kingdom of our Lord and of his Christ, and he will reign for ever and ever." (Rev 11:15)

Then I heard a loud voice in heaven say: "Now have come the salvation and the power and the kingdom of our God, and the authority of his Christ. For the accuser of our brothers, who accuses them before our God day and night, has been hurled down. (Rev 12:10)

These are those who did not defile themselves with women, for they kept themselves pure. They follow the Lamb wherever he goes. They were purchased from among men and offered as firstfruits to God and the Lamb. (Rev 14:4)

They will make war against the Lamb, but the Lamb will overcome them because he is Lord of lords and King of kings—and with him will be his called, chosen and faithful followers." (Rev 17:14)

I saw heaven standing open and there before me was a white horse, whose rider is called Faithful and True. With justice he judges and makes war. His eyes are like blazing fire, and on his head are many crowns. He has a name written on him that no one knows but he himself. Out of his mouth comes a sharp sword with which to strike down the nations. "He will rule them with an iron scepter." He treads the winepress of the fury of the wrath of God Almighty. On his robe and on his thigh he has this name written: KING OF KINGS AND LORD OF LORDS. (Rev 19:11-12, 15-16)

Blessed and holy are those who have part in the first resurrection. The second death has no power over them, but they will be priests of God and of Christ and will reign with him for a thousand years. (Rev 20:6)

3 (3:32-38) **Adamic Heir—Roots—Genealogy**: Jesus was the Adamic heir—He was qualified to be the Messianic High Priest, the Perfect High Priest who represents man before God and God before man. This was the very *function* of the High Priest: to represent men before God and God before men. The High Priest bore the name of God before men, and He carried the names of men before God (Ro.8:33-34; Heb.2:17; 9:24; 1 Jn.2:1-2; cp. Is.49:16). In relation to the Messiah, this meant two things.

1. The Messiah must *know man perfectly*, and He must *know God perfectly*. He must be the Perfect God-Man in Person, in Being, in Essence. He had to be Man, yes, but He also had to be God Incarnate in human flesh. He had to be born of Adam, that is, of Adam's seed, of human flesh; but He also had to possess the very nature of God. This was the only way man could ever have a Perfect High Priest. It was absolutely necessary—because of the very nature of a depraved world—that a Perfect High Priest be *Perfect God-Perfect Man.*

2. The Messiah must also *be able to represent God before man*, represent God perfectly; and He must *be able to represent man before God*, represent man perfectly. As Scripture says, the [Messiah must] be "faithful to the one who appointed Him" (Heb.3:2).

The Messiah had to live as Perfect God in order to represent God to man. The Messiah also had to live as Perfect Man (never sinning) in order to represent man before God (if man was to be represented as perfect before God).

Scripture declares that Jesus did live a perfect life, that He never sinned (2 Cor.5:21; Heb.4:15; 9:28; 3:5).

1. The Messianic High Priest was typified by two men or priests in the Old Testament.

a. By Melchizedek.

Then Melchizedek king of Salem brought out bread and wine. He was priest of God Most High, and he blessed Abram, saying, "Blessed be Abram by God Most High, Creator of heaven and earth. And blessed be God Most High, who delivered your enemies into your hand." Then Abram gave him a tenth of everything. (Gen 14:18-20)

The LORD has sworn and will not change his mind: "You are a priest forever, in the order of Melchizedek." (Psa 110:4)

b. By Aaron.

"Bring Aaron and his sons to the entrance to the Tent of Meeting and wash them with water. Then dress Aaron in the sacred garments, anoint him and consecrate him so he may serve me as priest. Bring his sons and dress them in tunics. Anoint them just as you anointed their father, so they may serve me as priests. Their anointing will be to a priesthood that will continue for all generations to come." (Exo 40:12-15)

2. The Messianic High Priest was prophesied.

Their leader will be one of their own; their ruler will arise from among them. I will bring him near and he will come close to me, for who is he who will devote himself to be close to me?' declares the LORD. "'So you will be my people, and I will be your God.'" (Jer 30:21-22. Note how the governor draws near in High Priestly fashion.)

Tell him this is what the LORD Almighty says: 'Here is the man whose name is the Branch, and he will branch out from his place and build the temple of the LORD. It is he who will build the temple of the LORD, and he will be clothed with majesty and will sit and rule on his throne. And he will be a priest on his throne. And there will be harmony between the two.' (Zec 6:12-13)

3. Jesus Christ is the Messianic High Priest.

Therefore, holy brothers, who share in the heavenly calling, fix your thoughts on Jesus, the apostle and high priest whom we confess. He was faithful to the one who appointed him, just as Moses was faithful in all God's house. (Heb 3:1-2)

Therefore, since we have a great high priest who has gone through the heavens, Jesus the Son of God, let us hold firmly to the faith we profess. For we do not have a high priest who is unable to sympathize with our weaknesses, but we have one who has been tempted in every way, just as we are—yet was without sin. Let us then approach the throne of grace with confidence, so that we may receive mercy and find grace to help us in our time of need. (Heb 4:14-16)

No one takes this honor upon himself; he must be called by God, just as Aaron was. So Christ also did not take upon himself the glory of becoming a high priest. But God said to him, "You are my Son; today I have become your Father." Although he was a son, he learned obedience from what he suffered and, once made perfect, he became the source of

eternal salvation for all who obey him (Heb 5:4-5, 8-9) (See outline—Heb 4:14-5:10 for overview. See outlines—Heb 4:14-7:28 for full picture.)

4 (3:38) **Jesus Christ, Prophet**: Jesus is the Godly heir—He was qualified to be the Messianic Prophet of God Himself. Jesus Christ Himself proclaimed what the Messianic Prophet of God was to do.

> **He went to Nazareth, where he had been brought up, and on the Sabbath day he went into the synagogue, as was his custom. And he stood up to read. The scroll of the prophet Isaiah was handed to him. Unrolling it, he found the place where it is written: "The Spirit of the Lord is on me, because he has anointed me to preach good news to the poor. He has sent me to proclaim freedom for the prisoners and recovery of sight for the blind, to release the oppressed, to proclaim the year of the Lord's favor." Then he rolled up the scroll, gave it back to the attendant and sat down. The eyes of everyone in the synagogue were fastened on him, and he began by saying to them, "Today this scripture is fulfilled in your hearing." (Luke 4:16-21)**

1. The Messianic Prophet of God was prophesied.

> **The LORD your God will raise up for you a prophet like me from among your own brothers. You must listen to him. (Deu 18:15)**
>
> **The people walking in darkness have seen a great light; on those living in the land of the shadow of death a light has dawned. (Isa 9:2)**
>
> **A shoot will come up from the stump of Jesse; from his roots a Branch will bear fruit. The Spirit of the LORD will rest on him— the Spirit of wisdom and of understanding, the Spirit of counsel and of power, the Spirit of knowledge and of the fear of the LORD—and he will delight in the fear of the LORD. He will not judge by what he sees with his eyes, or decide by what he hears with his ears; but with righteousness he will judge the needy, with justice he will give decisions for the poor of the earth. He will strike the earth with the rod of his mouth; with the breath of his lips he will slay the wicked. (Isa 11:1-4)**
>
> **"Here is my servant, whom I uphold, my chosen one in whom I delight; I will put my Spirit on him and he will bring justice to the nations. He will not shout or cry out, or raise his voice in the streets. A bruised reed he will not break, and a smoldering wick he will not snuff out. In faithfulness he will bring forth justice; he will not falter or be discouraged till he establishes justice on earth. In his law the islands will put their hope." (Isa 42:1-4)**
>
> **How beautiful on the mountains are the feet of those who bring good news, who proclaim peace, who bring good tidings, who proclaim salvation, who say to Zion, "Your God reigns!" (Isa 52:7)**
>
> **Look, there on the mountains, the feet of one who brings good news, who proclaims peace! Celebrate your festivals, O Judah, and fulfill your vows. No more will the wicked invade you; they will be completely destroyed. (Nahum 1:15)**

2. Jesus Christ was the Messianic Prophet of God (see above statement of Christ, Lk.4:16-21).

> **The crowds answered, "This is Jesus, the prophet from Nazareth in Galilee." (Mat 21:11)**
>
> **They were all filled with awe and praised God. "A great prophet has appeared among us," they said. "God has come to help his people." (Luke 7:16)**
>
> **In any case, I must keep going today and tomorrow and the next day—for surely no prophet can die outside Jerusalem! (Luke 13:33)**
>
> **For the one whom God has sent speaks the words of God, for God gives the Spirit without limit. (John 3:34)**
>
> **After the people saw the miraculous sign that Jesus did, they began to say, "Surely this is the Prophet who is to come into the world." (John 6:14)**
>
> **On hearing his words, some of the people said, "Surely this man is the Prophet." (John 7:40)**
>
> **"I have much to say in judgment of you. But he who sent me is reliable, and what I have heard from him I tell the world." So Jesus said, "When you have lifted up the Son of Man, then you will know that I am the one I claim to be and that I do nothing on my own but speak just what the Father has taught me. (John 8:26, 28)**
>
> **Finally they turned again to the blind man, "What have you to say about him? It was your eyes he opened." The man replied, "He is a prophet." (John 9:17)**
>
> **For I did not speak of my own accord, but the Father who sent me commanded me what to say and how to say it. I know that his command leads to eternal life. So whatever I say is just what the Father has told me to say." (John 12:49-50)**
>
> **Don't you believe that I am in the Father, and that the Father is in me? The words I say to you are not just my own. Rather, it is the Father, living in me, who is doing his work. He who does not love me will not obey my teaching. These words you hear are not my own; they belong to the Father who sent me. (John 14:10, 24)**
>
> **I no longer call you servants, because a servant does not know his master's business. Instead, I have called you friends, for everything that I learned from my Father I have made known to you. (John 15:15)**
>
> **For I gave them the words you gave me and they accepted them. They knew with certainty that I came from you, and they believed that you sent me. I have made you known to them, and will continue to make you known in order that the love you have for me may be in them and that I myself may be in them." (John 17:8, 26)**

CHAPTER 4

E. The Temptation of Jesus: Victory Over Temptation, 4:1-15
(Mt.4:1-11, 12-17; Mk.1:12-13, 14-15)

1 **Being prepared to serve God**DS1
  a. By being filled with the Spirit
  b. By spending time alone with God
  c. By being tried & tested
  d. By fasting & praying
2 **Tempt. 1: To meet the necessities of life by His own power**
  a. Satan's temptation: To misuse His power
  b. Jesus' answer: Man needs more than bread—he needs God's life or spiritual food
3 **Tempt. 2: To seek His ambition by compromise**
  a. Satan's enticement: He shows the world's possessions & glory
  b. Satan's claim: He controls world & its glory
  c. Satan's offer: He will give the world to anyone he wills
  d. Satan's condition: A person must worship & follow him
  e. Jesus' answer: He must worship & follow God alone
4 **Tempt. 3: To prove Himself through sensationalism**
  a. Satan's temptation
    1) To choose another way
    2) To misuse & twist the Scripture to suit his own ends
    3) To give people sensations—a religion of feelings
  b. Jesus' answer: God is not to be tempted— God's way alone is to be followed
5 **Conclusion: Satan left Jesus for a while**
  a. Jesus' great power
  b. Jesus' great fame
  c. Jesus' great ministry

Jesus, full of the Holy Spirit,
returned from the Jordan and
was led by the Spirit in the
desert,
2 Where for forty days he
was tempted by the devil. He
ate nothing during those days,
and at the end of them he was
hungry.
3 The devil said to him, "If
you are the Son of God, tell
this stone to become
bread."
4 Jesus answered, "It is
written: 'Man does not live
on bread alone.'"
5 The devil led him up to a
high place and showed him in
an instant all the kingdoms of
the world.
6 And he said to him, "I
will give you all their
authority and splendor, for
it has been given to me, and
I can give it to anyone I
want to.
7 So if you worship me, it
will all be yours."
8 Jesus answered, "It is
written: 'Worship the Lord
your God and serve him
only.'"
9 The devil led him to Jerusalem and had him stand on the
highest point of the temple.
"If you are the Son of God,"
he said, "throw yourself
down from here.
10 For it is written: "'He will
command his angels concerning you to guard you carefully;
11 They will lift you up in
their hands, so that you will
not strike your foot against a
stone.'"
12 Jesus answered, "It says:
'Do not put the Lord your
God to the test.'"
13 When the devil had finished all this tempting, he left
him until an opportune time.
14 Jesus returned to Galilee
in the power of the Spirit, and
news about him spread
through the whole countryside.
15 He taught in their synagogues, and everyone praised
him.

DIVISION II

THE SON OF MAN'S APPEARANCE, 3:1-4:15

E. The Temptation of Jesus: Victory Over Temptation, 4:1-15

(4:1-15) **Introduction**: victory over temptation is essential before we can live and minister for God. No temptation has ever confronted man that Jesus Christ has not confronted. This is seen in this passage. In His confrontation, Jesus reveals what lies behind each temptation and how to conquer it. Once it has been conquered, we can then live a victorious life and serve God effectively.

1. Being prepared to serve God (v.1-2).
2. Temptation 1: to meet the necessities of life by His own power (v.3-4).
3. Temptation 2: to seek His ambition through compromise (v.5-8).
4. Temptation 3: to prove Himself through sensationalism (v.9-12).
5. Conclusion: Satan left Jesus for a while (v. 13-15).

1 (4:1-2) **Ministry, Preparation—Service**: Jesus was being prepared to serve God. He was about to launch the most important work ever performed by man. His work was to determine the eternal fate of the world and of every man in the world. Jesus had to be strengthened and prepared perfectly, without flaw. Two things were involved in His preparation.

First, there was God's plan. Jesus had to be totally committed to carry out God's plan no matter what happened. God's plan was the cross, the way of sacrifice and suffering in order to help others. Jesus would always be tempted to choose the easier course of self, power, and glory. He needed to gain the victory *once-for-all.* Not that He would not be tempted again; He would. But He needed a strong moment of victory to show that He could conquer the temptation.

Second, Jesus' preparation involved a personal need for strength and assurance. The only way Jesus could be strengthened and gain assurance was to be tempted. He had to struggle against temptation to become tough and strong, and to be assured that He could conquer and be victorious over the trials of life.

Now, note the first two verses. They give the four essentials necessary for preparation. Jesus had to be prepared to serve God. (How much more do we!)

1. Jesus was "full of the Holy Spirit." Note the emphasis upon the Holy Spirit. He is mentioned twice.
   a. Jesus had a dramatic experience with the Spirit at His baptism (Lk.3:21-22).
   b. Jesus was "led by the Spirit" (egeto en toi pneumati). Note the Greek word "en." It means *in,* which means that Jesus was not only "led by the Spirit" He was led "in the Spirit," step by step and day by day. A man must be *in the Spirit* to be led by the Spirit.
2. Jesus was led to spend time alone with God. He was led to get all alone in the wilderness. Time alone with God is necessary for preparation.

3. Jesus was led to be tried and tested. Trials toughen us, make us stronger, and give us greater assurance so that we can face whatever lies ahead.

4. Jesus was led to fast and pray, two absolute essentials in one's preparation to do a great work for God.

DEEPER STUDY # 1

(4:1-2) **Temptation** (perirazo): the word temptation is used here in both a good and a bad sense. In the good sense it means to test, to try, to prove. It does not mean to seduce into sin. Its purpose is not to defeat or to destroy. The idea is not that one is tempted, seduced, enticed, and pulled into sin by the Holy Spirit (cp. Jas.1:13); but one is tested, proved, strengthened, reinforced, and purified through the trials of temptation.

In the bad sense, it means to tempt, to seduce, to entice, and to pull someone away from God into the way of sin, of self, and of Satan (Mt.4:1; 1 Cor.7:5; 1 Th.3:5; Gal.6:1; Jas.1:13-14).

Jesus was led into the wilderness by the Spirit *to be tested*. The Spirit did not seduce or entice Jesus to do evil, but He led Jesus into circumstances whereby He could learn obedience and discipline. Through such trials, Jesus was to be perfected and enabled to succor all those who suffer trials (Heb.4:15-16; 5:8). (See notes—Mt.4:2-4; 4:5-7; 4:8-10.)

Six things need to be said about overcoming temptation.

1. Temptation has its bottom root in passion and appetite (Mk.7:20-23; Jas.1:14). It comes directly from within, from man's heart, not from without. And it does not come from God. "For God cannot be tempted by evil; nor does he tempt anyone" (Jas.1:3). God does not tempt any man in a bad sense. What He does is look upon His people as they endure temptation, and He strengthens them to bear the temptation. By such He teaches them discipline and obedience for a greater work (Ro.8:28; 2 Cor.1:3-4; Heb.5:8; 1 Pt.1:6-7).

2. No man confronts any temptation that is not common to all men (1 Cor.10:13).

3. God does not allow the believer to be tempted beyond what he is able to bear. There is always a way to escape (1 Cor.10:13).

4. Jesus Christ understands temptation. He was tempted in all points just as all men are tempted, yet He never sinned (Heb.2:18; 4:15).

5. Jesus Christ is a sympathetic High Priest in helping the believer through temptation (Heb.2:17-18; 4:15).

6. Temptation is overcome (a) by submitting to God and resisting the devil (Jas.4:7-8; 1 Pt.5:8-9), and (b) by using and obeying Scripture to combat temptation (Lk.4:4; cp. Dt.4:8; 4:12; 6:13, 16; 8:3; 10:20).

2 (4:3-4) **Jesus Christ, Temptation—Self-Sufficient—Necessities**: the first temptation was for Jesus to meet the necessities of life by His own power. Note two things.

1. Satan's temptation was for Jesus to misuse His power and His ability. (See note—Mt.4:2-4.) Jesus was very hungry. He had the power to create food and to meet His need, and the tempter tempted Him to use His power upon Himself. But note the wrong in this temptation. Jesus would have been misusing His power by using it in an illegitimate way. His power had not been given to use upon Himself, but to demonstrate His deity by showing men that He was the Son of God. Never once did He use His power upon Himself nor for His own ends—not even when He was hanging upon the cross (cp.Mt.26:42; Lk.23:35). He always used His power to help men, thereby demonstrating and giving evidence that what He was claiming was true: He is the Son of God sent to save the world.

The point is just this: Satan wanted Jesus to prove His Messiahship by *centering* His attention and power upon Himself. If Jesus had used His power upon Himself...

- He would be trusting Himself and not the Father, acting completely independent of the Father and the Father's will.
- He would be saying that men could use their abilities to center upon themselves instead of helping a world lost in need.
- He would be teaching that men could use their abilities to build themselves up (pride) instead of honoring God and His will.

2. Jesus' answer was that something more than physical food was needed. Man needs to be fed spiritually. He needs his spiritual needs met. The point is that Jesus alone can meet man's spiritual needs; therefore He, the Son of God, must use His power only as God wills. (See note—Mt.4:2-4 for detailed discussion.)

Thought 1. A man has needs, the very necessities of life. There are the necessities of...

- food
- clothing
- shelter
- friends
- acceptance
- recognition
- self-esteem
- work
- rest and recreation

The necessities are legitimate. However, the problem arises when we are tempted...

- to use our ability independent of God, forgetting His will and doing our own thing.
- to focus our ability upon ourselves, getting and banking more and more instead of meeting the needs of a desperate world.
- to use our abilities to build ourselves up instead of acknowledging God as the Source of our abilities. Too many seek fame, honor, and praise for selfish ends. Too many want to be recognized as superior and better, as having more position, authority, clothes, houses, cars, lands, and looks.

The great wrong with this is twofold.

1) We misuse our ability. Forgetting God and His will, we focus upon self.
2) We live for the physical and not for the spiritual, for receiving and not for giving. There is a spiritual hunger that just is not met by bread, that is, the physical and material. (See note—Eph.1:3 for detailed discussion.)

"Come, all you who are thirsty, come to the waters; and you who have no money, come, buy and eat! Come, buy wine and milk without money and without cost. Why spend money on what is not bread, and your labor on what does not satisfy? Listen, listen to me, and eat what is good, and your soul will delight in the richest of fare. Give ear and come to me; hear me, that your soul may live. I will make an everlasting covenant with you, my faithful love promised to David. (Isa 55:1-3)

Then Jesus declared, "I am the bread

of life. He who comes to me will never go hungry, and he who believes in me will never be thirsty. (John 6:35)

But here is the bread that comes down from heaven, which a man may eat and not die. I am the living bread that came down from heaven. If anyone eats of this bread, he will live forever. This bread is my flesh, which I will give for the life of the world." (John 6:50-51)

"I tell you the truth, whoever hears my word and believes him who sent me has eternal life and will not be condemned; he has crossed over from death to life. (John 5:24)

I have not departed from the commands of his lips; I have treasured the words of his mouth more than my daily bread. (Job 23:12)

How sweet are your words to my taste, sweeter than honey to my mouth! (Psa 119:103)

When your words came, I ate them; they were my joy and my heart's delight, for I bear your name, O LORD God Almighty. (Jer 15:16)

3 (4:5-8) **Jesus Christ, Temptation—Compromise—Ambition**: the second temptation was for Jesus to seek His ambition (God's kingdom) through compromise. (See note—Mt.4:8-10.) Jesus had come to earth to seek and to save men *eternally*, to secure their loyalty for God, and to set up the Kingdom of God forever (see DEEPER STUDY # 3—Mt.19:23-24). This was the ambition of Jesus. The only way to fulfill His ambition was by the cross (freeing men from sin, death, and judgment). Note what happened in this temptation.

1. Satan enticed Jesus in a moment of time. Satan *flashed* across Jesus' mind all the kingdoms of the world in their enormous glory.

2. Satan claimed that he controlled the possessions and glory of the world. Sometime later, Jesus substantiated Satan's claim. Jesus said that Satan is "the prince of this world" (Jn.12:31; 14:30). Other Scriptures say that he is "the prince...the spirit who is now at work in those who are disobedient" (Eph.2:2) and the "god of this age" (2 Cor.4:4).

3. Satan offered Jesus all the possessions and glory of the world. The world was under His influence and control; therefore, he could give it to anyone whom he wished.

4. Satan, however, had one condition. Jesus had to worship Satan, that is, follow and obey the way of Satan's world. Jesus had to compromise Himself...

- by compromising His standards and behavior.
- by compromising His loyalty and faithfulness to God.
- by compromising His ministry and mission.

Note Jesus' answer: He was quick and decisive, totally dependent upon Scripture to conquer the temptation. "Worship the Lord your God and serve him only" (v.8). He must worship, follow, and serve God alone, not the way and standards and evil of the world. He would follow God even if it meant not realizing His ambition. There is a right way and a wrong way to achieve one's end and purpose; and He, the Son of God, would choose the right way.

Thought 1. The *power* and the *glory* of the world comes from many things. *Worldly power and glory* come from...

- houses
- lands
- wealth
- authority
- influence
- success
- cars
- possessions
- stimulation
- excitement
- fame
- position

A man is often taken up to a mountain by Satan and shown the power and glory of the world. The man is offered whatever he wants if he will do but one thing: worship Satan, that is, follow the path of *worldliness*. Man feels that if he compromises and goes along with the world (everyone else), he will get what he wants and move ahead much faster.

Thought 2. Note a significant point. There is nothing wrong with ambition and desiring to fulfill one's calling in life. There is nothing wrong with experiencing the power and the glory of whatever one's calling is. The wrong is found in following Satan (evil) when tempted to satisfy one's desires and ambitions instead of following God.

What good will it be for a man if he gains the whole world, yet forfeits his soul? Or what can a man give in exchange for his soul? (Mat 16:26)

Do not conform any longer to the pattern of this world, but be transformed by the renewing of your mind. Then you will be able to test and approve what God's will is—his good, pleasing and perfect will. (Rom 12:2)

Endure hardship with us like a good soldier of Christ Jesus. No one serving as a soldier gets involved in civilian affairs—he wants to please his commanding officer. (2 Tim 2:3-4)

Do not love the world or anything in the world. If anyone loves the world, the love of the Father is not in him. For everything in the world—the cravings of sinful man, the lust of his eyes and the boasting of what he has and does—comes not from the Father but from the world. (1 John 2:15-16)

For the grace of God that brings salvation has appeared to all men. It teaches us to say "No" to ungodliness and worldly passions, and to live self-controlled, upright and godly lives in this present age, (Titus 2:11-12)

4 (4:9-12) **Jesus Christ, Temptation—Sensationalism—Obedience**: this particular temptation was for Jesus to be sensational. The thought flashed across Jesus' mind that if He jumped off the pinnacle of the temple, God would cause angels to catch Him. God would never let Him be dashed to bits. Therefore, when the people saw the angels float Him to the ground, they would be stunned into belief and become His followers immediately. (Remember Jesus had not yet done a miracle. Satan had no idea of the miracles to come, nor that men would be slow to believe even with all the evidence of signs and wonders.) Note that Satan's temptation was threefold.

1. Satan tempted Jesus to choose some way other than God's way (see note and DEEPER STUDY # 1—Lk.9:23). God's way was the way of the cross and of identifying with man in his trials and sufferings (cp. Heb.4:15-16. Then cp. Heb.2:14-18 with Jn.3:16. Cp. also Heb.5:7-9.)

2. Satan tempted Jesus to misuse Scripture by twisting it to suit His purposes. Scripture did say that God would take care of His Son no matter what. The heavenly angels were given charge to help Him in everything.

3. Satan tempted Jesus to give people sensations, a religion of feelings. People do not want a life of self-denial and sacrifice, of too much discipline and control. They want the spectacular, something that will be a quick fix, something...

⇒ to stir their emotions and flesh.
⇒ to stimulate their feelings and give gratification.
⇒ to meet their needs with less and less effort.
⇒ to feed their body and soul without cost.

Jesus' answer was straightforward and decisive: "Do not put the Lord your God to the test." There is no way other than God's way; God's way alone is to be pursued and followed. And God's Word is not to be stretched or twisted (presumed upon) trying to make another way. Men must be taught the truth. The way to God is the way of the cross.

Thought 1. All men are tempted to by-pass God, to choose another way. The way of the cross is hard and difficult, yet it is the only way to God (see note and DEEPER STUDY # 1—Lk.9:23). Trying to devise another way to God only spells doom. (Cp. Jn.14:6; 1 Tim.1:15; 2:5-6; Tit.3:4-7).

Since we have now been justified by his blood, how much more shall we be saved from God's wrath through him! (Rom 5:9)

And through him to reconcile to himself all things, whether things on earth or things in heaven, by making peace through his blood, shed on the cross. (Col 1:20)

For the message of the cross is foolishness to those who are perishing, but to us who are being saved it is the power of God. For it is written: "I will destroy the wisdom of the wise; the intelligence of the intelligent I will frustrate." (1 Cor 1:18-19)

How much more, then, will the blood of Christ, who through the eternal Spirit offered himself unblemished to God, cleanse our consciences from acts that lead to death, so that we may serve the living God! (Heb 9:14)

For you know that it was not with perishable things such as silver or gold that you were redeemed from the empty way of life handed down to you from your forefathers, (1 Pet 1:18)

Thought 2. Some try to twist or stretch Scripture...
1) To allow them to do what they want (sin).
2) To devise some way to God other than the cross.

5 (4:13-15) **Ministry**: the conclusion to Jesus' temptations was striking. Satan left him until an opportune time. He left Jesus alone for a while. The victory was won; the temptation was conquered, and Satan was routed for a while. He would be back, but for now there was peace and freedom to carry on the ministry. Note the immediate result of the Lord's victory.

1. Jesus' great power was demonstrated.
2. Jesus' great fame was spread abroad.
3. Jesus' great ministry in the synagogue was admired.

Thought 1. Victory over temptation does not mean a person is freed forever from temptation. In this life temptation will always return. It did for Jesus; it will for us (see note and DEEPER STUDY # 1, 3—Mt.4:1-11).

Jesus said to his disciples: "Things that cause people to sin are bound to come, but woe to that person through whom they come. (Luke 17:1)

Thought 2. Victory over temptation will lead to great results in a person's life. It will give more power, a greater testimony, and a greater ministry.

Blessed is the man who perseveres under trial, because when he has stood the test, he will receive the crown of life that God has promised to those who love him. (James 1:12)

To him who overcomes, I will give the right to sit with me on my throne, just as I overcame and sat down with my Father on his throne. (Rev 3:21)

Since you have kept my command to endure patiently, I will also keep you from the hour of trial that is going to come upon the whole world to test those who live on the earth. (Rev 3:10)

Outline	Scripture
	III. THE SON OF MAN'S ANNOUNCED MISSION AND PUBLIC MINISTRY, 4:16-9:17 **A. Jesus Announces His Mission: A Graphic Picture of Rejection, 4:16-30** (cp. Mt.13:53-58; Mk.6:1-6)
1 A dramatic scene a. Jesus visited His hometown b. Jesus entered the synagogue—His custom on the Sabbath	16 He went to Nazareth, where he had been brought up, and on the Sabbath day he went into the synagogue, as was his custom. And he stood up to read.
2 Scene 1: Jesus' dramatic reading from the prophet Isaiah—concerned the Messiah a. The Messiah was to be anointed by the Spirit b. The Messiah was to preach the gospel (good news) c. The Messiah was to minister	17 The scroll of the prophet Isaiah was handed to him. Unrolling it, he found the place where it is written: 18 "The Spirit of the Lord is on me, because he has anointed me to preach good news to the poor. He has sent me to proclaim freedom for the prisoners and recovery of sight for the blind, to release the oppressed,
d. The Messiah was to preach the age of salvation	19 To proclaim the year of the Lord's favor."
3 Scene 2: Jesus' phenomenal claim a. The rapt attention of the people	20 Then he rolled up the scroll, gave it back to the attendant and sat down. The eyes of everyone in the synagogue were fastened on him,
b. The claim of Jesus to be the Messiah	21 And he began by saying to them, "Today this scripture is fulfilled in your hearing."
4 Scene 3: The people's declining response a. First: They were impressed b. Second: They questioned	22 All spoke well of him and were amazed at the gracious words that came from his lips. "Isn't this Joseph's son?" they asked.
c. Third: They demanded proof—insisted He heal (prove) Himself, that is, work miracles	23 Jesus said to them, "Surely you will quote this proverb to me: 'Physician, heal yourself! Do here in your hometown what we have heard that you did in Capernaum.'"
5 Scene 4: The people's painful rejection	24 "I tell you the truth," he continued, "no prophet is accepted in his hometown.
a. Illust. 1: Only one needy widow had her needs met in Elijah's day—because only one widow accepted Elijah	25 I assure you that there were many widows in Israel in Elijah's time, when the sky was shut for three and a half years and there was a severe famine throughout the land. 26 Yet Elijah was not sent to any of them, but to a widow in Zarephath in the region of Sidon.
b. Illust. 2: Only one needy leper was cleansed in Elisha's day—because only one leper accepted Elisha	27 And there were many in Israel with leprosy in the time of Elisha the prophet, yet not one of them was cleansed—only Naaman the Syrian."
6 Scene 5: The people's true spirit a. An insane wrath: A close-mindedness	28 All the people in the synagogue were furious when they heard this.
b. An insane assault: To silence Jesus	29 They got up, drove him out of the town, and took him to the brow of the hill on which the town was built, in order to throw him down the cliff.
c. The insane behavior of the people failed	30 But he walked right through the crowd and went on his way.

DIVISION III

THE SON OF MAN'S ANNOUNCED MISSION AND PUBLIC MINISTRY, 4:16-9:17

A. Jesus Announces His Mission: A Graphic Picture of Rejection, 4:16-30

(4:16-30) **Introduction**: Jesus Christ claimed to be the Messiah, and His claim was rejected by the people of His day. His claim is still rejected by people today. A graphic picture of rejection is painted in the present passage.

1. A dramatic scene (v.16).
2. Scene 1: Jesus' dramatic reading from the prophet Isaiah—concerned the Messiah (v.17-19).
3. Scene 2: Jesus' phenomenal claim (v.20-21).
4. Scene 3: the people's declining response (v.22-23).
5. Scene 4: the people's painful rejection (v.24-27).
6. Scene 5: the people's true spirit (v.28-30).

1 (4:16) **Jesus, Worship of**: this was a dramatic scene. Jesus visited His hometown of Nazareth where He had been reared (see DEEPER STUDY # 4, Nazareth—Mt.2:23). On the Sabbath He entered the synagogue for worship. Note it was His custom to worship on the Sabbath. He was faithful in His worship of God and faithful to the church. This was the very synagogue that Jesus had always attended as a child. It was a small community synagogue where everyone would know everyone else. Jesus and the congregation were neighors; some were close to His family.

The synagogue had no preachers or ministers as we know them (see DEEPER STUDY # 2, Synagogue—Mt.4:23). The leaders would simply invite some person to read and preach. They had been hearing a good deal about their neighbor Jesus, so they invited Him to read and preach this Sabbath.

2 (4:17-19) **Jesus Christ—Messiah, Ministry—Mission**: the first scene was Jesus' dramatic reading from the prophet Isaiah. The prophecy centered around the Messiah (cp. Is.61:1-2). Note six things.

1. Jesus stood to read the Scripture because of His reverence for the Scripture. (v.16).

Thought 1. There should always be reverence for the Scripture, both in hearing and in reading it (cp. Neh.8:5).

2. The Messiah was to be anointed by the Spirit (v.18). The Messiah was to be both *called* and *equipped* by the Spirit (cp. Lk.3:21-22).

Thought 1. When God calls, He anoints; He equips the messenger with His Spirit. The Holy Spirit goes with the messenger wherever God sends him.

3. The Messiah was to preach the "good news" (gospel). The words "good news" (gospel) (evaggelizesthai) mean to evangelize. Note the Messiah was to preach to two classes of people.

a. He was to preach to the poor. The "poor" means not only poor in material possessions but also *poor in spirit* (see DEEPER STUDY # 2—Mt.5:3).

b. He was to preach freedom to the prisoners (aichmalotois). This is a picture of prisoners of war. (See note, Redemption—Eph.1:7.)

4. The Messiah was to minister. A twofold ministry was mentioned.

a. He was to give sight to the *blind*, not only to those who were spiritually blind, but to those who were blind physically.

b. He was to release the *oppressed*. He was to set free those who were physically, mentally, emotionally, psychologically, and spiritually bruised—those who were...

- disabled
- injured
- wounded
- hurting
- afflicted
- battered

5. The Messiah was to preach the age of salvation. The term "the year of the Lord's favor" means the era, the age or day of salvation (cp. 2 Cor.6:2). It means that the age of the Messiah had come.

6. Note a significant point. Jesus was reading from Is.61:1-2, but He abruptly stopped in the middle of v.2. Why? Because the last part of the verse had to do with judgment and Jesus' present ministry was salvation, not judgment. His future ministry would be to judge the world (Is.61:2b). (Cp. Is.58:6.)

3 (4:20-21) **Jesus Christ, Claims—Messiah**: the second scene was Jesus' phenomenal claim. The scene was one of eager expectation. Jesus closed the book, handed it to the minister, and sat down; sitting was the posture for preaching in the synagogue. All eyes "were fastened on Him" (esan atenizontes autoi), a descriptive phrase meaning fixed, gazing, spellbound. They stared at Him in rapt attention; their eyes were locked upon Him eagerly waiting to see what He had to say.

His voice pierced the air: "Today this scripture is fulfilled in your hearing"—a phenomenal claim.

The word "today" is important. The people thought of the Messiah's coming and the Messianic age in terms of the future. Jesus proclaimed that He was the Messiah—that the Messianic Age was then and now—that all the Scripture of Isaiah was *fulfilled* in Him. He proclaimed...

- that He was the One upon whom the Spirit abode
- that He was the One anointed to preach the gospel to the poor and prisoners
- that He was the One who gave sight to the blind
- that He was the One who released the oppressed
- that He was the One who preached the year of the Lord's favor (the age of salvation)

"But what about you?" he asked. "Who do you say I am?" Simon Peter answered, "You are the Christ, the Son of the living God." Jesus replied, "Blessed are you, Simon son of Jonah, for this was not revealed to you by man, but by my Father in heaven. (Mat 16:15-17)

But Jesus remained silent. The high priest said to him, "I charge you under oath by the living God: Tell us if you are the Christ, the Son of God." "Yes, it is as you say," Jesus replied. "But I say to all of you: In the future you will see the Son of Man sitting at the right hand of the Mighty One and coming on the clouds of heaven." (Mat 26:63-64)

He said to them, "How foolish you are, and how slow of heart to believe all that the prophets have spoken! Did not the Christ have to suffer these things and then enter his glory?" (Luke 24:25-26)

The woman said, "I know that Messiah" (called Christ) "is coming. When he comes, he will explain everything to us." Then Jesus declared, "I who speak to you am he." (John 4:25-26)

So Jesus said, "When you have lifted up the Son of Man, then you will know that I am the *one I claim to be* and that I do nothing on my own but speak just what the Father has taught me. The one who sent me is with me; he has not left me alone, for I always do what pleases him." (John 8:28-29)

Jesus said to her, "I am the resurrection and the life. He who believes in me will live, even though he dies; and whoever lives and believes in me will never die. Do you believe this?" "Yes, Lord," she told him, "I believe that you are the Christ, the Son of God, who was to come into the world." (John 11:25-27)

Just as the Son of Man did not come to be served, but to serve, and to give his life as a ransom for many." (Mat 20:28)

For the Son of Man came to seek and to save what was lost." (Luke 19:10)

The thief comes only to steal and kill and destroy; I have come that they may have life, and have it to the full. (John 10:10)

Here is a trustworthy saying that deserves full acceptance: Christ Jesus came into the world to save sinners—of whom I am the worst. (1 Tim 1:15)

4 (4:22-23) **Jesus Christ, Response to—Signs**: the third scene was the people's declining response. Note how drastically the people's response declined.

1. First, they were impressed with His eloquence, His charm and winning words, and the power of His message. Note the word "amazed" (ethaumazon). It means they began to marvel and to be astonished at the gracious words flowing from His mouth. They were taking *pride* in one of their own neighbor's being so capable.

2. Second, they began to question. This was a quick reaction, a quick change. Sitting there listening, the questions

began to arise in their thoughts: "Is this Joseph's son?" Matthew is even more descriptive. The people were sitting there glancing around, asking in their minds, "Isn't this his mother, brothers and sisters who are with us?" (Mt.13:55-56). "And they took offense at him" (Mt.13:57). The word "offense" means they stumbled over Him. They could not imagine that someone from their own town—someone whom they had known since a child—could be the Messiah, the Son of God.

3. Third, they demanded proof, insisted that He had to heal, that is, prove Himself by working miracles in their midst. Remember, all this was still thoughts in their minds. They were still sitting there listening to Him, but their thoughts were *stumbling* over His claim to be the Messiah. Jesus knew their thoughts, so He stopped His message and directed a statement to them: "You are thinking, saying to me, Physician, heal, prove yourself. Prove yourself by doing the miracles you did in Capernaum."

The point is this: the response of the people to Jesus' claim deteriorated from being *impressed* to being *offended* to *demanding proof*.

> **Thought 1.** Many are impressed with Jesus Christ at first, but when they are presented with His claims and the cross, they become offended and demand proof. His claim to be the Incarnate God in human flesh—to be the virgin-born Son of God—who must die for man's sin by being crucified upon a vulgar cross, is offensive to some. Many refuse to accept such phenomenal claims and vulgar scenes. They want a religion of grand images, beautiful pictures, and soft words.
>
> **"Unless you people see miraculous signs and wonders," Jesus told him, "you will never believe." (John 4:48)**
>
> **Jews demand miraculous signs and Greeks look for wisdom, but we preach Christ crucified: a stumbling block to Jews and foolishness to Gentiles, (1 Cor 1:22-23)**

5 (4:24-27) **Jesus Christ, Rejection of—Salvation**: the fourth scene was the people's painful rejection. Jesus continued to speak, directing His remarks toward His hometown audience. But note: Jesus knew they had already rejected Him. Therefore, He would not gratify their curiosity and demand for signs, nor would He continue to preach; but rather He would give a twofold warning.

1. "No prophet is *accepted* in His hometown." They had rejected Him and He knew it. They could not hide the fact. They had (as is so often the case)...

- allowed familiarity to breed contempt.
- thought it farfetched that the claims of a hometown boy could be true.
- given in to envy among neighbors.

Note the words "His hometown." Jesus was bound to be thinking of all Israel as well as Nazareth. The Jewish nation would eventually reject Him, the true Messiah.

2. God would reject those who rejected His prophet, the Messiah. Jesus warned the people by recalling two well known stories in the history of Israel. The audience could not miss the point. In the past, God had not given His mercy to people who just *thought* they were "God's people" (the Jews), but God had given His mercy to those whose hearts were turned toward Him and who accepted Him.

a. There was the one needy widow in Elijah's day. She was the only widow who had her need met by God in the day of famine. There were many without food, destitute and starving, yet God sent His prophet to help only this one person; and she was a despised Gentile. Why? When there were so many others who *professed to be God's chosen people*, why would God help only this one poor widow? Why would God turn away from the Jews to another person? The point is clear. She was the only one whose heart was turned toward God and who accepted Him.

b. There was also the one leper who had his leprosy cleansed by Elisha. When God sent Elisha to heal Naaman, Elisha passed by many Jewish lepers, many who thought they were the chosen people of God. But the prophet stopped to help none of these. He was sent to heal the Syrian Gentile, the one person whose heart accepted God.

Thought 1. Salvation requires more than mere profession, more than just thinking one is chosen of God and that one will never be rejected by God. A person's heart must be turned toward God (repentance) and must accept God (belief) in order to be saved.

> **Whoever believes in him is not condemned, but whoever does not believe stands condemned already because he has not believed in the name of God's one and only Son. (John 3:18)**
>
> **Whoever believes in the Son has eternal life, but whoever rejects the Son will not see life, for God's wrath remains on him." (John 3:36)**
>
> **I told you that you would die in your sins; if you do not believe that I am the one I claim to be, you will indeed die in your sins." (John 8:24)**
>
> **See to it, brothers, that none of you has a sinful, unbelieving heart that turns away from the living God. (Heb 3:12)**

6 (4:28-30) **Jesus Christ, Rejection of**: the fifth scene was the people's true spirit. Note what Jesus said to the people sitting before Him.

1. Jesus said (predicted) that God would turn and give His mercy to someone else if the people rejected Him. God would turn to those who were responsive to Him. He would not continue to appeal to those who were always rejecting and hardening their hearts.

2. Jesus also made a much broader statement. He said that God would turn from Israel ("His hometown," v.24) if Israel continued to reject Him.

As a result of these two statements, the people's reaction grew hostile and violent. They "got up." Note three facts.

1. Their insane wrath: a close-mindedness.
2. Their insane assault: a violent attempt to silence Jesus.
3. Their insane behavior: a failure. Somehow Jesus was able to escape their assault. How? Perhaps the people were stricken with a moment of confusion, a moment of shock, or some temporary blindness which enabled Him to quickly escape.

> **Thought 1.** The Lord will not always contend with nor strive after a man, not forever. A person can go too far too often and face eternity without the pres-

ence of God. A person must surrender to the Spirit of God while there is still time.

Then the LORD said, "My Spirit will not contend with man forever, for he is mortal; his days will be a hundred and twenty years." (Gen 6:3)

Blessed is the man who always fears the LORD, but he who hardens his heart falls into trouble. (Prov 28:14)

A man who remains stiff-necked after many rebukes will suddenly be destroyed—without remedy. (Prov 29:1)

Or do you show contempt for the riches of his kindness, tolerance and patience, not realizing that God's kindness leads you toward repentance? But because of your stubbornness and your unrepentant heart, you are storing up wrath against yourself for the day of God's wrath, when his righteous judgment will be revealed. (Rom 2:4-5)

See to it, brothers, that none of you has a sinful, unbelieving heart that turns away from the living God. But encourage one another daily, as long as it is called Today, so that none of you may be hardened by sin's deceitfulness. We have come to share in Christ if we hold firmly till the end the confidence we had at first. (Heb 3:12-14)

Thought 2. A person or a people may wish to silence Jesus and His followers, but their efforts will be to no avail. The message of the gospel will never be silenced.

Simon Peter answered, "You are the Christ, the Son of the living God." And I tell you that you are Peter, and on this rock I will build my church, and the gates of Hades will not overcome it. (Mat 16:16, 18)

Heaven and earth will pass away, but my words will never pass away. (Luke 21:33; cp. Mat 5:18)

"Praise be to the LORD, who has given rest to his people Israel just as he promised. Not one word has failed of all the good promises he gave through his servant Moses. (1 Ki 8:56)

Simon Peter answered, "You are the Christ, the Son of the living The works of his hands are faithful and just; all his precepts are trustworthy. (Psa 111:7)

	B. Jesus Ministers and Makes an Amazing Impact: A Day in the Life of Jesus, 4:31-44 (Mt.8:14-17; Mk.1:21-39)	38 Jesus left the synagogue and went to the home of Simon. Now Simon's mother-in-law was suffering from a high fever, and they asked Jesus to help her.	**4 He cured the most needful** a. So needful, a great fever b. So needful, could not speak or seek Jesus for herself
1 Jesus went down to Capernaum	31 Then he went down to Capernaum, a town in Galilee, and on the Sabbath began to teach the people.	39 So he bent over her and rebuked the fever, and it left her. She got up at once and began to wait on them.	c. So needful, could not even come to Jesus d. So needful, He came & healed her; she arose & ministered
2 He taught in the morning service with authority **3 He delivered the most unclean** a. A man with an unclean spirit sat in worship	32 They were amazed at his teaching, because his message had authority. 33 In the synagogue there was a man possessed by a demon, an evil spirit. He cried out at the top of his voice,	40 When the sun was setting, the people brought to Jesus all who had various kinds of sickness, and laying his hands on each one, he healed them.	**5 He healed the diseases of those who sought Him out**
1) Evil spirits acknowledged Jesus' deity	34 "Ha! What do you want with us, Jesus of Nazareth? Have you come to destroy us? I know who you are—the Holy One of God!"	41 Moreover, demons came out of many people, shouting, "You are the Son of God!" But he rebuked them and would not allow them to speak, because they knew he was the Christ.	**6 He rebuked the evil spirits from making a false profession**
2) Jesus rebuked the evil acknowledgement 3) Jesus cast out the unclean spirit	35 "Be quiet!" Jesus said sternly. "Come out of him!" Then the demon threw the man down before them all and came out without injuring him.	42 At daybreak Jesus went out to a solitary place. The people were looking for him and when they came to where he was, they tried to keep him from leaving them.	**7 He sought to be alone, seeking the presence of God** a. He tried to get alone b. He was sought out & was begged to stay
b. The people were amazed	36 All the people were amazed and said to each other, "What is this teaching? With authority and power he gives orders to evil spirits and they come out!"	43 But he said, "I must preach the good news of the kingdom of God to the other towns also, because that is why I was sent."	**8 He persisted in His mission despite pressure to be sidetracked**
c. The people spread His fame	37 And the news about him spread throughout the surrounding area.	44 And he kept on preaching in the synagogues of Judea.	

DIVISION III

THE SON OF MAN'S ANNOUNCED MISSION AND PUBLIC MINISTRY, 4:16-9:17

B. Jesus Ministers and Makes an Amazing Impact: A Day in the Life of Jesus, 4:31-44

(4:31-44) **Introduction**: this is one of the most interesting passages in all of Scripture. This is the very beginning, the very launch of Jesus' ministry. What Luke does is paint the picture of a typical day so that the reader will have some idea of what a day was like in the life of Jesus. Note how busy and pressuring and tiring the day was, and note the powerful lessons applicable to our lives.

1. Jesus went down to Capernaum (v.31).
2. He taught in the morning service with authority (v.32).
3. He delivered the most unclean (v.33-37).
4. He cured the most needful (v.38-39).
5. He healed the diseases of those who sought Him out (v.40).
6. He rebuked the evil spirits from making a false profession (v.41).
7. He sought to be alone, seeking the presence of God (v.42).
8. He persisted in His mission despite pressure to be sidetracked (v.43-44).

1 (4:31) **Capernaum—Jesus' Headquarters**: Jesus went down to Capernaum, a city of Galilee. Note the exact wording and look at verse 44: "And he kept on preaching in the synagogues of Judea." Capernaum became the *headquarters* of Jesus. Nazareth was Jesus' hometown, but the city had rejected Him. He had to move elsewhere. The city He chose as the center of His operations was Capernaum. Capernaum was the manufacturing center of Palestine; therefore, it was strategically located, always flooded with travelling merchants. The major roads passed through its borders, roads which connected such metropolitan cities as Damascus, Jerusalem, and the great Syrian cities of Tyre and Sidon. The great caravan route leading to the Mediterranean Sea also ran through the city (cp. Is.9:1). It was an ideal location for the spread of the gospel, an ideal location for the Messiah to use as His base of operations. (See note, Capernaum—Mt.4:12-13.)

2 (4:32) **Preaching—Jesus Christ, Teaching of**: Jesus taught in the morning worship service with authority. His teaching was not ordinary, not the kind of teaching the people were used to hearing. They were astonished at His doctrine. It was what He taught that astounded them: "His message had authority."

⇒ His message had authority, the authority of God's Spirit.
⇒ His message had a commanding force to it.
⇒ His message had the power of God's Spirit upon it, *quickening* the Word to the hearts of the hearers. (See note—Mt.7:29.)

Jesus answered, "My teaching is not my own. It comes from him who sent me. If anyone chooses to do God's will, he will find out whether my teaching comes from God or whether I speak on my own. He who speaks on his own does so to gain honor for himself, but he who works for the honor of the one who sent him is a man of truth; there is nothing false about him. (John 7:16-18)

Don't you believe that I am in the Father, and that the Father is in me? The words I say to you are not just my own. Rather, it is the Father, living in me, who is doing his work. (John 14:10)

3 (4:33-37) **Unclean—Evil Spirit—Sin—Resisting**: Jesus delivered the most unclean. Note several facts. (See outline and notes—Mk.1:23-28.)

1. The man was "in the synagogue," actually attending the worship service; yet he was desperately unclean, as dirty as could be.

2. The man was possessed by a demon (an evil spirit). "Evil" (akathartou) means that the man was both morally and ceremonially unclean, dirty, dishevelled, filthy. He was worshipping, but he was morally unclean and corrupt; his life was all dishevelled.

3. The evil spirit *acknowledged* Jesus' deity. He knew three things. (See note, pt.2—Mk.1:23-24 for detailed discussion.)

a. He had nothing to do with Jesus. He was unclean, dirty, and sinful in comparison with Jesus.
b. He knew that he was to be destroyed by Jesus, that a day of judgment was coming.

He who does what is sinful is of the devil, because the devil has been sinning from the beginning. The reason the Son of God appeared was to destroy the devil's work. (1 John 3:8)

c. He knew that Jesus was "the Holy One of God." (Lk. 4:34). He knew and proclaimed that he stood face to face with the true Messiah, the Son of the living God.

Thought 1. The person who is morally unclean and dirty is in desperate straits. He is gripped by an evil force that cries out in the very face of God...

- What do you want with us, Jesus of Nazareth?
- Have you come to destroy us?
- I know who you are, the Holy One of God!"

"You stiff-necked people, with uncircumcised hearts and ears! You are just like your fathers: You always resist the Holy Spirit! (Acts 7:51)

They turned their backs to me and not their faces; though I taught them again and again, they would not listen or respond to discipline. (Jer 32:33)

"We will not listen to the message you have spoken to us in the name of the LORD! (Jer 44:16)

"But they refused to pay attention; stubbornly they turned their backs and stopped up their ears. (Zec 7:11)

3. Jesus rebuked the evil spirit's acknowledgement. This is a critical point: Jesus stopped the acknowledgement, the proclamation of the evil spirit. Jesus would not have the evil spirit's witnessing to His deity. Why? Because it was a false witness, a profession only. The evil spirit was not confessing from the heart nor from the will to follow Jesus. He had not been born again. The *only confession* Jesus accepted was the confession of a man who made a deliberate decision to follow Him *as Lord*. (See note—Mk.1:25-26.)

That if you confess with your mouth, "Jesus is Lord," and believe in your heart that God raised him from the dead, you will be saved. For it is with your heart that you believe and are justified, and it is with your mouth that you confess and are saved. As the Scripture says, "Anyone who trusts in him will never be put to shame." For there is no difference between Jew and Gentile—the same Lord is Lord of all and richly blesses all who call on him, for, "Everyone who calls on the name of the Lord will be saved." (Rom 10:9-13)

4. Jesus cast out the evil spirit and saved the man. How? By His Word, by simply saying, "Be quiet...come out of him!" Note the great power of the Lord's Word.

Then Jesus came to them and said, "All authority in heaven and on earth has been given to me. (Mat 28:18)

For you granted him authority over all people that he might give eternal life to all those you have given him. (John 17:2)

5. The evil spirit threw the man down, but he came out of the man and did not hurt him. (See note, pt.2—Mk.1:25-26 for detailed discussion.)

6. The people were amazed, astonished, shocked, stunned. Note what amazed them: His Word—the authority and power of His Word to cleanse even the most unclean.

7. The people spread His fame everywhere, witnessing to His cleansing and healing power. They could do no other, for they were witnessing a power never before seen.

Thought 1. The Lord has the power to save and cleanse anyone who comes to Him, no matter how possessed by evil.

For you granted him authority over all people that he might give eternal life to all those you have given him. (John 17:2)

I pray also that the eyes of your heart may be enlightened in order that you may know the hope to which he has called you, the riches of his glorious inheritance in the saints, and his incomparably great power for us who believe. That power is like the working of his mighty strength, (Eph 1:18-19)

"I know that you can do all things; no plan of yours can be thwarted. (Job 42:2)

4 (4:38-39) **Helpless, The—Needful, The—Ministering**: Jesus cured the most needful. After the worship service, Jesus went to Peter's home. Peter's mother-in-law was critically ill. Note these simple facts.

1. She was desperately needful, overtaken with a "high fever."
2. She was so helpless she could not even speak to ask Jesus for help.
3. She was so weakened she was unable to rise out of bed to seek the help of Jesus.
4. Jesus came to her and rebuked the fever by simply speaking the Word, and she arose and began to minister.

Thought 1. Jesus is the great hope of the most needful. No matter how *desperate or helpless or weakened*—Jesus will speak the Word of healing. All that is needed is a willing heart and mind.

Even if a person is so helpless that he is unable to speak verbally, that person can call upon the Lord by thought, and God will still save him.

For, "Everyone who calls on the name of the Lord will be saved." (Rom 10:13)

But so that you may know that the Son of Man has authority on earth to forgive sins." Then he said to the paralytic, "Get up, take your mat and go home." (Mat 9:6)

5 (4:40) **Helpless, The—Ministering**: Jesus healed all the diseases of those who sought Him out. Again, note several simple facts. (See outline and notes—Mk.1:32-34 for detailed discussion.)

1. It was early evening and the sun was setting. Jesus had been ministering rather extensively all day and was tired, yet He was approachable. He could be approached at all hours. There was never a closed door into His presence.
2. The people who came to Him were totally helpless. Every one of them had to be brought, yet someone cared enough to bring them.

Thought 1. Note two challenging lessons.
1) The most helpless can come or be brought to Jesus. He is always available to help.
2) There is a strong challenge to us. We need to care enough to bring the helpless to Jesus.

3. Jesus did not bypass or overlook a single one. He touched every one and healed every one. No matter the disease, they were healed.

Thought 1. No one, no matter how helpless, ever comes to Jesus that He does not help. Rich or poor, strong or weak, the Lord forbids no one.

When evening came, many who were demon-possessed were brought to him, and he drove out the spirits with a word and healed all the sick. This was to fulfill what was spoken through the prophet Isaiah: "He took up our infirmities and carried our diseases." (Mat 8:16-17)

Jesus answered them, "It is not the healthy who need a doctor, but the sick. I have not come to call the righteous, but sinners to repentance." (Luke 5:31-32)

How God anointed Jesus of Nazareth with the Holy Spirit and power, and how he went around doing good and healing all who were under the power of the devil, because God was with him. (Acts 10:38)

You have been a refuge for the poor, a refuge for the needy in his distress, a shelter from the storm and a shade from the heat. For the breath of the ruthless is like a storm driving against a wall (Isa 25:4)

Surely he took up our infirmities and carried our sorrows, yet we considered him stricken by God, smitten by him, and afflicted. (Isa 53:4)

6 (4:41) **Evil Spirits—Demons**: Jesus rebuked the demons from making false professions (see notes—Lk.4:33-37; Mk.1:25-26).

7 (4:42) **Jesus Christ, Prayer**: Jesus sought to be alone, seeking the presence of God. Jesus was exhausted and drained, spiritually as well as physically. Apparently, He had been ministering all day and night, that is, for almost twenty-four hours without a break.

1. He tried to get alone in a solitary place. He needed to be refreshed and revived in body and spirit. He wanted time alone with God.
2. He was sought out by the people who begged Him to stay. They were desperate and helpless.

Thought 1. Note two great lessons.
1) We need to seek the renewal of our bodies and spirits in the Lord's presence—seek renewal much more than most of us do.
2) We need to seek Him out and beg for His help while He may be found. When Jesus was on the earth in the body, He could help only those who surrounded Him. Now that He is in the Spirit and able to minister everywhere at once, so few of us are seeking Him out. What an example these people were in seeking Him!

Look to the LORD and his strength; seek his face always. (1 Chr 16:11)

Seek the LORD while he may be found; call on him while he is near. (Isa 55:6)

But as for me, it is good to be near God. I have made the Sovereign LORD my refuge; I will tell of all your deeds. (Psa 73:28)

The LORD is near to all who call on him, to all who call on him in truth. (Psa 145:18)

Let us draw near to God with a sincere heart in full assurance of faith, having our hearts sprinkled to cleanse us from a guilty conscience and having our bodies washed with pure water. (Heb 10:22)

8 (4:43-44) **Jesus Christ, Mission**: Jesus persisted in His *mission* despite the pressure of some persons to sidetrack Him. Jesus had to preach in other cities as well, so He could not stay with those clamoring after Him. He had to fulfill His mission. He could not be sidetracked. Everyone had to hear the Gospel. He had to give others the opportunity as well. He knew that the more He could reach and disciple, the more others would hear and be reached. So He set His face like a flint and marched on despite all who "tried to keep him from leaving them" (kateichon): tried to prevent, hinder, stop, hold Him back.

For the Son of Man came to seek and to save what was lost." (Luke 19:10)

As long as it is day, we must do the work of him who sent me. Night is coming, when no one can work. (John 9:4)

	CHAPTER 5 **C. Jesus Calls His First Disciples: Steps to Calling Men, 5:1-11** (Mt.4:18-22; Mk.1:16-20; Jn.1:35-51)
1 **Lake Gennesaret** 2 **Step 1: Seeing a vision of people who need to hear the Word of God**	One day as Jesus was standing by the Lake of Gennesaret, with the people crowding around him and listening to the word of God,
3 **Step 2: Seizing resources** a. Seeing the resources available	2 He saw at the water's edge two boats, left there by the fishermen, who were washing their nets.
b. Seeing a man: Simon c. Leading the man to serve	3 He got into one of the boats, the one belonging to Simon, and asked him to put out a little from shore. Then he sat down and taught the people from the boat.
4 **Step 3: Removing reluctant obedience**	4 When he had finished speaking, he said to Simon, "Put out into deep water, and let down the nets for a catch." 5 Simon answered, "Master, we've worked hard all night and haven't caught anything. But because you say so, I will let down the nets."
5 **Step 4: Demonstrating godly power** a. A great catch made b. A catch so great the net breaks	6 When they had done so, they caught such a large number of fish that their nets began to break.
c. A catch so great other help is needed d. A catch so great both boats are filled e. A catch so great the boats began to sink	7 So they signaled their partners in the other boat to come and help them, and they came and filled both boats so full that they began to sink.
6 **Step 5: Stirring a deep confession** a. Of sin, v.8 b. Of Christ as Lord, v.8	8 When Simon Peter saw this, he fell at Jesus' knees and said, "Go away from me, Lord; I am a sinful man!"
c. Of awe—reverence—fear	9 For he and all his companions were astonished at the catch of fish they had taken,
7 **Step 6: Challenging men to discipleship, that is, to catch other men**[DS1,2]	10 And so were James and John, the sons of Zebedee, Simon's partners. Then Jesus said to Simon, "Don't be afraid; from now on you will catch men."
8 **Step 7: Watching for the decision to forsake all**	11 So they pulled their boats up on shore, left everything and followed him.

DIVISION III

THE SON OF MAN'S ANNOUNCED MISSION AND PUBLIC MINISTRY, 4:16-9:17

C. Jesus Calls His First Disciples: Steps to Calling Men, 5:1-11

(5:1-11) **Introduction**: Jesus Christ set out to catch men, that is, to catch them for God. He desires to catch all men, but He is unable to catch everyone by Himself. He needs help, the help of all who will follow Him. The present passage is a descriptive picture of how Jesus goes about calling men to help Him in the enormous task of reaching the world.

1. Lake Gennesaret (v.1).
2. Step 1: seeing a vision of people who need to hear the Word of God (v.1).
3. Step 2: seizing resources (v.2-3).
4. Step 3: removing reluctant obedience (v.4-5).
5. Step 4: demonstrating godly power (v.6-7).
6. Step 5: stirring a deep confession (v.8-9).
7. Step 6: challenging men to discipleship, that is, to catch other men (v.10).
8. Step 7: watching for the decision to forsake all (v.11).

1 (5:1) **Lake Gennesaret**: the scene of this experience took place on Lake Gennesaret which was the same as the Sea of Galilee (see DEEPER STUDY # 1—Mk.1:16; Lk.8:22).

2 (5:1) **Word of God, Hunger for—Righteousness—Vision**: the first step to calling men is seeing a vision of people—people who need the Word of God. The people were actually "crowding around," "pressing" (epikeisthai) in upon Jesus. They gathered and crowded around Him. Note why: to hear the Word of God. They pressed and crowded in to hear the Word of God. They had a craving, a *hunger and thirst* after righteousness. Note two things.

1. Jesus met the hunger and thirst of people.

> **Blessed are those who hunger and thirst for righteousness, for they will be filled. (Mat 5:6)**
>
> **Blessed are you who hunger now, for you will be satisfied. Blessed are you who weep now, for you will laugh. (Luke 6:21)**
>
> **But whoever drinks the water I give him will never thirst. Indeed, the water I give him will become in him a spring of water welling up to eternal life." (John 4:14)**
>
> **On the last and greatest day of the Feast, Jesus stood and said in a loud voice, "If anyone is thirsty, let him come to me and drink. (John 7:37)**
>
> **Like newborn babies, crave pure spiritual milk, so that by it you may grow up in your salvation, now that you have tasted that the Lord is good. (1 Pet 2:2-3)**
>
> **Never again will they hunger; never again will they thirst. The sun will not beat upon them, nor any scorching heat. (Rev 7:16)**
>
> **The Spirit and the bride say, "Come!" And let him who hears say, "Come!" Whoever is thirsty, let him come; and whoever wishes, let him take the free gift of the water of life. (Rev 22:17)**
>
> **They feast on the abundance of your**

house; you give them drink from your river of delights. (Psa 36:8)

For he satisfies the thirsty and fills the hungry with good things. (Psa 107:9)

"Come, all you who are thirsty, come to the waters; and you who have no money, come, buy and eat! Come, buy wine and milk without money and without cost. (Isa 55:1)

The LORD will guide you always; he will satisfy your needs in a sun-scorched land and will strengthen your frame. You will be like a well-watered garden, like a spring whose waters never fail. (Isa 58:11)

2. Jesus saw that He could never meet the needs of all the people, not by Himself. He needed others to help.

He told them, "The harvest is plentiful, but the workers are few. Ask the Lord of the harvest, therefore, to send out workers into his harvest field. (Luke 10:2)

3 (5:2-3) **Resource—Opportunity, Serving**: the second step to calling men is seizing resources. Jesus had to find some way to handle the throng of people both then and later. The crowds were so large and their needs so many that He just could not handle their disorder. He could not meet the needs of everyone. Standing there and being confronted with the present problem, He scanned the horizon for some way to handle the matter.

As He looked around, He saw an opportunity and laid His plans. He saw a boat and a fisherman in the boat, and He needed both. The boat could be used as a pulpit, and the man could become a disciple. He asked the man to let Him use the boat as a pulpit and to steer the boat out from land a short distance. The point is this: Jesus seized and used the resources available. He had the vision of people's needing the Word of God, but He needed a pulpit and others to help, so He scanned the horizon and found both.

Do you not say, 'Four months more and then the harvest'? I tell you, open your eyes and look at the fields! They are ripe for harvest. Even now the reaper draws his wages, even now he harvests the crop for eternal life, so that the sower and the reaper may be glad together. (John 4:35-36)

4 (5:4-5) **Obedience—Reluctance**: the third step to calling men is the *removal of reluctant obedience.* As soon as Jesus finished His preaching, He decided to win Peter's loyalty and discipleship. But first, He had to humble Peter. He had to show Peter that He, the Messiah, could look after and take care of him. He told Peter to put out to sea and fish. Peter objected because he had fished all night and had caught nothing. However, he stopped right in the middle of his objection and obeyed Jesus. Note what had happened.

1. Peter was reluctant to obey Jesus. He objected to what Jesus asked. He was thoroughly *exhausted*, for he had "worked hard all night." He was *disappointed*, because he had caught nothing, and he had worked enough hours already. Despite needing to be home in bed, he had stayed to help the Lord in His preaching by loaning his boat to Him.

2. Peter caught himself in the middle of his objection and obeyed. What caused the switch, the change from reluctance to willing obedience? Probably two things.

a. Peter was pretty well convinced that Jesus was who He claimed to be, the Messiah.

b. Peter was drawn somewhat to follow Jesus. Therefore, when he began to object to Jesus' will, there was a prick of conscience, and he obeyed his conscience. He followed his heart...

- not his *mind*, thinking there were no fish.
- not his *experience*, having already tried and failed to catch fish.
- not his *body*, being too tired and exhausted, just incapable of going on.

Thought 1. Reluctance should always give in to obedience. We need the spirit that will *try* for God, no matter what the obstacles or how hopeless a situation may seem.

Thought 2. When a man is drawn to Christ, he desperately needs to obey his heart and to obey it immediately.

Never be lacking in zeal, but keep your spiritual fervor, serving the Lord. (Rom 12:11)

Therefore, my dear brothers, stand firm. Let nothing move you. Always give yourselves fully to the work of the Lord, because you know that your labor in the Lord is not in vain. (1 Cor 15:58)

We do not want you to become lazy, but to imitate those who through faith and patience inherit what has been promised. (Heb 6:12)

5 (5:6-7) **Jesus Christ, Power—Obedience, Results—Humility**: the fourth step to calling men is *demonstrating godly power.* Peter's obedience produced results; his obedience caught fish, and the catch was no ordinary catch. It was much more, so much more that there could be no question about Jesus. Jesus was behind the miracle; Jesus was demonstrating the power of God. (Remember this was the very purpose of Jesus, to win Peter's loyalty and willingness to become a disciple on a full-time basis.) What happened is a little humorous when we remember what Jesus was doing with Peter, and Peter's reluctance and objection, weariness and exhaustion. There was a sense in which the Lord was really laying it on Peter, really letting him have it. Peter thought he was tired, but he did not know what exhaustion was yet. The Lord must have stood to the side smiling to Himself. How our Lord loved this man Peter, even now! He was after Peter's loyalty, and He was going to get it even if He had to make Peter drop in his tracks (which was exactly what was to happen, v.8). At any rate, there was some humor in what began to happen to this man who was so reluctant, moaning and groaning about his tiredness. Just imagine Peter already bone weary, grumbling in his mind at this carpenter's telling him, the skilled fisherman, how to fish. Imagine Peter's exhaustion and weariness, reluctance and objection, moaning and groaning; and then all of a sudden a catch is made, a catch so great that he was going to have to work wearily along for hour upon hour.

⇒ Peter's net broke.
⇒ Peter had to call for another whole crew and boat to help.
⇒ Both boats were filled as full to capacity.
⇒ Then to top it off, both boats began to sink.

Jesus had His man! What else was Peter to do other than what followed? In all the humor of the situation, our Lord's heart was bound to be full of rejoicing because this big hunk of a fisherman, man though he was, was like a little child before the Lord. He was broken in humility before the Lord, and the experience was but the first of many experiences of brokenness yet to come.

> **"I know that you can do all things; no plan of yours can be thwarted. (Job 42:2)**
> **Yes, and from ancient days I am he. No one can deliver out of my hand. When I act, who can reverse it?" (Isa 43:13)**

6 (5:8-9) **Confession**: the fifth step to calling men is *stirring a deep confession.* Peter knew exactly what had happened. He had been reluctant and objected to the Lord's request, and he had not been too happy that the great catch had caused so much trouble. But he was a skilled fisherman, and he knew that the great catch was no ordinary catch; it was a miracle of the Lord, a miracle which the Lord was using to teach him that he was to obey without reluctance and objection.

Note exactly what happened. When Peter saw the boat's beginning to sink, he raced over to Jesus, fell upon his knees, and in a sense (continuing the humor) said, "Lord, I've had enough. Let me alone. I'll do anything." His confession was threefold.

1. He confessed his sin of disobedience and unbelief: of being reluctant to obey the Lord, of questioning the Lord's will and knowledge and power.
2. He confessed Jesus to be the *Lord.* Note that Peter had previously called Jesus "Master" (epistate, v.5), which is a word used to address anyone in authority. But Peter had learned better. He now called Jesus "Lord" (kurie). He is the Lord who is holy and convicting, who must be obeyed and followed.
3. He confessed a fear, a reverence, an awe for the Lord (cp. v.9-10).

> **"Woe to me!" I cried. "I am ruined! For I am a man of unclean lips, and I live among a people of unclean lips, and my eyes have seen the King, the LORD Almighty." (Isa 6:5)**
> **My ears had heard of you but now my eyes have seen you. Therefore I despise myself and repent in dust and ashes." (Job 42:5-6)**
> **Then Abraham spoke up again: "Now that I have been so bold as to speak to the Lord, though I am nothing but dust and ashes, (Gen 18:27)**
> **Then one who looked like a man touched my lips, and I opened my mouth and began to speak. I said to the one standing before me, "I am overcome with anguish because of the vision, my lord, and I am helpless. (Dan 10:16)**
> **That if you confess with your mouth, "Jesus is Lord," and believe in your heart that God raised him from the dead, you will be saved. For it is with your heart that you believe and are justified, and it is with your mouth that you confess and are saved. (Rom 10:9-10)**
> **If we confess our sins, he is faithful and just and will forgive us our sins and purify us from all unrighteousness. (1 John 1:9)**
> **Only acknowledge your guilt— you have rebelled against the LORD your God, you have scattered your favors to foreign gods under every spreading tree, and have not obeyed me,'" declares the LORD. (Jer 3:13)**
> **He who conceals his sins does not prosper, but whoever confesses and renounces them finds mercy. (Prov 28:13)**
> **Now make confession to the LORD, the God of your fathers, and do his will. Separate yourselves from the peoples around you and from your foreign wives." (Ezra 10:11)**

7 (5:10) **Call—Discipleship—Mission**: the sixth step to calling men is *challenging men to discipleship,* that is, to *catch other men.* Note two significant facts.

1. The words "don't be afraid" (me phobon) indicate that Peter was actually scared and frightened. Jesus was calming him, telling him to trust and stop fearing. He, the Lord, was in charge and looking after everything.
2. The call to Peter was to "catch men." The word "catch" (zogreo) means to *catch alive* or to *catch for life.* The idea is that Peter was no longer to catch (fish) for death, but he was to catch (men) for life.

> **"Come, follow me," Jesus said, "and I will make you fishers of men." (Mat 4:19)**
> **Be merciful to those who doubt; snatch others from the fire and save them; to others show mercy, mixed with fear—hating even the clothing stained by corrupted flesh. (Jude 1:22-23)**
> **You did not choose me, but I chose you and appointed you to go and bear fruit— fruit that will last. Then the Father will give you whatever you ask in my name. (John 15:16)**
> **But the Lord said to Ananias, "Go! This man is my chosen instrument to carry my name before the Gentiles and their kings and before the people of Israel. (Acts 9:15)**
> **Then I heard the voice of the Lord saying, "Whom shall I send? And who will go for us?" And I said, "Here am I. Send me!" (Isa 6:8)**
> **The word of the LORD came to me, saying, "Before I formed you in the womb I knew you, before you were born I set you apart; I appointed you as a prophet to the nations." (Jer 1:4-5)**
> **The fruit of the righteous is a tree of life, and he who wins souls is wise. (Prov 11:30)**
> **Those who are wise will shine like the brightness of the heavens, and those who lead many to righteousness, like the stars for ever and ever. (Dan 12:3)**

DEEPER STUDY # 1

(5:10) **James**: there were two disciples named James. (1) The James mentioned in this passage, the brother of John, was the son of Zebedee. He along with Peter and his brother John formed an inner circle around the Lord

(Mt.17:1; Mk.5:37; 9:2; 14:33). He is never mentioned apart from John. He was killed with the sword by Herod (Acts 12:2). (2) James the less was the son of Alphaeus (Mt.10:3). He was called *the less* because he was shorter of stature.

It should be noted that two other men named James are mentioned in the New Testament. (1) There is James the Lord's half-brother (Mt.13:55; Mk.6:3; Gal.1:19). He and the Lord's other brothers and sisters did not believe Jesus to be the Messiah until after Jesus' resurrection (Jn.7:5; Acts 1:14). James, however, became a great leader and pastor in the early church. He pastored the Jerusalem Church (Acts 12:17; 15:13; 21:18; Gal.1:19; 2:9, 12), and he wrote the Epistle of James. (2) There is also James who was the father of Judas (Lk.6:16; Acts 1:13, ASV).

DEEPER STUDY # 2
(5:10) **Apostle—Witnessing**: see DEEPER STUDY # 5—Mt.10:2. Cp. 2 Cor.5:19-20; Jn.20:21; Acts 1:8.

8 (5:11) **Decision—Dedication—Forsaking All**: the seventh step to calling men is *watching for the decision to forsake everything*. Note three things.

1. The men responded immediately.
2. The men left everything: their businesses, their professions, and the biggest catch they had ever seen.
3. The men followed Jesus. He was the Lord who had spoken, and they were to be His disciples who obeyed and followed.

> **Then he said to them all: "If anyone would come after me, he must deny himself and take up his cross daily and follow me. (Luke 9:23)**
>
> **"If anyone comes to me and does not hate his father and mother, his wife and children, his brothers and sisters—yes, even his own life—he cannot be my disciple. (Luke 14:26)**
>
> **In the same way, any of you who does not give up everything he has cannot be my disciple. (Luke 14:33)**
>
> **Whoever serves me must follow me; and where I am, my servant also will be. My Father will honor the one who serves me. (John 12:26)**

	D. Jesus Cleanses the Untouchable, 5:12-16 (Mt.8:1-4; Mk.1:40-45)	And immediately the leprosy left him. 14 Then Jesus ordered him, "Don't tell anyone, but go, show yourself to the priest and offer the sacrifices that Moses commanded for your cleansing, as a testimony to them."	said, "I am willing" b. The leper was cleansed **3 Jesus charged the newly cleansed man** a. To tell no man: Boast not; watch being prideful[DS2] b. To rush to obey God
1 Jesus was confronted by a desperate man, an untouchable a. He was full of leprosy[DS1] b. He saw Jesus: Fell on his face & called Jesus Lord; he begged for cleansing **2 Jesus cleansed the untouchable** a. Jesus touched him &	12 While Jesus was in one of the towns, a man came along who was covered with lep- rosy. When he saw Jesus, he fell with his face to the ground and begged him, "Lord, if you are willing, you can make me clean." 13 Jesus reached out his hand and touched the man. "I am willing," he said. "Be clean!"	15 Yet the news about him spread all the more, so that crowds of people came to hear him and to be healed of their sicknesses. 16 But Jesus often withdrew to lonely places and prayed.	**4 Jesus made an impact** a. His fame spread rapidly b. The crowds thronged to hear Him & to be healed by Him c. He withdrew into the wilderness to pray

DIVISION III

THE SON OF MAN'S ANNOUNCED MISSION AND PUBLIC MINISTRY, 4:16-9:17

D. Jesus Cleanses the Untouchable, 5:12-16

(5:12-16) **Introduction—Untouchable, The**: some persons are treated by society as though they are untouchable. Some persons are so gripped and enslaved, so depraved and destitute, so different and derelict, so down and out, so helpless and hopeless that they become untouchable to most people. But not to Jesus. And that is the whole thrust of this event. Jesus will touch the untouchable and He will cleanse the untouchable.

1. Jesus was confronted by a desperate man, an untouchable (v.12).
2. Jesus cleansed the untouchable (v.13).
3. Jesus charged the newly cleansed man (v.14).
4. Jesus made an impact (v.15-16).

1 (5:12) **Jesus Christ, Seeking—Sin, Terrible—Spiritual Cleansing**: Jesus was confronted by a desperate man, an untouchable.

1. The man was full of leprosy. The man was evidently covered with sores and extremely disfigured (see DEEPER STUDY # 1, Leprosy—Lk.5:12).
2. The man saw Jesus. He forgot all else...
   - forgot all the people surrounding Jesus.
   - forgot the shame of his condition.
   - forgot the embarrassment.
   - forgot that he was not to approach within six feet of anyone.

Nothing mattered but the *hope* he felt within, the possibility that Jesus would help him in his desperate condition. He rushed up to Jesus while people were scattering about, fearing the contagion of the disease. He fell upon his face and cried out, "Lord, if you are willing, you can make me clean." Note several things. (See outline and notes—Mt.8:1-4; Mk.1:40-45 for additional discussion.)

a. The man's determination to seek Jesus' help. Nothing and no one was going to stop him, not even the fear and threats of people whom he would be frightening with the contagiousness of his disease.
b. The man's humility. He actually prostrated himself, falling upon his face before Christ.
c. The man's confession of Christ. He called Jesus "Lord."
d. The man's request was to be cleansed, not healed. He was asking for both spiritual and physical cleansing. He knew he was dirty and defiled both within and without.

The LORD is close to the brokenhearted and saves those who are crushed in spirit. (Psa 34:18)

The sacrifices of God are a broken spirit; a broken and contrite heart, O God, you will not despise. (Psa 51:17)

Rend your heart and not your garments. Return to the LORD your God, for he is gracious and compassionate, slow to anger and abounding in love, and he relents from sending calamity. (Joel 2:13)

Yet I am poor and needy; may the Lord think of me. You are my help and my deliverer; O my God, do not delay. (Psa 40:17)

Wash away all my iniquity and cleanse me from my sin. (Psa 51:2)

Help us, O God our Savior, for the glory of your name; deliver us and forgive our sins for your name's sake. (Psa 79:9)

On hearing this, Jesus said to them, "It is not the healthy who need a doctor, but the sick. I have not come to call the righteous, but sinners." (Mark 2:17)

For we do not have a high priest who is unable to sympathize with our weaknesses, but we have one who has been tempted in every way, just as we are—yet was without sin. (Heb 4:15)

DEEPER STUDY # 1

(5:12) **Leprosy**: leprosy was the most terrible disease in the day of Jesus, and it was greatly feared. It was disfiguring and sometimes fatal. In the Bible leprosy is a type of sin.

1. The leper was considered *utterly unclean*—physically and spiritually. He could not approach within six feet of any person, including family members. "The person with such an infectious disease must wear torn clothes, let his hair be unkempt, cover the lower part of his face and cry out" (Lev.13:45).
2. He was judged as *dead—the living dead.* He had to wear a black garment so he could be recognized as from among the *dead.*
3. He was banished as an *outcast, totally ostracized* from society—considered without hope of going to heaven. "As long as he has the infection he remains unclean. He must live alone; he must live outside the camp"

(Lev.13:46). He could not live within the walls of any city; his dwelling had to be outside the city gates.

4. He was thought to be *polluted, incurable* by any human means whatsoever. Leprosy could be cured by God and His power alone. (Note how Christ proves His Messiahship and deity by healing the leper.)

Imagine the anguish and heartbreak of the leper's being completely cut off from family and friends and society. Imagine the emotional and mental pain. There are other recorded instances of lepers' being healed (cp. Mt.10:8; 11:5; Mk.1:40; Lk.7:22; 17:12; and perhaps Mt.26:6; cp. Mk.14:3).

2 (5:13) **Jesus Christ, Power—Salvation—Spiritual Cleansing**: Jesus cleansed the untouchable. Note several things.

1. Jesus was *moved with compassion*, deeply moved (Mk.1:41). The sight gripped Jesus' heart. The man's condition was wretched. Just imagine...

- his body full of sores
- his flesh eaten away
- his loneliness
- his alienation
- his emptiness
- his hopelessness
- his helplessness
- his desperation

2. Jesus reached out and touched the man, an unheard of act. The man was an untouchable, a man covered with leprosy, the most feared and dreaded and contagious disease known to the world of that day. Yet Jesus condescended, lowered Himself to touch the man. No other man would. The man had been a leper for years, so many years that he was now full of leprosy, a very advanced stage. During all those years no one could help him. He had not been touched by a human hand for so many years, he probably could not remember the softness of a tender touch.

3. Jesus said, "I am *willing*—I will make you clean."

Thought 1. Jesus wills for the untouchable to be cleansed and fully restored, restored within his own heart and restored within society. Jesus wishes to touch every man who has become untouchable.

When he saw the crowds, he had compassion on them, because they were harassed and helpless, like sheep without a shepherd. (Mat 9:36)

When Jesus landed and saw a large crowd, he had compassion on them and healed their sick. (Mat 14:14)

As a father has compassion on his children, so the LORD has compassion on those who fear him; (Psa 103:13)

In all their distress he too was distressed, and the angel of his presence saved them. In his love and mercy he redeemed them; he lifted them up and carried them all the days of old. (Isa 63:9)

4. Jesus spoke the word of cleansing, "Be clean!" Jesus saved the man spiritually, physically, and socially. The man was fully cleansed. But note how: he was cleansed by the *Word* of Jesus.

Thought 1. The Lord's Word is sufficient, able to save and heal unto the uttermost (Heb.7:25).

How God anointed Jesus of Nazareth with the Holy Spirit and power, and how he went around doing good and healing all who were under the power of the devil, because God was with him. (Acts 10:38)

Therefore he is able to save completely those who come to God through him, because he always lives to intercede for them. (Heb 7:25)

Has not my hand made all these things, and so they came into being?" declares the LORD. "This is the one I esteem: he who is humble and contrite in spirit, and trembles at my <u>word</u>. (Isa 66:2)

3 (5:14) **Warning—Believers, Duty**: Jesus charged the newly cleansed man to do two things (see note and DEEPER STUDY # 4—Mt.8:4; note—Mk.1:44 for additional discussion).

1. Jesus demanded: tell no man. The man had been saved from the depths and pit of defilement. Few ever go that deep and become so covered with leprosy (sin). He had been saved from so much, and he was now full of joy and rejoicing, bubbling over with happiness. He wanted to run all about telling the world, but there was a danger in this, the danger...

⇒ of pride and boasting within himself.

⇒ of jealousy and envy's arising within others toward him.

2. Jesus demanded: rush and obey God. The man first needed to worship and offer thanks to God and to learn to obey God's Word before doing anything else (see DEEPER STUDY # 2, <u>Leprosy</u>—Lk.5:14).

Like <u>newborn babies</u>, crave pure spiritual milk, so that by it you may grow up in your salvation, now that you have tasted that the Lord is good. (1 Pet 2:2-3)

Do your best to present yourself to God as one approved, a workman who does not need to be ashamed and who correctly handles the word of truth. (2 Tim 2:15)

Those who accepted his message were baptized, and about three thousand were added to their number that day. They devoted themselves to the apostles' teaching and to the fellowship, to the breaking of bread and to prayer. (Acts 2:41-42)

DEEPER STUDY # 2

(5:14) **Leprosy**: in the unlikely event a leper was ever cured, there was a detailed list of laws and rituals he had to go through. These rituals gave the priests time to confirm the cure and led the leper to make a thanksgiving offering to God (Lev.14:1-32; cp. 13:38-59). Jesus was charging the man to make his offering to God and to receive the certificate that he was cleansed.

4 (5:15-16) **Jesus Christ, Response—Prayer**: Jesus' impact was enormous. Great crowds thronged to hear Him and to be healed of their sicknesses.

1. Jesus had both the message of salvation and the power to heal sicknesses, but it was by Him and Him alone that both came.

2. Jesus knew the source of His message and power: God and prayer. Therefore, He often withdrew to get alone with God and to seek His face and commune with Him.

	E. Jesus Proves His Amazing Power to Forgive Sins, 5:17-26 (Mt.9:1-8; Mk.2:1-12)	21 The Pharisees and the teachers of the law began thinking to themselves, "Who is this fellow who speaks blasphemy? Who can forgive sins but God alone?"	**3 The power necessary to forgive sins: The power of God alone**
1 An investigative committee visited Jesus a. They were representatives from everywhere b. They were to investigate Jesus' claims c. Jesus' power was set to face the opposition	17 One day as he was teaching, Pharisees and teachers of the law, who had come from every village of Galilee and from Judea and Jerusalem, were sitting there. And the power of the Lord was present for him to heal the sick.	22 Jesus knew what they were thinking and asked, "Why are you thinking these things in your hearts? 23 Which is easier: to say, 'Your sins are forgiven,' or to say, 'Get up and walk'?	**4 The proof that Jesus can forgive sins, that He is the Son of Man**[DS2]
2 The approach necessary for forgiveness of sins a. Must seek help from others b. Must believe in Jesus' power. c. Must persist[DS1] d. Must seek forgiveness	18 Some men came carrying a paralytic on a mat and tried to take him into the house to lay him before Jesus. 19 When they could not find a way to do this because of the crowd, they went up on the roof and lowered him on his mat through the tiles into the middle of the crowd, right in front of Jesus. 20 When Jesus saw their faith, he said, "Friend, your sins are forgiven."	24 But that you may know that the Son of Man has authority on earth to forgive sins. . . ." He said to the paralyzed man, "I tell you, get up, take your mat and go home." 25 Immediately he stood up in front of them, took what he had been lying on and went home praising God. 26 Everyone was amazed and gave praise to God. They were filled with awe and said, "We have seen remarkable things today."	a. His Word: It works b. His claim: He is God, the Son of Man[DS3] c. His power: He saves & heals d. His impact 1) Upon the man: The man praised God 2) Upon the crowd: They were amazed & praised God & were filled with awe

DIVISION III

THE SON OF MAN'S ANNOUNCED MISSION AND PUBLIC MINISTRY, 4:16-9:17

E. Jesus Proves His Amazing Power to Forgive Sins, 5:17-26

(5:17-26) **Introduction**: this is a critical passage of Scripture. It deals with forgiveness of sins—the most important issue that ever confronts man. Can a man's sins be forgiven, truly forgiven? If so, is Jesus Christ the One who has the power to forgive sins?

1. An investigative committee visited Jesus (v.17).
2. The approach necessary for forgiveness (v.18-20).
3. The power necessary to forgive sins: the power of God alone (v.21).
4. The proof that Jesus can forgive sins, that He is the Son of Man (v.22-26).

1 (5:17) **Religionists—Criticism—Wayside—Commitment, Lack of**: an investigative committee of religionists visited Jesus. Note several facts.

1. The committee was comprised of representatives from all over the country. Every major area was represented.

2. The Pharisees and Scribes were the religious leaders of Israel (see DEEPER STUDY # 1—Lk.6:2; DEEPER STUDY # 2,3—Acts 23:8).

3. The committee had come to *sit there* (v.17), to investigate, to observe Jesus, not to participate in the services and ministry. They were "sitting by," not sitting at His feet and learning from Him.

4. Jesus' power was set to face the opposition. The power of God was upon Him, and He continued right on ministering. He did not let those who just *sat by* and were *critical* affect His preaching or ministry. He was immovable in His message and call.

Thought 1. Note three critical points.
1) There are always those who just *sit there,* who are just *spectators*, never really listening or learning, never becoming involved.
2) There are always those who are critical, who set themselves up as knowing best, who are censors and judges of what the preacher or teacher does. They listen and watch to make sure nothing is too different. If it is, they begin to criticize and judge.
3) The preacher or teacher must continue on in his call and ministry. "To his own Master he stands or falls" (Ro.14:4).

2 (5:18-20) **Forgiveness—Jesus Christ, Seeking—Faith—Persistence**: the approach necessary for forgiveness was clearly demonstrated. These men took four steps in seeking forgiveness and healing from Jesus. The same four steps are necessary for anyone to receive forgiveness of sin.

1. They *sought help*. The man had sought the help of his friends, and they were all seeking the help of Jesus. The man was unable to help himself, to secure forgiveness and wholeness by himself. He had to have help, the help of Jesus and of friends. The same was true of all the friends of the man. They were unable to provide forgiveness and wholeness to the sick man. They, too, knew that they needed the help of Jesus and of one another.

Thought 1. It is always necessary to seek Jesus' help. And it is often necessary to seek the help of friends as well.

2. They *believed* and had confidence in Jesus' power to forgive sins and to heal. They believed that, if they came, Jesus had the power to help and that He loved and cared enough to help. Therefore, they came to Jesus. And note the inconvenience and difficulty they faced in coming. The man was bedridden. They would have to pick up his bed and carry it through the streets. Also, the crowds would be huge, perhaps making it impossible to get the bed through the throng of people. What belief! What desperation! The very kind of desperation and belief necessary to secure forgiveness and healing.

3. They *persisted* despite enormous difficulty. Just as they had thought, the crowds were huge, much too large to get through to Jesus. But they did not give up. They went around to the side or back of the house and climbed up to the roof with the bed of the man. They removed some of the roof and used ropes to lower the man's bed below, right before the feet of Jesus. Of course sitting there, Jesus observed the whole scene, as surprised as everyone else that men would be so bold and persistent. But as with any of us, the spirit of their boldness and persistence and the reason for such a spirit made all the difference in the world. They were desperate; their need was great and they were helpless without Jesus' help. Such a spirit touched the Lord's heart and still touches His heart today.

4. They *sought forgiveness.* The man was definitely seeking forgiveness of sins as well as healing of body. The whole scene points to this fact. The man was paralyzed. There was the possibility that he had been injured or become diseased because of some foolish sin in the past. It was also the common belief of that day that suffering was due to sin. The man's mind was upon his sin as the *cause* of his problem; therefore, he wanted Jesus to forgive his sin as well as heal him.

Note three things.

1. Jesus saw "their faith," the faith of the friends as well as of the sick man. The faith of the friends had a large part in the man's sins being forgiven. What a lesson to us, for our families and friends!

We who are strong ought to bear with the failings of the weak and not to please ourselves. (Rom 15:1)

Carry each other's burdens, and in this way you will fulfill the law of Christ. (Gal 6:2)

Let us not become weary in doing good, for at the proper time we will reap a harvest if we do not give up. (Gal 6:9)

I was eyes to the blind and feet to the lame. I was a father to the needy; I took up the case of the stranger. (Job 29:15-16)

She opens her arms to the poor and extends her hands to the needy. (Prov 31:20)

But a Samaritan, as he traveled, came where the man was; and when he saw him, he took pity on him. He went to him and bandaged his wounds, pouring on oil and wine. Then he put the man on his own donkey, took him to an inn and took care of him. (Luke 10:33-34)

2. The faith Jesus saw was a faith that believed and persisted against all kinds of obstacles, a faith that really believed and persisted. This is crucial to remember in seeking forgiveness.

"So I say to you: Ask and it will be given to you; seek and you will find; knock and the door will be opened to you. For everyone who asks receives; he who seeks finds; and to him who knocks, the door will be opened. (Luke 11:9-10)

And without faith it is impossible to please God, because anyone who comes to him must believe that he exists and that he rewards those who <u>earnestly</u> seek him. (Heb 11:6)

But if from there you seek the LORD your God, you will find him if you look for him with all your heart and with all your soul. (Deu 4:29)

A righteous man may have many troubles, but the LORD delivers him from them all; he protects all his bones, not one of them will be broken. (Psa 34:19-20)

The LORD redeems his servants; no one will be condemned who takes refuge in him. (Psa 34:22)

Commit your way to the LORD; trust in him and he will do this: (Psa 37:5)

How great is your goodness, which you have stored up for those who fear you, which you bestow in the sight of men on those who take refuge in you. (Psa 31:19)

Trust in the LORD forever, for the LORD, the LORD, is the Rock eternal. (Isa 26:4)

You will seek me and find me when you seek me with all your heart. (Jer 29:13)

3. Jesus Himself forgave the man's sins. This is a critical fact to note. Jesus did not say, "Friend, God forgives your sins." He said, "Friend, I forgive your sins."

God exalted him to his own right hand as Prince and Savior that he might give repentance and forgiveness of sins to Israel. (Acts 5:31)

"Therefore, my brothers, I want you to know that through Jesus the forgiveness of sins is proclaimed to you. (Acts 13:38)

In him we have redemption through his blood, the forgiveness of sins, in accordance with the riches of God's grace (Eph 1:7)

DEEPER STUDY # 1

(5:19) **House**: many houses of Jesus' day had an outside stairway that climbed up to a second floor. The roof was easily reached from this stairway. The roof was flat and made of tile-like rocks matted together with a straw and clay-like substance. The roofs were sturdy enough for people to sit upon and carry on conversations and other activities (see note—Mt.24:17). These men dug and scooped out an opening through the roof. They were so sure of Jesus' power to help, nothing was going to prevent them from getting to Jesus—an unstoppable faith.

3 (5:21) **Forgiveness—Belief**: the power necessary to forgive sins was clearly stated to be found in God alone. Only God has the power to truly forgive sins. The religionists knew this; but they failed to see that Jesus Christ was One with God, the Son of God Himself—that He was One with God in being and nature, in exaltation and dominion, in love and compassion, in authority and power—all of which necessitated His coming to earth as the Incarnate God in human flesh (see notes—Jn.1:1-2; note and DEEPER STUDY # 1—1:14; note—Ph.2:7). They were seen standing before Jesus thinking and reasoning, but not speaking aloud. In their minds they were saying He was guilty of blasphemy, but at this point they did not charge Him publicly.

Thought 1. This is the very point over which so many religionists stumble: that Jesus Christ is God incarnate in human flesh, the Son of God who has come to save the world.

"For God so loved the world that he gave his one and only Son, that whoever believes in him shall not perish but have eternal life. (John 3:16)

What about the one whom the Father set apart as his very own and sent into the world? Why then do you accuse me of blasphemy because I said, 'I am God's Son'? (John 10:36)

4 (5:22-26) **Jesus Christ, Deity; Power; Impact—Forgiveness**: the proof that Jesus can forgive sins and is the Son of Man was clearly demonstrated. Jesus knew the thoughts of the religionists. He read their minds, giving evidence of His deity.

Thought 1. Jesus knows our thoughts, just what we are thinking, whether thoughts...
- of unbelief or belief
- of selfishness or unselfishness
- of worldliness or godliness
- of impurity or purity
- of deception or truth
- of wrong or right

"I know that you can do all things; no plan of yours can be thwarted. (Job 42:2)

Note how Jesus set out to prove His deity, His right and power to forgive sins.

1. His Word and the fact that it works proves His deity. He posed a test of God's power. He suggested that He merely *speak the Word*, "Get up and walk." *If His Word worked to heal the man, then His Word to forgive sins must work also*.

2. His claim proved His deity. He is God, the Son of Man (see DEEPER STUDY # 3—Mt.8:20). He was not afraid to put Himself to the test. He wanted all men to know and believe. Therefore, that "you may know that [I] the Son of Man has authority on earth to forgive sins," I purpose to prove My power in the lives of those who seek forgiveness.

Jesus heard that they had thrown him out, and when he found him, he said, "Do you believe in the Son of Man?" "Who is he, sir?" the man asked. "Tell me so that I may believe in him." Jesus said, "You have now seen him; in fact, he is the one speaking with you." (John 9:35-37)

Jesus said to her, "I am the resurrection and the life. He who believes in me will live, even though he dies; and whoever lives and believes in me will never die. Do you believe this?" "Yes, Lord," she told him, "I believe that you are the Christ, the Son of God, who was to come into the world." (John 11:25-27)

I have seen and I testify that this is the Son of God." (John 1:34)

3. His power proved His deity. Dramatically, Jesus spoke the Word, and the man arose. He was healed immediately. How? By the Word of the Lord. *God's Word* proved itself. When Jesus spoke the *Word of healing*, the man was healed; when Jesus spoke the *Word of forgiveness*, the man was forgiven.

Then Jesus came to them and said, "All authority in heaven and on earth has been given to me. (Mat 28:18)

How God anointed Jesus of Nazareth with the Holy Spirit and power, and how he went around doing good and healing all who were under the power of the devil, because God was with him. (Acts 10:38)

4. His impact proved His deity. The man praised God. The people were amazed, and they praised God and were filled with awe (fear and reverence).

Thought 1. The proofs of Jesus' deity should be studied closely by all religionists and skeptics.

Thought 2. Note four critical points.
1) Jesus is still *willing* to speak the Word of forgiveness and healing.
2) Jesus is the Son of Man and *purposes* to forgive the sins of all who are willing (see DEEPER STUDY # 3—Mt.8:20).
3) Jesus has both the power and will to speak the Word of forgiveness and healing to those who *seek* it.
4) The impact of Jesus' life upon so many is evidence of His deity. The fact that some are genuinely glorify- ing God and serving Him in awe and reverence is *strong evidence* that Jesus has the power to forgive sins.

DEEPER STUDY # 2
(5:23) **Sins—Forgiven**: the common belief of that day was that suffering was due to sin. Jesus' healing of the man was the proof that the man's sins were truly forgiven and that He had the power to forgive sins. The religionists could not logically deny this (see DEEPER STUDY # 4—Mt.26:28).

DEEPER STUDY # 3
(5:24) **Son of Man**: see DEEPER STUDY # 3—Mt.8:20.

	F. Jesus Reveals His Great Mission: The Greatest Mission of All, 5:27-39 (Mt.9:9-17; Mk.2:13-22)
1 The mission of calling outcasts[DS1] a. He went forth b. He saw c. He called	27 After this, Jesus went out and saw a tax collector by the name of Levi sitting at his tax booth. "Follow me," Jesus said to him,
d. The outcast left all & followed Jesus	28 And Levi got up, left everything and followed him.
e. The outcast reached his friends	29 Then Levi held a great banquet for Jesus at his house, and a large crowd of tax collectors and others were eating with them.
2 The mission of calling sinners to repentance a. The religionists questioned Jesus' associations	30 But the Pharisees and the teachers of the law who belonged to their sect complained to his disciples, "Why do you eat and drink with tax collectors and 'sinners'?"
b. Jesus' answer 1) He illustrated His mission	31 Jesus answered them, "It is not the healthy who need a doctor, but the sick.
2) He stated His mission	32 I have not come to call the righteous, but sinners to repentance."
3 The mission of bringing real joy a. The religionists questioned Jesus' behavior	33 They said to him, "John's disciples often fast and pray, and so do the disciples of the Pharisees, but yours go on eating and drinking."
b. Jesus' answer: His presence brings joy & vitality to life	34 Jesus answered, "Can you make the guests of the bridegroom fast while he is with them?
4 The mission of dying	35 But the time will come when the bridegroom will be taken from them; in those days they will fast."
5 The mission of launching a new life & spiritual movement a. Illustration 1: Not patching the old, but starting a new	36 He told them this parable: "No one tears a patch from a new garment and sews it on an old one. If he does, he will have torn the new garment, and the patch from the new will not match the old.
b. Illustration 2: Not put ting His teaching (wine) in old wineskins, but in a new wineskin	37 And no one pours new wine into old wineskins. If he does, the new wine will burst the skins, the wine will run out and the wineskins will be ruined. 38 No, new wine must be poured into new wineskins.
c. Illustration 3: The new is difficult to accept—it takes time	39 And no one after drinking old wine wants the new, for he says, 'The old is better.'"

DIVISION III

THE SON OF MAN'S ANNOUNCED MISSION AND PUBLIC MINISTRY, 4:16-9:17

F. Jesus Reveals His Great Mission: The Greatest Mission of All, 5:27-39

(5:27-39) **Introduction**: the greatest life ever lived on earth was the life of Jesus Christ. Therefore no mission can ever compare with the mission which He was sent to do. The great mission of Christ was…

- a quickening mission: to make people alive to God.
- an eternal mission: to give people life forever.
- a purposeful mission: to cause people to commit their lives to God unconditionally.

Luke's very purpose in this passage is to reveal the great mission of Christ. With the skillful mind of a man who knew the Lord intimately, he weaves several events together to spell out the great mission of the Lord.

1. The mission of calling outcasts (v.27-29).
2. The mission of calling sinners to repentance (v.30-32).
3. The mission of bringing real joy (v.33-34).
4. The mission of dying (v.35).
5. The mission of launching a new life and spiritual movement (v.36-39).

1 (5:27-29) **Jesus Christ, Mission—Ministers**: there was the mission of calling outcasts, those who are rejected by society. (See notes—Mt.9:9; note and DEEPER STUDY # 1—Mk.2:14 for additional discussion.)

1. Jesus "went out." There is deliberate purpose in this statement. Jesus got up and left either the house (Lk.5:19) or the city. He went out for the specific purpose of seeking the outcast (cp. Lk.19:10; Jn.20:21).

2. Jesus "saw a tax collecter by the name of Levi." He was an outcast, the most hated of men among the public (see DEEPER STUDY # 1, Tax Collector—Lk.5:27). Yet when Jesus saw him, He "saw a man named Levi [Matthew]," a sinner, a man who was hurting within, a man who needed a cause. (See note—Mt.9:9 for detailed discussion.)

3. Jesus called the outcast. Very simply, yet forcibly, Jesus said, "Follow me." Note two facts.

a. Note the great *love* and *compassion* of Jesus for the outcast. The man was despised. By associating with such an outcast, Jesus was exposing Himself to criticism and rejection by the *upper class*, the acceptable and social of society.

b. Note the great humility of Christ. He stooped down to reach an outcast; but remember, He had come to earth to save sinners, those who were outcasts from heaven.

Thought 1. Jesus' call is issued to all men, for all men are outcasts, the outcasts of heaven. However, there is a condition to becoming an acceptable person to God. A person must humble himself before Jesus, just as Jesus humbled Himself before us.

> **And he said: "I tell you the truth, unless you change and become like little children, you will never enter the kingdom of heaven. (Mat 18:3)**
>
> **Godly sorrow brings repentance that leads to salvation and leaves no regret, but worldly sorrow brings death. (2 Cor 7:10)**

And being found in appearance as a man, he humbled himself and became obedient to death— even death on a cross! (Phil 2:8; Cp. Ph2:6-9)

The LORD is close to the broken-hearted and saves those who are crushed in spirit. (Psa 34:18)

'Even now,' declares the LORD, 'return to me with all your heart, with fasting and weeping and mourning.' (Joel 2:12)

Thought 2. The person who is truly an outcast of society, who is rejected and despised by people, can be saved and delivered from emptiness and loneliness. Jesus Christ will save him. In fact, He longs to save and deliver the outcast, the empty and lonely of the earth.

"Come to me, all you who are weary and burdened, and I will give you rest. Take my yoke upon you and learn from me, for I am gentle and humble in heart, and you will find rest for your souls. For my yoke is easy and my burden is light." (Mat 11:28-30)

"Come, all you who are thirsty, come to the waters; and you who have no money, come, buy and eat! Come, buy wine and milk without money and without cost. (Isa 55:1)

"Come now, let us reason together," says the LORD. "Though your sins are like scarlet, they shall be as white as 33:11)

"Come, now; though they are red as crimson, they shall be like wool. (Isa 1:18)

Say to them, 'As surely as I live, declares the Sovereign LORD, I take no pleasure in the death of the wicked, but rather that they turn from their ways and live. Turn! Turn from your evil ways! Why will you die, O house of Israel?' (Ezek 33:11)

"Come, let us return to the LORD. He has torn us to pieces but he will heal us; he has injured us but he will bind up our wounds. (Hosea 6:1)

4. The outcast left all and followed Jesus. Matthew was very wealthy. This is the emphasis of Lukes' words, "left everything." (Note also v.29 where Matthew held a great banquet in his own house. The house itself must have been very large to hold so many people.)

This outcast "left everything," responding to Jesus immediately. How could a man such as Matthew give up so much to follow Jesus? Because money cannot buy happiness, peace, security, completeness, satisfaction, fulfillment, confidence, or assurance. Money can only buy things. Matthew had, as so many do, plenty of things: houses, land, clothes, food, furnishings. But he was *empty and restless* in heart, *incomplete and insecure* in spirit, *unfulfilled and dissatisfied* in life. When he confronted Jesus, he saw the possibility that Jesus could meet all his needs, really meet them.

Thought 1. It is hard for rich men to enter heaven, for they are attached to this material world. Matthew was one of the few who was willing to give up all in order to follow Jesus. Thus, the Kingdom of Heaven shall be his.

Then Jesus said to his disciples, "I tell you the truth, it is hard for a rich man to enter the kingdom of heaven. Again I tell you, it is easier for a camel to go through the eye of a needle than for a rich man to enter the kingdom of God." When the disciples heard this, they were greatly astonished and asked, "Who then can be saved?" Jesus looked at them and said, "With man this is impossible, but with God all things are possible." (Mat 19:23-26; cp. Mat 19:16-26)

In the same way, any of you who does not give up everything he has cannot be my disciple. (Luke 14:33)

For whoever wants to save his life will lose it, but whoever loses his life for me and for the gospel will save it. What good is it for a man to gain the whole world, yet forfeit his soul? (Mark 8:35-36)

5. The outcast reached his friends. This is a beautiful picture of the kind of witness every believer should be. Matthew's heart was filled immediately with the genuine joy for which he had ached. There was so much difference, so much love, joy, and peace; he just could not contain it. It burst forth. He had to tell his friends, but it would take so long to visit each one separately; he had to figure out a way to reach them sooner. How could he do it quicker? Having a feast came to his mind. So he held a feast for his friends to meet Jesus.

Matthew was excited about his faith. He knew the depth of emptiness from which he had come, and he was ever so appreciative and thankful. (Remember: Matthew, the outcast, was the one who wrote the gospel of Matthew.) He wanted his friends to meet Jesus personally and to come to know the salvation given by Christ.

Again Jesus said, "Peace be with you! As the Father has sent me, I am sending you." (John 20:21)

that God was reconciling the world to himself in Christ, not counting men's sins against them. And he has committed to us the message of reconciliation. We are therefore Christ's ambassadors, as though God were making his appeal through us. We implore you on Christ's behalf: Be reconciled to God. (2 Cor 5:19-20)

And the things you have heard me say in the presence of many witnesses entrust to reliable men who will also be qualified to teach others. (2 Tim 2:2)

DEEPER STUDY # 1

(5:27) **Tax Collector**: a tax collector was bitterly hated by the people. There were three reasons.

1. Tax collectors served the Roman conquerors. Most tax collectors were Jews, but in the people's eyes they had denied their Jewish heritage and betrayed their country. They were thus ostracized, completely cut off from Jewish society and excommunicated from Jewish religion and privileges.

2. They were cheats, dishonest and unjust men. Most tax collectors were extremely wealthy. The Roman government compensated tax collectors by allowing them to collect more than the percentage required for taxes. Tax collectors greedily abused their right, adding whatever per-

cent they wished and felt could be collected (see DEEPER STUDY # 1—Ro.13:6). They took bribes from the wealthy who wished to avoid taxes, fleeced the average citizen, and swindled the government when they could.

3. They were assuming rights that belonged only to God. God alone was King in the eyes of the Jews. This was a strong conviction of the Jews; therefore, God and the ruler appointed by God were considered to be the head of Jewish government. God was their God, and they were His people. Taxes were to be paid only to Him and His government, which was centered only in the temple of Judaism. To pay taxes to earthly rulers was an abuse and a denial of God's rights. Therefore, tax collectors were excommunicated from Jewish religion and privileges. They were accursed, anathema.

2 (5:30-32) **Jesus Christ, Mission**: there was the mission of calling sinners to repentance. Note two things.

1. The religionists questioned Jesus' association with the outcasts and sinners. They criticized and judged Him.

a. He was associating with those who were not socially acceptable. Sinners and outcasts had rejected society. They had forsaken the ways of acceptability. Why would Jesus associate with such outcasts and sinners who

b. He was associating with those who were religiously and ceremonially unclean. Many, if not all, had not sought religious and ceremonial cleansing. They were guilty of breaking every law of religion and decency.

2. Jesus answered their question by illustrating and stating His mission.

a. The sick (sinners) are the ones who need a physician (Him, the Savior). Note: a man may be sick…
   - and not know it; therefore his sickness is never cured.
   - and not call the physician; therefore, his sickness is never cured.

b. The mission of Jesus was not to call the righteous but sinners to repentance.

Thought 1. The righteous either do not know or do not accept the fact that they need repentance. Sinners do know, but they may not accept the depth of their need nor turn from their sin in order to be saved by Jesus.

For the Son of Man came to seek and to save what was lost." (Luke 19:10)

For God did not send his Son into the world to condemn the world, but to save the world through him. (John 3:17)

The thief comes only to steal and kill and destroy; I have come that they may have life, and have it to the full. (John 10:10)

"As for the person who hears my words but does not keep them, I do not judge him. For I did not come to judge the world, but to save it. (John 12:47)

Here is a trustworthy saying that deserves full acceptance: Christ Jesus came into the world to save sinners—of whom I am the worst. (1 Tim 1:15)

Here I am! I stand at the door and knock. If anyone hears my voice and opens the door, I will come in and eat with him, and he with me. (Rev 3:20)

3 (5:33-34) **Jesus Christ, Mission—Believer, Joy; Life—Fasting**: there was the mission of bringing real joy. The religionists questioned Jesus' loose behavior and the fact that He was teaching His disciples the same loose behavior. What is meant by *loose behavior*? Jesus' disciples were eating and drinking, actually feasting when they should have been fasting. By law religious Jews fasted twice a week, every Monday and Thursday (Lk.18:12). Jesus was not only religious, He was a religious teacher, and even more, He was claiming to be the Messiah Himself. Why was He not fasting? (See note—Mk.2:18-22 for detailed discussion.) Note something important. The religionists fasted as a ritual; their days for fasting were already determined. The ritual or the custom and tradition determined their fast. Their need for God, for a very special sense of God's presence had nothing to do with fasting. Fasting was purely a matter of ritual and custom.

Jesus' answer was revealing and of utmost importance. He claimed that He was the *Bridegroom*, and as long as He was with them, there was no need for them to fast. Now note what Jesus was saying. (See note—Mt.9:15; Mk.2:19.)

1. His presence brought joy and vitality to life, not ritual and ceremonial demands.

2. There was no need to be fasting for a special sense of God's presence, if the Bridegroom, the Son of God, was already present.

3. His mission was that of a Bridegroom, to bring joy and vitality to life.

I have told you this so that my joy may be in you and that your joy may be complete. (John 15:11)

Until now you have not asked for anything in my name. Ask and you will receive, and your joy will be complete. (John 16:24)

For the kingdom of God is not a matter of eating and drinking, but of righteousness, peace and joy in the Holy Spirit, (Rom 14:17)

Sorrowful, yet always rejoicing; poor, yet making many rich; having nothing, and yet possessing everything. (2 Cor 6:10)

Rejoice in the Lord always. I will say it again: Rejoice! (Phil 4:4)

Though you have not seen him, you love him; and even though you do not see him now, you believe in him and are filled with an inexpressible and glorious joy, (1 Pet 1:8)

You have made known to me the path of life; you will fill me with joy in your presence, with eternal pleasures at your right hand. (Psa 16:11)

They rejoice in your name all day long; they exult in your righteousness. (Psa 89:16)

With joy you will draw water from the wells of salvation. (Isa 12:3)

I delight greatly in the LORD; my soul rejoices in my God. For he has clothed me with garments of salvation and arrayed me in a robe of righteousness, as a bridegroom adorns his head like a priest, and as a bride adorns herself with her jewels. (Isa 61:10)

4 (5:35) **Jesus Christ, Mission; Death**: there was the mission of dying. Note two points.

Jesus said, "the Bridegroom will be taken from them." He meant that He was appointed to die. Dying upon the cross was His primary mission for coming to earth. Note three significant points.

1. His death enables His Spirit to be present with all believers around the world (Jn.14:16-18, 26; 15:26; 16:7, 13).

2. His death brings sorrow to the heart of any who see it and understand it. However, His death brings joy soon after, for there is the knowledge that Jesus lives forever (Jn.16:16-22; Heb.7:25; cp. Eph.1:19-23).

3. His death and its cleansing power can be *forgotten* (2 Pt.1:9). The Lord's presence can fade from our consciousness. We can become so busy and preoccupied with the affairs of the world that we lose our sensitivity to the Lord's presence. At such times we need to get alone with God. Our concern for God's presence should be so great that neither food nor sleep matter. Nothing matters except regaining the consciousness of God's presence. We need to fast and pray, and pray and fast.

Thought 1. His death caused the first disciples to fast; it ought to cause us to fast...

- when we first learn of His death and what it really means.

He told them, "This is what is written: The Christ will suffer and rise from the dead on the third day, (Luke 24:46)

"For God so loved the world that he gave his one and only Son, that whoever believes in him shall not perish but have eternal life. (John 3:16)

But God demonstrates his own love for us in this: While we were still sinners, Christ died for us. (Rom 5:8)

He himself bore our sins in his body on the tree, so that we might die to sins and live for righteousness; by his wounds you have been healed. (1 Pet 2:24)

For Christ died for sins once for all, the righteous for the unrighteous, to bring you to God. He was put to death in the body but made alive by the Spirit, (1 Pet 3:18)

- when we are reminded rather forcibly that He died for us. Such times should be heart-rending times, precious times of prayer and fasting.
- when we allow His presence to slip out of our mind for some length of time. We need to get alone and meditate upon His death, allowing nothing to interfere, including food.

"Watch and pray so that you will not fall into temptation. The spirit is willing, but the body is weak." (Mat 26:41)

Look to the LORD and his strength; seek his face always. (1 Chr 16:11)

Then Jesus told his disciples a parable to show them that they should always pray and not give up. (Luke 18:1)

He will call upon me, and I will answer him; I will be with him in trouble, I will deliver him and honor him. (Psa 91:15)

In the same way, the Spirit helps us in our weakness. We do not know what we ought to pray for, but the Spirit himself intercedes for us with groans that words cannot express. And he who searches our hearts knows the mind of the Spirit, because the Spirit intercedes for the saints in accordance with God's will. (Rom 8:26-27)

I was ashamed to ask the king for soldiers and horsemen to protect us from enemies on the road, because we had told the king, "The gracious hand of our God is on everyone who looks to him, but his great anger is against all who forsake him." So we fasted and petitioned our God about this, and he answered our prayer. (Ezra 8:22-23)

If my people, who are called by my name, will humble themselves and pray and seek my face and turn from their wicked ways, then will I hear from heaven and will forgive their sin and will heal their land. (2 Chr 7:14)

5 (5:36-39) **Jesus Christ, Mission**: there was the mission of a new life and a new spiritual movement. Jesus gave three points to illustrate what He meant.

Illustration 1: a patch of new cloth is not used to patch an old garment, for it fails to match the old garment. Jesus was saying that He was not patching up the old life, but starting a new life and a new movement (cp. v.36. See notes—Mt.9:16; Mk.2:21 for discussion.)

Illustration 2: the new wine is not put into old wineskins, for the new wine would burst the old wineskins. Jesus was saying that He was not putting His teaching into the old life and movement, but He was launching a new life and movement for God (cp. v.37. See notes—Mk.2:22.)

Illustration 3: the new wine is difficult to accept if one has been drinking old wine. Jesus was saying that His new life and spiritual movement would be difficult to accept; it would take time. Men were slow to give up the old, for they were too content with it (their religious ways and self-righteousness). Therefore, men would often refuse to even consider the new life and movement.

Therefore, if anyone is in Christ, he is a new creation; the old has gone, the new has come! (2 Cor 5:17)

You were taught, with regard to your former way of life, to put off your old self, which is being corrupted by its deceitful desires; to be made new in the attitude of your minds; (Eph 4:22-23)

And have put on the new self, which is being renewed in knowledge in the image of its Creator. (Col 3:10)

He saved us, not because of righteous things we had done, but because of his mercy. He saved us through the washing of rebirth and renewal by the Holy Spirit, (Titus 3:5)

For you have been born again, not of perishable seed, but of imperishable, through the living and enduring word of God. (1 Pet 1:23)

Everyone who believes that Jesus is the Christ is born of God, and everyone who loves the father loves his child as well. (1 John 5:1)

In reply Jesus declared, "I tell you the truth, no one can see the kingdom of God unless he is born again." (John 3:3)

1 **The Sabbath**
2 **Fact 1: Meeting man's real needs is more important than religion & ritual**
a. The need: The disciples were hungry, so they picked grain
b. The opposition: The religionists became upset because a religious rule was broken[DS1]
c. The answer of Jesus: An illustration
1) David hungered
2) David overrode the religious rules to meet a need[DS2]
d. The point: The Son of Man[DS3] is as great as David—He is the Lord of the Sabbath

CHAPTER 6

G. Jesus Teaches that Need Supersedes Religion, 6:1-11
(Mt.12:1-13; Mk.2:23-28; 3:1-6)

One Sabbath Jesus was go-
ing through the grainfields,
and his disciples began to
pick some heads of grain, rub
them in their hands and eat
the kernels.
2 Some of the Pharisees
asked, "Why are you doing
what is unlawful on the Sabbath?"
3 Jesus answered them,
"Have you never read what
David did when he and his
companions were hungry?
4 He entered the house of
God, and taking the consecrated bread, he ate what is
lawful only for priests to eat.
And he also gave some to his
companions."
5 Then Jesus said to them,
"The Son of Man is Lord of
the Sabbath."
6 On another Sabbath he
went into the synagogue and
was teaching, and a man was
there whose right hand was
shriveled.
7 The Pharisees and the
teachers of the law were
looking for a reason to accuse
Jesus, so they watched him
closely to see if he would
heal on the Sabbath.
8 But Jesus knew what they
were thinking and said to the
man with the shriveled hand,
"Get up and stand in front of
everyone." So he got up and
stood there.
9 Then Jesus said to them, "I
ask you, which is lawful on
the Sabbath: to do good or to
do evil, to save life or to destroy it?"
10 He looked around at them
all, and then said to the man,
"Stretch out your hand." He
did so, and his hand was
completely restored.
11 But they were furious and
began to discuss with one
another what they might do to
Jesus.

3 **Fact 2: Doing good & saving life are more important than religion & ritual**
a. The need: A man's right hand shriveled
b. The opposition by the religionists[DS4]
c. The question & challenge of Jesus
1) He perceived their thoughts
2) He challenged them to think honestly
3) He healed the man—doing good
d. The point: To do good and to save life supersedes rituals
e. The religionists' insane anger

DIVISION III

THE SON OF MAN'S ANNOUNCED MISSION AND PUBLIC MINISTRY, 4:16-9:17

G. Jesus Teaches That Need Supersedes Religion, 6:1-11

(6:1-11) **Introduction**: men have the tendency to institutionalize religion, to make it full of form and ritual, rules and regulations, ceremonies and services. Men, religionists and laymen alike, are too often guilty of "having a *form* of godliness but denying its power" (2 Tim.3:5). This is the very point Jesus is making in this passage. The power of godliness exists to meet the needs of man. Yet too often, religion is placed before man and his needs. Maintaining the religious organization and form, keeping things the way they have always been, is considered more important than meeting the needs of man.

1. The Sabbath (v.1).
2. Fact 1: meeting man's real needs is more important than religion and ritual (v.1-5).
3. Fact 2: doing good and saving life are more important than religion and ritual (v.6-11).

1 (6:1) **Sabbath**: note that both of these events took place on the Sabbath (v.1, 6). This is the very thrust of Luke: to show that religion and ritual must never be put before the needs of man. (See DEEPER STUDY # 1, Sabbath—Mt.12:1 for discussion.)

2 (6:1-5) **Necessities—Religion—Rituals—Jesus Christ, Deity**: first, *real needs* are more important than religion and rituals. The disciples had a real need: they were extremely hungry. They had not eaten since the day before (Mt.12:1; Mk.2:23). As they were passing by a grain field, they began to pick and eat some grain. They were not stealing the grain, for a hungry traveller was permitted by law to eat a few heads of grain when passing by a field (Dt.23:25). The crime was that the disciples *worked* by picking the heads of grain *on the Sabbath day*.

This was a serious offense to the orthodox Jew. Just how serious can be seen in the strict demands governing the Sabbath. Law after law was written to govern all activity on the Sabbath, laws which prohibited a person from contemplating any kind of work or activity. A good example of the legal restriction and the people's loyalty to it is seen in the women who witnessed Jesus' crucifixion. They would not even walk to His tomb to prepare the body for burial until the Sabbath was over (Mk.16:1f; Mt.28:1f).

It was a serious matter to break the Sabbath law. A person was condemned, and if the offence were serious enough, the person was to die.

This may seem harsh to some, but when dealing with the Jewish nation, one must remember that it was their religion that held them together as a nation through centuries and centuries of exile. Their religion (in particular their beliefs about God's call to their nation), the temple, and the Sabbath became the *binding force* that kept Jews together and maintained their distinctiveness as a people. It protected them from alien beliefs and from being swallowed up by other people through intermarriage. No matter where they were, they met and associated together and held on to their beliefs. A picture of this can be seen in the experience of Nehemiah when he led some Jews back to Jerusalem (Neh.13:15-22; cp. Jer.17:19-27; Ezk.46:1-7).

All the above explains to some degree why the religionists opposed Jesus with such hostility. Their problem was that they had allowed religion and ritual, ceremony and liturgy, position and security, recognition and livelihood to become more important than the basic essentials of human life: personal need and compassion, and the true worship and mercy of God. (See note and DEEPER STUDY # 1—Mt.12:10. This is an important note for this point.)

Note several things.

1. Jesus used David's experience to illustrate His point. David had eaten the bread of the Presence (Consecrated Bread) or the showbread in the tabernacle when he was hungry (see DEEPER STUDY # 2—Lk.6:4; Mk.2:25-27).

2. Jesus declared that "[He] the Son of Man is Lord of the Sabbath." This was His very point. He was as great as David, in fact, greater; for He was the Son of Man. Therefore He was the Lord over the Sabbath (see notes and thoughts—Mt.12:1-8; Mk.2:23-28 for detailed discussion).

> **"Therefore let all Israel be assured of this: God has made this Jesus, whom you crucified, both Lord and Christ." (Acts 2:36)**
>
> **God exalted him to his own right hand as Prince and Savior that he might give repentance and forgiveness of sins to Israel. (Acts 5:31)**
>
> **God, who has called you into fellowship with his Son Jesus Christ our Lord, is faithful. (1 Cor 1:9)**
>
> **Yet for us there is but one God, the Father, from whom all things came and for whom we live; and there is but one Lord, Jesus Christ, through whom all things came and through whom we live. (1 Cor 8:6)**
>
> **Then Jesus came to them and said, "All authority in heaven and on earth has been given to me. (Mat 28:18)**
>
> **And God placed all things under his feet and appointed him to be head over everything for the church, (Eph 1:22)**
>
> **[Jesus Christ] who has gone into heaven and is at God's right hand—with angels, authorities and powers in submission to him. (1 Pet 3:22)**

Thought 1. Christ shows that human needs are far more important than religious rituals and rules. However, two things must always be kept in mind.

1) The need must be a *real need* before religious rituals and rules are to be superseded. We are not to abuse, neglect, or ignore religious worship and ceremonies. Sometimes, however, a real need does arise that has to be taken care of immediately.
2) Jesus Christ is the Lord of the Sabbath (Sunday); therefore, He should be the One who says when a need should supersede a religious ceremony. We must be living closely enough to Him in fellowship and worship, sacrifice and ministry to sense what should be done.

> **Just as the Son of Man did not come to be served, but to serve, and to give his life as a ransom for many." (Mat 20:28)**
>
> **Again Jesus said, "Peace be with you! As the Father has sent me, I am sending you." (John 20:21)**
>
> **In everything I did, I showed you that by this kind of hard work we must help the weak, remembering the words the Lord Jesus himself said: 'It is more blessed to give than to receive.'" (Acts 20:35)**
>
> **We who are strong ought to bear with the failings of the weak and not to please ourselves. (Rom 15:1)**
>
> **Carry each other's burdens, and in this way you will fulfill the law of Christ. (Gal 6:2)**

DEEPER STUDY # 1

(6:2) **Teachers of the Law—Scribes—Scribal Law—Pharisees**: these Pharisees were probably Scribes, the teachers of the law. The Scribes were a profession of men sometimes called lawyers (see DEEPER STUDY # 1—Mt.22:35). They were some of the most devoted and committed men to religion in all of history and were of the sect known as the Pharisees. However, every Pharisee was not a Scribe. A Scribe was more of a scholar, more highly trained than the average Pharisee (see DEEPER STUDY # 3, Pharisees—Acts 23:8). They had two primary functions.

1. The Scribes copied the written law, the Old Testament Scriptures. In their copying function, they were strict copiers, meticulously keeping count of every letter in every word. This exactness was necessary, for God Himself had given the written law to the Jewish nation. Therefore, the law was not only the very Word of God, it was the greatest thing in the life of the Jewish nation. It was considered the most precious possession in all the world; consequently, the Jewish nation was committed to the preservation of the law (Neh.8:1-8). A young Jew could enter no greater profession than the profession of Scribes.

2. The Scribes studied, classified, and taught the moral law. This function brought about the Oral or Scribal Law that was so common in Jesus' day. It was the law of rules and regulations. There were, in fact, so many regulations that over fifty large volumes were required when they were finally put into writing. The great tragedy was that through the centuries, the Jews began to place the Oral law over the written law (see note—Mt.12:1-8; note and DEEPER STUDY # 1—12:10; note—15:1-20).

The Scribes felt that the law was God's final word. Everything God wanted man to do could be deduced from it; therefore, they drew out of the law every possible rule they could and insisted that life was to be lived in conformity to these rules. Rules were to be a way of life, the preoccupation of a man's thoughts. At first these rules and regulations were taught by word of mouth; however, in the third century after Christ, they were put into certain writings.

The Halachoth: rules that were to govern the ritual of worship.

The Talmud: made up of two parts.

⇒ The Mishnah: sixty-three discussions of various subjects of the law.

⇒ Germara: the sacred legends of the people.

Midrashim: the commentaries on the writings.

Hagada: thoughts on the commentaries.

DEEPER STUDY # 2

(6:4) **Consecrated Bread—The Bread of the Presence—Showbread**: the word means *the bread of the face* or *the bread of the Presence*. It symbolized the *Presence of God* who is the Bread of Life. The consecrated bread was twelve loaves of bread that were brought to the house of God as a symbolic offering to God. It was a thanksgiving offering expressing appreciation and praise to God for food. The loaves were to be taken to the Holy Place by the

Priest and placed on the table before the Lord. The loaves symbolized an everlasting covenant between God and His people: He would always see to it that His people had whatever food was necessary to sustain them (see outline—Mt.6:25-34). The loaves were to be changed every week. The old loaves became food for the priests and were to be eaten by them alone.

DEEPER STUDY # 3
(6:5) **Son of Man**: see DEEPER STUDY # 3—Mt.8:20.

3 (6:6-11) **Life, Saving—Needs—Jesus Christ, Deity; Power—Rituals**: second, doing good and saving life are more important than religious rituals.

1. The need was a man whose right hand was shriveled. The only thing we know about the man with the shriveled hand is just that: he had a shriveled hand. The gospels say nothing else about him. However, there is a dramatic background given by one of the books which was never accepted into the New Testament: *The Gospel According to the Hebrews*. This gospel says that the man was a carpenter who made his living with his hands. It adds that the man pleaded with Jesus to heal him that he might not have to beg for food in shame.

2. The religionists "watched" (pareterounto) Jesus. The meaning is that they watched closely just as an animal does its prey. Note their purpose was to accuse Him. (See note and DEEPER STUDY # 1—Mt.12:10. This is an important note for understanding why the religionists conflicted so much with Jesus.)

3. Jesus knew their thoughts, so He challenged them to think and contemplate the matter and to be honest in their conclusion. "Which is lawful on the Sabbath: to do good, or to do evil? to save life or to destroy it?" Note several facts.

   a. He knew their thoughts. This was evidence of His deity.
   b. Jesus was claiming to be the *Lord of good and the Lord of salvation*, the One who does good and the One who saves life.
   c. Jesus' love reached out even to those who opposed Him so violently, at least for a while, as long as there was some hope to reach them. He appealed to them to be open and honest, to think and reason, and to be willing to confess the truth. What He was doing was good and did save life. He was the Lord of good and the Lord of salvation.

4. Jesus' point was clear: to do good and to save life always supersedes religion and rituals. Picture the scene. Jesus stood there looking around upon the religionists; there was stone silence while He scanned His audience. He was awaiting their answer to His question (v.9). He longed for them to answer honestly, to confess Him as the Lord of good and the Lord of salvation, but there was only stone silence. All of a sudden with a thunderous voice He commanded: "Stretch out your hand. He [the man] did so, and his hand was completely restored."

Thought 1. The man's life had to be saved; his hand had to be restored. The man might never stand before the Lord again. Now was the day of salvation, not tomorrow.

> **For he says, "In the time of my favor I heard you, and in the day of salvation I helped you." I tell you, now is the time of God's favor, now is the day of salvation. (2 Cor 6:2)**

Thought 2. Doing good and saving life never abuses the Sabbath or Sunday. In fact, there is no better day to help and minister than on the Lord's day.

Thought 3. If we do not help people—no matter the day, even on the Sabbath—then we are *withholding good and doing evil to our neighbor*.

> **"Teacher, which is the greatest commandment in the Law?" Jesus replied: "'Love the Lord your God with all your heart and with all your soul and with all your mind.' This is the first and greatest commandment. And the second is like it: 'Love your neighbor as yourself.' (Mat 22:36-39)**
>
> **Love does no harm to its neighbor. Therefore love is the fulfillment of the law. (Rom 13:10)**
>
> **This is how we know what love is: Jesus Christ laid down his life for us. And we ought to lay down our lives for our brothers. If anyone has material possessions and sees his brother in need but has no pity on him, how can the love of God be in him? Dear children, let us not love with words or tongue but with actions and in truth. This then is how we know that we belong to the truth, and how we set our hearts at rest in his presence (1 John 3:16-19)**
>
> **He has showed you, O man, what is good. And what does the LORD require of you? To act justly and to love mercy and to walk humbly with your God. (Micah 6:8)**

5. The religionists became insanely mad. They were furious (eplesthesan anoias) which means insane rage. According to Mark, they immediately stormed out of the synagogue and joined forces with the Herodians in plotting how to kill Jesus (see notes and thoughts—Mk.3:6).

DEEPER STUDY # 4
(6:7) **Israel, History—Law—Legalism—Scribes—Pharisees**: in understanding the Scribes and Pharisees it is helpful to understand that the Jews were above all else *a people of God's Law*. Their nation was based on the Ten Commandments and the first five books of the Old Testament, known as the Law or Pentateuch (Genesis, Exodus, Leviticus, Numbers, Deuteronomy). This fact alone, that the nation was based upon God's Law, makes Israel unique among surviving nations of the world.

There are several significant stages in Israel's history that show just how dominating a force the Law was in the nation's survival.

1. The Jews were a people created by God in one man, Abraham (Gen.12:1-3). Abraham believed he was called by God to be the father of a great nation, and he passed the belief down to his son, Isaac.

2. The Jewish population grew enormously during the four-hundred years of slavery in Egypt, originating from the twelve sons of Jacob. They had been led to Egypt by Joseph to save the family during a life-threatening famine. Again, the significant fact was that the fathers passed on to their children the faith of Abraham: that they were the people of God, chosen to become the greatest of all nations.

3. The nation itself was officially formed at Mt. Sinai when God gave the Law to Moses. The nation was appointed for a spiritual purpose: to be the guardian of God's law. This event was extremely significant, for Israel was being appointed as the messenger of God to the rest of the world, as the people who were to bear testimony to the only living and true God and to His Law. They were to be God's missionary force to the world.

4. The Jewish people had been conquered and scattered all over the world time after time. In Old Testament history they had been conquered and scattered by the Assyrians, Babylonians, and Persians; yet they had survived attempt after attempt to annihilate them as a people. The one thing that bound the people together, enabling them to survive was the Law of God and their belief and practice of it (see notes and DEEPER STUDY # 1—Mt.12:10; 12:1-8).

5. A small remnant of the Jewish people had been allowed to return to rebuild the capital, Jerusalem, and to start over again under the leadership of Nehemiah and Ezra.

It was at this point in Israel's history that the birth of the Scribes took place (about B.C. 450). In a most dramatic moment in the nation's history, Ezra the Scribe took the Law (Genesis-Deuteronomy) and read it aloud to the handful of people who had returned. He then led the people to rededicate themselves to being the people of God's Law (Neh.8:1-8). The rededication was strong and meaningful. It had to be, for the nation had almost been wiped out, and there were but a few who had returned to begin the nation anew.

Therefore, the law became the greatest thing in the people's lives; and the most honored profession became the Scribe who was made responsible to study, teach, and preserve the law (see DEEPER STUDY # 1—Lk.6:2). Through the years the Scribes took the law of God and attempted to define every key phrase and word of the law. By so doing, they ended up with thousands and thousands of rules and regulations to govern the lives of the people. The people would thereby become distinct from all other people and be protected from intermarriage and from being swallowed up by the cultures of other nations. These rules and regulations were called the Scribal Law. Interestingly, when the Scribal Law was finally completed, it compiled more than fifty volumes.

The Pharisees were born as a group several hundred years later (about B.C. 175). Antiochus Epiphanes of Syria marched against Jerusalem and captured the nation and made a deliberate attempt to destroy the Jewish people. To prevent the annihilation of their life and nation as a people, a group of men dedicated themselves at all cost to keep every detail of the law (Scribal Law). The practice of the Scribal Law by these men soon became a profession, for working to keep thousands and thousands of laws just left no time for anything else. Very simply stated, the practice of the Scribal Law required more time than a man had; therefore, the profession of Pharisees was born—born to practice and preserve the law. A Pharisee genuinely believed that by obeying the law and imposing it upon the people, he was saving his people and their nation. It was the law that made the Jewish people, their religion, and their nation different from all other people. Therefore, the Pharisee had a consuming devotion to see that the law was taught and practiced among the people.

These two things, *extreme legalism and extreme devotion*, were the two major traits of the Pharisees. But the same two traits lying within a self-centered heart can lead to terrible abuse.

1. A man can become a stern legalist, laying burden after burden upon men. Such legalism knows little of the mercy and forgiveness of God.

2. A man can become monastic, separate from the people.

3. A man can become *super-religious*, or *super-spiritual*, with a *holier than thou* attitude and aire.

4. A man can become prideful because he belongs to a certain profession and holds a particular place or position or title or because he is more disciplined in keeping the rules. Thus, he feels more elevated than others, more honored, more religious, and more acceptable to God.

5. A man can become hypocritical. There is just no way to keep thousands and thousands of rules and regulations. Human nature militates against and prevents perfect obedience.

6. A man can become showy and ostentatious. Strict discipline and personal achievement put a desire within a person to show his achievements and to seek recognition.

7. A man can become hypocritical, publicly acting and preaching one thing, but privately practicing another.

Outline	Scripture	Scripture	Outline
	H. Jesus Chooses His Men: Who Is Chosen & Why, 6:12-19 (Mk.3:13-19)	16 Judas son of James, and Judas Iscariot, who became a traitor.	
1 He chose them after prayerful consideration—after praying all night	12 One of those days Jesus went out to a mountainside to pray, and spent the night praying to God.	17 He went down with them and stood on a level place. A large crowd of his disciples was there and a great number of people from all over Judea, from Jerusalem, and from the coast of Tyre and Sidon,	**5 He chose them to minister with Him** a. They ministered to two distinct groups 1) To followers 2) To the crowds b. They had a threefold ministry
2 He chose them from among His disciples **3 He chose them to be apostles**	13 When morning came, he called his disciples to him and chose twelve of them, whom he also designated apostles:	18 Who had come to hear him and to be healed of their diseases. Those troubled by evil spirits were cured,	1) To preach 2) To heal
4 He chose diverse personalities	14 Simon (whom he named Peter), his brother Andrew, James, John, Philip, Bartholomew, 15 Matthew, Thomas, James son of Alphaeus, Simon who was called the Zealot,	19 And the people all tried to touch him, because power was coming from him and healing them all.	3) To lead people to touch Jesus

DIVISION III

THE SON OF MAN'S ANNOUNCED MISSION AND PUBLIC MINISTRY, 4:16-9:17

H. Jesus Chooses His Men: Who Is Chosen and Why, 6:12-19

(6:12-19) **Introduction**: Jesus needs people. He needs men, women, boys, and girls who will carry His message of salvation to the world. This passage is a picture of how Jesus goes about choosing people to serve Him.

1. He chose them after prayerful consideration—after praying all night (v.12).
2. He chose them from among His disciples (v.13).
3. He chose them to be apostles (v.13).
4. He chose diverse personalities (v.14-16).
5. He chose them to minister with Him (v.17-19).

1 (6:12) **Prayer—Call**: Jesus chose His men after prayerful consideration. He had continued all night in prayer, discussing and sharing with God. It was a momentous decision. Think about it. The destiny of the world and the fate of mankind was to rest upon the shoulders of these men. They were to carry the message of salvation to the world. If they failed, the world would be lost and man would be eternally doomed. Jesus needed to know exactly who to choose. He needed to talk the matter over with His Father. He needed to be spiritually renewed; He needed His spirit and mind quick and sharp and full of God's presence as He made the *critical choices*. So He prayed, but He not *only* prayed, He wrestled with God *all night* in prayer. Note that He got all *alone* on top of a mountain where He would not be disturbed.

> **Thought 1.** In all honesty, how many minutes do we spend in prayer a day? Some say they pray all day as they go about their affairs. Praying as we walk throughout the day is good and commendable. We should "pray continually" (1 Th.5:17). Christ did. But praying throughout the day by flickering our minds over to God for a moment here and there is not *concentrated prayer*, not the kind of prayer that really moves and causes things to happen. Thinking and talking to God here and there is *fellowship prayer*. Fellowship prayer is easy. It is very common to share with God as we walk through the day. But what is needed and what the Bible means primarily by prayer is *concentrated prayer*, a time set aside when we get all alone with God and share specific matters with Him. Christ sets a dynamic example of *concentrated prayer* in this passage. (See notes—Mt.6:9-13.)
>
> **Very early in the morning, while it was still dark, Jesus got up, left the house and went off to a solitary place, where he prayed. (Mark 1:35)**
> **After leaving them, he went up on a mountainside to pray. (Mark 6:46)**
> **But Jesus often withdrew to lonely places and prayed. (Luke 5:16)**
> **Once when Jesus was praying in private and his disciples were with him, he asked them, "Who do the crowds say I am?" (Luke 9:18)**
> **He withdrew about a stone's throw beyond them, knelt down and prayed, (Luke 22:41)**

2 (6:13) **Disciple—Call**: Jesus chose His men from among His disciples. There were a large number of people following Jesus as disciples. A disciple was a learner. But a disciple in that day was much more than what we mean by a student who just studies a subject taught by a teacher. A disciple was a person who *attached* himself to his teacher and who followed his teacher wherever he went, studying and learning all he could from the teacher's life as well as from his word. (See note—Mt.28:19-20 for detailed discussion and application.)

Note that Jesus called His disciples to Him; He called all those who had attached themselves to Him. (It would be interesting to know who all these were.) Out of these disciples Jesus chose twelve to serve as His apostles and to join Him in His great mission and ministry. They were to serve with Him in a very, very special way (cp. v.17-19. See outline—Lk.5:27-39.)

And the things you have heard me say in the presence of many witnesses entrust to reliable men who will also be qualified to teach others. (2 Tim 2:2)

3 (6:13) **Apostle—Ministry—Believers—Ambassador**: Jesus chose His men to be apostles (see DEEPER STUDY # 5, Apostle—Mt.10:2). Note three things.

1. The word "apostle" (apostolos) means to send out. An apostle is a man chosen directly by the Lord Himself or by the Holy Spirit (cp. Mt.10:1-2; Mk.3:13-14; Lk.6:13; Acts 9:6, 15; 13:2; 22:10, 14-15; Ro.1:1). He was a man who had either seen or been a companion of the Lord Jesus.

2. Jesus called Himself an apostle (apesteilos, Jn.17:3), and He is called the *Apostle* and High Priest of our profession (Heb.3:1).

3. Others were also called apostles (Acts 14:4, 14, 17; 1 Th.2:6; 2 Cor.8:23; Ph.2:25; Gal.1:19; Ro.16:7). However, there is a distinct difference between all these and the twelve whom Christ chose. The first twelve were...

- chosen by the Lord Himself while on earth.
- chosen to *be with Him* during His earthly ministry (Mk.3:14).
- chosen to be trained by Him alone, personally.
- chosen to be the eyewitnesses of His resurrection (Acts 1:22).
- chosen to be the ones who were to carry forth His message which had come from His very own mouth.

There is a sense in which the gift of apostleship is still given and used in the ministry today (see DEEPER STUDY # 5, Apostle—Mt.10:2).

Thought 1. The believer is the ambassador for Christ, one who goes forth representing Christ Himself both by life and word. The believer is to *reflect* the very life of Christ.

That God was reconciling the world to himself in Christ, not counting men's sins against them. And he has committed to us the message of reconciliation. We are therefore Christ's ambassadors, as though God were making his appeal through us. We implore you on Christ's behalf: Be reconciled to God. (2 Cor 5:19-20)

Thought 2. The Lord does pick *a few* from among His followers (disciples) to serve Him in very special ways. Every church has to have its leaders; and every area, state, country, and generation has to have its leaders. God must have those who will go beyond in sacrificing and giving, serving and ministering in every place and generation.

There came a man who was sent from God; his name was John. (John 1:6)

Then I will give you shepherds after my own heart, who will lead you with knowledge and understanding. (Jer 3:15)

I will place shepherds over them who will tend them, and they will no longer be afraid or terrified, nor will any be missing," declares the LORD. (Jer 23:4)

The third time he said to him, "Simon son of John, do you love me?" Peter was hurt because Jesus asked him the third time, "Do you love me?" He said, "Lord, you know all things; you know that I love you." Jesus said, "Feed my sheep. (John 21:17)

Keep watch over yourselves and all the flock of which the Holy Spirit has made you overseers. Be shepherds of the church of God, which he bought with his own blood. (Acts 20:28)

Be shepherds of God's flock that is under your care, serving as overseers—not because you must, but because you are willing, as God wants you to be; not greedy for money, but eager to serve; (1 Pet 5:2)

"Come near me and listen to this: "From the first announcement I have not spoken in secret; at the time it happens, I am there." And now the Sovereign LORD has sent me, with his Spirit. (Isa 48:16)

4 (6:14-16) **Apostles**: Jesus chose diverse personalities. There were at least three businessmen: Peter, James, and John. All three were fishermen with rather large businesses (Mk.1:19-20; Lk.5:2-3). One apostle was perhaps wealthy: Matthew, the tax collector. His house must have been an estate, for it was large enough to handle a huge crowd for a large feast (Lk.5:27-29). One was a political nationalist, an insurrectionist, Simon the Zealot. The Zealots were pledged to overthrow the Roman government and to assassinate as many Roman officials and Jewish cohorts as possible (Lk.6:15; Acts 1:13). One was evidently deeply religious: Nathanael (Jn.1:48). So far as is known, there was no outstanding official or famous citizen among the apostles.

Their personalities were a strange mixture. Matthew, being a tax collector and ostracized by the Jewish community, was bound to be a hard-crusted, non-religious individual (Mt.9:9). The fishermen James and John were of a rough breed with thundering personalities (Mk.3:17). Simon the Zealot was possessed with a fanatical, nationalistic spirit (Lk.6:15; Acts 1:13). Peter was apparently a rough fisherman with a loud, rough-hewn personality (Mk.14:71). The power of Christ to give purpose and meaning to life and to bring peace among men is clearly seen in His ability to bring so diverse a group together under one banner. (See DEEPER STUDY # 4-15—Mk.3:16-19 for a discussion on each of the apostles.)

But God chose the foolish things of the world to shame the wise; God chose the weak things of the world to shame the strong. He chose the lowly things of this world and the despised things—and the things that are not—to nullify the things that are, so that no one may boast before him. (1 Cor 1:27-29)

5 (6:17-19) **Mission—Call—Ministry**: Jesus chose His men to carry out His mission with Him. Note that the twelve were now *with Him in a very special relationship.* Jesus "went down with them, and stood on a level place." Standing there, He and the twelve were faced with a crowd of people. The twelve were now to learn what their mission was to be.

1. Their mission was to learn to minister to two distinct groups: "a large crowd of His disciples" and a great number of people.

2. Their mission was to learn to carry out a threefold ministry.

a. The ministry of preaching to those who came to hear Jesus (v.18).

Thought 1. The minister and teacher of God is to preach and teach. He is to share with all those who went to hear Jesus.

> **Therefore go and make disciples of all nations, baptizing them in the name of the Father and of the Son and of the Holy Spirit, and teaching them to obey everything I have commanded you. And surely I am with you always, to the very end of the age." (Mat 28:19-20)**
>
> **He said to them, "Go into all the world and preach the good news to all creation. (Mark 16:15)**

b. The ministry of healing (v.17-18).

Thought 1. The minister and teacher of God is to minister to the diseased and brokenhearted of his community and world. In the name and power of Jesus, he is to heal the sick and mend the brokenhearted.

> **How God anointed Jesus of Nazareth with the Holy Spirit and power, and how he went around doing good and healing all who were under the power of the devil, because God was with him. (Acts 10:38)**
>
> **He heals the brokenhearted and binds up their wounds. (Psa 147:3)**
>
> **Again Jesus said, "Peace be with you! As the Father has sent me, I am sending you." (John 20:21)**

c. The ministry of leading people to *touch Jesus* in order to receive His power (dunamis) (v.19). The people were *touching Jesus* in order to receive His power.

Thought 1. The servant of God is to be an instrument of Jesus' power. Jesus' power is to flow through His servant and flow outward to men.

> **Then Jesus came to them and said, "All authority in heaven and on earth has been given to me. (Mat 28:18)**
>
> **But you will receive power when the Holy Spirit comes on you; and you will be my witnesses in Jerusalem, and in all Judea and Samaria, and to the ends of the earth." (Acts 1:8)**
>
> **Now to him who is able to do immeasurably more than all we ask or imagine, according to his power that is at work within us, (Eph 3:20)**
>
> **Preach the Word; be prepared in season and out of season; correct, rebuke and encourage—with great patience and careful instruction. (2 Tim 4:2)**

	I. Jesus Teaches the Perils of the Material World, 6:20-26 (Mt.5:3-12)	the Son of Man. 23 "Rejoice in that day and leap for joy, because great is your reward in heaven. For that is how their fathers treated the prophets.	2) The attitude to have while being persecuted: Rejoicing 3) Reward: To be great
1 The promise to those who reject materialism a. The poor: Will inherit the Kingdom of God	20 Looking at his disciples, he said: "Blessed are you who are poor, for yours is the kingdom of God.	24 "But woe to you who are rich, for you have already received your comfort.	**2 The judgment of those who follow materialism** a. The rich: Will want
b. The hungry: Will be filled c. The sorrowful: Will laugh	21 Blessed are you who hunger now, for you will be satisfied. Blessed are you who weep now, for you will laugh.	25 Woe to you who are well fed now, for you will go hungry. Woe to you who laugh now, for you will mourn and weep.	b. The full: Will hunger c. The merry: Will weep
d. The persecuted for Jesus' sake 1) The persecuted described: The hated, the ostracized, & the rejected	22 Blessed are you when men hate you, when they exclude you and insult you and reject your name as evil, because of	26 Woe to you when all men speak well of you, for that is how their fathers treated the false prophets.	d. The prideful & compromising: Will have earthly approval only

DIVISION III

THE SON OF MAN'S ANNOUNCED MISSION AND PUBLIC MINISTRY, 4:16-9:17

I. Jesus Teaches the Perils of the Material World, 6:20-26

(6:20-26) **Introduction**: this is a shocking passage to the world, for Jesus switches the world's values completely around. He rejects entirely the *materialism* (things) of the world and warns the worldly and materialistic that severe judgment is coming.

1. The promise to those who reject materialism (v.20-23).
2. The judgment to those who follow materialism (v.24-26).

1 (6:20-23) **Materialism—Worldliness—Righteousness—Persecution**: the promise to those who reject materialism.

1. Blessed are the poor. This does not mean that a man must be poverty-stricken and financially poor. Hunger, nakedness, and slums are not pleasing to God, especially in a world of plenty. Jesus is not talking about material poverty. He means what he adds in Matthew: "poor in spirit" (cp. Mt.5:3). "Poor in spirit" means several things.

   a. To acknowledge one's utter helplessness before God, one's spiritual poverty, one's spiritual need; acknowledging that one is solely dependent upon God to meet his need.
   b. To acknowledge one's utter lack in facing life and eternity apart from God; to acknowledge that the real blessings of life and eternity come only from a right relationship with God (see note—Eph.1:3; cp. Jn.10:10; Gal.5:22-23).
   c. To acknowledge one's utter lack of superiority before all others and one's spiritual deadness before God; to acknowledge that no matter what one has achieved in this world (fame, fortune, power), he is no better, no richer, no more superior than the next person. His attitude toward others is not proud and haughty, not superior and overbearing. To be "poor in spirit" means acknowledging that every human being is a real person just like everyone else—a person who has a significant contribution to make to society and to the world. The person who is "poor in spirit" approaches life in humility and appreciation, not as though life owes him, but as though he owes life. He has been given the privilege of living; thus, he journeys through life with a humble attitude, that is, with an attitude of being poor in spirit and contributing all he can out of a spirit of appreciation.

Two critical steps are taken by the person who truly acknowledges his spiritual poverty.

   a. He turns his primary attention away from the things of this world, knowing things can never make him rich in spirit.
   b. He turns his primary attention to God and His kingdom, knowing that God alone can make him rich in spirit (see note—Eph.1:3).

The opposite of being "poor in spirit" is having a spirit that is full of self. There is a world of difference between these two spirits. There is the difference of thinking one is righteous and acknowledging one has the need for righteousness. There is the difference of *having self-righteousness* and of having *another's righteousness*. Man must have *another's righteousness*. Self-righteousness goes no farther than self, that is, no farther than death. *Another's righteousness*, that is, Christ's righteousness, lives forever (2 Cor.5:21; Ph.3:9. See note—Ro.3:21-22; note and DEEPER STUDY # 1—Gal.2:15-16. See outline and notes—Ro.10:4.)

The promise to the *poor* is phenomenal. Note the exact words: "yours is the kingdom of God." The promise is not "yours will be," but "yours is." The poor in spirit receive the Kingdom of God *now* (see DEEPER STUDY # 3—Mt.19:23-24).

2. Blessed are the hungry. This is spiritual hunger, not physical hunger. Again, being physically hungry is not a blessing. It is often sad and tragic. Jesus is saying, "Blessed are they who hunger spiritually, who hunger after righteousness" (Mt.5:6). It means to have a starving spirit, a spirit that craves righteousness.

In the Bible righteousness means two simple but profound things. It means both *to be right and to do right.* (See DEEPER STUDY # 5, Righteousness—Mt.5:6 for more discussion.)

   a. There are those who stress *being righteous and neglect doing righteousness.* This leads to two serious errors.
      1) False security. It causes a person to stress that he is saved and acceptable to God because he

has *believed in* Jesus Christ. But he neglects doing good and living as he should. He neglects obeying God and serving man.

2) Loose living. It allows one to go out and do pretty much as he desires. He feels secure and comfortable in his *faith in Christ.* He knows that what he does may affect his fellowship with God and other believers, but he thinks his behavior will not affect his salvation. He thinks that no matter what he does he is still acceptable to God.

The problem with this stress is that it is a false righteousness. Righteousness in the Bible means being righteous and doing righteousness. The Bible knows nothing about being righteous without living righteously.

b. There are those who stress doing righteousness and neglect being righteous. This also leads to two serious errors.

1) Self-righteousness and legalism. It causes a person to stress that he is saved and acceptable to God because he does good. He works and behaves morally and keeps certain rules and regulations. He does the things a Christian should do by obeying the main laws of God. But he neglects the basic law: the law of love and acceptance—that God loves him and accepts him not because he does good but because he loves and trusts the righteousness of Christ (see note and DEEPER STUDY # 5—Mt.5:6).

2) Being judgmental and censorious. A person who stresses that he is righteous (acceptable to God) because he keeps certain laws often judges and censors others. He feels that rules and regulations can be kept, for *He* keeps them. Therefore, anyone who fails to keep them is judged, criticized, and censored.

The problem with this stress is that it, too, is a false righteousness. Again, righteousness in the Bible is both being righteous and doing righteousness. The Bible knows nothing of being acceptable to God without being made righteous in Christ Jesus (see notes and DEEPER STUDY # 5—Mt.5:6; Ro.5:1 for more discussion. Cp. 2 Cor.5:21.)

Note that Jesus does not say, "Blessed are the righteous," for no one is righteous (Ro.3:10). He says, "Blessed are those who hunger and thirst for righteousness." Man is not righteous, not perfectly righteous. His chance to be righteous is gone. He has already come short and missed the mark. He is already imperfect. Man has but one hope: that God will love him so much that He will somehow count him righteous. That is just what God does. God takes a man's "hunger and thirst for righteousness" and counts that hunger and thirst as righteousness (see DEEPER STUDY # 2—Ro.4:22).

The promise to those who hunger after righteousness is fulfilling. They will be filled with abundant life: love, joy, peace, longsuffering, gentleness, goodness, faith, meekness, temperance (Gal.5:22-23).

3. Blessed are the sorrowful, the persons who weep and mourn. The idea is a broken heart, a desperate, helpless weeping. It is weeping over sin; it is a broken heart over evil and suffering; it is a brokenness of self that comes from seeing Jesus on the cross and realizing that one's own sins put Him there (cp. Jas.4:9).

Who are they who mourn? Who are they so full of grief and sorrow that they cry and weep and utter groanings deep from within? There are three persons who mourn and utter such groanings.

a. The person who is *desperately sorry* for his sin and unworthiness before God. He has such a sense of sin that his heart is just broken (Lk.18:13).
b. The person who really *feels* the desperate plight and terrible suffering of others. The tragedies, the problems, the sinful behavior of others; the state, the condition, the lostness of the world—all weigh ever so heavily upon the heart of the mourner.
c. The person who *experiences* personal tragedy and intense trauma.

The promise to the one who weeps is that he will laugh (gelasete). The word means *loud laughter* that arises from a deep-seated joy and comfort. The laughter comes from two things.

a. It comes from seeing the end of sin and shame, sorrow and suffering, tragedy and trauma.
b. It comes from being comforted (paraclesia, see note—2 Cor.1:3). Note two glorious truths.
    1) There is a present comfort.
        ⇒ A settled peace: a relief, a solace, a consolation within.
        ⇒ An assurance of forgiveness and acceptance by God.
        ⇒ A fullness of joy: a sense of God's presence, care and guidance (Jn.14:26); a sense of His sovereignty, of His working all things out for good to those who love Him (Ro.8:28; cp. Jn.10:10; 15:11; 2 Cor.6:10; Ps.16:11).

    2) There is an eternal comfort.
        ⇒ A passing from death to life (Jn.3:16; Jn.5:24f).
        ⇒ A wiping away of all tears (Is.25:8; Rev.7:17; 21:4).

4. Blessed are the persecuted, the persons who are persecuted for Jesus' sake. The persecuted are those who endure suffering *for Christ*. Jesus spelled out what He meant by persecution. He means being hated, ostracized, reproached, and having one's name spoken against.

Note the attitude a person is to have while being persecuted. The person is to "rejoice" and "leap for joy." How is such possible? By keeping one's eyes on the reward. Note the words, "Rejoice in that day and leap for joy, because great is your reward in heaven" (Lk.6:23).

Believers are forewarned: they will suffer persecution (Jn.15:20; 16:4; Ph.1:29; 2 Tim.3:12; 1 Jn.3:13; 1 Pt.4:12f).

a. Believers suffer persecution because they do not belong to the world. They are called out of the world. They are *in the world*, but they are not *of the world*. They are separated from the behavior of the world; therefore, the world reacts against them (Jn.15:19).
b. Believers suffer persecution because they *strip away the world's cloak of sin*. They live and demonstrate a life of righteousness. Such exposes the sins of people (Jn.15:21, 24; cp. 15:18; 2 Tim.3:12).
c. Believers suffer persecution because the world does not know God or Christ. They want no God, no Lord other than themselves and their own

imaginations. They want to do just what they want, to fulfill their own desires and not what another Lord wishes and demands (Jn.15:21; 16:3).

d. Believers suffer persecution because the world is deceived in its concept and belief of God. The world conceives God to be the Person who fulfills their earthly desires and lusts (Jn.16:2-3). Man's idea of God is that of a *Supreme Grandfather.* He protects, provides, and gives, no matter one's behavior, just so the behavior is not too far out. God (the Supreme Grandfather) will accept and work all things out in the final analysis. But the true believer teaches against this. God is love, but He is also just and demands righteousness. The world rebels against this concept of God (Jn.16:2-3).

The promise to the persecuted is twofold. Their reward is great in heaven, and they are following in the footsteps (testimony) of the great prophets of the past.

1. The persecuted receive a great reward now.
   a. They experience a special honor (Acts 5:41).
   b. They experience a special consolation (2 Cor.1:5).
   c. They are given a very special closeness, a glow of the Lord's presence (see note—1 Pt.4:14).
   d. They become a greater witness for Christ (2 Cor. 1:4-6).
2. The persecuted will receive the Kingdom of Heaven eternally (Heb.11:35f; 1 Pt.4:12-13; see DEEPER STUDY # 3—Mt.19:23-24).

2 (6:24-26) **Judgment—Materialism**: the judgment to those who follow materialism.

1. The warning is strong to the rich. Who are the rich? Realistically, in comparison to what the vast majority of the world has, a rich person is anyone who has anything to put back beyond meeting the true needs of his own family. This is exactly what Christ and the Bible say time and again (cp. also Mk.12:41-44; Lk.21:1-4; Acts 4:34-35).

Why are the rich warned? Because wealth pulls a person away from the Kingdom of Heaven. It is difficult for a rich person to enter heaven. Christ made this statement because of the things that *pulled* the rich young ruler away from heaven. There is a lure, an attraction, a force, a power, a pull that reaches out and draws any of us who look at or possess wealth. There are pulls so forceful that they will enslave and doom any rich person who fails to turn and embrace God.

a. *Wealth creates the big "I".* The wealthy are usually esteemed, honored, and envied. Wealth brings position, power, and recognition. It boosts *ego,* making a person self-sufficient and independent in this world. As a result there is a tendency for the rich man to feel that he is truly independent and self-sufficient, that he needs nothing. And in such an atmosphere and world of thought, God is forgotten. The rich person forgets there are things that money cannot buy and events from which money cannot save. Peace, love, joy—all that really matter within the spirit of man—can never be bought. Neither can money save one from disaster, disease, accident, and death.

b. *Wealth tends to make one hoard.* The Bible lays down the principle of handling money for all men, even for the poor:

> **He who has been stealing must steal no longer, but must work, doing something useful with his own hands, that he may have something to share with those in need. (Eph 4:28)**
>
> **Honor your father and mother,' and 'love your neighbor as yourself.'" And the second is like it: 'Love your neighbor as yourself.' (Mat 19:19; 22:39)**

The world reels in desperate need. People are starving, sick, unhoused, and unclothed by the millions; and teeming millions are spiritually lost and without God in this world and doomed to die without ever knowing Him. When any of us sit still and objectively look at the world in its desperate plight, how can we keep from asking: "How can any man hoard and not help—even to the last available penny? Why would any man keep more than what he needs for himself and his family?"

As God looks at the rich, He is bound to ask the same questions. In fact, His questions are bound to be more pointed and forceful. This is exactly what Christ said to the rich young ruler:

> **Jesus answered, "If you want to be perfect, go, sell your possessions and give to the poor, and you will have treasure in heaven. Then come, follow me." (Mat 19:21)**

c. *Riches tend to make a man selfish.* For some unexplainable reason, the more we get, the more we want. When we taste the things of this world and become comfortable, we tend to fear loosing our possessions. We struggle to keep what we have and to get more. True, many are willing to make contributions, but only a certain amount, an amount that will not lower their overall estate or standing or level of comfort and possessions. There are few who give all they are and have to Christ to meet the needs of the world.

As Jesus said, "How hard it is for the rich [meaning those who have anything in comparison with most of the world] to enter the kingdom of God" (cp. Lk.18:24). If we do not have compassion and take care of our brothers (fellowman) when they are in desperate need, how can we expect God to have compassion and take care of us when we face the desperate need for heaven? It is foolish for us to think that a loving and just God will meet our need for eternal life when we would not meet the need of our fellowman for earthly life. The rich have the means to help and to save human life, *if they would.*

d. *Wealth attaches one to the world.* Wealth enables one to buy things that...

- make him comfortable
- please his taste
- expand his experience
- stir his ego
- challenge his mental pursuit
- stimulate his flesh
- stretch his self-image

If a man centers his life upon the things of the world, his attention is on the world not on God. He tends to become wrapped up in securing more and in protecting what he has. Too often, he gives little if any time and thought to heavenly matters. Wealth and the things it can provide usually consume the rich.

The judgment of the rich is their wealth on earth. The word received (apechete) means a receipt in full. Their only "comfort" (paraklesin, help, aid, encouragement) is to be on this earth—the wealth they have. There will be no consolation after this life—no help, no aid, no encouragement, no cheer. They are *paid in full*. They choose this life, so all the good they will receive is the good they now experience.

For we brought nothing into the world, and we can take nothing out of it. (1 Tim 6:7)

People who want to get rich fall into temptation and a trap and into many foolish and harmful desires that plunge men into ruin and destruction. (1 Tim 6:9)

Your gold and silver are corroded. Their corrosion will testify against you and eat your flesh like fire. You have hoarded wealth in the last days. (James 5:3)

And when your herds and flocks grow large and your silver and gold increase and all you have is multiplied, then your heart will become proud and you will forget the LORD your God, who brought you out of Egypt, out of the land of slavery. (Deu 8:13-14)

A flood will carry off his house, rushing waters on the day of God's wrath. (Job 20:28)

Though he heaps up silver like dust and clothes like piles of clay, (Job 27:16)

Man is a mere phantom as he goes to and fro: He bustles about, but only in vain; he heaps up wealth, not knowing who will get it. (Psa 39:6)

For all can see that wise men die; the foolish and the senseless alike perish and leave their wealth to others. (Psa 49:10)

Do not trust in extortion or take pride in stolen goods; though your riches increase, do not set your heart on them. (Psa 62:10)

Cast but a glance at riches, and they are gone, for they will surely sprout wings and fly off to the sky like an eagle. (Prov 23:5)

For riches do not endure forever, and a crown is not secure for all generations. (Prov 27:24)

A faithful man will be richly blessed, but one eager to get rich will not go unpunished. (Prov 28:20)

I hated all the things I had toiled for under the sun, because I must leave them to the one who comes after me. (Eccl 2:18)

Like a partridge that hatches eggs it did not lay is the man who gains riches by unjust means. When his life is half gone, they will desert him, and in the end he will prove to be a fool. (Jer 17:11)

2. The warning is strong to the full. The full are the opposite of those who hunger for righteousness. The full are those who are filled with all that the world has to offer; in essence they are full of themselves, their own desires, urges, and cravings. They have no hunger for righteousness at all. Scripture identifies the full as those who...

- fill their stomachs with the pods of the world (Lk.15:16).
- serve their own appetites and not the Lord Jesus Christ (Ro.16:18).
- indulge in the food (things, sins) of the world (1 Cor.6:13; cp. 6:9-13).
- make their god their stomachs (Ph.3:19).
- "They have become filled with every kind of wickedness, evil, greed and depravity. They are full of envy, murder, strife, deceit and malice. They are gossips, slanderers, God-haters, insolent, arrogant and boastful; they invent ways of doing evil; they disobey their parents; they are senseless, faithless, heartless, ruthless. Although they know God's righteous decree that those who do such things deserve death, they not only continue to do these very things but also approve of those who practice them" (Ro.1:29-32).

The judgment of the full will be hunger. This means they...

- will leave all that filled them behind when they die (Lk.12:20; 16:25).
- will have no desires filled after this life.
- will have no delights fulfilled throughout eternity.
- will hunger for good (righteousness) and for the good things throughout eternity.

You say, 'I am rich; I have acquired wealth and do not need a thing.' But you do not realize that you are wretched, pitiful, poor, blind and naked. (Rev 3:17)

They close up their callous hearts, and their mouths peak with arrogance. (Psa 17:10)

Now this was the sin of your sister Sodom: She and her daughters were arrogant, overfed and unconcerned; they did not help the poor and needy. (Ezek 16:49)

3. The warning is strong to the merry, to those who laugh now. This means three things.

Laughing now refers to those who have no sense of sin, no sorrow or regret over evil and suffering, no brokenness over the cross and their own sin. Their joy is carnal and sensual.

Laughing now refers to those who are laughing it up *in the world* with all its comfort and ease, pleasures and stimulations, recreations and pastimes. Their joy is the indulgence and entertaining of their flesh.

Laughing now refers to those who pay little or no attention to the reality of the world, a world suffering under the weight of evil and disaster, greed and selfishness, sin and death. Their joy is found in denying and ignoring the truth of the world or in giving a pittance of time or money to help in order to ease their consciences.

The warning and judgment to the merry is mourning and weeping. They are doomed because they refused to face the reality of a world lost in sin and evil, a world that needed their attention and help. They refused to help the needy, those who suffered and wept so much in this world. Therefore, they will be left alone in the next world to mourn and weep over their great loss.

That the mirth of the wicked is brief, the joy of the godless lasts but a moment. (Job 20:5)

Even in laughter the heart may ache,

and joy may end in grief. (Prov 14:13)

Like the crackling of thorns under the pot, so is the laughter of fools. This too is meaningless. (Eccl 7:6)

Joy and gladness are taken away from the orchards; no one sings or shouts in the vineyards; no one treads out wine at the presses, for I have put an end to the shouting. (Isa 16:10)

Come near to God and he will come near to you. Wash your hands, you sinners, and purify your hearts, you double-minded. Grieve, mourn and wail. Change your laughter to mourning and your joy to gloom. Humble yourselves before the Lord, and he will lift you up. (James 4:8-10)

4. The warning is strong to the prideful and compromising. These are the opposite of those who are persecuted for Christ's sake. The worldly speak well of those who live worldly...

- who live as they live
- who speak as they speak
- who compromise
- who seek their company and approval
- who never point out the truth of sin and death, judgment and hell

Worldly men want attention and esteem, position and place, honor and praise, recognition and applause. Men honor such ambitions and rewards. Therefore, they speak well of men who attain such. But note what Jesus said. He said that *false prophets* were those of whom the world spoke well, and this was their reward, all they would ever receive. They coveted worldly recognition and honor and they received it, but at the expense of heavenly recognition and honor.

Thought 1. We are not to be as false prophets, slapping men on the back, acknowledging and compromising with their worldliness. If we do, the world will speak well of us, but we will lose our reward. What the believer must do is tell the truth to all men: all men need a Savior and their eternal fate depends upon their coming to Him for salvation, seeking His righteousness.

I will show partiality to no one, nor will I flatter any man; (Job 32:21)

A gossip betrays a confidence; so avoid a man who talks too much. (Prov 20:19)

Whoever says to the guilty, "You are innocent"— peoples will curse him and nations denounce him. (Prov 24:24)

A lying tongue hates those it hurts, and a flattering mouth works ruin. (Prov 26:28)

Whoever flatters his neighbor is spreading a net for his feet. (Prov 29:5)

May the LORD cut off all flattering lips and every boastful tongue (Psa 12:3)

For the time will come when men will not put up with sound doctrine. Instead, to suit their own desires, they will gather around them a great number of teachers to say what their itching ears want to hear. (2 Tim 4:3)

They must be silenced, because they are ruining whole households by teaching things they ought not to teach—and that for the sake of dishonest gain. (Titus 1:11)

But there were also false prophets among the people, just as there will be false teachers among you. They will secretly introduce destructive heresies, even denying the sovereign Lord who bought them—bringing swift destruction on themselves. Many will follow their shameful ways and will bring the way of truth into disrepute. (2 Pet 2:1-2)

	J. Jesus Teaches the New Principles of Life, 6:27-38 (Mt.5:39, 43-48; 7:12)
1 The principles of life a. Governing relationships 1) Love & do good 2) Bless & pray	27 "But I tell you who hear me: Love your enemies, do good to those who hate you, 28 Bless those who curse you, pray for those who mistreat you.
3) Offer the other cheek	29 If someone strikes you on one cheek, turn to him the other also. If someone takes
b. Governing property 1) Deprive not	your cloak, do not stop him from taking your tunic.
2) Give 3) Do not demand material goods	30 Give to everyone who asks you, and if anyone takes what belongs to you, do not demand it back.
c. Governing behavior[DS1]	31 Do to others as you would have them do to you.
2 The argument: A disciple's behavior must surpass a sinner's a. In love	32 "If you love those who love you, what credit is that to you? Even 'sinners' love those who love them.
b. In doing good	33 And if you do good to those who are good to you, what credit is that to you? Even 'sinners' do that.
c. In lending	34 And if you lend to those from whom you expect repayment, what credit is that to you? Even 'sinners' lend to 'sinners,' expecting to be repaid in full.
3 The reward for living right a. Shall be great b. Shall be the children of the Most High	35 But love your enemies, do good to them, and lend to them without expecting to get anything back. Then your reward will be great, and you will be sons of the Most High, because he is kind to the ungrateful and wicked.
c. Shall be acting as God's children	36 Be merciful, just as your Father is merciful.
4 The promise: Reciprocal behavior—you will receive what you give a. In relationships	37 "Do not judge, and you will not be judged. Do not condemn, and you will not be condemned. Forgive, and you will be forgiven.
b. In property c. The principle: A person receives what he gives	38 Give, and it will be given to you. A good measure, pressed down, shaken together and running over, will be poured into your lap. For with the measure you use, it will be measured to you."

DIVISION III

THE SON OF MAN'S ANNOUNCED MISSION AND PUBLIC MINISTRY, 4:16-9:17

J. Jesus Teaches the New Principles of Life, 6:27-38

(6:27-38) **Introduction**: the principles spelled out by Jesus are shocking. They go against every grain of society and every fiber of a man's being. Man rebels by nature against what Jesus is saying; however the new principles must be heeded, for they are the salvation of society and the hope of man for life.

1. The principles of life (v.27-31).
2. The argument: a disciple's behavior must surpass a sinner's (v.32-34).
3. The reward for living right (v.35-36).
4. The promise: reciprocal behavior—you will receive what you give (v.37-38).

1 (6:27-31) **Life, Principles of—Believers, Behavior of**: there are the new principles of life. Two things should be noted immediately. Jesus was speaking to his disciples (v.20) and to those who would hear (v.27). He knew that all would not hear. Even if they were disciples, some just closed their ears if they did not like what they heard. And what Jesus was about to preach was a complete switch from the way men and society lived. He was about to say some things men had never heard or thought about. He knew some were going to shut their ears, so He warned them and encouraged them to guard against not listening.

1. There are the new principles governing human relationships. Jesus touched on five specific behaviors.

a. Love: "Love your enemies." Believers are to *love all men, even enemies*. They are to respect and honor all men (1 Pt.2:17). Every human being has something that is commendable, even if it is nothing but the fact that he is a fellow human being with a soul to be reached for God. Note two facts.

First, loving one's enemies is against human nature. The behavior of human nature is to react: to hate, strike back, and wish hurt. At best, human nature treats enemies with coldness and distance. The root of human reaction against enemies is self and bitterness. (Self-preservation is not evil of itself. See note and DEEPER STUDY # 1, Love—Mt.5:44. The section on agape love points out that love is not complacent acceptance of wickedness and license.)

Second, the one thing that a believer can have for enemies is mercy and compassion. Those who are enemies may choose to remain antagonistic, but the believer can still forgive in mercy and compassion. In fact, if the believer does not have compassion for those who hate him, he has gained nothing of the spirit of Christ (v.36).

b. Do good: "Do good to those who hate you." Imagine the impact of these words to the world of Jesus' day. They were an enslaved people conquered and hated by the Romans, yet Jesus was saying, "Do good to [them]." (See note, Love—Enemies—Mt.5:44 for more discussion.)

Note that *doing good* goes beyond words; it actually does things for the person who hates. It reaches out to him through his family and friends, employment and business. It searches for ways to do good to him, realizing that he needs to be reached for God. If no immediate way is found, then the Christian continues to bless him, ever waiting for the day when the hater will face one of the crises that comes to every human being. And then the believer goes and does good, ministering as Christ Himself ministered.

On the contrary: "If your enemy is hungry, feed him; if he is thirsty, give him something to drink. In doing this, you will heap burning coals on his head." (Rom 12:20)

Make sure that nobody pays back wrong for wrong, but lways try to be kind to each other and to everyone else. (1 Th 5:15)

If you see the donkey of someone who hates you fallen down under its load, do not leave it there; be sure you help him with it. (Exo 23:5)

If your enemy is hungry, give him food to eat; if he is thirsty, give him water to drink. (Prov 25:21)

c. Bless people: "Bless those who curse you." People do curse, and sometimes they curse other people. When someone curses a believer, the believer is to bless his curser, not rail back. He is to speak softly, to use kind and reconciling words.

Bless those who persecute you; bless and do not curse. (Rom 12:14)

Do not repay evil with evil or insult with insult, but with blessing, because to this you were called so that you may inherit a blessing. (1 Pet 3:9)

A gentle answer turns away wrath, but a harsh word stirs up anger. (Prov 15:1)

d. Pray for others: "Pray for those who mistreat you." Note this refers not only to those who speak abusively but those who *mistreat us*. It is an attempt to shame and to hurt both our name and body. Someone tries to shame, dishonor, disgrace and reproach us. And they go even farther; they misuse, mistreat, abuse, attack, and persecute us. What are we to do? Christ says, "Pray for them. When they despitefully use you, pray for them." (a) Pray for God to forgive the persecutor. (b) Pray for peace between one's self and the persecutor. (c) Pray for the persecutor's salvation and correction.

Jesus said, "Father, forgive them, for they do not know what they are doing." And they divided up his clothes by casting lots. (Luke 23:34)

Then he [Stephen] fell on his knees and cried out, "Lord, do not hold this sin against them." When he had said this, he fell asleep. (Acts 7:60)

Prayer for the persecutor will greatly benefit the believer. It will keep the believer from becoming bitter, hostile, and reactionary.

e. Offer the other cheek: "If someone strikes you on one cheek, turn to him the other also." The word for cheek (siagon) really means the jaw or jawbone. It is a strong blow, a punch, and not just a slap of contempt. Of course, there is contempt and bitterness, but there is also physical injury. Christ is saying that the believer is not to strike back, not to retaliate against...

- bitter insults or contempt.
- bodily threats or injury.

When suffering *for the gospel's sake*, for his personal testimony for Christ, the believer is to respond to physical abuse just as his Lord did. He is to demonstrate *moral strength through a quiet and meek spirit*, trusting God to touch the heart of his persecutors. (See notes—Mt.5:38-39 for more discussion.)

They spit on him, and took the staff and struck him on the head again and again. (Mat 27:30)

When Jesus said this, one of the officials nearby struck him in the face. "Is this the way you answer the high priest?" he demanded. (John 18:22)

Men open their mouths to jeer at me; they strike my cheek in scorn and unite together against me. (Job 16:10)

But the fruit of the Spirit is love, joy, peace, patience, kindness, goodness, faithfulness, gentleness and self-control. Against such things there is no law. (Gal 5:22-23)

Those who oppose him he must gently instruct, in the hope that God will grant them repentance leading them to a knowledge of the truth, (2 Tim 2:25)

Do not repay anyone evil for evil. Be careful to do what is right in the eyes of everybody. (Rom 12:17)

"'Do not seek revenge or bear a grudge against one of your people, but love your neighbor as yourself. I am the LORD. (Lev 19:18)

Do not say, "I'll pay you back for this wrong!" Wait for the LORD, and he will deliver you. (Prov 20:22)

Do not say, "I'll do to him as he has done to me; I'll pay that man back for what he did." (Prov 24:29)

Seek the LORD, all you humble of the land, you who do what he commands. Seek righteousness, seek humility; perhaps you will be sheltered on the day of the Lord's anger. (Zep 2:3)

2. There are the new principles governing property. Jesus touched upon two specific behaviors.

a. Deprive not: "If someone takes your cloak, do not stop him from taking your tunic." The Jews wore both an inner and an outer garment. If a man took the outer garment, the believer was to offer his inner garment as well. Jewish law allowed the inner garment to be taken as a debt or pledge, but never the outer garment. A man might have several underclothings, but only one outer garment (cp. Ex.22:26-27).

Giving one's cloak is difficult. It means the believer does not defend, stand up, or dispute the taking of his property. He forgives, and he gives more to the person who takes. He even gives his coat (tunic) if necessary. A believer does not get tied up and consumed with his rights and privileges in or out of court. He has time only to go about his duty. He is tied up and consumed with living—living to the fullest for Christ and reaching out to a world lost and consumed with *disputes and needing the peace which only God can bring*. (See note and thoughts—Mt.5:39-41 for additional discussion.)

b. Give: "Give to everyone who asks you." The believer is to help those who have need, and he is to readily help. Note that Christ allows no excuse. The picture is that the believer *gives and does not turn away* when a person asks. Note, however, the Bible does not say to give without discretion.

Good will come to him who is generous and lends freely, who conducts his affairs with justice. (Psa 112:5)

Thought 1. There are two significant attitudes to control the believer's giving.

1) The believer is to live in readiness—a readiness to give and to lend (cp. 2 Cor.8:11-15, esp. 11). He does not live for this earth and world. He lives for God and for heaven. His citizenship is in heaven, from whence he looks for the Savior (Ph.3:20). Thus, his attachment to earthly things is only for meeting the necessities of life and for helping others. He exists to help and to give.

Sell your possessions and give to the poor. Provide purses for yourselves that will not wear out, a treasure in heaven that will not be exhausted, where no thief comes near and no moth destroys. (Luke 12:33)

Share with God's people who are in need. Practice hospitality. (Rom 12:13)

Therefore, as we have opportunity, let us do good to all people, especially to those who belong to the family of believers. (Gal 6:10)

Command those who are rich in this present world not to be arrogant nor to put their hope in wealth, which is so uncertain, but to put their hope in God, who richly provides us with everything for our enjoyment. Command them to do good, to be rich in good deeds, and to be generous and willing to share. (1 Tim 6:17-18)

And do not forget to do good and to share with others, for with such sacrifices God is pleased. (Heb 13:16)

Now finish the work, so that your eager willingness to do it may be [giving] matched by your completion of it, [to give] according to your means. For if the willingness is there, the gift is acceptable according to what one has, not according to what he does not have. Our desire is not that others might be relieved while you are hard pressed, but that there might be equality. At the present time your plenty will supply what they need, so that in turn their plenty will supply what you need. Then there will be equality, as it is written: "He who gathered much did not have too much, and he who gathered little did not have too little." (2 Cor 8:11-15)

2) The believer is to work for two reasons: (1) to meet his own necessities; and (2) to have enough to help those in need.

He who has been stealing must steal no longer, but must work, doing something useful with his own hands, that he may have something to share with those in need. (Eph 4:28)

In everything I did, I showed you that by this kind of hard work we must help the weak, remembering the words the Lord Jesus himself said: 'It is more blessed to give than to receive.'" (Acts 20:35)

c. Demand not: "If anyone takes what belongs to you, do not demand it back." Often a person fails to pay back what he borrowed. He takes and keeps what he borrowed, whether tools, clothing, food, or money. The believer is not to demand them back, not if the person *needs* them and is going to be deprived and hurt if they are taken back. The believer has to consider two facts: first, the person's need; second, if the person has no need, the sin of allowing license and irresponsibility versus alienating and turning the person away from one's testimony of Christ. The believer must not allow license and irresponsibility, but he must be careful to not lose his chance of winning the person to Christ. No item, no amount of money is worth his soul.

Give to the one who asks you, and do not turn away from the one who wants to borrow from you. (Mat 5:42)

3. There is the new principle which governs all behavior, the Golden Rule itself: "Do to others as you would have them do to you." (See DEEPER STUDY # 1—Lk.6:31.)

DEEPER STUDY # 1

(6:31) **Golden Rule—Righteousness—Justice**: the golden rule is probably the most well-known thing Jesus ever said. It is the summit of ethics, of behavior, of righteousness, of godliness. It is a very practical statement of God's love; that is, God has done to us just as He wants us to do to Him. God has treated us just as He wants us to treat Him (and everyone else).

The golden rule reveals the heart of God. It shows us exactly how God's heart longs for us to live and act. It is a simple one-sentence statement revealing what love really is and what life in heaven (the perfect world) is to be like. It tells believers that, as citizens of both heaven and earth, they are to live as the golden rule dictates while still on the earth.

There are four significant facts that set the golden rule apart from all other teaching.

1. The golden rule is a simple one-sentence statement that embraces all human behavior. The fact that all law and all love can be stated in one simple sentence is amazing. The simple statement of the golden rule includes all "the Law and the Prophets" (Mt.7:12).

2. The golden rule *demands true law and justice.* Note the wording; it is not negative and passive, yet it tells man how not to behave. It restrains man. For example, the golden rule is teaching a man not to lie, steal, cheat, or injure; and it is teaching much more.

3. The golden rule is concerned with true love, that is, with positive, active behavior.

a. It is more than not doing wrong (lying, stealing, cheating).
b. It is more than just doing good (helping, caring, giving).
c. It is *looking, searching, seeking for ways to do the good* that you want others to do to you; and then doing that good to others.

4. The golden rule teaches the whole law, for the whole law is contained in the words: "Love your neighbor as yourself" (Mt.22:39-40). Every human being would like to have all others treat him perfectly: to love and care for him to the ultimate degree and to express that love and care. The believer is to so love and care while still on earth. He is to give earth a taste of heaven before all things end. Men, being treated so supremely and getting a taste of heaven, might then turn to God.

2 (6:32-34) **World, Behavior of—Self-Denial**: Jesus presented a logical argument for the believer to live as God says. The argument is strong: a believer's behavior must surpass a sinner's behavior.

⇒ Sinners love those who love them.
⇒ Sinners do good to those who do good to them.
⇒ Sinners lend to secure an interest or favor or some gain.

Note three points.

1. The shocking truth: believers who do not live as Christ says do no more than sinners.

2. The world sees virtue and goodness as love; they see doing good and lending as being neighborly. And it is good to love, to do good, and to lend.

3. But loving, doing good, and lending are not enough. It does not get a person into heaven. It is not what Christ did. Christ denied Himself in order to win the world. He loved His enemies and did good to those who hated Him. It might be said that He even loaned His life to the world.

> **Christ died for the ungodly. (Rom 5:6)**
> **While we were still sinners, Christ died for us. (Rom 5:8)**
> **when we were God's enemies, we were reconciled to him through the death of his Son, (Rom 5:10)**

The believer is to do the very same as Christ: deny and sacrifice himself to win the world and offer them the privilege of being saved to the utmost. It takes more than the virtue and goodness of love and doing good and lending among men to become a follower of Christ. It takes the denial and sacrifice of oneself for the sake of reaching the unlovely for Christ, those who are…

- enemies
- haters
- cursers
- borrowers
- persecutors
- thieves
- despiteful
- needful
- selfish

3 (6:35-36) **Reward**: the reward for living as Jesus said is challenging. The obedient believer shall receive a threefold reward.

1. He shall receive a *great reward.* All that the believer suffers and loses on earth will be restored. But note: what he lost will not only be restored, he will *receive well beyond* what he has lost. He will receive an *enormous reward* for having obeyed the Lord and for having sacrificed in order to meet the needs of a dying world. What will the *great reward* be? It will be at least twofold: eternal life and inheriting all that God the Father has.

> **"I tell you the truth, whoever hears my word and believes him who sent me has eternal life and will not be condemned; he has crossed over from death to life. (John 5:24)**
> **So that, having been justified by his grace, we might become heirs having the hope of eternal life. (Titus 3:7)**
> **Praise be to the God and Father of our Lord Jesus Christ! In his great mercy he has given us new birth into a living hope through the resurrection of Jesus Christ from the dead, and into an inheritance that can never perish, spoil or fade—kept in heaven for you, (1 Pet 1:3-4)**
> **"Then the King will say to those on his right, 'Come, you who are blessed by my Father; take your inheritance, the kingdom prepared for you since the creation of the world. (Mat 25:34. See DEEPER STUDY #3—Mat 10:23-24)**

Simply stated, the believer shall receive both *eternal life* and *an inheritance* for having obeyed Christ and having served so sacrificially while on earth. The believer shall have part in the glorious work of God that will be performed in the new heavens and earth, a work that will go on from glory to glory.

2. He shall be the child of the Most High Himself.

> **But when the time had fully come, God sent his Son, born of a woman, born under law, to redeem those under law, that we might receive the full rights of sons. Because you are sons, God sent the Spirit of his Son into our hearts, the Spirit who calls out, "Abba, Father." (Gal 4:4-6)**
> **The Spirit himself testifies with our spirit that we are God's children. Now if we are children, then we are heirs—heirs of God and co-heirs with Christ, if indeed we share in his sufferings in order that we may also share in his glory. (Rom 8:16-17)**

3. He shall be acting as God's child. What a privilege! The privilege of actually behaving as God behaves! The privilege of demonstrating and showing mercy! Acting as God acts, being merciful as God is merciful will do a great thing for us. It will stir great assurance and confidence within.

And now, dear children, continue in him, so that when he appears we may be confident and unashamed before him at his coming. (1 John 2:28)

4 (6:37-38) **Reward—Justice**: Jesus made a phenomenal promise to the disciple who lives as He said—the promise of reciprocal behavior, of receiving back just what he gave.

1. Personal relationships are involved in reciprocal behavior. Three specific behaviors are covered: judging, condemning, and forgiving others. Jesus was saying two things.

a. If we judge and condemn and are unforgiving of others, then both men and God will treat us the same. We shall be judged, condemned, and unforgiven both on earth and in heaven.

b. If we do not judge and condemn men, but rather forgive them, then God and most men will not judge and condemn us; they will also be forgiving.

2. Property matters are involved in reciprocal behavior. The believer is to give and to possess a spirit of giving and not to be selfish and hoarding. If he gives, he shall receive back much more. In fact, his cup shall be *running over*. God will pour all the good things of this earth into his life.

3. The principle is clear and challenging: a person receives what he gives. This is definitely true of God and usually true of men. What a man puts into life is what he gets out of life.

Is it not to share your food with the hungry and to provide the poor wanderer with shelter— when you see the naked, to clothe him, and not to turn away from your own flesh and blood? Then your light will break forth like the dawn, and your healing will quickly appear; then your righteousness will go before you, and the glory of the LORD will be your rear guard. (Isa 58:7-8)

	K. Jesus Teaches His Rules for Discipleship: The Need to Watch, 6:39-45 (Mt.7:3-5, 17-18; 10:25; 12:35	the speck out of your eye,' when you yourself fail to see the plank in your own eye? You hypocrite, first take the plank out of your eye, and then you will see clearly to remove the speck from your brother's eye.	c. The criticizer is a hypocrite d. Judging oneself enables one to see clearly & to see how to help others
1 Watch blindness: One's leaders & how one leads a. If both are in darkness b. Both stumble & fall	39 He also told them this parable: "Can a blind man lead a blind man? Will they not both fall into a pit?	43 "No good tree bears bad fruit, nor does a bad tree bear good fruit.	**4 Watch the fruit that a man brings forth**
2 Watch the Teacher (Lord) a. The student (disciple) must submit b. He will be like his teacher	40 A student is not above his teacher, but everyone who is fully trained will be like his teacher.	44 Each tree is recognized by its own fruit. People do not pick figs from thornbushes, or grapes from briers.	a. Every tree is known by its fruit b. Every tree reproduces after its nature or kind
3 Watch hypocrisy & criticism of others a. Both have a problem b. The criticizer has the biggest problem	41 "Why do you look at the speck of sawdust in your brother's eye and pay no attention to the plank in your own eye? 42 How can you say to your brother, 'Brother, let me take	45 The good man brings good things out of the good stored up in his heart, and the evil man brings evil things out of the evil stored up in his heart. For out of the overflow of his heart his mouth speaks.	c. Every man reproduces what is in his heart

DIVISION III

THE SON OF MAN'S ANNOUNCED MISSION AND PUBLIC MINISTRY, 4:16-9:17

K. Jesus Teaches His Rules for Discipleship: The Need to Watch, 6:39-45

(6:39-45) **Introduction**: man is to watch how he lives. Both the quality and fate of his life depend upon it.

⇒ God cares about the quality of a man's life. He wants every man to have the fullest life that he possibly can.

⇒ God cares about the destiny of a man, where a man will spend eternity. He wants every man to receive eternal life.

There are four rules, four warnings that must be watched if we are to live life to the fullest and be assured of eternal life.

1. Watch blindness: one's leaders and how one leads (v.39).
2. Watch the Teacher (the Lord Himself) (v.40).
3. Watch hypocrisy and the criticism of others (v.41-42).
4. Watch the fruit that a man brings forth (v.43-45).

1 (6:39) **Spiritual Blindness—Darkness**: the first rule is to watch blindness; watch one's leaders and how one leads. "Can a blind man lead a blind man?" Note several things.

1. Note who the blind are. They are the leaders: the preachers, teachers, parents—anyone who has influence or responsibility for anyone else. In fact, any person can be blind and lead someone else down the same path of blindness. But observe a significant fact. Jesus also says that the blind are those who follow: the pupil, learner, listener, seeker, child—anyone who looks up to someone else for guidance.

2. Note why people are blind. There are several clear reasons.

a. A person can be born blind. He can be handicapped, never having had the opportunity to see the *truth* of things, never having been exposed to the light.

b. A person can be blind because of some injury. He used to be able to see and had every opportunity to see, but now he is blind, blind because…

- he injured himself by some careless act. (He is guilty of blinding himself to the Light.)
- he was blinded by someone else, either deliberately or carelessly. (Others led him astray, led him off into the darkness.)
- he was blinded by nature. (Circumstances, heritage, location kept him from ever having the opportunity to escape the darkness.)

c. A person can be blind because he wants and chooses to be in the dark. The dark is his choice; he finds the dark is enjoyable and comfortable; therefore, he refuses to come out into the light and to see the truth of things.

d. A person can be blind because he closes his eyes or turns his head and looks away. He just refuses to see the light, the truth.

Jesus warned against being blind. He said blindness leads to two tragic results.

1. Both walk in darkness, both the leader and the follower. Being a leader does not guarantee that one walks in the light. A leader can be blind, and if the leader is blind, then the follower will remain blind. The leader must see and have his sight if the follower is to ever see. (Note the awesome responsibility upon leaders.)

2. Both stumble and fall "into a pit." Being a leader does not guarantee that one will not fall. The blind person will stumble and fall no matter who he is, leader or not. And note, a leader will especially stumble about and fall if he is on strange or unfamiliar terrain. The truth of Christ is totally unknown terrain to the blind teacher, no matter his profession.

Anyone who breaks one of the least of these commandments and teaches others to do the same will be called least in the kingdom of heaven, but whoever practices and teaches these commands will be called great in the kingdom of heaven. For I tell you that unless your righteousness surpasses that of the Pharisees and the teachers of the law, you will certainly not enter the kingdom of heaven. (Mat 5:19-20)

They want to be teachers of the law, but they do not know what they are talking about or what they so confidently affirm. (1 Tim 1:7)

If anyone teaches false doctrines and does not agree to the sound instruction of our Lord Jesus Christ and to godly teaching, he is conceited and understands nothing. He has an unhealthy interest in controversies and quarrels about words that result in envy, strife, malicious talk, evil suspicions and constant friction between men of corrupt mind, who have been robbed of the truth and who think that godliness is a means to financial gain. (1 Tim 6:3-5)

For the time will come when men will not put up with sound doctrine. Instead, to suit their own desires, they will gather around them a great number of teachers to say what their itching ears want to hear. They will turn their ears away from the truth and turn aside to myths. (2 Tim 4:3-4)

But there were also false prophets among the people, just as there will be false teachers among you. They will secretly introduce destructive heresies, even denying the sovereign Lord who bought them—bringing swift destruction on themselves. (2 Pet 2:1)

The light shines in the darkness, but the darkness has not understood it. (John 1:5)

This is the verdict: Light has come into the world, but men loved darkness instead of light because their deeds were evil. (John 3:19)

But if your eyes are bad, your whole body will be full of darkness. If then the light within you is darkness, how great is that darkness! (Mat 6:23)

And even if our gospel is veiled, it is veiled to those who are perishing. The god of this age has blinded the minds of unbelievers, so that they cannot see the light of the gospel of the glory of Christ, who is the image of God. (2 Cor 4:3-4)

So I tell you this, and insist on it in the Lord, that you must no longer live as the Gentiles do, in the futility of their thinking. They are darkened in their understanding and separated from the life of God because of the ignorance that is in them due to the hardening of their hearts. (Eph 4:17-18)

2 (6:40) **Self-Denial—Dedication**: the second rule is to watch the life of the Teacher, of the Lord Jesus Christ Himself. "A student is not above his teacher: but...will be like his teacher." Note several points.

1. The words "fully trained" (katertismenos) mean to complete, render fit, mend. It is a common word often used for mending, repairing, or restoring broken things such as nets (Mt.4:21) or men (Gal.6:1).

2. The point is forceful: "a student is not above his teacher" (see note, pt.1—Mt.10:24-25). The point is clear: the disciple is not better than his Lord; therefore, he cannot expect to be treated better, nor can he expect to receive more in this world than his Teacher. The disciple cannot expect to be better by having more honor, praise, recognition, or esteem. He cannot expect to have more comfort, rest, or pleasure. The Lord suffered, humbled, and denied Himself for the sake of the world and its needs. The disciple, as a follower of the Lord, does the same; he denies himself in order to reach the world for his Lord (see note and DEEPER STUDY # 1—Lk. 9:23).

That everyone who believes in him may have eternal life. (John 3:15)

Your attitude should be the same as that of Christ Jesus: Who, being in very nature God, did not consider equality with God something to be grasped, but made himself nothing, taking the very nature of a servant, being made in human likeness. And being found in appearance as a man, he humbled himself and became obedient to death— even death on a cross! (Phil 2:5-8)

Again Jesus said, "Peace be with you! As the Father has sent me, I am sending you." (John 20:21)

But you will receive power when the Holy Spirit comes on you; and you will be my witnesses in Jerusalem, and in all Judea and Samaria, and to the ends of the earth." (Acts 1:8)

3. The goal of the student (disciple) is to "be like his Teacher." The disciple of the Lord seeks to be like his Master: conformed, mended, repaired, restored (perfected) into His very image.

I want to know Christ and the power of his resurrection and the fellowship of sharing in his sufferings, *becoming like him in his death,* (Phil 3:10)

"You are my witnesses," declares the LORD, "and my servant whom I have chosen, so that *you may know and believe me and understand* that I am he." (Isa 43:10)

And we, who with unveiled faces all reflect the Lord's glory, are *being transformed into his likeness* with ever-increasing glory, which comes from the Lord, who is the Spirit. (2 Cor 3:18)

3 (6:41-42) **Criticism—Hypocrisy**: the third rule is to watch hypocrisy and criticism of others. Note a crucial fact: Jesus was speaking to everyone seated before Him. No matter how moral, decent, strong, religious, or free of visible sin, He was speaking to everyone seated in the audience. No one was exempt. Everyone was to watch out for hypocrisy and criticism of others. Why? Because whatever is in a person's eye, even if it is only a speck, is serious. Even a speck causes the eye to water, squint, blink, and close. The speck hinders a person's sight (life, walk), holding him back from full sight and service. Now note four points about the parable.

1. Both persons, the one being criticized and the criticizer, do have a problem. Both have a need to clean the dirt out of their eyes. Neither one is free of dirt. Not a single person serves in perfect obedience and ministry to the Lord. There is at least a speck in everyone's eye.

2. The criticizer has the biggest problem. This is usually overlooked. Criticism of others is a plank. If one has only a speck in his eye, when he begins to criticize others he immediately catches a plank in his own eye. *Criticism is the tree that strikes the eye and blinds one* to his own need, his need for continued confession and repentance. The criticizer becomes blinded to his constant need for the righteousness of Jesus Christ.

But if anyone does not have them, he is nearsighted and blind, and has forgotten that

he has been cleansed from his past sins. (2 Pet 1:9)

3. The criticizer is a hypocrite (see DEEPER STUDY # 2—Mt.23:13). He is but a man who is like all other men, full of ever so many faults and coming ever so short, yet he finds fault with others. He criticizes, grumbles, gripes, condemns, judges, and censors others while he too is guilty of so much in so many other areas. And note: his greatest fault is that he sets himself up as the *Judge*, as the one who has the right to judge men.

4. The disciple must examine himself first. Judging himself first will enable him to *see clearly* just how to help others. Rigid examination is required. Simple honesty and thought say that a man must clean the dirt out of his own eye before he can see clearly enough to help others clean their eyesight.

"Do not judge, or you too will be judged. (Mat 7:1)

Who are you to judge someone else's servant? To his own master he stands or falls. And he will stand, for the Lord is able to make him stand. (Rom 14:4)

Therefore let us stop passing judgment on one another. Instead, make up your mind not to put any stumbling block or obstacle in your brother's way. (Rom 14:13)

Therefore judge nothing before the appointed time; wait till the Lord comes. He will bring to light what is hidden in darkness and will expose the motives of men's hearts. At that time each will receive his praise from God. (1 Cor 4:5)

There is only one Lawgiver and Judge, the one who is able to save and destroy. But you—who are you to judge your neighbor? (James 4:12)

4 (6:43-45) **Fruit-Bearing—Words—Tongue**: watch the fruit that a man brings forth.

1. Every tree is known by its fruit, its nature. A good man is not judged by a bad piece of fruit here and there but by the good fruit he bears. Every tree produces some bad fruit, yet the tree is not cast away. A tree is not rejected unless it *leans toward* bad fruit. When testing and examining men, we must observe not single acts here and there; but the tenor, the lean, the whole behavior of their lives. How important! (See note—Mt.7:17 for detailed discussion.)

2. Every tree reproduces after its nature, after its kind. How can we tell if a man is false? There is one revealing mark: the fruit he gathers. A man is known by the fruit he feeds upon and the fruit he feeds to others (see outlines and notes—Jn.15:1-8). If he feeds himself on thorns and briars and not on grapes and figs, that is one way to tell. If he feeds thorns and briars to others instead of grapes and figs, that is another way to tell.

Thorns and briars are false food, worldliness (see DEEPER STUDY # 3—Mt.13:7, 22). Grapes and figs are true food. There is only one true food for the soul of man: the Lord Jesus Christ and His Word. (See note—Jn.6:1-71; outlines and notes—Jn.6:30-36; 6:41-51. Cp. all outlines and notes 6:1-71; DEEPER STUDY # 4—Jn.17:17; cp. 5:24; 1 Pt.2:2-3.) A man must feed on and feed others the truth of the Lord and His Word. Any other source of food for the human soul is false food: it is thorn and briar (worldliness). If eaten or served to others, it will choke the life out of the soul (Mt.13:7; cp. 1 Jn.2:15-16; 2 Cor.6:17-18; Ro.12:1-2).

3. Every man reproduces what is in his heart. Note that Jesus is dealing with a man's mouth, the *words* a man speaks. A man speaks what is in his heart. His words expose his heart, the kind of man he is. The idea is that words come out of an overflowing heart: "For out of the overflow of his heart his mouth speaks." A man's words expose five things about him.

⇒ A man's words expose his true nature: what he is really like beneath the surface.
⇒ A man's words expose what he is down deep within his heart: his motives, desires, ambitions, or the lack of initiative.
⇒ A man's words expose his true character: good or bad, kind or cruel.
⇒ A man's words expose his mind, what he thinks: pure or impure thoughts, dirty or clean thoughts.
⇒ A man's words expose his spirit, what he believes and pursues: the legitimate or illegitimate, the intelligent or ignorant, the true or false, the beneficial or wasteful.

Likewise every good tree bears good fruit, but a bad tree bears bad fruit. (Mat 7:17)

In the same way, faith by itself, if it is not accompanied by action, is dead. But someone will say, "You have faith; I have deeds." Show me your faith without deeds, and I will show you my faith by what I do. (James 2:17-18)

Live such good lives among the pagans that, though they accuse you of doing wrong, they may see your good deeds and glorify God on the day he visits us. (1 Pet 2:12)

The acts of the sinful nature are obvious: sexual immorality, impurity and debauchery; idolatry and witchcraft; hatred, discord, jealousy, fits of rage, selfish ambition, dissensions, factions and envy; drunkenness, orgies, and the like. I warn you, as I did before, that those who live like this will not inherit the kingdom of God. But the fruit of the Spirit is love, joy, peace, patience, kindness, goodness, faithfulness, gentleness and self-control. Against such things there is no law. (Gal 5:19-23)

	L. Jesus Teaches Two Foundations of Life: Genuine vs. Counterfeit Discipleship, 6:46-49 (Mt.7:24-27)	a house, who dug down deep and laid the foundation on rock. When a flood came, the torrent struck that house but could not shake it, because it was well built.	1) He builds a house 2) He digs deep 3) He lays a rock foundation c. Result: It stands
1 The foundation of discipleship is obedience	46 "Why do you call me, 'Lord, Lord,' and do not do what I say?	49 But the one who hears my words and does not put them into practice is like a man who built a house on the	**3 The false disciple: Lays no foundation** a. He hears, but does not obey b. He is like a builder
2 The true disciple: Lays a foundation a. He comes & hears & does b. He is like a builder	47 I will show you what he is like who comes to me and hears my words and puts them into practice. 48 He is like a man building	ground without a foundation. The moment the torrent struck that house, it collapsed and its destruction was complete."	1) Builds a house 2) Does not dig 3) Lays no foundation c. Result: A great fall

DIVISION III

THE SON OF MAN'S ANNOUNCED MISSION AND PUBLIC MINISTRY, 4:16-9:17

L. Jesus Teaches Two Foundations of Life: Genuine vs. Counterfeit Discipleship, 6:46-49

(6:46-49) **Introduction—Life—Foundation—Profession, False vs. True**: Jesus Christ was a carpenter by trade and profession. He knew houses; He knew the building trade.

Several important matters about building a house need to be noted here.

1. Hearing instructions. This is critical. Knowing how to build is critical.
    a. One must hear and follow (obey) the instructions.
    b. One must hear and build upon what he hears for future building. Builders must always be "They will lay treasure up for themselves as a firm foundation for the coming age" (1 Tim.6:19).
2. Selecting the foundation. This, too, is critical. Selecting the site and material determine the future of the house.
    a. One must build upon a solid foundation. There is only one foundation upon which to build: the rock (1 Cor.3:11).
    b. One must make his call and choice to build sure (2 Pt.1:10).
    c. One must know that building upon rock takes time and skill.
3. Counting the cost. This also is critical. The fact is brought out by Christ in another passage. Beginning and not finishing the house brings mockery and shame (Lk.14:28-30).

Several introductory applications are clearly seen in this picture of house building.

1. Every person has a house, a life to build. How he builds his life determines his destiny, not just for this life, but for eternity. How he builds his life makes all the difference between...
    - success and failure
    - life and death
    - reward and loss
    - acceptance and rejection
    - standing and falling
2. There is only One foundation for every life: Jesus Christ (1 Cor.3:11). He is the Rock upon which both individuals and churches are to build (Mt.16:18).
3. Everyone either builds upon this world or upon Christ, heaven itself. Jesus teaches that there are two kinds of builders.
    a. A wise builder: hears and obeys (v.47-48).
    b. A foolish builder: hears and does not obey (v.49).

1. The foundation of discipleship is obedience (v.46).
2. The true disciple: lays a foundation (v.47-48).
3. The false disciple: lays no foundation (v.49).

1 (6:46) **Profession—Foundation—Life**: the foundation of discipleship is *obedience, doing the things which Jesus says*. There is no substitute. If a person wishes to be a follower of Jesus Christ, that person has to do what Jesus says.

1. Both builders in this passage call Jesus "Lord." Both acknowledge Him as Lord. Both pray and call Him "Lord, Lord," and both witness before others that He is Lord. Both are known as followers of Jesus.
2. Jesus questions disobedience and disloyalty. He rebukes and warns anyone who calls Him Lord and does not do what He says. As Lord He is due allegiance and expects loyalty from all, especially those who call Him Lord.
3. A profession of words is not enough. Even repeating one's profession, "Lord, Lord," is not enough. One can cry before the world and still be questioned and warned by Christ: "Why do you not do what I say?"
4. A person is cheating himself to profess and not obey. Profession without obedience gives a false security; it makes one feel like he is acceptable to God when he is not. Christ says he is not, for the only foundation to discipleship, that is, the only way to be accepted by God, is to do the things which Christ says.

2 (6:47-48) **Foundation—Disciple—Trials**: the true disciple *lays a foundation*. Note three points.

1. The true disciple comes to Christ, hears Christ and does what Christ says. All three steps are essential.
2. The true disciple is like a builder.
    a. The disciple builds a house. Every person has a house to build, a life to build. Once in the world, we cannot escape the fact. We are building our lives, and how we build our lives determines our eternal destiny.

        God's own Son instructs a man how to build. A man hears and follows (obeys) the instructions or hears and rejects (disobeys) the instructions and builds his own way. The instructions, the words of Christ, are the materials which determine the structure and fate of our lives. Our lives and our destiny depend upon how we respond to the sayings of Christ.

b. The disciple digs deep to lay the foundation (footing). This is critical to note. The ground is not soil, it is rock. Great effort and energy are demanded. The most expensive and costly thing to a builder is *hitting rock*, yet rock is by far the best foundation.
   ⇒ This builder chooses the rock for his foundation. He did not just hit it while digging for his footing; he knew the rock was there and chose it as the right foundation for his house. He deliberately chose *the most sure and secure* foundation available.
   ⇒ This builder *dug deep*. He took no chances. He wanted to be absolutely sure and secure, as sure and secure as possible. So he *dug* as deep as possible.
   ⇒ This builder was willing to put both the *time and effort and cost* into digging rock. It was difficult, exhausting, and expensive; yet he did it. Why? Because it was *his house* and he wanted to be absolutely sure and secure.

c. He lays the foundation upon the rock. Christ is the only foundation upon which we can build and structure our lives. "For no one can lay any foundation other than the one already laid, which is Jesus Christ " (1 Cor. 3:11; cp. Eph.2:20; 1 Pt.2:4-5).

Thought 1. The Lord is not a lifeless rock, but "the living Stone" (1 Pt.2:4). When we come to Him as "the living Stone," we are "built into a spiritual house" (1 Pt.2:5).

Like newborn babies, crave pure spiritual milk, so that by it you may grow up in your salvation, now that you have tasted that the Lord is good. As you come to him, the living Stone—rejected by men but chosen by God and precious to him—you also, like living stones, are being built into a spiritual house to be a holy priesthood, offering spiritual sacrifices acceptable to God through Jesus Christ. (1 Pet 2:2-5)

3. The true disciple stands. The house (his life) he built stands against the storms of life and eternity. Now note: he is not exempt from the storms of life. Just because he built upon a rock does not mean storms will not come. In fact, it is because storms do come that he built upon the rock. This man (the true disciple) knows that it rains "on the righteous and on the unrighteous" (Mt.5:45). All kinds of storms will come, the storms of…

- sickness
- sin
- temptation
- suffering
- disappointment
- tension
- death
- accidents
- complaints
- mistreatments
- abuse
- hospitalization

Thought 1. A man must build upon Jesus Christ. There is no other foundation that can withstand the coming storms of trouble, problems, afflictions, evil, and death.

Jesus said to them, "Have you never read in the Scriptures: "'The stone the builders rejected has become the capstone ; the Lord has done this, and it is marvelous in our eyes'? (Mat 21:42)

For no one can lay any foundation other than the one already laid, which is Jesus Christ. (1 Cor 3:11)

Built on the foundation of the apostles and prophets, with Christ Jesus himself as the chief cornerstone. (Eph 2:20)

For in Scripture it says: "See, I lay a stone in Zion, a chosen and precious cornerstone, and the one who trusts in him will never be put to shame." (1 Pet 2:6)

He is "'the stone you builders rejected, which has become the capstone.' (Acts 4:11)

In this way they will lay up treasure for themselves as a firm foundation for the coming age, so that they may take hold of the life that is truly life. (1 Tim 6:19)

Nevertheless, God's solid foundation stands firm, sealed with this inscription: "The Lord knows those who are his," and, "Everyone who confesses the name of the Lord must turn away from wickedness." (2 Tim 2:19)

Thought 2. When the storms come, no man falls if he has built his life upon Christ.

1) God accepts us in Christ; He adopts us as a child of His.

But when the time had fully come, God sent his Son, born of a woman, born under law, to redeem those under law, that we might receive the full rights of sons. Because you are sons, God sent the Spirit of his Son into our hearts, the Spirit who calls out, "Abba, Father." (Gal 4:4-6)

He predestined us to be adopted as his sons through Jesus Christ, in accordance with his pleasure and will—to the praise of his glorious grace, which he has freely given us in the One he loves. (Eph 1:5-6)

2) God promises to provide the necessities of life.

But seek first his kingdom and his righteousness, and all these things will be given to you as well. (Mat 6:33; cp. Mat 6:25-34)

3) God promises to work out all things (all storms) for good to those who build wisely.

And we know that in all things God works for the good of those who love him, who have been called according to his purpose. (Rom 8:28)

4) God blesses those who "hear the word of God, and obey it" (Lk.11:28).
5) Christ promises joy to those who hear and receive the things He said.

I have told you this so that my joy may be in you and that your joy may be complete. (John 15:11; cp. John 13:17)

3 (6:49) **Foundation—Disciple**: the false disciple *lays no foundation*. Note three points.

1. The false disciple hears Christ but *does not do* what Christ says.
   ⇒ He ignores what Christ says.
   ⇒ He applies himself elsewhere.
   ⇒ He is too busy.
   ⇒ He does not think about the consequences.

2. The false disciple is like a builder.
   a. He does build a house, but note a very critical point. He hears the instructions of the Master Builder (through church, parents, radio, book, friends, television). He has been told how to build, and he knows where to build; therefore, he is expected to build according to instructions. In fact, it is shocking if he does not build a solid house (note the question and shock of Christ in v.46).
   b. He does not dig. How foolish! Here is the depth of man's foolishness well illustrated. Why does he not dig?
      ⇒ The rock is too time-consuming and demanding.
      ⇒ He fails to look ahead, to consider the future.
      ⇒ He wants to be doing something else.

   c. He lays no foundation, no footing. What a tragedy! He knew better, but he ignored the Master Builder's instructions. The false disciple heard what the prophets and righteous men of old desired to hear (Mt.13:17; 1 Pt.1:10). What a privilege he had! And how he abused that privilege! Week after week, day after day, year after year he heard; yet, he never followed the instructions on how to build his life.

3. The false disciple *falls*. The house (his life) he built collapses against the storms of life and eternity.
   a. "The torrent struck that house." Floods of trials do come. They cannot be stopped; the house without a foundation cannot stand. Note: "The moment the torrent struck that house, it collapsed and *its destruction was complete*."
   b. Every man's work shall be revealed. Our work is to be tested in this life through many, many trials, and in the next life by Christ. Great will be the fall of a life if it is not built upon Christ. The man who built his house upon sand *has to face* Christ in that day (1 Cor.3:13).

Thought 1. The person who builds upon sand clings to a *false trust*. His faith and trust are in the wrong thing.

Whoever trusts in his riches will fall, but the righteous will thrive like a green leaf. (Prov 11:28)

He who trusts in himself is a fool, but he who walks in wisdom is kept safe. (Prov 28:26)

You have trusted in your wickedness and have said, 'No one sees me.' Your wisdom and knowledge mislead you when you say to yourself, 'I am, and there is none besides me.' (Isa 47:10)

This is what the LORD says: "Cursed is the one who trusts in man, who depends on flesh for his strength and whose heart turns away from the LORD. (Jer 17:5)

Therefore tell those who cover it with whitewash that it is going to fall. Rain will come in torrents, and I will send hailstones hurtling down, and violent winds will burst forth. (Ezek 13:11)

My people come to you, as they usually do, and sit before you to listen to your words, but they do not put them into practice. With their mouths they express devotion, but their hearts are greedy for unjust gain. (Ezek 33:31)

Thought 2. The person who builds upon the sands of this world of sin shall fall.

The righteousness of the blameless makes a straight way for them, but the wicked are brought down by their own wickedness. (Prov 11:5)

Are they ashamed of their loathsome conduct? No, they have no shame at all; they do not even know how to blush. So they will fall among the fallen; they will be brought down when I punish them," says the LORD. (Jer 6:15)

His work will be shown for what it is, because the Day will bring it to light. It will be revealed with fire, and the fire will test the quality of each man's work. If what he has built survives, he will receive his reward. If it is burned up, he will suffer loss; he himself will be saved, but only as one escaping through the flames. (1 Cor 3:13-15)

For you know very well that the day of the Lord will come like a thief in the night. While people are saying, "Peace and safety," destruction will come on them suddenly, as labor pains on a pregnant woman, and they will not escape. (1 Th 5:2-3; cp. 2 Pet 3:4, 9-13)

See how the evildoers lie fallen—thrown down, not able to rise! (Psa 36:12)

Therefore disaster will overtake him in an instant; he will suddenly be destroyed—without remedy. (Prov 6:15)

How shall we escape if we ignore such a great salvation? This salvation, which was first announced by the Lord, was confirmed to us by those who heard him. (Heb 2:3)

CHAPTER 7

M. Jesus Finds Great Faith in a Soldier: Great Faith, What It Is, 7:1-10
(Mt.8:5-13)

When Jesus had finished saying all this in the hearing of the people, he entered Capernaum.
2 There a centurion's servant, whom his master valued highly, was sick and about to die.
3 The centurion heard of Jesus and sent some elders of the Jews to him, asking him to come and heal his servant.
4 When they came to Jesus, they pleaded earnestly with him, "This man deserves to have you do this,
5 Because he loves our nation and has built our synagogue."
6 So Jesus went with them. He was not far from the house when the centurion sent friends to say to him: "Lord, don't trouble yourself, for I do not deserve to have you come under my roof.
7 That is why I did not even consider myself worthy to come to you. But say the word, and my servant will be healed.
8 For I myself am a man under authority, with soldiers under me. I tell this one, 'Go,' and he goes; and that one, 'Come,' and he comes. I say to my servant, 'Do this,' and he does it."
9 When Jesus heard this, he was amazed at him, and turning to the crowd following him, he said, "I tell you, I have not found such great faith even in Israel."
10 Then the men who had been sent returned to the house and found the servant well.

1 Jesus returned to Capernaum

2 Great faith cares deeply for people[DS1]

3 Great faith feels unworthy in approaching Jesus Christ

4 Great faith seeks God in Jesus Christ

5 Great faith is centered
- a. In Jesus as Sovereign Lord
- b. In Jesus' supreme power & Word

6 Great faith stirs the great power of Jesus Christ
- a. Jesus marvelled
- b. Jesus commended the soldier
- c. Jesus healed the servant

DIVISION III

THE SON OF MAN'S ANNOUNCED MISSION AND PUBLIC MINISTRY, 4:16-9:17

M. Jesus Finds Great Faith in a Soldier: Great Faith, What It Is, 7:1-10

(7:1-10) **Introduction**: Jesus Christ meets the need of everyone—Gentile or Jew, rich or poor, leader or follower, ruler or slave. He bridges the gaps, prejudices, and divisions between men. The one essential for securing His help is faith. A person must have faith in Christ and His power. The fact is clearly demonstrated in what happened between this soldier and Jesus. Note that Jesus termed this man's faith "great faith."

1. Jesus returned to Capernaum (v.1).
2. Great faith cares deeply for people (v.2).
3. Great faith feels unworthy in approaching Jesus Christ (v.3).
4. Great faith seeks God (v.4-5).
5. Great faith is centered in Jesus Christ (v.6-8).
6. Great faith stirs the great power of Jesus Christ (v.9-10).

1 (7:1) **Jesus Christ, Headquarters**: Jesus returned to Capernaum. Capernaum was His headquarters where He now lived (see note—Lk.4:31).

2 (7:2) **Care**: great faith cares deeply for people. The soldier was a man who cared deeply for people. Note the words "valued highly" (entimos) meaning esteemed, honored, precious, prized. In the society of that day, a servant or slave was nothing, only a tool or a thing to be used as the owner wished. He had no rights whatsoever, not even the right to live. An owner could mistreat and kill a servant or slave without having to give an account. But this soldier loved his servant or slave. This reveals a deep concern and care for people. It would have been much less bother to dispose of the servant or slave or to ignore him and just let him die, but not this soldier. He cared. Note how he *personally* looked after the servant or slave, a person who meant nothing to the rest of society. But his arms and love were wide open to do all he could to help this person who was helpless. This alone, helping a person who meant nothing to society, was bound to affect Christ dramatically.

> **'Love your neighbor as yourself.' (Mat 22:39)**
> **My command is this: Love each other as I have loved you. (John 15:12)**
> **Love must be sincere. Hate what is evil; cling to what is good. (Rom 12:9)**
> **May the Lord make your love increase and overflow for each other and for everyone else, just as ours does for you. (1 Th 3:12)**
> **If you really keep the royal law found in Scripture, "Love your neighbor as yourself," you are doing right. (James 2:8)**

DEEPER STUDY # 1
(7:2) **Centurion**: see DEEPER STUDY # 1—Acts 23:23.

3 (7:3) **Rejection—Unworthiness**: great faith feels unworthy in approaching Jesus. The soldier was a man who had heard about Jesus and what he had heard made him feel unworthy. Note several things.

1. Luke's account differs from Matthew's. Luke says the centurion sent some religious leaders to approach Jesus, whereas Matthew says that the centurion approached Jesus. What needs to be remembered is that in a dictatorial soci-

ety, whatever a leader commands others to do is counted as his act, as he himself having done it. The leader's representatives act for him; thus, he is said to have done it.

2. The centurion was in a place where he could hear about Jesus. He was where he could hear the message of hope, and when the news came, he did not close his mind or ignore it. He responded.

3. The centurion, however, felt unworthy to approach Jesus himself. Why?

⇒ He was a soldier, trained to take life and probably guilty of having taken life. What he had heard about Christ was the message of love and brotherhood.

⇒ He was a sinner, a terrible sinner, a Roman heathen, *totally unworthy* and rejected in the eyes of most. He felt that Jesus, too, would count him unworthy and reject him.

4. The centurion requested help from others. He asked them to intercede for him. Note: he did not allow his sense of unworthiness and rejection to defeat him; neither was he too proud to ask for help, despite his superior position.

Thought 1. A man must expose himself to the gospel, be where the gospel is preached, and humble himself before the Lord if he wishes the blessings of God.

For by the grace given me I say to every one of you: Do not think of yourself more highly than you ought, but rather think of yourself with sober judgment, in accordance with the measure of faith God has given you. (Rom 12:3)

But he gives us more grace. That is why Scripture says: "God opposes the proud but gives grace to the humble." (James 4:6)

Humble yourselves before the Lord, and he will lift you up. (James 4:10)

The LORD is close to the brokenhearted and saves those who are crushed in spirit. (Psa 34:18)

Though the LORD is on high, he looks upon the lowly, but the proud he knows from afar. (Psa 138:6)

He has showed you, O man, what is good. And what does the LORD require of you? To act justly and to love mercy and to walk humbly with your God. (Micah 6:8)

For this is what the high and lofty One says— he who lives forever, whose name is holy: "I live in a high and holy place, but also with him who is contrite and lowly in spirit, to revive the spirit of the lowly and to revive the heart of the contrite. (Isa 57:15)

4 (7:4-5) **Seeking God—Jew—Gentile—Rejected—Prejudice**: great faith seeks God. The soldier was a man who sought God.

1. He was not a superficial religionist. He had heard about the God of Israel and accepted Him, rejecting the gods of Rome. This he did despite the hostility and rejection of the Jews. He was so drawn to God that he evidently was going to let nothing stop him from discovering the truth.

2. He was a man of faith (v.9), a man who loved God. The very reason he would love the Jewish nation (a people who despised him) and build a synagogue was because of his love for God. His faith and love had to be genuine. It was most unusual for a Gentile, especially a Gentile official, to care for the Jews. Anti-semitism was the common thing. The Jew and Gentile had no dealings with one another. (See notes—Mt.15:26-27; Mk.7:25; DEEPER STUDY # 1—7:27.) Note how far he went to serve God: he loved those who had formerly rejected and despised him, and he did what he could to edify and enhance the worship of God's people by building a synagogue. His love and faith were so strong and evident that those who had despised him now felt close to him—close enough to intercede for him.

And without faith it is impossible to please God, because anyone who comes to him must believe that he exists and that he rewards those who earnestly seek him. (Heb 11:6)

God did this so that men would seek him and perhaps reach out for him and find him, though he is not far from each one of us. (Acts 17:27)

Look to the LORD and his strength; seek his face always. (Psa 105:4)

5 (7:6-8) **Faith**: great faith is centered in Jesus Christ. The centurion was a man of faith. The centurion illustrated perfectly what faith is (Heb.11:6).

1. It is believing that "Christ exists": that He is sovereign Lord (Heb.11:6). All power is subject to Him.

2. It is believing that "[Christ] rewards those who earnestly seek Him" (Heb.11:6). He will use His power in behalf of those who do seek Him.

Note that the centurion had diligently sought Jesus, believing Jesus could meet his need. Many believers earnestly seek the Lord, but the centurion's faith was so much greater than most believers. Why? Because he believed that *the Word of Christ was all that was needed.* Jesus did not have to be present for the need to be met. As a centurion, he had authority over men. All he had to do was issue an order and it was carried out, whether he was present or not. He was a sovereign commander. He was saying, "How much more are you, O' Lord. But speak the word only, and my need shall be met." What a forceful and powerful lesson on faith for all!

Then Jesus came to them and said, "All authority in heaven and on earth has been given to me. (Mat 28:18)

Commit your way to the LORD; trust in him and he will do this: (Psa 37:5)

It is better to take refuge in the LORD than to trust in man. (Psa 118:8)

Trust in the LORD forever, for the LORD, the LORD, is the Rock eternal. (Isa 26:4)

Seek the LORD while he may be found; call on him while he is near. (Isa 55:6)

6 (7:9-10) **Faith—Jesus Christ, Power of**: great faith stirs the great power of Jesus. The centurion was a man who stirred the great power of Jesus.

1. Jesus marvelled. Only twice is Jesus said to have marvelled at people: at the centurion, and at the people in Nazareth because of their unbelief (Mk.6:6). What an impact this man made upon Jesus!

2. Jesus embraced and commended the soldier. He embraced him for his faith, not for who he was or for what he had done as a soldier. *Believing*, that is, true faith, is a rare thing. Not many believe; yet belief in Christ is one of the greatest qualities of human life—a quality ignored, neglected, and in some cases denied.

He commended him before others. There are times when recognition and commendation are to be given, but again, note for what. It is for spiritual graces, for spiritual strength. However, caution should always be exercised lest the temptation of pride and self-importance set in.

3. Jesus healed the servant, and His power to meet the centurion's request proved His Messiahship—that He was truly the Son of God.

> **Thought 1.** Jesus Christ has the power to meet our needs; however, there is one prerequisite: faith. We must believe that Jesus Christ *can* meet our needs.

> **"Have faith in God," Jesus answered. "I tell you the truth, if anyone says to this mountain, 'Go, throw yourself into the sea,' and does not doubt in his heart but believes that what he says will happen, it will be done for him. Therefore I tell you, whatever you ask for in prayer, believe that you have received it, and it will be yours. (Mark 11:22-24)**

> **But I know that even now God will give you whatever you ask." (John 11:22)**

> **Therefore he is able to save completely those who come to God through him, because he always lives to intercede for them. (Heb 7:25)**

Outline	Scripture	Scripture	Outline
	N. Jesus Raises a Widow's Son: Great Compassion & Power, 7:11-17	he said, "Don't cry."	giving assurance
		14 Then he went up and touched the coffin, and those carrying it stood still. He said, "Young man, I say to you, get up!"	**3 The great power of Jesus** a. To bypass traditional beliefs b. To stop the death processional c. To raise the dead
1 Jesus entered Nain—many were present to witness the conquest of death	11 Soon afterward, Jesus went to a town called Nain, and his disciples and a large crowd went along with him.	15 The dead man sat up and began to talk, and Jesus gave him back to his mother.	
2 The great compassion of Jesus: He was touched a. By death, a dead man b. By a broken heart c. By a loving, caring, beloved woman	12 As he approached the town gate, a dead person was being carried out—the only son of his mother, and she was a widow. And a large crowd from the town was with her.	16 They were all filled with awe and praised God. "A great prophet has appeared among us," they said. "God has come to help his people."	**4 The great awe of the people** a. They glorified God b. They believed Him to be a prophet
d. The Lord saw: Had compassion[DS1] & spoke,	13 When the Lord saw her, his heart went out to her and	17 This news about Jesus spread throughout Judea and the surrounding country.	c. They acknowledged God's dealing with them again d. They bore witness

DIVISION III

THE SON OF MAN'S ANNOUNCED MISSION AND PUBLIC MINISTRY, 4:16-9:17

N. Jesus Raises a Widow's Son: Great Compassion and Power, 7:11-17

(7:11-17) **Introduction—Resurrection, The**: the most phenomenal event in all history is the resurrection of the dead. It may be the fact of Jesus Himself being resurrected or the promise of believers' being raised someday, or of Jesus raising the dead—some men just have enormous difficulty believing such claims. Luke knew this, so he wanted to help unbelieving minds. In this event Luke shared the great compassion and power of Jesus to raise the dead.

1. Jesus entered Nain—many were present to witness the conquest of death (v.11).
2. The great compassion of Jesus: He was touched (v.12-13).
3. The great power of Jesus (v.14-15).
4. The great awe of the people (v.16-17).

1 (7:11) **Jesus Christ, Following—Seeking, Reasons**: Jesus entered Nain. This is the only time this city is named in the Bible. It was only about six miles from Nazareth and a day's journey from Capernaum. Note two facts.

1. It is the same area where Elisha raised the son of the Shunammite woman (2 Kings 4:18-37). Therefore, it became an area where the great compassion and power of God had been manifested.

2. Many were present to witness the great conquest of death. There were many of His disciples present, and there were crowds of other people, those who did not believe. The unbelievers were following Him for any number of reasons:

⇒ curiosity
⇒ neighborly fellowship
⇒ a belief in His ethics
⇒ a need for help
⇒ admiration
⇒ a desire for something to do
⇒ being impressed with His teaching
⇒ thinking Him to be a great prophet

2 (7:12-13) **Compassion**: the great compassion of Jesus is seen in that He was touched. Note four points.

1. Jesus was touched by death. Apparently, the sight of death always touched Him. The fact that men die is what brought Him to earth. Probably the whole scene of sin and death flashed across His mind—the scene of...

⇒ man's sin and death (Ro.5:12; 6:23; Heb.9:27).
⇒ the great cost of sin and death, that is, His own death in bearing the sins and death of the world (1 Pt.2:24; 1 Jn.2:1-2).

For this very reason, Christ died and returned to life so that he might be the Lord of both the dead and the living. (Rom 14:9)

2. Jesus was touched by a broken heart, the broken heart of the mother. Note her situation. She was a widow, apparently somewhat up in years with only one child, a grown son. He had just died, and now she was all alone in the world—a world that was harsh and rough on women, offering them little chance for earning a living and little help on a permanent basis. Hereafter, the woman would be without any permanent companion, provider, or protector; and there was no one to carry on the family line. The family name would die out with her death. She was brokenhearted, full of hurt and pain, without understanding and hope. When Jesus saw all this, He was touched and moved with compassion.

3. Jesus was touched by a loving and caring woman, a woman who was much beloved. Note that "A large crowd from the town was with her." This indicates that she had been a woman who *loved and cared* for others throughout the years. Therefore, others loved and cared for her. She was a beloved person. Jesus is always touched and moved to help those who have helped others (Lk.6:38).

Blessed are the merciful, for they will be shown mercy. (Mat 5:7)

Now note a fact: in this particular need, no one asked Jesus for help. He initiated the help Himself, acted purely out of His own compassion. Why did He not always do this? The woman seemed to be the difference. Her life was apparently so filled with love and care for others that she just stood out as a glorious example of what love for God is all about (Mt.22:38-39; Jn.13:34-35; 1 Jn.4:7).

4. The Lord saw and, having compassion, assured the woman. Note three striking facts.

a. It was "the Lord" who saw her. This is the first time Luke uses the title "the Lord" by itself, and it is striking. The point Luke is making is that "the Lord," the Sovereign Power of the universe, saw this woman who was utterly heartbroken. "The Lord" of all power actually saw her.

b. It was "the Lord" who had *compassion* upon her. His heart went out to her. The fact is shocking, for the sovereign power of the universe actually felt compassion for a simple woman. He was not just the sovereign power of a vast universe who was *way off in outer space someplace*, unattached and disinterested in this earth and its inhabitants. Contrariwise, He was vitally interested, interested enough to be looking and seeing; and He was concerned about what He saw, full of compassion for the heartbroken (see note—Lk.7:13).

c. It was "the Lord" who spoke and gave assurance. Again, the fact was shocking, for the sovereign power of the universe actually spoke and gave assurance to a simple woman. Luke is definitely stressing the staggering thought: "the Lord," the sovereign majesty of the universe, *speaks* to men; and *His Word* gives great assurance. The Lord is vitally interested in the affairs of men, even in the plight of a simple woman.

Who shall separate us from the love [compassion] of Christ? Shall trouble or hardship or persecution or famine or nakedness or danger or sword? (Rom 8:35)

For we do not have a high priest who is unable to sympathize with our weaknesses, but we have one who has been tempted in every way, just as we are—yet was without sin. (Heb 4:15)

Cast all your anxiety on him because he cares for you. (1 Pet 5:7)

He remembered that they were but flesh, a passing breeze that does not return. (Psa 78:39)

As a father has compassion on his children, so the LORD has compassion on those who fear him; (Psa 103:13)

But from everlasting to everlasting the Lord's love is with those who fear him, and his righteousness with their children's children— (Psa 103:17)

In all their distress he too was distressed, and the angel of his presence saved them. In his love and mercy he redeemed them; he lifted them up and carried them all the days of old. (Isa 63:9)

Because of the Lord's great love we are not consumed, for his compassions never fail. (Lam 3:22)

DEEPER STUDY # 1

(7:13) **Compassion** (esplagchnisthe): to be moved inwardly, to yearn with tender mercy, affection, pity, empathy, compassion. It is the very seat of a man's affections. It is the deepest movement of emotions possible; being moved within the deepest part of one's being.

3 (7:14-15) **Jesus Christ, Power—Resurrection, The**: the great power of Jesus. Three surprising acts are seen here.

1. The power of Jesus to bypass traditional beliefs. The people of that day believed that a person became polluted by touching a corpse. The person became ceremonially unclean, unacceptable to God. By touching the bier or body, Jesus was showing that He possessed the right and power to override religious laws and beliefs. He was the Sovereign Power even over religious beliefs and over death and life.

2. The power of Jesus to stop the death processional. Note the pallbearers stopped; they "stood still." They obeyed His touch.

Thought 1. Willingness and obedience on the part of the pallbearers and the mother were essential for Jesus to raise the dead son. We, too, must be willing and obedient if we wish to be raised from the dead.

And so, somehow, to attain to the resurrection from the dead. (Phil 3:11; cp. Phil 3:7-11)

3. The power of Jesus to raise the dead. It was the command, the simple yet powerful *Word* of Jesus, that raised the dead.

"I tell you the truth, whoever hears my word and believes him who sent me has eternal life and will not be condemned; he has crossed over from death to life. I tell you the truth, a time is coming and has now come when the dead will hear the voice of the Son of God and those who hear will live. For as the Father has life in himself, so he has granted the Son to have life in himself. And he has given him authority to judge because he is the Son of Man. "Do not be amazed at this, for a time is coming when all who are in their graves will hear his voice and come out—those who have done good will rise to live, and those who have done evil will rise to be condemned. (John 5:24-29)

The reason my Father loves me is that I lay down my life—only to take it up again. No one takes it from me, but I lay it down of my own accord. I have authority to lay it down and authority to take it up again. This command I received from my Father." (John 10:17-18)

Jesus said to her, "I am the resurrection and the life. He who believes in me will live, even though he dies; and whoever lives and believes in me will never die. Do you believe this?" "Yes, Lord," she told him, "I believe that you are the Christ, the Son of God, who was to come into the world." (John 11:25-27)

For he must reign until he has put all his enemies under his feet. The last enemy to be destroyed is death. (1 Cor 15:25-26)

For the Lord himself will come down from heaven, with a loud command, with the voice of the archangel and with the trumpet call of God, and the dead in Christ will rise first. After that, we who are still

alive and are left will be caught up together with them in the clouds to meet the Lord in the air. And so we will be with the Lord forever. Therefore encourage each other with these words. (1 Th 4:16-18)

When I saw him, I fell at his feet as though dead. Then he placed his right hand on me and said: "Do not be afraid. I am the First and the Last. I am the Living One; I was dead, and behold I am alive for ever and ever! And I hold the keys of death and Hades. (Rev 1:17-18)

He will swallow up death forever. The Sovereign LORD will wipe away the tears from all faces; he will remove the disgrace of his people from all the earth. The LORD has spoken. (Isa 25:8)

4 (7:16-17) **Jesus Christ, Response—God, Fear of**: the great awe of the people. The word "awe" (phobos) means a fear of reverence. Seeing the dead man sit up and speak struck the fear of God in their hearts.

1. They glorified God (edoxazon ton theon). The tense is imperfect active, they "praised God" and *continued* to praise God.
2. They believed Jesus to be a *great* prophet.
3. They acknowledged that God was dealing with them. There was a widespread revival going on throughout all Israel. The message of John the Baptist had been heard by multitudes, and Jesus was affecting the lives of scores of people. The people felt that God was now visiting and dealing with Israel once again.
4. They bore witness everywhere.

This is to my Father's glory, that you bear much fruit, showing yourselves to be my disciples. (John 15:8)

Giving thanks to the Father, who has qualified you to share in the inheritance of the saints in the kingdom of light. (Col 1:12)

Through Jesus, therefore, let us continually offer to God a sacrifice of praise—the fruit of lips that confess his name. (Heb 13:15)

But you are a chosen people, a royal priesthood, a holy nation, a people belonging to God, that you may declare the praises of him who called you out of darkness into his wonderful light. (1 Pet 2:9)

You who fear the LORD, praise him! All you descendants of Jacob, honor him! Revere him, all you descendants of Israel! (Psa 22:23)

My tongue will speak of your righteousness and of your praises all day long. (Psa 35:28)

O Lord, open my lips, and my mouth will declare your praise. (Psa 51:15)

Enter his gates with thanksgiving and his courts with praise; give thanks to him and praise his name. (Psa 100:4)

	O. Jesus Answers The Question of John the Baptist: Is Jesus the Messiah? 7:18-28 (Mt.11:1-15)		
1 John, in prison, heard of Jesus' loving works a. John was puzzled: Pictured a stern Messiah b. John sent two disciples to question Jesus' Messiahship	18 John's disciples told him about all these things. Calling two of them, 19 He sent them to the Lord to ask, "Are you the one who was to come, or should we expect someone else?" 20 When the men came to Jesus, they said, "John the Baptist sent us to you to ask, 'Are you the one who was to come, or should we expect someone else?'"	raised, and the good news is preached to the poor. 23 Blessed is the man who does not fall away on account of me." 24 After John's messengers left, Jesus began to speak to the crowd about John: "What did you go out into the desert to see? A reed swayed by the wind? 25 If not, what did you go out to see? A man dressed in fine clothes? No, those who wear expensive clothes and indulge in luxury are in palaces. 26 But what did you go out to see? A prophet? Yes, I tell you, and more than a prophet.	c. He preached the gospel of the Messiah d. He promised both the blessing & judgment of the Messiah **3 The forerunner, John himself, proved Jesus was the Messiah** a. His conviction & staunchness b. His self-denial & discipline c. His prophetic mission
2 The ministry & message of Jesus proved He was the Messiah a. He demonstrated the power & works of the Messiah b. He fulfilled the prophecies of the Messiah[DS1]	21 At that very time Jesus cured many who had diseases, sicknesses and evil spirits, and gave sight to many who were blind. 22 So he replied to the messengers, "Go back and report to John what you have seen and heard: The blind receive sight, the lame walk, those who have leprosy are cured, the deaf hear, the dead are	27 This is the one about whom it is written: "'I will send my messenger ahead of you, who will prepare your way before you.' 28 I tell you, among those born of women there is no one greater than John; yet the one who is least in the kingdom of God is greater than he."	d. His identity as the true forerunner **4 The Kingdom of God proved Jesus was the Messiah**

DIVISION III

THE SON OF MAN'S ANNOUNCED MISSION AND PUBLIC MINISTRY, 4:16-9:17

O. Jesus Answers the Question of John the Baptist: Is Jesus the Messiah? 7:18-28

(7:18-28) **Introduction—Messiah**: some question the Messiahship of Jesus Christ. It may be out of rebellion or in moments of weakness and despair, but the questions arise. John the Baptist had a moment of wondering. What we need to remember is that *honest* questions never disappoint God; only rebellion is judged by Him. God will meet and answer any honest question posed by a hurting or needful person. This passage gives Jesus' answer to John's question; this is the final proof of Jesus' Messiahship.

1. John, in prison, heard of Jesus' loving works (v.18-20).
2. The ministry and message of Jesus proved He was the Messiah (v.21-23).
3. The forerunner, John himself, proved Jesus was the Messiah (v.24-27).
4. The Kingdom of God proved Jesus was the Messiah (v.28).

1 (7:18-20) **Messiah, Misconceptions of—John the Baptist**: John was in prison (cp. Lk.3:19-20; 9:9). His disciples brought him word about Jesus' loving works. Apparently his disciples were allowed to visit him. He was anxious to hear about Jesus and the Messianic movement, so they related the wonderful miracles and teachings of Jesus. However, their report included nothing about eliminating the injustices of men nor freeing men from the tyranny and rule of others; nothing about fulfilling the hope of men for the great Messiah who was to take over the world and rule in righteousness, executing judgment upon all men and nations. In fact, the very opposite seemed to be taking place; for when the people were aroused to exalt Jesus as their King, He withdrew and discouraged their actions (Lk.5:16).

What John heard puzzled him, for Jesus seemed to be fulfilling only half of the prophecies concerning the Messiah, the half dealing with ministry. The prophecies dealing with righteousness and judgment were not being fulfilled (see notes—Mt.11:1-6; 11:2-3).

John needed assurance, so he sent two disciples to question Jesus' Messiahship: "Are you the one who was to come, or should we expect someone else?"

2 (7:21-23) **Messiah—Messiahship—Jesus Christ, Deity**: the ministry and message of Jesus proved He was the Messiah. Jesus gave four assurances to John, assurances that proved His Messiahship beyond question.

1. Jesus demonstrated the power and works of the Messiah (v.21). Note what happened when John's disciples approached Jesus and told Him that John needed assurance. Jesus turned and gave the two disciples an example of what His ministry was. They had only heard about His ministry; now they were to see for themselves. He cured many and gave sight to many. Apparently, He ministered for about an hour (v.21).

The point was this. Jesus was telling John not only to hear what He claimed (the claims of Messiahship) but also to look at what He was doing and judge Him by what He did for people. He did not just profess to be the Messiah, He was proving it. He was proving it by ministering to people in *the power of God*. In particular, He demonstrated two glorious truths.

a. He demonstrated that God truly exists and that He is sovereign. He is above and beyond nature, and He has the power to override the laws of nature by miraculously healing the sick.

b. He demonstrated that God loves and cares for man and has planned a way for man to be saved and delivered forever.

2. Jesus fulfilled the prophecies of the Messiah. After ministering to the people, Jesus turned to the two disciples of John and told them to go tell John what they had *seen* and *heard*. Note two things.

a. John was questioning Jesus' Messiahship. The reports he had heard said nothing about Jesus' mobilizing the people into a great army. Jesus was not plotting the strategy to free Israel from Roman domination and to set up the Kingdom of God. John had heard nothing about the Day of the Lord, about the Messianic fire of judgment, about cities' falling and sinners' being judged. And his time was running out. He would be tried and executed soon. The answer Jesus sent back to John was a totally new concept of Messiahship. It is God's idea of Messiahship, radically different from man's idea. It was a demonstration and proclamation of salvation, of God's care and love for persons. (See notes—Lk.3:24-31; DEEPER STUDY # 3—Jn.1:45 for discussion. Also see notes—Mt.1:1; DEEPER STUDY # 2—1:18; DEEPER STUDY # 3—3:11; notes—11:1-6; 11:2-3; DEEPER STUDY # 1—11:5; DEEPER STUDY # 2—11:6; DEEPER STUDY # 1—12:16; note—22:42.)

b. Jesus was saying that His power and concern (love) were the power and concern *predicted* for the Messiah, and both were unlimited (see DEEPER STUDY # 1—Lk.7:22. See note, pt.2—Mt.11:4-6 for detailed discussion.)

3. Jesus preached the gospel of the Messiah. The "poor" represented those who were "poor in spirit," those who had need and acknowledged their need. God's heart and compassion reached out to any who came and brought their need to Him. It was these, the poor in spirit, to whom He preached the good news. (See note, pt.4—Mt.11:4-6 for more discussion.)

4. Jesus promised both the blessing and judgment of the Messiah (see DEEPER STUDY # 2—Mt.11:6). Note the two facets of what Jesus promised—the two areas of work predicted about the Messiah.

a. The area of blessing, of the Spirit, of salvation, of God's care and love for people. This is the area Christ covered here. Today is the day of blessing.

> **Jesus replied, "Go back and report to John what you hear and see: The blind receive sight, the lame walk, those who have leprosy are cured, the deaf hear, the dead are raised, and the good news is preached to the poor. (Mat 11:4-5)**
>
> **"For God so loved the world that he gave his one and only Son, that whoever believes in him shall not perish but have eternal life. For God did not send his Son into the world to condemn the world, but to save the world through him. (John 3:16-17)**
>
> **"As for the person who hears my words but does not keep them, I do not judge him. For I did not come to judge the world, but to save it. (John 12:47)**
>
> **The grace of our Lord was poured out on me abundantly, along with the faith and love that are in Christ Jesus. Here is a trustworthy saying that deserves full acceptance: Christ Jesus came into the world to save sinners—of whom I am the worst. (1 Tim 1:14-15)**

b. The area of fire, of wrath, of judgment. The Messiah is to fulfill the judgment of God when He returns (see DEEPER STUDY # 2—Mt.1:18; DEEPER STUDY # 3—3:11; notes—11:1-6; 11:2-3; DEEPER STUDY # 2—11:6; DEEPER STUDY # 1—12:16; note—22:42 for discussion).

DEEPER STUDY # 1

(7:22) **Messiah, False Concepts**: Jesus was referring to Scripture in this verse. He was telling John that His actions were prophesied by the prophets (Is.35:5-6; 61:1-2; cp. Ps.72:2; 146:8; Zech.11:11). Note, however, that Jesus stressed the personal ministry and not the political. He omitted the phrases of Is.61:1 that could be interpreted that He was to be a political leader: "to proclaim freedom for the captives and release from darkness for the prisoners." He needed to get John's attention away from the wrong concept of the Messiah. He was reaching out in the power of the Spirit to individuals, saving and restoring them, not reaching out to mobilize people for the deliverance of Israel from the Roman enslavement.

3 (7:24-27) **Messiah—John the Baptist**: the forerunner, John himself, proved Jesus was the Messiah (see outline and notes—Mt.11:7-15 for detailed discussion). As soon as John's disciples were gone, Jesus turned His attention to the crowd. This was necessary, for the people had heard all that had happened. Some thought John had wavered in his faith. If the people were allowed to think this, they would soon question if John were really the prophet who was to pave the way for the Messiah. Then following upon the heels of this question would be the questioning of Jesus' being the true Messiah. If this kind of talk and questioning got started, it would affect not only the crowd, but those who had already believed. It would be devastating to the Lord's mission. Note something in all this: how fickle people really are and how easily people forget a prophet's real calling and strength and pick up the news of his weak moment.

What Jesus did was reprimand the crowd. He vindicated John and his mission. He reminded the forgetful and fickle that John was the forerunner, and He claimed that He was the true Messiah.

1. John was a man of conviction and staunchness. He was not like a reed shaken by the wind.

⇒ John's conviction that he was the forerunner proves Jesus is the Messiah.

⇒ John's conviction that the Messiah was coming proves Jesus is the Messiah.

⇒ John's conviction that He (Jesus) was the Lamb of God proves Jesus is the Messiah.

⇒ John's staunchness in standing up to the religionists proves Jesus is the Messiah.

⇒ John's staunchness in standing up to Herod proves Jesus is the Messiah.

> **Test everything. Hold on to the good. (1 Th 5:21)**
>
> **Therefore, my dear brothers, stand**

firm. Let nothing move you. Always give yourselves fully to the work of the Lord, because you know that your labor in the Lord is not in vain. (1 Cor 15:58)

Let us hold unswervingly to the hope we profess, for he who promised is faithful. (Heb 10:23)

2. John was a man of self-denial and sacrifice. He was not a man clothed in soft, extravagant, fashionable clothing. He denied himself and sacrificed the things of the world in order to carry out the work of God.

In the same way, any of you who does not give up everything he has cannot be my disciple. (Luke 14:33)

What is more, I consider everything a loss compared to the surpassing greatness of knowing Christ Jesus my Lord, for whose sake I have lost all things. I consider them rubbish, that I may gain Christ (Phil 3:8)

3. John was a prophet, a man sent on a prophetic mission. He proclaimed the Word of God, and his proclamation could not be denied. But John was more than a prophet.

a. He was the subject of prophecy as well as the messenger of it.
b. He was the herald who brought the message to the world that *the Lord had come*. In this John excelled over all other prophets. They only *foresaw* the Messiah's coming, but John *saw* Him come.

4. John was the true forerunner. Note two critical points.

a. Jesus was saying that John was definitely the forerunner of the Messiah, the messenger predicted by the Scripture.
b. Jesus was *claiming* to be the Messiah before whom John ran and prepared the way.

A voice of one calling: "In the desert prepare the way for the LORD ; make straight in the wilderness a highway for our God. (Isa 40:3)

"See, I will send my messenger, who will prepare the way before me. Then suddenly the Lord you are seeking will come to his temple; the messenger of the covenant, whom you desire, will come," says the LORD Almighty. (Mal 3:1)

In those days John the Baptist came, preaching in the Desert of Judea and saying, "Repent, for the kingdom of heaven is near." This is he who was spoken of through the prophet Isaiah: "A voice of one calling in the desert, 'Prepare the way for the Lord, make straight paths for him.'" (Mat 3:1-3)

And he will go on before the Lord, in the spirit and power of Elijah, to turn the hearts of the fathers to their children and the disobedient to the wisdom of the righteous—to make ready a people prepared for the Lord." (Luke 1:17)

And you, my child, will be called a prophet of the Most High; for you will go on before the Lord to prepare the way for him, (Luke 1:76)

4 (7:28) **Kingdom of God**: the Kingdom of God proved Jesus was the Messiah. Jesus' invasion into human history divided time and the ages. The period of history before Jesus came into the world is known as the age of promise. But since Jesus' coming, men are living in the time and age of God's kingdom. John lived in the age of promise, whereas the followers of Jesus live in the Kingdom of God. Therefore, the least in the Kingdom is greater than the greatest of prophets who lived in the age of promise. *Jesus Christ is the reason*: knowing Him personally makes all the difference in the privileges of a person. The citizen of God's kingdom knows the presence of Christ within his body in the Person of the Holy Spirit, and he knows the *active* rule and reign of God in life (1 Cor.6:19-20; cp. Jn.14:16-18, 20, 23). However, those who lived in the age of promise only had the hope of the promise (Ro.8:16-17; Gal.4:4-6). (See note—Mt.11:11 for more discussion.)

Though you have not seen him, you love him; and even though you do not see him now, you believe in him and are filled with an inexpressible and glorious joy, for you are receiving the goal of your faith, the salvation of your souls. Concerning this salvation, the prophets, who spoke of the grace that was to come to you, searched intently and with the greatest care, trying to find out the time and circumstances to which the Spirit of Christ in them was pointing when he predicted the sufferings of Christ and the glories that would follow. It was revealed to them that they were not serving themselves but you, when they spoke of the things that have now been told you by those who have preached the gospel to you by the Holy Spirit sent from heaven. Even angels long to look into these things. (1 Pet 1:8-12; cp. v.13-16)

Praise be to the God and Father of our Lord Jesus Christ! In his great mercy he has given us new birth into a living hope through the resurrection of Jesus Christ from the dead, and into an inheritance that can never perish, spoil or fade—kept in heaven for you, (1 Pet 1:3-4)

Grace and peace be yours in abundance through the knowledge of God and of Jesus our Lord. His divine power has given us everything we need for life and godliness through our knowledge of him who called us by his own glory and goodness. Through these he has given us his very great and precious promises, so that through them you may participate in the divine nature and escape the corruption in the world caused by evil desires. (2 Pet 1:2-4)

	P. Jesus Reveals God's Verdict Upon this Generation & Age, 7:29-35 (Mt.11:16-27)	generation? What are they like?	
		32 They are like children sitting in the marketplace and calling out to each other: "'We played the flute for you, and you did not dance; we sang a dirge, and you did not cry.'	**2 An age of childishness**
1 Reactions to John a. The people & tax collectors who were baptized: Vindicated John	29 (All the people, even the tax collectors, when they heard Jesus' words, acknowledged that God's way was right, because they had been baptized by John.	33 For John the Baptist came neither eating bread nor drinking wine, and you say, 'He has a demon.'	**3 An age of escapism: Seeking to escape responsibility**
b. The religionists who were not baptized: Rejected God's purpose	30 But the Pharisees and experts in the law rejected God's purpose for themselves, because they had not been baptized by John.)	34 The Son of Man came eating and drinking, and you say, 'Here is a glutton and a drunkard, a friend of tax collectors and "sinners."'	a. Accused John of conservatism: Too denying b. Accused Jesus of license: Too loose
c. Jesus warned His generation & age	31 "To what, then, can I compare the people of this	35 But wisdom is proved right by all her children."	**4 An age with only a few wise toward God**

DIVISION III

THE SON OF MAN'S ANNOUNCED MISSION AND PUBLIC MINISTRY, 4:16-9:17

P. Jesus Reveals God's Verdict Upon This Generation and Age, 7:29-35

(7:29-35) **Introduction**: Jesus gave the verdict upon His generation. In so doing He gave a glimpse of God's verdict upon every generation of men. (See outline and notes—Mt.11:16-27 for more discussion.)

1. Reactions to John (v.29-31).
2. A generation and age of childishness (v.32).
3. A generation and age of escapism (v.33-34).
4. A generation and age with only a few wise toward God (v.35).

1 (7:29-31) **John the Baptist—Religionists**: the reaction of the people to John was twofold. The common people and tax collectors accepted John and his ministry, but the religionists rejected him. Note several things.

1. The tax collectors were set apart from the people themselves. This was because they were so despised and ostracized. They were actually treated in a class all by themselves, a class of betrayers (usually wealthy) who had forsaken the common people. The tax collectors, of course, felt the sting of rejection; and in some cases sensed their sin and the need for repentance. These responded to John.

2. It was the people who heard Him "Jesus" who repented:

⇒ the people who wanted forgiveness of sin, sensing the need for repentance.
⇒ the people who believed his message that the Messiah was coming.

3. The people who repented "acknowledged that God's way was right." By repenting and being baptized, they vindicated John's ministry. They proclaimed that God is just and righteous and that they owed their lives to Him. They accepted God, repenting and changing their lives. Their repentance proved that both God and John were just and true.

4. The religionists (Pharisees and lawyers) rejected the counsel of God. The evidence was clearly seen in what they failed to do: they did not repent and were not baptized by John. Being the religious leaders, they were the very ones who should have responded, but they did not. And what a surprise! The Pharisees were the practitioners of religion, a whole sect of men who had given their lives to live out the law—even to the most minute detail (see DEEPER STUDY # 3—Acts 23:8). The lawyers (Scribes) were those who gave their lives to study and learn the law to the fullest extent possible (see DEEPER STUDY # 1—Lk.6:2; DEEPER STUDY # 1—Mt.22:35).

5. Jesus warned His generation. It was a religious generation...

- that should have known and been prepared for the prophet of God and his message.
- that had God's Word, yet ignored it.
- that had the worship of God and the ordinances of God, yet neglected them.
- to whom God sent His prophet, yet they rejected him.
- to whom God sent His Son, yet they rejected Him.
- that was smug in its own adequacy and sufficiency.

2 (7:32) **World—Generation—Perverse**: a generation of childishness. Note three things.

1. When looking at His own generation, Jesus asked: "To what, then, can I compare the people of this generation?" The most adequate illustration which came to His mind was that of children (see note—Mt.11:16-19). He was saying that His own generation was a *childish generation*. By childish He meant *perverse*. His generation was perverse. They turned away from that which was right and good to that which was corruptible; they acted contrary to the evidence; they were opposed to that which was right, reasonable, and acceptable; and they were obstinate in their opposition. They were mindless and contrary. They did not want the truth, so they made excuses for not receiving the truth.

2. The illustration Jesus used is clearly understood. Children are playing in the market place. A few begin to play wedding music on their pipes and cry out to others, "Let's play wedding." The others shout back, "No. We don't want to dance around today." So the first group, still wanting to play, begins to play funeral music and shout back, "Well, let's play funeral." "No. We don't want to play funeral either. We don't feel like acting sad."

3. Every generation is alike in that it has its privileges. The privileges are used by some and ignored and abused by others. Since the coming of Christ, God's very own Son, the greatest privilege in all the world has been the privilege of knowing Him personally and of being brought into a right relationship with God. As with all privileges, some have come to know Him personally, but the vast majority have ignored and abused Him.

> **"My people are fools; they do not know me. They are senseless children; they have no understanding. They are skilled in doing evil; they know not how to do good." (Jer 4:22)**
>
> **Then we will no longer be infants, tossed back and forth by the waves, and blown here and there by every wind of teaching and by the cunning and craftiness of men in their deceitful scheming. (Eph 4:14)**
>
> **Brothers, I could not address you as spiritual but as worldly—mere infants in Christ. I gave you milk, not solid food, for you were not yet ready for it. Indeed, you are still not ready. (1 Cor 3:1-2)**
>
> **When I was a child, I talked like a child, I thought like a child, I reasoned like a child. When I became a man, I put childish ways behind me. (1 Cor 13:11)**
>
> **In fact, though by this time you ought to be teachers, you need someone to teach you the elementary truths of God's word all over again. You need milk, not solid food! (Heb 5:12)**

3 (7:33-34) **Escapism—License vs. Liberty**: a generation of escapism, of always seeking an excuse to escape *personal* responsibility. The generation was contrary, mindless, playful; they were faultfinders who could not be pleased. The people found fault with whatever was suggested. They just could not accept anything that put restrictions upon their loose play. They found fault with a separatist approach to the gospel, and they also find fault with a sociable approach to the gospel.

1. They accused John of being too conservative and too self-denying. John came neither eating nor drinking; he was a separatist. He was from the desert; and he lived a strict, austere, highly disciplined life. He did not associate with people; he did not make friends. He just isolated himself, cut himself off from everyone and withdrew from society. His message was a gospel of repentance and of separation from the things of the world. Therefore, he was accused of having a "demon," of being mad and insane for choosing to live that way.

2. They accused Jesus of license, of being too loose. Jesus was the very opposite of John. He lived and preached a gospel of liberty, eating and drinking with people. He was with them in their social moments; and He moved among all sorts of people—mixing, being friendly and open and accessible to all, no matter how terrible they were thought to be. Therefore, He was accused of being a sinner Himself: a glutton, a winebibber, and an immoral friend of sinners.

God clearly used both approaches to righteousness (cp. 1 Cor.12:6-7). Jesus did not condemn John's approach, and John did not condemn Jesus' approach. They supported each other, but the majority of people rejected any attempt to restrict their *own play*. They wished to continue doing their own thing: seeking pleasure, intellectual pursuit, secular interest, religious commitment. Most were willing to go only so far in restricting their own desires, wills, and way. Few were willing to deny self completely (see note and DEEPER STUDY # 1—Lk.9:23).

> **So I told you, but you would not listen. You rebelled against the Lord's command and in your arrogance you marched up into the hill country. (Deu 1:43)**
>
> **A man who remains stiff-necked after many rebukes will suddenly be destroyed—without remedy. (Prov 29:1)**
>
> **This is what the Sovereign LORD, the Holy One of Israel, says: "In repentance and rest is your salvation, in quietness and trust is your strength, but you would have none of it. (Isa 30:15)**
>
> **But these men blaspheme in matters they do not understand. They are like brute beasts, creatures of instinct, born only to be caught and destroyed, and like beasts they too will perish. They will be paid back with harm for the harm they have done. Their idea of pleasure is to carouse in broad daylight. They are blots and blemishes, reveling in their pleasures while they feast with you. With eyes full of adultery, they never stop sinning; they seduce the unstable; they are experts in greed—an accursed brood! They have left the straight way and wandered off to follow the way of Balaam son of Beor, who loved the wages of wickedness. (2 Pet 2:12-15)**
>
> **But encourage one another daily, as long as it is called Today, so that none of you may be hardened by sin's deceitfulness. (Heb 3:13)**

4 (7:35) **Wise, The—Liberty vs. Ascetic**: a generation with only a few wise toward God. Note what Jesus said: "But wisdom is proved right by all her children."

1. Wisdom does have children, wise children.

2. Wise children will justify (declare wisdom) what is wise and right.

3. Therefore, the wise will declare that both John and Jesus were right. The way they lived and preached, the ascetic vs. the social, are both right. They were both of God, one the forerunner and the other the Messiah, the Son of God. (See note, pt.2—Mt.11:16-19 and DEEPER STUDY # 1—Mt.11:19 for a different understanding of this verse.)

4. The wise (children of wisdom) are the non-critical, the saved who know that God sent both John the ascetic and Jesus the Messiah. Very simply, the wise are the few who accept the ministry of both John and Jesus, both of whom fulfilled the *prophetic Word of God.*

> **It is because of him [God] that you are in Christ Jesus, who has become for us wisdom from God—that is, our righteousness, holiness and redemption. (1 Cor 1:30; cp. 1 Cor 1:24)**
>
> **In whom [Christ] are hidden all the treasures of wisdom and knowledge. (Col 2:3; cp. Is 11:2)**
>
> **And he said to man, 'The fear of the Lord—that is wisdom, and to shun evil is understanding.'" (Job 28:28; cp. Hos 14:9)**

	Q. Jesus Contrasts the Attitudes of the Repentant & Self-Righteous, 7:36-50	42 Neither of them had the money to pay him back, so he canceled the debts of both. Now which of them will love him more?"	b. A free forgiveness of both debtors c. A piercing question: Who appreciated & loved the most?
1 Simon, a Pharisee, invited Jesus to dinner & Jesus accepted	36 Now one of the Pharisees invited Jesus to have dinner with him, so he went to the Pharisee's house and reclined at the table.	43 Simon replied, "I suppose the one who had the bigger debt canceled." "You have judged correctly," Jesus said.	d. A begrudging answer
2 The attitude of the repentant: A woman prostitute a. She sensed a desperate need	37 When a woman who had lived a sinful life in that town learned that Jesus was eating at the Pharisee's house, she brought an alabaster jar of perfume,	44 Then he turned toward the woman and said to Simon, "Do you see this woman? I came into your house. You did not give me any water for my feet, but she wet my feet with her tears and wiped them with her hair.	**5 The need of the self-righteous: To really see Jesus, who the repentant say He is** a. He is the One who deserves more than common courtesies 1) Common vs. worshipful respect
b. She approached the Lord despite all c. She surrendered to the Lord in utter humility d. She loved much, giving her most precious possession	38 And as she stood behind him at his feet weeping, she began to wet his feet with her tears. Then she wiped them with her hair, kissed them and poured perfume on them.	45 You did not give me a kiss, but this woman, from the time I entered, has not stopped kissing my feet. 46 You did not put oil on my head, but she has poured perfume on my feet.	2) Common vs. humble greeting 3) Common vs. sacrificial gift
3 The attitude of the self-righteous a. He was a considerate man, but self-righteous b. He considered himself better than others c. He sensed no need for forgiveness	39 When the Pharisee who had invited him saw this, he said to himself, "If this man were a prophet, he would know who is touching him and what kind of woman she is—that she is a sinner."	47 Therefore, I tell you, her many sins have been forgiven—for she loved much. But he who has been forgiven little loves little." 48 Then Jesus said to her, "Your sins are forgiven."	b. He is the One who has the power to forgive sins
4 The two attitudes illustrated: The parable of two debtors	40 Jesus answered him, "Simon, I have something to tell you." "Tell me, teacher," he said.	49 The other guests began to say among themselves, "Who is this who even forgives sins?"	c. He is the One whom people need to ask about
a. One debtor owed much; the other little	41 "Two men owed money to a certain moneylender. One owed him five hundred denarii, and the other fifty.	50 Jesus said to the woman, "Your faith has saved you; go in peace."	d. He is the One who saves the repentant

DIVISION III

THE SON OF MAN'S ANNOUNCED MISSION AND PUBLIC MINISTRY, 4:16-9:17

Q. Jesus Contrasts the Attitudes of the Repentant and Self-Righteous, 7:36-50

(7:36-50) **Introduction**: the present passage contrasts the attitudes of the sinful (repentant) and the self-righteous. It needs to be studied carefully, for self-righteousness is a serious sin. It is both common and damning.

1. Simon, a Pharisee, invited Jesus to dinner and Jesus accepted (v.36).
2. The attitude of the repentant: a woman prostitute (v.37-38).
3. The attitude of the self-righteous (v.39).
4. The two attitudes illustrated: the parable of two debtors (v.40-43).
5. The need of the self-righteous: to really see Jesus, who the repentant say He is (v.44-50).

1 (7:36) **Jesus Christ, Seeking Man**: Simon, a Pharisee, invited Jesus to dinner. Note several things.

1. Simon invited Jesus to his house, but he did not extend to Jesus the common courtesies (v.44-46). He was rude to the Lord. He was not even sure Jesus was a prophet, much less the Messiah (v.39). Why then did he invite Jesus to his house? We do not know; nothing is said as to why. The best speculation is that Simon enjoyed the company of celebrities, and he had heard so much about Jesus that he wanted to meet and talk with Him on an informal and friendly basis.

2. Jesus ate with both sinners and religionists (Pharisees) (Lk.5:29-30). No one was excluded from His attention or love, even when they lacked the common everyday courtesies and respect (v.44-46). He sought every man.

3. The house of Simon was a house of the rich. The rich always had an open courtyard, usually in the center of the house. Sometimes the host would allow the public to stand around in the courtyard and listen to the discussions, in particular when a rabbi or some celebrity was the chief guest.

2 (7:37-38) **Repentance—Salvation—Humility—Jesus Christ, Seeking**: the attitude of the repentant. The woman was a sinner, a prostitute. She demonstrated what a sinner has to do in coming to Jesus.

1. She sensed a desperate need. She was either convicted of her sin while hearing Jesus or else she had heard Him before and came under heavy conviction. His plea for

men and women to repent and prepare for the Kingdom of God pierced her heart. She knew she was a sinner: unclean, lost, condemned. The guilt and weight of her sin was more than she could bear. She ached for forgiveness and cleansing, for freedom and liberty.

2. She approached the Lord despite all. She knew that the public scorned and gossiped about her, and the so-called decent people wanted nothing to do with her. What would Jesus do—He who said, "Come to me all you who are weary and burdened and I will give you rest...." (Mt.11:28-30)? She knew that if she were recognized, the Pharisee might throw her out of the house. He knew about her (v.39). She thought about the situation, and her thinking turned into hope, and her hope into belief. Surely He who offered such an invitation would receive her. Before anyone could stop her, she rushed to Jesus and stood behind Him at His feet. (Remember, in the East people reclined to eat. They rested on their left arm facing each other around the table with their body and feet extending out away from the table.)

3. She surrendered to the Lord in utter humility. Standing there, she was overcome with conviction and emotion. She fell at Jesus' feet weeping—so broken that tears just flowed from her eyes. She unwound her hair and wiped and kissed Jesus' feet. Seldom has such love and devotion been shown Jesus.

Now note: there was only one thing that could make a prostitute enter a Pharisee's home—desperation. She was gripped with a sense of lostness, of helplessness, of urgency. The loosening of her hair to wipe Jesus' feet was forbidden of women in public. She must have been so desperate she was totally oblivious to the onlookers. The point is this: she was surrendering her heart and life to the Lord, begging Him to forgive her. She was so broken she was unable to speak, but Jesus knew her heart. Words were not necessary (v.47-48).

4. She loved much, giving her most precious possession. Perfume was highly valued by women of that day (see note—Mt.26:8-9). Apparently, by describing the perfume as he does, Luke is stressing the expense of the perfume and the great sacrifice she was making. It was probably the most costly possession she had, so she was giving it to her Lord. However, there is something more important here. Note what she did with the perfume. She anointed her Lord; anointed His feet in a supreme act of humility and love and surrender (see note—Lk.7:44-50).

Thought 1. The person who comes to Christ must come with a broken and contrite heart.

> **"Come to me, all you who are weary and burdened, and I will give you rest. (Mat 11:28)**
>
> **For we do not have a high priest who is unable to sympathize with our weaknesses, but we have one who has been tempted in every way, just as we are—yet was without sin. Let us then approach the throne of grace with confidence, so that we may receive mercy and find grace to help us in our time of need. (Heb 4:15-16)**
>
> **The LORD is close to the brokenhearted and saves those who are crushed in spirit. (Psa 34:18)**
>
> **For this is what the high and lofty One says— he who lives forever, whose name is holy: "I live in a high and holy place, but also with him who is contrite and lowly in spirit, to revive the spirit of the lowly and to revive the heart of the contrite. (Isa 57:15)**
>
> **Has not my hand made all these things, and so they came into being?" declares the LORD. "This is the one I esteem: he who is humble and contrite in spirit, and trembles at my word. (Isa 66:2)**

3 (7:39) **Self-righteousness**: the attitude of the self-righteous. The behavior of the self-righteous man revealed several things.

1. The man was considerate, but self-righteous. Note, he only thought these things; he would not say them publicly lest he embarrass his guests. (How like the self-righteous!)

2. The man considered himself better. He felt he was better than the sinful woman, so he would never allow her to touch him. He would keep his distance, ignore, and have nothing to do with her. But note something else. He considered his judgment and knowledge, opinions and behavior to be better than others. He expected others (Jesus) to judge and act as he did. He thought that if Jesus only knew who the lady was, then He would reject her.

Thought 1. Many do live self-righteously. They feel that they live and act better than others. They feel and act superior because they have a...

- a better house
- a better profession
- a better education
- a better religion
- a better child
- a better heritage
- a better income
- a better discipline
- a better position
- more ability
- more success
- more recognition
- a better job
- better skills
- a better life

3. The man sensed no need for forgiveness and repentance. He thought of himself as *good enough* in two areas.

a. He was *good enough in religion.* Note he was a Pharisee, a man who had given his life to practice religion. If anyone were ever *good enough*, he should have been (see DEEPER STUDY # 3—Acts 23:8).

b. He was *good enough* in behavior. He was well behaved, decent and moral, just and equitable, respected and highly esteemed. He was not immoral; in fact, he would have nothing to do with immorality. He had not and never would commit a sin that would be publicly condemned. Therefore, he felt as though he had done nothing for which he needed forgiveness.

> **"Not everyone who says to me, 'Lord, Lord,' will enter the kingdom of heaven, but only he who does the will of my Father who is in heaven. (Mat 7:21)**
>
> **He replied, "Isaiah was right when he prophesied about you hypocrites; as it is written: "'These people honor me with their lips, but their hearts are far from me. (Mark 7:6)**
>
> **We do not dare to classify or compare ourselves with some who commend themselves. When they measure themselves by themselves and compare themselves with themselves, they are not wise. (2 Cor 10:12)**
>
> **They claim to know God, but by their actions they deny him. They are detestable, disobedient and unfit for doing anything good. (Titus 1:16)**

Dear children, let us not love with words or tongue but with actions and in truth. (1 John 3:18)

Many a man claims to have unfailing love, but a faithful man who can find? (Prov 20:6)

Those who are pure in their own eyes and yet are not cleansed of their filth; (Prov 30:12)

4 (7:40-43) **Jesus Christ, Deity; Knowledge**: the two attitudes illustrated. Jesus told a parable about two debtors. Note several things that say much to the self-righteous.

1. Jesus *announced* that He had something to say, something critically important. Undivided attention was needed. Every self-righteous person needs to listen and listen closely.

2. Jesus was a prophet and more—He was the Son of God; therefore, He not only knew the people who were sitting around Him, He knew their every thought. Note that from this point on, Jesus was answering the *thoughts* of Simon. Simon had never said a word about Jesus' not knowing who the woman was nor about his own question about Jesus' being a prophet. Simon had only been thinking these thoughts "to himself" (v.39).

Thought 1. Jesus is the Son of God; therefore, what a man thinks pales into insignificance when facing the One who knows all thoughts, including what one really thinks and feels *within*. Jesus knows the truth of every thought and feeling within a man. If a person is self-righteous, Jesus knows it. If a person is repentant, truly repentant, Jesus knows it. No one hides anything, no feeling, no thought from Him.

3. The meaning of the parable is strikingly clear. A glance at the verses and points in the outline show this. Note how clearly the parable illustrates the grace of God in freely forgiving sin (salvation) (cp. Eph.1:7; 2:8-9; 1 Jn.1:9; 2:1-2).

5 (7:44-50) **Self-Righteousness**: the need of the self-righteous—to really see Jesus, who the repentant say He is. Note what Jesus asked Simon, "Do you see this woman, this repentant?" The repentant had much to teach the self-righteous about Jesus. The repentant *really sees* Jesus, who He really is.

1. Jesus was the One who deserved more than common courtesies. The host usually showed respect by providing water for the guests to wash their dusty, sandaled feet. The kiss was the accepted greeting among friends, and oil was usually given for honored guests to refresh themselves after travelling under the hot sun. It was expensive, so it was usually reserved for honored guests.

a. Jesus deserved *more than common respect* (water); He deserved a worshipful respect. He was seen as Lord and was respected as Lord by the repentant. He was the One who alone could meet the needs of the human heart; therefore, He was the One who was to be worshipped. The self-righteous needed to learn this.

b. Jesus deserved *more than a common greeting*; He deserved a humble, brokenhearted greeting. He was approached with a sense of unworthiness and humility. The repentant saw the worthiness of Jesus and grasped something of His awesome person as the Son of God and as the sovereign Lord of the universe; therefore, He was the One to whom all men owed their allegiance, the One who alone had the power to forgive and accept men. The repentant saw Jesus as the One who alone could help her, the One who alone had the power to help, so the repentant approached Jesus and greeted Him with a deep sense of humility and unworthiness. The self-righteous needed to learn this.

c. Jesus deserved *more than a common gift*; He deserved a sacrificial gift. He was seen as the hope and Savior of one's life, so the repentant gave Jesus her life, all she was and had. The repentant surrendered her life and gave the most precious gift she had to anoint her Lord. The self-righteous needed to learn this.

2. Jesus was the One who had the power to forgive sins. Three simple facts are imporant here.

a. The woman's sins were many. Jesus did not overlook her sins, nor the seriousness of them. After all it was her sins and the sins of others that brought about *His humiliation*, His having to come to this sinful world and to die for the sins of men. However, He forgave her sins despite their awfulness. Every sinner should note this carefully.

b. Self-righteousness sensed the need for *little* forgiveness; therefore, the self-righteous loved little. The self-righteous had only a formal, distant relationship with God. His relationship was cold, having only a small sense of sin and sensing only a little need for forgiveness. It was enough to have Jesus present at his table (the table was about the only place many acknowledged His presence).

Thought 1. The self-righteous approach to God...

- has only a little sense of sin; therefore senses only a little need for forgiveness.
- is blinded to man's *state of sin*, to man's true being, that of being short of God's glory (Ro.3:23).
- has little sense of the need for special mercy and grace, is blinded to God's Sovereign Majesty and Person.
- has only a formal, distant relationship with God, has little personal relationship with God.
- gives little honor to God, makes little sacrifice for God.

c. Jesus forgave sin. He had the power to forgive the sins of this repentant.

Thought 1. The fact of forgiveness, the very knowledge that millions have been truly forgiven, is proof that Christ is the Son of God, the One to whom men are to go for forgiveness.

3. Jesus was the One whom people needed to ask about.

Thought 1. The very fact that Jesus claimed the right and power to forgive sins should cause every man to sit up, take notice and ask, "Who is this?"

God exalted him to his own right hand as Prince and Savior that he might give repentance and forgiveness of sins to Israel. (Acts 5:31)

"Therefore, my brothers, I want you to know that through Jesus the forgiveness of sins is proclaimed to you. (Acts 13:38)

In him we have redemption through his

blood, the forgiveness of sins, in accordance with the riches of God's grace (Eph 1:7)

Who forgives all your sins and heals all your diseases, (Psa 103:3)

But with you there is forgiveness; therefore you are feared. (Psa 130:4)

"I, even I, am he who blots out your transgressions, for my own sake, and remembers your sins no more. (Isa 43:25)

I have swept away your offenses like a cloud, your sins like the morning mist. Return to me, for I have redeemed you." (Isa 44:22)

Let the wicked forsake his way and the evil man his thoughts. Let him turn to the LORD, and he will have mercy on him, and to our God, for he will freely pardon. (Isa 55:7)

I will cleanse them from all the sin they have committed against me and will forgive all their sins of rebellion against me. (Jer 33:8)

4. Jesus was the One who did save the repentant. The woman believed Christ to be the Savior, the One who could forgive her sins. Therefore, Christ saved her.

> **"For God so loved the world that he gave his one and only Son, that whoever believes in him shall not perish but have eternal life. (John 3:16)**
>
> **Jesus answered, "I am the way and the truth and the life. No one comes to the Father except through me. (John 14:6)**
>
> **That if you confess with your mouth, "Jesus is Lord," and believe in your heart that God raised him from the dead, you will be saved. For it is with your heart that you believe and are justified, and it is with your mouth that you confess and are saved. (Rom 10:9-10)**
>
> **Here is a trustworthy saying that deserves full acceptance: Christ Jesus came into the world to save sinners—of whom I am the worst. (1 Tim 1:15)**

Outline	Scripture	Scripture	Outline
1 They supported a ministry of preaching[DS1,2] a. It reached out b. It was true to the gospel: The Kingdom of God **2 They supported a ministry of discipleship**	**CHAPTER 8** **R. Jesus & the Women Who Supported Him, 8:1-3** After this, Jesus traveled about from one town and village to another, proclaiming the good news of the kingdom of God. The Twelve were with him,	2 And also some women who had been cured of evil spirits and diseases:Mary (called Magdalene) from whom seven demons had come out; 3 Joanna the wife of Cuza, the manager of Herod's household; Susanna; and many others. These women were helping to support them out of their own means.	**3 They supported a ministry of salvation** a. Mary Magdalene: A dark past[DS3] b. Joanna: A lady of the King's court[DS4] c. Susanna:[DS5] An unnoticed follower d. Many others: Unknown[DS6]

DIVISION III

THE SON OF MAN'S ANNOUNCED MISSION AND PUBLIC MINISTRY, 4:16-9:17

R. Jesus and the Women Who Supported Him, 8:1-3

(8:1-3) **Introduction**: this is an interesting passage. It shows that Jesus received financial support for His ministry. There were some women, apparently well-off financially, who supported Him.

1. They supported a ministry of preaching (v.1).
2. They supported a ministry of discipleship (v.1).
3. They supported a ministry of salvation (v.2-3).

1 (8:1) **Preaching**: the women supported a preaching ministry. Preaching was Jesus' business; it was what He came to do, His primary call and mission. Note the words "after this" (en toi kathexes). The words mean one after the other, an orderly, successive step. The suggestion is that right after the banquet at Simon's home, Jesus got up and went about His primary task, that of preaching and proclaiming the gospel. He did not linger in fellowship or in any other pursuits, no matter their legitimacy or enjoyment. He was faithful and consistent in preaching and proclaiming the gospel. The point is this: the women supported a solid preaching ministry. They supported the Lord because He *preached* and was faithful to His call to preach. Note two facts in particular.

1. They supported a ministry that reached out. Jesus "traveled about from one town and village to another." He had an ache, a compassion for all, not willing that any should perish. He sought everyone *within His reach.* Note that He did not seek the limelight of the cities. He went out into the villages of the countryside as well. He had been sent to preach, and He preached anywhere and everywhere He could reach. The whole thrust of His being was to reach people for God, to reach everyone He could. This was the kind of ministry the women supported.

> **Just as the Son of Man did not come to be served, but to serve, and to give his life as a ransom for many." (Mat 20:28)**
>
> **"The Spirit of the Lord is on me, because he has anointed me to preach good news to the poor. He has sent me to proclaim freedom for the prisoners and recovery of sight for the blind, to release the oppressed, to proclaim the year of the Lord's favor." (Luke 4:18-19)**
>
> **But he said, "I must preach the good news of the kingdom of God to the other towns also, because that is why I was sent." (Luke 4:43)**
>
> **For the Son of Man came to seek and to save what was lost." (Luke 19:10)**
>
> **The thief comes only to steal and kill and destroy; I have come that they may have life, and have it to the full. (John 10:10)**
>
> **"As for the person who hears my words but does not keep them, I do not judge him. For I did not come to judge the world, but to save it. (John 12:47)**
>
> **"You are a king, then!" said Pilate. Jesus answered, "You are right in saying I am a king. In fact, for this reason I was born, and for this I came into the world, to testify to the truth. Everyone on the side of truth listens to me." (John 18:37)**
>
> **Here is a trustworthy saying that deserves full acceptance: Christ Jesus came into the world to save sinners—of whom I am the worst. (1 Tim 1:15)**
>
> **Here I am! I stand at the door and knock. If anyone hears my voice and opens the door, I will come in and eat with him, and he with me. (Rev 3:20)**

2. They supported a ministry that was *true* to the gospel, a ministry that proclaimed the glad tidings of the Kingdom of God (see DEEPER STUDY # 3—Mt.19:23-24). Note that Jesus did not preach religion and ritual, ceremony and ordinance, laws and rules, works and deeds, mind and spirit, soul and body, thinking and reasoning. He touched on all these, but they were not His prime message. His message was the *good news.*

> **"For God so loved the world that he gave his one and only Son, that whoever believes in him shall not perish but have eternal life. For God did not send his Son into the world to condemn the world, but to save the world through him. Whoever believes in him is not condemned, but whoever does not believe stands condemned already because he has not believed in the name of God's one and only Son. (John 3:16-18)**
>
> **"I tell you the truth, whoever hears my word and believes him who sent me has eternal life and will not be condemned; he has crossed over from death to life. (John 5:24)**

"My children, I will be with you only a little longer. You will look for me, and just as I told the Jews, so I tell you now: Where I am going, you cannot come. "A new command I give you: Love one another. As I have loved you, so you must love one another. (John 13:33-34)

And this is his command: to believe in the name of his Son, Jesus Christ, and to love one another as he commanded us. (1 John 3:23)

DEEPER STUDY # 1
(8:1) **Proclaim—Preach—Preaching** (kerusso): to proclaim, to publish, to be a herald, to preach the gospel as a herald.

DEEPER STUDY # 2
(8:1) **Proclaiming the Good News—Preaching** (euaggelizomenos): to preach glad tidings, to announce glad tidings, to declare good news, to proclaim the gospel of Jesus Christ. Note the Greek word, how it resembles the word *evangelism.* The English word *evangelism* comes from it. By the very nature of his work, the preacher is an evangelist. He is a herald who comes in the name of the King, representing the King (cp. 2 Cor.5:20). He proclaims *only* the message of the King; he has no message of his own. If and when he begins to proclaim his own message, he is no longer the representative or the spokesman of the King.

2 (8:1) **Discipleship—Stewardship**: they supported a ministry of discipleship. This was a critically important ministry, one which Christ stressed in His own life and practice. Making disciples of others was what He was doing with the twelve, and it was soon to be the *Great Commission* to all His followers. The support of the women in this ministry was critical, for it is doubtful that the disciples could have given their *full time* to Jesus without financial support. (See note—Mt.28:19-20 for detailed discussion.)

Therefore go and <u>make disciples</u> of all nations, baptizing them in the name of the Father and of the Son and of the Holy Spirit, and teaching them to obey everything I have commanded you. And surely I am with you always, to the very end of the age." (Mat 28:19-20)

Again Jesus said, "Peace be with you! As the Father has sent me, I am sending you." (John 20:21)

And the things you have heard me say in the presence of many witnesses entrust to reliable men who will also be qualified to teach others. (2 Tim 2:2)

3 (8:2-3) **Devotion—Stewardship**: they supported Jesus out of devotion. They were grateful for what He had done for them. Note that each one of them had been *reached and healed* by Jesus. They had received a very special touch from Him, and as a result they "were helping to support them out of their own means" (means, finances, property). Note the women who did minister (see DEEPER STUDY # 3-6—Lk.8:2-3).

DEEPER STUDY # 3
(8:2) **Mary Magdalene**: she was delivered from seven demons (Lk.8:2); was one of Jesus' primary financial supporters (Lk.8:3); was among the women who courageously stood at the cross (Mt.27:55-56); and was one to whom Jesus appeared after His resurrection (Mt.28:1; Mk.16:1; Lk.24:10; cp. Jn.20:11).

DEEPER STUDY # 4
(8:3) **Joanna**: her husband, Herod's steward, was the court official who looked after the king's estate and financial interests. Such was the task of the *steward.* The very nature of his job shows that he had to be a most-trusted official (cp. Lk.24:10).

DEEPER STUDY # 5
(8:3) **Susanna**: there is no other reference to Susanna. She represents the prominent disciple who is known by everyone but serves in a capacity that few ever notice. But note: she was such a devoted servant in giving, her name is known.

DEEPER STUDY # 6
(8:3) **Many others**: these represent the unknown and quiet, but all-important, followers of the Lord. They serve completely in the background, never up front; therefore, they are totally unknown. But note: they are faithful and do serve, consistently and faithfully.

	S. Jesus Teaches The Sure Fate of the Word: How People Receive the Word, 8:4-15 (Mt.13:1-23; Mk.4:1-20)
1 Crowds thronged Jesus—came from every town	4 While a large crowd was gathering and people were coming to Jesus from town after town, he told this par- able:
2 The parable: A farmer sowed seed a. Some fell by the path 1) Were trampled 2) Were devoured b. Some fell upon rock 1) Were withered & scorched 2) Had no moisture or depth c. Some fell among thorns: Were choked d. Some fell on good ground: Were fruitful	5 "A farmer went out to sow his seed. As he was scattering the seed, some fell along the path; it was trampled on, and the birds of the air ate it up. 6 Some fell on rock, and when it came up, the plants withered because they had no moisture. 7 Other seed fell among thorns, which grew up with it and choked the plants. 8 Still other seed fell on good soil. It came up and yielded a crop, a hundred times more than was sown." When he said this, he called out, "He who has ears to hear, let him hear."
3 The reason why Jesus spoke in parables a. To reveal the truth	9 His disciples asked him what this parable meant. 10 He said, "The knowledge

of the secrets of the kingdom of God has been given to you, but to others I speak in par- ables, so that, "'though see- ing, they may not see; though hearing, they may not under- stand.'	to open hearts b. To conceal the truth from closed minds
11 "This is the meaning of the parable: The seed is the word of God.	**4 The interpretation** a. The seed is the Word of God
12 Those along the path are the ones who hear, and then the devil comes and takes away the word from their hearts, so that they may not believe and be saved.	b. Some are by the path 1) They do hear 2) The devil snatches the Word away
13 Those on the rock are the ones who receive the word with joy when they hear it, but they have no root. They believe for a while, but in the time of testing they fall away.	c. Some are on rock 1) They do hear 2) They have no root: When tempted, they fall away
14 The seed that fell among thorns stands for those who hear, but as they go on their way they are choked by life's worries, riches and pleasures, and they do not mature.	d. Some are among thorns 1) They do hear 2) They are choked with materialism & pleasure
15 But the seed on good soil stands for those with a noble and good heart, who hear the word, retain it, and by perse- vering produce a crop.	e. Some are on rich soil 1) They keep the Word 2) They have honest & good hearts 3) They bear fruit

DIVISION III

THE SON OF MAN'S ANNOUNCED MISSION AND PUBLIC MINISTRY, 4:16-9:17

S. Jesus Teaches the Sure Fate of the Word: How People Receive the Word, 8:4-15

(8:4-15) **Introduction—Revival—Crowds—Worship—Church Attendance—Decision—Word of God**: the whole country was in a state of revival. It began with John the Baptist and continued with Jesus the Messiah. Multitudes of people were flocking to Jesus and being challenged to repent and follow God. The whole nation was charged with expectation, for the carpenter from Nazareth was not only claiming to be the Messiah, He was backing up His claims with a phenomenal demonstration of power—the power of God. But as Scripture says, "for [the Lord] knew what was in a man" (Jn.2:25). He knew that many were not really sincere. They did not have what it takes. They lacked...

- a real spirit of repentance
- a changed life
- an honest commitment
- a genuine faith
- a willingness to sacrifice
- a consistent obedience

Jesus knew that many were following Him not because they wanted to know God, not because they were genuine and sincere, but because of...

- family and friends
- the fellowship
- the social identification
- good feelings
- needs' being met

The insincerity of so many, of course, cut the heart of Jesus; but He still wanted to warn and reach as many as possible. This is what the parable of the seed is all about. Jesus wanted people to know that *hearing* the Word of God was not enough. There are many ways to hear the Word of God, but only one way bears fruit. Only one reception makes us acceptable to God. If we receive the Word of God any other way, then it becomes fruitless and does no good. It is snatched away or scorched or choked out. Only one reception will bear fruit.

Note how the parable speaks to every person. It is a *warning* to all hearers of the Word, especially to those who are not genuine followers of Christ. It gives great *assurance* to those who do hear: they shall definitely bear fruit. It is great encouragement to the preacher and teacher and to the lay witness. The seed they sow shall bear *some* fruit. (See outline and notes—Mt.13:1-9; Mk.4:1-20 for more discussion.)

1. Crowds thronged Jesus, coming from every town(v.4).
2. The parable: a farmer sowed seed (v.5-8).
3. The reason Jesus spoke in parables (v.9-10).
4. The interpretation (v.11-15).

1 (8:4) **Multitudes—Jesus Christ, Multitudes Follow—Revival**: the crowds thronged Jesus, coming from every city. Note the words "large crowd" and "town after town."

Thousands were now flocking to Jesus from everywhere. One can estimate the numbers on the basis of His having fed five thousand men on one occasion. This does not count the women and children, each of which would outnumber the men by far. We are probably safe to say, as we can in every generation, that more women followed Jesus than men; and families were larger than the average of four persons per family today. Apparently the crowd was well over twenty thousand.

2 (8:5-8) **Sower, Parable of—Word of God**: the parable was taken from an everyday happening. It concerned a sower, a farmer, who went out to sow seed. Note: he did go out and he did sow.

> **Thought 1.** How many *do not* go out? Of those who do, how many really sow the seed of the Word? It is so easy for the minister and believer...
> - to sit in the comfort of the home or office and rest and work administratively instead of going out and sowing.
> - to visit and care for the flock in their needs instead of going out into the fields to sow.

In sharing the parable, Jesus said four things happened to the seed when it was sown.

1. Some seed fell by the path or wayside, off to the side, out of the field upon the walking paths and roads. The paths and roads, of course, were trodden down and the soil was hard; therefore, the seed just lay on top and the birds came and devoured it.

2. Some seed fell upon a rock, that is, a large layer of rock lying right under the surface. This seed, of course, grew quickly because of the water's lying upon the rock right after a rain. But it soon withered away because the water was soon evaporated, leaving nothing but dry soil. The sun scorched the young plant.

3. Some seed fell among thorns. The seed sprouted, but the plants were soon choked to death by thorns.

4. Other seed fell on good ground. The seed sprang up and was very fruitful, bearing an hundredfold.

Now note what Jesus did. Immediately upon finishing the parable, He called out (ephonei) with a loud shout: "He who has ears to hear, let him hear." He warned: "Hear!"

3 (8:9-10) **Parables**: the reason why Jesus spoke in parables. Later, when Jesus and the disciples were all alone, the disciples asked Him to explain the parable. But Jesus used the occasion, first, to explain why He was now beginning to teach by parables. Up until now He had been teaching by direct statement and clear illustration, using few parables. But from now on, there was to be a difference. His primary method would be the parable. Why? Jesus gave two reasons.

1. Jesus wanted the *open hearts*, the persons who were really seeking God, to learn all they could about the *secrets or mysteries* of the Kingdom of God. Parables required much thought in order to grasp their meaning. A person who really sought after God would seek, strive, think, and ask until he could find the meaning to the parable. And then he would chew upon the meaning, drawing all the meaning he could out of the parable so that he could learn everything possible about God.

> **Thought 1.** What Christ said about seeking the truth is especially true of those who already know God personally. However, it is also true of the crowd, of any who are genuine in their search for God but have not yet found Him. Christ longs to reach any who are truly seeking Him. The parable is an excellent method to arouse interest and curiosity among men. Of course, if a man is genuinely sincere in knowing *the Truth*, he will search out the meaning (Truth), no matter how much time and effort are required.

2. Jesus wanted the truth concealed from closed minds. Closed minds are hardened and unwilling to consider the secrets or mysteries of the Kingdom of God. Sitting there in the audience, they heard and understood the words and the pictures which the words painted. But there was only a little interest in searching into the hidden meaning (secrets) of the parable. The time and effort required were not worth it. The closed minded and carnal were just not that interested. Jesus and His message were interesting, for He was a very capable preacher, full of charisma and practical help for living. However, as far as committing one's life totally to His cause and commandments, as far as denying self completely and sacrificing all one is and has, it was not worth it, not to the carnal. Therefore, the carnal were not willing to take the time or effort required to search out the meaning of the parable. Jesus actually said that He wanted the meaning hidden from the closed minded.

Note something else as well. The closed-minded, hardhearted, and carnal often *react* to the truth when the truth points a finger at them and their wrong. (See outline and notes—Mt.13:10-17 for a full outline on why Jesus spoke in parables.)

4 (8:11-15) **Word of God—Witnessing—Profession—Worldliness—Conversion, Dramatic**: the interpretation of the parable was given by Jesus. The sower is the Lord Jesus Christ or a servant of His. The servants of the Lord, ministers or laymen, are "God's fellow workers" (1 Cor.3:9). The seed is the Word of God or the Word of the kingdom. It is called (1) the "imperishable seed" (1 Pt.1:23), and (2) "the gospel that...bears fruit" (Col.1:5-6).

The ground upon which the seed is sown is the heart of the hearer. Jesus said two significant things about the ground. (1) There are different ways to hear and receive the Word (seed). And (2) He warns all hearers (all types of ground): the fate of the Word, how well it grows, depends upon the hearer.

> **Thought 1.** The success of the seed depends upon one thing alone; the condition of the soil (heart) to receive the seed (Word). If the ground (heart) is soft and rich, being full of the right minerals (spiritual qualities) and cleared of all junk and brush, ploughed and turned over, then it is ready to receive the seed.

1. The seed by the path or wayside. The person by the path does hear the Word of God. He is present, but he is off to the side, out of the way, not involved. He lets his mind wander and thinks little and involves himself even less. He respects Christ and the preacher and would not miss a service, but he is on the outer circle, paying little attention to the warnings and promises of the Word.

Note what happens. Before the person believes, the devil comes and snatches the Word away. It is taken from the person; the person never applies the Word to his life, never really lives sacrificially for Christ. (Cp. Judas Iscariot and cp. Herod who enjoyed listening to John the Baptist, Mk.6:20.)

For this people's heart has become calloused; they hardly hear with their ears, and they have closed their eyes. Otherwise they might see with their eyes, hear with their ears, understand with their hearts and turn, and I would heal them.' (Acts 28:27)

[The hardhearted] Having lost all sensitivity, they have given themselves over to sensuality so as to indulge in every kind of impurity, with a continual lust for more. (Eph 4:19)

But encourage one another daily, as long as it is called Today, so that none of you may be hardened by sin's deceitfulness. (Heb 3:13)

Blessed is the man who always fears the LORD, but he who hardens his heart falls into trouble. (Prov 28:14)

A man who remains stiff-necked after many rebukes will suddenly be destroyed—without remedy. (Prov 29:1)

But because of your stubbornness and your unrepentant heart, you are storing up wrath against yourself for the day of God's wrath, when his righteous judgment will be revealed. (Rom 2:5)

2. The seed on the rock. This person hears the Word, and becomes excited over it. He receives the Word, professes belief in Christ, and makes a profession of faith before the world. But he fails to count the cost, to consider the commitment, the self-denial, the sacrifice, the study, the learning, the hours and effort required. He does not apply himself to *learn Christ*; therefore, he does not become rooted and grounded in the Word. He is only a superficial believer.

Note what happens. When trials and temptations come, he falls away. His profession is scorched and consumed, burned up by the heat of the trial and temptation. (Cp. John Mark who at first failed to endure, Acts 13:13; Demas, Phile.1:24; and the men who discovered that following Christ just cost too much, Lk.9:57-62.)

Because of the increase of wickedness, the love of most will grow cold, (Mat 24:12)

But the one who hears my words and does not put them into practice is like a man who built a house on the ground without a foundation. The moment the torrent struck that house, it collapsed and its destruction was complete." (Luke 6:49)

Jesus replied, "No one who puts his hand to the plow and looks back is fit for service in the kingdom of God." (Luke 9:62)

But now that you know God—or rather are known by God—how is it that you are turning back to those weak and miserable principles [the world]? Do you wish to be enslaved by them all over again? (Gal 4:9)

But my righteous one will live by faith. And if he shrinks back, I will not be pleased with him." (Heb 10:38)

If they have escaped the corruption of the world by knowing our Lord and Savior Jesus Christ and are again entangled in it and overcome, they are worse off at the end than they were at the beginning. It would have been better for them not to have known the way of righteousness, than to have known it and then to turn their backs on the sacred command that was passed on to them. Of them the proverbs are true: "A dog returns to its vomit," and, "A sow that is washed goes back to her wallowing in the mud." (2 Pet 2:20-22)

Yet I hold this against you: You have forsaken your first love. Remember the height from which you have fallen! Repent and do the things you did at first. If you do not repent, I will come to you and remove your lampstand from its place. (Rev 2:4-5)

3. The seed among thorns. This is a person who receives the Word and *honestly tries* (professes) to live for Christ. Christ and His followers and the church and its activities appeal to him. So he joins right in, even professing Christ as he walks about his daily affairs. But there is one problem: the thorns or worldliness. He is unwilling to cut completely loose from the world: "[to] come out from them and be separate" (2 Cor.6:17-18). He lives a double life, trying to live for Christ and yet still live out in the world. He keeps right on growing in the midst of the thorns, giving his mind and attention to the *cares* and *riches* and *pleasures* of this world.

Note what happens. He bears fruit. Fruit does appear, but it never ripens; it is never able to be plucked. The thorns choke the life out of it. It never lives to be used. (Cp. the Rich Young Ruler, Lk.18:18f; Ananias and Sapphira, Acts 5:1f.)

Thought 1. Note the three areas that choke the life out of men.

1) The cares of this life.

"Therefore I tell you, do not worry about your life, what you will eat or drink; or about your body, what you will wear. Is not life more important than food, and the body more important than clothes? (Mat 6:25)

So do not worry, saying, 'What shall we eat?' or 'What shall we drink?' or 'What shall we wear?' (Mat 6:31)

And do not set your heart on what you will eat or drink; do not worry about it. (Luke 12:29)

"Be careful, or your hearts will be weighed down with dissipation, drunkenness and the anxieties of life, and that day will close on you unexpectedly like a trap. (Luke 21:34)

Do not be anxious about anything, but in everything, by prayer and petition, with thanksgiving, present your requests to God. (Phil 4:6)

Cast all your anxiety on him because he cares for you. (1 Pet 5:7)

Man is a mere phantom as he goes to and fro: He bustles about, but only in vain; he heaps up wealth, not knowing who will get it. (Psa 39:6)

In vain you rise early and stay up late, toiling for food to eat— for he grants sleep to those he loves. (Psa 127:2)

2) The riches of this life.

But the worries of this life, the deceitfulness of wealth and the desires for other things come in and choke the word, making it unfruitful. (Mark 4:19)

People who want to get rich fall into temptation and a trap and into many foolish and harmful desires that plunge men into ruin and destruction. (1 Tim 6:9)

Your gold and silver are corroded. Their corrosion will testify against you and eat your flesh like fire. You have hoarded wealth in the last days. (James 5:3)

Then Jesus said to his disciples, "I tell you the truth, it is hard for a rich man to enter the kingdom of heaven. (Mat 19:23)

For we brought nothing into the world, and we can take nothing out of it. (1 Tim 6:7)

And when your herds and flocks grow large and your silver and gold increase and all you have is multiplied, then your heart will become proud and you will forget the LORD your God, who brought you out of Egypt, out of the land of slavery. (Deu 8:13-14)

A flood will carry off his house, rushing waters on the day of God's wrath. (Job 20:28)

For all can see that wise men die; the foolish and the senseless alike perish and leave their wealth to others. (Psa 49:10)

Cast but a glance at riches, and they are gone, for they will surely sprout wings and fly off to the sky like an eagle. (Prov 23:5)

I hated all the things I had toiled for under the sun, because I must leave them to the one who comes after me. (Eccl 2:18)

Like a partridge that hatches eggs it did not lay is the man who gains riches by unjust means. When his life is half gone, they will desert him, and in the end he will prove to be a fool. (Jer 17:11)

3) The pleasures of this life.

And I'll say to myself, "You have plenty of good things laid up for many years. Take life easy; eat, drink and be merry." (Luke 12:19)

But the widow who lives for pleasure is dead even while she lives. (1 Tim 5:6)

But mark this: There will be terrible times in the last days. People will be lovers of themselves, lovers of money, boastful, proud, abusive, disobedient to their parents, ungrateful, unholy, treacherous, rash, conceited, lovers of pleasure rather than lovers of God— (2 Tim 3:1-2, 4)

At one time we too were foolish, disobedient, deceived and enslaved by all kinds of passions and pleasures. We lived in malice and envy, being hated and hating one another. (Titus 3:3)

You have lived on earth in luxury and self-indulgence. You have fattened yourselves in the day of slaughter. (James 5:5)

They will be paid back with harm for the harm they have done. Their idea of pleasure is to carouse in broad daylight. They are blots and blemishes, reveling in their pleasures while they feast with you. (2 Pet 2:13)

"Now then, listen, you wanton creature, lounging in your security and saying to yourself, 'I am, and there is none besides me. I will never be a widow or suffer the loss of children.' Both of these will overtake you in a moment, on a single day: loss of children and widowhood. They will come upon you in full measure, in spite of your many sorceries and all your potent spells. (Isa 47:8-9)

4. The seed on good ground. These are they who have an honest and good heart. Therefore, when they hear the Word, they keep it. Note several things.

a. Their hearts are "noble" (kalei). The word means fair, honest, and just. It has the idea of holding fast. These people are honest and fair; they are noble people in listening and considering the Word. They honestly seek to learn and know the truth, spiritually as well as physically.

Now the Bereans were of more noble character than the Thessalonians, for they received the message with great eagerness and examined the Scriptures every day to see if what Paul said was true. (Acts 17:11)

Those who accepted his message were baptized, and about three thousand were added to their number that day. (Acts 2:41)

And we also thank God continually because, when you received the word of God, which you heard from us, you accepted it not as the word of men, but as it actually is, the word of God, which is at work in you who believe. (1 Th 2:13)

b. Their hearts are "good" (agathei), meaning devoted, committed, given over to the truth. Once the truth is known, they hold fast to it.

But thanks be to God that, though you used to be slaves to sin, you wholeheartedly obeyed the form of teaching to which you were entrusted. (Rom 6:17)

Oh, that their hearts would be inclined to fear me and keep all my commands always, so that it might go well with them and their children forever! (Deu 5:29)

The LORD your God commands you this day to follow these decrees and laws; carefully observe them with all your heart and with all your soul. (Deu 26:16)

Do not let this Book of the Law depart from your mouth; meditate on it day and night, so that you may be careful to do everything written in it. Then you will be prosperous and successful. (Josh 1:8)

My heart is steadfast, O God, my heart is steadfast; I will sing and make music. (Psa 57:7)

I will give them a heart to know me, that I am the LORD. They will be my people, and I will be their God, for they will return to me with all their heart. (Jer 24:7)

I will give you a new heart and put a new spirit in you; I will remove from you

your heart of stone and give you a heart of flesh. (Ezek 36:26; cp. Ezek 11:19)

c. They keep the Word. They do not let the devil snatch it, nor the trials and temptations of life scorch it, nor the cares and riches and pleasures of this life choke it.

I tell you the truth, if anyone keeps my word, he will never see death." (John 8:51)

Jesus replied, "If anyone loves me, he will obey my teaching. My Father will love him, and we will come to him and make our home with him. (John 14:23)

"I have revealed you to those whom you gave me out of the world. They were yours; you gave them to me and they have obeyed your word. (John 17:6)

We know that we have come to know him if we obey his commands. (1 John 2:3)

I know your deeds. See, I have placed before you an open door that no one can shut. I know that you have little strength, yet you have kept my word and have not denied my name. (Rev 3:8)

d. They bear fruit with perseverance and *patience.* They endure and study, grow and serve more and more. They constantly water and pluck the weeds and thorns, and they continue to do so until the fruit is fully grown and plucked and *taken home* to the Master of the house.

Therefore, if anyone is in Christ, he is a new creation; the old has gone, the new has come! (2 Cor 5:17)

I tell you the truth, unless a kernel of wheat falls to the ground and dies, it remains only a single seed. But if it dies, it produces many seeds. (John 12:24)

"I am the vine; you are the branches. If a man remains in me and I in him, he will bear much fruit; apart from me you can do nothing. (John 15:5)

(For the fruit of the light consists in all goodness, righteousness and truth) (Eph 5:9)

Filled with the fruit of righteousness that comes through Jesus Christ—to the glory and praise of God. (Phil 1:11)

And we pray this in order that you may live a life worthy of the Lord and may please him in every way: bearing fruit in every good work, growing in the knowledge of God, (Col 1:10)

Planted in the house of the LORD, they will flourish in the courts of our God. They will still bear fruit in old age, they will stay fresh and green, (Psa 92:13-14)

Outline	Title	Scripture	Outline
	T. Jesus Teaches Three Fundamental Principles of Life, 8:16-18 (Mt.5:15-16; 10:26-27; 13:12; Mk.4:21-23; cp. Lk.11:33-36)	17 For there is nothing hidden that will not be disclosed, and nothing concealed that will not be known or brought out into the open.	**2 Secrecy is impossible: All things shall be found out**
1 A lamp (life) is for the purpose of giving light[DS1] a. It is not covered, not hid b. It is made conspicuous	16 "No one lights a lamp and hides it in a jar or puts it under a bed. Instead, he puts it on a stand, so that those who come in can see the light.	18 Therefore consider carefully how you listen. Whoever has will be given more; whoever does not have, even what he thinks he has will be taken from him."	**3 Truth is very narrow** a. A person must watch how he hears b. The reason: Truth shall be rewarded; but the "seemingly" true shall be stripped away

DIVISION III

THE SON OF MAN'S ANNOUNCED MISSION AND PUBLIC MINISTRY, 4:16-9:17

T. Jesus Teaches Three Fundamental Principles of Life, 8:16-18

(8:16-18) **Introduction**: Christ gives three fundamental principles of life, principles that speak clearly to all believers, both layman and preacher.

1. A lamp or life is for the purpose of giving light (v.16).
2. Secrecy is impossible: all things shall be found out (v.17).
3. Truth is very narrow (v.18).

1 (8:16) **Light—Purpose—Life**: a lamp, a life, is for the purpose of giving light. Note five simple facts about its purpose.

1. The lamp is a given lamp. It is not purchased or earned. God gives the lamp to every man. This is the key. The lamp is a gift from God. A man has it, but a man has to use it for it to be of any benefit. The lamp is a man's life, the life which he is given when he is born into the world.

2. The lamp is to be lit. The lamp just exists until it is lit; it is not fulfilling its primary function. Its function is to give light, but it may be used for other things, useful things such as…

- decorations to beautify (a life that beautifies).
- focussing attention upon an object (a life that focuses attention upon the desperate needs of the world).
- protection by illumintation an odd (a life that protects people from evil).
- an ornament to attract attention (a life that entices, centers on self).

Note a significant fact: in most of these cases the lamp or life of a person is helpful and useful; but the lamp has yet to fulfill its *primary* function, the very purpose for which it was made and formed. The lamp has to be lit before it can give light. The man himself is the one who has to take the initiative to have his lamp lit. He has to come to Christ, the Light of the World, and receive the quickening spark of His Light. A man has to reach out for the light that is Jesus Christ. Christ is the Light, but man has to put the lamp of his life up to the light of Christ in order to be lit, ignited, and quickened (Jn.1:9; Jn.8:12; 11:9-10; 12:36, 46; Eph.5:8).

3. The lamp is not to be hid. Once the lamp has been lit *no man* covers it with a vessel or puts it under a bed. Such is ludicrous, foolish, unreasonable. All the energy and effort as well as the purpose for lighting the lamp are wasted if it is slid under a bed or covered. The lamp and light are useless, of no purpose.

If anyone is ashamed of me and my words in this adulterous and sinful generation, the Son of Man will be ashamed of him when he comes in his Father's glory with the holy angels." (Mark 8:38)

For God did not give us a spirit of timidity, but a spirit of power, of love and of self-discipline. So do not be ashamed to testify about our Lord, or ashamed of me his prisoner. But join with me in suffering for the gospel, by the power of God, (2 Tim 1:7-8)

4. The lamp is to be conspicuous, placed high upon a lampstand. Every genuine believer has had his lamp ignited; he has touched Christ, the Light of the World, and Christ has given him light. Therefore, the believer burns and shows forth light. The only question is, how brightly does he shine? His light may be bright or dim, strong or weak, flickering or flaming, blinking or flooding, smoking or clear. Christ says it is foolish to have light and it not be turned on, conspicuously giving off light.

I eagerly expect and hope that I will in no way be ashamed, but will have sufficient courage so that now as always Christ will be exalted in my body, whether by life or by death. (Phil 1:20)

However, if you suffer as a Christian, do not be ashamed, but praise God that you bear that name. (1 Pet 4:16)

And now, dear children, continue in him, so that when he appears we may be confident and un-ashamed before him at his coming. (1 John 2:28)

Then I would not be put to shame when I consider all your commands. (Psa 119:6)

Because the Sovereign LORD helps me, I will not be disgraced. Therefore have I set my face like flint, and I know I will not be put to shame. (Isa 50:7)

You will have plenty to eat, until you are full, and you will praise the name of the LORD your God, who has worked wonders for you; never again will my people be shamed. (Joel 2:26)

5. The lamp is to be seen by all who enter. Note a critical point. This is the very purpose of *the lighted lamp, to*

provide light. And light does numerous things (see DEEPER STUDY # 1, Light, Purpose—Lk.8:16).

> **"You are the light of the world. A city on a hill cannot be hidden. Neither do people light a lamp and put it under a bowl. Instead they put it on its stand, and it gives light to everyone in the house. In the same way, let your light shine before men, that they may see your good deeds and praise your Father in heaven. (Mat 5:14-16)**
>
> **For we cannot help speaking about what we have seen and heard." (Acts 4:20)**
>
> **Do not get drunk on wine, which leads to debauchery. Instead, be filled with the Spirit. Speak to one another with psalms, hymns and spiritual songs. Sing and make music in your heart to the Lord, (Eph 5:18-19)**
>
> **But in your hearts set apart Christ as Lord. Always be prepared to give an answer to everyone who asks you to give the reason for the hope that you have. But do this with gentleness and respect, (1 Pet 3:15)**
>
> **I have posted watchmen on your walls, O Jerusalem; they will never be silent day or night. You who call on the LORD, give yourselves no rest, (Isa 62:6)**
>
> **"'The LORD has vindicated us; come, let us tell in Zion what the LORD our God has done.' (Jer 51:10)**
>
> **Come and listen, all you who fear God; let me tell you what he has done for me. (Psa 66:16)**

DEEPER STUDY # 1

(8:16) **Light—Purpose**: Christ said, "I am the Light of the world" (Jn.8:12; 9:5). Here He says the disciple is to be like Himself—"the light of the world." Therefore, the disciple is to undergo a radical transformation. He is to *become like Christ* more and more and *to reflect the light* of Christ (2 Cor.3:18; 4:6-7). Light is and does several things.

1. Light is clear and pure. It is clean, that is, good, right, and true (Eph.5:8f).
2. Light penetrates. It cuts through and eliminates darkness.
3. Light enlightens. It enlarges one's vision and knowledge of an area.
4. Light reveals. It opens up the truth of an area, a whole new world, and it clears the way so that a person can see the truth and the life (Jn.14:6).
5. Light guides (Jn.12:36, 46). It directs the way to go and leads along the right path.
6. Light strips away (Jn.3:19-20). It unclothes the darkness that blackens life.
7. Light routes the chaos (cp. Gen.1:2-3). It brings peace to the disturbance caused by walking in pitch darkness.
8. Light discriminates between the right way and the wrong way (see note—Eph.5:10; cp. 5:8-10).
9. Light warns. It warns of dangers that lie ahead in one's path.

2 (8:17) **Sin, Secret—Judgment**: secrecy is impossible. All things shall be found out. Three things are said in this verse.

1. Men try to hide things. They try to keep some things secret.

a. Men try to hide sin and shame. They sin in the dark and behind closed doors, when out and away from home and friends, and by keeping secret books or bank accounts.
b. Men try to hide possessions lest they have to give or spend more.
c. Men try to hide abilities and talents, lest they have to serve and use them. They prefer the ease and comfort of complacency and plenty instead of the rigors and sacrifice required to meet the needs of a suffering world.
d. Men try to hide the Light and the Truth they have come to know. They are lazy, complacent, embarrassed, apprehensive and fearful; or else they lack the vision, willingness, commitment, initiative, and endurance to set the Light and Truth out before men. They just keep quiet within their own world, unwilling to sacrifice and deny themselves in order *to go* and share with those in darkness and ignorance.

2. Men think they will never be found out. They think their secrets will be hid forever and never discovered...

- not by mom or dad
- not by friend or acquaintance
- not by preacher or God
- not by wife or children
- not by society or organization

Men feel they are safe with the secret. They feel bad consequences will never happen to them: suffering and punishment, bad and evil will never fall upon them. They will be able to keep the secret hid forever and escape punishment.

3. Christ said nothing—not a single thing—will be hid forever. Every secret thing will be revealed and opened up. The thing hidden is seen, if not by men then by God, and it will be revealed. God will reveal the truth in the day of judgment if not before. The deceptions, the cloaks, the disguises, the secrets, the hidden things of all men shall be stripped away and unveiled; then all shall see, for it shall be manifested for all to see (Ro.2:2, 6, 11, 16).

> **Therefore judge nothing before the appointed time; wait till the Lord comes. He will bring to light what is hidden in darkness and will expose the motives of men's hearts. At that time each will receive his praise from God. (1 Cor 4:5)**
>
> **This will take place on the day when God will judge men's secrets through Jesus Christ, as my gospel declares. (Rom 2:16)**
>
> **"But if you fail to do this, you will be sinning against the LORD; and you may be sure that your sin will find you out. (Num 32:23)**
>
> **If I sinned, you would be watching me and would not let my offense go unpunished. (Job 10:14)**
>
> **Surely then you will count my steps but not keep track of my sin. (Job 14:16)**
>
> **The heavens will expose his guilt; the earth will rise up against him. (Job 20:27)**
>
> **For God will bring every deed into judgment, including every hidden thing, whether it is good or evil. (Eccl 12:14)**
>
> **Although you wash yourself with soda and use an abundance of soap, the stain of your guilt is still before me," declares the Sovereign LORD. (Jer 2:22)**

My eyes are on all their ways; they are not hidden from me, nor is their sin concealed from my eyes. (Jer 16:17)

"I the LORD search the heart and examine the mind, to reward a man according to his conduct, according to what his deeds deserve." (Jer 17:10)

Can anyone hide in secret places so that I cannot see him?" declares the LORD. "Do not I fill heaven and earth?" declares the LORD. (Jer 23:24)

Then the Spirit of the LORD came upon me, and he told me to say: "This is what the LORD says: That is what you are saying, O house of Israel, but I know what is going through your mind. (Ezek 11:5)

But they do not realize that I remember all their evil deeds. Their sins engulf them; they are always before me. (Hosea 7:2)

For I know how many are your offenses and how great your sins. You oppress the righteous and take bribes and you deprive the poor of justice in the courts. (Amos 5:12)

"Therefore judge nothing before the time, until the Lord come, who both will bring to light the hidden things of darkness, and will make manifest the counsels of the hearts: and then shall every man have praise of God" (1 Cor.4:5).

3 (8:18) **Truth—Seeking**: truth is narrow, very narrow. This verse is a severe warning. It is referring back to the seed or the Word of God and the hearers. Very simply, Christ warns that we must hear and use what we hear if we want to be given things from God. If we hear and do not use what we hear, then what we have shall be taken away.

Note two points.

1. We must take heed *how* we hear. We can hear but hear wrongly. We can think and guess and suppose we know what we hear, but it is false and counterfeit and shall be stripped away. Note that we must "consider carefully," discern what we hear. We must make sure we have the truth. (See DEEPER STUDY # 1—Jn.1:9; DEEPER STUDY # 1—8:32; DEEPER STUDY # 2—14:6.)

2. The *reason* we need to watch how we hear is strikingly clear: the truth shall be rewarded, but the *seemingly true* shall be stripped away. If we use what we hear, we shall be given more; if we do not use what we have, even what we do possess will be taken away.

Seekers and achievers do receive and get more. The non-dreamer and complacent receive little and get less. This is a law of every realm.

1. It is the law of nature. The early get and survive. The early bird gets the worm; the late get little and suffer.

2. It is the law of man. Men reward energy and effort, production and results. They threaten and often take away from the lazy and inactive. Those who labor and practice and are diligent and persistent will always see and hear and get. They are in a position to get more and more and to be given more and more. But the lazy and non-worker, the neglectful and unfaithful will always lose.

All through life a man either gains or loses. He seldom, if ever, stands still. It all depends on the dreams, the effort, and the energy he is willing to exert.

3. It is the law of God.

Blessed are those who hunger and thirst for righteousness, for they will be filled. (Mat 5:6)

But seek first his kingdom and his righteousness, and all these things will be given to you as well. (Mat 6:33)

"Ask and it will be given to you; seek and you will find; knock and the door will be opened to you. For everyone who asks receives; he who seeks finds; and to him who knocks, the door will be opened. (Mat 7:7-8)

"Whoever can be trusted with very little can also be trusted with much, and whoever is dishonest with very little will also be dishonest with much. (Luke 16:10)

Then the LORD your God will make you most prosperous in all the work of your hands and in the fruit of your womb, the young of your livestock and the crops of your land. The LORD will again delight in you and make you prosperous, just as he delighted in your fathers, (Deu 30:9)

Thought 1. This verse is both a great encouragement and a realistic threat.

1) It is a great encouragement to the...
- faithful
- diligent
- stedfast
- toiling
- persevering
- consistent
- enduring
- hardworking
- hardpracticing
- beginner and finisher
- initiator and finalizer
- hardstudying

2) It is a realistic and understandable threat to the...
- lazy
- idle
- complacent
- inconsistent
- close-minded
- close-eyed
- close-eared
- self-satisfied
- sluggish
- slothful
- shiftless
- purposeless
- late sleeper
- late starter
- time waster
- misguided

We want each of you to show this same diligence to the very end, in order to make your hope sure. We do not want you to become lazy, but to imitate those who through faith and patience inherit what has been promised. (Heb 6:11-12)

Never be lacking in zeal, but keep your spiritual fervor, serving the Lord. (Rom 12:11; cp. Mat 25:24-27)

For even when we were with you, we gave you this rule: "If a man will not work, he shall not eat." We hear that some among you are idle. They are not busy; they are busybodies. Such people we command and urge in the Lord Jesus Christ to settle down and earn the bread they eat. (2 Th 3:10-12)

Because you did not serve the LORD your God joyfully and gladly in the time of prosperity, therefore in hunger and thirst, in nakedness and dire poverty, you will serve the enemies the LORD sends against you. He will put an iron yoke on your neck until he has destroyed you. (Deu 28:47-48)

He [the wicked man] wanders about—food for vultures ; he knows the day of darkness is at hand. (Job 15:23)

Allow no sleep to your eyes, no slumber to your eyelids. (Prov 6:4)

Go to the ant, you sluggard; consider

its ways and be wise! It has no commander, no overseer or ruler, yet it stores its provisions in summer and gathers its food at harvest. How long will you lie there, you sluggard? When will you get up from your sleep? A little sleep, a little slumber, a little folding of the hands to rest—and poverty will come on you like a bandit and scarcity like an armed man. (Prov 6:6-11)

He who gathers crops in summer is a wise son, but he who sleeps during harvest is a disgraceful son. (Prov 10:5)

The sluggard craves and gets nothing, but the desires of the diligent are fully satisfied. (Prov 13:4)

The way of the sluggard is blocked with thorns, but the path of the upright is a highway. (Prov 15:19)

One who is slack in his work is brother to one who destroys. (Prov 18:9)

Laziness brings on deep sleep, and the shiftless man goes hungry. (Prov 19:15)

The sluggard buries his hand in the dish; he will not even bring it back to his mouth! (Prov 19:24)

A sluggard does not plow in season; so at harvest time he looks but finds nothing. (Prov 20:4)

Do not love sleep or you will grow poor; stay awake and you will have food to spare. (Prov 20:13)

The sluggard's craving will be the death of him, because his hands refuse to work. All day long he craves for more, but the righteous give without sparing. (Prov 21:25-26)

The sluggard says, "There is a lion outside!" or, "I will be murdered in the streets!" (Prov 22:13)

For drunkards and gluttons become poor, and drowsiness clothes them in rags. (Prov 23:21)

I went past the field of the sluggard, past the vineyard of the man who lacks judgment; thorns had come up everywhere, the ground was covered with weeds, and the stone wall was in ruins. I applied my heart to what I observed and learned a lesson from what I saw: A little sleep, a little slumber, a little folding of the hands to rest—and poverty will come on you like a bandit and scarcity like an armed man. (Prov 24:30-34)

The sluggard says, "There is a lion in the road, a fierce lion roaming the streets!" As a door turns on its hinges, so a sluggard turns on his bed. The sluggard buries his hand in the dish; he is too lazy to bring it back to his mouth. The sluggard is wiser in his own eyes than seven men who answer discreetly. (Prov 26:13-16)

If a man is lazy, the rafters sag; if his hands are idle, the house leaks. (Eccl 10:18)

	U. Jesus Teaches the Basis of True Kinship, 8:19-21 (Mt.12:46-50; Mk.3:31-35)	20 Someone told him, "Your mother and brothers are standing outside, wanting to see you."	**2 True kinship is not based upon human relationships**
1 Jesus' family sought Him	19 Now Jesus' mother and brothers came to see him, but they were not able to get near him because of the crowd.	21 He replied, "My mother and brothers are those who hear God's word and put it into practice."	**3 True kinship is based upon the Word of God: Hearing & doing it**

DIVISION III

THE SON OF MAN'S ANNOUNCED MISSION AND PUBLIC MINISTRY, 4:16-9:17

U. Jesus Teaches the Basis of True Kinship, 8:19-21

(8:19-21) **Introduction**: the immediate family is generally looked upon as the closest bond on earth. Sometimes it is; sometimes it is not. It should always be very, very close. However, Christ teaches there is a closer tie than the family, the tie that binds Him and His followers together. This is the lesson of this passage, a lesson that teaches a phenomenal truth. (See outline and notes—Mt.12:46-50; Mk.3:31-35 for more discussion.)

1. Jesus' family sought Him (v.19).
2. True kinship is not based upon human relationships (v.20).
3. True kinship is based upon the Word of God: hearing and doing it (v.21).

1 (8:19) **Jesus Christ, Family—Accusations, Insane**: Jesus' family sought Him. It is interesting to observe what they were *not* doing.

1. They were not making a social call. It was not a friendly visit, not family members visiting family members. Jesus was preaching and holding a service, yet His family interrupted Him right in the middle of the service. However, Jesus did not stop preaching; He continued right on. In fact, He used the occasion to teach a great spiritual truth.

2. They were not visiting Jesus to hear Him preach nor to learn from Him. This is known from the fact that His brothers did not believe in Him and the fact that the family did not enter the service. Note also that the family was late for the service; they arrived while He was already preaching and conducting the service.

3. They did not make their way through the crowd to Him. Instead they sent word by someone else for Him to come outside to them (Mt.12:47; Mk.3:31). Apparently, they were too embarrassed for one of them to try to reach Him.

Why was Jesus' family seeking Him? Several facts need to be considered in answering the question.

1. At first, some of the family supported Jesus and followed His leadership. They went with Him and His disciples on one of His very first evangelistic tours to Capernaum and remained with Him for a long time, apparently helping out in both practical and ministerial duties (Jn.2:12).

2. Second, the family witnessed two *unbelievable events* at the beginning of Jesus' ministry when He visited their hometown, Nazareth. They heard Jesus, one of their very own, claim to be the Messiah, the very One who was the fulfillment of the Holy Scripture. Imagine the shock of hearing one's own brother claiming to be Messiah, the Savior of the world. Then they witnessed their own hometown neighbors reject and attempt to kill Jesus. They actually saw their closest neighbors and dearest friends become insanely violent against their brother. Again, imagine the shock and the fear for Jesus' welfare, and the embarrassment as they walked among their friends throughout the coming days and weeks. It would be very difficult to live and face one's neighbors and townfolk after such an incident (Lk.4:16-31).

3. Third, the family was under constant pressure from friends to bring Jesus home—friends who counted themselves dear enough to advise the family. The friends thought Jesus was *mad* and *insane* by going about making the claims He was making, claims which included being the Son of God. Apparently, the family at some point gave permission for some friends to go bring Jesus home (Mk.3:21).

4. Fourth, Jesus' brothers did not support nor believe in Him. In fact, their disbelief eventually declined into ridicule. This is seen happening about six months before the crucifixion (Jn.7:5). As a point of interest, the brothers never did believe in Him until after the resurrection.

What seems to have been happening was that Mary and the family were coming to take Jesus home. The brothers had become convinced that Jesus was either insane or else caught up in the frenzy and honor of the people, and Mary feared for His life and welfare. Acting out of a mother's love and concern, she wanted to be a responsible mother and bring Him home to help Him all she could. (See notes—Mt.12:46-50; Mk.3:31-35.)

2(8:20) **Brotherhood—Family**: true kinship is not based upon human relationships. Picture the scene. Jesus was standing before the crowd preaching, and all of a sudden He was interrupted, being told that His mother and brothers were outside *wanting to see Him*. Of course, Jesus knew why they had come, and in this event He saw a unique opportunity to teach a profound truth, the truth that *true kinship* is not based upon human relationships.

> **Thought 1.** A true family, a true kinship does not exist just because some people have common blood, genes, and traits. This is clearly seen in the pages of family histories every day. Too many families are in turmoil, divided and being torn apart. Too many families are in constant conflict ranging from mild verbal attacks to murderous assaults. There is...
> - parent against child
> - child against parent
> - brother against brother
> - sister against sister
> - relative against relative
> - husband against wife
>
> **Yet to all who received him, to those who believed in his name, he gave the right**

to become children of God—children born not of natural descent, nor of human decision or a husband's will, but born of God. (John 1:12-13)

For you have been born again, not of perishable seed, but of imperishable, through the living and enduring word of God. (1 Pet 1:23)

3 (8:21) **Brotherhood—Word of God—Believers**: true kinship is based upon the Word of God—hearing it and doing it. The emphasis, of course, is upon doing the Word of God. The person who is closest to God is the person who obeys God, who takes His Word seriously. Any honest person knows that the child who obeys is the child closest to his parent's heart.

The deepest relationships in life are not determined by blood, but by hearts and minds being meshed together. The deepest relationships are founded upon common purposes and cares and behavior. However, the Christian believer has something even beyond this: he has the very *Word of God Himself*. When the believer hears and does the Word, that is, the will of God, five things happen.

1. God takes the believer's heart and life and welds it together with the hearts and lives of other believers—spiritually and supernaturally. They become the adopted children of God; therefore, the persons who hear the Word of God and do it are spiritually bound together in the family of God.

a. Adoption by redemption.

But when the time had fully come, God sent his Son, born of a woman, born under law, to redeem those under law, that we might receive the full rights of sons. Because you are sons, God sent the Spirit of his Son into our hearts, the Spirit who calls out, "Abba, Father." (Gal 4:4-6)

Yet to all who received him, to those who believed in his name, he gave the right to become children of God— (John 1:12)

For you did not receive a spirit that makes you a slave again to fear, but you received the Spirit of sonship. And by him we cry, "Abba, Father." The Spirit himself testifies with our spirit that we are God's children. Now if we are children, then we are heirs—heirs of God and co-heirs with Christ, if indeed we share in his sufferings in order that we may also share in his glory. (Rom 8:15-17)

For through him we both have access to the Father by one Spirit. Consequently, you are no longer foreigners and aliens, but fellow citizens with God's people and members of God's household, (Eph 2:18-19)

But now, this is what the LORD says—he who created you, O Jacob, he who formed you, O Israel: "Fear not, for I have redeemed you; I have summoned you by name; you are mine. (Isa 43:1)

b. Adoption by separation.

"Therefore come out from them and be separate, says the Lord. Touch no unclean thing, and I will receive you." "I will be a Father to you, and you will be my sons and daughters, says the Lord Almighty." (2 Cor 6:17-18)

Both the one who makes men holy and those who are made holy are of the same family. So Jesus is not ashamed to call them brothers. (Heb 2:11)

For you are a people holy to the LORD your God. Out of all the peoples on the face of the earth, the LORD has chosen you to be his treasured possession. (Deu 14:2)

2. Believers become a people who search God's Word out, absorb it into their lives and do it. His Word becomes their life and behavior. Believers obey the three basic commandments.

a. The commandment of God.

And this is his command: to believe in the name of his Son, Jesus Christ, and to love one another as he commanded us. (1 John 3:23)

b. The commandment of Christ.

"I tell you the truth, whoever hears my word and believes him who sent me has eternal life and will not be condemned; he has crossed over from death to life. (John 5:24)

c. The greatest commandment.

"Teacher, which is the greatest commandment in the Law?" Jesus replied: "'Love the Lord your God with all your heart and with all your soul and with all your mind.' This is the first and greatest commandment. And the second is like it: 'Love your neighbor as yourself.' All the Law and the Prophets hang on these two commandments." (Mat 22:36-40)

3. Believers live obediently in a very special relationship to God and Christ.

Jesus declared, "Believe me, woman, a time is coming when you will worship the Father neither on this mountain nor in Jerusalem. (John 4:21)

Like newborn babies, crave pure spiritual milk, so that by it you may grow up in your salvation, now that you have tasted that the Lord is good. (1 Pet 2:2-3)

Do your best to present yourself to God as one approved, a workman who does not need to be ashamed and who correctly handles the word of truth. (2 Tim 2:15)

4. Believers act together and live together in *fellowship* within the church and society. They are knitted together by God's Word and God's true family. (See DEEPER STUDY # 3, Fellowship—Acts 2:42 for more discussion.)

They devoted themselves to the apostles' teaching and to the fellowship, to the breaking of bread and to prayer. (Acts 2:42)

So in Christ we who are many form one body, and each member belongs to all the others. (Rom 12:5)

> **Because there is one loaf, we, who are many, are one body, for we all partake of the one loaf. (1 Cor 10:17)**
> **The body is a unit, though it is made up of many parts; and though all its parts are many, they form one body. So it is with Christ. For we were all baptized by one Spirit into one body—whether Jews or Greeks, slave or free—and we were all given the one Spirit to drink. (1 Cor 12:12-13)**
> **Now you are the body of Christ, and each one of you is a part of it. (1 Cor 12:27)**
> **Until we all reach unity in the faith and in the knowledge of the Son of God and become mature, attaining to the whole measure of the fullness of Christ. (Eph 4:13)**

5. Believers become God's new community, new society, new race, new nation of people. They become His church, His new creation—spiritually and supernaturally born again—who comprise the true family of God. (See DEEPER STUDY # 8—Mt.21:43; note—Mk.3:34-35; DEEPER STUDY # 1—Jn.4:22; notes—Eph.2:11-18; pt.4—Eph.2:14-15; 2:15; 4:17-19; cp. 1 Pt.2:9-10; Rev.21:1f for discussion.)

> **For through him we both have access to the Father by one Spirit. Consequently, you are no longer foreigners and aliens, but fellow citizens with God's people and members of God's household, built on the foundation of the apostles and prophets, with Christ Jesus himself as the chief cornerstone. In him the whole building is joined together and rises to become a holy temple in the Lord. And in him you too are being built together to become a dwelling in which God lives by his Spirit. (Eph 2:18-22)**

	V. Jesus Calms a Storm: Jesus' Deity & Sovereignty, 8:22-25 (Mt.8:23-27; Mk.4:35-41)	were in great danger.	
		24 The disciples went and woke him, saying, "Master, Master, we're going to drown!" He got up and rebuked the wind and the raging waters; the storm subsided, and all was calm.	**4 Jesus' power & sovereignty: He was definitely God** a. The disciples despaired b. Jesus calmed the storm
1 Jesus crossed the Sea of Galilee **2 Jesus' humanity: He was definitely a man** a. He needed & requested the help of men b. He became tired & slept	22 One day Jesus said to his disciples, "Let's go over to the other side of the lake." So they got into a boat and set out. 23 As they sailed, he fell asleep. A squall came down on the lake, so that the boat	25 "Where is your faith?" he asked his disciples. In fear and amazement they asked one another, "Who is this? He commands even the winds and the water, and they obey him."	**5 Jesus' faith in God** a. He questioned the disciples' faith b. He stirred the disciples to question who He was
3 Jesus' confidence in His men	was being swamped, and they		

DIVISION III

THE SON OF MAN'S ANNOUNCED MISSION AND PUBLIC MINISTRY, 4:16-9:17

V. Jesus Calms a Storm: Jesus' Deity and Sovereignty, 8:22-25

(8:22-25) **Introduction**: this event is a clear demonstration of the deity and sovereignty of the Lord Jesus Christ. It shows clearly the sovereign power of Christ to calm the storms that arise in man's life.

1. Jesus crossed the Sea of Galilee (v.22).
2. Jesus' humanity: He was definitely a man (v.22-23).
3. Jesus' confidence in His men (v.23).
4. Jesus' power and sovereignty: He was definitely God (v.24).
5. Jesus' faith in God (v.25).

1 (8:22) **The Sea of Galilee**: Jesus crossed the Sea of Galilee (see note—Mk.1:16).

2 (8:22-23) **Jesus Christ, Humanity—God, Power of—Jesus Christ, Incarnation**: two pictures of Jesus' humanity are clearly seen in these verses.

First, Jesus needed and requested the help of the disciples. He wanted to cross the lake. He could have walked around the lake; it was only a mile's journey, but He wanted to go by boat in order to get away from the crowd. They had been pressing in upon Him most of the day now, demanding and needing help. The *pressure and physical strain* had gotten to Jesus, wearing Him down. He needed time away from the crowds. If He walked, they would follow Him, so He requested the seamanship skills of the disciples to cross the lake. He could get alone off to the side someplace on the boat, away even from the disciples.

Second, Jesus was tired and needed sleep. He was fully man, flesh and blood; therefore, He sometimes suffered exhaustion just as any hardworking man does.

Now note: when studying the deity of Jesus, it helps to see His humanity, the fact that He was fully man. Seeing Jesus as Man helps tremendously in understanding God, for Jesus' humanity (being fully Man) highlights God more. It highlights and sets off His deity in at least two ways.

1. Christ's humanity, His having to suffer through life as a man, shows us the great love of God. In Christ, God identifies with man, and He identifies fully in every way and in everything. He knows how we feel and suffer because He was fully man. He knows all the trials and experiences and day-to-day routines of life; therefore, He is able to save us from the depths to the uttermost.

For surely it is not angels he helps, but Abraham's descendants. For this reason he had to be made like his brothers in every way, in order that he might become a merciful and faithful high priest in service to God, and that he might make atonement for the sins of the people. Because he himself suffered when he was tempted, he is able to help those who are being tempted. (Heb 2:16-18)

For we do not have a high priest who is unable to sympathize with our weaknesses, but we have one who has been tempted in every way, just as we are—yet was without sin. Let us then approach the throne of grace with confidence, so that we may receive mercy and find grace to help us in our time of need. (Heb 4:15-16)

2. Christ's humanity shows us the great power of God.
   a. It shows God's power to actually become a man, to bring about the Incarnation. Standing before us as flesh and blood, Jesus Christ is a powerful demonstration of God's great sovereignty. God is sovereign; He can do anything, even become a Man. By partaking of flesh and blood, Jesus Christ shows the enormous power (Sovereignty) of God.

Therefore the Lord himself will give you a sign: The virgin will be with child and will give birth to a son, and will call him Immanuel. (Isa 7:14)

For to us a child is born, to us a son is given, and the government will be on his shoulders. And he will be called Wonderful Counselor, Mighty God, Everlasting Father, Prince of Peace. (Isa 9:6)

This is how the birth of Jesus Christ came about: His mother Mary was pledged to be married to Joseph, but before they came together, she was found to be with child through the Holy Spirit. Because Joseph her husband was a righteous man and did not want to expose her to public disgrace, he had in mind to divorce her qui-

etly. But after he had considered this, an angel of the Lord appeared to him in a dream and said, "Joseph son of David, do not be afraid to take Mary home as your wife, because what is conceived in her is from the Holy Spirit. She will give birth to a son, and you are to give him the name Jesus, because he will save his people from their sins." All this took place to fulfill what the Lord had said through the prophet: "The virgin will be with child and will give birth to a son, and they will call him Immanuel" —which means, "God with us." (Mat 1:18-23)

The Word became flesh and made his dwelling among us. We have seen his glory, the glory of the One and Only, who came from the Father, full of grace and truth. (John 1:14)

"Brothers, I can tell you confidently that the patriarch David died and was buried, and his tomb is here to this day. But he was a prophet and knew that God had promised him on oath that he would place one of his descendants on his throne. Seeing what was ahead, he spoke of the resurrection of the Christ, that he was not abandoned to the grave, nor did his body see decay. God has raised this Jesus to life, and we are all witnesses of the fact. (Acts 2:29-32)

Paul, a servant of Christ Jesus, called to be an apostle and set apart for the gospel of God—the gospel he promised beforehand through his prophets in the Holy Scriptures regarding his Son, who as to his human nature was a descendant of David, and who through the Spirit of holiness was declared with power to be the Son of God by his resurrection from the dead: Jesus Christ our Lord. (Rom 1:1-4)

For what the law was powerless to do in that it was weakened by the sinful nature, God did by sending his own Son in the likeness of sinful man to be a sin offering. And so he condemned sin in sinful man, (Rom 8:3)

But made himself nothing, taking the very nature of a servant, being made in human likeness. (Phil 2:7)

Beyond all question, the mystery of godliness is great: He appeared in a body, was vindicated by the Spirit, was seen by angels, was preached among the nations, was believed on in the world, was taken up in glory. (1 Tim 3:16)

Since the children have flesh and blood, he too shared in their humanity so that by his death he might destroy him who holds the power of death—that is, the devil— (Heb 2:14)

This is how you can recognize the Spirit of God: Every spirit that acknowledges that Jesus Christ has come in the flesh is from God, (1 John 4:2)

Many deceivers, who do not acknowledge Jesus Christ as coming in the flesh, have gone out into the world. Any such person is the deceiver and the antichrist. (2 John 1:7)

b. Christ's humanity shows God's power to control physical events. When Jesus the carpenter calms a storm and multiplies food, the power and sovereignty of God are stressed—stressed much more than when some mystical force or freak accident happens to intervene in physical events. When Jesus Christ stands and works a miracle before men's very eyes, *God's power is clearly seen.* It is visible and there is no question about it. The presence and power, the very Being and Sovereignty of God, are acting for all to see; and *only a hard and foolish heart would deny it.*

3 (8:23) **Ministers, Call—Believers—Trust**: Jesus demonstrated a very striking point. He had confidence in His men. He entrusted His life to them, which means He laid the completion of His mission into their hands. Note the enormous confidence He had in His men. He slept soundly, remaining off to the side even through the most fierce storm. The boat was filling with water. Note two things.

1. He was definitely trusting His men and their ability. He was entrusting His life and mission into their hands.
2. He was present, but not actively engaged in this particular task. The disciples had the natural skill to handle this work, so they were expected to do it themselves. And note: the task was difficult, demanding all the seamen's skills they had.

I thank Christ Jesus our Lord, who has given me strength, that he considered me faithful, appointing me to his service. (1 Tim 1:12)

Therefore, since through God's mercy we have this ministry, we do not lose heart. (2 Cor 4:1)

4 (8:24) **Jesus Christ, Power; Deity; Sovereignty**: Jesus' power and sovereignty are clearly seen in this event. He was definitely God, just as He was definitely man (cp. v.22).

1. The disciples came to Him crying out, "Master, Master, we're going to drown!"
   a. They had no problem realizing and acknowledging their need.
   b. They believed and were sure that He could save them.
   c. It was their cry—a desperate, fervent cry—that awakened Him and brought about the calm. He awakened to their need, and the danger and fear were relieved. The calm and stillness came because they cried in all earnestness.
2. Jesus rebuked the wind and raging water by simply speaking. It was His Word that removed the threat and that brought calm both within nature and within their fearful hearts (cp. Ps.89:9; Ph.4:6-7).
3. Jesus' mastery over the sea was absolute, clearly showing (revealing) that He was the Sovereign Lord of the universe. Moreover, Jesus' mastery over the fear of the human heart was absolute, clearly showing that He was the loving God so desperately needed by man.

Thought 1. Christ can calm the storms that so often confront man, the storms of...

- suffering
- bankruptcy
- temptation
- loss
- lust
- trouble
- trial
- anger

- hatred
- passion
- grief
- persecution

Thought 2. Bringing calm to the storms of life involves doing as the disciples did: coming to Christ.
1) Acknowledging that one is perishing.
2) Believing that Jesus can save.
3) Crying out for Jesus to save.

Thought 3. God's Word is the Source and Power that brings calmness to the storms of life.

Then Jesus came to them and said, "All authority in heaven and on earth has been given to me. (Mat 28:18)

Peace I leave with you; my peace I give you. I do not give to you as the world gives. Do not let your hearts be troubled and do not be afraid. (John 14:27)

"I have told you these things, so that in me you may have peace. In this world you will have trouble. But take heart! I have overcome the world." (John 16:33)

The Lord will rescue me from every evil attack and will bring me safely to his heavenly kingdom. To him be glory for ever and ever. Amen. (2 Tim 4:18)

So do not fear, for I am with you; do not be dismayed, for I am your God. I will strengthen you and help you; I will uphold you with my righteous right hand. (Isa 41:10)

'Call to me and I will answer you and tell you great and unsearchable things you do not know.' (Jer 33:3)

5 (8:25) **Faith—Jesus Christ, Deity**: Jesus' faith in God is demonstrated in this verse. Look carefully at Jesus' question, "Where is your faith?" He was contrasting His confidence with their confidence. He was trusting God (as Man); why were they not trusting God? Note three points.

1. Jesus was stressing the absolute necessity for His people to have faith in God. He demonstrated faith perfectly by sleeping in the midst of a storm. His life was in the hands of God; He had put it there. Therefore, His destiny was under God's control and at God's disposal. This was the lesson Christ wanted to teach His disciples.

2. Jesus was rebuking the disciples, their fear and lack of faith. They should not have been terrified and distrusting. They should have labored on against the storm knowing that He was nearby and would never have let them perish. They should have known that their lives and destiny were in His hands and under His love and care and power.

Note a crucial lesson. The faith of the disciples was to be used. Their faith was not to be dormant, lying within their hearts doing nothing. Faith existed for the purpose of struggling against the storm. They were to exercise their faith when the storm came.

Thought 1. The lesson is clear. The very time for us to use our faith is when the storms of life come. It is against the storms that our faith is to be aroused and exercised.

He replied, "Because you have so little faith. I tell you the truth, if you have faith as small as a mustard seed, you can say to this mountain, 'Move from here to there' and it will move. Nothing will be impossible for you." (Mat 17:20)

"'If you can'?" said Jesus. "Everything is possible for him who believes." (Mark 9:23)

In addition to all this, take up the shield of faith, with which you can extinguish all the flaming arrows of the evil one. (Eph 6:16)

And without faith it is impossible to please God, because anyone who comes to him must believe that he exists and that he rewards those who earnestly seek him. (Heb 11:6)

If any of you lacks wisdom, he should ask God, who gives generously to all without finding fault, and it will be given to him. But when he asks, he must believe and not doubt, because he who doubts is like a wave of the sea, blown and tossed by the wind. (James 1:5-6)

Early in the morning they left for the Desert of Tekoa. As they set out, Jehoshaphat stood and said, "Listen to me, Judah and people of Jerusalem! Have faith in the LORD your God and you will be upheld; have faith in his prophets and you will be successful." (2 Chr 20:20)

3. The disciples feared as those who stand in the presence of God Himself. They did not, of course, fully understand the Person of Christ. But they knew they stood in the presence of One who aroused the same fearful reverence due God. This is seen in three responses.
   a. They were afraid, stricken with awe and reverence.
   b. They were "amazed," that is, marvelled, at His enormous power and sovereignty.
   c. They asked, "Who is this?" This was just the question Jesus wanted them to ask. They needed to be thinking about who He was.

Do not be afraid of those who kill the body but cannot kill the soul. Rather, be afraid of the One who can destroy both soul and body in hell. (Mat 10:28)

His mercy extends to those who fear him, from generation to generation. (Luke 1:50)

But accepts men from every nation who fear him and do what is right. (Acts 10:35)

Since you call on a Father who judges each man's work impartially, live your lives as strangers here in reverent fear. (1 Pet 1:17)

And now, O Israel, what does the LORD your God ask of you but to fear the LORD your God, to walk in all his ways, to love him, to serve the LORD your God with all your heart and with all your soul, (Deu 10:12)

"Now fear the LORD and serve him with all faithfulness. Throw away the gods your forefathers worshiped beyond the River and in Egypt, and serve the LORD. (Josh 24:14)

Who, then, is the man that fears the LORD? He will instruct him in the way chosen for him. (Psa 25:12)

How great is your goodness, which you have stored up for those who fear you, which you bestow in the sight of men on

those who take refuge in you. (Psa 31:19)

Let all the earth fear the LORD; let all the people of the world revere him. (Psa 33:8)

In the council of the holy ones God is greatly feared; he is more awesome than all who surround him. (Psa 89:7)

Do not be wise in your own eyes; fear the LORD and shun evil. (Prov 3:7)

Now all has been heard; here is the conclusion of the matter: Fear God and keep his commandments, for this is the whole duty of man. (Eccl 12:13)

The LORD Almighty is the one you are to regard as holy, he is the one you are to fear, he is the one you are to dread, (Isa 8:13)

Who among you fears the LORD and obeys the word of his servant? Let him who walks in the dark, who has no light, trust in the name of the LORD and rely on his God. (Isa 50:10)

W. Jesus Casts out Demons in Gadara: Power to Free Men from Evil Spirits, 8:26-39
(Mt.8:28-34; Mk.5:1-20)

1 The character of evil spirits

26 They sailed to the region of the Gerasenes, which is across the lake from Galilee.

a. Possessed a man
b. Caused a man to lose his sense of shame & conscience
c. Caused alienation
d. Stripped a man of his necessities

27 When Jesus stepped ashore, he was met by a demon-possessed man from the town. For a long time this man had not worn clothes or lived in a house, but had lived in the tombs.

e. Became enraged against the Lord
   1) Knew Him
   2) Opposed Him
   3) Feared Him

28 When he saw Jesus, he cried out and fell at his feet, shouting at the top of his voice, "What do you want with me, Jesus, Son of the Most High God? I beg you, don't torture me!"

f. Seized a man
g. Hated restraint, cp. v.31

29 For Jesus had commanded the evil spirit to come out of the man. Many times it had seized him, and though he was chained hand and foot and kept under guard, he had broken his chains and had been driven by the demon into solitary places.

h. Were numerous, formidable

30 Jesus asked him, "What is your name?" "Legion," he replied, because many demons had gone into him.
31 And they begged him repeatedly not to order them to go into the Abyss.

i. Desired a body to inhabit for the purpose of working evil

32 A large herd of pigs was feeding there on the hillside. The demons begged Jesus to let them go into them, and he gave them permission.

j. Were subject to the Lord's command & power[DS1]

33 When the demons came out of the man, they went into the pigs, and the herd rushed down the steep bank into the lake and was drowned.

2 The reaction of a covetous people

34 When those tending the pigs saw what had happened, they ran off and reported this in the town and countryside,

a. Saw a great deliverance & good done: Feared the strange, what they could not understand

35 And the people went out to see what had happened. When they came to Jesus, they found the man from whom the demons had gone out, sitting at Jesus' feet, dressed and in his right mind; and they were afraid.

b. Feared the great loss of property

36 Those who had seen it told the people how the demon-possessed man had been cured.

   1) Rejected Jesus
   2) Feared Him & feared more loss

37 Then all the people of the region of the Gerasenes asked Jesus to leave them, because they were overcome with fear. So he got into the boat and left.

3 The spirit of a delivered man

a. He desired discipleship

38 The man from whom the demons had gone out begged to go with him, but Jesus sent him away, saying,

b. He was commissioned as a disciple—to his own hometown

39 "Return home and tell how much God has done for you." So the man went away and told all over town how much Jesus had done for him.

DIVISION III

THE SON OF MAN'S ANNOUNCED MISSION AND PUBLIC MINISTRY, 4:16-9:17

W. Jesus Casts Out Demons in Gadara: Power to Free Men from Evil Spirits, 8:26-39

(8:26-39) **Evil Spirits—Unclean Spirits—Devils—Demons** (daimonia): evil spirits are demons. There is only one devil (see DEEPER STUDY # 1, Satan, Diabolos—Rev.12:9). However, there are many evil or unclean spirits or demons, and the New Testament has much to say about them.

The characteristics of demons other than the ones given in the outline above are said to be as follows:

1. They are spirits (Mt.12:43-45).
2. They are Satan's emissaries (Mt.12:26-27).
3. They know their fate is to be eternal doom (Mt.8:29; Lk.8:31).
4. They affect man's health (Mt.12:22; 17:15-18; Lk.13:16). Apparently, demon-possession is to be distinguished from mental illness.
5. They seduce men to a false religion of asceticism (1 Tim.4:1-3).
6. They seduce men to depart from the faith (1 Tim.4:1).
7. They are cast out of people (exorcism) in the name of Jesus Christ (Acts 16:18).
8. They shall participate in the apocalyptic judgment which is coming upon the earth (Rev.9:1-11, 20).

Evil spirits are enemies of Christ and of man. As such, they oppress, possess, and obsess people. (1) They delude the world and blind people to Christ (Eph.2:2). (2) They attack theology (1 Tim.4:1-3). (3) They attack society (Rev.9:3, 20-21). (4) They attack individuals (Lk.8:29). (5) They influence people to commit the sins of demon-worship, idolatry, sorcery, fornication, theft, murder, and much more (Rev.9:20-21).

The believer's defense is the Lord. The believer must pray and fast and take on the armor of God in order to stand against their power (Mt.17:21; Eph.6:12f).

This passage is excellent for studying the character of evil spirits and the Lord's power to deliver men from evil spirits.

1. The character of evil spirits (v.26-33).
2. The reaction of a covetous people (v.34-37).
3. The spirit of a delivered man (v.38-39).

1 (8:26-33) **Evil Spirits—Demons—Devils**: the character of evil spirits. At least ten traits of evil spirits are seen in this passage. (See notes—Mt.8:28-31; Mk.5:2-5 for more discussion and thoughts for application.)

1. Evil spirits are enemies of man, possessing a man for long periods of time. They take hold of a man, controlling his faculties and causing him to act abnormally, hurting both himself and others.

2. Evil spirits cause men to lose their sense of shame and conscience. This man was driven to run around naked. The point is, evil spirits destroy man's sense of modesty, privacy, intimacy, and respect. Evil spirits cause men to enjoy the attention of public exposure and the embarrassment of others.

3. Evil spirits cause alienation, the loss of all friends and social life. They lead a man to be *cut off*, ostracized from others. They often force a man to withdraw into himself and away from others, including immediate family; or they cause society to push the man away, forcing him to live alone or with others like himself. Evil spirits often destroy a man by making him live as it were among the dead, among those who have no contact with the world of living men. This is seen in this man's being forced to live among the tombs of the dead.

4. Evil spirits are enraged against the Lord. Note three things in this verse. They knew that Jesus was the Son of the Most High God (cp. the Holy One of God, Mk.4:34). They also opposed Him and feared Him (see note—Mk.1:23-24; 5:6-7. Cp. Mt.8:31-32; Jas.2:19.)

5. Evil spirits seize men. Their influence and unrestrained nature seem to come and go, to lie calm and then to break forth in violence.

6. Evil spirits hate restraint and cause men to mistreat and oppose others. They drive men to struggle against morality and justice and against being governed, restricted, controlled, and disciplined. They drive men to live wild and loose lives, to do as they please. They cause men to become unclean, sullen, violent, and malicious (cp. Mt.8:28; 9:33; 10:1; 12:43; Mk.1:23; 5:3-5; 9:17-20; Lk.6:18; 9:39).

7. Evil spirits take away a man's name, his identity, and his recognition. They deprive a person of purpose, meaning, significance. They destroy his self-image and his public image.

Note that Christ asked the man what his name was. The Lord was stirring within the man fond memories of his name before he had become demon-possessed.

8. Evil spirits are numerous and formidable. The evil spirit cried out within the man that his name was *Legion*. The legion refers to the Roman military legion which included over six thousand men. This definitely indicates that the man's case was desperate; the evil spirits in him were formidable, just as a military legion was formidable. (Cp. Mary Magdalene who had been possessed by seven devils, Mk.16:9. Note how a specific number was known. Cp. also Mk.5:9 "many.")

9. Evil spirits desire a body to inhabit for the purpose of working evil. They desire to be malicious, violent, and destructive. The evil spirits are said to be the ones who are speaking here. They recognized Jesus' sovereignty. Note how the "evil spirits" thought and worked.

a. They were indwelling and hurting this man physically, mentally, and spiritually.
b. They wished (if exorcised from the human body) to hurt other men by damaging and destroying their property.
c. They wished (if exorcised) to keep other men from Christ by destroying property and having them blame God for the devastation and loss.

10. Evil spirits are subject to the Lord's power. Christ had the power of His Word. The devil's power may be great, but the Word of Christ is omnipotent (all powerful), for all power belongs to Him.

You, dear children, are from God and have overcome them, because the one who is in you is greater than the one who is in the world. (1 John 4:4)

If God is for us, who can be against us? (Rom 8:31f. Read this whole passage for a beautiful and powerful description of the Lord's love and might.)

There was the result of Jesus' Word: the man was saved; the evil spirits were cast out of the man. Christ had the power to deliver and save. All He had to do was say, "Go," and whatever evil indwelt the man was gone. The man was delivered from all evil: its presence, guilt, and consequences. The man was "saved completely" (Heb.7:25). (See note—Mk.5:8-13 for more discussion and thoughts for application.)

But so that you may know that the Son of Man has authority on earth to forgive sins" Then he said to the paralytic, "Get up, take your mat and go home." (Mat 9:6)

Jesus looked at them and said, "With man this is impossible, but with God all things are possible." (Mat 19:26)

Then Jesus came to them and said, "All authority in heaven and on earth has been given to me. (Mat 28:18)

For nothing is impossible with God." (Luke 1:37)

For you granted him authority over all people that he might give eternal life to all those you have given him. (John 17:2)

How God anointed Jesus of Nazareth with the Holy Spirit and power, and how he went around doing good and healing all who were under the power of the devil, because God was with him. (Acts 10:38)

Therefore he is able to save completely those who come to God through him, because he always lives to intercede for them. (Heb 7:25)

"I know that you can do all things; no plan of yours can be thwarted. (Job 42:2)

DEEPER STUDY # 1
(8:33) **Pigs**: a question is often asked about the pigs which were killed. This is discussed in Matthew (see DEEPER STUDY # 2—Mt.8:32).

2 (8:34-37) **Covetousness**: the reaction of a covetous people (see DEEPER STUDY # 2—Mt.8:32; Mk.5:14-17 for more discussion and application). Note three things.

1. The people saw the great deed done, the marvelous deliverance of the demon-possessed man. However, their response was not one of rejoicing; it was fear—fear of Christ's power. They had known the demon-possessed man, how desperately hopeless his condition had been; and here he sat, delivered and made whole. What enormous power this man Jesus had!

2. The people rejected Jesus, being overwhelmed "and afraid." They were bound to be gripped with a sense of judgment because of their pigs's being killed. They were also bound to be wondering if the proclaimed Messiah had

come to judge them ahead of time or to destroy more of their property. They definitely knew they were breaking the law of God by *keeping pigs* (cp. Lev.11:7; Is.65:3-4; 66:17). Because of this sin and other sins and their callousness toward the healed demonic, they were bound to be fearful standing there face to face with God's Son. They were unwilling to repent of their sins and to begin living for God. Thus, they could feel nothing else but fear.

3. Jesus did exactly what they asked. He left them. They chose the tasty, satisfying nourishment of the *pigs of the world* over the joy and salvation of Christ. And so far as we know, He left forever, never to return to those who coveted this world more than Him.

> **Do not love the world or anything in the world. If anyone loves the world, the love of the Father is not in him. For everything in the world—the cravings of sinful man, the lust of his eyes and the boasting of what he has and does—comes not from the Father but from the world. (1 John 2:15-16)**
>
> **What good will it be for a man if he gains the whole world, yet forfeits his soul? Or what can a man give in exchange for his soul? (Mat 16:26)**
>
> **But whoever disowns me before men, I will disown him before my Father in heaven. (Mat 10:33)**
>
> **If anyone is ashamed of me and my words in this adulterous and sinful generation, the Son of Man will be ashamed of him when he comes in his Father's glory with the holy angels." (Mark 8:38)**
>
> **Whoever loves money never has money enough; whoever loves wealth is never satisfied with his income. This too is meaningless. (Eccl 5:10)**
>
> **Why spend money on what is not bread, and your labor on what does not satisfy? Listen, listen to me, and eat what is good, and your soul will delight in the richest of fare. (Isa 55:2)**

3 (8:38-39) **Witnessing—Call**: the spirit of a delivered man. The man was a dynamic example. As soon as he was delivered, he begged to be "with him" [Christ], to travel all around, sharing the good news of Christ. He was *on fire* for the Lord and wanted to commit himself to the ministry. But note what Christ did. He redirected the man; He commissioned the man to go to his own hometown.

> **Thought 1.** Christ often redirects our fervor and willingness. He knows where we can best serve Him and the cause of His kingdom.
>
> **Thought 2.** Every man, when saved, should become a dynamic witness for the Lord and be willing to go anyplace.
>
> **Thought 3.** We should never let a redirection or a call to go elsewhere kill our fervor.
>
> > **In the same way, let your light shine before men, that they may see your good deeds and praise your Father in heaven. (Mat 5:16)**
> >
> > **Therefore go and make disciples of all nations, baptizing them in the name of the Father and of the Son and of the Holy Spirit, and teaching them to obey everything I have commanded you. And surely I am with you always, to the very end of the age." (Mat 28:19-20)**
> >
> > **He said to them, "Go into all the world and preach the good news to all creation. (Mark 16:15)**
> >
> > **But you will receive power when the Holy Spirit comes on you; and you will be my witnesses in Jerusalem, and in all Judea and Samaria, and to the ends of the earth." (Acts 1:8)**
> >
> > **He then brought them out and asked, "Sirs, what must I do to be saved?" They replied, "Believe in the Lord Jesus, and you will be saved—you and your household." (Acts 16:30-31)**
> >
> > **Those who had been scattered preached the word wherever they went. (Acts 8:4)**
> >
> > **But in your hearts set apart Christ as Lord. Always be prepared to give an answer to everyone who asks you to give the reason for the hope that you have. But do this with gentleness and respect, (1 Pet 3:15)**

	X. Jesus Raises Jairus' Daughter & Heals a Woman: The Reward of True Faith, 8:40-56 (Mt.9:18-26; Mk.5:21-43)
1 The Gadarenes rejected Jesus, but the Galileans welcomed Him	40 Now when Jesus returned, a crowd welcomed him, for they were all expecting him.
2 The faith of a desperate ruler a. His rank: A religious ruler b. His approach: He forgot pride & position—denied himself	41 Then a man named Jairus, a ruler of the synagogue, came and fell at Jesus' feet, pleading with him to come to his house
c. His faith: He believed Jesus could save His daughter d. The reward: Jesus went to help him	42 Because his only daughter, a girl of about twelve, was dying. As Jesus was on his way, the crowds almost crushed him.
3 The faith of an embarrassed, hopeless woman a. Her hopelessness b. Her shame: Ceremonially unclean & socially outcast	43 And a woman was there who had been subject to bleeding for twelve years, but no one could heal her.
c. Her unusual "touch of faith": Many touched Jesus but only she was healed	44 She came up behind him and touched the edge of his cloak, and immediately her bleeding stopped. 45 "Who touched me?" Jesus asked. When they all denied it, Peter said, "Master, the people are crowding and pressing against you."
d. Her fearful awe & honest trust	46 But Jesus said, "Someone touched me; I know that power has gone out from me." 47 Then the woman, seeing that she could not go unnoticed, came trembling and fell at his feet. In the presence of all the people, she told why she had touched him and how she had been instantly healed.
e. Her reward: Jesus' undivided attention & healing	48 Then he said to her, "Daughter, your faith has healed you. Go in peace."
4 The faith of stubborn, helpless parents a. The parents' helplessness: The daughter died	49 While Jesus was still speaking, someone came from the house of Jairus, the synagogue ruler. "Your daughter is dead," he said. "Don't bother the teacher any more."
b. The parents' need: A strong faith[DS1]	50 Hearing this, Jesus said to Jairus, "Don't be afraid; just believe, and she will be healed."
c. The parents' strong faith: They followed Jesus despite the mockery	51 When he arrived at the house of Jairus, he did not let anyone go in with him except Peter, John and James, and the child's father and mother. 52 Meanwhile, all the people were wailing and mourning for her. "Stop wailing," Jesus said. "She is not dead but asleep." 53 They laughed at him, knowing that she was dead.
d. The reward: Jesus' undivided attention & resurrection power	54 But he took her by the hand and said, "My child, get up!" 55 Her spirit returned, and at once she stood up. Then Jesus told them to give her something to eat.
e. The unusual command	56 Her parents were astonished, but he ordered them not to tell anyone what had happened.

DIVISION III

THE SON OF MAN'S ANNOUNCED MISSION AND PUBLIC MINISTRY, 4:16-9:17

X. Jesus Raises Jairus' Daughter and Heals a Woman: The Reward of True Faith, 8:40-56

(8:40-56) **Introduction**: true faith will be rewarded. This passage gives a glimpse into just how enormously faith will be rewarded.

1. The Gadarenes rejected Jesus, but the Galileans welcomed Him (v.40).
2. The faith of a desperate ruler (v.41-42).
3. The faith of an embarrassed, hopeless woman (v.43-48).
4. The faith of stubborn, helpless parents (v.49-56).

1 (8:40) **Minister—Jesus Christ, Rejection**: the Gadarenes rejected Jesus, but the Galileans welcomed Him. Note two points.

1. One people drove Him away; the other hoped in Him. One country was closed to Him; the other was opened to Him.

2. Jesus sought work to do. Note a crucial point. When He was rejected by a people…

- He did not retaliate, strike back.
- He did not begin to moan, grumble, or gripe.
- He did not slip into discouragement or depression.
- He did not quit.

What did He do? He immediately left the people, the country of those who rejected Him, but He sought to minister elsewhere.

2 (8:41-42) **Faith—Self-Denial—Care—Humility**: the faith of a desperate ruler. One of the persons waiting for Jesus was a man named Jairus.

1. Jairus was a religious ruler, probably the highest-ranking official in the area. He was the head of the synagogue, the very center of Jewish life in the city. He was evidently well-to-do and highly esteemed among the people.

2. Jairus approached Jesus willing to pay the ultimate price.

a. He laid his position on the line in order to secure Jesus' help. The religionists were now opposing Jesus with a fierceness seldom seen, and they were attacking Him publicly. By coming to Jesus, Jairus was running the risk of arousing the hostility of his peers and of being censored and losing his position.
b. He denied and forgot self completely, laying all pride aside. He ran up to Jesus and fell down at Jesus' feet begging for help (see note and DEEPER STUDY # 1—Lk.9:23).

For whoever wants to save his life will lose it, but whoever loses his life for me will save it. What good is it for a man to gain the whole world, and yet lose or forfeit his very self? If anyone is ashamed of me and my words, the Son of Man will be ashamed of him when he comes in his glory and in the glory of the Father and of the holy angels. (Luke 9:24-26)
But he gives us more grace. That is why Scripture says: "God opposes the proud but gives grace to the humble." (James 4:6)
Humble yourselves before the Lord, and he will lift you up. (James 4:10)

3. Jairus' concern was over someone else. He was running the risk of losing everything for the sake of someone else: his twelve-year-old daughter. She was his only child and she was dying. Note Jairus' faith. He pleaded with Jesus to help. He believed with all his heart that Jesus could save his daughter—if He would only come to his house.

He will call upon me, and I will answer him; I will be with him in trouble, I will deliver him and honor him. (Psa 91:15)
Then you will call, and the LORD will answer; you will cry for help, and he will say: Here am I. "If you do away with the yoke of oppression, with the pointing finger and malicious talk, (Isa 58:9)
'Call to me and I will answer you and tell you great and unsearchable things you do not know.' (Jer 33:3)

4. Jairus' faith was immediately rewarded. Jesus answered Jairus' plea. Jesus turned and began to move toward Jairus' house. The humble, self-denying approach of Jairus caused Jesus to turn and begin meeting his desperate need.

If you believe, you will receive whatever you ask for in prayer." (Mat 21:22)
You may ask me for anything in my name, and I will do it. (John 14:14)

3 (8:43-48) **Hopelessness—Faith—Jesus Christ, Work of**: the faith of an embarrassed, hopeless woman. Five simple points are brought out about this woman.

1. She was hopeless.

2. She was ashamed, extremely embarrassed over her problem. The reason was twofold. First, she was considered ceremonially unclean; that is, she was cut off from society and religious worship (Lev.15:19-33). She had even been divorced, for the law required it (Lev.15:25-27). Imagine a woman's having to live with the shame of being divorced because of a medical problem. Second, she was hesitant about letting anyone know about her condition. Her hemorrhaging was a personal, intimate matter for her, something she did not want to be known and discussed publicly.

3. Her unusual *touch of faith.* Note that many were crowding Jesus and touching Him, but only one touched Him in faith. The woman had an *expectant, believing attitude*. She believed that if she could only touch Him she would be made whole (v.47; cp. Mt.9:21), and she was: "Immediately her bleeding stopped" (este).

"'If you can'?" said Jesus. "Everything is possible for him who believes." (Mark 9:23)
How great is your goodness, which you have stored up for those who fear you, which you bestow in the sight of men on those who take refuge in you. (Psa 31:19)
Commit your way to the LORD; trust in him and he will do this: (Psa 37:5)

4. Her fearful awe and honest trust. Note what now happened.
a. Jesus knew what had happened. He had allowed the woman to be healed in order to help her in her embarrassment. However, secret discipleship was impossible. She had to confess her deliverance.

"I tell you, whoever acknowledges me before men, the Son of Man will also acknowledge him before the angels of God. (Luke 12:8)
"Whoever acknowledges me before men, I will also acknowledge him before my Father in heaven. (Mat 10:32)
That if you confess with your mouth, "Jesus is Lord," and believe in your heart that God raised him from the dead, you will be saved. For it is with your heart that you believe and are justified, and it is with your mouth that you confess and are saved. (Rom 10:9-10)

b. Serving and helping others cost Jesus, and cost Him dearly. Power (dunamin), spiritual power, flowed out from His being into the woman. It was that which healed her. Note that the disciples were unaware of what it cost Jesus to minister. They were insensitive to the spiritual energy He was exerting, ignorant of what Jesus was doing:
⇒ He was taking our infirmities upon Himself and bearing our sicknesses.

This was to fulfill what was spoken through the prophet Isaiah: "He took up our infirmities and carried our diseases." (Mat 8:17; cp. Is 53:4)

⇒ He was teaching that public confession of Him was essential.
Note what the woman did when she saw "that she could not go unnoticed." She knew that He who had such power knew who had touched Him, so she came as all should come in approaching the Lord: "trembling and fell at His feet," confessing all.

Thought 1. It is spiritual power that flows into and delivers any of us, the spiritual power of Christ.

5. The woman's faith was rewarded, wonderfully so. Her faith caused Jesus to meet her face to face; her faith did some wonderful things for her.

a. She was called, "Daughter." This was the only time Jesus ever called a woman, "Daughter." What a distinct privilege! It meant she had become a child of God's.

The Spirit himself testifies with our spirit that we are God's children. Now if we are children, then we are heirs—heirs of God and co-heirs with Christ, if indeed we share in his sufferings in order that we may also share in his glory. (Rom 8:16-17)

But when the time had fully come, God sent his Son, born of a woman, born under law, to redeem those under law, that we might receive the full rights of sons. Because you are sons, God sent the Spirit of his Son into our hearts, the Spirit who calls out, *"Abba,* Father." (Gal 4:4-6)

b. She was given comfort (tharsei), or more accurately, cheer, courage, confidence, and boldness in her faith and healing.

c. She was assured that she was whole permanently. Her deliverance would last.

d. She was given peace (see note—Jn.14:27).

Do not be anxious about anything, but in everything, by prayer and petition, with thanksgiving, present your requests to God. And the peace of God, which transcends all understanding, will guard your hearts and your minds in Christ Jesus. (Phil 4:6-7)

Peace I leave with you; my peace I give you. I do not give to you as the world gives. Do not let your hearts be troubled and do not be afraid. (John 14:27)

"I have told you these things, so that in me you may have peace. In this world you will have trouble. But take heart! I have overcome the world." (John 16:33)

4 (8:49-56) **Faith—Helplessness**: the faith of stubborn, helpless parents. Five points are seen in the suspense of this scene.

1. The helplessness of Jairus: his daughter died. It was while Jesus was still speaking to the hemorrhaging woman that the news came to Jairus: his daughter was dead. Note three things.

a. Jairus' faith had been sorely tried. His daughter was critically ill, and he was forced to wait while Jesus ministered to another patient. What he feared had happened. Jesus was too late; his daughter had died.

b. Jairus was pulled off to the side and told not to bother the Lord any more now; the Master was too busy to bother with his situation since his daughter was now dead.

c. Jesus' power was thought to be limited and ineffective in the face of death. So the messenger suggested that Jairus could now go home. The point is that Jairus was totally helpless, and the power of Jesus was thought to be limited to the living. The thought that Jesus' power would be effective in dealing with the dead never crossed this gloomy messenger's mind.

2. The parents' need: a strong, stubborn faith. Jesus did not even give Jairus a chance to speak. Jesus forcibly said:

⇒ "Don't be afraid" (me phobou): do not be gripped with terror, dread, fear, anxiety.

⇒ "Just believe" (see notes—Mk.11:22-23; DEEPER STUDY # 2—Jn.2:24; note—Ro.10:16-17; DEEPER STUDY # 1—Heb.10:38).

⇒ "And she will be healed" (swthesetai): restored, made alive, saved.

Imagine the strong faith required to believe simply because of Jesus' Word, because of what He said.

3. The parents' strong faith: they followed Jesus despite the mockery.

a. Jesus took only the parents and His inner circle into the house. The parents and daughter would need quiet and time to be reunited and to regain their joyful composure before seeing people. The inner circle would give enough witness to verify and record the incident for all generations.

b. The mourners who scorned Jesus would probably include relatives, friends, neighbors, and the professional mourners. The professional mourners were a custom in the East. Note how Jesus was scorned and ridiculed.

c. The girl was dead. Some readers stress Jesus' words, "she is not dead but asleep," saying that she was actually still alive (see DEEPER STUDY # 1, Death—Lk.8:50).

d. The parents' stubborn faith was rewarded, greatly so. Their faith caused Jesus to save their daughter, to actually raise her up from the dead. Her spirit returned to her body and she arose.

Note Jesus commanded that food be given to her. This activity would help her mother handle the emotion of the moment and help to strengthen the daughter.

Thought 1. *Stubborn faith* is desperately needed by many parents in behalf of their children. However, note what must precede stubborn faith: a desperate faith that forgets and denies oneself, seeking Jesus no matter the cost. Difficult cases require both a desperate faith and a stubborn faith. It is such faith that receives the *great* reward.

He replied, "Because you have so little faith. I tell you the truth, if you have faith as small as a mustard seed, you can say to this mountain, 'Move from here to there' and it will move. Nothing will be impossible for you." (Mat 17:20; cp. Mat 21:21)

"Have faith in God," Jesus answered. "I tell you the truth, if anyone says to this mountain, 'Go, throw yourself into the sea,' and does not doubt in his heart but believes that what he says will happen, it will be done for him. Therefore I tell you, whatever you ask for in prayer, believe that you have received it, and it will be yours. (Mark 11:22-24)

Hearing this, Jesus said to Jairus, "Don't be afraid; just believe, and she will be healed." (Luke 8:50)

Early in the morning they left for the Desert of Tekoa. As they set out, Jehoshaphat stood and said, "Listen to me, Judah and people of Jerusalem! Have faith in the LORD your God and you will be up-

held; have faith in his prophets and you will be successful." (2 Chr 20:20)

e. Jesus gave an unusual command. He was probably commanding the parents to keep silent about the matter because the crowds surrounding Him were already too large.

DEEPER STUDY # 1

(8:50) **Death—Sleep**: some argue that this girl was actually alive and that Jesus knew it. But note several facts. (See DEEPER STUDY # 1—Jn.11:13 for more discussion.)

1. Jesus and the Bible speak of death as nothing more than sleep. By sleep is meant *rest and comfort in God* (Mt.27:52; Acts 7:60; 1 Th.4:13-18). Many within the world think of death as annihilation or ceasing to exist. Jesus drew the contrast in order to say that death is not annihilation. Believers continue to exist, resting in the life and comfort of God.

2. Note that Jesus knew the girl was dead (v.53). He clearly said so.

3. Note the words "her spirit returned." The point is this: her spirit had left her body, and upon the command of Jesus, her spirit returned. Her life returned to the body immediately.

	CHAPTER 9
	Y. Jesus Commissions His Disciples, 9:1-9 (Mt.9:35-10:42; Mk.6:7-13)
1 Their call: To come together for ministry **2 Their equipment: Power & authority**	When Jesus had called the Twelve together, he gave them power and authority to drive out all demons and to cure diseases,
3 Their mission: To preach & minister	2 And he sent them out to preach the kingdom of God and to heal the sick.
4 Their method a. Not to seek success through personal appearance & materialism	3 He told them: "Take nothing for the journey—no staff, no bag, no bread, no money, no extra tunic.
b. To minister in the homes, to the interested & the hospitable[DS1]	4 Whatever house you enter, stay there until you leave that town.
c. To warn rejecters	5 If people do not welcome you, shake the dust off your feet when you leave their town, as a testimony against them."
5 Their obedience: They went forth preaching & ministering	6 So they set out and went from village to village, preaching the gospel and healing people everywhere.
6 Their effect a. Herod was disturbed by their message	7 Now Herod the tetrarch heard about all that was going on. And he was perplexed, because some were saying that John had been raised from the dead,
b. The people speculated about Jesus' identity	8 Others that Elijah had appeared, and still others that one of the prophets of long ago had come back to life.
c. Herod desired to know Jesus' identity	9 But Herod said, "I beheaded John. Who, then, is this I hear such things about?" And he tried to see him.

DIVISION III

THE SON OF MAN'S ANNOUNCED MISSION AND PUBLIC MINISTRY, 4:16-9:17

Y. Jesus Commissions His Disciples, 9:1-9

(9:1-9) **Introduction**: this was the first time Jesus sent His disciples out alone; therefore, it a significant event. The instructions given by Jesus to the early disciples are needed by every generation of believers. It is the only sure way the world can ever be reached and grounded in the Lord.

1. Their call: to come together for ministry (v.1).
2. Their equipment: power and authority (v.1).
3. Their mission: to preach and minister (v.2).
4. Their method (v.3-5).
5. Their obedience: they went forth preaching and ministering (v.6).
6. Their effect (v.7-9).

1 (9:1) **Ministers, Call—Unity—Jesus Christ, Ministry—Power**: the disciples' call was to come together for ministry. Jesus had to call His disciples back *together.* Note the word "together" (sunkalesamenos). The word reveals several things to us.

1. The disciples had families and responsibilities. We tend to glamorize the disciples and Jesus, forgetting the disciples were ordinary men with day-to-day duties. They were not with the Lord at this time. They had to spend some time at home taking care of their families and whatever other duties they had. No doubt they did spend most of their time with Jesus as travelling evangelists, but at certain times, they returned home in order to tend to family affairs.

2. The basic ingredient for ministry is *togetherness.* Note the words, "called...together." The very thrust of the words points to the importance of *coming together.*

> **"My children, I will be with you only a little longer. You will look for me, and just as I told the Jews, so I tell you now: Where I am going, you cannot come. "A new command I give you: Love one another. As I have loved you, so you must love one another. (John 13:33-34)**
>
> **Whatever happens, conduct yourselves in a manner worthy of the gospel of Christ. Then, whether I come and see you or only hear about you in my absence, I will know that you stand firm in one spirit, contending as one man for the faith of the gospel (Phil 1:27)**

3. The purpose for coming together is to minister. Jesus was completing His Galilean ministry. He was now ready to set His face toward Jerusalem (Lk.9:51). His ministry had been successful. Multitudes knew of His coming to earth, many had been helped and some did believe and trust. Now, before He left the area, He wanted to reach out one more time to those who were close to believing and to more deeply root and ground those who already believed.

4. The call of Jesus was for the disciples to have power to "drive out all demons', and to cure diseases."

a. "Power...to drive out all demons'." The word "all" means that the disciple was to have power over all kinds of evil, no matter how evil and enslaving, strong and fierce, subtle and undetected. It also points to the glorious purpose of Jesus. He had come to defeat and conquer the evil forces of this world, to rout and triumph over "all" of them.

> **For our struggle is not against flesh and blood, but against the rulers, against the authorities, against the powers of this dark world and against the spiritual forces of evil in the heavenly realms. (Eph 6:12)**
>
> **Now is the time for judgment on this world; now the prince of this world will be driven out. (John 12:31)**
>
> **For he has rescued us from the dominion of darkness and brought us into the**

kingdom of the Son he loves, in whom we have redemption, the forgiveness of sins. (Col 1:13-14)

And having disarmed the powers and authorities, he [Christ] made a public spectacle of them, triumphing over them by the cross. (Col 2:15)

Since the children have flesh and blood, he too shared in their humanity so that by his death he might destroy him who holds the power of death—that is, the devil—and free those who all their lives were held in slavery by their fear of death. (Heb 2:14-15)

He who does what is sinful is of the devil, because the devil has been sinning from the beginning. The reason the Son of God appeared was to destroy the devil's work. (1 John 3:8)

b. "Power...to cure diseases." This would demonstrate the great compassion of the Lord and draw people to Him (Jn.12:32). It would also help tremendously in confirming the faith of some.

2 (9:1) **Power—Authority**: the disciples' equipment was to be power and authority. Jesus equipped His disciples with power and with the authority to use that power. Power is the *gift*, the necessary resource to minister; authority is the *right* to minister. The disciple has to decide when and where to exercise his power (resource). The awesome responsibility for such power should help to keep the disciple on his face before God, acknowledging his total dependence upon God. It should also help the disciple to seek a closeness with God, a true sensitivity to the Spirit of God.

Thought 1. Think how little power is really seen in the lives and ministry of believers, lay and minister alike! How *displaced* or *misplaced* so many believers are. The *authority* to minister (where and when) has not been used as it should. The face of the Lord has not been sought, not to the point that a true closeness to His Spirit has directed our authority. We have taken the authority, the right to minister where we wish into our own hands. The evidence: after 2000 years so much of the world still has not heard the gospel.

Therefore go and make disciples of all nations, baptizing them in the name of the Father and of the Son and of the Holy Spirit, and teaching them to obey everything I have commanded you. And surely I am with you always, to the very end of the age." (Mat 28:19-20)

But you will receive power when the Holy Spirit comes on you; and you will be my witnesses in Jerusalem, and in all Judea and Samaria, and to the ends of the earth." (Acts 1:8)

With great power the apostles continued to testify to the resurrection of the Lord Jesus, and much grace was upon them all. (Acts 4:33)

My message and my preaching were not with wise and persuasive words, but with a demonstration of the Spirit's power, (1 Cor 2:4)

I thank Christ Jesus our Lord, who has given me strength, that he considered me faithful, appointing me to his service. (1 Tim 1:12)

He has made us competent as ministers of a new covenant—not of the letter but of the Spirit; for the letter kills, but the Spirit gives life. (2 Cor 3:6)

And God is able to make all grace abound to you, so that in all things at all times, having all that you need, you will abound in every good work. (2 Cor 9:8)

I can do everything through him who gives me strength. (Phil 4:13)

Now to him who is able to do immeasurably more than all we ask or imagine, according to his power that is at work within us, (Eph 3:20)

Because our gospel came to you not simply with words, but also with power, with the Holy Spirit and with deep conviction. You know how we lived among you for your sake. (1 Th 1:5)

For God did not give us a spirit of timidity, but a spirit of power, of love and of self-discipline. (2 Tim 1:7)

3 (9:2) **Ministers, Duty—Mission**: the disciples' mission was to preach and minister. Note three points.

1. They were sent on the very same mission as Christ.

Again Jesus said, "Peace be with you! As the Father has sent me, I am sending you." (John 20:21)

But the crowds learned about it and followed him. He welcomed them and spoke to them about the kingdom of God, and healed those who needed healing. (Luke 9:11)

2. They were to preach the Kingdom of God (see Deeper Study # 3—Mt.19:23-24). Preaching met the spiritual needs of the human soul.

For the Son of Man came to seek and to save what was lost." (Luke 19:10; cp. John 20:31)

3. They were to heal the sick. Healing met the physical needs of the human body.

Just as the Son of Man did not come to be served, but to serve, and to give his life as a ransom for many." (Mat 20:28)

Finally, all of you, live in harmony with one another; be sympathetic, love as brothers, be compassionate and humble. (1 Pet 3:8)

Be merciful to those who doubt; snatch others from the fire and save them; to others show mercy, mixed with fear—hating even the clothing stained by corrupted flesh. (Jude 1:22-23)

"This is what the LORD Almighty says: 'Administer true justice; show mercy and compassion to one another. (Zec 7:9)

He is able to deal gently with those who are ignorant and are going astray, since he himself is subject to weakness. (Heb 5:2)

4 (9:3-5) **Mission—Ministry—Method**: the disciples' method was threefold.

1. They were not to seek success through personal appearance and materialism. They were to live in utter simplicity and humility. This was the point of the things Christ listed (v.3. See note—Mk.6:8-13 for more discussion.) Christ was saying three things to the disciples.

a. The need and the hour were urgent. Concentrate on preaching and ministering. Do not get sidetracked.

Set your minds on things above, not on earthly things. (Col 3:2)

b. Learn to believe and trust God day by day. Become a living example of what is being preached: faith in God. Do not begin to trust in the things of the world. Learn to trust God daily, and then others can learn what is meant by "believing" and "trusting" God through your example.

But seek first his kingdom and his righteousness, and all these things will be given to you as well. (Mat 6:33)

c. Avoid the very appearance of evil. Having your mind upon the things of this world will distract from God and from the needs of men and from the ministry. Become attached to God and to His kingdom alone; not to money, houses, lands, cars, clothes, hairstyles, appearance, food, buying, selling, and accumulating. Be heavenly-minded and ministry-centered, so that men may know there is a far better land than what this earth offers.

Those who live according to the sinful nature have their minds set on what that nature desires; but those who live in accordance with the Spirit have their minds set on what the Spirit desires. The mind of sinful man is death, but the mind controlled by the Spirit is life and peace; (Rom 8:5-6)

All these people were still living by faith when they died. They did not receive the things promised; they only saw them and welcomed them from a distance. And they admitted that they were aliens and strangers on earth. People who say such things show that they are looking for a country of their own. If they had been thinking of the country they had left, they would have had opportunity to return. Instead, they were longing for a better country—a heavenly one. Therefore God is not ashamed to be called their God, for he has prepared a city for them. (Heb 11:13-16)

By faith Moses, when he had grown up, refused to be known as the son of Pharaoh's daughter. He chose to be mistreated along with the people of God rather than to enjoy the pleasures of sin for a short time. He regarded disgrace for the sake of Christ as of greater value than the treasures of Egypt, because he was looking ahead to his reward. (Heb 11:24-26)

2. They were to minister in the homes to the interested and the hospitable families (see DEEPER STUDY # 1—Lk.9:4).

3. They were to warn rejecters. If a community or city did not receive their witness and if a home could not be found that would receive them, then the disciple was to leave.

a. He was not to force the issue or create a bad situation either for the rejecters or for himself. There was to be no tongue-lashing, accusation, or divisiveness created.

b. He was simply to leave; and as he left, he was to give a *silent* testimony against them. He was to shake the very dust from his feet. This was a symbol of serious judgment. It meant that not even the dust of that place was worthy of the gospel of God, much less the people. The place and its people were *left* to themselves just as they had wished. They were left *without God* and His glorious news of salvation, so they were to be left alone to govern their own lives just as they had willed. God would *abandon* them to their own way and choice of life.

DEEPER STUDY # 1

(9:4) **Church, In Homes**: the method Christ chose for evangelizing was the method of home evangelism (cp. 10:5f). Note this, for it should speak loudly and clearly to us. The disciple was to carefully investigate and search out a receptive family and home. He was to make that home the center for ministry. Note several things about this method.

a. It emphasizes the family, making it the very hub of ministry.

b. It stresses stability, security, and settledness. Nothing on earth is to be any more secure and stable than the family. By placing the center of ministry in the home, the Kingdom of God becomes secure and stable.

c. It centers preaching and ministering in the community, right where people live and walk. It makes the presence of Christ visible to all in day-to-day living.

d. It serves as the center from which the message can move out in an ever-widening circle, spreading from family to family.

Thought 1. The most ideal form of evangelism is probably this method given by Christ: a selected home and family serving as the center of witness within a community or town. The early church was definitely centered in the homes of committed believers (Acts 5:42; 12:12; 16:40; 20:20; 1 Cor.16:19; Col.4:15; Phile.2).

5 (9:6) **Obedience**: they went forth and preached and ministered. The disciples did exactly what Christ had commissioned them to do. They did not fail in the least.

a. They departed. There was no hesitation, no question, no condition, no hanging back, no slowness to move.

b. They went through the towns. They reached a home and ministered to its surrounding community, ever moving farther and farther out into the whole town. And then they moved on to another town to bear witness to its people as well.

c. They preached and ministered "everywhere." They had an extensive ministry, very successful in its outreach, ministering to both soul (preaching) and body (healing).

Those who had been scattered preached the word wherever they went. (Acts 8:4)

Preach the Word; be prepared in season and out of season; correct, rebuke and encourage—with great patience and careful instruction. (2 Tim 4:2)

Jesus said to him, "Let the dead bury their own dead, but you go and proclaim the kingdom of God." (Luke 9:60)

"Go, stand in the temple courts," he said, "and tell the people the full message of this new life." (Acts 5:20)

6 (9:7-9) **Jesus Christ, Response to**: their effect was phenomenal. The message and ministry of Jesus and His apostles reached even into the halls of government. The impact of the message and ministry reached far and wide during these days. (See outline and notes—Mt.14:1-14; Mk.6:14-29 for detailed discussion.)

1. Herod became disturbed. He had murdered John the Baptist, and some were saying that Jesus was John the Baptist risen from the dead. Of course, Herod's conscience was bothering him, just as all men are nagged by questions (at least questions about reality and the hereafter). He thought he had gotten rid of John's convicting preaching. Was it possible that John had arisen or that another like John had come on the scene? Herod wished to know.

2. The people were speculating about Jesus' identity (see outline and notes—Jn.7:37-53).

	Z. Jesus Teaches How to Minister, 9:10-17 (Mt.14:15-21; Mk.6:30-44; Jn.6:1-14)
1 He demonstrated & taught the need for privacy & rest a. The twelve returned & reported to Jesus b. Jesus sought privacy with the disciples	10 When the apostles returned, they reported to Jesus what they had done. Then he took them with him and they withdrew by themselves to a town called Bethsaida,
2 He allowed the needy to interrupt the much needed privacy & rest **3 He met both spiritual & physical needs**	11 But the crowds learned about it and followed him. He welcomed them and spoke to them about the kingdom of God, and healed those who needed healing.
4 He challenged the disciples to meet the people's needs a. The wrong attitude: Let the people take care of themselves b. The right attitude: Let the disciples meet the peoples' needs c. The problem: Inadequate resources	12 Late in the afternoon the Twelve came to him and said, "Send the crowd away so they can go to the surrounding villages and countryside and find food and lodging, because we are in a remote place here." 13 He replied, "You give them something to eat." They answered, "We have only five loaves of bread and two fish—unless we go and buy food for all this crowd."
5 He approached needs in an orderly fashion	14 (About five thousand men were there.) But he said to his disciples, "Have them sit down in groups of about fifty each." 15 The disciples did so, and everybody sat down.
6 He looked to God in meeting needs a. He thanked God for what He had b. He broke & gave what He had c. He utilized all for future ministering & feeding	16 Taking the five loaves and the two fish and looking up to heaven, he gave thanks and broke them. Then he gave them to the disciples to set before the people. 17 They all ate and were satisfied, and the disciples picked up twelve basketfuls of broken pieces that were left over.

DIVISION III

THE SON OF MAN'S ANNOUNCED MISSION AND PUBLIC MINISTRY, 4:16-9:17

Z. Jesus Teaches How to Minister, 9:10-17

(9:10-17) **Introduction**: Jesus once said, "The Son of Man did not come to be served, but to serve" (cp. Mt. 20:28; Mark 10:45). So it is with the Lord's disciple. But how the disciple ministers is of vital concern, for how he ministers determines the eternal fate of men and the success or failure of the Lord's mission. In this passage Jesus teaches His followers *how to minister*. (See outlines and notes—Mt.14:15-21; Mk.6:30-44 for more discussion and applications.)

1. He demonstrated and taught the need for privacy and rest (v.10).
2. He allowed the needy to interrupt the much needed privacy and rest (v.11).
3. He met both spiritual and physical needs (v.11).
4. He challenged the disciples to meet the people's needs (v.12-13).
5. He approached needs in an orderly fashion (v.14-15).
6. He looked to God in meeting needs (v.16-17).

1 (9:10) **Devotion—Rest—Evaluation**: Jesus demonstrated and taught the need for privacy. The twelve returned from their mission and reported what had happened. Jesus had never needed time with them as much as He did now, for He was closing out His Galilean ministry. In fact, there was to be little public ministry hereafter. From this point onward He was to concentrate primarily on His disciples, giving them intensive training (see notes—Mt.16:13-20; 16:21-28; 17:1-13; 17:22; 17:24-27; 20:17; 20:20-28 to see the emphasis upon this intensive training).

1. Jesus needed to discuss their witnessing tour with them. As they reported, He needed to point out both the strengths and weaknesses of how they went about it. They must learn to minister in the most effective way possible. An evaluation session was needed.

2. The disciples needed to evaluate themselves; but they needed to do it in the presence of God alone so that they could restore both their spirits and bodies. They were physically exhausted and their spirits were drained.

What did Jesus do? "He took them with Him and they withdrew by themselves to a town called Bethsaida. Jesus had hoped to get some rest, some quietness, and privacy for Himself and His disciples. Note that they had apparently not entered the town, that they were in a *"remote place"* (v. 12).

The point was clearly demonstrated for the disciples. There is a time for ministry and for evaluating oneself and one's ministry; there is also a time for renewing one's spirit and body.

> **"Come to me, all you who are weary and burdened, and I will give you rest. (Mat 11:28)**
>
> **Then, because so many people were coming and going that they did not even have a chance to eat, he said to them, "Come with me by yourselves to a quiet place and get some rest." (Mark 6:31)**
>
> **"Six days you shall labor, but on the seventh day you shall rest; even during the plowing season and harvest you must rest. (Exo 34:21; cp. Ex.23:12; 31:15; 35:2)**
>
> **"'There are six days when you may work, but the seventh day is a Sabbath of rest, a day of sacred assembly. You are not to do any work; wherever you live, it is a Sabbath to the LORD. (Lev 23:3)**
>
> **I said, "Oh, that I had the wings of a dove! I would fly away and be at rest—I would flee far away and stay in the desert; Selah (Psa 55:6-7)**

The LORD replied, "My Presence will go with you, and I will give you rest." (Exo 33:14)

Be at rest once more, O my soul, for the LORD has been good to you. (Psa 116:7)

To whom he said, "This is the resting place, let the weary rest"; and, "This is the place of repose"— but they would not listen. (Isa 28:12)

This is what the Sovereign LORD, the Holy One of Israel, says: "In repentance and rest is your salvation, in quietness and trust is your strength, but you would have none of it. (Isa 30:15)

Be diligent in these matters; give yourself wholly to them, so that everyone may see your progress. (1 Tim 4:15)

Take my yoke upon you and learn from me, for I am gentle and humble in heart, and you will find rest for your souls. (Mat 11:29)

I will meditate on all your works and consider all your mighty deeds. (Psa 77:12)

May my meditation be pleasing to him, as I rejoice in the LORD. (Psa 104:34)

I meditate on your precepts and consider your ways. (Psa 119:15)

I remember the days of long ago; I meditate on all your works and consider what your hands have done. (Psa 143:5)

2 (9:11) **Ministry—Vision**: Jesus allowed the needy to interrupt the much needed privacy. The emphasis is on the words "thecrowds learned about it an dfollowed Him." (See note—Mk.6:33 for the drama of the scene.) The people were disturbing and interrupting the disciples' need for privacy, for rest and spiritual renewal. The disciples had been ministering, doing all they could, yet here the people were demanding more. Note the contrast between Jesus and the disciples. The disciples became irritated (v.12; cp. the rude statement, "unless we go and buy food for all this crowd" of v.13). Jesus, on the other hand, was filled with compassion for the people (cp. Mk.6:34). The disciples had a much needed lesson to learn, and they needed to learn the lesson more than they needed rest. The lesson was simple but dramatic: while one is resting the multitudes are still lost. They are as sheep without a shepherd (Mk.6:34). A disciple must not rest unless it is *absolutely necessary.* Too many are lost and hurting.

Do you not say, 'Four months more and then the harvest'? I tell you, open your eyes and look at the fields! They are ripe for harvest. (John 4:35)

As long as it is day, we must do the work of him who sent me. Night is coming, when no one can work. (John 9:4)

For we cannot help speaking about what we have seen and heard." (Acts 4:20)

Yet when I preach the gospel, I cannot boast, for I am compelled to preach. Woe to me if I do not preach the gospel! (1 Cor 9:16)

Preach the Word; be prepared in season and out of season; correct, rebuke and encourage—with great patience and careful instruction. (2 Tim 4:2)

For this reason I remind you to fan into flame the gift of God, which is in you through the laying on of my hands. (2 Tim 1:6)

Whatever your hand finds to do, do it with all your might, for in the grave, where you are going, there is neither working nor planning nor knowledge nor wisdom. (Eccl 9:10)

For Zion's sake I will not keep silent, for Jerusalem's sake I will not remain quiet, till her righteousness shines out like the dawn, her salvation like a blazing torch. (Isa 62:1)

But if I say, "I will not mention him or speak any more in his name," his word is in my heart like a fire, a fire shut up in my bones. I am weary of holding it in; indeed, I cannot. (Jer 20:9)

3 (9:11) **Heals—Healing**: Jesus met both spiritual and physical needs. The people did not need preaching alone; they also needed help physically. Both body and soul needed to be saved and restored. So Jesus...

- spoke (preached) unto them the Kingdom of God.
- healed them that had need of healing.

Note two points.

1. Jesus preached the Kingdom of God—of which God is the ruler and man is the subject, of which the Word of God is Law and the obedience of man is demanded.

2. Jesus healed the people "who needed healing." This is always true. A believer who really *needs healing* is blessed by God and healed. But note: *the need of healing is not always the greatest need of a person.* God sometimes uses the physical need to meet that which is far more important: the spiritual need and the glory of God. Therefore, not all believers are always healed. Sometimes the believer needs to learn love, joy, peace, endurance, prayer, trust, faith, and hope through his suffering. (See DEEPER STUDY # 3—Mt.8:1-4 for detailed discussion.)

However, there is and has been a problem with the truth of this down through the centuries. So many use the spiritual need as an excuse for not having the faith and godly power to be healed and to heal. As Jesus Himself said, it is much easier to tell a man his sins are forgiven than it is to tell him to take up his bed and walk. Jesus met both needs of a man, his spiritual needs and his physical needs: "[He] healed those who needed healing." (See DEEPER STUDY # 3—Mt.8:1-4 for detailed discussion.)

The disciples needed to learn that both the spiritual and physical needs of men were to be met.

How God anointed Jesus of Nazareth with the Holy Spirit and power, and how he went around doing good and healing all who were under the power of the devil, because God was with him. (Acts 10:38)

4 (9:12-13) **Resources—Ministering—Needs, Attitudes Toward**: Jesus challenged the disciples to meet the people's needs. The people had been listening to Jesus for hours. Sundown was soon to come. There was danger the people would be caught out in the desert in the dark, unable to get food before the next day. Some had already gone most of the day without food. It was time for Jesus to stop and let the people go; however, He gave no sign of stopping. So the disciples suggested He dismiss the crowd. Note the two attitudes toward meeting the needs of people.

1. The wrong attitude was illustrated by the disciples. They suggested that Jesus let the people go and take care of their own needs. Keep in mind that the crowd was not welcomed by the disciples, not this day. It was to have been a day of rest and spiritual renewal for them. The point is, the disciples had not sensed any personal responsibility for the *hunger* (physical or spiritual) of the crowd. They were willing, even wanting the crowd to go away, no matter the difficulty they would have in fending for themselves.

2. The right attitude was illustrated by Jesus. He emphatically said, "You give them something to eat." The "you" is emphatic in the Greek. Jesus was stressing that it was the disciples' responsibility. They were to take care of the people's needs. They were to "feed" the people (physically and spiritually). The people were not to be left to themselves. They could not fend nor provide for themselves.

Note something else: it was more important for the people to be hearing the gospel and receiving ministry than to be out seeking bread. "Man does not live on bread alone" (Lk.4:4). It is, of course, necessary to seek bread sometime in order to survive, but seeking spiritual food is absolutely essential. Seeking spiritual food must be interrupted only when necessary.

> **"Martha, Martha," the Lord answered, "you are worried and upset about many things, but only one thing is needed. Mary has chosen what is better [sitting at Jesus' feet learning], and it will not be taken away from her." (Luke 10:41-42)**
>
> **Then Jesus declared, "I am the bread of life. He who comes to me will never go hungry, and he who believes in me will never be thirsty. (John 6:35)**
>
> **I am the living bread that came down from heaven. If anyone eats of this bread, he will live forever. This bread is my flesh, which I will give for the life of the world." (John 6:51)**

3. The problem was inadequate resources. The disciples readily confessed that they had too little to meet the need of the people. Just think about the enormity of the situation for a moment. The crowd was huge; the task was *impossible*. There was no possibility the disciples could meet the need of the people. But note: they did exactly what needed to be done:

⇒ They told Jesus exactly what they did have.
⇒ They did the best thinking they could, giving the best solution they could.

What the disciples had was inadequate, but they did lay what they had before Jesus and discussed the only solution they knew (to go and buy food).

> **And I charged your judges at that time: Hear the disputes between your brothers and judge fairly, whether the case is between brother Israelites or between one of them and an alien. Do not show partiality in judging; hear both small and great alike. Do not be afraid of any man, for judgment belongs to God. Bring me any case too hard for you, and I will hear it. (Deu 1:16-17)**
>
> **On the first day of every week, each one of you should set aside a sum of money in keeping with his income, saving it up, so that when I come no collections will have to be made. (1 Cor 16:2)**
>
> **Give, and it will be given to you. A good measure, pressed down, shaken together and running over, will be poured into your lap. For with the measure you use, it will be measured to you." (Luke 6:38)**
>
> **Give to the one who asks you, and do not turn away from the one who wants to borrow from you. (Mat 5:42)**
>
> **In everything I did, I showed you that by this kind of hard work we must help the weak, remembering the words the Lord Jesus himself said: 'It is more blessed to give than to receive.'" (Acts 20:35)**

5 (9:14-15) **Organization**: Jesus approached needs in an orderly fashion. There were over five thousand men alone, not counting women and children. The need was so great, organization was necessary for the need to be met. The need was divided and spread about among the disciples by setting the people up in groups. Each group or company had fifty persons, or double rows of fifty each (Mk.6:40).

> **Thought 1.** The task is enormous. It can be met only by an orderly, organized approach.

6 (9:16-17) **Ministering**: Jesus looked to God in meeting needs. Note exactly what Jesus did.

1. Jesus looked up to heaven, giving thanks to God for what He did have. This is what is meant by the *blessing*.

2. Jesus broke and gave what He had. Note a crucial point. Jesus was doing what He could: looking up to God, giving thanks and then giving what He had. He could do no more.

> **Thought 1.** The lesson is clear for every believer. Once we do our part, God will multiply our resources.

3. Jesus utilized all. There was plenty to feed all, in fact more than enough.

> **Thought 1.** There will always be enough to feed all—if we will only confess our inadequate resources, give thanks for what we have, and then give what we have.
>
> **But seek first his kingdom and his righteousness, and all these things will be given to you as well. (Mat 6:33)**
>
> **Bring the whole tithe into the storehouse, that there may be food in my house. Test me in this," says the LORD Almighty, "and see if I will not throw open the floodgates of heaven and pour out so much blessing that you will not have room enough for it. (Mal 3:10)**
>
> **Of David. A psalm. The earth is the Lord's, and everything in it, the world, and all who live in it; (Psa 24:1)**
>
> **For the director of music. A psalm of David. Blessed is he who has regard for the weak; the LORD delivers him in times of trouble. (Psa 41:1)**

For every animal of the forest is mine, and the cattle on a thousand hills. (Psa 50:10)

A generous man will prosper; he who refreshes others will himself be refreshed. (Prov 11:25)

A generous man will himself be blessed, for he shares his food with the poor. (Prov 22:9)

He who gives to the poor will lack nothing, but he who closes his eyes to them receives many curses. (Prov 28:27)

Cast your bread upon the waters, for after many days you will find it again. (Eccl 11:1)

But the noble man makes noble plans, and by noble deeds he stands. (Isa 32:8)

And if you spend yourselves in behalf of the hungry and satisfy the needs of the oppressed, then your light will rise in the darkness, and your night will become like the noonday. (Isa 58:10)

'The silver is mine and the gold is mine,' declares the LORD Almighty. (Hag 2:8)

	IV. THE SON OF MAN'S INTENSIVE PREPARATION OF HIS DISCIPLES FOR JERUSALEM AND DEATH, 9:18-50	19 They replied, "Some say John the Baptist; others say Elijah; and still others, that one of the prophets of long ago has come back to life."	
		20 "But what about you?" he asked. "Who do you say I am?" Peter answered, "The Christ of God."	**3 The disciples' conviction: Jesus was Messiah**
	A. The First Prediction of Death: Who Jesus Really Is, 9:18-22 (Mt.16:13-23; Mk.8: 27-33)	21 Jesus strictly warned them not to tell this to anyone.	**4 The full meaning of the conviction** a. The full meaning: Was not yet grasped
1 Jesus was alone praying **2 The people's belief: Jesus was only a great man**	18 Once when Jesus was praying in private and his disciples were with him, he asked them, "Who do the crowds say I am?"	22 And he said, "The Son of Man must suffer many things and be rejected by the elders, chief priests and teachers of the law, and he must be killed and on the third day be raised to life."	b. The full meaning: Jesus was the suffering & conquering Savior[DS1]

DIVISION IV

THE SON OF MAN'S INTENSIVE PREPARATION OF HIS DISCIPLES FOR JERUSALEM AND DEATH, 9:18-50

A. The First Prediction of Death: Who Jesus Really Is, 9:18-22

(9:18-22) **Introduction**: Who is Jesus? The most critical time in a man's life is when he answers this question.
1. Jesus was alone praying (v.18).
2. The people's belief: Jesus was only a great man (v.18-19).
3. The disciples' conviction: Jesus was the Messiah (v.20).
4. The full meaning of the conviction (v.21-22).

1 (9:18) **Prayer**: Jesus was alone praying. He sensed a deep need for prayer.

1. He needed personal strength. Jesus resolutely set out for Jerusalem," which means that He was setting His face toward the cross where He was to die for the sins of men (Lk.9:51). The days ahead held excruciating suffering for Him.

2. The disciples needed a very special *quickening* from God. They, too, had to face the issue of the cross, that the Messiah had to die for the sins of the world in order to save men. This was a radically different concept of the Messiah than the popular concept. The popular concept said that the Messiah was to be the Son of David, the promised King who was to come and free Israel from her enemies and set up the Kingdom of God over all nations of the earth (see note—Mt.16:21-28).

The disciples also had an immediate need, the need for a very special *revelation* into His person. It was time for them to grasp and confess without any hesitation that He was the Messiah, the very Son of God. Jesus was now ready to examine their hearts and convictions about Him, so He went before God to beg a very *special insight*, a very special revelation of the Spirit for the disciples.

Thought 1. Three important lessons on prayer can be gleaned from what Christ was doing.
1) We must pray before momentous events.

"Ask and it will be given to you; seek and you will find; knock and the door will be opened to you. (Mat 7:7)

Is any one of you in trouble? He should pray. Is anyone happy? Let him sing songs of praise. (James 5:13)

'Call to me and I will answer you and tell you great and unsearchable things you do not know.' (Jer 33:3)

2) We must pray for others, that they might have special insight and the quickening power of the Spirit upon their lives.

And pray in the Spirit on all occasions with all kinds of prayers and requests. With this in mind, be alert and always keep on praying for all the saints. (Eph 6:18)

3) We must pray for strength to withstand severe trials, that we might be enabled to bear whatever cross lies ahead.

"Watch and pray so that you will not fall into temptation. The spirit is willing, but the body is weak." (Mat 26:41)

In the same way, the Spirit helps us in our weakness. We do not know what we ought to pray for, but the Spirit himself intercedes for us with groans that words cannot express. (Rom 8:26)

He will call upon me, and I will answer him; I will be with him in trouble, I will deliver him and honor him. (Psa 91:15)

"The poor and needy search for water, but there is none; their tongues are parched with thirst. But I the LORD will answer them; I, the God of Israel, will not forsake them. (Isa 41:17)

Then you will call, and the LORD will answer; you will cry for help, and he will say: Here am I. "If you do away with the yoke of oppression, with the pointing finger and malicious talk, (Isa 58:9)

Before they call I will answer; while they are still speaking I will hear. (Isa 65:24)

This third I will bring into the fire; I will refine them like silver and test them like gold. They will call on my name and I

will answer them; I will say, 'They are my people,' and they will say, 'The LORD is our God.'" (Zec 13:9)

2 (9:18-19) **Jesus Christ, Concept of—Man, Concept of Christ**: the people's belief was that Jesus was only a great man. The scene was that of Jesus' being off to the side, away from the disciples and all alone. He was seeking the face of God and agonizing in prayer. Then all of a sudden He quit praying and arose, and walked over to the disciples. Immediately He asked them, "Who do the crowds say I am?" Why did Christ ask this question? What was He doing?

1. The disciples' concept of the Messiah needed to be corrected. Their concept was the popular concept that saw the Messiah only as the greatest of men. They desperately needed to grasp and understand to the fullest measure who Jesus was. The very destiny of the world rested in their hands. Men were doomed and lost forever unless the disciples fully understood. Therefore, Jesus had to examine them to make sure they were thinking for themselves and rejecting the false ideas of Messiahship held by men.

2. The popular opinion of the Messiah was wrong. Most of the people honored Jesus highly, very highly. They saw Him as a great man; in fact, they saw Him as one of the greatest of men. However, such a concept would spell doom for the world if it were not corrected. Jesus had to make sure the people's idea had not influenced and corrupted the thinking of the disciples.

a. Some thought Jesus was John the Baptist, that is, the forerunner of the Messiah (Mal.4:5). Both John and Jesus were doing a unique and great work for God. Both were divinely chosen and gifted by God, and both proclaimed the Kingdom of God and prepared men for it. Therefore, when some looked at Jesus and His ministry, they thought Jesus was not the Messiah Himself, but the promised forerunner of the Messiah (Mal.4:5).

b. Some thought Jesus was Elijah. These were professing Jesus to be the greatest prophet and teacher of all time. Elijah was so considered, and Elijah was also predicted to be the forerunner of the coming Messiah (Mal.4:5). Even today the Jews expect Elijah to return before the Messiah. In celebrating the Passover they always leave a chair vacant for him to occupy. Elijah had also been used by God to miraculously feed a widow woman and her son (1 Ki.17:14). The people connected Elijah's miracle and Jesus' feeding of the multitude.

c. Some thought Jesus was one of the old prophets. These were professing Jesus to be a great prophet sent for their day and time. He was thought to be one of the great prophets brought back to life or one in whom the spirit of a great prophet dwelt (cp. Dt.18:15, 18).

Thought 1. Note that the same false confessions about Christ exist in every generation.

1) He was only a great man of righteousness, martyred for His faith. As such He leaves us a great example of how to live and stand up for what we believe.
2) He was one of the greatest teachers and prophets of all time.
3) He was a great man who revealed some very important things to us about God and religion. As such He can make a significant contribution to every man in His search for God.
4) He was a great man and prophet sent to the people (Jews) of His day; however, we can learn a great deal that will help us by studying His life.

Isn't this the carpenter? Isn't this Mary's son and the brother of James, Joseph, Judas and Simon? Aren't his sisters here with us?" And they took offense at him. (Mark 6:3)

He was in the world, and though the world was made through him, the world did not recognize him. He came to that which was his own, but his own did not receive him. (John 1:10-11)

Who is the liar? It is the man who denies that Jesus is the Christ. Such a man is the antichrist—he denies the Father and the Son. No one who denies the Son has the Father; whoever acknowledges the Son has the Father also. (1 John 2:22-23)

But every spirit that does not acknowledge Jesus is not from God. This is the spirit of the antichrist, which you have heard is coming and even now is already in the world. (1 John 4:3)

3 (9:20) **Jesus Christ, Concept—Man, Concept of Christ**: the disciples' conviction was that Jesus was the Messiah. Jesus sat and listened closely to what the disciples had to say about the people's ideas regarding the Messiah. Now He was ready for *the question...*

- the question whose answer determines a man's eternal salvation.
- the question which is the most significant question ever asked.

"But what about you...Who do you say I am?" The "you" is emphatic. Jesus stressed the *personal*, the importance of a personal response: "But *you*, who do *you* say I am?" Note several things.

1. The answer was immediate and forceful: *the Christ of God*. Peter was the spokesman for all, and he emphatically declared that Jesus was *the Christ of God*. It was a powerful statement—a statement profound in meaning.

2. The answer was profound in its meaning, for Jesus was "the Christ," that is, "the Messiah," *the anointed One of God* (see DEEPER STUDY # 2—Mt.1:18). This means three things.

a. Jesus was sent on a deliberate mission, the mission of saving man (Lk.19:10).

b. Jesus was *sent and qualified* by God to carry out that mission (Jn.3:16; 4:34; 5:23-24, 30, 36-38; 6:29, 38-40, 44, 57; 7:16, 18, 28-29; 8:16, 18, 26, 29, 42; 9:4; 10:36; 11:42; 12:45, 49; 14:24; 15:21; 16:5; 17:3, 18, 21, 23, 25; 20:21; 1 Jn.4:9-10, 14).

c. Jesus was the fulfillment of all the prophecies which promised the coming of the Messiah for man.

3. The question was very personal. It might even offend some. But Jesus meant the question to be personal. It had to be, for a man's eternal destiny and fate is determined by his answer. Jesus was not just a man as the popular idea of Him declared. He was more, much more. He was *the Christ of God*. Man's life, death, and eternal fate hinged on how he saw and confessed Christ.

"Whoever acknowledges me before men, I will also acknowledge him before my Father in heaven. But whoever disowns me before men, I will disown him before my Father in heaven. (Mat 10:32-33)

If anyone is ashamed of me and my words in this adulterous and sinful generation, the Son of Man will be ashamed of him when he comes in his Father's glory with the holy angels." (Mark 8:38)

"I tell you, whoever acknowledges me before men, the Son of Man will also acknowledge him before the angels of God. (Luke 12:8)

That if you confess with your mouth, "Jesus is Lord," and believe in your heart that God raised him from the dead, you will be saved. For it is with your heart that you believe and are justified, and it is with your mouth that you confess and are saved. (Rom 10:9-10)

No one who denies the Son has the Father; whoever acknowledges the Son has the Father also. (1 John 2:23)

If anyone acknowledges that Jesus is the Son of God, God lives in him and he in God. (1 John 4:15)

He who conceals his sins does not prosper, but whoever confesses and renounces them finds mercy. (Prov 28:13)

The first thing Andrew did was to find his brother Simon and tell him, "We have found the Messiah" (that is, the Christ). (John 1:41)

Philip found Nathanael and told him, "We have found [the Messiah] the one Moses wrote about in the Law, and about whom the prophets also wrote—Jesus of Nazareth, the son of Joseph." (John 1:45)

Then Nathanael declared, "Rabbi, you are the Son of God; you are the King of Israel." (John 1:49)

"Come, see a man who told me everything I ever did. Could this be the Christ?" (John 4:29)

We believe and know that you are the Holy One of God." (John 6:69)

"Yes, Lord," she told him, "I believe that you are the Christ, the Son of God, who was to come into the world." (John 11:27)

Thomas said to him, "My Lord and my God!" (John 20:28)

As they traveled along the road, they came to some water and the eunuch said, "Look, here is water. Why shouldn't I be baptized?" (Acts 8:36)

4 (9:21-22) **Messiah—Messiahship—Jesus Christ, Death; Resurrection**: the full meaning of the conviction. There are two significant points here.

1. The full meaning of the Messiah was not yet fully grasped. The disciples were yet to experience the death and resurrection of Jesus Christ. The prophecies of the Messiah which stuck out in their minds were those dealing with His exaltation, sovereignty, power, and glory. They saw His ruling and reigning over the earth and subjecting men to God by force. Their idea of the Messiah was that of an earthly rule within the bounds of the physical and material world. They had little if any idea of the spiritual world; therefore, they were not ready to share the truth of the Messiah (see note—Eph.1:3).They would be sharing an incomplete message, a false message; so Jesus had to charge them to tell no man, not yet, not until they understood the real meaning of the spiritual salvation which He was bringing to man. Note the importance of understanding the full meaning of the Messiah. Jesus charged them and then commanded them to say nothing until they did understand.

2. Jesus began to clearly reveal that the Messiah had to be both a suffering and a conquering Savior. For some time Jesus had been telling His disciples about His death and resurrection, but they had not understood. Why? There are two reasons:

⇒ The idea of a suffering Messiah differed radically from their own idea of the Messiah (see notes—Mt.1:1; DEEPER STUDY # 2—1:18; DEEPER STUDY # 3—3:11; notes—11:1-6; 11:2-3; DEEPER STUDY # 1—11:5; DEEPER STUDY # 2—11:6; DEEPER STUDY # 1—12:16; note—Lk.7:21-23).

⇒ The revelation had been hid in pictures and symbols.

Jesus answered them, "Destroy this temple, and I will raise it again in three days." (John 2:19)

Just as Moses lifted up the snake in the desert, so the Son of Man must be lifted up, (John 3:14)

I am the living bread that came down from heaven. If anyone eats of this bread, he will live forever. This bread is my flesh, which I will give for the life of the world." (John 6:51)

The difference now was that Jesus no longer spoke in pictures and symbols, but He told them in simple and direct words (Mt.20:18-20; Lk.18:31-33). A new stage in the revelation of God's plan for the world was now taking place: God's Son was to die and be raised again for the sins of the world. God's plan for saving the world was to take place through a suffering Messiah, not a conquering Messiah who was going to deliver a *materialistic* world into the hands of His followers. His death was to usher in the Kingdom of God, making it possible for His followers to live eternally in the very presence of God Himself (see DEEPER STUDY # 3—Mt.19:23-24; cp. Jn.3:16; 5:24f).

Note the word "must" (dei). It is strong; it means a constraint, an imperative, a necessity was laid upon Him. He had no choice. His death and resurrection had been planned and willed by God through all eternity. The prophets had so predicted. He must fulfill the will of God, for God had ordained His death. (See DEEPER STUDY # 3—Acts 2:23 for more discussion. Cp. Mt.26:54.)

Did not the Christ have to suffer these things and then enter his glory?" (Luke 24:26)

He told them, "This is what is written: The Christ will suffer and rise from the dead on the third day, and repentance and forgiveness of sins will be preached in his name to all nations, beginning at Jerusalem. (Luke 24:46-47)

DEEPER STUDY # 1

(9:22) **Jesus Christ, Opposition**: note the three Jewish groups who were to take the lead in killing Jesus. These were the three groups who made up the Sanhedrin, the supreme court of Jewish justice. It was comprised of seventy members (cp. the historical basis for this structure, 2 Chron.19:5-11).

1. The elders: these were the older, respected men of a community. The elders were judges of the civil courts, of temporal affairs (Ex.3:29; 12:21; 24:9; Num.11:25; 1 Sam.16:4; Ezra 10:14; Mt.27:12).

2. The chief priests: these were primarily leaders from among the Sadducees who held most of the high offices of Jewish government under Roman rule (see note—Acts 23:8). The chief priests were judges of religious affairs.

3. The teachers of the law [Scribes]: these were Pharisees who held the teaching positions of the nation (see DEEPER STUDY # 1—Lk.6:2).

	B. The Terms of Discipleship, 9:23-27 (Mt.16:24-28; Mk.8:34-9:1)	25 What good is it for a man to gain the whole world, and yet lose or forfeit his very self?	**3 The question for the materialist** a. If he gains the world b. And loses his life c. What does he gain?[DS2]
1 The terms of discipleship a. Must deny self b. Must take up the cross—daily[DS1] c. Must follow Jesus	23 Then he said to them all: "If anyone would come after me, he must deny himself and take up his cross daily and follow me.	26 If anyone is ashamed of me and my words, the Son of Man will be ashamed of him when he comes in his glory and in the glory of the Father and of the holy angels.	**4 The judgment of the materialist** a. The reason: He is ashamed of Jesus & His Words b. The judgment: Counted unsuitable for glory
2 The warning to the materialist a. Do not save life for self b. Spend life for Christ	24 For whoever wants to save his life will lose it, but whoever loses his life for me will save it.	27 I tell you the truth, some who are standing here will not taste death before they see the kingdom of God."	**5 The disciple's reward: God's kingdom**

DIVISION IV

THE SON OF MAN'S INTENSIVE PREPARATION OF HIS DISCIPLES FOR JERUSALEM ANDDEATH, 9:18-50

B. The Terms of Discipleship, 9:23-27

(9:23-27) **Introduction**: Jesus was to bear the cross for man. He had just discussed this fact with His disciples (Lk.9:22). Now He said there was another cross—a cross which man was to bear for Him. If a man wished to follow Christ, he had to bear this cross. There was no option. Discipleship demanded it.

1. The terms of discipleship (v.23).
2. The warning to the materialist (v.24).
3. The question for the materialist (v.25).
4. The judgment of the materialist (v.26).
5. The disciple's reward: God's kingdom (v.27).

1 (9:23) **Cross—Self-Denial—Death, to Self—Disciple ship**: there are three terms of discipleship if a person wills to follow Christ.

1. A person must deny himself. Man's tendency is to indulge himself and do exactly what he desires; but the believer is not to indulge himself, his comfort and ease, appetites and urges, thoughts and feelings, deceptions and enticements, plots and intrigues, pride and boastings, reactions and disturbances. The believer is to deny himself by discipline and control and by loving and caring, sacrificing and giving, helping and ministering.

2. A person must take up his cross and do it daily (see DEEPER STUDY # 1, Cross—Lk.9:23).

3. A person must follow Jesus. However, man's tendency is to follow someone else and to give one's first allegiance to something else. Within the world, there are many things available for a man to serve and to put first. There are…

- service organizations
- humanitarian needs
- religion (institutional)
- family
- recreation
- hobby
- education
- profession
- houses
- business
- clubs
- self (fame, honor)
- comfort
- clothing
- social acceptance
- pleasure
- health
- looks
- sports
- fleshy stimulation

When Jesus spoke again to the people, he said, "I am the light of the world. Whoever follows me will never walk in darkness, but will have the light of life." (John 8:12)

My sheep listen to my voice; I know them, and they follow me. I give them eternal life, and they shall never perish; no one can snatch them out of my hand. My Father, who has given them to me, is greater than all ; no one can snatch them out of my Father's hand. (John 10:27-29)

Whoever serves me must follow me; and where I am, my servant also will be. My Father will honor the one who serves me. (John 12:26)

So I say, live by the Spirit, and you will not gratify the desires of the sinful nature. (Gal 5:16)

Be imitators of God, therefore, as dearly loved children and live a life of love, just as Christ loved us and gave himself up for us as a fragrant offering and sacrifice to God. (Eph 5:1-2)

For of this you can be sure: No immoral, impure or greedy person—such a man is an idolater—has any inheritance in the kingdom of Christ and of God. (Eph 5:5)

So then, just as you received Christ Jesus as Lord, continue to live in him, (Col 2:6)

To this you were called, because Christ suffered for you, leaving you an example, that you should follow in his steps. (1 Pet 2:21)

Whoever claims to live in him must walk as Jesus did. (1 John 2:6)

DEEPER STUDY # 1

(9:23) **Cross—Discipleship**: people in Jesus' day knew what it meant to "take up" a cross. They saw scores of criminals bear the cross to the place where they were to be executed, and they witnessed scores of crucifixions, some even by the side of the roads that led in and out of the cities.

The cross does not mean merely bearing one's particular hardship in life, such as poor health, abuse, unemployment, invalid parents, an unsaved spouse, a wayward child. The cross is always an instrument of death, not just an object to carry or bear. The Christian is to die mentally and actively. He is to deny himself daily. He is to let the mind of Christ, the mind of humbling himself to the point of death, be in him and fill his thoughts every day (Ph.2:5-8;

2 Cor.10:3-5). He is to put his will, his desires, his wants, his ambitions to death. In their stead, he is to follow Jesus and to do His will all day long. Note this is not negative, passive behavior. It takes positive, active behavior to *will*, to *deny self*, to *take up* one's *cross*, to *follow* Christ. A person has to act, work, get to it, be diligent, consistent, and enduring in order to die to self.

There are several ways the believer dies to self. Romans 6:11-13 spells out the ways as clearly as they can be.

In the same way, count yourselves dead to sin but alive to God in Christ Jesus. Therefore do not let sin reign in your mortal body so that you obey its evil desires. Do not offer the parts of your body to sin, as instruments of wickedness, but rather offer yourselves to God, as those who have been brought from death to life; and offer the parts of your body to him as instruments of righteousness. (Rom 6:11-13; cp. Ro.6:2-10)

1. The believer reckons or counts himself crucified with Christ.

In the same way, count yourselves dead to sin. (Rom 6:11a)

For we know that our old self was crucified with him so that the body of sin might be done away with, that we should no longer be slaves to sin— (Rom 6:6)

I have been crucified with Christ and I no longer live, but Christ lives in me. The life I live in the body, I live by faith in the Son of God, who loved me and gave himself for me. (Gal 2:20)

Those who belong to Christ Jesus have crucified the sinful nature with its passions and desires. (Gal 5:24)

2. The believer reckons or counts himself dead to sin, but alive to God.

In the same way, count yourselves dead to sin but alive to God in Christ Jesus. (Rom 6:11)

As a result, he does not live the rest of his earthly life for evil human desires, but rather for the will of God. (1 Pet 4:2)

3. The believer does not let sin reign in his body.

Therefore do not let sin reign in your mortal body so that you obey its evil desires. (Rom 6:12)

Put to death, therefore, whatever belongs to your earthly nature: sexual immorality, impurity, lust, evil desires and greed, which is idolatry. (Col 3:5)

4. The believer does not yield the parts of his body to sin, as instruments of wickedness.

Do not offer the parts of your body to sin, as instruments of wickedness. (Rom 6:13a)

For if you live according to the sinful nature, you will die; but if by the Spirit you put to death the misdeeds of the body, you will live. (Rom 8:13)

5. The believer yields himself to God—as much as those who are alive from the dead are yielded to God.

But rather offer yourselves to God, as those who have been brought from death to life. (Rom 6:13b)

Therefore, I urge you, brothers, in view of God's mercy, to offer your bodies as living sacrifices, holy and pleasing to God—this is your spiritual act of worship. (Rom 12:1)

Rather, clothe yourselves with the Lord Jesus Christ, and do not think about how to gratify the desires of the sinful nature. (Rom 13:14)

6. The believer yields his body members as instruments of righteousness.

And offer the parts of your body to him as instruments of righteousness. (Rom 6:13c)

So I say, live by the Spirit, and you will not gratify the desires of the sinful nature. (Gal 5:16)

It should be noted that one's hardship or burden can bring a person to the place where the Lord can deal with him. It is then that the hardship becomes the cross and denial of self that Jesus is talking about. With an act of self-denial, the Christian can then count or reckon himself alive to God (Ro.6:13). He can then follow Jesus. This is an act which can be described as committing all that one is and has to Christ. It is an act that needs to be repeated every day (cp. Mt.10:38). (See outlines and notes—Mt.19:21-22; 19:23-26; 19:27-30.)

2 (9:24) **Life**: the warning to the materialist is clear. Note the word "life" (psuche). In this context it means the natural, animal life; the earthly life that quickly passess away; the fading, aging, decaying, corruptible life of the earth. The warning is twofold. (See note—Mt.16:25-28 for more discussion.)

1. Do not save your life for yourself. If a person saves his life, that is, works to please himself on this earth, he will lose his life eternally. A man does not have life…

- to indulge himself: getting all he can of the comforts and pleasures and interests of life.
- to hoard life: keeping all the good things of life and seldom becoming involved in giving and sacrificing to help those who do not have.

The seed that fell among thorns stands for those who hear, but as they go on their way they are choked by life's worries, riches and pleasures, and they do not mature. (Luke 8:14)

And I'll say to myself, "You have plenty of good things laid up for many years. Take life easy; eat, drink and be merry."' "But God said to him, 'You fool! This very night your life will be demanded from you. Then who will get what you have prepared for yourself?' "This is how it will be with anyone who stores up things for himself but is not rich toward God." (Luke 12:19-21)

But the widow who lives for pleasure is dead even while she lives. (1 Tim 5:6)

But these men blaspheme in matters they do not understand. They are like brute beasts, creatures of instinct, born only to be caught and destroyed, and like beasts they too will perish. They will be paid back with harm for the harm they have done. Their idea of pleasure is to carouse [riot, indulge, party] in broad daylight. They are blots and blemishes, reveling in their pleasures while they feast with you. With eyes full of adultery, they never stop sinning; they seduce the unstable; they are experts in greed—an accursed brood! (2 Pet 2:12-14)

The laborer's appetite works for him; his hunger drives him on. (Prov 16:26)

All man's efforts are for his mouth, yet his appetite is never satisfied. (Eccl 6:7)

As when a hungry man dreams that he is eating, but he awakens, and his hunger remains; as when a thirsty man dreams that he is drinking, but he awakens faint, with his thirst unquenched. So will it be with the hordes of all the nations that fight against Mount Zion. (Isa 29:8)

Blessed is the man who does this, the man who holds it fast, who keeps the Sabbath without desecrating it, and keeps his hand from doing any evil." (Isa 56:2)

2. Spend your life for Christ. Note the words "for me." The person who loses his life, that is, works to please Christ on this earth, shall save his life eternally.

a. A man has life to know God and fellowship with God.

We proclaim to you what we have seen and heard, so that you also may have fellowship with us. And our fellowship is with the Father and with his Son, Jesus Christ. (1 John 1:3)

"You are my witnesses," declares the LORD, "and my servant whom I have chosen, so that you may know and believe me and understand that I am he. Before me no god was formed, nor will there be one after me. (Isa 43:10)

b. A man has life to know men and fellowship with men.

The LORD God said, "It is not good for the man to be alone. I will make a helper suitable for him." (Gen 2:18)

But if we walk in the light, as he is in the light, we have fellowship with one another, and the blood of Jesus, his Son, purifies us from all sin. (1 John 1:7)

They devoted themselves to the apostles' teaching and to the fellowship, to the breaking of bread and to prayer. (Acts 2:42)

I am a friend to all who fear you, to all who follow your precepts. (Psa 119:63)

Two are better than one, because they have a good return for their work: If one falls down, his friend can help him up. But pity the man who falls and has no one to help him up! (Eccl 4:9-10)

Then those who feared the LORD talked with each other, and the LORD listened and heard. A scroll of remembrance was written in his presence concerning those who feared the LORD and honored his name. (Mal 3:16)

c. A man has life to help save a world lost in sin and shame and suffering.

Just as the Son of Man did not come to be served, but to serve, and to give his life as a ransom for many." (Mat 20:28)

For the Son of Man came to seek and to save what was lost." (Luke 19:10)

Again Jesus said, "Peace be with you! As the Father has sent me, I am sending you." (John 20:21)

We who are strong ought to bear with the failings of the weak and not to please ourselves. (Rom 15:1)

3 (9:25) **Materialism—Worldliness—Wealth—Soul—Life**: the materialist is questioned. The man who seeks to save his life, who works to please himself, is challenged to think honestly. Christ asks one question of the materialist, but it has two parts or pictures. (See note—Mt.16:25-28 for more discussion.)

1. The picture of gaining the *whole* world. Note that Christ did not say this: what if a man could gain and own all the land of Texas, or all of the wealth of Africa. He said what if a man could gain the *whole world*, all the world's...

- land
- honor
- gold
- wealth
- pleasure
- satisfaction

Imagine for a moment: What if a man could gain the whole world? No man can or will gain it all; but many pursue and some do gain a great deal of land, wealth, honor, pleasure, and carnal satisfaction.

2. The picture of losing or forfeiting one's' life, of being cast away. Note that this is a stated fact, an inevitable and sure result. The man who seeks to please himself is doomed to "lose himself" or to "forfeit His very [life]," or to "be cast away." He *tried to find himself* here on earth, but he never did. He *lost himself.* He lost the greatest things in all the world: certainty, assurance, confidence, and satisfaction of knowing that he is eternally secure and destined to live and serve God forever.

What good is it for a man to gain the whole world, and yet lose or forfeit his very self? (Luke 9:25)

I say to you that many will come from the east and the west, and will take their places at the feast with Abraham, Isaac and Jacob in the kingdom of heaven. But the subjects of the kingdom will be thrown outside, into the darkness, where there will be weeping and gnashing of teeth." (Mat 8:11-12)

'Friend,' he asked, 'how did you get in here without wedding clothes [righteousness]?' The man was speechless. "Then the king told the attendants, 'Tie him hand and foot, and throw him outside,

into the darkness, where there will be weeping and gnashing of teeth.' (Mat 22:12-13)

And throw that worthless servant outside, into the darkness, where there will be weeping and gnashing of teeth.' (Mat 25:30)

You did not choose me, but I chose you and appointed you to go and bear fruit—fruit that will last. Then the Father will give you whatever you ask in my name. (John 15:16)

No, I beat my body and make it my slave so that after I have preached to others, I myself will not be disqualified for the prize. (1 Cor 9:27)

"Be careful, or your hearts will be weighed down with dissipation, drunkenness and the anxieties of life, and that day will close on you unexpectedly like a trap. (Luke 21:34)

DEEPER STUDY # 2
(9:25) Forfeit his very self(zemiotheis): to suffer the loss of, to forfeit, to lose what is of greatest value, to be punished by forfeiting and losing.

4 (9:26) **Judgment—Jesus Christ, Coming Again—Ashamed, of Christ—Rejection, of Christ**: the judgment of the materialist is tragic. He did not have to suffer the judgment of God, but the materialist chose the world and its things and pleasures over Christ. Why is the materialist to be judged?

1. There is basically one reason: the materialist is ashamed of *Jesus and His words*. He is embarrassed and ashamed by such things as…

- being known as a true believer.
- following and obeying Christ completely.
- witnessing and standing up for Christ and morality.
- living less extravagantly than others.
- having less because of giving so much.
- associating with the needy to help them.
- driving a cheaper car.
- living in a less expensive home.
- not socializing with the worldly.
- not compromising and going along.
- not having the things others have.
- not joining in off-colored talk and jokes.

Simply stated, the man *loved* the acceptance and recognition of society, the comfort and pleasure of the world too much—he loved it all too much to give up his life and bear the reproach of Christ. He misjudged, counting the few years (ten to thirty years) of plenty on this earth as worth the unending years of the new earth and heavens.

2. Judgment is the most tragic event imaginable in the life of the materialist. He is counted unsuitable for glory.

a. The Lord is coming. It is stated without equivocation. It is definite, even fixed. Jesus said He shall come.

b. The Lord is coming in a threefold glory.

⇒ There is His own glory, exalted as the Messiah, the Christ of God (Ph.2:9-11).

⇒ There is the glory of God in all the brilliance and splendor of His person (1 Tim.6:16; 1 Jn.1:5; Rev.22:15).

⇒ There is the glory of the angels in their magnificence of being and brightness. They shall accompany Jesus when He returns to judge the earth.

The point is clear: when Jesus comes in His glory, the materialist will not join Him. He will not be welcomed into the glory of the Lord. Why? Christ will be *ashamed* of him. He will be embarrassed by the man, too embarrassed to acknowledge that He knows the man. The man is…

- not properly dressed (with the righteousness of God).
- not employed (in the things of God).
- too dirty (morally and righteously).
- too poor (in the spirit).
- too immoral (not repenting).
- too unjust (not changing).
- too disliked (by being obstinate in unbelief).
- too different (from the children of God).
- too uneducated (in the things of God).

Then I will tell them plainly, 'I never knew you. Away from me, you evildoers!' (Mat 7:23)

"But he replied, 'I tell you the truth, I don't know you.' (Mat 25:12)

But he who disowns me before men will be disowned before the angels of God. (Luke 12:9)

"But he will reply, 'I don't know you or where you come from. Away from me, all you evildoers!' (Luke 13:27)

5 (9:27) **Reward—Kingdom of God**: the reward of the disciple is God's kingdom. The believer enters the Kingdom of God immediately upon believing (see DEEPER STUDY # 3—Mt.19:23-24). Standing there in the crowd before Christ, some were to be eye-witnesses of the death and resurrection of Christ and the coming of the Holy Spirit. They were to taste and experience the Kingdom of God. Since that day, many have been saved and have seen the Kingdom of God before experiencing *physical death* (cp. Jn.3:16; 5:24; 8:52; Heb.2:9, 14-15).

	C. The Events of the Transfiguration: A Glimpse into Glory, 9:28-36 (Mt.17:1-13; Mk.9:2-13)	they became fully awake, they saw his glory and the two men standing with him.	a. Peter, James, & John
		33 As the men were leaving Jesus, Peter said to him, "Master, it is good for us to be here. Let us put up three shelters—one for you, one for Moses and one for Elijah." (He did not know what he was saying.)	b. They desired to retain the experience
1 Jesus took three disciples up into a mountain **2 Event 1: Jesus was praying**	28 About eight days after Jesus said this, he took Peter, John and James with him and went up onto a mountain to pray.		
3 Event 2: The countenance & clothing of Jesus were changed— as bright as lightning	29 As he was praying, the appearance of his face changed, and his clothes became as bright as a flash of lightning.	34 While he was speaking, a cloud appeared and enveloped them, and they were afraid as they entered the cloud.	**6 Event 5: A cloud overshadowed them**
4 Event 3: Two men appeared and talked with Jesus a. Moses, the lawgiver; Elijah, the great prophet	30 Two men, Moses and Elijah, 31 Appeared in glorious splendor, talking with Jesus.	35 A voice came from the cloud, saying, "This is my Son, whom I have chosen; listen to him."	**7 Event 6: A voice spoke to them**
b. They discussed His death	They spoke about his departure, which he was about to bring to fulfillment at Jerusalem.	36 When the voice had spoken, they found that Jesus was alone. The disciples kept this to themselves, and told no one at that time what they had seen.	**8 Event 7: A stunned silence fell upon them**
5 Event 4: Three disciples witnessed the event	32 Peter and his companions were very sleepy, but when		

DIVISION IV

THE SON OF MAN'S INTENSIVE PREPARATION OF HIS DISCIPLES FOR JERUSALEM AND DEATH, 9:18-50

C. The Events of the Transfiguration: A Glimpse into Glory, 9:28-36

(9:28-36) **Introduction—Transfiguration**: there were at least seven reasons for the transfiguration.

1. Jesus needed a very special strength to face the pressure of the cross. In the transfiguration and in the Garden of Gethsemane, God is shown strengthening His Son in a marvelous way. Jesus was enabled to become the sin-bearer for the world (2 Cor.5:21).

2. The disciples needed their faith strengthened to face what lay ahead. Therefore, God gave them a glimpse of the glory of Jesus, that He is "the radiance of God's glory and the exact representation of His being" (Heb.1:3).

3. The disciples needed the quickening power and insight of God's Spirit, for Jesus was to be killed (Mt.16:21; cp. Mt.17:1-2). After the resurrection, the disciples' memory would need to be *quickened* to understand the spiritual significance of the cross. They would thereby become dynamic witnesses for Him. Remembering the transfiguration would stir their conviction.

4. The disciples needed to know that Jesus was more than a great lawgiver and a great prophet. In fact, He was the very Son of God who fulfilled all the Law and the Prophets (the Old Testament). He was the One who was to usher in the New Testament or covenant between God and man (see outline and notes—Mt.5:17-18; 2 Cor.3:6-18; cp. Mt.9:16-17).

5. The disciples needed to see into the glory of the spiritual world and into the reality of life after death. The disciples needed to understand God's purpose in Christ: to save man eternally and to make it possible for man to be transferred from this world into the next upon death. The Messiah of the cross was God's way, not a messiah of power and dominion.

6. The disciples would need to be reminded of the glory of Christ in the future, for the cross was an ugly sight because of the blood and suffering and sin and death. But it was also a glorious event planned by God, through which He revealed His love and grace and through which He saves the world. (See outline and notes—Mt.16:21-28.)

7. The disciples needed some glimpse into the glory that will be experienced when all believers are raised and transformed into the Lord's image. By seeing Moses and Elijah, the disciples saw two Old Testament believers who were *still living*, and they were living in a glorious state (v.30-31). They also knew that Christ had power over life and death. He could raise whom He wished from the dead to be in glory with Him.

The transfiguration was a striking event, an event that both interests and intrigues men. But, as has already been seen, intrigue was not its purpose. We should learn from the transfiguration, learn more about who Jesus really is and more about the life we are to live.

1. Jesus took three disciples up onto a mountain (v.28).
2. Event 1: Jesus was praying (v.28).
3. Event 2: Jesus' countenance and clothing were changed—as bright as lightning (v.29).
4. Event 3: two men appeared and talked with Jesus (v.30-31).
5. Event 4: three disciples witnessed the event (v.32-33).
6. Event 5: a cloud overshadowed them (v.34).
7. Event 6: a voice spoke to them (v.35).
8. Event 7: a stunned silence fell upon them (v.36).

1 (9:28) **Inner Circle**: Jesus took three disciples up onto a mountain. The disciples were Peter, James, and John—His inner circle (see DEEPER STUDY # 1, Inner Circle—Mk.9:2). Why did He take just these three disciples? The answer is not given. Perhaps it was for the same reason that leaders sometimes need to be alone with only a few of their closest friends.

⇒ There is the need for supportive companionship and prayer because of severe pressure.
⇒ There is the need to guard what is happening from spreading out into the public before it should.

The leader knows that the fewer witnesses to an event the less likely something will spread. In Jesus' case, He was under severe pressure, and the transfiguration and the glory of His person could not be understood until after the cross and the resurrection. He had to keep the matter quiet for now (cp. v.36).

2 (9:28) **Jesus Christ, Prayer of—Prayer**: the first event was Jesus' praying. The transfiguration was a spectacular event—one that met the special needs of Jesus Christ. Note that Jesus went up onto the mountain for the express purpose of praying (v.28). At least two things drove Him to pray at this time.

1. The cross lay right before Him. The *weight* and *load* of bearing the sin of the world was closing in on Him, and the pressure was almost more than He could bear. The terrifying strain and pressure are seen in three significant events that lay just ahead: the need for Moses and Elijah to talk with Him about His death; the excruciating pressure of Gethsemane; and the terrifying cry on the cross (Mt.26:36-46; see note—Mt.27:46-49).

2. The disciples had so much to learn and time was short. Jesus faced a tremendous problem: how to make them understand that God's way was not the way of earthly power and might (see notes—Mt.1:1; DEEPER STUDY # 2—1:18; DEEPER STUDY # 3—3:11; notes—11:1-6; 11:2-3; DEEPER STUDY # 1—11:5; DEEPER STUDY # 2—11:6; DEEPER STUDY # 1—12:16; note—Lk.7:21-23), but the way of spiritual and eternal salvation (Jn.3:16; 2 Cor.5:21; 1 Pt.2:24; 3:18).

Jesus had no choice with such pressure and responsibility bearing in upon Him. He had to seek God and trust God to meet His need, and God did—in a most remarkable and encouraging way. While He met Jesus' need, God also met the needs of the three disciples who accompanied Him.

Thought 1. God will always meet the needs of the person who prays and seeks His help.

He will call upon me, and I will answer him; I will be with him in trouble, I will deliver him and honor him. (Psa 91:15)

"The poor and needy search for water, but there is none; their tongues are parched with thirst. But I the LORD will answer them; I, the God of Israel, will not forsake them. (Isa 41:17)

Then you will call, and the LORD will answer; you will cry for help, and he will say: Here am I. "If you do away with the yoke of oppression, with the pointing finger and malicious talk, (Isa 58:9)

Before they call I will answer; while they are still speaking I will hear. (Isa 65:24)

'Call to me and I will answer you and tell you great and unsearchable things you do not know.' (Jer 33:3)

"So I say to you: Ask and it will be given to you; seek and you will find; knock and the door will be opened to you. For everyone who asks receives; he who seeks finds; and to him who knocks, the door will be opened. (Luke 11:9-10)

You may ask me for anything in my name, and I will do it. (John 14:14)

If you remain in me and my words remain in you, ask whatever you wish, and it will be given you. (John 15:7)

And receive from him anything we ask, because we obey his commands and do what pleases him. (1 John 3:22)

3 (9:29) **Jesus Christ, Deity—Glory**: the second event was the change of Jesus' countenance and clothing. Note three points.

1. His countenance or face was altered and became different. "His face shone like the sun" (Mt.17:2). Imagine being as bright "as the sun!"

2. His clothing was altered and became different, a glittering or dazzling white. The words "bright as a flash of lightning" (exastrapton) means to flash like lightning, to gleam, brighten, be radiant.

White as the light. (Mat 17:2)

Whiter than anyone...could bleach them. (Mark 9:3)

Bright as a flash of lightning. (Luke 9:29)

3. Jesus was praying when these changes took place. Apparently, He was concentrating so intensely and was so wrapped up in God that God transformed Him, that is, allowed His Godly nature to shine right through Him.

Thought 1. Note several lessons.
1) The divine nature of Christ is seen in this event. God is showing man that Christ is definitely His Son. There is no excuse for unbelief.
2) The need of Christ was desperate, so God was meeting His need in a very special way. When our need is desperate, God will meet our need in a very special way if we will come to Him in intense prayer.

Thought 2. When a genuine believer prays with intensity and heavy concentration, his countenance is sometimes changed. He experiences a precious glow, a brightness, a light about his whole countenance.

And we, who with unveiled faces all reflect the Lord's glory, are being transformed into his likeness with ever-increasing glory, which comes from the Lord, who is the Spirit. (2 Cor 3:18)

So that you may become blameless and pure, children of God without fault in a crooked and depraved generation, in which you shine like stars in the universe (Phil 2:15)

"Yet if you devote your heart to him and stretch out your hands to him, if you put away the sin that is in your hand and allow no evil to dwell in your tent, then you will lift up your face without shame; you will stand firm and without fear. You will surely forget your trouble, recalling it only as waters gone by. Life will be brighter than noonday, and darkness will become like morning. (Job 11:13-17)

Those who look to him [God] are radiant; their faces are never covered with

shame. (Psa 34:5)

Who is like the wise man? Who knows the explanation of things? Wisdom brightens a man's face and changes its hard appearance. (Eccl 8:1)

Those who are wise will shine like the brightness of the heavens, and those who lead many to righteousness, like the stars for ever and ever. (Dan 12:3)

4 (9:30-31) **Jesus Christ, Death—Moses—Elijah—Exodus—Salvation**: the third event was the two men who appeared and talked with Jesus. Note two things.

1. Moses and Elijah appeared and talked with Jesus. Moses was the great lawgiver and Elijah was the greatest of the prophets. These two men were honoring and ministering to Jesus. By such they were *symbolizing* that the law and the prophets found their fulfillment in Jesus. Jesus was the One of whom the law and the prophets spoke; He was the One to whom they pointed (cp. Lk.24:26-27; 1 Pt.1:11).

2. The conversation concerned the death of Jesus. Jesus was sensing extreme pressure in thinking about His death, and the thought probably never left His mind. Death for Him meant so much more than the death of men. He was going to die for the sins of all men of all generations, and God was going to separate Himself from Jesus. The pressure and suffering were to be unbearable (see note—Mt.20:19; Mk.10:33). He desperately needed to be strengthened—inwardly and spiritually—to bear the suffering of the cross.

Apparently, Jesus needed a very special kind of encouragement, an encouragement from two Old Testament believers—believers who had lived in the faith and expectation of His coming to save them. Sharing their love for Him and their trust and hope in His dying for them, they would stir Him to continue on for the sake of mankind. It must have been a precious moment for all three. Luke gives some hint of this. His word for "departure" (exodos) means exodus. There stood Moses sharing how God had so miraculously saved and delivered the children of Israel out of bondage and how the exodus (deliverance) was only a picture of the marvelous deliverance that He, God's Son, was to accomplish for man. Jesus was to accomplish a new exodus, a new *saving deliverance*, except this time it was to be for all men. All men were to be delivered from the bondage of sin and death, from the devil and hell—delivered into the glorious liberty of God and life, both abundant and eternal life. Jesus' dying was to be well worth it, Moses and Elijah stressed. Note: the very encouragement that our Lord needed as Man was given by two who had believed and hoped in His coming. Being reminded of the marvelous deliverance (exodus) that had happened so long ago was bound to strengthen and lift the heart of Christ. Just seeing Moses and Elijah stand there, two who had trusted and believed and hoped, was bound to cause the Lord's spirit to rise. He was greatly encouraged and knew that He could not fail these men who had trusted and hoped in Him so much.

Elijah's stress, of course, would have been the many prophecies concerning the sufferings of Jesus and the glory that should follow. Again, Luke hints at this in the word "fulfillment" (pleroo).

Jesus took the Twelve aside and told them, "We are going up to Jerusalem, and everything that is written by the prophets about the Son of Man will be fulfilled. (Luke 18:31; cp. Lk.12:50; 22:37.))

Concerning this salvation, the prophets, who spoke of the grace that was to come to you, searched intently and with the greatest care, trying to find out the time and circumstances to which the Spirit of Christ in them was pointing when he predicted the sufferings of Christ and the glories that would follow. (1 Pet 1:10-11)

Thought 1. Our faith and hope are realized and fulfilled in Christ. He is our Deliverer or Exodus out of the grip of sin and death, the devil and hell. We can be free in Christ, free to live abundantly and eternally.

"I tell you the truth, whoever hears my word and believes him who sent me has eternal life and will not be condemned; he has crossed over from death to life. (John 5:24)

Who gave himself for our sins to rescue us from the present evil age, according to the will of our God and Father, (Gal 1:4)

Who gave himself for us to redeem us from all wickedness and to purify for himself a people that are his very own, eager to do what is good. (Titus 2:14)

Since the children have flesh and blood, he too shared in their humanity so that by his death he might destroy him who holds the power of death—that is, the devil—and free those who all their lives were held in slavery by their fear of death. (Heb 2:14-15)

And from Jesus Christ, who is the faithful witness, the firstborn from the dead, and the ruler of the kings of the earth. To him who loves us and has freed us from our sins by his blood, (Rev 1:5)

Therefore, there is now no condemnation for those who are in Christ Jesus, because through Christ Jesus the law of the Spirit of life set me free from the law of sin and death. For what the law was powerless to do in that it was weakened by the sinful nature, God did by sending his own Son in the likeness of sinful man to be a sin offering. And so he condemned sin in sinful man, in order that the righteous requirements of the law might be fully met in us, who do not live according to the sinful nature but according to the Spirit. (Rom 8:1-4)

Thought 2. Discussing death should not be feared, not if we are genuine believers. Sharing with other believers will encourage us in our faith and hope.

5 (9:32-33) **Spiritual Experiences—Glory**: the fourth event was the presence of three disciples to witness the event. Apparently it was night (v.37). The three had fallen asleep. Suddenly something woke them—more than likely the brilliance of the light, the Shekinah glory upon Christ. The three were *tasting glory*. They were in the very presence of God Himself and were tasting some of heaven's perfection: joy, peace, security, fulfillment. They did not want to leave this hallowed ground.

Note what Peter did.

1. Peter offered to build three *shelters* (skenas) for Jesus and the two prophets. By this act he hoped to extend the stay of the heavenly guests and the glorious experience. The shelters offered were the booths made of branches and grass which could be quickly built, the kind often built by travellers on their stops along the road night by night.

2. Peter said, "Let us." Even in a moment as glorious as this, Peter would not act against His Lord's will. Imagine the devotion and loyalty.

> **Thought 1.** There is always a pull to live in the glory and forget the human need, to experience the high and neglect the low. We must always remember: it is the discipline of serving where there is need and ministering to the low that results in glory and the experiences of highs.
>
> **Is it not [your purpose] to share your food with the hungry and to provide the poor wanderer with shelter— when you see the naked, to clothe him, and not to turn away from your own flesh and blood? (Isa 58:7)**
>
> **In everything I did, I showed you that by this kind of hard work we must help the weak, remembering the words the Lord Jesus himself said: 'It is more blessed to give than to receive.'" (Acts 20:35)**
>
> **We who are strong ought to bear with the failings of the weak and not to please ourselves. (Rom 15:1)**
>
> **Carry each other's burdens, and in this way you will fulfill the law of Christ. (Gal 6:2)**
>
> **Remember those in prison as if you were their fellow prisoners, and those who are mistreated as if you yourselves were suffering. (Heb 13:3)**
>
> **Religion that God our Father accepts as pure and faultless is this: to look after orphans and widows in their distress and to keep oneself from being polluted by the world. (James 1:27)**
>
> **Finally, all of you, live in harmony with one another; be sympathetic, love as brothers, be compassionate and humble. (1 Pet 3:8)**

6 (9:34) **Jesus Christ, Deity—Covenants—Law vs. Grace**: the fifth event was the cloud that overshadowed them. The cloud and the voice of God terrified the disciples and caused them to fall immediately upon their faces, prostrate and unable to look up. As mortal men they were crouched in fear, and paralyzed in terror. Note three facts.

1. The cloud was "a bright cloud." This was the Shekinah glory, the cloud that symbolized God's presence. It was the cloud that guided Israel out of Egypt and that rested upon the tabernacle and above the Mercy Seat in the Most Holy Place (Ex.40:34-38). God "who alone is immortal and who lives in unapproachable light, whom no onehas seen orcan see" (1 Tim.6:16). God dwells in unapproachable light upon which no man can look. Peter later called it "the Majestic Glory" (2 Pt.1:17).

2. The "bright cloud" overshadowing Christ was a sharp contrast to the dark and threatening cloud that overshadowed the giving of the old covenant to Moses, that is, the law (Ex.19:18; 20:21). There is a point to be made here. The law (old covenant) was dark and threatening (see notes—Gal.3:10). The new covenant (the love of Christ) is bright: it is given to save and bless, not to threaten and condemn (Heb.12:18-24. Cp. Heb.8:6-13.)

3. The voice which spoke actually said, "This is My Son, the Beloved One" (Greek). Note the two facts stressed: Christ is God's Son, and He is the Beloved One. The idea is that Christ is the *only begotten Son* who was to be given for the world.

> **"For God so loved the world that he gave his one and only Son, that whoever believes in him shall not perish but have eternal life. (John 3:16)**
>
> **He who did not spare his own Son, but gave him up for us all—how will he not also, along with him, graciously give us all things? (Rom 8:32)**

7 (9:35) **Jesus Christ, Deity**: the sixth event was the voice that spoke out of the cloud. The message was clear: "This is my Son, whom I have chosen [ho huios mou, ho eklelegmenos], listen to him!" "Listen to Him, for He is my Son, my chosen One." God was both telling and warning the disciples to listen to Christ...

- He was God's Son, the beloved and chosen One.
- What Jesus spoke was the truth, even when He predicted His death and resurrection.

> **Thought 1.** God warns every living man to listen to Christ for the same two reasons.
>
> **We accept man's testimony, but God's testimony is greater because it is the testimony of God, which he has given about his Son. Anyone who believes in the Son of God has this testimony in his heart. Anyone who does not believe God has made him out to be a liar, because he has not believed the testimony God has given about his Son. And this is the testimony: God has given us eternal life, and this life is in his Son. He who has the Son has life; he who does not have the Son of God does not have life. (1 John 5:9-12)**
>
> **"I have much to say in judgment of you. But he who sent me is reliable, and what I have heard from him I tell the world." (John 8:26)**
>
> **For I did not speak of my own accord, but the Father who sent me commanded me what to say and how to say it. (John 12:49)**
>
> **Don't you believe that I am in the Father, and that the Father is in me? The words I say to you are not just my own. Rather, it is the Father, living in me, who is doing his work. (John 14:10)**
>
> **He who does not love me will not obey my teaching. These words you hear are not my own; they belong to the Father who sent me. (John 14:24)**
>
> **For I gave them the words you gave me and they accepted them. They knew with certainty that I came from you, and they believed that you sent me. (John 17:8)**
>
> **For Moses said, 'The Lord your God will raise up for you a prophet [Christ] like me from among your own people; you must listen to everything he tells you. (Acts 3:22)**

8 (9:36) **Quietness**: the seventh event was the stunned silence. Jesus was standing there all alone. There was stone silence. No one said anything, not even Jesus. We can picture the silence throughout the night. They were apparently on the mountain all night (v.37). Note the disciples said nothing about the experience during those days (see note, Inner Circle—Lk.9:28).

Thought 1. There is a time for silence, for being still and meditating upon the Lord.

In your anger do not sin; when you are on your beds, search your hearts and be silent. *Selah* (Psa 4:4)

"Be still, and know that I am God; I will be exalted among the nations, I will be exalted in the earth." (Psa 46:10)

Now then, stand here, because I am going to confront you with evidence before the LORD as to all the righteous acts performed by the LORD for you and your fathers. (1 Sam 12:7)

If only you would be altogether silent! For you, that would be wisdom. (Job 13:5)

"Listen to this, Job; stop and consider God's wonders. (Job 37:14)

When words are many, sin is not absent, but he who holds his tongue is wise. (Prov 10:19)

Even a fool is thought wise if he keeps silent, and discerning if he holds his tongue. (Prov 17:28)

A time to tear and a time to mend, a time to be silent and a time to speak, (Eccl 3:7)

But the LORD is in his holy temple; let all the earth be silent before him." (Hab 2:20)

Be silent before the Sovereign LORD, for the day of the LORD is near. The LORD has prepared a sacrifice; he has consecrated those he has invited. (Zep 1:7)

Be still before the LORD, all mankind, because he has roused himself from his holy dwelling." (Zec 2:13)

Therefore, since these facts are undeniable, you ought to be quiet and not do anything rash. (Acts 19:36)

Make it your ambition to lead a quiet life, to mind your own business and to work with your hands, just as we told you, (1 Th 4:11)

Instead, it should be that of your inner self, the unfading beauty of a gentle and quiet spirit, which is of great worth in God's sight. (1 Pet 3:4)

D. The Second Prediction of Death: A Rebuke of the Present Generation, 9:37-45
(Mt.17:14-23; Mk.9:14-32)

37 The next day, when they
came down from the moun-
tain, a large crowd met him.
38 A man in the crowd called
out, "Teacher, I beg you to
look at my son, for he is my
only child.
39 A spirit seizes him and he
suddenly screams; it throws
him into convulsions so that
he foams at the mouth. It
scarcely ever leaves him and
is destroying him.
40 I begged your disciples to
drive it out, but they could
not."
41 "O unbelieving and perverse
generation," Jesus replied,
"how long shall I stay with
you and put up with you?
Bring your son here."
42 Even while the boy was
coming, the demon threw him
to the ground in a convulsion.
But Jesus rebuked the evil
spirit, healed the boy and
gave him back to his father.
43 And they were all amazed
at the greatness of God.
While everyone was marvel-
ing at all that Jesus did, he
said to his disciples,
44 "Listen carefully to what I
am about to tell you: The Son
of Man is going to be be-
trayed into the hands of men."
45 But they did not understand what this meant. It was
hidden from them, so that
they did not grasp it, and they
were afraid to ask him about it.

1 The next day after the transfiguration
- a. Jesus was met by a crowd
- b. A man cried out in desperation
  - 1) For his only son
  - 2) The problem: An evil spirit possessed him[DS1]
- c. The disciples were powerless

2 Rebuke 1: A lack of faith & a wayward heart[DS2,3]

3 Rebuke 2: A lack of God's power
- a. Jesus rebuked the disciples' lack of power by His own act of healing
- b. The people were amazed

4 Rebuke 3: A slowness to grasp the Messiah's death

DIVISION IV

THE SON OF MAN'S INTENSIVE PREPARATION OF HIS DISCIPLES FOR JERUSALEM AND DEATH, 9:18-50

D. The Second Prediction of Death: A Rebuke of the Present Generation, 9:37-45

(9:37-45) **Introduction**: Jesus was rebuking His generation (v.41). They deserved to be rebuked—so does any generation which stands guilty of such unbelief and perverse living.

1. The next day after the transfiguration (v.37-40).
2. Rebuke 1: unbelief and a perverse heart(v.41).
3. Rebuke 2: a lack of God's power (v.42-43).
4. Rebuke 3: a slowness to grasp the Messiah's death (v.44-45).

1 (9:37-40) **Powerlessness—Seeking Christ**: it was the next day after the transfiguration. Jesus and the three disciples were coming down from having spent the night on the mountain. A huge crowd ran to meet Jesus, and from their midst a man broke forth, elbowing his way up to Jesus (Mt.17:14; Mk.9:15).

1. The man called out in desperation: "Teacher, I beg you." The words "called" and "beg" are strong; he shouted and begged for Jesus to meet his need.

"Look at my son, for he is my only child." The word for "look at" (epiblepsai) is a medical term. It means to carefully examine the patient, to look upon with pity. The son had an evil spirit that abused him physically (see DEEPER STUDY # 1—Lk.9:39).

2. The disciples were powerless in helping the man, despite his desperate need. This was tragic, for it meant that the power of God had left them. They had just demonstrated the power to cast out demons on their preaching tour (Lk.9:1-6, 10), but now they had no power. There was something wrong in their lives, some sin, some lack which was blocking the power of God. Jesus later told them they had not been praying and fasting as they should (Mt.17:21).

DEEPER STUDY # 1

(9:39) **Evil Spirits**: the son's illness seemed to have been both physical and spiritual. The description of the illness in Mark points toward what is known today as epilepsy and demon-possession (Mt.17:15; Mk.9:17-18). The demon-possession in particular seems to have heightened and aggravated the condition, perhaps causing some suicidal tendencies (Mt.17:15; Mk.9:22). Throughout the gospels this seems to be one of the major works of evil spirits: to *heighten and aggravate* existing conditions.

2 (9:41) **Unbelief—Heart,Perverse**: the first rebuke was for unbelief and a perverse heart. Note three things.

1. Jesus spoke to His whole generation. He enlarged His comments beyond the disciples. They had no power; neither did anyone else in His generation. What the disciples lacked was lacked by all. Their sins were the sins of all, the sins of *unbelief and being perverse* (see DEEPER STUDY # 2,3—Lk.9:41).

2. Jesus actually said that His presence would not always be available; He would not be patient with man's unbelief forever. Note: there is a point of coming judgment in this statement.

3. Jesus was looked upon only as a great prophet and minister...
- not as the very presence of God in their midst.
- not as the true Messiah before whom a person must repent.
- not as the Christ to whom a person owed his life and service.

Thus, the generation of people were walking around in unbelief and perverse before God, as powerless and helpless as ever.

He said to his disciples, "Why are you so afraid? Do you still have no faith?" (Mark 4:40)

And without faith it is impossible to

please God, because anyone who comes to him must believe that he exists and that he rewards those who earnestly seek him. (Heb 11:6)

"If you are the Christ, " they said, "tell us." Jesus answered, "If I tell you, you will not believe me, (Luke 22:67)

I tell you the truth, we speak of what we know, and we testify to what we have seen, but still you people do not accept our testimony. (John 3:11)

The Jews gathered around him, saying, "How long will you keep us in suspense? If you are the Christ, tell us plainly." Jesus answered, "I did tell you, but you do not believe. The miracles I do in my Father's name speak for me, (John 10:24-25)

Even after Jesus had done all these miraculous signs in their presence, they still would not believe in him. (John 12:37)

Who has believed our message and to whom has the arm of the LORD been revealed? (Isa 53:1)

DEEPER STUDY # 2
(9:41) **Unbelief—Faithless** (apistos): disbelieving; being without faith; being out of faith; not keeping faith, (cp. Tit.1:15).

DEEPER STUDY # 3
(9:41) **Perverse** (diastrepho): to distort, to twist, to turn aside or away, to be torn in two, to be corrupted (cp. Acts 20:30; Ph.2:15).

So that you may become blameless and pure, children of God without fault in a crooked and depraved generation, in which you shine like stars in the universe (Phil 2:15)

Even from your own number men will arise and distort the truth in order to draw away disciples after them. (Acts 20:30)

And constant friction between men of corrupt mind, who have been robbed of the truth and who think that godliness is a means to financial gain. (1 Tim 6:5)

The integrity of the upright guides them, but the unfaithful are destroyed by their duplicity. (Prov 11:3)

A man is praised according to his wisdom, but men with warped minds are despised. (Prov 12:8)

The tongue that brings healing is a tree of life, but a deceitful tongue crushes the spirit. (Prov 15:4)

Better a poor man whose walk is blameless than a rich man whose ways are perverse. (Prov 28:6)

3 (9:42-43) **Minister, Duty**: the second rebuke was for a lack of God's power. Note two significant points.

1. Jesus rebuked the disciples' lack of power by His own act of healing.
   a. Jesus healed the boy while the evil spirit was actually attacking the boy, while he was at his very worst. The Lord's power was clearly demonstrated.

But so that you may know that the Son of Man has authority on earth to forgive sins." Then he said to the paralytic, "Get up, take your mat and go home." (Mat 9:6)

Then Jesus came to them and said, "All authority in heaven and on earth has been given to me. (Mat 28:18)

For nothing is impossible with God." (Luke 1:37)

How God anointed Jesus of Nazareth with the Holy Spirit and power, and how he went around doing good and healing all who were under the power of the devil, because God was with him. (Acts 10:38)

"I know that you can do all things; no plan of yours can be thwarted. (Job 42:2)

   b. Jesus rebuked the spirit, broke the devil's power by *His Word*. Satan could not stand before God's Word. Jesus had purposed to spoil principalities and powers.

Now is the time for judgment on this world; now the prince of this world will be driven out. (John 12:31)

For he has rescued us from the dominion of darkness and brought us into the kingdom of the Son he loves, in whom we have redemption, the forgiveness of sins. (Col 1:13-14)

And having disarmed the powers and authorities, he made a public spectacle of them, triumphing over them by the cross. (Col 2:15)

Since the children have flesh and blood, he too shared in their humanity so that by his death he might destroy him who holds the power of death—that is, the devil—and free those who all their lives were held in slavery by their fear of death. (Heb 2:14-15)

He who does what is sinful is of the devil, because the devil has been sinning from the beginning. The reason the Son of God appeared was to destroy the devil's work. (1 John 3:8)

   c. Jesus showed tenderness for men. He delivered the little boy to his father.

2. The people were all amazed (exeplessonto depantes). They marvelled, were astonished at "the greatness of God." The Greek word is "megaleioteti," which means majesty. They marvelled at "the majesty of God." Note that Jesus brought honor to God, not to Himself.

Thought 1. Powerlessness is inexcusable. Why? Because Christ has revealed how the believer can possess the power and strength of God.

He replied, "Because you have so little faith. I tell you the truth, if you have faith as small as a mustard seed, you can say to this mountain, 'Move from here to there' and it will move. Nothing will be impossible for you." (Mat 17:20)

To this John replied, "A man can receive only what is given him from heaven. (John 3:27)

"I am the vine; you are the branches. If a man remains in me and I in him, he will bear much fruit; apart from me you can do nothing. (John 15:5)

Not that we are competent in ourselves to claim anything for ourselves, but our competence comes from God. (2 Cor 3:5)

But you will receive power when the Holy Spirit comes on you; and you will be my witnesses in Jerusalem, and in all Judea and Samaria, and to the ends of the earth." (Acts 1:8. See outline—Ro.8:1-17.)

4 (9:44-45) **Dullness—Understanding, Lack of**: the third rebuke was for a slowness to grasp the Messiah's death. Apparently, the disciples began to think about the earthly reign of Jesus. The power of God demonstrated that Jesus had the power to conquer the earth and subject all men to Himself. Their hopes were stirred.

But note what Jesus did. He rebuked their thoughts of a physical and material Messiah. He again had to show them that God's Messiah had to die in order to save the world.

1. Jesus strongly exhorted: "Listen carefully to what I am about to tell you." The Greek is, "Put these sayings into your ears." Give special attention to them.

2. The word "betrayed" (paradidosthai) means to be ordained, predetermined in the counsel and plan of God. (See note—Mt.17:22.)

This man was handed over to you by God's set purpose and foreknowledge; and you, with the help of wicked men, put him to death by nailing him to the cross. (Acts 2:23)

He who did not spare his own Son, but gave him up for us all—how will he not also, along with him, graciously give us all things? (Rom 8:32)

3. The disciples did not grasp the Messiah's death. They just did not understand. Note why: it was hidden from them, so that they could not perceive it.

Why was it hid from them? Certainly not because of God. The reason had to be because of their unbelief and perverseness. They just refused to see it. They were spiritually dull, lacking a sensitivity to spiritual truth.

He said to them, "How foolish you are, and how slow of heart to believe all that the prophets have spoken! (Luke 24:25)

Hypocrites! You know how to interpret the appearance of the earth and the sky. How is it that you don't know how to interpret this present time [the day and age of Christ]? (Luke 12:56)

Why is my language not clear to you? Because you are unable to hear what I say. (John 8:43)

For this people's heart has become calloused; they hardly hear with their ears, and they have closed their eyes. Otherwise they might see with their eyes, hear with their ears, understand with their hearts and turn, and I would heal them.' (Acts 28:27)

There is no one who understands, no one who seeks God. (Rom 3:11)

The man without the Spirit does not accept the things that come from the Spirit of God, for they are foolishness to him, and he cannot understand them, because they are spiritually discerned. (1 Cor 2:14)

Always learning but never able to acknowledge the truth. (2 Tim 3:7)

We have much to say about this, but it is hard to explain because you are slow to learn. (Heb 5:11)

I will instruct you and teach you in the way you should go; I will counsel you and watch over you. Do not be like the horse or the mule, which have no understanding but must be controlled by bit and bridle or they will not come to you. (Psa 32:8-9)

A man who has riches without understanding is like the beasts that perish. (Psa 49:20)

When its twigs are dry, they are broken off and women come and make fires with them. For this is a people without understanding; so their Maker has no compassion on them, and their Creator shows them no favor. (Isa 27:11)

"My people are fools; they do not know me. They are senseless children; they have no understanding. They are skilled in doing evil; they know not how to do good." (Jer 4:22)

Hear this, you foolish and senseless people, who have eyes but do not see, who have ears but do not hear: Should you not fear me?" declares the LORD. "Should you not tremble in my presence? I made the sand a boundary for the sea, an everlasting barrier it cannot cross. The waves may roll, but they cannot prevail; they may roar, but they cannot cross it. But these people have stubborn and rebellious hearts; they have turned aside and gone away. They do not say to themselves, 'Let us fear the LORD our God, who gives autumn and spring rains in season, who assures us of the regular weeks of harvest.' (Jer 5:21-24)

But they do not know the thoughts of the LORD; they do not understand his plan, he who gathers them like sheaves to the threshing floor. (Micah 4:12)

	E. The Way of Greatness: Humility, 9:46-50 (Mt.18:1-4; Mk.9:33-41)	child in my name welcomes me; and whoever welcomes me welcomes the one who sent me. For he who is least among you all—he is the greatest."	a. Welcoming a child in Jesus' name b. Reward 1) Will receive Jesus 2) Will receive God 3) Will be the greatest
1 The desire for greatness: Wanting place, recognition & power	46 An argument started among the disciples as to which of them would be the greatest.	49 "Master," said John, "we saw a man driving out demons in your name and we tried to stop him, because he is not one of us."	**4 The right to greatness: Not an exclusive right**
2 The picture of greatness a. Jesus took a child b. Jesus held the child	47 Jesus, knowing their thoughts, took a little child and had him stand beside him.	50 "Do not stop him," Jesus said, "for whoever is not against you is for you."	
3 The right concept of greatness	48 Then he said to them, "Whoever welcomes this little		

DIVISION IV

THE SON OF MAN'S INTENSIVE PREPARATION OF HIS DISCIPLES FOR JERUSALEM AND DEATH, 9:18-50

E. The Way of Greatness: Humility, 9:46-50

(9:46-50) **Introduction**: people are interested in greatness to varying degrees. It is enough for some people to simply be accepted and approved by friends and neighbors; that is enough *greatness* for them. Others want more: to be elevated to a particular position, to live in a particular neighborhood, to own a certain kind of car, to hold a particular club membership—they want something that gives them greater recognition and greater prestige. They crave for more greatness than others. Some crave the greatness of authority and rule, of power and fame, of position and wealth. They want the prestige and honor and recognition far above the ordinary.

Note another fact: the nature of a person determines whether he secures his greatness by hook or crook or by respect and honesty, by meanness and depravity or by right and goodness. A man's heart determines whether people are blessed or hurt by his greatness. A good neighbor or ruler blesses others. A bad neighbor or ruler hurts others.

Jesus teaches the way to greatness.

1. The desire for greatness: wanting place, recognition, and power (v.46).
2. The picture of greatness (v.47).
3. The right concept of greatness (v.48).
4. The right to greatness is not an exclusive right (v.49-50).

1 (9:46) **Greatness—Worldliness—Material vs. Spiritual—Selfishness**: the disciples desired greatness in the Kingdom of Christ. They desired places of honor, recognition, and power.

1. The disciples were actually arguing over the highest positions in the Lord's kingdom. The word "argument" (dialogismos) means a dispute, or debate. They were maneuvering for positions of leadership. Later, James and John were even to manipulate their mother into asking Jesus for the highest positions.

2. The disciples were thinking of an earthly kingdom, a physical and material rule right here on earth. Their desire was for worldly position, name, recognition, honor, authority, challenge, duties, pleasure, and wealth. They were not thinking in terms of goodness or character. They did not mean the greatest in love and care, in ministry and help, but in position and rule, name and recognition.

3. The disciples were full of self, just as all men are. They were thinking of self, not of others, not how they could be great in helping others. They were not even thinking of Jesus. And remember, He had just been revealing that He was to *give* His life for the salvation of the world (v.44. Cp. Mk.9:33-34.) Their thoughts should have been on Jesus and the meaning of what He had said. They should have been seeking to encourage Him and to learn all they could from Him. Instead they were so full of self, they could think of nothing but themselves.

> **Thought 1.** It is difficult to admit that we are full of self, that is, self-centered and selfish. The fact hurts; we revolt against it. But the truth has to be faced before we can become what we should be.
>
> **For whoever exalts himself will be humbled, and whoever humbles himself will be exalted. (Mat 23:12)**
>
> **How can you believe if you accept praise from one another, yet make no effort to obtain the praise that comes from the only God ? (John 5:44)**
>
> **For by the grace given me I say to every one of you: Do not think of yourself more highly than you ought, but rather think of yourself with sober judgment, in accordance with the measure of faith God has given you. (Rom 12:3)**
>
> **Live in harmony with one another. Do not be proud, but be willing to associate with people of low position. Do not be conceited. (Rom 12:16)**
>
> **If anyone thinks he is something when he is nothing, he deceives himself. (Gal 6:3)**
>
> **Do nothing out of selfish ambition or vain conceit, but in humility consider others better than yourselves. Each of you should look not only to your own interests, but also to the interests of others. (Phil 2:3-4)**
>
> **So, because you are lukewarm—neither hot nor cold—I am about to spit you out of my mouth. You say, 'I am rich; I have acquired wealth and do not need a thing.' But you do not realize that you are wretched, pitiful, poor, blind and naked. (Rev 3:16-17)**
>
> **He boasts of the cravings of his heart; he blesses the greedy and reviles the LORD. (Psa 10:3)**
>
> **Those who trust in their wealth and**

boast of their great riches? No man can redeem the life of another or give to God a ransom for him— (Psa 49:6-7)

Like clouds and wind without rain is a man who boasts of gifts he does not give. (Prov 25:14)

You have trusted in your wickedness and have said, 'No one sees me.' Your wisdom and knowledge mislead you when you say to yourself, 'I am, and there is none besides me.' (Isa 47:10)

Though you soar like the eagle and make your nest among the stars, from there I will bring you down," declares the LORD. (Oba 1:4)

4. The disciples did not understand what the Kingdom of Heaven was. They still saw an earthly and temporal kingdom and not a spiritual and eternal kingdom. They still thought in terms of getting all they could for a few short years while on this earth. They had not grasped the hope and reality of the spiritual world, of eternal life and blessings. (See DEEPER STUDY # 3—Mt.19:23-24; Eph.1:3 for more discussion.)

2 (9:47) **Greatness—Salvation—Deliverance—Freedom—Bondage**: the picture of greatness was acted out by Jesus. Note that He pictured what greatness was before He explained the right concept. The picture involved two acts. First, He reached out and took a child; and second, He set the child by His side. What was Jesus doing?

Very simply, Jesus was *showing* the disciples what greatness was. A person is great when he takes a child and brings that child to Jesus. Greatness surrounds Christ and children, children who are *willing* to be brought to Christ. Greatness is setting children, the people of the world, by the side of Christ, beside the One who can meet all their needs.

1. Greatness is bringing people to the One who can give them freedom from the bondages of this world. Imagine how great the person is who shows men how to be liberated from…

- sin
- guilt
- drunkenness
- immorality
- oppression
- loneliness
- suffering
- lying
- stealing
- emptiness
- death
- laziness
- cursing
- selfishness
- hatred

2. Greatness is bringing people to the One who can give them the right to live, to live abundantly on this earth and eternally when entering the next world.

Yet to all who received him, to those who believed in his name, he gave the right to become children of God— (John 1:12)

"For God so loved the world that he gave his one and only Son, that whoever believes in him shall not perish but have eternal life. (John 3:16)

"I tell you the truth, whoever hears my word and believes him who sent me has eternal life and will not be condemned; he has crossed over from death to life. (John 5:24)

And this is the testimony: God has given us eternal life, and this life is in his Son. He who has the Son has life; he who does not have the Son of God does not have life. I write these things to you who believe in the name of the Son of God so that you may know that you have eternal life. (1 John 5:11-13)

So that, having been justified by his grace, we might become heirs having the hope of eternal life. (Titus 3:7)

The Spirit himself testifies with our spirit that we are God's children. Now if we are children, then we are heirs—heirs of God and co-heirs with Christ, if indeed we share in his sufferings in order that we may also share in his glory. (Rom 8:16-17)

The fruit of the righteous is a tree of life, and he who wins souls is wise. (Prov 11:30)

Those who are wise will shine like the brightness of the heavens, and those who lead many to righteousness, like the stars for ever and ever. (Dan 12:3)

3 (9:48) **Greatness**: the right concept of greatness is explained. Greatness is *welcoming* a child, that is, a person, in the name of Jesus. To welcome a child means at least three things.

1. It means doing just what Jesus did: we *reach out and welcome and accept* a person into our arms. This sounds easy—taking a child into our arms—but it is not always so. Sometimes a person…

- is unkempt, dirty, even filthy.
- is acting ugly, mean, misbehaving.
- is disliked, rejected, unacceptable to others.

And there is always the threat that welcoming a person will cause our own friends to withdraw their friendship because the person is unacceptable to them.

2. It means sharing the best news that we have: the *good news of God's kingdom.* Note: Jesus did not say that greatness is *just* welcoming a child. He adds that the child must be welcomed *in His name*. The name of Jesus has to be shared with the person. The person is to be told and shown that we act in the name and cause of Jesus. The kingdom of God is to be shared with the child (the person welcomed).

3. It means that we help the person in every way possible, no matter the cost. We do our best to meet his…

- physical and mental needs.
- material and social needs.
- spiritual and godly needs.

Just as the Son of Man did not come to be served, but to serve, and to give his life as a ransom for many." (Mat 20:28)

Again Jesus said, "Peace be with you! As the Father has sent me, I am sending you." (John 20:21)

In everything I did, I showed you that by this kind of hard work we must help the weak, remembering the words the Lord Jesus himself said: 'It is more blessed to give than to receive.'" (Acts 20:35)

We who are strong ought to bear with the failings of the weak and not to please ourselves. (Rom 15:1)

Carry each other's burdens, and in this way you will fulfill the law of Christ. (Gal 6:2)

Now, note what Jesus covered in this point. He revealed what the reward will be for welcoming people in His name. This stresses the importance of welcoming people. It is close to His heart, the very purpose for which He came to earth (Mt.20:28). It is the thing His followers are to be doing, the very thing to which we are to commit our lives. Therefore, He wants to challenge His followers to get to it. There is no better challenge than to lay the reward out in front of them. The reward is threefold for the man who welcomes persons *in the name of Jesus Christ*.

1. The disciple welcomes Christ. Note, it is in the very act of welcoming others that we receive Christ. This means that the disciple welcomes a very special presence of Christ, an abiding presence, a presence that cares for and looks after and guides and directs his life.

Another way to see what Christ is saying is this…

- Welcoming our neighbor *equals* welcoming Christ.
- Loving our neighbor *equals* loving Christ.

If anyone says, "I love God [Christ]," yet hates his brother, he is a liar. For anyone who does not love his brother, whom he has seen, cannot love God, whom he has not seen. (1 John 4:20. Cp. Mt.22:36-39.)

2. The disciple welcomes God. Again, this is active, that is, it is *in the very act* of welcoming Christ that we welcome God. God enters the disciple's life *at the very moment* the disciple welcomes Christ.

But love your enemies, do good to them, and lend to them without expecting to get anything back. Then your reward will be great, and you will be sons of the Most High, because he is kind to the ungrateful and wicked. Be merciful, just as your Father is merciful. (Luke 6:35-36)

3. The disciple shall be the greatest. Note: Jesus did not say *great*; He said "greatest." Every one who serves by bringing men to Christ by welcoming others *in the name of Christ* shall be the greatest.

Note a crucial point. It is the person who welcomes others and who is actually reaching out to others in the name of Jesus who *receives Christ*. Reaching and welcoming others is the evidence that one has welcomed Christ. A person's heart has to be opened both to Christ and to others before Christ can ever enter his life. To open one's heart to Christ is to open one's heart to others. There is no such thing as an open heart to God and a closed hand to man. It is out of the heart that man acts. If his heart belongs to God, then his hand (life) belongs to man. He will do all he can to love and help man, welcoming and welcoming every child who will be brought to Christ. That person "shall be the greatest."

And if anyone gives even a cup of cold water to one of these little ones because he is my disciple, I tell you the truth, he will certainly not lose his reward." (Mat 10:42)

Then the righteous will shine like the sun in the kingdom of their Father. He who has ears, let him hear. (Mat 13:43)

And everyone who has left houses or brothers or sisters or father or mother or children or fields for my sake will receive a hundred times as much and will inherit eternal life. (Mat 19:29)

"His master replied, 'Well done, good and faithful servant! You have been faithful with a few things; I will put you in charge of many things. Come and share your master's happiness!' (Mat 25:23)

Whoever serves me must follow me; and where I am, my servant also will be. My Father will honor the one who serves me. (John 12:26)

But glory, honor and peace for everyone who does good: first for the Jew, then for the Gentile. (Rom 2:10)

The Spirit himself testifies with our spirit that we are God's children. Now if we are children, then we are heirs—heirs of God and co-heirs with Christ, if indeed we share in his sufferings in order that we may also share in his glory. (Rom 8:16-17)

But our citizenship is in heaven. And we eagerly await a Savior from there, the Lord Jesus Christ, who, by the power that enables him to bring everything under his control, will transform our lowly bodies so that they will be like his glorious body. (Phil 3:20-21)

When Christ, who is your life, appears, then you also will appear with him in glory. (Col 3:4)

If we endure, we will also reign with him. If we disown him, he will also disown us; (2 Tim 2:12)

You sympathized with those in prison and joyfully accepted the confiscation of your property, because you knew that you yourselves had better and lasting possessions. (Heb 10:34)

He regarded disgrace for the sake of Christ as of greater value than the treasures of Egypt, because he was looking ahead to his reward. (Heb 11:26)

And when the Chief Shepherd appears, you will receive the crown of glory that will never fade away. (1 Pet 5:4)

I am coming soon. Hold on to what you have, so that no one will take your crown. (Rev 3:11)

4 (9:49-50) **Tolerance**: the right to greatness is not an exclusive right. John knew that the apostles had done just what Christ had demonstrated they should not do. They had just failed to receive a man; in fact, they had rejected the man. And to top it off, the man was ministering in the name of Christ. John wanted to find out if they were right in forbidding others to preach in Jesus' name. John felt there were bound to be limits to what Jesus was saying—certainly not everyone was to be welcomed and welcomed and brought to Jesus—some people "are not one of us." They were…

- different
- untrained
- uneducated
- immoral
- doctrinally unsound
- unruly
- unauthorized
- too far right
- too far left

What Jesus said is pointed and clear, yet it is difficult for some to accept.

⇒ "Do not stop him."

⇒ "Whoever is not against you is for you."

Note: Jesus said, "against you." Jesus and His followers are one. The man who stands against us stands against Jesus, and he who stands against Jesus stands against us. A person's attitude and behavior are to be watched. The way he acts toward Christ and His followers determines whether we weclome him or not. A person who is against Jesus and His followers is not to be welcomed . The person who welcomes Jesus and His followers is to be welcomed (cp. Lk.9:5; 10:10-11). (See outline and notes—Mk.9:38-41 for more discussion.)

"Whatever town or village you enter, search for some worthy person there and stay at his house until you leave. As you enter the home, give it your greeting. If the home is deserving, let your peace rest on it; if it is not, let your peace return to you. If anyone will not welcome you or listen to your words, shake the dust off your feet when you leave that home or town. I tell you the truth, it will be more bearable for Sodom and Gomorrah on the day of judgment than for that town. (Mat 10:11-15)

I have other sheep that are not of this sheep pen. I must bring them also. They too will listen to my voice, and there shall be one flock and one shepherd. (John 10:16)

It is true that some preach Christ out of envy and rivalry, but others out of goodwill. The latter do so in love, knowing that I am put here for the defense of the gospel. The former preach Christ out of selfish ambition, not sincerely, supposing that they can stir up trouble for me while I am in chains. But what does it matter? The important thing is that in every way, whether from false motives or true, Christ is preached. And because of this I rejoice. Yes, and I will continue to rejoice, (Phil 1:15-18)

"He who listens to you listens to me; he who rejects you rejects me; but he who rejects me rejects him who sent me." (Luke 10:16)

"He who is not with me is against me, and he who does not gather with me, scatters. (Luke 11:23)

"No servant can serve two masters. Either he will hate the one and love the other, or he will be devoted to the one and despise the other. You cannot serve both God and Money." (Luke 16:13)

When you sin against your brothers in this way and wound their weak conscience, you sin against Christ. (1 Cor 8:12)

	V. THE SON OF MAN'S GREAT JOURNEY TO JERUSALEM (STAGE I): HIS MISSION AND PUBLIC CHALLENGE, 9:51-13:21	52 And he sent messengers on ahead, who went into a Samaritan village to get things ready for him;	**2 His mission misunderstood** a. He sent forerunners to prepare the way
		53 But the people there did not welcome him, because he was heading for Jerusalem.	b. He was rejected by the Samaritans[DS2]
	A. The Son of Man's Mission: Jesus' Mission Misunderstood, 9:51-56	54 When the disciples James and John saw this, they asked, "Lord, do you want us to call fire down from heaven to destroy them?"	c. The disciples reacted against the Samaritans
1 His mission: To secure salvation a. By the ascension[DS1] b. By death: He set His face toward Jerusalem	51 As the time approached for him to be taken up to heaven, Jesus resolutely set out for Jerusalem.	55 But Jesus turned and rebuked them, 56 And they went to another village.	**3 His mission explained,** v.55 a. He did not come to use His power to destroy men's lives b. He came to use His power to save men

DIVISION V

THE SON OF MAN'S GREAT JOURNEY TO JERUSALEM (STAGE I): HIS MISSION AND PUBLIC CHALLENGE, 9:51-13:21

A. The Son of Man's Mission: Jesus' Mission Misunderstood, 9:51-56

(9:51-19:28) **DIVISION OVERVIEW: Jesus' Purpose**: this passage marks a significant turning point in Jesus' ministry. Chapters 9:51-19:28 have no parallel in the other Gospels. Most of the events are recorded by Luke alone. The thrust of the passage is that Jesus set his face, resolutely set out for Jerusalem.

Luke divides this journey of Jesus into three stages. Each stage begins by strongly emphasizing Jesus' journey toward Jerusalem (Lk.9:51, 53; 13:22; 17:11). There are also several passages that hint or mention the journey (Lk.9:53, 57; 10:1, 38; 13:33; 14:25; 18:31; 19:11, 28).

(9:51-56) **Introduction**: Jesus turned and set His face, resolutely set out for Jerusalem and death. This was one of the turning points of His life. As He launched forth in this new direction, the first subject covered is His mission. The mission of the Son of Man is seen in clear terms—terms so clear that the follower of the Lord cannot miss the meaning.

1. His mission: to secure salvation (v.51).
2. His mission misunderstood (v.52-54).
3. His mission explained (v.55-56).

1 (9:51) **Jesus Christ, Mission**: Jesus' mission upon earth was to secure salvation. Jesus knew His mission; He knew why He had come to earth. He also knew that the time for Him to die for the salvation of men was at hand. Note the words, "as the time approached." He was fully aware that the time had come (Lk.9:22, 27, 31). Therefore, He turned around and " resolutely set out for Jerusalem."

What is so significant about Jerusalem? Very simply, it was in Jerusalem that Jesus was to die for the salvation of men and be received up, that is, ascend into heaven. When Jesus "resolutely set out for Jerusalem ," Jerusalem symbolized the death, resurrection, and ascension of our Lord. It was in Jerusalem that He secured salvation for man through His death, resurrection, and ascension.

1. Jesus Christ secured salvation by His ascension (see DEEPER STUDY # 1, Ascension—Lk.9:51 for discussion).
2. Jesus Christ secured salvation by His death.

But God demonstrates his own love for us in this: While we were still sinners, Christ died for us. (Rom 5:8)

Christ redeemed us from the curse of the law by becoming a curse for us, for it is written: "Cursed is everyone who is hung on a tree." (Gal 3:13)

For [God] he has rescued us from the dominion of darkness and brought us into the kingdom of the Son he loves, in whom we have redemption, the forgiveness of sins. (Col 1:13-14)

This is good, and pleases God our Savior, who wants all men to be saved and to come to a knowledge of the truth. For there is one God and one mediator between God and men, the man Christ Jesus, who gave himself as a ransom for all men—the testimony given in its proper time. (1 Tim 2:3-6)

But we see Jesus, who was made a little lower than the angels, now crowned with glory and honor because he suffered death, so that by the grace of God he might taste death for everyone. (Heb 2:9)

So Christ was sacrificed once to take away the sins of many people; and he will appear a second time, not to bear sin, but to bring salvation to those who are waiting for him. (Heb 9:28)

He himself bore our sins in his body on the tree, so that we might die to sins and live for righteousness; by his wounds you have been healed. (1 Pet 2:24; cp. 1 Pet 3:18)

But he was pierced for our transgressions, he was crushed for our iniquities; the punishment that brought us peace was upon him, and by his wounds we are healed. (Isa 53:5)

DEEPER STUDY # 1

(9:51) **Jesus Christ, Ascension**: the words "taken up" (analempseos) mean received. They refer to the ascension of Christ (cp. analambano, Acts 1:2, 11, 22; 1 Tim.3:16). Salvation was to be secured by the ascension of Christ. How? The Ascended Lord means at least four things.

1. It means *the Risen Lord*. The ascension means that Christ arose from the dead. If He had remained in the grave, He would still be there in the form of dust. He could not have ascended. If He were to be "taken up," He

had to be *raised up—quickened—made alive—taken up*. No one can be *taken up* without first being raised up. Therefore, to speak of the ascension is to mean that Christ is risen. Death is conquered; man can now be saved from death.

But if it is preached that Christ has been raised from the dead, how can some of you say that there is no resurrection of the dead? If there is no resurrection of the dead, then not even Christ has been raised. And if Christ has not been raised, our preaching is useless and so is your faith. More than that, we are then found to be false witnesses about God, for we have testified about God that he raised Christ from the dead. But he did not raise him if in fact the dead are not raised. For if the dead are not raised, then Christ has not been raised either. And if Christ has not been raised, your faith is futile; you are still in your sins. Then those also who have fallen asleep in Christ are lost. If only for this life we have hope in Christ, we are to be pitied more than all men. But Christ has indeed been raised from the dead, the firstfruits of those who have fallen asleep. For since death came through a man, the resurrection of the dead comes also through a man. For as in Adam all die, so in Christ all will be made alive. But each in his own turn: Christ, the firstfruits; then, when he comes, those who belong to him. Then the end will come, when he hands over the kingdom to God the Father after he has destroyed all dominion, authority and power. (1 Cor 15:12-24)

But made himself nothing, taking the very nature of a servant, being made in human likeness. And being found in appearance as a man, he humbled himself and became obedient to death— even death on a cross! Therefore God exalted him to the highest place and gave him the name that is above every name, (Phil 2:7-9)

The words "it was credited to him" were written not for him alone, but also for us, to whom God will credit righteousness—for us who believe in him who raised Jesus our Lord from the dead. He was delivered over to death for our sins and was raised to life for our justification. (Rom 4:23-25)

2. It means *the Advocate or Representative Lord.* On earth Christ lived a perfect life; He was without sin (2 Cor.5:21; Heb.4:15; 1 Pt.1:19; 2:22; Jn.8:46). He was "obedient to death, even death on a cross. Therefore God exalted Him" (Ph.2:8-9). He is "seated at the right hand of God (Col.3:1). He is "Jesus Christ the Righteous One," therefore, He is our "advocate with the Father," the One who speaks to the Father in our defense" (1 Jn.2:1). He is able to represent us before God because He has lived upon earth and secured a perfect righteousness. He is the Ideal Man (see note—Mt.5:17-18), our advocate, the One who is qualified to plead our case before God and see to it that we are saved.

Therefore he is able to save completely those who come to God through him, because he always lives to intercede for them. (Heb 7:25)

3. It means *the Priestly or Intercessory Lord.* Every man suffers while on earth: suffers pain, trial, need, want, temptation, loss, illness, and eventually death. We are incapable of even knowing how to pray as we ought in order to secure the help we need. But Christ knows and understands. He has been to earth and suffered just as we suffer. Therefore, He knows how to intercede for us and how to deliver us.

Therefore, since we have a great high priest who has gone through the heavens, Jesus the Son of God, let us hold firmly to the faith we profess. For we do not have a high priest who is unable to sympathize with our weaknesses, but we have one who has been tempted in every way, just as we are—yet was without sin. Let us then approach the throne of grace with confidence, so that we may receive mercy and find grace to help us in our time of need. (Heb 4:14-16)

For surely it is not angels he helps, but Abraham's descendants. For this reason he had to be made like his brothers in every way, in order that he might become a merciful and faithful high priest in service to God, and that he might make atonement for the sins of the people. Because he himself suffered when he was tempted, he is able to help those who are being tempted. (Heb 2:16-18)

Who will bring any charge against those whom God has chosen? It is God who justifies. Who is he that condemns? Christ Jesus, who died—more than that, who was raised to life—is at the right hand of God and is also interceding for us. (Rom 8:33-34)

4. It means *the exalted Lord.* Christ has ascended to be exalted, to rule and reign over the universe for God. There is a great day of judgment coming upon the world, a day when all men shall bow the knee and acknowledge that Jesus is Lord, the Son of the living God.

Therefore God exalted him to the highest place and gave him the name that is above every name, that at the name of Jesus every knee should bow, in heaven and on earth and under the earth, and every tongue confess that Jesus Christ is Lord, to the glory of God the Father. (Phil 2:9-11)

And his incomparably great power for us who believe. That power is like the working of his mighty strength, which he exerted in Christ when he raised him from the dead and seated him at his right hand in the heavenly realms, far above all rule and authority, power and dominion, and every title that can be given, not only in the present age but also in the one to come. And God placed all things under his feet and appointed him to be head over everything for the church, which is his body, the fullness of him who fills everything in every way. (Eph 1:19-23)

Then the end will come, when he hands over the kingdom to God the Father after he has destroyed all dominion, authority and power. For he must reign until he has

put all his enemies under his feet. The last enemy to be destroyed is death. (1 Cor 15:24-26)

DEEPER STUDY # 2
(9:53) **Samaritans**: see DEEPER STUDY # 2—Lk.10:33.

2 (9:52-54) **Jesus Christ, Mission**: Jesus' mission upon earth was misunderstood. Note three things of vital importance.

1. Jesus sent some disciples to run ahead of Him, to prepare the way for His coming. Apparently, this was the *method* Christ used to let the people of an area know He was soon to enter their city. Those who had interest could thereby be prepared for His coming.
2. Jesus was rejected by the Samaritans. Why? Because He was heading for Jerusalem, going to a place they despised. The Jews were unacceptable to them; therefore, they would have nothing to do with Jesus if He were going to minister in Jerusalem. Jerusalem had its own worship and priests, and the Samaritans had theirs. If Jesus would be theirs alone, they would gladly receive Him; if not, then He was not welcomed in their circles. (See DEEPER STUDY # 2, Samaritans—Lk.10:33 for more detailed discussion.)
3. James and John were upset, fiery and angry over such rejection. They asked Jesus if they should destroy the village by calling fire from heaven to consume the people. Note two crucial points.
   a. The faith of James and John in Jesus was strong. They believed without question that Jesus had the authority to control the power of heaven, either through Himself or through them.
   b. The wrong understanding of Jesus' mission that James and John had was also strong. They thought in terms of a Messianic Ruler on earth, subjecting men and forcing them to worship and serve God. They saw the Messiah's judging those who rejected Him.

      Note that James and John were guilty of the very some error that the Samaritans had just committed. They were full of bitterness, wrath, and vengeance, reacting against the Samaritans just as the Samaritans had reacted against the Jews and Jesus. They wanted to destroy the Samaritans because the Samaritans were not willing to worship (Jesus) and live as James and John wished.

For God did not send his Son into the world to condemn the world, but to save the world through him. (John 3:17)

"As for the person who hears my words but does not keep them, I do not judge him. For I did not come to judge the world, but to save it. (John 12:47)

3 (9:55-56) **Jesus Christ, Mission**: Jesus' mission explained. Jesus' mission was not to destroy life, but to save it. This is repeated time and time again.

For the Son of Man came to seek and to save what was lost." (Luke 19:10)

"I tell you the truth, whoever hears my word and believes him who sent me has eternal life and will not be condemned; he has crossed over from death to life. (John 5:24)

The thief comes only to steal and kill and destroy; I have come that they may have life, and have it to the full. (John 10:10)

Therefore, there is now no condemnation for those who are in Christ Jesus, (Rom 8:1)

Who is he that condemns? Christ Jesus, who died—more than that, who was raised to life—is at the right hand of God and is also interceding for us. (Rom 8:34)

Here is a trustworthy saying that deserves full acceptance: Christ Jesus came into the world to save sinners—of whom I am the worst. (1 Tim 1:15)

Thought 1. Note several facts.

1) Christ proclaimed that today is the day of salvation, and He proclaimed it loudly and clearly.

For he says, "In the time of my favor I heard you, and in the day of salvation I helped you." I tell you, now is the time of God's favor, now is the day of salvation. (2 Cor 6:2)

Here I am! I stand at the door and knock. If anyone hears my voice and opens the door, I will come in and eat with him, and he with me. (Rev 3:20)

For the Son of Man came to seek and to save what was lost." (Luke 19:10)

2) Scripture pronounces that judgment is *to come*. There is a day "when man is destined to die once, and after that to face judgment."

Just as man is destined to die once, and after that to face judgment, (Heb 9:27)

1 A person must count the cost a. The man offered himself b. Jesus offered no luxury, no materialism—only self-denial & sacrifice[DS1] **2 A person must follow immediately**	**B. The Great Cost of Discipleship, 9:57-62** (Mt.8:18-22) 57 As they were walking along the road, a man said to him, "I will follow you wher- ever you go." 58 Jesus replied, "Foxes have holes and birds of the air have nests, but the Son of Man has no place to lay his head." 59 He said to another man, "Follow me." But the man	replied, "Lord, first let me go and bury my fa- ther." 60 Jesus said to him, "Let the dead bury their own dead, but you go and proclaim the kingdom of God." 61 Still another said, "I will follow you, Lord; but first let me go back and say good-by to my family." 62 Jesus replied, "No one who puts his hand to the plow and looks back is fit for serv- ice in the kingdom of God."	a. Jesus invited the man b. The man had divided attention c. Jesus' demand 1) A sense of urgency 2) Go now & preach **3 A person must not look back** a. Another man offered himself b. The man's double allegiance c. Jesus' judgment: Looking back disqualifies a person

DIVISION V

THE SON OF MAN'S GREAT JOURNEY TO JERUSALEM (STAGE I): HIS MISSION AND PUBLIC CHALLENGE, 9:51-13:21

B. The Great Cost of Discipleship, 9:57-62

(9:57-62) **Introduction**: some people desire to follow Christ; therefore, they attach themselves to Him and join the church. Yet they come ever so short and miss eternal life. Why? Because they never knew the price of discipleship. They were to pay a great price, but they knew nothing about it or else were unwilling to pay the price. True discipleship costs everything a person is and has.

1. One must count the cost (v.57-58).
2. One must follow immediately (v.59-60).
3. One must not look back (v.61-62).

1 (9:57-58) **Discipleship**: one must count the cost. A man offered to become a follower of Jesus, and he made an unusual promise: he would follow Jesus wherever He led. Why? For the same reasons so many are attracted to the Lord.

⇒ He enjoyed the presence of the Lord and His followers.

⇒ He was motivated by the Lord's wisdom and teaching.

⇒ He appreciated the good the Lord did.

Jesus' reply was to the point. The man had to count the cost, for Jesus offered no luxury and no material comfort—only self-denial. The man had to deny himself and sacrifice all he was and had. Note several facts. (See note—Mt.8:19-20 for more discussion.)

1. Jesus Himself was the prime example. He denied Himself completely. He sacrificed and gave all, both Himself and all He had. He did not even have a place to lay His head. The animals of the world did; the birds had their nests and the foxes had their holes, but Jesus had no place. He gave all to meet the needs of a dying and desperate world.

2. Jesus told the man to count the cost. A profession was not enough. Being *willing to follow* was not enough. The man must deny himself completely, sacrificing and giving all he was and had to meet the needs of a lost and desperate world (see note and DEEPER STUDY # 1—Lk.9:23 for discussion).

3. Jesus called Himself the Son of Man (see DEEPER STUDY # 1—Lk.9:58 for discussion). This pictures exactly who He was. The man was to follow Jesus, accepting Him as the Son of Man. He was to accept Jesus as the Ideal Servant of man, the Ideal Man who loved and cared and ministered and felt for all, and who did it perfectly.

Thought 1. Some persons are willing and determined to go to the ends of the earth. However Jesus said that *He—the Son of Man, His pattern of life*—must be accepted.

Many are committed, but their commitments are *self-commitments*, not Christ-centered commitments. We must realize that self-commitments can arise from (1) strong wills, (2) strong determinations, and (3) strong discipline. And the person can follow through in a great way. But self-commitment is not enough for Christ. There has to be a total commitment to the Son of Man, abandoning all of self and all of the world.

Then he said to them all: "If anyone would come after me, he must deny himself and take up his cross daily and follow me. (Luke 9:23)

To this you were called, because Christ suffered for you, leaving you an example, that you should follow in his steps. (1 Pet 2:21)

Your attitude should be the same as that of Christ Jesus: Who, being in very nature God, did not consider equality with God something to be grasped, but made himself nothing, taking the very nature of a servant, being made in human likeness. And being found in appearance as a man, he humbled himself and became obedient to death— even death on a cross! (Phil 2:5-8)

For we who are alive are always being given over to death for Jesus' sake, so that his life may be revealed in our mortal body. (2 Cor 4:11)

For you know the grace of our Lord Jesus Christ, that though he was rich, yet for your sakes he became poor, so that you through his poverty might become rich. (2 Cor 8:9)

DEEPER STUDY # 1

(9:58) **Son of Man**: Jesus was not only what an ordinary man is, a son of man; but Jesus was what every man ought to be, the Son of Man Himself. As such, He has become the *Ideal Man*, the *Representative Man*, the *Perfect Man*, the *Pattern*, the *Embodiment* of everything a man ought to be (see DEEPER STUDY # 3—Mt.1:16). Jesus Christ is the *perfect picture* of a man. Everything God wants a man to be is seen perfectly in Jesus Christ (cp. Jn.1:14; Col.2:9-10; Heb.1:3). The title also means the *Ideal Servant* of man. It stresses His sympathy for the poor, the brokenhearted, the captives, the blind, the bruised, the outcasts, the bereaved (cp. Lk.4:18). Jesus is the pattern, the model, the perfect example of concern and caring. He served just like every man ought to serve others.

Jesus called Himself "the Son of Man" about eighty times. It was His favorite term. The title *Son of Man* is probably based upon the Son of Man of Daniel 7:13-14. There is a picture of Jesus as the heavenly Son of Man contrasted with Adam as the earthly Man in 1 Cor.15:45-47. Each served as a Representative Man in God's plan for world history.

2 (9:59-60) **Discipleship—Decision—Call**: one must follow Jesus immediately. Note three things.

1. It was Jesus who invited the man to follow Him. There was something very special within the man that caught Jesus' eye, and Jesus was moved to call him. In fact, the *specialness* within the man was of such quality that Jesus stayed after the man even after the man hesitated. The man was of too much value to let go, so Jesus pleaded and argued and even commanded, "Go and proclaim the kindom of God."

Thought 1. Note two important points.
1) Every person is of extreme value to Jesus. Therefore, the Spirit stays after a man as long as the man allows Him, despite man's selfishness.
2) Every person who is called by Christ to "preach" must take heed and respond immediately. The Lord's call is to be the primary thrust of a person's life.

2. The man had divided attention. The call of God came to this man, yet he hesitated (see note—Mt.8:21). Note two facts.
a. The man's hesitation was legitimate. Caring for parents is essential. His father was either already dead or on the verge of death. He was legitimately needed at home.
b. The man's problem was *divided attention*. When he felt God's call, he looked at his situation and did not yield immediately. What happened so often happens. His circumstances and problems overwhelmed him, so he wanted to wait and handle them. As soon as the problems were handled, he would leave and follow Jesus.

"If anyone comes to me and does not hate his father and mother, his wife and children, his brothers and sisters—yes, even his own life—he cannot be my disciple. And anyone who does not carry his cross and follow me cannot be my disciple. (Luke 14:26-27)

Peter said to him, "We have left everything to follow you!" "I tell you the truth," Jesus replied, "no one who has left home or brothers or sisters or mother or father or children or fields for me and the gospel will fail to receive a hundred times as much in this present age (homes, brothers, sisters, mothers, children and fields—and with them, persecutions) and in the age to come, eternal life. (Mark 10:28-30)

And the things you have heard me say in the presence of many witnesses entrust to reliable men who will also be qualified to teach others. Endure hardship with us like a good soldier of Christ Jesus. No one serving as a soldier gets involved in civilian affairs—he wants to please his commanding officer. (2 Tim 2:2-4)

And the Lord's servant must not quarrel; instead, he must be kind to everyone, able to teach, not resentful. Those who oppose him he must gently instruct, in the hope that God will grant them repentance leading them to a knowledge of the truth, and that they will come to their senses and escape from the trap of the devil, who has taken them captive to do his will. (2 Tim 2:24-26)

But you, keep your head in all situations, endure hardship, do the work of an evangelist, discharge all the duties of your ministry. (2 Tim 4:5)

3. Jesus demanded that the man act now and not wait. Jesus saw through the man's partial commitment. He saw through the man's lack of trust in God. Jesus expects us to take care of our parents (1 Tim.5:3-8), but He demands first loyalty and immediate response. He demands two things in particular.
a. A sense of urgency. Imagine! Jesus refused to give the man time to bury the dead. Why? Because the need is so great, and men are dying every hour without Christ. Nothing can be done for the dead (his father), but the living can be reached and snatched out of the grip of death and saved unto eternal life. If we hesitate, for whatever reason, some whom we might have reached will die and be doomed. The point is forceful: the hour is urgent.

"Come, follow me," Jesus said, "and I will make you fishers of men." At once they left their nets and followed him. (Mark 1:17-18)

"My food," said Jesus, "is to do the will of him who sent me and to finish his work. (John 4:34)

As long as it is day, we must do the work of him who sent me. Night is coming, when no one can work. (John 9:4)

And do this, understanding the present time. The hour has come for you to wake up from your slumber, because our salvation is nearer now than when we first believed. The night is nearly over; the day is almost here. So let us put aside the deeds of darkness and put on the armor of light. (Rom 13:11-12)

What I mean, brothers, is that the time is short. From now on those who have wives should live as if they had none; (1 Cor 7:29)

Making the most of every opportunity, because the days are evil. (Eph 5:16)

Be wise in the way you act toward outsiders; make the most of every opportunity. (Col 4:5)

For this reason I remind you to fan into flame the gift of God, which is in you through the laying on of my hands. (2 Tim 1:6)

I think it is right to refresh your memory as long as I live in the tent of this body, (2 Pet 1:13)

Those whom I love I rebuke and discipline. So be earnest, and repent. (Rev 3:19)

Teach us to number our days aright, that we may gain a heart of wisdom. (Psa 90:12)

Remember your Creator in the days of your youth, before the days of trouble come and the years approach when you will say, "I find no pleasure in them"— (Ecc1 12:1)

b. Go and preach the Kingdom of God. Note that Christ tells His messengers what to preach, yet how little the real message of God's kingdom is preached (see note—Mt.19:23-24).

For we cannot help speaking about what we have seen and heard." (Acts 4:20)

When Silas and Timothy came from Macedonia, Paul devoted himself exclusively to preaching, testifying to the Jews that Jesus was the Christ. (Acts 18:5)

Yet when I preach the gospel, I cannot boast, for I am compelled to preach. Woe to me if I do not preach the gospel! (1 Cor 9:16)

Preach the Word; be prepared in season and out of season; correct, rebuke and encourage—with great patience and careful instruction. (2 Tim 4:2)

But if I say, "I will not mention him or speak any more in his name," his word is in my heart like a fire, a fire shut up in my bones. I am weary of holding it in; indeed, I cannot. (Jer 20:9)

The lion has roared— who will not fear? The Sovereign LORD has spoken— who can but prophesy? (Amos 3:8)

3 (9:61-62) **Decision—Discipleship**: one must not look back. Note three things.

1. This man offered himself to Jesus. He was *willing* to follow Jesus. Something about the Lord touched his heart or else the Lord's teaching and ministry appealed to him. He saw the enormous benefit to men and to society as Christ ministered to the needs of men. In either case, he made a decision to follow Jesus. He was *willing*.

2. The man had a *double allegiance*. Note the words "but" and "first." The man had thought through his decision and concluded that he was willing to follow Christ, *but* something else needed to be handled *first*: a family affair, a business affair, an employment affair, a financial affair—some other concern was put first (as is the case with so many).

Something else could have been concerning the man. He may have wanted his family's counsel and advice, to see how they felt about his decision. Perhaps he felt their approval was needed. Then again, he could have been putting his love for family before his love for Christ. Perhaps he was attached to his family more than he was attached to Christ. Family should be our *first* attachment *after* our attachment to Christ. Christ is to be first in our lives.

But seek first his kingdom and his righteousness, and all these things will be given to you as well. (Mat 6:33)

"He who is not with me is against me, and he who does not gather with me scatters. (Mat 12:30)

"Then the King will say to those on his right, 'Come, you who are blessed by my Father; take your inheritance, the kingdom prepared for you since the creation of the world. For I was hungry and you gave me something to eat, I was thirsty and you gave me something to drink, I was a stranger and you invited me in, I needed clothes and you clothed me, I was sick and you looked after me, I was in prison and you came to visit me.' (Mat 25:34-36)

"Which of these three do you think was a neighbor to the man who fell into the hands of robbers?" The expert in the law replied, "The one who had mercy on him." Jesus told him, "Go and do likewise." (Luke 10:36-37)

In the same way, any of you who does not give up everything he has cannot be my disciple. (Luke 14:33)

"No servant can serve two masters. Either he will hate the one and love the other, or he will be devoted to the one and despise the other. You cannot serve both God and Money." (Luke 16:13)

When they had finished eating, Jesus said to Simon Peter, "Simon son of John, do you truly love me more than these?" "Yes, Lord," he said, "you know that I love you." Jesus said, "Feed my lambs." Again Jesus said, "Simon son of John, do you truly love me?" He answered, "Yes, Lord, you know that I love you." Jesus said, "Take care of my sheep." The third time he said to him, "Simon son of John, do you love me?" Peter was hurt because Jesus asked him the third time, "Do you love me?" He said, "Lord, you know all things; you know that I love you." Jesus said, "Feed my sheep." (John 21:15-17)

What is more, I consider everything a loss compared to the surpassing greatness of knowing Christ Jesus my Lord, for whose sake I have lost all things. I consider them rubbish, that I may gain Christ (Phil 3:8)

Be shepherds of God's flock that is under your care, serving as overseers—not because you must, but because you are willing, as God wants you to be; not greedy for money, but eager to serve; (1 Pet 5:2)

And now, O Israel, what does the LORD your God ask of you but to fear the LORD your God, to walk in all his ways, to love him, to serve the LORD your God with all your heart and with all your soul, (Deu 10:12)

"Now fear the LORD and serve him with all faithfulness. Throw away the gods

your forefathers worshiped beyond the River and in Egypt, and serve the LORD. (Josh 24:14)

But Samuel replied: "Does the LORD delight in burnt offerings and sacrifices as much as in obeying the voice of the LORD? To obey is better than sacrifice, and to heed is better than the fat of rams. (1 Sam 15:22)

Elijah went before the people and said, "How long will you waver between two opinions? If the LORD is God, follow him; but if Baal is God, follow him." But the people said nothing. (1 Ki 18:21)

"And you, my son Solomon, acknowledge the God of your father, and serve him with wholehearted devotion and with a willing mind, for the LORD searches every heart and understands every motive behind the thoughts. If you seek him, he will be found by you; but if you forsake him, he will reject you forever. (1 Chr 28:9)

Serve the LORD with fear and rejoice with trembling. (Psa 2:11)

"Stand at the gate of the Lord's house and there proclaim this message: "'Hear the word of the LORD, all you people of Judah who come through these gates to worship the LORD. (Jer 7:2)

"Son of man, I have made you a watchman for the house of Israel; so hear the word I speak and give them warning from me. (Ezek 3:17)

3. Jesus' judgment was descriptively stated—stated in such a way that once heard or read, it would be difficult to forget: "No one who puts his hand to the plow and looks back is fit for service in the kingdom of God." The man got the point, and he probably never forgot it. It more than likely pricked his conscience and disturbed him often as the saying flashed across his mind. He had willed to follow Christ, but he "had looked back"; therefore, he was not fit for the Kingdom of God.

The idea is this. A man who begins to plough and then looks back...

- ploughs a crooked row. No row (person) is ever straight, not like it should be. (Each row or person receives only partial teaching.)
- ploughs an inconsistent field. The field under his care is never matured; it never receives consistent work.
- ploughs in a spirit lacking total commitment. He may turn away at any time, leaving a job unfinished.
- ploughs but allows distractions and disruptions which affect the crops (the plants are not cared for).

"Not everyone who says to me, 'Lord, Lord,' will enter the kingdom of heaven, but only he who does the will of my Father who is in heaven. (Mat 7:21)

But everyone who hears these words of mine and does not put them into practice is like a foolish man who built his house on sand. The rain came down, the streams rose, and the winds blew and beat against that house, and it fell with a great crash." (Mat 7:26-27)

Jesus answered, "If you want to be perfect, go, sell your possessions and give to the poor, and you will have treasure in heaven. Then come, follow me." When the young man heard this, he went away sad, because he had great wealth. Then Jesus said to his disciples, "I tell you the truth, it is hard for a rich man to enter the kingdom of heaven. (Mat 19:21-23)

"That servant who knows his master's will and does not get ready or does not do what his master wants will be beaten with many blows. (Luke 12:47)

The Spirit gives life; the flesh counts for nothing. The words I have spoken to you are spirit and they are life. Yet there are some of you who do not believe." For Jesus had known from the beginning which of them did not believe and who would betray him. He went on to say, "This is why I told you that no one can come to me unless the Father has enabled him." From this time many of his disciples turned back and no longer followed him. "You do not want to leave too, do you?" Jesus asked the Twelve. Simon Peter answered him, "Lord, to whom shall we go? You have the words of eternal life. We believe and know that you are the Holy One of God." Then Jesus replied, "Have I not chosen you, the Twelve? Yet one of you is a devil!" (John 6:63-70)

So then, each of us will give an account of himself to God. (Rom 14:12)

I am astonished that you are so quickly deserting the one who called you by the grace of Christ and are turning to a different gospel—which is really no gospel at all. Evidently some people are throwing you into confusion and are trying to pervert the gospel of Christ. (Gal 1:6-7)

But now that you know God—or rather are known by God—how is it that you are turning back to those weak and miserable principles? Do you wish to be enslaved by them all over again? (Gal 4:9)

But my righteous one will live by faith. And if he shrinks back, I will not be pleased with him." (Heb 10:38)

Consider him who endured such opposition from sinful men, so that you will not grow weary and lose heart. (Heb 12:3)

He is a double-minded man, unstable in all he does. (James 1:8)

Come near to God and he will come near to you. Wash your hands, you sinners, and purify your hearts, you double-minded. (James 4:8)

Anyone, then, who knows the good he ought to do and doesn't do it, sins. (James 4:17)

If they have escaped the corruption of the world by knowing our Lord and Savior Jesus Christ and are again entangled in it and overcome, they are worse off at the end than they were at the beginning. (2 Pet 2:20)

Therefore, dear friends, since you already know this, be on your guard so that

you may not be carried away by the error of lawless men and fall from your secure position. (2 Pet 3:17)

They went out from us, but they did not really belong to us. For if they had belonged to us, they would have remained with us; but their going showed that none of them belonged to us. (1 John 2:19)

Yet I hold this against you: You have forsaken your first love. Remember the height from which you have fallen! Repent and do the things you did at first. If you do not repent, I will come to you and remove your lampstand from its place. (Rev 2:4-5)

"A curse on him who is lax in doing the Lord's work! A curse on him who keeps his sword from bloodshed! (Jer 48:10)

1 Jesus appointed seventy disciples to prepare the way for Him
a. Had many disciples
b. Sent two by two
c. Saw tremendous need
d. Sent as forerunners
2 First, pray for more laborers
3 Second, go into an antagonistic world
4 Third, trust God & sense the hour's urgency
5 Fourth, guard the message—do not force it upon people
6 Fifth, accept compensation, but do not seek luxury
7 Sixth, be accommodating & adaptable

CHAPTER 10

C. The Seventy Sent Forth: Great Purpose, 10:1-16
(cp. Mt.10)

After this the Lord appointed
seventy-two others and sent
them two by two ahead of
him to every town and
place where he was about to
go.
2 He told them, "The harvest
is plentiful, but the workers
are few. Ask the Lord of the
harvest, therefore, to send out
workers into his harvest
field.
3 Go! I am sending you out
like lambs among wolves.
4 Do not take a purse or bag
or sandals; and do not greet
anyone on the road.
5 "When you enter a house,
first say, 'Peace to this house.'
6 If a man of peace is there,
your peace will rest on him;
if not, it will return to you.
7 Stay in that house, eating
and drinking whatever they
give you, for the worker deserves
his wages. Do not move
around from house to house.
8 "When you enter a town
and are welcomed, eat what
is set before you
9 Heal the sick who are there
and tell them, 'The kingdom
of God is near you.'
10 But when you enter a
town and are not welcomed,
go into its streets and say,
11 'Even the dust of your
town that sticks to our
feet we wipe off against
you. Yet be sure of this:
The kingdom of God is
near.'
12 I tell you, it will be more
bearable on that day for
Sodom than for that town.
13 "Woe to you, Korazin!
Woe to you, Bethsaida! For if
the miracles that were performed
in you had been performed
in Tyre and Sidon,
they would have repented
long ago, sitting in sackcloth
and ashes.
14 But it will be more bearable
for Tyre and Sidon at the
judgment than for you.
15 And you, Capernaum, will
you be lifted up to the skies?
No, you will go down to the
depths.
16 "He who listens to you
listens to me; he who rejects
you rejects me; but he who
rejects me rejects him who
sent me."

a. Identify with people
b. Minister to people
c. Proclaim the Kingdom of God
8 Seventh, walk away from rejecters
a. Any town & people who reject
1) Symbolize God's rejection by wiping off the very dust of the city
2) Reason: Kingdom of God came near, but they rejected it
3) Judgment: Shall be greater than Sodom's
b. Any who *only profess* to be God's people*DS1*
1) Illustrated. by two Jewishtowns
2) The reason: The works of Christ were seen, yet He was rejected
3) The judgment: To be more terrible
c. Any who have a constant witness but reject: To receive the greatest judgment—hell
9 Eighth, know that the Christian laborer represents the Lord

DIVISION V

THE SON OF MAN'S GREAT JOURNEY TO JERUSALEM (STAGE I): HIS MISSION AND PUBLIC CHALLENGE, 9:51-13:21

C. The Seventy Sent Forth: Great Purpose, 10:1-16

(10:1-16) **Introduction**: this passage tells the Christian laborer how he is to work and tells the hearer how he is to treat the laborer of God.

1. Jesus appointed seventy disciples to prepare the way for Him (v.1).
2. First, pray for more laborers (v.2).
3. Second, go into an antagonistic world (v.3).
4. Third, trust God and sense the hour's urgency (v.4).
5. Fourth, guard the message—do not force it upon people (v.5-6).
6. Fifth, accept compensation, but do not seek luxury (v.7).
7. Sixth, be accommodating and adaptable (v.8-9).
8. Seventh, walk away from rejecters (v.10-15).
9. Eighth, know that the Christian laborer represents the Lord (v.16).

1 (10:1) **Apostles—Disciples—Jesus Christ, Followers—Witnessing**: Jesus appointed seventy disciples to prepare the way for Him. The number seventy is disputed, for some very good manuscripts say seventy-two were appointed. No matter which number is adopted, the number is held to be symbolic just as the appointment of twelve apostles is said to be symbolic. The twelve apostles are said to symbolize…

- the twelve patriarchs.
- the twelve tribes of Israel.
- the twelve leaders of the tribes.

The seventy are said to symbolize…

- the nations of the world (cp. Gen.10 where seventy names are listed; seventy-two in the Septuagint Greek Version of the Old Testament). The point in the symbolism is that the gospel is to go into all the world.
- the seventy elders who saw the glory of God (Ex.24:1, 9).
- the seventy elders of Israel (Num.11:16f).
- the seventy palm trees at Elim (Ex.15:27). (Note there were also twelve wells of water at Elim said to represent the twelve apostles.)
- the great Sanhedrin, the ruling body of the Jews, which had seventy members.

Whatever the case may be, the verse does point out four significant things.

1. Jesus had many disciples, many more than just the twelve often pictured. There were at least seventy disciples who followed Jesus so closely that He could send them out as witnesses for Him. Peter spoke of the witnesses as "men who have been with us the whole time the Lord Jesus went in and out among us" (Acts 1:21; cp.1:15).

2. Jesus sent them out two by two for mutual encouragement and help.

3. Jesus saw a tremendous need, a need so great that a great corps of witnesses was needed.

4. Jesus sent the seventy forth as forerunners. They were to prepare the people for His coming (cp. Tit.2:12-13).

> **Thought 1.** All four points are applicable to us. Think them through. How many of us follow Christ so closely that He can send us out as witnesses for Him?

2 (10:2) **Prayer—World—Ministers—Vision—Laborers**: first, pray for more laborers (see outline and notes—Mt.9:37-38 for more discussion). This was the very first duty. There were not enough laborers because the need was so overwhelming. (We must always be praying diligently for laborers.) Jesus gave four reasons.

1. There was a great harvest of precious souls to be reached with the gospel. The number was staggering, and the vast majority were without Jesus, reeling to and fro under the weight of the problems of a sinful and dying world.

> **Do you not say, 'Four months more and then the harvest'? I tell you, open your eyes and look at the fields! They are ripe for harvest. Even now the reaper draws his wages, even now he harvests the crop for eternal life, so that the sower and the reaper may be glad together. (John 4:35-36)**
>
> **Let us not become weary in doing good, for at the proper time we will reap a harvest if we do not give up. (Gal 6:9)**

2. The laborers were few, very few.

3. The need was urgent: the crop was ripe, ready for *harvest*. Some wanted the *gospel*, the answer to life. They were actually ready to be reaped, wanting purpose, meaning, and significance in their lives. They might not know what was causing the longing and aching within their hearts; they might not know how to identify it, but they were ready to listen and grab hold of the answer. And Jesus was the answer.

4. God was the One who had to send forth laborers. He was the Source of laborers, and prayer was the method He used to send them forth.

> **Thought 1.** Note a crucial point. A generation's concern determines how well that generation gets along under God's care. A generation that longs for God—that seeks after God to send forth laborers—will have laborers and see a good deal of righteousness prevail during its life. A generation that ignores God finds immorality and ungodliness, injustice and evil getting worse and worse. The answer to a solid generation, to a moral and just generation is prayer—prayer for laborers to be sent forth to reap the precious harvest of souls. If voices are not proclaiming love and morality and justice, then sin and death will reign.
>
> **As soon as the grain is ripe, he puts the sickle to it, because the harvest has come." (Mark 4:29)**
>
> **Those who sow in tears will reap with songs of joy. He who goes out weeping, carrying seed to sow, will return with songs of joy, carrying sheaves with him. (Psa 126:5-6)**
>
> **Sow for yourselves righteousness, reap the fruit of unfailing love, and break up your unplowed ground; for it is time to seek the LORD, until he comes and showers righteousness on you. (Hosea 10:12)**

3 (10:3) **Persecution—Sheep—Wolves**: second, go into an antagonistic world (see note, pt.2—Mt.10:16 for more discussion). Note two points.

1. The threat or danger of persecution. Jesus said that some men would be as wolves...

- protecting their territory, snarling and putting down the messenger of God, trying to scare him away from trying to tame the world.
- growling and threatening the believer who opposes the way of the world.
- hungry and ready to hunt down, attack and consume.

2. The spirit of the Christian laborer. He was to be as a sheep: meek, harmless, and non-combative.

> **Keep watch over yourselves and all the flock of which the Holy Spirit has made you overseers. Be shepherds of the church of God, which he bought with his own blood. I know that after I leave, savage wolves will come in among you and will not spare the flock. Even from your own number men will arise and distort the truth in order to draw away disciples after them. So be on your guard! Remember that for three years I never stopped warning each of you night and day with tears. (Acts 20:28-31)**
>
> **Remember the words I spoke to you: 'No servant is greater than his master.' If they persecuted me, they will persecute you also. If they obeyed my teaching, they will obey yours also. (John 15:20)**
>
> **"All this I have told you so that you will not go astray. They will put you out of the synagogue; in fact, a time is coming when anyone who kills you will think he is offering a service to God. They will do such things because they have not known the Father or me. I have told you this, so that when the time comes you will remember that I warned you. I did not tell you this at first because I was with you. (John 16:1-4)**
>
> **For it has been granted to you on behalf of Christ not only to believe on him, but also to suffer for him, (Phil 1:29)**
>
> **So that no one would be unsettled by these trials. You know quite well that we were destined for them. (1 Th 3:3)**
>
> **In fact, everyone who wants to live a godly life in Christ Jesus will be persecuted, (2 Tim 3:12)**
>
> **Dear friends, do not be surprised at the painful trial you are suffering, as though something strange were happening to you. But rejoice that you participate in the sufferings of Christ, so that you may be overjoyed when his glory is revealed. If you are insulted because of the name of Christ, you**

are blessed, for the Spirit of glory and of God rests on you. If you suffer, it should not be as a murderer or thief or any other kind of criminal, or even as a meddler. However, if you suffer as a Christian, do not be ashamed, but praise God that you bear that name. (1 Pet 4:12-16)

Do not be like Cain, who belonged to the evil one and murdered his brother. And why did he murder him? Because his own actions were evil and his brother's were righteous. (1 John 3:12)

Do not be afraid of what you are about to suffer. I tell you, the devil will put some of you in prison to test you, and you will suffer persecution for ten days. Be faithful, even to the point of death, and I will give you the crown of life. (Rev 2:10)

"Be on your guard against men; they will hand you over to the local councils and flog you in their synagogues. (Mat 10:17)

4 (10:4) **Conversation—Trust—Necessities—Minister**: third, trust God and sense the hour's urgency. The charge was twofold.

1. Trust God. They were not to carry a money-bag (purse, ballantion) or a traveller's bag (pera) or two pair of sandals. They were to trust God for provisions, not worrying about money for food, housing, or clothing (Mt.6:24-34). Worrying about such things would be cumbersome, taking away precious time that should be spent in ministering. Also, they were preaching a message of faith and trust in God. They needed to live what they were preaching and become a living picture of the dependency that God wants from every man.

But seek first his kingdom and his righteousness, and all these things will be given to you as well. (Mat 6:33)

I am not saying this because I am in need, for I have learned to be content whatever the circumstances. I know what it is to be in need, and I know what it is to have plenty. I have learned the secret of being content in any and every situation, whether well fed or hungry, whether living in plenty or in want. I can do everything through him who gives me strength. (Phil 4:11-13)

Trust in the LORD and do good; dwell in the land and enjoy safe pasture. Commit your way to the LORD; trust in him and he will do this: (Psa 37:3, 5)

You who fear him, trust in the LORD— he is their help and shield. (Psa 115:11)

It is better to take refuge in the LORD than to trust in man. (Psa 118:8)

Trust in the LORD with all your heart and lean not on your own understanding; (Prov 3:5)

You will keep in perfect peace him whose mind is steadfast, because he trusts in you. Trust in the LORD forever, for the LORD, the LORD, is the Rock eternal. (Isa 26:3-4)

Who among you fears the LORD and obeys the word of his servant? Let him who walks in the dark, who has no light, trust in the name of the LORD and rely on his God. (Isa 50:10)

2. Act now, the hour is urgent. They were not to waste time by stopping along the way and carrying on needless conversation. Such time was to be spent in ministry or prayer. Their mission was focused upon another world that lasted forever, a world into which every man was to eventually enter. Man desperately needed to sense the urgency and commitment necessary to enter the Kingdom of God. This world and its needless affairs were not to be engaged in by the Christian laborer. (Note: all affairs are not needless, but so many often are.)

As long as it is day, we must do the work of him who sent me. Night is coming, when no one can work. (John 9:4)

What I mean, brothers, is that the time is short. From now on those who have wives should live as if they had none; (1 Cor 7:29)

Making the most of every opportunity, because the days are evil. (Eph 5:16)

Be wise in the way you act toward outsiders; make the most of every opportunity. (Col 4:5)

Teach us to number our days aright, that we may gain a heart of wisdom. (Psa 90:12)

5 (10:5-6) **Peace**: fourth, guard the message, do not force it upon people. Three points were stressed by Jesus.

1. The message of the laborer was peace (see note, Peace—Jn.14:27 for discussion)...

- the peace with God.
- the peace of God dwelling within a person's heart.
- the peace between men.

Therefore, since we have been justified through faith, we have peace with God through our Lord Jesus Christ, (Rom 5:1)

And how can they preach unless they are sent? As it is written, "How beautiful are the feet of those who bring good news!" (Rom 10:15)

But now in Christ Jesus you who once were far away have been brought near through the blood of Christ. For he himself is our peace, who has made the two one and has destroyed the barrier, the dividing wall of hostility, by abolishing in his flesh the law with its commandments and regulations. His purpose was to create in himself one new man out of the two, thus making peace, and in this one body to reconcile both of them to God through the cross, by which he put to death their hostility. He came and preached peace to you who were far away and peace to those who were near. (Eph 2:13-17)

And with your feet fitted with the readiness that comes from the gospel of peace. (Eph 6:15)

2. The laborer was to proclaim peace to whatever house he entered. If "a man of peace," that is, the head of the household, was a man of peace, then the message of peace was to be continued. But if the message of peace was not accepted, then it was to be taken away. The disciple was not to proclaim the message of peace to anyone who was not willing to receive it. Neither the messenger nor the message was to be forced upon anyone.

> **As you enter the home, give it your greeting. If the home is deserving, let your peace rest on it; if it is not, let your peace return to you. If anyone will not welcome you or listen to your words, shake the dust off your feet when you leave that home or town. I tell you the truth, it will be more bearable for Sodom and Gomorrah on the day of judgment than for that town. (Mat 10:12-15)**

3. The method Christ used was *house evangelism* (see DEEPER STUDY # 1—Lk.9:4 for discussion).

6 (10:7) **Stewardship—Minister, Compensation**: fifth, accept compensation, but do not seek luxury. There were three things being stressed.

1. "The worker deserves his wages"; therefore, he should be given compensation and taken care of (1 Tim.5:18). Scripture says the worker is really worth double compensation and such appreciation should be expressed to him (1 Tim.5:17). He is never to be taken advantage of. He is to be looked after by seeing that he has a house, food, and drink—all the necessities of life.

> **In the same way, the Lord has commanded that those who preach the gospel should receive their living from the gospel. (1 Cor 9:14)**
>
> **Anyone who receives instruction in the word must share all good things with his instructor. (Gal 6:6)**
>
> **Yet it was good of you to share [give] in my troubles. (Phil 4:14)**
>
> **For the Scripture says, "Do not muzzle the ox while it is treading out the grain," and "The worker deserves his wages." (1 Tim 5:18)**
>
> **Command those who are rich in this present world not to be arrogant nor to put their hope in wealth, which is so uncertain, but to put their hope in God, who richly provides us with everything for our enjoyment. Command them to do good, to be rich in good deeds, and to be generous and willing to share. (1 Tim 6:17-18)**

2. The worker was to accept compensation. He was not to be self-conscious or embarrassed in receiving payment for his work.

3. *However*, he was not to seek luxury, going from house to house and person to person seeking more and more of the better things of life. *The worker was to live in simplicity, giving all that he had beyond his own needs—giving all to meet the needs of others.* He was to seek to meet the needs of men, not to secure the things of this world. What a contrast of value: things vs. people. How mixed up men allow their values to become.

> **Since, then, you have been raised with Christ, set your hearts on things above, where Christ is seated at the right hand of God. Set your minds on things above, not on earthly things. (Col 3:1-2)**
>
> **Those who live according to the sinful nature have their minds set on what that nature desires; but those who live in accordance with the Spirit have their minds set on what the Spirit desires. The mind of sinful man is death, but the mind controlled by the Spirit is life and peace; (Rom 8:5-6)**
>
> **All these people were still living by faith when they died. They did not receive the things promised; they only saw them and welcomed them from a distance. And they admitted that they were aliens and strangers on earth. People who say such things show that they are looking for a country of their own. If they had been thinking of the country they had left, they would have had opportunity to return. Instead, they were longing for a better country—a heavenly one. Therefore God is not ashamed to be called their God, for he has prepared a city for them. (Heb 11:13-16)**
>
> **By faith Moses, when he had grown up, refused to be known as the son of Pharaoh's daughter. He chose to be mistreated along with the people of God rather than to enjoy the pleasures of sin for a short time. He regarded disgrace for the sake of Christ as of greater value than the treasures of Egypt, because he was looking ahead to his reward. (Heb 11:24-26)**

7 (10:8-9) **Missions—Missionaries**: sixth, be hospitable, accommodating, and adaptable. Jesus gave three charges that will help His messenger reach those to whom he goes.

1. Identify with the people. This is the point Jesus was making. He simply used the most sensitive and basic thing to stress its importance, that of food. If necessary, God's messenger was to change his customs and habits to reach the people. He was to accommodate and adapt himself to the people he was trying to reach, even down to the food eaten. The people were to see that he accepted and received them into his life and heart.

> **Rather he must be hospitable, one who loves what is good, who is self-controlled, upright, holy and disciplined. (Titus 1:8)**
>
> **Keep on loving each other as brothers. Do not forget to entertain strangers, for by so doing some people have entertained angels without knowing it. (Heb 13:1-2)**
>
> **Offer hospitality to one another without grumbling. (1 Pet 4:9)**
>
> **The second is this: 'Love your neighbor as yourself.' There is no commandment greater than these." (Mark 12:31; cp. Gal.5:14; Jas.2:8)**
>
> **Love does no harm to its neighbor. Therefore love is the fulfillment of the law. (Rom 13:10)**
>
> **Each of us should please his neighbor for his good, to build him up. (Rom 15:2)**

2. Minister to the people. The messenger was to minister to the people's physical needs, even to the point of healing the sick.

> **Just as the Son of Man did not come to be served, but to serve, and to give his life as a ransom for many." (Mat 20:28)**
>
> **Again Jesus said, "Peace be with you! As the Father has sent me, I am sending you." (John 20:21)**
>
> **How God anointed Jesus of Nazareth with the Holy Spirit and power, and how he went around doing good and healing all who were under the power of the devil, because God was with him. (Acts 10:38)**
>
> **In everything I did, I showed you that by this kind of hard work we must help the weak, remembering the words the Lord Jesus himself said: 'It is more blessed to give than to receive.'" (Acts 20:35)**
>
> **We who are strong ought to bear with the failings of the weak and not to please ourselves. (Rom 15:1)**
>
> **Carry each other's burdens, and in this way you will fulfill the law of Christ. (Gal 6:2)**

3. Proclaim the Kingdom of God. Note: the message was given by Christ; it was not created in the mind of the messenger. Note also that the kingdom was near people, right before them. The opportunity to receive the kingdom was present, right then and there (see DEEPER STUDY # 3, Kingdom of God—Mt.19:23-24 for discussion).

> **From that time on Jesus began to preach, "Repent, for the kingdom of heaven is near." (Mat 4:17)**
>
> **As you go, preach this message: 'The kingdom of heaven is near.' (Mat 10:7)**
>
> **But he said, "I must preach the good news of the kingdom of God to the other towns also, because that is why I was sent." (Luke 4:43)**
>
> **After this, Jesus traveled about from one town and village to another, proclaiming the good news of the kingdom of God. The Twelve were with him, (Luke 8:1)**
>
> **And he sent them out to preach the kingdom of God and to heal the sick. (Luke 9:2)**
>
> **"The Law and the Prophets were proclaimed until John. Since that time, the good news of the kingdom of God is being preached, and everyone is forcing his way into it. (Luke 16:16)**
>
> **Even so, when you see these things happening, you know that the kingdom of God is near. (Luke 21:31)**
>
> **After his suffering, he showed himself to these men and gave many convincing proofs that he was alive. He appeared to them over a period of forty days and spoke about the kingdom of God. (Acts 1:3)**
>
> **But when they believed Philip as he preached the good news of the kingdom of God and the name of Jesus Christ, they were baptized, both men and women. (Acts 8:12)**
>
> **"Now I know that none of you among whom I have gone about preaching the kingdom will ever see me again. (Acts 20:25)**
>
> **They arranged to meet Paul on a certain day, and came in even larger numbers to the place where he was staying. From morning till evening he explained and declared to them the kingdom of God and tried to convince them about Jesus from the Law of Moses and from the Prophets. (Acts 28:23)**

8 (10:10-15) **Rejection—Judgment, Degrees of—Profession Only**: seventh, walk away from rejecters. This, of course, protected the messenger from harm, at least to some degree. It also served as an immediate warning to any who rejected, perhaps causing them to think about the matter more deeply and changing their minds and hearts toward Jesus. Jesus discussed three classes of rejecters.

1. There would be towns that would reject Him (v.10-12). The messenger was to symbolize God's rejection of them by shaking the dust off his feet. This was a silent testimony that God was doing just what they wanted, leaving them alone to walk through life as they desired (see note, pt.3—Lk.9:3-5 for more discussion).

The reason for God's judgment was that they rejected the Kingdom of God. The kingdom came near them; the opportunity was there, but they rejected it. They shut their doors to God. Their judgment was, therefore, to be greater than Sodom's (see DEEPER STUDY # 4—Mt.10:15; DEEPER STUDY # 4—11:23 for more discussion).

2. There would be those who *only professed* to be God's people. These were illustrated by two towns that were heavily populated by Jewish people who professed to be the people of God. Yet they *only professed.* They rejected God's Son, despite the mighty works done among them. Therefore, they were to be judged. Their profession was profession only. Therefore, their judgment was to be greater than the judgment which was to come upon the heathen. Why? Because they had the opportunity to accept Christ, an opportunity that the heathen never had (Tyre and Sidon). Note the degrees of judgment taught. (See outline and notes—Mt.11:20-24; Ro.2:11-15 for more discussion.)

3. There would be those who had a constant witness. These were to receive the greatest judgment of all, hell itself. Capernaum was the *chosen* town and headquarters of Christ (Mt.9:1), yet they rejected Christ. (See outline and notes—Mt.11:20-24 for more discussion.)

Thought 1. Judgment is definitely coming, and everyone who rejects the Lord Jesus Christ will be condemned.

> **If anyone is ashamed of me and my words in this adulterous and sinful generation, the Son of Man will be ashamed of him when he comes in his Father's glory with the holy angels." (Mark 8:38)**
>
> **But the one who does not know and does things deserving punishment will be beaten with few blows. From everyone who has been given much, much will be demanded; and from the one who has been entrusted with much, much more will be asked. (Luke 12:48)**
>
> **This is the verdict: Light has come into the world, but men loved darkness instead of light because their deeds were evil. (John 3:19)**
>
> **But because of your stubbornness and your unrepentant heart, you are storing up**

wrath against yourself for the day of God's wrath, when his righteous judgment will be revealed. (Rom 2:5)

So then, each of us will give an account of himself to God. (Rom 14:12)

And give relief to you who are troubled, and to us as well. This will happen when the Lord Jesus is revealed from heaven in blazing fire with his powerful angels. He will punish those who do not know God and do not obey the gospel of our Lord Jesus. (2 Th 1:7-8)

But encourage one another daily, as long as it is called Today, so that none of you may be hardened by sin's deceitfulness. (Heb 3:13)

They think it strange that you do not plunge with them into the same flood of dissipation, and they heap abuse on you. But they will have to give account to him who is ready to judge the living and the dead. (1 Pet 4:4-5)

Enoch, the seventh from Adam, prophesied about these men: "See, the Lord is coming with thousands upon thousands of his holy ones to judge everyone, and to convict all the ungodly of all the ungodly acts they have done in the ungodly way, and of all the harsh words ungodly sinners have spoken against him." (Jude 1:14-15)

Fathers shall not be put to death for their children, nor children put to death for their fathers; each is to die for his own sin. (Deu 24:16)

A man who remains stiff-necked after many rebukes will suddenly be destroyed—without remedy. (Prov 29:1)

While you were doing all these things, declares the LORD, I spoke to you again and again, but you did not listen; I called you, but you did not answer. Therefore, what I did to Shiloh I will now do to the house that bears my Name, the temple you trust in, the place I gave to you and your fathers. I will thrust you from my presence, just as I did all your brothers, the people of Ephraim.' (Jer 7:13-15)

Instead, everyone will die for his own sin. (Jer 31:30)

The soul who sins is the one who will die. (Ezek 18:20)

DEEPER STUDY # 1
(10:13) **Woe**: not a call for vengeance, but an expression of deep regret, of warning (cp. 6:24).

9 (10:16) **Ministers, Rejection; Acceptance; Treatment of**: eighth, know that the messenger represents the Lord. This stresses two critical points.

1. The messenger's position and message were of the highest value. The messenger represented Christ and was to be given the most serious hearing possible. He was counted as though Christ Himself were speaking.
2. The rejection of the messenger was the most serious offense. It was counted as the rejection of God Himself.

"He who receives you receives me, and he who receives me receives the one who sent me. (Mat 10:40)

"And whoever welcomes a little child [believer] like this in my name welcomes me. (Mat 18:5)

"The King will reply, 'I tell you the truth, whatever you did for one of the least of these brothers of mine, you did for me.' (Mat 25:40)

"He will reply, 'I tell you the truth, whatever you did not do for one of the least of these, you did not do for me.' "Then they will go away to eternal punishment, but the righteous to eternal life." (Mat 25:45-46)

Meanwhile, Saul was still breathing out murderous threats against the Lord's disciples. He went to the high priest and asked him for letters to the synagogues in Damascus, so that if he found any there who belonged to the Way, whether men or women, he might take them as prisoners to Jerusalem. As he neared Damascus on his journey, suddenly a light from heaven flashed around him. He fell to the ground and heard a voice say to him, "Saul, Saul, why do you persecute me?" (Acts 9:1-4)

When you sin against your brothers in this way and wound their weak conscience, you sin against Christ. (1 Cor 8:12)

Outline	Scripture	Scripture (cont.)	Outline (cont.)
	D. The Seventy Return (Part I): Great Power, 10:17-20	fall like lightning from heaven.	**has power over Satan**
		19 I have given you authority to trample on snakes and scorpions and to overcome all the power of the enemy;	**3 The Christian laborer has power over all enemies: perfect security**
1 The seventy returned a. With joy b. With great results & a testimony of power	17 The seventy-two returned with joy and said, "Lord, even the demons submit to us in your name."	nothing will harm you. 20 However, do not rejoice that the spirits submit to you, but rejoice that your names are written in heaven."	**4 The Christian laborer is to rejoice in his salvation, not in his power**
2 The Christian laborer	18 He replied, "I saw Satan		

DIVISION V

THE SON OF MAN'S GREAT JOURNEY TO JERUSALEM (STAGE I): HIS MISSION AND PUBLIC CHALLENGE, 9:51-13:21

D. The Seventy Return (Part I): Great Power, 10:17-20

(10:17-20) **Introduction**: Christ gives great power to the person who truly works for Him. The presence of God's power in the laborer's life is a wonderful thing; however, it is something that can be misunderstood and abused. When the seventy returned, Jesus used the occasion to teach a much needed lesson on the power of God in a person's life.

1. The seventy returned (v.17).
2. The Christian laborer has power over Satan (v.18).
3. The Christian laborer has power over all enemies—perfect security (v.19).
4. The Christian laborer is to rejoice in his salvation, not in his power (v.20).

1 (10:17) **Power—Ministry, Results; Praise for**: the seventy returned. The testimony of their return has several significant lessons for every generation of Christian laborers.

1. They returned with joy (chara). The word means joy and rejoicing, a heart full of gladness. Frankly, their spirit was different from what so many express after an arduous ministry. They were not sharing and reveling in...

- how much they had done for Christ.
- how taxing the work had been.
- how strong the opposition and enemy had fought.

The very opposite was true. They were filled with joy and were rejoicing in Christ over the phenomenal power of Christ's name.

2. They returned with astounding results—results that were wrought through the name of Christ. The seventy expressed surprise: "Lord, even the demons submit to us in your name." But note two facts.

a. The power had come *through Christ's name.*

> **Salvation is found in no one else, for there is no other name under heaven given to men by which we must be saved." (Acts 4:12)**

b. Their shock at such power or results led to a confession of their own weakness and nothingness before Christ. They knew and readily confessed that the power to do the work had not come from them. Only the name of Christ could give genuine power and results.

3. They returned giving glory to Christ. They praised Him for the glorious experience He had granted them "in your [His] name." They were not in any sense of the term drawing attention to themselves. They were lifting up Christ and praising Him. The demons were submitted to them through *Christ's name.*

4. They returned having ministered to both body and soul. Men's bodies were healed (v.9), and they were freed spiritually when the demons and forces of evil were cast out of their lives. (See outline and notes—Mt.8:28-34 for more discussion and thoughts.)

2 (10:18) **Power—Satan, Defeat of**: there was power over Satan (see DEEPER STUDY # 1, Satan—Rev.12:9). Satan "fell like lightning from heaven" means falling from the height and the summit of power. The word "saw" (etheoroun) means that Jesus thought upon, gave full attention to, contemplated, envisioned Satan's falling from his summit of power as the *god and prince* of this world (see DEEPER STUDY # 1, Satan—Rev.12:9). The idea is that Jesus saw the seventy's victorious mission as a sign of the total defeat of Satan that was now beginning.

1. Jesus saw Satan defeated in the souls of men.

> **As for you, you were dead in your transgressions and sins, in which you used to live when you followed the ways of this world and of the ruler of the kingdom of the air, the spirit who is now at work in those who are disobedient. (Eph 2:1-2;cp. v.3-10)**
>
> **For he [God] has rescued us from the dominion of darkness [Satan] and brought us into the kingdom of the Son he loves, in whom we have redemption, the forgiveness of sins. (Col 1:13-14)**

2. Jesus saw Satan defeated through the spread of the gospel.

> **Now is the time for judgment on this world; now the prince of this world will be driven out. But I, when I am lifted up from the earth, will draw all men to myself." (John 12:31-32)**
>
> **But I tell you the truth: It is for your good that I am going away. Unless I go away, the Counselor will not come to you; but if I go, I will send him to you. When he comes, he will convict the world of guilt in regard to sin and righteousness and judgment: in regard to sin, because men do not believe in me; in regard to righteousness, because I am going to the Father, where you can see me no longer; and in regard to judgment, because the prince of this world now stands condemned. (John 16:7-11)**

The god of this age has blinded the minds of unbelievers, so that they cannot see the light of the gospel of the glory of Christ, who is the image of God. (2 Cor 4:4)

3. Jesus saw Satan defeated in the daily strategies and struggles which he wages against the individual believer (See note—Ro.8:2-4.)

He who does what is sinful is of the devil, because the devil has been sinning from the beginning. The reason the Son of God appeared was to destroy the devil's work. (1 John 3:8)

Finally, be strong in the Lord and in his mighty power. Put on the full armor of God so that you can take your stand against the devil's schemes. For our struggle is not against flesh and blood, but against the rulers, against the authorities, against the powers of this dark world and against the spiritual forces of evil in the heavenly realms. (Eph 6:10-12cp. v. 13-18)

4. Jesus saw Satan defeated in His power over death.

The last enemy to be destroyed is death. (1 Cor 15:26)

5. Jesus saw Satan defeated through His death on the cross.

And having disarmed the powers and authorities, he made a public spectacle of them, triumphing over them by the cross. (Col 2:15)

He himself bore our sins in his body on the tree, so that we might die to sins and live for righteousness; by his wounds you have been healed. (1 Pet 2:24; cp. Jn. 12:32)

6. Jesus saw Satan defeated in the end of the world, in the consummation of the ages and time. (See outlines and notes—Rev.20:1-3; 20:7-10.)

And the devil, who deceived them, was thrown into the lake of burning sulfur, where the beast and the false prophet had been thrown. They will be tormented day and night for ever and ever. (Rev 20:10)

Thought 1. We are to "observe" the power of God in the same way that Christ "observed" it. God's power is for the purpose of defeating Satan, of delivering men from the power of Satan.

3 (10:19) **Power—Deliverance—Satan, Power Over**: the Christian believer has power over all enemies; he has perfect security. Are the words "authority to trample on snakes and scorpions" to be taken literally or figuratively? (Cp. Mk.16:15-18.)

1. There is a literal meaning in this sense. If it is God's purpose to continue using His servant, then God will protect His servant no matter the threat or injury, whether by shipwreck (Acts 28:14f) or snake bite (Acts 28:3-5). The life of a genuine believer is in the hands of God every moment of his life, and God looks after the believer. Whatever befalls him is under the will and care of God (Ro.8:28f; cp. 2 Cor.11:23-30 for a descriptive picture of what does befall God's servant and a picture of how God delivers until He is ready to take His servant home.)

But note a crucial point. A man does not test God; he does not presume upon the power of God. The true servant of God does not put himself in *harm's way* where he will be threatened. Such a person is busy at the wrong thing. The servant is to be busy reaching people for Christ, not proving his ability with animals or his immunity to their bites.

2. There is a spiritual meaning. Power is given over the enemy (Satan). Note five points.

a. The enemy does have power; the idea is that he has enormous power.

For our struggle is not against flesh and blood, but against the rulers, against the authorities, against the powers of this dark world and against the spiritual forces of evil in the heavenly realms. (Eph 6:12)

b. The Lord's power is greater, much greater.

What, then, shall we say in response to this? If God is for us, who can be against us? (Rom 8:31)

The one who is in you is greater than the one who is in the world. (1 John 4:4; Heb.2:14-15; 1 Jn.3:8).)

c. The Lord gives His power to His laborer.

When Jesus had called the Twelve together, he gave them power and authority to drive out all demons and to cure diseases, (Luke 9:1)

For God did not give us a spirit of timidity, but a spirit of power, of love and of self-discipline. (2 Tim 1:7)

d. The laborer's power is over *all* the power of the enemy.

And his incomparably great power for us who believe. That power is like the working of his mighty strength, (Eph 1:19)

Now to him who is able to do immeasurably more than all we ask or imagine, according to his power that is at work within us, (Eph 3:20)

e. The laborer is *perfectly secure* against all enemies. No spiritual power shall by any means be able to touch him. He is secure in the hands of God.

My Father, who has given them to me, is greater than all ; no one can snatch them out of my Father's hand. (John 10:29; cp. Eph.6:10-18)

I will remain in the world no longer, but they are still in the world, and I am coming to you. Holy Father, protect them by the power of your name—the name you gave me—so that they may be one as we are one. (John 17:11)

Being confident of this, that he who began a good work in you will carry it on to completion until the day of Christ Jesus. (Phil 1:6)

But the Lord is faithful, and he will strengthen and protect you from the evil one. (2 Th 3:3)

That is why I am suffering as I am. Yet I am not ashamed, because I know whom I have believed, and am convinced that he is able to guard what I have entrusted to him for that day. (2 Tim 1:12)

The Lord will rescue me from every evil attack and will bring me safely to his heavenly kingdom. To him be glory for ever and ever. Amen. (2 Tim 4:18)

Who [believers] through faith are shielded by God's power until the coming of the salvation that is ready to be revealed in the last time. (1 Pet 1:5)

To him who is able to keep you from falling and to present you before his glorious presence without fault and with great joy— to the only God our Savior be glory, majesty, power and authority, through Jesus Christ our Lord, before all ages, now and forevermore! Amen. (Jude 1:24-25)

I am with you and will watch over you wherever you go, and I will bring you back to this land [promised land, heaven]. I will not leave you until I have done what I have promised you." (Gen 28:15)

4 (10:20) **Joy—Book of Life—Salvation**: the Christian laborer is to rejoice in his salvation, not in his power. Note two points.

1. The real basis for joy is not power, but salvation. The great privilege of a believer is not his work and ministry, but the fact that he is a child of God's and has been given eternal life.

⇒ He has been adopted as a son or daughter of God.

But when the time had fully come, God sent his Son, born of a woman, born under law, to redeem those under law, that we might receive the full rights of sons. Because you are sons, God sent the Spirit of his Son into our hearts, the Spirit who calls out, "Abba, Father." (Gal 4:4-6)

"Therefore come out from them and be separate, says the Lord. Touch no unclean thing, and I will receive you." "I will be a Father to you, and you will be my sons and daughters, says the Lord Almighty." (2 Cor 6:17-18)

⇒ He has received the Spirit of adoption which gives him open access into the very presence of God.

For you did not receive a spirit that makes you a slave again to fear, but you received the Spirit of sonship. And by him we cry, "Abba, Father." (Rom 8:15)

In the same way, the Spirit helps us in our weakness. We do not know what we ought to pray for, but the Spirit himself intercedes for us with groans that words cannot express. (Rom 8:26)

Until now [before Jesus' death, salvation] you have not asked for anything in my name. Ask and you will receive, and your joy will be complete. (John 16:24)

⇒ He has been made an heir of God and, unbelievably, an equal heir with Christ.

The Spirit himself testifies with our spirit that we are God's children. Now if we are children, then we are heirs—heirs of God and co-heirs with Christ, if indeed we share in his sufferings in order that we may also share in his glory. (Rom 8:16-17)

So that, having been justified by his grace, we might become heirs having the hope of eternal life. (Titus 3:7)

Praise be to the God and Father of our Lord Jesus Christ! In his great mercy he has given us new birth into a living hope through the resurrection of Jesus Christ from the dead, and into an inheritance that can never perish, spoil or fade—kept in heaven for you, (1 Pet 1:3-4)

2. The believer's name is written down in heaven (cp. Rev.13:8; 17:8; 20:12; 22:19).

He who overcomes will, like them, be dressed in white. I will never blot out his name from the book of life, but will acknowledge his name before my Father and his angels. (Rev 3:5)

Yes, and I ask you, loyal yokefellow, help these women who have contended at my side in the cause of the gospel, along with Clement and the rest of my fellow workers, whose names are in the book of life. (Phil 4:3)

But you have come to Mount Zion, to the heavenly Jerusalem, the city of the living God. You have come to thousands upon thousands of angels in joyful assembly, to the church of the firstborn, whose names are written in heaven. You have come to God, the judge of all men, to the spirits of righteous men made perfect, (Heb 12:22-23)

Nothing impure will ever enter it [heaven], nor will anyone who does what is shameful or deceitful, but only those whose names are written in the Lamb's book of life. (Rev 21:27)

But now, please forgive their sin—but if not, then blot me out of the book you have written." The LORD replied to Moses, "Whoever has sinned against me I will blot out of my book. (Exo 32:32-33)

May they be blotted out of the book of life and not be listed with the righteous. (Psa 69:28; cp. Jer17:13)

"At that time Michael, the great prince who protects your people, will arise. There will be a time of distress such as has not happened from the beginning of nations until then. But at that time your people--everyone whose name is found written in the book--will be delivered. (Dan 12:1)

E. The Seventy Return (Part II): Great Privileges, 10:21-24
(Mt.11:25-27)

1 Jesus rejoiced
2 Privilege 1: The spiritual insight into truth
a. Into "these things"
b. God hides truth from the wise & learned
c. God reveals truth to babes
d. Such action is well pleasing to God
3 Privilege 2: The knowledge of God & of His only Son
a. God & the Son alone know one another
b. The Son reveals God to some
4 Privilege 3: The insight & privilege of learning God's full revelation

21 At that time Jesus, full of
joy through the Holy Spirit,
said, "I praise you, Father,
Lord of heaven and earth, because you have hidden these
things from the wise and
learned, and revealed them to
little children. Yes, Father,
for this was your good pleasure.
22 "All things have been
committed to me by my Fa-
ther. No one knows who the
Son is except the Father, and
no one knows who the Father
is except the Son and those to
whom the Son chooses to reveal him."
23 Then he turned to his
disciples and said privately,
"Blessed are the eyes that see
what you see.
24 For I tell you that many
prophets and kings wanted to
see what you see but did not
see it, and to hear what you
hear but did not hear it."

DIVISION V

THE SON OF MAN'S GREAT JOURNEY TO JERUSALEM (STAGE I): HIS MISSION AND PUBLIC CHALLENGE, 9:51-13:21

E. The Seventy Return (Part II): Great Privileges, 10:21-24

(10:21-24) **Introduction**: the Christian laborer has three great privileges. Jesus was filled with such a joy over these privileges that He broke forth in praise to God. How the Lord's heart longs to share these privileges with every person.

1. Jesus rejoiced (v.21).
2. Privilege 1: the spiritual insight into truth (v.21).
3. Privilege 2: the knowledge of God and of His only Son (v.22).
4. Privilege 3: the insight and privilege of learning God's full revelation (v.23-24).

1 (10:21) **Joy—Rejoicing**: Jesus rejoiced (egalliasato): He was "full of joy through the Holy Spirit." The words "full of joy through the Holy Spirit" are much stronger than the English *rejoice*. The Greek means great joy and exultation. It means to be filled with joy or thrilled with joy. There is the idea of *victorious joy* because of the glorious triumph over the arch-enemy Satan (v.18-20). Note: this joy comes only from the Spirit; it cannot be worked up. It is a joy of confidence and assurance that arises from down deep within—a confidence and assurance that all is well with God and the victory is won over evil. This was the joy experienced by Christ when the seventy returned. Souls had been snatched from the grip of sin and death, for the power of God over evil had been exercised by men. Satan's fall was assured. God would be victorious within the world as the gospel was carried forth by His servants; the Spirit of God stirred Jesus to rejoice greatly over the victory won.

> **"Looking unto Jesus the author and finisher of our faith; who for the joy that was set before him endured the cross, despising the shame, and is set down at the right hand of the throne of God" (Heb.12:2).**

2 (10:21) **Truth—Self-Sufficient—Predestination—Humanism—Unbelief—"Babes"—"Wise and Prudent of World"**: first, there is the privilege of spiritual insight into truth. The Christian laborer is able to grasp the spiritual truth of things. Note four points.

1. The term "these things" refers to the gospel of the Lord Jesus Christ. More specifically, however, it refers to the truth which the seventy had learned (v.19-20); that is, that God is active in the world. God saves men and cares for men, giving them power over the forces of evil and writing their names in heaven. Note an important fact: knowing "these things" is the greatest knowledge in all the world. No other knowledge could ever surpass knowing God in such a personal way, knowing...

- that He has saved us.
- that He cares and looks after us.
- that He delivers us from the power of evil.
- that He infuses us with assurance and confidence and perfect security.

2. God hides "these things" from the wise and learned. Such people are those who think themselves wise and intelligent. They are the self-sufficient, the proud, the wise of this world (1 Cor.1:21, 25-29; 2:14). These are blind to the Lord of heaven and earth and to the truth. The proud and self-sufficient by their very nature sense no need for help and refuse to receive help. They rest in their own ability and achievements.

a. Spiritual truth is *hid*. Where? In God. God has done the logical thing. He has taken spiritual truth and locked it up in Himself. The only access to truth is through God. The only key to spiritual truth is faith and trust in God.

The man who considers himself wise and intelligent and sufficient enough without God never comes to God. Therefore, a personal relationship with God is never known. The self-sufficient person never comes to know God nor the spiritual truth *hid* in God (Ro.1:18-22). God and His presence and His plan for the ages are foreign to the self-sufficient person. He does not believe God—not enough to come to Him. Therefore, the things of the Spirit and of the gospel are hid from him. However, God's heart and truths are open to the one who comes in dependency and trust.

Note a crucial point. What Christ condemns is not intelligence and wisdom, but intellectual pride and self-sufficiency. God made man to think and reason and seek and search in order to discover and build, but God expects man "Do not think of yourself more highly than you ought" (Ro.12:3; cp. Ph.2:3-4). A man is to walk humbly during his short stay on earth, knowing from whom he has come and to whom he is going. He is to trust God, putting his time and destiny in God's hands.

b. God is helpless to reveal truth to the "wise and learned" of this world. Why? Because they *rest* in their own ability and achievements and *sense no need* beyond themselves. They sense no need for God. They…
   ⇒ keep God out of their lives.
   ⇒ push God away.
   ⇒ deny God's existence.
   ⇒ question the value of God.
   ⇒ believe they have no need for God, not now.
   ⇒ believe God is irrelevant in a scientific, technological world.

c. God is not the Author of man's self-sufficiency and pride. Man is the one who makes himself his own *god* and creates the religion of humanism (that man is sufficient unto himself). God has no choice. He has to do two things.

   First, God has to leave such persons to themselves. God cannot force man to worship Him, for forced behavior would be making robots out of man. And God wants to be loved and worshipped by men because men *choose* to worship Him. Therefore, man's sin becomes his punishment; his rejection becomes harder and harder, and he is removed farther and farther away from God—exactly what the man had desired (Jn.12:39-40; Ro.1:18-32. Cp. Acts 28:26-27; Ro.11:7-8.) Second, God has to hide the truth from such persons because their *evil hearts* would only corrupt the truth. They would mix the truth with their own *rationalized and humanistic ideas.* Note another fact: if the self-sufficient knew the truth, they would be honored as the creators of the truth. They would lift man up as the source of truth. Unfortunately, this is exactly the claim made by so many. However, God will not share the honor due His Son with anyone. His Son, the only Son He has, is to receive all the honor and praise of this earth. Why? Because He is the One who has loved perfectly, loved so much that He laid down His life to save the world.

d. If a man honors God with what he has (his intelligence, abilities, and achievements), God will give "these things" to that man. But if the man takes what he has and claims to be self-sufficient, then God has no choice but to hide "these things" from his understanding.

"And he spake this parable unto certain which trusted in themselves that they were righteous" (Lk.18:9).

"Jesus said unto them, If God were your Father, ye would love me: for I proceeded forth and came from God; neither came I of myself, but he sent me. Why do ye not understand my speech? even because ye cannot hear my word" (Jn.8:42-43).

"Which of you convinceth me of sin? And if I say the truth, why do ye not believe me? He that is of God heareth God's words: ye therefore hear them not, because ye are not of God" (Jn.8:46-47).

"Therefore they could not believe, because that Esaias said again, He hath blinded their eyes, and hardened their heart; that they should not see with their eyes, nor understand with their heart, and be converted, and I should heal them" (Jn.12:39-40).

"And if any man hear my words, and believe not, I judge him not: for I came not to judge the world, but to save the world. He that rejecteth me, and receiveth not my words, hath one that judgeth him: the word that I have spoken, the same shall judge him in the last day. For I have not spoken of myself; but the Father which sent me, he gave me a commandment, what I should say, and what I should speak. And I know that his commandment is life everlasting: whatsoever I speak therefore, even as the Father said unto me, so I speak" (Jn.12:47-50).

"He that loveth me not keepeth not my sayings: and the word which ye hear is not mine, but the Father's which sent me" (Jn.14:24).

"For the invisible things of him from the creation of the world are clearly seen, being understood by the things that are made, even his eternal power and Godhead; so that they are without excuse: because that, when they knew God, they glorified him not as God, neither were thankful; but became vain in their imaginations, and their foolish heart was darkened. Professing themselves to be wise, they became fools" (Ro.1:20-22; cp. v.18-32).

"Be of the same mind one toward another. Mind not high things, but condescend to men of low estate. Be not wise in your own conceits" (Ro.12:16).

"For the preaching of the cross is to them that perish foolishness; but unto us which are saved it is the power of God. For it is written, I will destroy the wisdom of the wise, and will bring to nothing the understanding of the prudent. Where is the wise? where is the scribe? where is the disputer of this world? hath not God made foolish the wisdom of this world? For after that in the wisdom of God the world by wisdom knew not God, it pleased God by the foolishness of preaching to save them that believe" (1 Cor.1:18-21; cp. 1 Cor.3:19-21).

"And if any man think that he knoweth any thing, he knoweth nothing yet as he ought to know" (1 Cor.8:2).

"Wherefore let him that thinketh he standeth take heed lest he fall" (1 Cor.10:12).

"For if a man think himself to be something, when he is nothing, he deceiveth himself" (Gal.6:3).

"And the afflicted people thou wilt save: but thine eyes are upon the haughty, that thou mayest bring them down" (2 Sam.22:28).

"Be not wise in thine own eyes: fear the LORD, and depart from evil" (Pr.3:7).

"Most men will proclaim every one his own goodness: but a faithful man who can find?" (Pr.20:6).

"Seest thou a man wise in his own conceit? There is more hope of a fool than of him" (Pr.26:12).

"He that trusteth in his own heart is a fool: but whoso walketh wisely, he shall be delivered" (Pr.28:26).

"Woe unto them that are wise in their own eyes, and prudent in their own sight!" (Is.5:21).

"The earth mourneth and fadeth away, the world languisheth and fadeth away, the haughty people of the earth do languish" (Is.24:4).

"Therefore hear now this, thou that art given to pleasures, that dwellest carelessly, that sayest in thine heart, I am, and none else beside me; I shall not sit as a widow, neither shall I know the loss of children: but these two things shall come to thee in a moment in one day, the loss of children, and widowhood: they shall come upon thee in their perfection for the multitude of thy sorceries and for the great abundance of thine enchantments. For thou hast trusted in thy wickedness: thou hast said, None seeth me. Thy wisdom and thy knowledge, it hath perverted thee; and thou hast said in thine heart, I am, and none else beside me" (Is.47:8-10).

"Ye have plowed wickedness, ye have reaped iniquity; ye have eaten the fruit of lies: because thou didst trust in thy way, in the multitude of thy mighty men" (Hos.10:13).

"The pride of thine heart hath deceived thee, thou that dwellest in the clefts of the rock, whose habitation is high; that saith in his heart, Who shall bring me down to the ground? though thou exalt thyself as the eagle, and though thou set thy nest among the stars, thence will I bring thee down, saith the LORD" (Obad.3-4).

"This is the rejoicing city that dwelt carelessly, that said in her heart, I am, and there in none beside me: how is she become a desolation, a place for beasts to lie down in! every one that passeth by her shall hiss, and wag his hand" (Zeph.2:15).

3. God reveals "these things" to little children (see DEEPER STUDY # 4—Mk.10:14). The babes are the humble before God, those who acknowledge…

- that this world is not all there is.
- that a few short years of life are not all there is.
- that they have an inadequacy in solving the *seed of corruption*, that is, the seed of sin and death in the world.
- that God is, and that He is their Father.
- that God is, and that He is a rewarder of those who diligently seek Him (Heb.11:6).

The *"little children"* are those who look up to God as their Father because they are…

- open and receptive within their spirits.
- dependent and trusting spiritually.
- responsive and submissive to spiritual truth.
- teachable and obedient to God.
- loving and forgiving toward others (Mt.22:36-40; 1 Jn.4:20-21; Mt.6:14-15).

(See Pt.1 of this note to see what it is that God reveals to "little children".)

4. It pleases God enormously that He is able to reveal "these things" to the "little children" of the earth.

"Then said Jesus to those Jews which believed on him, If ye continue in my word, then are ye my disciples indeed; and ye shall know the truth, and the truth shall make you free" (Jn.8:31-32).

"Ye are my friends, if ye do whatsoever I command you. Henceforth I call you not servants; for the servant knoweth not what his lord doeth: but I have called you friends; for all things that I have heard of my Father I have made known unto you" (Jn.15:14-15).

"But as it is written, Eye hath not seen, nor ear heard, neither have entered into the heart of man, the things which God hath prepared for them that love him. But God hath revealed them unto us by his Spirit: for the Spirit searcheth all things, yea, the deep things of God" (1 Cor.2:9-10).

"As newborn "little children", desire the sincere milk of the word, that ye may grow thereby: if so be ye have tasted that the Lord is gracious" (1 Pt.2:2-3).

3 (10:22) **Revelation—Spiritual World—Jesus Christ, Deity; Knows God; Sovereignty**: second, there is the privilege of knowing God and Christ in a very personal way. Four things are being said by Christ.

1. Christ holds the supreme place in the universe. All things have been delivered into the hands of God's Son, for all things have been made for God's Son (Col.1:16-17). Jesus Christ is the supreme Authority over the universe; therefore, He is to oversee and rule the universe. However, His sovereignty is not seen, not right now, not by the vast majority of men. He was not understood nor accepted by the people of His day, nor is He understood and accepted by the people of today (Jn.1:10-11). But the truth will be obvious some day, for the day is coming when the Son of God will be revealed to the world.

"Because he hath appointed a day, in the which he will judge the world in righteousness by that man whom he hath ordained; whereof he hath given assurance unto all men, in that he hath raised him from the dead" (Acts 17:31).

"Then cometh the end, when he shall have delivered up the kingdom to God, even the Father; when he shall have put down all rule and all authority and power. For he must reign, till he hath put all enemies under his feet" (1 Cor.15:24-25).

"And to you who are troubled rest with us, when the Lord Jesus shall be revealed from heaven with his mighty angels, in flaming fire taking vengeance on them that know not God, and that obey not the gospel of our Lord Jesus Christ: who shall be punished with everlasting destruction from the presence of the Lord, and from the glory of his power; when he shall come to the glorified in his saints, and to be admired in all them that believe (because our testimony among you was believed) in that day" (2 Th.1:7-10).

"And being found in fashion as a man, he humbled himself, and became obedient unto death, even the death of the cross. Wherefore God also hath highly exalted him, and given him a name which is above every name: that at the name of Jesus every knee should bow, of things in heaven, and things in earth, and things under the earth; and that every tongue should confess that Jesus Christ is Lord, to the glory of God the Father" (Ph.2:8-11).

2. God and Christ alone have perfect knowledge. Therefore, a complete knowledge of God can be grasped only by the Son, and a complete knowledge of the Son can be grasped only by God the Father.

"Then cried Jesus in the temple as he taught, saying, Ye both know me, and ye know whence I am: and I am not come of myself, but he that sent me is true, whom ye know not. But I know him: for I am from him, and he hath sent me" (Jn.7:28-29).

"Jesus answered, If I honour myself, my honour is nothing: it is my Father that honoureth me; of whom ye say, that he is your God: yet ye have not known him; but I know him: and if I should say, I know him not, I shall be a liar like unto you: but I know him, and keep his saying" (Jn.8:54-55).

"As the Father knoweth me, even so know I the Father: and I lay down my life for the sheep" (Jn.10:15).

"O righteous Father, the world hath not known thee: but I have known thee, and these have known that thou hast sent me" (Jn.17:25).

3. God is Spirit (Jn.4:24). He is of another dimension of being entirely. If man is to know the spiritual world, then God must reveal that spiritual world and the things of that world to man. This is what Jesus is profoundly claiming. He and God alone know each other; but He has chosen to reveal the Father, who is Spirit, to some. Passages such as v.21 show that the persons chosen to receive this revelation are the humble who truly seek God and trust the Son's testimony. (See outline and notes—1 Cor.2:6-13; 2:14—3:4; Jn.4:23-24.)

"Howbeit we speak wisdom among them that are perfect: yet not the wisdom of this world, nor of the princes of this world, that come to nought: but we speak the wisdom of God in a mystery, even the hidden wisdom, which God ordained before the world unto our glory: which none of the princes of this world knew: for had they known it, they would not have crucified the Lord of glory" (1 Cor.2:6-8).

"But the natural man receiveth not the things of the Spirit of God: for they are foolishness unto him: neither can he know them, because they are spiritually discerned. But he that is spiritual judgeth all things, yet he himself is judged of no man. For who hath known the mind of the Lord, that he may instruct him? But we have the mind of Christ" (1 Cor.2:14-16).

4. The persons chosen to receive this revelation are the "little children" who truly seek God and trust the *Son's* testimony (see note, Truth, pt.3—Lk.10:21).

4 (10:23-24) **Revelation—Knowledge, Hidden—Prophets, Salvation Predicted**: third, there is the privilege of seeing and learning God's full revelation. Note several things.

1. Jesus shared this point with His disciples alone. What He said is understood only by His disciples.

2. Jesus said that He himself was the great salvation which the godly prophets and kings of old desired to see and hear. Jesus was claiming to be the Messiah, the Son of the Living God. He was the One promised by God down through the ages. (Cp. Is.53:1f.)

"I have waited for thy salvation, O LORD" (Gen.49:18).

"And now I [Paul] stand and am judged for the hope of the promise made of God unto our fathers: unto which promise our twelve tribes, instantly serving God day and night, hope to come. For which hope's sake, king Agrippa, I am accused of the Jews. Why should it be thought a thing incredible with you, that God should raise the dead?" (Acts 26:6-8).

"Which in other ages was not made known unto the sons of men, as it is now revealed unto his holy apostles and prophets by the Spirit" (Eph.3:5).

"Of which salvation the prophets have enquired and searched diligently, who prophesied of the grace that should come unto you: searching what, or what manner of time the Spirit of Christ which was in them did signify, when it testified beforehand the sufferings of Christ, and the glory that should follow. Unto whom it was revealed, that not unto themselves, but unto us they did minister the things, which are now reported unto you by them that have preached the gospel unto you with the Holy Ghost sent down from heaven; which things the angels desire to look into" (1 Pt.1:10-12).

3. Jesus was saying that His disciples were highly privileged to know Him, to see and hear Him and the truth which He revealed.

"Verily, verily, I say unto you, He that heareth my word, and believeth on him that sent me, hath everlasting life, and shall not come into condemnation; but is passed from death and life" (Jn.5:24; cp. 1 Pt. 1:10-13).

1 **A lawyer (an expert in the law) tempted Jesus**

2 **Question 1: How do we inherit eternal life?**[DS1]
a. First, the law has the answer
b. Second, love God supremely
c. Third, love your neighbor as yourself
d. Fourth, obey & you shall live

3 **Question 2: Who is my neighbor?**
a. The traveller: Was foolish & irresponsible
1) Travelled alone
2) Was robbed
3) Was assaulted & left half-dead

F. The Parable of the Good Samaritan: The Two Supreme Questions of Life, 10:25-37
(cp. Mt.22:34-40; Mk.12:28-34)

25 On one occasion an expert in the law stood up to test Jesus. "Teacher," he asked, "what must I do to inherit eternal life?"
26 "What is written in the Law?" he replied. "How do you read it?"
27 He answered: "'Love the Lord your God with all your heart and with all your soul and with all your strength and with all your mind' ; and, 'Love your neighbor as yourself.'"
28 "You have answered correctly," Jesus replied. "Do this and you will live."
29 But he wanted to justify himself, so he asked Jesus, "And who is my neighbor?"
30 In reply Jesus said: "A man was going down from Jerusalem to Jericho, when he fell into the hands of robbers. They stripped him of his clothes, beat him and went away, leaving him half dead.
31 A priest happened to be going down the same road, and when he saw the man, he passed by on the other side.
32 So too, a Levite, when he came to the place and saw him, passed by on the other side.
33 But a Samaritan, as he traveled, came where the man was; and when he saw him, he took pity on him.
34 He went to him and bandaged his wounds, pouring on oil and wine. Then he put the man on his own donkey, took him to an inn and took care of him.
35 The next day he took out two silver coins and gave them to the innkeeper. 'Look after him,' he said, 'and when I return, I will reimburse you for any extra expense you may have.'
36 "Which of these three do you think was a neighbor to the man who fell into the hands of robbers?"
37 The expert in the law replied, "The one who had mercy on him." Jesus told him, "Go and do likewise."

b. The priest: Placed work above people
1) Saw the injured traveller
2) Rushed by him
c. The Levite: Placed safety before compassion
1) Saw him
2) Stopped & looked
d. The Samaritan:[DS2] Placed compassion before prejudice & opinion
1) Gave his heart: Compassion
2) Sacrificed his work, time, energy, goods, and money
3) Saw to it that continued care was given
e. The Lord's commission: Go & do likewise

DIVISION V

THE SON OF MAN'S GREAT JOURNEY TO JERUSALEM (STAGE I): HIS MISSION AND PUBLIC CHALLENGE, 9:51-13:21

F. The Parable of the Good Samaritan: The Two Supreme Questions of Life, 10:25-37

(10:25-37) **Introduction**: there are two supreme questions of life, questions that could revolutionize the world if men would ask them and then heed their answers.

1. A lawyer (an expert in the law) tempted Jesus (v.25).
2. Question 1: how do we inherit eternal life (v.25-28)?
3. Question 2: who is my neighbor (v.29-37)?

1 (10:25) **Jesus Christ, Questioned**: a lawyer, an expert in the law, tempted Jesus (see DEEPER STUDY # 1, Lawyer—Mt.22:35). The lawyer was not seeking the truth. He was not really trying to discover the way to God. His purpose was to trip Jesus, to lead Jesus to discredit Himself by giving some unusual answer that would arouse the people against Him.

2 (10:25-28) **Eternal Life—Love**: the first supreme question of life is: How do we inherit eternal life? Note that the lawyer's question stressed works. He asked, "What must I do?" To him, salvation was by works. God was going to accept him because he was or could become *good enough*. He had no concept of the part that God's love and grace played in salvation (cp. Eph.2:8-8; Tit.3:5-7 for a description of what he failed to see).

Note how clearly Jesus led the conversation to spell out the steps to eternal life.

1. First, the law has the answer to eternal life. If a man wishes eternal life, he must look into the law of God. Note Jesus' instructions to the lawyer, "How do you read it?" The lawyer had a little leather box called a phylactery. Several passages of Scripture were in the box, two of which were Dt.6:3 and Dt.6:11. These were the two verses which he quoted.

> **Thought 1.** God has given us the answer to eternal life in clear terms—so clear we are left without excuse.
> 1) He has given us the answer in written words. It is in black and white, certain and unmistakable.
> 2) He has given us the answer in the life of Christ Himself. God has caused the words to be lived out in a human life, giving us the example of the Ideal Life (see DEEPER STUDY # 1, Jesus Christ, The Word—Jn.1:1-5).

2. Second, love God supremely.
   a. "Love the Lord your God." Love God as *your* very own God. This is a personal relationship, not a distant relationship. God is not impersonal, not

far out in space someplace, distant and removed. God is personal, ever so close, and we are to be personally involved with God as though face to face. The command is to *"love the Lord your God."* Loving God is alive and active, not dead and inactive. We are, therefore, to maintain a personal relationship with God that is alive and active.

b. Love God with all that you are, with all of your being, all of your nature. Jesus breaks our being into three parts: the heart, the soul, and the mind (see notes—Mk.12:29-31 for more discussion).

May the Lord direct your hearts into God's love and Christ's perseverance. (2 Th 3:5)

Keep yourselves in God's love as you wait for the mercy of our Lord Jesus Christ to bring you to eternal life. (Jude 1:21)

Love the LORD your God with all your heart and with all your soul and with all your strength. (Deu 6:5)

And now, O Israel, what does the LORD your God ask of you but to fear the LORD your God, to walk in all his ways, to love him, to serve the LORD your God with all your heart and with all your soul, (Deu 10:12)

Love the LORD your God and keep his requirements, his decrees, his laws and his commands always. (Deu 11:1)

But be very careful to keep the commandment and the law that Moses the servant of the LORD gave you: to love the LORD your God, to walk in all his ways, to obey his commands, to hold fast to him and to serve him with all your heart and all your soul." (Josh 22:5)

Love the LORD, all his saints! The LORD preserves the faithful, but the proud he pays back in full. (Psa 31:23)

3. Third, love your neighbor as yourself. If a man wishes eternal life, he has to love his *neighbor*. The first commandment, "Love God," is abstract; it cannot be seen or understood standing by itself. There has to be a *demonstration, an act, something done* for love to be seen and understood. A profession of love without demonstration is empty. It is profession only. Love is not known without showing it. Several important things need to be said about love at this point.

a. Love is an active experience, not inactive and dormant. This was the point Jesus was making. Love for God *acts*. Love acts by showing and demonstrating itself. It is inaccurate and foolish for a man to say, "I love God," and then be inactive and dormant, doing nothing for God. If he truly loves God, he will *do things* for God. Any person who loves does things for the one loved.

b. The *primary thing* God wants from us is to love our neighbor, not to do religious things. Doing religious things is good, but it is not the first thing God wants. God wants us to make loving our neighbor the first order of our lives. To do religious things is only dealing with things such as rituals, observances, ordinances, laws. Such things are lifeless, unfeeling and unresponsive. They are material objects; therefore, they are not helped by our doing them. Only we are helped. They make us feel good and religious, which is beneficial to our growth, but religious things are not what demonstrate our love for God. Loving our neighbor is what proves our love for God. A man may say he loves God, but if he hates and acts unkindly toward his neighbor, everyone knows his religion is profession only. (See note—Mt.22:39 for more discussion.)

4. Fourth, obey and you shall live eternally.

We know that we have passed from death to life, because we love our brothers. Anyone who does not love remains in death. (1 John 3:14)

If anyone says, "I love God," yet hates his brother, he is a liar. For anyone who does not love his brother, whom he has seen, cannot love God, whom he has not seen. And he has given us this command: Whoever loves God must also love his brother. (1 John 4:20-21)

But I tell you: Love your enemies and pray for those who persecute you, (Mat 5:44)

The second is this: 'Love your neighbor as yourself.' There is no commandment greater than these." (Mark 12:31)

The crowd spoke up, "We have heard from the Law that the Christ will remain forever, so how can you say, 'The Son of Man must be lifted up'? Who is this 'Son of Man'?" Then Jesus told them, "You are going to have the light just a little while longer. Walk while you have the light, before darkness overtakes you. The man who walks in the dark does not know where he is going. (John 12:34-35)

My command is this: Love each other as I have loved you. (John 15:12)

Love must be sincere. Hate what is evil; cling to what is good. (Rom 12:9)

Let no debt remain outstanding, except the continuing debt to love one another, for he who loves his fellowman has fulfilled the law. The commandments, "Do not commit adultery," "Do not murder," "Do not steal," "Do not covet," and whatever other commandment there may be, are summed up in this one rule: "Love your neighbor as yourself." Love does no harm to its neighbor. Therefore love is the fulfillment of the law. (Rom 13:8-10)

The entire law is summed up in a single command: "Love your neighbor as yourself." (Gal 5:14)

May the Lord make your love increase and overflow for each other and for everyone else, just as ours does for you. (1 Th 3:12)

Keep on loving each other as brothers. (Heb 13:1)

If you really keep the royal law found in Scripture, "Love your neighbor as yourself," you are doing right. (James 2:8)

Now that you have purified yourselves by obeying the truth so that you have sincere love for your brothers, love one another deeply, from the heart. (1 Pet 1:22)

Dear friends, let us love one another, for love comes from God. Everyone who loves has been born of God and knows

God. Whoever does not love does not know God, because God is love. This is how God showed his love among us: He sent his one and only Son into the world that we might live through him. This is love: not that we loved God, but that he loved us and sent his Son as an atoning sacrifice for our sins. Dear friends, since God so loved us, we also ought to love one another. (1 John 4:7-11)

The alien living with you must be treated as one of your native-born. Love him as yourself, for you were aliens in Egypt. I am the LORD your God. (Lev 19:34)

DEEPER STUDY # 1
(10:25) **Eternal Life**: see DEEPER STUDY # 2—Jn.1:4; DEEPER STUDY # 1—10:10; DEEPER STUDY # 1—17:2-3.

3 (10:29-37) **Love—Brotherhood—Compassion—Ministering —Care**: the second supreme question of life is: Who is my neighbor? Note the lawyer sought to "justify himself." He sensed that Jesus was saying that he had not done the law; he had failed to love his neighbor. So he asked the logical question, "Who is my neighbor?" Jesus answered and drove the point home to the human heart by doing what He had so often done—He gave an illustration.

1. There was a traveller who was foolish and irresponsible. He was foolish because he travelled the road between Jerusalem and Jericho that was known for its danger. It was about twenty one miles in distance, in a wild country, a rugged, rocky pass much of the way. It was a favorite habitat for marauding thieves, so much so it was called *the Way of Blood.* Travellers never journeyed there alone. They always travelled with caravans. Therefore, this traveller was irresponsible, foolish, and reckless. Some would even argue that such foolishness was undeserving of help.

Thought 1. How many are foolish and reckless in life, exposing and destroying their bodies by walking where they should not and by doing what they should not?

A prudent man sees danger and takes refuge, but the simple keep going and suffer for it. (Prov 22:3)

Who is wise? He will realize these things. Who is discerning? He will understand them. The ways of the LORD are right; the righteous walk in them, but the rebellious stumble in them. (Hosea 14:9)

2. There was the priest who placed his religious work and ceremony before the welfare of the man. Note this was a religionist, and he did not even make a move toward helping the man. He "passed by on the other side" which means he rushed away. The priest was probably hurrying to meet his evening religious duties. The trip was a day's journey, and he would have to rush to make it. There was also a religious rule that made a person unclean for seven days after touching a dead body. This ceremonial ritual caused a priest to lose his turn of duty at the temple. The priest was not about to sacrifice his primary work and privilege for the man.

Thought 1. How many put work, even religious works, and *busyness* before helping others?

Thought 2. How many put their church and its ceremony and ritual before the needs of desperate men? How much less would be invested in buildings and facilities if men were seen as half dead travellers who needed our compassion and help?

"Then he will say to those on his left, 'Depart from me, you who are cursed, into the eternal fire prepared for the devil and his angels. For I was hungry and you gave me nothing to eat, I was thirsty and you gave me nothing to drink, I was a stranger and you did not invite me in, I needed clothes and you did not clothe me, I was sick and in prison and you did not look after me.' (Mat 25:41-43)

"That servant who knows his master's will and does not get ready or does not do what his master wants will be beaten with many blows. (Luke 12:47)

Anyone, then, who knows the good he ought to do and doesn't do it, sins. (James 4:17)

For I desire mercy, not sacrifice, and acknowledgment of God rather than burnt offerings. (Hosea 6:6)

He has showed you, O man, what is good. And what does the LORD require of you? To act justly and to love mercy and to walk humbly with your God. (Micah 6:8)

3. There was the Levite who placed safety before compassion. The Levite was touched with enough feeling to walk over and look upon the man. But he shrank from helping. Perhaps He...

- feared being identified with the robbers.
- feared that the robbers might still be lurking behind the shadows of the surrounding cliffs.
- felt that meddling with the poor soul was just too much bother to undergo.

"There was a rich man who was dressed in purple and fine linen and lived in luxury every day. At his gate was laid a beggar named Lazarus, covered with sores and longing to eat what fell from the rich man's table. Even the dogs came and licked his sores. "The time came when the beggar died and the angels carried him to Abraham's side. The rich man also died and was buried. In hell, where he was in torment, he looked up and saw Abraham far away, with Lazarus by his side. (Luke 16:19-23)

What good is it, my brothers, if a man claims to have faith but has no deeds? Can such faith save him? Suppose a brother or sister is without clothes and daily food. If one of you says to him, "Go, I wish you well; keep warm and well fed," but does nothing about his physical needs, what good is it? (James 2:14-16)

If anyone has material possessions and sees his brother in need but has no pity on him, how can the love of God be in him?

Dear children, let us not love with words or tongue but with actions and in truth. (1 John 3:17-18)

For he never thought of doing a kindness, but hounded to death the poor and the needy and the brokenhearted. He loved to pronounce a curse— may it come on him; he found no pleasure in blessing— may it be far from him. (Psa 109:16-17)

If a man shuts his ears to the cry of the poor, he too will cry out and not be answered. (Prov 21:13)

Rescue those being led away to death; hold back those staggering toward slaughter. If you say, "But we knew nothing about this," does not he who weighs the heart perceive it? Does not he who guards your life know it? Will he not repay each person according to what he has done? (Prov 24:11-12)

You have not strengthened the weak or healed the sick or bound up the injured. You have not brought back the strays or searched for the lost. You have ruled them harshly and brutally. (Ezek 34:4; cp. v.5-10)

4. The good Samaritan placed compassion before everything: prejudice, opinion, work, time, energy, and money. The *good Samaritan* teaches beyond question who our neighbor is. The good Samaritan gave his heart, his compassion, his all in order to help the desperate man.

a. The injured man was a Jew. The good Samaritan and the Jew were of different races—races who hated and despised each other. No prejudice has ever run any deeper than the prejudice between these two (see note—Lk.10:33). Yet the good Samaritan had a sense of *common humanity*. He was a man who saw another man—not as a Jew and not as an enemy. This was most strange, for the Jews cursed the Samaritans, and there was the likelihood that the injured Jew would curse the Samaritan when he had recovered. However, despite all, the good Samaritan saw a fellow human being in desperate need, and he was moved with compassion for him.

b. The good Samaritan gave up his work, time, and energy to help the man. Note what he did. Each step is significant in showing how we are to love our neighbors.

⇒ He went to him: went forth, reached out personally to help.

⇒ He bandaged up his wounds: eased his pain.

⇒ He poured oil and wine into his wounds: gave of his own goods.

⇒ He set him on his own donkey: sacrificed his own comfort.

⇒ He provided rooming for him: provided the basic necessities.

⇒ He took care of him: nursed, looked after him personally.

Note the time, energy, and money involved in this. Showing love to one's neighbor is putting love into action; and putting love into action requires time, energy, and money. Love is not just an idea or a feeling toward God. It is *practical acts and commitment* to help any who need help.

c. The good Samaritan saw to it that continued compassion and care were given. Two silver coins (*two denarii)* amounted to somewhere between twenty-four to forty-eight days of room and board, a considerable sum. And note: the good Samaritan said that if it cost more, he would pay it when he returned. The good Samaritan saw a desperate need and did *all he could* to help.

5. The Lord's commission was forceful: go and do likewise. Note a striking point: Christ still did not answer the lawyer (an expert in the law). There was no need. The answer was strikingly clear. If the lawyer wished eternal life, he had to "go and do likewise." He now knew who his neighbor was: it was any man who needed mercy, whether a friend or just an acquaintance or even an enemy. The lawyer was forced to admit this. However, more than just confession was needed. Love was needed. The lawyer and all of us need to demonstrate love as we go about our daily affairs. We must help our neighbors—all those around us who hurt and are suffering.

For I was hungry and you gave me something to eat, I was thirsty and you gave me something to drink, I was a stranger and you invited me in, I needed clothes and you clothed me, I was sick and you looked after me, I was in prison and you came to visit me.' "Then the righteous will answer him, 'Lord, when did we see you hungry and feed you, or thirsty and give you something to drink? When did we see you a stranger and invite you in, or needing clothes and clothe you? When did we see you sick or in prison and go to visit you?' "The King will reply, 'I tell you the truth, whatever you did for one of the least of these brothers of mine, you did for me.' (Mat 25:35-40)

In everything I did, I showed you that by this kind of hard work we must help the weak, remembering the words the Lord Jesus himself said: 'It is more blessed to give than to receive.'" (Acts 20:35)

On the contrary: "If your enemy is hungry, feed him; if he is thirsty, give him something to drink. In doing this, you will heap burning coals on his head." (Rom 12:20)

Carry each other's burdens, and in this way you will fulfill the law of Christ. (Gal 6:2)

Remember those in prison as if you were their fellow prisoners, and those who are mistreated as if you yourselves were suffering. (Heb 13:3)

"If you come across your enemy's ox or donkey wandering off, be sure to take it back to him. (Exo 23:4)

"'If one of your countrymen becomes poor and is unable to support himself among you, help him as you would an alien or a temporary resident, so he can continue to live among you. (Lev 25:35)

For the LORD your God is God of gods and Lord of lords, the great God, mighty and awesome, who shows no partiality and accepts no bribes. He defends the cause of

the fatherless and the widow, and loves the alien, giving him food and clothing. And you are to love those who are aliens, for you yourselves were aliens in Egypt. (Deu 10:17-19)

Do not gloat when your enemy falls; when he stumbles, do not let your heart rejoice, (Prov 24:17)

If your enemy is hungry, give him food to eat; if he is thirsty, give him water to drink. In doing this, you will heap burning coals on his head, and the LORD will reward you. (Prov 25:21-22)

"Is not this the kind of fasting [religion] I have chosen: to loose the chains of injustice and untie the cords of the yoke, to set the oppressed free and break every yoke? Is it not to share your food with the hungry and to provide the poor wanderer with shelter— when you see the naked, to clothe him, and not to turn away from your own flesh and blood? (Isa 58:6-7)

DEEPER STUDY # 2

(10:33) **Samaritans**: Samaria was the central part of Palestine. Palestine was a small country, reaching only one hundred twenty miles north to south. The country was divided into three sections:

⇒ Judea, the southern section
⇒ Galilee, the northern section
⇒ Samaria, the central section, lying right between the two

There was bitter hatred between the Jews and the Samaritans. Two things in particular caused this hatred.

1. The Samaritans were mongrel or half-Jews, a mixed breed by birth. What had happened was this. Centuries before (about 720 B.C.), the King of Assyria had captured the ten tribes of Israel and deported a large number of the people, scattering them throughout Media (cp. 2 Ki.17:6-41). He then took people from all over the Assyrian empire and transplanted them into Samaria to repopulate the land. The result was only natural. Intermarriage took place and the people became a mixed breed, a breed including...

- the transplanted people
- the weak of the land who had been left behind
- the outcast and irreligious who had intermarried with the original Samaritans

The fact of a mixed breed, of course, infuriated the strict Jews who held to a pure race.

2. The Samaritans were mongrel or half-Jews, a mixed breed by religion as well as by birth. The transplanted heathen, of course, brought their gods with them. The God of Israel eventually won out, but the religion of the Samaritans never became pure Judaism. Three things happened to cause this.

a. When Ezra led the Jews back from exile in Babylon, the first thing the Jews did was to start rebuilding their temple. The Samaritans offered to help them but the Jews rejected their help, declaring that the Samaritans, through intermarriage and worship of false gods, had lost their purity and forfeited their right to worship the only true God. This severe denunciation, of course, embittered the Samaritans against the Jews in Jerusalem.

b. The Samaritans built a rival temple on Mount Gerizim to stand in competition with the Jewish temple at Jerusalem (cp. Jn.4:20-21).

c. The Samaritans twisted both the Scripture and history to favor their own people and nation.

⇒ They twisted Scripture by accepting only the first five books of the Bible, the Pentateuch. Just imagine! They missed all the richness and depth of the Psalms and prophets.
⇒ They twisted history by claiming that three great events took place on Mt. Gerizim, events that set it apart as a place of worship. It was the place where Abraham offered Isaac, where Melchizedek met Abraham, and where Moses built his first altar after leading Israel out of Egyptian bondage.

	G. The One Thing Needed: To Sit at Jesus' Feet, 10:38-42	40 But Martha was distracted by all the preparations that had to be made. She came to him and asked, "Lord, don't you care that my sister has left me to do the work by myself? Tell her to help me!"	**3 Martha's problem: She was distracted** a. Distracted by serving b. Distracted by material things: Food, necessities & the cares of the world
1 Jesus entered a village **2 Two strong characters** a. Martha's character 1) Giving 2) Courageous 3) Caring & loving b. Mary's character 1) Loving & humble 2) Gripped with a spiritual hunger	38 As Jesus and his disciples were on their way, he came to a village where a woman named Martha opened her home to him. 39 She had a sister called Mary, who sat at the Lord's feet listening to what he said.	41 "Martha, Martha," the Lord answered, "you are worried and upset about many things, 42 But only one thing is needed. Mary has chosen what is better, and it will not be taken away from her."	**4 Martha's one need: To sit quietly & listen to Jesus' words**

DIVISION V

THE SON OF MAN'S GREAT JOURNEY TO JERUSALEM (STAGE I): HIS MISSION AND PUBLIC CHALLENGE, 9:51-13:21

G. The One Thing Needed: To Sit at Jesus' Feet, 10:38-42

(10:38-42) **Introduction—Devotion**: this event is historically misplaced, for Mary and Martha lived in Bethany, a suburb two to three miles outside of Jerusalem. Why then does Luke place it here on Jesus' journey to Jerusalem? Perhaps he feared the Parable of the Good Samaritan might be construed to teach salvation by works. Mary and Martha's experience teaches that waiting and sitting at Jesus' feet is much more important than running to and fro trying to work one's way into God's favor. There is one basic essential in life, and that is sitting at Jesus' feet and hearing His Word.

1. Jesus entered a village (v.38).
2. Two strong characters (v.38-39).
3. Martha's problem: she was distracted (v.40).
4. Martha's one need: to sit quietly and listen to Jesus' words (v.41-42).

1 (10:38) **Bethany**: Jesus entered a certain village. The village was Bethany which was a suburb of Jerusalem only about two miles away (see note, Bethany—Mt.21:17; cp. Jn.11:1).

2 (10:38-39) **Spiritual Hunger—Character—Mary—Martha**: the scene pictures two strong characters.

1. Martha is the first person seen, and she has a highly commendable character. It is said that "Jesus loved Martha" (Jn.11:5). Therefore, it is important to see the strong points of her character and to see what it was that caused a person who was so strong to fail.

   a. Martha was a *giving* person. Note that she owned a house so large she could give lodging to Jesus and His apostles. Taking care of so many was expensive, yet she willingly entertained them. The next two traits also show how giving she was.
   b. Martha was a *courageous* person. It was now dangerous to associate too closely with Jesus, especially around Jerusalem. The authorities were seeking some way to kill Jesus (see Jn.7:25, 30, 32). Many of His own disciples had forsaken Him (Jn.5:66) and others were now speaking against Him (Jn.7:20, 43-44). Even His own family had rejected Him (Jn.7:3-5). Nevertheless, Martha welcomed Him; she was willing to let the world know of her devotion to Him.
   c. Martha was a caring and loving person. She loved and cared for her sister Mary. Note that Mary was living with Martha and that her brother Lazarus was also living there (Jn.11:1f). For some unknown reason, Martha was taking care of them both. She felt a deep devotion for her family, loving and caring for them very much. This was apparent even in the midst of the disturbance she felt toward Mary (v.40).

2. Mary also had a commendable character. (Her name was *Miriam* in the Hebrew.)

   a. She was loving and humble. Note how she loved Jesus; she attached herself to Him. Her love and devotion ran deep, so deep that nothing else mattered except being right next to Him. Note also her humility. She *sat* at His feet, not by His side and not in front of Him. The room or courtyard was large enough to entertain a large crowd, so she could have chosen to sit elsewhere. Mary definitely had a devoted love and a sense of humility toward her Lord.
   b. She had a spiritual hunger for the Word of the Lord: she "sat...listening to what he said." She sat there, fixing her eyes and attention upon Him. She centered her mind upon what He said, listening and concentrating and hearingevery word. She did not take His message lightly. She hungered for the Word of Christ, so she *absorbed* His words and took them to heart. This means that she had...
      - a spiritual hunger
      - a readiness to hear
      - a desire to surrender
      - willingness to do

3 (10:40) **Service—Ministry, Burdened Down—Stress—Pressure—Busyness—Murmuring—Complaining**: Martha's problem was that she became distracted. The word "distracted" (periespato) means to draw around, to twist, to be drawn here and there. The idea is that Martha was drawn around and twisted with anxiety and worry. She was distracted, running here and there, being drawn by the cares of this person and that person. There are two ways Martha's distraction can be viewed and applied to our lives.

1. She was distracted by "all the preparations." She loved others; so she ministered to them, helping whomever and wherever she could, even using her own home as a center for caring. But Martha had a problem. She was "distracted," loaded down with the cares and needs of others. She became so weighed and burdened down, so tired and fatigued, so pressured and tense…

- that she lost sight of her priority
- that she became aggravated and critical of those who were not helping

2. Martha could also be distracted by material things, by the food and necessities and cares of this world. Martha had wealth, which is indicated by her entertaining Jesus and His large group. Apparently, she was a very active lady, possessing initiative and some management ability. She had much to look after, including a brother and sister who lived with her. It was the things of this world—food, necessities, cares, and social entertaining—that had distracted her.

As any lady of the house would do, she felt a keen responsibility for taking care of the guests and meeting their needs. When Jesus and His large group arrived, she naturally expected her sister to help with the preparation of the meals and lodging. The problem in her mind was that even Jesus did not suggest that Mary help. Martha was disturbed with Jesus as well as with Mary.

Martha had a legitimate complaint, and that legitimacy points out the importance of sitting at Jesus' feet and hearing His Word (v.39). No matter *how* important anything else is, sitting at Jesus' feet is the one thing that is to be given priority.

The fact that Martha owned a house, entertained Jesus and His large group, and took care of her sister shows that Martha was loving and concerned about people. But evidently she had become too busy. Perhaps her wealth, initiative, hospitality, social status, and management ability were the things that had priority in her mind and life. As good as they were, they were not enough, for they did not meet the one basic essential in life: having her spiritual hunger fed with the Word of Christ Himself.

Thought 1. Man needs food and necessities and some social entertainment. But he is not to be distracted by these. He is not to be choked by the cares of this world.

The seed that fell among thorns stands for those who hear, but as they go on their way they are choked by life's worries, riches and pleasures, and they do not mature. (Luke 8:14)

And do not set your heart on what you will eat or drink; do not worry about it. (Luke 12:29)

"Be careful, or your hearts will be weighed down with dissipation, drunkenness and the anxieties of life, and that day will close on you unexpectedly like a trap. (Luke 21:34)

No one serving as a soldier gets involved in civilian affairs—he wants to please his commanding officer. (2 Tim 2:4)

Thought 2. We should seek out opportunities to serve, working to meet the needs of a desperate world. But we must not become distracted and burdened down to the point…

- that the pressure gets to us
- that we become critical of others

"Stop grumbling among yourselves," Jesus answered. (John 6:43)

And do not grumble, as some of them did—and were killed by the destroying angel. (1 Cor 10:10)

Do everything without complaining or arguing, so that you may become blameless and pure, children of God without fault in a crooked and depraved generation, in which you shine like stars in the universe (Phil 2:14-15)

Man is a mere phantom as he goes to and fro: He bustles about, but only in vain; he heaps up wealth, not knowing who will get it. (Psa 39:6)

A man's own folly ruins his life, yet his heart rages against the LORD. (Prov 19:3)

Yet when I surveyed all that my hands had done and what I had toiled to achieve, everything was meaningless, a chasing after the wind; nothing was gained under the sun. (Eccl 2:11)

I hated all the things I had toiled for under the sun, because I must leave them to the one who comes after me. (Eccl 2:18)

Why should any living man complain when punished for his sins? (Lam 3:39)

4 (10:41-42) **Devotions—Worship—Quiet Time—Anxiety—Busyness**: Martha's one need was to sit quietly and listen to Jesus' words. Note four things.

1. Jesus loved and was tender toward Martha despite her failure. This is seen in His double address, "Martha, Martha." Jesus was deeply concerned for her. She was under stress and pressure and she had become disturbed. So many men had moved in upon her, and she was trying her best to meet the needs of all. Jesus' heart went out to her, wanting to ease the pressuring and stressful situation and her sense of anger with Mary (cp. Lk.22:31; Acts 9:4 for double addresses tenderly spoken).

2. Jesus reproved her because she was anxious and troubled about "many things." The word "worried" (merimnais) means to be anxious. It has the idea of being inwardly torn and divided in two, of being distracted from what one's mind and heart and life should be focused upon. The word "upset" (thorubazei) means to be disturbed, agitated, in turmoil, stirred up, ruffled. Martha sought to please Jesus with her service and ministering, but two things were wrong.

⇒ She was looking after "many things," too many. She was trying to do *too much* for so many.
⇒ She had become worried and upset.

3. Jesus said, "One thing is needful." What was the one thing? He clearly said that it was the *good part* which Mary chose. And in the words of Scripture, "*Mary…sat at the Lord's feet, listening to what he said.*" Martha's mistake was failing to do what Mary did. She let "many things" distract her from her *devotion* to the Lord, from sitting at His feet and listening to His Word. Note what Jesus meant by the "many things," what it actually was that distracted Martha from her devotions:

⇒ giving lodging and food to those who needed such
⇒ preparing the food for those who needed it
⇒ serving the hungry
⇒ making the needy comfortable

(Remember that Jesus was poor in worldly goods, having no place to lay His head, and apparently He sometimes had no money for food. Yet, He still stressed the spiritual over the physical.)

4. Jesus said that the "letter" chosen by Mary would not be taken away. The hunger and thirst after righteousness (God's Word) would be filled and never taken away (Mt.5:6).

> **Thought 1.** Our devotion to Christ is a daily affair (Lk.9:23). Therefore, seeking to hear His Word is to be a daily experience. Every believer should have what is commonly called *daily devotions*, a time set aside every day when he gets alone with God and sits at God's feet to seek His Word.
>
> **Very early in the morning, while it was still dark, Jesus got up, left the house and went off to a solitary place, where he prayed. (Mark 1:35)**
>
> **And then was a widow until she was eighty-four. She never left the temple but worshiped night and day, fasting and praying. (Luke 2:37)**
>
> **Now the Bereans were of more noble character than the Thessalonians, for they received the message with great eagerness and examined the Scriptures every day to see if what Paul said was true. (Acts 17:11)**
>
> **For everything that was written in the past was written to teach us, so that through endurance and the encouragement of the Scriptures we might have hope. (Rom 15:4)**
>
> **Be diligent in these matters; give yourself wholly to them, so that everyone may see your progress. (1 Tim 4:15)**
>
> **It is to be with him, and he is to read it all the days of his life so that he may learn to revere the LORD his God and follow carefully all the words of this law and these decrees (Deu 17:19)**
>
> **Do not let this Book of the Law depart from your mouth; meditate on it day and night, so that you may be careful to do everything written in it. Then you will be prosperous and successful. (Josh 1:8)**
>
> **But his delight is in the law of the LORD, and on his law he meditates day and night. He is like a tree planted by streams of water, which yields its fruit in season and whose leaf does not wither. Whatever he does prospers. (Psa 1:2-3)**
>
> **In your anger do not sin; when you are on your beds, search your hearts and be silent. Selah (Psa 4:4)**
>
> **In the morning, O LORD, you hear my voice; in the morning I lay my requests before you and wait in expectation. (Psa 5:3)**
>
> **May the words of my mouth and the meditation of my heart be pleasing in your sight, O LORD, my Rock and my Redeemer. (Psa 19:14)**
>
> **Evening, morning and noon I cry out in distress, and he hears my voice. (Psa 55:17)**
>
> **I will remember the deeds of the LORD; yes, I will remember your miracles of long ago. I will meditate on all your works and consider all your mighty deeds. (Psa 77:11-12; cp. Psa. 104:34; 119:15-16; 119:47; 119:96-100; 119:148; 127:1-2; 143:5)**
>
> **You will keep in perfect peace him whose mind is steadfast, because he trusts in you. Trust in the LORD forever, for the LORD, the LORD, is the Rock eternal. (Isa 26:3-4)**
>
> **Now when Daniel learned that the decree had been published, he went home to his upstairs room where the windows opened toward Jerusalem. Three times a day he got down on his knees and prayed, giving thanks to his God, just as he had done before. (Dan 6:10)**

1 **Jesus prayed**
  a. The disciples asked Jesus to teach them how to pray
  b. John had taught his disciples to pray

2 **Jesus' model prayer**
  a. Thank God
    1) For being our Father
    2) For heaven
  b. Praise His name
  c. Pray
    1) For His kingdom
    2) For daily bread
    3) For forgiveness
    4) For deliverance

3 **Man's part in prayer**[DS1]
  a. The illustration: Man is to persevere & endure in prayer

CHAPTER 11

H. The Great Subject of Prayer, 11:1-13
(cp. Mt.6:5-15; cp. Mk.11:20-26)

One day Jesus was praying
in a certain place. When he
finished, one of his disciples
said to him, "Lord, teach us
to pray, just as John taught
his disciples."
2 He said to them, "When
you pray, say: "'Father,
hallowed be your name, your
kingdom come.
3 Give us each day our daily
bread.
4 Forgive us our sins, for we
also forgive everyone who
sins against us. And lead us
not into temptation.'"
5 Then he said to them,
"Suppose one of you has a
friend, and he goes to him at
midnight and says, 'Friend,
lend me three loaves of
bread,
6 Because a friend of mine
on a journey has come to me,
and I have nothing to set before him.'
7 "Then the one inside answers, 'Don't bother me. The
door is already locked, and
my children are with me in
bed. I can't get up and give
you anything.'
8 I tell you, though he will
not get up and give him the
bread because he is his friend,
yet because of the man's
boldness he will get up and
give him as much as he needs.
9 "So I say to you: Ask and it
will be given to you; seek
and you will find; knock and
the door will be opened to
you.
10 For everyone who asks
receives; he who seeks finds;
and to him who knocks, the
door will be opened.
11 "Which of you fathers, if
your son asks for a fish, will
give him a snake instead?
12 Or if he asks for an egg,
will give him a scorpion?
13 If you then, though you
are evil, know how to give
good gifts to your children,
how much more will your
Father in heaven give the
Holy Spirit to those who ask
him!"

  b. The point: Perseverance & endurance receive what is requested
  c. The exhortation
    1) Ask—shall be given
    2) Seek—shall find
    3) Knock—shall be opened
  d. The answer assured

4 **God's part in prayer**
  a. The illust.: God is not evil, but He is good—He is just like a father
  b. The point: God is *most* willing to give—especially the Holy Spirit to dwell within man's heart & life

DIVISION V

THE SON OF MAN'S GREAT JOURNEY TO JERUSALEM STAGE I): HIS MISSION AND PUBLIC CHALLENGE, 9:51-13:21

H. The Great Subject of Prayer, 11:1-13

(11:1-13) **Introduction**: this is one of the most thorough passages in all of Scripture dealing with the great subject of prayer. It is a passage that should be studied time and again.

1. Jesus prayed (v.1).
2. Jesus' model prayer (v.2-4).
3. Man's part in prayer (v.5-10).
4. God's part in prayer (v.11-13).

1 (11:1) **Jesus Christ, Prayer Life**: Jesus prayed. It had been predicted that He would give Himself to prayer (Ps.109:4), and He was always praying. (See Introduction, Special Features, pt.7 for a complete list of Jesus' recorded prayer times.)

⇒ He prayed at His baptism (Lk.3:21).
⇒ He prayed during His temptation (Lk.5:16).
⇒ He continued all night in prayer (Lk.6:12).
⇒ He was alone praying (Lk.9:18).
⇒ He went up into a mountain to pray (Lk.9:28).
⇒ He was now praying in a certain place (Lk.11:1).

While Jesus prayed, something caught the eye and ear of the disciples. Apparently, they were off to the side someplace but within sight and hearing. Three things stirred them to ask Jesus to teach them to pray.

1. Jesus often prayed, and He emphasized prayer as one of the greatest needs of human life. He always insisted that it was the source of His strength in living and serving God. Therefore, the disciples were aroused to hunger after the same strength for life and service.

2. Jesus prayed as a Son to His Father, and such intimacy stirred the disciples to want the same kind of relationship with God.

3. John had taught His disciples to pray. It was a common practice for a teacher to instruct his disciples in prayer. Jesus' disciples used this as the basis to ask Him: "Lord, teach us to pray."

2 (11:2-4) **Prayer**: Jesus' model prayer. Naturally, Jesus will teach anyone to pray—anyone who is really sincere and wants to begin praying. Note what Jesus did. He said, "When you pray, say...." or "This, then, is how you should pray" or "Pray then like this." He was giving a *model prayer* upon which we are to base our praying. It is a guide, the points of which are to be *prayed through*. The believer is to develop the points as He prays. (See note—Mt.6:9-13 for more discussion.)

1. Thank God for two things.
   a. Thank God for being our "Father." This is a personal relationship, a family relationship, the relationship of a child to a parent. It is a family relationship wrought by a person's being born anew (Jn.1:12-13; 2 Cor.6:17-18. Cp. Gal.4:4-7.) A person needs to thank God for being his Father,

for creating the family of God and allowing him to be a part of so glorious a family.

b. Thank God for heaven. Heaven is the spiritual dimension of being; it is the real world, incorruptible and undefiled, and it does not fade away. More importantly, it is where God is, and it is where we shall be. We need to thank God for heaven, that He is there and that we shall be in heaven with Him.

2. Praise God. His name is hallowed, set apart, different. God is holy, righteous, pure, loving, kind, merciful, gracious. Therefore, God is to be praised for who He is.

3. Request four things in particular. But note: these should be prayed for only after we have thanked and praised God.

a. Pray for God's kingdom to come. Christ needs to be enthroned, His rule and reign established on earth. His will needs to be done in all of our lives just as it is done in heaven. We need to pray for such to come. (See DEEPER STUDY # 3—Mt.19:23-24 for a discussion of the kingdom which shows that for which we should pray.)

b. Pray for daily bread, that is, for the necessities of life. People are hungry, starving both physically and spiritually. We all need to be fed both without and within. We need to pray both for our bodies and spirits—*daily* (cp. Mt.6:24-32).

c. Pray for forgiveness. We should pray for the Father to forgive our sins, and we need to take some time in discussing the matter with our Father. But note the word "our." We are to ask God to forgive "our sins," the sins of our family, neighbors, city, state, nation, and world. Sin is a shame, an affront to God. Sin is the most serious matter and most tragic event to ever occur in the universe. It is to be discussed with the Father every day—not just our own sins, but the world's sins. Intercessory prayer for the sinners of the world is to be a daily event in the life of every believer. But note a crucial fact: old sins that have been confessed and covered by the blood of Christ are not to be brought back up to God. They are already forgiven, hid and cast away by God. He does not want them remembered anymore. They are too painful and hurtful. However, there are new sins—new things committed every day—so many within our hearts and throughout the world that it would stagger the human mind. We are ever so short of God's glory—*unconformed* to the image of Christ, undeveloped and immature—so far short of what we should be. It is these and the unconfessed sins of the world and the new sins of the human heart that need to be forgiven. The believer needs to come every day begging for a fresh experience of forgiveness both for himself and for the world.

Note there is a condition for forgiveness. We must forgive those who sin against us. We sin and sin often against God. If we expect Him to forgive us, we have to forgive those who offend us.

For if you forgive men when they sin against you, your heavenly Father will also forgive you. But if you do not forgive men their sins, your Father will not forgive your sins. (Mat 6:14-15)

And when you stand praying, if you hold anything against anyone, forgive him, so that your Father in heaven may forgive you your sins." (Mark 11:25)

d. Pray for deliverance. The idea of God's leading men into temptation bothers some people. God tempts no one to do evil (Jas.1:13). What this request means is, "Pray for God to deliver us from temptation and from the evil one, Satan" (cp. Lk.22:40; 1 Cor.10:13).

3 (11:5-10) **Prayer**: man's part in prayer. No clearer explanation of man's part in prayer could be given than what is taught here.

1. Jesus *illustrated* very simply what man's part is. The story explains itself.

2. Jesus drove *the point* home: perseverance and endurance receives what it asks. The believer shall get what he asks if he...

- will not leave the throne of God
- will not go away
- will not let God alone

The whole point is that the person who prays must be sincere, fervent, constant, persistent, persevering, and enduring in seeking the face of God for whatever he wants.

3. Jesus gave an exhortation, a mini-sermon, to persevere and endure in prayer, and he stated it perfectly in two ways.

a. The person who prays is to continue asking for what he needs.

⇒ Ask, and it will be given you. But if asking does not receive it, then...

⇒ seek, and ye will find. But if seeking does not receive it, then...

⇒ knock, and it will be opened unto you.

The point is: we must mean what we pray, and the way we show God our sincerity is by continuing to ask for what we need.

b. The verbs ask, seek, and knock are all *continuous action*. We are to keep on asking and seeking and knocking, ever beseeching God to hear us.

4. The answer is assured. God will hear and answer the person who perseveres and endures in prayer. The believer always receives the need desired. In the parable shared by Jesus, the friend was occupied with a very needed and worthy matter—he was rejuvenating his body with sleep. The point is this: most have experienced being disturbed while sleeping (whether by a crying child or some other noise) and being slow to arise. Few arise unless the beckoning call persists. But one always arises if the child coughs or cries enough or the noise repeats itself enough. Persistence proves one's sincerity. There are certain requests that need a *continual coming* (Lk.18:5). (See note and DEEPER STUDY # 1—Mt.7:7.)

God is most willing to give. The child of God can rest assured that when the circumstances of life become hard, God will give the presence and power of the Holy Spirit to see His child through.

Now note another fact: God is not only willing to answer, He is *most willing* to answer. He loves and cares for man in all his needs. This must always be remembered. (See DEEPER STUDY # 1—Lk.11:5-10.) Note something else: God always answers our prayers, but sometimes the answer has to be "no." Why? Because what we asked is not always for our good, and God is always going to do what is best for us.

"Watch and pray so that you will not fall into temptation. The spirit is willing, but the body is weak." (Mat 26:41)

Then Jesus told his disciples a parable to show them that they should always pray and not give up. (Luke 18:1)

Be always on the watch, and pray that you may be able to escape all that is about to happen, and that you may be able to stand before the Son of Man." (Luke 21:36)

And pray in the Spirit on all occasions with all kinds of prayers and requests. With this in mind, be alert and always keep on praying for all the saints. (Eph 6:18)

Do not be anxious about anything, but in everything, by prayer and petition, with thanksgiving, present your requests to God. (Phil 4:6)

Devote yourselves to prayer, being watchful and thankful. (Col 4:2)

Pray continually; (1 Th 5:17)

But if from there you seek the LORD your God, you will find him if you look for him with all your heart and with all your soul. (Deu 4:29)

Look to the LORD and his strength; seek his face always. (1 Chr 16:11)

Seek the LORD while he may be found; call on him while he is near. (Isa 55:6)

You will seek me and find me when you seek me with all your heart. (Jer 29:13)

Look to the LORD and his strength; seek his face always. (Psa 105:4)

I love those who love me, and those who seek me find me. (Prov 8:17)

DEEPER STUDY # 1

(11:5-10) **Prayer—Fellowship**: Why does God not always answer our prayers immediately? Why is it necessary to ask and seek and knock and to keep on asking and seeking and knocking? Why do we need to ask at all when God knows our needs even before we ask?

There are at least four reasons.

1. Prayer teaches us to communicate and fellowship with God and to trust and seek after God more and more. When God back holds the giving, we keep coming to talk and share with Him more and more. Just as a human father longs for such fellowship and trust, our heavenly Father longs for such fellowship and trust.

2. Prayer teaches us both patience and hope in God and His promises. When God does not give immediately, we patiently (enduringly) keep coming into His presence, waiting for and hoping in what He has promised us (Mt.21:22; Jn.14:26; 1 Jn.5:14-15).

3. Prayer teaches us to love God as our Father more and more. Knowing that what we ask is coming and having to wait on it causes us to draw closer and closer to God and His gifts. And then when the gift is given, our hearts are endeared ever so much more to Him.

4. Prayer demonstrates how deeply we trust God and how much we love and depend upon Him. A person who really trusts God—who really knows that what he asks is going to be received—will bring more and more to God. He will come to God in prayer more and more. But the person who is not quite sure about receiving will only occasionally come, usually only in emergencies. God easily sees how much we really love and trust Him by our prayer life.

4 (11:11-13) **Prayer**: God's part in prayer. No clearer explanation of God's part in prayer could be given than what is taught here.

1. Jesus illustrated what God's part is. God is not evil; He is good just as an earthly father is good. Jesus stressed the point with three simple illustrations. Note all three illustrations had to do with a father and his son.

2. Jesus drove the point home: God is most willing to give. Note two points.

a. Man is evil, full of selfishness and sin, yet he gives to his child when asked. (Note the enormous contrast being made between evil man and God, who is perfectly good. If evil man gives, it is impossible that God, who is good, would not give.)

b. Our heavenly Father gives us the very Source of all good things, the Holy Spirit Himself. Just imagine the very presence of God dwelling within our hearts and bodies! If He dwells within us, then every good thing is assured. Once we have the Holy Spirit, we do not have to pray to God who is *way off* in outer space somewhere. We do not have to wait upon His gifts to arrive. We have His presence within...

- to accompany and be with us.

But I tell you the truth: It is for your good that I am going away. Unless I go away, the Counselor will not come to you; but if I go, I will send him to you. (John 16:7)

- to look after and care for us.

But the fruit of the Spirit is love, joy, peace, patience, kindness, goodness, faithfulness, gentleness and self-control. Against such things there is no law. (Gal 5:22-23)

- to direct and guide us.

Because those who are led by the Spirit of God are sons of God. (Rom 8:14)

But when he, the Spirit of truth, comes, he will guide you into all truth. He will not speak on his own; he will speak only what he hears, and he will tell you what is yet to come. (John 16:13)

- to assure and comfort us.

But the Counselor, the Holy Spirit, whom the Father will send in my name, will teach you all things and will remind you of everything I have said to you. (John 14:26)

For you did not receive a spirit that makes you a slave again to fear, but you received the Spirit of sonship. And by him we cry, "Abba, Father." The Spirit himself testifies with our spirit that we are God's children. Now if we are children, then we are heirs—heirs of God and co-heirs with Christ, if indeed we share in his sufferings in order that we may also share in his glory. (Rom 8:15-17)

- to pray and intercede for us.

In the same way, the Spirit helps us in our weakness. We do not know what we ought to pray for, but the Spirit himself intercedes for us with groans that words cannot express. (Rom 8:26)

Thought 1. God does answer prayer.

If you believe, you will receive whatever you ask for in prayer." (Mat 21:22)

Therefore I tell you, whatever you ask for in prayer, believe that you have received it, and it will be yours. (Mark 11:24)

And I will do whatever you ask in my name, so that the Son may bring glory to the Father. You may ask me for anything in my name, and I will do it. (John 14:13-14)

If you remain in me and my words remain in you, ask whatever you wish, and it will be given you. (John 15:7)

Until now you have not asked for anything in my name. Ask and you will receive, and your joy will be complete. (John 16:24)

If any of you lacks wisdom, he should ask God, who gives generously to all without finding fault, and it will be given to him. But when he asks, he must believe and not doubt, because he who doubts is like a wave of the sea, blown and tossed by the wind. (James 1:5-6)

And receive from him anything we ask, because we obey his commands and do what pleases him. (1 John 3:22)

This is the confidence we have in approaching God: that if we ask anything according to his will, he hears us. And if we know that he hears us—whatever we ask—we know that we have what we asked of him. (1 John 5:14-15)

If my people, who are called by my name, will humble themselves and pray and seek my face and turn from their wicked ways, then will I hear from heaven and will forgive their sin and will heal their land. (2 Chr 7:14)

He will call upon me, and I will answer him; I will be with him in trouble, I will deliver him and honor him. (Psa 91:15)

"The poor and needy search for water, but there is none; their tongues are parched with thirst. But I the LORD will answer them; I, the God of Israel, will not forsake them. (Isa 41:17)

Then you will call, and the LORD will answer; you will cry for help, and he will say: Here am I. "If you do away with the yoke of oppression, with the pointing finger and malicious talk, (Isa 58:9)

Before they call I will answer; while they are still speaking I will hear. (Isa 65:24)

'Call to me and I will answer you and tell you great and unsearchable things you do not know.' (Jer 33:3)

This third I will bring into the fire; I will refine them like silver and test them like gold. They will call on my name and I will answer them; I will say, 'They are my people,' and they will say, 'The LORD is our God.'" (Zec 13:9)

	I. The Proof that Jesus is the Messiah, 11:14-28 (Mt.12:22-30; Mk.3:22-30)
1 Jesus proved He was the Messiah—He cast a demon out of a man a. The people were amazed: Who was Jesus? b. Some accused Him: He was a deceiver, of Beelzebub c. Some tested Him: Sought a sign	14 Jesus was driving out a demon that was mute. When the demon left, the man who had been mute spoke, and the crowd was amazed. 15 But some of them said, "By Beelzebub, the prince of demons, he is driving out demons." 16 Others tested him by asking for a sign from heaven.
2 Illust.1: A kingdom & a house—He claimed to be of another kingdom & house than Satan's kingdom & house	17 Jesus knew their thoughts and said to them: "Any kingdom divided against itself will be ruined, and a house divided against itself will fall. 18 If Satan is divided against himself, how can his kingdom stand? I say this because you claim that I drive out demons by Beelzebub.
3 Illust.2: Religious exorcist—He claimed the right to be respected, at least as much as other ministers	19 Now if I drive out demons by Beelzebub, by whom do your followers drive them out? So then, they will be your judges.
4 Illust.3: The finger of God—He claimed to possess the power to usher in the Kingdom of God	20 But if I drive out demons by the finger of God, then the kingdom of God has come to you.
5 Illust.4: A stronger man—He claimed to be stronger than Satan	21 "When a strong man, fully armed, guards his own house, his possessions are safe. 22 But when someone stronger attacks and overpowers him, he takes away the armor in which the man trusted and divides up the spoils.
6 Illust.5: A shepherd & a flock—He claimed to be the pivotal figure of history	23 "He who is not with me is against me, and he who does not gather with me, scatters.
7 Illust.6: An empty house—He claimed that a man must turn from self-reformation to Him & be infilled with His very presence	24 "When an evil spirit comes out of a man, it goes through arid places seeking rest and does not find it. Then it says, 'I will return to the house I left.' 25 When it arrives, it finds the house swept clean and put in order. 26 Then it goes and takes seven other spirits more wicked than itself, and they go in and live there. And the final condition of that man is worse than the first."
8 Conclusion: The necessary thing—to hear the Word of God & keep it	27 As Jesus was saying these things, a woman in the crowd called out, "Blessed is the mother who gave you birth and nursed you." 28 He replied, "Blessed rather are those who hear the word of God and obey it."

DIVISION V

THE SON OF MAN'S GREAT JOURNEY TO JERUSALEM (STAGE I): HIS MISSION AND PUBLIC CHALLENGE, 9:51-13:21

I. The Proof that Jesus is the Messiah, 11:14-28

(11:14-28) **Introduction**: Jesus has been rejected, denied, and cursed by most men. Yet there is enormous evidence that He is just who He claimed to be. Jesus Himself gave some of the indisputable evidence in this passage.

1. Jesus proved that He was the Messiah—He cast a demon out of a man (v.14-16).
2. Illustration.1: a kingdom and a house—He claimed to be of another kingdom and house than Satan's kingdom and house (v.17-18).
3. Illustration 2: religious exorcist—He claimed the right to be respected, at least as much as other ministers (v.19).
4. Illustration 3: the finger of God—He claimed to possess the power to usher in the Kingdom of God (v.20).
5. Illustration 4: a stronger man—He claimed to be stronger than Satan (v.21-22).
6. Illustration 5: a shepherd and a flock—He claimed to be the pivotal or decisive figure of history (v.23).
7. Illustration 6: an empty house—He claimed that a man must turn from self-reformation to Him and be infilled with His very presence (v.24-26).
8. Conclusion: the necessary thing—to hear the Word of God and keep it (v.27-28).

1 (11:14-16) **Signs, Seeking—Jesus Christ, Charges Against**: Jesus proved that He was the Messiah by casting a demon out of a man. He demonstrated that He…

- was waging war against the spiritual forces of evil in this dark world (Eph.6:12).
- had come to destroy the works of the devil (Jn.3:8).

Jesus saw a man gripped by evil, by some spirit that made him mute and blind (cp. Mt.12:22). Jesus' heart went out to the man, and He was moved with compassion for him. Jesus cast out the evil spirit and healed the man. By doing so, He demonstrated to all that He was the true Messiah, the One who possessed the power of God perfectly. The response of the people was threefold.

1. Some were amazed and astonished, wondering just who Jesus might be.

2. Others immediately rejected Jesus. But note they did not question His power. They had to admit He possessed the power to do marvelous things. The tragedy of their rejection was this: they said the power was of Beelzebub, the prince of the demons. (See DEEPER STUDY # 1—Mk.3:22 for more discussion.)

3. Others sought fleshly, carnal signs that would satisfy their worldly desires. To confess Christ would cost them

everything they had, both wealth and friends (see note and DEEPER STUDY # 1—Lk.9:23; note—Mt.19:16-22). There was already plenty of evidence that Jesus was the true Messiah; they were just unwilling to give all they had to meet the needs of a desperate world and to be ridiculed and abused by the world (see note—Mt.16:2-4). Therefore, they demanded a sign—a sign so great that it would convert everyone and everything all at once. If everything could be miraculously converted all at once, then heaven would be on earth and all man's carnal desires would be met. (See outline and notes—Jn.6:22-29, esp. 6:26-27, 30.) Therefore, they asked for a sign from heaven, a sign that would convert all men. (Note: if God did this, it would be treating us as robots, eliminating our freedom of choice and will.)

> **Thought 1.** Men think that if they had a spectacular sign, then all men would believe and two things would happen. (1)There would be no abuse, ridicule, or persecution by friends or neighbors or anyone else. (2) The whole world would be converted. The Kingdom of God would come to earth and there would be plenty for everyone. There would be no need to protect what one has nor to fear the selfishness and evil of others. This, of course, is untrue, for man is *selfish and self-centered*, seeking to control his own life. Man would still disbelieve and distrust God and would still choose to do what he desired instead of God's will.
>
> **The heart is deceitful above all things and beyond cure. Who can understand it? (Jer 17:9)**

Jesus knew the thoughts of the unbelievers standing there, so He delivered a crushing blow to their thoughts and unbelief. He did so by giving six illustrations.

2 (11:17-18) **Jesus Christ, Deity—Messiah, Proof of—Satan, Purpose of**: Illustration 1—a kingdom. Jesus claimed to be of another kingdom and house than Satan's. Note several facts.

1. Jesus used a very simple illustration to make His claim, that of a divided kingdom and a house. It is an illustration that is clearly understood by all because everyone knows of kingdoms and houses that are divided and that crumble every day.

2. Jesus assumed the existence of Satan and his kingdom, both of which struggle against righteousness and good. He did not deny Satan's existence nor try to correct man's *mistaken notion* about the devil and his kingdom. Why? Because the devil and his kingdom are not *mistaken notions*. They are very, very real (see DEEPER STUDY # 1—Rev.12:9).

3. Jesus said Satan is not divided against himself. He is not going to do good nor is he going to build up God's kingdom. The very opposite is true. Satan is going to build his own kingdom, his own rule and reign. He desires to oppose and exalt himself against God. He wants men to follow him and his way of evil and by such to cut the heart of God. He wants God to hurt, and he knows that God hurts when man goes astray and turns from God's kingdom (see DEEPER STUDY # 3—Mt.19:23-24). Therefore, Satan seeks to lead men into evil by enticing them through the fleshly and carnal desires of human nature. Satan knows that sin leads to disease and to the destruction of the human body and family. He knows that such destruction causes great pain and hurt and suffering for God, which apparently is his ultimate motive.

The point is clear: Satan is not going to be casting out evil. Therefore, the power of Christ has to be of God. His power is good; it casts out evil. Therefore He, the Messiah, is of God's kingdom and house, not of Satan's kingdom and house.

> **Whoever believes in him is not condemned, but whoever does not believe stands condemned already because he has not believed in the name of God's one and only Son. (John 3:18)**
>
> **What about the one whom the Father set apart as his very own and sent into the world? Why then do you accuse me of blasphemy because I said, 'I am God's Son'? Do not believe me unless I do what my Father does. But if I do it, even though you do not believe me, believe the miracles, that you may know and understand that the Father is in me, and I in the Father." (John 10:36-38)**
>
> **How much more severely do you think a man deserves to be punished who has trampled the Son of God under foot, who has treated as an unholy thing the blood of the covenant that sanctified him, and who has insulted the Spirit of grace? (Heb 10:29)**

3 (11:19) **Jesus Christ, Response to**: Illustration 2—religious exorcists. Jesus claimed the right to be respected, at least as much as other ministers. This is a simple argument. There were Jewish exorcists, sons of the Jewish nation, who tried to cast out demons in the name of God. Jesus argued that they were not accused of hellish power. Why was He being accused? The question is pointed and instructive, for Jesus always healed and was always successful in casting out evil. Certainly He should be respected as much if not more than other ministers.

> **Thought 1.** The mistake of the Jews was that they exalted priests (ministers) and religion above God. Many do the same today. They read, quote, and use other ministers as their source much more than they use Jesus and the Holy Scripture.
>
> **Thought 2.** Jesus Christ should be exalted as the Messiah, the Son of God who alone can cast out evil. Therefore, He must be read, quoted, and preached day in and day out. Jesus Christ must be honored by every man.
>
> **That all may honor the Son just as they honor the Father. He who does not honor the Son does not honor the Father, who sent him. "I tell you the truth, whoever hears my word and believes him who sent me has eternal life and will not be condemned; he has crossed over from death to life. (John 5:23-24)**
>
> **You diligently study the Scriptures because you think that by them you possess eternal life. These are the Scriptures that testify about me, (John 5:39; cp. v.40-47)**
>
> **Simon Peter answered him, "Lord, to whom shall we go? You have the words of**

eternal life. (John 6:68)

"No one ever spoke the way this man does," the guards declared. (John 7:46)

Jesus replied, "If anyone loves me, he will obey my teaching. My Father will love him, and we will come to him and make our home with him. He who does not love me will not obey my teaching. These words you hear are not my own; they belong to the Father who sent me. (John 14:23-24)

We know that we have come to know him if we obey his commands. (1 John 2:3)

I know your deeds. See, I have placed before you an open door that no one can shut. I know that you have little strength, yet you have kept my word and have not denied my name. (Rev 3:8)

Ascribe to the LORD the glory due his name; worship the LORD in the splendor of his holiness. (Psa 29:2)

Glorify the LORD with me; let us exalt his name together. (Psa 34:3)

Let the redeemed of the LORD say this— those he redeemed from the hand of the foe, (Psa 107:2)

O LORD, you are my God; I will exalt you and praise your name, for in perfect faithfulness you have done marvelous things, things planned long ago. (Isa 25:1)

4 (11:20) **Kingdom of God—Messiah**: Illustration 3—the finger of God. Jesus claimed to possess the power to usher in the Kingdom of God. The finger of God is the same as the Spirit of God (cp. Mt.12:28). The power that cast out demons is the power of God. It comes from God and from no one else (see note, pt.3—Lk.11:17-18).

Now note something of crucial importance. Jesus said, "If I possess the power of God, then I am bringing the Kingdom of God to you. Wherever the power of God is, there is the Kingdom of God, for the power of God is used to bring about the rule and reign of God. Therefore, the Kingdom of God is come to you and is beginning in this day and age. The power of evil is now being cast out." Jesus is, of course, urging that no one miss the Kingdom of God. He is ushering the kingdom in, but it has to be accepted (see DEEPER STUDY # 3—Mt.19:23-24).

"The Law and the Prophets were proclaimed until John. Since that time, the good news of the kingdom of God is being preached, and everyone is forcing his way into it. (Luke 16:16)

Once, having been asked by the Pharisees when the kingdom of God would come, Jesus replied, "The kingdom of God does not come with your careful observation, nor will people say, 'Here it is,' or 'There it is,' because the kingdom of God is within you." (Luke 17:20-21)

After John was put in prison, Jesus went into Galilee, proclaiming the good news of God. "The time has come," he said. "The kingdom of God is near. Repent and believe the good news!" (Mark 1:14-15)

I tell you the truth, anyone who will not receive the kingdom of God like a little child will never enter it." (Mark 10:15)

Looking at his disciples, he said: "Blessed are you who are poor, for yours is the kingdom of God. (Luke 6:20)

In reply Jesus declared, "I tell you the truth, no one can see the kingdom of God unless he is born again."...Jesus answered, "I tell you the truth, no one can enter the kingdom of God unless he is born of water and the Spirit. (John 3:3, 5)

When Jesus saw that he had answered wisely, he said to him, "You are not far from the kingdom of God." And from then on no one dared ask him any more questions. (Mark 12:34)

"I tell you the truth," Jesus said to them, "no one who has left home or wife or brothers or parents or children for the sake of the kingdom of God will fail to receive many times as much in this age and, in the age to come, eternal life." (Luke 18:29-30)

For the kingdom of God is not a matter of eating and drinking, but of righteousness, peace and joy in the Holy Spirit, (Rom 14:17)

5 (11:21-22) **Satan—Jesus Christ, Destroys Satan**: Illustration 4—a stronger man. Jesus claimed to be stronger than Satan.

1. Satan is the strong man. Note he is armed.
2. Satan's "possessions" are men who are subjected to him: men who follow the way of the world, that is, selfishness, the rejection of God, and rebellion against righteousness.
3. Satan works to keep his palace (kingdom) and "possessions" in peace, that is, under his rule and reign. There is some *peace and comfort* in Satan's realm. Satan will give pleasures to secure a person in his kingdom. But note, it is only for a season (Heb.11:25; 9:27).
4. The stronger Man is Jesus Christ.
   ⇒ Jesus Christ came upon Satan.

He who does what is sinful is of the devil, because the devil has been sinning from the beginning. The reason the Son of God appeared was to destroy the devil's work. (1 John 3:8)

Since the children have flesh and blood, he too shared in their humanity so that by his death he might destroy him who holds the power of death—that is, the devil— and free those who all their lives were held in slavery by their fear of death. (Heb 2:14-15)

⇒ Jesus Christ overcame Satan.

And having disarmed the powers and authorities, he made a public spectacle of them, triumphing over them by the cross. (Col 2:15)

For he has rescued us from the dominion of darkness and brought us into the kingdom of the Son he loves, in whom we have redemption, the forgiveness of sins. (Col 1:13-14)

⇒ Jesus Christ delivered men from Satan's strategies.

Finally, be strong in the Lord and in

his mighty power. Put on the full armor of God so that you can take your stand against the devil's schemes. (Eph 6:10-11; cp. v.12-18).

⇒ Jesus Christ divided Satan's spoils: the spoils of a clear mind, clean body, pure heart, and the gifts of the Spirit.

This is why it says: "When he ascended on high, he led captives in his train and gave gifts to men." (What does "he ascended" mean except that he also descended to the lower, earthly regions ? He who descended is the very one who ascended higher than all the heavens, in order to fill the whole universe.) It was he who gave some to be apostles, some to be prophets, some to be evangelists, and some to be pastors and teachers, (Eph 4:8-11; cp. Gal.5:22-23)

6 (11:23) **Shepherd—Decision—History, Pivotal Point of**: Illustration 5—a shepherd and a flock. Jesus claimed to be the pivotal or decisive figure of history. Gathering and scattering is a picture of the shepherd and his flock. The person who does not stand with Christ does not gather, but scatters the flock. Where a person stands in relation to Jesus Christ determines the success and impact of his life. Jesus Christ is the decisive figure of history that determines a person's destiny (see note—Lk.7:28).

There is *no neutrality* with Christ: a person is either with Him or against Him. A person either fights against evil or against righteousness, either fights for the Kingdom of God or for the kingdom of evil. Standing still is impossible, for standing still is doing nothing for God. Standing still, being neutral, is working for evil by allowing evil to continue and to grow without opposition. A voice of silence is a voice for evil.

You cannot drink the cup of the Lord and the cup of demons too; you cannot have a part in both the Lord's table and the table of demons. (1 Cor 10:21)

He is a double-minded man, unstable in all he does. (James 1:8)

Come near to God and he will come near to you. Wash your hands, you sinners, and purify your hearts, you double-minded. (James 4:8)

Jesus replied, "No one who puts his hand to the plow and looks back is fit for service in the kingdom of God." (Luke 9:62)

"No servant can serve two masters. Either he will hate the one and love the other, or he will be devoted to the one and despise the other. You cannot serve both God and Money." (Luke 16:13)

See, I set before you today life and prosperity, death and destruction. (Deu 30:15)

This day I call heaven and earth as witnesses against you that I have set before you life and death, blessings and curses. Now choose life, so that you and your children may live (Deu 30:19)

Elijah went before the people and said, "How long will you waver between two opinions? If the LORD is God, follow him; but if Baal is God, follow him." But the people said nothing. (1 Ki 18:21)

They worshiped the LORD, but they also served their own gods in accordance with the customs of the nations from which they had been brought. (2 Ki 17:33)

Their heart is deceitful, and now they must bear their guilt. The LORD will demolish their altars and destroy their sacred stones. (Hosea 10:2)

7 (11:24-26) **Reformation—Regeneration—New Birth**: Illustration 6—an empty house. Jesus claimed that a man must turn from self-reformation to Him and be infilled with His very presence. Note three things.

1. What happens when a man casts the evil (spirit) out of his life?

   a. A man experiences many "arid places." No matter where he goes or what he does, there is an emptiness, a void. Nothing seems to fill the evil (spirit) put out of his life.
   b. The evil (spirit) that was in man and has been put aside seeks rest, but finds none. Man's evil spirit, when it is subdued or cast aside, becomes restless. It goes about in *restless wanderings*, yet it finds no rest.
   c. A man always experiences the craving of the evil to return. The evil (spirit) says, "I will return." Note the words, "to the house I left," the place that was so comfortable, that made him feel so good and at ease. He says in essence, "I will return to that which always looked good, tasted good, and felt good."

2. All the above has to do with a man's reforming and cleaning up his life. However, note what happened when the evil (spirit) returned to the man and knocked on the door of his thoughts and pried at the windows of his desires.

   a. He found the house empty and *unoccupied.*
   b. He found the house swept; it was clean and put in order—ready for occupancy. The man had removed all the rubbish and swept out all the dirt. He had cleaned the house (his life), but he had not invited the *tenant* (the Lord Jesus Christ) to move in and occupy the premises.

3. What happened when the evil (spirit) found the house empty and unoccupied?

   a. The evil swarmed and flooded in with more force than ever. The man indulged much more than before.
   b. The evil brought more evil with him—launched out and did more evil than ever.
   c. The evil *dwelt* there. It is unlikely the man would ever clean his house again.

Because of the increase of wickedness, the love of most will grow cold, (Mat 24:12)

Formerly, when you did not know God, you were slaves to those who by nature are not gods. But now that you know God—or rather are known by God—how is it that you are turning back to those weak and miserable principles? Do you wish to be enslaved by them all over again? You are observing special days and months and seasons and years [religious ritual]! (Gal 4:8-10)

While evil men and impostors will go from bad to worse, deceiving and being deceived. (2 Tim 3:13)

If they have escaped the corruption of the world by knowing our Lord and Savior Jesus Christ and are again entangled in it and overcome, they are worse off at the end than they were at the beginning. It would have been better for them not to have known the way of righteousness, than to have known it and then to turn their backs on the sacred command that was passed on to them. (2 Pet 2:20-21)

Yet I hold this against you: You have forsaken your first love. (Rev 2:4)

Thought 1. The answer to being infilled with the presence of Christ is not reformation—not the changing of the outside or the external—but the transformation or regeneration of man's heart. It is the filling of the human heart and of society with Christ Himself and with acts of Christian love and care. The message and acts of love and care are to be carried to a world suffering and reeling in pain and war, doomed to die and to be without God's presence forever.

8 (11:27-28) **Word of God**: the necessary thing is to hear the Word of God and keep it. Luke is the only Gospel writer to mention this incident. Apparently what happened was that some woman in the crowd was caught up in Jesus' teaching and presence. She just exclaimed that a woman who could bear One like Jesus was to be blessed. But note what Jesus said. There is a greater blessing than what even Mary had. Imagine! A greater blessing than being able to testify that one had given birth to Jesus! What is it? "Blessed rather are those who hear the Word of God and obey it" (v.28).

Whoever has my commands and obeys them, he is the one who loves me. He who loves me will be loved by my Father, and I too will love him and show myself to him." (John 14:21)

But the man who looks intently into the perfect law that gives freedom, and continues to do this, not forgetting what he has heard, but doing it—he will be blessed in what he does. (James 1:25)

And receive from him anything we ask, because we obey his commands and do what pleases him. (1 John 3:22)

"Blessed are those who wash their robes, that they may have the right to the tree of life and may go through the gates into the city. (Rev 22:14)

Now if you obey me fully and keep my covenant, then out of all nations you will be my treasured possession. Although the whole earth is mine, (Exo 19:5)

When you are in distress and all these things have happened to you, then in later days you will return to the LORD your God and obey him. For the LORD your God is a merciful God; he will not abandon or destroy you or forget the covenant with your forefathers, which he confirmed to them by oath. (Deu 4:30-31)

Oh, that their hearts would be inclined to fear me and keep all my commands always, so that it might go well with them and their children forever! (Deu 5:29)

And if you walk in my ways and obey my statutes and commands as David your father did, I will give you a long life." (1 Ki 3:14)

If they obey and serve him, they will spend the rest of their days in prosperity and their years in contentment. (Job 36:11)

He who keeps the law is a discerning son, but a companion of gluttons disgraces his father. (Prov 28:7)

	J. The Great Proof that Jesus is the Messiah: The Resurrection, 11:29-36 (Mt.5:14-16; 12:38-42; Mk.4:21-22; cp.Lk.8:16)	stand up at the judgment with this generation and condemn it; for they repented at the preaching of Jonah, and now one greater than Jonah is here.	with Christ's preaching (as Nineveh)
1 The crowds thronged Jesus a. Jesus charged: This is an evil generation b.The reason: They sought a sign **2 The one & only sign: The sign of Jonah, that is, the resurrection**	29 As the crowds increased, Jesus said, "This is a wicked generation. It asks for a miraculous sign, but none will be given it except the sign of Jonah. 30 For as Jonah was a sign to the Ninevites, so also will the Son of Man be to this generation.	33 "No one lights a lamp and puts it in a place where it will be hidden, or under a bowl. Instead he puts it on its stand, so that those who come in may see the light. 34 Your eye is the lamp of your body. When your eyes are good, your whole body also is full of light. But when they are bad, your body also is full of darkness.	**4 The sign's (resurrection) visibility: It is as clearly seen as a shining lamp** a. A fact: A shining lamp is not hid but is placed where it gives light b. A choice: To see the sign (resurrection) with a healthy eye or a diseased eye
3 The sign's (resurrection) effect: It will condemn this evil generation a. Because. they did not seek Christ (as the queen sought wisdom)	31 The Queen of the South will rise at the judgment with the men of this generation and condemn them; for she came from the ends of the earth to listen to Solomon's wisdom, and now one greater than Solomon is here.	35 See to it, then, that the light within you is not darkness. 36 Therefore, if your whole body is full of light, and no part of it dark, it will be completely lighted, as when the	c. A warning: Beware of a diseased eye, of a body full of darkness d. A promise: A healthy eye will give great light
b. Because they did not repent	32 The men of Nineveh will	light of a lamp shines on you."	

DIVISION V

THE SON OF MAN'S GREAT JOURNEY TO JERUSALEM (STAGE I): HIS MISSION AND PUBLIC CHALLENGE, 9:51-13:21

J. The Great Proof that Jesus is the Messiah: The Resurrection, 11:29-36

(11:29-36) **Introduction**: the great proof that Jesus Christ is the Messiah, the Son of the living God, is the resurrection. Men may seek for other proofs and other signs, but God has given this one supreme sign. No other sign will ever be given to man. The resurrection leaves man without excuse.

1. The crowds thronged Jesus (v.29).
2. The one and only sign: the sign of Jonah, that is, the resurrection (v.29-30).
3. The sign's (resurrection) effect: it will condemn this evil generation (v.31-32).
4. The sign's (resurrection) visibility: it is as clearly seen as a shining lamp (v.33-36).

1 (11:29) **Man, Unbelief—Jesus Christ, Deity—Signs**: crowds thronged Jesus. As soon as the crowd settled down, Jesus began to preach, and what He had to say was strong. He made a serious charge against His generation: "This is a wicked generation." Why? They sought a sign.

1. What is wrong with seeking a sign, with seeking some proof that Jesus is who He claims to be? Nothing. There is nothing wrong with seeking evidence that Jesus is the Son of God. The problem is not in seeking evidence; the problem is in seeking *more and more* evidence. Think for a moment. What greater sign could God have given than to *reveal Himself* to man? The greatest sign in all the world was to have God's very own Son stand in the presence of men so that they could see and touch Him.

> **The Word became flesh and made his dwelling among us. We have seen his glory, the glory of the One and Only, who came from the Father, full of grace and truth. John testifies concerning him. He cries out, saying, "This was he of whom I said, 'He who comes after me has surpassed me because he was before me.'" From the fullness of his grace we have all received one blessing after another. (John 1:14-16)**
>
> **That which was from the beginning, which we have heard, which we have seen with our eyes, which we have looked at and our hands have touched—this we proclaim concerning the Word of life. The life appeared; we have seen it and testify to it, and we proclaim to you the eternal life, which was with the Father and has appeared to us. We proclaim to you what we have seen and heard, so that you also may have fellowship with us. And our fellowship is with the Father and with his Son, Jesus Christ. (1 John 1:1-3)**

2. What greater evidence could God give that Jesus is His Son? God met *all the needs of men* while Jesus was among them. The greatest evidence in all the world is seeing Jesus demonstrate the *love and power* of God...

- by feeding the hungry.
- by calming both nature and the fear of men.
- by preaching and teaching as no other man has ever done.
- by healing all manner of sicknesses and infirmities.
- by casting out evil spirits.
- by raising the dead.

> **Blessed are those who hunger and thirst for righteousness, for they will be filled. (Mat 5:6)**
>
> **But whoever drinks the water I give**

him will never thirst. Indeed, the water I give him will become in him a spring of water welling up to eternal life." (John 4:14)

On the last and greatest day of the Feast, Jesus stood and said in a loud voice, "If anyone is thirsty, let him come to me and drink. (John 7:37)

And my God will meet all your needs according to his glorious riches in Christ Jesus. (Phil 4:19)

They feast on the abundance of your house; you give them drink from your river of delights. (Psa 36:8; cp. Ps. 23:1f)

The LORD will guide you always; he will satisfy your needs in a sun-scorched land and will strengthen your frame. You will be like a well-watered garden, like a spring whose waters never fail. (Isa 58:11)

3. What greater proof (sign) could God give that He was bringing salvation to man? God sent His Son into the world to personally save man. What greater evidence could God give than…

- to have His Son live as a Man, living a perfect and sinless life, and by His perfection to secure righteousness for man.
- to have His Son die *for men*.
- to raise His Son from the dead.

The Jews and all men are totally unjustified in seeking additional signs. God has given the greatest signs that could ever be given. If a man rejects the signs already given, he will reject any sign no matter what the sign might be. Signs and evidence are not man's problem. Man's problem is twofold.

1. Man just does not believe because he does not want to believe. He wants to live like he wants, to do his own thing. Man wants no Lord over him, not One who demands all he is and has. Man's heart is hard, and he is obstinate in his unbelief (see notes—Lk.10:21; DEEPER STUDY # 4—Mt.12:24; note—12:31-32).

2. Man does not understand the love and the faith of God, that is, the true religion of God. He fails to see what God is after and has always been after: faith and love, not signs and works. God wants a man to simply believe and love Him because of who He is and because of what He does for man. The true religion of God is not a religion of works and signs, but of faith and love in Christ Jesus, His own Son (see DEEPER STUDY # 2—Jn.2:24; DEEPER STUDY # 1—4:22; note—4:48-49; DEEPER STUDY # 1—Ro.4:1-25; note—4:4-5. Cp. Acts 2:22.)

2 (11:29-30) **Jesus Christ, Deity—Resurrection**: the one and only sign—the sign of Jonah, that is, of the resurrection (cp. v.32). The sign of Jonah pointed to the resurrection of Jesus from the dead (see note—Mt.12:38-40). The resurrection is the *great proof* that Jesus is the Messiah, the Savior of the world. He is "declared with power to be the Son of God…by his resurrection from the dead" (Ro.1:4).

Jesus claimed to be greater than Jonah. He claimed to be the greatest messenger who had ever come, the Messiah Himself. Since His coming, all men are definitely without excuse. The worst sinners in history repented at the preaching of a mere man, the prophet Jonah. Now the Messiah Himself, God's own Son, has come. And He has preached and announced that the Kingdom of God itself is at hand. Every person is now, beyond question, without excuse.

3 (11:31-32) **Jesus Christ, Deity; Resurrection—Queen of Sheba—Seeking Jesus—Wisdom**: the sign's (resurrection) effect—it will condemn this wicked generation. There are two reasons for this:

1. This wicked generation did not seek Jesus, the One who knew the truth. Jesus gave a prime example in the Queen of Sheba of what He meant (cp. 1 Ki.10:1f; 2 Chron.9:1f). The Queen of Sheba demonstrated how a person is to seek the truth and how important it is to seek Christ. She had to seek as diligently and go through as much as anyone ever has in seeking the truth.

a. She had a long and perilous search. She had to travel from "the ends of the earth" to seek the truth.

b. She had extreme responsibility. She was a queen with demanding duties and a busy schedule as the Head of State. As with all Heads of State, she had much demanding her time and presence and depending upon her care, yet she let nothing stop her search for the truth.

c. She had uncertain seeking. Her search was a gamble, uncertain in at least two senses.

⇒ She could not be absolutely certain that Solomon was as wise in the truth as he was said to be. Reputations become exaggerated when spread by word of mouth, and she knew this.

⇒ She had no personal invitation to visit Solomon. Fame flatters men and causes them to become inaccessible in order to enhance their fame of being busy and laden with heavy responsibility and of being surrounded with greatness. She could not be sure he would see her nor grant much time to her.

d. She had to bear terrible prejudice. She was a woman in a man's world. In her day women were nothing more than chattel property, possessed and used by men for their own pleasure as they so desired.

The Queen of Sheba will be used as a testimony in the day of judgment. Her diligent seeking will stand as a testimony against all who fail to seek after Christ. Her seeking will leave all without excuse. There is no distance too far, no road too perilous, no responsibility so important, no question so weighty, no prejudice or opposition so strong that it should keep a person from seeking after Christ. The Queen of Sheba faced all this, yet despite all, she sought the truth. It was the primary drive of her life; therefore, her example leaves everyone without excuse.

But seek first his kingdom and his righteousness, and all these things [provisions] will be given to you as well. (Mat 6:33)

"So I say to you: Ask and it will be given to you; seek and you will find; knock and the door will be opened to you. For everyone who asks receives; he who seeks finds; and to him who knocks, the door will be opened. (Luke 11:9-10; cp. v.5-8)

From one man he made every nation of men, that they should inhabit the whole earth; and he determined the times set for them and the exact places where they should live. God did this so that men would seek him and perhaps reach out for him and find him, though he is not far from each one of us. (Acts 17:26-27)

But if from there you seek the LORD your God, you will find him if you look for

him with all your heart and with all your soul. (Deu 4:29)

"But where can wisdom be found? Where does understanding dwell? (Job 28:12; cp. v. 13-27)

And he said to man, 'The fear of the Lord—that is wisdom, and to shun evil is understanding.'" (Job 28:28)

Look to the LORD and his strength; seek his face always. (Psa 105:4)

And if you call out for insight and cry aloud for understanding, and if you look for it as for silver and search for it as for hidden treasure, then you will understand the fear of the LORD and find the knowledge of God. (Prov 2:3-5)

Seek the LORD while he may be found; call on him while he is near. (Isa 55:6)

For I know the plans I have for you," declares the LORD, "plans to prosper you and not to harm you, plans to give you hope and a future. Then you will call upon me and come and pray to me, and I will listen to you. You will seek me and find me when you seek me with all your heart. (Jer 29:11-13)

This is what the LORD says to the house of Israel: "Seek me and live; (Amos 5:4)

Sow for yourselves righteousness, reap the fruit of unfailing love, and break up your unplowed ground; for it is time to seek the LORD, until he comes and showers righteousness on you. (Hosea 10:12)

Seek the LORD, all you humble of the land, you who do what he commands. Seek righteousness, seek humility; perhaps you will be sheltered on the day of the Lord's anger. (Zep 2:3)

Note that Jesus claimed to be greater than Solomon. He claimed to be the way, the truth, and the life. Imagine! He claimed to be *life* itself (Jn.14:6). He claimed to be the One whom all men must seek and find or else face condemnation.

Since His coming, all men are definitely without excuse. The most improbable person (the Queen of Sheba) went to the farthest extremes possible to seek after the truth from a mere man, Solomon. Now the Messiah, who is *the truth* Himself, has come and revealed the truth of God. Beyond question, every person is now without excuse.

The Word became flesh and made his dwelling among us. We have seen his glory, the glory of the One and Only, who came from the Father, full of grace and truth. (John 1:14)

Jesus answered, "I am the way and the truth and the life. No one comes to the Father except through me. (John 14:6)

Jesus answered: "Don't you know me, Philip, even after I have been among you such a long time? Anyone who has seen me has seen the Father. How can you say, 'Show us the Father'? Don't you believe that I am in the Father, and that the Father is in me? The words I say to you are not just my own. Rather, it is the Father, living in me, who is doing his work. Believe me when I say that I am in the Father and the Father is in me; or at least believe on the evidence of the miracles themselves. (John 14:9-11)

For there is one God and one mediator between God and men, the man Christ Jesus, (1 Tim 2:5)

But the ministry Jesus has received is as superior to theirs as the covenant of which he is mediator is superior to the old one, and it is founded on better promises. (Heb 8:6)

For this reason Christ is the mediator of a new covenant, that those who are called may receive the promised eternal inheritance—now that he has died as a ransom to set them free from the sins committed under the first covenant. (Heb 9:15)

For Christ did not enter a man-made sanctuary that was only a copy of the true one; he entered heaven itself, now to appear for us in God's presence. (Heb 9:24)

To Jesus the mediator of a new covenant, and to the sprinkled blood that speaks a better word than the blood of Abel. See to it that you do not refuse him who speaks. If they did not escape when they refused him who warned them on earth, how much less will we, if we turn away from him who warns us from heaven? (Heb 12:24-25)

My dear children, I write this to you so that you will not sin. But if anybody does sin, we have one who speaks to the Father in our defense—Jesus Christ, the Righteous One. (1 John 2:1)

2. This wicked generation did not repent with Jesus' preaching. Note several things.

a. A whole generation can be evil and adulterous—so evil and adulterous that its life-style and dominant character can be called "wicked and adulterous" (Mt.12:39).
b. The Ninevites gave a prime example of *repentance* and just how essential repentance is. A person must repent or else he shall be condemned.
c. There is a day of judgment out in the future. Note the words, "at the judgment." This phrase points to a definite day of judgment.
d. The Ninevites' repentance will be used as a testimony in the day of judgment. The people of Nineveh are the prime example of people's turning to God from the depth of sin. They had fallen into the pit of sin, as deeply as a people can fall. Yet, they repented at the preaching of Jonah.
e. The Ninevites' repentance leaves all *without excuse*. Why? There is no one who has fallen any deeper into sin than they did, yet they repented. They show that anyone can turn to God from sin no matter how terrible his sin is. No man has an excuse for not turning to God.

Blessed are those who mourn, for they will be comforted. (Mat 5:4)

I tell you, no! But unless you repent, you too will all perish. (Luke 13:3)

Peter replied, "Repent and be baptized, every one of you, in the name of Jesus Christ for the forgiveness of your sins. And you will receive the gift of the Holy Spirit. (Acts 2:38)

Repent, then, and turn to God, so that your sins may be wiped out, that times of re-

freshing may come from the Lord, (Acts 3:19)

Repent of this wickedness and pray to the Lord. Perhaps he will forgive you for having such a thought in your heart. (Acts 8:22)

In the past God overlooked such ignorance, but now he commands all people everywhere to repent. (Acts 17:30)

If my people, who are called by my name, will humble themselves and pray and seek my face and turn from their wicked ways, then will I hear from heaven and will forgive their sin and will heal their land. (2 Chr 7:14)

Let the wicked forsake his way and the evil man his thoughts. Let him turn to the LORD, and he will have mercy on him, and to our God, for he will freely pardon. (Isa 55:7)

Go, proclaim this message toward the north: "'Return, faithless Israel,' declares the LORD, 'I will frown on you no longer, for I am merciful,' declares the LORD, 'I will not be angry forever. (Jer 3:12)

"But if a wicked man turns away from all the sins he has committed and keeps all my decrees and does what is just and right, he will surely live; he will not die. (Ezek 18:21)

Therefore tell the people: This is what the LORD Almighty says: 'Return to me,' declares the LORD Almighty, 'and I will return to you,' says the LORD Almighty. (Zec 1:3)

f. Jesus claimed to be greater, to be superior to Jonah (see note—Lk.11:30).

4 (11:33-36) **Jesus Christ, Resurrection**: the sign's (resurrection) visibility. It is as clearly seen as a shining lamp. Note four points.

1. A fact: a lit lamp is not hid but placed where it can give light and be seen. Jesus said that the lit lamp, the *resurrection*, would not be done in secret nor would it be hidden. Jesus was resurrected openly and publicly so that all who were to "come in may see the light" and be convinced that He is the true Messiah.

2. A choice: to see the sign (resurrection) with a healthy eye or a diseased eye. The healthy eye is the good eye, the eye that concentrates on seeing the light, the way of God and righteousness. The diseased eye is the bad eye, the eye which centers upon the world and material things, the flesh and passion, pleasure and stimulation, self and wealth. Note: the one sign that God has given is dramatically clear: it is the resurrection. God has not kept the sign a secret nor has He hidden it. The sign can be seen just as clearly as a lamp lit in the dark of midnight. The only conceivable thing that can prevent a person from seeing it is an unhealthy or bad eye; and if a person's eye is bad, his whole body is full of darkness, that is, full of evil and death.

3. A warning: beware of a diseased eye, of a body full of darkness. Every man thinks he sees light and has light, sees truth and has truth. Simply said, every man thinks that what he sees (believes) and embraces is the truth. The warning is clear.See to it, then to...

- make sure that what you see is seen with a healthy eye.
- make sure that what is in you is light and not darkness.

The *resurrection is the light of God. Seeing any other light or truth is darkness.* It is looking for light and truth with a diseased eye.

4. A promise: a healthy eye will give great light. Very simply, if a man is "full of light"...

- from having seen the resurrection,
- and allows no part of darkness (doubt, unbelief, false belief) to enter...

...then his whole being shall be full of light. He will be as full of light as the brightest light of a lamp.

Thought 1. Jesus Christ is the Light of the world; He is the Light to which men must open the door of their dark hearts. He is the light which men must take into their sinful lives and world of darkness.

In him was life, and that life was the light of men. (John 1:4)

The true light that gives light to every man was coming into the world. (John 1:9)

When Jesus spoke again to the people, he said, "I am the light of the world. Whoever follows me will never walk in darkness, but will have the light of life." (John 8:12)

Then Jesus told them, "You are going to have the light just a little while longer. Walk while you have the light, before darkness overtakes you. The man who walks in the dark does not know where he is going. (John 12:35)

I have come into the world as a light, so that no one who believes in me should stay in darkness. (John 12:46)

For God, who said, "Let light shine out of darkness," made his light shine in our hearts to give us the light of the knowledge of the glory of God in the face of Christ. (2 Cor 4:6)

For you were once darkness, but now you are light in the Lord. Live as children of light (Eph 5:8)

For it is light that makes everything visible. This is why it is said: "Wake up, O sleeper, rise from the dead, and Christ will shine on you." (Eph 5:14)

So that you may become blameless and pure, children of God without fault in a crooked and depraved generation, in which you shine like stars in the universe (Phil 2:15)

Yet I am writing you a new command; its truth is seen in him and you, because the darkness is passing and the true light is already shining. (1 John 2:8)

The city does not need the sun or the moon to shine on it, for the glory of God gives it light, and the Lamb is its lamp. (Rev 21:23)

The people walking in darkness have seen a great light; on those living in the land of the shadow of death a light has dawned. (Isa 9:2)

"I, the LORD, have called you in righteousness; I will take hold of your hand. I will keep you and will make you to be a covenant for the people and a light for the Gentiles, to open eyes that are blind, to free captives from prison and to release from the dungeon those who sit in darkness. (Isa 42:6-7; cp. Mt.4:14-16; Lk.1:79)

	K. The Severe Charges Against Religionists, 11:37-54 (cp. Mt.23:13-36; Mk.12: 38-40)	46 Jesus replied, "And you experts in the law, woe to you, because you load people down with burdens they can hardly carry, and you yourselves will not lift one finger to help them.	a. A lawyer's (an expert in the law) spiritual blindness b. Jesus' charge
1 A Pharisee invited Jesus to dine a. Jesus accepted the invitation	37 When Jesus had finished speaking, a Pharisee invited him to eat with him; so he went in and reclined at the table.	47 "Woe to you, because you build tombs for the prophets, and it was your forefathers who killed them.	**7 Charge 6: Religionists honor the true prophets of God—so long as they are dead**
b. Jesus was questioned about ceremonial cleanliness	38 But the Pharisee, noticing that Jesus did not first wash before the meal, was surprised.	48 So you testify that you approve of what your forefathers did; they killed the prophets, and you build their tombs.	a. The honor of the past servants of God
2 Charge 1: Religionists are ceremonially clean, but inwardly unclean a. They clean the outside & not the inside	39 Then the Lord said to him, "Now then, you Pharisees clean the outside of the cup and dish, but inside you are full of greed and wickedness.	49 Because of this, God in his wisdom said, 'I will send them prophets and apostles, some of whom they will kill and others they will persecute.'	b. The rejection of the present servants of God
b. God made both the outside & the inside (heart) of man	40 You foolish people! Did not the one who made the outside make the inside also?		
c. The giving of one's heart cleanses everything	41 But give what is inside the dish to the poor, and everything will be clean for you.	50 Therefore this generation will be held responsible for the blood of all the prophets that has been shed since the beginning of the world,	
3 Charge 2: Religionists obey God in tithing but ignore justice & love	42 "Woe to you Pharisees, because you give God a tenth of your mint, rue and all other kinds of garden herbs, but you neglect justice and the love of God. You should have practiced the latter without leaving the former undone.	51 From the blood of Abel to the blood of Zechariah, who was killed between the altar and the sanctuary. Yes, I tell you, this generation will be held responsible for it all.	c. The judgment to be required[DS1,2]
4 Charge 3: Religionists crave prominence & honor	43 "Woe to you Pharisees, because you love the most important seats in the synagogues and greetings in the marketplaces.	52 "Woe to you experts in the law, because you have taken away the key to knowledge. You yourselves have not entered, and you have hindered those who were entering."	**8 Charge 7: Religionists have taken away the key to the truth about God**
5 Charge 4: Religionists mislead others, causing them to become unclean & corrupt	44 "Woe to you, because you are like unmarked graves, which men walk over without knowing it."	53 When Jesus left there, the Pharisees and the teachers of the law began to oppose him fiercely and to besiege him with questions,	**9 Conclusion: A reaction of hostility and opposition toward Jesus**
6 Charge 5: Religionists burden men with rules & regulations	45 One of the experts in the law answered him, "Teacher, when you say these things, you insult us also."	54 Waiting to catch him in something he might say.	

DIVISION V

THE SON OF MAN'S GREAT JOURNEY TO JERUSALEM (STAGE I):HIS MISSION AND PUBLIC CHALLENGE, 9:51-13:21

K. The Severe Charges Against Religionists, 11:37-54

(11:37-54) **Introduction**: most people feel they are *religious*. For that reason, the religious person needs to pay close attention to what Jesus says in this passage. The religious person needs to examine his heart and life to make sure his religion is genuine. Jesus was severe in His charges against false religionists. (See outline and notes—Mt.23:1-12; 23:13-36; Lk.15:25-32; 18:9-12; Ro.2:17-29 for more discussion and application.)

1. A Pharisee invited Jesus to dine (v.37-38).
2. Charge 1: religionists are ceremonially clean, but inwardly unclean (v.39-41).
3. Charge 2: religionists obey God in tithing, but ignore justice and love (v.42).
4. Charge 3: religionists crave prominence and honor (v.43).
5. Charge 4: religionists mislead others to become unclean and corrupted (v.44).
6. Charge 5: religionists burden men with rules and regulations (v.45-46).
7. Charge 6: religionists honor the true prophets of God—so long as they are dead (v.47-51).
8. Charge 7: religionists have taken away the key to the truth about God (v.52).
9. Conclusion: a reaction of hostility (v.53-54).

1 (11:37-38) **Scribal Law—Washing the Hands**: a Pharisee invited Jesus to dine with him. The Pharisee had probably been in the audience of Jesus and had become interested in Jesus' teaching. He wanted to talk personally with Jesus, so he invited Him to a meal. What happened was this. When Jesus entered the man's home, He went straight to the food and sat down to eat; He did not wash His hands. This astonished the Pharisee, for it was a serious violation of religious law. It had nothing to do with cleanliness, but with ceremonial purity. It was taught that a person's hands had been in contact with a sinful world; therefore, the person was to wash his hands before eating to prevent impurity from entering into his body. The Pharisee (religionist) was thinking to himself that Jesus had seriously violated the law of purity. Jesus, of course, knew His thoughts and began to reply. His reply was in the form of seven severe charges.

2 (11:39-41) **Religionists—Heart, Good vs. Evil—Depravity—Ritual—Self-righteousness**: the first charge was that religionists were clean ceremonially but unclean within. They kept their religious ceremonies, but they did nothing about the human heart.

1. Religionists cleaned the outside and not the inside. They treated religion like a person who would be washing dishes. The person washed the outside of the cup and platter but left the inside dirty. The heart of the religionist was full of...

- greed (harpazo), which means plunder, seizing, extortion, robbery, taking by force.
- wickedness (ponerias).

Most religionists deny, just as they did in the day of Jesus, that they plunder and do wickedness. But note: Jesus said that a religionist not only does these things but he is full of plunder and wickedness. What did Jesus mean? A religionist is *plundering* the way of God, trying to *seize* God's kingdom his own way instead of following the way of God. He is committing extortion against God by robbing God of the salvation He has set up. The religionist is "full of...wickedness," that is, disobeying God and refusing to follow Jesus, who is the way of righteousness established by God (Ro.10:3-4; Ph.3:9). Instead of coming to God by the Messiah, a religionist comes to God by his own righteousness. He tries to make himself clean by keeping the religious ceremonies and worship. (See note—Mt.23:25-26 for more discussion and a different explanation.)

Thought 1. Note two critical lessons that must be heeded by the religionists.

1) Jesus Christ is God's righteousness.

Since they did not know the righteousness that comes from God and sought to establish their own, they did not submit to God's righteousness. Christ is the end of the law so that there may be righteousness for everyone who believes. Moses describes in this way the righteousness that is by the law: "The man who does these things will live by them." (Rom 10:3-5)

But now a righteousness from God, apart from law [and works], has been made known, to which the Law and the Prophets testify. This righteousness from God comes through faith in Jesus Christ to all who believe. There is no difference, for all have sinned and fall short of the glory of God, and are justified freely by his grace through the redemption that came by Christ Jesus. God presented him as a sacrifice of atonement, through faith in his blood. He did this to demonstrate his justice, because in his forbearance he had left the sins committed beforehand unpunished— (Rom 3:21-25)

[That I may] be found in him, not having a righteousness of my own that comes from the law, but that which is through faith in Christ—the righteousness that comes from God and is by faith. (Phil 3:9)

2) A man, religious or non-religious, cannot establish his own righteousness. He cannot make himself clean enough to approach God: not by works, nor by religious ceremony and worship, nor by cleaning up the outside of his platter or life.

For I tell you that unless your righteousness surpasses that of the Pharisees and the teachers of the law, you will certainly not enter the kingdom of heaven. (Mat 5:20)

Many will say to me on that day, 'Lord, Lord, did we not prophesy in your name, and in your name drive out demons and perform many miracles?' Then I will tell them plainly, 'I never knew you. Away from me, you evildoers!' (Mat 7:22-23)

Therefore no one will be declared righteous in his sight by observing the law; rather, through the law we become conscious of sin. (Rom 3:20)

Know that a man is not justified by observing the law, but by faith in Jesus Christ. So we, too, have put our faith in Christ Jesus that we may be justified by faith in Christ and not by observing the law, because by observing the law no one will be justified. (Gal 2:16)

For it is by grace you have been saved, through faith—and this not from yourselves, it is the gift of God—not by works, so that no one can boast. (Eph 2:8-9)

Who has saved us and called us to a holy life—not because of anything we have done but because of his own purpose and grace. This grace was given us in Christ Jesus before the beginning of time, (2 Tim 1:9)

But when the kindness and love of God our Savior appeared, he saved us, not because of righteous things we had done, but because of his mercy. He saved us through the washing of rebirth and renewal by the Holy Spirit, whom he poured out on us generously through Jesus Christ our Savior, so that, having been justified by his grace, we might become heirs having the hope of eternal life. (Titus 3:4-7)

2. God made both the outside and the inside (the heart) of man. Jesus said the outside is not all that is unclean. The inside is also unclean and must be cleansed to become acceptable to God. Note that He calls religionists "foolish people." God made the whole man, the heart as well as the body. A man has to give God a clean heart and a clean body, a spiritual heart as well as a religious body.

Thought 1. The heart is the source of evil; therefore, it has to be cleansed by Christ—even the heart of the religionist.

For from within, out of men's hearts, come evil thoughts, sexual immorality, theft, murder, adultery, (Mark 7:21)

See to it, brothers, that none of you has a sinful, unbelieving heart that turns away from the living God. (Heb 3:12)

But there were also false prophets among the people, just as there will be false teachers among you. They will secretly introduce destructive heresies, even denying the sovereign Lord who bought them—bringing swift destruction on themselves. Many will follow their shameful ways and will bring the way of truth into disrepute. In their greed these teachers will exploit you with stories they have made up. Their condemnation has long been hanging over them, and their destruction has not been sleeping....[These false teachers] have left the straight way and wandered off to follow the way of Balaam son of Beor, who loved the wages of wickedness. (2 Pet 2:1-3,15; cp. v. 1-22)

This is the evil in everything that happens under the sun: The same destiny overtakes all. The hearts of men, moreover, are full of evil and there is madness in their hearts while they live, and afterward they join the dead. (Eccl 9:3)

The heart is deceitful above all things and beyond cure. Who can understand it? (Jer 17:9)

3. The giving of one's heart cleanses everything. Note what Jesus said: "Give what is inside the dish to the poor." The one thing that a man has which he can give is his heart. If he gives his heart to God, then he will become clean in all things. He will be giving instead of taking, giving to God and giving to men. Simply stated, Jesus said that a man is...

- to give *all he is* to God, by which he *will become* clean within.
- to give *all he has* to God, by which he *will demonstrate* that he is clean within.

That if you confess with your mouth, "Jesus is Lord," and believe in your heart that God raised him from the dead, you will be saved. For it is with your heart that you believe and are justified, and it is with your mouth that you confess and are saved. (Rom 10:9-10)

But thanks be to God that, though you used to be slaves to sin, you wholeheartedly obeyed the form of teaching to which you were entrusted. You have been set free from sin and have become slaves to righteousness. When you were slaves to sin, you were free from the control of righteousness. What benefit did you reap at that time from the things you are now ashamed of? Those things result in death! But now that you have been set free from sin and have become slaves to God, the benefit you reap leads to holiness, and the result is eternal life. For the wages of sin is death, but the gift of God is eternal life in Christ Jesus our Lord. (Rom 6:17-18, 20-23)

But the seed on good soil stands for those with a noble and good heart, who hear the word, retain it, and by persevering produce a crop. (Luke 8:15)

Let us draw near to God with a sincere heart in full assurance of faith, having our hearts sprinkled to cleanse us from a guilty conscience and having our bodies washed with pure water. Let us hold unswervingly to the hope we profess, for he who promised is faithful. (Heb 10:22-23)

He [a lawyer] answered: "'Love the Lord your God with all your heart and with all your soul and with all your strength and with all your mind' ; and, 'Love your neighbor as yourself.'" "You have answered correctly," Jesus replied. "Do this and you will live." (Luke 10:27-28)

3 (11:42) **Tithe—Justice—God, Love of—Poor—Oppressed**: the second charge was that religionists obeyed God in tithing but ignored justice and love. Note several things.

1. The religionists took tithing very seriously. Tithing is the command of God and was meant to be a joyful experience (Dt.14:22-23; Lev.27:30). The religionists wanted to make sure they did exactly what God wanted, so they went beyond what God required. They tithed every little thing, even the plants of their gardens and the little potted plants they might have in their homes. (See DEEPER STUDY # 6, Tithe—Mt.23:23 for more discussion.)

2. Jesus did not say that going beyond the tithe is wrong. In fact, God demands everything (see outline and notes—Mt.19:16-22. Cp. Lk.9:23.) Jesus was not discussing the tithe; He was simply using the tithe to illustrate His point.

3. The point was that religionists stressed outward duties such as tithing and ceremony, ritual and ordinances, works and form; but they neglected the inward duties such as *justice and love of God.*

⇒ *Justice* is the way we treat others. Religionists and their church organizations are the recipients of the tithe and offerings of God's people. The monies and gifts are too often coveted for oneself and the building of one's organization more than for ministering to the poor, the oppressed, and the lost. Too often monies are kept for extravagant buildings and livelihoods and personal comfort—monies that God wants used to feed the hungry, clothe the naked, house the orphan, care for the widows and reach the lost. Such extravagance and misuse of the tithe reveals an unjust heart. It is cheating the needy of the world. It is as Jesus said, passing over justice. It is overlooking what is right and just in a world that just reels under the weight of millions who are in desperate need.

⇒ *The love of God* is both the love He has given us in Christ and the love we are to have for Him and others.

Jesus answered, "If you want to be perfect, go, sell your possessions and give to the poor, and you will have

treasure in heaven. Then come, follow me." (Mat 19:21)

And the second is like it: 'Love your neighbor as yourself.' (Mat 22:39)

Love must be sincere. Hate what is evil; cling to what is good. (Rom 12:9)

Let no debt remain outstanding, except the continuing debt to love one another, for he who loves his fellow-man has fulfilled the law. (Rom 13:8)

Masters, provide your slaves with what is right and fair, because you know that you also have a Master in heaven. (Col 4:1)

Suppose a brother or sister is without clothes and daily food. If one of you says to him, "Go, I wish you well; keep warm and well fed," but does nothing about his physical needs, what good is it? (James 2:15-16)

Do not take advantage of a hired man [employee] who is poor and needy, whether he is a brother Israelite or an alien living in one of your towns. (Deu 24:14)

If there is a poor man among your brothers in any of the towns of the land that the LORD your God is giving you, do not be hardhearted or tightfisted toward your poor brother. (Deu 15:7)

Follow justice and justice alone, so that you may live and possess the land the LORD your God is giving you. (Deu 16:20)

For the director of music. A psalm of David. Blessed is he who has regard for the weak; the LORD delivers him in times of trouble. (Psa 41:1)

Do not trust in extortion or take pride in stolen goods; though your riches increase, do not set your heart on them. (Psa 62:10)

Defend the cause of the weak and fatherless; maintain the rights of the poor and oppressed. (Psa 82:3)

He who despises his neighbor sins, but blessed is he who is kind to the needy. (Prov 14:21)

He who oppresses the poor shows contempt for their Maker, but whoever is kind to the needy honors God. (Prov 14:31)

He who is kind to the poor lends to the LORD, and he will reward him for what he has done. (Prov 19:17)

To do what is right and just is more acceptable to the LORD than sacrifice. (Prov 21:3)

If a man shuts his ears to the cry of the poor, he too will cry out and not be answered. (Prov 21:13)

He who oppresses the poor to increase his wealth and he who gives gifts to the rich—both come to poverty. (Prov 22:16)

To show partiality is not good— yet a man will do wrong for a piece of bread. (Prov 28:21)

If you see the poor oppressed in a district, and justice and rights denied, do not be surprised at such things; for one official is eyed by a higher one, and over them both are others higher still. (Eccl 5:8)

This is what the LORD says: "Maintain justice and do what is right, for my salvation is close at hand and my righteousness will soon be revealed. (Isa 56:1)

He defended the cause of the poor and needy, and so all went well. Is that not what it means to know me?" declares the LORD. (Jer 22:16)

"This is what the LORD Almighty says: 'Administer true justice; show mercy and compassion to one another. Do not oppress the widow or the fatherless, the alien or the poor. In your hearts do not think evil of each other.' (Zec 7:9-10)

4 (11:43) **Self-seeking—Tithes—Honor—Position**: the third charge was that religionists crave prominence and honor. Jesus mentioned two things.

1. Religionists loved the most prominent positions and seats. In the synagogues they sat at the front, facing the congregation. Every church has its individuals who seek prominent positions and seats.

2. They loved the titles that honored and recognized them. In Jesus' day it was "Rabbi" or "Teacher." In our day it is the various titles we give to honor a man above others. However, Jesus did not say that position or title is wrong. It is the *love* of these that is condemned. But we must be open with ourselves and search our hearts honestly.

How can you believe if you accept praise from one another, yet make no effort to obtain the praise that comes from the only God? (John 5:44)

For, "All men are like grass, and all their glory is like the flowers of the field; the grass withers and the flowers fall, (1 Pet 1:24)

I wrote to the church, but Diotrephes, who loves to be first, will have nothing to do with us. (3 John 1:9)

But man, despite his riches, does not endure; he is like the beasts that perish. This is the fate of those who trust in themselves, and of their followers, who approve their sayings. Selah (Psa 49:12-13)

For he will take nothing with him when he dies, his splendor will not descend with him. (Psa 49:17)

Man's fate is like that of the animals; the same fate awaits them both: As one dies, so dies the other. All have the same breath ; man has no advantage over the animal. Everything is meaningless. (Eccl 3:19)

Therefore the grave enlarges its appetite and opens its mouth without limit; into it will descend their nobles and masses with all their brawlers and revelers. (Isa 5:14)

5 (11:44) **Sin, Misleading Others—Hypocrisy**: the fourth charge was that religionists misled others and made them unclean and corrupt. Again, Jesus was talking about ceremonial and religious uncleanness. A man was considered to be unclean and corrupt if he walked over a grave. Therefore, men were walking over them and not aware of the defilement and corruption they were picking up. Note exactly what Jesus said. Religionists were as graves, as men declared dead and buried, but their graves were unmarked. People could not look at the religionists and tell that they were misleading people and corrupting them. (See note—Mt.23:27-28 for more discussion.)

> **In the same way, on the outside you appear to people as righteous but on the inside you are full of hypocrisy and wickedness. (Mat 23:28)**
>
> **Meanwhile, when a crowd of many thousands had gathered, so that they were trampling on one another, Jesus began to speak first to his disciples, saying: "Be on your guard against the yeast of the Pharisees, which is hypocrisy. There is nothing concealed that will not be disclosed, or hidden that will not be made known. (Luke 12:1-2)**
>
> **For it is shameful even to mention what the disobedient do in secret. (Eph 5:12)**
>
> **The Spirit clearly says that in later times some will abandon the faith and follow deceiving spirits and things taught by demons. Such teachings come through hypocritical liars, whose consciences have been seared as with a hot iron. (1 Tim 4:1-2)**
>
> **They claim to know God, but by their actions they deny him. They are detestable, disobedient and unfit for doing anything good. (Titus 1:16)**

6 (11:45-46) **Burdens—Rules and Regulations—Word of God, Adding to**: the fifth charge was that religionists burdened men with rules and regulations. Note three things.

1. A lawyer or legal expert, up to this point, had excluded himself and his profession. He was applying all that Jesus was saying to someone else. It never dawned upon him that Jesus could be talking to him! All of a sudden something struck the lawyer's mind, and he felt Jesus was including his profession. Jesus proceeded to leave no doubt in anyone's mind. He was speaking to all who put religion, ritual, ceremony, heritage, and anything else before God. Man's duty, even the duty of religionists, is to turn his heart and being over to God.

2. Jesus now charged the religionist with creating man-made rules and regulations. Jesus was speaking of the Scribal law (see DEEPER STUDY # 1—Lk.6:2). The Scribal law was considered even more important than the Word of God itself. In the minds of the religionists, the law of God was sometimes hard to understand, but not the rules and regulations of the religionists. Therefore, any breaking of the Scribal law was considered deliberate and much more serious. Jesus also charged the religionists with failing to lift one finger to help a man in keeping the law. Instead of helping the man, the religionist condemned the man.

> **But everyone who hears these words of mine and does not put them into practice is like a foolish man who built his house on sand. The rain came down, the streams rose, and the winds blew and beat against that house, and it fell with a great crash." (Mat 7:26-27)**
>
> **"That servant who knows his master's will and does not get ready or does not do what his master wants will be beaten with many blows. (Luke 12:47)**
>
> **Anyone, then, who knows the good he ought to do and doesn't do it, sins. (James 4:17)**
>
> **You, then, who teach others, do you not teach yourself? You who preach against stealing, do you steal? (Rom 2:21)**

3. Jesus said that the Law, the Word of God, was adequate by itself. Man did not have to add rules and regulation to it. (See note—Mt.23:4 for more discussion.)

7 (11:47-51) **Heritage—Roots**: the sixth charge was that religionists honored the true prophets of God as long as they were dead.

1. The religionists honored the past. They showed great respect for the prophets of old—renovating, adorning, and looking after their tombs and relics. They took great pride in their roots.

> **Produce fruit in keeping with repentance. And do not begin to say to yourselves, 'We have Abraham as our father.' For I tell you that out of these stones God can raise up children for Abraham. (Luke 3:8)**
>
> **They answered him, "We are Abraham's descendants and have never been slaves of anyone. How can you say that we shall be set free?" (John 8:33)**
>
> **"Abraham is our father," they answered. "If you were Abraham's children," said Jesus, "then you would do the things Abraham did. (John 8:39)**
>
> **Then they hurled insults at him and said, "You are this fellow's disciple! We are disciples of Moses! (John 9:28)**

2. The religionists, however, rejected the present. They *rejected the teaching and godly lives* of the prophets and apostles whom God sent. They reverenced the past—Abraham and Moses, Jeremiah and Zachariah—but they rejected God's very own Son. In rejecting Him, they bore witness that they were just as their father's were: murderers (v.48).

> **Then the Pharisees went out and began to plot with the Herodians how they might kill Jesus. (Mark 3:6)**
>
> **The chief priests and the teachers of the law heard this and began looking for a way to kill him, for they feared him, because the whole crowd was amazed at his teaching. (Mark 11:18)**
>
> **Now the Passover and the Feast of Unleavened Bread were only two days away, and the chief priests and the teachers of the law were looking for some sly way to arrest Jesus and kill him. "But not during the Feast," they said, "or the people may riot." (Mark 14:1-2)**

3. The judgment upon religionists will be more severe than upon others. The blood of all the prophets, ranging from Abel to Zechariah, will fall upon their head. Why the blood of all? Because Jesus' generation had the greatest privilege and opportunity known to man. God's Son Himself, the summit of the prophets, now stood before the world, in particular before the religionists. To reject Him was to reject all the prophets. He was *the One Prophet* who embraced all prophets, the One to whom all prophets had looked. (See notes—-Mt.23:29-33; 23:34-36; DEEPER STUDY # 10, 11—23:35; DEEPER STUDY # 12—23:36.)

> **For the Son of Man is going to come in his Father's glory with his angels, and then he will reward each person according to what he has done. (Mat 16:27)**
>
> **But because of your stubbornness and your unrepentant heart, you are storing up wrath against yourself for the day of God's wrath, when his righteous judgment will be revealed. God "will give to each person according to what he has done." (Rom 2:5-6)**
>
> **For we must all appear before the judgment seat of Christ, that each one may receive what is due him for the things done while in the body, whether good or bad. (2 Cor 5:10)**
>
> **Since you call on a Father who judges each man's work impartially, live your lives as strangers here in reverent fear. (1 Pet 1:17)**
>
> **I will strike her children dead. Then all the churches will know that I am he who searches hearts and minds, and I will repay each of you according to your deeds. (Rev 2:23)**
>
> **And I saw the dead, great and small, standing before the throne, and books were opened. Another book was opened, which is the book of life. The dead were judged according to what they had done as recorded in the books. (Rev 20:12; cp. Rev 22:12)**
>
> **And that you, O Lord, are loving. Surely you will reward each person according to what he has done. (Psa 62:12)**
>
> **If you say, "But we knew nothing about this," does not he who weighs the heart perceive it? Does not he who guards your life know it? Will he not repay each person according to what he has done? (Prov 24:12)**
>
> **"I the LORD search the heart and examine the mind, to reward a man according to his conduct, according to what his deeds deserve." (Jer 17:10)**
>
> **Great are your purposes and mighty are your deeds. Your eyes are open to all the ways of men; you reward everyone according to his conduct and as his deeds deserve. (Jer 32:19)**
>
> **"Therefore, O house of Israel, I will judge you, each one according to his ways, declares the Sovereign LORD. Repent! Turn away from all your offenses; then sin will not be your downfall. (Ezek 18:30)**

DEEPER STUDY # 1
(11:51) **Zechariah**: see DEEPER STUDY # 11—Mt.23:35.

DEEPER STUDY # 2
(11:51) **Abel**: cp. Gen.4:8.

8 (11:52) **Religionists—Stumbling Block—Teachers, False**: the seventh charge was that religionists had taken away the key to the truth about God. They had taken away the key that unlocked the Scriptures and the way to God.

⇒ They stressed the external, the ceremony, the religious form over the heart and repentance, the Scripture and obedience.

⇒ They turned men away from the Scripture to their own ideas and thoughts, rules and regulations.

> **Jesus replied, "You are in error because you do not know the Scriptures or the power of God. (Mat 22:29)**
>
> **Unlike so many, we do not peddle the word of God for profit. On the contrary, in Christ we speak before God with sincerity, like men sent from God. (2 Cor 2:17)**
>
> **He writes the same way in all his [Paul's] letters, speaking in them of these matters. His letters contain some things that are hard to understand, which ignorant and unstable people distort, as they do the other Scriptures, to their own destruction. (2 Pet 3:16)**

Note that some persons were entering into the truth until the religionists got hold of them. The religionist stopped them from entering.

> **"Woe to you, teachers of the law and Pharisees, you hypocrites! You shut the kingdom of heaven in men's faces. You yourselves do not enter, nor will you let those enter who are trying to. (Mat 23:13)**
>
> **"For the lips of a priest ought to preserve knowledge, and from his mouth men should seek instruction—because he is the messenger of the LORD Almighty. But you have turned from the way and by your teaching have caused many to stumble; you have violated the covenant with Levi," says the LORD Almighty. (Mal 2:7-8)**

9 (11:53-54) **Jesus Christ, Response to**: the conclusion was hostility and opposition. The religionists could not accept the truth. They were incensed and set aflame against Jesus. They tried to trap Him so they could arrest and stop Him.

	CHAPTER 12 **L. The Things Men Should Fear, 12:1-12**
1 Many thousands of people gathered around Jesus	Meanwhile, when a crowd of many thousands had gath- ered, so that they were trampling on one another, Je-
2 Message 1: To the disciples—fear hypocrisy[DS1]	sus began to speak first to his disciples, saying: "Be on your guard against the yeast of the Pharisees, which is hypocrisy.
a. Deeds are to be exposed	2 There is nothing concealed that will not be disclosed, or hidden that will not be made known.
b. Words are to be exposed	3 What you have said in the dark will be heard in the day- light, and what you have whispered in the ear in the inner rooms will be pro- claimed from the roofs.
3 Message 2: To the friends of Christ—what to fear[DS2] a. Do not fear men, but God and God alone	4 "I tell you, my friends, do not be afraid of those who kill the body and after that can do no more. 5 But I will show you whom you should fear: Fear him who, after the killing of the body, has power to throw you into hell. Yes, I tell you, fear him.
b. Do not fear the lack of necessities: God cares	6 Are not five sparrows sold for two pennies ? Yet not one of them is forgotten by God. 7 Indeed, the very hairs of your head are all numbered. Don't be afraid; you are worth more than many sparrows.
c. Fear the spirit of disloyalty, of denying Christ	8 "I tell you, whoever ac- knowledges me before men, the Son of Man will also ac- knowledge him before the angels of God. 9 But he who disowns me before men will be disowned before the angels of God.
d. Fear the unpardonable sin	10 And everyone who speaks a word against the Son of Man will be forgiven, but anyone who blasphemes against the Holy Spirit will not be forgiven.
e. Do not fear persecution & trials: The Holy Spirit empowers	11 "When you are brought before synagogues, rulers and authorities, do not worry about how you will defend yourselves or what you will say, 12 For the Holy Spirit will teach you at that time what you should say."

DIVISION V

THE SON OF MAN'S GREAT JOURNEY TO JERUSALEM (STAGE I): HIS MISSION AND PUBLIC CHALLENGE, 9:51-13:21

L. The Things Men Should Fear, 12:1-12

(12:1-12) **Introduction**: there are things to fear in life, some very serious things. However, there is a vast difference between what men usually fear and what God says to fear. The things men fear are usually of their own making, and men would not have to fear them if they trusted God (war, deception, evil, stealing, bankruptcy, and other fears of men).

Jesus covered what men *should* fear. Note: He spoke first to the disciples (v.1-3), then to His *friends* (v.4-12). There was one thing in particular that His disciples needed to fear, and that one thing needs to be feared by everyone. That one thing is hypocrisy.

1. Many thousands of people gathered around Jesus (v.1).
2. Message 1: to the disciples—fear hypocrisy (v.1-3).
3. Message 2: to the friends of Christ—what to fear (v.4-12).

1 (12:1) **Jesus Christ, Crowds Followed**: a vast crowd now gathered around Jesus, a crowd so large it could not be numbered. Many thousands (muriadon) is the Greek word. Note: so many had gathered that they were pushing and stepping upon each other. They were so eager to hear the Word of God that they were trying to get as close as possible.

> **Thought 1.** What a lesson for modern man—to be so hungry for the Word of God that we flock to His preaching and struggle to get up front!

2 (12:1-3) **Hypocrisy—Sin, Exposed**: the first message was to the disciples of Christ. He said, "Fear hypocrisy." Hypocrisy was the leaven or yeast of the religionists. (See DEEPER STUDY # 3—Mt.16:12; note and DEEPER STUDY # 1,2—Mk.8:15 for more discussion and application.)

1. The religionists, surprisingly, were the ones who were guilty of hypocrisy, that is, saying one thing and doing another. (See DEEPER STUDY # 2, Hypocrisy—Mt.23:13.) They claimed to be followers of God, to lead men to God…

- in their ceremony and ritual.
- in their form of worship and teaching.
- in their doctrine and preaching.

However, Jesus said that what the religionists were doing was hypocrisy, for religious form is not God's way of salvation.

> **You hypocrites! Isaiah was right when he prophesied about you: "'These people honor me with their lips, but their hearts are far from me. They worship me in vain; their teachings are but rules taught by men.'" (Mat 15:7-9)**
>
> **"Woe to you, teachers of the law and Pharisees, you hypocrites! You shut the kingdom of heaven in men's faces. You yourselves do not enter, nor will you let those enter who are trying to. (Mat 23:13)**

In the same way, on the outside you appear to people as righteous but on the inside you are full of hypocrisy and wickedness. (Mat 23:28)

"Why do you look at the speck of sawdust in your brother's eye and pay no attention to the plank in your own eye? How can you say to your brother, 'Brother, let me take the speck out of your eye,' when you yourself fail to see the plank in your own eye? You hypocrite, first take the plank out of your eye, and then you will see clearly to remove the speck from your brother's eye. "No good tree bears bad fruit, nor does a bad tree bear good fruit. (Luke 6:41-43)

Hypocrites! You know how to interpret the appearance of the earth and the sky. How is it that you don't know how to interpret this present time? "Why don't you judge for yourselves what is right? (Luke 12:56-57)

I urge you, brothers, to watch out for those who cause divisions and put obstacles in your way that are contrary to the teaching you have learned. Keep away from them. For such people are not serving our Lord Christ, but their own appetites. By smooth talk and flattery they deceive the minds of naive people. (Rom 16:17-18)

The Spirit clearly says that in later times some will abandon the faith and follow deceiving spirits and things taught by demons. Such teachings come through hypocritical liars, whose consciences have been seared as with a hot iron. (1 Tim 4:1-2)

They claim to know God, but by their actions they deny him. They are detestable, disobedient and unfit for doing anything good. (Titus 1:16)

For he is the kind of man who is always thinking about the cost. "Eat and drink," he says to you, but his heart is not with you. (Prov 23:7)

2. The religionists' hypocrisy was like yeast or leaven (see DEEPER STUDY # 1, Yeast—Leaven—Lk.12:1).

Then they understood that he was not telling them to guard against the yeast used in bread, but against the teaching of the Pharisees and Sadducees. (Mat 16:12)

See to it that no one takes you captive through hollow and deceptive philosophy, which depends on human tradition and the basic principles of this world rather than on Christ. (Col 2:8)

Do not be carried away by all kinds of strange teachings. It is good for our hearts to be strengthened by grace, not by ceremonial foods, which are of no value to those who eat them. (Heb 13:9)

The disciples of Jesus were the ones in particular who were to fear hypocrisy. Why? Because they were the teachers, the preachers of righteousness. They were both to proclaim the truth and live the truth.

1. The disciples' deeds were to be exposed. There is nothing covered or hid that will remain so. Every act—whether done behind closed doors, in the dark, placed in a file or deposit box, or written in a book, pamphlet or letter—will be revealed and known.

2. The disciples' words were to be exposed. There is no word that will not be heard and proclaimed for all to hear. Every word—whether spoken in the dark or whispered in the ear of someone or just conceived in the mind—will come to light.

For there is nothing hidden that will not be disclosed, and nothing concealed that will not be known or brought out into the open. (Luke 8:17)

But they will not get very far because, as in the case of those men, their folly will be clear to everyone. (2 Tim 3:9)

Therefore judge nothing before the appointed time; wait till the Lord comes. He will bring to light what is hidden in darkness and will expose the motives of men's hearts. At that time each will receive his praise from God. (1 Cor 4:5)

"But if you fail to do this, you will be sinning against the LORD; and you may be sure that your sin will find you out. (Num 32:23)

If I sinned, you would be watching me and would not let my offense go unpunished. (Job 10:14)

Surely then you will count my steps but not keep track of my sin. (Job 14:16)

The heavens will expose his guilt; the earth will rise up against him. (Job 20:27)

"His eyes are on the ways of men; he sees their every step. (Job 34:21)

For a man's ways are in full view of the LORD, and he examines all his paths. (Prov 5:21)

For God will bring every deed into judgment, including every hidden thing, whether it is good or evil. (Eccl 12:14)

Although you wash yourself with soda and use an abundance of soap, the stain of your guilt is still before me," declares the Sovereign LORD. (Jer 2:22)

My eyes are on all their ways; they are not hidden from me, nor is their sin concealed from my eyes. (Jer 16:17)

Great are your purposes and mighty are your deeds. Your eyes are open to all the ways of men; you reward everyone according to his conduct and as his deeds deserve. (Jer 32:19)

Then the Spirit of the LORD came upon me, and he told me to say: "This is what the LORD says: That is what you are saying, O house of Israel, but I know what is going through your mind. (Ezek 11:5)

For I know how many are your offenses and how great your sins. You oppress the righteous and take bribes and you deprive the poor of justice in the courts. (Amos 5:12)

DEEPER STUDY # 1

(12:1)**Yeast (leaven)**: leaven is inserted in dough, and once it is, it does at least four things.

1. Yeast (leaven) penetrates, seeps, and works its way through the dough. It cannot be seen, but it still works.

2. Yeast (leaven) spreads. It spreads slowly, but once it is inserted, it cannot be stopped. It continues to spread until the whole dough is risen.

3. Yeast (leaven)swells the dough. It puffs dough up, making dough look much larger than it really is. Note: it does not add to the dough. It only changes its appearance.

4. Yeast (leaven)ferments and sours the dough. It changes the dough's very nature.

3 (12:4-12) **Fear—God, Care of—Unpardonable Sin—Jesus Christ, Son of Man**: the second message was to the friends of Jesus. He told them what to fear.

1. Do not fear men, but God alone. The reason is logical: men can only kill the body. God can cast both body and soul "into hell." (See DEEPER STUDY # 2, <u>Fear</u>—Lk.12:4; note and DEEPER STUDY # 1—Mt.10:28; DEEPER STUDY # 2—5:22.)

2. Do not fear the lack of necessities. Note the word "forgotten." The friend of the Lord is not forgotten, no matter the circumstance. There is something very precious here, yet there is a revelation of power as well.

⇒ There is a preciousness in the thought that every sparrow, no matter how common or forgotten or ignored, is very dear to God.

⇒ There is power in that God knows every single sparrow on the earth, and not a single one falls but what He knows about its injury. The idea is that injury to the sparrow causes pain and hurt which God feels. Suffering is due to the corruption and evil in the world, and corruption and evil always cause pain for God.

a. There is God's providence. God sees, knows, cares, and oversees all the events and happenings on earth—even for the little sparrow that is so common and forgotten.

> **"Therefore I tell you, do not worry about your life, what you will eat or drink; or about your body, what you will wear. Is not life more important than food, and the body more important than clothes? Look at the birds of the air; they do not sow or reap or store away in barns, and yet your heavenly Father feeds them. Are you not much more valuable than they? (Mat 6:25-26)**
>
> **Cast all your anxiety on him because he cares for you. (1 Pet 5:7)**

b. There is God's knowledge (omniscience). God knows every little happening and all that is, even to the most minute detail. He knows when a single sparrow falls to the ground. He knows every hair of a person's head, even the number of hairs.

> **Do not be like them [heathen], for your Father knows what you need before you ask him. (Mat 6:8)**
>
> **Now we can see that you know all things and that you do not even need to have anyone ask you questions. This makes us believe that you came from God." (John 16:30)**
>
> **And again, "The Lord knows that the thoughts of the wise are futile." So then, no more boasting about men! <u>All things are yours</u>, (1 Cor 3:20-21)**
>
> **"Do not keep talking so proudly or let your mouth speak such arrogance, for the LORD is a God who knows, and by him deeds are weighed. (1 Sam 2:3)**
>
> **Do you not know? Have you not heard? The LORD is the everlasting God, the Creator of the ends of the earth. He will not grow tired or weary, and his understanding no one can fathom. (Isa 40:28)**

c. There is God's power (omnipotence). God is able to control the events that happen to the believer, no matter how detailed and minute. He can control and work them out for good to such an extent that there is no need for the believer to fear.

> **And we know that in all things God works for the good of those who love him, who have been called according to his purpose. (Rom 8:28)**
>
> **For our light and momentary troubles are achieving for us an eternal glory that far outweighs them all. (2 Cor 4:17)**
>
> **But he said to me, "My grace is sufficient for you, for my power is made perfect in weakness." Therefore I will boast all the more gladly about my weaknesses, so that Christ's power may rest on me. (2 Cor 12:9)**

d. There is God's love. Nothing can separate us from the love of Christ and of God.

> **Who shall separate us from the love of Christ? Shall trouble or hardship or persecution or famine or nakedness or danger or sword? For I am convinced that neither death nor life, neither angels nor demons, neither the present nor the future, nor any powers, neither height nor depth, nor anything else in all creation, will be able to separate us from the love of God that is in Christ Jesus our Lord. (Rom 8:35, 38-39)**

3. Fear the spirit of disloyalty, of denying Christ. Note three points.

a. Men shall be judged before the angels of God. Angels will witness either our acceptance or rejection by God.

b. The judgment will be executed by the Son of Man Himself. He alone is the One Man who lived and experienced all the temptations and trials of life, yet He never sinned. He alone has been through it all and conquered all. He alone is worthy to judge. He alone knows…

- what a man is
- what a man believes and does not believe
- what a man can and can not do
- what a man does and fails to do

> **All the nations will be gathered before him [Christ], and he will separate the people one from another as a shepherd separates the sheep from the goats. (Mat 25:32)**
>
> **Moreover, the Father judges no one, but has entrusted all judgment to the Son, (John 5:22)**
>
> **He commanded us to preach to the people and to testify that he is the one**

whom God appointed as judge of the living and the dead. (Acts 10:42)

For he has set a day when he will judge the world with justice by the man he has appointed. He has given proof of this to all men by raising him from the dead." (Acts 17:31)

This will take place on the day when God will judge men's secrets through Jesus Christ, as my gospel declares. (Rom 2:16)

You, then, why do you judge your brother? Or why do you look down on your brother? For we will all stand before God's judgment seat. (Rom 14:10)

In the presence of God and of Christ Jesus, who will judge the living and the dead, and in view of his appearing and his kingdom, I give you this charge: (2 Tim 4:1)

c. The basis of judgment is a man's attitude toward the Son of Man (see note—Mt.8:20).
   ⇒ The man who truly confesses (lives for) Christ before men, shall be confessed (given life) before the angels of God.

"Whoever acknowledges me before men, I will also acknowledge him before my Father in heaven. (Mat 10:32)

That if you confess with your mouth, "Jesus is Lord," and believe in your heart that God raised him from the dead, you will be saved. For it is with your heart that you believe and are justified, and it is with your mouth that you confess and are saved. (Rom 10:9-10)

No one who denies the Son has the Father; whoever acknowledges the Son has the Father also. (1 John 2:23)

If anyone acknowledges that Jesus is the Son of God, God lives in him and he in God. (1 John 4:15)

   ⇒ The man who denies (fails to live for) Christ before men shall be denied (not given life) before the angels of God.

But whoever disowns me before men, I will disown him before my Father in heaven. (Mat 10:33)

If anyone is ashamed of me and my words in this adulterous and sinful generation, the Son of Man will be ashamed of him when he comes in his Father's glory with the holy angels." (Mark 8:38)

If we endure, we will also reign with him. If we disown him, he will also disown us; (2 Tim 2:12)

They claim to know God, but by their actions they deny him. They are detestable, disobedient and unfit for doing anything good. (Titus 1:16)

But there were also false prophets among the people, just as there will be false teachers among you. They will secretly introduce destructive heresies, even denying the sovereign Lord who bought them—bringing swift destruction on themselves. (2 Pet 2:1)

Who is the liar? It is the man who denies that Jesus is the Christ. Such a man is the antichrist—he denies the Father and the Son. (1 John 2:22)

4. Fear the unpardonable sin. Note two crucial points.
   a. Blasphemy against Christ, the Son of Man, can be forgiven. If a person is guilty of cursing Christ and he really wants forgiveness, he can ask for forgiveness and God will forgive him if he repents.
   b. Blasphemy against the Holy Spirit is not forgiven. This sin is not referring to just speaking words against the Spirit. It means setting one's mind and heart and life against the Spirit. It means that the words spoken against the Spirit come from a heart set against the Spirit and the work of the Spirit (see note—Mt.12:31-32 for more discussion).

5. Do not fear persecution and trials. Why? Because the Holy Spirit empowers the believer. This point has to do with persecution, whether mild ridicule or physical abuse and martyrdom. The Holy Spirit will give power to the Lord's friend (follower), the strength to bear and the words to speak.

Very simply, God is to be trusted in the hour of trial, trusted for the strength to bear whatever men may do to us. This does not mean we should not be praying and thinking, but it means that God is to be trusted for the defense. There is a reason for this. Only God knows the heart of the persecutors and any others who are present. Thus, He alone knows what needs to be said to touch their hearts or else to serve as a witness against them in the future.

But when they arrest you, do not worry about what to say or how to say it. At that time you will be given what to say, (Mat 10:19)

For I will give you words and wisdom that none of your adversaries will be able to resist or contradict. (Luke 21:15)

This is what we speak, not in words taught us by human wisdom but in words taught by the Spirit, expressing spiritual truths in spiritual words. (1 Cor 2:13)

Now go; I will help you speak and will teach you what to say." (Exo 4:12)

The Sovereign LORD has given me an instructed tongue, to know the word that sustains the weary. He wakens me morning by morning, wakens my ear to listen like one being taught. (Isa 50:4)

I have put my words in your mouth and covered you with the shadow of my hand— I who set the heavens in place, who laid the foundations of the earth, and who say to Zion, 'You are my people.'" (Isa 51:16)

Therefore this is what the LORD God Almighty says: "Because the people have spoken these words, I will make my words in your mouth a fire and these people the wood it consumes. (Jer 5:14)

DEEPER STUDY # 2

(12:4) **Fear—Persecution**: fear of man is a terrible thing. It is a subject that needs to be looked at closely. Jesus said that fear can cost a person his eternal destiny, even if the person is a friend, a follower, of His. (Note that Jesus is addressing His "friends," His followers, v.4.)

1. The fear of men causes several things.
   ⇒ It causes a person to become disturbed within heart and mind: the loss of peace.
   ⇒ It causes a person to lose fervor: the loss of commitment.
   ⇒ It causes a person to be either sidetracked from or to give up what he knows to be God's will: the loss of mission and meaning and purpose.

For God did not give us a spirit of timidity, but a spirit of power, of love and of self-discipline. (2 Tim 1:7)

There is no fear in love. But perfect love drives out fear, because fear has to do with punishment. The one who fears is not made perfect in love. (1 John 4:18)

So do not fear, for I am with you; do not be dismayed, for I am your God. I will strengthen you and help you; I will uphold you with my righteous right hand. (Isa 41:10)

But now, this is what the LORD says— he who created you, O Jacob, he who formed you, O Israel: "Fear not, for I have redeemed you; I have summoned you by name; you are mine. When you pass through the waters, I will be with you; and when you pass through the rivers, they will not sweep over you. When you walk through the fire, you will not be burned; the flames will not set you ablaze. For I am the LORD, your God, the Holy One of Israel, your Savior; I give Egypt for your ransom, Cush and Seba in your stead. (Isa 43:1-3)

2. There are several reasons why men are not to be feared.
   a. Men can only kill the body, not the soul. Their power is limited; they can go no further. They cannot touch a person's soul or life.
   b. Men can only send us out of this world, not out of heaven. [To] "be with Christ...is better by far" anyway (Ph.1:23; 3:20-21).
   c. Men can only separate us from this world, not from life. We have eternal life. Death is not a part of the experience of the believer, for the believer will not "taste" death. Christ "tasted," that is, experienced, death for the believer (Heb.2:9). The believer has already passed from death to life and lives forever (Jn.5:24). When he faces death, he is merely transferred from this world, from the physical dimension of being, into the next world, the heavenly or spiritual dimension of being (see DEEPER STUDY # 1—2 Tim.4:18).

"I tell you the truth, whoever hears my word and believes him who sent me has eternal life and will not be condemned; he has crossed over from death to life. (John 5:24)

But we see Jesus, who was made a little lower than the angels, now crowned with glory and honor because he suffered death, so that by the grace of God he might taste death for everyone. In bringing many sons to glory, it was fitting that God, for whom and through whom everything exists, should make the author of their salvation perfect through suffering. Both the one who makes men holy and those who are made holy are of the same family. So Jesus is not ashamed to call them brothers. (Heb 2:9-11; cp. v.12-18)

The Lord will rescue me from every evil attack and will bring me safely to his heavenly kingdom. To him be glory for ever and ever. Amen. (2 Tim 4:18)

   d. Men can only cut us off from the unbelievers and believers of this earth, not from the love of God and the saints in glory.

Who shall separate us from the love of Christ? Shall trouble or hardship or persecution or famine or nakedness or danger or sword? As it is written: "For your sake we face death all day long; we are considered as sheep to be slaughtered." No, in all these things we are more than conquerors through him who loved us. For I am convinced that neither death nor life, neither angels nor demons, neither the present nor the future, nor any powers, neither height nor depth, nor anything else in all creation, will be able to separate us from the love of God that is in Christ Jesus our Lord. (Rom 8:35-39)

3. There are two *primary* reasons why we should not fear men and persecution.
   a. God has given us a great and glorious cause: to reach men for Christ. Very practically some men do not want to be reached; therefore, they rail and react and become our persecutors. But some do want to be saved, and the fact that they can receive eternal life is so glorious that it is worth whatever price we have to pay in order to see them saved.

Remember this: Whoever turns a sinner from the error of his way will save him from death and cover over a multitude of sins. (James 5:20)

"For God so loved the world that he gave his one and only Son, that whoever believes in him shall not perish but have eternal life. For God did not send his Son into the world to condemn the world, but to save the world through him. (John 3:16-17)

For the wages of sin is death, but the gift of God is eternal life in Christ Jesus our Lord. (Rom 6:23)

The mind of sinful man is death, but the mind controlled by the Spirit is life and peace; (Rom 8:6)

Therefore he is able to save completely those who come to God through him, because he always lives to intercede for them. (Heb 7:25)

There is no fear in love. But perfect love drives out fear, because fear has to do with punishment. The one who fears is not made perfect in love. (1 John 4:18)

b. God has given us a great hope (see thought—Mt.10:26-27).

I tell you the truth, if anyone keeps my word, he will never see death." (John 8:51)

And whoever lives and believes in me will never die. Do you believe this?" (John 11:26)

And I have the same hope in God as these men, that there will be a resurrection of both the righteous and the wicked. So I strive always to keep my conscience clear before God and man. (Acts 24:15-16)

To those who by persistence in doing good seek glory, honor and immortality, he will give eternal life. (Rom 2:7)

Now we know that if the earthly tent we live in is destroyed, we have a building from God, an eternal house in heaven, not built by human hands. (2 Cor 5:1)

The faith and love that spring from the hope that is stored up for you in heaven and that you have already heard about in the word of truth, the gospel (Col 1:5)

But our citizenship is in heaven. And we eagerly await a Savior from there, the Lord Jesus Christ, who, by the power that enables him to bring everything under his control, will transform our lowly bodies so that they will be like his glorious body. (Phil 3:20-21)

While we wait for the blessed hope—the glorious appearing of our great God and Savior, Jesus Christ, (Titus 2:13)

Because God wanted to make the unchanging nature of his purpose very clear to the heirs of what was promised, he confirmed it with an oath. God did this so that, by two unchangeable things in which it is impossible for God to lie, we who have fled to take hold of the hope offered to us may be greatly encouraged. We have this hope as an anchor for the soul, firm and secure. It enters the inner sanctuary behind the curtain, where Jesus, who went before us, has entered on our behalf. He has become a high priest forever, in the order of Melchizedek. (Heb 6:17-20)

Praise be to the God and Father of our Lord Jesus Christ! In his great mercy he has given us new birth into a living hope through the resurrection of Jesus Christ from the dead, and into an inheritance that can never perish, spoil or fade—kept in heaven for you, (1 Pet 1:3-4)

4. There is a remedy to keep us from fearing men: God. God is to be feared (see note—Mt.10:28). Note several things.

a. God can destroy us, both body and soul, and put both "in hell" (see DEEPER STUDY # 2—Mt.5:22). By "destroy" Jesus did not mean our body and soul would cease to exist, but they would live a worthless existence, be ruined and suffer in ruin forever (see DEEPER STUDY # 1—Mt.10:28).

b. Jesus was speaking to believers in this passage. God is to be feared much more and much sooner than men. The terror of men pales into absolute insignificance in comparison to God's terror. Imagine this one fact alone. Man's terror is but for a short while at most, but God's terror is *forever.* The Bible says it never ends. The point is clear: before caving in to man's persecution, we need to remember the *fear of God.*

c. The destruction of the soul comes from God, not from man. The power to destroy the soul is God's power alone. How fearful we must be of God—even we who are believers (see note—Mt.10:28)!

Do not be afraid of those who kill the body but cannot kill the soul. Rather, be afraid of the One who can destroy both soul and body in hell. (Mat 10:28)

Since you call on a Father who judges each man's work impartially, live your lives as strangers here in reverent fear. (1 Pet 1:17)

Show proper respect to everyone: Love the brotherhood of believers, fear God, honor the king. (1 Pet 2:17)

And, "If it is hard for the righteous to be saved, what will become of the ungodly and the sinner?" (1 Pet 4:18)

He said in a loud voice, "Fear God and give him glory, because the hour of his judgment has come. Worship him who made the heavens, the earth, the sea and the springs of water." (Rev 14:7)

Now let the fear of the LORD be upon you. Judge carefully, for with the LORD our God there is no injustice or partiality or bribery." (2 Chr 19:7)

	M. The Parable of the Rich Fool: The Man of Wealth & What He Should Fear, 12:13-21		
1 A request for Jesus to give a judicial decision a. Brother's desire for an inheritance & wealth b. Jesus' stern refusal	13 Someone in the crowd said to him, "Teacher, tell my brother to divide the inheritance with me." 14 Jesus replied, "Man, who appointed me a judge or an arbiter between you?"	17 He thought to himself, 'What shall I do? I have no place to store my crops.' 18 "Then he said, 'This is what I'll do. I will tear down my barns and build bigger ones, and there I will store all my grain and my goods. 19 And I'll say to myself, "You have plenty of good things laid up for many years. Take life easy; eat, drink and be merry."'	d. The big mistake: Self-indulgence & extravagant living
2 Fear this: Life does not consist in things a. The serious charge: Watch out!—beware b. The big sin: Greed or Covetousness[DS1] c. The big "I" (6 times, 16-19[a]): Aggressively self-centered	15 Then he said to them, "Watch out! Be on your guard against all kinds of greed; a man's life does not consist in the abundance of his possessions." 16 And he told them this parable: "The ground of a certain rich man produced a good crop.	20 "But God said to him, 'You fool! This very night your life will be demanded from you. Then who will get what you have prepared for yourself?' 21 "This is how it will be with anyone who stores up things for himself but is not rich toward God."	**3 Fear this: Your life may be required & demanded tonight** **4 Fear this: Wealth is not a permanent possession—someone else gets it**

DIVISION V

THE SON OF MAN'S GREAT JOURNEY TO JERUSALEM STAGE I): HIS MISSION AND PUBLIC CHALLENGE, 9:51-13:21

M. The Parable of the Rich Fool: The Man of Wealth and What He Should Fear, 12:13-21

(12:13-21) **Introduction**: the man of wealth is often self-sufficient, but there are some things he needs to fear.

1. A request for Jesus to give a judicial decision (v.13-14).
2. Fear: life does not consist in things (v.15-19).
3. Fear: the soul may be required and demanded tonight (v.20).
4. Fear: wealth is not a permanent possession—someone else gets it (v.20-21).

1 (12:13-14) **Worldliness—Materialism**: there was a request for Jesus to give a judicial decision. A man was having a dispute with his brother over the inheritance of his father's estate. The law gave two-thirds to the older son and one third to the younger son. The man felt he was not getting his legal share, so he appealed to Jesus for help in getting his share. It was a common practice for Rabbis or Teachers to settle legal disputes. Note five things.

1. The man was in the congregation listening to Jesus preach. There is a strong possibility that the man was even a follower of Jesus. This is seen in that Jesus had apparently paused for a brief rest between sermons, and the man knew Jesus well enough to approach Him about the matter in the midst of a huge crowd.

2. What the man wanted was significant. He wanted material wealth, money, and property. Note: he appealed to Jesus for help in getting what had probably been *stolen from him*. More than likely the property was rightfully his anyway. It would have been an act of justice to straighten out the inheritance.

3. Jesus refused rather sternly. He forcefully addressed the man as a stranger: "Man." He treats the man as one who is alien to the Lord and His purpose on earth. Jesus refused to become involved in worldly affairs, in settling property and money disputes.

4. The man exposed a serious flaw in his spiritual life. Jesus had just preached a message on trusting God for the necessities of life, for God cares and will provide. Apparently, the man *had not heard the message*. He was bodily present, but he was too preoccupied with the thoughts of property and money to really hear the Word and receive the message.

> **Thought 1.** Listening to the Word's being preached does not mean that we "hear the Word," nor that we learn from it. The Word, salvation, and spiritual maturity do not *rub off on a wandering mind or on a worldly life.*

5. The contrast between the mind and attitude of the man and of Jesus is significant. The man's mind was set on the things of the earth and the world, on property and money, wealth and selfishness. The Lord's mind was set on the higher and more noble, on salvation and life, on heaven and eternity. The mission of Jesus was not to give man property, but to give man life, both abundant and eternal. Property is nothing without life.

2 (12:15-19) **Fear—Worldliness—Selfishness—Indulgence**: fear—life does not consist in things. Note four points.

1. The charge of Jesus was strong. There was a double warning: "*Watch out! Be on your guard.*" The warning was to be given close attention. The words "be on your guard" (phulassesthe) means to beware, to guard oneself from some enemy.

2. The big sin of man is *greed or covetousness* (see Deeper Study # 1—Lk.12:15; Deeper Study # 1—Jas.4:1-3 for more discussion). This is the big sin of the world—desiring more and more. However, a man's happiness and comfort, soul and body do not depend upon what he has; *many poor people* are happy and comfortable with healthy souls and bodies. Life does not consist in possessions—a beautiful home, the latest clothes, a new car, property, money, wealth.

3. The *big "I"* shows that the greedy man is *aggressively self-centered.* Note how Jesus gets the fact of man's greed across. He shares a parable about a man who was also *aggressively self-centered.* In just three short verses describing his thoughts, the rich man in the parable said, "I" six times and "my" five times. The man's attention was solely upon himself. Now note the parable.

a. The man was blessed materially, tremendously blessed, but he did not *thank God* for his blessing.
b. The man called the fruits of the ground and the possessions he had, *"my crops"* and *"my goods"* (v.17-18).
c. The man said that he had plenty of good things, that he could take life easy, eat drink and be merry. There is no indication he had given his soul to God.
d. He became *puffed up*, prideful with what he had done. He began to think of *bigger and bigger*, of *I and I*, of *my and my*.

4. The big mistake of man is *selfishness*, self-indulgence, and extravagant living (see DEEPER STUDY # 1—Lk.16:19-21). Note the sole purpose of man is to be at ease, to have plenty to eat and drink, and to enjoy life as he wishes. Note several facts about the man in the parable.

a. He thought only of self, of living at ease and in comfort, of indulging self and being as extravagant as he wished. He gave no thought to helping others. He forgot that he lived in a needy world that was lost and dying.
b. He put off living and enjoying life until he got his barns built. The idea is that he was a *workaholic*, who was consumed with the passion to get what he wanted. (How many are just like him when they want something!)
c. Now note the most shocking point: he only *thought* these things. He never did them; they were only thoughts of his heart.

Be careful that you do not forget the LORD your God, failing to observe his commands, his laws and his decrees that I am giving you this day. Otherwise, when you eat and are satisfied, when you build fine houses and settle down, and when your herds and flocks grow large and your silver and gold increase and all you have is multiplied, then your heart will become proud and you will forget the LORD your God, who brought you out of Egypt, out of the land of slavery. (Deu 8:11-14)

One man gives freely, yet gains even more; another withholds unduly, but comes to poverty. (Prov 11:24)

If a man shuts his ears to the cry of the poor, he too will cry out and not be answered. (Prov 21:13)

Rescue those being led away to death; hold back those staggering toward slaughter. If you say, "But we knew nothing about this," does not he who weighs the heart perceive it? Does not he who guards your life know it? Will he not repay each person according to what he has done? (Prov 24:11-12)

He who gives to the poor will lack nothing, but he who closes his eyes to them receives many curses. (Prov 28:27)

Woe to you who add house to house and join field to field till no space is left and you live alone in the land. (Isa 5:8)

I have seen a grievous evil under the sun: wealth hoarded to the harm of its owner, (Eccl 5:13)

And when you were eating and drinking, were you not just feasting for yourselves? (Zec 7:6)

Then Jesus said to his disciples, "I tell you the truth, it is hard for a rich man to enter the kingdom of heaven. (Mat 19:23)

For I was hungry and you gave me nothing to eat, I was thirsty and you gave me nothing to drink, I was a stranger and you did not invite me in, I needed clothes and you did not clothe me, I was sick and in prison and you did not look after me.' (Mat 25:42-43)

But the worries of this life, the deceitfulness of wealth and the desires for other things come in and choke the word, making it unfruitful. (Mark 4:19)

People who want to get rich fall into temptation and a trap and into many foolish and harmful desires that plunge men into ruin and destruction. (1 Tim 6:9)

If anyone has material possessions and sees his brother in need but has no pity on him, how can the love of God be in him? (1 John 3:17)

DEEPER STUDY # 1

(12:15) **Greed—Covetousness** (pleonexia): a craving, a desire for more. It is greediness, a dissatisfaction with what is enough. It includes the cravings for both material things and fleshly indulgence. It is desiring what belongs to others; snatching at something that belongs to others; a love of having, a cry of *give me, give me* (cp. 2 Pt.2:14).

⇒ It is a lust so deep within a man that he finds his happiness in things instead of in God.

⇒ It is a greed or covetousness so deep that it desires the power that things bring more than the things themselves.

⇒ It is an intense appetite for gain; a passion for the pleasure that things can bring. It goes beyond the pleasure of possessing things for their own sakes.

"Do not store up for yourselves treasures on earth, where moth and rust destroy, and where thieves break in and steal. But store up for yourselves treasures in heaven, where moth and rust do not destroy, and where thieves do not break in and steal. For where your treasure is, there your heart will be also. (Mat 6:19-21)

"No one can serve two masters. Either he will hate the one and love the other, or he will be devoted to the one and despise the other. You cannot serve both God and Money. (Mat 6:24)

What good will it be for a man if he gains the whole world, yet forfeits his soul? Or what can a man give in exchange for his soul? (Mat 16:26)

But among you there must not be even a hint of sexual immorality, or of any kind of impurity, or of greed, because these are improper for God's holy people. For of this you can be sure: No immoral, impure or greedy person—such a man is an idolater—

has any inheritance in the kingdom of Christ and of God. (Eph 5:3, 5)

Put to death, therefore, whatever belongs to your earthly nature: sexual immorality, impurity, lust, evil desires and greed, which is idolatry. Because of these, the wrath of God is coming. (Col 3:5-6)

For, as I have often told you before and now say again even with tears, many live as enemies of the cross of Christ. Their destiny is destruction, their god is their stomach, and their glory is in their shame. Their mind is on earthly things. (Phil 3:18-19)

Now the overseer [minister] must be above reproach....not a lover of money. (1 Tim 3:2-3; cp. Tit 1:7)

For we brought nothing into the world, and we can take nothing out of it. But if we have food and clothing, we will be content with that. People who want to get rich fall into temptation and a trap and into many foolish and harmful desires that plunge men into ruin and destruction. For the love of money is a root of all kinds of evil. Some people, eager for money, have wandered from the faith and pierced themselves with many griefs. (1 Tim 6:7-10)

Command those who are rich in this present world not to be arrogant nor to put their hope in wealth, which is so uncertain, but to put their hope in God, who richly provides us with everything for our enjoyment. (1 Tim 6:17)

People will be lovers of themselves, lovers of money, boastful, proud, abusive, disobedient to their parents, ungrateful, unholy, (2 Tim 3:2)

Keep your lives free from the love of money and be content with what you have, because God has said, "Never will I leave you; never will I forsake you." (Heb 13:5)

You want something but don't get it. You kill and covet, but you cannot have what you want. You quarrel and fight. You do not have, because you do not ask God. When you ask, you do not receive, because you ask with wrong motives, that you may spend what you get on your pleasures. (James 4:2-3)

Now listen, you rich people, weep and wail because of the misery that is coming upon you. Your wealth has rotted, and moths have eaten your clothes. Your gold and silver are corroded. Their corrosion will testify against you and eat your flesh like fire. You have hoarded wealth in the last days. (James 5:1-3;cp. v.4-6)

Be shepherds of God's flock that is under your care, serving as overseers—not because you must, but because you are willing, as God wants you to be; not greedy for money, but eager to serve; (1 Pet 5:2)

In their greed these [false] teachers will exploit you with stories they have made up. Their condemnation has long been hanging over them, and their destruction has not been sleeping. (2 Pet 2:3)

[False teachers] With eyes full of adultery, they never stop sinning; they seduce the unstable; they are experts in greed—an accursed brood! (2 Pet 2:14)

"You shall not covet your neighbor's house. You shall not covet your neighbor's wife, or his manservant or maidservant, his ox or donkey, or anything that belongs to your neighbor." (Exo 20:17)

"If I have put my trust in gold or said to pure gold, 'You are my security,' if I have rejoiced over my great wealth, the fortune my hands had gained, then these also would be sins to be judged, for I would have been unfaithful to God on high. (Job 31:24-25, 28)

He boasts of the cravings of his heart; he blesses the greedy and reviles the LORD. (Psa 10:3)

Do not trust in extortion or take pride in stolen goods; though your riches increase, do not set your heart on them. (Psa 62:10)

Turn my heart toward your statutes and not toward selfish gain. (Psa 119:36)

A greedy man brings trouble to his family, but he who hates bribes will live. (Prov 15:27)

The sluggard's craving will be the death of him, because his hands refuse to work. All day long he craves for more, but the righteous give without sparing. (Prov 21:25-26)

He who oppresses the poor to increase his wealth and he who gives gifts to the rich—both come to poverty. (Prov 22:16)

Do not wear yourself out to get rich; have the wisdom to show restraint. Cast but a glance at riches, and they are gone, for they will surely sprout wings and fly off to the sky like an eagle. (Prov 23:4-5)

For riches do not endure forever, and a crown is not secure for all generations. (Prov 27:24)

He who leads the upright along an evil path will fall into his own trap, but the blameless will receive a good inheritance. (Prov 28:10)

A faithful man will be richly blessed, but one eager to get rich will not go unpunished. (Prov 28:20)

Keep falsehood and lies far from me; give me neither poverty nor riches, but give me only my daily bread. (Prov 30:8)

Whoever loves money never has money enough; whoever loves wealth is never satisfied with his income. This too is meaningless. (Eccl 5:10)

Your rulers are rebels, companions of thieves; they all love bribes and chase after gifts. They do not defend the cause of the fatherless; the widow's case does not come before them. (Isa 1:23)

They are dogs with mighty appetites; they never have enough. They are shepherds who lack understanding; they all turn to their own way, each seeks his own gain. (Isa 56:11)

I was enraged by his sinful greed; I punished him, and hid my face in anger, yet he kept on in his willful ways. (Isa 57:17)

"From the least to the greatest, all are greedy for gain; prophets and priests alike, all practice deceit. (Jer 6:13; cp. Jer 8:10)

"But your eyes and your heart are set only on dishonest gain, on shedding innocent blood and on oppression and extortion." (Jer 22:17)

You who live by many waters and are rich in treasures, your end has come, the time for you to be cut off. (Jer 51:13)

In you men accept bribes to shed blood; you take usury and excessive interest and make unjust gain from your neighbors by extortion. And you have forgotten me, declares the Sovereign LORD. (Ezek 22:12)

My people come to you, as they usually do, and sit before you to listen to your words, but they do not put them into practice. With their mouths they express devotion, but their hearts are greedy for unjust gain. (Ezek 33:31)

They covet fields and seize them, and houses, and take them. They defraud a man of his home, a fellowman of his inheritance. (Micah 2:2)

Her leaders judge for a bribe, her priests teach for a price, and her prophets tell fortunes for money. Yet they lean upon the LORD and say, "Is not the LORD among us? No disaster will come upon us." (Micah 3:11)

Both hands are skilled in doing evil; the ruler demands gifts, the judge accepts bribes, the powerful dictate what they desire— they all conspire together. (Micah 7:3)

"Woe to him who builds his realm by unjust gain to set his nest on high, to escape the clutches of ruin! You have plotted the ruin of many peoples, shaming your own house and forfeiting your life. (Hab 2:9-10)

You have planted much, but have harvested little. You eat, but never have enough. You drink, but never have your fill. You put on clothes, but are not warm. You earn wages, only to put them in a purse with holes in it." (Hag 1:6)

3 (12:20) **Death—Fear—Judgment**: fear—your life may be required and demanded tonight. Note several things.

1. It was God who now spoke. It was God who knew the thoughts of the man. It was God who knew the man was to die that very night. The man did not know it, nor did anyone else.

2. The man was to die that night. Everyone has his night (day) to die, and this was his night.

3. The man's "life" was required. God required and demanded it. His soul was not going to cease existing. It was to exist in another world. Existence was not over for the man. The man's soul was simply to be in another world, in the spiritual dimension of existence.

4. The man was called a "fool" by God. He had lived as a fool, lived entirely for himself. He had refused to think about the truth, about the uncertainty of life. There was a good possibility that he might not live as long as he wished to live.

But understand this: If the owner of the house had known at what hour the thief was coming, he would not have let his house be broken into. You also must be ready, because the Son of Man will come at an hour when you do not expect him." (Luke 12:39-40)

What benefit did you reap at that time from the things you are now ashamed of? Those things result in death! (Rom 6:21)

But land that produces thorns and thistles is worthless and is in danger of being cursed. In the end it will be burned. (Heb 6:8)

The end of all things is near. Therefore be clear minded and self-controlled so that you can pray. (1 Pet 4:7)

For it is time for judgment to begin with the family of God; and if it begins with us, what will the outcome be for those who do not obey the gospel of God? And, "If it is hard for the righteous to be saved, what will become of the ungodly and the sinner?" (1 Pet 4:17-18)

These men are springs without water and mists driven by a storm. Blackest darkness is reserved for them. (2 Pet 2:17)

They are wild waves of the sea, foaming up their shame; wandering stars, for whom blackest darkness has been reserved forever. (Jude 1:13)

But the cowardly, the unbelieving, the vile, the murderers, the sexually immoral, those who practice magic arts, the idolaters and all liars—their place will be in the fiery lake of burning sulfur. This is the second death." (Rev 21:8)

The wicked return to the grave, all the nations that forget God. (Psa 9:17)

For like the grass they will soon wither, like green plants they will soon die away. (Psa 37:2)

A little while, and the wicked will be no more; though you look for them, they will not be found. (Psa 37:10)

I have seen a wicked and ruthless man flourishing like a green tree in its native soil, but he soon passed away and was no more; though I looked for him, he could not be found. (Psa 37:35-36)

But you, O God, will bring down the wicked into the pit of corruption; bloodthirsty and deceitful men will not live out half their days. But as for me, I trust in you. (Psa 55:23)

That though the wicked spring up like grass and all evildoers flourish, they will be forever destroyed. (Psa 92:7)

The wicked man will see and be vexed, he will gnash his teeth and waste away; the longings of the wicked will come to nothing. (Psa 112:10)

For a man's ways are in full view of the LORD, and he examines all his paths. The evil deeds of a wicked man ensnare him; the cords of his sin hold him fast. He will die for lack of discipline, led astray by his own great folly. (Prov 5:21-23)

In the evening, sudden terror! Before the morning, they are gone! This is the portion of those who loot us, the lot of those who plunder us. (Isa 17:14)

Do I take any pleasure in the death of the wicked? declares the Sovereign LORD. Rather, am I not pleased when they turn from their ways and live? (Ezek 18:23)

4 (12:20-21) **Spiritual Dimension—Death—Judgment—Wealth**: fear—wealth is not a permanent possession; someone else gets it. The man left every penny behind. He took nothing with him. Now note why. This is a point seldom thought about. *He could take nothing with him because the strength, the energy, the power, the life of his body had left*. The Bible reveals…

- that the life of a man's body is his spirit.
- that the spirit lives forever.

Note: when the spirit left, the man's strength and energy and power were gone. His body had to lie down. Note something else: *his spirit was spiritual*, of another dimension of being. It belonged to another world, another life. Therefore, all *material* possessions had to be left behind.

For we brought nothing into the world, and we can take nothing out of it. (1 Tim 6:7)

By faith Moses, when he had grown up, refused to be known as the son of Pharaoh's daughter. He chose to be mistreated along with the people of God rather than to enjoy the pleasures of sin for a short time. (Heb 11:24-25)

Your gold and silver are corroded. Their corrosion will testify against you and eat your flesh like fire. You have hoarded wealth in the last days. (James 5:3)

So, because you are lukewarm—neither hot nor cold—I am about to spit you out of my mouth. You say, 'I am rich; I have acquired wealth and do not need a thing.' But you do not realize that you are wretched, pitiful, poor, blind and naked. (Rev 3:16-17)

A flood will carry off his house, rushing waters on the day of God's wrath. (Job 20:28)

Man is a mere phantom as he goes to and fro: He bustles about, but only in vain; he heaps up wealth, not knowing who will get it. (Psa 39:6)

For all can see that wise men die; the foolish and the senseless alike perish and leave their wealth to others. (Psa 49:10)

I hated all the things I had toiled for under the sun, because I must leave them to the one who comes after me. (Eccl 2:18)

To the man who pleases him, God gives wisdom, knowledge and happiness, but to the sinner he gives the task of gathering and storing up wealth to hand it over to the one who pleases God. This too is meaningless, a chasing after the wind. (Eccl 2:26)

Like a partridge that hatches eggs it did not lay is the man who gains riches by unjust means. When his life is half gone, they will desert him, and in the end he will prove to be a fool. (Jer 17:11)

Now this is what the LORD Almighty says: "Give careful thought to your ways. You have planted much, but have harvested little. You eat, but never have enough. You drink, but never have your fill. You put on clothes, but are not warm. You earn wages, only to put them in a purse with holes in it." (Hag 1:5-6)

	N. The Genuine Believer: Worry Not About Necessities, 12:22-34 (Mt.6:25-34)
1 Do not be anxious about food & clothing	22 Then Jesus said to his disciples: "Therefore I tell you, do not worry about your life, what you will eat; or about your body, what you will wear.
a. Illust.1: Life & body—mean more than things	23 Life is more than food, and the body more than clothes.
b. Illust.2: The ravens—are fed by God	24 Consider the ravens: They do not sow or reap, they have no storeroom or barn; yet God feeds them. And how much more valuable you are than birds!
c. Illust.3: A man's height—is not altered an inch by worry	25 Who of you by worrying can add a single hour to his life ? 26 Since you cannot do this very little thing, why do you worry about the rest?
d. Illust.4: The lilies & grass—are clothed by God	27 "Consider how the lilies grow. They do not labor or spin. Yet I tell you, not even Solomon in all his splendor was dressed like one of these. 28 If that is how God clothes the grass of the field, which is here today, and tomorrow is thrown into the fire, how much more will he clothe
e. A tragic truth: Little faith[DS1]	you, O you of little faith!
2 Do not be wrapped up in seeking food & drink, nor in doubting God's care a. Such is worldliness	29 And do not set your heart on what you will eat or drink; do not worry about it. 30 For the pagan world runs after all such things, and your
b. God knows your needs	Father knows that you need them.
3 Seek the Kingdom of God a. God provides necessities	31 But seek his kingdom, and these things will be given to you as well.
b. God gives you the kingdom	32 "Do not be afraid, little flock, for your Father has been pleased to give you the kingdom.
c. God gives treasures that do not age, fail, corrupt—nor can they be stolen	33 Sell your possessions and give to the poor. Provide purses for yourselves that will not wear out, a treasure in heaven that will not be exhausted, where no thief comes near and no moth destroys.
d. God warns: Your heart will be where your treasure is	34 For where your treasure is, there your heart will be also.

DIVISION V

THE SON OF MAN'S GREAT JOURNEY TO JERUSALEM (STAGE I): HIS MISSION AND PUBLIC CHALLENGE, 9:51-13:21

N. The Genuine Believer: Worry Not About Necessities, 12:22-34

(12:22-34) **Introduction**: this message is not for the world; it is for disciples, the followers of Jesus. Jesus spoke "to His disciples" (v.22). "Do not worry" (merimnan), that is, take thought, being anxious and overly concerned, is a constant problem among men. It is not to be so among God's people. (See outline and notes—Mt.6:25-34 for more discussion and application.)

1. Do not be anxious about food and clothing (v.22-28).
2. Do not be wrapped up in seeking food and drink, nor in doubting God's care (v.29-30).
3. Seek the Kingdom of God (v.31-34).

1 (12:22-28) **Necessities—Food—Clothing—Body—Life—Birds**: do not be anxious about food and clothing. One of the great sins of men is their desire for better and better things, such as food and clothing, houses and furnishings, position and recognition, property and wealth. The sin is greed or covetousness (v.15). It is so common that Jesus warned His disciples not to be taken in by it. They were not to be anxious and worrying over such things. Jesus drove the point home with four illustrations.

1. The first illustration was that of the life and the body. The life and the body mean much more than the food we eat and the clothes we wear. Think for a moment. What means the most? A steak or one's life? A dress or one's body? The answer is clear. Therefore, a person's concern needs to be his life and his body, not delicious foods and the latest styles in clothes. He needs to give his time, energy, and effort to taking care of his life and body, not the delicious and stylish things of the world. Note two points.

a. A *healthy body* will extend a person's time on earth, and a *well-kept life* will assure a person of living forever in the presence of God. The life and body are to be the concern of man, not food and clothing. (See note—Mt.6:25 for more discussion.)

b. Jesus did not say we are not to think and plan for the necessities of life. He said we are not to worry and be anxious over the necessities of life. Everything in life takes some thought and some planning, but nothing should be so coveted that it causes anxiety and worry for us.

2. The second illustration was that of the ravens (crows). They were fed by God. Jesus said, "Consider"—think about the birds. Learn from what happens to them.

⇒ They do not sow or reap their food.
⇒ They do not store up their food.
⇒ Yet, God provides food for them.
⇒ They are able to pluck up the food that they need.

Learn that the believer is of much more value than the birds.

a. He is a higher being, on a much higher level of creation. He is more noble and excellent, a spiritual being capable of a personal relationship with God (Job 35:11; Jn.3:16).

b. The believer is a child of God. God is the Creator of birds, but He is the Father of believers (Ro.8:15-16; Gal.4:4-6).

c. The believer is an heir of God. He is to receive all that God possesses in that glorious day of redemption (Ro.8:16-17; Tit.3:7; 1 Pt.1:3-4).

Again, however, Jesus was not pampering His followers. He was talking about worrying and being anxious over food and clothing and shelter. God does not put up with laziness and slothfulness, nor with lack of planning and initiative and effort. Jesus planned ahead (Jn.12:6) and preached industriousness (Lk.16:8; cp. 1-10). The Bible is clear about man's faithfully working at his employment, even working for extra in order to have enough to give and to help meet the needs of a desperate world (Eph.4:28). (See note—Mt.6:25-34.)

What good is it for a man to gain the whole world, and yet lose or forfeit his very self? (Luke 9:25)

Do not be anxious about anything, but in everything, by prayer and petition, with thanksgiving, present your requests to God. And the peace of God, which transcends all understanding, will guard your hearts and your minds in Christ Jesus. (Phil 4:6-7)

I would like you to be free from concern [anziety, to be free from care]. (1 Cor 7:32)

You will keep in perfect peace him whose mind is steadfast, because he trusts in you. (Isa 26:3)

Trust in the LORD forever, for the LORD, the LORD, is the Rock eternal. (Isa 26:4)

How great is your goodness, which you have stored up for those who fear you, which you bestow in the sight of men on those who take refuge in you. (Psa 31:19)

Now this is what the LORD Almighty says: "Give careful thought to your ways. (Hag 1:5)

Thought 1. The believer who truly trusts Jesus Christ shall never be forsaken by God. This does not mean the believer will never suffer nor that the believer will never have to face martyrdom. Suffering is sometimes necessary for the growth of the believer's faith and as a testimony to the world (see notes—Mt.5:10-12; 10:24-25). However, God never forsakes the believer. He takes care of the believer no matter what circumstances confront him. God cares for the believer and feeds him far more quickly than He feeds the ravens of the air.

And he directed the people to sit down on the grass. Taking the five loaves and the two fish and looking up to heaven, he gave thanks and broke the loaves. Then he gave them to the disciples, and the disciples gave them to the people. They all ate and were satisfied, and the disciples picked up twelve basketfuls of broken pieces that were left over. (Mat 14:19-20)

I am not saying this because I am in need, for I have learned to be content whatever the circumstances. I know what it is to be in need, and I know what it is to have plenty. I have learned the secret of being content in any and every situation, whether well fed or hungry, whether living in plenty or in want. I can do everything through him who gives me strength. (Phil 4:11-13)

And my God will meet all your needs according to his glorious riches in Christ Jesus. (Phil 4:19)

Trust in the LORD and do good; dwell in the land and enjoy safe pasture. (Psa 37:3)

You care for the land and water it; you enrich it abundantly. The streams of God are filled with water to provide the people with grain, for so you have ordained it. (Psa 65:9)

Praise be to the Lord, to God our Savior, who daily bears our burdens. Selah (Psa 68:19; cp. Ps.107:31-38; 114:11-15 for the basis of God's blessings)

Even to your old age and gray hairs I am he, I am he who will sustain you. I have made you and I will carry you; I will sustain you and I will rescue you. (Isa 46:4)

"But blessed is the man who trusts in the LORD, whose confidence is in him. He will be like a tree planted by the water that sends out its roots by the stream. It does not fear when heat comes; its leaves are always green. It has no worries in a year of drought and never fails to bear fruit." (Jer 17:7-8)

3. The third illustration was that of a man's life. The word "life [span]" (helikia) means height, quality, or status gained by growth; but sometimes it also means age. The word "hour" (pechus) literally means measure of space, or distance (approximately 18 inches i.e. the forearm); but it can also mean a measure of time or age (Jn.9:21). So the verse can read either "who can add a single hour to his life" or "one minute to his life span."

The point is striking: worry is senseless—just as senseless as trying to add to one's height or lengthen a minute to one's life span (when it is time for one to pass on). All statures and all bodies are not normal and perfectly formed. The world is corruptible and imperfect (see note—Mt.6:19-20). But there is a glorious hope in God—a hope that acknowledges that God does love and does care and has promised a new heavens and earth that shall be perfect. In that perfect heavens and earth, all bodies shall be normal and perfectly formed. God shall "wipe every tear from their eyes" (Rev.21:4; cp. 1-7).

But our citizenship is in heaven. And we eagerly await a Savior from there, the Lord Jesus Christ, who, by the power that enables him to bring everything under his control, will transform our lowly bodies so that they will be like his glorious body. (Phil 3:20-21)

So will it be with the resurrection of the dead. The body that is sown is perishable, it is raised imperishable; it is sown in dishonor, it is raised in glory; it is sown in weakness, it is raised in power; it is sown a natural body, it is raised a spiritual body. If there is a natural body, there is also a spiritual body. (1 Cor 15:42-44)

And just as we have borne the likeness of the earthly man, so shall we bear the likeness of the man from heaven. (1 Cor 15:49)

Meanwhile we groan, longing to be clothed with our heavenly dwelling, (2 Cor 5:2)

But those who are considered worthy of

taking part in that age and in the resurrection from the dead will neither marry nor be given in marriage, and they can no longer die; for they are like the angels. They are God's children, since they are children of the resurrection. (Luke 20:35-36)

For the Lamb at the center of the throne will be their shepherd; he will lead them to springs of living water. And God will wipe away every tear from their eyes." (Rev 7:17)

He will wipe every tear from their eyes. There will be no more death or mourning or crying or pain, for the old order of things has passed away." (Rev 21:4)

Thought 1. Note the rich fool could not add one minute to his life. There was a night (day) appointed for his death, and he could not change that night (cp. Lk.12:16-21).

Very practically, some do have imperfect or abnormal bodies. How do they keep from being anxious and worrying?

1) There is a glorious hope for all (see note—Mt.6:27 for discussion).
2) There is the assuring promise of God to work all things out for good to those who truly love God.

And we know that in all things God works for the good of those who love him, who have been called according to his purpose. (Rom 8:28)

3) There is the strong challenge to be content with one's state or lot in life.

Nevertheless, each one should retain the place in life that the Lord assigned to him and to which God has called him. This is the rule I lay down in all the churches....Each one should remain in the situation which he was in when God called him...Brothers, each man, as responsible to God, should remain in the situation God called him to. (1 Cor 7:17, 20, 24; cp. v. 7-24)

I am not saying this because I am in need, for I have learned to be content whatever the circumstances. I know what it is to be in need, and I know what it is to have plenty. I have learned the secret of being content in any and every situation, whether well fed or hungry, whether living in plenty or in want. I can do everything through him who gives me strength. (Phil 4:11-13)

The brother in humble circumstances ought to take pride in his high position. But the one who is rich should take pride in his low position, because he will pass away like a wild flower. For the sun rises with scorching heat and withers the plant; its blossom falls and its beauty is destroyed. In the same way, the rich man will fade away even while he goes about his business. (James 1:9-11)

4) There is the challenge to trust God's care.

Cast all your anxiety on him because he cares for you. (1 Pet 5:7)

In vain you rise early and stay up late, toiling for food to eat— for he grants sleep to those he loves. (Psa 127:2)

4. The fourth illustration was that of the lilies and the grass. They are clothed by God. Again Jesus said, "Consider"—look at and think about the lilies of the field. Learn from what happens to them.

⇒ Lilies do not toil for money to buy their clothing.
⇒ Lilies do not spin to make their clothing.
⇒ Yet, lilies are more arrayed than Solomon in all his glory.
⇒ Lilies pass away almost overnight, yet God cares enough for them to clothe them.

Learn that you are of much more value than lilies. God will clothe you.

There are three concerns surrounding clothing. (Sometimes the concern becomes so strong it turns into a literal fear.)

1. The concern of popularity. A person fears not having the right clothing necessary to make him popular. Sometimes the concern is so great that he refuses to go to a particular function without the proper clothing.

2. The concern of style and fashion. A person is concerned with the very latest in style and fashion. He cannot accept his clothing being the least bit outdated.

3. The concern of acceptability. Most adults would fall into this category. Clothing is a matter that actually involves inward feelings. The concern is really there. Time and thought and effort are expended to stay in style, at least enough to be acceptable.

The point Jesus was making is this: fret not, worry not, be not anxious over clothing. But seek ye first—center your life and thoughts and efforts upon God and His righteousness and not upon popularity, fashion and acceptability—and then all these things (clothing) will be added unto you (Mt.6:33).

The one who received the seed that fell among the thorns is the man who hears the word, but the worries of this life and the deceitfulness of wealth choke it, making it unfruitful. (Mat 13:22)

I also want women to dress modestly, with decency and propriety, not with braided hair or gold or pearls or expensive clothes, but with good deeds, appropriate for women who profess to worship God. (1 Tim 2:9-10)

When they [husbands] see the purity and reverence of your lives. Your beauty should not come from outward adornment, such as braided hair and the wearing of gold jewelry and fine clothes. Instead, it should be that of your inner self, the unfading beauty of a gentle and quiet spirit, which is of great worth in God's sight. For this is the way the holy women of the past who put their hope in God used to make themselves beautiful. They were submissive to their own husbands, (1 Pet 3:2-5)

Always be clothed in white, [cleaned, washed] and always anoint your head with oil [well-groomed, cared for]. (Eccl 9:8)

A woman must not wear men's clothing, nor a man wear women's clothing, for the LORD your God detests anyone who

does this. (Deu 22:5)

The LORD says, "The women of Zion are haughty, walking along with outstretched necks, flirting with their eyes, tripping along with mincing steps, with ornaments jingling on their ankles. Therefore the Lord will bring sores on the heads of the women of Zion; the LORD will make their scalps bald." In that day the Lord will snatch away their finery: the bangles and headbands and crescent necklaces, the earrings and bracelets and veils, the headdresses and ankle chains and sashes, the perfume bottles and charms, the signet rings and nose rings, the fine robes and the capes and cloaks, the purses and mirrors, and the linen garments and tiaras and shawls. Instead of fragrance there will be a stench; instead of a sash, a rope; instead of well-dressed hair, baldness; instead of fine clothing, sackcloth; instead of beauty, branding. (Isa 3:16-24)

DEEPER STUDY # 1
(12:28) **"O You of Little Faith"**: see DEEPER STUDY # 1—Mt.6:30 for discussion.

2 (12:29-30) **Worldliness—Materialism**: do not be wrapped up in seeking food and drink, nor in doubting God's care. Note a significant fact: this is not a challenge; *it is a command.* The believer is to center his mind and life upon the Lord and the work God has given him to do, not upon *making a living and eating and drinking.* There are two reasons Jesus commands this.

1. Being wrapped up in seeking food and drink is worldliness. It is what the nations of the world, the Gentiles, the heathen, the lost, do. They center their whole life around getting more and more of the things of this world. They talk and talk, think and think about food and drink and clothing. It consumes their whole beings. All they know is getting more of what the world has to offer. Life to them is food and drink and possessions (houses, furnishings, position, promotion, recognition, money, the latest styles, keeping up with everyone else). The believer is not to be seeking after these things. He is different. He is to be seeking the Kingdom of God and not doubting God's care and provision.

For the pagans run after all these things, and your heavenly Father knows that you need them. (Mat 6:32)

What good will it be for a man if he gains the whole world, yet forfeits his soul? Or what can a man give in exchange for his soul [life]? (Mat 16:26)

"Be careful, or your hearts will be weighed down with dissipation, drunkenness and the anxieties of life, and that day will close on you unexpectedly like a trap. (Luke 21:34)

Set your minds on things above, not on earthly things. (Col 3:2)

It teaches us to say "No" to ungodliness and worldly passions, and to live self-controlled, upright and godly lives in this present age, while we wait for the blessed hope—the glorious appearing of our great God and Savior, Jesus Christ, (Titus 2:12-13)

You adulterous people, don't you know that friendship with the world is hatred toward God? Anyone who chooses to be a friend of the world becomes an enemy of God. (James 4:4)

2. God knows that the believer has needs. The believer is...

- to know that God knows about his needs.
- not to have a *doubtful* and *anxious mind.*
- to trust God and His ability to meet the need for food and clothing (the necessities of life).

"'If you can'?" said Jesus. "Everything is possible for him who believes." (Mark 9:23)

For everyone born of God overcomes the world. This is the victory that has overcome the world, even our faith. (1 John 5:4)

The LORD redeems his servants; no one will be condemned who takes refuge in him. (Psa 34:22)

Commit your way to the LORD; trust in him and he will do this: (Psa 37:5)

The LORD remembers us and will bless us: He will bless the house of Israel, he will bless the house of Aaron, (Psa 115:12)

It is better to take refuge in the LORD than to trust in man. (Psa 118:8)

Trust in the LORD with all your heart and lean not on your own understanding; (Prov 3:5)

Trust in the LORD forever, for the LORD, the LORD, is the Rock eternal. (Isa 26:4)

Who among you fears the LORD and obeys the word of his servant? Let him who walks in the dark, who has no light, trust in the name of the LORD and rely on his God. (Isa 50:10)

3 (12:31-34) **Service—Giving—Wealth, True**: seek the Kingdom of God (see DEEPER STUDY # 3—Mt.19:23-24). The believer is not to seek after the things of the world. He is to focus his life upon the Kingdom of God and the work God has given him to do. He is to leave his welfare in the hands of God. Jesus made three great promises and one significant warning.

1. God will provide the necessities of life for the person who seeks God first.

"So I say to you: Ask and it will be given to you; seek and you will find; knock and the door will be opened to you. For everyone who asks receives; he who seeks finds; and to him who knocks, the door will be opened. "Which of you fathers, if your son asks for a fish, will give him a snake instead? Or if he asks for an egg, will give him a scorpion? If you then, though you are evil, know how to give good gifts to your children, how much more will your

Father in heaven give the Holy Spirit to those who ask him!" (Luke 11:9-13)

And will not God bring about justice for his chosen ones, who cry out to him day and night? Will he keep putting them off? (Luke 18:7)

You may ask me for anything in my name, and I will do it. (John 14:14)

2. God will give the kingdom to His "little flock," those who truly seek God's kingdom first and trust Him to care for them. Note the term "little flock." It tells us two things.

a. The number is small. Only a few really seek God's kingdom first.

But small is the gate and narrow the road that leads to life, and only a few find it. (Mat 7:14)

"For many are invited, but few are chosen." (Mat 22:14)

"Blessed are the poor in spirit, for theirs is the kingdom of heaven. (Mat 5:3)

"Then the King will say to those on his right, 'Come, you who are blessed by my Father; take your inheritance, the kingdom prepared for you since the creation of the world. For I was hungry and you gave me something to eat, I was thirsty and you gave me something to drink, I was a stranger and you invited me in, (Mat 25:34-35)

For the kingdom of God is not a matter of eating and drinking, but of righteousness, peace and joy in the Holy Spirit, (Rom 14:17)

I declare to you, brothers, that flesh and blood cannot inherit the kingdom of God, nor does the perishable inherit the imperishable. (1 Cor 15:50)

Listen, my dear brothers: Has not God chosen those who are poor in the eyes of the world to be rich in faith and to inherit the kingdom he promised those who love him? (James 2:5)

b. The care of God is sure. He is the Shepherd and His true followers are the sheep of *His pasture*.

The watchman opens the gate for him, and the sheep listen to his voice. He calls his own sheep by name and leads them out. When he has brought out all his own, he goes on ahead of them, and his sheep follow him because they know his voice. (John 10:3-4)

"I am the good shepherd; I know my sheep and my sheep know me—I have other sheep that are not of this sheep pen. I must bring them also. They too will listen to my voice, and there shall be one flock and one shepherd. (John 10:14, 16)

A psalm of David. The LORD is my shepherd, I shall not be in want. (Psa 23:1; cp. v. 2-6)

3. God gives treasures that do not age, fail, nor corrupt; neither can they be stolen. What Jesus said is revolutionary: "Sell your possessions, and give to the poor." Very simply, once our needs have been met, we do not need more. We can do nothing more with it...

- unless we waste it.
- unless we store it up.

This is exactly what Jesus preached against so strongly. When we live in a world so full of needs, a world lost and dying, once we have met our needs, we are to give what is left to meet the needs of others. It does not matter what position or profession or kind of income we have, once we meet our needs, we are to begin meeting the needs of the world. In fact, the believer is commanded to seek the *good professions and jobs* so that he can have *more* to give to the needy (Eph.4:28). Note the purpose: it is not to hold a reputable position nor to gain wealth. It is for the purpose of seeking God's kingdom, of spreading the love of God by meeting the needs of others.

a. The believer is to fill his bag (billfold, pocket, bank account) with the *gifts or giving* of money and *deeds* of helps. Such will never age.

Give to the one who asks you, and do not turn away from the one who wants to borrow from you. (Mat 5:42)

John answered, "The man with two tunics should share with him who has none, and the one who has food should do the same." (Luke 3:11)

In everything I did, I showed you that by this kind of hard work we must help the weak, remembering the words the Lord Jesus himself said: 'It is more blessed to give than to receive.'" (Acts 20:35)

Share with God's people who are in need. Practice hospitality. (Rom 12:13)

Therefore, as we have opportunity [to give], let us do good to all people, especially to those who belong to the family of believers. (Gal 6:10)

He who has been stealing must steal no longer, but must work, doing something useful with his own hands, that he may have something to share with those in need. (Eph 4:28)

Command them to do good, to be rich in good deeds, and to be generous and willing to share. (1 Tim 6:18)

And do not forget to do good and to share with others, for with such sacrifices God is pleased. (Heb 13:16)

b. The believer is to secure the treasures of God's approval and of souls won in heaven. These treasures will never fail nor corrupt nor be stolen.

For what is our hope, our joy, or the crown in which we will glory in the presence of our Lord Jesus when he comes? Is it not you? (1 Th 2:19)

Everything on this earth ages, fails, corrupts, and can be stolen. But the man who uses only what he needs and then gives the rest fills his bag with *real money and real treasure*, money and treasure that shall...

- never age
- never fail
- never corrupt
- never be stolen

What is more, I consider everything a loss compared to the surpassing greatness of knowing Christ Jesus my Lord, for whose sake I have lost all things. I consider them rubbish, that I may gain Christ (Phil 3:8)

In this way they will lay up treasure for themselves as a firm foundation for the coming age, so that they may take hold of the life that is truly life. (1 Tim 6:19)

Praise be to the God and Father of our Lord Jesus Christ! In his great mercy he has given us new birth into a living hope through the resurrection of Jesus Christ from the dead, and into an inheritance that can never perish, spoil or fade—kept in heaven for you, (1 Pet 1:3, 4)

I counsel you to buy from me gold refined in the fire, so you can become rich; and white clothes to wear, so you can cover your shameful nakedness; and salve to put on your eyes, so you can see. (Rev 3:18)

4. Jesus warned His followers: their hearts would be where their treasure is. If their treasure is in the world, if they live indulgent and extravagant lives, their hearts will be in the world.

But store up for yourselves treasures in heaven, where moth and rust do not destroy, and where thieves do not break in and steal. (Mat 6:20)

"The kingdom of heaven is like treasure hidden in a field. When a man found it, he hid it again, and then in his joy went and sold all he had and bought that field. (Mat 13:44)

Jesus answered, "If you want to be perfect, go, sell your possessions and give to the poor, and you will have treasure in heaven. Then come, follow me." (Mat 19:21)

Do not love the world or anything in the world. If anyone loves the world, the love of the Father is not in him. For everything in the world—the cravings of sinful man, the lust of his eyes and the boasting of what he has and does—comes not from the Father but from the world. The world and its desires pass away, but the man who does the will of God lives forever. (1 John 2:15-17)

	O. The Parable of the Faithful & Unfaithful Manager: A Strong Warning—Be Prepared, 12:35-48 (Mt.24:37-25:30)	42 The Lord answered, "Who then is the faithful and wise manager, whom the master puts in charge of his servants to give them their food allowance at the proper time?	b. There is a faithful & wise manager 1) He is a manager
1 The charge: Be watching—be ready for the Lord's return a. Because the Lord is returning	35 "Be dressed ready for service and keep your lamps burning, 36 Like men waiting for their master to return from a wedding banquet, so that when he comes and knocks they can immediately open the door for him.	43 It will be good for that servant whom the master finds doing so when he returns. 44 I tell you the truth, he will put him in charge of all his possessions. 45 But suppose the servant says to himself, 'My master is taking a long time in coming,' and he then begins to beat the menservants and maidservants and to eat and drink and get drunk.	2) He is a servant 3) He is found "doing": Serving faithfully 4) He is to be rewarded: Made a ruler, put in charge c. There is an unfaithful & unwise manager 1) He says there is "plenty of time" 2) He does his own will, his own thing
b. Because you will be served by Christ Himself	37 It will be good for those servants whose master finds them watching when he comes. I tell you the truth, he will dress himself to serve, will have them recline at the table and will come and wait on them.	46 The master of that servant will come on a day when he does not expect him and at an hour he is not aware of. He will cut him to pieces and assign him a place with the unbelievers.	3) He is to be judged with the unbelievers
c. Because you will be blessed (It will be good for you)	38 It will be good for those servants whose master finds them ready, even if he comes in the second or third watch of the night.	47 "That servant who knows his master's will and does not get ready or does not do what his master wants will be beaten with many blows.	d. There is the unfaithful manager identified 1) The 1st class of unfaithful managers: Sinned deliberately—knew the Lord's will
d. Because Christ will come suddenly, unexpectedly	39 But understand this: If the owner of the house had known at what hour the thief was coming, he would not have let his house be broken into.	48 But the one who does not know and does things deserving punishment will be beaten with few blows. From everyone who has been given much, much will be demanded; and from the one who has been entrusted with much, much more will be asked.	2) The 2nd class of unfaithful managers: Sinned in ignorance—did not know the Lord's will 3) The principle of judgment: Having much requires giving much
e. Because Christ will come when least expected	40 You also must be ready, because the Son of Man will come at an hour when you do not expect him."		
2 The parable of the manager a. There is Peter's question	41 Peter asked, "Lord, are you telling this parable to us, or to everyone?"		

DIVISION V

THE SON OF MAN'S GREAT JOURNEY TO JERUSALEM (STAGE I): HIS MISSION AND PUBLIC CHALLENGE, 9:51-13:21

O. The Parable of the Faithful and Unfaithful Manager: A Strong Warning—Be Prepared, 12:35-48

(12:35-48) **Introduction**: Jesus was still dealing with the subject of men who want things—wealth and riches and plenty. He was still dealing with covetousness (Lk.12:13-21; 12:22-34). The believer's mind is to be upon purity of life and service, not upon possessions and cares of this world. Jesus strongly warned: be prepared.

1. The charge: be watching—be ready for the Lord's return (v.35-40).
2. The parable of the manager (v.41-48).

1 (12:35-40) **Jesus Christ, Return**: the charge—be watching, be ready for the Lord's return. Jesus shared a striking illustration. The picture was that of a Lord who had gone off to attend a great marriage celebration. His servants had been left behind to look after the household and to wait for his return. The servants should be full of joy and rejoicing for their master's privilege in celebrating the marriage. They may not be, but they should be, and they should be looking after everything with all diligence until he returns. Jesus took the picture and applied it to Himself and His disciples.

The believer is to be in a state of readiness. He is always to be prepared, always watching and waiting for his Lord's return.

⇒ He is to be fully dressed, even to having his belt tight around his waist. This refers to personal preparation: purity of heart and life and keeping one's body ready to move and meet the Lord. In the East men wore robes that had to be tied with a belt at the waist or else the loose robes hampered movement and work. It was impossible to move quickly and freely without the belt being tight.

⇒ The Lord's servant is to have the lights burning, never allowing them to go out. Keeping the lights burning refers to serving and laboring for the Lord. He is to keep the lights of labor burning by faithfully serving and working for the Lord.

The idea with both the belt and the light is, of course, *readiness*: being prepared in body and labor, being pure and faithful. The believer must never lie down or slumber, never be caught off guard or unprepared. Jesus gave six reasons for living in a state of readiness, of purity and faithfulness.

1. The believer is to stay ready because the Lord is returning. He is the Head of the house; He owns the property. He did not desert the house and the property. He left to attend a great marriage feast. He will be returning to *His home and His property* (world). Note: the word "your" is emphatic (v.35). No matter what others may do, "be dressed...your lamps" must be prepared. You must be like men who wait and stay awake and look and are prepared for their Lord. You must be *ready* to open the door *immediately* when He knocks, for He is going to return and knock. His return is an absolute certainty (cp. Jn.14:2-3; Tit.2:12-13).

> **But Jesus remained silent and gave no answer. Again the high priest asked him, "Are you the Christ, the Son of the Blessed One?" "I am," said Jesus. "And you will see the Son of Man sitting at the right hand of the Mighty One and coming on the clouds of heaven." (Mark 14:61-62)**
>
> **At that time they will see the Son of Man coming in a cloud with power and great glory. (Luke 21:27)**
>
> **"Men of Galilee," they said, "why do you stand here looking into the sky? This same Jesus, who has been taken from you into heaven, will come back in the same way you have seen him go into heaven." (Acts 1:11)**
>
> **Brothers, we do not want you to be ignorant about those who fall asleep, or to grieve like the rest of men, who have no hope. We believe that Jesus died and rose again and so we believe that God will bring with Jesus those who have fallen asleep in him. According to the Lord's own word, we tell you that we who are still alive, who are left till the coming of the Lord, will certainly not precede those who have fallen asleep. For the Lord himself will come down from heaven, with a loud command, with the voice of the archangel and with the trumpet call of God, and the dead in Christ will rise first. After that, we who are still alive and are left will be caught up together with them in the clouds to meet the Lord in the air. And so we will be with the Lord forever. Therefore encourage each other with these words. (1 Th 4:13-18)**
>
> **So Christ was sacrificed once to take away the sins of many people; and he will appear a second time, not to bear sin, but to bring salvation to those who are waiting for him. (Heb 9:28)**

Thought 1. There is a message on salvation here as well. A person must be ready to open the door of his heart immediately when Jesus knocks.

> **Here I am! I stand at the door and knock. If anyone hears my voice and opens the door, I will come in and eat with him, and he with me. (Rev 3:20)**

2. The believer is to stay ready because he will be served by Christ Himself. This is a most precious and wonderful promise, a most unusual promise. Imagine the Lord of the universe *serving* us at a banquet, yet it is the promise made by Jesus! Why would such a promise be made to the believer?

God has only one Son, and God loves His only Son *so much* that He promises to elevate to the highest position any man who honors His Son. Any man who honors God's Son will be highly honored by God.

> **Whoever serves me must follow me; and where I am, my servant also will be. My Father will honor the one who serves me. (John 12:26)**

The person who honors God's Son is adopted as a child of God's, and that person becomes a brother to Christ and an heir of God.

> **But when the time had fully come, God sent his Son, born of a woman, born under law, to redeem those under law, that we might receive the full rights of sons. Because you are sons, God sent the Spirit of his Son into our hearts, the Spirit who calls out, "Abba, FatherSo you are no longer a slave, but a son; and since you are a son, God has made you also an heir. (Gal 4:4-7)**
>
> **For you did not receive a spirit that makes you a slave again to fear, but you received the Spirit of sonship. And by him we cry, "Abba, Father." The Spirit himself testifies with our spirit that we are God's children. Now if we are children, then we are heirs—heirs of God and co-heirs with Christ, if indeed we share in his sufferings in order that we may also share in his glory. I consider that our present sufferings are not worth comparing with the glory that will be revealed in us. (Rom 8:15-18)**
>
> **In my Father's house are many rooms; if it were not so, I would have told you. I am going there to prepare a place for you. And if I go and prepare a place for you, I will come back and take you to be with me that you also may be where I am. (John 14:2-3)**
>
> **Therefore judge nothing before the appointed time; wait till the Lord comes. He will bring to light what is hidden in darkness and will expose the motives of men's hearts. At that time each will receive his praise from God. (1 Cor 4:5)**

The believer is to stay ready because the very thing for which he has been working is Christ's return. When Christ gathers us all together, His heart will be so overflowing with love and joy (as will ours) that He will begin serving us immediately: conforming us to His image, explaining and discussing everything with us, assigning us our eternal duties.

> **But our citizenship is in heaven. And we eagerly await a Savior from there, the Lord Jesus Christ, who, by the power that enables him to bring everything under his control, will transform our lowly bodies so that they will be like his glorious body. (Phil 3:20-21)**

When Christ, who is your life, appears, then you also will appear with him in glory. (Col 3:4)

May he strengthen your hearts so that you will be blameless and holy in the presence of our God and Father when our Lord Jesus comes with all his holy ones. (1 Th 3:13)

Dear friends, now we are children of God, and what we will be has not yet been made known. But we know that when he appears, we shall be like him, for we shall see him as he is. (1 John 3:2)

3. The believer is to stay ready because he will be blessed. The phrase "it will be good" (makarioi) means to pronounce a person happy or blessed. The idea is that Christ is going to make the believer happy and blessed. Happiness and blessedness will become a state of being, the constant experience of the believer. But note two points.

a. It is conditional. The believer must be watching and ready for the Lord's coming (pure and faithful) if he is to be blessed.

b. The Lord is not returning in the first watch. His return is going to be in the second or third watch. The night was divided into four watches by the Romans and into three watches by the Jews. The point is the importance of being ready: the hour of His return is unknown, but He is returning. It may be immediately; it may be later. The idea is that no one knows the time, but be ready—be prepared—if you wish to be blessed.

Let your gentleness be evident to all. The Lord is near. (Phil 4:5)

You too, be patient and stand firm, because the Lord's coming is near. (James 5:8)

I am coming soon. Hold on to what you have, so that no one will take your crown. (Rev 3:11)

4. The believer is to stay ready because Christ will come unexpectedly. The parable is clear: the hour of the Lord's return is not known; His return is going to be unexpected. The believer...

- must not be careless: get tired of waiting up, get sleepy, be caught off guard, begin to disbelieve. (All of this can happen to a houseowner waiting on a burglar.)
- must watch: secure, sit up, stay awake, listen, look, take notice of all noises and sights (signs). (The burglar always comes in an unexpected hour.)

The believer must watch and be prepared as much as a houseowner would watch and prepare if he knew a burglar were coming.

For as lightning that comes from the east is visible even in the west, so will be the coming of the Son of Man. (Mat 24:27)

"No one knows about that day or hour, not even the angels in heaven, nor the Son, but only the Father. (Mat 24:36)

"Therefore keep watch because you do not know when the owner of the house will come back—whether in the evening, or at midnight, or when the rooster crows, or at dawn. (Mark 13:35)

5. The believer is to stay ready because Christ will come when *least* expected. Jesus could not have stated it any clearer; He could not have spoken any plainer. "When you do not expect him," He will come. He will be coming when we least expect Him to come. "You must also be ready."

So you also must be ready, because the Son of Man will come at an hour when you do not expect him. (Mat 24:44)

"But while they were on their way to buy the oil, the bridegroom arrived. The virgins who were ready went in with him to the wedding banquet. And the door was shut. "Later the others also came. 'Sir! Sir!' they said. 'Open the door for us!' "But he replied, 'I tell you the truth, I don't know you.' "Therefore keep watch, because you do not know the day or the hour. (Mat 25:10-13; cp. v. 6-9)

For you know very well that the day of the Lord will come like a thief in the night. (1 Th 5:2)

Remember, therefore, what you have received and heard; obey it, and repent. But if you do not wake up, I will come like a thief, and you will not know at what time I will come to you. (Rev 3:3)

"Behold, I come like a thief! Blessed is he who stays awake and keeps his clothes with him, so that he may not go naked and be shamefully exposed." (Rev 16:15)

2 (12:41-48) **Manager—Dedication—Faithfulness vs. Unfaithfulness—Rewards—Punishment, Degrees**: the parable of the manager.

1. Peter wanted to know if the message on *watching and readiness* was for the disciples only or did it apply to the world as well. Jesus answered by giving a parable known as the parable of the manager.

2. There was a faithful and wise manager. Jesus said four things about this manager.

a. He was a manager. A manager was just what Jesus said he was: a man who was made ruler over his Lord's household. He was the manager of the Lord's estate, responsible for all of it.

"Again, it will be like a man [Christ] going on a journey, who called his servants and entrusted his property to them. To one he gave five talents of money, to another two talents, and to another one talent, each according to his ability. Then he went on his journey. (Mat 25:14-15)

So he called ten of his servants and gave them ten minas. 'Put this money to work,' he said, 'until I come back.' (Luke 19:13)

b. He was a slave or servant (doulos), a bond-slave, a man under the Lord's will entirely. He was possessed by the Lord and his very life depended upon doing everything the Lord said (see note, Servant—Slave—Ro.1:1).

c. He was found "doing," that is, serving faithfully when the Lord returned. The Lord found him doing exactly what he should have been doing (1 Cor.4:2).

⇒ He was overseeing the Master's household.

You were bought at a price. Therefore honor God with your body. (1 Cor 6:20)

Therefore, my dear brothers, stand firm. Let nothing move you. Always give yourselves fully to the work of the Lord, because you know that your labor in the Lord is not in vain. (1 Cor 15:58)

Serve wholeheartedly, as if you were serving the Lord, not men, (Eph 6:7)

Obey your leaders and submit to their authority. They keep watch over you as men who must give an account. Obey them so that their work will be a joy, not a burden, for that would be of no advantage to you. (Heb 13:17)

Timothy, guard what has been entrusted to your care. Turn away from godless chatter and the opposing ideas of what is falsely called knowledge, (1 Tim 6:20)

Guard the good deposit that was entrusted to you—guard it with the help of the Holy Spirit who lives in us. (2 Tim 1:14)

Be shepherds of God's flock that is under your care, serving as overseers—not because you must, but because you are willing, as God wants you to be; not greedy for money, but eager to serve; not lording it over those entrusted to you, but being examples to the flock. (1 Pet 5:2-3)

⇒ He was feeding the Master's family faithfully.

When they had finished eating, Jesus said to Simon Peter, "Simon son of John, do you truly love me more than these?" "Yes, Lord," he said, "you know that I love you." Jesus said, "Feed my lambs." (John 21:15; cp. v.16-17)

Now it is required that those who have been given a trust must prove faithful. (1 Cor 4:2)

Watch your life and doctrine closely. Persevere in them, because if you do, you will save both yourself and your hearers. (1 Tim 4:16)

Each one should use whatever gift he has received to serve others, faithfully administering God's grace in its various forms. (1 Pet 4:10)

d. He was to be rewarded, made *ruler* and *put in charge of* that the Lord had. The idea is that the faithful and wise believer will be placed as highly as he can be placed. He will be given all that the Master and Lord has, that is, a complete estate to manage (see notes—Lk.16:10-12; 19:15-23; 22:28-30).

"His master replied, 'Well done, good and faithful servant! You have been faithful with a few things; I will put you in charge of many things. Come and share your master's happiness!' (Mat 25:23)

"Then the King will say to those on his right, 'Come, you who are blessed by my Father; take your inheritance, the kingdom prepared for you since the creation of the world. (Mat 25:34)

But love your enemies, do good to them, and lend to them without expecting to get anything back. Then your reward will be great, and you will be sons of the Most High, because he is kind to the ungrateful and wicked. (Luke 6:35)

"'Well done, my good servant!' his master replied. 'Because you have been trustworthy in a very small matter, take charge of ten cities.' (Luke 19:17)

You are those who have stood by me in my trials. And I confer on you a kingdom, just as my Father conferred one on me, (Luke 22:28-29)

For if, by the trespass of the one man, death reigned through that one man, how much more will those who receive God's abundant provision of grace and of the gift of righteousness reign in life through the one man, Jesus Christ. (Rom 5:17)

Do you not know that the saints will judge [rule, have authority over] the world? (1 Cor 6:2)

If we endure, we will also reign with him. If we disown him, he will also disown us; (2 Tim 2:12)

And from Jesus Christ, who is the faithful witness, the firstborn from the dead, and the ruler of the kings of the earth. To him who loves us and has freed us from our sins by his blood, and has made us to be a kingdom and priests to serve his God and Father—to him be glory and power for ever and ever! Amen. (Rev 1:5-6)

To him who overcomes, I will give the right to sit with me on my throne, just as I overcame and sat down with my Father on his throne. (Rev 3:21)

I saw thrones on which were seated those who had been given authority to judge. And I saw the souls of those who had been beheaded because of their testimony for Jesus and because of the word of God. They had not worshiped the beast or his image and had not received his mark on their foreheads or their hands. They came to life and reigned with Christ a thousand years. (Rev 20:4)

There will be no more night. They will not need the light of a lamp or the light of the sun, for the Lord God will give them light. And they will reign for ever and ever. (Rev 22:5)

3. There was an unfaithful, an unwise manager (manager). Jesus said three things about this manager.

a. The unfaithful manager said there is *plenty of time*. Why? Because the Lord had delayed His coming; therefore, the manager thought the Lord's return was a long way off. Note: he did not doubt the Lord's return. He knew the Lord was returning, but he did not think it would be soon.

And I'll say to myself, "You have plenty of good things laid up for many years. Take life easy; eat, drink and be merry."' (Luke 12:19)

As Paul discoursed on righteousness, self-control and the judgment to come, Felix was afraid and said, "That's enough for now! You may leave. When I find it convenient, I will send for you." (Acts 24:25)

Now listen, you who say, "Today or tomorrow we will go to this or that city, spend a year there, carry on business and make money." Why, you do not even know what will happen tomorrow. What is your life? You are a mist that appears for a little while and then vanishes. (James 4:13-14)

Do not boast about tomorrow, for you do not know what a day may bring forth. (Prov 27:1)

"Come," each one cries, "let me get wine! Let us drink our fill of beer! And tomorrow will be like today, or even far better." (Isa 56:12)

b. He did his own will, his own thing. He mistreated and abused others, both male and female, using and misusing, deceiving and taking advantage as he willed. And he lived a worldly life, indulging in the fleshly pleasures of partying and carousing, eating and drinking.

The seed that fell among thorns stands for those who hear, but as they go on their way they are choked by life's worries, riches and pleasures, and they do not mature. (Luke 8:14)

"Whoever can be trusted with very little can also be trusted with much, and whoever is dishonest with very little will also be dishonest with much. (Luke 16:10)

But the widow who lives for pleasure is dead even while she lives. (1 Tim 5:6)

But mark this: There will be terrible times in the last days. People will be lovers of themselves, lovers of money, boastful, proud, abusive, disobedient to their parents, ungrateful, unholy, without love, unforgiving, slanderous, without self-control, brutal, not lovers of the good, treacherous, rash, conceited, lovers of pleasure rather than lovers of God— (2 Tim 3:1-4)

At one time we too were foolish, disobedient, deceived and enslaved by all kinds of passions and pleasures. We lived in malice and envy, being hated and hating one another. (Titus 3:3)

You have lived on earth in luxury and self-indulgence. You have fattened yourselves in the day of slaughter. (James 5:5)

They will be paid back with harm for the harm they have done. Their idea of pleasure is to carouse in broad daylight. They are blots and blemishes, reveling in their pleasures while they feast with you. (2 Pet 2:13)

Do not take advantage of a hired man who is poor and needy, whether he is a brother Israelite or an alien living in one of your towns. (Deu 24:14)

Do not trust in extortion or take pride in stolen goods; though your riches increase, do not set your heart on them. (Psa 62:10)

"How long will you defend the unjust and show partiality to the wicked? Selah (Psa 82:2)

Do not envy a violent man or choose any of his ways, (Prov 3:31)

He who oppresses the poor shows contempt for their Maker, but whoever is kind to the needy honors God. (Prov 14:31)

He who oppresses the poor to increase his wealth and he who gives gifts to the rich—both come to poverty. (Prov 22:16)

If you see the poor oppressed in a district, and justice and rights denied, do not be surprised at such things; for one official is eyed by a higher one, and over them both are others higher still. (Eccl 5:8)

c. He was to be judged with the unbelievers. The Lord was very clear about this.
   ⇒ The unfaithful manager will be caught by the Lord, caught *unaware*, "in a day when he does not expect Him."

"Be careful, or your hearts will be weighed down with dissipation, drunkenness and the anxieties of life, and that day will close on you unexpectedly like a trap. For it will come upon all those who live on the face of the whole earth. (Luke 21:34-35)

Moreover, no man knows when his hour will come: As fish are caught in a cruel net, or birds are taken in a snare, so men are trapped by evil times that fall unexpectedly upon them. (Eccl 9:12)

For in the days before the flood, people were eating and drinking, marrying and giving in marriage, up to the day Noah entered the ark; and they knew nothing about what would happen until the flood came and took them all away. That is how it will be at the coming of the Son of Man. (Mat 24:38-39)

   ⇒ The Lord will "cut him to pieces." This means he will be condemned to death, cut off from among the living, exiled from eternal life. Most tragic, he will be *cut to pieces, cut off* from God's presence.
   ⇒ The Lord will assign him a place with the unbelievers. Why? Because he was not genuine. He was a hypocrite.

He will cut him to pieces and assign him a place with the hypocrites, where there will be weeping and gnashing of teeth. (Mat 24:51)

When he has filled his belly, God will vent his burning anger against him and rain down his blows upon him....The heavens will expose his

guilt; the earth will rise up against him. A flood will carry off his house, rushing waters on the day of God's wrath. Such is the fate God allots the wicked, the heritage appointed for them by God." (Job 20:23, 27-29)

On the wicked he will rain fiery coals and burning sulfur; a scorching wind will be their lot. (Psa 11:6)

This is your lot, the portion I have decreed for you," declares the LORD, "because you have forgotten me and trusted in false gods. I will pull up your skirts over your face that your shame may be seen—your adulteries and lustful neighings, your shameless prostitution! I have seen your detestable acts on the hills and in the fields. Woe to you, O Jerusalem! How long will you be unclean?" (Jer 13:25-27)

4. There was the unfaithful manager identified. Note that Jesus answered Peter's question in these two verses. He was speaking to both believers and unbelievers. Who is to be watching and living in a state of readiness? Who is to be served by Christ and greatly blessed? The answer is clear: the faithful manager, not the unfaithful manager. Who then is the unfaithful manager? There are two classes named:

a. Class 1: the *servant* who knew the Lord's will and did not prepare himself (v.35), nor did he do the Lord's will (cp. 1 Jn.3:23). This servant's judgment is tragic, for he knew God's will, but deliberately rejected it. Therefore, he will be beaten with many stripes, that is, due much more judgment and punishment.

"Then they will go away to eternal punishment, but the righteous to eternal life." (Mat 25:46; cp. v.25-45)

But whoever blasphemes against the Holy Spirit will never be forgiven; he is guilty of an eternal sin." (Mark 3:29)

His [Christ's] winnowing fork is in his hand to clear his threshing floor and to gather the wheat into his barn, but he will burn up the chaff with unquenchable fire." (Luke 3:17)

But for those who are self-seeking and who reject the truth and follow evil, there will be wrath and anger. There will be trouble and distress for every human being who does evil: first for the Jew, then for the Gentile; (Rom 2:8-9)

And give relief to you who are troubled, and to us as well. This will happen when the Lord Jesus is revealed from heaven in blazing fire with his powerful angels. He will punish those who do not know God and do not obey the gospel of our Lord Jesus. They will be punished with everlasting destruction and shut out from the presence of the Lord and from the majesty of his power (2 Th 1:7-9)

How much more severely do you think a man deserves to be punished who has trampled the Son of God under foot, who has treated as an unholy thing the blood of the covenant that sanctified him, and who has insulted the Spirit of grace? For we know him who said, "It is mine to avenge; I will repay," and again, "The Lord will judge his people." (Heb 10:29-30)

If this is so, then the Lord knows how to rescue godly men from trials and to hold the unrighteous for the day of judgment, while continuing their punishment. (2 Pet 2:9)

If anyone's name was not found written in the book of life, he was thrown into the lake of fire. (Rev 20:15)

But the cowardly, the unbelieving, the vile, the murderers, the sexually immoral, those who practice magic arts, the idolaters and all liars—their place will be in the fiery lake of burning sulfur. This is the second death." (Rev 21:8)

b. Class 2: the men who did not know the Lord's will; therefore, they were not able to prepare themselves as they should have, nor were they able to faithfully serve the Lord.

However, note a critical point. Even the managers committed things worthy of punishment. Therefore, they will be judged and condemned as well, but not as severely (cp. Ro.1:20f; 2:11-16).

The principle of judgment is perfect justice: having many gifts and possessing much wealth means a person is to serve and give much. A person is to use and give all he is and has—holding nothing back. Note that degrees of rewards and punishment are being taught. (See Master Subject Index, Rewards.)

P. The Three Gross Misconceptions of Man, 12:49-59

Outline	Scripture	Scripture (cont.)	Outline
1 Misconception 1: The Messiah was to bring peace on earth a. Truth 1: He came to bring judgment, v.49 b. Truth 2: He came to suffer & die c. Truth 3: He came to bring division **2 Misconception 2: The**	49 "I have come to bring fire on the earth, and how I wish it were already kindled! 50 But I have a baptism to undergo, and how distressed I am until it is completed! 51 Do you think I came to bring peace on earth? No, I tell you, but division. 52 From now on there will be five in one family divided against each other, three against two and two against three. 53 They will be divided, father against son and son against father, mother against daughter and daughter against mother, mother-in-law against daughter-in-law and daughter-in-law against mother-in-law." 54 He said to the crowd:	"When you see a cloud rising in the west, immediately you say, 'It's going to rain,' and it does. 55 And when the south wind blows, you say, 'It's going to be hot,' and it is. 56 Hypocrites! You know how to interpret the appearance of the earth and the sky. How is it that you don't know how to interpret this present time? 57 "Why don't you judge for yourselves what is right? 58 As you are going with your adversary to the magistrate, try hard to be reconciled to him on the way, or he may drag you off to the judge, and the judge turn you over to the officer, and the officer throw you into prison. 59 I tell you, you will not get out until you have paid the last penny."	**Messiah has not yet come** a. Truth 1: People discern the weather, i.e. earthly events b. Truth 2: People do not discern the signs of the times, the Messianic age c. Truth 3: People do not discern spiritual matters **3 Misconception 3: Men have no need to make peace with God** a. Truth 1: People have a bad case before God, the Judge. b. Truth 2: The time is urgent—"try hard" c. Truth 3: The surety of payment, that is, judgment

DIVISION V

THE SON OF MAN'S GREAT JOURNEY TO JERUSALEM (STAGE I): HIS MISSION AND PUBLIC CHALLENGE, 9:51-13:21

P. The Three Gross Misconceptions of Man, 12:49-59

(12:49-59) **Introduction**: forcibly, Jesus covered three gross misconceptions of man.

1. Misconception 1: the Messiah was to bring peace on earth (v.49-53).
2. Misconception 2: the Messiah has not yet come (v.54-57).
3. Misconception 3: men have no need to make "peace with God" (v.58-59).

1 (12:49-53) **Peace—Judgment—Jesus Christ, Work—Sin**: the first misconception is that the Messiah came to bring peace on earth. Men usually think of Christ as having brought the message of peace to earth, and He did. He brought *peace with God* to a man's heart and the *peace of God* to a man's life (see note, Peace—Jn.14:27). But note three significant truths about what Christ says in this point.

1. Christ brought not only peace but fire on the earth, that is, judgment. Fire is usually the symbol of judgment (cp. the term *fire of hell*). This is the clearest meaning here, for Christ was talking about His death (v.50).

   a. The Greek word "ti" can be and probably should be translated *how*,: "how I wish the [fire] were already kindled." (Mt.5:22;18:9) Christ was wishing that the cross was already over with. The judgment as the *sin-bearer* of the world was almost too much for Him to bear (cp. Lk.22:39-46, Gethsemane).

   b. It was Christ's death that brought the fire of judgment to the world.

   ⇒ His death judged (condemned) sin in the flesh or body.

> **For what the law was powerless to do in that it was weakened by the sinful nature, God did by sending his own Son in the likeness of sinful man to be a sin offering. And so he condemned sin in sinful man, (Rom 8:3)**
>
> **For Christ died for sins once for all, the righteous for the unrighteous, to bring you to God. He was put to death in the body but made alive by the Spirit, (1 Pet 3:18)**

⇒ His death judged (condemned) the prince of this world.

> **Now is the time for judgment on this world; now the prince of this world will be driven out. But I, when I am lifted up from the earth, will draw all men to myself." (John 12:31-32)**
>
> **And in regard to judgment, because the prince of this world now stands condemned. (John 16:11)**

⇒ His death caused men to judge themselves to be sinners, sinners who were spiritually dead to God.

> **For Christ's love compels us, because we are convinced that one died for all, and therefore all died. And he died for all, that those who live should no longer live for themselves but for him who died for them and was raised again. (2 Cor 5:14-15)**
>
> **He himself bore our sins in his body on the tree, so that we might die to sins and live for righteousness; by**

his wounds you have been healed. (1 Pet 2:24)

⇒ His death caused men to judge themselves in the flesh or body, that is, to judge their flesh as being weak and subject to sin. The flesh of men needs to be controlled and denied and brought into subjection to Christ.

I know that nothing good lives in me, that is, in my sinful nature. For I have the desire to do what is good, but I cannot carry it out. For what I do is not the good I want to do; no, the evil I do not want to do—this I keep on doing. Now if I do what I do not want to do, it is no longer I who do it, but it is sin living in me that does it. (Rom 7:18-20)

But if we judged ourselves, we would not come under judgment. (1 Cor 11:31)

For we know that our old self was [Greek] crucified with him so that the body of sin might be done away with, that we should no longer be slaves to sin—The death he died, he died to sin once for all; but the life he lives, he lives to God. In the same way, count yourselves dead to sin but alive to God in Christ Jesus. Therefore do not let sin reign in your mortal body so that you obey its evil desires. Do not offer the parts of your body to sin, as instruments of wickedness, but rather offer yourselves to God, as those who have been brought from death to life; and offer the parts of your body to him as instruments of righteousness. (Rom 6:6, 10-13)

Then he said to them all: "If anyone would come after me, he must deny himself and take up his cross daily and follow me. (Luke 9:23)

2. Christ came to suffer and die, that is, to be baptized with the judgment of death and to be separated from God. The term "a baptism to undergo" refers to Christ's death. He was to be immersed, placed into a state of death, of separation from God *for man.* His suffering in bearing the judgment of God was to be beyond imagination. Note that He used the metaphor of both *fire and baptism* to describe His death. Note also that He was *distressed,* pressured to get the ordeal of the judgment over, to have the judgment accomplished and man's salvation completed.

They were on their way up to Jerusalem, with Jesus leading the way, and the disciples were astonished, while those who followed were afraid. Again he took the Twelve aside and told them what was going to happen to him. "We are going up to Jerusalem," he said, "and the Son of Man will be betrayed to the chief priests and teachers of the law. They will condemn him to death and will hand him over to the Gentiles, who will mock him and spit on him, flog him and kill him. Three days later he will rise." "You don't know what you are asking," Jesus said. "Can you drink the cup I drink or be baptized with the baptism I am baptized with?" (Mark 10:32-34, 38)

3. Christ came to bring division to the earth. (See outline and notes—Mt.10:34-37 for more discussion and application.) Note three things.

a. It is Christ who *sets* a family member against his family. It is important to see this. Christ calls a person out of the world: to be separate from the world and to go about correcting the sin and evil of the world. If a family continues to live in sin and to walk ever onward toward the grave without turning to God and a life of righteousness, two things usually happen.
   1) The believer struggles to witness to his loved ones, no matter the cost and opposition he may face.
   2) The family members often rebel against the righteousness and efforts of the believer.

b. The believer is called to a life of righteousness and to a warfare against sin and evil. If a member of his family is engaged on the side of evil, there is *a natural conflict* between the believer and the family member.
   1) The family member is still of the earth and living primarily to satisfy his earthly desires. The thought of God is repressed and subdued so that he can pursue his physcal and material desires.
   2) The believer is of the earth, but he is also of heaven. He is physical and spiritual, and more importantly, he is living primarily for God and His righteousness, to reach men with the glorious gospel of Christ.

   The two natures differ drastically. They are diametrically opposed to one another. The person of the world primarily talks about the world and lives for the pursuit of the world. The person of the spirit makes God the primary force of his life: he talks about God and the things of righteousness, and he pursues God and His righteousness.

c. A believer is to love his family, but he is to love God first and foremost. Our first loyalty is to God. Two terrible things happen when we put our family before God.
   1) Our families cannot be what they should be without God. No family can reach its full potential without God. There will be a lack of spiritual growth and strength, of conviction and commitment, of confi-dence and assurance, of purpose and meaning, of life and God—a lack of all—it will be for eternity. There will be no sense, no assurance of anything beyond this life.
   2) Our families cannot be looked after by God unless God is given His rightful place in the family. If the family takes control over its own life, ignoring God and His control, then what happens to the family is in its hands. God is put off to the side, excluded and shut out. He has no say so over the welfare of the family. The family is left all to itself, and all kinds of trouble usually follows. There is certainly a lack of spiritual strength to face the trials and crises that confront every family during life.

   What these two facts teach is this: we must love God supremely, putting Him before all—even before our families. When we do, our families are assured of being everything they should be and of being looked after and cared for by God (Mt.6:33). Therefore, a man's decision to follow Christ, no matter the sacrifice to his family, is a wise decision; in fact, it is the only reasonable decision.

"Do not suppose that I have come to bring peace to the earth. I did not come to bring peace, but a sword. For I have come to turn "'a man against his father, a daughter against her mother, a daughter-in-law against her mother-in-law—a man's enemies will be the members of his own household.' "Anyone who loves his father or mother more than me is not worthy of me; anyone who loves his son or daughter more than me is not worthy of me; (Mat 10:34-37)

Therefore, I urge you, brothers, in view of God's mercy, to offer your bodies as living sacrifices, holy and pleasing to God—this is your spiritual act of worship. Do not conform any longer to the pattern of this world, but be transformed by the renewing of your mind. Then you will be able to test and approve what God's will is—his good, pleasing and perfect will. (Rom 12:1-2)

Jesus replied: "'Love the Lord your God with all your heart and with all your soul and with all your mind.' This is the first and greatest commandment. (Mat 22:37-38)

Keep yourselves in God's love as you wait for the mercy of our Lord Jesus Christ to bring you to eternal life. (Jude 1:21)

Love the LORD your God with all your heart and with all your soul and with all your strength. (Deu 6:5)

And now, O Israel, what does the LORD your God ask of you but to fear the LORD your God, to walk in all his ways, to love him, to serve the LORD your God with all your heart and with all your soul, (Deu 10:12)

2 (12:54-57) **Messiah—Unbelief—Incarnation**: the second misconception is that the Messiah has not yet come. People in Jesus' day did not believe that He was the Messiah, and people today do not believe that He is the Messiah. Jesus stated two truths to all unbelievers.

1. People discern the weather, that is, physical matters of the world. Man's natural senses can be very discerning and sharp. He is skillful in studying and experimenting and in drawing conclusions from the natural world. Weather is the example Christ used; but the subject could be finances, medicine, society, or any other earthly subject. Jesus said people are very capable in interpreting the material and physical matters of their world.

2. People do not discern spiritual matters. When it comes to the spiritual senses, man is dead and unable to interpret. He does not take time to observe nor to experience the spiritual world, not really.

a. People had *failed to discern the time*, that is, the coming of the Messiah. The signs that pointed to Jesus' being the Messiah were visible. A thoughtful and genuinely spiritual person could see the signs, and some had seen them such as Simeon and Anna (Lk.3:25f). Some of the signs were as follows:
   ⇒ The sceptre, that is, the lawgiver had actually come from Judah in the person of Jesus Christ (Mt.1:2).
   ⇒ The weeks and ages predicted by Daniel were closing out (see note and DEEPER STUDY # 1—Mt.24:15).
   ⇒ The prophet Elijah, the forerunner of the Messiah, had come and proclaimed the Messiah to be Jesus (Mt.3:1-12).
   ⇒ The baby Jesus had been born in Bethlehem (Mt.2:1).
   ⇒ Many throughout the world were expecting the coming of some great person, some Messiah (Mt.1:18).
   ⇒ Many godly Jews were looking for the coming of the Messiah, God's great Deliverer of Israel (Lk.2:25f).
   ⇒ The message and works of Jesus were great evidence, phenomenal miracles given by God to substantiate His claims (see note and DEEPER STUDY # 1—Jn.14:11).

   In addition to these what greater signs could God give than the signs which change lives, radically change them? Unbelief is without excuse. The problem is that men want signs of their own choosing, not the signs which God has chosen to give. Men are always wanting God to deal with them through some...
   - spectacular sign
   - brilliant sight
   - astounding truth
   - irrefutable argument
   - miraculous experience
   - unbelievable deliverance

   God's great concern is not *signs from heaven*, not signs outside man. God's great concern is meeting people in their lives, within their hearts, where they really need help. People must discern the times if they are to live abundantly while on this earth and live eternally in the next world. God wants to meet people in their sickness and sorrow and lostness. Meeting man in the areas of his need are irrefutable signs given to every generation.

b. They *failed to discern and judge what was right.* This was one of the most honest, thought-provoking, and revealing questions ever asked of man. It takes a man who is honestly open—a man who is willing to have his heart exposed for what it really is—to answer the question. "Why...don't you judge for yourselves what is right?"

Thought 1. Why do men not discern, not judge what is right?
1) Why do men not discern that God *is*, that He exists?

In the beginning God. (Gen 1:1)

You alone are the LORD. You made the heavens, even the highest heavens, and all their starry host, the earth and all that

is on it, the seas and all that is in them. You give life to everything, and the multitudes of heaven worship you. (Neh 9:6)

You were shown these things so that you might know that the LORD is God; besides him there is no other. (Deu 4:35)

Hear, O Israel: The LORD our God, the LORD is one. Love the LORD your God with all your heart and with all your soul and with all your strength. (Deu 6:4-5)

Let them know that you, whose name is the LORD— that you alone are the Most High over all the earth. (Psa 83:18)

For you are great and do marvelous deeds; you alone are God. (Psa 86:10)

I, even I, am the LORD, and apart from me there is no savior. I have revealed and saved and proclaimed— I, and not some foreign god among you. You are my witnesses," declares the LORD, "that I am God. (Isa 43:11-12)

"This is what the LORD says— Israel's King and Redeemer, the LORD Almighty: I am the first and I am the last; apart from me there is no God. (Isa 44:6)

For this is what the LORD says— he who created the heavens, he is God; he who fashioned and made the earth, he founded it; he did not create it to be empty, but formed it to be inhabited— he says: "I am the LORD, and there is no other. (Isa 45:18)

"The most important one," answered Jesus, "is this: 'Hear, O Israel, the Lord our God, the Lord is one. Love the Lord your God with all your heart and with all your soul and with all your mind and with all your strength.' (Mark 12:29-30)

So then, about eating food sacrificed to idols: We know that an idol is nothing at all in the world and that there is no God but one. (1 Cor 8:4)

There is one body and one Spirit— just as you were called to one hope when you were called—one Lord, one faith, one baptism; one God and Father of all, who is over all and through all and in all. (Eph 4:4-6)

For there is one God and one mediator between God and men, the man Christ Jesus, who gave himself as a ransom for all men—the testimony given in its proper time. (1 Tim 2:5-6)

For there are three that testify: (1 John 5:7)

2) Why do men not discern that Jesus Christ is truly the Son of God.

Then those who were in the boat worshiped him, saying, "Truly you are the Son of God." (Mat 14:33)

The beginning of the gospel about Jesus Christ, the Son of God. (Mark 1:1)

I have seen and I [John the Baptist] testify that this is the Son of God." (John 1:34)

"For God so loved the world that he gave his one and only Son, that whoever believes in him shall not perish but have eternal life. For God did not send his Son into the world to condemn the world, but to save the world through him. Whoever believes in him is not condemned, but whoever does not believe stands condemned already because he has not believed in the name of God's one and only Son. (John 3:16-18)

Jesus heard that they had thrown him out, and when he found him, he said, "Do you believe in the Son of Man?" "Who is he, sir?" the man asked. "Tell me so that I may believe in himJesus said, "You have now seen him; in fact, he is the one speaking with you." (John 9:35-37)

What about the one whom the Father set apart as his very own and sent into the world? Why then do you accuse me of blasphemy because I said, 'I am God's Son'? (John 10:36)

Jesus said to her, "I am the resurrection and the life. He who believes in me will live, even though he dies; and whoever lives and believes in me will never die. Do you believe this?" "Yes, Lord," she told him, "I believe that you are the Christ, the Son of God, who was to come into the world." (John 11:25-27)

How much more severely do you think a man deserves to be punished who has trampled the Son of God under foot, who has treated as an unholy thing the blood of the covenant that sanctified him, and who has insulted the Spirit of grace? (Heb 10:29)

If anyone acknowledges that Jesus is the Son of God, God lives in him and he in God. (1 John 4:15)

3) Why do men not discern that righteousness is the way for men to live and the way for communities and the world to conduct their affairs.

For I tell you that unless your righteousness surpasses that of the Pharisees and the teachers of the law, you will certainly not enter the kingdom of heaven. (Mat 5:20)

For the kingdom of God is not a matter of eating and drinking, but of righteousness, peace and joy in the Holy Spirit, (Rom 14:17)

Come back to your senses as you ought, and stop sinning; for there are some who are ignorant of God—I say this to your shame. (1 Cor 15:34)

For the love of money is a root of all kinds of evil. Some people, eager for money, have wandered from the faith and pierced themselves with many griefs. But you, man of God, flee from all this, and pursue righteousness, godliness, faith, love, endurance and gentleness. Fight the good fight of the faith. Take hold of the eternal life to which you were called when you made your good confession in the presence of many witnesses. (1 Tim 6:10-12)

It teaches us to say "No" to ungodliness and worldly passions, and to live self-controlled, upright and godly lives in this

present age, while we wait for the blessed hope—the glorious appearing of our great God and Savior, Jesus Christ, (Titus 2:12-13)

The Lord is not slow in keeping his promise, as some understand slowness. He is patient with you, not wanting anyone to perish, but everyone to come to repentance. But the day of the Lord will come like a thief. The heavens will disappear with a roar; the elements will be destroyed by fire, and the earth and everything in it will be laid bare. Since everything will be destroyed in this way, what kind of people ought you to be? You ought to live holy and godly lives as you look forward to the day of God and speed its coming. That day will bring about the destruction of the heavens by fire, and the elements will melt in the heat. But in keeping with his promise we are looking forward to a new heaven and a new earth, the home of righteousness. So then, dear friends, since you are looking forward to this, make every effort to be found spotless, blameless and at peace with him. (2 Pet 3:9-14)

Jesus was saying that the signs of the times—the signs of every generation—the signs of nature itself—are enough to point toward God in all His love and righteousness. "Why...don't you judge for yourselves what is right?"

3 (12:58-59) **Messiah, Misconception—Man, Need**: the third misconception is that men have no need to make *peace with God.* Jesus used an earthly illustration to stress three truths.

1. Men have a bad case before God, the Judge.
2. When a man has a hopeless case with an adversary, the best thing for him to do is to hasten for *settlement out of court.*
3. Otherwise, he is going to be to judged in court and have to *pay every penny.*

So it is with God. The hour is urgent. Man needs to make peace with God; he needs to give all diligence to the effort immediately. If he fails to make peace, then he will have to pay the most severe penalty, to the very last mite.

"You snakes! You brood of vipers! How will you escape being condemned to hell? (Mat 23:33)

So when you, a mere man, pass judgment on them and yet do the same things, do you think you will escape God's judgment? (Rom 2:3)

While people are saying, "Peace and safety," destruction will come on them suddenly, as labor pains on a pregnant woman, and they will not escape. (1 Th 5:3)

How shall we escape if we ignore such a great salvation? This salvation, which was first announced by the Lord, was confirmed to us by those who heard him. (Heb 2:3)

See to it that you do not refuse him who speaks. If they did not escape when they refused him who warned them on earth, how much less will we, if we turn away from him who warns us from heaven? (Heb 12:25)

Be sure of this: The wicked will not go unpunished, but those who are righteous will go free. (Prov 11:21)

The LORD detests all the proud of heart. Be sure of this: They will not go unpunished. (Prov 16:5)

Therefore this is what the LORD says: 'I will bring on them a disaster they cannot escape. Although they cry out to me, I will not listen to them. (Jer 11:11)

Woe to you who long for the day of the LORD! Why do you long for the day of the LORD? That day will be darkness, not light. It will be as though a man fled from a lion only to meet a bear, as though he entered his house and rested his hand on the wall only to have a snake bite him. Will not the day of the LORD be darkness, not light— pitch-dark, without a ray of brightness? (Amos 5:18-20)

Though they dig down to the depths of the grave, from there my hand will take them. Though they climb up to the heavens, from there I will bring them down. (Amos 9:2)

CHAPTER 13

Q. The Truth About Suffering and Sin: The Great Need for All to Repent, 13:1-9
(cp. Mt.21:18-21; Mk.11: 12-14, 20-26; Is.5:1-7)

1 Men do not suffer because they are greater sinners than others[DS1]
a. Event 1: The latest news of a horrible murderous event
1) Did not suffer because they were greater sinners
2) *All* must repent or perish
b. Event 2: The latest news of a terrible tragedy

Now there were some present
at that time who told Jesus
about the Galileans whose
blood Pilate had mixed with
their sacrifices.
2 Jesus answered, "Do you
think that these Galileans
were worse sinners than all
the other Galileans because
they suffered this way?
3 I tell you, no! But unless
you repent, you too will all
perish.
4 Or those eighteen who died
when the tower in Siloam fell
on them—do you think they
were more guilty than all the
others living in Jerusalem?
5 I tell you, no! But unless
you repent, you too will all
perish."
6 Then he told this parable:
"A man had a fig tree,
planted in his vineyard, and
he went to look for fruit on it,
but did not find any.
7 So he said to the man who
took care of the vineyard,
'For three years now I've
been coming to look for fruit
on this fig tree and haven't
found any. Cut it down! Why
should it use up the soil?'
8 "'Sir,' the man replied,
'leave it alone for one more
year, and I'll dig around it
and fertilize it.
9 If it bears fruit next year,
fine! If not, then cut it
down.'"

1) Did not suffer because they were greater sinners
2) *All* must repent or perish

2 Men must bear fruit or else they will perish
a. The fig tree's privilege: In the vineyard
b. The fig tree's purpose: To bear fruit
c. The day for reaping came
1) Found no fruit
2) Found that the tree was using up space on the ground & producing nothing
d. The mercy of God
1) Gave another chance
2) Fertilized & fed
e. The judgment was based on fruit

DIVISION V

THE SON OF MAN'S GREAT JOURNEY TO JERUSALEM (STAGE I): HIS MISSION AND PUBLIC CHALLENGE, 9:51-13:21

Q. The Truth About Suffering and Sin: The Great Need for All to Repent, 13:1-9

(13:1-9) **Introduction**: one of the world's most perplexing problems is, why do men suffer? Some say that men suffer because they are greater sinners. The result, too often, is that many who suffer feel this is true; consequently, they end up with all sorts of guilt and emotional problems. They think their suffering is due to some great sin they have committed and that God is punishing them because they have been such great sinners. It is this subject that is dealt with in this passage.

1. Men do not suffer because they are *greater sinners* (v.1-5).
2. Men must bear fruit or else they will perish (v.6-9).

1 (13:1-5) **Suffering—Sin—Repentance**: men do not suffer because they are *greater sinners* than others. Jesus used two of the latest news events of His day to teach this lesson.

1. Some shared with Jesus the latest news of a horrible massacre. Some Galileans were in the temple in the midst of worship, offering their sacrifices to God, when Herod had them attacked and slaughtered by his soldiers (see DEEPER STUDY # 1—Lk.13:1-5). The crowd was being harsh and making a very harsh judgment. They were saying the Galileans were murdered because they were *great sinners.* The crowd was responding to what Jesus had taught, that men must make peace with God before it is too late (Lk.12:58-59). They were saying the Galileans were swept down upon, just like Jesus had described; therefore, they must have been great sinners.

Jesus was pointed and clear in refuting their thoughts. Note: the people had not spoken their thoughts; they had *only related* the story. However, the thought in their minds was that the Galileans had suffered such a horrible death because they were great sinners, or to express it as it is so often stated: suffering is due to sin.

Jesus said, "No! But unless you repent, you too will all perish!" Such an argument has its basis in self-righteousness. The point is unmistakable: all men must repent of sin, for all men are sinners, just as sinful as the Galileans.

2. Now note: the subject is so important and men need to grasp its lesson so much that Jesus referred to another late-news event—the terrible tragedy of a tower's falling on eighteen construction workers. It is significant that Jesus used a tragedy as a second illustration instead of an event similar to the murderous act just discussed. His point is unquestionable; suffering is not necessarily due to sin or to degrees of sin. If suffering were due to sin, then there would be no life whatsoever. Why? Because *all men are so sinful* that they are worthy of only the most horrible suffering—death itself. Thus, Jesus made His point: all men must repent or else perish. (See DEEPER STUDY # 2—Lk.5:23; note—Jn.9:1-3.)

Note what Jesus had said.

1. Suffering is not always due to *greater sins.*

> **How can you say to your brother, 'Let me take the speck out of your eye,' when all the time there is a plank in your own eye? (Mat 7:4)**
> **When the islanders saw the snake hanging from his hand, they said to each other, "This man must be a murderer; for though he escaped from the sea, Justice has not allowed him to live." (Acts 28:4; see outline and notes—1 Cor.1:3-11; 1:3-4 for more discussion and verses)**

2. All men are guilty of great sin, sin great enough to perish.

> **As it is written: "There is no one righteous, not even one; there is no one who un-**

derstands, no one who seeks God. All have turned away, they have together become worthless; there is no one who does good, not even one." "Their throats are open graves; their tongues practice deceit." "The poison of vipers is on their lips." "Their mouths are full of cursing and bitterness." "Their feet are swift to shed blood; ruin and misery mark their ways, and the way of peace they do not know." "There is no fear of God before their eyes." (Rom 3:10-18)

For all have sinned and fall short of the glory of God, (Rom 3:23)

The acts of the sinful nature are obvious: sexual immorality, impurity and debauchery; idolatry and witchcraft; hatred, discord, jealousy, fits of rage, selfish ambition, dissensions, factions and envy; drunkenness, orgies, and the like. I warn you, as I did before, that those who live like this will not inherit the kingdom of God. (Gal 5:19-21)

3. All men are doomed to perish.

For the wages of sin is death, but the gift of God is eternal life in Christ Jesus our Lord. (Rom 6:23)

The mind of sinful man is death, but the mind controlled by the Spirit is life and peace; (Rom 8:6)

But the cowardly, the unbelieving, the vile, the murderers, the sexually immoral, those who practice magic arts, the idolaters and all liars—their place will be in the fiery lake of burning sulfur. This is the second death." (Rev 21:8)

The soul who sins is the one who will die. The son will not share the guilt of the father, nor will the father share the guilt of the son. The righteousness of the righteous man will be credited to him, and the wickedness of the wicked will be charged against him. (Ezek 18:20)

4. There is only one way to keep from perishing: repent.

Peter replied, "Repent and be baptized, every one of you, in the name of Jesus Christ for the forgiveness of your sins. And you will receive the gift of the Holy Spirit. (Acts 2:38)

Repent, then, and turn to God, so that your sins may be wiped out, that times of refreshing may come from the Lord, (Acts 3:19)

Repent of this wickedness and pray to the Lord. Perhaps he will forgive you for having such a thought in your heart. (Acts 8:22)

In the past God overlooked such ignorance, but now he commands all people everywhere to repent. (Acts 17:30)

DEEPER STUDY # 1

(13:1-5) **Suffering—Galileans—Construction Workers**: Who were the Galileans slaughtered by Herod and the construction workers upon whom the tower fell? There is no sure record of either group other than what is given here. The best *guesses* are these.

Two suggestions are made about the Galileans. First, they were followers of Judas of Galilee who opposed taxation imposed by the Romans (Acts 5:37). Herod either knew that some of Judas' followers were in the temple worshipping or mistook some group of Galileans as his followers and had them slaughtered. This much is known. Pilate set out to build a new water system for Jerusalem. It was a huge construction project, and to finance the work, Pilate had to insist that the money be taken from the temple finances. This of course enraged the Jews, for the temple monies were gifts to God and belonged to God. The Galileans were an inflammable people; therefore, they were usually in the forefront of trouble. Second, some commentators think that the slaughtered Galileans were revolutionaries who had moved into the city to carry out terrorist acts against the government. Herod knew about it and caught them off guard while they were worshipping. Note they were caught so much by surprise that their blood actually flowed and mingled with the blood of the animal sacrifices they were offering to God.

The construction workers are thought by most to have been repairing one of the towers which served as part of the fortifications on the walls of Jerusalem. It is thought to have been near the pool of Siloam.

2 (13:6-9) **Fruit-Bearing**: men must bear fruit or else they shall perish. Jesus wanted to drive home the need for repentance by sharing the parable of a man's seeking fruit. The man represents God; the vineyard keeper represents Christ; the vineyard represents either the world or Israel. Note these facts about the fig tree.

1. The fig tree was greatly privileged. It was *in the vineyard*, which meant several things.

a. It was planted (born) by the vineyard keeper (God or Christ) himself. God causes every man to be born into the world. He stands behind every person as that person's Creator and Lord.

'For in him we live and move and have our being.' As some of your own poets have said, 'We are his offspring.' (Acts 17:28)

The Spirit of God has made me; the breath of the Almighty gives me life. (Job 33:4)

Know that the LORD is God. It is he who made us, and we are his ; we are his people, the sheep of his pasture. (Psa 100:3)

That you forget the LORD your Maker, who stretched out the heavens and laid the foundations of the earth, that you live in constant terror every day because of the wrath of the oppressor, who is bent on destruction? For where is the wrath of the oppressor? (Isa 51:13)

Have we not all one Father? Did not one God create us? Why do we profane the covenant of our fathers by breaking faith with one another? (Mal 2:10)

b. It was planted in the vineyard itself, right where there were other trees bearing fruit. It had the same soil, nourishment, rain, and sun from heaven. This is true of all persons who are born in nations where the gospel is freely preached.

"Listen to another parable: There was a landowner who planted a vineyard. He put a wall around it, dug a winepress in it and built a watchtower. Then he rented the vineyard to some farmers and went away on a journey. (Mat 21:33)

2. The fig tree's purpose was to bear fruit. It had been *planted* to bear fruit and it *existed* to bear fruit. It was by nature a *fruit* tree; therefore, it was supposed to bear fruit. It had no other purpose for existing. So it is with man (Lk.10:27; Gal.5:22-23. See DEEPER STUDY # 1—Jn.15:1-8.)

Produce fruit in keeping with repentance. (Mat 3:8)

"For the kingdom of heaven is like a landowner who went out early in the morning to hire men to work in his vineyard. (Mat 20:1)

This is to my Father's glory, that you bear much fruit, showing yourselves to be my disciples. (John 15:8)

You did not choose me, but I chose you and appointed you to go and bear fruit—fruit that will last. Then the Father will give you whatever you ask in my name. (John 15:16)

3. The day for reaping came. Jesus said five things about the day of reaping.

a. The vineyard owner, God Himself, was the One who came looking for fruit. The reaper was not someone else; it was God Himself.

⇒ He planted the tree to get fruit (God put man on earth to bear fruit).

⇒ He expected fruit, for He was the One who had planted the tree.

Likewise every good tree bears good fruit, but a bad tree bears bad fruit. (Mat 7:17)

"I am the vine; you are the branches. If a man remains in me and I in him, he will bear much fruit; apart from me you can do nothing. (John 15:5)

But the fruit of the Spirit is love, joy, peace, patience, kindness, goodness, faithfulness, gentleness and self-control. Against such things there is no law. (Gal 5:22-23)

b. The vineyard owner found no fruit. The tree was bare.

⇒ It failed in its purpose. (So many have all the privileges, yet so few ever honor God or bear fruit as they should.)

⇒ The investment in the life of the tree was wasted.

The one who received the seed that fell among the thorns is the man who hears the word, but the worries of this life and the deceitfulness of wealth choke it, making it unfruitful. (Mat 13:22)

He dug it up and cleared it of stones and planted it with the choicest vines. He built a watchtower in it and cut out a winepress as well. Then he looked for a crop of good grapes, but it yielded only bad fruit. (Isa 5:2)

But you have planted wickedness, you have reaped evil, you have eaten the fruit of deception. Because you have depended on your own strength and on your many warriors, (Hosea 10:13)

c. The vineyard owner had waited a long time. He had come time after time looking for fruit.

⇒ The tree had plenty of time to bear fruit if it were ever going to bear fruit.

⇒ The Owner's patience was extremely long-suffering.

The Lord is not slow in keeping his promise, as some understand slowness. He is patient with you, not wanting anyone to perish, but everyone to come to repentance. (2 Pet 3:9)

d. The tree was wasting and misusing space. The purpose of the vineyard, the very reason for its existence, was to produce fruit for the Owner.

⇒ All space was needed for fruit.

⇒ No space could be allowed to be wasted, not forever.

⇒ The tree was hurting the production of the vineyard. The example of false believers affects the whole vineyard. They cheapen the vineyard (world, church), causing others not to want its fruit.

For he has set a day when he will judge the world with justice by the man he has appointed. He has given proof of this to all men by raising him from the dead." (Acts 17:31)

You who brag about the law, do you dishonor God by breaking the law? As it is written: "God's name is blasphemed among the Gentiles because of you." (Rom 2:23-24)

Many will follow their shameful ways and will bring the way of truth into disrepute. (2 Pet 2:2)

e. The tree was to be cut down. The Owner pronounced judgment.

Do not be deceived: God cannot be mocked. A man reaps what he sows. The one who sows to please his sinful nature, from that nature will reap destruction; the one who sows to please the Spirit, from the Spirit will reap eternal life. (Gal 6:7-8)

For the wages of sin is death, but the gift of God is eternal life in Christ Jesus our Lord. (Rom 6:23)

All the nations will be gathered before him, and he will separate the people one from another as a shepherd separates the sheep from the goats. (Mat 25:32)

4. The mercy of God. The vineyard keeper interceded for the unfruitful tree. He asked for another year, one last chance for the tree.

⇒ God granted one last chance, one last opportunity.
⇒ Next year, however, was to be the last chance, the last opportunity for the tree.

Who is he that condemns? Christ Jesus, who died—more than that, who was raised to life—is at the right hand of God and is also *interceding for us*. (Rom 8:34)

Therefore he is able to save completely those who come to God through him, because he always lives to intercede for them. (Heb 7:25)

Jesus said, "Father, forgive them, for they do not know what they are doing." And they divided up his clothes by casting lots. (Luke 23:34)

Their vine comes from the vine of Sodom and from the fields of Gomorrah. Their grapes are filled with poison, and their clusters with bitterness. (Their wine is the venom of serpents, the deadly poison of cobras. "Have I not kept this in reserve and sealed it in my vaults? It is mine to avenge; I will repay. In due time their foot will slip; their day of disaster is near and their doom rushes upon them." (Deu 32:32-35)

5. The judgment was based upon fruit (see outline and notes—Jn.15:1-8; Gal.5:22-23).

The ax is already at the root of the trees, and every tree that does not produce good fruit will be cut down and thrown into the fire. (Mat 3:10)

If anyone does not remain in me, he is like a branch that is thrown away and withers; such branches are picked up, thrown into the fire and burned. (John 15:6)

But land that produces thorns and thistles is worthless and is in danger of being cursed. In the end it will be burned. (Heb 6:8)

	R. People vs. Religion: Which is More Important? 13:10-17	the synagogue ruler said to the people, "There are six days for work. So come and be healed on those days, not on the Sabbath."	a. He became angry with the people b. He corrupted God's Word[DS2] c. He rejected Christ
1 Jesus taught in the synagogue on the Sabbath	10 On a Sabbath Jesus was teaching in one of the synagogues,	15 The Lord answered him, "You hypocrites! Doesn't each of you on the Sabbath untie his ox or donkey from the stall and lead it out to give it water?	d. He was hypocritical 1) He placed animals above people[DS3]
2 The woman was a worshipper of God a. She was worshipping b. She had a curvature of the spine c. She was seen & called by Jesus	11 And a woman was there who had been crippled by a spirit for eighteen years. She was bent over and could not straighten up at all. 12 When Jesus saw her, he called her forward and said to her, "Woman, you are set free from your infirmity."	16 Then should not this woman, a daughter of Abraham, whom Satan has kept bound for eighteen long years, be set free on the Sabbath day from what bound her?"	2) He placed religion above people
d. She received Jesus' word & touch e. She glorified God first	13 Then he put his hands on her, and immediately she straightened up and praised God.	17 When he said this, all his opponents were humiliated, but the people were delighted with all the wonderful things he was doing.	**4 The effect of Jesus' works & words** a. The opponents: Were humiliated b. The crowds: Rejoiced
3 The ruler (religionist) was a worshipper of God[DS1]	14 Indignant because Jesus had healed on the Sabbath,		

DIVISION V

THE SON OF MAN'S GREAT JOURNEY TO JERUSALEM (STAGE I): HIS MISSION AND PUBLIC CHALLENGE, 9:51-13:21

R. People vs. Religion: Which is More Important? 13:10-17

(13:10-17) **Introduction**: one of the great tragedies of religion is that religion is so often placed before man and his needs. Jesus met this problem head-on.

1. Jesus taught in the synagogue on the Sabbath (v.10).
2. The woman was a worshipper of God (v.11-13).
3. The ruler (religionist) was a worshipper of God (v.14-16).
4. The effect of Jesus' works and words (v.17).

1 (13:10) **Jesus Christ, Worship of**: Jesus taught in the synagogue on the Sabbath. Three significant facts need to be seen in this point.

1. This was the last time Jesus was ever in a synagogue as far as we know. From this point on He was such a controversial figure that no synagogue would allow Him in the pulpit.

2. This healing miracle took place on the Sabbath, and healing was not allowed on the Sabbath. It was considered work unless it was a matter of life and death. The fact that Jesus broke the Sabbath law was what caused the present dispute.

3. Note that both the woman and the religionist were worshippers of God (v.11-16).

> **Thought 1.** Jesus was worshipping on the Sabbath, doing exactly what He should have been doing.

> **Thought 2.** There is a difference between worshippers. This is seen in the woman and the man (v.11-16). She sought to draw near the Lord for deliverance, whereas the man only practiced his ceremony and ritual.

2 (13:11-13) **Salvation—Worship—Jesus Christ, Heals—Compassion**: the woman was a worshipper of God. Note five things about her.

1. She was worshipping. It was her habit to worship, to seek the face of God in looking after her life. Therefore, she was where she was supposed to be on this particular Sabbath: in worship. And because she was there, she was to receive a very special touch from God. She did not know it yet, but she was. Why her? Because she was sincere, ever so sincere in seeking God and His care.

> **Jesus said to him, "Away from me, Satan! For it is written: 'Worship the Lord your God, and serve him only.'" (Mat 4:10)**
>
> **God is spirit, and his worshipers must worship in spirit and in truth." (John 4:24)**
>
> **Ascribe to the LORD the glory due his name. Bring an offering and come before him; worship the LORD in the splendor of his holiness. (1 Chr 16:29)**
>
> **Surely goodness and love will follow me all the days of my life, and I will dwell in the house of the LORD forever. (Psa 23:6)**
>
> **I love the house where you live, O LORD, the place where your glory dwells. (Psa 26:8)**
>
> **One thing I ask of the LORD, this is what I seek: that I may dwell in the house of the LORD all the days of my life, to gaze upon the beauty of the LORD and to seek him in his temple. (Psa 27:4)**
>
> **Blessed are those you choose and bring near to live in your courts! We are filled with the good things of your house, of your holy temple. (Psa 65:4)**
>
> **My soul yearns, even faints, for the courts of the LORD; my heart and my flesh cry out for the living God. (Psa 84:2)**
>
> **Better is one day in your courts than a thousand elsewhere; I would rather be a doorkeeper in the house of my God than**

dwell in the tents of the wicked. (Psa 84:10)
A song of ascents. Of David. I rejoiced with those who said to me, "Let us go to the house of the LORD." (Psa 122:1)

2. She had a curvature of the spine. This sounds like some form of arthritis where the joints of the spine fuse together. Luke, the physician, gives the medical description of his day for the disease. She had been deformed for eighteen yars. Two facts need to be noted.

a. She had been afflicted with "a spirit." Jesus said the spirit was a *satanic spirit*: "[She was] a daughter…whom Satan has bound" (v.16). Thus, the woman needed spiritual healing as well as physical healing.
b. She was in worship *despite* her deformity, and note her deformity was severe. She was all bent over and nable to rise up. The pain was sometimes severe. Yet, her habit was to attend worship and to seek the favor and help of God upon her life.

But seek first his kingdom and his righteousness, and all these things will be given to you as well. (Mat 6:33)
"So I say to you: Ask and it will be given to you; seek and you will find; knock and the door will be opened to you. For everyone who asks receives; he who seeks finds; and to him who knocks, the door will be opened. (Luke 11:9-10)
God did this so that men would seek him and perhaps reach out for him and find him, though he is not far from each one of us. (Acts 17:27)
Look to the LORD and his strength; seek his face always. (Psa 105:4)
This is what the LORD says to the house of Israel: "Seek me and live; (Amos 5:4)

3. She was seen and called by Jesus. The woman's faithfulness in the worship of God, despite deformity and pain, attracted Jesus. He knew both her condition with all its pain and inconvenience and the great sacrifice she made to worship God. He was moved with compassion. Note: she did not have to call to Him for help; Jesus called her *to Him*.

But from everlasting to everlasting the Lord's love is with those who fear him, and his righteousness with their children's children— (Psa 103:17)
In all their distress he too was distressed, and the angel of his presence saved them. In his love and mercy he redeemed them; he lifted them up and carried them all the days of old. (Isa 63:9)
For we do not have a high priest who is unable to sympathize with our weaknesses, but we have one who has been tempted in every way, just as we are—yet was without sin. (Heb 4:15)
Who shall separate us from the love of Christ? Shall trouble or hardship or persecution or famine or nakedness or danger or sword? (Rom 8:35)
Cast all your anxiety on him because he cares for you. (1 Pet 5:7)
Because of the Lord's great love we are not consumed, for his compassions never fail. (Lam 3:22)

4. She received Jesus' Word and touch. This was crucial. Jesus had "called her forward [to Him]." She had to respond to His call; He could not come for her. She had to take the step of coming herself. When she obeyed, Jesus spoke the Word, the *good news* to her: "Woman, you are set free from your infirmity." (Keep in mind that her problem had been both spiritual and physical.) Jesus reached out and touched her and she "straightened up." She stood upright. *She experienced both the power of Jesus' Word and touch.* But note: it was because she came when Jesus called, and she was able to hear Jesus' call because she was worshipping God, seeking His grace and care.

Thought 1. The Lord alone can heal those who are bowed down.

The LORD gives sight to the blind, the LORD lifts up those who are bowed down, the LORD loves the righteous. (Psa 146:8)

Thought 2. Souls that are bent or bowed down can be lifted up by Jesus, no matter what it is that has caused the bowing:

⇒ humiliation and shame
⇒ sin
⇒ lack of education
⇒ loss of everything
⇒ accident
⇒ disease
⇒ appearance & looks
⇒ personality

I am bowed down and brought very low; all day long I go about mourning. My back is filled with searing pain; there is no health in my body. I am feeble and utterly crushed; I groan in anguish of heart. All my longings lie open before you, O Lord; my sighing is not hidden from you. My heart pounds, my strength fails me; even the light has gone from my eyes. (Psa 38:6-10)
Just as the Son of Man did not come to be served, but to serve, and to give his life as a ransom for many." (Mat 20:28)
When evening came, many who were demon-possessed were brought to him, and he drove out the spirits with a word and healed all the sick. This was to fulfill what was spoken through the prophet Isaiah: "He took up our infirmities and carried our diseases." (Mat 8:16-17)
Jesus answered them, "It is not the healthy who need a doctor, but the sick. I have not come to call the righteous, but sinners to repentance." (Luke 5:31-32)
How God anointed Jesus of Nazareth with the Holy Spirit and power, and how he went around doing good and healing all who were under the power of the devil, because God was with him. (Acts 10:38)
You have been a refuge for the poor, a refuge for the needy in his distress, a shelter from the storm and a shade from the heat. For the breath of the ruthless is like a storm driving against a wall (Isa 25:4)
Surely he took up our infirmities and carried our sorrows, yet we considered him stricken by God, smitten by him, and afflicted. (Isa 53:4)

5. She glorified God first. Note the word "immediately."

> **But thanks be to God! He gives us the victory through our Lord Jesus Christ. (1 Cor 15:57)**
> **You were bought at a price. Therefore honor God with your body. (1 Cor 6:20)**
> **Thanks be to God for his indescribable gift! (2 Cor 9:15)**
> **Always giving thanks to God the Father for everything, in the name of our Lord Jesus Christ. (Eph 5:20)**
> **Give thanks in all circumstances, for this is God's will for you in Christ Jesus. (1 Th 5:18)**
> **Through Jesus, therefore, let us continually offer to God a sacrifice of praise—the fruit of lips that confess his name. (Heb 13:15)**
> **But you are a chosen people, a royal priesthood, a holy nation, a people belonging to God, that you may declare the praises of him who called you out of darkness into his wonderful light. (1 Pet 2:9)**
> **Give thanks to the LORD, call on his name; make known among the nations what he has done. (1 Chr 16:8)**
> **Sing praises to the LORD, enthroned in Zion; proclaim among the nations what he has done. (Psa 9:11)**
> **Sacrifice thank offerings to God, fulfill your vows to the Most High, (Psa 50:14)**
> **May the peoples praise you, O God; may all the peoples praise you. (Psa 67:3)**
> **Praise be to the Lord, to God our Savior, who daily bears our burdens. Selah (Psa 68:19)**
> **A psalm. A song. For the Sabbath day. It is good to praise the LORD and make music to your name, O Most High, (Psa 92:1)**

3 (13:14-16) **Religionists—Tradition—Hypocrisy**: the ruler (religionist) was a worshipper of God. He was the head of the synagogue (see DEEPER STUDY # 2—Mt.4:23; 9:18-19). He was a different kind of worshipper than the deformed woman. Whereas the woman sought God *through her need and dependency* to favor and help her personally, the ruler sought God *through form and ritual*, ceremony and rules. There is a vast difference between the two approaches. The one thing God teaches is that a man has to approach Him as a child, dependent and needy. Note four faults or sins of the religionist. (See outline and notes—Mt.12:1-8; 12:9-13 for more discussion and application.)

1. The ruler got angry with people. In fact, the very people with whom he became angry were his neighbors, the very persons who sat in worship with him every week. He allowed his temper to get out of control. The people were merely seeking help, for they were in desperate need, especially the woman; and he knew it. However, because he differed with them, he flared up against them.

> **Thought 1.** How many have hot tempers! How many strike out when they differ! How few control themselves!
>
> **Thought 2.** Note two things.
>
> 1) The man lost his temper in the presence of Jesus. Every flare-up is seen by God, and He knows the sin being committed.
> 2) The man was really upset with Jesus as well as the people. However, he *feared* to take Jesus on, for he felt Jesus was stronger and more able than himself. So he struck out against the weaker persons. How like the *angry* person!

2. The ruler misunderstood and corrupted God's law (Sabbath). In his mind, Jesus had committed a serious crime. He had healed on the Sabbath day (see DEEPER STUDY # 1, 2—Lk.13:14 for discussion).

3. He refused to acknowledge the Messiah, God's Son, who actually stood right before him (see outline and notes—Ro.11:28-29; 1 Th.2:15-16 for discussion).

> **"Not everyone who says to me, 'Lord, Lord,' will enter the kingdom of heaven, but only he who does the will of my Father who is in heaven. (Mat 7:21)**
> **"Whoever acknowledges me before men, I will also acknowledge him before my Father in heaven. But whoever disowns me before men, I will disown him before my Father in heaven. (Mat 10:32-33)**
> **Jesus answered, "I am the way and the truth and the life. No one comes to the Father except through me. (John 14:6)**
> **For there is one God and one mediator between God and men, the man Christ Jesus, who gave himself as a ransom for all men—the testimony given in its proper time. (1 Tim 2:5-6)**
> **And this is his command: to believe in the name of his Son, Jesus Christ, and to love one another as he commanded us. (1 John 3:23)**

4. He was hypocritical. He placed both animals and *man-made* religious rules above people. He allowed tradition and ritual, ceremony and rules to become more important than meeting the basic needs of human life: the need for God and the need for spiritual, physical, and mental help—all were to take a back seat to religious form. The religionist's offense was serious. Note the woman was...

- a "daughter of Abraham," a professed believer in God.
- a woman who had a spiritual need. She had been bound by Satan.
- a woman who had suffered for eighteen years.

> **If you had known what these words mean, 'I desire mercy, not sacrifice,' you would not have condemned the innocent. For the Son of Man is Lord of the Sabbath." (Mat 12:7-8)**
> **"Teacher, which is the greatest commandment in the Law?" Jesus replied: "'Love the Lord your God with all your heart and with all your soul and with all your mind.' This is the first and greatest commandment. And the second is like it: 'Love your neighbor as yourself.' (Mat 22:36-39)**
> **"Woe to you, teachers of the law and Pharisees, you hypocrites! You clean the outside of the cup and dish, but inside they are full of greed and self-indulgence. Blind**

Pharisee! First clean the inside of the cup and dish, and then the outside also will be clean. "Woe to you, teachers of the law and Pharisees, you hypocrites! You are like whitewashed tombs, which look beautiful on the outside but on the inside are full of dead men's bones and everything unclean. In the same way, on the outside you appear to people as righteous but on the inside you are full of hypocrisy and wickedness. (Mat 23:25-28)

He replied, "Isaiah was right when he prophesied about you hypocrites; as it is written: "'These people honor me with their lips, but their hearts are far from me. They worship me in vain; their teachings are but rules taught by men.' You have let go of the commands of God and are holding on to the traditions of men." And he said to them: "You have a fine way of setting aside the commands of God in order to observe your own traditions! (Mark 7:6-9)

"Why do you call me, 'Lord, Lord,' and do not do what I say? (Luke 6:46)

Love does no harm to its neighbor. Therefore love is the fulfillment of the law. (Rom 13:10)

See to it that no one takes you captive through hollow and deceptive philosophy, which depends on human tradition and the basic principles of this world rather than on Christ. (Col 2:8)

Having a form of godliness but denying its power. Have nothing to do with them. (2 Tim 3:5)

They claim to know God, but by their actions they deny him. They are detestable, disobedient and unfit for doing anything good. (Titus 1:16)

This testimony is true. Therefore, rebuke them sharply, so that they will be sound in the faith and will pay no attention to Jewish myths or to the commands of those who reject the truth. (Titus 1:13-14)

Religion that God our Father accepts as pure and faultless is this: to look after orphans and widows in their distress and to keep oneself from being polluted by the world. (James 1:27)

This is how we know what love is: Jesus Christ laid down his life for us. And we ought to lay down our lives for our brothers. If anyone has material possessions and sees his brother in need but has no pity on him, how can the love of God be in him? Dear children, let us not love with words or tongue but with actions and in truth. This then is how we know that we belong to the truth, and how we set our hearts at rest in his presence (1 John 3:16-19)

For I desire mercy, not sacrifice, and acknowledgment of God rather than burnt offerings. (Hosea 6:6)

He has showed you, O man, what is good. And what does the LORD require of you? To act justly and to love mercy and to walk humbly with your God. (Micah 6:8)

DEEPER STUDY # 1

(13:14) **Sabbath Law—Religionists**: the crime committed by Jesus was "breaking the sabbath law," that is, *working* on the Sabbath day. This was a serious matter to the orthodox Jew. Just how serious can be seen in the strict demands governing the Sabbath. Law after law was written to govern all activity on the Sabbath. A person could not travel, fast, cook, buy, sell, draw water, walk beyond a certain distance, lift anything, fight in a war, or heal on the sabbath unless life was at stake. A person was not even to contemplate any kind of work or activity. A good example of the legal restriction and the people's loyalty to it is seen in the women who witnessed Jesus' crucifixion. Despite their enormous love for Him, they would not even walk to His tomb to prepare the body for burial until the Sabbath was over (Mk.16:1f, Mt.28:1f).

It was a serious matter to break the Sabbath law. A person who broke the law was condemned, and if the offence were serious enough, the person was to die.

This may seem harsh to some. But when dealing with the Jewish nation, one must remember that it was their religion that held them together as a nation through centuries and centuries of exile. Their religion—in particular their beliefs about God's call to their nation, the temple, and the Sabbath—became the *binding force* that kept Jews together and maintained their distinctiveness as a people. It protected them from alien beliefs and from being swallowed up by other people through intermarriage. No matter where they were, they met together and associated together and held on to their beliefs. A picture of this can be seen in the insistence of Nehemiah when he led some Jews back to Jerusalem (Neh.13:15-22; cp. Jer.17:19-27; Ezk.46:1-7).

All the above explains to some degree why the religionists opposed Jesus with such hostility. Their problem was that they had allowed religion and ritual, ceremony and liturgy, and probably position, security, and recognition to become more important than the basic essentials of human life: personal need and compassion, and the true worship and mercy of God. (See note and DEEPER STUDY # 1—Mt.12:10. This is an important note for more discussion on this point.)

DEEPER STUDY # 2

(13:14) **Religionists—Word of God**: the religionists (Jewish teachers) corrupted God's Word. There are two ways this is done (Rev.22:18-19; Pr.30:6).

1. By taking away from the words of God's Scripture. A person takes away from God's Word by denying sections that he does not like or understand, by neglecting to live the whole counsel of God, and by interpreting some command-ments too loosely.

2. By adding to the words of God's Scripture. A person adds to God's Word by interpreting and living too strictly. Such exalts the flesh and is nothing more than extreme discipline and self-control. Of course, both discipline and self-control are commendable and are qualities demanded by God's Word, but they are not an end in themselves.

God's Word is practical and leads to an abundant life, to real living. It is not cold, harsh, restrictive, monastic, unrealistic, or impractical. God did not give His Word for a select group (clergy); He gave it for the common man. "His commandments are not burdensome" (1 Jn.5:3).

The Sadducees were especially guilty of taking away from God's Word, whereas the Pharisees and Scribes were especially guilty of adding to God's Word (see DEEPER STUDY # 2—Acts 23:8; DEEPER STUDY # 1—Lk.6:2).

I tell you the truth, until heaven and earth disappear, not the smallest letter, not the least stroke of a pen, will by any means disappear from the Law until everything is accomplished. (Mat 5:18)

And if anyone takes words away from this book of prophecy, God will take away from him his share in the tree of life and in the holy city, which are described in this book. (Rev 22:19)

Do not add to what I command you and do not subtract from it, but keep the com

mands of the LORD your God that I give you. (Deu 4:2)

See that you do all I command you; do not add to it or take away from it. (Deu 12:32)

"Every word of God is flawless; he is a shield to those who take refuge in him. Do not add to his words, or he will rebuke you and prove you a liar. (Prov 30:5-6)

DEEPER STUDY # 3

(13:15-16) **Man, Deceived**: the ruler became angry with Jesus, but he camouflaged it by attacking the people over a religious tradition. His life had become so routine that it was warped: he showed more concern for animals than he did for human beings. Jesus' frontal rebuke indicates that the man had probably never even thought of his plight. If he had, Jesus would probably have tried to stir him to a proper decision.

4 (13:17) **Jesus Christ, Impact**: the effect of Jesus' work and words was the humiliation of those who opposed Him and the rejoicing of those who were open to Him.

       1 The Kingdom of God illustrated **2 It is like a mustard seed**[DS1] a. It is planted by God	**S. The Parables of the Mustard Seed and Yeast (Leaven): The Kingdom of God, 13:18-21** (Mt.13:31-33; Mk.4: 30-32) 18 Then Jesus asked, "What is the kingdom of God like? What shall I compare it to? 19 It is like a mustard seed, which a man took and	planted in his garden. It grew and became a tree, and the birds of the air perched in its branches." 20 Again he asked, "What shall I compare the kingdom of God to? 21 It is like yeast that a woman took and mixed into a large amount of flour until it worked all through the dough."	1) As a seed 2) In His garden b. It grows to be great[DS2] c. It is lodging for all **3 It is like yeast's (leaven's) working in bread**[DS3,4] a. It is taken & placed in meal b. It works until the whole is changed

DIVISION V

THE SON OF MAN'S GREAT JOURNEY TO JERUSALEM (STAGE I): HIS MISSION AND PUBLIC CHALLENGE, 9:51-13:21

S. The Parables of the Mustard Seed and Yeast (Leaven): The Kingdom of God, 13:18-21

(13:18-21) **Introduction**: Jesus was still in the synagogue teaching. Some had rejected Him; others had accepted Him (v.17). This stirred His mind to think about the Kingdom of God, a subject that people needed to understand fully.

1. The Kingdom of God illustrated (v.18).
2. It is like a mustard seed (v.19).
3. It is like yeast's (leaven's) working in bread (v.20-21).

1 (13:18) **Kingdom of God**: the Kingdom of God illustrated. Jesus stirred thought about the kingdom by asking two questions.

1. What is the Kingdom of God like?
2. To what shall the Kingdom of God be compared?

2 (13:19) **Kingdom of God—Christianity, Growth of—Mustard Seed**: the Kingdom of God is like a mustard seed. Jesus said three things about this particular mustard seed.

1. The mustard seed was planted by God. The man in the parable is God or Christ. Note the word "took" (labon, having taken). It means to deliberately take, to take with purpose and thought. The seed was not planted by chance; it did not just happen. With purpose and thought God planted and nourished the seed (kingdom).
   a. He planted it as a small seed (see DEEPER STUDY # 1, Mustard Seed—Lk.13:19 for discussion).
   b. He planted it in His garden. God's garden is the world, the creation of His own hand.

> **In the beginning God created the heavens and the earth. (Gen 1:1)**
> **You alone are the LORD. You made the heavens, even the highest heavens, and all their starry host, the earth and all that is on it, the seas and all that is in them. You give life to everything, and the multitudes of heaven worship you. (Neh 9:6)**
> **In the beginning you laid the foundations of the earth, and the heavens are the work of your hands. (Psa 102:25)**

2. The mustard seed grew to be great. This is really the major point of Luke, to show how the kingdom was to grow from a few persons into a great movement. Imagine the scene. There stood Jesus in the synagogue with only a few persons who truly believed that He was bringing the Kingdom of God to earth. In fact, most of the ones sitting before Him did not believe in Him at all; they opposed Him. But He knew something. God was planting the kingdom on earth through Him; therefore the kingdom was destined to grow and succeed. (See DEEPER STUDY # 2, Christianity—Lk.13:19.)

> **When the Gentiles heard this, they were glad and honored the word of the Lord; and all who were appointed for eternal life believed. (Acts 13:48)**
> **"Therefore I want you to know that God's salvation has been sent to the Gentiles, and they will listen!" (Acts 28:28)**
> **So that the Gentiles may glorify God for his mercy, as it is written: "Therefore I will praise you among the Gentiles; I will sing hymns to your name." (Rom 15:9)**
> **He redeemed us in order that the blessing given to Abraham might come to the Gentiles through Christ Jesus, so that by faith we might receive the promise of the Spirit. (Gal 3:14)**
> **This mystery is that through the gospel the Gentiles are heirs together with Israel [Jewish believers], members together of one body, and sharers together in the promise in Christ Jesus. (Eph 3:6)**
> **Let grain abound throughout the land; on the tops of the hills may it sway. Let its fruit flourish like Lebanon; let it thrive like the grass of the field. (Psa 72:16)**
> **Of the increase of his government and peace there will be no end. He will reign on David's throne and over his kingdom, establishing and upholding it with justice and righteousness from that time on and forever. The zeal of the LORD Almighty will accomplish this. (Isa 9:7)**
> **For you will spread out to the right and to the left; your descendants will dispossess nations and settle in their desolate cities. (Isa 54:3)**
> **Surely you will summon nations you know not, and nations that do not know you will hasten to you, because of the LORD your God, the Holy One of Israel, for he has endowed you with splendor." (Isa 55:5)**
> **Then you will look and be radiant, your heart will throb and swell with joy;**

the wealth on the seas will be brought to you, to you the riches of the nations will come. (Isa 60:5)

The least of you will become a thousand, the smallest a mighty nation. I am the LORD; in its time I will do this swiftly." (Isa 60:22)

3. The mustard bush provided lodging for the birds' of the air. The birds flocking to the tree is a picture of the people and nations of the earth seeking refuge in the covering of Christianity.

a. Some say the birds are those in the world who find their lodging in the kingdom—the kingdom (the church, Christianity) that had so small a beginning but is now growing into a stately movement. Many in the world, believers and non-believers alike, have found help and safety under its branches. To a large extent laws and institutions of mercy, justice, and honor have evolved from this magnificent movement. This interpretation relies heavily upon the picture painted by the Old Testament. A great empire is said to be like a tree, and conquered nations are said to be like birds who lodge under its shadow (Ezk.17:22-24; 31:6; Dan.4:14).

b. Others say the birds are the children of the evil one who see the lodging facilities and protective covering of the kingdom and seek lodging therein.

"The Law and the Prophets were proclaimed until John. Since that time, the good news of the kingdom of God is being preached, and everyone is forcing his way into it. (Luke 16:16)

DEEPER STUDY # 1

(13:19) **Mustard Seed**: the mustard seed was not actually the smallest seed known in Jesus' day, but the seed was small and the mustard bush grew as large as some trees. It has been reported that a rider on horseback could find shade under its branches. The fact that such a small seed could produce such huge results caused people to use the mustard seed as a proverbial saying to describe smallness.

DEEPER STUDY # 2

(13:19) **Christianity—Kingdom of God**: there are several facts that show just how small the beginning of the kingdom or of Christianity really was.

1. It began in the soul of a single person. Jesus launched the movement all by Himself. The idea, the dream, was in no one else's soul but His. He moved out alone—in God's strength.

2. It was born in the soul of a carpenter from an obscure village, Nazareth, and from an obscure and despised nation, Israel (see note—Mt.8:5-13; Lk.7:4-5).

3. It was carried forth by men with no position and no prestige. There were no mighty, no noble, no famous persons among its early followers. They were but common folk, some from honorable professions such as the fishing industry (Mt.4:18-21), and some from despised professions such as tax collecting (Mt.9:9). (Cp. 1 Cor.1:26.)

4. It grew from just a few persons who had very *little faith* (cp. Mt.14:31; Lk.12:32).

5. It was formed as a church and numbered only one hundred and twenty in the very beginning (Acts 1:15).

3 (13:20-21) **Kingdom of God—Christianity—Leaven—Yeast**: the Kingdom of God is like yeast's (leaven's) working in bread. Quickly note what Jesus said: the Kingdom of God is like yeast which is placed in meal (the world) until the whole (world) is changed. Note two major points.

1. The yeast (kingdom) is taken and placed into the meal (world).

a. The kingdom or gospel is deliberately taken and placed into the world. The kingdom and the gospel of God are not by chance (see DEEPER STUDY # 2, pt.1, Kingdom of God—Lk.13:19).

"For God so loved the world that he gave his one and only Son, that whoever believes in him shall not perish but have eternal life. (John 3:16)

But God demonstrates his own love for us in this: While we were still sinners, Christ died for us. (Rom 5:8)

For there is no difference between Jew and Gentile—the same Lord is Lord of all and richly blesses all who call on him, (Rom 10:12)

Who wants all men to be saved and to come to a knowledge of the truth. (1 Tim 2:4)

He is the atoning sacrifice for our sins, and not only for ours but also for the sins of the whole world. (1 John 2:2)

"Turn to me and be saved, all you ends of the earth; for I am God, and there is no other. (Isa 45:22)

b. The purpose of the kingdom is to work like yeast, that is, to change the whole of an individual and of society itself.

⇒ It seeks to change individuals: to penetrate them with the gospel until the *whole* being is transformed.

⇒ It seeks to change society as a whole: to penetrate society with the gospel until the whole of society is transformed.

Therefore, if anyone is in Christ, he is a new creation; the old has gone, the new has come! (2 Cor 5:17)

Neither circumcision nor uncircumcision means anything; what counts is a new creation. (Gal 6:15)

To be made new in the attitude of your minds; and to put on the new self, created to be like God in true righteousness and holiness. (Eph 4:23-24)

And have put on the new self, which is being renewed in knowledge in the image of its Creator. (Col 3:10)

c. Yeast (leaven) has a changing, transforming, fulfilling, and satisfying power (see DEEPER STUDY # 3—Lk.1:21 for discussion).

2. The yeast (leaven) (kingdom) works until the whole (world) is changed. (See DEEPER STUDY # 4, Yeast—Leaven—Lk.13:21 for discussion.)

Jesus said to them, "I tell you the truth, it is not Moses who has given you the

bread from heaven, but it is my Father who gives you the true bread from heaven. For the bread of God is he who comes down from heaven and gives life to the world." (John 6:32-33)

Then Jesus declared, "I am the bread of life. He who comes to me will never go hungry, and he who believes in me will never be thirsty. I am the bread of life. Your forefathers ate the manna in the desert, yet they died. But here is the bread that comes down from heaven, which a man may eat and not die. I am the living bread that came down from heaven. If anyone eats of this bread, he will live forever. This bread is my flesh, which I will give for the life of the world." (John 6:48-51)

This is the bread that came down from heaven. Your forefathers ate manna and died, but he who feeds on this bread will live forever." (John 6:58)

The thief comes only to steal and kill and destroy; I have come that they may have life, and have it to the full. (John 10:10)

And to know this love that surpasses knowledge—that you may be filled to the measure of all the fullness of God. (Eph 3:19)

Who [the Lord] satisfies your desires with good things so that your youth is renewed like the eagle's. (Psa 103:5)

For he satisfies the thirsty and fills the hungry with good things. (Psa 107:9)

DEEPER STUDY # 3

(13:21) **Yeast—Leaven—Transformation—Gospel—Kingdom of God**: yeast (leaven) changes and transforms bread. Bread made from water is hard, dry, and not too nourishing; but yeast, mixed in with dough, changes and transforms bread tremendously. It does at least four things for bread.

1. Yeast (leaven) makes bread soft, no longer hard. The yeast of the gospel does the same: it penetrates the heart of man and softens the hardness of his life. Thereby the man becomes much softer toward the Lord and toward the needs of others. He becomes a more caring and giving person. Softness is definitely one of the trademarks of a transformed person.

2. Yeast (leaven) makes bread porous and moist, no longer dry. The yeast of the gospel does the same: it penetrates the dryness of a man's heart and life. Thereby the gospel penetrates, creates pores in his life, and moistens his heart so that he can grow into a moist or fruitful person.

3. Yeast (leaven) makes bread satisfying, no longer dissatisfying. Again, the gospel does the same for the man who lives a dissatisfied life with no purpose, meaning, or significance. The gospel changes, that is, transforms a person's heart and life, giving purpose and joy and hope—all the satisfaction a person could ever desire.

4. Yeast (leaven) makes bread nourishing, no longer of little benefit. The yeast of the gospel does the same thing for the man who seems to accomplish so little in life. The gospel not only gives *purpose* but it *inspires*, *commissions*, and causes a man to *feed others*. A person transformed by the gospel is able to feed the truth to the world. The gospel is able to explain the reasons for the emptiness and loneliness of the human heart and God's provision for such.

DEEPER STUDY # 4

(13:21) **Leaven—Yeast**: note several important facts about how yeast (leaven) works.

1. Yeast (leaven) works quietly and silently. It works without fanfare and the spectacular. There is a thoughtful lesson here on how the gospel should be presented (see outline and notes—Mt.4:5-7; 12:38-40).

And the Lord's servant must not quarrel; instead, he must be kind to everyone, able to teach, not resentful. Those who oppose him he must gently instruct, in the hope that God will grant them repentance leading them to a knowledge of the truth, (2 Tim 2:24-25)

To slander no one, to be peaceable and considerate, and to show true humility toward all men. (Titus 3:2)

Who is wise and understanding among you? Let him show it by his good life, by deeds done in the humility that comes from wisdom. (James 3:13)

But in your hearts set apart Christ as Lord. Always be prepared to give an answer to everyone who asks you to give the reason for the hope that you have. But do this with gentleness and respect, (1 Pet 3:15)

2. Yeast (leaven) finishes its work. Once it is inserted into the dough, nothing can stop it or ever pluck it out. It will transform the dough. This is a great lesson on the security of the person who genuinely allows the gospel to penetrate his heart and life.

I give them eternal life, and they shall never perish; no one can snatch them out of my hand. (John 10:28)

Being confident of this, that he who began a good work in you will carry it on to completion until the day of Christ Jesus. (Phil 1:6)

That is why I am suffering as I am. Yet I am not ashamed, because I know whom I have believed, and am convinced that he is able to guard what I have entrusted to him for that day. (2 Tim 1:12)

But the Lord is faithful, and he will strengthen and protect you from the evil one. (2 Th 3:3)

Who through faith are shielded by God's power until the coming of the salvation that is ready to be revealed in the last time. (1 Pet 1:5)

To him who is able to keep you from falling and to present you before his glorious presence without fault and with great joy—to the only God our Savior be glory, majesty, power and authority, through Jesus Christ our Lord, before all ages, now and forevermore! Amen. (Jude 1:24-25)

Since you have kept my command to endure patiently, I will also keep you from the hour of trial that is going to come upon the whole world to test those who live on the earth. (Rev 3:10)

I will remain in the world no longer, but they are still in the world, and I am coming to you. Holy Father, protect them by the power of your name—the name you

gave me—so that they may be one as we are one. (John 17:11)

I am with you and will watch over you wherever you go, and I will bring you back to this land. I will not leave you until I have done what I have promised you." (Gen 28:15)

The LORD watches over you— the LORD is your shade at your right hand; the sun will not harm you by day, nor the moon by night. The LORD will keep you from all harm— he will watch over your life; the LORD will watch over your coming and going both now and forevermore. (Psa 121:5-8)

3. Yeast (leaven) works slowly and gradually, yet consistently. It takes time for it to cause the whole lump to rise. The believer can learn at least two lessons from this fact.

a. It will take time for him to personally grow in the gospel. Just as a child grows physically through proper nourishment, so the believer will grow spiritually if he receives proper nourishment. His spiritual growth will take time; but it will be consistent and sure.

"Now I commit you to God and to the word of his grace, which can build you up and give you an inheritance among all those who are sanctified. (Acts 20:32)

Like newborn babies, crave pure spiritual milk, so that by it you may grow up in your salvation, now that you have tasted that the Lord is good. (1 Pet 2:2-3)

Do your best to present yourself to God as one approved, a workman who does not need to be ashamed and who correctly handles the word of truth. (2 Tim 2:15)

All Scripture is God-breathed and is useful for teaching, rebuking, correcting and training in righteousness, (2 Tim 3:16)

b. It will take time for his own witnessing and work to produce bread. Yet his role as yeast (service and ministry) will change the lump of meal (people) he handles and works.

4. Yeast (leaven) changes the quality, not the substance, of the dough. It is still dough, yet it is changed. A man who receives the gospel remains a man; but he is a changed man, a man of quality, a man of God.

5. Yeast (leaven) changes the whole lump. It permeates every pore of the dough's being. So it is with a man. Once the gospel honestly penetrates, it permeates and affects all of his life (cp. 2 Cor.5:17; Gal.6:15; Eph.4:23-24; Col.3:10).

	VI. THE SON OF MAN'S GREAT JOURNEY TO JERUSALEM (STAGE II): HIS TEACHING AND PUBLIC CONFLICT, 13:22-17:10 **A. The Saved Discussed, 13:22-30**
1 Jesus journeyed toward Jerusalem a. Taught in the cities & villages b. Along the way someone questioned Jesus about salvation	22 Then Jesus went through the towns and villages, teaching as he made his way to Jerusalem. 23 Someone asked him, "Lord, are only a few people going to be saved?" He said to them,
2 The saved make every effort to enter the narrow door	24 "Make every effort to enter through the narrow door, because many, I tell you, will try to enter and will not be able to.
3 The saved act soon enough: A man can move too late	25 Once the owner of the house gets up and closes the door, you will stand outside

knocking and pleading, 'Sir, open the door for us.' "But he will answer, 'I don't know you or where you come from.'	
26 "Then you will say, 'We ate and drank with you, and you taught in our streets.'	**4 The saved are not the citizens of so-called Christian nations nor members of certain fellowships**
27 "But he will reply, 'I don't know you or where you come from. Away from me, all you evildoers!' 28 "There will be weeping there, and gnashing of teeth, when you see Abraham, Isaac and Jacob and all the prophets in the kingdom of God, but you yourselves thrown out.	**5 The saved shall be separated from the lost, & the lost shall see them enter God's Kingdom**[DS1,2]
29 People will come from east and west and north and south, and will take their places at the feast in the kingdom of God. 30 Indeed there are those who are last who will be first, and first who will be last."	**6 The saved will come from all nations & classes of society**

DIVISION VI

THE SON OF MAN'S GREAT JOURNEY TO JERUSALEM (STAGE II): HIS TEACHING AND PUBLIC CONFLICT, 13:22-17:10

A. The Saved Discussed, 13:22-30

(13:22-30) **Introduction**: Who are the saved? Will many be saved? Christ answers these questions in this passage. However, He does not answer the questions to satisfy curiosity. He answers them to challenge us so that we will make sure we are saved.

1. Jesus journeyed toward Jerusalem (v.22-23).
2. The saved struggle to enter the narrow door (v.24).
3. The saved act soon enough: a man can move too late (v.25).
4. The saved are not the citizens of so-called Christian nations nor members of certain fellowships (v.26).
5. The saved shall be separated from the lost, and the lost shall see them enter God's Kingdom (v.27-28).
6. The saved will come from all nations and classes of society (v.29-30).

1 (13:22-23) **Jesus Christ, Cross—Salvation**: Jesus journeyed toward Jerusalem. This is the second stage of Jesus' great journey to the cross. (See DEEPER STUDY # 1—Lk.9:51; cp. Lk.17:11.) Note: as He travelled along, He taught wherever He was. He kept on doing what God sent Him to do, not slacking off nor forgetting His call and mission. Whether he was in a large city or a small village, it did not matter; He reached out to as many as He could reach.

Somewhere along the way, someone asked Him point blank: "Lord, are only a few people going to be saved?" The man was not asking how he might be saved but if the saved would be many or few. His question was probably one of two things. It was a question of curiosity, a question often discussed among people: Are most people saved or lost? However, it could have been a legitimate question asking for clarification. The Jews taught that all would be saved just because they were Jews by birth and circumcision. But Jesus taught that nationality and ritual had nothing to do with salvation, and He was always stressing that many are called, but few are chosen. Perhaps the man was asking how to reconcile the two teachings. Note: Jesus used the occasion to speak "to them" all, the whole crowd.

> **Thought 1.** Many are curious, but not curious enough to really seek after the Lord for personal salvation. They are ready and willing to discuss *religious subjects* but unwilling to deny themselves and to diligently seek after God.

> **Thought 2.** Birth and ritual are not enough to save a person, not even if the ritual is circumcision (for the Jew) or baptism (for the Christian). Baptism no more saves a person *born within Christian circles* than circumcision saved a Jew *born within Jewish circles*.

2 (13:24) **Salvation—Narrow Gate—Narrow Door—Jesus Christ, Mediator—Seeking**: the saved struggle to enter the narrow door. Note three significant facts.

1. The entrance to salvation is a *narrow door*. This means at least three things.
   a. The way to salvation is specific, very specific.
   b. The way to salvation is the only way. There are not many ways to be saved; there is only one way.

> **Jesus answered, "I am the way and the truth and the life. No one comes to the Father except through me. (John 14:6)**
>
> **Salvation is found in no one else, for there is no other name under heaven given to men by which we must be saved." (Acts 4:12)**
>
> **For there is one God and one mediator**

between God and men, the man Christ Jesus, Who gave himself as a ransom for all men—the testimony given in its proper time. (1 Tim 2:6)

But the ministry Jesus has received is as superior to theirs as the covenant of which he is mediator is superior to the old one, and it is founded on better promises. (Heb 8:6)

For this reason Christ is the mediator of a new covenant, that those who are called may receive the promised eternal inheritance—now that he has died as a ransom to set them free from the sins committed under the first covenant. (Heb 9:15)

To Jesus the mediator of a new covenant, and to the sprinkled blood that speaks a better word than the blood of Abel. (Heb 12:24)

My dear children, I write this to you so that you will not sin. But if anybody does sin, we have one who speaks to the Father in our defense—Jesus Christ, the Righteous One. (1 John 2:1)

c. The way to salvation is straight. It is not crooked in direction or purpose or morals. It is the straight way.

2. A person has to *"struggle, make every effort"* (agonizesthe) to be saved. The word means to agonize, struggle, contend, exert to the fullest, labor fervently. *Whole-hearted dedication and effort* are required. But note a critical point: the idea is not that a person works for his salvation, but that he *diligently seeks* God. He casts himself totally upon the *belief that God is*, that God actually exists (cp. Heb.11:6). It is the spirit, the attitude, the heart that sets itself upon God, refusing to be diverted or to be committed to anything else. It is the total commitment of one's life to God for salvation.

"So I say to you: Ask and it will be given to you; seek and you will find; knock and the door will be opened to you. For everyone who asks receives; he who seeks finds; and to him who knocks, the door will be opened. (Luke 11:9-10)

God did this so that men would seek him and perhaps reach out for him and find him, though he is not far from each one of us. (Acts 17:27; cp. v.24-28)

And without faith it is impossible to please God, because anyone who comes to him must believe that he exists and that he rewards those who earnestly seek him. (Heb 11:6)

But if from there you seek the LORD your God, you will find him if you look for him with all your heart and with all your soul. (Deu 4:29)

Seek the LORD while he may be found; call on him while he is near. (Isa 55:6)

You will seek me and find me when you seek me with all your heart. (Jer 29:13)

Sow for yourselves righteousness, reap the fruit of unfailing love, and break up your unplowed ground; for it is time to seek the LORD, until he comes and showers righteousness on you. (Hosea 10:12)

This is what the LORD says to the house of Israel: "Seek me and live; (Amos 5:4)

Seek the LORD, all you humble of the land, you who do what he commands. Seek righteousness, seek humility; perhaps you will be sheltered on the day of the Lord's anger. (Zep 2:3)

3. Many will seek to enter the door of salvation but "will not be able to." The reason is what Jesus said. One must *"struggle, make every effort"* to enter and few are willing to pay the price of self-denial. It costs too much for them to give up the world (see note and DEEPER STUDY # 1—Lk.9:23).

Then he said to them all: "If anyone would come after me, he must deny himself and take up his cross daily and follow me. For whoever wants to save his life will lose it, but whoever loses his life for me will save it. (Luke 9:23-24)

3 (13:25) **Salvation—Decision—Accepted Time**: the saved act soon enough; a man can move too late. The parable is simple and clearly understood. Note three things.

1. The person who strives *now* can enter salvation. This is seen in the words "will try" (v.24). The words are in the future tense; that is, it is in the future that many "will try to enter, and will not be able." Right now, all who "struggle, make every effort" to enter salvation can be saved.

For he says, "In the time of my favor I heard you, and in the day of salvation I helped you." I tell you, now is the time of God's favor, now is the day of salvation. (2 Cor 6:2)

Then I acknowledged my sin to you and did not cover up my iniquity. I said, "I will confess my transgressions to the LORD"—and you forgave the guilt of my sin. Selah Therefore let everyone who is godly pray to you while you may be found; surely when the mighty waters rise, they will not reach him. You are my hiding place; you will protect me from trouble and surround me with songs of deliverance. Selah (Psa 32:5-7)

But I pray to you, O LORD, in the time of your favor; in your great love, O God, answer me with your sure salvation. (Psa 69:13)

For he is our God and we are the people of his pasture, the flock under his care. Today, if you hear his voice, (Psa 95:7)

This is what the LORD says: "In the time of my favor I will answer you, and in the day of salvation I will help you; I will keep you and will make you to be a covenant for the people, to restore the land and to reassign its desolate inheritances, (Isa 49:8)

2. The Owner shall rise up and shut the door to salvation. There is a time limit to salvation. The door will not always be opened.

a. It is shut at a person's death. No man who is presently living has yet had the door shut; but for some, the door will be shut within the very next minute, the next hour, the next day (Heb.9:27).

b. It is shut when the Lord returns and the great day of judgment takes place. The age of grace and the day of salvation will be closed for the whole world, for every man and woman and child who is of responsible age.

3. Many shall rise up and knock at the closed door and beg to enter. This is the scene painted by Christ: men's rising up and crying for mercy and salvation after it is too late. Once a man dies, it is too late. Once Christ returns, it will be too late.

> **For everyone who has will be given more, and he will have an abundance. Whoever does not have, even what he has will be taken from him. And throw that worthless servant outside, into the darkness, where there will be weeping and gnashing of teeth.' (Mat 25:29-30; cp. v.24-30)**
>
> **"Then he will say to those on his left, 'Depart from me, you who are cursed, into the eternal fire prepared for the devil and his angels. For I was hungry and you gave me nothing to eat, I was thirsty and you gave me nothing to drink, I was a stranger and you did not invite me in, I needed clothes and you did not clothe me, I was sick and in prison and you did not look after me.' "They also will answer, 'Lord, when did we see you hungry or thirsty or a stranger or needing clothes or sick or in prison, and did not help you?' "He will reply, 'I tell you the truth, whatever you did not do for one of the least of these, you did not do for me.' "Then they will go away to eternal punishment, but the righteous to eternal life." (Mat 25:41-46)**
>
> **Just as man is destined to die once, and after that to face judgment, (Heb 9:27)**
>
> **Afterward, as you know, when he wanted to inherit this blessing, he was rejected. He could bring about no change of mind, though he sought the blessing with tears. (Heb 12:17)**
>
> **"The harvest is past, the summer has ended, and we are not saved." (Jer 8:20)**

4 (13:26) **False Profession—Heritage—Christian Nation**: the saved are not the citizens of so-called Christian nations nor members of certain fellowships or churches. Note the exact words of men when they stand before Christ in that day:

1. "We ate and drank with you." They were…
   - where He was, in His very presence (in church, in the presence of believers).
   - where His Word was taught.
   - where His works were performed.

2. "You taught in our streets."
   - They were citizens of nations which allowed His teaching.
   - They allowed His teaching in their own streets, neighborhoods, cities, and homes.

However, they are *only professing believers*; they are not genuine believers. They are people who had all the privileges of the gospel; some are even baptized church members and moral persons, but they never dedicated their whole being's to *strive* after salvation (see outline and notes—Jn.1:12-13; Ph.3:7-11). They continued to live worldly and unrighteous lives, seeking the comforts and possessions of this world.

> **"Not everyone who says to me, 'Lord, Lord,' will enter the kingdom of heaven, but only he who does the will of my Father who is in heaven. (Mat 7:21)**
>
> **He replied, "Isaiah was right when he prophesied about you hypocrites; as it is written: "'These people honor me with their lips, but their hearts are far from me. (Mark 7:6)**
>
> **"Why do you call me, 'Lord, Lord,' and do not do what I say? (Luke 6:46)**
>
> **They claim to know God, but by their actions they deny him. They are detestable, disobedient and unfit for doing anything good. (Titus 1:16)**
>
> **Dear children, let us not love with words or tongue but with actions and in truth. (1 John 3:18)**
>
> **They remembered that God was their Rock, that God Most High was their Redeemer. (Psa 78:35)**
>
> **My people come to you [the prophet, the preacher], as they usually do, and sit before you to listen to your words, but they do not put them into practice. With their mouths they express devotion, but their hearts are greedy for unjust gain. Indeed, to them you are nothing more than one who sings love songs with a beautiful voice and plays an instrument well, for they hear your words but do not put them into practice. (Ezek 33:31-32)**

5 (13:27-28) **Judgment—Lost, Rejected by God**: the saved shall be separated from the lost, and the lost shall see them enter God's kingdom. (See DEEPER STUDY # 3, Kingdom of God—Mt.19:23-24.) Note several tragic facts.

1. The Owner or Master will not know the lost nor from where they came. They had lived in a different life and realm, a different world of thought and behavior than He had. They will have come from a different background entirely than the Owner or Master. Therefore, He will not know them nor from where they came.

> **For I tell you that unless your righteousness surpasses that of the Pharisees and the teachers of the law, you will certainly not enter the kingdom of heaven. (Mat 5:20)**
>
> **And he said: "I tell you the truth, unless you change and become like little children, you will never enter the kingdom of heaven. (Mat 18:3; cp. Mk.10:15)**
>
> **Do you not know that the wicked will not inherit the kingdom of God? Do not be deceived: Neither the sexually immoral nor idolaters nor adulterers nor male prostitutes nor homosexual offenders (1 Cor 6:9; cp. Gal.5:19-21; cp. v.22-23)**
>
> **I declare to you, brothers, that flesh and blood cannot inherit the kingdom of**

God, nor does the perishable inherit the imperishable. (1 Cor 15:50)

Nothing impure will ever enter it, nor will anyone who does what is shameful or deceitful, but only those whose names are written in the Lamb's book of life. (Rev 21:27)

2. The Owner or Master will have to reject the lost, because they have been "doing evil" (cp. Ps.6:8).

Many will say to me on that day, 'Lord, Lord, did we not prophesy in your name, and in your name drive out demons and perform many miracles? Then I will tell them plainly, 'I never knew you. Away from me, you evildoers!' (Mat 7:22-23)

Let both grow together until the harvest. At that time I will tell the harvesters: First collect the weeds and tie them in bundles to be burned; then gather the wheat and bring it into my barn.'" (Mat 13:30)

This is how it will be at the end of the age. The angels will come and separate the wicked from the righteous (Mat 13:49)

Two men will be in the field; one will be taken and the other left. Two women will be grinding with a hand mill; one will be taken and the other left. (Mat 24:40-41; cp. Lk.17:34-36)

"Later the others also came. 'Sir! Sir!' they said. 'Open the door for us!' "But he replied, 'I tell you the truth, I don't know you.' (Mat 25:11-12)

"Then they will go away to eternal punishment, but the righteous to eternal life." (Mat 25:46)

And besides all this, between us and you a great chasm has been fixed, so that those who want to go from here to you cannot, nor can anyone cross over from there to us.' (Luke 16:26)

3. The lost will weep and gnash their teeth (see DEEPER STUDY # 1, 2—Lk.13:28). Note the reason: they will actually see their fathers, godly men from whose roots they came, enter God's kingdom; but they themselves shall be thrust out. Note: the lost are able to see believers in heaven, in God's kingdom (see note, pt.2—Lk.16:23-31).

Thought 1. How many will see godly parents, children, friends, neighbors, and acquaintences enter God's kingdom and find themselves shut out? There will be weeping and gnashing of teeth in that tragic day. Why? Simply because they (the lost) would neither "struggle nor make every effort" to enter salvation. They would not deny themselves (see note and DEEPER STUDY # 1—Lk.9:23).

DEEPER STUDY # 1
(13:28) **Weeping**: loud grief, mourning, groaning, wailing, floods and floods of tears.

DEEPER STUDY # 2
(13:28) **Gnashing** (brugmos): grinding; biting in hostility and bitterness and indignation; spitefully snapping the teeth; rage, fury, and despair because nothing can be done. A person's state is permanently determined (cp. Is.51:20).

6 (13:29-30) **Gentile, Conversion—Salvation, Universal—Reward**: the saved will come from all nations and classes of society. This is a prediction of the great Gentile revival and conversion to take place. We are, of course, in the midst of this great revival today. Note three facts.

1. The saved will come from the four corners of the world. Salvation is not from one corner nor from one nation of the earth. It is of God, who rules over all the earth, and it is by faith, by *struggling and making every effort* to enter God's kingdom (see notes—Ro.4:11-12. See outline and DEEPER STUDY # 1—Ro.4:1-25.)

Go to the street corners and invite to the banquet anyone you find.' (Mat 22:9)

Therefore go and make disciples of all nations, baptizing them in the name of the Father and of the Son and of the Holy Spirit, and teaching them to obey everything I have commanded you. And surely I am with you always, to the very end of the age." (Mat 28:19-20)

On the last and greatest day of the Feast, Jesus stood and said in a loud voice, "If <u>anyone</u> is thirsty, let him come to me and <u>drink.</u> (John 7:37)

For there is no difference between Jew and Gentile—the same Lord is Lord of all and richly blesses all who call on him, (Rom 10:12)

The Spirit and the bride say, "Come!" And let him who hears say, "Come!" Whoever is thirsty, let him come; and <u>whoever</u> wishes, let him take the free gift of the water of life. (Rev 22:17)

"Turn to me and be saved, all you ends of the earth; for I am God, and there is no other. (Isa 45:22)

"Come, all you who are thirsty, come to the waters; and you who have no money, come, buy and eat! Come, buy wine and milk without money and without cost. (Isa 55:1)

2. The saved will sit down in the Kingdom of God. The picture is that of the great marriage supper of the Messiah. (See outline and notes—Lk.14:15-24; Mt.22:1-14 for discussion.)

To him who overcomes, I will give the right to sit with me on my throne, just as I overcame and sat down with my Father on his throne. (Rev 3:21)

3. The saved come from all classes, even from those who are classified as "last" by men. *Classes* do not matter to God. He is no respecter of persons. He saves any man who *struggles and makes every effort* to enter salvation. Thus, many who are first (safe and secure) in the minds of themselves and others will be last (lost), and many considered as last will be first.

Then Peter began to speak: "I now realize how true it is that God does not show favoritism but accepts men from every nation who fear him and do what is

right. (Acts 10:34-35)

But glory, honor and peace for everyone who does good: first for the Jew, then for the Gentile. For God does not show favoritism. (Rom 2:10-11)

For there is no difference between Jew and Gentile—the same Lord is Lord of all and richly blesses all who call on him, (Rom 10:12)

As for those who seemed to be important—whatever they were makes no difference to me; God does not judge by external appearance—those men added nothing to my message. (Gal 2:6)

He has brought down rulers from their thrones but has lifted up the humble. (Luke 1:52)

Woe to you who are well fed now, for you will go hungry. Woe to you who laugh now, for you will mourn and weep. (Luke 6:25)

	B. The Tragic Rejection of Jesus, 13:31-35 (Mt.23:37-39; cp. Lk.19:41-44)	and the next day—for surely no prophet can die outside Jerusalem!	continue" c. His death must be diligently pursued in Jerusalem
1 Some Pharisees warned Jesus about a plot to kill Him	31 At that time some Pharisees came to Jesus and said to him, "Leave this place and go somewhere else. Herod wants to kill you."	34 "O Jerusalem, Jerusalem, you who kill the prophets and stone those sent to you, how often I have longed to gather your children together, as a hen gathers her chicks under her wings, but you were not willing!	**3 The rejection by the religionists & the people** a. They killed God's prophets & messengers b. They rejected the Messiah's salvation
2 The rejection by political leaders a. His ministry will be completed	32 He replied, "Go tell that fox, 'I will drive out demons and heal people today and tomorrow, and on the third-day I will reach my goal.'	35 Look, your house is left to you desolate. I tell you, you will not see me again until you say, 'Blessed is he who comes in the name of the Lord.'"	**4 The warning to all those who reject Jesus** a. They will be forsaken by God b. There will be a day when Jesus will return & rule supremely
b. His walk today, tomorrow, & the day after "must	33 In any case, I must keep going today and tomorrow		

DIVISION VI

THE SON OF MAN'S GREAT JOURNEY TO JERUSALEM (STAGE II): HIS TEACHING AND PUBLIC CONFLICT, 13:22-17:10

B. The Tragic Rejection of Jesus, 13:31-35

(13:31-35) **Introduction**: Jesus Christ has always been rejected and opposed by men. He has been and still is opposed by the ordinary man, the religionist, and the ruler. There is not a single class of men who flocks to Christ, not in *true* belief. The opposition to Jesus ranges from ignoring Him to trying to stamp out His witness through His followers. Some people ridicule and abuse the followers of the Lord, while others persecute and kill them. This passage deals with persons who rejected Jesus Christ.

1. Some Pharisees warned Jesus about Herod's plot to kill Him (v.31).
2. The rejection by political leaders (v.31-33).
3. The rejection by the religionists and the people (v.34).
4. The warning to all those who reject Jesus (v.35).

(13:31-35) **Another Outline**. Some Unusual Things About Jesus.

1. Some Pharisees cared for Jesus (v.31).
2. Herod plotted against Jesus (v.31).
3. Jesus used sharp language: "That fox" (v.32).
4. Jesus knew the duration of His life (v.33).
5. Jesus knew the place of His death (v.33).
6. Jesus deliberately walked into the murderous trap set for Him (v.33).
7. Jesus lamented over those who rejected Him (v.34).
8. Jesus foretold a future day of Godly supremacy (v.35).

1 (13:31) **Pharisees**: some Pharisees warned Jesus about Herod's plot. This verse shows that some Pharisees respected Jesus and were not hostile toward Him. Apparently, the vast majority did reject and stand against Him, but there were a few who *truly* loved and believed God. Therefore, they would never think of plotting to kill a man, much less to kill Jesus. When they looked at Jesus, they felt He was a good man—perhaps a prophet, maybe even the Messiah. We do know that some Pharisees did accept Jesus as the Messiah (Acts 6:7; 15:5; 18:8, 17). It was probably some of these who warned Jesus against Herod.

2 (13:31-33) **Jesus Christ, Rejection**: the rejection by political leaders. Herod plotted to kill Jesus. This is a fact seldom considered, but the plot was real and dangerous. The Lord's words to Herod show this (v.32). Remember the scene. Jesus was in Herod's territory, Galilee, and thousands were following Him throughout the whole area. The whole country was aroused with the rumor of the Messiah. And when the subject of a Jewish Messiah arose, the authorities paid close attention. Usually when a man claimed to be a Messiah, an uprising of some sort took place. Herod was bound to be paying close attention and keeping watch over Jesus and His movements.

> **Thought 1.** The Pharisees who warned Jesus bucked the tide. What they did was not popular among their peers, but they did what they knew to be the right thing. They *stood up for Christ*.

Another factor is known about Herod. He had reacted against the righteousness of John the Baptist and had him killed. Herod fell sway to what so many political leaders experience:

⇒ The fear of the people's *first* loyalty going to God instead of the state. (Government leaders often fail to see that Christ's kingdom is not of this earth and that God demands loyalty to the state. See notes—Lk.20:19-26; Mt.22:15-22; 17:24-27.)
⇒ The fear of the teaching of Christ: the responsibility of men to God.
⇒ The fear of *true* righteousness and justice and love. (Such virtues often run contrary to what government leaders really want.)

It is for these reasons that men try to stamp out the witness of Christ. Note that Jesus called Herod "that fox." The *fox* was a symbol of...

- a sly man
- a subtle man
- a base man
- a crafty man
- a treacherous man
- a destructive man
- a worthless man

Men will attack the witness of Christ by being...

- sly
- subtle
- base
- crafty
- treacherous
- destructive
- worthless

Jesus said three revealing things about the attack against His witness.

1. His ministry and witness will be *"completed"* (teleioumai). The word means completed and finished. His ministry of delivering men spiritually and physically (casting out evil spirits and healing) will not be stopped by any man, even rulers such as Herod.

The words "on the third day I will reach my goal" mean that His witness and delivering power will be completed and finished. There is a *definite time* for it, then His witness will stop. It will be no more. But until that day, nothing can stop His ministry and witness. This is, of course, a reference to Jesus' death and His resurrection on the third day. Note that His resurrection is the goal, the completion of His ministry. It is by arising from the dead that death is conquered and man's salvation is completed.

> **You disowned the Holy and Righteous One and asked that a murderer be released to you. You killed the author of life, but God raised him from the dead. We are witnesses of this. (Acts 3:14-15)**
>
> **"We are witnesses of everything he did in the country of the Jews and in Jerusalem. They killed him by hanging him on a tree, but God raised him from the dead on the third day and caused him to be seen. He was not seen by all the people, but by witnesses whom God had already chosen—by us who ate and drank with him after he rose from the dead. (Acts 10:39-41)**
>
> **And who through the Spirit of holiness was declared with power to be the Son of God by his resurrection from the dead: Jesus Christ our Lord. (Rom 1:4)**
>
> **But Christ has indeed been raised from the dead, the firstfruits of those who have fallen asleep. For since death came through a man, the resurrection of the dead comes also through a man. For as in Adam all die, so in Christ all will be made alive. But each in his own turn: Christ, the firstfruits; then, when he comes, those who belong to him. (1 Cor 15:20-23)**
>
> **Because we know that the one who raised the Lord Jesus from the dead will also raise us with Jesus and present us with you in his presence. (2 Cor 4:14)**
>
> **But also for us, to whom God will credit righteousness—for us who believe in him who raised Jesus our Lord from the dead. He was delivered over to death for our sins and was raised to life for our justification. (Rom 4:24-25)**
>
> **That if you confess with your mouth, "Jesus is Lord," and believe in your heart that God raised him from the dead, you will be saved. (Rom 10:9)**
>
> **We believe that Jesus died and rose again and so we believe that God will bring with Jesus those who have fallen asleep in him. (1 Th 4:14)**
>
> **Praise be to the God and Father of our Lord Jesus Christ! In his great mercy he has given us new birth into a living hope through the resurrection of Jesus Christ from the dead, and into an inheritance that can never perish, spoil or fade—kept in heaven for you, (1 Pet 1:3-4)**

2. His walk today and tomorrow and the day after *"must be."* The word "must" (dei) means necessary, being necessary by the very nature of the case. The witness of Jesus was a divine necessity overseen and ordained by God, and it could not be stopped. Jesus' walk and witness were directed by God.

> **This man was handed over to you by God's set purpose and foreknowledge; and you, with the help of wicked men, put him to death by nailing him to the cross. But God raised him from the dead, freeing him from the agony of death, because it was impossible for death to keep its hold on him. (Acts 2:23-24. See DEEPER STUDY # 3, Determinate Counsel—Acts 2:23)**
>
> **As his custom was, Paul went into the synagogue, and on three Sabbath days he reasoned with them from the Scriptures, explaining and proving that the Christ had to suffer and rise from the dead. "This Jesus I am proclaiming to you is the Christ, " he said. (Acts 17:2-3)**

Thought 1. Note two critical questions.

1. How many of us know the *divine necessity* of God to witness?
2) How many of us walk *today and tomorrow* under the direction (divine necessity) of God?

3. His death *must be in Jerusalem.* Jerusalem was the capital of the nation, the symbolic center of the people's government, religion, and hopes. It was there that their temple stood and that their ruling body (the Sanhedrin) governed and judged the nation. If a prophet were to die, the decision for death was made in Jerusalem. Therefore, Jesus was saying this about His death:

⇒ When the people kill Him (God's Son), He must be killed in the place that symbolized all the hopes and activities of man (government and religion). Why? Because He was to die for all men everywhere: for all their corruptions in government and religion and for all their injustices in both. They did not understand the reason yet, but they soon would.

> **He himself bore our sins in his body on the tree, so that we might die to sins and live for righteousness; by his wounds you have been healed. (1 Pet 2:24)**
>
> **For Christ died for sins once for all, the righteous for the unrighteous, to bring you to God. He was put to death in the body but made alive by the Spirit, (1 Pet 3:18)**

3 (13:34) **Jesus Christ, Rejection**: the rejection by the religionists and the people. When Jesus looked upon Jerusalem, He wept. He wept because he saw the city as the symbol of all formal religion and of all men who rejected His witness. (See note, pt.3—Lk.13:31-33.) It is because of this that this passage is known as Jesus' lament over Jerusalem (see outline and notes—Mt.23:37-39 for more discussion).

1. The religionists and people rejected, ridiculed, abused, persecuted, and killed God's prophets and messengers. Something needs to be remembered by people who abuse God's messengers. God holds His messengers very dear to His heart; and He is extremely protective of them. To ridicule and abuse one of His true followers is a very serious offense. Jerusalem and the people of Israel were guilty of many sins, but it was this sin that Jesus pointed out as the *most condemning*. In conjunction with this thought is the fact that it was primarily the *grumbling* of Israel in the wilderness against Moses and God that caused God to judge that generation so severely.

Scripture says:

> **Who are you to judge someone else's servant? To his own master he stands or falls. And he will stand, [for the Lord] is able to make him stand. (Rom 14:4) (See note, Jews, Sins of—Mt.23:37 for a list of the prophets abused by the people.)**

2. The people rejected the Messiah's salvation.
   a. Note the enormous patience of God. Despite continued rejection and even murder of the godly, God kept after the people.
   b. Note the continued patience and love of Christ. "How often I have longed to gather [you]." He would have saved the people time and again, for He desired to save them, not to condemn them.

> **For the Son of Man came to seek and to save what was lost." (Luke 19:10)**
>
> **For God did not send his Son into the world to condemn the world, but to save the world through him. (John 3:17)**
>
> **The thief comes only to steal and kill and destroy; I have come that they may have life, and have it to the full. (John 10:10)**
>
> **"As for the person who hears my words but does not keep them, I do not judge him. For I did not come to judge the world, but to save it. (John 12:47)**
>
> **"You are a king, then!" said Pilate. Jesus answered, "You are right in saying I am a king. In fact, for this reason I was born, and for this I came into the world, to testify to the truth. Everyone on the side of truth listens to me." (John 18:37)**
>
> **Here is a trustworthy saying that deserves full acceptance: Christ Jesus came into the world to save sinners—of whom I am the worst. (1 Tim 1:15)**

   c. Note the tragic words, "You were not willing." He would save them, but they would not be saved. The people had every privilege and opportunity imaginable. They heard Christ and learned of Him, yet they rejected Him. Their rejection was a *deliberate decision.*

> **He came to that which was his own, but his own did not receive him. (John 1:11)**
>
> **I have come in my Father's name, and you do not accept me; but if someone else comes in his own name, you will accept him. (John 5:43)**
>
> **There is a judge for the one who rejects me and does not accept my words; that very word which I spoke will condemn him at the last day. (John 12:48)**

4 (13:35) **Jesus Christ, Exaltation—Judgment—Rejection**: the warning to all those who reject Christ is twofold.

1. They and their house are to be forsaken by God. The house may be a literal house, a nation, a religious body, a city, a local group—it does not matter—if they reject Christ time after time, reject the privileges they have, God will leave them all alone. They will be deserted, left without the presence of God. And a place without the presence of God is like a wilderness or a desert—deserted and left all alone to waste away. (See outlines and notes—Mt.23:38-39; Ro.1:24-32.)

> **But the subjects of the kingdom will be thrown outside, into the darkness, where there will be weeping and gnashing of teeth." (Mat 8:12)**
>
> **"Then the king told the attendants, 'Tie him hand and foot, and throw him outside, into the darkness, where there will be weeping and gnashing of teeth.' (Mat 22:13)**
>
> **And throw that worthless servant outside, into the darkness, where there will be weeping and gnashing of teeth.' (Mat 25:30)**
>
> **If anyone does not remain in me, he is like a branch that is thrown away and withers; such branches are picked up, thrown into the fire and burned. (John 15:6)**
>
> **But God turned away and gave them over to the worship of the heavenly bodies [cp. astrology]. (Acts 7:42)**
>
> **Therefore God gave them over in the sinful desires of their hearts to sexual impurity for the degrading of their bodies with one another. They exchanged the truth of God for a lie, and worshiped and served created things rather than the Creator—who is forever praised. Amen. Because of this, God gave them over to shameful lusts. Even their women exchanged natural relations for unnatural ones. In the same way the men also abandoned natural relations with women and were inflamed with lust for one another. Men committed indecent acts with other men, and received in themselves the due penalty for their perversion. Furthermore, since they did not think it worthwhile to retain the knowledge of God, he gave them over to a depraved mind, to do what ought not to be done. They have become filled with every kind of wickedness, evil, greed and depravity. They are full of envy, murder, strife, deceit and malice. They are gossips, slanderers, God-haters, insolent, arrogant and boastful; they invent ways of doing evil; they disobey their parents; they are senseless, faithless, heartless, ruthless. Although they know God's righteous decree that those who do such things deserve death, they not only continue to do these very things but also approve of those who practice them. (Rom 1:24-32)**
>
> **For I told him that I would judge his family forever because of the sin he knew about; his sons made themselves con-**

temptible, and he failed to restrain them. (1 Sam 3:13)

Do not be like your fathers and brothers, who were unfaithful to the LORD, the God of their fathers, so that he made them an object of horror, as you see. (2 Chr 30:7)

"But my people would not listen to me; Israel would not submit to me. So I gave them over to their stubborn hearts to follow their own devices. (Psa 81:12)

"Then they will call to me but I will not answer; they will look for me but will not find me. Since they hated knowledge and did not choose to fear the LORD, since they would not accept my advice and spurned my rebuke, they will eat the fruit of their ways and be filled with the fruit of their schemes. For the waywardness of the simple will kill them, and the complacency of fools will destroy them; but whoever listens to me will live in safety and be at ease, without fear of harm." (Prov 1:28-33)

Ephraim is joined to idols; leave him alone! (Hosea 4:17)

2. There is to be a day when He will return and rule supremely. This is a definite reference to Jesus' return to earth (cp. Ps.118:26). Note: every one who rejected Jesus Christ will see Him return, but then it will be too late. He will be returning in judgment, to bow the knee of all those who rejected His supremacy.

Therefore God exalted him to the highest place and gave him the name that is above every name, that at the name of Jesus every knee should bow, in heaven and on earth and under the earth, and every tongue confess that Jesus Christ is Lord, to the glory of God the Father. (Phil 2:9-11)

It teaches us to say "No" to ungodliness and worldly passions, and to live self-controlled, upright and godly lives in this present age, while we wait for the blessed hope—the glorious appearing of our great God and Savior, Jesus Christ, (Titus 2:12-13)

After the Lord Jesus had spoken to them, he was taken up into heaven and he sat at the right hand of God. (Mark 16:19)

But from now on, the Son of Man will be seated at the right hand of the mighty God." (Luke 22:69)

"The one who comes from above is above all; the one who is from the earth belongs to the earth, and speaks as one from the earth. The one who comes from heaven is above all. (John 3:31)

"You call me 'Teacher' and 'Lord,' and rightly so, for that is what I am. (John 13:13)

"Therefore let all Israel be assured of this: God has made this Jesus, whom you crucified, both Lord and Christ." (Acts 2:36)

Let us therefore make every effort to do what leads to peace and to mutual edification. (Rom 14:19)

For he must reign until he has put all his enemies under his feet. (1 Cor 15:25)

Which he exerted in Christ when he raised him from the dead and seated him at his right hand in the heavenly realms, (Eph 1:20)

Who has gone into heaven and is at God's right hand—with angels, authorities and powers in submission to him. (1 Pet 3:22)

Then I looked and heard the voice of many angels, numbering thousands upon thousands, and ten thousand times ten thousand. They encircled the throne and the living creatures and the elders. In a loud voice they sang: "Worthy is the Lamb, who was slain, to receive power and wealth and wisdom and strength and honor and glory and praise!" Then I heard every creature in heaven and on earth and under the earth and on the sea, and all that is in them, singing: "To him who sits on the throne and to the Lamb be praise and honor and glory and power, for ever and ever!" The four living creatures said, "Amen," and the elders fell down and worshiped. (Rev 5:11-14)

	CHAPTER 14 **C. The Religionists & Their Error, 14:1-6** (cp. Mt.12:9-13)	and experts in the law, "Is it lawful to heal on the Sabbath or not?" 4 But they remained silent. So taking hold of the man, he healed him and sent him away.	**religious form more important than healing men** **4 The religionists refused to confess the truth taught by Jesus**
1 The religionists watched Jesus critically	One Sabbath, when Jesus went to eat in the house of a prominent Pharisee, he was being carefully watched.	5 Then he asked them, "If one of you has a son or an ox that falls into a well on the Sabbath day, will you not immediately pull him out?"	**5 The religionists failed to see the inconsistency of their belief & behavior**
2 The religionists overlooked what was really needful **3 The religionists made**	2 There in front of him was a man suffering from dropsy. 3 Jesus asked the Pharisees	6 And they had nothing to say.	**6 Conclusion: The religionists were silenced**

DIVISION VI

THE SON OF MAN'S GREAT JOURNEY TO JERUSALEM (STAGE II): HIS TEACHING AND PUBLIC CONFLICT, 13:22-17:10

C. The Religionists and Their Error, 14:1-6

(14:1-6) **Introduction**: a chief Pharisee invited Jesus to a meal on the Sabbath. Some commentators think the invitation was deceptive, a plot to entrap Jesus into breaking the Sabbath law and to disqualify Him in the eyes of the people as a lawbreaker. However, we are not told this; and usually when the religionists were trying to entrap Jesus, the gospel writer said so. This much is known: Jesus was sitting at the meal surrounded by religionists, and He saw a unique opportunity to point out the errors of the religionists. The same errors are common to every generation of religionists.

1. The religionists watched Jesus critically (v.1).
2. The religionists overlooked what was really needful (v.2).
3. The religionists made religious form more important than healing men (v.3).
4. The religionists refused to confess the truth taught by Jesus (v.4).
5. The religionists failed to see the inconsistency of their belief and behavior (v.5).
6. The conclusion: the religionists were silenced (v.6).

1 (14:1) **Religionists, Error—Denial**: the religionists "watched" Jesus with critical eyes. The word "watched" (parateroumenoi) means to observe with a sinister purpose: to look for something wrong, to search for the incorrect, to watch for error. It means to look with critical and cynical eyes. The religionists sat there watching Jesus, looking for some mistake, some wrong He might do.

Thought 1. Men should be trying to learn of Christ, but too often they search for ways to deny Him. They seek for error in His Word and for wrong in His behavior in order to deny His claim upon their lives. They feel that if they can disprove His Word and Person, they are then free to live as they wish.

Some of them were looking for a reason to accuse Jesus, so they watched him closely to see if he would heal him on the Sabbath. (Mark 3:2)

Keeping a close watch on him, they sent spies, who pretended to be honest. They hoped to catch Jesus in something he said so that they might hand him over to the power and authority of the governor. (Luke 20:20)

The wicked lie in wait for the righteous, seeking their very lives; (Psa 37:32)

The ruthless will vanish, the mockers will disappear, and all who have an eye for evil will be cut down— (Isa 29:20)

I hear many whispering, "Terror on every side! Report him! Let's report him!" All my friends are waiting for me to slip, saying, "Perhaps he will be deceived; then we will prevail over him and take our revenge on him." But the LORD is with me like a mighty warrior; so my persecutors will stumble and not prevail. They will fail and be thoroughly disgraced; their dishonor will never be forgotten. O LORD Almighty, you who examine the righteous and probe the heart and mind, let me see your vengeance upon them, for to you I have committed my cause. Sing to the LORD! Give praise to the LORD! He rescues the life of the needy from the hands of the wicked. (Jer 20:10-13)

2 (14:2) **Religionists, Errors of—Need**: the religionists overlooked what was really needful. The man with dropsy was not an invited guest; he just appeared. He either came on his own, hoping for help from Jesus, or he had been planted there by the religionists to see if Jesus would break the Sabbath law. In either case, a real failure of the religionists is seen. They did not see the *need* of the man. He was a reject, an abnormal person who was *down and out* in society, a man who was in desperate need. However, the religionists failed to see his need and to reach out to help him. If they had planted him, then their failure was even more severe, for they were using him for their own purposes instead of reaching out to help him.

Thought 1. There are two serious failures seen in this event.

1) The failure of going about one's business and not reaching out to help the needy. In this case, it was the religionists who were going about their religious business.
2) The using of the needy for one's own purpose. The purpose may be to show that one is benevolent, or to ease one's conscience, or to add to one's statistics by bringing them into church.

Whatever the case, the motive is impure and regretful.

Thought 2. This point forces several critical questions that should touch the heart of every person who has had a roof over his head and a hot meal in the last twelve hours.

1) How many within the church ever *see* the needful? How many *overlook* the needful? How many of the needful, of those who are *down and out*, walk into the church and have others *sit away* from them? How many have come to church for help and been sent away empty?
2) How many churches sit empty for days upon days and are not in use while so many walk the streets cold and freezing? Are they being overlooked deliberately? Or are the churches just ignoring and neglecting them?
3) How many believers and churches have nice houses and buildings and plenty of food, yet their own communities or cities are full of needy people who are hungry and unclothed and unsheltered?
4) How many ever think about a world full of teeming millions who are desperately needful? Who are suffering and lost, never having heard the gospel?

Is it not [your purpose] to share your food with the hungry and to provide the poor wanderer with shelter— when you see the naked, to clothe him, and not to turn away from your own flesh and blood? (Isa 58:7)

[Religionists] who say, 'Keep away; don't come near me, for I am too sacred for you!' Such people are smoke in my nostrils, a fire that keeps burning all day. (Isa 65:5)

3 (14:3) **Religionists, Errors of—Ritual—Ceremony—Need**: the religionists made their religious form more important than *healing* men. Note: the man stood "in front of" Jesus, and Jesus was touched by the man's needs. Jesus knew it was the Sabbath, the day when the Jews allowed no work whatsoever (see DEEPER STUDY # 1, Sabbath—Lk.13:14). He saw a unique opportunity to teach a much needed truth: the truth that healing and helping a needy man is much more important than religious form and ceremony, than religious ritual and rules.

Note the question of Jesus: "Is it lawful to heal on the Sabbath or not?" The law said absolutely not. No work whatsoever, not even the healing of a man could be done on the Sabbath. (See DEEPER STUDY # 1—Lk.13:14; note and DEEPER STUDY # 1—Mt.12:10 for a clear understanding of this discussion.)

What Jesus did was show that the very purpose of God is the *healing of man*. God is seeking to save man, to reconcile man unto Himself. Therefore, the very object of true religion becomes the *healing of man*, not form and ceremony, not ritual and rules.

Thought 1. Religionists are always putting their *form and practices* of religion before meeting the healing needs of men. People can be desperately in need within a few miles of a church, yet the religionists...

- will shelter their religious services for only a few hours each week (no matter the cost) while so many never have shelter.
- will feed their own flocks three meals a day while so many eat less than one meal a day, and multitudes starve to death every day of the week.
- will clothe their own flocks in the latest fashion while so many go cold, some even freezing to death.
- will fill their own religious buildings with the finest facilities and warmth while so many are so desperately needful.
- will preach and teach the man, exalting messages of self-help and social improvement, while so many are dying without ever hearing of God's personal salvation for the human soul.
- will observe their worship and ritual, their rules and ceremonies without ever reaching out to help those who surround them and are in such desperate need.

If you had known what these words mean, 'I desire mercy, not sacrifice,' you would not have condemned the innocent. For the Son of Man is Lord of the Sabbath." (Mat 12:7-8)

And the second is like it: 'Love your neighbor as yourself.' (Mat 22:39)

And he said to them: "You have a fine way of setting aside the commands of God in order to observe your own traditions! (Mark 7:9)

Love does no harm to its neighbor. Therefore love is the fulfillment of the law. (Rom 13:10)

They claim to know God, but by their actions they deny him. They are detestable, disobedient and unfit for doing anything good. (Titus 1:16)

This is how we know what love is: Jesus Christ laid down his life for us. And we ought to lay down our lives for our brothers. If anyone has material possessions and sees his brother in need but has no pity on him, how can the love of God be in him? (1 John 3:16-17)

Thought 2. A religionist will observe his religious worship and form without ever repenting of his sin and turning to God in complete surrender and self-denial. Too often he places his trust in his baptism, religious ceremony, church membership, worship attendance, rules, and regulations instead of in Christ Himself.

4 (14:4) **Religionists, Errors of—Church, Problems**: the religionists refused to confess the truth taught by Jesus. Jesus had asked if it were lawful to heal a man on the Sabbath day. "They remained silent." They said nothing in reply to Jesus' question. No matter how they answered the question, they would offend a large number of people and run the risk of losing their loyalty. Therefore, they said nothing.

⇒ They could have agreed with Christ and said "Yes, it is lawful to help a man before keeping one's religious rule." But if they had answered "Yes," other religionists would have charged them with disloyalty and with being loose with the law.

⇒ They could have said, "No, it is not lawful to help a man on the Sabbath, unless he is dying, no matter how serious his case." This answer would have caused honest and thoughtful people to charge them with being *hard and indifferent* to human suffering.

Therefore, the religionists said nothing. They sat there ignoring Jesus. It seemed ridiculous, for Jesus was there, and He had just asked a question of them. Yet they refused to answer lest they entrap themselves. After a long silence and some pause in activity, Jesus apparently took the man into His arms and healed him.

Thought 1. There are reasons why the religionist refuses to confess the truth taught by Jesus, reasons why religious form and the present order of things are put before man and the meeting of his real needs.

1) Too many of us slip into a routine, a way of doing things, and just continue in it because it is comfortable.
2) Too many of us fear change lest we lose some people and their support.
3) Too many of us fear the loss of position and security.
4) Too many of us fear failure, the weakening of what we already have, of losing the loyalty of our followers to our own religious position and practices.

Thought 2. Nothing should keep us from meeting man's needs, from putting him and his needs first, before all religious ritual and form.

1) It is the only way the heart of man can be reached and satisfied (Col.2:9-10; Jn.10:10).
2) It is the only way we can stop the loss of people who are being lost by the droves. As the saying goes: they come in the front door and leave just as quickly by the back door. Why? Their needs are not being met.
   Something else needs to be asked of our hearts. Are that many really coming? Are people really accepting Christ by the droves? Why not? Did not the Lord say the fields are white unto *harvest*? Could it be we are so steeped in *religion* that we are putting religion before meeting the real needs of men?

Thought 3. Man's basic need is to know and worship God in a personal way. Yet we put worship and form and order and ritual before trying to reach out to man and actually meeting his need. Too often, we act as though...

⇒ man exists for religion, instead of religion's existing for man.
⇒ man exists for worship services, instead of worship services' existing for man.
⇒ man exists for maintaining the organization, instead of the organization's existing for man.
⇒ man exists for the rules and rituals instead of the rules and rituals' existing for man.

Just as the Son of Man did not come to be served, but to serve, and to give his life as a ransom for many." (Mat 20:28)

In everything I did, I showed you that by this kind of hard work we must help the weak, remembering the words the Lord Jesus himself said: 'It is more blessed to give than to receive.'" (Acts 20:35)

We who are strong ought to bear with the failings of the weak and not to please ourselves. (Rom 15:1)

Carry each other's burdens, and in this way you will fulfill the law of Christ. (Gal 6:2)

5(14:5) **Religionists, Errors of—Needs**: the religionists failed to see the inconsistency in their belief and behavior. The illustration by Christ was powerful. A man would set aside his religious rule to help his oxen out of a ditch. His oxen or personal property was quickly put before his religious rule. Why then should a man who was in need not be put before religious rules?

Thought 1. The world reels with teeming millions' dying from starvation and disease, from the elements of nature and war, from spiritual ignorance and eternal death while religionists who profess belief in God...

- build newer buildings to be used for only a few hours a week.
- stress attendance to church services instead of stressing Christ.
- preach and teach physical well-being instead of spiritual salvation and peace of heart and mind.
- covet the latest styles in cars and clothing, hairdo's and furnishings.
- desire better houses and positions, more pay and security.

"Not everyone who says to me, 'Lord, Lord,' will enter the kingdom of heaven, but only he who does the will of my Father who is in heaven. (Mat 7:21)

He replied, "Isaiah was right when he prophesied about you hypocrites; as it is written: "'These people honor me with their lips, but their hearts are far from me. (Mark 7:6)

My people come to you, as they usually do, and sit before you to listen to your words, but they do not put them into practice. With their mouths they express devotion, but their hearts are greedy for unjust gain. (Ezek 33:31)

6(14:6) **Religionists, Errors of—Guilt**: the conclusion is that the religionists were silenced. What can any of us say against what Christ has just taught if we are truly honest and thoughtful?

Outline	Scripture	Scripture (cont.)	Outline (cont.)
	D. The Importance of Humility, 14:7-14	up to a better place.' Then you will be honored in the presence of all your fellow guests.	2) Is rewarded with a higher position 3) Is honored by all
1 Jesus attended a banquet a. He noticed some choosing the best seats b. He shared a parable	7 When he noticed how the guests picked the places of honor at the table, he told them this parable:	11 For everyone who exalts himself will be humbled, and he who humbles himself will be exalted."	**3 The parable's point** a. Self-exaltation humbles b. Humility exalts[DS1]
2 The parable: The ambitious guest a. The first man: Seeks the place of honor 1) Is displaced 2) Finds all other seats already taken 3) Has to take the lowest seat 4) Is embarrassed	8 "When someone invites you to a wedding feast, do not take the place of honor, for a person more distinguished than you may have been invited. 9 If so, the host who invited both of you will come and say to you, 'Give this man your seat.' Then, humiliated, you will have to take the least important place.	12 Then Jesus said to his host, "When you give a luncheon or dinner, do not invite your friends, your brothers or relatives, or your rich neighbors; if you do, they may invite you back and so you will be repaid. 13 But when you give a banquet, invite the poor, the crippled, the lame, the blind,	**4 The demonstration of humility** a. Humility is not serving those who can repay b. Humility is serving those who are needy & cannot repay
b. The second man: Takes the lowest place of honor 1) Is acknowledged	10 But when you are invited, take the lowest place, so that when your host comes, he will say to you, 'Friend, move	14 And you will be blessed. Although they cannot repay you, you will be repaid at the resurrection of the righteous."	c. Humility shall be rewarded

DIVISION VI

THE SON OF MAN'S GREAT JOURNEY TO JERUSALEM (STAGE II): HIS TEACHING AND PUBLIC CONFLICT, 13:22-17:10

D. The Importance of Humility, 14:7-14

(14:7-14) **Introduction**: the importance of humility is the thrust of this passage.

1. Jesus attended a banquet (v.7).
2. The parable: the ambitious guest (v.8-10).
3. The parable's point (v.11).
4. The demonstration of humility (v.12-14).

1 (14:7) **Jesus Christ, Social Life**: Jesus was still at the banquet of the chief Pharisee (v.1). It was time for everyone to be seated for the meal, and Jesus noticed how some guests scrambled for the chief seats. Today we usually place the names of the most honored guests at the plates. However, in Jesus' day the highest seat of honor was on the right of the host and the next highest on his left, and so the ranking continued alternating back and forth until the lowest ranked person sat the farthest away from the host. Very simply, the closer one sat to the host, the higher the honor. When Jesus saw how some quickly moved up close to the host, He saw an opportunity to teach the great importance of humility. The phrase "the places of honor" (tas protoklisias) means the best seats.

2 (14:8-10) **Ambition—Self-Seeking—Parable**: the parable is that of the ambitious guest. Jesus spoke directly to the man of ambition, the man who wants more recognition, honor, and position. Jesus said something that is very practical and should be clearly seen even by the ambitious man: the ambitious man should not sit in a seat that is higher than his position or capability lest a man more honorable enters and replace hims. If the ambitious man takes a higher seat, four things are likely to happen.

1. He will be displaced.
2. He will then find all the other seats taken.
3. He will have to take a lower seat.
4. He will be embarrassed.

What the ambitious man should take is the lowest seat and place of honor. Three things happen when he does.

1. His presence is acknowledged by the host.
2. He is rewarded, moved up to a higher seat and position.
3. He is recognized and honored by all, no matter how high or how far from the top the position is.

The point of the parable is twofold: self-exaltation humbles and humility exalts.

3 (14:11) **Self-Exaltation—Pride—Arrogance—Self-Seeking—Ambition**: the parable's point is clearly contrary to the ambitions and behavior of most men. The man who exalts himself shall be humbled. It is not just a possibility; he *will* be humbled. Jesus said so.

1. The man who exalts himself does at least four things.
   a. He debases others. He has to treat others as less and lower than himself in order to exalt himself.
      ⇒ He degrades others: downplaying their ability or person, position or performance, appearance or acceptance.
      ⇒ He demeans others: trying to wound and injure, shame and humiliate.
      ⇒ He debases others: trying to tear down, hurt, lower, and damage.

   b. He acts self-sufficient. He may not be self-sufficient, but if he is going to exalt himself, he is forced to act...
      • in control
      • in charge
      • very capable
      • independent
      • above others

   Note: the great problem with being self-sufficient is that a person feels he does not even need God in his life. He may be religious, but he does not live a changed life that demonstrates a true trust and dependency upon God for salvation and life.

c. He corrupts morality and justice. The man who exalts himself governs all things by whatever moves him ahead and gives him the greatest position and recognition. True morality and justice may be thought about, but they are set aside if needed. The ambitious man who exalts himself often has to...

- lie
- steal
- cheat
- abuse
- ridicule
- shame
- not give due recognition
- hold others back or down
- hurt, damage or kill

d. He lives a life of struggle. He always feels torn within to maneuver and outdo others in order to get the highest seat or recognition possible. He seldom knows peace within, no matter the appearance given.

2. The man who exalts himself is to be humbled. As mentioned above, it is not just a possibility; it is a sure thing. He shall be humbled. The likelihood is that he will be humbled in this life, but if not, then he will be humbled by God in eternity (cp. v.14). Four things will happen to him.

a. He will be displaced. He will be removed from his seat of position and recognition. It probably will happen in this world, for people can be fooled and misused for only so long. Eventually they catch on and react. More tragically, the self-exalting (prideful) man will be displaced by God. He will lose his place in heaven and be put out of heaven.

b. He will find all other seats and positions already taken. There will be no room for him. This often happens in business when a man is demoted or released. A suitable position cannot be found to match his ability and true worth. The same will happen in heaven. If a man has exalted himself, he will find all available seats taken. His name will not be written by any seat in heaven. He will move farther and farther down the line, finding no empty seat.

c. He will have to take the lowest seat. Note: this man was invited to the feast and he responded. He walked in he midst of all the guests. But he had a problem. He exalted himself, so he had to be moved down to the lowest seat. The lowest seat was the place of the least recognition and honor, doomed to be the seat for all hypocrites (cp. Mt.25:41. See note, pt.3—Lk.12:41-48.)

d. He will be embarrassed and shamed by being debased.

Live in harmony with one another. Do not be proud, but be willing to associate with people of low position. Do not be conceited. (Rom 12:16)

The man who thinks he knows something does not yet know as he ought to know. (1 Cor 8:2)

If anyone thinks he is something when he is nothing, he deceives himself. (Gal 6:3)

For everything in the world—the cravings of sinful man, the lust of his eyes and the boasting of what he has and does—comes not from the Father but from the world. (1 John 2:16)

You save the humble, but your eyes are on the haughty to bring them low. (2 Sam 22:28)

In his arrogance the wicked man hunts down the weak, who are caught in the schemes he devises. (Psa 10:2)

When pride comes, then comes disgrace, but with humility comes wisdom. (Prov 11:2)

Pride only breeds quarrels, but wisdom is found in those who take advice. (Prov 13:10)

Pride goes before destruction, a haughty spirit before a fall. (Prov 16:18)

Haughty eyes and a proud heart, the lamp of the wicked, are sin! (Prov 21:4)

Do you see a man wise in his own eyes? There is more hope for a fool than for him. (Prov 26:12)

A greedy man stirs up dissension, but he who trusts in the LORD will prosper. (Prov 28:25)

Woe to those who are wise in their own eyes and clever in their own sight. (Isa 5:21)

The earth dries up and withers, the world languishes and withers, the exalted of the earth languish. (Isa 24:4)

Though you soar like the eagle and make your nest among the stars, from there I will bring you down," declares the LORD. (Oba 1:4)

"See, he is puffed up; his desires are not upright— but the righteous will live by his faith— (Hab 2:4)

On that day you will not be put to shame for all the wrongs you have done to me, because I will remove from this city those who rejoice in their pride. Never again will you be haughty on my holy hill. (Zep 3:11)

DEEPER STUDY # 1

(14:11) **Humility—Exaltation**: the man who humbles himself shall be exalted. Exaltation is a certainty, and a man can ask for nothing more than to be assured that he will be exalted.

Humility (tareinophrosune) means lowliness of mind. It is a word that was coined by Christianity. Before Christ, a humble man was looked upon as a coward: a cringing, unappealing, effeminate type of person. However after Christ, humility was elevated to the most praise-worthy level. When men looked at Christ, they saw the strength of humility through the influence of One Who was perfect in meekness and lowliness of heart. Humility means five things.

1. To *walk* as a servant to others, always ready and willing to help (cp. Ph.2:8).

2. To *behave* in an unassuming manner, not being showy or pretentious, prideful or haughty, arrogant or assertive.

Therefore, whoever humbles himself like this child is the greatest in the kingdom of heaven. (Mat 18:4)

For by the grace given me I say to every one of you: Do not think of yourself more highly than you ought, but rather

think of yourself with sober judgment, in accordance with the measure of faith God has given you. (Rom 12:3)

3. To *assume* a spirit of lowliness and submission, of oneness and identification with others, not showing conceit or superiority or being boastful.

Jesus called them together and said, "You know that the rulers of the Gentiles lord it over them, and their high officials exercise authority over them. Not so with you. Instead, whoever wants to become great among you must be your servant, and whoever wants to be first must be your slave—just as the Son of Man did not come to be served, but to serve, and to give his life as a ransom for many." (Mat 20:25-28)

Jesus said to them, "The kings of the Gentiles lord it over them; and those who exercise authority over them call themselves Benefactors. But you are not to be like that. Instead, the greatest among you should be like the youngest, and the one who rules like the one who serves. (Luke 22:25-26)

I served the Lord with great humility and with tears, although I was severely tested by the plots of the Jews. (Acts 20:19)

Young men, in the same way be submissive to those who are older. All of you, clothe yourselves with humility toward one another, because, "God opposes the proud but gives grace to the humble." Humble yourselves, therefore, under God's mighty hand, that he may lift you up in due time. (1 Pet 5:5-6)

4. To *possess* a sense of lowliness and unworthiness, to have a modest opinion of oneself, knowing that others are just as significant and valuable.

Do nothing out of selfish ambition or vain conceit, but in humility consider others better than yourselves. Each of you should look not only to your own interests, but also to the interests of others. (Phil 2:3-4)

As a prisoner for the Lord, then, I urge you to live a life worthy of the calling you have received. Be completely humble and gentle; be patient, bearing with one another in love. (Eph 4:1-2)

Therefore, as God's chosen people, holy and dearly loved, clothe yourselves with compassion, kindness, humility, gentleness and patience. (Col 3:12)

5. To *come* to God on a regular basis and confess one's spiritual need and unworthiness.

Humble yourselves before the Lord, and he will lift you up. (James 4:10)

Humility is a problem to most men. Why? Because the world looks upon humility as a sign of weakness and cowardice. They see a humble person as a person who cowers and cringes before others, as a person who the world takes and…

- uses and misuses
- overlooks and bypasses
- ignores and neglects
- enslaves and abuses
- shuns and despises

Men fear humility. They fear humility will make them the object of contempt and abuse, causing them to be passed over. However, the very opposite is true. Humility leads a person…

- to Christ and to conversion.
- to realize his full potential.
- to evaluate himself and to work at improving himself.
- to become all that he can and should be.
- to develop more healthy relationships with people.
- to a stronger and more productive community and world.

When men consider others (humble themselves), they win friends and influence people. They build and strengthen everyone and everything involved.

The results of humility are threefold.

1. The humble man will be acknowledged. Both men and God will notice his spirit and energy in serving others, no matter how lowly his position. His putting others first, whether person, project, work or company, will not go unnoticed for long. His dedication to serving and working and helping others will be seen and acknowledged.

2. The humble man will be rewarded. He will be approached; and his presence, energy, and effort will be desired and promoted and placed where he can serve to the maximum.

3. The humble man will be honored by all. He will have lived to serve and help others; therefore, when he is exalted, all will rejoice with him.

Humility and the fear of the LORD bring wealth and honor and life. (Prov 22:4)

A man's pride brings him low, but a man of lowly spirit gains honor. (Prov 29:23)

For this is what the high and lofty One says— he who lives forever, whose name is holy: "I live in a high and holy place, but also with him who is contrite and lowly in spirit, to revive the spirit of the lowly and to revive the heart of the contrite. (Isa 57:15)

Therefore, whoever humbles himself like this child is the greatest in the kingdom of heaven. (Mat 18:4)

"I tell you that this man, rather than the other, went home justified before God. For everyone who exalts himself will be humbled, and he who humbles himself will be exalted." (Luke 18:14)

Humility comes from three things. (These ideas come from William Barclay in his *Letters to the Galatians and Ephesians,* Eph.4:1-3.)

a. Humility comes from measuring ourselves against

the Lord Jesus. When a man measures himself against Christ, he measures himself against Perfection, for Christ was without sin (Jn.8:46; 2 Cor.5:21; Heb.4:15; 7:26; 1 Pt.1:19; 2:22). When measured against other men, a man may be morally good, but God demands that every man measure himself against the perfection of Christ. Against such a One and such a demand, there is no room for pride. (See DEEPER STUDY # 3—Mt.8:20.)

b. Humility comes from a continued consciousness of God's presence. No man has anything, not in reality: not air, not food, not clothing—nothing. All we have and all we know deteriorates and decays, even our own bodies. And all that crosses our path is held but for a short time, for the end of all things comes ever so quickly. We are completely dependent upon God who has given all and controls all and, in the end, shall take all. Before Him we can only walk humbly.

c. Humility comes from knowing ourselves, just who we really are. It comes from an honest appraisal of ourselves. It takes courage to look at ourselves and it takes honesty to see ourselves as we really are: basically self-centered, a bundle of self-admiration and self-love. We tend to dramatize ourselves. We tend to see ourselves through rose-colored glasses. We see ourselves...

- at the center of action.
- as the hero of some spectacular rescue.
- as the great politician marching to victory.
- as the reknown sportsman saving the game in the last second or bagging a record catch.
- as the beauty queen dazzling the crowds.
- as the laborer of brilliance.
- as Prince Charming or Cinderella sweeping others off their feet.

We are always at the center of the picture. Humility begins to come when we honestly face ourselves and admit our self-centeredness. Self-centeredness weakens and limits and destroys relationships and achievements. Humility reaches its height when we lose our lives in the cause of Christ and welfare of others.

4 (14:12-14) **Humility—Ministry—Service—Needy, The**: the demonstration of humility was clearly stated by Jesus. He addressed His words to the chief Pharisee, the most proud and ambitious man present. What He said was forceful; it served as a strong warning, for no man can enter the Kingdom of Heaven without true humility.

1. Humility is not serving or centering one's life around those who can repay. Jesus used the banquet as an illustration. If the host courts the presence of those who can repay him for his favor, then the host has received his reward. He will receive their favors, but that is all he will receive. He will not have God's favor; he will be left with only human favor.

Note: Jesus was not downgrading normal social life and Christian fellowship. He was saying that the host had not shown humility and lowliness of mind, the giving of himself and his goods to those who really needed his gifts and services. The host served only those who could repay by adding to his welfare. He had not humbled himself to help anyone who really needed help.

2. Humility is serving those who are needy and cannot repay. Now, if a man serves the poor, the maimed, the lame, the blind—that man demonstrates humility. His motive is pure; he has a lowly spirit, a spirit willing to get down with a needy person and help him. By *"host"* Jesus means any man who is able to help others because he has the health, position, or finances. When he gives himself and his goods to help those who need help, he is demonstrating humility. Man lives in a world full of desperate needs; therefore, a man should live being kind and giving generously. But note the crucial point: he should not be giving to receive back, but rather to help and to encourage and to build others up.

Jesus answered, "If you want to be perfect, go, sell your possessions and give to the poor, and you will have treasure in heaven. Then come, follow me." (Mat 19:21)

Give, and it will be given to you. A good measure, pressed down, shaken together and running over, will be poured into your lap. For with the measure you use, it will be measured to you." (Luke 6:38)

He who is kind to the poor lends to the LORD, and he will reward him for what he has done. (Prov 19:17)

For the director of music. A psalm of David. Blessed is he who has regard for the weak; the LORD delivers him in times of trouble. (Psa 41:1)

He who despises his neighbor sins, but blessed is he who is kind to the needy. (Prov 14:21)

He who gives to the poor will lack nothing, but he who closes his eyes to them receives many curses. (Prov 28:27)

And if you spend yourselves in behalf of the hungry and satisfy the needs of the oppressed, then your light will rise in the darkness, and your night will become like the noonday. (Isa 58:10)

3. Humility shall be rewarded. Note when: at the resurrection of the just.

a. A humble person is a *just* and righteous person, a person who does what is right.

b. A humble person shall be raised from the dead to live eternally with all the other just persons and, of 0course, with God Himself who is the very embodiment of righteousness. (See note, pts.2, 3—Lk.14:11.)

Leave your gift there in front of the altar. First go and be reconciled to your brother; then come and offer your gift. "Settle matters quickly with your adversary who is taking you to court. Do it while you are still with him on the way, or he may hand you over to the judge, and the judge may hand you over to the officer, and you may be thrown into prison. (Mat 5:24-25)

For my Father's will is that everyone who looks to the Son and believes in him shall have eternal life, and I will raise him up at the last day." (John 6:40)

Jesus said to her, "I am the resurrection and the life. He who believes in me will

live, even though he dies; (John 11:25)

And I [Paul] have the same hope in God as these men, that there will be a resurrection of both the righteous and the wicked. (Acts 24:15)

Because we know that the one who raised the Lord Jesus from the dead will also raise us with Jesus and present us with you in his presence. (2 Cor 4:14)

And so, somehow [I, Paul], to attain to the resurrection from the dead. (Phil 3:11)

For the Lord himself will come down from heaven, with a loud command, with the voice of the archangel and with the trumpet call of God, and the dead in Christ will rise first. After that, we who are still alive and are left will be caught up together with them in the clouds to meet the Lord in the air. And so we will be with the Lord forever. Therefore encourage each other with these words. (1 Th 4:16-18)

It teaches us to say "No" to ungodliness and worldly passions, and to live self-controlled, upright and godly lives in this present age, while we wait for the blessed hope—the glorious appearing of our great God and Savior, Jesus Christ, (Titus 2:12-13)

	E. The Parable of the Great Banquet: The Invitation and Man's Excuses, 14:15-24 (cp. Mt.22:1-14)	19 "Another said, 'I have just bought five yoke of oxen, and I'm on my way to try them out. Please excuse me.'	b. Excuse 2: Too wrapped up in new purchases
		20 "Still another said, 'I just got married, so I can't come.'	c. Excuse 3: Too wrapped up with family
1 Jesus was still at the feast of the chief Pharisee (v.1) a. A Pharisee's joy b. Jesus' parable: A great supper	15 When one of those at the table with him heard this, he said to Jesus, "Blessed is the man who will eat at the feast in the kingdom of God."	21 "The servant came back and reported this to his master. Then the owner of the house became angry and ordered his servant, 'Go out quickly into the streets and alleys of the town and bring in the poor, the crippled, the blind and the lame.'	**4 The Lord becomes angry at the busy guests who reject** **5 The Lord sends invitations to outsiders—quickly**
2 The invitation to "God's Great Banquet" goes out to many guests	16 Jesus replied: "A certain man was preparing a great banquet and invited many guests. 17 At the time of the banquet he sent his servant to tell those who had been invited, 'Come, for everything is now ready.'	22 "'Sir,' the servant said, 'what you ordered has been done, but there is still room.' 23 "Then the master told his servant, 'Go out to the roads and country lanes and make them come in, so that my house will be full.	a. He has a difficult time filling the kingdom even then b. He demands a double, strenuous effort
3 The invited guests make excuses a. Excuse 1: Too involved in business	18 "But they all alike began to make excuses. The first said, 'I have just bought a field, and I must go and see it. Please excuse me.'	24 I tell you, not one of those men who were invited will get a taste of my banquet.'"	**6 The guests who rejected are excluded**

DIVISION VI

THE SON OF MAN'S GREAT JOURNEY TO JERUSALEM (STAGE II): HIS TEACHING AND PUBLIC CONFLICT, 13:22-17:10

E. The Parable of the Great Banquet: The Invitation and Man's Excuses, 14:15-24

(14:15-24) **Introduction**: this passage gives a clear picture of the Lord's great invitation to mankind and the flimsy excuses men give for not accepting His invitation. The scene is known as *The Great Supper of God*. The Great Marriage Feast of Matthew should be compared with this passage. There are some similarities, but the differences are many (see outline and note—Mt.22:1-14).

1. Jesus was still at the feast of the chief Pharisee (v.15).
2. The invitation to God's Great Supper went out to many guests (v.16-17).
3. The invited guests make excuses (v.18-20).
4. The Lord becomes angry at the guests who reject (v.21).
5. The Lord sends invitations to outsiders—"quickly" (v.21-23).
6. The guests who rejected are excluded (v.24).

1 (14:15) **Great Supper of God**: Jesus was still at the feast of the chief Pharisee (v.1). When Jesus mentioned the resurrection (v.14), all of a sudden one of the Pharisees broke forth in joyful praise: "Blessed is the man who will eat at the feast" (v.15). What the Pharisee meant was the Jewish picture of the great Messianic Feast. The Feast was to be given by God for His people when He set up His kingdom on earth.

The Pharisee saw himself and the Jewish nation only as being invited to God's Great Banquet. No outsider, no Gentile or serious sinner, would ever be an invited guest. Jesus knew what was in the mind of the Pharisee, so He sets out to correct his misconception of the Great Banquet of God. Note three things.

1. *The Great Banquet of God* will be held. The Pharisee was right in his picture of a great gathering and feast at "the resurrection" (v.14).

2. *The Great Banquet of God* will include guests from the roads and country lanes of the world, not just Jews. The Pharisee was wrong about this. It was this that Jesus set out to correct.

3. The parable can apply to Israel in verses 16-22 and to the Gentiles in verses 23-24. However, the parable has a strong personal message to all men everywhere: men are saved by responding to God's invitation, and they are lost by making excuses. Note something else of significance: God is planning a *Great Banquet* where all who accept His invitation will be gathered together. Once the guest list is filled, time will be no more; all things will end. The doors to His banquet hall will be closed forever.

2 (14:16-17) **Invitation—Decision**: the invitation to *God's Great Banquet* goes out to many. Note four things.

1. "Everything is now ready" (v.17). Christ has purchased salvation for every man through His death and resurrection. The provisions for God's Great Banquet have now been secured and are waiting for the guests to accept.

2. The invitation is to "many." The many are those who hear the gospel...

- in church
- from a preacher
- from a witnessing believer
- over television or radio
- by reading
- through conscience

The many are all those who hear, see, or read the gospel and who sense a personal invitation to join God at His great feast.

3. The invitation is given more than once; it comes in the future as well as in the past. This is seen in v.16-17.

The invitation was sent out to inform people of the upcoming banquet. Then it was followed up as soon as "everything is now ready." (See note—Mt.22:3-7 for application to Israel.)

4. The invitation is accepted by all. Note this, for this is a most critical point. The servant was sent "to tell those who had been invited" They had already accepted; now they were being told to come, for the day of the Supper had arrived. The point is this: these claim to have accepted God's invitation, but they have only professed. They are not preparing to attend, not cleaning up or getting dressed (Tit.3:5; 2 Cor.5:21).

> **"For many are invited, but few are chosen." (Mat 22:14)**
> **He replied, "Isaiah was right when he prophesied about you hypocrites; as it is written: "'These people honor me with their lips, but their hearts are far from me. (Mark 7:6)**
> **They claim to know God, but by their actions they deny him. They are detestable, disobedient and unfit for doing anything good. (Titus 1:16)**
> **Whoever believes in him is not condemned, but whoever does not believe stands condemned already because he has not believed in the name of God's one and only Son. (John 3:18)**

3 (14:18-20) **Excuses—Decision**: the invited guests make excuses.

1. Excuse 1: one man said he was too involved in business. The man had bought a piece of ground and needed to look after it. A man can become too involved in any business, not just the business of developing property and farming. A person's business, profession, and affairs must not be allowed to consume his life. God is to be the center of a person's life, and God is to be the one around whom all else revolves.

> **What good will it be for a man if he gains the whole world, yet forfeits his soul? Or what can a man give in exchange for his soul? (Mat 16:26)**
> **The seed that fell among thorns stands for those who hear, but as they go on their way they are choked by life's worries, riches and pleasures, and they do not mature. (Luke 8:14)**
> **And do not set your heart on what you will eat or drink; do not worry about it. (Luke 12:29)**
> **No one serving as a soldier gets involved in civilian affairs—he wants to please his commanding officer. (2 Tim 2:4)**
> **He makes Lebanon skip like a calf, Sirion like a young wild ox. (Psa 29:6)**
> **So my heart began to despair over all my toilsome labor under the sun. (Eccl 2:20)**

2. Excuse 2: another man said that he was too wrapped up in new purchases. The oxen had just been purchased. They were a new possession, and the owner wanted to *try them out*. So it is with new purchases such as houses, lands, cars, bikes, records, books, radios, televisions, and a host of other material things. However, this is the point: things should never keep us from God.

> **"Be careful, or your hearts will be weighed down with dissipation, drunkenness and the anxieties of life, and that day will close on you unexpectedly like a trap. (Luke 21:34)**
> **Do not conform any longer to the pattern of this world, but be transformed by the renewing of your mind. Then you will be able to test and approve what God's will is—his good, pleasing and perfect will. (Rom 12:2)**
> **It teaches us to say "No" to ungodliness and worldly passions, and to live self-controlled, upright and godly lives in this present age, (Titus 2:12)**
> **You adulterous people, don't you know that friendship with the world is hatred toward God? Anyone who chooses to be a friend of the world becomes an enemy of God. (James 4:4)**
> **Do not love the world or anything in the world. If anyone loves the world, the love of the Father is not in him. For everything in the world—the cravings of sinful man, the lust of his eyes and the boasting of what he has and does—comes not from the Father but from the world. (1 John 2:15-16)**
> **You say, 'I am rich; I have acquired wealth and do not need a thing.' But you do not realize that you are wretched, pitiful, poor, blind and naked. (Rev 3:17)**
> **Jeshurun grew fat and kicked; filled with food, he became heavy and sleek. He abandoned the God who made him and rejected the Rock his Savior. (Deu 32:15)**
> **They close up their callous hearts, and their mouths speak with arrogance. (Psa 17:10)**
> **"Now then, listen, you wanton creature, lounging in your security and saying to yourself, 'I am, and there is none besides me. I will never be a widow or suffer the loss of children.' (Isa 47:8)**
> **And have grown fat and sleek. Their evil deeds have no limit; they do not plead the case of the fatherless to win it, they do not defend the rights of the poor. (Jer 5:28)**

3. Excuse 3: still another man said that he was too wrapped up with his family. This man had just been married, and it is true that marriage is ordained by God. However, it is not to be put before God. The man should have prepared for *The Great Banquet* before marrying. Nothing—family, friends, or important social functions—should be put before attending *The Great Banquet of God.*

> **In the same way, any of you who does not give up everything he has [friends, family] cannot be my disciple. (Luke 14:33)**
> **When they had finished eating, Jesus said to Simon Peter, "Simon son of John, do you truly love me more than these?" "Yes, Lord," he said, "you know that I love you." Jesus said, "Feed my lambs." Again Jesus said, "Simon son of John, do you truly love me?" He answered, "Yes, Lord, you know that I love you." Jesus said, "Take care of my sheep." The third time he said to him, "Simon son of John,**

do you love me?" Peter was hurt because Jesus asked him the third time, "Do you love me?" He said, "Lord, you know all things; you know that I love you." Jesus said, "Feed my sheep. (John 21:15-17)

And now, O Israel, what does the LORD your God ask of you but to fear the LORD your God, to walk in all his ways, to love him, to serve the LORD your God with all your heart and with all your soul, (Deu 10:12)

4 (14:21) **Jesus Christ, Rejected—Response**: the Lord becomes angry at the *busy* guests who make excuses. Note three things.

1. The guests who rejected showed both unconcern and contempt for the invitation.
   a. They showed unconcern over the *great cost* to God in preparing and providing "all things" (Christ's death, v.17). The great cost and price He paid was of little, if any, concern to them.
   b. They showed contempt in that they deceived the Lord. They accepted the first invitation, but they never began to clean themselves nor to dress properly for the feast.
2. The Lord had reason to be angry. The guests who had rejected His invitation had deceived and shown the utmost contempt, giving no thought to the great price He had paid for them.
3. Note a critical fact. Not a single one of the guests who rejected His invitation were allowed to *taste of His supper* (v.24).

For of this you can be sure: No immoral, impure or greedy person—such a man is an idolater—has any inheritance in the kingdom of Christ and of God. Let no one deceive you with empty words, for because of such things God's wrath comes on those who are disobedient. (Eph 5:5-6)

The wrath of God is being revealed from heaven against all the godlessness and wickedness of men who suppress the truth by their wickedness, (Rom 1:18)

But for those who are self-seeking and who reject the truth and follow evil, there will be wrath and anger. (Rom 2:8)

5 (14:21-23) **Evangelism—Witnessing—Decision—Invitation**: the Lord sends invitations to outsiders *quickly*. Note several facts.

1. The Lord will not allow His plan to be halted. He has planned a feast and no one will be allowed to stop it.
2. The Lord is going to fill His banquet hall quickly. Note: He sends His servant forth saying, "Go out quickly." (What a challenge to all believers! God wants the job done quickly. What excitement to think of being with Him at *The Great Banquet* soon!)
3. The Lord's servant is to "go out" into the streets and and alleys of the town. He is to leave the homes of the rich and luxurious, the self-sufficient and worldly-minded, the religionists and self-righteous. He is to "go out" from among the acceptable and established to reach out to the people of the streets and the highways.
4. The Lord's servant is to go to those who will need assistance in order to come; he is to go to those who know and readily admit that they need help. Note the servant is to "bring in" these to whom he is now sent.
   a. He is to bring in the poor, those who will need new and appropriate clothing. Some of the poor will accept the clothing.

God made him who had no sin to be sin for us, so that in him we might become the righteousness of God. (2 Cor 5:21)

"Blessed are the poor in spirit, for theirs is the kingdom of heaven. (Mat 5:3)

   b. He is to bring in the crippled and the lame, those who will need to be supported and perhaps carried to the banquet hall.
   c. He is to bring in the blind, those who will need to be guided and directed.

Note: some of these know their need. Their need is evident, and they readily *confess their need and accept the help*.

Now note two critical points.

1. The Lord's servant still has a difficult time in getting enough people to accept the invitation. Some of the poor, crippled, lame, and blind care nothing about coming. They are too prideful or bitter, too embarrassed or ashamed, too self-centered or self-pitying to receive help or to accept an invitation that is being rejected by so many.
2. The Lord demands a double, strenuous effort. He sends His servant into the roads and country lanes to invite whomever he can find. Note three facts.
   a. This refers either to the Gentiles or to the greatest of sinners, depending on how a person is approaching the passage.
   b. The Lord says, "make them come." This does not mean to compel by physical force but by the force of preaching and persuasion, by the power of the Holy Spirit.

Since, then, we know what it is to fear the Lord, we try to persuade men. What we are is plain to God, and I hope it is also plain to your conscience. (2 Cor 5:11)

For I know your eagerness to help, and I have been boasting about it to the Macedonians, telling them that since last year you in Achaia were ready to give; and your enthusiasm has stirred most of them to action. (2 Cor 9:2)

Preach the Word; be prepared in season and out of season; correct, rebuke and encourage—with great patience and careful instruction. (2 Tim 4:2)

As you go, preach this message: 'The kingdom of heaven is near.' (Mat 10:7)

What I tell you in the dark, speak in the daylight; what is whispered in your ear, proclaim from the roofs. (Mat 10:27)

He said to them, "Go into all the world and preach the good news to all creation. (Mark 16:15)

Jesus said to him, "Let the dead bury their own dead, but you go and proclaim the kingdom of God." (Luke 9:60)

"Go, stand in the temple courts," he said, "and tell the people the full message of this new life." (Acts 5:20)

c. The Lord says, "My house will be full." Remember the command "go out quickly." Connect the command to this promise, and the time frame seems to be soon. However, we must keep in mind that a thousand years is as one day to the Lord
(2 Pt.3:8).

On the last and greatest day of the Feast, Jesus stood and said in a loud voice, "If anyone is thirsty, let him come to me and drink. (John 7:37)

For, "Everyone who calls on the name of the Lord will be saved." (Rom 10:13)

Who wants all men to be saved and to (1 Tim 2:4)

**The Spirit and the bride say, "Come!" And let him who hears say, "Come!" Whoever is thirsty, let him come; and whoever wishes, let him take the free gift of the water of life.
(Rev 22:17)**

"Come, all you who are thirsty, come to the waters; and you who have no money, come, buy and eat! Come, buy wine and milk without money and without cost. (Isa 55:1)

6 (14:24) **Judgment—Salvation, Rejected**: the rejecters are excluded. This is a tragic pronouncement, but a very deserving verdict. The Lord says that not a single rejecter "will get a taste of my banquet." There is no second chance.

"But while they were on their way to buy the oil, the bridegroom arrived. The virgins who were ready went in with him to the wedding banquet. And the door was shut. (Mat 25:10)

I tell you the truth, anyone who will not receive the kingdom of God like a little child will never enter it." (Mark 10:15)

Do you not know that the wicked will not inherit the kingdom of God? Do not be deceived: Neither the sexually immoral nor idolaters nor adulterers nor male prostitutes nor homosexual offenders nor thieves nor the greedy nor drunkards nor slanderers nor swindlers will inherit the kingdom of God. (1 Cor 6:9-10)

I declare to you, brothers, that flesh and blood cannot inherit the kingdom of God, nor does the perishable inherit the imperishable. (1 Cor 15:50)

Nothing impure will ever enter it, nor will anyone who does what is shameful or deceitful, but only those whose names are written in the Lamb's book of life. (Rev 21:27)

Your wrongdoings have kept these away; your sins have deprived you of good. (Jer 5:25)

My God will reject them because they have not obeyed him; they will be wanderers among the nations. (Hosea 9:17)

	F. The Cost of Discipleship, 14:25-35 (cp. Mt.5:13; cp. Mt.10:37-39; Mk.9:50)	to build and was not able to finish.' 31 "Or suppose a king is about to go to war against another king. Will he not first sit down and consider whether he is able with ten thousand men to oppose the one coming against him with twenty thousand? 32 If he is not able, he will send a delegation while the other is still a long way off and will ask for terms of peace.	b. Illust.2: A king at war—must count the consequences
1 Huge crowds followed Jesus & He challenged them	25 Large crowds were traveling with Jesus, and turning to them he said:		
2 A man must put Christ first: Before family & even before himself	26 "If anyone comes to me and does not hate his father and mother, his wife and children, his brothers and sisters—yes, even his own life—he cannot be my disciple.		
3 A man must bear the cross of death: Death to self	27 And anyone who does not carry his cross and follow me cannot be my disciple.	33 In the same way, any of you who does not give up everything he has cannot be my disciple.	c. The point: A man must pay the ultimate price—give up everything
4 A man must give thought to discipleship: Count the cost & the consequences	28 "Suppose one of you wants to build a tower. Will he not first sit down and estimate the cost to see if he has enough money to complete it?	34 "Salt is good, but if it loses its saltiness, how can it be made salty again?	**5 A man must have the salt of discipleship: The salt of self-denial**
a. Illust.1: A builder—must count his resources	29 For if he lays the foundation and is not able to finish it, everyone who sees it will ridicule him, 30 Saying, 'This fellow began	35 It is fit neither for the soil nor for the manure pile; it is thrown out. "He who has ears to hear, let him hear."	a. A half-hearted choice 1) Is worthless 2) Is to be cast out b. An invitation: Hearing is a choice

DIVISION VI

THE SON OF MAN'S GREAT JOURNEY TO JERUSALEM (STAGE II): HIS TEACHING AND PUBLIC CONFLICT, 13:22-17:10

F. The Cost of Discipleship, 14:25-35

(14:25-35) **Introduction**: Christ is not interested in cheap invitations and discipleship. Too often the call to discipleship is to receive the great benefits and advantages offered by God. There are eternal benefits and advantages, but salvation and discipleship involve much more. They involve an unbelievable cost, the supreme sacrifice. A person must pay the ultimate price, all that one *is and has* to follow Christ. Just what does it cost to follow Christ? This is the all important subject of this passage.

1. Huge crowds followed Jesus and He challenged them (v.25).
2. A man must put Christ first: before family, even before self (v.26).
3. A man must bear the cross of death: death to self (v.27).
4. A man must give thought to discipleship: count the cost and the consequences (v.28-33).
5. A man must have the salt of discipleship: the salt of self-denial (v.34-35).

(14:25-35) **Another Outline**: *The cost or conditions of discipleship* might be outlined as follows.

1. Renunciation (v.26).
2. Self-denial (v.27).
3. Thoughtfulness—counting the cost (v.28-32).
4. Forsaking all—giving up everything (v.33-35).

There are three other *conditions for discipleship* given by Christ elsewhere.

1. Love to others: "By this shall all men know that ye are my disciples, if ye have love one to another" (Jn.13:35; cp. 34).
2. Stedfastness: "If you hold to my teachings, then you are really my disciples" (Jn.8:31).
3. Fruitfulness: "This is to my Father's glory, that you bear much fruit, showing yourselves to be my disciples" (Jn.15:8).

1 (14:25) **Discipleship**: huge crowds were following Jesus. The cross and the desperate needs of the world were upon His mind (v.27). The enormous sacrifice and cost it was going to take to reach the world consumed His thoughts. He must have followers who would sacrifice themselves totally if the message of salvation were to be carried to the world. He could not have second best. God would not accept any place other than first place in a man's life. He must make clear what it meant and what it cost to be His disciple.

2 (14:26) **Family—Self-Denial—Dedication—Discipleship**: a man must put Christ first, even before his family and himself. (See outline and note—Mt.10:35-37.) The words "does not hate" (ou misei) are strong. They mean not showing preference, indifference, aversion, disregard (cp. Gen.29:31, 33; Dt.21:15). Christ was not saying that one's family and one's self were to be literally hated. The true believer is to love *even* his enemies (Lk.6:27). What then did Christ mean? Very simply…

⇒ Christ is to be *first* in a person's life: before family, even before self.
⇒ Christ is to be put before family: even if one's family opposes his decision to follow Christ.
⇒ Christ is to be put *first*: before the companionship and comfort and pleasure of family and home.

⇒ All—even family and self—are to be put behind Christ and His mission. All must be denied and put behind a person's love and devotion to Christ and His cause.

> **Peter said to him, "We have left everything to follow you!" (Mark 10:28)**
> **So they pulled their boats up on shore, left everything and followed him. (Luke 5:11)**
> **After this, Jesus went out and saw a tax collector by the name of Levi sitting at his tax booth. "Follow me," Jesus said to him, (Luke 5:27)**
> **"I tell you the truth," Jesus said to them, "no one who has left home or wife or brothers or parents or children for the sake of the kingdom of God will fail to receive many times as much in this age and, in the age to come, eternal life." (Luke 18:29-30)**
> **What is more, I consider everything a loss compared to the surpassing greatness of knowing Christ Jesus my Lord, for whose sake I have lost all things. I consider them rubbish, that I may gain Christ (Phil 3:8)**

3 (14:27) **Self-denial**: a man must bear the cross of death—to self. (See notes and DEEPER STUDY # 1—Lk.9:23; Mt.16:24 for discussion and application.)

4 (14:28-33) **Decision—Discipleship—Thought—Mind**: a man must think and give thought to discipleship; he must count the cost and the consequences. Christ used two parables to get His point across.

1. A man who wants to build a tower, first sits down to *think* about the project and to count the cost. Does he have *sufficient resources*, enough of what it takes to finish the task? He has to make sure, or else he will not be able to finish the task and will end up being mocked. The point is clear: before a person begins to follow Christ, Christ wants that person to think about it. He wants the person to be sure, absolutely sure. Can he afford to follow through; does he have what it takes to build the tower (life)? Why? Because a false profession damages the Kingdom of God.

A false profession causes...
- the world to mock and charge true believers with being hypocritical.
- prospective believers to turn sour.
- believers to be hampered and hindered in their ministry.
- some believers to become discouraged.

2. The second parable concerned two kings at war. The king being attacked had only ten thousand soldiers, whereas the king marching against him had twenty thousand soldiers. The defending king sat down and thought long and hard about his resources and the consequences. He was forced to think about the loss of life and property even if he did win. Note: this king had to make a decision. He was being invaded. He had to decide to fight against the invading king or to surrender. He had to *think through the consequences both ways*, the consequences of fighting or surrendering. (Cp. the invading king to Christ and the defending king to the individual.)

The point of the two parables is clear: a man must pay the ultimate price. He must forsake all, renounce and give up all that he *is and has*; or else "he cannot be my disciple." When a man counts the cost of following Christ, he needs to think about two things.

1. It will cost him *all he is*. The man must be willing to center his life around Christ and His mission to reach a world lost and full of desperate needs. It will cost the man...
- his heart: total devotion and commitment.
- his mind: being permeated and controlled by Christ.
- his eyes: watching what he looks at.
- his ears: watching what he listens to.
- his hands: watching what he touches and picks up.
- his feet: watching where he goes.
- his mouth: watching what he eats and drinks and says.
- his desires: watching, controlling, and changing his urges and desires.
- his energy: committing his strength, initiative, and will to Christ.
- his effort and work: dedicating and centering all in Christ, using his efforts and work in the cause of Christ.

> **For we know that our old self was crucified with him so that the body of sin might be done away with, that we should no longer be slaves to sin— (Rom 6:6)**
> **Therefore, I urge you, brothers, in view of God's mercy, to offer your bodies as living sacrifices, holy and pleasing to God—this is your spiritual act of worship. (Rom 12:1)**
> **It is better not to eat meat or drink wine or to do anything else that will cause your brother to fall. (Rom 14:21)**
> **Do you not know that your body is a temple of the Holy Spirit, who is in you, whom you have received from God? You are not your own; you were bought at a price. Therefore honor God with your body. (1 Cor 6:19-20)**
> **Nobody should seek his own good, but the good of others. (1 Cor 10:24)**
> **"Therefore come out from them and be separate, says the Lord. Touch no unclean thing, and I will receive you." "I will be a Father to you, and you will be my sons and daughters, says the Lord Almighty." (2 Cor 6:17-18)**
> **I have been crucified with Christ and I no longer live, but Christ lives in me. The life I live in the body, I live by faith in the Son of God, who loved me and gave himself for me. (Gal 2:20)**
> **Those who belong to Christ Jesus have crucified the sinful nature with its passions and desires. (Gal 5:24)**
> **For you died, and your life is now hidden with Christ in God. (Col 3:3)**

2. It will cost him *all he has*. The man must be willing to give everything he has to Christ, without watering down the cost. It is this point that will cause so many to be lost and doomed (see outline and notes—Lk.18:18-30; Mt.10:16-22). To really follow Christ will cost...

- family: being put after Christ.
- friends: being put after Christ and centered around Christ.
- home: all the comforts and extravagances.
- job: being centered around Christ and being used to earn enough to give to those who do not have (Eph.4:28).
- cars: not being extravagant, so as to have more to give to a needful world.
- investments: using for God's cause.
- money: taking care of personal necessities and then using the rest for God's cause.

Whatever a person has, it will cost him. He must surrender it to Christ, which is to say, he must be willing to use it in the Lord's mission, the mission of helping a world lost and reeling under the weight of enormous needs.

When a man counts the cost of following Christ, he must think about the consequences of both fighting against Christ and surrendering to Christ. If the man chooses to reject Christ, to struggle against Him, the man will...

- never experience abundant life, deep satisfaction (Jn.10:10).
- never know God, His love and care, on a daily basis.
- never have an *eternal sense* of purpose, meaning, and significance.
- never know nor have the assurance of eternal life.
- never be free from the uncertainty of life.
- never be free from the dread and fear of death.
- never be free of some sense of judgment and of what lies ahead.
- never be freed from a sense of false security.

The consequences of surrendering to Christ are, of course, the very opposite of the above.

> **Jesus answered, "If you want to be perfect, go, sell your possessions and give to the poor, and you will have treasure in heaven. Then come, follow me." (Mat 19:21; cp. Lk.18:22)**
>
> **But the worries of this life, the deceitfulness of wealth and the desires for other things come in and choke the word, making it unfruitful. (Mark 4:19)**
>
> **Sell your possessions and give to the poor. Provide purses for yourselves that will not wear out, a treasure in heaven that will not be exhausted, where no thief comes near and no moth destroys. For where your treasure is, there your heart will be also. (Luke 12:33-34)**
>
> **But Zacchaeus stood up and said to the Lord, "Look, Lord! Here and now I give half of my possessions to the poor, and if I have cheated anybody out of anything, I will pay back four times the amount." (Luke 19:8)**
>
> **Even as I try to please everybody in every way. For I am not seeking my own good but the good of many, so that they may be saved. (1 Cor 10:33)**
>
> **For you know the grace of our Lord Jesus Christ, that though he was rich, yet for your sakes he became poor, so that you through his poverty might become rich. (2 Cor 8:9)**
>
> **People who want to get rich fall into temptation and a trap and into many foolish and harmful desires that plunge men into ruin and destruction. (1 Tim 6:9)**
>
> **If anyone has material possessions and sees his brother in need but has no pity on him, how can the love of God be in him? (1 John 3:17)**

5 (14:34-35) **Decision, Half-hearted—Dedication**: a man must have the salt of discipleship which is self-denial, renunciation, the sacrifice and giving, of all one is and has. (See notes—Mt.5:13; Mk.9:50 for more discussion.) Christ said three very pointed things.

1. A half-hearted choice is worthless. It *cannot season or penetrate*; it cannot help anything or anyone.

> **Jesus replied, "No one who puts his hand to the plow and looks back is fit for service in the kingdom of God." (Luke 9:62)**

2. A half-hearted choice is to be cast out. Salt that is worthless and useless is always thrown out, for it is good for nothing.

> **But the subjects of the kingdom will be thrown outside, into the darkness, where there will be weeping and gnashing of teeth." (Mat 8:12)**
>
> **"Then the king told the attendants, 'Tie him hand and foot, and throw him outside, into the darkness, where there will be weeping and gnashing of teeth.' (Mat 22:13)**
>
> **And throw that worthless servant outside, into the darkness, where there will be weeping and gnashing of teeth.' (Mat 25:30)**
>
> **"But he will reply, 'I don't know you or where you come from. Away from me, all you evildoers!' (Luke 13:27)**
>
> **If anyone does not remain in me, he is like a branch that is thrown away and withers; such branches are picked up, thrown into the fire and burned. (John 15:6)**
>
> **Anyone who receives instruction in the word must share all good things with his instructor. Do not be deceived: God cannot be mocked. A man reaps what he sows. The one who sows to please his sinful nature, from that nature will reap destruction; the one who sows to please the Spirit, from the Spirit will reap eternal life. (Gal 6:6-8)**
>
> **But my righteous one will live by faith. And if he shrinks back, I will not be pleased with him." But we are not of those who shrink back and are destroyed, but of those who believe and are saved. (Heb 10:38-39)**
>
> **If they have escaped the corruption of the world by knowing our Lord and Savior Jesus Christ and are again entangled in it and overcome, they are worse off at the end than they were at the beginning. (2 Pet 2:20)**

3. A man with ears needs to hear the invitation. Hearing spiritual truth is a choice which a man must make. He chooses whether to hear or not to hear the truth.

"Therefore everyone who hears these words of mine and puts them into practice is like a wise man who built his house on the rock. The rain came down, the streams rose, and the winds blew and beat against that house; yet it did not fall, because it had its foundation on the rock. But everyone who hears these words of mine and does not put them into practice is like a foolish man who built his house on sand. The rain came down, the streams rose, and the winds blew and beat against that house, and it fell with a great crash." (Mat 7:24-27)

But the seed on good soil stands for those with a noble and good heart, who hear the word, retain it, and by persevering produce a crop. (Luke 8:15)

"He said to him, 'If they do not listen to Moses and the Prophets, they will not be convinced even if someone rises from the dead.'" (Luke 16:31)

And we also thank God continually because, when you received the word of God, which you heard from us, you accepted it not as the word of men, but as it actually is, the word of God, which is at work in you who believe. (1 Th 2:13)

Anyone who listens to the word but does not do what it says is like a man who looks at his face in a mirror and, after looking at himself, goes away and immediately forgets what he looks like. (James 1:23-24)

He who listens to a life-giving rebuke will be at home among the wise. (Prov 15:31)

	CHAPTER 15
	G. The Parable of the Lost Sheep: The Lost Sinner Out in the World, 15:1-7 (cp. Mt.18:11-14)
1 Tax collectors & sinners drew near Jesus	Now the tax collectors and "sinners" were all gathering around to hear him.
a. The religionists: Grumbled against Jesus associating with "sinners"	2 But the Pharisees and the teachers of the law muttered, "This man welcomes sinners and eats with them."
b. Jesus: Shared a parable	3 Then Jesus told them this parable:
2 The sheep was lost[DS1]	4 "Suppose one of you has a hundred sheep and loses one of them.
3 The sheep was lost because of self	Does he not leave
4 The sheep was lost in the wilderness or open country	the ninety-nine in the open country and go after the lost
5 The sheep was sought until found	sheep until he finds it?
6 The sheep, once found, brings great joy	5 And when he finds it, he joyfully puts it on his shoulders 6 And goes home. Then he calls his friends and neighbors together and says, 'Rejoice with me; I have found my lost sheep.'
7 The sheep represented a repentant sinner	7 I tell you that in the same way there will be more rejoicing in heaven over one sinner who repents than over ninety-nine righteous per-sons who do not need to repent.

DIVISION VI

THE SON OF MAN'S GREAT JOURNEY TO JERUSALEM (STAGE II): HIS TEACHING AND PUBLIC CONFLICT, 13:22-17:10

G. The Parable of the Lost Sheep: The Lost Sinner Out in the World, 15:1-7

(15:1-7) **Introduction**: Chapter 15 is one of the most important chapters in all the Bible. It includes three of the most famous parables ever told. The parables deal with the lost sinner and the great love of God in seeking and receiving the lost sinner when the sinner repents and returns home. The first parable is that of the Lost Sheep in the wilderness of the world.

1. Tax collectors and sinners drew near Jesus (v.1-3).
2. The sheep was lost (v.4).
3. The sheep was lost because of self (v.4).
4. The sheep was lost "in the wilderness or open country" (v.4).
5. The sheep was sought until found (v.4).
6. The sheep, once found, brought great joy (v.5-6).
7. The sheep represented a repentant sinner (v.7).

1 (15:1-3) **Separation—Spiritual Hunger**: tax-collectors and sinners drew near Jesus. Note they "all" drew near to Him. This shows two things.

1. They were hungry for His message. They were not coming out of curiosity, nor to observe, nor to seek physical blessings; they were coming out of a spiritual need, out of the need to receive His message of salvation.

2. They acknowledged their great need. Publicans, that is, tax-collectors, worked for the Roman government, the nation that had conquered Israel. Therefore, they were considered traitors to both Israel and God. Consequently, they were despised by the people and were cut off and shut out by the religionists. Sinners were the rank immoral and unjust who did not keep the law, such as harlots (cp. Mt.21:32), liars, thieves, murderers. All these were *sinners*, traitors to both God and man, and they knew it. So when Christ came along preaching deliverance from sin and hope of the Kingdom of God, they flocked to Him.

The attitude of the religionists was tragic. They grumbled against Jesus because He associated and ate with such terrible sinners. They felt it was beneath the dignity of any respectable person to associate with such vile sinners. Note an important point: Christ was not *of the world*, but He was *out in the world* trying to reach men for God. It is this that is often overlooked by both the liberals and the separatists.

⇒ The true believer is to "come out from them [the world] and be separate, says the Lord. Touch no unclean thing, and I will receive you. I will be a Father to you, and you will be my sons and daughters, says the Lord Almighty." (2 Cor.6:17-18). He is not to be out in the world with sinners doing worldly things and carrying on worldly conversation (Eph.4:29; Col.4:6).

⇒ The true believer is to "go into all the world and preach the good news to all creation [sinners]" (Mk.16:15). The believer *goes*; he does not sit back and wait on sinners to come to him and the church. He goes out where the sinners are.

Thought 1. If the *whole gospel—all of the good news—* were preached today in power and authority, how many would be flocking to hear…

- the gospel of salvation from sin and death?
- the gospel of the hope for the Kingdom of God (see DEEPER STUDY # 3, Kingdom of God—Mt.19:23-24)?

Christ answered the religionists by sharing three great parables. The first parable is one of the most-loved stories ever told, the parable of the lost sheep.

2 (15:4) **Sheep**: the sheep was lost. The sheep represents the unbeliever, the sinner who wanders out in the wilderness (open country) of the world, the person who has gone astray and is lost to God. Note the meaning of the word lost (see Deeper Study # 1, Lost—Lk.15:4).

DEEPER STUDY # 1
(15:4) **Lost (apollumi)**: to perish, to destroy, to lose, to lose eternal life, to be spiritually destitute, to be cut off.

3 (15:4) **Sheep, Lost—Man, Lost**: the sheep was lost because of self. A sheep loses itself in one of five ways.

1. The sheep is attracted by something out "in the open country (wilderness)," away from the flock of the shepherd. What the sheep sees is more attractive and appealing. It tempts and seduces him, and he lusts after it ("the cravings of sinful man: the lust of the flesh" and the lust of the eyes, 1 Jn.2:16).

2. The sheep is aimless, not paying attention to what is going on. It aimlessly wanders off, and while it is *getting lost*, the sheep does not know it is losing its way. The sheep is already lost when it discovers it has lost its way.

3. The sheep refuses to heed the warnings of the shepherd and the example of the other sheep ("the boasting of what he has and does", 1 Jn.2:16).

4. The sheep is not attached enough to the shepherd or to the other sheep. There is not the bond or union there should be. Therefore, he stays off by himself, eating and resting and working alone until eventually he wanders off without anyone's knowing it, including himself (Heb.10:25).

5. The sheep does not trust the shepherd. It does not think the shepherd will take care and see that there is satisfying food. It goes astray in search of *greener pasture and more satisfying food* (see note—Mt.18:14 for the help of others needed by the shepherd to care for the sheep).

> **We all, like sheep, have gone astray, each of us has turned to his own way; and the LORD has laid on him the iniquity of us all. (Isa 53:6)**
>
> **A man who strays from the path of understanding comes to rest in the company of the dead. (Prov 21:16)**
>
> **Like a bird that strays from its nest is a man who strays from his home. (Prov 27:8)**
>
> **Now they grope through the streets like men who are blind. They are so defiled with blood that no one dares to touch their garments. (Lam 4:14)**
>
> **"My people have committed two sins: They have forsaken me, the spring of living water, and have dug their own cisterns, broken cisterns that cannot hold water. (Jer 2:13)**
>
> **You have rejected me," declares the LORD. "You keep on backsliding. So I will lay hands on you and destroy you; I can no longer show compassion. (Jer 15:6)**
>
> **Because of the increase of wickedness, the love of most will grow cold, (Mat 24:12)**
>
> **But my righteous one will live by faith. And if he shrinks back, I will not be pleased with him." (Heb 10:38)**
>
> **They have left the straight way and wandered off to follow the way of Balaam son of Beor, who loved the wages of wickedness. (2 Pet 2:15)**
>
> **They are wild waves of the sea, foaming up their shame; wandering stars, for whom blackest darkness has been reserved forever. (Jude 1:13)**

4 (15:4) **World—Worldliness—Open Country—Wilderness—Lost**: the sheep was lost in the open country or wilderness. The open country had an excitement about it. The unknown and the risk aroused the emotions; but once the sheep ventured out into the open country, he found its terrain rugged, full of narrow ridges and deep ravines and crevices. It was rough going, heavy with thick underbrush, pricking thorns, dangerous footing; and, if the way out were never found, it would sap the sheep's strength and age him ever so rapidly. Eventually the open country would take its life.

The open country and thrills of the world do attract a person. The world has much to offer.

1. The world gives a man...
   - occupation and purpose
   - lifestyle and acceptance
   - ego and self-esteem
   - recognition and privilege
   - more and more honor
   - position and image
   - plenty and wealth
   - opportunity and satisfaction
   - authority and power
2. The world stimulates and arouses a man, causing...
   - his blood to rush
   - his heart to beat faster
   - goose bumps
   - butterflies
   - desires
   - cravings
   - escape
   - relaxation

> **Do not love the world or anything in the world. If anyone loves the world, the love of the Father is not in him. For everything in the world—the cravings of sinful man, the lust of his eyes and the boasting of what he has and does—comes not from the Father but from the world. (1 John 2:15-16)**
>
> **The acts of the sinful nature are obvious: sexual immorality, impurity and debauchery; idolatry and witchcraft; hatred, discord, jealousy, fits of rage, selfish ambition, dissensions, factions and envy; drunkenness, orgies, and the like. I warn you, as I did before, that those who live like this will not inherit the kingdom of God. (Gal 5:19-21)**
>
> **"My people have been lost sheep; their shepherds have led them astray and caused them to roam on the mountains. They wandered over mountain and hill and forgot their own resting place. (Jer 50:6)**
>
> **My sheep wandered over all the mountains and on every high hill. They were scattered over the whole earth, and no one searched or looked for them. (Ezek 34:6)**
>
> **When he saw the crowds, he had compassion on them, because they were harassed and helpless, like sheep without a shepherd. (Mat 9:36)**

5 (15:4) **Ministry—Seeking Lost**: the sheep was sought until found. Note four things.

1. The lost sheep was sought (v.4). The shepherd left the ninety-nine to seek the one lost sheep. The ninety-nine were safe; they were already in the shepherd's fold. But the one sheep was lost. It was the one that needed to be sought. It was this sheep that needed the attention of the shepherd and was to occupy the time, energy, and effort of the shepherd. As long as the sheep was lost, seeking it was the primary purpose and reason for the shepherd. (What a lesson for the church and ministers!)

2. The search was urgent. The shepherd *went after* the lost sheep (v.4). He was gripped with concern. He went

after the one lost sheep as though it were the only one. Note the shepherd's dedication and commitment to seeking the lost.

3. The shepherd sought until he found the sheep. He did not seek complacently or slowly, as though there were plenty of time. Nor did he give up, despite the difficulties that lay along the rough terrain and the weariness of the long hours and the tediousness of running into dead end after dead end. He sought and kept on seeking until he found the lost sheep. He never slackened, never backed off, never gave up.

4. When the shepherd found the sheep, he embraced the sheep and threw it over his shoulders. He received it...

- with arms wide open
- embracing it
- rejoicing in heart
- supporting and carrying it to his home (v.6)

Surely he took up our infirmities and carried our sorrows, yet we considered him stricken by God, smitten by him, and afflicted. But he was pierced for our transgressions, he was crushed for our iniquities; the punishment that brought us peace was upon him, and by his wounds we are healed. We all, like sheep, have gone astray, each of us has turned to his own way; and the LORD has laid on him the iniquity of us all. (Isa 53:5-6)

For you were like sheep going astray, but now you have returned to the Shepherd and Overseer of your souls. (1 Pet 2:25)

I have strayed like a lost sheep. Seek your servant, for I have not forgotten your commands. (Psa 119:176)

6 (15:5-6) **Salvation, Results**: once found, the sheep bought great joy. Note what the shepherd did.

1. He called all his neighbors together. He wanted everyone to know that the lost sheep had been found. Everyone had been so concerned—praying, hoping, waiting. They wanted to join in the rejoicing.

2. Everyone rejoiced because the shepherd's labor was not in vain.

3. The shepherd tenderly called the lost sheep "my lost sheep"—"my sheep which was lost." It was his, no matter how dirty, filthy, unclean, destitute, depraved, ugly or lost it had been. It was still the shepherd's sheep.

Note that God did not send an angel as a servant, but He sent His Son to seek the lost (cp. Is.53:4-6, 10-12).

"For God so loved the world that he gave his one and only Son, that whoever believes in him shall not perish but have eternal life. (John 3:16)

He himself bore our sins in his body on the tree, so that we might die to sins and live for righteousness; by his wounds you have been healed. For you were like sheep going astray, but now you have returned to the Shepherd and Overseer of your souls. (1 Pet 2:24-25)

For the Son of Man came to seek and to save what was lost." (Luke 19:10)

7 (15:7) **Repentance**: the sheep represents a repentant sinner. A sinner must repent (see note and DEEPER STUDY # 1—Acts 17:29-30).

Peter replied, "Repent and be baptized, every one of you, in the name of Jesus Christ for the forgiveness of your sins. And you will receive the gift of the Holy Spirit. (Acts 2:38)

Repent, then, and turn to God, so that your sins may be wiped out, that times of refreshing may come from the Lord, (Acts 3:19)

Let the wicked forsake his way and the evil man his thoughts. Let him turn to the LORD, and he will have mercy on him, and to our God, for he will freely pardon. (Isa 55:7)

"But if a wicked man turns away from all the sins he has committed and keeps all my decrees and does what is just and right, he will surely live; he will not die. (Ezek 18:21)

	H. The Parable of the Lost Coin: The Lost Sinner Within the Home, 15:8-10
1 The coin was lost **2 The coin was lost because of others** **3 The coin was lost in the house** **4 The coin was sought until found** **5 The coin, once found, brought great joy**	8 "Or suppose a woman has ten silver coins and loses one. Does she not light a lamp, sweep the house and search carefully until she finds it? 9 And when she finds it, she calls her friends and neighbors together and says, 'Rejoice with me; I have found my lost coin.'
6 The coin represented a repentant sinner	10 In the same way, I tell you, there is rejoicing in the presence of the angels of God over one sinner who repents."

DIVISION VI

THE SON OF MAN'S GREAT JOURNEY TO JERUSALEM (STAGE II): HIS TEACHING AND PUBLIC CONFLICT, 13:22-17:10

H. The Parable of the Lost Coin: The Lost Sinner Within the Home, 15:8-10

(15:8-10) **Introduction**: this passage is often preached and taught right along with the Parable of the Lost Sheep (Lk.15:1-7). The lost sheep was lost out in the wilderness or open country of the world, whereas the lost coin was lost in the house. Note the points are the same for each parable, but the application is different.

1. The coin was lost (v.8).
2. The coin was lost because of others (v.8).
3. The coin was lost in the house (v.8).
4. The coin was sought until found (v.9).
5. The coin, once found, brought great joy (v.9).
6. The coin represented a repentant sinner (v.10)

1 (15:8) **Lost—Coin**: the lost coin represents the unbeliever, the sinner who is lost within the house, the family member who has gone astray and is lost both to God and to the mother. Note two facts.

1. The coin was silver, of extreme worth, and greatly desired.

2. The coin was lost and doomed to be lost forever if not found (see DEEPER STUDY # 1, Lost—Lk.15:4 for discussion).

2 (15:8) **Lost—Family—Witnessing**: the coin was lost because of others. This is a striking picture of the responsibility family members have for one another. A coin (person) within the home is lost in one of four ways.

1. Ignoring the coin. It is set aside and forgotten. Once it has been brought into the house, little if any thought is given to it. Being too busy, not knowing its value, and confusing priorities can cause a coin to be ignored.

2. Neglecting the coin. A person can know the coin is there and know its value, yet neglect it. He can just fail to pay attention to the coin for such a long period of time that he forgets where it is.

3. Carelessly handling the coin. It is badly handled, dropped, and lost.

4. Unconsciously placing the coin someplace. Placing the coin can be unplanned; therefore, little attention is given to it. A person just goes about his daily affairs without ever planning any use for the coin. Eventually, it is forgotten.

Then they can train the younger women to love their husbands and children, to be self-controlled and pure, to be busy at home, to be kind, and to be subject to their husbands, so that no one will malign the word of God. (Titus 2:4-5)

When they had finished eating, Jesus said to Simon Peter, "Simon son of John, do you truly love me more than these?" "Yes, Lord," he said, "you know that I love you." Jesus said, "Feed my lambs." (John 21:15)

Now I am ready to visit you for the third time, and I will not be a burden to you, because what I want is not your possessions but you. After all, children should not have to save up for their parents, but parents for their children. (2 Cor 12:14)

Impress them on your children. Talk about them [God's Word] when you sit at home and when you walk along the road, when you lie down and when you get up. (Deu 6:7)

Teach them [God's Word] to your children, talking about them when you sit at home and when you walk along the road, when you lie down and when you get up. (Deu 11:19)

Train a child in the way he should go, and when he is old he will not turn from it. (Prov 22:6)

"Who is it he is trying to teach? To whom is he explaining his message? To children weaned from their milk, to those just taken from the breast? (Isa 28:9)

The living, the living—they praise you, as I am doing today; fathers tell their children about your faithfulness. (Isa 38:19)

Arise, cry out in the night, as the watches of the night begin; pour out your heart like water in the presence of the Lord. Lift up your hands to him [God} for the lives of your children, who faint from

hunger at the head of every street. (Lam 2:19)

3 (15:8) **Lost—Family—Witnessing**: the coin was lost in the house. Note three points.

1. The coin, although lost in the house, was lost in the dust and dirt of the floor. It was not clean like the other nine coins sitting on the dresser. The dust and dirt was slowly covering and tarnishing it in its filth.

2. The coin's experience, although in the house, was terrible. Being lost, it was…

- useless: unable to contribute to family needs.
- helpless: unable to fulfill its purpose.
- gone: not present to participate in family functions.
- bypassed: not seen, it could not be polished and cared for.
- stepped upon and walked upon: down upon the floor covered with dust and dirt, it was not seen; therefore, it was misused and abused.

The rod of correction imparts wisdom, but a child left to himself disgraces his mother. (Prov 29:15)

The younger one said to his father, 'Father, give me my share of the estate.' So he divided his property between them. "Not long after that, the younger son got together all he had, set off for a distant country and there squandered his wealth in wild living. (Luke 15:12-13)

Prompted by her mother, she said, "Give me here on a platter the head of John the Baptist." (Mat 14:8)

For I told him [Eli] that I would judge his family forever because of the sin he knew about; his sons made themselves contemptible, and he failed to restrain them. (1 Sam 3:13)

But his sons did not walk in his ways. They turned aside after dishonest gain and accepted bribes and perverted justice. (1 Sam 8:3)

He did evil in the eyes of the LORD, because he walked in the ways of his father and mother and in the ways of Jeroboam son of Nebat, who caused Israel to sin. (1 Ki 22:52)

He too walked in the ways of the house of Ahab, for his mother encouraged him in doing wrong. (2 Chr 22:3)

Instead, they have followed the stubbornness of their hearts; they have followed the Baals, as their fathers taught them." (Jer 9:14)

I said to their children in the desert, "Do not follow the statutes of your fathers or keep their laws or defile yourselves with their idols. I am the LORD your God; follow my decrees and be careful to keep my laws. (Ezek 20:18-19)

3. The coin was not aware it was lost. Note three things.

a. A family member may have no consciousness or sensation of being lost. There may be no discomfort, distress, or anxiety; however, there is still personal responsibility. Everyone, no matter who he is, is responsible for his own life and salvation. He cannot blame his parents, mother, father, brother, sister, son or daughter. The family member who sins is responsible for his own behavior. He is the one who is lost in the dirt of the earth.

b. There is no excuse for following peers and stronger personalities. There is no excuse for being passive, weak, or easily misled. A family member is eventually responsible for his own life.

c. The other family members may not know the *truth* about the love of God and Christ, about the privilege of being saved and having one's sins forgiven and inheriting eternal life. Therefore, a family member is responsible to get out and seek the truth from those who do know the truth.

So you must obey them and do everything they tell you. But do not do what they do, for they do not practice what they preach. (Mat 23:3)

And after they have been destroyed before you, be careful not to be ensnared by inquiring about their gods, saying, "How do these nations serve their gods? We will do the same." (Deu 12:30)

They rejected his decrees and the covenant he had made with their fathers and the warnings he had given them. They followed worthless idols and themselves became worthless. They imitated the nations around them although the LORD had ordered them, "Do not do as they do," and they did the things the LORD had forbidden them to do. (2 Ki 17:15)

This is what the LORD says: "For three sins of Judah, even for four, I will not turn back my wrath. Because they have rejected the law of the LORD and have not kept his decrees, because they have been led astray by false gods, the gods their ancestors followed, (Amos 2:4)

4 (15:9) **Witnessing—Lost, Seeking**: the coin was sought until found. There are several significant facts in this point.

1. The woman changed the whole atmosphere of the house. She lit a lamp, for the houses of that day were very dark. Most had only one small window less than two feet across. The woman's only hope of finding the coin was to secure light.

The light represents Christ, the Light of the World (see DEEPER STUDY # 1—Jn.8:12). The woman turned to Christ to bring light to her dark house. Note she used the light in her search, looking behind every door, under every table, in every drawer, and everywhere else. She went nowhere without the Light. (The light also represents the light of her life, that is, her trust in the righteousness of God. See notes—Mt.5:14; DEEPER STUDY # 5—Jn.12:35:36.)

2. The woman swept throughout the house. She swept all the loose and clinging dirt and filth out of her house (cp. sin in the house). She knew two things.

a. As long as there was loose dirt and filth in the house (sin), she might never find her precious coin.

b. If she did not clean out all the loose dirt and filth (sin), she might lose another coin.

3. The woman searched for the coin immediately and urgently. The longer the coin stayed lost...
- the dirtier it became
- the more scarred it became
- the more it settled in the dirt
- the harder it was to find

4. The woman searched diligently for the coin until she found it. There was great loss felt, as though there were no other silver piece. There was no comfort in knowing the other pieces were safe. So much depended upon finding this one lost coin.

The coin's very purpose and usefulness in life depended upon being found and saved from the dirt of the earth, so one thing was set: she would not give up until she had found it.

⇒ She *willed* to find the coin: dedicated and committed her life to finding it, always praying for God's direction and trusting Him for His help.

⇒ She *labored* diligently: poured all the thought and energy and effort of her being into seeking her lost coin. Seeking the coin became the focus of her life until she found it.

⇒ She *endured*: the work was tedious and hard, for it involved sweeping away the dirt and filth under everything and in every little corner and unseen place.

She looked and prayed while walking upright, bowing, bending, and kneeling. Despite the inconvenience and difficulty, she shifted, removed, and rearranged all the furniture in order to clean and reach out to unnoticed areas—all in an attempt to reach and find the lost coin.

For the Son of Man came to seek and to save what was lost." (Luke 19:10)

Later Jesus found him at the temple and said to him, "See, you are well again. Stop sinning or something worse may happen to you." (John 5:14)

To this they replied, "You were steeped in sin at birth; how dare you lecture us!" And they threw him out. Jesus heard that they had thrown him out, and when he found him, he said, "Do you believe in the Son of Man?" (John 9:34-35)

"As for the person who hears my words but does not keep them, I do not judge him. For I did not come to judge the world, but to save it. (John 12:47)

Those whom I love I rebuke and discipline. So be earnest, and repent. Here I am! I stand at the door and knock. If anyone hears my voice and opens the door, I will come in and eat with him, and he with me. (Rev 3:19-20)

But in keeping with his promise we are looking forward to a new heaven and a new earth, the home of righteousness. So then, dear friends, since you are looking forward to this, make every effort to be found spotless, blameless and at peace with him. (2 Pet 3:13-14)

"Return home and tell how much God has done for you." So the man went away and told all over town how much Jesus had done for him. (Luke 8:39)

For I could wish that I myself were cursed and cut off from Christ for the sake of my brothers, those of my own race, (Rom 9:3)

5 (15:9) **Salvation—Joy—Witnessing**: the coin, once found, brought great joy. Note several things.

1. The woman's prayers and efforts payed off. She found her lost coin. Such prayer and diligence are rewarded by God.

2. The woman called her friends and neighbors together for a glorious celebration. Her lost coin had been found. It was a joyous moment, and she wanted those dearest to her to share in the joyful moment.

3. This is critical to remember. Note her words, "I have found my lost coin." She had been the one who had lost the coin. Why had she lost it? Note that the lamp had not been lit. The house had only natural light shining through a small man-made window. The light of the lamp (Christ) did not shine throughout the house.

4. The woman could now rejoice because...
- she had secured light (Christ)
- she had swept all the dirt and filth out of her house
- she had prayed and sought diligently for her lost coin
- her efforts and prayer led her to the coin

6 (15:10) **Repentance**: the coin represented a repentant sinner. Note two simple but profound points.

1. The sinner who is found is a man who repents (see note and DEEPER STUDY # 1—Acts 17:29-30).

2. God and all the angels rejoice greatly when one sinner repents.

Peter replied, "Repent and be baptized, every one of you, in the name of Jesus Christ for the forgiveness of your sins. And you will receive the gift of the Holy Spirit. (Acts 2:38)

Let the wicked forsake his way and the evil man his thoughts. Let him turn to the LORD, and he will have mercy on him, and to our God, for he will freely pardon. (Isa 55:7)

1 **He said, "Give me"**
a. My inheritance[DS1]
b. My independence
c. The result: He wasted his life in wild living
2 **He met the day when he suffered & was in need**
a. He suffered being destitute
b. He suffered natural disaster
c. He suffered humiliation[DS2]
d. He suffered hunger
e. He suffered the loss of friends
3 **He came to his senses & snapped out of his insanity, back to reality**
a. Thought of his father

I. The Parable of the Prodigal Son: The Lost Son, 15:11-24

11 Jesus continued: "There
was a man who had two sons.
12 The younger one said to
his father, 'Father, give me
my share of the estate.' So he
divided his property between
them.
13 "Not long after that, the
younger son got together all
he had, set off for a distant
country and there squandered
his wealth in wild living.
14 After he had spent everything, there was a severe
famine in that whole country,
and he began to be in need.
15 So he went and hired
himself out to a citizen of that
country, who sent him to his
fields to feed pigs.
16 He longed to fill his stomach with the pods that the
pigs were eating, but no one
gave him anything.
17 "When he came to his
senses, he said, 'How many of
my father's hired men have
food to spare, and here I am
starving to death!
18 I will set out and go back
to my father and say to him:
Father, I have sinned against
heaven and against you.
19 I am no longer worthy to
be called your son; make me
like one of your hired men.'
20 So he got up and went to
his father. "But while he was
still a long way off, his father
saw him and was filled with
compassion for him; he ran to
his son, threw his arms
around him and kissed him.
21 "The son said to him,
'Father, I have sinned against
heaven and against you. I am
no longer worthy to be called
your son.'
22 "But the father said to his
servants, 'Quick! Bring the
best robe and put it on him.
Put a ring on his finger and
sandals on his feet.
23 Bring the fattened calf
and kill it. Let's have a feast
and celebrate.
24 For this son of mine was
dead and is alive again; he
was lost and is found.' So
they began to celebrate.

& his enormous provision
b. Thought of his plight
c. Thought of humbling himself:
1) Of repenting
2) Of confessing his sin & unworthiness
4 **He got up & returned to his father**
a. He repented—turned from his sinful life
b. He was accepted even before he confessed
c. He confessed
5 **He was accepted when he returned to the father**
a. The father restored him
b. The father fed the son & celebrated his son's return
c. The father proclaimed his son's new life

DIVISION VI

THE SON OF MAN'S GREAT JOURNEY TO JERUSALEM (STAGE II): HIS TEACHING AND PUBLIC CONFLICT, 13:22-17:10

I. The Parable of the Prodigal Son: The Lost Son, 15:11-24

(15:11-24) **Introduction**: the parable of the Prodigal Son is the greatest and most-beloved story ever told in human language. God loves and reaches out to the most prodigal of men, and He runs to embrace any prodigal son who *repents and returns home*. God forgives His prodigal son and restores him, no matter how terrible the sin and failure of the prodigal.

1. He said, "Give me" (v.11-13).
2. He met the day when he suffered and was in need(v.14-16).
3. He came to his senses and snapped out of his insanity, back to reality (v.17-19).
4. He got up and returned to his father (v.20-21).
5. He was accepted when he returned to the father (v.22-24).

1 (15:11-13) **Selfishness—Hardness—Independence—Self—Stubborn—Worldliness**: the prodigal said, "Give me." Note the son was a child of the father's by birth. He belonged to the estate (world) of the father's by natural birth. But it is clear from what follows that the son did not belong to the father *in heart*, *mind*, or *spirit*. The prodigal wanted two things.

1. He said, "*Give me* my inheritance." He wanted money and the things and possessions of the estate (world) which he was to inherit. He wanted to get all the Father would give him so that he could enjoy it now.

a. He had not earned it, not yet; therefore, he did not deserve it.
b. He was selfish and self-centered, rude and unkind. He said, "Give me," not "Please" nor "May I have." The effect upon his father and the estate was of little, if any, concern to the prodigal (the lost son). The father could be hurt and the estate could suffer from the loss of the money and goods; it mattered little to the prodigal.

But the worries of this life, the deceitfulness of wealth and the desires for other things come in and choke the word, making it unfruitful. (Mark 4:19)

Then he said to them, "Watch out! Be on your guard against all kinds of greed; a man's life does not consist in the abundance of his possessions." (Luke 12:15)

People who want to get rich fall into temptation and a trap and into many foolish and harmful desires that plunge men into ruin and destruction. For the love of money is a root of all kinds of evil. Some people, eager for money, have wandered from the faith and pierced themselves with many griefs. (1 Tim 6:9-10)

But mark this: There will be terrible times in the last days. People will be lovers of themselves, lovers of money, boastful,

proud, abusive, disobedient to their parents, ungrateful, unholy, (2 Tim 3:1-2)

If anyone has material possessions and sees his brother in need but has no pity on him, how can the love of God be in him? (1 John 3:17)

Israel was a spreading vine; he brought forth fruit for himself. As his fruit increased, he built more altars; as his land prospered, he adorned his sacred stones. (Hosea 10:1)

"From the least to the greatest, all are greedy for gain; prophets and priests alike, all practice deceit. (Jer 6:13)

And when you were eating and drinking, were you not just feasting for yourselves? (Zec 7:6)

2. He said, "Give me my independence." This is what the prodigal, the lost son, was really after, the right to his own life. He was tied down to the father's property and was held responsible for the care of the property. He wanted to *cut loose—to be away* from the father and to be relieved of the responsibility of the property. He wanted to live his own life, to do his own thing (Lk.15:12).

The prodigal rejected and turned from the father and his way of life because he felt the father would...

- demand and require too much work
- curtail and limit his freedom
- disallow and restrict his fun and pleasure
- be unfair and not understand
- control and discipline too much
- keep an eye and hand upon him

Note a crucial point: the father gave the son his freedom and possessions. The son was able to do what he wanted with his life and goods (abilities, talents, money, things). All was placed into the son's hands. He could use his life and what he had as he wished without any interference from the father. Since he was an adult son, he wanted to be free from the father and the father respected his adulthood. The father could do nothing about the choice of life chosen by the son. He had to let him go and live as he wished.

"You stiff-necked people, with uncircumcised hearts and ears! You are just like your fathers: You always resist the Holy Spirit! (Acts 7:51)

This is especially true of those [the wicked] who follow the corrupt desire of the sinful nature and despise authority. Bold and arrogant, these men are not afraid to slander celestial beings [authority]; (2 Pet 2:10)

"I have seen these people," the LORD said to Moses, "and they are a stiff-necked people. (Exo 32:9)

Although the LORD sent prophets to the people to bring them back to him, and though they testified against them, they would not listen. (2 Chr 24:19)

Do not be stiff-necked, as your fathers were; submit to the LORD. Come to the sanctuary, which he has consecrated forever. Serve the LORD your God, so that his fierce anger will turn away from you. (2 Chr 30:8)

To whom he said, "This is the resting place, let the weary rest"; and, "This is the place of repose"— but they would not listen. (Isa 28:12)

This is what the Sovereign LORD, the Holy One of Israel, says: "In repentance and rest is your salvation, in quietness and trust is your strength, but you would have none of it. (Isa 30:15)

Do not be like the horse or the mule, which have no understanding but must be controlled by bit and bridle or they will not come to you. (Psa 32:9)

Blessed is the man who always fears the LORD, but he who hardens his heart falls into trouble. (Prov 28:14)

A man who remains stiff-necked after many rebukes will suddenly be destroyed—without remedy. (Prov 29:1)

Listen to me, you stubborn-hearted, you who are far from righteousness. (Isa 46:12)

For I knew how stubborn you were; the sinews of your neck were iron, your forehead was bronze. (Isa 48:4)

They turned their backs to me and not their faces; though I taught them again and again, they would not listen or respond to discipline. (Jer 32:33)

"We will not listen to the message you have spoken to us in the name of the LORD! (Jer 44:16)

"But they refused to pay attention; stubbornly they turned their backs and stopped up their ears. (Zec 7:11)

If you do not listen, and if you do not set your heart to honor my name," says the LORD Almighty, "I will send a curse upon you, and I will curse your blessings. Yes, I have already cursed them, because you have not set your heart to honor me. (Mal 2:2)

3. The prodigal, the lost son, wasted his life in wild living.

a. He left his father—he rebelled and revolted and journeyed to a *distant country*. He chose a country that was drastically different from his father's, a country that was full of carousing and drunkenness, partying and immorality, selfishness and greed, sin and shame, death and hell.

b. He lived a worldly, fleshly life—living for the pleasure of this life only. "Wild living" means loose, reckless, wild, extravagant living. It means...
   - careless spending
   - carousing in the forbidden bed
   - drunkenness
   - being loose
   - cursing
   - telling off-colored jokes
   - gluttonous eating
   - drinking
   - partying
   - dressing to attract
   - having a foul mouth

The seed that fell among thorns stands for those who hear, but as they go on their way they are choked by life's worries, riches and pleasures, and they do not mature. (Luke 8:14)

And I'll say to myself, "You have plenty of good things laid up for many years. Take life easy; eat, drink and be

merry."' (Luke 12:19)

The acts of the sinful nature are obvious: sexual immorality, impurity and debauchery; idolatry and witchcraft; hatred, discord, jealousy, fits of rage, selfish ambition, dissensions, factions and envy; drunkenness, orgies, and the like. I warn you, as I did before, that those who live like this will not inherit the kingdom of God. (Gal 5:19-21)

But the widow who lives for pleasure is dead even while she lives. (1 Tim 5:6)

But mark this: There will be terrible times in the last days. People will be lovers of themselves, lovers of money, boastful, proud, abusive, disobedient to their parents, ungrateful, unholy, treacherous, rash, conceited, lovers of pleasure rather than lovers of God— (2 Tim 3:1-2, 4)

At one time we too were foolish, disobedient, deceived and enslaved by all kinds of passions and pleasures. We lived in malice and envy, being hated and hating one another. (Titus 3:3)

You have lived on earth in luxury and self-indulgence. You have fattened yourselves in the day of slaughter. (James 5:5)

They will be paid back with harm for the harm they have done. Their idea of pleasure is to carouse in broad daylight. They are blots and blemishes, reveling in their pleasures while they feast with you. (2 Pet 2:13)

Wisdom is better than weapons of war, but one sinner destroys much good. (Eccl 9:18)

"Now then, listen, you wanton creature, lounging in your security and saying to yourself, 'I am, and there is none besides me. I will never be a widow or suffer the loss of children.' (Isa 47:8)

DEEPER STUDY # 1
(15:12) **Inheritance**: by law the younger son received one-third and the older son two-thirds of a father's estate when the father died. However, if the father wished, he could make gifts to his children throughout his life. The prodigal son was asking for a huge gift amounting to what his final inheritance would be.

2 (15:14-16) **Worldliness—Sin—Enslavement—Bondage—Suffering—Friends—Dissatisfaction—Emptiness—Destitute— Spiritual Poverty**: the prodigal son met the day when he suffered and was in need. He suffered five things.

1. He suffered being *destitute*. He "spent everything." He squandered and wasted and misused...

- his money
- his property
- his talents
- his purpose
- his opportunities
- his mind
- his thoughts
- his hands
- his body
- his soul

He misused all these in the lust of his flesh (sinful nature). Note: all these things, ranging from his money to his soul, came from God. They had been given to the son from the Father, either through nature at birth or through a direct gift. The son owed everything to the Father. He should have been working to hold up the name of the Father, serving and repaying the Father for all His marvelous gifts. But instead, the son became a rebel, a prodigal and "spent everything" upon "wild living."

The point is this: the prodigal had nothing on earth to help him. He had wrapped his life up in the pleasure and security of the world; but now, when they were all gone, there was nothing left to help him. He stood *bare*, *empty*, *alone*, and *destitute*. All that he had based his life upon was now gone. He now knew that the world was corruptible and that it passed away. Note: he had cut himself off from his Father (God), so he had no security from God. He was completely void of the confidence and spiritual strength that God would look after him and help him recover. He had not looked to God nor trusted and honored God with his life and goods. Therefore, he was destitute of all spiritual help, left out in the world all alone, having "spent everything."

What benefit did you reap at that time from the things you are now ashamed of? Those things result in death! For the wages of sin is death, but the gift of God is eternal life in Christ Jesus our Lord. (Rom 6:21, 23)

The truly righteous man attains life, but he who pursues evil goes to his death. (Prov 11:19)

Remember that at that time you were separate from Christ, excluded from citizenship in Israel and foreigners to the covenants of the promise, <u>without hope</u> and <u>without God</u> in the world. (Eph 2:12)

You say, 'I am rich; I have acquired wealth and do not need a thing.' But you do not realize that you are wretched, pitiful, poor, blind and naked. (Rev 3:17)

But as for me, my feet had almost slipped; I had nearly lost my foothold. (Psa 73:2)

But rebels and sinners will both be broken, and those who forsake the LORD will perish. "You will be ashamed because of the sacred oaks in which you have delighted; you will be disgraced because of the gardens that you have chosen. You will be like an oak with fading leaves, like a garden without water. (Isa 1:28-30)

O LORD, do not your eyes look for truth? You <u>struck</u> them, but they felt no pain; you <u>crushed</u> them, but they refused correction. They made their faces harder than stone and refused to repent. I thought, "These are only the <u>poor</u>; they are foolish, for they do not know the way of the LORD, the requirements of their God. (Jer 5:3-4)

But you have planted wickedness, you have reaped evil, you have eaten the fruit of deception. Because you have depended on your own strength and on your many warriors, (Hosea 10:13)

"The days are coming," declares the Sovereign LORD, "when I will send a famine through the land— not a famine of food or a thirst for water, but a famine of hear-

ing the words of the LORD. Men will stagger from sea to sea and wander from north to east, searching for the word of the LORD, but they will not find it. (Amos 8:11-12)

2. He suffered *natural disaster*. A famine struck. This refers to all the severe trials and disasters in life because of the very nature of the world. It may be storm, sickness, accident, death. Whatever it is, it is disastrous and causes great loss. Again, the prodigal son was all alone without God's presence; therefore, he had to face the disaster without God's care and help.

But everyone who hears these words of mine and does not put them into practice is like a foolish man who built his house on sand. The rain came down, the streams rose, and the winds blew and beat against that house, and it fell with a great crash." (Mat 7:26-27)

His work will be shown for what it is, because the Day will bring it to light. It will be revealed with fire, and the fire will test the quality of each man's work. (1 Cor 3:13)

"And every one that heareth these sayings of mine, and doeth them not, shall be likened unto a foolish man, which built his house upon the sand: and the rain descended, and the floods came, and the winds blew, and beat upon that house; and it fell: and great was the fall of it" (Mt.7:26-27).

"Every man's work shall be made manifest: for the day shall declare it, because it shall be revealed by fire; and the fire shall try every man's work of what sort it is" (1 Cor.3:13).

3. He suffered *enslavement and humiliation* (see DEEPER STUDY # 2—Lk.15:15 for discussion).

4. He suffered hunger. The world's garbage (wild living) will always leave a man empty and hungry. The world, its pleasures and wealth and styles, will please the body but leave the soul empty. The world cannot permanently...

- satisfy
- fill
- nourish
- provide
- supply
- please

The world will leave a man (deep within, within his soul)...

- dissatisfied
- unfulfilled
- unnourished
- empty
- unsupplied
- displeased

In contrast, only the man who hungers and thirsts after righteousness will be filled and bear the fruit of God's Spirit (see outlines, notes, and DEEPER STUDY # 5,6—Mt.5:6; Gal.5:22-23).

Jesus answered, "Everyone who drinks this water will be thirsty again, but whoever drinks the water I give him will never thirst. Indeed, the water I give him will become in him a spring of water [earthly water, pleasures] welling up to eternal life." (John 4:13-14)

The tempter came to him and said, "If you are the Son of God, tell these stones to become bread." (Mat 4:3)

"They will say, 'The fruit you longed for is gone from you. All your riches and splendor have vanished, never to be recovered.' (Rev 18:14)

"Food for the stomach and the stomach for food"—but God will destroy them both. The body is not meant for sexual immorality, but for the Lord, and the Lord for the body. (1 Cor 6:13)

He wanders about—food for vultures ; he knows the day of darkness is at hand. (Job 15:23)

All man's efforts are for his mouth, yet his appetite is never satisfied. (Eccl 6:7)

He feeds on ashes, a deluded heart misleads him; he cannot save himself, or say, "Is not this thing in my right hand a lie?" (Isa 44:20)

Why spend money on what is not bread, and your labor on what does not satisfy? Listen, listen to me, and eat what is good, and your soul will delight in the richest of fare. (Isa 55:2; cp. Is.29:8; 65:13)

5. He suffered *the loss of friends*. The *so-called friends* who surrounded him when he had plenty were now gone. Note two things.

a. When he had plenty and was able to maintain the same social class as his friends, they were all glad to call him friend. But when he was not able to *keep up* with their standard of living, he was not welcomed. They were *above* him, and he was *below* them. He was, in fact, an embarrassment to them. They did not want him around lest others associate them with a person who was unsuccessful and a failure.

b. The friends, at least some of them, were feeling the pinch of the famine as well. Note the selfishness of the world: "no one gave him anything." How like the vast majority of people today! And so many have so much that could be given!

All my intimate friends detest me; those I love have turned against me. (Job 19:19)

My friends and companions avoid me because of my wounds; my neighbors stay far away. (Psa 38:11)

I lie awake; I have become like a bird alone on a roof. (Psa 102:7)

Look to my right and see; no one is concerned for me. I have no refuge; no one cares for my life. (Psa 142:4)

Do not trust a neighbor; put no confidence in a friend. Even with her who lies in your embrace be careful of your words. (Micah 7:5)

DEEPER STUDY # 2

(15:15) **Sin**: a Jew was forbidden by law to be attached to a Gentile, a man of a "distant country." But even disregarding this prohibition, the humiliation of cleaning hog pens was a horrible pain for a formerly fine rich young man to suffer. There are three pictures here.

1. The picture of being spiritually and emotionally and mentally drained. He ran out of spiritual strength, spent his inheritance.

2. The picture of attaching himself and becoming enslaved to a person of a "distant country." Being spiritually drained, he sought refuge with a man of a "distant country," a man away from God.

3. The picture of sin's leading and enslaving a man to the "hog pens" of the world.

> **Jesus replied, "I tell you the truth, everyone who sins is a slave to sin. (John 8:34)**
>
> **Don't you know that when you offer yourselves to someone to obey him as slaves, you are slaves to the one whom you obey—whether you are slaves to sin, which leads to death, or to obedience, which leads to righteousness? (Rom 6:16; cp. Rom. 6:21)**
>
> **But I see another law at work in the members of my body, waging war against the law of my mind [which tells me better] and making me a prisoner of the law of sin at work within my members. (Rom 7:23)**
>
> **They promise them freedom, while they themselves are slaves of depravity—for a man is a slave to whatever has mastered him. (2 Pet 2:19)**
>
> **If a man cleanses himself from the latter, he will be an instrument for noble purposes, made holy, useful to the Master and prepared to do any good work. (2 Tim 2:21)**
>
> **The evil deeds of a wicked man ensnare him; the cords of his sin hold him fast. (Prov 5:22)**
>
> **Therefore my people will go into exile for lack of understanding; their men of rank will die of hunger and their masses will be parched with thirst. (Isa 5:13)**

3 (15:17-19) **Sin—Repentance—Thinking**: the prodigal came to his senses, snapped out of his insanity, back to reality. Note the words "came to his senses." Jesus considers a person away from God to be *mad, insane, living in an unreal world.*

> **This is the evil in everything that happens under the sun: The same destiny overtakes all. The hearts of men, moreover, are full of evil and there is madness in their hearts while they live, and afterward they join the dead. (Eccl 9:3)**

Two things are indicated about repentance.

⇒ Repentance is the beginning of sanity and reality, the very basis for building a sound life.

⇒ The beginning of repentance is thought, thinking about one's need to repent and turn back to God.

Note the words, "When he came to his senses, he said"; that is, he began to think to himself. He thought long and hard upon these things.

1. He thought upon his Father (God) and His enormous provision.

a. The Father's "many hired men" would be the believers, the children of God.

b. The Father's "food" was enough to feed all, and then there was even more to spare.

The prodigal remembered how his father had been able to provide for all. He remembered the sense of belonging, of being a family and of fellowshipping together among all the servants of God, the great provision of love and joy and peace, of purpose and meaning and significance. His father had it all and more to spare.

2. He thought upon his plight: "I am starving to death!" (v.17). The meaning is both now and future.

a. He was starving now: empty, lonely, unhappy, humiliated, destitute, without purpose, meaning, or significance, without family or friend.

b. He was doomed to starve, to perish eternally (Jn.3:16; see DEEPER STUDY # 1—Heb.9:27).

3. He thought about humbling himself. Humbling himself would involve two significant steps.

a. Repenting. Note the prodigal would have to "get up," that is, turn from and leave the distant country, and go to his father. These are the steps involved in repentance...

- arising, getting up
- turning away from one's sinful life
- turning toward and moving toward God

Note that repentance is simply a changed life, a life that turns from sin to righteousness, from self to God, from this world to heaven, from the temporal to the eternal.

b. Confessing. The prodigal would have to confess...

- his sin
- his unworthiness to be called God's son

Thought 1. Note that the prodigal was only thinking of these things, not doing them—not yet. However, the desire and longing to return to his father was gnawing at his heart deeply.

> **Blessed are those who hunger and thirst for righteousness, for they will be filled. (Mat 5:6; cp. Lk.6:21)**
>
> **On the last and greatest day of the Feast, Jesus stood and said in a loud voice, "If anyone is thirsty, let him come to me and drink. (John 7:37)**
>
> **I spread out my hands to you; my soul thirsts for you like a parched land. Selah (Psa 143:6; cp. Ps.42:2; 38:9; 63:1; 119:174)**
>
> **"Come, all you who are thirsty, come to the waters; and you who have no money, come, buy and eat! Come, buy wine and milk without money and without cost. (Isa 55:1)**

4 (15:20-21) **Repentance—Confession—God, Seeking Men—Contrition**: the prodigal got up and returned to his father. This was the greatest of moments for the prodigal, the most momentous event in the life of any sinner. It is the summit of human experience. The prodigal returned to God: he sought reconciliation with his Father.

1. He repented: he did get up and turn from his sinful life and go to his Father. He was no longer just thinking about it; he was now repenting and going to the Father.

> **Blessed are those who mourn, for they will be comforted. (Mat 5:4)**
>
> **Repent, then, and turn to God, so that your sins may be wiped out, that times of refreshing may come from the Lord, (Acts 3:19)**

> **Repent of this wickedness and pray to the Lord. Perhaps he will forgive you for having such a thought in your heart. (Acts 8:22)**
>
> **Godly sorrow brings repentance that leads to salvation and leaves no regret, but worldly sorrow brings death. (2 Cor 7:10)**
>
> **Let the wicked forsake his way and the evil man his thoughts. Let him turn to the LORD, and he will have mercy on him, and to our God, for he will freely pardon. (Isa 55:7)**
>
> **Rid yourselves of all the offenses you have committed, and get a new heart and a new spirit. Why will you die, O house of Israel? (Ezek 18:31)**
>
> **Say to them, 'As surely as I live, declares the Sovereign LORD, I take no pleasure in the death of the wicked, but rather that they turn from their ways and live. Turn! Turn from your evil ways! Why will you die, O house of Israel?' (Ezek 33:11; cp. Joel 2:12)**
>
> **Therefore tell the people: This is what the LORD Almighty says: 'Return to me,' declares the LORD Almighty, 'and I will return to you,' says the LORD Almighty. (Zec 1:3; cp. Mal.3:7)**

2. He was accepted even before he confessed. This is a significant point to note. Repentance is the sign that we are sincere when we confess, and God knows we are sincere when He sees us actually turn from our wicked ways. He forgives when we repent, when we truly want Him to forgive. This is the reason the Father runs to meet His son. The son had turned away from the distant country and *had come* to the Father. Note:

⇒ the Father's eyes were merciful and compassionate: no matter what He had seen, He wanted to have mercy.

⇒ the Father's heart was merciful and compassionate: He wanted to reach out in compassion to the sinning son.

⇒ the Father's feet were merciful and compassionate: He wanted to run and meet and *escort* the sinner home.

⇒ the Father's arms were merciful and compassionate: He wanted to embrace the prodigal son and weep with him.

⇒ the Father's lips were merciful and compassionate: He wanted to welcome the prodigal son home with all the tenderness of a true Father.

> **The LORD is close to the brokenhearted and saves those who are crushed in spirit. (Psa 34:18)**
>
> **The sacrifices of God are a broken spirit; a broken and contrite heart, O God, you will not despise. (Psa 51:17)**
>
> **Sing the glory of his name; make his praise glorious! (Psa 66:2)**
>
> **Rend your heart and not your garments. Return to the LORD your God, for he is gracious and compassionate, slow to anger and abounding in love, and he relents from sending calamity. (Joel 2:13)**

3. He confessed. He needed to confess his terrible evil: that he had rebelled, rejected, and sinned against the Father. He had sinned against heaven, all that heaven stood for in all its righteousness and godliness; and sinned in the sight of God, going against all that the Father stood for and knew to be best.

> **If we confess our sins, he is faithful and just and will forgive us our sins and purify us from all unrighteousness. (1 John 1:9)**
>
> **Now make confession to the LORD, the God of your fathers, and do his will. Separate yourselves from the peoples around you and from your foreign wives." (Ezra 10:11)**
>
> **He who conceals his sins does not prosper, but whoever confesses and renounces them finds mercy. (Prov 28:13)**
>
> **Only acknowledge your guilt— you have rebelled against the LORD your God, you have scattered your favors to foreign gods under every spreading tree, and have not obeyed me,'" declares the LORD. (Jer 3:13)**
>
> **Then he [God] comes to men and says, 'I sinned, and perverted what was right, but I did not get what I deserved. He redeemed my soul from going down to the pit, and I will live to enjoy the light.' (Job 33:27-28)**

5 (15:22-24) **Forgiveness—Restoration**: the prodigal was accepted and restored. But note: he would not have been accepted and restored if he had not returned. The key to being accepted by God is *repentance*. We must always remember this fact, a fact which determines our eternal destiny.

1. The father restored him.
   a. The "*robe*" restored him to a position of sonship and honor. It symbolized being clothed with the righteousness of Christ.

> **God made him who had no sin to be sin for us, so that in him we might become the righteousness of God. (2 Cor 5:21)**
>
> **Rather, clothe yourselves with the Lord Jesus Christ, and do not think about how to gratify the desires of the sinful nature. (Rom 13:14)**
>
> **And to put on the new self, created to be like God in true righteousness and holiness. (Eph 4:24)**
>
> **And have put on the new self, which is being renewed in knowledge in the image of its Creator. (Col 3:10)**

   b. The "*ring*" restored him to a position of authority. The son was now to represent the father and his kingdom.

> **Because you are sons, God sent the Spirit of his Son into our hearts, the Spirit who calls out, "Abba, Father." So you are no longer a slave, but a son; and since you are a son, God has made you also an heir. (Gal 4:6-7)**
>
> **To him who overcomes, I will give the right to sit with me on my throne, just as I overcame and sat down with my Father on his throne. (Rev 3:21)**

For you did not receive a spirit that makes you a slave again to fear, but you received the Spirit of sonship. And by him we cry, "Abba, Father." The Spirit himself testifies with our spirit that we are God's children. Now if we are children, then we are heirs—heirs of God and co-heirs with Christ, if indeed we share in his sufferings in order that we may also share in his glory. (Rom 8:15-17)

So that, having been justified by his grace, we might become heirs having the hope of eternal life. (Titus 3:7)

c. The "*sandals*" immediately restored and elevated him above servanthood, which means he became a *free man*. The son was now fitted with sandals to carry the gospel of peace wherever he went (cp. Eph 6:15).

Then you will know the truth, and the truth will set you free." (John 8:32)

You have been set free from sin and have become slaves to righteousness. (Rom 6:18)

Because through Christ Jesus the law of the Spirit of life set me free from the law of sin and death. (Rom 8:2)

Now the Lord is the Spirit, and where the Spirit of the Lord is, there is freedom. (2 Cor 3:17)

For you know the grace of our Lord Jesus Christ, that though he was rich, yet for your sakes he became poor, so that you through his poverty might become rich. (2 Cor 8:9)

You, my brothers, were called to be free. But do not use your freedom to indulge the sinful nature ; rather, serve one another in love. (Gal 5:13)

And with your feet fitted with the readiness that comes from the gospel of peace. (Eph 6:15)

Live as free men, but do not use your freedom as a cover-up for evil; live as servants of God. (1 Pet 2:16)

d. The "*celebration*" pictures reconciliation, full acceptance, and the great joy of the occasion.

But when the kindness and love of God our Savior appeared, he saved us, not because of righteous things we had done, but because of his mercy. He saved us through the washing of rebirth and renewal by the Holy Spirit, whom he poured out on us generously through Jesus Christ our Savior, so that, having been justified by his grace, we might become heirs having the hope of eternal life. (Titus 3:4-7)

2. The father fed the son and celebrated his son's return. Both facts are important. All that the son needed was fed to him. He was fully accepted into the family; therefore, all the food of heaven was laid out before him. It was there to nourish him. But even more: there was celebration and great joy over the son's return. The whole household celebrated in joy.

In order that in the coming ages he might show the incomparable riches of his grace, expressed in his kindness to us in Christ Jesus. (Eph 2:7)

And my God will meet all your needs according to his glorious riches in Christ Jesus. (Phil 4:19)

The grace of our Lord was poured out on me abundantly, along with the faith and love that are in Christ Jesus. (1 Tim 1:14)

With me are riches and honor, enduring wealth and prosperity. (Prov 8:18)

The blessing of the LORD brings wealth, and he adds no trouble to it. (Prov 10:22)

3. The Father proclaimed His son's new life.

a. He "was dead and is alive again."

"For God so loved the world that he gave his one and only Son, that whoever believes in him shall not perish but have eternal life. (John 3:16)

"I tell you the truth, whoever hears my word and believes him who sent me has eternal life and will not be condemned; he has crossed over from death to life. (John 5:24)

As for you, you were dead in your transgressions and sins, (Eph 2:1)

For you have been born again, not of perishable seed, but of imperishable, through the living and enduring word of God. (1 Pet 1:23)

b. "He was lost and is found."

We all, like sheep, have gone astray, each of us has turned to his own way; and the LORD has laid on him the iniquity of us all. (Isa 53:6)

And goes home. Then he calls his friends and neighbors together and says, 'Rejoice with me; I have found my lost sheep.' And when she finds it, she calls her friends and neighbors together and says, 'Rejoice with me; I have found my lost coin.' (Luke 15:6, 9)

For the Son of Man came to seek and to save what was lost." (Luke 19:10)

He himself bore our sins in his body on the tree, so that we might die to sins and live for righteousness; by his wounds you have been healed. For you were like sheep going astray, but now you have returned to the Shepherd and Overseer of your souls. (1 Pet 2:24-25)

	J. The Parable of the Older Son: The Self-Righteous Religionist, 15:25-32	29 But he answered his father, 'Look! All these years I've been slaving for you and never disobeyed your orders. Yet you never gave me even a young goat so I could celebrate with my friends.	**3 Fault 3: He was self-righteous** a. He claimed to be religious b. He claimed to be moral & just c. He felt he deserved more, that he was not recognized enough
1 Fault 1: He was in the field away from home	25 "Meanwhile, the older son was in the field. When he came near the house, he heard music and dancing. 26 So he called one of the servants and asked him what was going on. 27 'Your brother has come,' he replied, 'and your father has killed the fattened calf because he has him back safe and sound.'	30 But when this son of yours who has squandered your property with prostitutes comes home, you kill the fattened calf for him!'	**4 Fault 4: He lacked compassion & the understanding of sinners**
		31 "'My son,' the father said, 'you are always with me, and everything I have is yours. 32 But we had to celebrate and be glad, because this brother of yours was dead and is alive again; he was lost and is found.'"	**5 Fault 5: He failed to see two critical facts** a. He had the same blessings available b. His brother was truly saved
2 Fault 2: He shut himself out	28 "The older brother became angry and refused to go in. So his father went out and pleaded with him.		

DIVISION VI

THE SON OF MAN'S GREAT JOURNEY TO JERUSALEM (STAGE II): HIS TEACHING AND PUBLIC CONFLICT, 13:22-17:10

J. The Parable of the Older Son: The Self-Righteous Religionist, 15:25-32

(15:25-32) **Introduction**: this passage is about the second son of the father (v.11, 25). The older son represents the self-righteous religionist—the moral, the just, the good—the man who has never committed gross and visible sin. He is religious and does religious works; therefore, he feels and believes he is acceptable to God. In this parable Jesus pointed out five faults with the self-righteous religionist. (See outlines and notes—Lk.11:37-54; 18:9-12; Ro.2:17-29 for more discussion.)

1. Fault 1: he was in the field away from home (v.25-27).
2. Fault 2: he shut himself out (v.28).
3. Fault 3: he was self-righteous (v.29).
4. Fault 4: he lacked compassion and the understanding of sinners (v.30).
5. Fault 5: he failed to see two critical facts (v.31-32).

1 (15:25-27) **Religionists—Errors of**: the first fault of the religionist is his tragic position. He was "in the field" away from the house. He was in the field of religion, but not in the house of salvation. He was unaware of his father's affairs (v.26-27).

1. The older son was *in the field* of his father. He was working diligently, looking after the responsibilities of the field. So it is with the religionist. He is working diligently at the field of religious things: services, rituals, ceremonies, ordinances, prayers. He even uses religious talk and terms in his daily conversation. He attends services and prays and talks as much as he needs to satisfy his conscience.

The point is this: the religionist is "in the field" of religion. He professes to know God and to be a follower of religion. Just how much religion he practices depends upon how much religion he needs to salve his conscience and to feel acceptable to God. Most men want to feel acceptable to God, so they do whatever amount of religion makes them feel acceptable.

> **Thought 1.** How much religion does a man need to salve his conscience and make him feel acceptable to God?
>
> 1) Some men sense the need for *very little religious activity*.
> 2) Other men sense the need for *a great deal of religious activity*, even to becoming professional ministers.

2. The older son was in the field, not in the house of his father.

⇒ He did not know what was going on in the house (of salvation and repentance), only what was happening in the field (of religion).
⇒ When he looked at the *celebration* of repentant sinners, he questioned. He did not understand.
⇒ He had to ask what the celebration meant (what the celebration of repentance and salvation meant).

> **Having a form of godliness but denying its power. Have nothing to do with them. (2 Tim 3:5)**
>
> **"Woe to you, teachers of the law and Pharisees [religionists], you hypocrites! You give a tenth of your spices—mint, dill and cummin. But you have neglected the more important matters of the law—justice, mercy and faithfulness. You should have practiced the latter, without neglecting the former. (Mat 23:23)**
>
> **You are observing special days and months and seasons and years! I fear for you, that somehow I have wasted my efforts on you. (Gal 4:10-11)**
>
> **For it is by grace you have been saved, through faith—and this not from yourselves, it is the gift of God—not by works, so that no one can boast. (Eph 2:8-9)**
>
> **[God] who has saved us and called us to a holy life—not because of anything we have done but because of his own purpose and grace. This grace was given us in Christ Jesus before the beginning of time, (2 Tim 1:9)**

But when the kindness and love of God our Savior appeared, he saved us, not because of righteous things we had done, but because of his mercy. He saved us through the washing of rebirth and renewal by the Holy Spirit, whom he poured out on us generously through Jesus Christ our Savior, so that, having been justified by his grace, we might become heirs having the hope of eternal life. (Titus 3:4-7)

2 (15:28) **Religionists—Jealousy—Unbelief**: the second fault of the religionist is his tragic rejection of God. He shuts himself out. Note the son in the field became angry at the repentant son who was now in the father's house. He did not understand repentance, how a man who had been so immoral, dirty, and unclean could change so much. The claims of being safe and secure and the sound of celebration and testimony disturbed the son from the field. So it is with the religionist. He does not understand such claims as...

- being saved
- being saved *by God Himself*
- being filled with power
- being filled with joy
- being delivered *immediately* from enslaved habits (such as alcohol, smoking, immorality, cursing, covetousness, selfishness)
- being healed
- being indwelt and given power by the Holy Spirit

The religionist reacts against such claims. How? He wants nothing to do with such a *house of repentance and salvation*. He shuts himself out. Sometimes he even talks against and criticizes such a celebration and house.

"Woe to you, teachers of the law and Pharisees, you hypocrites! You shut the kingdom of heaven in men's faces. You yourselves do not enter, nor will you let those enter who are trying to. (Mat 23:13)

The Lord says: "These people come near to me with their mouth and honor me with their lips, but their hearts are far from me. Their worship of me is made up only of rules taught by men....Therefore once more I will astound these people with wonder upon wonder; the wisdom of the wise will perish, the intelligence of the intelligent will vanish." (Isa 29:14; cp. Mk.7:6)

"For the lips of a priest ought to preserve knowledge, and from his mouth men should seek instruction—because he is the messenger of the LORD Almighty. But you have turned from the way and by your teaching have caused many to stumble; you have violated the covenant with Levi," says the LORD Almighty. (Mal 2:7-8)

Note a significant fact: the religionist *shut himself out*. God does not shut him out. The *father* "went...out and pleaded with him" to come in. The father does even more for the religionist in that he comes seeking him, whereas the prodigal had to return home before the father could run out to meet him. The father came out and begged the religious son to understand repentance and salvation and to come in. (The religionist is already in the field of religion and close to the gospel, whereas the prodigal son is out in the field of the world far removed from the church and the gospel.)

Note the terrible jealousy and envy in the heart of the older son. He was jealous of the treatment, of the fruit and blessing's being given to the prodigal son. (See DEEPER STUDY # 1, Fruit-bearing—Jn.15:1-8; cp. Gal.5:22-23 for more discussion.)

3 (15:29) **Religionists—Self-righteousness**: the third fault of the religionist is his tragic self-righteousness. Note the older son claimed three things.

1. He claimed to be religious: "I've been slaving for you." A religionist does serve God through religious things: he worships, prays, tithes, witnesses, reads his Bible, and teaches.

2. He claimed to be moral and just: "[I] never disobeyed your orders." He never committed immorality, not any other dirty or unclean act that could be visibly or publicly seen. He never stole, cheated, lied, or cursed. He was obedient to his parents and responsible in his work and duties both to God and man.

3. He felt he deserved more, that he was not recognized enough: "You never gave me even a young goat," that is, the spiritual food of power, love, joy, peace, confidence, joy, and the absolute assurance of heaven and eternal life. He felt he did not get enough, that he deserved more than those who were now filled with so much spiritual food and celebration.

Note what the religionist lacks: *faith* (Mt.23:23). He just does not *trust* the Father's love and judgment, His plan of salvation and repentance *for all*.

You say, 'I am innocent; he is not angry with me.' But I will pass judgment on you because you say, 'I have not sinned.' (Jer 2:35)

Many will say to me on that day, 'Lord, Lord, did we not prophesy in your name, and in your name drive out demons and perform many miracles?' Then I will tell them plainly, 'I never knew you. Away from me, you evildoers!' (Mat 7:22-23)

Know that a man is not justified by observing the law, but by faith in Jesus Christ. So we, too, have put our faith in Christ Jesus that we may be justified by faith in Christ and not by observing the law, because by observing the law no one will be justified. (Gal 2:16)

"Woe to you, teachers of the law and Pharisees, you hypocrites! You clean the outside of the cup and dish, but inside they are full of greed and self-indulgence. (Mat 23:25)

In the same way, on the outside you appear to people as righteous but on the inside you are full of hypocrisy and wickedness. (Mat 23:28)

4 (15:30) **Self-righteousness—Compassion, Lack of—Hardness—Pride**: the fourth fault of the religionist is his tragic lack of compassion and the understanding of God's spiritual feast. Note three things about the older son.

1. He did not call the prodigal son his brother. He said with arrogance, "this son of yours." He felt *above* and *better* than the prodigal son, despite the change of heart

and life that existed within the repentant son. He felt no compassion or joy whatsoever. But note something: his statement was true. The repentant son was *God's true son.*

2. He focused on the prodigal's faults, especially his immoral past. He ignored the prodigal son's repentance, his return home, and the glorious reunion. He ignored God's...

- great love
- great forgiveness
- great joy

3. He did not understand God's spiritual feast. The fatted calf would symbolize the spiritual food God gives to the repentant sinner.

a. There was the food of absolute assurance of salvation and eternal life.

For you did not receive a spirit that makes you a slave again to fear, but you received the Spirit of sonship. And by him we cry, "Abba, Father." The Spirit himself testifies with our spirit that we are God's children. Now if we are children, then we are heirs—heirs of God and co-heirs with Christ, if indeed we share in his sufferings in order that we may also share in his glory. (Rom 8:15-17)

But when the time had fully come, God sent his Son, born of a woman, born under law, to redeem those under law, that we might receive the full rights of sons. Because you are sons, God sent the Spirit of his Son into our hearts, the Spirit who calls out, "Abba, Father." (Gal 4:4-6)

b. There was the food of love, joy, and peace.

But the fruit of the Spirit is love, joy, peace, patience, kindness, goodness, faithfulness, gentleness and self-control. Against such things there is no law. (Gal 5:22-23)

"Not everyone who says to me, 'Lord, Lord,' will enter the kingdom of heaven, but only he who does the will of my Father who is in heaven. (Mat 7:21)

Dear children, let us not love with words or tongue but with actions and in truth. (1 John 3:18)

And this is his command: to believe in the name of his Son, Jesus Christ, and to love one another as he commanded us. (1 John 3:23)

5 (15:31-32) **Religionists—Blindness—Unbelief—Rejection**: the fifth fault of the religionist is his tragic blindness. He fails to see two critical facts.

1. The religionist has the same privileges as the repentant prodigal. Note the words, "Everything I have is yours." He has the worship, the Word, the promises, the preaching, and the teaching. He has constant exposure to all that is God's (see outline and notes—Ro.9:4-5 for more discussion). He can enter God's "house of salvation" anytime. All he has to do is repent, turn from trusting the field of religion, and enter God's house. He simply needs to believe in and trust the love of God. He is to stop opposing God's love to the prodigal sinner and come in himself.

2. The salvation of the repentant prodigal was real.

⇒ This brother of yours was dead, but he is now alive.

"I tell you the truth, whoever hears my word and believes him who sent me has eternal life and will not be condemned; he has crossed over from death to life. (John 5:24)

As for you, you were dead in your transgressions and sins, (Eph 2:1)

For you have been born again, not of perishable seed, but of imperishable, through the living and enduring word of God. (1 Pet 1:23)

"For God so loved the world that he gave his one and only Son, that whoever believes in him shall not perish but have eternal life. (John 3:16)

⇒ This brother of yours was lost, but now he is found.

We all, like sheep, have gone astray, each of us has turned to his own way; and the LORD has laid on him the iniquity of us all. (Isa 53:6)

And goes home. Then he calls his friends and neighbors together and says, 'Rejoice with me; I have found my lost sheep.' And when she finds it, she calls her friends and neighbors together and says, 'Rejoice with me; I have found my lost coin.' (Luke 15:6, 9)

For the Son of Man came to seek and to save what was lost." (Luke 19:10)

He himself bore our sins in his body on the tree, so that we might die to sins and live for righteousness; by his wounds you have been healed. For you were like sheep going astray, but now you have returned to the Shepherd and Overseer of your souls. (1 Pet 2:24-25)

1 The unjust manager
- a. He was charged with embezzlement, with wasting the Lord's possessions.
- b. He was required to prepare a final accounting
- c. He knew he was guilty and was unwilling to change and cry for mercy
- d. He decided what to do: He would forget the Lord and court the favor and rewards of men[DSI]

CHAPTER 16

K. The Parable of the Unjust Manager: Man and Money, 16:1-13

Jesus told his disciples: "There was a rich man whose manager was accused of wasting his possessions.
2 So he called him in and asked him, 'What is this I hear about you? Give an account of your management, because you cannot be manager any longer.'
3 "The manager said to himself, 'What shall I do now? My master is taking away my job. I'm not strong enough to dig, and I'm ashamed to beg—
4 I know what I'll do so that, when I lose my job here, people will welcome me into their houses.'
5 "So he called in each one of his master's debtors. He asked the first, 'How much do you owe my master?'
6 "'Eight hundred gallons of olive oil,' he replied. "The manager told him, 'Take your bill, sit down quickly, and make it four hundred.'
7 "Then he asked the second, "'A thousand bushels of wheat,' he replied. "He told him, 'Take your bill and make it eight hundred.'
8 "The master commended the dishonest manager because he had acted shrewdly. For the people of this world are more shrewd in dealing with their own kind than are the people of the light.
9 I tell you, use worldly wealth to gain friends for yourselves, so that when it is gone, you will be welcomed into eternal dwellings.
10 "Whoever can be trusted with very little can also be trusted with much, and whoever is dishonest with very little will also be dishonest with much.
11 So if you have not been trustworthy in handling worldly wealth, who will trust you with true riches?
12 And if you have not been trustworthy with someone else's property, who will give you property of your own?
13 "No servant can serve two masters. Either he will hate the one and love the other, or he will be devoted to the one and despise the other. You cannot serve both God and Money."

2 The worldly are more wise in their material pursuits than God's people are in their spiritual pursuits

3 The Christian is to use material wealth for good
- a. Wealth will fail—at death
- b. Giving will be reciprocated

4 The Christian is to be faithful in handling possessions: Will determine what he will be trusted with eternally
- a. Money is the least trust
- b. Unfaithfulness disqualifies one from true, heavenly riches
- c. Unfaithfulness disqualifies one from all he would receive

5 The Christian cannot serve two masters: Must choose God or riches

DIVISION VI

THE SON OF MAN'S GREAT JOURNEY TO JERUSALEM (STAGE II): HIS TEACHING AND PUBLIC CONFLICT, 13:22-17:10

K. The Parable of the Unjust Manager: Man and Money, 16:1-13

(16:1-13) **Introduction—Unjust Manager**: this passage is looked upon as one of the most difficult passages in all of Scripture to understand. Verse eight is the primary reason. In studying the passage, two overall approaches can be taken. A person can read the parable and the comments about the parable made by Christ and take it only for what it says, that is, without adding any comment or seeing any application in it. However, a person can also see application in the parable as well as in the points taught by Christ. To help those interested in the latter approach, some application is given to the points of the parable.

The manager was a trusted slave who was put in charge of the landowner's estate. He was highly regarded and esteemed, considered to be completely trustworthy. The term "*manager*" is applied to ministers (1 Cor.4:1) and to believers in general (1 Pt.4:10; Lk.16:1). (See note, pt.2—Lk.12:41-48.)

1. The unjust manager (v.1-7).
2. The worldly are more wise in their material pursuits than God's people are in their spiritual pursuits (v.8).
3. The Christian is to use material wealth for good (v.9).
4. The Christian is to be faithful in handling possessions: how he handles his possessions will determine what he will be trusted with eternally (v.10-12).
5. The Christian cannot serve two masters: he must choose God or riches (v.13).

1 (16:1-7) **Parable, Unjust Manager**: in the parable itself Jesus said four things about the unjust manager.

1. The manager was charged with embezzlement, with *wasting the Lord's "possessions."* The manager was in charge of the Lord's property, of all the Lord's possession. Therefore, it was easy for him to use the possessions for his own purposes just as he desired. The point is, God has given every man some "possessions": life, talents, house, property, money, duty, a sense of responsibility, conscience, family, and a host of other possessions. Every man is charged with embezzlement, with misusing the possessions to some degree.

> **"Again, it will be like a man going on a journey, who called his servants and en-**

trusted his property to them. To one he gave five talents of money, to another two talents, and to another one talent, each according to his ability. Then he went on his journey. (Mat 25:14-15, cp. Rom.12:6-8; 1 Cor 12:7f)

So he called ten of his servants and gave them ten minas. 'Put this money to work,' he said, 'until I come back.' (Luke 19:13)

Now it is required that those who have been given a trust must prove faithful. (1 Cor 4:2)

Each one should use whatever gift he has received to serve others, faithfully administering God's grace in its various forms. (1 Pet 4:10)

2. The manager was required to prepare a final accounting. Two facts are important in this point.

a. The Lord hears that the manager has been misusing His "possessions." Note: the Lord had only *heard* about the embezzlement. The full evidence against the manager was not yet fully known. The Lord gave the manager a chance to prove his trust and faithfulness. The accounting did not mean that the manager would be dismissed from the Lord's estate (eaven, Kingdom of God), only that he must prove his trust and faithfulness. Of course, if the manager had not been faithful in looking after the Lord's possessions, then he would be dismissed: "You cannot be manager any longer."

b. The final accounting is at death (Heb.9:27). If the manager is found to have been untrustworthy, he will be *dismissed and discharged* from the Lord's estate (kingdom, heaven, eternal life. See DEEPER STUDY # 3—Mt.19:23-24.)

Thought 1. Death will take us away from all our earthly possessions. If our accounting justifies us, then we shall be given a much greater responsibility, an eternal responsibility, for the Lord.

"Therefore, the kingdom of heaven is like a king who wanted to settle accounts with his servants. (Mat 18:23)

When the harvest time approached, he sent his servants to the tenants to collect his fruit. (Mat 21:34)

"After a long time the master of those servants returned and settled accounts with them. (Mat 25:19)

"He was made king, however, and returned home. Then he sent for the servants to whom he had given the money, in order to find out what they had gained with it. (Luke 19:15)

So then, each of us will give an account of himself to God. (Rom 14:12)

Just as man is destined to die once, and after that to face judgment, (Heb 9:27)

They think it strange that you do not plunge with them into the same flood of dissipation, and they heap abuse on you. (1 Pet 4:4)

3. The manager knew he was guilty and was unwilling to change or ask for mercy. Note two things.

a. The words "What shall I do...?" The manager knew he was guilty and that the Lord was going to dismiss him.

b. The manager thought over what he should do. He reasoned out two courses of action.

⇒ He could dig. However, he was not willing to dig, not willing to be demoted to a field laborer and to serve in such a low capacity.

⇒ He could beg. However, he was *too proud* to leave the Lord and openly beg. He would be ashamed.

Now note something not mentioned. He was too proud to beg forgiveness of the Lord, too proud to be known as a repentant embezzler (sinner). This is the dominant point, although not mentioned. Begging for forgiveness was the manager's only hope. He considered every course of action but this one.

He who conceals his sins does not prosper, but whoever confesses and renounces them finds mercy. (Prov 28:13)

Woe to those who go to great depths to hide their plans from the LORD, who do their work in darkness and think, "Who sees us? Who will know?" (Isa 29:15)

"Woe to the obstinate children," declares the LORD, "to those who carry out plans that are not mine, forming an alliance, but not by my Spirit, heaping sin upon sin; (Isa 30:1)

4. The manager decided what to do: he would forget the Lord and court the favor and returns of men. He did what he could to secure the acceptance and favor of men.

a. He led them to be dishonest, to dismiss and lower their debts to the Lord. They were led to *embezzle and hold back* some of their possessions. Note: the manager was in a responsible position (a religionist) and misled others.

Thought 1. How many religionists mislead others through false teaching, causing so many not to use their lives and gifts for God.

b. This act *stole* from the Lord; it stole the possessions (life and gifts) of others from the Lord.

c. The manager misled others to benefit himself, to secure his position and livelihood. And he did it in a most shrewd way, a way that was pleasing and profitable to the debtors. Anyone of them would gladly help the manager when he needed their support. (See DEEPER STUDY # 1—Lk.16:6-7.)

But you have turned from the way and by your teaching have caused many to stumble; you have violated the covenant with Levi," says the LORD Almighty. (Mal 2:8)

Therefore let us stop passing judgment on one another. Instead, make up your mind not to put any stumbling block or obstacle in your brother's way. (Rom 14:13)

DEEPER STUDY # 1

(16:6-7) **Measure—Oil—Wealth**: Eight hundred gallons of oil. Therefore, the payment was a sizeable 800 gallons. The measure of wheat (koros) was about 10 bushels. This too was sizeable, about 1,000 bushels.

2 (16:8) **Dedication—Worldly—Materialism**: the worldly are more wise in their material pursuits than God's people are in their spiritual pursuits. Note two points.

1. Jesus said the unjust manager acted "shrewdly."
   ⇒ He looked out for himself, his personal welfare. In this he was very wise.
   ⇒ He was dedicated and sold out to taking care of his future.

Jesus was not commending the manager for his cunning deceit. He commended him for his concern about the future and his dedication and energy. The manager was *sold out* to pursuing a goal, and that part of his life was commendable. His mistake was being sold out to pursuing material wealth and comfort instead of Christ.

2. Jesus said the worldly are more shrewd in dealing with the world and its wealth" than believers. Why? Because they dedicate so much energy and effort to caring for their earthly welfare.

The point is clear. Every disciple should be just as dedicated and sold out in spiritual pursuits as the worldly are in their material pursuits. The disciple is not to be outdone in the exertion of energy and dedication.

Thought 1. Note how much more initiative and energy this man of the world exerted in his pursuits than many Christians exert in theirs.

But the one who received the seed that fell on good soil is the man who hears the word and understands it. He produces a crop, yielding a hundred, sixty or thirty times what was sown." (Mat 13:23)

Then he said to them all: "If anyone would come after me, he must deny himself and take up his cross daily and follow me. For whoever wants to save his life will lose it, but whoever loses his life for me will save it. (Luke 9:23-24)

Therefore, I urge you, brothers, in view of God's mercy, to offer your bodies as living sacrifices, holy and pleasing to God—this is your spiritual act of worship. (Rom 12:1)

Trust in the LORD with all your heart and lean not on your own understanding; (Prov 3:5)

My son, give me your heart and let your eyes keep to my ways, (Prov 23:26)

3 (16:9) **Managership—Wealth—Riches—Materialism**: the Christian is to use material wealth for good. The Christian is not being told to seek the friendship of the wealthy; he is being told to use his wealth to help others. By so helping, the disciple will gain friends and influence them for Christ. Then when the disciple finds himself without resources in this life, he will more likely be helped by those whom he helped.

But seek first his kingdom and his righteousness, and all these things will be given to you as well. (Mat 6:33)

"I tell you the truth," Jesus said to them, "no one who has left home or wife or brothers or parents or children for the sake of the kingdom of God will fail to receive many times as much in this age and, in the age to come, eternal life." (Luke 18:29-30)

Worship the LORD your God, and his blessing will be on your food and water. I will take away sickness from among you, (Exo 23:25)

Bring the whole tithe into the storehouse, that there may be food in my house. Test me in this," says the LORD Almighty, "and see if I will not throw open the floodgates of heaven and pour out so much blessing that you will not have room enough for it. (Mal 3:10)

Note another significant point: if the Christian is not helped in this life, then at death he will certainly be welcomed abundantly into heaven. His compassionate initiative in helping others will assure God's approval. (See note—Jas.1:10-11 for more discussion.)

But store up for yourselves treasures in heaven, where moth and rust do not destroy, and where thieves do not break in and steal. (Mat 6:20)

Jesus answered, "If you want to be perfect, go, sell your possessions and give to the poor, and you will have treasure in heaven. Then come, follow me." (Mat 19:21)

Sell your possessions and give to the poor. Provide purses for yourselves that will not wear out, a treasure in heaven that will not be exhausted, where no thief comes near and no moth destroys. (Luke 12:33)

In the same way, any of you who does not give up everything he has cannot be my disciple. (Luke 14:33)

Now we know that if the earthly tent we live in is destroyed, we have a building from God, an eternal house in heaven, not built by human hands. (2 Cor 5:1)

What is more, I consider everything a loss compared to the surpassing greatness of knowing Christ Jesus my Lord, for whose sake I have lost all things. I consider them rubbish, that I may gain Christ (Phil 3:8)

In this way they will lay up treasure for themselves as a firm foundation for the coming age, so that they may take hold of the life that is truly life. (1 Tim 6:19)

Therefore, my brothers, be all the more eager to make your calling and election sure. For if you do these things, you will never fall, and you will receive a rich welcome into the eternal kingdom of our Lord and Savior Jesus Christ. (2 Pet 1:10-11)

I counsel you to buy from me gold refined in the fire, so you can become rich; and white clothes to wear, so you can cover your shameful nakedness; and salve to put on your eyes, so you can see. (Rev 3:18)

4 (16:10-12) **Rewards**: the Christian is to be faithful in handling possessions, for his faithfulness determines what he will be trusted with eternally.

1. Money and possessions are the least trust given a person (v.10). They are nothing compared to eternal salvation and to love, joy, peace, and the absolute assurance and confidence of life eternal. They are nothing compared to the presence and companionship, the power and leadership of the Holy Spirit. They are nothing compared to possessing the Word of God and the promises of God. They are nothing compared to knowing God personally and to being made an heir of God and a joint heir with Christ.

2. Unfaithfulness in the use of money and possessions disqualifies a person from true, heavenly riches. A person may think his life and possessions are his own to do with as he wills, but they are not. His life and possessions are God's. God has trusted the person with life and possessions only as long as he is on this earth. The holder is only a manager of all he is and has. He cannot take his life or possessions with him out of this world when he dies. He has both life and possessions only temporarily—as a trust. If he handles his life and possessions badly, he shows he is not fit to be trusted with responsibility in the new heavens and earth.

Scripture says that the *true heavenly riches* and rewards are beyond comprehension:

Rewards Dealing with our Nature or State of Being

⇒ Being adopted as a son of God (Gal.4:4-7; 1 Jn.3:1).
⇒ Being made blameless and harmless (Ph.2:15).
⇒ Being given eternal life (Jn.3:16; 1 Tim.6:19).
⇒ Being given better and lasting possessions (Heb.10:34).
⇒ Being given a glorious body (Ph.3:11, 21; 1 Cor.15:42-44).
⇒ Being given eternal glory and honor and peace (Ro.2:10).
⇒ Being given eternal rest and peace (Heb.4:9; Rev.14:13).
⇒ Being given the blessings of the Lord (Pr.10:22).
⇒ Being given the knowledge of Christ Jesus (Ph.3:8).
⇒ Being given enduring wealth and prosperity(Pr.8:18).
⇒ Being made priests (Rev.20:6).
⇒ Being given a crown of that will last forever (1 Cor.9:25).
⇒ Being given the crown of righteousness (2 Tim.4:8).
⇒ Being given the crown of life (Jas.1:12).
⇒ Being given the crown of glory (1 Pt.5:4).

Rewards Dealing with Work or Position or Rule

⇒ Being made exalted beings (Rev.7:9-12).
⇒ Being put in charge of many things (Mt.25:23).
⇒ Being given the Kingdom of God (Jas.2:5; Mt.25:34).
⇒ Being given a position or rule and authority (Lk.12:42-44; Lk.22:28-29; 1 Cor.6:2-3).
⇒ Being given eternal responsibility and joy (Mt.25:21, 23).
⇒ Being given rule and authority over cities (Lk.19:17, 19).
⇒ Being given thrones and the privilege of reigning forever (Rev.20:4; 22:5).
⇒ Being given the privilege of surrounding the throne of God (Rev.7:9-13; 20:4).
⇒ Being made priests (Rev.20:6).
⇒ Being made kings (Rev.1:5; 5:10).

Rewards Dealing with our Inheritance or Wealth

⇒ Being made an heir of God (Ro.8:16-17; Tit.3:7).
⇒ Being given an inheritance that can never perish, spoil or fade inheritance (1 Pt.1:3-4).
⇒ Being given the blessings of the Lord (Pr.10:22).
⇒ Being given enduring wealth and prosperity (Pr.8:18).
⇒ Being given unsearchable riches (Eph.3:8).
⇒ Being given treasures in heaven (Mt.19:21; Lk.12:33).

3. Unfaithfulness disqualifies a person from all he would receive. The other man in verse 12 refers to God. Our lives and possessions are His. If we are not faithful in using them, how can we expect to be compensated? Note a person never has all he would have if he fails to pursue God and to give others what is due them. (Cp. Mt.19:29; Mk.10:29-30; Lk.18:30.)

> **Well then, you should have put my money on deposit with the bankers, so that when I returned I would have received it back with interest. "'Take the talent from him and give it to the one who has the ten talents. For everyone who has will be given more, and he will have an abundance. Whoever does not have, even what he has will be taken from him. (Mat 25:27-29)**
>
> **What good is it for a man to gain the whole world, yet forfeit his soul? (Mark 8:36)**
>
> **his work will be shown for what it is, because the Day will bring it to light. It will be revealed with fire, and the fire will test the quality of each man's work. If what he has built survives, he will receive his reward. If it is burned up, he will suffer loss; he himself will be saved, but only as one escaping through the flames. (1 Cor 3:13-15)**
>
> **Your wrongdoings have kept these away; your sins have deprived you of good. (Jer 5:25)**

5 (16:13) **Decision—Spiritual Struggle**: the Christian cannot serve two masters; he must choose God or money. Note three significant points.

1. There are two masters in life, either God or the things and money of this world.

2. A person serves one of the two masters. He gives himself either to one or the other...

- He focuses himself upon the things and money of the world or upon God.
- He turns himself over to the things and money of the world or to God.
- He thinks primarily upon the things of the world or upon God.
- He gives his time, energy, and effort to the things of the world or to God.
- He allows his worldly pursuits to control Christ, or Christ to control his pursuits.

3. A person struggles against God or else struggles against the things and money of the world. No man can serve both God and money.

⇒ He hates the one and loves the other.
⇒ He holds to one and despises the other.

Jesus said to him, "Away from me, Satan! For it is written: 'Worship the Lord your God, and serve him only.'" (Mat 4:10)

Jesus looked at him and loved him. "One thing you lack," he said. "Go, sell everything you have and give to the poor, and you will have treasure in heaven. Then come, follow me." (Mark 10:21)

You cannot drink the cup of the Lord and the cup of demons too; you cannot have a part in both the Lord's table and the table of demons. (1 Cor 10:21)

He chose to give us birth through the word of truth, that we might be a kind of firstfruits of all he created. (James 1:18)

Come near to God and he will come near to you. Wash your hands, you sinners, and purify your hearts, you double-minded. (James 4:8)

See, I set before you today life and prosperity, death and destruction. (Deu 30:15)

But if serving the LORD seems undesirable to you, then choose for yourselves this day whom you will serve, whether the gods your forefathers served beyond the River, or the gods of the Amorites, in whose land you are living. But as for me and my household, we will serve the LORD." (Josh 24:15)

Elijah went before the people and said, "How long will you waver between two opinions? If the LORD is God, follow him; but if Baal is God, follow him." But the people said nothing. (1 Ki 18:21)

Outline	Text	Text (cont.)	Outline (cont.)
	L. The Misunderstanding About Wealth and God's Kingdom, 16:14-18	were proclaimed until John. Since that time, the good news of the kingdom of God is being preached, and everyone is forcing his way into it.	**2 The misunderstanding of the new kindgom & world or social order** a. It is of God, not of earth b. It is for "everyone"
1 The misunderstanding of money & possessions a. Man tends to use his possessions to justify himself b. God knows the heart c. God detests men who center their esteem around money & possessions	14 The Pharisees, who loved money, heard all this and were sneering at Jesus. 15 He said to them, "You are the ones who justify yourselves in the eyes of men, but God knows your hearts. What is highly valued among men is detestable in God's sight. 16 "The Law and the Prophets	17 It is easier for heaven and earth to disappear than for the least stroke of a pen to drop out of the Law. 18 "Anyone who divorces his wife and marries another woman commits adultery, and the man who marries a divorced woman commits adultery.	**3 The misunderstanding of the law** a. It is not destroyed by the new kingdom b. Marriage is an example of the unfailing law in both kingdoms

DIVISION VI

THE SON OF MAN'S GREAT JOURNEY TO JERUSALEM (STAGE II): HIS TEACHING AND PUBLIC CONFLICT, 13:22-17:10

L. The Misunderstanding About Wealth and God's Kingdom, 16:14-18

(16:14-18) **Introduction**: three of the greatest misunderstandings among men are covered in this passage. This is a critical message. It needs to be heeded by men so they can correct their misunderstanding.

1. The misunderstanding of money and possessions (v.14-15).
2. The misunderstanding of the new kingdom and world or social order (v.16).
3. The misunderstanding of the law (v.17-18).

1 (16:14-15) **Money—Wealth—Materialism—Heart**: the misunderstanding of money and possessions. Jesus had just said: "No servant can serve two masters. Either he will hate the one and love the other, or he will be devoted to the one and despise the other. You cannot serve both God and money" (Lk.16:13).

The religionists and others standing before Jesus could not believe what they were hearing.

⇒ Jesus was saying that a man's energy and effort in seeking and looking after money was wrong, that a man could not seek money and at the same time keep his mind and thoughts upon God. It was impossible to concentrate on both. Jesus was demanding total allegiance, all of one's mind and thoughts, energy and effort. Those who heard Jesus knew exactly what He was saying.

⇒ Jesus was saying that a man must not give himself to seek the comfort and ease and pleasures and possessions of the world.

⇒ Jesus was going against the philosophy of the world, a philosophy that had even permeated religious circles: that money and possessions are a sign of the blessings of God.

What Jesus was teaching bothered men, in particular the religionists. The reason has to do with the nature of man. By nature, men want money and possessions, comfort and ease, acceptance and recognition; and at the same time, they want to be known as *close to God*. A man wants to fit in and be acceptable to the world and, at the same time, to feel acceptable to God. Therefore, a man becomes disturbed, sometimes extremely disturbed, when he is told...

⇒ that he cannot give his mind and thought, energy and effort to both God and money (the possessions of the world).

⇒ that he cannot serve both God and money at the same time.

⇒ that God demands a person's total allegiance, all of a person's mind and thoughts, energy and effort.

Note four things.

1. Men can be both religious and greedy; in fact, the most covetous men are sometimes the most religious. These men who were ridiculing Jesus were Pharisees, probably the most religious sect who had ever lived, yet they were said to be greedy. They wanted things of the world and the things of God at the same time.

> **"No one can serve two masters. Either he will hate the one and love the other, or he will be devoted to the one and despise the other. You cannot serve both God and Money. (Mat 6:24)**
>
> **For, as I have often told you before and now say again even with tears, many live as enemies of the cross of Christ. Their destiny is destruction, their god is their stomach, and their glory is in their shame. Their mind is on earthly things. (Phil 3:18-19)**
>
> **For the love of money is a root of all kinds of evil. Some people, eager for money, have wandered from the faith and pierced themselves with many griefs. (1 Tim 6:10)**

2. Jesus said that men tend to use their money to justify themselves before other men.

a. They use their money to court the favor and honor of men and women. Even if they secured their money unjustly, they compensate for it by being generous, by entertaining, or by giving to some worthy need or project. And unfortunately, men and women alike give in to and go along with the wealthy.

b. Some rich persons are conscious of their need for a right relationship with God and of their obligation to help people. Therefore, they live strict religious lives and use some of their money to court the favor and honor of people through religious causes. The world, including the religious world, honors such benevolent giving by the wealthy.

He replied, "Isaiah was right when he prophesied about you hypocrites; as it is written: "'These people honor me with their lips, but their hearts are far from me. (Mark 7:6)

We do not dare to classify or compare ourselves with some who commend themselves. When they measure themselves by themselves and compare themselves with themselves, they are not wise. (2 Cor 10:12)

They claim to know God, but by their actions they deny him. They are detestable, disobedient and unfit for doing anything good. (Titus 1:16)

Dear children, let us not love with words or tongue but with actions and in truth. (1 John 3:18)

Many a man claims to have unfailing love, but a faithful man who can find? (Prov 20:6)

Those who are pure in their own eyes and yet are not cleansed of their filth; (Prov 30:12)

3. Jesus said, "But God knows your hearts." What did He mean?

a. A man is acceptable to God because his heart is right before God, not because he has a lot of money. Money does not mean that a man is greatly blessed by God. God's blessings are not in material things.
   ⇒ Some people are wealthy, yet they are as ungodly and dirty as they can be.
   ⇒ Some people are poor, yet they are very godly, having little money and few things of the world.
   ⇒ Some people have some money and possessions, yet they are very godly.

   The point is this: the heart is that which *makes* a man acceptable to God, not money. Money does not mean that a man is blessed by God. It is the heart of a man that shows the blessings of God. God's blessings are not material things, they are spiritual things (see notes—Mt.19:25; Eph.1:3).

Then Jesus said to his disciples, "I tell you the truth, it is hard for a rich man to enter the kingdom of heaven. Again I tell you, it is easier for a camel to go through the eye of a needle than for a rich man to enter the kingdom of God." When the disciples heard this, they were greatly astonished and asked, "Who then can be saved?" (Mat 19:23-25)

Praise be to the God and Father of our Lord Jesus Christ, who has blessed us in the heavenly realms with every spiritual blessing in Christ. (Eph 1:3)

b. Note another important fact. When Jesus said that a man cannot serve both God and money, He did not mean that a man's mind and thought could not be put upon his profession and work.

Finally, brothers, whatever is true, whatever is noble, whatever is right, whatever is pure, whatever is lovely, whatever is admirable—if anything is excellent or praiseworthy—think about such things. (Phil 4:8)

We demolish arguments and every pretension that sets itself up against the knowledge of God, and we take captive every thought to make it obedient to Christ. (2 Cor 10:5)

The Scripture is very clear about this. A person's profession and the beneficial activities of life are included in the things of God. The legitimate things of life are true and honest. Therefore, a man is to live and work well. Living and working well are a great testimony to God's name; therefore, a genuine believer should be the very best at living and working, demonstrating that God's people are the most true and honest, pure and lovely people on earth.

c. When dealing with the money and possessions of the world, we are to provide adequately for our families. But after adequate provision, the question arises, what are we to do? God is clear in His instructions: we are to work in order to have enough to help the needy. We are to help meet the needs of a desperate world.

Jesus answered, "If you want to be perfect, go, sell your possessions and give to the poor, and you will have treasure in heaven. Then come, follow me." (Mat 19:21)

He who has been stealing must steal no longer, but must work, doing something useful with his own hands, that he may have something to share with those in need. (Eph 4:28)

4. God detests the esteem of men being centered around money and things. God wants men to center their lives and esteem around the things of the heart, not around the things they possess. Material possessions pass away; spiritual possessions endure forever (see note—Eph.1:3. See outlines and notes—Mt.19:16-22; 19:23-26; 19:27-30 for more discussion on Christ's teaching concerning money and wealth.)

But store up for yourselves treasures in heaven, where moth and rust do not destroy, and where thieves do not break in and steal. (Mat 6:20)

Sell your possessions and give to the poor. Provide purses for yourselves that will not wear out, a treasure in heaven that will not be exhausted, where no thief comes near and no moth destroys. (Luke 12:33)

2 (16:16) **Kingdom of God—Wealth—New Order—Old and New Testaments**: the misunderstanding of the new kingdom and order. Note three things.

1. Jesus sees the *period of Israel* (the law and the prophets) lasting up to and including the ministry of John the Baptist. As God's Messiah He ushered in a *new period and social order*, that is, the Kingdom of God. The Kingdom of God is presently a spiritual kingdom that occurs within a man and takes effect in the acts and behavior of men. Since Jesus has come, every man is to let God rule and reign in his heart and life (see DEEPER STUDY # 3—Mt.19:23-24 for more discussion).

2. The kingdom is now preached, a message which does not value what a man has, but what a man is—what he is within his heart. The message now centers upon the individual and his eternal potential in God, not upon material and temporal blessings. (See DEEPER STUDY # 3—Mt.19:23-24; note—Eph.1:3.)

> **Once, having been asked by the Pharisees when the kingdom of God would come, Jesus replied, "The kingdom of God does not come with your careful observation, nor will people say, 'Here it is,' or 'There it is,' because the kingdom of God is within you." (Luke 17:20-21)**
>
> **"The time has come," he said. "The kingdom of God is near. Repent and believe the good news!" (Mark 1:15)**
>
> **Looking at his disciples, he said: "Blessed are you who are poor, for yours is the kingdom of God. (Luke 6:20)**
>
> **For the kingdom of God is not a matter of eating and drinking, but of righteousness, peace and joy in the Holy Spirit, (Rom 14:17)**

3. Everyone tries to force his way into the kingdom. The Kingdom of God is not for any single race; the kingdom is for all people everywhere. When people hear the glorious message of the kingdom, they press and struggle to get into it. They no longer want a cheap, formal religion and an easy message. They cannot be content with such, not when they *really get a glimpse* of the Kingdom of God. Once they have seen the glory and value of God's kingdom, they press and struggle to enter, no matter the odds.

> **Blessed are those who hunger and thirst for righteousness, for they will be filled. (Mat 5:6)**
>
> **But I, when I am lifted up from the earth, will draw all men to myself." (John 12:32)**
>
> **Now the Bereans were of more noble character than the Thessalonians, for they received the message with great eagerness and examined the Scriptures every day to see if what Paul said was true. (Acts 17:11)**
>
> **Sow for yourselves righteousness, reap the fruit of unfailing love, and break up your unplowed ground; for it is time to seek the LORD, until he comes and showers righteousness on you. (Hosea 10:12)**
>
> **My soul yearns for you in the night; in the morning my spirit longs for you. When your judgments come upon the earth, the people of the world learn righteousness. (Isa 26:9)**

3 (16:17-18) **Old Testament—Law, The—Word of God Enslaves**: the misunderstanding of the law. In this point Jesus dealt with a very serious question—a question that bothers men. Is there a *higher law*, a law of God to which men are to subject their lives? Since Christ has come, since there is now a new order and a New Testament, what about the Old Testament, the law and the prophets? Is the Old Testament and its laws still to be used and followed by us? What is the place of the law? Is it erased? Does it have a place in God's new kingdom? Jesus said that there is a *higher law*, a law of God that is given in the Old Testament. It is not erased; it has a place in the new order. In fact, the Old Testament is fulfilled in the new kingdom, and it shall outlast heaven and earth. An example is the law governing marriage. It is the law for both social orders. It never changes. (See note—Mt.5:17-18; DEEPER STUDY # 2—Ro.8:3 for detailed discussion of Christ fulfilling the law; see DEEPER STUDY # 1—Mt.19:1-12 for detailed discussion of marriage.)

> **Thought 1.** There is a *higher law*, a law of God given by God in the Old Testament, that is, in the old dispensa-tion. It has been fulfilled in Christ; therefore, all men are to obey *the Law of God.* (Again, see note—Mt.5:17-18. This is an extremely important note to see how the Old Testament law was fulfilled in Christ.)

> **"Do not think that I have come to abolish the Law or the Prophets; I have not come to abolish them but to fulfill them. I tell you the truth, until heaven and earth disappear, not the smallest letter, not the least stroke of a pen, will by any means disappear from the Law until everything is accomplished. (Mat 5:17-18)**
>
> **Heaven and earth will pass away, but my words will never pass away. (Mat 24:35)**
>
> **But the word of the Lord stands forever." And this is the word that was preached to you. (1 Pet 1:25)**
>
> **Your word, O LORD, is eternal; it stands firm in the heavens. (Psa 119:89)**
>
> **Long ago I learned from your statutes that you established them to last forever. (Psa 119:152)**
>
> **The grass withers and the flowers fall, but the word of our God stands forever." (Isa 40:8)**

	M. The Rich Man and Lazarus: The Self-Indulgent vs. The Man of Faith, 16:19-31
1 A difference in life[DS1] a. Rich man nameless; Lazarus named b. Rich man wealthy; Lazarus poor c. Rich man healthy; Lazarus disabled d. Rich man lived in luxury and extravagance; Lazarus begged, being helpless	19 "There was a rich man who was dressed in purple and fine linen and lived in luxury every day. 20 At his gate was laid a beggar named Lazarus, covered with sores 21 And longing to eat what fell from the rich man's table. Even the dogs came and licked his sores.
2 A difference in death: Lazarus died & was escorted to Paradise; rich man died & was buried[DS2]	22 "The time came when the beggar died and the angels carried him to Abraham's side. The rich man also died and was buried.
3 A difference in eternity a. Rich man in hell;[DS3] Lazarus in Paradise b. Rich man *saw* glory; Lazarus was *in* glory c. Rich man was alone; Lazarus had fellowship d. Rich man had burning sensation; Lazarus had water e. Rich man tormented;[DS] Lazarus comforted	23 In hell, where he was in torment, he looked up and saw Abraham far away, with Lazarus by his side. 24 So he called to him, 'Father Abraham, have pity on me and send Lazarus to dip the tip of his finger in water and cool my tongue, because I am in agony in this fire.'
f. Rich man remembered his former life; Lazarus was silent	25 "But Abraham replied, 'Son, remember that in your lifetime you received your good things, while Lazarus received bad things, but now he is comforted here and you are in agony.
g. Rich man was fixed in hell; Lazarus was fixed in Paradise	26 And besides all this, between us and you a great chasm has been fixed, so that those who want to go from here to you cannot, nor can anyone cross over from there to us.'
h. Rich man agonized for loved ones; Lazarus was settled in eternity	27 "He answered, 'Then I beg you, father, send Lazarus to my father's house, 28 For I have five brothers. Let him warn them, so that they will not also come to this place of torment.' 29 "Abraham replied, 'They have Moses and the Prophets; let them listen to them.'
i. Rich man begged for another chance; Lazarus was silently at peace	30 "'No, father Abraham,' he said, 'but if someone from the dead goes to them, they will repent.'
j. Rich man was unable to intercede for his family; Lazarus was at rest in God's promises	31 "He said to him, 'If they do not listen to Moses and the Prophets, they will not be convinced even if someone rises from the dead.'"

DIVISION VI

THE SON OF MAN'S GREAT JOURNEY TO JERUSALEM (STAGE II): HIS TEACHING AND PUBLIC CONFLICT, 13:22-17:10

M. The Rich Man and Lazarus: The Self-Indulgent vs. the Man of Faith, 16:19-31

(16:19-31) **Introduction**: note two things. Jesus identified Lazarus; Lazarus was named. When giving a parable, Jesus never named a character—not even once. Also note: Jesus did not say that this was a parable. These two facts, plus the language used to begin the account, point to it as an actual experience. Of course, it must always be remembered that spiritual and eternal truths have to be described with human and earthly language. This does not in any way lessen the blessing nor the terror of the truth; contrariwise, the eternal truth is *much more blessed* and *much more terrifying* than any mere human description.

1. A difference in life (v.19-21).
2. A difference in death: Lazarus died and was escorted to paradise; the rich man died and was buried (v.22).
3. A difference in eternity (v.23-31).

1 (16:19-21) **Life—Christians**: there is a difference in life. The differences are fourfold.

1. There was one main difference between Lazarus and the rich man: the rich man was nameless, but Lazarus was named. The difference is ever so important. It is the difference between being known and honored by God and not being known or honored by God. The rich man did not know God; therefore, he was unknown to God and God was not able to honor him. He was nameless to God. Lazarus knew God and was known by God. His very name, Lazarus, means *God is my Help or Helper.* He trusted God to look after him, and his eyes were upon heaven and the blessings of heaven, not upon the earth. The Latin word for "rich" is Dives. This is the reason the rich man is often called *Dives*. However, we must always remember it was not his name; he was a nameless man to God.

> **"I am the good shepherd; I know my sheep and my sheep know me— (John 10:14; cp. Jn.10:27)**
>
> **But the man who loves God is known by God. (1 Cor 8:3)**
>
> **Now we see but a poor reflection as in a mirror; then we shall see face to face. Now I know in part; then I shall know fully, even as I am fully known. (1 Cor 13:12)**
>
> **Formerly, when you did not know God, you were slaves to those who by nature are not gods. But now that you know God—or rather are known by God—how is it that you are turning back to those weak and miserable principles? Do you wish to be enslaved by them all over again? (Gal 4:8-9)**

2. The rich man was wealthy; Lazarus was poor. (See DEEPER STUDY # 1, Sin—Lk.16:19-21 for discussion.)

3. The rich man was healthy; Lazarus was disabled. Lazarus was full of ulcerated sores, unable to work and

earn a living. He was either carried to the rich man's gate or else barely able to walk to the gate. He was what is called a *street person*—not by choice, but by being handicapped and without a family or friends who loved enough to care for him. How tragic! What an indictment against *men*. Note the charge is against the rich man and not *society*. Society is only an *idea*; men are a reality. The term or *idea of society* allows some men, including some social workers, to escape responsibility and to build up good salaries, healthy standards of living, and personal wealth while the needful continue to suffer. Each man is personally responsible for the poor and needy of the earth. That is Christ's point. In this case the rich man was responsible for Lazarus.

4. The rich man lived in luxury and extravagance; Lazarus had to beg because he was helpless. The picture is that of Lazarus' lying at the rich man's gate (most people would not allow this). The rich man was too occupied with his own estate, interests and pleasures; he ignored Lazarus' lying at his gate. The rich man neither helped nor seemed to care. While Lazarus waited for the crumbs from the rich man's table, too weak to fight off the dogs from licking his sores, he found hope and peace in God. The wealthy used large pieces of bread to wipe their hands and then threw the large pieces away. It was this bread that Lazarus waited for.

DEEPER STUDY # 1

(16:19-21) **Sin**: the sin of the rich man would not be a sin in the eyes of most societies. There is no record of a vicious, glaring sin; no record of a vulgar, public sin. He was not cruel—he never ordered Lazarus from his gate nor refused Lazarus the crumbs from his table. He was not a tyrant; not an oppressor of the poor, not a monstrous member of society. Rather, he was socially responsible, an upright citizen, respected and well-liked. No earthly court would ever think of arresting or condemning him. In society's eyes he was honored and highly esteemed. People liked him and spoke well of him. What then was his sin?

1. The word "luxury" (lampros) means that he was flamboyant, displaying his wealth in materialistic ways.

2. The "gate" was a large gate indicating that his home was a large house or a mansion.

3. The purple and fine linen show that he had the latest styles and the ultimate in luxury.

4. The words "every day" show that he feasted every day. His sin was *self-indulgence*, *comfort*, *ease*, *luxury*, *extravagant living*. He sought the things and pleasures of this world. He was complacent, hoarding and allowing money to lie around making more and more for himself and his estate while needs lay all around him—right at his gate. He neglected and ignored others, most significantly, Lazarus. The needs of a degenerate world concerned him little, if at all. He wanted what others in the world had, plenty for themselves and more. The world acknowledged and honored those who had plenty, and he wanted such recognition and honor for himself. He wanted what others had and he wanted to keep up with them.

I was a stranger and you did not invite me in, I needed clothes and you did not clothe me, I was sick and in prison and you did not look after me.' (Mat 25:43)

If anyone has material possessions and sees his brother in need but has no pity on him, how can the love of God be in him? (1 John 3:17)

But the worries of this life, the deceitfulness of wealth and the desires for other things come in and choke the word, making it unfruitful. (Mark 4:19)

People who want to get rich fall into temptation and a trap and into many foolish and harmful desires that plunge men into ruin and destruction. (1 Tim 6:9)

And when you were eating and drinking, were you not just feasting for yourselves? (Zec 7:6)

If there is a poor man among your brothers in any of the towns of the land that the LORD your God is giving you, do not be hardhearted or tightfisted toward your poor brother. (Deu 15:7)

2 (16:22) **Death**: there was a difference in death. Lazarus died and was escorted to Paradise; the rich man died and was buried. Note the only words said about the rich man's death: "He also died and was buried." What a terrible and disappointing legacy for a man to leave behind. The rich man was probably buried in state in the finest clothes and within the very best grave and cemetary. He had a most impressive funeral—a funeral well attended by the upper social class of his community. The words spoken over him were probably words of praise, words that recognized his respectability and contribution to society in providing so much for his community and religion. An expensive monument was probably set over his grave. However, the *tragedy of tragedies* was his experience. He knew *nothing* about it. He was not there to enjoy it. He just died and was buried.

However, note what is said about Lazarus. He "died and the angels carried him to Abraham's side" (see DEEPER STUDY # 2, Abraham's Bosom—Lk.16:22) or Paradise. Three facts are important here.

1. Lazarus lived on despite his body's being dead. His being—his spirit and soul—did not die, nor cease to exist, nor fall into a state of sleep.

2. Lazarus' soul was immediately met by angels. Instantaneously—as quick as the blinking of an eye—when Lazarus died, the angels stood by his body and carried his soul into Paradise.

3. Lazarus was carried into the very place where the *Source* of all wealth is, where all who have trusted God are, the place where Abraham is: the Paradise of God Himself. (See DEEPER STUDY # 3, Paradise—Lk.16:23 for discussion.)

"For God so loved the world that he gave his one and only Son, that whoever believes in him shall not perish but have eternal life. (John 3:16)

Whoever believes in the Son has eternal life, but whoever rejects the Son will not see life, for God's wrath remains on him." (John 3:36)

"I tell you the truth, whoever hears my word and believes him who sent me has eternal life and will not be condemned; he has crossed over from death to life. (John 5:24)

For our light and momentary troubles are achieving for us an eternal glory that far outweighs them all. (2 Cor 4:17)

The one who sows to please his sinful nature, from that nature will reap destruc-

tion; the one who sows to please the Spirit, from the Spirit will reap eternal life. (Gal 6:8)

Therefore, my brothers, be all the more eager to make your calling and election sure. For if you do these things, you will never fall, and you will receive a rich welcome into the eternal kingdom of our Lord and Savior Jesus Christ. (2 Pet 1:10-11)

DEEPER STUDY # 2

(16:22) **Abraham's Side**: this refers to Paradise. It is a term that expressed the happiness that believers could expect upon death. It had the idea of sitting down and feasting with Abraham in Paradise. The side of Abraham was referred to because he was the father of the Jewish nation.

3 (16:23-31) **Eternal Life**: there was a difference in eternity. Ten facts are contrasted here.

1. The rich man was in hell; Lazarus was in Paradise (see DEEPER STUDY # 3, Hell—Lk.16:23).

a. Death snatched the rich man from his comfort and pleasures and from the material goods and wealth of this life. And he was immediately in hell, the place of misery and torment. (See DEEPER STUDY # 3, Hell—Lk.16:23.)

"Then they will go away to eternal punishment, but the righteous to eternal life." (Mat 25:46)

And the smoke of their torment rises for ever and ever. There is no rest day or night for those who worship the beast and his image, or for anyone who receives the mark of his name." (Rev 14:11)

b. The rich man was unfit for Paradise. Why? Because he had lived in a *worldly paradise* while others were hungry and starving, diseased and helpless, cold and unclothed, unsaved and dying. He had possessed the "good things" of life while others had nothing; and he had kept back, banked, and hoarded beyond what he really needed—all for the sake of recognition from people. Justice had to be executed. He was unfit to live in a paradise of justice and love. He deserved to be tormented and left without the "good things," for he had added to and refused to ease the torments of others while on earth.

If a man shuts his ears to the cry of the poor, he too will cry out and not be answered. (Prov 21:13)

2. The rich man only saw glory: Lazarus was sharing in and experiencing glory. Note three things.

a. The rich man was able to see Paradise, but it was far, far off and way out of reach.

b. The rich man was able to see into Paradise, able to see both Abraham and Lazarus there. He saw all the glory and comfort, perfection and joy of Paradise. He saw the man Lazarus whom he had neglected and treated so lowly. He saw Lazarus in all the glory and perfection of heaven, and he envied and regretted what he saw.

"There will be weeping there, and gnashing of teeth, when you see Abraham, Isaac and Jacob and all the prophets in the kingdom of God, but you yourselves thrown out. (Luke 13:28)

c. Note that Lazarus seemed to be totally unaware of hell. He lived only in Paradise, only in the glory and perfection of God.

For the perishable must clothe itself with the imperishable, and the mortal with immortality. (1 Cor 15:53)

3. The rich man was painfully alone; Lazarus had companionship. Nothing is said about another soul around the rich man. He stood all alone, talking to no one else in hell. He only saw those in Paradise. What a drastic difference from what is so often pictured and expressed by the lost of this world, thinking they will have plenty of company in hell. The true picture painted by Christ is that a person will be tormented with loneliness, that the person will...

- be all alone
- see no one
- sense no one
- be cut off from others
- be desolate
- be bleak

Lazarus had the company of Abraham and of the saints in glory. Christ had earlier taught the same point to the "evildoers":

"There will be weeping there, and gnashing of teeth, when you see Abraham, Isaac and Jacob and all the prophets in the kingdom of God, but you yourselves [workers of iniquity] thrown out. (Luke 13:28)

4. The rich man had a burning sensation; Lazarus had water. The contrast here is dramatic. The rich man was burning with such misery and pain from the "fire" (the wrath of God) that he begged for mercy: if he could not be freed from the flame and the misery, then he begged for just a drop of water to feel a momentary coolness. However, look at Lazarus. He had water; he had the coolness of whatever he needed to refresh his body.

...but he will burn up the chaff with unquenchable fire." (Luke 3:17)

Then the angel showed me the river of the water of life, as clear as crystal, flowing from the throne of God and of the Lamb (Rev 22:1)

5. The rich man was tormented; Lazarus was comforted (see DEEPER STUDY # 4, Hell—Lk.16:24).

But the subjects of the kingdom will be thrown outside, into the darkness, where there will be weeping and gnashing of teeth." (Mat 8:12)

They will throw them into the fiery furnace, where there will be weeping and gnashing of teeth. (Mat 13:42)

If anyone's name was not found written in the book of life, he was thrown into the lake of fire. (Rev 20:15)

6. The rich man remembered his former life; Lazarus was silent.

a. Note the word "your." It is emphatic. The rich man had what *he* chose to have when on earth. He had received *his* "good things" (what he considered "good") in *his* lifetime, and he *saw* to it that Lazarus had "bad things." Now note: he did not beat, injure, or persecute Lazarus; *but he did not help Lazarus either*. He could have helped, for he had an estate and a bank full of money; but he did not help. Therefore, he *kept* Lazarus down and destitute in this world. He saw to it that Lazarus had "bad things" when he could have seen to it that Lazarus was helped.

b. Lazarus was not responsible for the bad things that came upon him. Lazarus was *dished out* the bad things of this world by circumstances and by men like the rich man who neglected, ignored, and abused him.

c. The rich man remembered...
- his sins (comfort, ease, indulgence, pleasure, extravagance).
- his missed opportunities (to help Lazarus).
- his deaf ear to conscience, God, the Word, Lazarus, and all others who were so needy.
- his failure to seek the truth (Heb.11:6).
- his rejection of warning after warning.

7. The rich man was fixed in hell; Lazarus was fixed in Paradise. There was no passing from hell into Paradise or from Paradise into hell. There was a permanent gulf, and it was there for the *purpose* of keeping one from passing over. The sinner, who chooses to be cut off from God and Paradise, has his wish. He is cut off.

Let both grow together until the harvest. At that time I will tell the harvesters: First collect the weeds and tie them in bundles to be burned; then gather the wheat and bring it into my barn.'" (Mat 13:30)

This is how it will be at the end of the age. The angels will come and separate the wicked from the righteous (Mat 13:49)

"Then they will go away to eternal punishment, but the righteous to eternal life." (Mat 25:46)

8. The rich man agonized for loved ones; Lazarus was settled in eternity. The rich man had five brothers. He had set such a bad example for them they were also heading for hell. Note that the rich man was saying two things.

a. Hell is such a horrible place that it is not worth all the wealth and comfort and ease and pleasure of this world. Christ had said the same thing:

What good is it for a man to gain the whole world, yet forfeit his soul? (Mark 8:36)

b. Hell is such a horrible place that the world must be told to flee it. (Note that Christ is sharing how terrible hell is and how desperately we must seek to avoid it.)

The rich man was told that his brothers had the Scriptures, the Word of God, which explained and warned them of the future. They were to hear the Scripture, for the Scripture is a sufficient witness.

Lazarus was settled in eternity. He was a great contrast with the rich man's brothers. Why? Because he had believed the Scriptures, trusting God and His promises.

"I tell you the truth, whoever hears my word and believes him who sent me has eternal life and will not be condemned; he has crossed over from death to life. (John 5:24)

9. The rich man begged for another chance as Lazarus was silently at peace as the Scriptures promised. This is seen by looking behind the words of the rich man. If Abraham were to allow one to arise to tell the living, the rich man could then plead less opportunity. He, too, would be entitled to another chance, to a sensational and miraculous sign, or so he felt.

Note that Lazarus was at peace just as the Scriptures had promised. Lazarus had believed and was thereby saved.

10. The rich man was unable to intercede for his family; Lazarus rested in God's presence. Note the words, "They will not be convinced even if someone rises from the dead."

a. A Man, the Lord Jesus Christ, has risen from the dead, yet men do not believe. Man's unbelief is not due to lack of signs; it is due to their love for the world with all its creature comforts and recognition, indulgence and selfishness, pleasures and honors.

But because of your stubbornness and your unrepentant heart, you are storing up wrath against yourself for the day of God's wrath, when his righteous judgment will be revealed. (Rom 2:5)

b. The Scriptures and their testimony of the Lord's resurrection are much greater testimony than a dead man's standing before us in some *ghostly, mysterious form.*

You diligently study the Scriptures because you think that by them you possess eternal life. These are the Scriptures that testify about me, (John 5:39)

But also for us, to whom God will credit righteousness—for us who believe in him who raised Jesus our Lord from the dead. He was delivered over to death for our sins and was raised to life for our justification. (Rom 4:24-25)

DEEPER STUDY # 3

(16:23) **Paradise—Hell (Hades)**: the Greek word Hades is the same as the Hebrew word Sheol (see DEEPER STUDY # 3—Gen.37:35). The picture of Hades revealed by Jesus is that of the other world: the unseen world, the spiritual world, the spiritual dimension of being. Jesus says that Hades is a place which is divided into two huge areas or sections or compartments. The two areas are separated by a great gulf that is impassible (v.26). One area is the place of sorrow (v.23-24, 28). The other area is the place of Paradise where believers go. To say that a person is dead is to say that one is in hades, in the other world.

Note a critical fact: the other world, the spiritual world and the spiritual dimension of being, does exist. And there are two areas or two places in the other world: Paradise, the place of glory, and hell, the place of torment. Jesus said they both actually exist. (Cp. 22-23, see outline and notes—Lk.16:19-31; see DEEPER STUDY # 4—Lk.16:24; notes—Mt.27:52-53; Eph.4:8-10; DEEPER STUDY # 1—1 Pt.3:19-20.)

DEEPER STUDY # 4

(16:24) **Hell—Torment**: to be anguished, tortured, and greatly distressed; to suffer pain and sorrow. The Bible unquestionably teaches there is to be a torment for unbelievers in fire. However, it must be remembered that the fire we know is material and temporal; it is not spiritual or eternal. Earthly fire does not last forever. Nothing on earth does. Earthly fire is of the physical dimension of being. The fire of hell, whatever its nature and qualities, is spiritual and eternal. It never ends. And men must face this; they must not shrink from the truth of hell. Why? Because hell, that is, separation from God, is much worse than any experience here on earth. It will be much worse than any physical experience imaginable. This is the teaching of Scripture. This is the point Jesus was making. Man absolutely must flee from hell. Man absolutely must flee to Christ for salvation (see DEEPER STUDY # 2—Mt.5:22). (Cp. Mt.5:22, 29; 10:28; 18:9; 23:15, 33; 25:41; Mk.9:43-48; Lk.12:5; 16:23; 2 Th.1:8-9; 2 Pt.2:4; Rev.14:10-11; 16:10; 18:10; 19:20; 20:10-15; 21:8.)

	CHAPTER 17 **N. The Christian Disciple and Four Laws, 17:1-10** (cp. Mt.18:6, 15; 17:20)
1 Law 1: Leading another to sin brings judgment a. Sin is inevitable b. Leading others to sin is terrible c. Leading others to sin is condemned[DS1]	Jesus said to his disciples: "Things that cause people to sin are bound to come, but woe to that person through whom they come. 2 It would be better for him to be thrown into the sea with a millstone tied around his neck than for him to cause one of these little ones to sin.
2 Law 2: Forgiving others is essential a. If one sins, he is to be rebuked b. If one repents, he is to be forgiven c. How often: Time after time	3 So watch yourselves. "If your brother sins, rebuke him, and if he repents, for- give him. 4 If he sins against you seven times in a day, and seven times comes back to you and says, 'I repent,' forgive him." 5 The apostles said to the Lord, "Increase our faith!"
3 Law 3: Having faith is essential—one of most powerful forces in the world[DS2]	6 He replied, "If you have faith as small as a mustard seed, you can say to this mul- berry tree, 'Be uprooted and planted in the sea,' and it will obey you.
4 Law 4: Obeying God is a duty, not a service a. The illust.: A servant is a slave who serves his master 1) To serve all day 2) To serve all evening 3) To serve until all others have retired 4) To serve whether or not one is thanked or appreciated b. The believer is to serve & obey until all of God's commandments are done c. The believer is to be humble in his service for the Lord	7 "Suppose one of you had a servant plowing or looking after the sheep. Would he say to the servant when he comes in from the field, 'Come along now and sit down to eat'? 8 Would he not rather say, 'Prepare my supper, get yourself ready and wait on me while I eat and drink; af- ter that you may eat and drink'? 9 Would he thank the servant because he did what he was told to do? 10 So you also, when you have done everything you were told to do, should say, 'We are unworthy servants; we have only done our duty.'"

DIVISION VI

THE SON OF MAN'S GREAT JOURNEY TO JERUSALEM (STAGE II): HIS TEACHING AND PUBLIC CONFLICT, 13:22-17:10

N. The Christian Disciple and Four Laws, 17:1-10

(17:1-10) **Introduction**: there are four laws in this passage that could revolutionize society. They are to revolutionize the believer's life. The believers are to "watch themselves" and to pay attention to the laws (v.3).

1. Law 1: leading another into sin brings judgment (v.1-2).
2. Law 2: forgiving others is essential (v.3-4).
3. Law 3: having faith is essential: one of the most powerful forces in the world (v.5-6).
4. Law 4: obeying God is a duty, not a service (v.7-10).

1 (17:1-2) **Sin, Leading Others—Stumbling Blocks**: the first law is a severe warning: leading another person into sin brings heavy judgment. Note several facts.

1. The Lord was speaking to His disciples. The disciple had to guard against this grave sin. He was always subject to temptation, and if he yielded, he was going to mislead others. No sin will be condemned any more than the sin of misleading others into sin.

2. Sin is inevitable. Note the exact words of Jesus, "Things that cause people to sin are bound to come."

> **Thought 1.** Sin enters the world. Sin enters the business, the office, the marketplace, the play field, the club, even the home and the church. No place ever escapes sin, for no person is perfect. Wherever a person is, there is sin. No person is without sin.

3. Committing sin is a terrible thing, but leading others to sin is even more terrible. The phrase "cause...to sin" means to be a stumbling block; to bait, lure, and trip someone (see note, —Mt.17:27 for more discussion). Who are these, the ones who cause others to stumble? In one simple statement, it is anyone who *practices sin*, who *continues in sin*.

a. A stumbling block is anyone who *seduces others to sin*. Many persons seduce others into the sins…
- of grumbling, complaining, and criticizing
- of taking sides against others
- of being worldly and materialistic
- of craving more and more
- of being conceited and prideful
- of living loose and immoral lives
- of cursing and talking filthy

b. A stumbling block is anyone who *makes a false profession*, anyone who claims to be a follower of Christ, but who is not. The person who makes a false profession scandalizes the name of Christ. He is a hypocrite who causes others to stay away and to detest Christ and the church. False professors not only shut themselves out of the kingdom, but they lead their children into a false, hypocritical religion which shuts them out. The false professor causes others to say they want nothing to do with the church because it is full of hypocrites.

c. A stumbling block is anyone who *discourages a person* from following and serving Christ by…
- word or deed
- abuse or neglect
- persecution or injury
- gossip or slander
- anger or hostility

4. Leading others to sin is heavily condemned (see DEEPER STUDY # 1—Lk.17:2).

> **"And if anyone causes one of these little ones who believe in me to sin, it would be better for him to be thrown into the sea**

with a large millstone tied around his neck. (Mark 9:42)

Therefore let us stop passing judgment on one another. Instead, make up your mind not to put any stumbling block or obstacle in your brother's way. (Rom 14:13)

If your brother is distressed because of what you eat, you are no longer acting in love. Do not by your eating destroy your brother for whom Christ died. (Rom 14:15)

It is better not to eat meat or drink wine or to do anything else that will cause your brother to fall. (Rom 14:21)

Do not cause anyone to stumble, whether Jews, Greeks or the church of God— (1 Cor 10:32)

We put no stumbling block in anyone's path, so that our ministry will not be discredited. (2 Cor 6:3)

Whoever loves his brother lives in the light, and there is nothing in him to make him stumble. (1 John 2:10)

DEEPER STUDY # 1
(17:2) **Millstone** (monos onikos): the word *onos* is the word for a donkey. The word *mulos* is the word for the millstone that the donkey pulled around and around to grind the grain. Thus, the millstone Jesus spoke of is the huge millstone, not the small hand millstone used by the women to grind a little grain at a time. Note: the very fact that Jesus chose the huge millstone shows how great this sin is. The person would be held to the bottom of the sea by the most awful and terrible weight. The sin of leading others astray is the most awful sin that can be committed. Jesus is stressing that its condemnation will be awful and terrible.

2 (17:3-4) **Forgiveness—Church, Discipline—Rebuke**: the second law is that forgiving others is essential. Note the words, "watch yourselves." What Jesus said was of critical importance. If a person sins against us, we are to rebuke him; but if he repents, we are to forgive him. The point is strong. There is to be no sense of unforgiveness among God's people, no matter how grave the sin against us, no matter how big a stumbling block is put in our path (cp. v.1-2).

The word "rebuke" (epitimeson) is important. It means to charge, to be emphatic with. The believer is to confront the person who *offends* and puts a *stumbling block* in his way. We are to do what we can to correct an offending brother, but the correction is to be done in love and compassion, not in a censoring and judgmental spirit. The whole theme of this instruction is forgiveness, which means that a spirit of love and compassion exists. The instruction does not mean that the believer is weak or indifferent to sin, but rather that he responds to being mistreated by being loving and compassionate.

Thought 1. Believers are to correct those who sin against them and do them wrong. To allow sin to continue is to indulge and to give license to sin, and the last thing God wants is for sin to be indulged in and given the license to run wild.

Have nothing to do with the fruitless deeds of darkness, but rather expose them. (Eph 5:11)

And we urge you, brothers, <u>warn those who are idle</u>, encourage the timid, <u>help the weak</u>, be patient with everyone. (1 Th 5:14)

Yet do not regard him as an enemy, but warn him as a brother. (2 Th 3:15)

Do not rebuke an older man harshly, but exhort him as if he were your father. Treat younger men as brothers, older women as mothers, and younger women as sisters, with absolute purity. (1 Tim 5:1-2)

Preach the Word; be prepared in season and out of season; <u>correct, rebuke</u> and encourage—with great <u>patience and careful</u> instruction. (2 Tim 4:2)

These, then, are the things you should teach. Encourage and rebuke with all authority. Do not let anyone despise you. (Titus 2:15)

Warn a divisive person once, and then warn him a second time. After that, have nothing to do with him. (Titus 3:10)

And you have forgotten that word of encouragement that addresses you as sons: "My son, do not make light of the Lord's discipline, and do not lose heart when he rebukes you, (Heb 12:5)

The world cannot hate you, but it hates me because I testify that what it does is evil. (John 7:7)

I am not writing this to shame you, but to warn you, as my dear children. (1 Cor 4:14)

Let a righteous man strike me—it is a kindness; let him rebuke me—it is oil on my head. My head will not refuse it. Yet my prayer is ever against the deeds of evildoers; (Psa 141:5)

Since you ignored all my advice and would not accept my rebuke, (Prov 1:25)

He who heeds discipline shows the way to life, but whoever ignores correction leads others astray. (Prov 10:17)

Whoever loves discipline loves knowledge, but he who hates correction is stupid. (Prov 12:1)

A fool spurns his father's discipline, but whoever heeds correction shows prudence. (Prov 15:5)

Stern discipline awaits him who leaves the path; he who hates correction will die. (Prov 15:10)

A man who remains stiff-necked after many rebukes will suddenly be destroyed—without remedy. (Prov 29:1)

It is better to heed a wise man's rebuke than to listen to the song of fools. (Eccl 7:5)

You hate the one who reproves in court and despise him who tells the truth. (Amos 5:10)

The command to forgive is also strong. In fact, this is one of the most beautiful pictures of God's unlimited forgiveness. He continues to forgive and forgive. True, the believer does not have license to sin; the Bible is very clear about this (Ro.6:1-2; Gal.5:13; 1 Pt.2:16). The believer is not to take advantage of the forgiveness of God, for judgment awaits the person who so abuses the grace of God. However, the Bible is equally strong in proclaiming that

God forgives and forgives the believer who truly repents—even if he sins time and again. It is God's unlimited forgiveness that requires the believer to forgive anyone who offends him and truly repents—even if the believer has to forgive the offender seven times a day for having wronged him. (See DEEPER STUDY # 4—Mt.26:28.)

> **Blessed are the merciful, for they will be shown mercy. (Mat 5:7)**
>
> **And when you stand praying, if you hold anything against anyone, forgive him, so that your Father in heaven may forgive you your sins." (Mark 11:25)**
>
> **Be merciful, just as your Father is merciful. (Luke 6:36)**
>
> **Be kind and compassionate to one another, forgiving each other, just as in Christ God forgave you. (Eph 4:32)**
>
> **Bear with each other and forgive whatever grievances you may have against one another. Forgive as the Lord forgave you. (Col 3:13)**
>
> **Let love and faithfulness never leave you; bind them around your neck, write them on the tablet of your heart. (Prov 3:3)**
>
> **A kind man benefits himself, but a cruel man brings trouble on himself. (Prov 11:17)**
>
> **But you must return to your God; maintain love and justice, and wait for your God always. (Hosea 12:6)**
>
> **He has showed you, O man, what is good. And what does the LORD require of you? To act justly and to love mercy and to walk humbly with your God. (Micah 6:8)**

3 (17:5-6) **Faith—Boldness**: the third law is that faith is essential; faith is a powerful force. The disciples realized something: their faith was weak—too weak to ever live like Jesus was talking about. He was insisting on a faith so strong that they would...

- be free from ever causing another person to stumble.
- be so loving and compassionate they could forgive a person time and again, even seven times in a single day.

They knew that they desperately needed greater faith in the power and love of Christ, that the power and love of Christ would infill and permeate their whole beings. They knew that they had to believe and trust His presence more and more. Note what Jesus answered.

1. Genuine faith is what is needed, not great faith. The stress is not quantity, not on how much faith a person has. It is not a matter of *increasing faith*; it is a matter of *possessing* and *having* faith. It is a matter of *genuine* faith. The very smallest amount of genuine faith, a faith as small as a mustard seed, can do the impossible. Nothing is impossible to him who has a faith that is genuine, even if the faith is the smallest amount possible. (See DEEPER STUDY # 2, Mustard Seed—Lk.17:6.)

2. Boldness is needed. It takes boldness to walk up to a tree and tell it to be removed. Imagine—to really believe that the request is done! We either believe it or not. It is not a matter of how much belief; it is a matter of genuine belief. If one's belief is genuine, then it is done.

> **Jesus replied, "I tell you the truth, if you have faith and do not doubt, not only can you do what was done to the fig tree, but also you can say to this mountain, 'Go, throw yourself into the sea,' and it will be done. If you believe, you will receive whatever you ask for in prayer." (Mat 21:21-22)**
>
> **"'If you can [believe]'?" said Jesus. "Everything is possible for him who believes." (Mark 9:23)**
>
> **Now faith is being sure of what we hope for and certain of what we do not see. (Heb 11:1)**
>
> **And without faith it is impossible to please God, because anyone who comes to him must believe that he exists and that he rewards those who earnestly seek him. (Heb 11:6)**
>
> **How great is your goodness, which you have stored up for those who fear you, which you bestow in the sight of men on those who take refuge in you. (Psa 31:19)**
>
> **Commit your way to the LORD; trust in him and he will do this: (Psa 37:5)**

DEEPER STUDY # 2

(17:6) **Mustard Seed—Faith**: What did Jesus mean by "faith as small as a mustard seed"? The mustard seed was known for its small size, yet it grew to be a very large bush (see note—Mt.13:32). Picture a mustard seed lying in one's hand. It is *real and very small*, yet imagine the potential for *growth and use*. So is "faith as small as a mustard seed." Faith is *real and small*, yet it has enormous power for growth and ministry.

4(17:7-10) **Service—Ministry—Faithfulness—Labor—Steadfastness**: the fourth law concerns obedience: to obey God is a duty not a service. There is danger that believers will become prideful and puffed up because of the gifts and power God gives, especially if they begin to live victoriously in faith as just described (v.5-6). Jesus used an illustration, making three points to combat this danger.

1. The believer is a servant, and a servant is a slave who serves his Master. (The parable is clear, but see note, Servant—Ro.1:1 for more discussion.)

2. The believer is to serve and obey the commandments of God until all the work is done. He is to feed the cattle and plough the fields, then in the evenings he is to serve the household by feeding and waiting on tables. Ploughing and feeding are tough work, requiring a sound and disciplined body and spirit. They require endurance. Note that the servant works all day and all through the evening until all others have gone to bed. He goes to bed *after* all others have retired, and he get upgets up *before* all others get up. *The servant serves his Master.* (What a lesson Christ lays out for the believer! How few serve the Lord so diligently! How many get up before others in order to spend time alone with the Lord, and then spend the last minutes of a day with the Lord after all others have retired?)

> **Not so with you. Instead, whoever wants to become great among you must be your servant, and whoever wants to be first must be slave of all. (Mark 10:43-44)**
>
> **"My food," said Jesus, "is to do the will of him who sent me and to finish his work. (John 4:34)**

As long as it is day, we must do the work of him who sent me. Night is coming, when no one can work. (John 9:4)

They arranged to meet Paul on a certain day, and came in even larger numbers to the place where he was staying. From morning till evening he explained and declared to them the kingdom of God and tried to convince them about Jesus from the Law of Moses and from the Prophets. (Acts 28:23)

Never be lacking in zeal, but keep your spiritual fervor, serving the Lord. (Rom 12:11)

Therefore, my dear brothers, stand firm. Let nothing move you. Always give yourselves fully to the work of the Lord, because you know that your labor in the Lord is not in vain. (1 Cor 15:58)

Let us not become weary in doing good, for at the proper time we will reap a harvest if we do not give up. Therefore, as we have opportunity, let us do good to all people, especially to those who belong to the family of believers. (Gal 6:9-10)

For this reason I remind you to fan into flame the gift of God, which is in you through the laying on of my hands. (2 Tim 1:6)

But you, keep your head in all situations, endure hardship, do the work of an evangelist, discharge all the duties of your ministry. (2 Tim 4:5)

We want each of you to show this same diligence to the very end, in order to make your hope sure. We do not want you to become lazy, but to imitate those who through faith and patience inherit what has been promised. (Heb 6:11-12)

Therefore, since we are surrounded by such a great cloud of witnesses, let us throw off everything that hinders and the sin that so easily entangles, and let us run with perseverance the race marked out for us. (Heb 12:1)

Therefore, dear friends, since you already know this, be on your guard so that you may not be carried away by the error of lawless men and fall from your secure position. (2 Pet 3:17)

Whatever your hand finds to do, do it with all your might, for in the grave, where you are going, there is neither working nor planning nor knowledge nor wisdom. (Eccl 9:10)

3. The believer is to be humble in his service for the Lord. No matter what we do for Christ, it is our *duty* to do it. We are unworthy of the privilege to serve Him. We are to count ourselves *"unworthy servants."* No man can claim he has done all he should; we know this. We all come short, no matter how much we do or how great the work. There is no room for pride or arrogance or boasting. God commands perfection; therefore, He expects humility.

Be perfect, therefore, as your heavenly Father is perfect. (Mat 5:48)

Therefore, whoever humbles himself like this child is the greatest in the kingdom of heaven. (Mat 18:4)

"I tell you that this man, rather than the other, went home justified before God. For everyone who exalts himself will be humbled, and he who humbles himself will be exalted." (Luke 18:14)

Granted. But they were broken off because of unbelief, and you stand by faith. Do not be arrogant, but be afraid. (Rom 11:20)

For by the grace given me I say to every one of you: Do not think of yourself more highly than you ought, but rather think of yourself with sober judgment, in accordance with the measure of faith God has given you. (Rom 12:3)

Do nothing out of selfish ambition or vain conceit, but in humility consider others better than yourselves. Each of you should look not only to your own interests, but also to the interests of others. Your attitude should be the same as that of Christ Jesus: Who, being in very nature God, did not consider equality with God something to be grasped, but made himself nothing, taking the very nature of a servant, being made in human likeness. And being found in appearance as a man, he humbled himself and became obedient to death— even death on a cross! (Phil 2:3-8)

Humble yourselves before the Lord, and he will lift you up. (James 4:10)

Young men, in the same way be submissive to those who are older. All of you, clothe yourselves with humility toward one another, because, "God opposes the proud but gives grace to the humble." (1 Pet 5:5)

	VII. THE SON OF MAN'S GREAT JOURNEY TO JERUSALEM (STAGE III): HIS LESSONS AND WARNINGS, 17:11-19:27	pity on us!" 14 When he saw them, he said, "Go, show yourselves to the priests." And as they went, they were cleansed.	d. There was perseverance e. There was believing, being tested, obeying
	A. The Lesson on Need and Gratitude, 17:11-19	15 One of them, when he saw he was healed, came back, praising God in a loud voice. 16 He threw himself at Jesus' feet and thanked him—and he was a Samaritan.	**3 The lesson on gratitude** a. All were blessed b. One gave thanks 1) Praised God 2) Worshipped Jesus 3) Was a Samaritan
1 Jesus went toward Jerusalem	11 Now on his way to Jerusalem, Jesus traveled along the border between Samaria and Galilee.	17 Jesus asked, "Were not all ten cleansed? Where are the other nine?	c. Most did not give thanks
2 The lesson on need: Ten lepers were healed[DS1] a. There was desperation b. There was humility c. There was a cry for mercy	12 As he was going into a village, ten men who had leprosy met him. They stood at a distance 13 And called out in a loud voice, "Jesus, Master, have	18 Was no one found to return and give praise to God except this foreigner?" 19 Then he said to him, "Rise and go; your faith has made you well."	d. The one who was the most rejected was the most thankful e. The thankful one shall be the one assured of salvation

DIVISION VII

THE SON OF MAN'S GREAT JOURNEY TO JERUSALEM (STAGE III): HIS LESSONS AND WARNINGS, 17:11-19:27

A. The Lesson on Need and Gratitude, 17:11-19

(17:11-19) **Introduction**: this passage teaches two powerful lessons, one on how to have needs met and the other on gratitude.

1. Jesus went toward Jerusalem (v.11).
2. The lesson on need: ten lepers are healed (v.12-14).
3. The lesson on gratitude (v.15-19).

1 (17:11) **Jesus Christ, Purpose**: Jesus went toward Jerusalem. His face was set to fulfill His purpose on earth: to die *for* man (see DEEPER STUDY # 1—Lk.9:51; note—13:22).

2 (17:12-14) **Need—Cleansing—Faith—Perseverance—Prayer, Answer**: the lesson on need—ten lepers are healed. (See DEEPER STUDY # 1, Leper—Lk.17:12-14.) There were five things that led to their need's being met.

1. There was desperation. The men had leprosy, the most feared disease of that day (see DEEPER STUDY # 1, Leprosy—Lk.17:12-14). They met Jesus as He was entering the city, coming in from a long journey. The lepers had no idea where He was going: He could have been heading for an important meeting, or He could have been tired and exhausted, or He could have had no time for interruptions; but the lepers did not care. They were so desperate they would interrupt Him no matter what.

> **Thought 1.** One thing is basic to having a need met: a sense of desperation. When we sense a need so desperately that nothing can stop us from reaching Jesus, our needs will be met.
>
> **Look to the LORD and his strength; seek his face always. (Psa 105:4)**
> **This is what the LORD says to the house of Israel: "Seek me and live; (Amos 5:4)**
> **Seek the LORD while he may be found; call on him while he is near. (Isa 55:6)**

2. There was humility. Note: they "stood at a distance." They respected the law which demanded they stand at least six feet away from a person. These lepers were, of course, many yards away from Jesus because of the large crowd's following Him. They showed a great respect for the law by remaining on the outskirts of the crowd. On other occasions those seeking healing had ignored the law, bursting through crowds and running up to Jesus. Jesus was bound to note their humility and their acknowledgment of being unclean.

> **Thought 1.** Every man must recognize his uncleanness in approaching Jesus. He must come in humility...
> ⇒ *confessing unworthiness* to approach One so holy.
>
> **Humble yourselves before the Lord, and he will lift you up. (James 4:10)**
> **The LORD is close to the brokenhearted and saves those who are crushed in spirit. (Psa 34:18)**
> **For this is what the high and lofty One says— he who lives forever, whose name is holy: "I live in a high and holy place, but also with him who is contrite and lowly in spirit, to revive the spirit of the lowly and to revive the heart of the contrite. (Isa 57:15)**
>
> ⇒ *confessing need* for the cleansing touch of the Holy One of God, even the Lord Jesus Christ.

3. There was a cry for mercy. Note two things.
   a. They called Jesus "Master." The Greek word for "Master" is not *Rabbi*, the Teacher; but it is *epistata*, which means the Chief, the Commander, the Overseer, the One who has the power to meet needs. Note: the need is not for instruction (Rabbi) but for healing. By healing, they meant both the cleansing of their physical bodies and the spiritual sin which had caused their disease. The Jews always connected leprosy with sin, so this is definitely what they meant. They recognized Jesus to

be the Master who could cleanse both the body and spirit, who could give them both healing and forgiveness of sins.

b. They cried out for mercy. They did not ask only for physical healing; they asked for spiritual healing, for the forgiveness of sins as well. They cried out for mercy upon all of their being.

For we do not have a high priest who is unable to sympathize with our weaknesses, but we have one who has been tempted in every way, just as we are—yet was without sin. Let us then approach the throne of grace with confidence, so that we may receive mercy and find grace to help us in our time of need. (Heb 4:15-16)

For the director of music. With stringed instruments. According to sheminith. A psalm of David. O LORD, do not rebuke me in your anger or discipline me in your wrath. Be merciful to me, LORD, for I am faint; O LORD, heal me, for my bones are in agony. (Psa 6:1-2)

Hear my voice when I call, O LORD; be merciful to me and answer me. (Psa 27:7)

This poor man called, and the LORD heard him; he saved him out of all his troubles. (Psa 34:6)

For the director of music. A psalm of David. When the prophet Nathan came to him after David had committed adultery with Bathsheba. Have mercy on me, O God, according to your unfailing love; according to your great compassion blot out my transgressions. (Psa 51:1)

Show us your unfailing love, O LORD, and grant us your salvation. (Psa 85:7)

I will maintain my love to him forever, and my covenant with him will never fail. (Psa 89:28)

The LORD is compassionate and gracious, slow to anger, abounding in love. (Psa 103:8)

But from everlasting to everlasting the Lord's love is with those who fear him, and his righteousness with their children's children— (Psa 103:17)

Let your compassion come to me that I may live, for your law is my delight. (Psa 119:77)

As the eyes of slaves look to the hand of their master, as the eyes of a maid look to the hand of her mistress, so our eyes look to the LORD our God, till he shows us his mercy. (Psa 123:2)

Have mercy on us, O LORD, have mercy on us, for we have endured much contempt. We have endured much ridicule from the proud, much contempt from the arrogant. (Psa 123:3-4)

Let the wicked forsake his way and the evil man his thoughts. Let him turn to the LORD, and he will have mercy on him, and to our God, for he will freely pardon. (Isa 55:7)

4. There was perseverance. Jesus did not notice them immediately. He ignored their cry in order to test them. They needed to cry and cry for mercy in order to show their sincerity and to build up their sense of need. These two things are important to note. God does not always answer our prayers immediately. Sometimes we need to learn to trust Him more or to build up a greater sense of need and desperation. Forcing us to seek and knock and persevere does both. Once God answers our prayer, we learn to trust Him more. There is another crucial matter as well. Forcing us to stay on our knees and to persevere in prayer day after day keeps us in His presence. Deep concentrated prayer provides some of the sweetest communion and fellowship ever experienced, and such communion and fellowship is what God is after.

"So I say to you: Ask and it will be given to you; seek and you will find; knock and the door will be opened to you. (Luke 11:9)

But if from there you seek the LORD your God, you will find him if you look for him with all your heart and with all your soul. (Deu 4:29)

You will seek me and find me when you seek me with all your heart. (Jer 29:13)

5. There was *believing and obeying*. Jesus did not heal the lepers immediately. There were things they had to do, instructions that had to be obeyed, to have their needs met. They were to obey the law, go to the priest and report that they had been cleansed. If they obeyed the law and believed the Lord's Word (promise of cleansing), they would be cleansed. Now note: they were cleansed "as they went." This was a great legacy of faith to leave for succeeding generations (cp. Heb.11:7f). Think about the great belief they had in Jesus' word and power! They had to strike out for the temple to be inspected and pronounced cleansed—and they were not even healed yet! While they were obeying the Jewish law of cleansing, they were to be healed (Lev.14:1f).

Jesus replied, "You may go. Your son will live." The man took Jesus at his word and departed. (John 4:50)

And without faith it is impossible to please God, because anyone who comes to him must believe that he exists and that he rewards those who earnestly seek him. (Heb 11:6)

And, once made perfect, he became the source of eternal salvation for all who obey him (Heb 5:9)

How great is your goodness, which you have stored up for those who fear you, which you bestow in the sight of men on those who take refuge in you. (Psa 31:19)

The LORD redeems his servants; no one will be condemned who takes refuge in him. (Psa 34:22)

Commit your way to the LORD; trust in him and he will do this: (Psa 37:5)

DEEPER STUDY # 1

(17:12-14) **Leprosy**: leprosy was the most terrible disease in the day of Jesus; it was greatly feared. It was disfiguring and sometimes fatal. In the Bible, leprosy is a type of sin.

1. The leper himself was considered *utterly unclean*—physically and spiritually. He could not approach within six feet of any person including family members. "The person with such an infectious disease must wear torn clothes, let

his hair be unkempt, cover the lower part of his face and cry out, 'Unclean! Unclean!' (Lev.13:45).

2. He was judged to be *dead—the living dead.* He had to wear a black garment so he could be recognized as from among the dead.

3. He was banished as an outcast, totally ostracized from society—earthly and heavenly. As long as he has the infection he remains unclean. He must live alone; he must live outside the camp(Lev.13:46). He could not live within the walls of any city; his dwelling had to be outside the city gates.

4. He was thought to be polluted, incurable by any human means whatsoever. Leprosy could be cured by God and His power alone. (Note how Jesus proved His Messiahship and deity by healing the leper.)

Imagine the anguish and heartbreak of the leper, being completely cut off from family and friends and society. Imagine the emotional and mental pain. There are other recorded instances of lepers' being healed (cp. Lk.7:22; Mt.8:1; 10:8; 11:5; Mk.1:40; and perhaps Mt.26:6; cp. Mk.14:3).

3 (17:15-19) **Gratitude**: there are five points to note on the lesson of gratitude.

1. All the lepers were blessed and should have been thankful. This was true of the ten lepers, and it should be true of every man. Every one of the ten should have turned back and given thanks. They had all been blessed by Christ. Note they had all…

- recognized their need.
- shown humility.
- cried for mercy.
- persevered.
- believed and obeyed.

Their need had been met: they had all been healed. They now needed to turn back to give thanks and show appreciation.

> **In the same way, let your light shine before men, that they may see your good deeds and praise your Father in heaven. (Mat 5:16)**
> **So that with one heart and mouth you may glorify the God and Father of our Lord Jesus Christ. (Rom 15:6)**
> **You were bought at a price. Therefore honor God with your body. (1 Cor 6:20)**
> **Through Jesus, therefore, let us continually offer to God a sacrifice of praise—the fruit of lips that confess his name. (Heb 13:15)**
> **Sing praises to the LORD, enthroned in Zion; proclaim among the nations what he has done. (Psa 9:11)**
> **My tongue will speak of your righteousness and of your praises all day long. (Psa 35:28)**
> **May the peoples praise you, O God; may all the peoples praise you. (Psa 67:3)**

2. One did give thanks. He was a Samaritan, the most despised and rejected of the men. (See DEEPER STUDY # 2, Samaritan—Lk.10:33.) Note what he did.

a. He praised God immediately. He shouted at the top of his lungs with the loudest voice possible. He *witnessed* for God. God had cleansed him and he wanted all to know the great mercy and love of God.

b. He worshipped Jesus. Note that he fell down on his face at the feet of Jesus. This was both humility and recognition of the power of God in Christ, two essentials for true spiritual cleansing (salvation, v.19).

3. Most did not give thanks. They kept going about their business at hand. They did not stop what they were doing nor return to the Lord to give thanks. But note something: they did return to their former world, the lives they used to live.

> **Thought 1.** There is a lesson in the behavior of the lepers. Christ expects us to return to Him continually, to return, glorify, and worship Him as the Source of our power and strength for life.
>
> **People will be lovers of themselves, lovers of money, boastful, proud, abusive, disobedient to their parents, ungrateful, unholy, (2 Tim 3:2)**
> **For although they knew God, they neither glorified him as God nor gave thanks to him, but their thinking became futile and their foolish hearts were darkened. (Rom 1:21)**
> **Is this the way you repay the LORD, O foolish and unwise people? Is he not your Father, your Creator, who made you and formed you? (Deu 32:6)**

4. The most rejected was the most thankful. Note the word "foreigner" (allogenes, v.18). It means that he was a foreigner "to the covenants of promise, without hope, and without God in the world" (Eph.2:12). He had felt his need more keenly and deeply. He knew he needed to be saved, genuinely saved—spiritually as well as physically. Despite the fact that he had never known the real promises of God and that he had been without God in this world, he now knew God. His heart just broke forth to give glory to God. Jesus had saved him from so much.

> **Giving thanks to the Father, who has qualified you to share in the inheritance of the saints in the kingdom of light. (Col 1:12)**
> **But you are a chosen people, a royal priesthood, a holy nation, a people belonging to God, that you may declare the praises of him who called you out of darkness into his wonderful light. (1 Pet 2:9)**
> **Give thanks in all circumstances, for this is God's will for you in Christ Jesus. (1 Th 5:18)**

5. The thankful man shall be the one truly saved—spiritually. The verb "made well" (sesoken) is literally "has saved you." The man was clearly whole in body. This could be easily seen, but one could not see the spiritual and inward cleansing. Jesus was telling the man that his sins were forgiven; He was giving the man the assurance of salvation.

Now note an important question. Had the nine been spiritually cleansed as well as physically cleansed? Or was it lack of being spiritually cleansed that kept them from returning to give thanks? Or was Jesus just giving this man a strong assurance of salvation?

We are not told, but one crucial factor is known. This man, the grateful and thankful leper, was the man who received *assurance of being cleansed and of having his sins forgiven*. The others did not. They failed to be grateful and thankful.

Another important fact to note is this: gratitude and praise bring assurance to the heart. They stir Christ to speak to the human heart, giving assurance of acceptance and cleansing.

Therefore, if anyone is in Christ, he is a new creation; the old has gone, the new has come! (2 Cor 5:17)

He saved us, not because of righteous things we had done, but because of his mercy. He saved us through the washing of rebirth and renewal by the Holy Spirit, (Titus 3:5)

For you have been born again, not of perishable seed, but of imperishable, through the living and enduring word of God. (1 Pet 1:23)

I said, "O LORD, have mercy on me; heal me, for I have sinned against you." (Psa 41:4)

But he was pierced for our transgressions, he was crushed for our iniquities; the punishment that brought us peace was upon him, and by his wounds we are healed. (Isa 53:5)

	B. The Coming Day of God's Kingdom and Jesus' Return, 17:20-37 (cp. Mt.24; Mk.13)
1 The coming of God's Kingdom a. It cannot be observed	20 Once, having been asked by the Pharisees when the kingdom of God would come, Jesus replied, "The kingdom of God does not come with your careful observation,
b. It is within	21 Nor will people say, 'Here it is,' or 'There it is,' because the kingdom of God is within you."
2 The day will be longed for	22 Then he said to his disciples, "The time is coming when you will long to see one of the days of the Son of Man, but you will not see it.
3 The day is unknown; it is coming suddenly & visibly	23 Men will tell you, 'There he is!' or 'Here he is!' Do not go running off after them. 24 For the Son of Man in his day will be like the lightning, which flashes and lights up the sky from one end to the other.
4 The day cannot come until some things happen first	25 But first he must suffer many things and be rejected by this generation.
5 The day will be as the days of Noah & Lot: Men will be occupied with normal, routine affairs a. The days of Noah 1) Normal affairs will be going on 2) Suddenly, unexpectedly, judgment will fall	26 "Just as it was in the days of Noah, so also will it be in the days of the Son of Man. 27 People were eating, drinking, marrying and being given in marriage up to the day Noah entered the ark. Then the flood came and destroyed them all.
b. The days of Lot 1) Normal affairs will be going on 2) Suddenly, unexpectedly, judgment will fall	28 "It was the same in the days of Lot. People were eating and drinking, buying and selling, planting and building. 29 But the day Lot left Sodom, fire and sulfur rained down from heaven and destroyed them all.
c. The day of the Son of Man will be the same: Sudden, unexpected	30 "It will be just like this on the day the Son of Man is revealed.
6 The day will be a day of urgency for all men a. The urgency illust.	31 On that day no one who is on the roof of his house, with his goods inside, should go down to get them. Likewise, no one in the field should go back for anything.
b. The doom of turning back illustrated	32 Remember Lot's wife!
c. The one essential: Total abandonment	33 Whoever tries to keep his life will lose it, and whoever loses his life will preserve it.
7 The day will be a day of separation	34 I tell you, on that night two people will be in one bed; one will be taken and the other left. 35 Two women will be grinding grain together; one will be taken and the other left."[36]
8 The day will be universal, worldwide	37 "Where, Lord?" they asked. He replied, "Where there is a dead body, there the vultures will gather."

DIVISION VII

THE SON OF MAN'S GREAT JOURNEY TO JERUSALEM (STAGE III): HIS LESSONS AND WARNINGS, 17:11-19:27

B. The Coming Day of God's Kingdom and Jesus' Return, 17:20-37

(17:20-37) **Introduction**: the religionists (Pharisees) asked when the Kingdom of God was going to come. The Kingdom of God was the focus of Jesus' preaching and conversation. It was the topic of conversation being buzzed about by everyone. The Messiah had come and the Kingdom of God was to be ushered in. The religionists (Pharisees) in particular were interested.

⇒ They had heard Jesus preach, "Repent, for the kingdom of God is near" (Mt.4:17). They wanted to know when it was coming, for it meant great blessings both for Israel and for them personally as religious leaders.

⇒ They had heard Jesus instruct His disciples to pray for the Kingdom of God to come. Their curiosity was aroused, and they wanted to know when to expect it.

Jesus answered their question in a very simple statement of two verses (v.20-21). Then, note what He did. He turned to His disciples (v.22) and gave them a dynamic message on *the coming day of God's Kingdom and on His own return*. It is important to see two things (see DEEPER STUDY # 3—Mt.19:23-24 for more discussion).

⇒ Two stages of God's kingdom are covered here: the spiritual kingdom that is within a person (v.20-21), and the coming kingdom to be set up on earth when Christ returns (v.24).

⇒ The Kingdom of God and of the Lord (Son of Man) refer to the same kingdom (v.20-21, 24, 26, 30).

1. The coming of God's Kingdom (v.20-21).
2. The day will be longed for (v.22).
3. The day is unknown; it is coming suddenly and visibly (v.23-24).

---

36 Two men will be in the field; one will be taken and the other left.

4. The day cannot come until some things happen first (v.25).
5. The day will be as the days of Noah and Lot: men will be occupied with normal, routine affairs (v.26-30).
6. The day will be a day of urgency for all men (v.31-33).
7. The day will be a day of separation (v.34-35).
8. The day will be universal, worldwide (v.37).

1 (17:20-21) **Kingdom of God**: the coming of God's kingdom. When will it come?

1. The Kingdom of God cannot be observed (paratereseos). The word means to watch closely, to give close observation to (as in astronomical observations). The kingdom cannot be seen with the naked eye. This means at least two things.
   a. The Kingdom of God does not come with an outward, dramatic, thunderous show. It does not come in such a way that men say, "Here it is! or there it is!" It comes with a silent, pervasive influence. It is coming, and its coming will permeate the whole world; but its coming is to be silent, not showy (cp. the leaven which silently permeates the whole lump, see note—Mt.13:33).
   b. The Kingdom of God cannot be seen with the naked eye. The Lord's kingdom is not of this world, not of the physical and material dimension of being. It is not the kind of kingdom men see when they observe the nations of the world.

2. The Kingdom of God is "within you" (entos humon). Some say this should be translated "among you." If so, then Christ is saying that He is the embodiment of the Kingdom of God. He is setting up the Kingdom of God among them, there and then. God is already beginning to rule and reign in the lives He is touching.

Others say the words mean "within you." If so, then the kingdom is to be looked for within the hearts and lives of people. The Kingdom of God is spiritual; it is the changing of hearts, the rule and reign of God within men's lives. It is the power of God to change a sinful, immoral, and unjust man into a servant of God.

> **After John was put in prison, Jesus went into Galilee, proclaiming the good news of God. "The time has come," he said. "The kingdom of God is near. Repent and believe the good news!" (Mark 1:14-15)**
>
> **Looking at his disciples, he said: "Blessed are you who are poor, for yours is the kingdom of God. (Luke 6:20)**
>
> **For the kingdom of God is not a matter of eating and drinking, but of righteousness, peace and joy in the Holy Spirit, (Rom 14:17)**

2 (17:22) **Jesus Christ, Return—Kingdom of God**: the day will be longed for. Note: from this point on Jesus began to speak to the disciples, but He was still dealing with the same subject: the coming of the Son of Man and of God's kingdom.

1. The Kingdom of God is internal, but it is to be external also.
   ⇒ The term the "days of the Son of Man" refers to the Messianic kingdom.
   ⇒ The Son of Man is the title used by Daniel when describing the kingdom of the Messiah (cp. Dan.7:13-14).

2. Men cannot control the Kingdom of God. This is a crucial point to note. They may wish to see the kingdom...
   • as being prepared by the hands of men,
   • as being close at hand, coming soon,
   • as being now—existing on earth with God's ruling and reigning,

...but man has nothing to do with its control. No matter how much men may "long to see one of the days," they do not control even one day of it. They cannot create a single day of the kingdom so that they can see it.

3. What is it that makes a believer ache to see the Son of Man and to be with Him in His kingdom (heaven)?
   ⇒ tough and terrible trials
   ⇒ persecution, personal abuse, and mistreatment
   ⇒ divisions, torn families and social groups
   ⇒ death, separation from family and dear friends
   ⇒ worship, a close sense and deep experience with God

Now note something ever so wonderful and precious. In every one of the above situations, God takes His dear child and meets his need. God draws his dear child near Him to give His child a sense of His presence and care and love. Even if the moment for the child's death and entrance into heaven has arrived, God draws near and carries His child in His arms of love, carries him through the "valley of the shadow of death" (Ps.23:4). However, the point made by Jesus is not the closeness of His presence in the death of the believer. It is the closeness of His presence through the great trials and troubles of life that causes the believer to ache for heaven. God does infuse a deep desire for heaven into the heart of the genuine believer, and He does it often. Such a consciousness of God's presence causes the genuine believer to long and ache for God's presence all the time.

> **As you look forward to the day of God and speed its coming. That day will bring about the destruction of the heavens by fire, and the elements will melt in the heat. But in keeping with his promise we are looking forward to a new heaven and a new earth, the home of righteousness. (2 Pet 3:12-13)**
>
> **Find rest, O my soul, in God alone; my hope comes from him. (Psa 62:5)**

3 (17:23-24) **Jesus Christ, Return—Kingdom of God**: the day is unknown; it is coming suddenly. Some men will always be saying the kingdom has come and is present on earth. The kingdom...

• is there, "There he is!"
• is here, "Here he is!"

Jesus said there is an *internal kingdom*, a kingdom "within you" which is the rule and reign of God within the human heart (v.21). But there is also an *external kingdom*, a heaven for which men shall long and not be able to see (v.22). The external kingdom is coming "in His day" (v.24). When that day comes, it shall come suddenly and visibly, just as quickly and visibly as a flash of lightning.

Jesus was teaching an important lesson here. Since the day cannot be known, believers are to be busy about their labor for the Lord.

> **Therefore, my dear brothers, stand firm. Let nothing move you. Always give yourselves fully to the work of the Lord,**

because you know that your labor in the Lord is not in vain. (1 Cor 15:58)

For as lightning that comes from the east is visible even in the west, so will be the coming of the Son of Man. (Mat 24:27)

So then, dear friends, since you are looking forward to this [God's kingdom], make every effort to be found spotless, blameless and at peace with him. (2 Pet 3:14)

4 (17:25) **Jesus Christ, Return**: the day cannot come until some things happen first. This was, of course, a reference to the Lord's death. Before the Kingdom of God could ever come to earth, He had to suffer and die. It was His death that would make it possible for His kingdom to come to earth.

And being found in appearance as a man, he humbled himself and became obedient to death— even death on a cross! Therefore God exalted him to the highest place and gave him the name that is above every name, that at the name of Jesus every knee should bow, in heaven and on earth and under the earth, and every tongue confess that Jesus Christ is Lord, to the glory of God the Father. (Phil 2:8-11; cp. 1 Cor.15:22-24)

"Do not let your hearts be troubled. Trust in God ; trust also in me. In my Father's house are many rooms; if it were not so, I would have told you. I am going there to prepare a place for you. And if I go and prepare a place for you, I will come back and take you to be with me that you also may be where I am. (John 14:1-3)

5 (17:26-30) **Noah—Lot—Jesus Christ, Return—Judgment**: the day will be as the days of Noah and Lot; men will be occupied with normal, routine affairs.

1. The affairs listed are the routine affairs of every day life. Men...

- ate
- drank
- married
- bought
- sold
- planted
- built

This is just the point. Men will be going about their daily lives without giving any attention to God or to the warnings of coming judgment (see note—Mt.24:37-39. Cp. 1 Pt.3:18-22; Gen.6:1f; 7:11f.)

2. Noah and Lot were not men who had reached spiritual maturity. They were not examples of spiritual men for others to follow. However, they did one thing which others failed to do: they believed God's Word when God said to prepare for the flood and for the coming judgment of fire. Despite all their shortcomings and failures, all their sensual and loose living, when the Word came to prepare, they *believed* and they *prepared.*

3. The people of Noah's and Lot's day did not believe and did not prepare. They went right on with their normal routine, living and focusing their minds upon...

- the world and its things.
- the flesh and its pleasures.

4. The people of Noah's and Lot's day were caught unaware. Unexpectedly—suddenly...

- "Then the flood came and destroyed them all" (v.27).
- "Fire and sulfur rained down from heaven, and destroyed them all" (v.29).

5. God took care of Noah and Lot, the two who really believed His warning and prepared. He saved them from the coming judgment.

6. This is the crucial point. When the Son of Man returns, the world will be the same as it was in the days of Noah and Lot.

a. Men will be going about their routine day-to-day affairs.
b. Men will not believe God's warnings.
c. Men will be caught unaware. Unexpectedly, suddenly Christ will appear and men will be judged.
d. True believers who have really prepared themselves will be saved and delivered.

It teaches us to say "No" to ungodliness and worldly passions, and to live self-controlled, upright and godly lives in this present age, while we wait for the blessed hope—the glorious appearing of our great God and Savior, Jesus Christ, (Titus 2:12-13)

Since everything will be destroyed in this way, what kind of people ought you to be? You ought to live holy and godly lives (2 Pet 3:11)

May God himself, the God of peace, sanctify you through and through. May your whole spirit, soul and body be kept blameless at the coming of our Lord Jesus Christ. (1 Th 5:23)

And this is his command: to believe in the name of his Son, Jesus Christ, and to love one another as he commanded us. (1 John 3:23)

To keep this command without spot or blame until the appearing of our Lord Jesus Christ, (1 Tim 6:14)

6 (17:31-33) **Jesus Christ, Return—Judgment—Decision**: the day will be a day of urgency for all men. These verses are applied by some to the destruction of Jerusalem and by others to the return of Christ. They are applicable to both.

1. "On that day" when God gives the indication that His return is imminent, a man must act quickly, not wasting a moment's time. When is the Lord's return imminent? When are we to prepare and act?

Jesus said *now*: "Behold, I am coming soon (cp. Rev.3:11; 22:7,12)." Since He is coming soon, there are no "goods inside" [the house] (v.31)—no possessions—worth our attention and loyalty. Christ and Christ alone is worthy of our devotion and attention.

2. "Remember Lot's wife." She illustrates the doom of turning back. She came close to being saved; she had prepared. She was faithful to her husband, listening to his spiritual warnings, walking with him through the sinful city (world), and walking toward God's designated safety. But she walked behind her husband, not by his side; therefore, she was able to look back upon her sensual experiences in the world of Sodom. When she did, she perished with the worldly. "Remember Lot's wife" who came so close but

who tried to hang on to the delights of the world (Gen. 19:26).

> **Jesus replied, "No one who puts his hand to the plow and looks back is fit for service in the kingdom of God." (Luke 9:62)**
>
> **But my righteous one will live by faith. And if he shrinks back, I will not be pleased with him." (Heb 10:38)**
>
> **If they have escaped the corruption of the world by knowing our Lord and Savior Jesus Christ and are again entangled in it and overcome, they are worse off at the end than they were at the beginning. (2 Pet 2:20)**

3. The one essential is total abandonment to Christ and the warnings of judgment to come. We must not try to save (live) our lives for this world in its worldly ways. We must not do as Lot's wife and the people in the days of Noah and Lot. We must lose our lives for *Christ and His coming kingdom*. (See outline and notes—Lk.9:24 for more discussion.)

> **And everyone who has left houses or brothers or sisters or father or mother or children or fields for my sake will receive a hundred times as much and will inherit eternal life. (Mat 19:29)**
>
> **Then he said to them all: "If anyone would come after me, he must deny himself and take up his cross daily and follow me. (Luke 9:23)**
>
> **I tell you the truth, unless a kernel of wheat falls to the ground and dies, it remains only a single seed. But if it dies, it produces many seeds. (John 12:24)**
>
> **What is more, I consider everything a loss compared to the surpassing greatness of knowing Christ Jesus my Lord, for whose sake I have lost all things. I consider them rubbish, that I may gain Christ (Phil 3:8)**

7 (17:34-35) **Jesus Christ, Return**: the day will be a day of separation. The point is clear: the day will come when all men will be going about their affairs, working or resting as usual. Then all of a sudden, unexpectedly, one here and there will be taken and the other left behind. The believer who has truly prepared himself will be taken home to the Lord. All who reject and oppose the Lord will be left behind. (See outline and notes—1 Th.4:13-5:3.)

> **Let both grow together until the harvest. At that time I will tell the harvesters: First collect the weeds and tie them in bundles to be burned; then gather the wheat and bring it into my barn.'" (Mat 13:30)**
>
> **This is how it will be at the end of the age. The angels will come and separate the wicked from the righteous (Mat 13:49)**
>
> **And throw them into the fiery furnace, where there will be weeping and gnashing of teeth. "Have you understood all these things?" Jesus asked. "Yes," they replied. (Mat 13:50-51)**
>
> **All the nations will be gathered before him, and he will separate the people one from another as a shepherd separates the sheep from the goats. (Mat 25:32)**
>
> **And give relief to you who are troubled, and to us as well. This will happen when the Lord Jesus is revealed from heaven in blazing fire with his powerful angels. (He will punish those who do not know God and do not obey the gospel of our Lord Jesus. They will be punished with everlasting destruction and shut out from the presence of the Lord and from the majesty of his power on the day he comes to be glorified in his holy people and to be marveled at among all those who have believed. This includes you, because you believed our testimony to you. (2 Th 1:7-10)**

8 (17:37) **Jesus Christ, Return**: the day will be universal, that is, worldwide. Note the disciples asked where His return and kingdom was to take place. Jesus used an illustration to teach that His return would be universal. The "vultures" (hoi aetoi) can mean either eagle or vulture. It probably should be translated vulture here, for they are the ones who gather universally as scavengers over dead bodies. Vultures gather where the dead are and feast upon them. Since death is universal, vultures are found everywhere. Therefore, the coming of Jesus Christ and of God's kingdom will be the same as the coming of vultures. He shall come to the whole earth, to the place where men die. The moral corruption throughout the world necessitates the Lord's return in divine judgment (see note—Mt.24:25-28; cp. Job 39:27-30).

> **"At that time the sign of the Son of Man will appear in the sky, and all the nations of the earth will mourn. They will see the Son of Man coming on the clouds of the sky, with power and great glory. (Mat 24:30)**
>
> **Look, he is coming with the clouds, and every eye will see him, even those who pierced him; and all the peoples of the earth will mourn because of him. So shall it be! Amen. (Rev 1:7)**

	CHAPTER 18	But finally he said to himself, 'Even though I don't fear God or care about men,	He was hard & harsh
	C. The Parable of the Unjust Judge: The Secret of Prayer—Persistence, 18:1-8	5 Yet because this widow keeps bothering me, I will see that she gets justice, so that she won't eventually wear me out with her coming!'"	d. The point: The judge honored her request because she continued to come
1 The great duty to persevere in prayer	Then Jesus told his disciples a parable to show them that they should always pray and not give up.	6 And the Lord said, "Listen to what the unjust judge says. 7 And will not God bring about justice for his chosen ones,	**3 The lesson on persevering prayer** a. Hear this point b. God avenges the elect who persevere in prayer[DS1]
2 The parable of persevering prayer a. The unjust judge b. The poor widow: Was all alone & persecuted	2 He said: "In a certain town there was a judge who neither feared God nor cared about men. 3 And there was a widow in that town who kept coming to him with the plea, 'Grant me justice against my adversary.'	who cry out to him day and night? Will he keep putting them off? 8 I tell you, he will see that they get justice, and quickly.	c. He waits & bears long with unbelievers; puts off justice for a while d. God will quickly bring about justice.
c. The silence of the judge:	4 "For some time he refused.	However, when the Son of Man comes, will he find faith on the earth?"	**4 The great tragedy: In the last days few will persevere in prayer & faith**

DIVISION VII

THE SON OF MAN'S GREAT JOURNEY TO JERUSALEM (STAGE III): HIS LESSONS AND WARNINGS, 17:11-19:27

C. The Parable of the Unjust Judge: The Secret of Prayer—Persistence, 18:1-8

(18:1-8) **Introduction**: the secret to prayer is persistence. This is the great lesson Jesus taught in this passage.

1. The great duty to persevere in prayer (v.1).
2. The parable of persevering prayer (v.2-5).
3. The lesson on persevering prayer (v.6-7).
4. The great tragedy: in the last days few will persevere in prayer and faith (v.8).

1 (18:1) **Prayer—Perseverance—Jesus Christ, Return**: the great duty to persevere in prayer. Jesus was strong and forceful in stressing the believer's duty to persevere in prayer.

1. This discussion follows the passage dealing with the return of Christ. There is need for perseverance in prayer, for praying over a long period of time and not giving in and becoming discouraged. God's people are to pray and keep on praying until Christ returns, no matter how long He may be delayed.

2. The word "should" has the idea of necessity. It is absolutely necessary that men persevere in prayer.

3. The word "always" means at all times. The believer is to develop a constant spirit of prayer, to maintain an unbroken consciousness of God's presence, to practice the very presence of God, to walk in a constant state of prayer.

4. The words "not to give up" (me egkakein) mean not to lose heart, not to turn coward, or give up, or give in to evil.

> **Look to the LORD and his strength; seek his face always. (1 Chr 16:11)**
>
> **You will seek me and find me when you seek me with all your heart. (Jer 29:13)**
>
> **"Ask and it will be given to you; seek and you will find; knock and the door will be opened to you. For everyone who asks receives; he who seeks finds; and to him who knocks, the door will be opened. (Mat 7:7-8)**
>
> **"Watch and pray so that you will not fall into temptation. The spirit is willing, but the body is weak." (Mat 26:41)**
>
> **And pray in the Spirit on all occasions with all kinds of prayers and requests. With this in mind, be alert and always keep on praying for all the saints. (Eph 6:18)**
>
> **Do not be anxious about anything, but in everything, by prayer and petition, with thanksgiving, present your requests to God. (Phil 4:6)**
>
> **Devote yourselves to prayer, being watchful and thankful. (Col 4:2)**
>
> **Pray continually; (1 Th 5:17)**

2 (18:2-5) **Prayer—Perseverance**: the parable of persevering prayer. The parable shows clearly the *power of persistence* even in the business and judicial affairs of men.

1. There was the unjust judge. He had no fear of God and cared even less for what men said. The idea is that he took bribes and gave favors to persons who held position and authority. He did not care for conscience or law, for morality or justice. He was out to fill his pockets and to gain honor and esteem, recognition and position from those who were influential, those who held position, power, and wealth (cp. Eccl.3:16).

2. There was the poor widow.

⇒ She was poor, without money to bribe the judge.

⇒ She was a widow, a woman all alone in a man's world, with no man and no money to secure legal counsel to plead her case.

⇒ She held no position or authority, no rights to commend her to the judge.

⇒ She was persecuted, being taken advantage of and abused by some adversary.

Note what she did: she let none of this stop her. She came to the judge and asked him to avenge her, to get rid of her adversary.

3. There was the silence of the judge. The judge did not move to help her. His heart was hard and harsh; he had no interest in helping anyone who would not benefit his career or fill his pockets.

4. The point is this: the judge gave in. For sometime he refused, but the poor widow kept on coming and coming, pleading and pleading. She would not let the judge rest. Now note the stress. The judge…

- did not fear God,
- did not regard man's opinions,

…yet he gave in to the widow, granting her justice against her adversary.

Why? Because of her *continual coming*. He could not get rid of her. She would not accept silence nor take *no* for an answer. She kept coming and coming. The judge said, "So that she won't eventually wear me out with her coming." (hina me hupopiazei me). The literal meaning is unless she "give me a black eye." The word can mean to *annoy* or to *damage a reputation*. She was persistent—refusing to let the judge go!

3 (18:6-7) **Believers, Avenged—Judgment—Prayer, Persevering**: the lesson on persevering prayer. The lesson has four points.

1. Hear the lesson. The unjust judge holds a great lesson for believers. Hear, give attention and thought to what he teaches.

2. God avenges and brings justice to His chosen ones who persevere in prayer.

a. The chosen ones are God's "chosen ones," the followers of His dear Son (see DEEPER STUDY # 1, Chosen ones—Lk.18:7).

b. God will avenge and bring justice to His chosen ones. This indicates that they are in trouble; they need to be avenged and delivered from being…

- ridiculed
- ignored
- slandered
- cursed
- criticized
- abused
- passed over
- persecuted
- injured

c. The reason God avenges and brings justice to His chosen ones is because they persevere in prayer. They pray *day and night*.

⇒ They have great need.

⇒ They recognize that God alone can meet their need.

Therefore, they go before God as the just Judge of the universe. They are one of His own chosen ones, and they cry day and night to be avenged of their adversaries (spiritual as well as human adversaries). They plead and plead their case before God. They do not let God remain silent nor let Him refuse His delivering power.

"Watch and pray so that you will not fall into temptation. The spirit is willing, but the body is weak." (Mat 26:41)

Be always on the watch, and pray that you may be able to escape all that is about to happen, and that you may be able to stand before the Son of Man." (Luke 21:36)

If you remain in me and my words remain in you, ask whatever you wish, and it will be given you. (John 15:7)

He will call upon me, and I will answer him; I will be with him in trouble, I will deliver him and honor him. (Psa 91:15)

Before they call I will answer; while they are still speaking I will hear. (Isa 65:24)

'Call to me and I will answer you and tell you great and unsearchable things you do not know.' (Jer 33:3)

This third I will bring into the fire; I will refine them like silver and test them like gold. They will call on my name and I will answer them; I will say, 'They are my people,' and they will say, 'The LORD is our God.'" (Zec 13:9)

3. God waits and bears a long time; He puts off justice for a time. He is *long-suffering* toward unbelievers. This is part of His purpose: to have mercy upon all who can be reached, not willing that any should perish (2 Pt.3:9). Note a significant point: the believer, bearing up under trial and persecution, is a dynamic witness of the strength of Christ. Some unbelievers are reached, and eventually they turn to Christ because of the strong witness of suffering believers. The point is this: God does not always answer the cry of a believer immediately. God allows the believer to suffer trial.

a. A believer is allowed to suffer in order to be a dynamic witness to others. The presence and power of Christ is sufficient to help the believer stand faithfully.

The Lord is not slow in keeping his promise, as some understand slowness. He is patient with you, not wanting anyone to perish, but everyone to come to repentance. (2 Pet 3:9)

These have come so that your faith—of greater worth than gold, which perishes even though refined by fire—may be proved genuine and may result in praise, glory and honor when Jesus Christ is revealed. (1 Pet 1:7)

[God] who comforts us in all our troubles, so that we can comfort those in any trouble with the comfort we ourselves have received from God. (2 Cor 1:4)

Wives, in the same way be submissive to your husbands so that, if any of them do not believe the word, they may be won over without words by the behavior of their wives, when they see the purity and reverence of your lives. (1 Pet 3:1-2)

b. A believer is allowed to suffer in order to become stronger and stronger in trusting and hoping in God (see note—Ro.5:3-5).

Not only so, but we also rejoice in our sufferings, because we know that suffering produces perseverance; perseverance, character; and character, hope. And hope does not disappoint us, because God has poured out his love into our hearts by the Holy Spirit, whom he has given us. (Rom 5:3-5)

Consider it pure joy, my brothers, whenever you face trials of many kinds, because you know that the testing of your faith develops perseverance. Perseverance must finish its work so that you may be mature and complete, not lacking anything. (James 1:2-4)

4. God will will quickly bring about justice for His chosen ones speedily; that is, in God's time He will act quickly, suddenly, and without hesitation. He will avenge His chosen ones. His wrath will come upon the world.

> **Do not take revenge, my friends, but leave room for God's wrath, for it is written: "It is mine to avenge; I will repay," says the Lord. On the contrary: "If your enemy is hungry, feed him; if he is thirsty, give him something to drink. In doing this, you will heap burning coals on his head." (Rom 12:19-20)**
>
> **He has delivered us from such a deadly peril, and he will deliver us. On him we have set our hope that he will continue to deliver us, as you help us by your prayers. Then many will give thanks on our behalf for the gracious favor granted us in answer to the prayers of many. (2 Cor 1:10-11)**
>
> **The Lord will rescue me from every evil attack and will bring me safely to his heavenly kingdom. To him be glory for ever and ever. Amen. (2 Tim 4:18)**
>
> **And give relief to you who are troubled, and to us as well. This will happen when the Lord Jesus is revealed from heaven in blazing fire with his powerful angels. He will punish those who do not know God and do not obey the gospel of our Lord Jesus. (2 Th 1:7-8)**
>
> **And free those who all their lives were held in slavery by their fear of death. (Heb 2:15)**
>
> **They cried to you and were saved; in you they trusted and were not disappointed. (Psa 22:5)**
>
> **In you, O LORD, I have taken refuge; let me never be put to shame. (Psa 71:1)**
>
> **The prospect of the righteous is joy, but the hopes of the wicked come to nothing. (Prov 10:28)**
>
> **Even to your old age and gray hairs I am he, I am he who will sustain you. I have made you and I will carry you; I will sustain you and I will rescue you. (Isa 46:4)**
>
> **Do not be afraid of them, for I am with you and will rescue you," declares the LORD. (Jer 1:8)**

DEEPER STUDY # 1

(18:7) **Chosen ones** (eklektos): the chosen, the person picked out. The chosen ones are the believers, the disciples of Christ, the people who genuinely belong to God (Mt.24:22, 24, 31; Mk.13:20, 22, 27; Ro.8:33; Col.3:12; 2 Tim.2:10; Tit.1:1; 1 Pt.1:1; 2:9. Also cp. where the word is translated "*chosen,*" Mt.20:16; 22:14; Ro.16:13; 2 Jn.1:1, 13; Rev.17:14.)

The focus of the word is upon God's choice. There is no doubt about this, for the word itself means that God does the choosing and the picking out. But note: the choosing is for service, not for salvation or position (Jn.15:16). The believer is chosen to bear fruit (see DEEPER STUDY # 1—Jn.15:1-8).

4 (18:8) **Prayer, Persevering**: the great tragedy is this: in the last days few will persevere in prayer and faith. Most will fall away. This is the implication of Christ. Note three significant facts.

1. Faith is the one thing Christ is after. He wants trust and belief in Him, in His Word, in His promises and warnings.
2. The greatest evidence of faith is persevering prayer. Faith and persevering prayer are tied together. The person who truly believes will be talking and sharing, communing and fellowshipping, living and moving with God day and night. The person will be praying always.
3. There will be few men of faith and prayer when He returns to earth. There will be some, but the number will be few.

> **The Spirit clearly says that in later times some will abandon the faith and follow deceiving spirits and things taught by demons. (1 Tim 4:1)**
>
> **But mark this: There will be terrible times in the last days. People will be lovers of themselves, lovers of money, boastful, proud, abusive, disobedient to their parents, ungrateful, unholy, without love, unforgiving, slanderous, without self-control, brutal, not lovers of the good, treacherous, rash, conceited, lovers of pleasure rather than lovers of God—having a form of godliness but denying its power. Have nothing to do with them. (2 Tim 3:1-5)**
>
> **First of all, you must understand that in the last days scoffers will come, scoffing and following their own evil desires. They will say, "Where is this 'coming' he promised? Ever since our fathers died, everything goes on as it has since the beginning of creation." (2 Pet 3:3-4)**
>
> **Dear children, this is the last hour; and as you have heard that the antichrist is coming, even now many antichrists have come. This is how we know it is the last hour. (1 John 2:18)**
>
> **They said to you, "In the last times there will be scoffers who will follow their own ungodly desires." (Jude 1:18)**
>
> **The LORD looks down from heaven on the sons of men to see if there are any who understand, any who seek God. All have turned aside, they have together become corrupt; there is no one who does good, not even one. (Psa 14:2-3)**
>
> **I look but there is no one— no one among them to give counsel, no one to give answer when I ask them. (Isa 41:28)**
>
> **He saw that there was no one, he was appalled that there was no one to intervene; so his own arm worked salvation for him, and his own righteousness sustained him. (Isa 59:16)**
>
> **I looked, but there was no one to help, I was appalled that no one gave support; so my own arm worked salvation for me, and my own wrath sustained me. (Isa 63:5)**
>
> **"I looked for a man among them who would build up the wall and stand before me in the gap on behalf of the land so I would not have to destroy it, but I found none. (Ezek 22:30)**

	D. The Parable of the Pharisee and the Tax-Collector: The Spirit Needed for Prayer, 18:9-14	other men—robbers, evildoers, adulterers—or even like this tax collector.	b. He thanks God for making him what he is
		12 I fast twice a week and give a tenth of all I get.'	c. He rededicates himself—he reaffirms his commitment
		13 "But the tax collector	**4 The sinner prays**
1 A parable of warning a. To the self-righteous b. To those who despise or look down on other people	9 To some who were confident of their own righteousness and looked down on everybody else, Jesus told this parable:	stood at a distance. He would not even look up to heaven, but beat his breast and said, 'God, have mercy on me, a sinner.'	a. He stands "at a distance" b. He feels unworthy to face God c. He cries for mercy
2 The scene: Two men are praying in the temple a. One is a Pharisee b. One is a sinner	10 "Two men went up to the temple to pray, one a Pharisee and the other a tax collector.	14 "I tell you that this man, rather than the other, went home justified before God. For everyone who exalts himself will be humbled, and	**5 The major lesson: Justification** a. A humble approach is heard
3 The religionist prays a. He stands—prays only with himself	11 The Pharisee stood up and prayed about himself: 'God, I thank you that I am not like	he who humbles himself will be exalted."	b. A proud approach is not heard

DIVISION VII

THE SON OF MAN'S GREAT JOURNEY TO JERUSALEM (STAGE III): HIS LESSONS AND WARNINGS, 17:11-19:27

D. The Parable of the Pharisee and the Tax-collector: The Spirit Needed for Prayer, 18:9-14

(18:9-14) **Introduction**: two striking things are seen in this passage—both the spirit needed for prayer and the spirit needed for one to be saved.

1. A parable of warning (v.9).
2. The scene: two men are praying in the temple (v.10).
3. The religionist prays (v.11-12).
4. The sinner prays (v.13).
5. The major lesson: justification (v.14).

1 (18:9) **Self-righteousness—Religionists—Self-sufficient**: this parable is directed to three self-centered persons.

1. Those who trust (peitho) in themselves; that is, those who feel they are completely self-sufficient and have no need for anyone else. They feel all they need dwells within their own bodies and minds. There is a feeling that neither God nor anyone else is really needed—not too often, if ever—as one ploughs through life. Note the pride and conceit in the self-sufficient.

> **The man who thinks he knows something does not yet know as he ought to know. (1 Cor 8:2)**
> **So, if you think you are standing firm, be careful that you don't fall! (1 Cor 10:12)**
> **If anyone thinks he is something when he is nothing, he deceives himself. (Gal 6:3)**
> **Do you see a man wise in his own eyes? There is more hope for a fool than for him. (Prov 26:12)**
> **Woe to those who are wise in their own eyes and clever in their own sight. (Isa 5:21)**
> **But you have planted wickedness, you have reaped evil, you have eaten the fruit of deception. Because you have depended on your own strength and on your many warriors, (Hosea 10:13)**

2. Those who are self-righteous. (See notes—Lk.11:37-54; 15:25-32; note and DEEPER STUDY # 1—Ro.2:17-29 for more discussion.) The self-righteous differ from the self-sufficient in that they are interested in righteousness and in God. The self-righteous can be divided into two classes.

a. There are those who feel they are *good enough* for God as they are. They have done and are doing enough good for God to accept them. They think that when they stand face to face with God, He will never reject them. True, they do wrong; but not that much wrong, not enough for God to reject and condemn them, not for eternity. They go about life living as they wish, worshipping God only enough to satisfy their consciences.

Thought 1. The vast majority of people are in this class of self-righteousness. Few men believe they will be rejected by God and refused entrance into heaven. They feel they have enough *goodness* to make them acceptable to God.

> **We do not dare to classify or compare ourselves with some who commend themselves. When they measure themselves by themselves and compare themselves with themselves, they are not wise. (2 Cor 10:12)**
> **Even if I were innocent, my mouth would condemn me; if I were blameless, it would pronounce me guilty. (Job 9:20)**
> **'I am pure and without sin; I am clean and free from guilt. (Job 33:9)**
> **"Do you think this is just? You say, 'I will be cleared by God.' (Job 35:2)**
> **All a man's ways seem innocent to him, but motives are weighed by the LORD. (Prov 16:2)**
> **Many a man claims to have unfailing love, but a faithful man who can find? (Prov 20:6)**
> **All a man's ways seem right to him, but the LORD weighs the heart. (Prov 21:2)**
> **He who trusts in himself is a fool, but he who walks in wisdom is kept safe. (Prov 28:26)**
> **Those who are pure in their own eyes**

and yet are not cleansed of their filth; (Prov 30:12)

You say, 'I am innocent; he is not angry with me.' But I will pass judgment on you because you say, 'I have not sinned.' (Jer 2:35)

b. There are those who have a sensitive conscience and feel the need to give themselves to *good works* as much as is humanly possible. They work and do good in order to secure the favor of God. They believe their good works are what make them *good and righteous* and build them up in the eyes of God. Thus, they labor all their lives trying to build up virtue and merit before God. They try their best to make themselves acceptable to God.

For I tell you that unless your righteousness surpasses that of the Pharisees and the teachers of the law, you will certainly not enter the kingdom of heaven. (Mat 5:20)

Many will say to me on that day, 'Lord, Lord, did we not prophesy in your name, and in your name drive out demons and perform many miracles?' Then I will tell them plainly, 'I never knew you. Away from me, you evildoers!' (Mat 7:22-23)

Therefore no one will be declared righteous in his sight by observing the law; rather, through the law we become conscious of sin. (Rom 3:20)

Know that a man is not justified by observing the law, but by faith in Jesus Christ. So we, too, have put our faith in Christ Jesus that we may be justified by faith in Christ and not by observing the law, because by observing the law no one will be justified. (Gal 2:16)

For it is by grace you have been saved, through faith—and this not from yourselves, it is the gift of God—not by works, so that no one can boast. (Eph 2:8-9)

Who has saved us and called us to a holy life—not because of anything we have done but because of his own purpose and grace. This grace was given us in Christ Jesus before the beginning of time, (2 Tim 1:9)

But when the kindness and love of God our Savior appeared, he saved us, not because of righteous things we had done, but because of his mercy. He saved us through the washing of rebirth and renewal by the Holy Spirit, whom he poured out on us generously through Jesus Christ our Savior, so that, having been justified by his grace, we might become heirs having the hope of eternal life. (Titus 3:4-7)

3. Those who look down on and despise others. The word "look down on or despise" (exouthenountas) means to set at naught; to count as nothing, as unimportant and insignificant. Such persons feel and act as though they are above and better, more important and significant than others. They shy away from, ignore and neglect, pass by and downgrade, criticize and talk about...

- the poor
- the unfortunate
- the poorly dressed
- the homeless
- the downcast
- the derelict
- the undernourished
- the sinner

"'Look, you scoffers, wonder and perish, for I am going to do something in your days that you would never believe, even if someone told you.'" (Acts 13:41)

Or do you show contempt for the riches of his kindness, tolerance and patience, not realizing that God's kindness leads you toward repentance? (Rom 2:4)

Anyone who rejected the law of Moses died without mercy on the testimony of two or three witnesses. How much more severely do you think a man deserves to be punished who has trampled the Son of God under foot, who has treated as an unholy thing the blood of the covenant that sanctified him, and who has insulted the Spirit of grace? (Heb 10:28-29)

Now note: it is these people to whom Jesus directed this parable. He both appealed to and warned the self-sufficient, the self-righteous, and the man who looks down on others.

2 (18:10) **Seeking God—Prayer**: two men are praying in the temple. One was a Pharisee, a religionist; the other was a tax collector who was a great sinner. Note two points.

1. Both men went to the most prominent place to pray, to the temple, the house of prayer itself. There is no better place to pray, no better place to seek God's face. Both men were seeking God's face right where they should have been.

2. Both men went to pray in order to please God. They were both seeking God, wanting God to accept them and to be present with them throughout all their life.

But if from there you seek the LORD your God, you will find him if you look for him with all your heart and with all your soul. (Deu 4:29)

3 (18:11-12) **Self-Righteousness—Religionists**: there is the prayer of the religionist.

1. The religionist stood and prayed only "about himself." Standing was the posture used for public prayer in that day. But note the significant fact: he prayed only, " that is, only to himself. He called "God" by name and addressed his words to God, but his words were not going up to God. They were not a true prayer. He was speaking only with himself and perhaps to others who could hear him. His time and words were wasted except for their personal value, that is, to build his self-confidence and social acceptance. As far as God was concerned, no prayer was being offered to Him. The man's so-called prayer was only a *formal prayer.* There was no true worship or personal communion in it.

We know that God does not listen to sinners. He listens to the godly man who does his will. (John 9:31)

When you ask, you do not receive, because you ask with wrong motives, that you may spend what you get on your pleasures.

(James 4:3)

If I had cherished sin in my heart, the Lord would not have listened; (Psa 66:18)

"Then they will call to me but I will not answer; they will look for me but will not find me. (Prov 1:28)

If a man shuts his ears to the cry of the poor, he too will cry out and not be answered. (Prov 21:13)

If anyone turns a deaf ear to the law, even his prayers are detestable. (Prov 28:9)

When you spread out your hands in prayer, I will hide my eyes from you; even if you offer many prayers, I will not listen. Your hands are full of blood; (Isa 1:15)

But your iniquities have separated you from your God; your sins have hidden his face from you, so that he will not hear. (Isa 59:2)

Then they will cry out to the LORD, but he will not answer them. At that time he will hide his face from them because of the evil they have done. (Micah 3:4)

2. The religionist thanked God for making him what he was. Note several things that should be eye-openers to us. (See note—Lk.18:9 for Scripture on the self-righteous attitude.)

a. He *thanked God that he had been kept* from the sins which people counted as *public sins* or *scandalous sins*. God had kept him from falling into the *great public sins*. He acknowledged that "but for the grace [strength] of God, there go I," and he thanked God that he had been kept from such terrible sins.

b. He said that other men had fallen and committed such sins. He said that...
   - God had His hand upon his life and had kept him from sin, so he thanked God for keeping him.
   - God did not have His hand upon the lives of sinners, so he thanked God that he was not like such men.
   - God looked upon him as the favored one and upon the sinner as the unfavored one.

c. He listed some of the *more serious* public or scandalous sins that he had not fallen into. He thanked God that he was not...
   - a robber: in dealing with others he had always been fair and just, kind and giving, rather than coming across as not being fair or as taking advantage of others.
   - an evildoer: he treated all men justly by recognizing, commending, and promoting them and their welfare. He moved to the side himself and pushed others ahead rather than running the risk of appearing unjust and demonstrating a bad testimony.
   - an adulterer: he was faithful and moral, never going astray in his behavior.
   - a betrayer or non-religious person: he was not as the tax collectors who sold their loyalty and religious privileges to serve the Roman empire, by which they betrayed their own nation (see DEEPER STUDY # 1, Tax Collector—Lk.5:27).

d. He listed two very positive and worshipful acts which he did.
   ⇒ He fasted twice a week. Imagine going without food two days every week just to seek to worship and please God. The religionist was as sincere as he could be about God and righteousness.
   ⇒ He tithed not only ten percent of his income but also ten percent of all that he possessed. Imagine!

(Again, see note—Lk.18:9 for Scripture on the self-righteous attitude.)

4 (18:13) **Lost, The—Confession—Mercy**: there is the prayer of the sinner. Note three significant points.

1. The sinner stood "at a distance ." He was ashamed and embarrassed by his sin. He felt cut off both by God and man. He felt isolated and alone, estranged and separated, dirty and unclean. He also knew that others were embarrassed and shamed by his sin, and he did not want them to be, so he kept his distance: he stood "at a distance." But note: he is genuinely worshipping God, even if he is standing "at a distance."

2. The sinner felt he was unworthy to face God. This is seen in two acts.

a. He would not so much as lift his eyes up to heaven. He did lift his heart, but not his eyes. His sins weighed him down ever so heavily, for he had fallen into gross sin. He was a terrible sinner and he knew it. He was unworthy of the least of God's favors and he knew it. He did not deserve God's forgiveness and acceptance, and he knew it. He could not lift up his eyes, for he had hurt God too much.

b. He beat upon his breast and did it often. Why? Because he could not help it. Sometimes he was disappointed in himself and angry at himself; at other times his heart burst with tears of pleading, begging God to forgive him. He was so unworthy that the tension, emotions, and strain burst forth.

"All things have been committed to me by my Father. No one knows the Son except the Father, and no one knows the Father except the Son and those to whom the Son chooses to reveal him. (Mat 11:27)

On hearing this, Jesus said to them, "It is not the healthy who need a doctor, but the sick. I have not come to call the righteous, but sinners." (Mark 2:17)

For we do not have a high priest who is unable to sympathize with our weaknesses, but we have one who has been tempted in every way, just as we are—yet was without sin. Let us then approach the throne of grace with confidence, so that we may receive mercy and find grace to help us in our time of need. (Heb 4:15-16)

Humble yourselves before the Lord, and He will lift you up. (James 4:10)

The LORD is close to the brokenhearted and saves those who are crushed in spirit. (Psa 34:18)

Yet I am poor and needy; may the Lord think of me. You are my help and my deliverer; O my God, do not delay. (Psa 40:17)

Wash away all my iniquity and cleanse me from my sin. (Psa 51:2)

The sacrifices of God are a broken spirit; a broken and contrite heart, O God,

you will not despise. (Psa 51:17)

Help us, O God our Savior, for the glory of your name; deliver us and forgive our sins for your name's sake. (Psa 79:9)

For this is what the high and lofty One says— he who lives forever, whose name is holy: "I live in a high and holy place, but also with him who is contrite and lowly in spirit, to revive the spirit of the lowly and to revive the heart of the contrite. (Isa 57:15)

Has not my hand made all these things, and so they came into being?" declares the LORD. "This is the one I esteem: he who is humble and contrite in spirit, and trembles at my word. (Isa 66:2)

Rend your heart and not your garments. Return to the LORD your God, for he is gracious and compassionate, slow to anger and abounding in love, and he relents from sending calamity. (Joel 2:13)

3. The sinner cried for mercy. There are two things to note.

a. He called himself *"a sinner"* (to hamartolo). This is critical: he did not feel he was just "a sinner" like everyone else, which would mean he was also as good as everyone else. He no doubt felt he was *the sinner*, the one who had hurt and shamed God more than anyone else, the one who was more undeserving than anyone else. There was nothing *good* within him, nothing to commend him to God, nothing to make him acceptable to God.

b. He cried for mercy. The word "mercy" (hilastheti) is really the word for *"propitiated" or "atonement."* He prayed for God to remove His anger and judgment from him. He deserved God's anger and judgment, but he begged God to turn His anger and judgment away. He felt he would die from the pressure within his chest unless God forgave him and gave him peace and assurance of forgiveness. He wanted to be reconciled to God; he wanted God to remove His judgment from him and to accept him.

Now note: he knew the only way he could ever be accepted by God was for God to have mercy upon him and to forgive his sins. He had *no good* thing about him, no righteousness to offer God. If he were going to be saved by God, God had to accept him simply because he came to God in all the desperation and sin-cerity of his heart and begged God for mercy. God alone was his hope, and mercy alone was all he could plead.

His mercy extends to those who fear him, from generation to generation. (Luke 1:50)

He saved us, not because of righteous things we had done, but because of his mercy. He saved us through the washing of rebirth and renewal by the Holy Spirit, (Titus 3:5; cp. v. 4-7)

But because of his great love for us, God, who is rich in mercy, made us alive with Christ even when we were dead in transgressions—it is by grace you have been saved. (Eph 2:4-5)

Who is a God like you, who pardons sin and forgives the transgression of the remnant of his inheritance? You do not stay angry forever but delight to show mercy. (Micah 7:18)

5 (18:14) **Justification—Salvation**: the major lesson of these verses is justification. The words of Jesus are shocking, contrary to what the world teaches, contrary to the opinions of men, and even contrary to the way many believers act. The *scandalous sinner is the one "justified"* in the sight of God. Why? There are two reasons given by Jesus.

1. Because of what justification means. It means that a person...

- acknowledges his sinfulness and unworthiness.
- cries for God to have mercy.

The justified person is *not righteous*, but he is *counted righteous* by God. The justified person has genuinely cried for mercy and turned from his sin to God. Because of his cry and repentance, God has taken his cry and counted it as righteousness. He has accepted the person because his heart was really set upon God. (See DEEPER STUDY # 2, Justification—Ro.4:22; 5:1. Cp. Ro.4:5; 4:1-3; 4:1-25 for more discussion.)

On hearing this, Jesus said to them, "It is not the healthy who need a doctor, but the sick. I have not come to call the righteous, but sinners." (Mark 2:17)

This is why "it [faith] was credited to him as righteousness." (Rom 4:22)

But also for us, to whom God will credit righteousness—for us who believe in him who raised Jesus our Lord from the dead. He was delivered over to death for our sins and was raised to life for our justification. (Rom 4:24-25)

Therefore, since we have been justified through faith, we have peace with God through our Lord Jesus Christ, (Rom 5:1)

2. Because a proud approach is not heard (see note and DEEPER STUDY # 1—Lk.14:11 for complete discussion).

For everyone who exalts himself will be humbled, and he who humbles himself will be exalted." (Luke 14:11)

A man's pride brings him low, but a man of lowly spirit gains honor. (Prov 29:23)

1 **Little children were brought to Jesus** a. By parents b. For Jesus to touch c. Against the disciples' judgment	**E. The Little Children and Jesus, 18:15-17** (Mt.19:13-15; Mk.10: 13-16) 15 People were also bringing babies to Jesus to have him touch them. When the disciples saw this, they rebuked them.	16 But Jesus called the children to him and said, "Let the little children come to me, and do not hinder them, for the kingdom of God belongs to such as these. 17 I tell you the truth, anyone who will not receive the kingdom of God like a little child will never enter it."	**2 Jesus wanted to receive little children & He called them to Him** **3 Little children are in the Kingdom of God** **4 Only children are in the Kingdom of God**

DIVISION VII

THE SON OF MAN'S GREAT JOURNEY TO JERUSALEM (STAGE III): HIS LESSONS AND WARNINGS, 17:11-19:27

E. The Little Children and Jesus, 18:15-17

(18:15-17) **Introduction**: What is it that makes a man acceptable to God? The answer had just been given by Jesus in the story of the Pharisee and the tax collector (Lk.18:9-14). Now Jesus gave a living demonstration. He took a few small children into His arms and sat them upon His lap, and He told everyone exactly what they must do to be acceptable to God.

1. Little children were brought to Jesus (v.15).
2. Jesus wanted to receive little children and He called them to Him (v.16).
3. Little children are in the Kingdom of God (v.16).
4. Only children are in the Kingdom of God. (v.17).

1 (18:15) **Children—Parents**: little children were brought to Jesus. Note three things.

1. The children were brought by their parents. It is not actually said that the parents brought the children, but it was certainly their parents. They were brought by parents who had already been blessed by Jesus, parents who had already heard Him and been touched by Him. They had been so deeply touched that they wanted their children to be touched.

> **Thought 1.** The point is clear. Parents need to expose themselves to the gospel; they need to be touched by Christ. Parents need to experience true repentance and salvation, and then they need to bring their children to Christ.

2. The children were brought to Jesus for Him to touch. The parents cared for their children and cared deeply. They believed that the thing needed by their children was the *touch* of Jesus. They believed that His touch would bring blessings to their children's lives. But the children were unable to come by themselves. The children would not receive the touch of Jesus unless the parents brought them. To these parents, the touch of Jesus was powerful.

> **When they had finished eating, Jesus said to Simon Peter, "Simon son of John, do you truly love me more than these?" "Yes, Lord," he said, "you know that I love you." Jesus said, "Feed my lambs." (John 21:15)**
>
> **Now I am ready to visit you for the third time, and I will not be a burden to you, because what I want is not your possessions but you. After all, children should not have to save up for their parents, but parents for their children. (2 Cor 12:14)**
>
> **Fathers, do not exasperate your children; instead, bring them up in the training and instruction of the Lord. (Eph 6:4)**
>
> **Only be careful, and watch yourselves closely so that you do not forget the things your eyes have seen or let them slip from your heart as long as you live. Teach them to your children and to their children after them. (Deu 4:9)**
>
> **Impress them on your children. Talk about them when you sit at home and when you walk along the road, when you lie down and when you get up. (Deu 6:7)**

3. The disciples rebuked the parents, refusing to let them reach Jesus. They probably felt the parents were only trying to show off their children, and Jesus was just too busy for such frivolous pride. They made two serious errors in stopping children from coming to Jesus.

a. They were determining who could and who could not be touched by Jesus. Of course, no man has the right to dictate who can and cannot be touched by Jesus.

b. They were not grasping the importance of Jesus' touch, even for little children. Their understanding of the blessing and power of God was immature. No one should ever be stopped or discouraged from coming or from being brought to Jesus.

2 (18:16) **Children—Man, Growth Process—Creation**: Jesus wanted to receive little children and He called them to Him. There are at least two reasons for this.

1. Little children were formed in the mind of God. God is the One who planned for a person to grow from a little child. God cares about every stage of the process of human growth. Therefore, He cares for every single child. As the song says, "He holds the tiny little baby in His hands."

2. Jesus is love, and as love He cares for all, no matter the size or age, looks or appearance, abilities or capabilities. Jesus loves the person even if the person is only a *baby* who has to be carried in the arms of a parent.

> **'For in him we live and move and have our being.' As some of your own poets have said, 'We are his offspring.' (Acts 17:28)**
>
> **The Spirit of God has made me; the breath of the Almighty gives me life. (Job 33:4)**
>
> **Know that the LORD is God. It is he who made us, and we are his ; we are his**

people, the sheep of his pasture. (Psa 100:3)

Sons are a heritage from the LORD, children a reward from him. (Psa 127:3)

Here am I, and the children the LORD has given me. We are signs and symbols in Israel from the LORD Almighty, who dwells on Mount Zion. (Isa 8:18)

Everyone who is called by my name, whom I created for my glory, whom I formed and made." (Isa 43:7)

The people I formed for myself that they may proclaim my praise. (Isa 43:21)

This is what the LORD says— he who made you, who formed you in the womb, and who will help you: Do not be afraid, O Jacob, my servant, Jeshurun, whom I have chosen. (Isa 44:2)

"Before I formed you in the womb I knew you, before you were born I set you apart; I appointed you as a prophet to the nations." (Jer 1:5)

This is the word of the LORD concerning Israel. The LORD, who stretches out the heavens, who lays the foundation of the earth, and who forms the spirit of man within him, declares: (Zec 12:1)

3 (18:16) **Children—Kingdom of God**: little children are in the Kingdom of God. Jesus was saying at least two significant things.

1. Little children are in the *keeping* hands and care of God. "For the Kingdom of God belongs to such as these [little children]." God is looking after little children, loving and caring for them, at least until they reach the point of deliberately rejecting Him and His righteousness.

2. Little children possess the traits that exist in heaven. (See notes—Mt.18:3; DEEPER STUDY # 5—Mk.10:15 for more discussion.)

a. A child is usually dependent and trusting. He knows little and can do little in taking care of himself. To him *big people*, especially mommy and daddy, know everything and can do everything. The child trusts everyone; anyone can take the child into his arms, for the child has not learned to suspect the world. Everyone is a friend; no one is an enemy, and few are strangers.

Be imitators of God, therefore, as dearly loved children (Eph 5:1)

Come, my children, listen to me; I will teach you the fear of the LORD. (Psa 34:11)

But I have stilled and quieted my soul; like a weaned child with its mother, like a weaned child is my soul within me. (Psa 131:2)

Young men and maidens, old men and children. Let them praise the name of the LORD, for his name alone is exalted; his splendor is above the earth and the heavens. (Psa 148:12-13)

Remember your Creator in the days of your youth, before the days of trouble come and the years approach when you will say, "I find no pleasure in them"— (Eccl 12:1)

I said to their children in the desert, "Do not follow the statutes of your fathers or keep their laws or defile yourselves with their idols. I am the LORD your God; follow my decrees and be careful to keep my laws. (Ezek 20:18-19)

b. A child is usually responsive and submissive. A child responds to an adult. He will come, go, pick up, do whatever is suggested to him. He will drop whatever he is doing, surrender whatever is occupying his thoughts and behavior and respond.

If you obey my commands, you will remain in my love, just as I have obeyed my Father's commands and remain in his love. You are my friends if you do what I command. (John 15:10, 14)

But you are not to be like that. Instead, the greatest among you should be like the youngest, and the one who rules like the one who serves. (Luke 22:26)

Young men, in the same way be submissive to those who are older. All of you, clothe yourselves with humility toward one another, because, "God opposes the proud but gives grace to the humble." Humble yourselves, therefore, under God's mighty hand, that he may lift you up in due time. (1 Pet 5:5-6)

Even a child is known by his actions, by whether his conduct is pure and right. (Prov 20:11)

c. A child is usually obedient and learning. He will do exactly what he is asked to do and learn by it. He has not yet learned too much pride nor to act too independently—not while small and innocent. The terrible tragedy is, he is soon taught to be self-centered and pridefully independent just by the example of adults.

Then we will no longer be infants, tossed back and forth by the waves, and blown here and there by every wind of teaching and by the cunning and craftiness of men in their deceitful scheming. (Eph 4:14)

Children, obey your parents in the Lord, for this is right. "Honor your father and mother"—which is the first commandment with a promise—"that it may go well with you and that you may enjoy long life on the earth." (Eph 6:1-3)

Children, obey your parents in everything, for this pleases the Lord. (Col 3:20)

Like newborn babies, crave pure spiritual milk, so that by it you may grow up in your salvation, (1 Pet 2:2)

Come, my children, listen to me; I will teach you the fear of the LORD. (Psa 34:11)

Listen to your father, who gave you life, and do not despise your mother when she is old. (Prov 23:22)

He has showed you, O man, what is good. And what does the LORD require of you? To act justly and to love mercy and to walk humbly with your God. (Micah 6:8)

d. A child is usually humble and forgiving. He is not interested in prominence, fame, power, wealth, or position. He does not push himself forward. He does not want to *sit around* in the midst of a group of adults. He has not been taught to think in terms of *self-importance*, not yet. The child also forgives ever so easily. He can be disciplined, neglected, even abused; and before the adult turns around the child forgives and forgets (unless, of course, it is extreme abuse. We must remember that Christ is talking about the child in a normal, healthy environment.)

Blessed are the peacemakers, for they will be called sons of God. (Mat 5:9)

Brothers, stop thinking like children. In regard to evil be infants, but in your thinking be adults. (1 Cor 14:20)

And you have forgotten that word of encouragement that addresses you as sons: "My son, do not make light of the Lord's discipline, and do not lose heart when he rebukes you, because the Lord disciplines those he loves, and he punishes everyone he accepts as a son." (Heb 12:5-6)

4 (18:17) **Children—Kingdom of God**: only children are in the Kingdom of God. This point is critical to see, for Christ used strong words about some persons not being able to enter the Kingdom of Heaven: "[Some persons] will never enter it." There is nothing, absolutely nothing that can get a man into the Kingdom of Heaven except receiving the kingdom like a little child. There is no one in heaven except little children, people who have become children of God. (See note, Child—Mt.18:3 for more explanation of this fact.)

And if he finds it, I tell you the truth, he is happier about that one sheep than about the ninety-nine that did not wander off. (Mat 18:13)

Yet to all who received him, to those who believed in his name, he gave the right to become children of God—children born not of natural descent, nor of human decision or a husband's will, but born of God. (John 1:12-13)

In reply Jesus declared, "I tell you the truth, no one can see the kingdom of God unless he is born again." (John 3:3)

Because those who are led by the Spirit of God are sons of God. For you did not receive a spirit that makes you a slave again to fear, but you received the Spirit of sonship. And by him we cry, "Abba, Father." The Spirit himself testifies with our spirit that we are God's children. (Rom 8:14-16)

"Therefore come out from them and be separate, says the Lord. Touch no unclean thing, and I will receive you." "I will be a Father to you, and you will be my sons and daughters, says the Lord Almighty." (2 Cor 6:17-18)

(Cp. also Gal.4:4-7; Ph.2:15; 1 Jn.3:1.)

	F. The Rich Young Ruler: The Cost of Eternal Life, 18:18-30 (Mt.19:16-30; Mk.10: 17-31)	23 When he heard this, he became very sad, because he was a man of great wealth.	d. He rejects sorrowfully
1 Example 1: The ruler a. He must acknowledge Jesus as God 1) Ruler called Him "Good Teacher" 2) God is the only good one 3) Jesus asked: Are you calling me God? b. He must keep the commandments c. He must *give up* all that he has	18 A certain ruler asked him, "Good teacher, what must I do to inherit eternal life?" 19 "Why do you call me good?" Jesus answered. "No one is good—except God alone. 20 You know the commandments: 'Do not commit adultery, do not murder, do not steal, do not give false testimony, honor your father and mother.'" 21 "All these I have kept since I was a boy," he said. 22 When Jesus heard this, he said to him, "You still lack one thing. Sell everything you have and give to the poor, and you will have treasure in heaven. Then come, follow me."	24 Jesus looked at him and said, "How hard it is for the rich to enter the kingdom of God! 25 Indeed, it is easier for a camel to go through the eye of a needle than for a rich man to enter the kingdom of God." 26 Those who heard this asked, "Who then can be saved?" 27 Jesus replied, "What is impossible with men is possible with God." 28 Peter said to him, "We have left all we had to follow you!" 29 "I tell you the truth," Jesus said to them, "no one who has left home or wife or brothers or parents or children for the sake of the kingdom of God 30 Will fail to receive many times as much in this age and, in the age to come, eternal life."	**2 Example 2: The Wealthy** a. It is difficult for a wealthy person to enter God's Kingdom b. The misconception about wealthy persons c. The only possible way for wealthy persons to be saved: God **3 Example 3: The disciples** a. They left all to follow Christ b. They & all other followers shall be greatly rewarded 1) In this world: "Much more" 2) In the world to come: "eternal Life"

DIVISION VII

THE SON OF MAN'S GREAT JOURNEY TO JERUSALEM (STAGE III): HIS LESSONS AND WARNINGS, 17:11-19:27

F. The Rich Young Ruler: The Cost of Eternal Life, 18:18-30

(18:18-30) **Introduction**: many people think that eternal life is free, that it costs nothing. This is a false concept. Eternal life does cost. It costs a man everything he is and has. The message of this passage is probably the most demanding message ever preached.

1. Example 1: the ruler (v.18-23).
2. Example 2: the wealthy (v.24-27).
3. Example 3: the disciples (v.28-30).

1 (18:18-23) **Eternal Life—Jesus Christ, Deity—Needs—Self-Denial**: the first example is that of the rich young ruler. When the other gospel accounts of this event are compared, the ruler is seen to be young and rich. But it does not matter, not for the purpose Luke is stressing. The cost of eternal life is the *same* for all persons, rich or poor, young or old.

1. The person who seeks eternal life must acknowledge Jesus as God. The ruler called Jesus "Good Teacher." The word "good" was a word that was ascribed only to God. It was never used in reference to a man. This is critical to see, for it meant that the ruler was calling Jesus "good" in the sense that God would be called "good." He saw something in Jesus *like God*. It was not just flattery; he esteemed Jesus highly, probably believing or else coming close to believing Jesus' claim to be the Son of God.

Now note what Jesus did. The man had called Him "good," a word used only in addressing God. Jesus asked the man, "Why do you call me good? God alone is good. Are you saying I am God?" Jesus is unquestionably claiming to be God. He was saying, "If I am a mere man, a good teacher, then I am not good and do not have the words of eternal life. But if I am God, then you can truly call me good, and I do have the words of eternal life." The point is this: Jesus told the man how to receive eternal life. He was claiming to be God, the One who could give eternal life to a person.

> **"For God so loved the world that he gave his one and only Son, that whoever believes in him shall not perish but have eternal life. (John 3:16)**
>
> **Simon Peter answered him, "Lord, to whom shall we go? You have the words of eternal life. (John 6:68)**
>
> **I told you that you would die in your sins; if you do not believe that I am the one I claim to be, you will indeed die in your sins." (John 8:24)**
>
> **Jesus answered, "I am the way and the truth and the life. No one comes to the Father except through me. If you really knew me, you would know my Father as well. From now on, you do know him and have seen him." (John 14:6-7)**
>
> **Salvation is found in no one else, for there is no other name under heaven given to men by which we must be saved." (Acts 4:12)**
>
> **For there is one God and one mediator between God and men, the man Christ Jesus, who gave himself as a ransom for all**

men—the testimony given in its proper time. (1 Tim 2:5-6)

2. The man must keep the commandments. He had asked, "What must I do to inherit eternal life?" In his mind he had to do something, some great work—and he did. He had to trust and love God so much that he would keep God's commandments. He had to keep the commandments *after* he had accepted Jesus as God.

Jesus said to the man, "I am good, just as God is good; therefore, I am God. Now, once accepting this fact, you must obey the commandments and learn to love your neighbor. First, trust and love God, then trust and love your neighbor." Note two facts.

a. The man had to see that Jesus was God, and as God He was to be trusted and loved. Then he had to see that he was to love his neighbor *as* himself. Jesus was simply covering the two great commandments with the man, and He was going to show the man how desperately short he was. (See outlines and notes—Mt.22:34-40.)

"Not everyone who says to me, 'Lord, Lord,' will enter the kingdom of heaven, but only he who does the will of my Father who is in heaven. (Mat 7:21)

Whoever has my commands and obeys them, he is the one who loves me. He who loves me will be loved by my Father, and I too will love him and show myself to him." (John 14:21)

Jesus replied, "If anyone loves me, he will obey my teaching. My Father will love him, and we will come to him and make our home with him. (John 14:23)

If you obey my commands, you will remain in my love, just as I have obeyed my Father's commands and remain in his love. You are my friends if you do what I command. (John 15:10, 14)

"Blessed are those who wash their robes, that they may have the right to the tree of life and may go through the gates into the city. (Rev 22:14)

b. The man made a phenomenal claim: he had kept all these commandments from his youth up. He, of course, had not kept them, not like he should. He was sincere, but this picture of God was a surface picture. He was not perfect in all his dealings with men and women, not in the eyes of God. In fact, it was just this, the way he looked at men and the desperate needs of the world, that was his problem. He was not *giving* to help the needs of the world like he should. It was this that was keeping him out of heaven.

3. The man must *give up* all he had. This is exactly what Jesus said, "Sell everything you have, and give to the poor." Was this unreasonable? Did Jesus really mean it? Could such radical action be demanded even by God?

Why not? Why would God *not* demand just this? Especially when the world is full of little children (and men and women) who are starving and diseased, without shelter or clothing, and dying being doomed to hell? And why are they in such a condition when there is enough of everything to go around, and the gospel that can save them is known? Let no one ever say that God does not demand the giving of all after a man has taken care of his own necessities. And let no one ever think that the doom of God will not fall upon the man…

- who shuts his eyes to the massive needs of the world.
- who hoards and banks his money.
- who lets money just sit and sit, doing nothing except causing men to say "My, what a rich man."

How empty words really are. There is but one question for the man who builds up and keeps: "Who do you think you are, God? Beware of God if you think He does not demand the giving of all you are and have to help the desperate millions of this earth." Jesus hit the very nerve of the man's problem: coveting—lusting after money, material goods, possessions, and wealth—instead of longing to help the needy of the world.

Note the glorious promise: give all you have and you shall have treasure in heaven and be allowed to follow Christ. It is *only after* we give all we have (beyond our own true needs) that we are allowed to enter heaven. That is the Word of Christ, His answer to the question, "How do I inherit eternal life?"

The man rejected Jesus—Jesus had asked too much. The man was unwilling to give all he was and had; he was very sad, sorrowful about his decision, but he did reject.

Then he said to them all: "If anyone would come after me, he must deny himself and take up his cross daily and follow me. (Luke 9:23)

But store up for yourselves treasures in heaven, where moth and rust do not destroy, and where thieves do not break in and steal. (Mat 6:20)

Sell your possessions and give to the poor. Provide purses for yourselves that will not wear out, a treasure in heaven that will not be exhausted, where no thief comes near and no moth destroys. (Luke 12:33)

In the same way, any of you who does not give up everything he has cannot be my disciple. (Luke 14:33)

What is more, I consider everything a loss compared to the surpassing greatness of knowing Christ Jesus my Lord, for whose sake I have lost all things. I consider them rubbish, that I may gain Christ (Phil 3:8)

Command those who are rich in this present world not to be arrogant nor to put their hope in wealth, which is so uncertain, but to put their hope in God, who richly provides us with everything for our enjoyment. Command them to do good, to be rich in good deeds, and to be generous and willing to share. In this way they will lay up treasure for themselves as a firm foundation for the coming age, so that they may take hold of the life that is truly life. (1 Tim 6:17-19)

I counsel you to buy from me gold refined in the fire, so you can become rich; and white clothes to wear, so you can cover your shameful nakedness; and salve to put on your eyes, so you can see. (Rev 3:18)

2 (18:24-27) **Wealth—Rich—Salvation—Needy**: the second example is that of wealthy persons. Jesus made three striking points.

1. It is extremely difficult, almost impossible, for a rich person to enter heaven. It is as difficult as a camel's going through the eye of a needle. Why? Because the rich man has kept his wealth, hoarded and stored it up. He has not served God by *loving his neighbor as himself.* The rich man has used his talents to make money so that he could buy the *latest styles and be called rich* by other men. He failed to use his talents to make money to meet the desperate needs of children (and men and women). The world desperately needs food, shelter, clothes, medicine, and above all, the gospel. It is no wonder a rich man will not enter heaven when most of the world is in such desperate need. Why would God accept a man who has wealth when that man would not take the time to seek and reach out to the child who was starving and dying both physically and spiritually?

Attempts are sometimes made to lessen the cost of the Lord's demands.

⇒ Some say that what Christ means is this: a man *must be willing* to give his wealth, not actually give it. This is tragic, for there is *no meaning in willingness*—no act, no true decision, no work, no evidence, no proof, no demonstration. Willingness is nothing more than a word. It is empty without action to back it up. A man who is truly willing does something. Conversely, a man is *not really willing* if he does not do something.

⇒ Others try to explain away the impossibility of a camel's going through the eye of a needle. They say that a sewing needle is not what is meant (see note, Camel—Mt.19:24). Again, this view misses the whole point. Jesus is saying this: a man who does not give all his wealth (beyond his true necessities) to meet the needs of the world shall find it no easier entering heaven than a camel does going through the eye of a needle.

Thought 1. Let none of us miss heaven or cause another to miss heaven by trying to lessen the demand of Christ. Any honest man—if he were responsible for overseeing the children of the world—would condemn another person who had the money but who let a child die of starvation or exposure.

Thought 2. It is time for us to be honest and let the Savior of the world speak with the force with which He spoke. The world is desperate. Children and their mothers and fathers are dying from the agonizing pain of hunger and disease, and the terrorizing elements of nature. They are dying without ever having heard of the eternal salvation that is in Christ. The rich, who have the talents to earn more than they need, must use their talents to earn more to save the children and adults of the world who are in such a desperate plight. Jesus said no rich man shall enter heaven who does not give all he has.

For where your treasure is, there your heart will be also. (Mat 6:21)

Jesus answered, "If you want to be perfect, go, sell your possessions and give to the poor, and you will have treasure in heaven. Then come, follow me." (Mat 19:21)

And the second is like it: 'Love your neighbor as yourself.' (Mat 22:39)

For you know the grace of our Lord Jesus Christ, that though he was rich, yet for your sakes he became poor, so that you through his poverty might become rich. (2 Cor 8:9)

He who has been stealing must steal no longer, but must work, doing something useful with his own hands, that he may have something to share with those in need. (Eph 4:28)

"Here now is the man who did not make God his stronghold but trusted in his great wealth and grew strong by destroying others!" (Psa 52:7)

Whoever trusts in his riches will fall, but the righteous will thrive like a green leaf. (Prov 11:28)

2. The misconception about wealth. The disciples were shocked, thoroughly dismayed. Jesus was saying something diametrically opposed to what they and everyone else had always thought. They had always been taught (as have succeeding generations, even the church):

⇒ that prosperity (wealth, comfort, and things) is God's blessing.

⇒ that a person receives because God is blessing him.

⇒ that prosperity is the reward of righteousness and obedience.

⇒ that God blesses a person with the things of this earth if he is righteous and obedient.

However, Jesus was saying the very opposite: that a prosperous person will most likely never enter heaven; that prosperity poses such a dangerous threat to a person that his eternal doom is almost assured. The disciples knew that God would never put a person in such a precarious, dangerous position. They knew that Jesus was attacking the world's most cherished and ardent belief: be good (righteous) and you will be blessed by God (and the thought of blessing is always of material blessing. See note—Eph.1:3.)

They were shocked, thoroughly dismayed: Who then can be saved? The vast majority of people were threatening their own eternal destiny. They were dooming themselves. Since prosperity is not the reward (sign) for righteousness and the rich are barred from heaven, that means that the poor, too, are barred; for they are spending most of their time in dreaming about and seeking prosperity.

But the worries of this life, the deceitfulness of wealth and the desires for other things come in and choke the word, making it unfruitful. (Mark 4:19)

And I'll say to myself, "You have plenty of good things laid up for many years. Take life easy; eat, drink and be merry."' "But God said to him, 'You fool! This very night your life will be demanded from you. Then who will get what you have prepared for yourself?' (Luke 12:19-20)

People who want to get rich fall into temptation and a trap and into many foolish and harmful desires that plunge men into ruin and destruction. (1 Tim 6:9)

Command those who are rich in this present world not to be arrogant nor to put their hope in wealth, which is so uncertain, but to put their hope in God, who richly provides us with everything for our enjoyment. (1 Tim 6:17)

And when your herds and flocks grow large and your silver and gold increase and all you have is multiplied, then your heart

will become proud and you will forget the LORD your God, who brought you out of Egypt, out of the land of slavery. (Deu 8:13-14)

The wealth of the rich is their fortified city; they imagine it an unscalable wall. (Prov 18:11)

3. The only possibility for wealthy persons to be saved is God. Very simply…
   - it is impossible for a rich man to save himself.
   - the rich man must turn to God and love God and do God's will by loving his neighbor as himself. God alone can save a rich man.
   - the decision is up to the rich man. He can turn to be *with God* in eternity, or he can continue to live for himself now and can suffer eternal condemnation.

For nothing is impossible with God." (Luke 1:37)

"I know that you can do all things; no plan of yours can be thwarted. (Job 42:2)

Command those who are rich in this present world not to be arrogant nor to put their hope in wealth, which is so uncertain, but to put their hope in God, who richly provides us with everything for our enjoyment. Command them to do good, to be rich in good deeds, and to be generous and willing to share. In this way they will lay up treasure for themselves as a firm foundation for the coming age, so that they may take hold of the life that is truly life. (1 Tim 6:17-19)

For no one can lay any foundation other than the one already laid, which is Jesus Christ. (1 Cor 3:11)

3 (18:28-30) **Reward**: the third example is that of the disciples. Note two points.

1. The disciples were examples of what Christ meant. They had left all to follow Christ. (See note and DEEPER STUDY # 1—Lk.9:23 for discussion.)

2. The disciples and all other followers of Christ will be richly rewarded. Note three points.

   a. The reason for the reward is clearly stated. They left all, gave up all for Christ in order to meet the desperate needs of the world, and they gave up the most cherished things on earth: their property and family.

   b. Their reward in this world was to be *much more.* The Gospel of Mark makes it clear that Christ was speaking of present reward on earth (Mk.10:21). No true follower of Christ has ever forsaken persons or things and then been left alone and destitute by Christ. Christ rewards His true follower manyfold. Note: the reward is both human and material.

      1) The human reward is most fulfilling: a real and true fellowship among genuine believers. Christ knows when a follower of His has been turned against by those whom He loves ever so deeply. He knows when to send someone into the life of His followers, when to meet the aching need of His follower for true friendship. He more than abundantly meets the need.

We proclaim to you what we have seen and heard, so that you also may have fellowship with us. And our fellowship is with the Father and with his Son, Jesus Christ. (1 John 1:3)

But if we walk in the light, as he is in the light, we have fellowship with one another, and the blood of Jesus, his Son, purifies us from all sin. (1 John 1:7)

They devoted themselves to the apostles' teaching and to the fellowship, to the breaking of bread and to prayer. (Acts 2:42)

I am a friend to all who fear you, to all who follow your precepts. (Psa 119:63)

Then those who feared the LORD talked with each other, and the LORD listened and heard. A scroll of remembrance was written in his presence concerning those who feared the LORD and honored his name. (Mal 3:16)

      2) The material reward is most assuring: the meeting of necessities and whatever else God wants us to have so that we can help meet the needs of others.

      The idea that Christ was conveying is that of perfect care and security. Fear and insecurity cause us to crave and to be greedy for more, and fear and insecurity are most unhealthy and destabilizing. When we forsake all to genuinely follow Christ, He gives us the greatest peace and security possible: Himself and His power to provide our necessities. We never have to worry or be anxious again (see notes—Lk.16:10-12; Mt.6:25-34. Cp. Lk.18:30; Mk.10:30; Eph.4:28.) There is much more in Christ than in any amount of possessions or worldly companionship and friendship. In Christ the believer has…

- happiness
- peace
- assurance
- satisfaction
- fulfillment
- joy
- security
- confidence
- completeness

But seek first his kingdom and his righteousness, and all these things will be given to you as well. (Mat 6:33; cp. Mt.6:25-34)

The thief comes only to steal and kill and destroy; I have come that they may have life, and have it to the full. (John 10:10)

And my God will meet all your needs according to his glorious riches in Christ Jesus. (Phil 4:19)

Worship the LORD your God, and his blessing will be on your food and water. I will take away sickness from among you, (Exo 23:25)

Praise be to the Lord, to God our Savior, who daily bears our burdens. Selah (Psa 68:19)

He will also send you rain for the seed you sow in the ground, and the food that comes from the land will be rich and plentiful. In that day your cattle will graze in broad meadows. (Isa 30:23)

You will have plenty to eat, until you are full, and you will praise the name of the LORD your God, who has worked wonders for you; never again will my people be shamed. (Joel 2:26)

Bring the whole tithe into the storehouse, that there may be food in my house. Test me in this," says the LORD Almighty, "and see if I will not throw open the floodgates of heaven and pour out so much blessing that you will not have room enough for it. (Mal 3:10)

c. Their reward in the world to come is to be "eternal life" (see DEEPER STUDY # 1—Jn.17:2-3; cp. Jn.1:4 and Mt.19:28. Cp. Ro.8:16-18.)

Jesus looked at him and loved him. "One thing you lack," he said. "Go, sell everything you have and give to the poor, and you will have treasure in heaven. Then come, follow me." (Mark 10:21)

"I tell you the truth, whoever hears my word and believes him who sent me has eternal life and will not be condemned; he has crossed over from death to life. (John 5:24)

	G. The Prediction of the Cross, 18:31-34 (Mt.20:17-19; Mk.10: 32-34)		
1 The purpose of Jesus: To fullfill the Scripture	31 Jesus took the Twelve aside and told them, "We are going up to Jerusalem, and everything that is written by the prophets about the Son of Man will be fulfilled.	32 He will be handed over to the Gentiles. They will mock him, insult him, spit on him, flog him and kill him. 33 On the third day he will rise again." 34 The disciples did not understand any of this. Its meaning was hidden from them, and they did not know what he was talking about.	**2 The prophecies to be fulfilled** a. He was to be tortured & disgraced b. He was to be put to death c. He was to rise again[DS1] **3 The disciples' response: Confusion**

DIVISION VII

THE SON OF MAN'S GREAT JOURNEY TO JERUSALEM (STAGE III): HIS LESSONS AND WARNINGS, 17:11-19:27

G. The Prediction of the Cross, 18:31-34

(18:31-34) **Jesus' Death—Bible**: note that Jesus pulled the twelve disciples off to the side. He wanted to continue drilling into them the fact of His death and resurrection. It was through these two phenomenal events that He was to save the world; therefore, they had to be indoctrinated with the glorious truth of the two events.

1. The purpose of Jesus: to fulfill Scripture (v.31).
2. The prophecies to be fulfilled (v.32-33).
3. The disciples' response: confusion (v.34).

1 (18:31) **Jesus Christ, Mission—Purpose—Scripture—Prophecy**: the purpose of Jesus was to fulfill Scripture. Note three points.

1. Jesus said, "We are going to Jerusalem." This was His purpose, to set His face toward Jerusalem. By this He meant His death and His sufferings. The focus of His purpose on earth was to suffer for the salvation of men (see notes—Lk.9:51-13:21; 9:51-56).

2. Jesus claimed to be the Son of Man. He said that all things written concerning the Son of Man would be fulfilled in Him. He was the One who was sent to fulfill God's purposes on earth (see DEEPER STUDY # 3—Mt.8:20).

3. Jesus said that His sufferings were the prophetic fulfillment of Scripture. In Him all the prophecies of Scripture are to be fulfilled. Note how this supports both the truth of the Scripture and of Christ. The Scriptures have to be fulfilled, and they have to be fulfilled in Christ. Not one jot or tittle can fail. Jesus was the Son of Man, the very One of whom Scripture spoke and the very One in whom all Scripture was to be fulfilled.

> **I tell you the truth, until heaven and earth disappear, not the smallest letter, not the least stroke of a pen, will by any means disappear from the Law until everything is accomplished. (Mat 5:18)**
>
> **Heaven and earth will pass away, but my words will never pass away. (Luke 21:33)**
>
> **The works of his hands are faithful and just; all his precepts are trustworthy. (Psa 111:7)**
>
> **But I the LORD will speak what I will, and it shall be fulfilled without delay. For in your days, you rebellious house, I will fulfill whatever I say, declares the Sovereign LORD.'" (Ezek 12:25)**

2 (18:32-33) **Prophecy—Scripture**: the prophecies to be fulfilled. Note the reference to the Gentiles. Jesus was to be delivered to the Gentiles. The Jews were going to be the ones to deliver Him into Gentile hands. This fact was to symbolize both the religionists and the world—both were going to reject and put God's Son to death. Neither could accept Him and His message of total self-denial. There were three prophecies in particular to be fulfilled. (Cp. Ps.22:1f; Is.53:1f.)

1. Jesus was to be tortured and disgraced, injured and insulted. There were four forms of disgrace and torture mentioned.
   a. To mock: to ridicule, scorn, insult, humiliate, defy, jeer.
   b. To insult (hubristhsetai): to reproach; to treat with insolence and contempt; to be outraged; to treat shamefully and despitefully.
   c. To spit upon: a sign of monstrous disrespect and gross insult.
   d. To flog: to beat with a rod or a whip weighted with either jagged metal or bone chips. Thirty-nine or forty lashes were inflicted. The whole purpose of scourging was to inflict severe pain.

2. Jesus was to be put to death. In this passage He was predicting His death. We, of course, look back upon it. Jesus bore the sins of men, suffering the ultimate degree of pain. He suffered pain in an absolute sense.
   a. Mentally, while He was being tortured, His mind was bound to be upon why He was suffering. He was thinking about the sin of man and the problem sin had caused God. Imagine all the world's sin, the enormity and awfulness of it, consuming His mind. He was suffering mentally to the ultimate degree.
   b. Spiritually, His heart was being broken. Those whom He loved so much were committing a sin so horrendous it defied imagination. They were rebelling against God so much that they were killing God's own Son.

      Even more terrible, His own Father, God Himself, was to turn His back upon Him. Because of sin, God was forced to separate Himself from His Son (see notes—Mt.27:46-49; Mk.15:34). Jesus was going to bear spiritual pain in an absolute sense (1 Pt.2:24; 2 Cor.5:21. Cp. Is.53:4-7 for a descriptive account of His bearing our sin.)
   c. Physically, the pain of the crucifixion was to be more severe because of the mental and spiritual pressure He was having to bear. There is also

truth to the fact that the more ridicule within a persecutor's heart, the more he tortures his victim (cp. the crown of thorns, royal robe, and excessive mockery of the soldiers). The fact that Jesus claimed to be the Son of God aroused the heart of the persecutors to inflict more scorn and torture.

"I am the good shepherd. The good shepherd lays down his life for the sheep. (John 10:11)

Just as the Father knows me and I know the Father—and I lay down my life for the sheep. (John 10:15)

The reason my Father loves me is that I lay down my life—only to take it up again. No one takes it from me, but I lay it down of my own accord. I have authority to lay it down and authority to take it up again. This command I received from my Father." (John 10:17-18)

Who gave himself for our sins to rescue us from the present evil age, according to the will of our God and Father, (Gal 1:4)

And live a life of love, just as Christ loved us and gave himself up for us as a fragrant offering and sacrifice to God. Husbands, love your wives, just as Christ loved the church and gave himself up for her (Eph 5:2, 25)

Who gave himself for us to redeem us from all wickedness and to purify for himself a people that are his very own, eager to do what is good. (Titus 2:14)

He himself bore our sins in his body on the tree, so that we might die to sins and live for righteousness; by his wounds you have been healed. (1 Pet 2:24)

For Christ died for sins once for all, the righteous for the unrighteous, to bring you to God. He was put to death in the body but made alive by the Spirit, (1 Pet 3:18)

This is how we know what love is: Jesus Christ laid down his life for us. And we ought to lay down our lives for our brothers. (1 John 3:16)

And from Jesus Christ, who is the faithful witness, the firstborn from the dead, and the ruler of the kings of the earth. To him who loves us and has freed us from our sins by his blood, (Rev 1:5)

3. Jesus was to rise from the dead (see DEEPER STUDY # 1—Lk.18:33).

This man was handed over to you by God's set purpose and foreknowledge; and you, with the help of wicked men, put him to death by nailing him to the cross. But God raised him from the dead, freeing him from the agony of death, because it was impossible for death to keep its hold on him. (Acts 2:23-24)

You disowned the Holy and Righteous One and asked that a murderer be released to you. You killed the author of life, but God raised him from the dead. We are witnesses of this. (Acts 3:14-15)

With great power the apostles continued to testify to the resurrection of the Lord Jesus, and much grace was upon them all. (Acts 4:33)

"We are witnesses of everything he did in the country of the Jews and in Jerusalem. They killed him by hanging him on a tree, but God raised him from the dead on the third day and caused him to be seen. He was not seen by all the people, but by witnesses whom God had already chosen—by us who ate and drank with him after he rose from the dead. (Acts 10:39-41)

He was delivered over to death for our sins and was raised to life for our justification. (Rom 4:25)

That if you confess with your mouth, "Jesus is Lord," and believe in your heart that God raised him from the dead, you will be saved. (Rom 10:9)

For what I received I passed on to you as of first importance : that Christ died for our sins according to the Scriptures, that he was buried, that he was raised on the third day according to the Scriptures, (1 Cor 15:3-4)

Then he appeared to James, then to all the apostles, (1 Cor 15:7)

And he died for all, that those who live should no longer live for themselves but for him who died for them and was raised again. (2 Cor 5:15)

Which he exerted in Christ when he raised him from the dead and seated him at his right hand in the heavenly realms, (Eph 1:20)

We believe that Jesus died and rose again and so we believe that God will bring with Jesus those who have fallen asleep in him. (1 Th 4:14)

Praise be to the God and Father of our Lord Jesus Christ! In his great mercy he has given us new birth into a living hope through the resurrection of Jesus Christ from the dead, (1 Pet 1:3)

For Christ died for sins once for all, the righteous for the unrighteous, to bring you to God. He was put to death in the body but made alive by the Spirit, (1 Pet 3:18)

DEEPER STUDY # 1

(18:33) **Jesus Christ, Resurrection**: Jesus was to be raised from the dead. Covering the resurrection in the same discussion with His death did three major things.

1. It drove the point of the resurrection into the minds of the disciples. They must forever remember the resurrection. The death of Jesus was not the final word.

Remember Jesus Christ, raised from the dead, descended from David. This is my gospel, (2 Tim 2:8)

2. It foreshadowed the power of God. After His resurrection the disciples would remember, and the glorious

truth of God's power would be reinforced in their minds and hearts forever.

a. The power of God was victorious.

"Where, O death, is your victory? Where, O death, is your sting?" But thanks be to God! He gives us the victory through our Lord Jesus Christ. (1 Cor 15:55, 57)

b. The power of God did triumph.

And having disarmed the powers and authorities, he made a public spectacle of them, triumphing over them by the cross. (Col 2:15)

c. The power of God did conquer.

No, in all these things we are more than conquerors through him who loved us. (Rom 8:37)

Since the children have flesh and blood, he too shared in their humanity so that by his death he might destroy him who holds the power of death—that is, the devil—and free those who all their lives were held in slavery by their fear of death. (Heb 2:14-15)

3. It foreshadowed the stirring that God's power was going to work in their lives.

a. The power to encourage and motivate.

And his incomparably great power for us who believe. That power is like the working of his mighty strength, which he exerted in Christ when he raised him from the dead and seated him at his right hand in the heavenly realms, (Eph 1:19-20)

For God did not give us a spirit of timidity, but a spirit of power, of love and of self-discipline. (2 Tim 1:7)

b. The power to assure and build confidence.

Then he said to Thomas, "Put your finger here; see my hands. Reach out your hand and put it into my side. Stop doubting and believe." Thomas said to him, "My Lord and my God!" Then Jesus told him, "Because you have seen me, you have believed; blessed are those who have not seen and yet have believed." (John 20:27-29)

c. The power to give courage and boldness.

Now, Lord, consider their threats and enable your servants to speak your word with great boldness. Stretch out your hand to heal and perform miraculous signs and wonders through the name of your holy servant Jesus." (Acts 4:29-30)

So do not be ashamed to testify about our Lord, or ashamed of me his prisoner. But join with me in suffering for the gospel, by the power of God, who has saved us and called us to a holy life—not because of anything we have done but because of his own purpose and grace. This grace was given us in Christ Jesus before the beginning of time, (2 Tim 1:8-9)

3 (18:34) **Jesus Christ, Death, Misunderstood**: the disciples' response was that of confusion. (See notes—Mt.17:22; Lk.9:44-45 for more discussion.) Note an interesting fact. This verse says the same thing over and over in three different ways. The disciples were totally confused.

⇒ They understood none of these things. They *would not* accept nor understand the death of Christ literally. They refused to take His words at face value; therefore, they *did not* understand these things.

⇒ His meaning was hidden from them. Since they *would not* literally accept His words, they *could not* understand. What He said was a puzzle, a mystery, a riddle. The meaning was completely hidden from them. The word "hidden" (kekrummenon) has the sense of completion in it.

⇒ They did not know the things which were spoken. They did not perceive, and they *kept on* not perceiving.

The disciples were familiar with the Old Testament, but they had never seen *within* the passages that predicted the Messiah's death. They were so intent on the predicted blessings that the Messiah was to bring that they were blind to the predicted sufferings. They could see nothing that could be accomplished by the disgrace of death; therefore, they had only a partial grasp of prophetic truth. (See note—Mk.10:32.)

Thought 1. When the Scriptures are not taken at face value—when they are not accepted for exactly what they say—the result for anyone is always...

- not understanding *any of this.*
- having the *meaning* hidden from them.
- not knowing what He is talking about.

He said to them, "How foolish you are, and how slow of heart to believe all that the prophets have spoken! (Luke 24:25)

The man without the Spirit does not accept the things that come from the Spirit of God, for they are foolishness to him, and he cannot understand them, because they are spiritually discerned. (1 Cor 2:14)

A man who has riches without understanding is like the beasts that perish. (Psa 49:20)

But they do not know the thoughts of the LORD; they do not understand his plan, he who gathers them like sheaves to the threshing floor. (Micah 4:12)

	H. The Healing of a Blind Beggar: Steps to Getting Help from God, 18:35-43 (cp. Mt.20:29-34; Mk.10:46-52)	39 Those who led the way rebuked him and told him to be quiet, but he shouted all the more, "Son of David, have mercy on me!"	**4 A man had a persistence in seeking Jesus that would not quit**
		40 Jesus stopped and ordered the man to be brought to him. When he came near, Jesus asked him,	**5 A man had the boldness to ask great things of God** a. Jesus stood still & called for him
1 Jesus approached Jericho **2 A man had great need** a. He was blind b. He was poor	35 As Jesus approached Jericho, a blind man was sitting by the roadside begging.	41 "What do you want me to do for you?" "Lord, I want to see," he replied.	b. The man expressed his longing
3 A man had great hope in Jesus	36 When he heard the crowd going by, he asked what was happening.	42 Jesus said to him, "Receive your sight; your faith has healed you."	c. The man was saved by faith
a. He believed the reports he had heard about Jesus b. He acknowledged Jesus as the Messiah[DS1] c. He cried for mercy	37 They told him, "Jesus of Nazareth is passing by." 38 He called out, "Jesus, Son of David, have mercy on me!"	43 Immediately he received his sight and followed Jesus, praising God. When all the people saw it, they also praised God.	**6 A man had the appreciation to praise God**

DIVISION VII

THE SON OF MAN'S GREAT JOURNEY TO JERUSALEM (STAGE III): HIS LESSONS AND WARNINGS, 17:11-19:27

H. The Healing of a Blind Beggar: Steps to Getting Help from God, 18:35-43

(18:35-43) **Introduction**:the blind Beggar demonstrated ever so clearly how men can get help from God.

1. Jesus approached Jericho (v.35).
2. A man had great need (v.35).
3. A man had great hope in Jesus (v.36-38).
3. A man had a persistence in seeking Jesus that would not quit (v.39).
4. A man had the boldness to ask great things of God (v.40-42).
5. A man had the appreciation to praise God (v.43).

1 (18:35) **Scripture, Discrepancies**: Jesus was near Jericho, about to enter the city. He was on His way to Jerusalem where He was to die. His face was set to accomplish the purpose for which God had sent Him into the world. (See DEEPER STUDY # 1—Lk.9:51.) Jericho was only about seventeen miles from Jerusalem, so the journey was about over. The cross was ever near, hanging immediately before His face.

There are two apparent conflicts among the three gospel accounts of this event that need to be mentioned.

1. The actual location where the healing of Bartimaeus took place. Luke said it took place as Jesus "approached" Jericho; Matthew and Mark said the event took place as He "departed from Jericho." What happened was apparently what often happens in a big city. There was an old Jericho (the one so often mentioned in the Old Testament), and a new Jericho built by Herod the Great; or as we might say today, an old section of town and a new section. Matthew and Mark were apparently referring to the old or new city Jesus was leaving and Luke to the other city He was entering. There is also the possibility that the two blind men began to cry as Jesus entered the city. However, since they needed their faith strengthened by persisting, Jesus waited until they were close to leaving the city before hearing their cry.

2. The number of blind men involved. Matthew said there were two; Mark and Luke said one, and Mark gave his name as Bartimaeus. The simplest explanation of what happened is what often happens in an ordinary conversation when an event is being explained: the spokesman or prominent person is the only one mentioned. In this particular case, the prominent person was Bartimaeus. Therefore, Bartimaeus is the only blind man referred to by Mark and Luke.

Note: we do not know what actually happened. However when we get to heaven, God will reveal that what *appeared* to be discrepancies were only that, apparent discrepancies that gave us another opportunity to trust Him and His Word.

2 (18:35) **Needy, The**: a man had great need. The blind man was as needful as he could be, desperately needful. He had been blind for years, perhaps for life, with no hope of ever seeing. All he knew about things and people was what he could imagine from touching and hearing and tasting. The only places he could go were the places where people led him or else where he could safely feel his way along. Even then he would sometimes stumble and fall. He was doomed to live in total darkness, never to see anything but pitch black as long as he lived. The worst fact of all was that he knew it. He had to live with the knowledge that he was doomed to a world of darkness. It preyed and preyed upon his mind. He knew that he could never be normal, never fit in, and never be fully accepted by normal people.

He was also poor. He had to beg to survive, and he suffered the humiliation of being a beggar every day. There was no one to care for him—not family or neighbor or social group. He was left entirely alone in fending for himself and struggling for survival. How many days he must have gone to bed hungry, his stomach suffering sharp pains or nausea from lack of food. He was desperately needful, and he knew it.

3 (18:36-38) **Seeking Jesus—Hope**: a man had great hope in Jesus. As the blind man sat by the wayside, he heard all kinds of commotion throughout the day. The road was a major highway, one of the major commercial routes of the day. During this particular time, pilgrims from all over the known world were flooding the road; therefore the commotion was noisier and more hectic than usual. All of a sudden, the blind man heard a huge throng of people passing by. When he asked about the crowd, someone told him Jesus of Nazareth was coming.

1. The blind man had heard about Jesus of Nazareth, and he had *believed the reports* about Him. Apparently the blind man hoped for "the consolation of Israel" (Lk. 2:25). As soon as he heard that Jesus of Nazareth was passing by, he knew who Jesus was and he began to cry out immediately. This tells us that he had already been thinking about the possibility of Jesus' coming his way. Hope had already risen in his heart, and now, despite the fact that he could not see, the opportunity of his life stared him in the face. The point to note is this: he had already *believed the report* that the Messiah had come. Belief had already been stirred in his heart—at least to some degree.

> **Who has believed our message and to whom has the arm of the LORD been revealed? (Isa 53:1; cp. Jn.12:38; Ro.10:16)**
>
> **For he says, "In the time of my favor I heard you, and in the day of salvation I helped you." I tell you, now is the time of God's favor, now is the day of salvation. (2 Cor 6:2)**

2. The blind man acknowledged Jesus as Messiah. He called Jesus "Son of David." This term is used only two times in Luke (cp. Lk.20:41). It was a title of the Messiah. (See notes—Lk.3:24-31; DEEPER STUDY # 1—18:38; note—7:21-23.) It was an inadequate concept of Jesus, although it was a true fact. He was the Son of David predicted from the beginning, but He was more, much more. He was the very Son of God Himself. But note: the blind man approached Jesus with what knowledge he had. He used what he understood and cried out to Jesus in his desperate need.

Thought 1. All a man needs to do is *use what knowledge* he has and call out to God. God will help a man grow in knowledge as the man continues to seek God's help, no matter the need.

> **God did this so that men would seek him and perhaps reach out for him and find him, though he is not far from each one of us. (Acts 17:27)**
>
> **Look to the LORD and his strength; seek his face always. (Psa 105:4)**
>
> **Seek the LORD, all you humble of the land, you who do what he commands. Seek righteousness, seek humility; perhaps you will be sheltered on the day of the Lord's anger. (Zep 2:3)**
>
> **Seek the LORD while he may be found; call on him while he is near. (Isa 55:6)**

3. The blind man cried for mercy. This is significant. He was blind and poor and he had to beg for daily survival. But note: he did not cry for food, clothing, or shelter. The basic necessities of life were not his primary concern. The mercy of God upon his life was his concern.

> **His mercy extends to those who fear him, from generation to generation. (Luke 1:50)**
>
> **"But the tax collector stood at a distance. He would not even look up to heaven, but beat his breast and said, 'God, have mercy on me, a sinner.' "I tell you that this man, rather than the other, went home justified before God. For everyone who exalts himself will be humbled, and he who humbles himself will be exalted." (Luke 18:13-14)**
>
> **But because of his great love for us, God, who is rich in mercy, made us alive with Christ even when we were dead in transgressions—it is by grace you have been saved. (Eph 2:4-5)**
>
> **Be merciful to me, LORD, for I am faint; O LORD, heal me, for my bones are in agony. My soul is in anguish. How long, O LORD, how long? (Psa 6:2-3)**
>
> **Hear my voice when I call, O LORD; be merciful to me and answer me. (Psa 27:7)**
>
> **For the director of music. A psalm of David. When the prophet Nathan came to him after David had committed adultery with Bathsheba. Have mercy on me, O God, according to your unfailing love; according to your great compassion blot out my transgressions. (Psa 51:1)**
>
> **Show us your unfailing love, O LORD, and grant us your salvation. (Psa 85:7)**
>
> **Let your compassion come to me that I may live, for your law is my delight. (Psa 119:77)**
>
> **Rend your heart and not your garments. Return to the LORD your God, for he is gracious and compassionate, slow to anger and abounding in love, and he relents from sending calamity. (Joel 2:13)**
>
> **Do not gloat over me, my enemy! Though I have fallen, I will rise. Though I sit in darkness, the LORD will be my light. (Micah 7:8)**

DEEPER STUDY # 1

(18:38) **Jesus Christ, Titles, Son of David**: the title the Son of David is a common title throughout the Bible. (Cp. Mt.12:23; 15:22; 20:30-31; 21:9, 15; Acts 2:29-36; Ro.1:3; 2 Tim.2:8; Rev.22:16.) It was the common title and popular concept of the Messiah. Generation after generation of Jews longed and looked for the promised deliverer of Israel. The people expected Him to be a great general who would deliver and restore the nation to its greatness. In fact, they expected Him to make the nation the center of universal rule. Under God, He would conquer the world and center the glory and majesty of God Himself in Jerusalem. From His throne, the throne of David, He (the Son of David, the Messiah) would execute "the Messianic fire of judgment" upon the nations and people of the world (see DEEPER STUDY # 2—Mt.1:18; DEEPER STUDY # 3—3:11; notes—11:1-6; 11:2-3; DEEPER STUDY # 1—11:5; DEEPER STUDY # 2—11:6; DEEPER STUDY # 1—12:16; 22:42; Lk.7:21-23. Referring to these notes will show what the Jewish concept of the Messiah was.)

4 (18:39) **Persistence**: a man had a persistence that would not quit. This is an excellent example of the kind of persistence that gets help from God.

1. Some of the people with Jesus rebuked the blind man. They tried to silence stop him from crying out to the

Lord. Why we are not told, but they did oppose him. He had every reason to be discouraged, for he was blind and could not see to make his way through the crowd. All he could do was shout out, and some were even trying to stop him from doing that. He could have easily quit and given up, for it seemed so useless.

2. Note what he did: he "shouted all the more." He would not quit and would not be silenced. Jesus was his hope, the only chance he had for mercy. No other man could have mercy upon him or meet his need. They might feed, clothe, and house him; but they could not meet the crying need of his heart, the blindness of his eyes and spirit. His faith in Jesus was strong; therefore, he was not to be stopped. His faith fought against all odds: the opposition of the crowd and the noise above which he had to be heard. His faith cried out louder and louder, desperately hoping that God would help Jesus hear.

> **"Ask and it will be given to you; seek and you will find; knock and the door will be opened to you. (Mat 7:7)**
>
> **But if from there you seek the LORD your God, you will find him if you look for him with all your heart and with all your soul. (Deu 4:29)**
>
> **This is what the LORD says to the house of Israel: "Seek me and live; (Amos 5:4)**

> **Thought 1.** Perseverance—resisting and standing against all odds—is the answer to being helped by God. God cannot turn a deaf ear to the persevering cry of a desperate need, not if the person cries and cries for help, never quitting. God has promised to hear and answer *undying perseverance* (cp. Lk.11:8-13; 18:1-8).

5 (18:40-42) **Prayer—Seeking**: a man had the boldness to ask great things of God. Note three significant facts.

1. The man's persistence caused Jesus to stop and to stand still. Imagine the scene. Jesus heard the cry and its sound of desperation. He stopped and looked about, standing perfectly still with a hush sweeping over the crowd until there was nothing but stone silence. Then piercing through the silence, the desperate cry came: "Jesus, Son of David, have mercy on me."

> **Thought 1.** There is symbolism in the scene: the great need for quietness and silence for Jesus to hear us. There are times when the crowd must be silenced, hushed so that Christ can hear our cries for mercy. Nothing should ever be allowed to interfere with our daily *quiet time* with the Lord. How many of our needs would be met so much quicker if we persevered daily in a *quiet time*, crying out to the Lord for mercy.

> **"Be still, and know that I am God; I will be exalted among the nations, I will be exalted in the earth." (Psa 46:10)**
>
> **But the LORD is in his holy temple; let all the earth be silent before him." (Hab 2:20)**
>
> **Be still before the LORD, all mankind, because he has roused himself from his holy dwelling." (Zec 2:13)**

2. The blind man asked for a great thing to be done. Imagine—being truly blind and asking a man standing there to heal your eyes. An unbelievable thing, yet the blind man believed. He believed in the One who stood before Him, *believing what he had heard*: that this Jesus was the Messiah who possessed the very power of God. He was able to do anything, so the blind man asked for the greatest need in his life to be met. There was no need to ask for anything less, for Jesus was the One possessing the power of God. And Jesus had called him to come forward and to ask for whatever he needed. It was a time for courage, the kind of courage that asks great things of God, even if they seem impossible.

> **If you believe, you will receive whatever you ask for in prayer." (Mat 21:22)**
>
> **And I will do whatever you ask in my name, so that the Son may bring glory to the Father. (John 14:13)**
>
> **If you remain in me and my words remain in you, ask whatever you wish, and it will be given you. (John 15:7)**
>
> **Until now you have not asked for anything in my name. Ask and you will receive, and your joy will be complete. (John 16:24)**
>
> **This is the confidence we have in approaching God: that if we ask anything according to his will, he hears us. And if we know that he hears us—whatever we ask—we know that we have what we asked of him. (1 John 5:14-15)**
>
> **Before they call I will answer; while they are still speaking I will hear. (Isa 65:24)**
>
> **'Call to me and I will answer you and tell you great and unsearchable things you do not know.' (Jer 33:3)**

3. Jesus granted his request. He gave him sight and saved him. The blind man had taken three critical steps. He had...

- believed the reports that Jesus was the promised Messiah (Ro.10:13-17, esp. 16).
- cried out for mercy.
- persevered and persisted and refused to give up despite all kinds of odds.

Therefore, Jesus saved him by giving him sight and saving his soul. This was a complete healing that included both the inner and outer person: the spirit as well as the body (see note—Mt.14:36).

> **Therefore he is able to save completely those who come to God through him, because he always lives to intercede for them. (Heb 7:25)**
>
> **And without faith it is impossible to please God, because anyone who comes to him must believe that he exists and that he rewards those who earnestly seek him. (Heb 11:6)**
>
> **Commit your way to the LORD; trust in him and he will do this: (Psa 37:5)**
>
> **Trust in the LORD with all your heart and lean not on your own understanding; (Prov 3:5)**
>
> **Trust in the LORD forever, for the LORD, the LORD, is the Rock eternal. (Isa 26:4)**

6 (18:43) **Witnessing—Courage**: a man had the appreciation to praise God, the courage to become a witness for Christ.

1. Note that he followed Christ immediately.

> **Then he said to them all: "If anyone would come after me, he must deny himself and take up his cross daily and follow me. (Luke 9:23)**
>
> **My sheep listen to my voice; I know them, and they follow me. (John 10:27)**
>
> **Whoever serves me must follow me; and where I am, my servant also will be. My Father will honor the one who serves me. (John 12:26)**
>
> **Be imitators of God, therefore, as dearly loved children (Eph 5:1)**
>
> **So then, just as you received Christ Jesus as Lord, continue to live in him, (Col 2:6)**
>
> **To this you were called, because Christ suffered for you, leaving you an example, that you should follow in his steps. (1 Pet 2:21)**

2. Note that he praised and glorified God and caused others to praise God.

> **In the same way, let your light shine before men, that they may see your good deeds and praise your Father in heaven. (Mat 5:16)**
>
> **So that with one heart and mouth you may glorify the God and Father of our Lord Jesus Christ. (Rom 15:6)**
>
> **You were bought at a price. Therefore honor God with your body. (1 Cor 6:20)**
>
> **We pray this so that the name of our Lord Jesus may be glorified in you, and you in him, according to the grace of our God and the Lord Jesus Christ. (2 Th 1:12)**
>
> **Through Jesus, therefore, let us continually offer to God a sacrifice of praise—the fruit of lips that confess his name. (Heb 13:15)**
>
> **But you are a chosen people, a royal priesthood, a holy nation, a people belonging to God, that you may declare the praises of him who called you out of darkness into his wonderful light. (1 Pet 2:9)**
>
> **Sing praises to the LORD, enthroned in Zion; proclaim among the nations what he has done. (Psa 9:11)**
>
> **May the peoples praise you, O God; may all the peoples praise you. (Psa 67:3)**

	CHAPTER 19 **I. The Conversion of Zacchaeus: The Meaning of Conversion, 19:1-10**
1 Zacchaeus, the chief tax-collector—a man who was very rich	Jesus entered Jericho and was passing through. 2 A man was there by the name of Zacchaeus; he was a chief tax collector and was wealthy.
2 First, being desperate to see Jesus: Who He is a. He was thrust back b. He persisted	3 He wanted to see who Jesus was, but being a short man he could not, because of the crowd. 4 So he ran ahead and climbed a sycamore-fig tree to see him, since Jesus was coming that way.
3 Second, receiving the invitation of Jesus a. Jesus saw him b. Jesus called him by name c. Jesus asked to be received d. Zacchaeus obeyed	5 When Jesus reached the spot, he looked up and said to him, "Zacchaeus, come down immediately. I must stay at your house today." 6 So he came down at once and welcomed him gladly.
4 Third, repenting, that is, changing one's whole way of life a. He was a sinner b. He repented, changed his life	7 All the people saw this and began to mutter, "He has gone to be the guest of a 'sinner.'" 8 But Zacchaeus stood up and said to the Lord, "Look, Lord! Here and now I give half of my possessions to the poor, and if I have cheated anybody out of anything, I will pay back four times the amount."
5 Fourth, looking to Jesus as the Savior a. The One who proclaims salvation b. The One who seeks & saves the lost	9 Jesus said to him, "Today salvation has come to this house, because this man, too, is a son of Abraham. 10 For the Son of Man came to seek and to save what was lost."

DIVISION VII

THE SON OF MAN'S GREAT JOURNEY TO JERUSALEM (STAGE III): HIS LESSONS AND WARNINGS, 17:11-19:27

I. The Conversion of Zacchaeus: The Meaning of Conversion, 19:1-10

(19:1-10) **Introduction**: the meaning of conversion is clearly illustrated in the experience of Zacchaeus. The fact that man can be converted should stir hope within every heart that truly senses need and wants to meet God as though face to face.

1. Zacchaeus, the chief tax-collector—a man who was very rich (v.1-2).
2. First, being desperate to see Jesus: who He is (v.3-4).
3. Second, receiving the invitation of Jesus (v.5-6).
4. Third, repenting, that is, changing one's whole way of life (v.7-8).
5. Fourth, looking to Jesus as the Savior (v.9-10).

1 (19:1-2) **Tax-Collector**: Zacchaeus, the chief tax-collector, was a very rich man. This is the only time the title "chief" is used with a tax-collector. Its meaning is not known. It probably refers to the head of the local taxation office; therefore, Zacchaeus would be responsible to the Roman government for the employment and management of the local tax-collectors and their monies. (See DEEPER STUDY # 1—Lk.5:27.) Note two things about Zacchaeus.

1. He had all the pleasures and comforts of life which money could buy.

2. He was a man who would find it very difficult to enter the Kingdom of Heaven. His money was a serious threat to his salvation, as it is with all rich men. It was going to be difficult to give up all he had to follow Christ. A man tends to *love* his money and the things it does for him (see outline and notes—Lk.18:24-27).

2 (19:3-4) **Seeking Jesus—Conversion**: first, conversion is being desperate to see Jesus, just who He is. Note three facts.

1. Zacchaeus showed a desperation in trying to see Jesus. Despite his wealth and the pleasures and comfort enjoyed by wealth, he was apparently empty and lonely within his heart. This can be imagined because tax-collectors were bitterly hated by the people. (See DEEPER STUDY # 1—Lk.5:27.) Zacchaeus was also small of stature, which means that he was probably self-conscious and felt inferior and had a low self-image. Being so little in stature, it was dangerous for him to be out in the midst of a crowd that despised him. From all indications he was denied passage through the crowd, probably being shoved back and abused. Therefore, his desperate determination and persistence is even more evident.

> **But if from there you seek the LORD your God, you will find him if you look for him with all your heart and with all your soul. (Deu 4:29)**
> **Seek the LORD while he may be found; call on him while he is near. (Isa 55:6)**
> **You will seek me and find me when you seek me with all your heart. (Jer 29:13)**
> **Sow for yourselves righteousness, reap the fruit of unfailing love, and break up your unplowed ground; for it is time to seek the LORD, until he comes and showers righteousness on you. (Hosea 10:12)**

2. Zacchaeus persevered in his attempt to see Jesus, and he had to humble himself to do it. Imagine Zacchaeus, a man of position and wealth, climbing a tree just to see an important person pass by. He wanted to see Jesus so badly he forgot everyone around and humbled himself to climb a tree. He was determined to see the Lord, and nothing was going to stop him.

3. Zacchaeus had most likely experienced the stirring of faith within his heart for some time. He had heard reports about, Jesus' being the Messiah and perhaps had heard about Jesus' saving and calling Matthew, another tax-collector, to be one of His apostles. Zacchaeus had begun to *believe the reports* or at least to wonder and hope that

the reports were true. His efforts to see Jesus and what follows are evidence of some stirring, of some hope that drove him to seek Jesus.

> **"Come, all you who are thirsty, come to the waters; and you who have no money, come, buy and eat! Come, buy wine and milk without money and without cost. (Isa 55:1)**
>
> **"Come to me, all you who are weary and burdened, and I will give you rest. (Mat 11:28)**
>
> **For we do not have a high priest who is unable to sympathize with our weaknesses, but we have one who has been tempted in every way, just as we are—yet was without sin. Let us then approach the throne of grace with confidence, so that we may receive mercy and find grace to help us in our time of need. (Heb 4:15-16)**

3 (19:5-6) **Conversion**: second, conversion is receiving the invitation of Jesus. Note several points.

1. Jesus "looked up, and said to him." Jesus sees every man, no matter where he is: in the dark places of his sin and shame, in his home and work and play, in his seeking to know the truth. Jesus sees everything about a man, but there is one person in particular whom he sees. He sees the man who is seeking Him. Jesus sees him in the sense of knowing about his need and reaching out to meet that need.

Zacchaeus is an example. He was desperate to see Jesus, so he had struggled against the odds and found a place where he could see Jesus. Even though the place he chose meant humiliating himself and exposing himself to people who were bitterly opposed to him, he was willing to suffer whatever it took to get a look at the Savior. And, because Zacchaeus sought so diligently to see Jesus, Jesus saw him.

2. Jesus knew and called him by name. This was bound to strike Zacchaeus and be very meaningful to him. When anyone, especially a stranger, calls us by name, our ears perk up and our senses become more alert. Jesus knows every man's name (cp. Jn.1:48; Is.43:1). He wants to address every one of us by name, but we must let Him. We have to do as Zacchaeus did: seek to find the place and vantage point where we can see Jesus, then Jesus will see us and call us by name.

> **And he brought him to Jesus. Jesus looked at him and said, "You are Simon son of John. You will be called Cephas" (which, when translated, is Peter). (John 1:42)**
>
> **The watchman opens the gate for him, and the sheep listen to his voice. He calls his own sheep by name and leads them out. (John 10:3)**
>
> **"I am the good shepherd; I know my sheep and my sheep know me— (John 10:14)**
>
> **But the man who loves God is known by God. (1 Cor 8:3)**
>
> **But now that you know God—or rather are known by God—how is it that you are turning back to those weak and miserable principles? Do you wish to be enslaved by them all over again? (Gal 4:9)**
>
> **Nevertheless, God's solid foundation stands firm, sealed with this inscription: "The Lord knows those who are his," and, "Everyone who confesses the name of the Lord must turn away from wickedness." (2 Tim 2:19)**
>
> **But now, this is what the LORD says—he who created you, O Jacob, he who formed you, O Israel: "Fear not, for I have redeemed you; I have summoned you by name; you are mine. (Isa 43:1)**

3. Jesus asked to be received and to be received with haste. He was set for Jerusalem and must not delay too long. There was no time to waste. Jesus wanted to be welcomed, received, and entertained by Zacchaeus; but Zacchaeus had to act then and there. Jesus had only a couple of hours before He had to move on to fulfill His purpose. The moment of opportunity was then and there, that day. The next day it would be gone. There would be no pull, no struggle, no spirit of seeking within Zacchaeus' heart.

> **"Come to me, all you who are weary and burdened, and I will give you rest. (Mat 11:28)**
>
> **Here I am! I stand at the door and knock. If anyone hears my voice and opens the door, I will come in and eat with him, and he with me. (Rev 3:20)**
>
> **We proclaim to you what we have seen and heard, so that you also may have fellowship with us. And our fellowship is with the Father and with his Son, Jesus Christ. (1 John 1:3)**
>
> **God, who has called you into fellowship with his Son Jesus Christ our Lord, is faithful. (1 Cor 1:9)**
>
> **The Spirit and the bride say, "Come!" And let him who hears say, "Come!" Whoever is thirsty, let him come; and whoever wishes, let him take the free gift of the water of life. (Rev 22:17)**
>
> **"Come now, let us reason together," says the LORD. "Though your sins are like scarlet, they shall be as white as snow; though they are red as crimson, they shall be like wool. (Isa 1:18)**
>
> **"Come, all you who are thirsty, come to the waters; and you who have no money, come, buy and eat! Come, buy wine and milk without money and without cost. (Isa 55:1)**

4. Zacchaeus *obeyed*; he made haste and received Christ joyfully.

> **Yet to all who received him, to those who believed in his name, he gave the right to become children of God— (John 1:12)**
>
> **For he says, "In the time of my favor I heard you, and in the day of salvation I helped you." I tell you, now is the time of God's favor, now is the day of salvation. (2 Cor 6:2)**

4 (19:7-8) **Conversion—Repentance—Restitution**: third, conversion is repenting, that is, changing one's whole way of life.

1. Zacchaeus was a sinner. Note "the people...began to mutter." Everyone knew that Zacchaeus was a betrayer of

his country, serving the alien power of Rome. And Zacchaeus himself knew that he was a sinner, both a betrayer and a thief, having stolen much from many. The point is twofold.

a. Zacchaeus knew he was a sinner and readily confessed his need for the Savior.

> **"Whoever acknowledges me before men, I will also acknowledge him before my Father in heaven. (Mat 10:32)**
>
> **That if you confess with your mouth, "Jesus is Lord," and believe in your heart that God raised him from the dead, you will be saved. (Rom 10:9)**
>
> **No one who denies the Son has the Father; whoever acknowledges the Son has the Father also. (1 John 2:23)**
>
> **If anyone acknowledges that Jesus is the Son of God, God lives in him and he in God. (1 John 4:15)**

b. The crowd, that is, the general populace, demonstrated self-righteousness. They did not like Jesus' eating and associating with a known and confessed sinner. Note: their sin was murmuring and grumbling and complaining—the great sins of Israel in the wilderness. They just misunderstood Jesus' purpose for coming to earth, that of saving sinners.

> **Jesus answered them, "It is not the healthy who need a doctor, but the sick. I have not come to call the righteous, but sinners to repentance." (Luke 5:31-32)**
>
> **But God demonstrates his own love for us in this: While we were still sinners, Christ died for us. (Rom 5:8)**
>
> **Here is a trustworthy saying that deserves full acceptance: Christ Jesus came into the world to save sinners—of whom I am the worst. (1 Tim 1:15)**

2. Zacchaeus repented and changed his whole life; he completely turned around from his sinful life to God and His way of righteousness.

a. He gave half his possessions to the poor. He did exactly what Jesus had said time after time, and he did exactly what the rich young ruler had refused to do (Lk.18:18-24).

> **Then he said to them all: "If anyone would come after me, he must deny himself and take up his cross daily and follow me. For whoever wants to save his life will lose it, but whoever loses his life for me will save it. What good is it for a man to gain the whole world, and yet lose or forfeit his very self? (Luke 9:23-25)**
>
> **But give what is inside the dish to the poor, and everything will be clean for you. (Luke 11:41)**
>
> **Sell your possessions and give to the poor. Provide purses for yourselves that will not wear out, a treasure in heaven that will not be exhausted, where no thief comes near and no moth destroys. (Luke 12:33)**
>
> **When Jesus heard this, he said to him, "You still lack one thing. Sell everything you have and give to the poor, and you will have treasure in heaven. Then come, follow me." (Luke 18:22)**
>
> **He who has been stealing must steal no longer, but must work, doing something useful with his own hands, that he may have something to share with those in need. (Eph 4:28)**
>
> **Command those who are rich in this present world not to be arrogant nor to put their hope in wealth, which is so uncertain, but to put their hope in God, who richly provides us with everything for our enjoyment. Command them to do good, to be rich in good deeds, and to be generous and willing to share. (1 Tim 6:17-18)**

b. He gave back to those whom he had cheated; he gave *four times* what he had taken. *Restitution* became the thrust of his life for the next while. Think of the people he had cheated, stealing everything he could from them. Imagine the list of people and how long it would take to track them down.

> **When he thus sins and becomes guilty, he must return what he has stolen or taken by extortion, or what was entrusted to him, or the lost property he found, (Lev 6:4)**
>
> **Yet if he is caught, he must pay sevenfold, though it costs him all the wealth of his house. (Prov 6:31)**
>
> **I will search for the lost and bring back the strays. I will bind up the injured and strengthen the weak, but the sleek and the strong I will destroy. I will shepherd the flock with justice. (Ezek 34:16; cp. 1 Ki.20:34; 2 Ki.8:6; Neh.5:12)**

The point is that this sinner, Zacchaeus, truly repented. He was serious about following Christ and living righteously. (See notes and DEEPER STUDY # 1, Repentance—Acts 17:29-30.)

> **I tell you, no! But unless you repent, you too will all perish. (Luke 13:3)**
>
> **Repent, then, and turn to God, so that your sins may be wiped out, that times of refreshing may come from the Lord, (Acts 3:19)**
>
> **Repent of this wickedness and pray to the Lord. Perhaps he will forgive you for having such a thought in your heart. (Acts 8:22)**
>
> **Let the wicked forsake his way and the evil man his thoughts. Let him turn to the LORD, and he will have mercy on him, and to our God, for he will freely pardon. (Isa 55:7)**
>
> **"But if a wicked man turns away from all the sins he has committed and keeps all my decrees and does what is just and right, he will surely live; he will not die. (Ezek 18:21)**

5 (19:9-10) **Jesus Christ, Mission**: fourth, conversion is looking to Jesus as the Savior.

1. Jesus is the One who proclaims salvation. He proclaimed two things:

a. That repentance saved Zacchaeus, and that Zacchaeus would bring the message of salvation to his whole household.

Whoever believes and is baptized will be saved, but whoever does not believe will be condemned. (Mark 16:16)

He then brought them out and asked, "Sirs, what must I do to be saved?" They replied, "Believe in the Lord Jesus, and you will be saved—you and your household." (Acts 16:30-31)

b. That Zacchaeus was a true son of Abraham, a spiritual son.

And he [Abraham] received the sign of circumcision, a seal of the righteousness that he had by faith while he was still uncircumcised. So then, he is the father of all who believe but have not been circumcised, in order that righteousness might be credited to them. (Rom 4:11)

For we maintain that a man is justified by faith apart from observing the law. (Rom 3:28)

2. Jesus is the One who seeks and saves the lost.

a. The lost are the ones who are perishing, being destroyed, losing eternal life, and being cut off from God. The lost are spiritually destitute.

b. Jesus, the One who seeks and saves the lost, is the One who sought Zacchaeus. Zacchaeus put himself in a position to see Jesus, but Jesus did the speaking to Zacchaeus' heart, asking Zacchaeus to receive him. Note: only after Zacchaeus received Jesus did Jesus save him. (See notes—Ro.10:16-17; note and DEEPER STUDY # 1—1 Cor.1:18 for more discussion.)

"Suppose one of you has a hundred sheep and loses one of them. Does he not leave the ninety-nine in the open country and go after the lost sheep until he finds it? (Luke 15:4)

Jesus heard that they had thrown him out, and when he found him, he said, "Do you believe in the Son of Man?" "Who is he, sir?" the man asked. "Tell me so that I may believe in him." Jesus said, "You have now seen him; in fact, he is the one speaking with you." (John 9:35-37)

But not all the Israelites accepted the good news. For Isaiah says, "Lord, who has believed our message?" Consequently, faith comes from hearing the message, and the message is heard through the word of Christ. (Rom 10:16-17)

	J. The Parable of the Pounds or Ten Minas: Every Man is Being Tested, 19:11-27
1 Jesus tried to correct a wrong idea about the Kingdom of God	11 While they were listening to this, he went on to tell them a parable, because he was near Jerusalem and the people thought that the kingdom of God was going to appear at once.
2 He went to a distant coun try to receive a kingdom, but He will return	12 He said: "A man of noble birth went to a distant country to have himself appointed king and then to return.
3 He insisted: Work until I come[DS1,2]	13 So he called ten of his servants and gave them ten minas. 'Put this money to work,' he said, 'until I come back.'
4 The citizens of the world hate Him & reject His rule	14 "But his subjects hated him and sent a delegation after him to say, 'We don't want this man to be our king.'
5 His servants are to be rewarded according to the percent of their labor[DS3]	15 "He was made king, however, and returned home. Then he sent for the servants to whom he had given the money, in order to find out what they had gained with it.
a. The believer who works 1000 percent receives 1000 percent	16 "The first one came and said, 'Sir, your mina has earned ten more.' 17 "'Well done, my good servant!' his master replied. 'Because you have been trustworthy in a very small matter, take charge of ten cities.'
b. The believer who works 500 percent receives 500 percent	18 "The second came and said, 'Sir, your mina has earned five more.' 19 "His master answered, 'You take charge of five cities.'
c. The believer who does not work receives nothing	20 "Then another servant came and said, 'Sir, here is your mina; I have kept it laid away in a piece of cloth. 21 I was afraid of you, because you are a hard man. You take out what you did not put in and reap what you did not sow.' 22 "His master replied, 'I will judge you by your own words, you wicked servant! You knew, did you, that I am a hard man, taking out what I did not put in, and reaping what I did not sow? 23 Why then didn't you put my money on deposit, so that when I came back, I could have collected it with interest?'
6 The servant who labors 1000 percent will be given the reward of the unfaith ful plus his own reward a. Other servants wonder why b. Because the servant was so faithful—ever increasing, 1 Cor.15:58	24 "Then he said to those standing by, 'Take his mina away from him and give it to the one who has ten minas.' 25 "'Sir,' they said, 'he already has ten!' 26 "He replied, 'I tell you that to everyone who has, more will be given, but as for the one who has nothing, even what he has will be taken away.
7 The citizens who are enemies of His rule are to be slain	27 But those enemies of mine who did not want me to be king over them—bring them here and kill them in front of me.'"

DIVISION VII

THE SON OF MAN'S GREAT JOURNEY TO JERUSALEM (STAGE III): HIS LESSONS AND WARNINGS, 17:11-19:27

J. The Parable of the Pounds or Ten Minas: Every Man is Being Tested, 19:11-27

(19:11-27) **Introduction**: the Lord trusts us; He believes in us. He gives us gifts and responsibilities to look after until He returns. He longs for us to be faithful and diligent in doing our duty, and He is going to greatly reward those who are faithful. But He is going to severely judge those who do nothing to help a lost and needful world. (See outline and notes—Mt.25:14-30 for more discussion.)

1. Jesus tried to correct a wrong idea about the Kingdom of God (v.11).
2. He went to a far country to receive a kingdom, but He will return (v.12).
3. He insisted: work until I come (v.13).
4. The citizens of the world hate Him and reject His rule (v.14).
5. His servants are to be rewarded according to the percent of their labor (v.15-23).
6. The servant who labors 1000 percent shall be given the reward of the unfaithful plus his own reward (v.24-26).
7. The citizens who are enemies of His rule are to be slain (v.27).

1 (19:11) **Kingdom of God—Messiah, Misconception of**: Jesus tried to correct a wrong idea about the Kingdom of God. Jesus was near Jerusalem. The disciples and people with Him believed that the capital of God's kingdom was to be set up in Jerusalem. They were very aware of how He had been talking about Jerusalem and setting His face like a flint for the city. They also thought that the kingdom "should appear at once." They believed that as soon as they reached Jerusalem, Jesus was going to usher in the Kingdom of God, freeing Israel from Roman domination and establishing the rule of God over all the earth. In their minds the climax of human history and the beginning of God's reign upon earth was at hand. They knew that with His power, He could do whatever was necessary to subdue the nations of the earth and bring God's righteousness to earth.

Now note, all their thoughts were upon this earth: upon the temporal and the worldly, the physical and the material. They saw themselves in positions of leadership and honor, as the princes and counsellors of state (cp. Lk.22:24-30; Mt.20:20-28; Mk.9:33-37). There is a problem with this concept: at most a person would enjoy an earthly kingdom for only a few short years of a life time. The disciples were just not thinking in terms of the spiritual world:

⇒ an eternal life which lives on forever.
⇒ an eternal world which actually exists.
⇒ an eternal world in another dimension of being.
⇒ an eternal world which is the real world.
⇒ an eternal world which is much more real than this physical world which fades away in its corruption.

Jesus had to correct their misconcept and teach them the truth about the Kingdom of God. In the parable, Jesus is the nobleman; the citizens are the unbelievers of the world; the servants are the professing believers of the Lord.

2 (19:12) **Jesus Christ, Return**: the Lord went to a "distant country" to receive a kingdom, but He will return. The following facts are important.

1. The "distant country" indicates He will be gone for a while. It takes time to travel a long distance and handle the affairs and return.

2. He has gone to receive a kingdom from the King of the *whole realm of the universe*, God Himself. The picture is that of Jesus' sitting at the right hand of God in glory while He and God discuss the kingdom and its affairs.

3. He is to return. He will be gone a long time, for the "distant country" is a long way off. The discussions surrounding His kingdom, His rule, and His reign will take time; but He will return. The day of His arrival will come. (See DEEPER STUDY # 3, Kingdom of Heaven—Mt.19:23-24.)

> **In my Father's house are many rooms; if it were not so, I would have told you. I am going there to prepare a place for you. And if I go and prepare a place for you, I will come back and take you to be with me that you also may be where I am. (John 14:2-3)**
>
> **But Jesus remained silent. The high priest said to him, "I charge you under oath by the living God: Tell us if you are the Christ, the Son of God." "Yes, it is as you say," Jesus replied. "But I say to all of you: In the future you will see the Son of Man sitting at the right hand of the Mighty One and coming on the clouds of heaven." (Mat 26:63-64)**
>
> **At that time they will see the Son of Man coming in a cloud with power and great glory. (Luke 21:27)**
>
> **So Christ was sacrificed once to take away the sins of many people; and he will appear a second time, not to bear sin, but to bring salvation to those who are waiting for him. (Heb 9:28)**

3 (19:13) **Dedication—Ministering—Service**: the Lord insisted, "Work until I come." Note what He did.

1. He called His servants. They were already His servants and already belonged to His household; therefore, He believed in them, feeling that He could trust them. They were supposed to be responsible persons, completely trustworthy, for they belonged to the household of the Lord Himself.

2. He put His business affairs into their hands while He was gone. Jesus illustrated this with money (see DEEPER STUDY # 1, Pound—Lk.19:13). The Lord said, "Work until I come." That was all He said: four exact, straightforward, and powerful words. Yet, they were so full of meaning. The servant of God is to take what Jesus has given him and use it until Jesus returns. The word "work" (pragmateuomai) is a word of diligent action. It is from the root word meaning to walk, to set in motion, and to continue in motion. The servant is to labor diligently, never letting up and using all the Lord has given him to look after (see DEEPER STUDY # 2, Work—Lk.19:13).

> **Thought 1.** Every believer is called and gifted by Christ to serve (cp. Ro.12:3f; 1 Cor.12:7f; Eph.4:11f; 1 Pt.4:10).
>
> **Do you not say, 'Four months more and then the harvest'? I tell you, open your eyes and look at the fields! They are ripe for harvest. (John 4:35)**
>
> **As long as it is day, we must do the work of him who sent me. Night is coming, when no one can work. (John 9:4)**
>
> **Now it is required that those who have been given a trust must prove faithful. (1 Cor 4:2)**
>
> **You were bought at a price. Therefore honor God with your body. (1 Cor 6:20)**
>
> **Each one should use whatever gift he has received to serve others, faithfully administering God's grace in its various forms. (1 Pet 4:10)**
>
> **For this reason I remind you to fan into flame the gift of God, which is in you through the laying on of my hands. (2 Tim 1:6)**
>
> **Recalling your tears, I long to see you, so that I may be filled with joy. (2 Tim 1:4)**
>
> **Whatever your hand finds to do, do it with all your might, for in the grave, where you are going, there is neither working nor planning nor knowledge nor wisdom. (Eccl 9:10)**

DEEPER STUDY # 1

(19:13) **Minas—Pound**: the word in the Greek testament is *mna.* The minas was about three months wages. This means that a Greek coin was worth about one hundred drachmai. One drachmai was about one days' wage for a laborer.

DEEPER STUDY # 2

(19:13) **Work** (pragmateuomai): to do business; to get busy; to work for gain; to trade. This is the only time the word is used in the New Testament (cp. Is.35:3; Heb.12:28; 12:12).

4 (19:14) **Jesus Christ, Response to—Unbelief**: the citizens of the world hate Him and reject His rule. This, of course, describes the unbeliever who refuses to acknowledge Christ and surrender his life to the rule of Christ. It can also apply to Israel's rejection of Christ. Men are rejecting Christ every day. Why? Very simply because they will not let Him rule over them. They want to control their own lives, do their own thing just as they wish.

> **He came to that which was his own, but his own did not receive him. (John 1:11)**
>
> **I have come in my Father's name, and you do not accept me; but if someone else comes in his own name, you will accept him. How can you believe if you accept praise from one another, yet make no effort to obtain the praise that comes from the only God? (John 5:43-44)**
>
> **There is a judge for the one who rejects me and does not accept my words; that very word which I spoke will condemn him at the last day. (John 12:48)**
>
> **To whom he said, "This is the resting place, let the weary rest"; and, "This is the place of repose"— but they would not listen. (Isa 28:12)**
>
> **This is what the Sovereign LORD, the Holy One of Israel, says: "In repentance and rest is your salvation, in quietness and trust is your strength, but you would have none of it. (Isa 30:15)**

5 (19:15-23) **Faithfulness—Dedication—Gifts—Unfaithfulness—Service**: the Lord's servants are to be rewarded according to the percent of their labor. The story is clear, but note these points.

1. Scripture is clear about judgment: there is to be a day of judgment.

> **For the Son of Man is going to come in his Father's glory with his angels, and then he will reward each person according to what he has done. (Mat 16:27)**
>
> **"When the Son of Man comes in his glory, and all the angels with him, he will sit on his throne in heavenly glory. All the nations will be gathered before him, and he will separate the people one from another as a shepherd separates the sheep from the goats. (Mat 25:31-32)**
>
> **So then, each of us will give an account of himself to God. (Rom 14:12)**
>
> **For we must all appear before the judgment seat of Christ, that each one may receive what is due him for the things done while in the body, whether good or bad. (2 Cor 5:10)**
>
> **In the presence of God and of Christ Jesus, who will judge the living and the dead, and in view of his appearing and his kingdom, I give you this charge: (2 Tim 4:1)**

2. In the parable the Lord did return. The day of accounting did arrive. Every servant was called to report on what he had done with the gifts Christ had given him.

3. Only the servants of the Lord are pictured as appearing before the Lord. The three results illustrate the three courses of action taken by God's servants: being very faithful, faithful, and unfaithful.

4. The first two servants were both faithful. Both labored diligently, but there was a difference. One labored ever so diligently: daily, hourly, every day and every hour. He was always walking with the Lord, never slacking up or allowing the trials of life to hinder his work. He worked to increase the Lord's property regardless of circumstances. He was 1000 percent faithful. The other servant was not quite as sold out; he did not strain and sacrifice as much. He was 500 percent faithful.

> **Then he said to them all: "If anyone would come after me, he must deny himself and take up his cross daily and follow me. (Luke 9:23)**
>
> **"Whoever can be trusted with very little can also be trusted with much, and whoever is dishonest with very little will also be dishonest with much. (Luke 16:10)**
>
> **Therefore, I urge you, brothers, in view of God's mercy, to offer your bodies as living sacrifices, holy and pleasing to God—this is your spiritual act of worship. (Rom 12:1)**
>
> **Never be lacking in zeal, but keep your spiritual fervor, serving the Lord. (Rom 12:11)**
>
> **Therefore, my dear brothers, stand firm. Let nothing move you. Always give yourselves fully to the work of the Lord, because you know that your labor in the Lord is not in vain. (1 Cor 15:58)**
>
> **Serve wholeheartedly, as if you were serving the Lord, not men, (Eph 6:7)**
>
> **We want each of you to show this same diligence to the very end, in order to make your hope sure. We do not want you to become lazy, but to imitate those who through faith and patience inherit what has been promised. (Heb 6:11-12)**
>
> **Be shepherds of God's flock that is under your care, serving as overseers—not because you must, but because you are willing, as God wants you to be; not greedy for money, but eager to serve; not lording it over those entrusted to you, but being examples to the flock. (1 Pet 5:2-3)**
>
> **Therefore, my brothers, be all the more eager to make your calling and election sure. For if you do these things, you will never fall, (2 Pet 1:10)**
>
> **So then, dear friends, since you are looking forward to this, make every effort to be found spotless, blameless and at peace with him. (2 Pet 3:14)**

5. The two faithful servants were rewarded. But note three facts.

a. The servant who labored 1000 percent was commended by the Lord, "Well done, my good servant." The servant who served 500 percent was not personally commended.

b. The servants were rewarded *exactly* as they worked. A city for each minas. *Perfect justice* was executed. Each servant determined exactly what his own reward would be. The amount or the percent of energy and labor put into increasing the Lord's property determined his reward.

c. The reward involved responsibility, the assigning of duties to perform for the Lord. The two faithful believers reigned with the Lord: they were put in charge of certain territories that included several cities or kingdoms. The point to see is this: they were definitely assigned certain areas of responsibility to oversee *for the Lord*, and the areas of responsibility were based upon how trustworthy they had been while He had been gone. This is the picture of rewards always painted by the Lord and Scripture (see Rev.2:26).

"His master replied, 'Well done, good and faithful servant! You have been faithful with a few things; I will put you in charge of many things. Come and share your master's happiness!' (Mat 25:23)

"Then the King will say to those on his right, 'Come, you who are blessed by my Father; take your inheritance, the kingdom prepared for you since the creation of the world. (Mat 25:34)

But love your enemies, do good to them, and lend to them without expecting to get anything back. Then your reward will be great, and you will be sons of the Most High, because he is kind to the ungrateful and wicked. (Luke 6:35)

You are those who have stood by me in my trials. And I confer on you a kingdom, just as my Father conferred one on me, (Luke 22:28-29)

For if, by the trespass of the one man, death reigned through that one man, how much more will those who receive God's abundant provision of grace and of the gift of righteousness reign in life through the one man, Jesus Christ. (Rom 5:17)

Do you not know that the saints will judge [reign over, hold authority over] the world? And if you are to judge the world, are you not competent to judge trivial cases? Do you not know that we will judge angels? How much more the things of this life! (1 Cor 6:2-3)

If we endure, we will also reign with him. If we disown him, he will also disown us; (2 Tim 2:12)

And from Jesus Christ, who is the faithful witness, the firstborn from the dead, and the ruler of the kings of the earth. To him who loves us and has freed us from our sins by his blood, and has made us to be a kingdom and priests to serve his God and Father—to him be glory and power for ever and ever! Amen. (Rev 1:5-6)

To him who overcomes and does my will to the end, I will give authority over the nations— (Rev 2:26)

To him who overcomes, I will give the right to sit with me on my throne, just as I overcame and sat down with my Father on his throne. (Rev 3:21)

There will be no more night. They will not need the light of a lamp or the light of the sun, for the Lord God will give them light. And they will reign for ever and ever. (Rev 22:5)

6. The servant who did not work received nothing. Note two facts.

a. The unfaithful servant did nothing, absolutely nothing with what Christ had given him.
   - ⇒ He had no vision of what could be done.
   - ⇒ He had no sense of responsibility to the Lord.
   - ⇒ He had no concern for the growth of the Lord's kingdom and property.
   - ⇒ He felt the gift given him did not matter that much and was not needed that much.
   - ⇒ He did not look for the blessed moment of his Lord's return.
   - ⇒ He had a *false security*, believing the Lord would accept him and understand even if he did fail to use the gifts.

b. He tried to justify his behavior. He accused the Lord of being "a hard man" (austeros), which means sharp, stringent. He felt the Lord was too demanding and strict, that if he committed himself to the Lord's affairs, he would lose out on too much of the pleasures and comforts of life. But note: this was merely an excuse for his failure. He had chosen to live a life of selfishness and comfort and worldliness in the kingdom of the Lord without paying the price of helping to build it. He had been complacent and idle, doing very little. He had to cover up his failure or else face judgment, but his excuse was unacceptable. Perfect justice was executed again. "I will judge you by your own words." The very excuse as well as the life of the unfaithful servant determined his judgment.

Note the unfaithful servant is called "you wicked servant." He was not being condemned for what he did, but for what he *had not* done. He was moral and decent, a good and ethical person, but he failed to use his gifts for the Lord in building up the Lord's kingdom. His sin was the sin of omission, not the sin of commission. He was not actively working with the faithful servants of the Lord. He felt the Lord required too much, that the Lord was too strict.

But everyone who hears these words of mine and does not put them into practice is like a foolish man who built his house on sand. The rain came down, the streams rose, and the winds blew and beat against that house, and it fell with a great crash." (Mat 7:26-27)

The seed that fell among thorns stands for those who hear, but as they go on their way they are choked by life's worries, riches and pleasures, and they do not mature. (Luke 8:14)

Then he told this parable: "A man had a fig tree, planted in his vineyard, and he went to look for fruit on it, but did not find any. (Luke 13:6)

"Be careful, or your hearts will be weighed down with dissipation, drunkenness and the anxieties of life, and that day will close on you unexpectedly like a trap. For it will come upon all those who live on the face of the whole earth. (Luke 21:34-35)

Anyone, then, who knows the good he ought to do and doesn't do it, sins. (James 4:17)

You have lived on earth in luxury and self-indulgence. You have fattened yourselves in the day of slaughter. (James 5:5)

They will be paid back with harm for the harm they have done. Their idea of pleasure is to carouse in broad daylight. They are blots and blemishes, reveling in

their pleasures while they feast with you. (2 Pet 2:13)

But you have planted wickedness, you have reaped evil, you have eaten the fruit of deception. Because you have depended on your own strength and on your many warriors, (Hosea 10:13)

DEEPER STUDY # 3

(19:15-19) **Rewards—Responsibility**: moneymaking was not the purpose of the servants (see note 3—Lk.19:13). The purpose was to test them, to show how capable and responsible they were. Could they be trusted with responsibility, with the authority of God? The leaders who are needed to rule God's universe in the coming kingdom and world order must be strong and responsible. The dominant idea is that of testing, a time of trial. The Nobleman's purpose is to develop distinguished rulers: leaders that are decisive, firm, and strong.

It is interesting that the Lord spoke in the hundreds of percent—interesting that the one who really pleased the Lord exerted not 100 percent energy but 1000 percent, and the one who showed some fruitfulness worked not just 50 percent but 500 percent. Is there some significance in these percentages? Some message for God's people? Is there a servant who dares to waste a moment of time after studying what the Lord said?

6 (19:24-26) **Reward**: the Lord's servant who labors 1000 percent shall be given the reward of the unfaithful. Why? Very simply, because he has proven he can handle any amount of responsibility. He had taken a little (one mina) and used it to the maximum. He was as responsible as he could be. He could and would handle and oversee whatever the Lord gave him to oversee.

Note: there were some who objected. Who it was that objected is not known. Jesus simply answered that he who had labored ever so diligently to increase would receive more and more. But the person who did not work to increase would lose even what he had (cp. 1 Cor.15:58). If a man does not use his gift, he will lose it just as a man would lose his arm if he did not use it.

Those who are wise will shine like the brightness of the heavens, and those who lead many to righteousness, like the stars for ever and ever. (Dan 12:3)

And if anyone gives even a cup of cold water to one of these little ones because he is my disciple, I tell you the truth, he will certainly not lose his reward." (Mat 10:42)

"His master replied, 'Well done, good and faithful servant! You have been faithful with a few things; I will put you in charge of many things. Come and share your master's happiness!' (Mat 25:23)

But love your enemies, do good to them, and lend to them without expecting to get anything back. Then your reward will be great, and you will be sons of the Most High, because he is kind to the ungrateful and wicked. (Luke 6:35)

Because you know that the Lord will reward everyone for whatever good he does, whether he is slave or free. (Eph 6:8)

7 (19:27) **Judgment**: the citizens who are enemies of the Lord's rule are to be slain. There are two points to note here.

1. The man who rejects Christ and His reign over his life is an enemy of Christ. He opposes and stands against Christ.

2. The enemy of Christ will be condemned *before Christ*. He shall suffer doom be killed, put to death, and be separated from God eternally and spiritually (see DEEPER STUDY # 1, Death—Heb.9:27).

But the subjects of the kingdom will be thrown outside, into the darkness, where there will be weeping and gnashing of teeth." (Mat 8:12)

And throw that worthless servant outside, into the darkness, where there will be weeping and gnashing of teeth.' (Mat 25:30)

"Then he will say to those on his left, 'Depart from me, you who are cursed, into the eternal fire prepared for the devil and his angels. (Mat 25:41)

"Then they will go away to eternal punishment, but the righteous to eternal life." (Mat 25:46)

But because of your stubbornness and your unrepentant heart, you are storing up wrath against yourself for the day of God's wrath, when his righteous judgment will be revealed. (Rom 2:5)

And give relief to you who are troubled, and to us as well. This will happen when the Lord Jesus is revealed from heaven in blazing fire with his powerful angels. He will punish those who do not know God and do not obey the gospel of our Lord Jesus. (2 Th 1:7-8)

Outline	Section heading & Scripture (vv.28-32)	Scripture (vv.32-40)	Outline
	VIII. THE SON OF MAN'S DRAMATIC ENTRANCE INTO JERUSALEM: HIS CLAIM AND CONFLICT, 19:28-21:4	as he had told them. 33 As they were untying the colt, its owners asked them, "Why are you untying the colt?"	
		34 They replied, "The Lord needs it."	d. He accepted the recognition of the disciples
	A. The Triumphal Entry: Jesus' Claim to be King, 19:28-40 (Mt.21:1-11; Mk.11: 1-11; Jn.12:12-19)	35 They brought it to Jesus, threw their cloaks on the colt and put Jesus on it. 36 As he went along, people spread their cloaks on the road.	**3 There was the people's proclaiming Him to be King**
1 There was the constraint to go to Jerusalem: To suffer & die	28 After Jesus had said this, he went on ahead, going up to Jerusalem.	37 When he came near the place where the road goes down the Mount of Olives, the whole crowd of disciples began joyfully to praise God in loud voices for all the miracles they had seen:	
2 There was the deliberate claim to be King[DS1,2]	29 As he approached Bethphage and Bethany at the hill called the Mount of Olives, he sent two of his disciples, saying to them,		
a. He planned a dramatic demonstration in detail[DS3]	30 "Go to the village ahead of you, and as you enter it, you will find a colt tied there, which no one has ever ridden. Untie it and bring it here.	38 "Blessed is the king who comes in the name of the Lord!" "Peace in heaven and glory in the highest!"	
b. He used the title "the Lord" in laying claim to men's property	31 If anyone asks you, 'Why are you untying it?' tell him, 'The Lord needs it.'"	39 Some of the Pharisees in the crowd said to Jesus, "Teacher, rebuke your disciples!"	**4 There was the insistent claim of Jesus; He was to be proclaimed King by the people** a. The religionists rebuked Him
c. His instructions were carefully followed	32 Those who were sent ahead went and found it just	40 "I tell you," he replied, "if they keep quiet, the stones will cry out."	b. Jesus insisted that proclaiming Him King was inevitable

DIVISION VIII

THE SON OF MAN'S DRAMATIC ENTRANCE INTO JERUSALEM: HIS CLAIM AND CONFLICT, 19:28-21:4

A. The Triumphal Entry: Jesus' Claim to be King, 19:28-40

(19:28-40) **Introduction**: this was a dramatic picture. Jesus' arrival into Jerusalem began the last week of His life. It is what we call *Holy Week* or *Palm Sunday*. Jesus was unquestionably claiming to be King, but He was claiming to be a different kind of King, a King who was different from what men usually conceived. He was claiming to be the King of Peace, the King whose kingdom is not of this earth (Jn.19:36).

1. There was the constraint to go to Jerusalem: to suffer and die (v.28).
2. There was the deliberate claim to be King (v.29-35).
3. There was the people's proclaiming Him to be King (v.36-38).
4. There was the insistent claim of Jesus: He was to be proclaimed King by the people (v.39-40).

1 (19:28) **Jesus Christ, Death**: there was the constraint, the drive to suffer and die. Right after Jesus had finished sharing the parable of the pounds, He felt the driving constraint to move on toward Jerusalem. There the climax of His purpose was to take place. He was to suffer and die for man. Jesus was constrained, compelled with an iron determination, to complete His purpose. Jesus was driven to die for man. His whole spirit is pictured in the words, "Therefore have I set my face like flint" (Is.50:7. See DEEPER STUDY # 1—Lk.9:51; Mk.10:32.) Remember, Jerusalem was only about seventeen miles away. The final events were now to begin.

2 (19:29-35) **Jesus Christ, Claim—Messiah**: there was the deliberate claim to be King. Note four things. (See notes—Mt.21:2-5 for more discussion.)

1. Jesus planned a dramatic demonstration in detail. The whole scene was to center around His riding into the city on a colt (see DEEPER STUDY # 3—Lk.19:30 for discussion).
2. Jesus used the title "the Lord" in laying claim upon men and their property. "The Lord" (o kurios) is a strong expression; it is the same as saying Jehovah. Jesus was claiming the right to use the colt because He was "the Lord." The owner was bound to have been a disciple who would allow "the Lord" to borrow his animals. A man of the world might not allow the claim of the Lord to affect him.
3. Jesus' instructions were followed carefully.

> **Thought 1.** Note a crucial point. The task given to the two disciples to go and secure the colt may have seemed small, but no task is small in the proclamation of Jesus as King. Fetching the colt was extremely important if Christ were to be proclaimed as King before the people. The task was essential.

4. Jesus accepted the recognition of the disciples. The disciples knew exactly what Jesus was doing. They acknow-ledged His claim by three acts.
   ⇒ They obeyed His instructions explicitly.
   ⇒ They used their own garments as a saddle.
   ⇒ They sat Jesus upon the colt.

The point is this: Jesus accepted their homage and thereby claimed to be the Messiah.

DEEPER STUDY # 1
(19:29) **Bethphage**: means *House of Figs.* It was a suburb of Jerusalem, lying toward the Mount of Olives. Note that Jesus arrived in Bethphage by foot. This pictures the great humiliation to which the Son of God subjected Himself in order to come to earth and save man. While on earth, He had no means of travelling except by walking.

DEEPER STUDY # 2
(19:29) **Bethany**: it was a suburb of Jerusalem, about two miles east. The city was the home of Lazarus, Mary, and Martha. Jesus stayed with the family when ministering in and around Jerusalem. One must remember that Jesus apparently had no home of His own. His immediate family did not believe in His claims (Jn.7:1-5, esp.5). He Himself said, "Foxes have holes and birds of the air have nests, but the Son of Man has no place to lay his head" (Mt.8:20). The only housing He had was the home of others such as Martha and Mary (Jn.11:1f; cp. Lk.11:1f; Lk.10:38-42; Jn.12:1f).

DEEPER STUDY # 3
(19:30) **Colt**: in ancient days the colt or donkey was a noble animal. It was used as a beast of service to carry the burdens of men. More significantly, it was used by Kings and their emissaries when they entered a city in peace. They rode a colt to symbolize their peaceful intentions (cp. the judges of Israel and the chieftains throughout the land, Judges 5:10; 10:4). This differed dramatically from a conquering King. When a King entered a city as a conqueror, he rode a stallion.

Jesus was dramatically demonstrating two things: first, He was unquestionably the promised King, the Savior of the people; and second, He was not coming as the people expected. He was not coming as a conquering king or as a worldly potentate in pomp and ceremony, nor as the leader of an army to kill, injure, and maim. Therefore, the people must change their concept of the Messiah, for He was coming as the Savior of Peace. He was coming to save men not to destroy them. He was coming to show men that God is the God of love and reconciliation.

1. The colt was a symbol of peace. Jesus came to bring peace, as pointed out in the above discussion.

2. The colt symbolized service. It was a noble animal, an animal used in the service of men to carry their burdens. Jesus came upon the colt symbolizing that He came to serve men, to bear their burdens for them.

3. The colt symbolized sacredness, for it had never been ridden before (v.2). Animals and things used for sacred or religious purposes had to be animals and things that had never been used before (Num.10:2; Dt.21:3; 1 Sam.6:7). This detail points to the sacredness of the event. It pictured that Jesus was deliberately taking every precaution to proclaim that *He is the sacred hope*, the promised Messiah of the people.

3 (19:36-38) **Messiah, Misconceptions**: there was the people's proclaiming Him to be King. Three facts need to be noted in this point.

1. The people praised God for all the mighty works they had seen. There were teeming thousands lining the roadway, throwing their cloaks down ahead of Him. (See note—Mt.21:8-9 for more discussion.) The people had just recently seen miracle after miracle including the raising of Lazarus from the dead. The whole atmosphere was electric with excitement and expectation. The people knew Jesus had the power to do anything: He could bring the Kingdom of God to earth.

> **How God anointed Jesus of Nazareth with the Holy Spirit and power, and how he went around doing good and healing all who were under the power of the devil, because God was with him. (Acts 10:38)**
>
> **"I know that you can do all things; no plan of yours can be thwarted. (Job 42:2)**
>
> **Our God is in heaven; he does whatever pleases him. (Psa 115:3)**

2. They proclaimed Jesus to be "the King who comes in the name of the Lord." They thought the hour had arrived. Jesus was going to usher in the Kingdom of God *now.* (See note—Lk.19:11.) God was going…

- to free all the nations of the earth from Roman domination.
- to set up the throne of Jesus in Jerusalem from which the rule and reign of righteousness would be executed.
- to establish Israel as the leading nation of the earth.

> **While they were listening to this, he went on to tell them a parable, because he was near Jerusalem and the people thought that the kingdom of God was going to appear at once. (Luke 19:11)**

3. The people failed to see several things.

a. They failed to see that Jesus was riding a colt, coming as the King of Peace.

> **Because of the tender mercy of our God, by which the rising sun [Christ] will come to us from heaven to shine on those living in darkness and in the shadow of death, to guide our feet into the path of peace." (Luke 1:78-79)**
>
> **"Glory to God in the highest, and on earth peace to men on whom his favor rests." (Luke 2:14)**
>
> **Peace I leave with you; my peace I give you. I do not give to you as the world gives. Do not let your hearts be troubled and do not be afraid. (John 14:27; cp. John 16:33)**
>
> **For the kingdom of God is not a matter of eating and drinking, but of righteousness, peace and joy in the Holy Spirit, (Rom 14:17)**
>
> **The LORD gives strength to his people; the LORD blesses his people with peace. (Psa 29:11)**

b. They failed to see that Jesus was riding the animal of burdens, coming as the King who wished to bear the burdens of men.

> **For this reason he had to be made like his brothers in every way, in order that he might become a merciful and faithful high priest in service to God, and that he might**

make atonement for the sins of the people. Because he himself suffered when he was tempted, he is able to help those who are being tempted. (Heb 2:17-18)

For we do not have a high priest who is unable to sympathize with our weaknesses, but we have one who has been tempted in every way, just as we are—yet was without sin. Let us then approach the throne of grace with confidence, so that we may receive mercy and find grace to help us in our time of need. (Heb 4:15-16)

c. They failed to see that Jesus was riding the animal that symbolized sacredness, coming for the purpose of saving the people spiritually. (See note—Eph.1:1-3.)
d. They failed to see that Jesus was riding the animal that symbolized gentleness, coming as the King of gentleness.

"Come to me, all you who are weary and burdened, and I will give you rest. Take my yoke upon you and learn from me, for I am gentle and humble in heart, and you will find rest for your souls. (Mat 11:28-29)

When they hurled their insults at him, he did not retaliate; when he suffered, he made no threats. Instead, he entrusted himself to him who judges justly. He himself bore our sins in his body on the tree, so that we might die to sins and live for righteousness; by his wounds you have been healed. (1 Pet 2:23-24)

4 (19:39-40) **Jesus Christ, Claim—Praise**: there was the insistent claim of Jesus. He was to be proclaimed King by the people. The religious authorities were hostile. They had already given the word to hunt Jesus down and arrest Him (Jn.11:57). Despite this threat, Jesus publicly and triumphantly entered Jerusalem. The great weight and importance of His mission, "to seek and save what was lost,"(Lk. 19:10) is clearly seen in such courageous behavior. (See notes—Mk.11:1-11.)

Then Nathanael declared, "Rabbi, you are the Son of God; you are the King of Israel." (John 1:49)

"You are a king, then!" said Pilate. Jesus answered, "You are right in saying I am a king. In fact, for this reason I was born, and for this I came into the world, to testify to the truth. Everyone on the side of truth listens to me." (John 18:37)

Note the clear declaration to deity that Jesus made: "I tell you...If they [the praising crowds] keep quiet, the stones will cry out." Nature did cry out when He hung upon the cross. The world and the disciples had forsaken Him, but the sun hid its face and the earth split asunder in a demonstration of the cry of nature (cp. Mt.27:45, 51-52).

Let heaven and earth praise him, the seas and all that move in them, (Psa 69:34)

Sing for joy, O heavens, for the LORD has done this; shout aloud, O earth beneath. Burst into song, you mountains, you forests and all your trees, for the LORD has redeemed Jacob, he displays his glory in Israel. (Isa 44:23)

Shout for joy, O heavens; rejoice, O earth; burst into song, O mountains! For the LORD comforts his people and will have compassion on his afflicted ones. (Isa 49:13)

	B. The Dramatic Prediction: Judgment Upon Jerusalem, 19:41-44 (cp. Mt.23:37-39; Lk.13:34-35)	from your eyes. 43 The days will come upon you when your enemies will build an embankment against you and encircle you and hem you in on every side.	**2 The terrible fate of the city foretold** a. Was to be encircled
1 The great love of Jesus for the city a. He wept over the city b. The city had rejected the way of peace; that is, it rejected the Messiah[DS1]	41 As he approached Jerusalem and saw the city, he wept over it 42 And said, “If you, even you, had only known on this day what would bring you peace—but now it is hidden	44 They will dash you to the ground, you and the children within your walls. They will not leave one stone on another, because you did not recognize the time of God’s coming to you.”	b. Was to be utterly destroyed c. Was to be personally judged **3 The cause of the city’s doom**

DIVISION VIII

THE SON OF MAN’S DRAMATIC ENTRANCE INTO JERUSALEM: HIS CLAIM AND CONFLICT, 19:28-21:4

B. The Dramatic Prediction: Judgment Upon Jerusalem, 19:41-44

(19:41-44) **Introduction**: this passage is covered only by Luke. It is full of prophecy and compassion, the prediction of Jerusalem’s terrible fate and the compassion of our Lord for a people doomed to utter destruction. The truth of Scripture is also demonstrated in this passage, the truth that Scripture is God’s Word. There is also the truth that sin dooms a nation, but righteousness exalts a nation and its people.

1. The great love of Jesus for the city (v.41-42).
2. The terrible fate of the city foretold (v.43-44).
3. The cause for the city’s doom (v.44).

(19:41-48) **Another Outline**. A Look at Jesus.

1. The compassion of Jesus (v.41-44).
2. The anger of Jesus (v.45-46).
3. The courage of Jesus (v.47-48).

1 (19:41-42) **Jerusalem—Jesus Christ, Compassion**: the city was greatly loved by Jesus (see outline and notes—Mt.23:37-39; Lk.13:34-35).

1. Jesus wept over the city. Note three facts.
   a. The word “wept” (eklausen) means to burst into tears, to weep out loud, to sob, to wail, to mourn. Jesus was literally heartbroken over Jerusalem.
   b. The words “saw the city” mean He was looking and gazing upon the city with deep intensity. He was looking upon, considering, regarding the city in all its tragic state.
   c. Jesus was weeping while the city was engaged in the excitement of feasting and fellowshipping in a jovial, party-like spirit. The whole atmosphere was like that of a present-day convention. The scene can be imagined. But while the people were in such a partying mood, Jesus was off on the hillside weeping over the city and its people.
2. The reason for Jesus’ weeping was stated by Jesus Himself: the city and its people had rejected the way of peace, that is, the Messiah Himself. Another way to say it is, they had rejected the things which make for peace.
   a. Jesus was not weeping because He was to suffer and die in the city. He was not weeping over Himself, not yet. He was weeping over the city and its people, weeping because they did not know the way of peace.
   b. There are things which make for peace, things which bring peace both to the hearts of men and to the society and world of men (see DEEPER STUDY # 1—Lk.19:42 for discussion).
   c. The things that bring peace are “hidden from [the people’s] eyes.” This statement has two possible meanings. First, the people closed their eyes to Jesus and His message of peace. They refused to see; therefore, they did not see. Second, God counted Jerusalem as having lost its opportunity. He had shown patience for generation after generation (see outline and notes—Mt.23:37); now the time for judgment had come. God hid from their eyes the things that would bring peace. He turned Jerusalem over to their blindness (see notes, Judicial Judgment—Mt.13:13-15; DEEPER STUDY # 1—Jn.12:39-41; note—Ro.1:24-25; DEEPER STUDY # 2—11:7-10).

For this people’s heart has become calloused; they hardly hear with their ears, and they have closed their eyes. Otherwise they might see with their eyes, hear with their ears, understand with their hearts and turn, and I would heal them.’ (Mat 13:15)

DEEPER STUDY # 1

(19:42) **Peace** (eriene): to bind together, to join and weave together. It means that one is bound, woven, joined together with himself and with God and with others.

The Hebrew word is *shalom.* It means freedom from trouble and much, much more. It means experiencing the highest good, enjoying the very best, possessing all the inner good possible.

There are two kinds of peace mentioned in the Scripture.

1. There is the *peace of the world.* This is a peace of escapism, of avoiding trouble, of refusing to face things, of unreality.
2. There is the *peace of Christ and of God.* This is a *bosom peace*, a peace deep within. It is a tranquility of mind, a composure, a peace that settles and strengthens the believer even through the most terrible circumstances and situations. It is more than feelings, even more than attitude and thought.
   a. God’s bosom peace is the *peace of conquest.* It is the peace independent of conditions and environment; the peace which no sorrow, danger, suffering, or experience can take away.

Peace I leave with you; my peace I give you. I do not give to you as the world gives.

Do not let your hearts be troubled and do not be afraid. (John 14:27)

"I have told you these things, so that in me you may have peace. In this world you will have trouble. But take heart! I have overcome the world." (John 16:33)

b. God's bosom peace is the *peace of perfect assurance*. It is the peace of unquestionable confidence; the peace with a sure knowledge that a person's life is in the hands of God and that all things will work out for good to those who love God and are called according to His purpose.

And we know that in all things God works for the good of those who love him, who have been called according to his purpose. (Rom 8:28)

Being confident of this, that he who began a good work in you will carry it on to completion until the day of Christ Jesus. (Phil 1:6)

That is why I am suffering as I am. Yet I am not ashamed, because I know whom I have believed, and am convinced that he is able to guard what I have entrusted to him for that day. (2 Tim 1:12)

c. God's bosom peace is the *peace of intimacy with God*. It is the peace of the highest good. It is the peace that settles the mind, strengthens the will, and establishes the heart.

Therefore, since we have been justified through faith, we have peace with God through our Lord Jesus Christ, (Rom 5:1; cp. v. 2-5)

Do not be anxious about anything, but in everything, by prayer and petition, with thanksgiving, present your requests to God. And the peace of God, which transcends all understanding, will guard your hearts and your minds in Christ Jesus. (Phil 4:6-7)

There is *the source of peace*. Peace is always born out of reconciliation. Its source is found only in the reconciliation wrought by Jesus Christ. Peace always has to do with personal relationships: a man's relationship to himself, to God, and to his fellow man. A man must be bound, woven, and joined together with himself, with God, and with his fellow man (cp. Eph.2:13-14).

Man secures peace in the following manner.

1. By justification (Ro.5:1)
2. By loving God's Word (Ps.119:165; Jn.16:33)
3. By praying about everything (Ph.4:7)
4. By being spiritually minded (Ro.8:6)
5. By keeping his mind upon God (Is.26:3; Ph.4:8)
6. By keeping God's commandments (Is.48:18; Ph.4:9)

The *subject of peace* is often divided as (1) Peace with God (Ro.5:1; Eph.2:14-17), (2) the Peace of God (Lk.7:50; Ph.4:6-7), and (3) Peace from God (Ro.1:7; 1 Cor.1:3).

2(19:43-44) **Jerusalem—Judgment, Upon Nations**: the city's terrible fate. Three major things were to be involved in Jerusalem's destruction.

1. The city was to have a trench dug around it, completely encircling the city. The ditch and dirt mound shoveled from it served as a protective wall for the Roman army. Sharp-pointed wooden stakes were driven into the mound of dirt, sticking up facing the encircled city in the event that the city's army launched a counterattack. The city was to have an army launched against it in a full-fledged military attack.

2. The city was to be utterly destroyed. It was to be completely demolished and razed to the ground; not one stone was to be left upon another.

3. The people were to be *personally* judged. Note the words, "The children within "your walls" will be dashed to the ground. Also note that the word "you" is used ten times in three verses (v.42-44). The prediction is very personal. Cities and nations may fall under the judgment of God, but it is the people who are at fault and who shall be personally judged.

What Christ said was literally fulfilled by the attack of Titus in 70 A.D. In 66 A.D. the Jews revolted and the Roman army was swift to attack, but the city was difficult to take, primarily for two reasons. It sat upon a hill, well protected by the terrain, and the leaders of the revolt were religious fanatics. Well over a million people had fled into the city behind its protective walls.

As the siege wore on, the predictions of Christ were literally fulfilled. Outside the walls sat the Roman army with all the maiming and killing of war. Inside the walls neighbor after neighbor faced famine, pestilence, false deliverers (messiahs), betrayal, murder, revolt, rebellion, and hatred—and all took their toll. Josephus says over 1,000,000 people died and 97,000 were taken captive. He describes well the horrors of the siege (see notes—Mt.24:7; 24:10; 24:11. See Flavius Josephus. *Josephus Complete Works*, translated by William Whiston. Grand Rapids, MI: Kregel, 1960. Wars. 5. 12:3; 6. 3:4; 6. 8:5.)

"It appears to me that the misfortunes of all men, from the beginning of the world, if they be compared to these of the Jews, are not so considerable as they were" (Josephus, Wars. Preface 4). (See outline and notes—Mt.24:1-14 for a descriptive picture of the utter destruction of Jerusalem.)

Thought 1. Jerusalem is a prime example of the fate of a nation that rejects God. It is doomed to fall.

Whoever believes in the Son has eternal life, but whoever rejects the Son will not see life, for God's wrath remains on him." (John 3:36)

I told you that you would die in your sins; if you do not believe that I am the one I claim to be, you will indeed die in your sins." (John 8:24)

But concerning Israel he says, "All day long I have held out my hands to a disobedient and obstinate people." (Rom 10:21)

Through the blessing of the upright a city is exalted, but by the mouth of the wicked it is destroyed. (Prov 11:11)

Righteousness exalts a nation, but sin is a disgrace to any people. (Prov 14:34)

Kings detest wrongdoing, for a throne is established through righteousness. (Prov 16:12)

Remove the wicked from the king's presence, and his throne will be established through righteousness. (Prov 25:5)

3 (19:44) **Jerusalem—Judgment Upon Nations**: the cause of the city's doom. The people rejected the day of the Messiah or the day of their salvation.

1. Their day of visitation came. God had always visited Israel; they had the revelation...

- of God Himself down through the centuries.
- of God's Word, the Scriptures of the Old Testament.
- of God's messengers and prophets.
- of God's active presence in the lives of believers.

Now they had the very presence of God's Messiah, the Son of God Himself (cp. Ro.9:4-5).

2. They did not know Him, and there was no excuse, for they could clearly see that God was at work once again among His people. It had been three to four hundred years since the Old Testament had closed and the last prophet had appeared. The evidence was clear and strong that the day of prophecy had been opened once again. The promised Messiah, the day of Israel's salvation had come, but the people rejected the evidence. They were doomed by their rejection, and Jesus wept because they refused to see the day of their salvation.

> **"O Jerusalem, Jerusalem, you who kill the prophets and stone those sent to you, how often I have longed to gather your children together, as a hen gathers her chicks under her wings, but you were not willing! Look, your house is left to you desolate. I tell you, you will not see me again until you say, 'Blessed is he who comes in the name of the Lord.'" (Luke 13:34-35)**

	C. The Cleansing of the Temple: The Righteous Anger of Jesus, 19:45-48 (Mt.21:12-16; Mk.11:15-19; cp. Jn.2:13-16)	house of prayer; 'but you have made it 'a den of robbers.'"	a. The place of His presence & dwelling b. The place of prayer c. The place for teaching the Word of God
1 **How He cleansed the temple: Drove people out** a. Those who profaned b. Those who exploited	45 Then he entered the temple area and began driving out those who were selling.	47 Every day he was teaching at the temple. But the chief priests, the teachers of the law and the leaders among the people were trying to kill him.	3 **The results of His cleansing the temple** a. The leaders: Sought to destroy Him
2 **Why He cleansed the temple**	46 "It is written," he said to them, "'My house will be a	48 Yet they could not find any way to do it, because all the people hung on his words.	b. The people: Listened to Him attentively

DIVISION VIII

THE SON OF MAN'S DRAMATIC ENTRANCE INTO JERUSALEM: HIS CLAIM AND CONFLICT, 19:28-21:4

C. The Cleansing of the Temple: The Righteous Anger of Jesus, 19:45-48

(19:45-48) **Introduction**: the anger of Jesus is seen in this passage. It is important to note what angered Him: the abuse of God's temple.

⇒ The believer's body is the temple of God, and it angered Him to see the body abused (1 Cor.6:19-20).

⇒ The church is the temple of God, and it angered Him to see the church abused (see note—1 Cor.3:16; 3:17).

The church is the temple of God. This fact is often de-emphasized by believers and overlooked by the world. But no matter how man treats the church, Jesus proclaims the church to be God's, to be His holy temple. The church is the place that is set apart for prayer, worship, and communion with God.

1. How He cleansed the temple: drove people out (v.45).
2. Why He cleansed the temple (v.46).
3. The results of His cleansing the temple (v.47-48).

1 (19:45) **Temple—Church**: How did Jesus cleanse the temple? He "drove out" those who profaned and exploited the temple. This took place in the outer court of the temple, the court of the Gentiles, which was where Gentiles worshipped. It was tragically abused. It had become nothing more than a commercial marketplace owned, and in many cases, operated by the priests. It was used for the selling and buying of sacrificial animals which included oxen and sheep as well as smaller doves and pigeons. It was also used for the inspection of the animals' purity and for the exchanging of foreign currencies. Every Passover season found thousands of pilgrims coming to the temple from all over the world travelling great distances. It was usually impossible for a pilgrim to bring his own animal for sacrifice; but if he did, he had to get it by the inspector, which often cost a fee. The bickering back and forth created an atmosphere of utter chaos that apparently gave off the sound of a human volcanic uproar. Picture a modern-day trade show—large, crowded, extremely noisy—and add to that the presence of animals and the exchanging of thousands of coins (see note, pt.2—Eph.2:14-15).

Hundreds of thousands of animals were sold at the great feasts, and unfortunately, the High Priest and other priests were often in the middle of the commercialism. It is this commercialism and secularism of religion that Jesus lashed out against. (See note—Mt.21:12-16 for detailed discussion and thoughts.)

To those who sold doves he said, "Get these out of here! How dare you turn my Father's house into a market!" (John 2:16)

Don't you have homes to eat and drink in [businesses to buy and sell in]? Or do you despise the church of God and humiliate those who have nothing? What shall I say to you? Shall I praise you for this? Certainly not! (1 Cor 11:22)

"'Observe my Sabbaths and have reverence for my sanctuary. I am the LORD. (Lev 19:30)

Guard your steps when you go to the house of God. Go near to listen rather than to offer the sacrifice of fools, who do not know that they do wrong. (Eccl 5:1)

"'The people of Judah have done evil in my eyes, declares the LORD. They have set up their detestable idols in the house that bears my Name and have defiled it. (Jer 7:30)

Her prophets are arrogant; they are treacherous men. Her priests profane the sanctuary and do violence to the law. (Zep 3:4)

2 (19:46-47) **Temple**: Why did Jesus cleanse the temple? Jesus' attitude toward the temple is clearly seen in this verse. The same attitude, of course, would be true of the church. He held the temple in the highest regard.

1. Jesus called the temple (church) "My house." This says at least two things to people of every generation.

a. The temple or church is the place where He dwells and lives: it is the place where His presence is. However, considering that God is omnipresent (everywhere) what could Jesus have meant? Very simply, the church is a place that has been *set apart* (sanctified) especially for Him. The church is the very special place designated for Him; it is the place that is different from all other places, different in that it is the place set aside for God's very own presence to be known.

Note: Jesus said in another place that the temple is related so closely to God that it actually *reveals and reflects God's nature*. This is seen in His demand that men not swear by the temple.

Why? Because the temple or church is God's, of His plan and purpose; therefore, the church is of Him, of His very nature (Mt.23:16f).

God is spirit, and his worshipers must worship in spirit and in truth." (John 4:24)

But you are to seek the place the LORD your God will choose from among all your tribes to put his Name there for his dwelling. To that place you must go; (Deu 12:5)

I love the house where you live, O LORD, the place where your glory dwells. (Psa 26:8)

One thing I ask of the LORD, this is what I seek: that I may dwell in the house of the LORD all the days of my life, to gaze upon the beauty of the LORD and to seek him in his temple. (Psa 27:4)

Blessed are those you choose and bring near to live in your courts! We are filled with the good things of your house, of your holy temple. (Psa 65:4)

b. The word "My" is possessive: the temple is the Lord's; it belongs to Him. He possesses and owns it. The people in the temple are only ministers, not owners; therefore, whatever is done in the temple is to be what He wants done. His house is to be operated as He wills, and His servants are to do His bidding, not violating, profaning, or exploiting His house. (See note—1 Cor.3:16; 3:17.)

Surely goodness and love will follow me all the days of my life, and I will dwell in the house of the LORD forever. (Psa 23:6)

Better is one day in your courts than a thousand elsewhere; I would rather be a doorkeeper in the house of my God than dwell in the tents of the wicked. (Psa 84:10)

A song of ascents. Of David. I rejoiced with those who said to me, "Let us go to the house of the LORD." (Psa 122:1)

2. Jesus called the temple "a house of prayer." Jesus' words are actually a quotation from two Scriptures.

These I will bring to my holy mountain and give them joy in my house of prayer. Their burnt offerings and sacrifices will be accepted on my altar; for my house will be called a house of prayer for all nations." (Isa 56:7)

Has this house, which bears my Name, become a den of robbers to you? But I have been watching! declares the LORD. (Jer 7:11)

Note three points.

a. The temple or church is called "a house of prayer," not a house of sacrifice, nor a house of offerings, teaching, prophecy, or preaching. Everything done within the House of God is to lead to prayer, the *worship of and communion with* the Father.

b. The temple or church is to be the house of prayer. Men are to pray everywhere, but they are to go to the church to pray also. The church is the very special place *set aside* for God. It is the place where all of God's people come together; therefore, it is a very special place for prayer.

He went to Nazareth, where he had been brought up, and on the Sabbath day he went into the synagogue, as was his custom. And he stood up to read. (Luke 4:16)

Then they worshiped him and returned to Jerusalem with great joy. And they stayed continually at the temple, praising God. (Luke 24:52-53)

Ascribe to the LORD the glory due his name. Bring an offering and come before him; worship the LORD in the splendor of his holiness. (1 Chr 16:29)

Ascribe to the LORD the glory due his name; worship the LORD in the splendor of his holiness. (Psa 29:2)

Come, let us bow down in worship, let us kneel before the LORD our Maker; (Psa 95:6)

Worship the LORD in the splendor of his holiness; tremble before him, all the earth. (Psa 96:9)

Exalt the LORD our God and worship at his footstool; he is holy. (Psa 99:5)

And the inhabitants of one city will go to another and say, 'Let us go at once to entreat the LORD and seek the LORD Almighty. I myself am going.' (Zec 8:21)

c. The temple or church is not to be used as a commercial place. It is not to be a place of buying and selling, marketing and retailing, stealing and cheating. It is not to be profaned. The church is the House of God, God's House of Prayer. It is to be a place of sanctity, refined and purified by God Himself. It is to be a place of quietness and meditation, a place set aside for worship, not for buying and selling and securing gain.

"'Observe my Sabbaths and have reverence for my sanctuary. I am the LORD. (Lev 19:30)

"Do not come any closer," God said. "Take off your sandals, for the place where you are standing is holy ground." (Exo 3:5)

In the council of the holy ones God is greatly feared; he is more awesome than all who surround him. (Psa 89:7)

But the LORD is in his holy temple; let all the earth be silent before him." (Hab 2:20)

3. Christ used the temple as a place for teaching. Note three things.

a. He taught daily in the temple. It was the place where the people had gathered for the purpose of hearing the Word of God, so He met their need and fulfilled that purpose.

b. It was not enough to cleanse the temple. He was compelled to be about God's business, that of proclaiming God's Word in God's house.

c. He was about God's business while others were still misusing the temple and plotting against His life. He was busy carrying out the purpose of the temple while others were profaning and misusing it. He used the temple as the house of teaching, teaching which led men into prayer and worship and communion with God.

"Why were you searching for me [in the temple]?" he asked. "Didn't you know

I had to be in my Father's house?" (Luke 2:49)

Many peoples will come and say, "Come, let us go up to the mountain of the LORD, to the house of the God of Jacob. He will teach us his ways, so that we may walk in his paths." The law will go out from Zion, the word of the LORD from Jerusalem. (Isa 2:3)

Many nations will come and say, "Come, let us go up to the mountain of the LORD, to the house of the God of Jacob. He will teach us his ways, so that we may walk in his paths." The law will go out from Zion, the word of the LORD from Jerusalem. (Micah 4:2)

3 (19:47-48) **Temple—Church**: the results of Christ's cleansing the temple were twofold.

1. The leaders sought to destroy Christ. The leaders were the chief priests and Scribes, that is, those who were *professional religionists*. There were also "the leaders among the people," that is, lay leaders and people from among the ruling class.

Note two things.

a. The leaders were actively seeking to "kill" (apolesai) Christ. The word means to *utterly destroy*. (Imagine *religious leaders'* being so disturbed that they seek to destroy and ruin the ministry of a person.)
b. The reason why the leaders were so disturbed was twofold: first, they were losing control of the temple; and second, they were losing control of the people. Jesus had invaded their temple by cleansing it, and He was teaching the true gospel of the Kingdom of God and righteousness. They were losing money because Jesus had cast out the vendors, and their own personal ideas and control were being undermined. They were unwilling to accept the truth personally and to surrender their lives to Jesus. (See notes—Mt.12:1-8; note and DEEPER STUDY # 1—12:10 for more discussion.)

Thought 1. The leaders were making the same two mistakes made by men of every generation.

1) They were letting their *greed* keep them from Christ.

For the love of money is a root of all kinds of evil. Some people, eager for money, have wandered from the faith and pierced themselves with many griefs. (1 Tim 6:10)

Your gold and silver are corroded. Their corrosion will testify against you and eat your flesh like fire. You have hoarded wealth in the last days. (James 5:3)

Better a little with righteousness than much gain with injustice. (Prov 16:8)

Like a partridge that hatches eggs it did not lay is the man who gains riches by unjust means. When his life is half gone, they will desert him, and in the end he will prove to be a fool. (Jer 17:11)

2) They were letting their self-confidence and self-righteousness keep them from Christ. Just think about it! Not a single leader, civil or religious, thought God would ever reject him or keep him out of heaven. Every one of them thought he was good enough to be acceptable to God, yet not a single one is in heaven today.

"Not everyone who says to me, 'Lord, Lord,' will enter the kingdom of heaven, but only he who does the will of my Father who is in heaven. (Mat 7:21)

He replied, "Isaiah was right when he prophesied about you hypocrites; as it is written: "'These people honor me with their lips, but their hearts are far from me. (Mark 7:6)

They claim to know God, but by their actions they deny him. They are detestable, disobedient and unfit for doing anything good. (Titus 1:16)

Many a man claims to have unfailing love, but a faithful man who can find? (Prov 20:6)

Those who are pure in their own eyes and yet are not cleansed of their filth; (Prov 30:12)

But you have planted wickedness, you have reaped evil, you have eaten the fruit of deception. Because you have depended on your own strength and on your many warriors, (Hosea 10:13)

The pride of your heart has deceived you, you who live in the clefts of the rocks and make your home on the heights, you who say to yourself, 'Who can bring me down to the ground?' Though you soar like the eagle and make your nest among the stars, from there I will bring you down," declares the LORD. (Oba 1:3-4)

2. The people listened to Jesus. The word "hung" (exekremeto) means they were attentive, gave Him rapt attention, were struck by Him. The picture is this: since the Triumphal Entry the day before, *teeming thousands* were clinging to Him, anxious to hear His word as much as they could. Note: it was His popularity among the people that kept the leaders from arresting Him. They just could not find a time or place to carry out their terrible scheme without causing an uprising among the people.

Thought 1. How many give rapt attention to Jesus today? If we were truly concentrating our attention upon Him like we should, would there be so much opposition to the gospel? Would society be different? Would evil be held back and controlled more?

My soul yearns for you in the night; in the morning my spirit longs for you. When your judgments come upon the earth, the people of the world learn righteousness. (Isa 26:9)

Blessed are those who hunger and thirst for righteousness, for they will be filled. (Mat 5:6)

All my longings lie open before you, O Lord; my sighing is not hidden from you. (Psa 38:9; cp. Ps.63:1)

Outline	Scripture	Scripture	Outline
	CHAPTER 20	3 He replied, "I will also ask you a question. Tell me,	d. Jesus appealed to the logic of men: Was John the Baptist from God or from men?
	D. The Question of Authority: Who is Jesus? 20:1-8 (Mt.21:23-27; Mk.11: 27-33)	4 John's baptism—was it from heaven, or from men?" 5 They discussed it among themselves and said, "If we say, 'From heaven,' he will ask, 'Why didn't you believe him?'	**2 Possibility 1: His authority was from God**
1 The unbelief of men vs. Jesus a. Jesus taught & preached the gospel b. Unbelief caused men to close their ears to the gospel c. Unbelief caused men to question the authority of Jesus	**O**ne day as he was teaching the people in the temple courts and preaching the gospel, the chief priests and the teachers of the law, together with the elders, came up to him. 2 "Tell us by what authority you are doing these things," they said. "Who gave you this authority?"	6 But if we say, 'From men,' all the people will stone us, because they are persuaded that John was a prophet." 7 So they answered, "We don't know where it was from." 8 Jesus said, "Neither will I tell you by what authority I am doing these things."	**3 Possibility 2: His authority was from men** **4 Possibility 3: Indecision & silence**

DIVISION VIII

THE SON OF MAN'S DRAMATIC ENTRANCE INTO JERUSALEM: HIS CLAIM AND CONFLICT, 19:28-21:4

D. The Question of Authority: Who is Jesus? 20:1-8

(20:1-8) **Introduction**: this passage begins a series of attacks upon Jesus. Question after question was asked Him in an attempt to discredit His claim to be the true Messiah, the Son of God. But the questions were to no avail. The present passage is basic; it is the question of authority: Who is Jesus?

1. The unbelief of men vs. Jesus (v.1-4).
2. Possibility 1: His authority was from God (v.5).
3. Possibility 2: His authority was from men (v.6).
4. Possibility 3: indecision and silence (v.7-8).

1 (20:1-4) **Unbelief**: there was unbelief vs. Jesus. This is a striking picture.

1. Jesus was teaching and preaching the gospel. He shared the good news about the Kingdom of God and the great hope for man through repentance. A large crowd hung on his words (Lk.19:48), soaking up every word He said and having the hope of God stirred within their hearts. The words of the Lord were being driven home to the need of the human heart.

2. But note what happened. Unbelief caused men to close their ears to the gospel. The religionists were standing there listening to Jesus just as so many others were, yet their motives differed from the crowd. They were not seeking God beyond their own ideas of religion. They had...

- critical and unbelieving hearts.
- a fear of worldly ridicule, disapproval, and unacceptance.
- a concern for livelihood, security, profession, and position.

They were not interested in discovering the truth about Jesus. They were only interested in tricking Him and discrediting Him before the people. They wanted the people's loyalty to their own *religious position*. The truth mattered little. Their ears were closed and their eyes were blinded to the truth because of their obstinate unbelief.

3. Note another fact about unbelief. Unbelief caused men to question the authority of Jesus, just who He really was. This was the basic question to ask, a question that probed into the very nature of Jesus. What was His authority, who sent Him, who empowered Him, who gave Him the right to do as He was doing? Where had He come from? Just who was He?

The leaders wanted to know what right He had to interfere with their lives and area of responsibility. They were the authorized guardians and rulers of the temple and of the people. He was interfering with their management and had no right to do so. They asked Him two questions.

a. What was the authority for His works? "Tell us by what authority you are doing these things?" He had marched triumphantly into the city of Jerusalem as a King, receiving the homage of the Messianic King from the people; He had cast the market traders out of the temple; He had healed the blind and lame (Mt.21:14); and He had accepted the homage of small children proclaiming Him to be the Messiah. What authority did He have to do such things?

Thought 1. The leaders were asking the basic question that needed to be asked. It is the question that every man needs to ask: What is the authority, the explanation for the works of Christ? The works of...

- ministry
- healing
- teaching
- raising the dead
- rising again
- preaching
- calming the storms of nature
- foretelling the future
- dying and fulfilling Scripture
- ascending into heaven

b. What was the authority of His person: "Who gave you this authority?" He *was claiming...*

- to be the promised Messianic King by entering the city as He did.
- to be the Head, the God of the Temple: "My house."
- to be the Light of the world to the blind and the Messianic Healer to the lame (Mt.21:14).

- to be the Messianic fulfillment of Scripture by receiving the praise of the children.

The authorities knew who Jesus was claiming to be. They just rejected His claim and refused to believe. They chose the course of obstinate unbelief, still refusing to believe despite having proof upon proof.

There were two possible answers to the question of who Jesus was.

⇒ Jesus could have claimed to be acting by His own authority, saying that His power was His own. This, of course, would have made Him an ego-maniac or a great imposter (the greatest in history). Of course, if He had claimed to act by His own authority, they would have discredited Him immediately and arrested Him for causing so much havoc.

⇒ Jesus could have claimed to be acting by the authority of God, to be of and from God. Now note: this was the claim that Jesus made time and again. But if He had made it then and there in the face of the authorities, they would have arrested Him immediately for blasphemy. They would claim that God would never give orders to cause such turmoil in the temple.

Again the leaders were asking the basic question that needs to be asked by every man. *Who gave Jesus* His authority? Who is He: a mere man or truly the Son of God? Is He *of man* or *of God*? Is His authority of men or inherent, that is, from within, of His very own nature as God?

4. Very simply, Jesus appealed to the truth and logic of John the Baptist: "Was [John] from heaven, or from men?"

2 (20:5) **Jesus Christ, Deity—Unbelief**: the first possibility was that Jesus' authority was *from God. John pointed* toward Christ and proclaimed...

- "Behold the Lamb of God" (Jn.1:29).
- "I have seen and I testify that this is the Son of God" (Jn.1:34).

If John were from God, a true messenger of God, then Jesus was the true Messiah, the Son of God. This would mean that Jesus' message of the Kingdom of God, of hope for man through repentance, was true. Man could be saved from sin, death, and hell.

Note the words, "they discussed it among themselves." They discussed the matter among themselves. However, they were not searching their hearts and seeking for the truth. Their minds were already made up. Their preconceived ideas were not going to be set aside, not even by the truth. They were deliberately rejecting Jesus, being obstinate in their unbelief.

Thought 1. Christ and His message were from God; therefore, there is great hope for man. Man can be saved eternally, saved for the Kingdom of God. However, man has a twofold problem.

1) There is the problem of obstinate unbelief.

Whoever believes in him is not condemned, but whoever does not believe stands condemned already because he has not believed in the name of God's one and only Son. (John 3:18)

Whoever believes in the Son has eternal life, but whoever rejects the Son will not see life, for God's wrath remains on him." (John 3:36)

I told you that you would die in your sins; if you do not believe that I am the one I claim to be, you will indeed die in your sins." (John 8:24)

See to it, brothers, that none of you has a sinful, unbelieving heart that turns away from the living God. (Heb 3:12)

A man who remains stiff-necked after many rebukes will suddenly be destroyed—without remedy. (Prov 29:1)

2) There is the problem of being unwilling to give up this world, of being unwilling to deny oneself, one's own desires and preconceived ideas. Man loves the money, acceptance, positions, and possessions of the world too much.

"No one can serve two masters. Either he will hate the one and love the other, or he will be devoted to the one and despise the other. You cannot serve both God and Money. (Mat 6:24)

But the worries of this life, the deceitfulness of wealth and the desires for other things come in and choke the word, making it unfruitful. (Mark 4:19)

For, as I have often told you before and now say again even with tears, many live as enemies of the cross of Christ. Their destiny is destruction, their god is their stomach, and their glory is in their shame. Their mind is on earthly things. (Phil 3:18-19)

People who want to get rich fall into temptation and a trap and into many foolish and harmful desires that plunge men into ruin and destruction. (1 Tim 6:9)

3 (20:6) **Jesus Christ, Deity—Unbelief**: the second possibility was that Jesus' authority was *from men*. Again, whatever was true of John was true of Jesus. However, if John's ministry were of men, how could so many *changed lives* be accounted for? Thousands had repented and been transformed, turning their lives completely around and following God with a new vigor. To say that John was *not from God*, that he had received his power and his authority from men, was foolish and absurd (cp. Lk.7:29; Jn.10:41-42).

The authorities knew that if they publicly held this position, the people would rise up against them. They would lose whatever grip they had over the people, for the people believed that John was a great prophet of God.

Thought 1. Down through the centuries thousands of lives have been changed by Christ. Thousands would lay down their lives in testimony of His transforming power. No greater evidence exists for the deity of Christ. The changed lives of many proclaim the glorious truth of the gospel. Christ is the true Messiah, the Son of God.

(All the people, even the tax collectors, when they heard Jesus' words, acknowledged that God's way was right, because they had been baptized by John. (Luke 7:29)

Jesus answered, "I did tell you, but you do not believe. The miracles I do in my Father's name speak for me, (John 10:25)

> **What about the one whom the Father set apart as his very own and sent into the world? Why then do you accuse me of blasphemy because I said, 'I am God's Son'? Do not believe me unless I do what my Father does. But if I do it, even though you do not believe me, believe the miracles, that you may know and understand that the Father is in me, and I in the Father." (John 10:36-38)**
>
> **And many people came to him. They said, "Though John never performed a miraculous sign, all that John said about this man was true." And in that place many believed in Jesus. (John 10:41-42)**
>
> **Don't you believe that I am in the Father, and that the Father is in me? The words I say to you are not just my own. Rather, it is the Father, living in me, who is doing his work. (John 14:10)**

4 (20:7-8) **Jesus Christ, Deity—Unbelief**: the third possibility was indecision and silence. This was tragic. It is always tragic when a person's concern is to save face not to discover the truth. It is always tragic when a person is so concerned with his position, esteem, and security that he ignores or denies the truth. This was the very response of these men, and it is often the response of men to Christ.

1. They chose expediency, to be deliberately ignorant. They feared being shamed, embarrassed, and ridiculed. To confess Jesus would have meant confessing they had been wrong all along. It would have meant denying self completely and doing so publicly.

2. They denied Jesus. To confess that John was of God would have forced them to acknowledge Jesus, and they were not willing to confess Him. They feared the loss of all they possessed: position, power, wealth, esteem, image, security, and livelihood.

> **Then he said to them all: "If anyone would come after me, he must deny himself and take up his cross daily and follow me. For whoever wants to save his life will lose it, but whoever loses his life for me will save it. (Luke 9:23-24)**
>
> **What good is it for a man to gain the whole world, yet forfeit his soul? (Mark 8:36)**

Thought 1. The tragedy of tragedies is that most men...

- choose expediency rather than principle.
- choose to play it safe rather than to stand for the truth.
- choose to say "I don't know" rather than to speak the truth.

> **If anyone is ashamed of me and my words in this adulterous and sinful generation, the Son of Man will be ashamed of him when he comes in his Father's glory with the holy angels." (Mark 8:38)**
>
> **If we endure, we will also reign with him. If we disown him, he will also disown us; (2 Tim 2:12)**
>
> **But there were also false prophets among the people, just as there will be false teachers among you. They will secretly introduce destructive heresies, even denying the sovereign Lord who bought them—bringing swift destruction on themselves. (2 Pet 2:1)**
>
> **Who is the liar? It is the man who denies that Jesus is the Christ. Such a man is the antichrist—he denies the Father and the Son. (1 John 2:22)**

	E. The Parable of the Wicked Tenants: The Overview of World History, 20:9-18 (Mt.21:33-46; Mk.12:1-12; cp. Is.5:1-7)	do? I will send my son, whom I love; perhaps they will respect him.' 14 "But when the tenants saw him, they talked the matter over. 'This is the heir,' they said. 'Let's kill him, and the inheritance will be ours.'	a. He sent His own Son to collect the fruit b. The tenants saw the Son c. The tenants plotted the Son's death d. The tenants planned to seize the inheritance
1 A man founded a vineyard a. Leased it to tenants b. Went to a far country	9 He went on to tell the people this parable: "A man planted a vineyard, rented it to some farmers and went away for a long time.	15 So they threw him out of the vineyard and killed him. "What then will the owner of the vineyard do to them?	e. The tenants rejected & killed the Son **4 A just judgment was pronounced**
2 A day of accounting came a. He sent servants to collect	10 At harvest time he sent a servant to the tenants so they would give him some of the fruit of the vineyard. But the tenants beat him and sent him away empty-handed.	16 He will come and kill those tenants and give the vineyard to others." When the people heard this, they said, "May this never be!"	a. He shall come to destroy them b. He shall give the world to others
b. The husbandmen mistreated His servants & refused to pay them	11 He sent another servant, but that one also they beat and treated shamefully and sent away empty-handed.	17 Jesus looked directly at them and asked, "Then what is the meaning of that which is written: 'The stone the builders rejected has become the capstone ?'	**5 A sure proof of coming judgment was given: Scripture** a. Jesus' solemn look b. The rejected Stone's exaltation
c. He showed patience	12 He sent still a third, and they wounded him and threw him out.	18 Everyone who falls on that stone will be broken to pieces, but he on whom it falls will be crushed."	c. The rejected Stone's destructive power
3 A special appeal was made to the tenants	13 "Then the owner of the vineyard said, 'What shall I		

DIVISION VIII

THE SON OF MAN'S DRAMATIC ENTRANCE INTO JERUSALEM: HIS CLAIM AND CONFLICT, 19:28-21:4

E. The Parable of the Wicked Tenants: The Overview of World History, 20:9-18

(20:9-18) **Introduction—World**: the parable was directed to Israel, but it is a panoramic view of world history as well. (See note—Mt.21:33-46 for the interpretation of Israel.) In the view of world history, God is the man who founded the world; the tenants are men and nations responsible for certain areas of production; the servants are God's messengers sent to secure His fruit; the Son is Jesus Christ Himself. Every man or nation who rejects God's Son finds God turning elsewhere and giving the vineyard and the responsibility to others.

1. A man founded a vineyard (v.9).
2. A day of accounting came (v.10-12).
3. A special appeal was made to the tenants (v.13-15).
4. A just judgment was pronounced (v.15-16).
5. A sure proof of coming judgment was given: Scripture (v.17-18).

1 (20:9) **Labor—Man, Duty—World**: a man (God) founded a vineyard. He planted the world; He also planted Israel. He leased the world to men, and Israel to the Jews. Now note two critical facts.

1. It was God, not man, who created the world and created Israel. Neither the world nor Israel happened by chance. God made both, each one for a very specific purpose.

> **'For in him we live and move and have our being.' As some of your own poets have said, 'We are his offspring.' (Acts 17:28)**
>
> **The Spirit of God has made me; the breath of the Almighty gives me life. (Job 33:4)**
>
> **Know that the LORD is God. It is he who made us, and we are his ; we are his people, the sheep of his pasture. (Psa 100:3)**
>
> **That you forget the LORD your Maker, who stretched out the heavens and laid the foundations of the earth, that you live in constant terror every day because of the wrath of the oppressor, who is bent on destruction? For where is the wrath of the oppressor? (Isa 51:13)**
>
> **Have we not all one Father ? Did not one God create us? Why do we profane the covenant of our fathers by breaking faith with one another? (Mal 2:10)**

2. God has given man the highest of privileges: the privilege of life and the privilege of caring for His world. (See DEEPER STUDY # 1—Jn.4:22 for Israel's privilege and purpose.) God has given man life and the potential of the earth in which to live, and He has placed both life and the earth into man's hands. The world is in no one else's hands; therefore, man is responsible for the world, to manage it for God and to give God the fruit of his hands. The point is simply this: man is to labor ever so vigorously, making every contribution He can both for God and for his fellow man (society). Why? Because he is privileged ever so highly, privileged with life and privileged with the beauty and potential of the earth. He is to labor out of love and appreciation for all God has given him.

> **So God created man in his own image, in the image of God he created him; male and female he created them. God blessed them and said to them, "Be fruitful and increase in number; fill the earth and subdue**

it. Rule over the fish of the sea and the birds of the air and over every living creature that moves on the ground." (Gen 1:27-28)

You made him ruler over the works of your hands; you put everything under his feet: (Psa 8:6)

"Again, it will be like a man going on a journey, who called his servants and entrusted his property to them. (Mat 25:14)

Now it is required that those who have been given a trust must prove faithful. (1 Cor 4:2)

Timothy, guard what has been entrusted to your care. Turn away from godless chatter and the opposing ideas of what is falsely called knowledge, (1 Tim 6:20)

So he called ten of his servants and gave them ten minas. 'Put this money to work,' he said, 'until I come back.' (Luke 19:13)

2 (20:10-12) **Judgment**: a day of accounting came; the day for payment came. Note the words "at harvest time." The season came when fruit was to be offered up to God.

1. God sent servants to collect. Fruit was expected, and it was time for payment. God *sent* servants to ask for the fruit. Every man was *expected* to pay his dues, to contribute for the wonderful privilege of living in the beautiful vineyard of the world.

Produce fruit in keeping with repentance. (Mat 3:8)

Then he told this parable: "A man had a fig tree, planted in his vineyard, and he went to look for fruit on it, but did not find any. (Luke 13:6)

He cuts off every branch in me that bears no fruit, while every branch that does bear fruit he prunes so that it will be even more fruitful. (John 15:2)

This is to my Father's glory, that you bear much fruit, showing yourselves to be my disciples. (John 15:8)

You did not choose me, but I chose you and appointed you to go and bear fruit—fruit that will last. Then the Father will give you whatever you ask in my name. (John 15:16)

So, my brothers, you also died to the law through the body of Christ, that you might belong to another, to him who was raised from the dead, in order <u>that we might bear fruit to God</u>. (Rom 7:4)

And we pray this in order that you may live a life worthy of the Lord and may please him in every way: bearing fruit in every good work, growing in the knowledge of God, (Col 1:10)

2. God's servants were mistreated and were refused payment. Note three things.

a. Man deliberately rebels against God. Man wants to rule the vineyard himself. He wants to be the king of the kingdom, the ruler of the earth, and even the head of the church. He wants things to go his way, to rule and reign as he desires and wills. He wants no authority above him. He wants to live as he wishes and do things as he wishes. He wants to claim the fruits for himself.

b. Man wants his own way so much that he criticizes, ridicules, slanders, persecutes and even murders the true servants of God.

Was there ever a prophet your fathers did not persecute? They even killed those who predicted the coming of the Righteous One. And now you have betrayed and murdered him—(Acts 7:52; cp. Mt.23:34-37; Heb 11:36-38.)

c. The servant of God must understand that he is called to suffer (see DEEPER STUDY # 2—Mt.20:22-23).

For it has been granted to you on behalf of Christ not only to believe on him, but also to suffer for him, (Phil 1:29)

In fact, everyone who wants to live a godly life in Christ Jesus will be persecuted, (2 Tim 3:12)

Dear friends, do not be surprised at the painful trial you are suffering, as though something strange were happening to you. But rejoice that you participate in the sufferings of Christ, so that you may be overjoyed when his glory is revealed. (1 Pet 4:12-13; cp. 1 Pt.2:21; 4:5-6; Mt.19:29; Ro.8:16-17)

3. God showed patience. He did not strike out in anger at the first sign of rebellion, even when men brutally attacked His servants. He continued to send messengers to Israel (the world), giving man chance after chance.

Was there ever a prophet your fathers did not persecute? They even killed those who predicted the coming of the Righteous One. And now you have betrayed and murdered him— (Acts 7:52. Cp. Mt.23:34-37; Heb.11:36-38.)

So he said to the man who took care of the vineyard, 'For three years now I've been coming to look for fruit on this fig tree and haven't found any. Cut it down! Why should it use up the soil?' "'Sir,' the man replied, 'leave it alone for one more year, and I'll dig around it and fertilize it. If it bears fruit next year, fine! If not, then cut it down.'" (Luke 13:7-9)

The Lord is not slow in keeping his promise, as some understand slowness. He is patient with you, not wanting anyone to perish, but everyone to come to repentance. (2 Pet 3:9)

For my own name's sake I delay my wrath; for the sake of my praise I hold it back from you, so as not to cut you off. (Isa 48:9)

3(20:13-15) **Jesus Christ, Rejection of**: a special appeal was made to the tenants. This was a very special appeal. It was God's sending His own "Son, whom I loved" into the world to collect the fruit. Five significant facts are spelled out.

1. Jesus claimed to be God's Son. He was different from all the servants sent before. He was more than another man-servant; He was God's very own Son. There

was no question that Jesus was clearly making this unique claim for Himself.

2. The Tenants saw God's Son. There were all kinds of evidence: Old Testament prophecies, the testimony of John the Baptist, the claims of Jesus Himself, the miraculous works, the signs of the times (Gal.4:4). There was a feeling that He wasthe promised Messiah even among those who now opposed Him (see note—Jn.3:2; cp. Jn.11:47-52). This was the tragic indictment against the Jews. Down deep within, they had a sense that Jesus really was the Messiah; but sin or greed for position, esteem, power, and security kept them from acknowledging Him. Their unbelief was deliberate—obstinate (see outline and notes—Mt.21:23-27).

3. The Tenants plotted His death (cp. Mt.12:14; Jn.11:53).

4. The Tenants planned to seize His inheritance. Man wants to possess the kingdom, the nation, the property, the power, the rule, the reign, the position, the esteem, the fame, the recognition, the wealth. Whatever the possession is, man always wants the possession himself. He will deny, deceive, lie, cheat, steal, and even kill to get it. (See note—Mt.12:1-8; note and DEEPER STUDY # 1—12:10; note—15:1-20; DEEPER STUDY # 2—15:6-9.)

5. The Tenants murdered the Son. They committed the worst crime of human history: they killed the Son of God Himself. Note two things: (1) Jesus was predicting His death, and (2) His death was to be a voluntary act on His part. He knew death lay ahead and could have escaped, but He chose to die. It was in "God's set purpose and foreknowledge" (Acts 2:23).

> **"For God so loved the world that he gave his one and only Son, that whoever believes in him shall not perish but have eternal life. (John 3:16)**
>
> **But God demonstrates his own love for us in this: While we were still sinners, Christ died for us. (Rom 5:8)**
>
> **But because of his great love for us, God, who is rich in mercy, made us alive with Christ even when we were dead in transgressions—it is by grace you have been saved. (Eph 2:4-5)**
>
> **For he [God] has rescued us from the dominion of darkness and brought us into the kingdom of the Son he loves, (Col 1:13)**

4 (20:15-16) **Judgment**: a just judgment was pronounced. The crime was the most terrible and tragic crime in all the universe: the rejection and killing of God's *only* Son. Therefore, the judgment was to be the most tragic and extreme judgment in all the universe.

1. The rebellious tenants will be destroyed (see note—Lk.20:17-18).

2. The vineyard (world) will be given to others. The vineyard will not be left uncultivated; it will not be left untended to bear no fruit. God will raise up a new people to care for it (the church, the new creation of God. See notes—Eph.2:11-18; pt.4, 2:14-15; 4:17-19.)

When the Jews heard this statement, they knew what Jesus meant. They could not believe their ears. There was no chance whatsoever that they could be rejected by God, not in their minds. They burst forth in outrage, interrupting His warning, "May this never be!"

> **The ax is already at the root of the trees, and every tree that does not produce good fruit will be cut down and thrown into the fire. (Mat 3:10)**
>
> **If anyone does not remain in me, he is like a branch that is thrown away and withers; such branches are picked up, thrown into the fire and burned. (John 15:6)**
>
> **But land that produces thorns and thistles is worthless and is in danger of being cursed. In the end it will be burned. (Heb 6:8)**

5 (20:17-18) **Judgment**: a sure proof of coming judgment was given—the proof of Scripture. Note His solemn look, "Jesus looked directly at them and asked...'What is the meaning of that which is written: "The stone the builders rejected has become the capstone.'"The stone is a symbol of Jesus Christ. Note two facts.

1. The rejected Stone's exaltation. Christ is the Capstone, the Head or Chief Cornerstone, the Foundation Stone. He is the Foundation, the Stone upon which every man must build his life. There is no other Foundation upon which man can build and be secure. Similarly, He is the Foundation and Cornerstone of the church (see DEEPER STUDY # 6—Mt.21:42).

> **For no one can lay any foundation other than the one already laid, which is Jesus Christ. (1 Cor 3:11)**
>
> **Built on the foundation of the apostles and prophets, with Christ Jesus himself as the chief cornerstone. In him the whole building is joined together and rises to become a holy temple in the Lord. And in him you too are being built together to become a dwelling in which God lives by his Spirit. (Eph 2:20-22)**
>
> **As you come to him, the living Stone—rejected by men but chosen by God and precious to him—you also, like living stones, are being built into a spiritual house to be a holy priesthood, offering spiritual sacrifices acceptable to God through Jesus Christ. (1 Pet 2:4-5)**

2. The rejected Stone's destructive power. The destructive power of a stone against flesh and blood is well-known. A man who stumbles or falls over the stone, Jesus Christ, is hurt. A man upon whom the huge stone, Jesus Christ, falls is ground to powder, utterly destroyed—permanently. (See DEEPER STUDY # 6—Mt.21:42; DEEPER STUDY # 8, 9—21:44 for more discussion.)

> **The righteousness of the blameless makes a straight way for them, but the wicked are brought down by their own wickedness. (Prov 11:5)**
>
> **Are they ashamed of their loathsome conduct? No, they have no shame at all; they do not even know how to blush. So they will fall among the fallen; they will be brought down when I punish them," says the LORD. (Jer 6:15)**
>
> **"Say to them, 'This is what the LORD says: "'When men fall down, do they not get up? When a man turns away, does he not return? (Jer 8:4)**
>
> **A people without understanding will come to ruin! (Hosea 4:14)**

	F. The Question of Government and Religion: Which is Supreme? 20:19-26 (Mt.22:15-22; Mk.12: 13-17)	21 So the spies questioned him: "Teacher, we know that you speak and teach what is right, and that you do not show partiality but teach the way of God in accordance with the truth.	3) Through deception & flattery
1 The cause of the question: The religionists sought to destroy Jesus a. Their reason: They feared losing control of the people	19 The teachers of the law and the chief priests looked for a way to arrest him immediately, because they knew he had spoken this parable against them. But they were afraid of the people.	22 Is it right for us to pay taxes to Caesar or not?" 23 He saw through their duplicity and said to them,	**2 The two false concepts of citizenship**
b. Their method: They sought to discredit Him 1) Before the people 2) Before Rome: Committing treason	20 Keeping a close watch on him, they sent spies, who pretended to be honest. They hoped to catch Jesus in something he said so that they might hand him over to the power and authority of the governor.	24 "Show me a denarius. Whose portrait and inscription are on it?" 25 "Caesar's," they replied. He said to them, "Then give to Caesar what is Caesar's, and to God what is God's." 26 They were unable to trap him in what he had said there in public. And astonished by his answer, they became silent.	**3 The image stamped on coins is the government's image** a. The government owns some things b. The government is due some things **4 The image stamped upon man is God's image** **5 Conclusion: The religionists were silenced**

DIVISION VIII

THE SON OF MAN'S DRAMATIC ENTRANCE INTO JERUSALEM: HIS CLAIM AND CONFLICT, 19:28-21:4

F. The Question of Government and Religion: Which is Supreme? 20:19-26

(20:19-26) **Introduction**: one of the major questions throughout history has dealt with government and religion—Which is supreme? Jesus deals with the subject in this passage.

1. The cause of the question: the religionists sought to destroy Jesus (v.19-21).
2. The two false concepts of citizenship (v.22-23).
3. The image stamped on coins is the government's image (v.24-25).
4. The image stamped upon man is God's image (v.25).
5. Conclusion: the religionists were silenced (v.26).

1 (20:19-21) **Religionists, Opposed Jesus**: the cause of the question. The religionists sought to destroy Jesus. Note how institutionalized and political Jewish religion had become. The priesthood had begun with Aaron right after Moses had led the Israelites out of Egyptian bondage. Now, after just a few centuries, the priests were seen manuevering to discredit and destroy Jesus just like secular rulers seek to destroy political opponents. There is no testimony of godliness in their lives. The very persons who were to be God's testimony in righteousness had become engrossed in selfish ambition and political intrigue.

The religionists feared they were losing their control over the people. The people were flocking to Jesus by the droves (Lk.19:37), and Jesus had...

- proclaimed Himself to be the Messiah (Lk.19:30, 37, 46; 20:2-6, 13, 17-18).
- cleansed the temple, accusing them of misusing it (Lk.19:25).
- confounded their attempt to discredit Him (Lk.20:7-8).
- accused them of being wicked tenants who had failed to care for God's vineyard (Lk.20:9-18).

If the people rose up against the leaders and proclaimed Jesus to be the Messiah, the Romans would step in to put down the revolt. The leaders would lose their position, authority, livelihood—everything. They felt they must stop Jesus at any cost.

The method they chose to stop Jesus was to pose trick questions to Him. If they could get Jesus to take some position against the people, the people would forsake Him. He could then be arrested and destroyed. On the other hand, if they could get Him to take some position against Rome, He would be arrested for preaching treason.

Note the deception and drooling flattery used on Jesus (v.21). It turns the reader's stomach, yet how characteristic of men who seek their own ends. (Cp. Job 15:5; Ps.5:9; Pr.12:3; 29:5.)

Thought 1. Too often religion becomes institutionalized and political. God's people must always guard against seeking...

- recognition
- honor
- position
- power
- worldly security
- selfish loyalty

How can you believe if you accept praise from one another, yet make no effort to obtain the praise that comes from the only God? (John 5:44)

Jesus called them together and said, "You know that the rulers of the Gentiles lord it over them, and their high officials exercise authority over them. Not so with you. Instead, whoever wants to become great among you must be your servant, and whoever wants to be first must be your slave—(Mat 20:25-27)

The greatest among you will be your servant. For whoever exalts himself will be humbled, and whoever humbles himself will be exalted. (Mat 23:11-12)

2 (20:22-23) **Citizenship—State—Caesar**: the two false concepts of citizenship are seen in this question.

1. There was the concept of the religionists who were asking the question. They believed religion was supreme. They believed strongly in the heavenly, spiritual world. They believed all obedience and loyalty were due God and God alone. In fact, all things on earth were due God. The state and all other power and authority were to be subject to religious rule. Therefore, they were strongly against paying taxes to a foreign king. Paying taxes was an infringement upon God's right.

2. There was the concept of the secularist or humanist. These believed the state was supreme. They did not hold to the supernatural, not in the sense that a Supreme Being was the creator and sovereign power who was to be actively involved in the affairs of men. Religion, if it were to be practiced at all, was to be subject to the state. Religion existed to serve and benefit the state. God was either ignored or denied, viewed only as a tool to benefit the state.

> **Thought 1.** Both concepts are always present among men. There will always be those who hold religion to be supreme and those who hold humanism and secularism to be supreme.
>
> **For, "All men are like grass, and all their glory is like the flowers of the field; the grass withers and the flowers fall, (1 Pet 1:24)**
> **For he will take nothing with him when he dies, his splendor will not descend with him. (Psa 49:17)**
> **Therefore the grave enlarges its appetite and opens its mouth without limit; into it will descend their nobles and masses with all their brawlers and revelers. (Isa 5:14)**
> **Hear the word of the LORD, you who tremble at his word: "Your brothers who hate you, and exclude you because of my name, have said, 'Let the LORD be glorified, that we may see your joy!' Yet they will be put to shame. (Isa 66:5)**
> **"And you, son of man, on the day I take away their stronghold, their joy and glory, the delight of their eyes, their heart's desire, and their sons and daughters as well— (Ezek 24:25)**
> **The more the priests increased, the more they sinned against me; they exchanged their Glory for something disgraceful. (Hosea 4:7)**

Note that Christ saw through the deception and flattery. He was the Son of God, so He knew *their craftiness* and knew…

- every self-seeking ambition
- every deception and flattering word
- every pretension to honor Him
- every man who ignored and denied Him
- every secular and humanistic claim

3 (20:24-25) **Citizenship—State**: the image stamped on coins is the government's image. As Jesus pointed to the image on the coin, this could not be denied. The government had made the coin and stamped its inscription on it. God did not make the coin; therefore, the government owned the coin and the government could demand the coin. The point was clear.

1. The coin and some other things produced by the state belonged to the state, things such as roads, buildings, sewage, and public transportation.

2. The government was due some things. In particular, the state was due a man's allegiance and support. A man was a citizen of this world as long as he was in the world. The world provided him with everything necessary to sustain physical life; and the government under which he lived provided protection, roads, water, and laws. Therefore, man owed his *due share* to the state. (See note—Ro.13:1-7 for more discussion.)

> **Everyone must submit himself to the governing authorities, for there is no authority except that which God has established. The authorities that exist have been established by God. (Rom 13:1)**
> **"But so that we may not offend them, go to the lake and throw out your line. Take the first fish you catch; open its mouth and you will find a four-drachma coin. Take it and give it to them for my tax and yours." (Mat 17:27)**
> **Remind the people to be subject to rulers and authorities, to be obedient, to be ready to do whatever is good, (Titus 3:1)**
> **Submit yourselves for the Lord's sake to every authority instituted among men: whether to the king, as the supreme authority, or to governors, who are sent by him to punish those who do wrong and to commend those who do right. For it is God's will that by doing good you should silence the ignorant talk of foolish men. (1 Pet 2:13-15)**
> **Show proper respect to everyone: Love the brotherhood of believers, fear God, honor the king. (1 Pet 2:17)**
> **Whoever does not obey the law of your God and the law of the king must surely be punished by death, banishment, confiscation of property, or imprisonment. (Ezra 7:26)**
> **Obey the king's command, I say, because you took an oath before God. (Eccl 8:2)**

4 (20:25) **Citizenship—State—Man, Image of God**: the image stamped upon man is God's image. The Jews frantically held that God created man and that He stamped His very image upon man. Therefore, man owed his total obedience to God and to no one other than God. What they failed to grasp was what Jesus was pointing out. Man is presently a citizen of two worlds: this world (cosmos) and the world of God or of the Spirit. Therefore, man owes to Caesar whatever carries Caesar's stamp, and he owes to God whatever carries God's stamp.

1. The stamp of God is upon *man's life*; therefore man owes God his life—life that was made to exist with God forever.

> **"For God so loved the world that he gave his one and only Son, that whoever believes in him shall not perish but have eternal life. (John 3:16)**
> **Now this is eternal life: that they may know you, the only true God, and Jesus Christ, whom you have sent. (John 17:3)**
> **The one who sows to please his sinful nature, from that nature will reap destruc-**

tion; the one who sows to please the Spirit, from the Spirit will reap eternal life. (Gal 6:8)

2. The stamp of God is upon *man's life*; therefore man owes God his world—a world that is ever so beautiful and needs to be looked after and cared for by man.

So God created man in his own image, in the image of God he created him; male and female he created them. God blessed them and said to them, "Be fruitful and increase in number; fill the earth and subdue it. Rule over the fish of the sea and the birds of the air and over every living creature that moves on the ground." (Gen 1:27-28)

This is to my Father's glory, that you bear much fruit, showing yourselves to be my disciples. (John 15:8)

You did not choose me, but I chose you and appointed you to go and bear fruit—fruit that will last. Then the Father will give you whatever you ask in my name. (John 15:16)

3. The stamp of God is upon *man's life*; therefore man owes God his spirit—a spirit that can be *born again* and live a self-denying life of love and peace for the sake of all men everywhere.

Now that you have purified yourselves by obeying the truth so that you have sincere love for your brothers, love one another deeply, from the heart. For you have been born again, not of perishable seed, but of imperishable, through the living and enduring word of God. (1 Pet 1:22-23)

Then he said to them all: "If anyone would come after me, he must deny himself and take up his cross daily and follow me. For whoever wants to save his life will lose it, but whoever loses his life for me will save it. (Luke 9:23-24)

We proclaim him, admonishing and teaching everyone with all wisdom, so that we may present everyone perfect in Christ. (Col 1:28)

The thief comes only to steal and kill and destroy; I have come that they may have life, and have it to the full. (John 10:10)

4. The stamp of God is upon man's mind and body; therefore man owes God his mind and body—a mind and body that have the power to produce for the betterment of all mankind.

Therefore, I urge you, brothers, in view of God's mercy, to offer your bodies as living sacrifices, holy and pleasing to God—this is your spiritual act of worship. Do not conform any longer to the pattern of this world, but be transformed by the renewing of your mind. Then you will be able to test and approve what God's will is—his good, pleasing and perfect will. (Rom 12:1-2)

Do you not know that your body is a temple of the Holy Spirit, who is in you, whom you have received from God? You are not your own; you were bought at a price. Therefore honor God with your body. (1 Cor 6:19-20)

But the fruit of the Spirit is love, joy, peace, patience, kindness, goodness, faithfulness, gentleness and self-control. Against such things there is no law. (Gal 5:22-23)

"Whoever sheds the blood of man, by man shall his blood be shed; for in the image of God has God made man. (Gen 9:6)

A man ought not to cover his head, since he is the image and glory of God; but the woman is the glory of man. (1 Cor 11:7)

And have put on the new self, which is being renewed in knowledge in the image of its Creator. (Col 3:10)

5 (20:26) **Citizenship**: the conclusion was that the religionsts were silenced. Two things happened: first, they were unable to discredit Jesus; and second, they were struck with amazement. They marvelled at His answer.

Thought 1. Men have to stand in amazement at the Lord's concept of dual citizenship. A man is to be a citizen both of this world and of heaven: rendering to Caesar what is due him, and rendering to God what is due Him.

Fear God, honor the king. (1 Pet 2:17)

	G. The Question of the Resurrection: The Two Worlds—Earth & Heaven—Differ, 20:27-38 (Mt.22:23-33; Mk.12:18-27)	too. 33 Now then, at the resurrection whose wife will she be, since the seven were married to her?”	c. They asked an egotistical & blind question
		34 Jesus replied, “The people of this age marry and are given in marriage.	**2 Marriage is different** a. This world: There is marriage
1 The Sadducees, the liberal-minded, tried to discredit Jesus[DS1]	27 Some of the Sadducees, who say there is no resurrection, came to Jesus with a question.	35 But those who are considered worthy of taking part in that age and in the resurrection from the dead will neither marry nor be given in marriage,	b. Next world: There is no marriage **3 Entrance is different: Must be counted worthy**
a. They referred to Levrite marriage[DS2]	28 “Teacher,” they said, “Moses wrote for us that if a man’s brother dies and leaves a wife but no children, the man must marry the widow and have children for his brother.	36 And they can no longer die; for they are like the angels. They are God’s children, since they are children of the resurrection.	**4 Death is different: No longer can die** **5 Personal being (nature) is different** a. Are like angels b. Are children of God
b. They presented a logical situation	29 Now there were seven brothers. The first one married a woman and died childless. 30 The second 31 And then the third married her, and in the same way the seven died, leaving no children. 32 Finally, the woman died	37 But in the account of the bush, even Moses showed that the dead rise, for he calls the Lord ‘the God of Abraham, and the God of Isaac, and the God of Jacob.’ 38 He is not the God of the dead, but of the living, for to him all are alive.”	**6 Life is different: It is a resurrected life** a. It is life after death b. Illustrated by Moses c. Purpose: To live for God

DIVISION VIII

THE SON OF MAN’S DRAMATIC ENTRANCE INTO JERUSALEM: HIS CLAIM AND CONFLICT, 19:28-21:4

G. The Question of the Resurrection: The Two Worlds (Earth and Heaven) Differ, 20:27-38

(20:27-38) **Introduction**: this world and the other world—earth and heaven—differ. They differ drastically. Jesus used the attack of the Sadducees to discuss the differences.

1. Sadducees, the liberal-minded, tried to discredit Jesus(v.27-33).
2. Marriage is different (v.34-35).
3. Entrance is different: must be counted worthy (v.35).
4. Death is different: no longer can die (v.36).
5. Personal being (nature) is different (v.36).
6. Life is different: it is a resurrected life (v.37-38).

1 (20:27-33) **Religionists, Oppose Christ—Question**: The Sadducees, the liberal-minded, tried to discredit Jesus. Note three points.

1. They referred to Levrite marriage (see DEEPER STUDY # 2—Lk.20:28).

2. They presented a logical situation: there were seven brothers. The first brother married but died without having children. Each of the other brothers obeyed the law, but each brother *died before having children.* Finally the woman died also. The point was logical, but most unlikely. (See DEEPER STUDY # 2—Lk.20:28 for discussion of the Levrite law.)

3. They asked an egotistical and blind question. The question was logical, but note two things:

a. The spirit that lay behind the questioning. The situation was absurd; the spirit was cold and coarse, egotistical and unbelieving, regrettable and revolting. The unbeliever’s spirit is often self-incriminating and self-condemning.

b. The blindness and human frailty of the question. The human mind *cannot know* the spiritual world apart from *revelation.* The Sadducees were thinking that the spiritual world would be just like the physical world, that it would be nothing more than a continuation of this world both in *its nature and in its relationships.*

> **The man without the Spirit does not accept the things that come from the Spirit of God, for they are foolishness to him, and he cannot understand them, because they are spiritually discerned. (1 Cor 2:14)**

DEEPER STUDY # 1

(20:27) **Sadducees**: these were the religious and political liberals of Jesus’ day. They were the wealthy, the aristocratic, the governing class of leaders in Israel. Many Sadducees served on the nation’s governing body, the Sanhedrin. The Chief Priest himself was usually a Sadducee who presided over the Sanhedrin. The Sanhedrin ruled the people in behalf of the Roman empire (Acts 4:1-2; 5:27). The Romans readily saw to it that the Sadducees held the positions of leadership in the nation, for the Sadducees favored Greek customs over Jewish customs. They willingly aided the Romans in doing away with religious practices and instituting Greek and Roman customs (Hellenism).

The Sadducees are thought to have arisen out of the same struggle as the Pharisees around 175 B.C. However, they were always the fewest in number among the various sects of Jewish belief.

Several things should be noted.

1. The Sadducees were secular and materialistic. They were the independent thinkers, the rationalists of their day.

2. They were heavily entrenched in the priesthood of Jesus' day (cp. Acts 4:1-2; 5:17). They readily collaborated with the Roman government in order to protect their position, power, and wealth.

3. They denied the supernatural to a great degree: the resurrection and miracles, life after death, and the existence of beings in other dimensions such as angels and spirits (Mt.22:23; Acts 23:8). To them there was no heaven or hell, no existence whatsoever except on this earth. A man died and was annihilated; he ceased to exist. There was no such thing as rewards or punishment in an afterlife; there was no such thing as life that continued eternally. (See notes—Mt.22:23-33.)

4. The only Scripture they accepted was the Pentateuch, the first five books of the Old Testament. They felt these books were the only Scripture that was binding. They rejected the Oral and Scribal Law. They did not accept the prophets nor the poetic books of the Scripture.

5. By practice, they bordered on being humanists, believing that man was in control of his own life and destiny. God had little if anything to do with life, for there was no afterlife. Whatever was achieved was to be done by man's own will and energy and effort.

6. They were diametrically opposed to the Pharisees.

The liberal position of the Sadducees caused two things.

1. It caused them to stumble at the spiritual and supernatural. They ridiculed and scorned both. Therefore, in their minds, the teachings of Jesus were the teachings of an unthinking and illogical man, lacking philosophical analysis and natural proof.

2. Their liberal position caused them to feel threatened and to oppose Jesus. The people were flocking to Jesus and soaking up His teachings. This meant the Sadducees were losing their grip on the people. Their position and wealth were being jeopardized; therefore, they were compelled to attack and discredit Him before the people.

DEEPER STUDY # 2

(20:28) **Levrite Marriage**: when a husband died without a son, the Levrite law said that his brother was to marry his wife and bear a son. By law, the son was considered the first-born son of the deceased brother. This assured two things: (a) that the family name continued, and (2) that the property holdings were kept in the family. This was a law that had been given to help preserve and enlarge the nation of Israel (cp. Ruth 4:5).

2 (20:34-35) **Heaven—Marriage—Resurrection**: marriage differs in the two worlds. In this world there is marriage, but in the other world there will be no marriage. There is a very special and wonderful reason why there is no marriage in the other world: *love is perfected.* Future life and relationships will exceed earthly relationships, even the bond of marital relationships. The strong union and bond of earthly marriage will not be less, it will be greater and stronger in heaven, but so will all other relationships.

In heaven our relationships will cease to be as they are on earth. They will be changed in an absolute sense: selfishness and sin will not affect our love and lives. Our love will be perfected; therefore, we will love everyone perfectly. A wife on this earth will not be loved as she was on this earth—imperfectly. She will be loved more, *loved perfectly*. Everyone will love everyone else perfectly. God will change all relationships into perfection, even as the relationships between angels and God are perfected.

3 (20:35) **Worthy—Justification—Heaven—World**: entrance into the two worlds differs. A man has nothing to do with his entrance into this world. He is conceived and born by the act of a man and a woman. But note three facts about the next world.

1. Only those who are *considered, accounted worthy* shall obtain that world. This is significant. A man does not work or earn his way into the next world. He is not worthy; he is only *counted* worthy. Worthiness is accounted to him, merely laid to his account. Scripture says that it is his *faith* that is counted as making him worthy. God takes a man's faith and counts, credits it as "righteousness" (see DEEPER STUDY # 2, Justification—Ro.4:22; 5:1. Cp. Ro.4:5; 4:1-3; 4:1-25.)

> **Therefore, since we have been justified through faith, we have peace with God through our Lord Jesus Christ, (Rom 5:1)**
>
> **The words "it [righteousness] was credited to him" were written not for him alone, but also for us, to whom God will credit righteousness—for us who believe in him who raised Jesus our Lord from the dead. He was delivered over to death for our sins and was raised to life for our justification. (Rom 4:23-25)**
>
> **Consider Abraham: "He believed God, and it was credited to him as righteousness." (Gal 3:6)**

2. Jesus was speaking of the resurrection of believers only. He did not say "the resurrection of the dead" which would mean all the dead, but He said "the resurrection from the dead" which means the resurrection of believers *from among* the dead.

> **I tell you the truth, a time is coming and has now come when the dead will hear the voice of the Son of God and those who hear will live. (John 5:25)**
>
> **For my Father's will is that everyone who looks to the Son and believes in him shall have eternal life, and I will raise him up at the last day." (John 6:40)**
>
> **And I have the same hope in God as these men, that there will be a resurrection of both the righteous and the wicked. (Acts 24:15)**
>
> **Blessed and holy are those who have part in the first resurrection. The second death has no power over them, but they will be priests of God and of Christ and will reign with him for a thousand years. (Rev 20:6)**

3. Every man continues to exist after this world, but all will not enter "that age," that is, heaven. Those who have not lived a life of faith in Christ, who are not counted worthy, will not enter "that age," but will enter hell (see DEEPER STUDY # 4—Lk.16:24; DEEPER STUDY # 2—Mt.5:22).

> **So he called to him, 'Father Abraham, have pity on me and send Lazarus to dip the tip of his finger in water and cool my**

tongue, because I am in agony in this fire.' (Luke 16:24)

"Do not be amazed at this, for a time is coming when all who are in their graves will hear his voice and come out—those who have done good will rise to live, and those who have done evil will rise to be condemned. (John 5:28-29)

And I have the same hope in God as these men, that there will be a resurrection of both the righteous and the wicked. (Acts 24:15)

Multitudes who sleep in the dust of the earth will awake: some to everlasting life, others to shame and everlasting contempt. (Dan 12:2)

4 (20:36) **Death—Eternal Life**: death differs in the two worlds. In the next world there is no death (see Deeper Study # 1, Death—Heb.9:27 for more discussion). Note: Jesus said a man "can no longer die." A man is locked in, given an incorruptible body and existence, living forever with God. (See DEEPER STUDY # 1—Jn.17:2-3. Cp. Jn.1:4.)

After that, we who are still alive and are left will be caught up together with them in the clouds to meet the Lord in the air. And so we will be with the Lord forever. (1 Th 4:17)

For the perishable must clothe itself with the imperishable, and the mortal with immortality. When the perishable has been clothed with the imperishable, and the mortal with immortality, then the saying that is written will come true: "Death has been swallowed up in victory." (1 Cor 15:53-54)

The Lord will rescue me from every evil attack and will bring me safely to his heavenly kingdom. To him be glory for ever and ever. Amen. (2 Tim 4:18)

5 (20:36) **Believers, Nature—Reward—Eternal Life—Heaven**: personal being, that is, man's nature, differs in the two worlds. Two things are said about believers.

1. Believers shall be "like the angels." The Greek word *isangelloi* means that believers shall have a nature like the angels: be glorified, be their peers, living in the joy of working and serving God just as the angels do. It means believers will have all the glorious being and privileges and responsibilities that angels have.

So will it be with the resurrection of the dead. The body that is sown is perishable, it is raised imperishable; it is sown in dishonor, it is raised in glory; it is sown in weakness, it is raised in power; it is sown a natural body, it is raised a spiritual body. If there is a natural body, there is also a spiritual body. (1 Cor 15:42-44)

And just as we have borne the likeness of the earthly man, so shall we bear the likeness of the man from heaven. I declare to you, brothers, that flesh and blood cannot inherit the kingdom of God, nor does the perishable inherit the imperishable. Listen, I tell you a mystery: We will not all sleep, but we will all be changed—in a flash, in the twinkling of an eye, at the last trumpet. For the trumpet will sound, the dead will be raised imperishable, and we will be changed. For the perishable must clothe itself with the imperishable, and the mortal with immortality. (1 Cor 15:49-53)

2. But there is even more than what angels have. Believers are the children of God, the adopted children of God. (See note—Gal.4:5-6.)

For you did not receive a spirit that makes you a slave again to fear, but you received the Spirit of sonship. And by him we cry, "Abba, Father." The Spirit himself testifies with our spirit that we are God's children. Now if we are children, then we are heirs—heirs of God and co-heirs with Christ, if indeed we share in his sufferings in order that we may also share in his glory. (Rom 8:15-17)

But when the time had fully come, God sent his Son, born of a woman, born under law, to redeem those under law, that we might receive the full rights of sons. Because you are sons, God sent the Spirit of his Son into our hearts, the Spirit who calls out, "Abba, Father." So you are no longer a slave, but a son; and since you are a son, God has made you also an heir. (Gal 4:4-7)

So that, having been justified by his grace, we might become heirs having the hope of eternal life. (Titus 3:7)

6 (20:37-38) **Life—Eternal Life—Heaven**: life differs in the two worlds. In the other world, it is a *resurrected life*, a real life, a life that is more real than the life of this world. It is a perfect life that lives for God perfectly. Note three facts.

1. God is the God of Abraham, Isaac, and Jacob. Jesus meant at least two things in this point.

a. God's relationships are active relationships, not inactive. God says, "I am the God of...." not, "I was the God of...." His relationships with His subjects are maintained even after departing this world. God is eternal; therefore, He creates and maintains eternal, active relationships. God's subjects enter into the spiritual realm of His presence and actively relate to Him. The resurrection is a fact.

b. God's relationships are good and rewarding. The patriarchs of old were promised very personal rewards (cp. Heb.11:13-16). There has to be a resurrection if our relationship with God is good and rewarding. To die and to be left dead as a decayed corpse is not good nor rewarding. Abraham, Isaac, and Jacob have a good and rewarding relationship with God. They are more alive today than they were while on earth, for they are perfected and eternal. They are with God Himself, and so shall we be. The resurrection is a fact.

2. *God is—God exists*. Note the two simple words in v.38. The fact that *God is*, that God exists, proves the resurrection. The Greek (ego eimi) means the self-existent, eternal One (see DEEPER STUDY # 1—Jn.6:20; note—18:4-6).

'I am the God (Mat 22:32)

Anyone who comes to him must believe that he exists. (Heb 11:6)

Since God exists, He is God with omnipotent power—power that is perfect and eternal. God can do anything and all things, perfectly and eternally. He can call the elements of a decayed body back together again and raise it up to live in the spiritual dimension, both perfectly and eternally.

Note carefully: *God exists* (lives)—the argument is irrefutable. Note carefully the great passage in Ephesians dealing with the spiritual blessings that are ours in Christ.

> **In him we were also chosen, having been predestined according to the plan of him who works out everything in conformity with the purpose of his will, in order that we, who were the first to hope in Christ, might be for the praise of his glory. (Eph 1:11-12)**

The resurrection is a fact. It will be experienced by all men of all ages because *God is*. God has willed to give us an inheritance—an inheritance *to be*, that is, *to live eternally* with Him. We will undergo a transformation of nature, a transformation of perfection and permanency. For this reason, we need to pay close attention to what Scripture says.

> **And without faith it is impossible to please God, because anyone who comes to him must believe that he [God] exists and that he rewards those who earnestly seek him. (Heb 11:6)**

We must believe that *God is* and that *He rewards* those who earnestly seek Him; that is, He rewards all of us who seek to live eternally with Him.

> **And so, somehow, to attain to the resurrection from the dead. (Phil 3:11)**
>
> **It teaches us to say "No" to ungodliness and worldly passions, and to live self-controlled, upright and godly lives in this present age, while we wait for the blessed hope—the glorious appearing of our great God and Savior, Jesus Christ, (Titus 2:12-13)**
>
> **Dear friends, now we are children of God, and what we will be has not yet been made known. But we know that when he appears, we shall be like him, for we shall see him as he is. (1 John 3:2)**
>
> **Then I saw a new heaven and a new earth, for the first heaven and the first earth had passed away, and there was no longer any sea. He who was seated on the throne said, "I am making everything new!" Then he said, "Write this down, for these words are trustworthy and true." (Rev 21:1, 5)**

3. God is not the God of the dead but of the living. God is the God of Abraham, Isaac, and Jacob, not the God of dead and decayed corpses. When Moses wrote these words, the three patriarchs had been dead for centuries. If they were dead, God was not their God. Since He was their God, they were alive; they were living in God's presence and in a relationship to Him that was perfect and eternal. There is to be a resurrection.

> **For none of us lives to himself alone and none of us dies to himself alone. If we live, we live to the Lord; and if we die, we die to the Lord. So, whether we live or die, we belong to the Lord. For this very reason, Christ died and returned to life so that he might be the Lord of both the dead and the living. (Rom 14:7-9)**

One simple fact comes to the forefront ever so clearly in these points made by Jesus: *since God is*, God is not the God of the dead but of the living.

> **Why should any of you consider it incredible that God raises the dead? (Acts 26:8)**
>
> **And I have the same hope in God as these men, that there will be a resurrection of both the righteous and the wicked. (Acts 24:15)**

Note also that all believers live. They live unto God, for God is the God of the living. Death cannot break the believer's relationship to God. The believer goes to live with the Lord forever. (See notes, Reward—Lk.12:41-48; 16:10-12; DEEPER STUDY # 3—19:15-19 for more discussion.)

	H. The Question of David's Son: Two Misunderstandings Corrected, 20:39-47 (Mt.22:41-46; 23:6-7, 14; Mk.12:35-40)	your enemies a footstool for your feet."' 43 David calls him 'Lord.' How then can he be his son?" 44 While all the people were listening, Jesus said to his disciples,	b. David himself called the Messiah "Lord"
1 The response of the religionists to Jesus a. Some were impressed b. All were silenced	39 Some of the teachers of the law responded, "Well said, teacher!" 40 And no one dared to ask him any more questions.	45 "Beware of the teachers of the law. They like to walk around in flowing robes and love to be greeted in the marketplaces and have the most important seats in the synagogues and the places of honor at banquets.	**3 Misunderstanding 2: Religionists are genuine** a. Their desire & love: Self-esteem & praise
2 Misunderstanding 1: The Messiah is David's Son*DS1* a. David said that God called the Messiah "Lord"	41 Then Jesus said to them, "How is it that they say the Christ is the Son of David? 42 David himself declares in the Book of Psalms: "'The Lord said to my Lord: "Sit at my right hand until I make	47 They devour widows' houses and for a show make lengthy prayers. Such men will be punished most severely."	b. Their terrible sin: Devour widows c. Their condemnation: Is to be more severe

DIVISION VIII

THE SON OF MAN'S DRAMATIC ENTRANCE INTO JERUSALEM: HIS CLAIM AND CONFLICT, 19:28-21:4

H. The Question of David's Son: Two Misunderstandings Corrected, 20:39-47

(20:39-47) **Introduction**: there are two ideas among men that desperately need correcting. It is absolutely essential that they be corrected, for they both lead to gross error and damnation (v.47). What are the erroneous ideas?

1. The response of the religionists to Jesus (v.39-40).
2. Misunderstanding 1: the Messiah is David's Son (v.41-44).
3. Misunderstanding 2: religionists are genuine (v.45-47).

1 (20:39-40) **Religionists, Response to Jesus**: the response of the religionists to Jesus was twofold.

1. Some were impressed with the Lord's answers to their questions (cp. Lk.19:47-20:38). They shared very honestly with Him, "Well said, teacher!" This was an amazing statement, for remember, the religionists were out to kill Jesus. They had engaged Him in argument time and again, trying to entrap Him in His words. They tried their best to turn the people against Him. They had to break His hold on the people before they dared arrest Him. But He had answered their questions so wisely and with so much authority, some of the very ones engaged in the plot were impressed.

2. All the religionists were silenced. They had been so routed and embarrassed before the people, that they dared not ask any more questions.

2 (20:41-44) **Messiah—Jesus Christ, Claims**: the first misunderstanding was that the Messiah was David's Son. Many believed that Jesus was a mere man, of human origin. The idea that the Messiah might be of divine origin, of God Himself, was unacceptable, and still is unacceptable, to some people. However, Jesus makes Himself perfectly clear. He is not the son of David, not born of man. He is the Lord from heaven. His argument is *forceful*.

1. David said in Scripture that God called the Messiah, "Lord." Note four facts.
   a. Fact 1: David called the Messiah "Lord" in the Psalms. That is, David's words are recorded in Scripture under the *inspiration of the Spirit*. God was directing him (cp. Mt.22:43; 2 Pt.1:21; 1 Cor.12:3).
   b. Fact 2: David said that "the Lord [Jehovah God] said to my Lord [the Messiah]." David unquestionably called the Messiah *"My Lord."*
   c. Fact 3: David said that *my* Lord "is at [God's] right hand." The Messiah is *Lord*, for He is *exalted* by God.

[God's mighty power] which he exerted in Christ when he raised him from the dead and seated him at his right hand in the heavenly realms, (Eph 1:20)

Therefore God exalted him to the highest place and gave him the name that is above every name, (Phil 2:9)

The point of what we are saying is this: We do have such a high priest, who sat down at the right hand of the throne of the Majesty in heaven, (Heb 8:1)

   d. Fact 4: David said that my Lord's "enemies are to be made His footstool." The Messiah is Lord, for all His enemies are to be subjected under Him (Ph.2:10-11).

2. David himself called Messiah "Lord." Jesus asked a pointed question. How could the Messiah be both David's Lord and his Son? Jesus was doing at least two things by asking this question.
   a. Jesus was saying this: to think of the Messiah only in human terms is totally inadequate. It is not enough to think in terms of earthly power, of national, political, military, and institutional leadership. There is no way a mere man can bring perfect deliverance, leadership, and utopia to this earth. The Messiah is not only man; He is the Lord from heaven.
   b. Jesus was claiming to be the Son of God Himself. Man's concept has to go beyond the mere human and physical. Man's idea has to stretch upward into God's very own heart. God loves this earth;

therefore, God sent His Son to earth, sacrificing Him in order to save it and all those within it.

"For God so loved the world that he gave his one and only Son, that whoever believes in him shall not perish but have eternal life. (John 3:16)

But God demonstrates his own love for us in this: While we were still sinners, Christ died for us. (Rom 5:8)

Simon Peter answered, "You are the Christ, the Son of the living God." (Mat 16:16)

The woman said, "I know that Messiah" (called Christ) "is coming. When he comes, he will explain everything to us." Then Jesus declared, "I who speak to you am he." (John 4:25-26)

"You do not want to leave too, do you?" Jesus asked the Twelve. Simon Peter answered him, "Lord, to whom shall we go? You have the words of eternal life. We believe and know that you are the Holy One of God." (John 6:67-69)

I told you that you would die in your sins; if you do not believe that I am the one I claim to be, you will indeed die in your sins." (John 8:24)

So Jesus said, "When you have lifted up the Son of Man, then you will know that I am the one I claim to be and that I do nothing on my own but speak just what the Father has taught me. (John 8:28)

DEEPER STUDY # 1

(20:41) **Messiah—Son of David**: The common title for the Messiah was *the Son of David.* The Old Testament definitely said the Messiah was to come from the line of David. It was from such passages as these that the Messiah was known as *the Son of David.* (See notes—Lk.3:24-31; DEEPER STUDY # 3—Jn.1:45 for most verses and their fulfillment dealing with the Messiah's being the Son of David.)

Once for all, I have sworn by my holiness— and I will not lie to David—that his line will continue forever and his throne endure before me like the sun; (Psa 89:35-36)

For to us a child is born, to us a son is given, and the government will be on his shoulders. And he will be called Wonderful Counselor, Mighty God, Everlasting Father, Prince of Peace. Of the increase of his government and peace there will be no end. He will reign on David's throne and over his kingdom, establishing and upholding it with justice and righteousness from that time on and forever. The zeal of the LORD Almighty will accomplish this. (Isa 9:6-7)

A shoot will come up from the stump of Jesse; from his roots a Branch will bear fruit. The Spirit of the LORD will rest on him— the Spirit of wisdom and of understanding, the Spirit of counsel and of power, the Spirit of knowledge and of the fear of the LORD—and he will delight in the fear of the LORD. He will not judge by what he sees with his eyes, or decide by what he hears with his ears; but with righteousness he will judge the needy, with justice he will give decisions for the poor of the earth. He will strike the earth with the rod of his mouth; with the breath of his lips he will slay the wicked. Righteousness will be his belt and faithfulness the sash around his waist. (Isa 11:1-5)

The Messiah was to do four specific things. (See notes—Mt.1:1; DEEPER STUDY # 2—1:18; DEEPER STUDY # 3—3:11; notes—11:1-6; 11:2-3; DEEPER STUDY # 1—11:5; DEEPER STUDY # 2—11:6; DEEPER STUDY # 1—12:16; notes—22:42; Lk.7:21-23. These notes will help in understanding concept of the Messiah.)

1. He was to free Israel from all enslavement. Enslavement was to be abolished and all men set free under God's domain.
2. He was to give victory over all enemies. Israel was to be established as the seat of His rule. This, of course, meant Israel was to be the leading nation of the world.
3. He was to bring peace to earth. All were to serve God under the government established by the Messiah.
4. He was to provide plenty for all. The Messiah was to bring all the benefits of both God's rule and care in providing the necessities of life and in bringing utopia (the Kingdom of God) to earth.

3 (20:45-47) **Religionists—Widows—Dress**: the second misunderstanding was that religionists were genuine. Jesus was forceful in this fact. He said to all men: "Beware of the [teachers of the law]" (religionists).

1. Their desire was self-esteem and praise.
   a. They draw attention to themselves. There were two ways this was done.

      First, a person could desire to wear the clothing of the extravagant and wasteful. The long robe was the dress of the nobility, the rich, the well-known, the person of style. It was a long robe reaching to the ground. A man was unable to work in it; therefore, it was the sign of *higher society* and of a man of leisure. Note: Jesus was not speaking against fine clothing. What He said was, "Beware of [those] who love to go in flowing robes" (fine clothing). He condemned the person who was extravagant and wasteful, whose mind was on attracting attention, on self, on appearance.

Thought 1. A person's mind is not to be on clothing, but...

Finally, brothers, whatever is true, whatever is noble, whatever is right, whatever is pure, whatever is lovely, whatever is admirable—if anything is excellent or praiseworthy—think about such things. (Phil 4:8)

Thought 2. A man's life consists not in the things he has, but in the service he renders to others. The world is desperate, swamped with enormous needs. God wills for all persons to be wrapped up in meeting the needs of others and not wrapped up in clothing—especially the believer. The believer's concern is to be righteousness. He is to work for Christ and His kingdom, not for expensive, flamboyant, ostentatious clothing (cp. 1 Pt.3:3-4).

He who has been stealing must steal no longer, but must work, doing something useful with his own hands, that he may have something to share with those in need. (Eph 4:28)

Second, a person can change his clothing and his appearance *in order to attract attention.* He desires and loves the attention, so he seeks to attract by being different and by making himself stand out. This was a prominent sin of the religionists in Jesus' day.

⇒ They wore phylacteries. These were little leather-type boxes which contained a piece of parchment with four passages of Scripture written on it. The scriptures were Ex.13:1-10; 13:11-16; Dt.6:4-9; and 11:13-21. The use of the phylacteries seems to have arisen from a literal translation of Ex.13:9 and Pr.7:3. However, the true meaning of these two passages seems to be that we are to have the Word of God in our minds just as clearly as if we had them before our eyes. The great fault of these religionists was that they not only interpreted the passages literally and wore the little leather boxes, but they enlarged the boxes to draw attention to themselves as being religious.

⇒ They also enlarged the borders of their garments; that is, they wore tassels on their outside robes. God had instructed the Jews to make fringes or tassles on the borders of their outer robes. When a person noticed them, he was to be reminded to keep God's commandments. Again, the error was that the religionist changed his appearance from others; he enlarged his tassels, drawing attention to his being more religious than others.

Thought 1. A person can wear clothes to attract attention by either overdressing or underdressing. A person can overdress to attract and focus attention upon himself, and a person can wear clothes that expose the body, that actually attract attention to certain parts of the body. A person can wear clothes that are too tight, too low cut, too high cut, too thin. A person can wear too little clothing and clothing that fails to cover enough of the body.

Jesus very simply says to beware of dressing to attract attention. The religionists did it to appear *righteous*. Others do it to appear *worldly* (appealing).

Do not offer the parts of your body to sin, as instruments of wickedness, but rather offer yourselves to God, as those who have been brought from death to life; and offer the parts of your body to him as instruments of righteousness. (Rom 6:13)

I also want women to dress modestly, with decency and propriety, not with braided hair or gold or pearls or expensive clothes, but with good deeds, appropriate for women who profess to worship God. (1 Tim 2:9-10)

Your beauty should not come from outward adornment, such as braided hair and the wearing of gold jewelry and fine clothes. Instead, it should be that of your inner self, the unfading beauty of a gentle and quiet spirit, which is of great worth in God's sight. For this is the way the holy women of the past who put their hope in God used to make themselves beautiful. They were submissive to their own husbands, (1 Pet 3:3-5)

b. The religionists loved the greetings and titles that exalted men with honor. Note: the title was "Rabbi" which meant teacher or master. It was only a simple title, yet some loved and revelled in the recognition above other men. It took a man that was supposed to be God's messenger and said, "Here he is; this is he." It honored the man and not the Lord.

For whoever exalts himself will be humbled, and whoever humbles himself will be exalted. (Mat 23:12)

Though you soar like the eagle and make your nest among the stars, from there I will bring you down," declares the LORD. (Oba 1:4)

For, "All men are like grass, and all their glory is like the flowers of the field; the grass withers and the flowers fall, (1 Pet 1:24)

But man, despite his riches, does not endure; he is like the beasts that perish. (Psa 49:12)

c. The religionists loved the front seats and high places in the synagogues and feasts that were seen, admired, and showed their prominence. In the synagogue the leaders and distinguished persons sat on a bench in front of the ark (where the Scripture was kept), and they sat facing the congregation. No leader could be missed. On social occasions the most honored sat at the right hand of the host, then the next honored at his left hand, and so on, alternating from the right to the left down the table. Position and recognition were set.

Thought 1. Some love the titles and esteem, the special seats and places of recognition. There are those who love the restricted neighborhoods and clubs, the preferred lists. They love the preeminence. Note what is condemned: not being in these positions and places, but the *love* of them. Someone has to hold the upper positions and fill the major places. It is the *love* and feeling of pride because of the title and the place and position that is wrong.

How can you believe if you accept praise from one another, yet make no effort to obtain the praise that comes from the only God ? (John 5:44)

But man, despite his riches, does not endure; he is like the beasts that perish. (Psa 49:12)

I wrote to the church, but Diotrephes, who loves to be first, will have nothing to do with us. (3 John 1:9)

2. The terrible sin of the religionists was that they devoured widows' houses; that is, they used widows for gain. This was and is a gross sin, and it is common. There are some preachers and leaders, professing hypocrites, who court the attention and favor of people (especially widows)

for the purpose of securing money. They seek large donations, endowments, trusts, investments, and gifts *to promote themselves and their institution.* The great tragedy is that such false and hypocritical hearts use the guise of religion to promote themselves and their false ideas. Their call to people is to institutional religion, not to the honor of God and the spirit of self-denial. Vain men, of course, are succeptible to such appeals; but widows in particular are exposed to those who seem to be so devoted to God.

3. The condemnation of religionists and any one else who is guilty of such sins is to be greater. There are some sins more horrible than others. Using religion for selfish ends is one of them. Such will receive a greater damnation. A fact should be noted here: widows hold a special place in God's heart. He has always instructed His people to care for them in a very special way.

He defends the cause of the fatherless and the widow, and loves the alien, giving him food and clothing. (Deu 10:18)

"Cursed is the man who withholds justice from the alien, the fatherless or the widow." Then all the people shall say, "Amen!" (Deu 27:19)

A father to the fatherless, a defender of widows, is God in his holy dwelling. (Psa 68:5)

Learn to do right! Seek justice, encourage the oppressed. Defend the cause of the fatherless, plead the case of the widow. (Isa 1:17)

And there was a widow in that town who kept coming to him with the plea, 'Grant me justice against my adversary.' "For some time he refused. But finally he said to himself, 'Even though I don't fear God or care about men, yet because this widow keeps bothering me, I will see that she gets justice, so that she won't eventually wear me out with her coming!'" And the Lord said, "Listen to what the unjust judge says. And will not God bring about justice for his chosen ones, who cry out to him day and night? Will he keep putting them off? (Luke 18:3-7)

	CHAPTER 21 **I. The Widow's Offering or Gift: The Question of Giving, 21:1-4** (Mk.12:41-44)
1 Jesus sat & restedDS1 a. Saw the rich give b. Saw a poor widow give	As he looked up, Jesus saw the rich putting their gifts into the temple treasury.
2 Giving must be in the right spirit	2 He also saw a poor widow put in two very small copper coins.
3 Giving must not be based on the amount given, but on the amount kept back	3 "I tell you the truth," he said, "this poor widow has put in more than all the others.
4 Giving must be sacrificial, given because a person has need	4 All these people gave their gifts out of their wealth; but she out of her poverty put in all she had to live on."

DIVISION VIII

THE SON OF MAN'S DRAMATIC ENTRANCE INTO JERUSALEM: HIS CLAIM AND CONFLICT, 19:28-21:4

I. The Widow's Offering or Gift: The Question of Giving, 21:1-4

(21:1-4) **Introduction—Stewardship**: giving to the church and charity is a thorn in the side of many. Most persons give a little money or a few worn out or unwanted items, but few give much of value. However, if the needs of a world that reels in desperation are to be met, many must begin to give and to give sacrificially. Something needs to be seen: giving may be debated among men, but it is not debatable with Jesus. Jesus answered the questions about giving, and He did so strongly—without hesitation and debate. Every person must give *everything he is and has* to meet the needs of a world that has thousands *dying every day*, dying because they lack the very necessities of life and have never heard the gospel of His glorious love and deliverance.

1. Jesus sat and rested (v.1-2).
2. Giving must be in the right spirit (v.2).
3. Giving must not be based on the amount given, but on the amount kept back (v.3).
4. Giving must be sacrificial, given because a person has need (v.4).

1 (21:1-2) **Jesus Christ, Tired—Vision**: Jesus sat and rested. He had suffered a great deal of pressure and tension over the past few hours. The authorities had baited Him time and again with trick questions, trying to trap and discredit Him before the people (Lk.20:1-47). He was tired and mentally exhausted. Note the words, "As He looked up." He had walked out of the court of the Gentiles into the court of the women and sat down to rest over by the treasury (see DEEPER STUDY # 1—Lk.21:1). His elbows were upon His knees and His face and head were resting in the palms of His hands. Sitting there with His eyes closed and resting, He heard the clanging of the money being dropped into the collection boxes. At some point Jesus looked up and saw what must have been an impressive sight. It was Passover week and teeming thousands would be streaming by the boxes making their contributions. In fact, Mark says "rich people threw in large amounts" (Mk.12:41). Jesus saw the rich making their contributions. In some cases the gifts were very large. Then all of a sudden out of nowhere, something caught Jesus' eye. A poor widow cast in "two very small copper coins," which were the smallest coins—coins that had the least value in that day.

The point is this: Jesus saw in the widow's offering a timely illustration, an illustration that would answer man's question about giving to the work of God and meeting the desperate needs of the world.

DEEPER STUDY # 1

(21:1) **Temple—Treasury**: the treasury (gazophulakion) was in the court of the women. A section of the court had thirteen trumpet shaped collection boxes. Each box had written on it the purpose for which the offerings were to be used. People simply dropped their offerings into the box of the ministry they wished to support.

2 (21:2) **Stewardship—Tithing**: giving must be in the right spirit. The widow was very poor. Jesus used two different words for "poor" to describe just how poor the woman really was. In verse two the word is *penichran* which means a person who earns only a meager, pitiful wage. In verse three the word is *ptoche* which means abject poverty, utter destitution, poverty that is visible and unquestionable. It is the poverty that forces one to beg and seek alms in order to survive. In that day there was little work for a widow. Poor widows had to struggle for their very survival. Such was the case of this poor widow; she was desperately poor. Note: she had cast in two small copper coins, and the two coins were all she had (v.4).

1. She was giving to God's work because she wanted to give. She wanted God to have what she had to use in His service. She did not give grudgingly or reluctantly, but willingly.

Each man should give what he has decided in his heart to give, not reluctantly or under compulsion, for God loves a cheerful giver. (2 Cor 9:7)

For if the willingness is there, the gift is acceptable according to what one has, not according to what he does not have. (2 Cor 8:12)

2. Her trust was not in money. Her trust was in God. She literally gave all she had to God. Her spirit was right; it was reaching out to God, saying that all she had belonged to God. Both she and her possessions were the Lord's.

But give what is inside the dish to the poor, and everything will be clean for you. (Luke 11:41)

Command those who are rich in this present world not to be arrogant nor to put their hope in wealth, which is so uncertain, but to put their hope in God, who richly provides us with everything for our enjoyment. (1 Tim 6:17)

The LORD redeems his servants; no one will be condemned who takes refuge in him. (Psa 34:22)

Commit your way to the LORD; trust in him and he will do this: (Psa 37:3, 5)

You will keep in perfect peace him whose mind is steadfast, because he trusts in you. (Isa 26:3)

"But blessed is the man who trusts in the LORD, whose confidence is in him. (Jer 17:7)

3 (21:3) **Stewardship—Tithing**: giving must not be based on the amount given, but on the amount kept back. This is difficult for men to accept, in particular rich men, but it is definitely one of the points Jesus was making. Wealth and money are not for the purpose of hoarding and storing and banking, not in a world reeling with poverty and need, sin and death. The needs of all men must be met and the message of salvation and eternal life must to be proclaimed. The imperative of the need and command of God is unequivocal and irrevocable.

Note what Jesus said. She "has put in more than all the others." Jesus was not saying that she cast in more than any *one* of them, but she cast in more than *all of them put together*. This was shocking! How could He make such a statement, for some had cast in much more money than she? And all the rich combined had cast in an enormous sum. Very simply, God measured what was kept back, not how much was given.

⇒ The widow had less remaining; the others still had much.

⇒ The widow had given more of what she had; the others had given less of what they had.

⇒ The widow had sacrificed more; the others had sacrificed less.

In proportion to what she had, the widow gave a larger percent. The others gave a much smaller percent. After they had given, they still had 85 percent or 95 percent to spend on themselves.

For where your treasure is, there your heart will be also. (Mat 6:21)

Sell your possessions and give to the poor. Provide purses for yourselves that will not wear out, a treasure in heaven that will not be exhausted, where no thief comes near and no moth destroys. (Luke 12:33)

When Jesus heard this, he said to him, "You still lack one thing. Sell everything you have and give to the poor, and you will have treasure in heaven. Then come, follow me." (Luke 18:22)

But Zacchaeus stood up and said to the Lord, "Look, Lord! Here and now I give half of my possessions to the poor, and if I have cheated anybody out of anything, I will pay back four times the amount." (Luke 19:8)

If I give all I possess to the poor and surrender my body to the flames, but have not love, I gain nothing. (1 Cor 13:3)

And God is able to make all grace abound to you, so that in all things at all times, having all that you need, you will abound in every good work. (2 Cor 9:8)

4 (21:4) **Stewardship—Tithing**: giving must be sacrificial—given because a person has need. This is a critical point, a truth that must be heeded by all givers of every generation.

1. The rich gave *out of their wealth*. They believed in God and trusted Him, and they were appreciative and thankful for the blessings of God. They were even concerned about the needs and welfare of God's work, concerned enough to give *sizable offerings*. It is important to see this fact in order to clearly see what Jesus was saying. The rich were giving and giving much because they cared deeply about the work of God.

2. The widow gave sacrificially; she gave "out of her poverty." She "gave all she had to live on." Why? Because she had a need, a great need. She desperately needed food, clothing, and shelter. She was so desperate she seldom knew where her next meal was coming from. The pressure and pain of being destitute and hungry and exposed to the elements was a daily experience for her, and no one cared or helped. But she knew something: God cared. She could trust God, so she took her need and gave it to God. Her need was financial, so she took what money she had and gave it all to God. She simply said, "God, I have need, the need for money. I do not even have enough money to buy food. If I am to eat, you have to provide—somehow, some way. I have worked as hard as I can at the jobs I have been able to find. Here is all I have. Take it; use it in your kingdom. I cast myself upon You. You take care of me."

She knew the great principle that God would take care of those who give all they *are and have* to Him. She knew that if she were to be *assured* of God's care, she had to give *all* to God. If she gave *all*, God would not deny anything to her. He would provide all the necessities of life (Mt.6:33). She took her need and all that was involved in it and gave it to God. She sought God to meet her need by giving to God *all that she had.*

Note another fact. Two needs are present and being met.

1. God's temple (church) had need. The widow, though poor, gave to help the temple carry on the ministry of God.

2. The poor widow had need. She gave believing God would see to it that she had food, clothing, and shelter. And note: God saw her, and although we are not told about how He did it, He took her under His wing and took care of her.

But seek first his kingdom and his righteousness, and all these things will be given to you as well. (Mat 6:33)

Bring the whole tithe into the storehouse, that there may be food in my house. Test me in this," says the LORD Almighty, "and see if I will not throw open the floodgates of heaven and pour out so much blessing that you will not have room enough for it. (Mal 3:10)

Of David. A psalm. The earth is the Lord's, and everything in it, the world, and all who live in it; (Psa 24:1)

For the director of music. A psalm of David. Blessed is he who has regard for the weak; the LORD delivers him in times of trouble. (Psa 41:1)

A generous man will prosper; he who refreshes others will himself be refreshed. (Prov 11:25)

A generous man will himself be blessed, for he shares his food with the poor.
(Prov 22:9)

But the noble man makes noble plans, and by noble deeds he stands. (Isa 32:8)

And if you spend yourselves in behalf of the hungry and satisfy the needs of the oppressed, then your light will rise in the darkness, and your night will become like the noonday. (Isa 58:10)

1 The disciples admired the temple's beauty a. Jesus predicted the temple's utter destruction	**IX. THE SON OF MAN'S PROPHETIC SIGNS: HIS PREDICTION CONCERNING THE FATE OF JERUSALEM AND THE WORLD,**[DS1] **21:5-38** (Mt.24-25; Mk.13) **A. The Predicted Signs of the Present Age, 21:5-11** (Mt.24:1-14; Mk.13:1-13) 5 Some of his disciples were remarking about how the temple was adorned with beautiful stones and with gifts dedicated to God. But Jesus said, 6 "As for what you see here, the time will come when not one stone will be left on an- other; every one of them will be thrown down."	7 "Teacher," they asked, "when will these things hap- pen? And what will be the sign that they are about to take place?" 8 He replied: "Watch out that you are not deceived. For many will come in my name, claiming, 'I am he,' and, 'The time is near.' Do not follow them. 9 When you hear of wars and revolutions, do not be fright- ened. These things must hap- pen first, but the end will not come right away." 10 Then he said to them: "Nation will rise against na- tion, and kingdom against kingdom. 11 There will be great earth- quakes, famines and pesti- lences in various places, and fearful events and great signs from heaven.	b. The disciples asked two questions 1) When was it to be destroyed 2) What were the signs c. The warning: Be not deceived **2 Sign 1: False Christs** **3 Sign 2: Conflict of nations** **4 Sign 3: Natural disasters**

DIVISION IX

THE SON OF MAN'S PROPHETIC SIGNS: HIS PREDICTION CONCERNING THE FATE OF JERUSALEM AND THE WORLD, 21:5-38

A. The Predicted Signs of the Present Age, 21:5-11

(21:5-38) **DIVISION OVERVIEW:** this chapter is known as the *Olivet Discourse* (see outlines and notes—Mt.24:1-25:46; DEEPER STUDY # 1,2,3—Mk.13:1-37 for more discussion). It deals with *three great subjects* that lay out in the future when they were predicted by Christ.

1. The destruction of Jerusalem (v.6-7; cp. Mt.24:2-3).
2. The Lord's return (v.7; cp. Mt.24:3).
3. The end of the world (v.7; cp. Mt.24:3).

Matthew and Mark's account of what happens in this passage should be read along with Luke for a clearer understanding.

DEEPER STUDY # 1

(21:5-38) **End Time**: four things will help in understanding what Jesus was doing in the discussion of the end times.

1. It will help to remember that Jesus was preparing His disciples for His death and departure from this world and preparing them to carry on after He was gone. His immediate disciples were to face some terrible times, ranging all the way from personal trials brought on by their witness for Jesus to national trials involving the utter destruction of their nation. In addition, it would be generations stretching into centuries before He returned to earth. No one knew this at that time, but He did. Therefore, He needed to prepare His future disciples as well, for they too were going to face all kinds of trials. There was the danger that His disciples might tire waiting for His return; moreover, they were to see and experience so much trouble in the world, their faith might falter. They, along with many in the world, might begin to ask:

> **They will say, "Where is this 'coming' he promised? Ever since our fathers died, everything goes on as it has since the beginning of creation." (2 Pet 3:4)**

What Jesus did was use this occasion to reveal some of the events that were to take place upon the earth during these "*last days,*" the days of the church (Acts 2:16-17; 1 Jn.2:18). By knowing some of the events, His disciples would be better prepared to endure and to keep their hope for His return alive.

⇒ They would know that God is never caught off guard. God is still on the throne and still in control of all world events.

⇒ They would not be caught off guard themselves. They would know what to expect in this corruptible and sinful world. Therefore, when the events happened, they would not be as likely to become discouraged.

⇒ They would be challenged to *keep themselves* ever so close to God in order to be as strong as possible to face the trials coming upon earth.

⇒ They would be encouraged to place their hope in God and in the new heavens and earth and not in this corruptible world. They will be "waiting for the blessed hope—the glorious appearing of the great God and our Savior Jesus Christ" (Tit.2:13).

2. Remembering that Jesus was dealing with two questions will also help in understanding what was being said. He was answering the questions: When will the temple be destroyed, and what shall be the sign of His return and of the end of the world?

Note something: Jesus was dealing with *the end of the temple and with the end of the world, the destruction of the temple and the destruction of the world.* He was covering the signs, the events that cause and occur during the judgment of *both the temple and the world.* What is the point? Simply this. Scripture teaches that the same sins and events cause the judgment of anything. That is, the events (sins)

(sins) that cause judgment upon one thing are the same events that will bring judgment upon everything else. Therefore, the signs that surrounded the destruction of Jerusalem are much the same as the signs that will surround the end of the world. What Jesus was saying has a double meaning and application (see notes—Mt.24:1-14; 24:15-28. Both notes will help to see the double application.)

The Lord's words applied both to the disciples of His day and to all disciples who were to follow in succeeding generations. As long as the earth stands, the disciples of "the last days" (or ages) will face many of the same signs faced by those who experienced the destruction of Jerusalem. However, there is to be one difference. At the end of the world, the signs will *increase and intensify*. The day is coming; it will be so terrible that it can be called *the beginning of birth pains* [sorrows] (Mt.24:8) and the *great distress* (Mt.24:21). (See notes—Mt.24:1-28; 24:15-28 for a discussion of these two lessons.)

3. The present age is considered by God to be "the age of the last days" or "the last time." According to God's timetable, the history of the church, its presence on earth takes place in "the last days" or during "the last times."

> **No, this is what was spoken by the prophet Joel: "'In the last days, God says, I will pour out my Spirit on all people. Your sons and daughters will prophesy, your young men will see visions, your old men will dream dreams. (Acts 2:16-17)**
>
> **But [God] in these last days he has spoken to us by his Son, whom he appointed heir of all things, and through whom he made the universe. (Heb 1:2)**
>
> **Dear children, this is the last hour; and as you have heard that the antichrist is coming, even now many antichrists have come. This is how we know it is the last hour. (1 John 2:18)**

4. A quick overview of the passages in this chapter also helps in understanding what Jesus was doing.

a. The signs of the present age (Lk.21:5-11).
b. The tragic sign prior to the end: persecution (Lk.21:12-19).
c. The destruction of Jerusalem (Lk.21:20-24).
d. The Coming of the Son of Man (Lk.21:25-28).
e. The Parable of the Fig Tree: the signs are clearly seen (Lk.21:29-33).

(21:5-11) **Introduction—End Time**: there is a matter of critical importance when looking at the end time. In understanding what Jesus was saying, we have to be very careful not to add to or take away from what He said. Both mistakes were made by religionists concerning Jesus' first coming (Mt.2:4-6).

A major fact to keep in mind is this. The disciples *did think* that all three events (Jerusalem's destruction, the Lord's return, and the world's end) would happen at about the same time. They did think in terms of the Messianic Kingdom of God. Comparing Acts 1:6 with the Jewish concept of the Messiah shows this. (See notes—Mt.1:1; DEEPER STUDY # 2—1:18; DEEPER STUDY # 3—3:11; notes—11:1-6; 11:2-3; DEEPER STUDY # 1—11:5; DEEPER STUDY # 2—11:6; DEEPER STUDY # 1—12:16; notes—22:42; Lk.7:23-23.) When Jesus said that the temple would be destroyed, the disciples assumed it would happen at the same time that He returned to end the world, thereby restoring the kingdom to Israel.

Jesus, however, gave no timetable. He did not say when the three events would occur. What He did was give signs that would occur before the events, signs that would point toward His return and toward the end of Jerusalem and toward the end of the world.

It is also important to keep in mind that most of the signs happen *all through history*. However, there is this difference: the signs increase and intensify right before the end of Jerusalem and the end of the world. There will be a period known as *the beginning of birth pains* or sorrows (Mt.24:8) and a period launched by *the abomination that causes desolation* known as the "great distress [tribulation], unequaled from the beginning of the world until now..." (Mt.24:21).

The signs of the present age are three.

1. The disciples admired the temple's beauty (v.5-8).
2. Sign 1: false Christs (v.8).
3. Sign 2: conflict of nations (v.9-10).
4. Sign 3: natural disasters (v.11).

1 (21:5-8) **End Time**: the disciples admired the temple's beauty. The temple was magnificent. It sat upon the towering summit of Mount Zion. It was built of white marble plated with gold. The temple was a massive structure that could hold thousands of people. (Cp. Acts 4:4 which perhaps took place in the temple. Five thousand men were saved among a crowd which probably numbered many thousands more.) The temple had several porches such as Solomon's Porch and the Royal Porch that were supported with huge, towering pillars. The pillars were so large that it took three to four men's reaching arm to arm to encircle each one. The temple was a striking sight, one of the building wonders of the world. The disciples apparently stood some place where the temple in all its magnificent beauty struck them with awe, and they wanted Jesus to see the beautiful sight. When they drew His attention to it, three things happened.

1. Jesus used the occasion to arouse the disciples' interest in coming events. He predicted the temple's utter destruction.

2. The disciples were shocked and aroused to ask two questions of the Lord. To understand the questions, the beliefs of the disciples must be remembered. Their thoughts were filled with the idea of Israel's glory as the greatest nation upon earth. They had finally accepted the fact that Jesus was the Messiah, God's appointed instrument to free Israel and to raise the nation to its destined glory. Therefore, when Jesus began to talk about the temple's being razed to the ground, they were utterly shocked. "Teacher, when will these things happen?" They could hardly believe their ears. The thought that flashed across their minds was *the end time*. "These things will occur in the end time, will they not, Master? Just when will they take place? What signs will there be to show they are about to take place?" (Cp. Mt.24:1-3, 15-31.) In their minds the temple could not possibly be destroyed until the end of all things came about. They were thinking that the glory of Israel was to be set up when all of a sudden, Jesus began to talk about the utter destruction of the temple, the very center of their nation. They wanted to know two things.

⇒ When was the temple to be destroyed?
⇒ What will be the sign "that they are about to take place," that is, the destruction of Jerusalem, the end of the world, and the Lord's return (see DEEPER STUDY # 1—Lk.21:5-38)?

3. Jesus warned His disciples not to be deceived. This can mean one or two things.

a. A person can be easily deceived when dealing with end time prophecies.
b. A person can be easily deceived when facing the end time events. He can be deceived into thinking that certain cataclysmic events are infallible signs that the end is at hand. Too often cataclysmic events result in wild guesses about the end time. They result in...
   - universal predictions.
   - the deceiving of others.
   - discouragement of one's faith when the end does not come.

2 (21:8) **Messiah, False**: the first sign will be *false messiahs*. Jesus said three things about this sign.

1. There will be *many*, not just a few but *many,* false messiahs.
2. They will make two claims.
   a. The claim of deity. Note the words, "I Am" (eimi). This is the name which was used by God to reveal Himself to Moses. It is the most basic name of Deity. "I Am" equals *Being*, the most basic Being of the Universe. It is the claim used by God to tell man that He is the Supreme Being of the universe, the Messiah, the Deliverer of all mankind (see note—Jn.6:20).
   b. The claim that the end time—the Messianic Age, the age when Israel and the world are to be delivered—*is at hand.* (How often this claim is made, even by some well-meaning men! But note what Jesus said in the next point.)
3. "Do not follow them." They are false messiahs. The real Messiah has already come, Jesus Christ, the Son of God Himself. It is He and He alone who has "the words of eternal life." As Peter exclaimed:

Simon Peter answered him, "Lord, to whom shall we go? You have the words of eternal life. (John 6:68)

Thought 1. Note to whom Christ was speaking: His disciples. Disciples can be misled by false teachers and prophets.

"Watch out for false prophets. They come to you in sheep's clothing, but inwardly they are ferocious wolves. (Mat 7:15)

For many will come in my name, claiming, 'I am the Christ, ' and will deceive many. (Mat 24:5)

And many false prophets will appear and deceive many people. (Mat 24:11)

For false Christs and false prophets will appear and perform great signs and miracles to deceive even the elect—if that were possible. (Mat 24:24; cp.Mk.13:22)

Even from your own number men will arise and distort the truth in order to draw away disciples after them. (Acts 20:30)

For such people are not serving our Lord Christ, but their own appetites. By smooth talk and flattery they deceive the minds of naive people. (Rom 16:18)

For such men are false apostles, deceitful workmen, masquerading as apostles of Christ. (2 Cor 11:13)

Then we will no longer be infants, tossed back and forth by the waves, and blown here and there by every wind of teaching and by the cunning and craftiness of men in their deceitful scheming. (Eph 4:14)

The Spirit clearly says that in later times some will abandon the faith and follow deceiving spirits and things taught by demons. Such teachings come through hypocritical liars, whose consciences have been seared as with a hot iron. (1 Tim 4:1-2)

While evil men and impostors will go from bad to worse, deceiving and being deceived. (2 Tim 3:13)

For the time will come when men will not put up with sound doctrine. Instead, to suit their own desires, they will gather around them a great number of teachers to say what their itching ears want to hear. They will turn their ears away from the truth and turn aside to myths. (2 Tim 4:3-4)

For there are many rebellious people, mere talkers and deceivers, especially those of the circumcision group. They must be silenced, because they are ruining whole households by teaching things they ought not to teach—and that for the sake of dishonest gain. (Titus 1:10-11)

But there were also false prophets among the people, just as there will be false teachers among you. They will secretly introduce destructive heresies, even denying the sovereign Lord who bought them—bringing swift destruction on themselves. (2 Pet 2:1)

Dear children, this is the last hour; and as you have heard that the antichrist is coming, even now many antichrists have come. This is how we know it is the last hour. They went out from us, but they did not really belong to us. For if they had belonged to us, they would have remained with us; but their going showed that none of them belonged to us. (1 John 2:18-19)

Who is the liar? It is the man who denies that Jesus is the Christ. Such a man is the antichrist—he denies the Father and the Son. (1 John 2:22)

Many deceivers, who do not acknowledge Jesus Christ as coming in the flesh, have gone out into the world. Any such person is the deceiver and the antichrist. (2 John 1:7)

3 (21:9-10) **World Violence—War**: the second sign will be *conflict of nations*. Four things were said here.

1. Believers will hear of wars and revolutions (akatastasias), which means tumults, uproars, riots, terrorism, insurrections, treasons, confusions of governments. There will be uprisings within governments, and governments will be overthrown. Believers can become extremely disturbed over the news.
2. Believers are not to be "frightened" (ptoethete). They are not to let their hearts "be troubled" (Jn.14:1). World violence can trouble people; but the believer's heart and

life are to be centered upon God, trusting His presence, care, and security—eternally.

> **"Do not let your hearts be troubled. Trust in God; trust also in me. In my Father's house are many rooms; if it were not so, I would have told you. I am going there to prepare a place for you. (John 14:1-2)**
>
> **"I have told you these things, so that in me you may have peace. In this world you will have trouble. But take heart! I have overcome the world." (John 16:33)**
>
> **"I tell you, my friends, do not be afraid of those who kill the body and after that can do no more. But I will show you whom you should fear: Fear him who, after the killing of the body, has power to throw you into hell. Yes, I tell you, fear him. (Luke 12:4-5)**

3. World violence "must happen first." It does not happen at first because God destines it, but because men's hearts are gripped by passion, lust, greed, and evil.

> **"Woe to the world because of the things that cause people to sin! Such things must come, but woe to the man through whom they come! (Mat 18:7)**
>
> **What causes fights and quarrels among you? Don't they come from your desires that battle within you? You want something but don't get it. You kill and covet, but you cannot have what you want. You quarrel and fight. You do not have, because you do not ask God. When you ask, you do not receive, because you ask with wrong motives, that you may spend what you get on your pleasures. (James 4:1-3)**

4. World violence can so dominate the news that men are led to believe that the end is at hand. However, Jesus warned, "The end will not come right away," not yet. Remember the words just spoken, "Watch out that you are not deceived."

> **One nation was being crushed by another and one city by another, because God was troubling them with every kind of distress. But as for you, be strong and do not give up, for your work will be rewarded." (2 Chr 15:6-7)**
>
> **"Come out of her, my people! Run for your lives! Run from the fierce anger of the LORD. Do not lose heart or be afraid when rumors are heard in the land; one rumor comes this year, another the next, rumors of violence in the land and of ruler against ruler. (Jer 51:45-46)**
>
> **"Be careful, or your hearts will be weighed down with dissipation, drunkenness and the anxieties of life, and that day will close on you unexpectedly like a trap. (Luke 21:34)**
>
> **Do not be anxious about anything, but in everything, by prayer and petition, with thanksgiving, present your requests to God. (Phil 4:6)**
>
> **Cast all your anxiety on him because he cares for you. (1 Pet 5:7)**

4 (21:11) **Nature—Earthquakes—Famines—Pestilence**: the fourth sign will be *natural disasters*. Five disasters in nature were mentioned in particular.

1. Earthquakes. Great earthquakes cause enormous damage to buildings, disrupting and destroying the lives of people, cities, and communitites. Earthquakes are one of the most alarming and frightening disasters among men. Josephus records the fulfillment of Jesus' prophecy. He even hints that the natural disasters which happened were a sign of coming destruction.

> *"...there broke out a prodigious storm in the night, with the utmost violence, and very strong winds, with the largest showers of rain, and continual lightnings, terrible thunderings, and amazing concussions and bellowings of the earth, that was in an earthquake. These things were a manifest indication that some destruction was coming upon men, when the system of the world was put into this disorder; and any one would guess that these wonders forshowed some grand calamities that were coming"* (Josephus, Wars. 4. 4:5).

Earthquakes will occur in many places during the last days of the earth (Rev.6:12; 11:12-13, 19; 16:17-19).

2. Famines. Food is one of the most basic necessities of men. Without food men die. Jesus said that in the last days, right before Jerusalem's fall and right before the end of the world, there shall be terrible famine. Scripture speaks of a "severe famine over the entire Roman world during the reign of Claudius" (Acts 11:28-30). Josephus describes the famine as being so terrible that when flour "was brought into the temple...not one of the priests was so hardy as to eat one crumb of it... while so great a distress was upon the land" (Josephus, Ant. 3. 15:3). He says in another place, "A famine did oppress them [Jerusalem]...and many people died for want of what was necessary to procure food" (Josephus, Ant. 20:25).

In the very last days before Jerusalem's fall, Josephus speaks of another terrible famine:

> *"It was now a miserable case, and a sight that would justly bring tears into our eyes, how men stood to their food, while the more powerful had more than enough, and the weaker were lamenting (for want of it)" (Josephus, Wars. 5. 10:3).*
>
> *"Then did the famine widen its progress, and devoured the people by whole houses and families; the upper rooms were full of women and children that were dying by famine; and the lanes of the city were full of the dead bodies of the aged; the children also and the young men wandered about the marketplaces like shadows, all swelled with famine, and fell down dead wheresoever their misery seized them"* (Josephus, Wars. 5. 12:3).

There is evidently to be terrible famine in the last days. The black horse of the four horsemen of the Apocalypse indicates terrible famine (see note—Rev.6:5-6). The unbearable pain and terrible evil that hunger can cause is graphically described by Scripture.

> **Those killed by the sword are better off**

than those who die of famine; racked with hunger, they waste away for lack of food from the field. With their own hands compassionate women have cooked [boiled] their own children, who became their food when my people were destroyed. (Lam 4:9-10)

Luke adds a third disaster of nature: pestilence. Earthquakes and famines, of course, cause disease and pestilence (see note—Mt.24:7).

3. Pestilence. Disease is often the result of war and widespread disasters such as earthquakes. Pestilence shows no partiality. The rich may be able to buy food during a famine, but they cannot buy their way out of an epidemic of disease. Death by disease and other natural causes shows no partiality.

Josephus' record of a great pestilence that struck during the days of Herod is evidence of the fact.

> *"When he [Herod] was in the way, there arose a pestilential disease, and carried off the greatest part of the multitude, and of his best and most esteemed friends [the wealthy]"* (Josephus, Ant. 15. 7:7).

Pestilence will also be one of the terrible sufferings at the end time. Part of the suffering caused by the pale horse of the four horsemen of the Apocalypse includes pestilences.

I looked, and there before me was a pale horse! Its rider was named Death, and Hades was following close behind him. They were given power over a fourth of the earth to kill by sword [war], famine [hunger] and plague [pestilence resulting from war and famine], and by the wild beasts of the earth. (Rev 6:8; see note—Rev.6:8).

4. Astronomical happenings. There will be "fearful events and great signs" happening in the sky at the end of the world. Very practically, such astronomical happenings occur now. The earth is sometimes darkened by dust from earthly catastrophes such as volcanic eruptions, wind storms, and smoke from huge fires. Of course, whatever darkens the sun, hides the light of the moon from earth. The stars, that is, meteorites of varying sizes, fall through space often. The point is, the events of the end time are going to trigger astronomical happenings worldwide, universally. (See notes—Mk.13:24; Mk.13:24-25 for more discussion.)

"But in those days, following that distress, "'the sun will be darkened, and the moon will not give its light; the stars will fall from the sky, and the heavenly bodies will be shaken.' (Mark 13:24-25)

But the day Lot left Sodom, fire and sulfur rained down from heaven and destroyed them all. "It will be just like this on the day the Son of Man is revealed. (Luke 17:29-30)

"There will be signs in the sun, moon and stars. On the earth, nations will be in anguish and perplexity at the roaring and tossing of the sea. Men will faint from terror, apprehensive of what is coming on the world, for the heavenly bodies will be shaken. (Luke 21:25-26)

I will show wonders in the heaven above and signs on the earth below, blood and fire and billows of smoke. The sun will be turned to darkness and the moon to blood before the coming of the great and glorious day of the Lord. (Acts 2:19-20)

I watched as he opened the sixth seal. There was a great earthquake. The sun turned black like sackcloth made of goat hair, the whole moon turned blood red, and the stars in the sky fell to earth, as late figs drop from a fig tree when shaken by a strong wind. The sky receded like a scroll, rolling up, and every mountain and island was removed from its place. Then the kings of the earth, the princes, the generals, the rich, the mighty, and every slave and every free man hid in caves and among the rocks of the mountains. They called to the mountains and the rocks, "Fall on us and hide us from the face of him who sits on the throne and from the wrath of the Lamb! For the great day of their wrath has come, and who can stand?" (Rev 6:12-17)

	B. The Tragic Sign Prior to the End: Persecution, 21:12-19 (Mt.24:9-10, 13; Mk.13:9, 11-12)	14 But make up your mind not to worry beforehand how you will defend yourselves. 15 For I will give you words and wisdom that none of your adversaries will be able to resist or contradict.	d. The preparation 1) Do not prepare a defense 2) A supernatural answer will be given
1 The persecution of believers a. The persecutors: Religious & civil authorities b. The reason: Believers are followers of Christ c. The result: A glorious testimony	12 "But before all this, they will lay hands on you and persecute you. They will deliver you to synagogues and prisons, and you will be brought before kings and governors, and all on account of my name. 13 This will result in your being witnesses to them.	16 You will be betrayed even by parents, brothers, relatives and friends, and they will put some of you to death. 17 All men will hate you because of me. 18 But not a hair of your head will perish. 19 By standing firm you will gain life.	**2 The betrayers of believers** a. Relatives b. All men **3 The promise to believers** a. God is in control b. Eternal security: If endure

DIVISION IX

THE SON OF MAN'S PROPHETIC SIGNS: HIS PREDICTION CONCERNING THE FATE OF JERUSALEM AND THE WORLD, 21:5-38

B. The Tragic Sign Prior to the End: Persecution, 21:12-19

(21:12-19) **Introduction**: the discussion of the present passage focuses upon the signs of the end time (see Deeper Study # 1—Lk.21:5-38). There is one sign of the end time that must be proclaimed to all believers. It is the sign of *persecution*. It is true that believers are persecuted in every generation, but right before the end time there will be a great intensification of persecution throughout the whole world. Believers will be persecuted as never before. Note the words, "But before all this, they will lay hands on you, and persecute you." Believers must be prepared. This is the purpose of the present passage. The passage can be applied to believers in every generation to prepare them for facing persecution.

1. The persecution of believers (v.12-15).
2. The betrayers and traitors of believers (v.16-17).
3. The promise to believers (v.18-19).

1 (21:12-15) **Persecution, Reasons; Results**: the persecution of believers. Note three facts.

1. The persecution will be carried out by both civil and religious authorities. Both the government and religion will persecute true believers right before the end time. The idea is, of course, an intensification of persecution in the end time (see note—Lk.21:5-8). This is the very reason Jesus made a distinction between the end time and the church age persecutors. Right before the end of the world, believers will be opposed, abused, arrested, tried, and martyred as never before in human history. Both the courts of the world and the councils of religion will take believers and rake them over the hot coals of persecution. Believers will be...

- afflicted (cp. Acts 4:3; 8:1; 12:4; 13:50; 14:19; 2 Cor.11:23-25).
- killed (Acts 7:59; 12:2).
- hated by all nations (Acts 28:22. See outline and notes—Mt.10:16-23. Cp. Jn.15:20; 16:2.)

2. The reason believers will be persecuted is clearly stated by Jesus: "*On account of my name.*" The world will try to stamp out and silence believers because they are true followers of Christ. Their intense hatred of the believer will be due to at least three reasons.

a. The standard of true godliness. The believer sets before the world a different standard—the standard of true godliness. The world is not godly nor is its standard godly. Therefore by his *very nature*, any man who lives for the world and does not wish to change opposes godliness.

"Therefore come out from them and be separate, says the Lord. Touch no unclean thing, and I will receive you." "I will be a Father to you, and you will be my sons and daughters, says the Lord Almighty." (2 Cor 6:17-18)

Do not love the world or anything in the world. If anyone loves the world, the love of the Father is not in him. For everything in the world—the cravings of sinful man, the lust of his eyes and the boasting of what he has and does—comes not from the Father but from the world. (1 John 2:15-16)

b. The life of purity. The genuine believer lives a life of purity, clean and just. True morality and godliness controls the mind, dresses modestly, converses respectfully, and behaves justly. The worldly live to fulfill the lust of their flesh and to have possessions as they wish. Therefore, the believer is opposed by any person who does not wish to live a pure and just life.

The acts of the sinful nature are obvious: sexual immorality, impurity and debauchery; idolatry and witchcraft; hatred, discord, jealousy, fits of rage, selfish ambition, dissensions, factions and envy; drunkenness, orgies, and the like. I warn you, as I did before, that those who live like this will not inherit the kingdom of God. But the fruit of the Spirit is love, joy, peace, patience, kindness, goodness, faithfulness, gentleness and self-control. Against such things there is no law. Those who belong to Christ Jesus have crucified the sinful nature with its passions and desires. (Gal 5:19-24)

c. The message of repentance and of self-denial. The genuine believer proclaims the message of Christ: repentance and self-denial. Very practically, few men are willing to change (repent) to the degree that self is totally denied (person and possessions) in order to meet the needs of desperate people. Therefore most, even the religious, oppose the idea that men are to live sacrificially in order to save a starving and dying world (both a physically and spiritually starving and dying world). (See outline and notes—Mt.19:21-22; 19:23-26.)

Then he said to them all: "If anyone would come after me, he must deny himself and take up his cross daily and follow me. For whoever wants to save his life will lose it, but whoever loses his life for me will save it. (Luke 9:23-24)

For if you live according to the sinful nature, you will die; but if by the Spirit you put to death the misdeeds of the body, you will live, (Rom 8:13)

Jesus answered, "If you want to be perfect, go, sell your possessions and give to the poor, and you will have treasure in heaven. Then come, follow me." (Mat 19:21)

It is better not to eat meat or drink wine or to do anything else that will cause your brother to fall. (Rom 14:21)

Nobody should seek his own good, but the good of others. (1 Cor 10:24)

3. The result of the persecution will be a glorious witness for the Lord. The persecutors will try to silence the believer, but the very persecution itself will turn out to be a glorious witness for the Lord. How? The believer, standing there suffering, will show such loyalty and supernatural strength that some, even some of the persecutors, will be attracted to Christ. The believer will show that Christ and eternity are real, and he will be a testimony even as he receives the beatings and the swords of the persecutors.

I will show him how much he must suffer for my name." (Acts 9:16)

Praise be to the God and Father of our Lord Jesus Christ, the Father of compassion and the God of all comfort, who comforts us in all our troubles, so that we can comfort those in any trouble with the comfort we ourselves have received from God. (2 Cor 1:3-4)

For we who are alive are always being given over to death for Jesus' sake, so that his life may be revealed in our mortal body. (2 Cor 4:11)

4. The preparation of a defense will not be necessary. When the genuine believer has to give an answer or a defense to his persecutors, God will fill his heart and mouth with a reply. The believer will be so filled with wisdom that his persecutors will not be able to resist his defense.

Note: Jesus was not promising the believer that he would be freed. He was promising a strong, unanswerable testimony. It will be time for many believers to go on home with the Lord. The end time will be filled with the blood of many martyrs for the Lord.

At my first defense, no one came to my support, but everyone deserted me. May it not be held against them. But the Lord stood at my side and gave me strength, so that through me the message might be fully proclaimed and all the Gentiles might hear it. And I was delivered from the lion's mouth. The Lord will rescue me from every evil attack and will bring me safely to his heavenly kingdom. To him be glory for ever and ever. Amen. (2 Tim 4:16-18)

So we say with confidence, "The Lord is my helper; I will not be afraid. What can man do to me?" (Heb 13:6)

So do not fear, for I am with you; do not be dismayed, for I am your God. I will strengthen you and help you; I will uphold you with my righteous right hand. (Isa 41:10)

It is the Sovereign LORD who helps me. Who is he that will condemn me? They will all wear out like a garment; the moths will eat them up. (Isa 50:9)

2 (21:16-17) **Persecution**: the betrayal of believers will be heartrending. Believers will be betrayed by their *own families and relatives*, friends and neighbors. Some believers will even be put to death because of their betrayal. Note three points.

1. Jesus was speaking of the end time. Betrayal by loved ones will intensify in the end time.

2. The reason for the betrayal will cut the human heart. Families and friends will hate the believer because of Christ (v.17). The believer will stand for the name and righteousness of Christ; therefore, loved ones will betray him...

- to save their own lives
- to secure some favor
- to escape embarrassment
- to secure vengeance
- to escape persecution themselves
- to gain the favor of authorities
- to escape fear
- to preserve selfish honor or position

"Brother will betray brother to death, and a father his child; children will rebel against their parents and have them put to death. (Mat 10:21)

3. *All* shall hate the believer. Few will be kind, tender, and loving; dissension and division will prevail in the last days. Most will begrudge what another has or is doing or is not doing. Unfortunately, such behavior has been the case down through the centuries, and too often the church has experienced one person's disliking and opposing another person. Envy, greed, and concern for security and recognition—all the sins of selfishness—have caused too many to stand against another person's position, beliefs, abilities, and leadership. Criticism and judging, dissension and division among believers have been and are some of the most visible traits of the church, both locally and universally. Jesus said that such hatred will increase and intensify in the end time.

"Be on your guard against men; they will hand you over to the local councils and flog you in their synagogues. (Mat 10:17)

"Then you will be handed over to be persecuted and put to death, and you will

be hated by all nations because of me. (Mat 24:9;cp. Lk.21:12-13)

Remember the words I spoke to you: 'No servant is greater than his master.' If they persecuted me, they will persecute you also. If they obeyed my teaching, they will obey yours also. (John 15:20)

"All this I have told you so that you will not go astray. They will put you out of the synagogue; in fact, a time is coming when anyone who kills you will think he is offering a service to God. They will do such things because they have not known the Father or me. (John 16:1-3)

In fact, everyone who wants to live a godly life in Christ Jesus will be persecuted, (2 Tim 3:12)

A shiggaion of David, which he sang to the LORD concerning Cush, a Benjamite. O LORD my God, I take refuge in you; save and deliver me from all who pursue me, (Psa 7:1)

My times are in your hands; deliver me from my enemies and from those who pursue me. (Psa 31:15)

All your commands are trustworthy; help me, for men persecute me without cause. (Psa 119:86)

The enemy pursues me, he crushes me to the ground; he makes me dwell in darkness like those long dead. (Psa 143:3)

3 (21:18-19) **Persecution**: the promise is glorious and assuring to the believer. It is twofold.

1. First, the promise is that God is in control of the believer's life, total control. "Not a hair of your head will perish." Jesus meant, of course, spiritual security. He had just said some would "be put to death" (v.16). God knows every hair on the believer's head (Lk.12:7); God is in total control of every single thing concerning the believer. Therefore, if the believer is persecuted, he is under God's care; and if he is being killed, he is under God's care. No matter the persecution and suffering…

- God sees and is in control. He holds the believer in His hands.
- God turns the suffering into a "an eternal glory [and reward] that far overweighs them all" (2Cor.4:17). (2 Cor.4:17).

2. Second, the promise is the eternal security of the believer's soul. If the believer endures the persecution, he shall possess his soul eternally. The idea is that endurance to the end is *required.* The genuine beliver *will* stand fast and endure. He will *not deny* his Lord; he could never give in to such, for he knows the presence and salvation (deliverance) of the Lord. (See note—Mk.13:13.)

Very simply, persecution is not to be feared by the Christian believer. Persecution, even martyrdom, is nothing in light of eternity (cp. Rev.6:9-11). Despite death (v.16) and hatred (v.17), Jesus promised "not a hair of your head will perish" (v.18). The believer is secure in the arms of Jesus eternally.

Do not be afraid of what you are about to suffer. I tell you, the devil will put some of you in prison to test you, and you will suffer persecution for ten days. Be faithful, even to the point of death, and I will give you the crown of life. (Rev 2:10)

To those who by persistence in doing good seek glory, honor and immortality, he will give *eternal life.* But for those who are self-seeking and who reject the truth and follow evil, there will be wrath and anger. There will be trouble and distress for every human being who does evil: first for the Jew, then for the Gentile; (Rom 2:7-9)

Blessed is the man who perseveres under trial [trial], because when he has stood the test, he will receive the crown of life that God has promised to those who love him. (James 1:12)

As you know, we consider blessed those who have persevered. You have heard of Job's perseverance and have seen what the Lord finally brought about. The Lord is full of compassion and mercy. (James 5:11)

But you are a chosen people, a royal priesthood, a holy nation, a people belonging to God, that you may declare the praises of him who called you out of darkness into his wonderful light. (1 Pet 2:9)

	C. The Destruction of Jerusalem, 21:20-24 (Mt.24:15-28; Mk.13: 14-23)	22 For this is the time of punishment in fulfillment of all that has been written.	**3 A time of punishment**
		23 How dreadful it will be in those days for pregnant women and nursing mothers!	**4 A time of woe: Distress & wrath, death & captivity**
1 A sign for which to look: Jerusalem surrounded by armies	20 "When you see Jerusalem being surrounded by armies, you will know that its desolation is near.	There will be great distress in the land and wrath against this people.	
2 A time to flee	21 Then let those who are in Judea flee to the mountains, let those in the city get out, and let those in the country not enter the city.	24 They will fall by the sword and will be taken as prisoners to all the nations. Jerusalem will be trampled on by the Gentiles until the times of the Gentiles are fulfilled.	**5 A time numbered by the Gentiles**

DIVISION IX

THE SON OF MAN'S PROPHETIC SIGNS: HIS PREDICTION CONCERNING THE FATE OF JERUSALEM AND THE WORLD, 21:5-38

C. The Destruction of Jerusalem, 21:20-24

(21:20-24) **Introduction—End Time**: this passage is definitely dealing with the destruction of Jerusalem in A.D. 70 and with the Jewish nation throughout history (v.24).

⇒ The desolation mentioned is the desolation of Jerusalem, not the *abomination that causes desolation* (that is, the antichrist spoken of by Matthew and Mark, Mt.24:15; Mk.13:14).

⇒ Verse 24 makes it clear that the period covered by Jesus stretches from the time "when you see Jerusalem being surrounded armies" (v.20) "until the times of the Gentiles are fulfilled" (v.24).

However, the points of this Scripture can also be applied to the end time as well. Matthew and Mark definitely give a double meaning to the words of Jesus. The disciples had asked two questions. First, when was Jerusalem to be destroyed? They thought it could be destroyed only in the end time. Second, what were the signs of the end time, or the destruction and remaking of all things which would usher in the Kingdom of God? (See note—Lk.21:5-8. Cp. notes—Lk.21:5-38 for more discussion.) What Jesus says in Matthew and Mark can be applied here in Luke. The fall of Jerusalem is judgment upon sin, and the fall of the world will be judgment upon sin. The questions asked by the disciples (v.7) refer to similar conditions that bring about judgment. Therefore, the signs of both the fall of Jerusalem and the end of the world are similar. The only difference is that there will be an intensification of the signs in the end time (see notes—Mt.24:15-28; Mk.13:14-23).

1. A sign for which to look: Jerusalem surrounded by armies (v.20).
2. A time to flee (v.21).
3. A time of punishment (v.22).
4. A time of woe, distress and wrath, death and captivity (v.23).
5. A time numbered by the Gentiles (v.24).

1 (21:20) **Jerusalem**: a sign to look for is that of Jerusalem's being surrounded by armies. In A.D. 66-70 Jerusalem experienced one of the most terrible sieges in history. In A.D. 66 the Jews revolted and the Roman army was swift to attack. However, the city was difficult to take primarily for two reasons. It sat upon a hill, well protected by the terrain, and the leaders of the revolt were religious fanatics. Well over a million people had fled into the city behind its protective walls.

Jesus made two points.

1. Some standing there with Him were to *see* and be witnesses of the sign. They were to actually see judgment fall upon Jerusalem.

2. All of His followers were to be *looking* for and alert to the sign. They were to be prepared at all times for the coming judgment.

> **Thought 1.** The point is clear. We are to be prepared for the coming judgment of the end time. Some of us will be the actual witnesses of the sign. (See outline, note, and DEEPER STUDY # 1—Mt.24:15 for more discussion and application.)

2 (21:21) **End Time—Judgment**: the sign of Jerusalem's being surrounded will be a time to flee. Jesus warned His disciples to flee and to flee immediately. The danger would be imminent and urgency would be needed. Believers...

- in the *surrounding areas* around Jerusalem are to flee to the mountains.
- in the *midst* of Jerusalem are to get out and leave the city immediately.
- in other countries are to stay away and give no thought to entering Jerusalem (Israel).

Note two things.

1. The believers did heed the warning of Jesus. They fled Jerusalem before the attack, sometime around A.D. 66. They fled to a small town called *Pella* in the district of Decapolis.

2. Matthew points out that Jesus said to forget all comfort of home and personal possessions, that the danger was so close and terrible that believers should think only about escaping. Nothing else mattered, nothing except fleeing the coming judgment.

> **Thought 1.** Too many minds are centered upon comfort and possessions, the world and money. The coming judgment is so close and terrible, it alone should consume our thoughts. We must flee to Christ for safety when the signs are seen, and they are definitely seen today. We who live in these "last days" must heed the warning of Christ even as believers of the first century heeded.

Thought 2. The judgment that fell upon Jerusalem is a picture of the coming judgment upon the world. We must be prepared to flee to Christ for safety.

> **"Therefore everyone who hears these words of mine and puts them into practice is like a wise man who built his house on the rock. The rain came down, the streams rose, and the winds blew and beat against that house; yet it did not fall, because it had its foundation on the rock. (Mat 7:24-25)**
>
> **In this way they will lay up treasure for themselves as a firm foundation for the coming age, so that they may take hold of the life that is truly life. (1 Tim 6:19)**
>
> **Nevertheless, God's solid foundation stands firm, sealed with this inscription: "The Lord knows those who are his," and, "Everyone who confesses the name of the Lord must turn away from wickedness." (2 Tim 2:19)**
>
> **Keep your lives free from the love of money and be content with what you have, because God has said, "Never will I leave you; never will I forsake you." (Heb 13:5)**

3 (21:22) **Judgment—End Time**: the sign of Jerusalem's being surrounded will be a time of punishment and vengeance. Note two points.

1. "The time of punishment" will be the fulfillment of Scripture, the days of God's wrath (see DEEPER STUDY # 1, Vengeance—Lk.21:22). God had been patient and longsuffering with Israel for generations, in fact, from the very beginning of their history. But Israel had always rejected God's pleadings. Therefore, the predicted judgment had to fall. What Israel had sown was to be reaped. (See DEEPER STUDY # 1—Jn.4:22.)

2. The terrible desolation that took place upon Jerusalem and that is to take place at the end of the world—all the desolation—is due to sin. Jerusalem committed the most heinous sin in human history: the people rejected God for centuries and eventually killed God's very own Son. Therefore, Jerusalem was utterly destroyed.

Thought 1. There is a severe warning here for believers and nations. Sin results in desolation. Rejection of God's Son will bring judgment upon any person and any nation of people.

DEEPER STUDY # 1

(21:22)**Punishment—Vengeance** (ekdikeseos): executing perfect justice, retribution, satisfaction. It is judgment that flows out of righteousness and justice. It is not the retaliation that flows from human anger and hurt feelings. There is no self-gratification or selfish reaction in the word at all. It is judgment that executes perfect justice. It is judgment that makes things right, exactly as they should be.

> **Do not take revenge, my friends, but leave room for God's wrath, for it is written: "It is mine to avenge; I will repay," says the Lord. (Rom 12:19)**
>
> **And give relief to you who are troubled, and to us as well. This will happen when the Lord Jesus is revealed from heaven in blazing fire with his powerful angels. He will punish those who do not know God and do not obey the gospel of our Lord Jesus. (2 Th 1:7-8)**
>
> **For we know him who said, "It is mine to avenge; I will repay," and again, "The Lord will judge his people." It is a dreadful thing to fall into the hands of the living God. (Heb 10:30-31)**
>
> **It is mine to avenge; I will repay. In due time their foot will slip; their day of disaster is near and their doom rushes upon them." (Deu 32:35)**
>
> **O LORD, the God who avenges, O God who avenges, shine forth. Rise up, O Judge of the earth; pay back to the proud what they deserve. (Psa 94:1-2)**
>
> **I will carry out great vengeance on them and punish them in my wrath. Then they will know that I am the LORD, when I take vengeance on them.'" (Ezek 25:17)**
>
> **I will take vengeance in anger and wrath upon the nations that have not obeyed me." (Micah 5:15)**
>
> **The LORD is a jealous and avenging God; the LORD takes vengeance and is filled with wrath. The LORD takes vengeance on his foes and maintains his wrath against his enemies. (Nahum 1:2)**

4 (21:23) **End Time—Judgment**: the sign of Jerusalem's being surrounded will be a time of woe, distress and wrath, death and captivity. Four pictures are painted to describe the awfulness of the hour.

1. Women who were pregnant and carrying small children would find it difficult to flee. They would be too slow to escape the onrushing judgment.

2. There would be great "distress" in the land. As the siege wore on, the predictions of Jesus were literally fulfilled. There was the killing and maiming of loved ones in war, the famine and pestilence and false deliverers (messiahs). There was the betrayal and murder of neighbors in stealing food and seeking the favor of authorities in order to survive. Everyone was fending for himself. There was the utter chaos and collapse of order. There was the pressure and tension, the suffering and pain that one's nation and people were about to be wiped off the face of the earth. Distress swept over the whole land.

3. The wrath of man (Rome) and the wrath of God fell upon the people.

4. An unbelievable number fell by the sword; over one million people died and about ninety-seven thousand were taken captive (see notes—Mt.24:7; 24:10; 24:11. See Josephus, Wars 5. 12:3; 6. 3:4; 6. 8:5.)

> *"It appears to me that the misfortunes of all men, from the beginning of the world, if they be compared to these of the Jews, are not so considerable as they were"* (Josephus, Wars. Preface 4).

In the end time, the world will experience great distresses, great tribulations—unparalleled in history. Note that Jesus did not describe the great trials beyond what He had already said in these verses. A quick glance at the great distess or tribulation period covered in Revelation will give some idea of the trials (see outlines and notes—all of the following. Cp. Dan.12:1-2.)

⇒ Thunderings, lightnings, and an earthquake (Rev.8:5; cp. 8:1-5).
⇒ Natural catastrophes (Rev.8:6-12).
⇒ Demonic-like locust or plagues (Rev.8:13-9:11).
⇒ Demonic-like army (Rev.9:12-21).
⇒ Nations angry, destroying the earth (Rev.11:18; cp. 11:14-19).
⇒ An evil political ruler (Rev.13:1-10).
⇒ A false religious ruler (Rev.13:11-18).
⇒ Terrible destruction and suffering both upon nature and men (Rev.16:1-21).
⇒ An evil, deceptive world power (Rev.17:1-18:24).

5 (21:24) **Gentiles, Times of**: the sign of Jerusalem's being surrounded will be a time numbered by the Gentiles. The Jewish nation was to be scattered and Jerusalem trodden down until "the times of the Gentiles are fulfilled." Note two things.

1. The word "fulfilled" (plerothosin) means that God is in control of the times. There is a purpose to "the times of the Gentiles" and to what has happened and is yet to happen to Israel. God is in control of history.

> **"The time has come," he said. "The kingdom of God is near. Repent and believe the good news!" (Mark 1:15)**
>
> **But when the time had fully come, God sent his Son, born of a woman, born under law, to redeem those under law, that we might receive the full rights of sons. Because you are sons, God sent the Spirit of his Son into our hearts, the Spirit who calls out, "Abba, Father." (Gal 4:4-6)**
>
> **To be put into effect when the times will have reached their fulfillment—to bring all things in heaven and on earth together under one head, even Christ. (Eph 1:10)**
>
> **For there is one God and one mediator between God and men, the man Christ Jesus, who gave himself as a ransom for all men—the testimony given in its proper time. (1 Tim 2:5-6)**
>
> **A faith and knowledge resting on the hope of eternal life, which God, who does not lie, promised before the beginning of time, and at his appointed season he brought his word to light through the preaching entrusted to me by the command of God our Savior, (Titus 1:2-3)**

2. There is to be an end to the Jews' captivity and to Jerusalem's being trodden down. The nation will be restored to its land. When? When "the times of the Gentiles are fulfilled." (See outline and notes, Israel's Restoration—Ro.11:25-36; note and DEEPER STUDY # 1—11:25-26 for more discussion.)

> **I do not want you to be ignorant of this mystery, brothers, so that you may not be conceited: Israel has experienced a hardening in part until the full number of the Gentiles has come in. And so all Israel will be saved, as it is written: "The deliverer will come from Zion; he will turn godlessness away from Jacob. And this is my covenant with them when I take away their sins." (Rom 11:25-27)**

	D. The Coming of Jesus: The Son of Man, 21:25-28 (Mt.24:29-31; Mk.13: 24-27)	apprehensive of what is coming on the world, for the heavenly bodies will be shaken.	& fearing d. Reason re-emphasized: Heavenly bodies shaken
		27 At that time they will see the Son of Man coming in a cloud with power and great glory.	2 **The actual coming of Jesus, the Son of Man**
1 **The signs of astronomical happenings & their results** a.Anguish of nations b. Oceans affected c. Men faint from terror	25 “There will be signs in the sun, moon and stars. On the earth, nations will be in anguish and perplexity at the roaring and tossing of the sea. 26 Men will faint from terror,	28 When these things begin to take place, stand up and lift up your heads, because your redemption is drawing near.”	3 **The great encouragement to the believer: Look up—your redemption is near**

DIVISION IX

THE SON OF MAN'S PROPHETIC SIGNS: HIS PREDICTION CONCERNING THE FATE OF JERUSALEM AND THE WORLD, 21:5-38

D. The Coming of Jesus: The Son of Man, 21:25-28

(21:25-28) **Introduction**: the Lord now begins to cover the most significant event yet to occur in human history: His own personal return. The language points toward the Lord's personal return to earth (Lk.21:27, 35). The point is this: there are signs that precede His coming, signs that will enable His followers to be prepared and strengthened to the utmost in endurance.

1. The signs of astronomical happenings and their results (v.25-26).
2. The actual coming of Jesus, the Son of Man (v.27).
3. The great encouragement to the believer: look up—your redemption is near (v.28).

1 (21:25-26) **End Time—Jesus Christ, Return—Heavenly Bodies—Outer Space**: the signs of astronomical happenings and their results. There shall be signs in the sun, moon, and stars. What will happen is described in both Matthew and Mark (Mt.24:29; Mk.13:24). Mark says...

- "The sun will be darkened."
- "The moon will not give its light."
- "The stars of heaven will fall from the sky."
- "The heavenly bodies will be shaken."

Very practically, such astronomical happenings occur now. The earth is sometimes darkened by dust from earthly catastrophes such as volcanic eruptions, wind storms, and smoke from huge fires. Of course, whatever darkens the sun, hides the light of the moon from earth. The stars, that is, meteorites of varying sizes, fall throughout space often. "The heavenly bodies" being shaken could mean the heavenly bodies outside our solar system that are called by the Bible "the heavenly array" (Dt.4:19).

Something should be mentioned about the power of the atom. The atom exploded on earth is powerful enough to darken the sun and moon from earth's view. Worldwide atomic warfare would cause so much dust and pollution it would be difficult for any man to see anything in outer space. But as the atom is known today, it could not affect the axis or rotation (the falling or shaking) of the sun and moon and stars unless there were to be an inter-galactical war of some sort way out in the future, and unless there was a power much greater than what we know today. This is not to say that atomic warfare will never happen. There will be wars and rumors of war as long as the earth stands. But what the Bible teaches is that God is going to end all things, not man. When the world ends, it will be God's ending it by His own will and act.

An extreme literalism needs to be avoided when interpreting these verses, for there is so much we do not know about the laws (powers) of nature and the forces God has put in motion throughout the universe. However, there is absolutely no reason for not understanding the Lord's words as actual or literal events.

What the present passage seems to mean is that the whole universe is going to be affected by Christ's coming to earth. The sun and moon, the stars and powers (laws) of heaven will be affected in the sense that they will *open up and receive Him* and serve notice that He is the Creator, the Son of Man, God's very own Son, who is now coming to earth in great power and glory. Imagine a spectacular universal fireworks display, and perhaps what Christ is saying is being pictured. A simple question is: Why would not everything, including the heavenly bodies, put on a display (that would be terrifying to man) when its Creator, the Son of God, returns?

The astronomical bodies are affected because of the *evil of men and the wrath of God.* The scene of falling stars (meteorites) will not be for man to witness a spectacular event; it will be to point to the Son of God, to His judgment falling upon the earth. Every man is going to know beyond any doubt that Jesus Christ is coming in all the power and the glory of God Himself. As Jesus said, "with power and great glory" He is coming. He is coming "that at the name of Jesus every knee should bow, in heaven and on earth and under the earth, and every tounge confess that Jesus Christ is Lord to the glory of God the Father (Ph.2:10-11). (See notes—Mt.24:29 for more discussion.)

The astronomical happenings will, of course, have devastating results upon earth. These results are the very point of Luke.

⇒ There will be distress and perplexity of nations. The picture is that of leaders' and governments' meeting and trying to figure out what is happening to the heavenly bodies in the sky above. However, they will not know nor be able to cope. They are perplexed and distressed, sensing the doom of the universe.

⇒ There will be the roaring effect upon the oceans and the upheaval of their waves and tides. This, of course, is to be expected since the oceans are controlled by the heavenly bodies.

⇒ There will be men fainting from terror; men will be gripped by fear, a desperate fear, sensing the end of the world is at hand. And note: the end *will* be at hand.

"But in those days, following that distress, "'the sun will be darkened, and the moon will not give its light; the stars will fall from the sky, and the heavenly bodies will be shaken.' (Mark 13:24-25)

But the day Lot left Sodom, fire and sulfur rained down from heaven and destroyed them all. "It will be just like this on the day the Son of Man is revealed. (Luke 17:29-30)

"There will be signs in the sun, moon and stars. On the earth, nations will be in anguish and perplexity at the roaring and tossing of the sea. Men will faint from terror, apprehensive of what is coming on the world, for the heavenly bodies will be shaken. (Luke 21:25-26)

I will show wonders in the heaven above and signs on the earth below, blood and fire and billows of smoke. The sun will be turned to darkness and the moon to blood before the coming of the great and glorious day of the Lord. (Acts 2:19-20)

I watched as he opened the sixth seal. There was a great earthquake. The sun turned black like sackcloth made of goat hair, the whole moon turned blood red, and the stars in the sky fell to earth, as late figs drop from a fig tree when shaken by a strong wind. The sky receded like a scroll, rolling up, and every mountain and island was removed from its place. Then the kings of the earth, the princes, the generals, the rich, the mighty, and every slave and every free man hid in caves and among the rocks of the mountains. They called to the mountains and the rocks, "Fall on us and hide us from the face of him who sits on the throne and from the wrath of the Lamb! For the great day of their wrath has come, and who can stand?" (Rev 6:12-17)

The stars of heaven and their constellations will not show their light. The rising sun will be darkened and the moon will not give its light. I will punish the world for its evil, the wicked for their sins. I will put an end to the arrogance of the haughty and will humble the pride of the ruthless. I will make man scarcer than pure gold, more rare than the gold of Ophir. Therefore I will make the heavens tremble; and the earth will shake from its place at the wrath of the LORD Almighty, in the day of his burning anger. (Isa 13:10-13)

Terror and pit and snare await you, O people of the earth. Whoever flees at the sound of terror will fall into a pit; whoever climbs out of the pit will be caught in a snare. The floodgates of the heavens are opened, the foundations of the earth shake. The earth is broken up, the earth is split asunder, the earth is thoroughly shaken. The earth reels like a drunkard, it sways like a hut in the wind; so heavy upon it is the guilt of its rebellion that it falls—never to rise again. In that day the LORD will punish the powers in the heavens above and the kings on the earth below. They will be herded together like prisoners bound in a dungeon; they will be shut up in prison and be punished after many days. (Isa 24:17-22)

I will show wonders in the heavens and on the earth, blood and fire and billows of smoke. The sun will be turned to darkness and the moon to blood before the coming of the great and dreadful day of the LORD. (Joel 2:30-31)

The sun and moon will be darkened, and the stars no longer shine. The LORD will roar from Zion and thunder from Jerusalem; the earth and the sky will tremble. But the LORD will be a refuge for his people, a stronghold for the people of Israel. (Joel 3:15-16)

2 (21:27) **Jesus Christ, Return**: the actual coming of Jesus, the Son of Man. There are three significant points in this verse.

1. It will be the Son of Man who comes. Jesus claimed to be the Son of Man, God's very own Son incarnate in human flesh as Perfect Man (see DEEPER STUDY # 3—Mt.8:20). In that day, there will be no doubt about who He is (cp. Mk.14:61-62). Right now He is recognized only by believers, but then His identity will be unmistakable: He is the Son of Man.

2. Every eye, all men, shall see Him return. This is what is meant by "they." Matthew actually says, "All the nations of the earth will mourn. They will see the Son of Man coming" (Mt.24:30). His return will be visible to every man on earth, and every man shall then acknowledge Him to be Lord, God's very own Son (Ph.2:9-11; cp. Rev.1:7).

3. He is coming "in a cloud with power and great glory." Picture the scene. The backdrop of heaven is pitch dark, without any major light from the sun and moon. And then, suddenly, as quickly as the flash of lightning, the most brilliant focus of light ever known to man appears. The Shekinah glory of God will shine in the person of Jesus Christ as He appears to the world. The Son of Man is there, in the clouds, having returned in power and great glory just as He said He would.

"Men of Galilee," they said, "why do you stand here looking into the sky? This same Jesus, who has been taken from you into heaven, will come back in the same way you have seen him go into heaven." (Acts 1:11)

And give relief to you who are troubled, and to us as well. This will happen when the Lord Jesus is revealed from heaven in blazing fire with his powerful angels. He will punish those who do not know God and do not obey the gospel of our Lord Jesus. They will be punished with everlasting destruction and shut out from the presence of the Lord and from the majesty of his power on the day he comes to be glorified in his holy people and to be marveled at among all those who have believed. This includes you, because you believed our testimony to you. (2 Th 1:7-10)

And then the lawless one will be revealed, whom the Lord Jesus will over

with the breath of his mouth and destroy by the splendor of his coming. (2 Th 2:8)

Look, he is coming with the clouds, and every eye will see him, even those who pierced him; and all the peoples of the earth will mourn because of him. So shall it be! Amen. (Rev 1:7)

I saw heaven standing open and there before me was a white horse, whose rider is called Faithful and True. With justice he judges and makes war. His eyes are like blazing fire, and on his head are many crowns. He has a name written on him that no one knows but he himself. He is dressed in a robe dipped in blood, and his name is the Word of God. The armies of heaven were following him, riding on white horses and dressed in fine linen, white and clean. Out of his mouth comes a sharp sword with which to strike down the nations. "He will rule them with an iron scepter." He treads the winepress of the fury of the wrath of God Almighty. On his robe and on his thigh he has this name written: KING OF KINGS AND LORD OF LORDS. (Rev 19:11-16)

3 (21:28) **Jesus Christ, Return**: the great encouragement to the believer. What a glorious hope the believer has! When the terrible events come in the heavens and upon the earth, he is...

- not to be distressed and perplexed, as the nations will be.
- not to fear and have a failing heart, as men will have.

Believers are not to be discouraged, but encouraged. They are to look up and lift up their heads, for their redemption draweth near. The consummation of their salvation and hope is about to take place.

It teaches us to say "No" to ungodliness and worldly passions, and to live self-controlled, upright and godly lives in this present age, while we wait for the blessed hope—the glorious appearing of our great God and Savior, Jesus Christ, who gave himself for us to redeem us from all wickedness and to purify for himself a people that are his very own, eager to do what is good. (Titus 2:12-14)

In whom we have redemption, the forgiveness of sins. (Col 1:14)

Once you were alienated from God and were enemies in your minds because of your evil behavior. But now he has reconciled [redeemed] you by Christ's physical body through death to [eternally] present you holy in his sight, without blemish and free from accusation— (Col 1:21-22)

While we wait for the blessed hope—the glorious appearing of our great God and Savior, Jesus Christ, who gave himself for us to redeem us [eternally] from all wickedness and to purify for himself a people that are his very own, eager to do what is good. (Titus 2:13-14)

For this reason Christ is the mediator of a new covenant, that those who are called may receive the promised eternal inheritance—now that he has died as a ransom to set them free from the sins committed under the first covenant. (Heb 9:15)

And they sang a new song: "You are worthy to take the scroll and to open its seals, because you were slain, and with your blood you purchased men for God from every tribe and language and people and nation. You have made them to be a kingdom and priests to serve our God, and they will reign on the earth." (Rev 5:9-10)

A song of ascents. I lift up my eyes to the hills— where does my help come from? (Psa 121:1)

Praise the LORD. Praise, O servants of the LORD, praise the name of the LORD. (Psa 113:1)

"To whom will you compare me? Or who is my equal?" says the Holy One. Lift your eyes and look to the heavens: Who created all these? He who brings out the starry host one by one, and calls them each by name. Because of his great power and mighty strength, not one of them is missing. (Isa 40:25-26)

Outline	Text	Text (cont.)	Outline
	E. The Parable of the Fig Tree: The Signs are Clearly Seen, 21:29-33 (Mt.24:32-35; Mk.13: 28-34)	and know that summer is near. 31 Even so, when you see these things happening, you know that the kingdom of God is near.	b. Will show the Kingdom of God is near
		32 "I tell you the truth, this generation will certainly not pass away until all these things have happened.	**2 The signs will occur within one generation**
1 The signs can be seen—are discernable a. Will be seen just as the leaves of a fig tree are seen when they first appear	29 He told them this parable: "Look at the fig tree and all the trees. 30 When they sprout leaves, you can see for yourselves	33 Heaven and earth will pass away, but my words will never pass away.	**3 The signs are sure—eternally set**

DIVISION IX

THE SON OF MAN'S PROPHETIC SIGNS: HIS PREDICTION CONCERNING THE FATE OF JERUSALEM AND THE WORLD, 21:5-38

E. The Parable of the Fig Tree: The Signs are Clearly Seen, 21:29-33

(21:29-33) **Introduction**: when will Christ return to earth? The signs covered in v.5-28 will be clearly seen. The day and hour are known only by God, but believers are to be ready. There will be no excuse for being caught off guard.

1. The signs can be seen—are discernable (v.29-31).
2. The signs will occur within one generation (v.32).
3. The signs are sure—eternally set (v.33).

1 (21:29-31) **End Time—Jesus Christ, Return**: the signs can be seen; they are discernable. Jesus said two things.

1. The signs are to be just as clear as the leaves appearing on a fig tree. Note exactly what Jesus said.
   a. Behold the fig tree and all the other trees. Observe and study this truth. If a person is not looking and thinking about the fact, he will miss the truth. Looking, observing, studying, thinking about the fact is essential in order to see the truth.
   b. When the leaves shoot forth, if a person sees and notices them, he *knows* something. Summer is *now* near.

2. The signs will show that the Kingdom of God is near, that Jesus Christ is ready to return to earth and set up the Kingdom of God (see DEEPER STUDY # 3, Kingdom of God—Mt.19:23-24). Note that Jesus used the word "know." When the signs are seen, believers are to *know* that the end is at hand and not question, wonder, doubt, disbelieve, or fall away.

⇒ When believers see false messiahs and prophets arise, they can *know* that a large number of the lost and carnal will be tragically deceived.

⇒ When believers see conflict of nations, they can *know* terrible times lie ahead.

⇒ When believers see natural disasters, they can *know* that the worst periods of human suffering ever experienced are about to occur.

⇒ When believers see intensified persecution, they can *know* God is about to straighten out the injustices and crimes of men.

⇒ When believers see armies amassing against Jerusalem, they can *know* the time of the Gentiles is about to end and Israel restored once-for-all.

⇒ When believers see astronomical happenings, they can *know* the Lord's return is at hand.

The point is strikingly clear: signs are just that, signs. And signs do at least four things.

1. They point toward an object, helping us to see the object (Christ) and to anticipate knowing the object (Christ).
2. They focus attention upon an object (Christ). Signs keep our thoughts upon Christ and His glorious return.
3. They give direction, keeping us on the right track, helping to guard and protect us from going astray.
4. They give assurance and confidence, assurance that we will not be caught off guard and taken by surprise.

2 (21:32) **End Time—Jesus Christ, Return**: the signs will occur in one generation. Jesus warned: the events will occur rapidly. They will happen in one generation. Just what is meant by "generation" is often disputed, but it must *always* be kept in mind that the disciples had asked two questions: one about Jerusalem's destruction and one about the end of the world. In answering their questions, Jesus nowhere drew a definite line between the two questions. The signs and events that precede one shall precede the other. Therefore, just as the signs and destruction of Jerusalem took place within a generation, the signs and destruction of the world will also occur within a generation. (See DEEPER STUDY # 2, pt.2—Mt.24:1-31 for more discussion.)

3 (21:33) **End Time—Jesus Christ, Return**: the signs are sure, eternally set. The events are sure and irrevocable. Jesus was definite about what He had said. "Heaven and earth will pass away, but my words will never pass away." Note two things.

1. Heaven and earth shall pass away. Jesus was saying they were actually going to be done away with (2 Pt.3:10-11).

2. All that He had said—all about the great distress or tribulation and His return—would happen. The great tribulation and His return were more sure than heaven and earth.

In the eyes of men, it has been a long, long time since Jesus spoke these words; and an innumerable list of events have happened. Therefore, they assume the whole idea of the second coming is a fable, the figment of hopeful imagination. God knew this would happen.

> **First of all, you must understand that in the last days scoffers will come, scoffing and following their own evil desires. They will say, "Where is this 'coming' he promi-**

ised? Ever since our fathers died, everything goes on as it has since the beginning of creation." But do not forget this one thing, dear friends: With the Lord a day is like a thousand years, and a thousand years are like a day. The Lord is not slow in keeping his promise, as some understand slowness. He is patient with you, not wanting anyone to perish, but everyone to come to repentance. But the day of the Lord will come like a thief. The heavens will disappear with a roar; the elements will be destroyed by fire, and the earth and everything in it will be laid bare. Since everything will be destroyed in this way, what kind of people ought you to be? You ought to live holy and godly lives as you look forward to the day of God and speed its coming. That day will bring about the destruction of the heavens by fire, and the elements will melt in the heat. But in keeping with his promise we are looking forward to a new heaven and a new earth, the home of righteousness. (2 Pet 3:3-4, 8-13)

Three things are certain to happen in human history:
⇒ "the beginning of birth pains [sorrows]" (Mt.24:8).
⇒ "the great distress [tribulation], unequealed from the beginning of the world" ((Mt.24:21).
⇒ "the Son of Man coming in a cloud with power and great glory" (Lk.21:27).

Heaven and earth shall pass away but not the words Jesus spoke, not what He said would happen. What He said would happen will happen. The three events are certain.

But the day of the Lord will come like a thief. The heavens will disappear with a roar; the elements will be destroyed by fire, and the earth and everything in it will be laid bare. (2 Pet 3:10)

Then I saw a new heaven and a new earth, for the first heaven and the first earth had passed away, and there was no longer any sea. (Rev 21:1)

The world and its desires pass away, but the man who does the will of God lives forever. (1 John 2:17)

Those who use the things of the world, as if not engrossed in them. For this world in its present form is passing away. (1 Cor 7:31)

So we fix our eyes not on what is seen, but on what is unseen. For what is seen is temporary, but what is unseen is eternal. (2 Cor 4:18)

In the beginning you laid the foundations of the earth, and the heavens are the work of your hands. They will perish, but you remain; they will all wear out like a garment. Like clothing you will change them and they will be discarded. (Psa 102:25-26)

The earth dries up and withers, the world languishes and withers, the exalted of the earth languish. (Isa 24:4)

All the stars of the heavens will be dissolved and the sky rolled up like a scroll; all the starry host will fall like withered leaves from the vine, like shriveled figs from the fig tree. (Isa 34:4)

Lift up your eyes to the heavens, look at the earth beneath; the heavens will vanish like smoke, the earth will wear out like a garment and its inhabitants die like flies. But my salvation will last forever, my righteousness will never fail. (Isa 51:6)

And I'll say to myself, "You have plenty of good things laid up for many years. Take life easy; eat, drink and be merry."' "But God said to him, 'You fool! This very night your life will be demanded from you. Then who will get what you have prepared for yourself?' (Luke 12:19-20)

	F. The Warning: Watch & Pray for The Day of Jesus' Return, 21:34-36 (Mt.24:42-44; Mk.13: 35-37)
1 It demands taking care a. By not engaging in worldliness 1) Partying & drunkenness 2) Anxieties of life b. Reason: Lest the believer be caught unaware—snared—trapped[DS1]	34 "Be careful, or your hearts will be weighed down with dissipation, drunkenness and the anxieties of life, and that day will close on you unexpectedly like a trap. 35 For it will come upon all those who live on the face of the whole earth.
2 It demands watching & praying always a. To be counted worthy b. To escape the things coming to earth c. To stand justified	36 Be always on the watch, and pray that you may be able to escape all that is about to happen, and that you may be able to stand before the Son of Man."

DIVISION IX

THE SON OF MAN'S PROPHETIC SIGNS: HIS PREDICTION CONCERNING THE FATE OF JERUSALEM AND THE WORLD, 21:5-38

F. The Warning: Watch and Pray for the Day of Jesus' Return, 21:34-36

(21:34-36) **Introduction**: the universe is to suffer much in coming days. Sometime out in the future, the world will experience disasters and calamities as never before. There will be an increase...

- in wars and conflicts of nations (v.9-10).
- in natural disasters such as earthquakes, famines, disease (v.11).
- in persecution of believers (v.12-19).
- in attacks upon Israel (v.20-24).
- in astronomical happenings (v.25-26).
- in distress of nations (v.25).
- in ocean disturbances (v.25).
- in men's hearts' failing and fearing (v.26).

Jesus warned the believer. The believer must watch and pray for that day.

1. It demands taking care (v.34-35).
2. It demands watching and praying always (v.36).

1 (21:34-35) **End Time—Jesus Christ, Return—Indulgence—Drunkenness—Worldliness**: that day (the end time and the day of the Lord's return) demands taking heed. The word "careful" (prosexete) means to give attention, to focus one's mind, to guard, to beware, to take care. Note the believer is to *be careful*, that is, to guard his life. *How*? By not engaging in worldliness. His heart is not to be weighed down (barethosin): heavy, burdened, overcharged overloaded, filled up, indulged. Three worldly acts in particular are mentioned.

1. Dissipation or careless ease (kraipale). The words mean to be lighthearted, silly, frivolous, giddy. Medically, it referred to drunken nausea or headaches. It is the kind of lightheartedness, silliness, frivolity, and giddiness that comes from partying and drinking. It is the loose, giddy, suggestive movements and talk that take place...

- at parties
- at social gatherings
- on dates
- behind closed doors
- at luncheons & dinner engagements
- at dances
- at clubs
- on business trips
- in the dark (cp. 1 Th.5:5-10)

2. Drunkenness (methei). The word comes from the word meaning *wine* (methu). It means to be drunk with wine (or any other strong drink or drug), to be intoxicated. Drinking wine (or any other strong drink or drug) has several bad effects:

⇒ It indulges the lust, the appetite of the flesh.
⇒ It *loosens up* a person's moral restraints and allows the indulging of sexual and immoral cravings.
⇒ It dulls the mind to responsibility.
⇒ It burdens the heart and conscience and causes guilt, at least until a person becomes hardened in his sin.
⇒ It deadens feelings for spouses and loved ones, causing distance and withdrawal (such is seldom, if ever, regained).
⇒ It harms the body.

Let us behave decently, as in the daytime, not in orgies and drunkenness [revelling, carousing, partying, not in sexual immorality and debauchery [sensuality, licentiousness], not in dissension and jealousy. (Rom 13:13)

The acts of the sinful nature are obvious: sexual immorality, impurity and debauchery; and envy; drunkenness, orgies, and the like. I warn you, as I did before, that those who live like this will not inherit the kingdom of God. (Gal 5:19, 21)

Do not get drunk on wine, which leads to debauchery. Instead, be filled with the Spirit. (Eph 5:18)

3. Anxieties or cares of this life. This means to indulge one's cravings for more and more of the things of this world. Man too often gives his attention and focuses his mind upon more and more of this world. *He desires far more than what he needs*, more...

- food and delicacies
- clothes and the latest styles
- houses and furnishings
- property and holdings
- cars and other vehicles
- free time and recreation
- money and wealth
- recognition and esteem

For you have spent enough time in the past doing what pagans choose to do—living in debauchery, lust, drunkenness, orgies, carousing and detestable idolatry. They think it strange that you do not plunge with them into the same flood of dissipation, and they heap abuse on you. (1 Pet 4:3-4)

But these men blaspheme in matters they do not understand. They are like brute beasts, creatures of instinct, born only to be caught and destroyed, and like beasts they too will perish. They will be paid back with harm for the harm they have done. Their idea of pleasure is to carouse in broad daylight. They are blots and blemishes, reveling in their pleasures while they feast with you. (2 Pet 2:12-13)

Why is the believer to be careful, to guard himself against these things? The point is crucial. The believer can be focusing upon the things and possessions of the world so much that he is caught unaware, snared and entrapped in the end time. That day, the day of the Lord's return, can catch him unexpectedly and unprepared.

For in the days before the flood, people were eating and drinking, marrying and giving in marriage, up to the day Noah entered the ark; and they knew nothing about what would happen until the flood came and took them all away. That is how it will be at the coming of the Son of Man. (Mat 24:38-39)

Moreover, no man knows when his hour will come: As fish are caught in a cruel net, or birds are taken in a snare, so men are trapped by evil times that fall unexpectedly upon them. (Eccl 9:12)

DEEPER STUDY # 1

(21:34)**Trap—Snare—End Time—Jesus Christ, Return—World, Judgment Upon**: the word "trap" (pagis) means to snare as in a net. That day, the end time, is going to catch the whole world unprepared. The terrible events and calamities of the end times are going to fall upon the earth and entrap all. All who dwell upon the earth shall be caught in the disastrous events, the destruction and devastation, distress and misery, misfortune and loss, suffering and affliction. (See outline and notes—Lk.21:5-33.)

Jesus warned the believer. He must "be careful," for in the end time the world will experience great tribulations unparalleled in history. A quick glance at the great distress or tribulation period covered in Revelation will give some idea of the trials (see outlines and notes—all of the following. Cp. Dan.12:1-2.)

⇒ Thunderings, lightnings, and an earthquake (Rev.8:5; cp. 8:1-5).
⇒ Natural catastrophes (Rev. 8:6-12).
⇒ Demonic-like locust or plagues (Rev.8:13-9:11).
⇒ Demonic-like army (Rev.9:12-21).
⇒ Nations angry and destroying the earth (Rev.11:18; cp. 11:14-19).
⇒ An evil political ruler (Rev.13:1-10).
⇒ A false and evil religious ruler (Rev.13:11-18).
⇒ Terrible destruction and suffering both upon nature and men (Rev.16:1-21).
⇒ An evil, deceptive world power (Rev.17:1-18:24).

2 (21:36) **End Times—Watching—Praying—Believers, Duties**: that day (the end time and the day of the Lord's return) demands watching and praying *always*. The word "watch" (agrupneite) means to be sleepless, awake, on guard. It means a spirit of being wakeful, of being restless, of guarding.

Praying always means the believer is to live in a spirit of prayer...

- praying all day, as he walks throughout the day.
- praying on all occasions and about everything.
- praying at appointed times, times set aside for nothing but prayer and devotions or quiet times.

There are three reasons why the believer is to watch and pray.

1. Watching and praying cause God to count the believer "worthy." The man who watches and prays for the Lord's return truly believes in the Lord, and God takes that man's belief and counts it worthy. Note: God does not *make* the man worthy; He counts the man worthy. The man's faith, his watching and praying, are counted as righteousness. (See note, Justification—Lk.20:35; DEEPER STUDY # 2—Ro.4:22; 5:1. Cp. Ro.4:5 and 4:1-3; 4:1-25.)

2. Watching and praying cause the believer to escape the things coming to earth (see DEEPER STUDY # 1, Snare—Lk.21:35). This can mean...

- to escape the presence of the coming judgments altogether (by being raptured away).
- to escape the sufferings of the judgments (by being supernaturally protected; for example, Israel was protected during the Egyptian plagues, Exodus 5:1f).

3. Watching and praying cause the believer to stand justified before the Son of Man (see DEEPER STUDY # 3, Son of Man—Mt.8:20). The picture is that the faithful believer will have no fear or dread, no apprehension or hesitation in facing the Son of Man. He will stand before his Lord...

- justified.
- ready to be "transormed just like His glorious body" (Ph.3:21).
- ready "to be conformed to His image" (Ro.8:29).
- ready to "see the face of the Father" (Mt.18:10).
- ready to "serve Him [God] day and night in His temple" or world (Rev.7:15).

"Therefore keep watch, because you do not know the day or the hour. (Mat 25:13)

It will be good for those servants whose master finds them watching when he comes. I tell you the truth, he will dress

himself to serve, will have them recline at the table and will come and wait on them. (Luke 12:37)

You are all sons of the light and sons of the day. We do not belong to the night or to the darkness. So then, let us not be like others, who are asleep, but let us be alert and self-controlled. (1 Th 5:5-6)

I am coming soon. Hold on to what you have, so that no one will take your crown. (Rev 3:11)

"Behold, I come like a thief! Blessed is he who stays awake and keeps his clothes with him, so that he may not go naked and be shamefully exposed." (Rev 16:15)

"Watch and pray so that you will not fall into temptation. The spirit is willing, but the body is weak." (Mat 26:41)

So, if you think you are standing firm, be careful that you don't fall! (1 Cor 10:12)

Devote yourselves to prayer, being watchful and thankful. (Col 4:2)

Be self-controlled and alert. Your enemy the devil prowls around like a roaring lion looking for someone to devour. (1 Pet 5:8)

	G. The Daily Ministry of Jesus, 21:37-38
1 The daytime: Jesus taught in the temple	37 Each day Jesus was teaching at the temple, and each
2 The night: Jesus was alone with God[DS1]	evening he went out to spend the night on the hill called the Mount of Olives,
3 The morning: Jesus began early in the morning	38 And all the people came early in the morning to hear him at the temple.

DIVISION IX

THE SON OF MAN'S PROPHETIC SIGNS: HIS PREDICTION CONCERNING THE FATE OF JERUSALEM AND THE WORLD, 21:5-38

G. The Daily Ministry of Jesus, 21:37-38

(21:37-38) **Introduction**: this passage very simply tells how Jesus spent His days and nights during the last days of His life. The picture is both interesting and informative.

1. The daytime: Jesus taught in the temple (v.37).
2. The night: Jesus was alone with God (v.37).
3. The morning: Jesus began early in the morning (v.38).

1 (21:37) **Jesus Christ, Teaching**: during the daytime Jesus taught in the temple. Several facts are seen in this point.

1. Jesus was a tireless teacher. He taught not only on Sunday, but every day of the week. He taught at every opportunity, and He made as many opportunities as He could. He taught all through the day. He sought the chance to teach, using day-to-day events and experiences to teach. He never tired of teaching even in the face of exhaustion. (Cp. all that happened during this last week of His life, beginning with the Triumphal Entry. Despite the pressure, tension, and fatigue, He continued to teach.)

> **"Why were you searching for me?" he asked. "Didn't you know I had to be in my Father's house?" (Luke 2:49)**
> **Every day he was teaching at the temple. But the chief priests, the teachers of the law and the leaders among the people were trying to kill him. (Luke 19:47)**
> **"My food," said Jesus, "is to do the will of him who sent me and to finish his work. (John 4:34)**
> **As long as it is day, we must do the work of him who sent me. Night is coming, when no one can work. (John 9:4)**

2. Jesus was a fearless teacher. The authorities were seeking to arrest and kill Him. The opposition was constant: questioning, arguing, plotting, and threatening. However, He did not flee, nor did He retaliate. He simply went about fulfilling God's will, teaching those who so desperately needed God's message.

> **Every day he was teaching at the temple. But the chief priests, the teachers of the law and the leaders among the people were trying to kill him. Yet they could not find any way to do it, because all the people hung on his words. (Luke 19:47-48)**

3. Jesus was a faithful teacher, ever meeting the needs of people. Men needed the gospel of God, needed to hear the glorious message of the Kingdom of God. The only way they could ever know how to live day by day was to be taught. Christ wanted to grasp every opportunity He could before He departed this world. (See DEEPER STUDY # 3, Kingdom of God—Mt.19:23-24.)

> **What I mean, brothers, is that the time is short. From now on those who have wives should live as if they had none; (1 Cor 7:29)**
> **Making the most of every opportunity, because the days are evil. (Eph 5:16)**

4. Jesus was a teacher of conviction. Note where He taught: in the temple. The temple was corrupt, being misused and abused and made into a center of commercialism. Yet, the temple was supposed to be God's house of prayer. Jesus refused to desert it; He used the temple as it should be used, making it the center for teaching the gospel of God.

> **His disciples remembered that it is written: "Zeal for your house will consume me." (John 2:17)**

2 (21:37) **Devotion—Mount of Olives—Preparation**: during the night, Jesus got all alone with God. This is a striking point, for it is information about our Lord that deeply moves and touches the heart. "Each evening, He went out, to spend the night on a hill called the Mount of Olives." He was facing so much, the final preparation of His disciples and His own final hours on earth, and He was facing it all in just *one week's time*. He needed time alone with God, a very special time, for He needed great strength, and the source of His strength was God. Every muscle in His body and every thought of His mind must have been craving for God's presence and wisdom and strength. He needed...

- to make maximum use of time in teaching the disciples, teaching exactly what they needed in these final hours.
- to have His own heart prepared to the maximum, ready to bear all the punishment of sin that was to be laid upon Him.

> **Very early in the morning, while it was still dark, Jesus got up, left the house and**

went off to a solitary place, where he prayed. (Mark 1:35)

After leaving them, he went up on a mountainside to pray. (Mark 6:46)

But Jesus often withdrew to lonely places and prayed. (Luke 5:16)

Once when Jesus was praying in private and his disciples were with him, he asked them, "Who do the crowds say I am?" (Luke 9:18)

He withdrew about a stone's throw beyond them, knelt down and prayed, (Luke 22:41)

He will call upon me, and I will answer him; I will be with him in trouble, I will deliver him and honor him. (Psa 91:15)

'Call to me and I will answer you and tell you great and unsearchable things you do not know.' (Jer 33:3)

In the same way, the Spirit helps us in our weakness. We do not know what we ought to pray for, but the Spirit himself intercedes for us with groans that words cannot express. (Rom 8:26)

DEEPER STUDY # 1

(21:37) **Mount of Olives or Olivet**: the mountain range was a little more than one-half mile from the city limits of Jerusalem. The range of mountains lie on the east of Jerusalem and stretch only about one or two miles across. The mountain range was loved by Jesus. It was...

- where Jesus often resorted (Lk.22:39).
- where Jesus often spent the night when in Jerusalem (Jn.7:53-8:1).
- where Jesus spent the nights of His last week on earth—praying and seeking God (Lk.29:37).
- where Jesus first went when He approached Jerusalem to face His last week on earth (Mt.21:1f; Mk.11:1f).
- where the great sermon on the end time was preached (Mt.24:3f; Mk.13:3f).
- where (at the descent) the Triumphal Entry began (Lk.19:37f).
- where Jesus' terrible agony in the Garden of Gethsemane took place. The Garden of Gethsemane was on the side of the mountain (Mt.26:30f; Mk.14:26).
- where the ascension took place (Acts 1:12).

3 (21:38) **Teaching—Prayer**: Jesus began early in the morning. Note four significant facts.

1. The first thing Jesus did after prayer and spending time alone with God was teach.

2. Jesus spent time alone with God before teaching. The *presence and power* of God was necessary before teaching.

In the morning, O LORD, you hear my voice; in the morning I lay my requests before you and wait in expectation. (Psa 5:3)

Evening, morning and noon I cry out in distress, and he hears my voice. (Psa 55:17)

Awake, my soul! Awake, harp and lyre! I will awaken the dawn. (Psa 57:8)

I rise before dawn and cry for help; I have put my hope in your word. (Psa 119:147)

Night and day we pray most earnestly that we may see you again and supply what is lacking in your faith. (1 Th 3:10; cp. Dan.6:10)

3. The first duty of Jesus after prayer was teaching the gospel. He did not seek relaxation, recreation, fellowship or some social function. After praying, He sought to teach the message of the glorious gospel.

Jesus replied, "Let us go somewhere else—to the nearby villages—so I can preach there also. That is why I have come." (Mark 1:38)

But he said, "I must preach the good news of the kingdom of God to the other towns also, because that is why I was sent." (Luke 4:43)

4. The people hungered and thirsted for righteousness. Note the word "all." All the people came early in the morning to hear Him.

Thought 1. What a difference between the people of that day and other generations! Why? Is it because people's hearts no longer cry out for righteousness? Or, is it because ministers do not seek the face of God *all night* in prayer like Jesus was doing?

Blessed are you who hunger now, for you will be satisfied. Blessed are you who weep now, for you will laugh. (Luke 6:21)

But whoever drinks the water I give him will never thirst. Indeed, the water I give him will become in him a spring of water welling up to eternal life." (John 4:14)

On the last and greatest day of the Feast, Jesus stood and said in a loud voice, "If anyone is thirsty, let him come to me and drink. (John 7:37)

All my longings lie open before you, O Lord; my sighing is not hidden from you. (Psa 38:9)

For he satisfies the thirsty and fills the hungry with good things. (Psa 107:9)

"Come, all you who are thirsty, come to the waters; and you who have no money, come, buy and eat! Come, buy wine and milk without money and without cost. (Isa 55:1)

Outline	Scripture	Scripture (cont.)	Outline
	CHAPTER 22 **X. THE SON OF MAN'S LAST SUPPER: HIS TRAITOR, INSTRUCTIONS AND WARNINGS, 22:1-38** **A. The Plot Against Jesus, 22:1-6** (Mt.26:14-16; Mk.14: 1-2, 10-11)	the teachers of the law were looking for some way to get rid of Jesus, for they were afraid of the people.	a. Used deception b. Feared the people
		3 Then Satan entered Judas, called Iscariot, one of the Twelve.	**3 Satan: Used an available disciple**
		4 And Judas went to the chief priests and the officers of the temple guard and discussed with them how he might be- tray Jesus. 5 They were delighted and agreed to give him money. 6 He consented, and watched for an opportunity to hand Je- sus over to them when no crowd was present.	**4 A covetous man: Went his own way** a. Was a professing disciple b. Communed with world c. Made the enemies of Jesus glad d. Coveted money e. Made a covenant with the world
1 The Passover is tied to the death of Christ[DS1]	Now the Feast of Unleavened Bread, called the Passover, was approaching,		
2 The unbelieving religionists[DS2]	2 And the chief priests and		

DIVISION X

THE SON OF MAN'S LAST SUPPER: HIS TRAITOR, INSTRUCTIONS AND WARNINGS, 22:1-38

A. The Plot Against Jesus, 22:1-6

(22:1-6) **Introduction—Jesus Christ, Opposition**: Jesus Christ was seriously opposed by formidable foes. The religionists rejected Him lest they lose the favor, security, and position of the world. Satan opposed His work of salvation lest men give their lives and worship to God. Men rebelled against His demand for self-denial, for the commitment of all one is and has to the cause of God.

1. The Passover is tied to the death of Christ (v.1).
2. The unbelieving religionists (v.2).
3. Satan: used an available man (v.3).
4. A covetous man: went his own way (v.4-6).

1 (22:1) **Passover**: the Passover is tied to the death of Christ. This passage begins the final stage of Jesus' life before He was killed. In dramatic fashion Luke sets the stage for what was coming. He mentions the Passover and then points out those who are plotting Jesus' death, two scenes as opposite from one another as can be imagined. The Passover was a feast, a joyous and festive occasion. It was a feast when all of God's people were to be celebrating God's glorious deliverance of Israel out of the bondage of Egypt. However, during the very days of this joyous celebration, Jesus' murder was being plotted. Tragically, it was being plotted by religionists, the very people who should have been taking the lead in the Passover. On the one hand is the celebration of deliverance, the saving of life; on the other hand is the plotting of death, the taking of life. This passage deliberately sets the stage for what was to come. (See DEEPER STUDY # 1, Passover—Mt.26:2.)

DEEPER STUDY # 1
(22:1) **Feast of Unleavened Bread**: this feast is another name for the Passover Feast (see Lev.23:5-8; Lk.22:1). However on the first day of the Passover week, the Feast of Unleavened Bread had special significance. It was the day that all preparations were made to celebrate the Passover. (See DEEPER STUDY # 1—Mt.26:2; cp. Ex.12:1-51, esp. v.11-28 for the background of the Passover.) Preparations included securing the lamb and taking it to the temple to be sacrificed. Preparations also included securing the items of food and drink necessary for the Passover and arranging the room for the Feast. However, there were two preparations from which the Feast of Unleavened Bread received its name.

1. There was the baking of unleavened bread, of bread without yeast. On the night of the Passover, God had told Israel to make final preparations for being delivered from Egyptian bondage. However, the Israelites did not have time to bake bread with yeast. They had to bake bread without yeast because of the time it takes for bread with yeast to rise. The Feast of Unleavened Bread is simply one of the Passover ceremonies by which Israel remembered God's glorious deliverance of their forefathers from Egyptian bondage. (See DEEPER STUDY # 1—Mt.26:2.)

2. There was a ceremony by which all yeast within the house had to be removed. It must be remembered that yeast was a symbol of evil to the Jews. In removing all yeast, they were picturing the need for putting evil out of their lives and household. There was an actual search made throughout the rooms of the house. The people looked for any crumb of yeast that might have fallen upon the floor and under or between some furniture. Whatever yeast was found, no matter how small a crumb, it was removed from the house. By removing all yeast from their households, the Jews were saying they wanted to be included among the faithful of their forefathers. They wanted to be counted as the faithful who purified and cleansed their lives and households for the journey of deliverance from bondage and slavery.

2 (22:2) **Religionists**: the first opponents to Jesus were unbelieving religionists. Luke paints a dramatic picture. While the people were in the streets openly preparing to praise God for His delivering power and the saving of life, the religionists were behind closed doors plotting to murder the very One who had come to be their great Deliverer (Savior). Note two facts.

1. The religionists plotted to use deception and lies (Mt.26:4; Mk.14:1).

"Their throats are open graves; their tongues practice deceit." "The poison of vipers is on their lips." (Rom 3:13)

Do you not know that the wicked will not inherit the kingdom of God? Do not be deceived: Neither the sexually immoral nor idolaters nor adulterers nor male prostitutes nor homosexual offenders (1 Cor 6:9)

Do not be deceived: God cannot be mocked. A man reaps what he sows. (Gal 6:7)

Let no one deceive you with empty words, for because of such things God's wrath comes on those who are disobedient. (Eph 5:6)

Dear children, do not let anyone lead you astray. He who does what is right is righteous, just as he is righteous. He who does what is sinful is of the devil, because the devil has been sinning from the beginning. The reason the Son of God appeared was to destroy the devil's work. (1 John 3:7-8)

Do not merely listen to the word, and so deceive yourselves. Do what it says. (James 1:22)

For in his own eyes he flatters himself too much to detect or hate his sin. (Psa 36:2)

All a man's ways seem innocent to him, but motives are weighed by the LORD. (Prov 16:2)

All a man's ways seem right to him, but the LORD weighs the heart. (Prov 21:2)

those who are pure in their own eyes and yet are not cleansed of their filth; (Prov 30:12)

Many a man claims to have unfailing love, but a faithful man who can find? (Prov 20:6)

Friend deceives friend, and no one speaks the truth. They have taught their tongues to lie; they weary themselves with sinning. (Jer 9:5)

The heart is deceitful above all things and beyond cure. Who can understand it? (Jer 17:9)

2. The reason they sought to get rid of Jesus was because they feared the people. This means that they feared both losing the support of the people and the reaction of the people against them if the people knew they were killing Jesus. (See DEEPER STUDY # 2, Religionists—Lk.22:2 for more discussion and application as to why the religionists opposed Jesus.)

DEEPER STUDY # 2

(22:2) **Religionists**: the religionists' conflict with Jesus is often misunderstood. This is because so much of the conflict had to do with rules and regulations that seem petty and meaningless to modern minds (cp. Mk.2:23-28; 3:1-6; 3:22-30. See notes—Mt.12:1-8; note and DEEPER STUDY # 1—12:10; note—15:1-20; DEEPER STUDY # 2—15:6-9.) Four facts will help in understanding why the conflicts happened and were life threatening, ending in the murder of Jesus Christ.

1. The Jewish nation had been held together by their religious beliefs. Through the centuries the Jewish people had been conquered by army after army, and by the millions they had been deported and scattered over the world. Even in the day of Jesus, they were enslaved by Rome. Their religion was the binding force that kept Jews together, in particular...

⇒ tinctive people (who worshipped the only true and living God).

⇒ their rules governing the Sabbath and the temple.

This belief and these rules protected them from alien beliefs and from being swallowed up by other peoples through intermarriage. Their religion was what maintained their distinctiveness as a people and as a nation.

Jewish leaders knew this. They knew that their religion was the binding force that held their nation together. Therefore, they opposed anyone or anything that threatened or attempted to break the laws of their religion.

2. The religionists were men of deep conviction. They were strong in their beliefs. Therefore, they became steeped in religious belief and practice, law and custom, tradition and ritual, ceremony and liturgy, rules and regulations. To break any law or rule governing any belief or practice was a serious offense, for it taught loose behavior. And loose behavior, once it had spread enough, would weaken their religion which was the binding force that held their people together. Therefore, Jesus was committing a great offense by breaking their law. He was weakening their religion and threatening their nation.

3. The religionists were men who had profession, position, recognition, esteem, livelihood and security. Anyone who went contrary to what they believed and taught was a threat to all they had. Some religionists felt that Jesus was a threat to them. Every time Jesus broke their law, He was undermining their very position and security.

4. The religionists were exposed by Jesus. In order for the religionists and the people to know the truth, Jesus had to point out where they were wrong and what they needed to do to get right with God. Both the sin of men and the truth of God had to be proclaimed. The religionists could not take it. They refused to accept the fact that they were unacceptable to God. They were, after all, the religious of the day, the very ones who professed God. They felt they had no sin, at least not enough sin to bar them from God. Anyone who accused them of being so wrong and so depraved could not conceivably be of God. He must be of Beelzebub (see outline and note—Mk.3:22-30).

There were at least four responses to Jesus by the religionists.

1. Some were sincere men of deep conviction. They actually thought Jesus was an imposter, a deceiver, a false messiah. Paul, Saul of Tarsus, would be an example of this position.

2. Some were open-minded enough to seek the truth about Jesus. They observed and reasoned, being honest enough to consider what He was saying, and they sought Him out to find the truth. Nicodemus is an example of this.

3. Some did believe and trust Christ (see note—Lk.13:31; pt.4—Mt.23:13-36).

4. Some were just professional priests and ministers who looked upon Jesus as a threat. They held the position because of the prestige, comfort, livelihood, and security they received from it. Therefore, they opposed Christ rather vehemently. Caiaphas and Annas are examples of this response.

The error of the religionists was fourfold.

1. They misinterpreted and corrupted God's Word (see notes—Mt.12:1-3; DEEPER STUDY # 1—Jn.4:22; cp. Ro.9:4).

2. They committed serious sin after serious sin in God's eyes (see notes—1 Th.2:15-16; cp. Ro.2:17-29).

3. They rejected God's way of righteousness, God's Messiah, which is Jesus Christ (see notes—Ro.11:18;

1 Th.2:15-16; cp. Ro.10:1-21, esp. 1-4, 19-21).

4. They allowed religion in its tradition and ritual, ceremony and rules, to become more important than meeting the basic needs of human life: the need for God and the need for spiritual, mental, and physical health. Jesus, being the true Messiah, was bound to expose such error. Therefore, the battle lines were drawn.

The Messiah had to liberate people from such enslaving behavior. He had to liberate them so they could be saved and worship God in freedom of spirit. The religionists had to oppose anyone who broke their law. They had to oppose Jesus because He was a threat to their nation and to their own personal position and security.

3 (22:3) **Satan, Work of**: the second opponent to Jesus was Satan. Satan is the spiritual being who is out to destroy the relationship between God and men. In wrath and bitter hostility he opposes God. (See DEEPER STUDY # 1, Satan—Rev.12:9 for more discussion on just who Satan is and on his terrible work.) Satan is seen entering Judas, stirring him to strike up a bargain to betray Jesus. Later Satan will enter Judas again and urge him to go ahead and finish his work of betrayal (Jn.13:27. See note, pt.4—Mk.14:10-11.) The point is, if Satan could destroy Jesus, keep Him from fulfilling His work on earth, then man could never be saved. Satan, of course, had no idea that God was going to save the world through the death of Jesus. Satan is not omniscient; he could not know the future any more than anyone else. Therefore, he had attempted to have Jesus killed time and again, even as a child (Mt.2:13, 16, 22; Lk.4:8, 29). Satan's opposition to God and man is clearly seen in Scripture.

1. He tempts to disobey God (Gen.3:4-5; Mt.4:4; 1 Th.3:5).
2. He snatches the Word out of man's heart (Mt.13:19).
3. He plants unbelievers in the midst of believers, the church (Mt.13:38-39).
4. He afflicts people with sickness and disease (Job 2:7;Lk.13:16).
5. He tries to sift, shake men in their faith (Lk.22:31).
6. He causes murder and killing (Jn.8:44; 1 Jn.3:12).
7. He lies and is the father of lies (Jn.8:44).
8. He enters men's lives (Lk.22:3; Jn.13:27).
9. He plants evil into the hearts of men (Jn.13:2).
10. He leads men to steal from God (Acts 5:3).
11. He tempts married couples sexually (1 Cor.7:5).
12. He tries to keep people from forgiving others (2 Cor.2:10-11).
13. He blinds the minds of unbelievers lest they believe(2 Cor.4:4).
14. He deceives the minds of men (2 Cor.11:3).
15. He transforms himself into a messenger of light to deceive man (2 Cor.11:14).
16. He transforms some ministers into ministers of righteousness to deceive men (2 Cor.11:15).
17. He works in the disobedient (Eph.2:2).
18. He launches powerful strategies against believers (Eph.6:11).
19. He rules the rulers, authorities powers of this dark world, and forces of evil in the heavenly realms (Eph.6:12; Col.2:15).
20. He hinders the work of believers (1 Th.2:18).
21. He works with power and signs and lying wonders (2 Th.2:9).
22. He leads men to blaspheme (1 Tim.1:20).
23. He condemns men and causes men to condemn themselves (1 Tim.3:6).
24. He snares and traps people (1 Tim.3:7; 2 Tim.2:26).
25. He turns people aside to go after him (1 Tim.5:15).
26. He did hold the power of death (Heb.2:14).
27. He seeks to prey upon men and devour them (1 Pt.5:8).
28. He sins and works against men and God (1 Jn.3:8).
29. He opposes the angels of God (Jude 6).
30. He possesses, rules, and controls some churches and worship centers (Rev.2:9; 3:9).
31. He causes believers to be cast into prison (Rev.2:10).
32. He deceives the whole world (Rev.12:9; 20:7-8, 10).
33. He accuses believers before God (Rev.12:10).
34. He causes great havoc upon the earth (Rev.12:12).

(See notes, Satan—Col.2:15; DEEPER STUDY # 1—Jas.4:7; DEEPER STUDY # 1—Rev.12:9 for more discussion.)

4 (22:4-6) **Judas—Unbeliever—Devil—Apostasy:** the third opponent to Jesus was a covetous man, a man who went his own way in life. Judas was such a man. Several facts show this.

1. Judas was a professing disciple. In fact, he was one of the twelve apostles. Just think about the fact: Judas had been personally chosen by Jesus. Judas had some great potential, some unique qualities that attracted the Lord, and the Lord gave Judas the most honored opportunity in all the world to develop his abilities, the privilege of walking with Him personally.

⇒ Judas knew Jesus face to face.
⇒ Judas walked with Jesus day after day.
⇒ Judas heard most, if not all, that Jesus taught.
⇒ Judas saw most, if not all, that Jesus did—miracles and wondrous works.
⇒ Judas was trained to be an apostle by Jesus Himself.
⇒ Judas served as an apostle even on witnessing tours under Jesus' personal command (Mk.6:7f).
⇒ Judas was warned of sin's consequences by Jesus Himself.

Despite all this, Judas' life was a terrible tragedy. He was so gifted and had so much opportunity, yet he lost it all. Why? Simply because he turned his back on the Lord Jesus Christ. He went to the chief priests of this earth and put his fate into their hands instead of placing his life into the hands of Jesus. He had allowed his craving for more and more to blind him to the truth about Jesus—that He was truly the Son of God who demanded loyalty—even when man cannot understand the events and happenings that surround Him (see note—Mt.26:14. This note will explain what is behind this statement.) Judas simply did not believe that Jesus was truly God's Son. Therefore, he did not give his heart and life to Jesus—not really. He was a follower of Jesus; he was even one of the first twelve apostles, but he was not a genuine believer who entrusted his life to Jesus.

Then he said to them all: "If anyone would come after me, he must deny himself and take up his cross daily and follow me. For whoever wants to save his life will lose it, but whoever loses his life for me will save it. (Luke 9:23-24)

2. Judas communed with the world. He was definitely worldly; his mind and heart were upon worldly acceptance, position, recognition, prestige, influence, power, and wealth. Note: he approached and communed with the world, the chief priests of the world. He thought they who were of the world were the winning side and could offer much more than Jesus.

> **Not so with you. Instead, whoever wants to become great among you must be your servant, and whoever wants to be first must be your slave—just as the Son of Man did not come to be served, but to serve, and to give his life as a ransom for many." (Mat 20:26-28)**
>
> **For whoever exalts himself will be humbled, and whoever humbles himself will be exalted. (Mat 23:12)**
>
> **How can you believe if you accept praise from one another, yet make no effort to obtain the praise that comes from the only God ? (John 5:44)**

3. Judas coveted the world and its money. Judas' gnawing sin was greed and the love of money. Various commentators pose different reasons why Judas may have betrayed Jesus, but the Scripture pointedly says that the reason was greed: "What are you willing to give me if I hand Him over to you?" (Mt.26:15)

Judas' gnawing greed was a growing sin. This is seen by looking at what is said about him in the Scripture.

a. Judas was chosen by Jesus to be an apostle (Mt.10:4). Therefore, we know he was sincere in the beginning. There was something within Judas—qualities that attracted Jesus, qualities that Jesus knew could mean a lot to the Kingdom of God.

b. Judas was a gifted man in financial affairs. Apparently he was even more gifted in financial affairs than Matthew, the wealthy tax collector, and the businessmen who were among the apostles such as Peter, James, and John (see Subject Index under each name for references to notes on their business background). Among all these, Judas was placed in charge of the Lord's funds and the purchasing of whatever was needed (Jn.12:6; 13:29; cp. Lk.8:2-3 for some who supported Jesus' ministry). His appointment from among so many was bound to be due to unusual spiritual qualities as well as financial management.

c. Judas, at some unknown point, began to embezzle from the Lord's funds. John says unmistakably that Judas was a thief (Jn.12:6). John relates this fact when he says that Judas was greatly disturbed with Mary, the sister of Martha. Mary used some very expensive perfume to annoint Jesus instead of selling it to secure money for the Lord's treasury. John says the reason for Judas' disturbance was because Judas was a thief and could have embezzled some of the money (Jn.12:5-6).

d. Judas refused to repent, and he hardened his heart more and more in his sin. Jesus knew of Judas' embezzlement and hinted at it, giving Judas opportunity time and again to repent.

> **Yet there are some of you who do not believe." For Jesus had known from the beginning which of them did not believe and who would betray him. Then Jesus replied, "Have I not chosen you, the Twelve? Yet one of you is a devil!" (He meant Judas, the son of Simon Iscariot, who, though one of the Twelve, was later to betray him.) (John 6:64; 70-71)**

Judas was bound to feel the pangs of guilt at such times, yet he continued to deceive himself, believing that Jesus did not really know and had no real proof. Judas kept right on taking what he felt he could safely embezzle, hardening his heart more and more.

e. Judas apparently followed Jesus out of a heart of greed and worldly ambition, not out of a heart of love and faith in Him as the Son of God. This seems to be indicated by two facts.

1) He felt that wealth, power, and position would be his when Jesus set up his kingdom. The other apostles thought the same, but there was a vast difference. They mistook the Messiah's method of saving the world, not His person. Judas mistook both the Lord's method and person. He did not believe and trust the Lord to be the Son of God, whereas the others did.

2) He apparently was disillusioned in Jesus after the triumphal entry. Jesus did not immediately set up His kingdom, and as the days passed, the fact that He was not going to set up His kingdom became more and more apparent. The authorities were mobilizing against Jesus to kill Him, and it seemed as though they were going to be successful. Jesus had even been teaching that they were to be successful. He was to be killed by their hands (Mt.16:21).

Judas became convinced he had been mistaken about Jesus. Jesus was not the real Messiah; He was just another mistaken self-proclaimed messiah; He was doomed and there was no way out. Judas experienced his dreams of wealth and power and position with Jesus being shattered. Therefore, what he was trying to do was to get what he could out of the situation. He wanted to be in good standing with the winning side and to secure a sizeable amount of money for betraying Jesus. Note: Judas apparently expected to get much more from the religionists than he got. Once he had approached the religionists, he had to follow through with the betrayal and accept whatever they offered.

f. Judas filled his heart with the lust for more and more instead of filling it with Jesus. He went too long without repenting and letting Jesus into his life, and the devil was able to fill his being. The devil blinded and took control of his rationale, hence Judas was able to justify his betrayal in his own mind. He was, after all, helping the religious body and himself. Therefore, he betrayed Jesus of Nazareth who apparently in Judas' mind was just another mistaken self-proclaimed messiah.

> **Then he said to them, "Watch out! Be on your guard against all kinds of greed; a man's life does not consist in the abundance of his possessions." (Luke 12:15)**
>
> **For the love of money is a root of all kinds of evil. Some people, eager for money, have wandered from the faith and pierced themselves with many griefs. (1 Tim 6:10)**

> **Your gold and silver are corroded. Their corrosion will testify against you and eat your flesh like fire. You have hoarded wealth in the last days. (James 5:3)**
>
> **Whoever loves money never has money enough; whoever loves wealth is never satisfied with his income. This too is meaningless. (Eccl 5:10)**

4. Judas makes a covenant with the world. Note the words, "He consented, and watched for an opportunity to hand Jesus over to them." Judas made a covenant with the world, a pact to betray Jesus. The picture is that of being on the prowl, searching and seeking, looking here and there for the right moment. Judas' heart was set, full of intrigue, plotting evil and planning its strategy. He did not believe, but unbelief was not enough. He willed to do evil against Jesus, to hurt Him, to destroy Him. And he sought opportunity to do so. Just how deceitful Judas was can be seen by noticing that immediately after bargaining with the authorities, he sat down to eat with Jesus. He sat at the very table where the Lord's Supper was being instituted.

Thought 1. Judas not only rejected but sought to destroy Jesus. Many reject Christ, but not all seek to harm and destroy Him. Some do, but not all.

⇒ Some curse and curse Him, consciously and unconsciously dishonoring His name.
⇒ Some talk and teach against His divine nature, saying that He is not the Son of God.
⇒ Some talk and teach against the written revelation of Himself and the truth, that is, the Word.
⇒ Some talk and teach against His active presence in the life of the genuine believer.

> **"Watch out for false prophets. They come to you in sheep's clothing, but inwardly they are ferocious wolves. (Mat 7:15)**
>
> **The Spirit clearly says that in later times some will abandon the faith and follow deceiving spirits and things taught by demons. Such teachings come through hypocritical liars, whose consciences have been seared as with a hot iron. But mark this: There will be terrible times in the last days. People will be lovers of themselves, lovers of money, boastful, proud, abusive, disobedient to their parents, ungrateful, unholy, without love, unforgiving, slanderous, without self-control, brutal, not lovers of the good, treacherous, rash, conceited, lovers of pleasure rather than lovers of God—having a form of godliness but denying its power. Have nothing to do with them. (2 Tim 3:1-5)**

B. The Lord's Supper, 22:7-23
(Mt.26:17-30; Mk.14: 12-25; Jn.13)

1 The great purpose of the Lord's Supper[DS1]
a. To show how Christ fulfilled the Passover Feast: Delivers man from judgment
b. To stress the need to remember & celebrate the Lord's death
1) Despite obstacles
2) The prearranged sign
c. To stress the need for cautious preparations in approaching Christ & His death

7 Then came the day of Unleavened Bread on which the
Passover lamb had to be
sacrificed.
8 Jesus sent Peter and John,
saying, "Go and make preparations for us to eat the
Passover."
9 "Where do you want us to
prepare for it?" they asked.
10 He replied, "As you enter
the city, a man carrying a jar
of water will meet you. Follow him to the house that he
enters,
11 And say to the owner of
the house, 'The Teacher asks:
Where is the guest room,
where I may eat the Passover
with my disciples?'
12 He will show you a large
upper room, all furnished.
Make preparations there."
13 They left and found things
just as Jesus had told them.
So they prepared the Passover.
14 When the hour came, Jesus and his apostles reclined
at the table.
15 And he said to them, "I
have eagerly desired to eat
this Passover with you before
I suffer.
16 For I tell you, I will not
eat it again until it finds fulfillment in the kingdom of
God."
17 After taking the cup, he
gave thanks and said, "Take
this and divide it among you.
18 For I tell you I will not
drink again of the fruit of the
vine until the kingdom of
God comes."
19 And he took bread, gave
thanks and broke it, and gave
it to them, saying, "This is
my body given for you; do
this in remembrance of me."
20 In the same way, after the
supper he took the cup, saying, "This cup is the new
covenant in my blood, which
is poured out for you.
21 But the hand of him who
is going to betray me is with
mine on the table.
22 The Son of Man will go
as it has been decreed, but
woe to that man who betrays
him."
23 They began to question
among themselves which of
them it might be who would
do this.

2 The great significance of the Lord's Supper
a. It is tied to the Lord's death & the Passover
b. It pictures a greater supper, a glorious promise

3 The great meaning of the Lord's Supper[DS2]
a. The Bread: Symbolizes Christ's body, broken for us
b. The Cup: Symbolizes Christ's blood, shed for us

4 The great appeal of the Lord's Supper
a. It is used to appeal to a sinner
b. It is used to warn a sinner
c. It is used to stir the searching of hearts

DIVISION X

THE SON OF MAN'S LAST SUPPER: HIS TRAITOR, INSTRUCTIONS, AND WARNINGS, 22:1-38

B. The Lord's Supper, 22:7-23

(22:7-23) **Introduction**: this is a great passage on the subject of the Lord's Supper.

1. The great purpose of the Lord's Supper (v.7-14).
2. The great significance of the Lord's Supper (v.15-18).
3. The great meaning of the Lord's Supper (v.19-20).
4. The great appeal of the Lord's Supper (v.21-23).

1 (22:7-14) **Lord's Supper**: the great purpose of the Lord's Supper is threefold.

1. It shows how Jesus fulfilled the great Passover Feast (see DEEPER STUDY # 1—Lk.22:7).

2. It stresses the great need and helps a person to remember the Lord's death. Scripture is pointedly clear about this. The Lord's Supper helps us to keep our minds upon Christ, and at the same time it demonstrates that our minds are upon Him.

> **Do this in remembrance of me." (Luke 22:19; 1 Cor 11:24-25)**
> **For whenever you eat this bread and drink this cup, you proclaim the Lord's death until he comes. (1 Cor 11:26)**

The Lord's Supper is to be kept even in the *face of difficulty*. Note the difficulty Jesus faced. There were those who were seeking to find out where He was so they might arrest and kill Him. Even one of His own disciples had betrayed Him and was only waiting for an opportunity to inform the authorities where He was and where He could be quietly arrested. However, despite this terrible difficulty, Jesus was determined to observe the celebration. (What an indictment against *loose attitudes and approaches* to the Lord's Supper! Believers are to be obedient to the religious ordinances despite difficulty.)

3. It stresses the need for cautious preparation in approaching Christ and His death. Note the words "prepared" in all three gospels.

> **They left and found things just as Jesus had told them. So they *prepared* the Passover. (Luke 22:13)**
> **So the disciples did as Jesus had directed them and *prepared* the Passover. (Mat 26:19)**
> **The disciples left, went into the city and found things just as Jesus had told them. So they *prepared* the Passover. (Mark 14:16)**

The point is this: detailed preparations were required for observing the Passover (see DEEPER STUDY # 1—Lk.22:7). The stringent preparations taught that God was to be *approached carefully*, exactly as prescribed. Why? Because God is holy, and there is only one way to approach Him—through the blood of the Passover Lamb. Three acts in this passage stress the need for approaching Christ carefully.

⇒ He went to great pains to keep the Passover despite extreme danger.
⇒ He had personally made preparations for the observance (v.9-12).
⇒ The disciples found the arrangements made just as He had said and did their part in preparing the observance.

Thought 1. Christ kept the Passover even in the face of death. How few value the Lord's Supper enough! How many observe it too little! How many could care less if it is observed or not! How many place the comfort of home, recreation, and the doing of one's own thing before observing the Lord's Supper!

DEEPER STUDY # 1

(22:7) **Passover—Lord's Supper**: historically, the Passover refers back to the time when God delivered Israel from Egyptian bondage (Ex.11:1f). He had pronounced judgment, the taking of the firstborn, upon the people of Egypt for their injustices. As He prepared to execute the final judgment, those who believed God were instructed to slay a pure lamb and sprinkle its blood over the door posts of their homes. The blood of the innocent lamb would then serve as a sign that the coming judgment had already been carried out upon the sacrificial lamb. When seeing the blood, God would *pass over* that house. Those who believed God applied the blood to their homes and were saved, but those who did not believe did not apply the blood to their homes, and they were destroyed.

Symbolically, the Passover pictured the coming of Jesus Christ as the Savior. The *lamb without blemish* pictured His sinless life (cp. Jn.1:29), and the *blood sprinkled on the door posts* pictured His blood shed for the believer. It was a sign that the life and blood of the innocent lamb had been substituted for the firstborn. The "eating of the lamb" pictured the need for spiritual nourishment gained by feeding on Christ, the Bread of Life. The unleavened bread (bread without yeast) pictured the need for putting evil out of one's life and household. (See DEEPER STUDY # 1, Feast of Unleavened Bread—Mt.26:17.)

In addition to the lamb and unleavened bread, the Jewish Passover Feast was celebrated by using four food and drink items. (1) A bowl of salt water was conspicuously placed on the table to remind the family of the tears shed by their forefathers in their 430 years of Egyptian bondage. (2) A bitter salad-like plate was to remind them of their forefather's bitter experiences of slavery. (3) A paste-like mixture of fruit (charosheth) with cinnamon sticks was to remind them of their forefather's toil in making bricks from clay and straw for the Egyptian cities and buildings. (4) Four cups of wine were used to remind them of God's four promises in Ex.6:6-8 to deliver their forefathers from Egyptian slavery.

The one thing to be noted about the Passover celebration is that it is all historical. It is celebrating an act of the past, whereas the Lord's Supper is much more than mere history. It is a celebration of the living Christ in the heart and life of the believer until He returns. It is a remembrance of the potential power of the living Christ within the life of the believer right now—an explosive power that is made possible through the cross (cp. 1 Cor.11:26).

2 (22:15-18) **Lord's Supper**: the great significance of the Lord's Supper is shown by two things.

1. The Lord's Supper is tied to the Lord's death. Note the Lord's words:

⇒ "Before I suffer" (v.15).
⇒ "I will not eat it again, *until....*" (v.16).
⇒ "I will not drink again of the fruit of the vine, *until....*" (v.18).

Jesus was definitely tying both the Passover and the Lord's Supper to His death. And, of course, His death is what the Lord's Supper is all about (see DEEPER STUDY # 2—Lk.22:19-20).

2. The Lord's Supper pictures a great supper, a glorious promise (v.16-18). Note carefully the promise of Jesus. He said He was going to eat and drink again when all things were fulfilled "in the kingdom of God." Jesus was *promising* to celebrate the Supper with His followers in the future. Believers shall sit down with Christ at the great *Marriage Feast of the Lamb* (see outline and notes—Mt.20:1-16; 20:2). It is the promise of sitting with Christ in His glorious kingdom, of being a part of the new heavens and earth, of being perfected and living forever (see DEEPER STUDY # 3, Kingdom of God—Mt.19:23-24; Rewards—Lk.16:10-12).

The Spirit himself testifies with our spirit that we are God's children. Now if we are children, then we are heirs—heirs of God and co-heirs with Christ, if indeed we share in his sufferings in order that we may also share in his glory. (Rom 8:16-17)

When Christ, who is your life, appears, then you also will appear with him in glory. (Col 3:4)

For our light and momentary troubles are achieving for us an eternal glory that far outweighs them all. (2 Cor 4:17)

To the elders among you, I appeal as a fellow elder, a witness of Christ's sufferings and one who also will share in the glory to be revealed: (1 Pet 5:1)

And you will receive a rich welcome into the eternal kingdom of our Lord and Savior Jesus Christ. (2 Pet 1:11)

3 (22:19-20) **Lord's Supper**: the great meaning of the Lord's Supper.

1. There is the meaning of the bread. Jesus took the bread and broke it. This symbolized His broken body. His body was broken, that is, sacrificed, as a victim for man's deliverance (Is.53:5). This act was so significant that the early church sometimes called the Lord's Supper simply *the breaking of bread* (Acts 2:42, 46; 1 Cor.10:16). Under the Old Testament the broken bread pictured the sufferings of the Israelites. Now, under the New Testament, the bread was to picture the broken body of Christ (1 Cor.11:24).

Note: Jesus said His body was broken and given for us. He suffered and died *for us*: in our behalf, in our stead, in our place. He bore the judgment of God against sin by dying *for us*.

But here is the bread that comes down from heaven, which a man may eat and not

die. I am the living bread that came down from heaven. If anyone eats of this bread, he will live forever. This bread is my flesh, which I will give for the life of the world." (John 6:50-51)

And when he had given thanks, he broke it and said, "This is my body, which is for you; do this in remembrance of me." (1 Cor 11:24)

But he was pierced for our transgressions, he was crushed for our iniquities; the punishment that brought us peace was upon him, and by his wounds we are healed. (Isa 53:5)

2. There is the meaning of the cup. Jesus identified the cup as His blood of the New Testament. He simply meant that His blood establishes a new covenant with God; His blood allows a new relationship between God and man. Note the Lord's exact words.

a. "This is my blood": His blood, which was shed or poured out from His body, was to become the sign or symbol of the new covenant. His blood was to take the place of the sacrifice of animals.

b. "The newcovenant": His blood, the sacrifice of His life established a New Testament, a new covenant between God and man (cp. Heb.9:11-15). Faith in His blood and sacrifice is the way man is now to approach God. Under the Old Testament, a man who wanted a right relationship with God approached God through the sacrifice of the animal's blood. The Old Testament believer believed that God accepted him because of the sacrifice of the animal. Now, under the New Testament, the believer believes that God accepts him because of the sacrifice of Christ. This is what Jesus said: "This is my blood of the New Covenant, which is poured out for many" (Mk.14:24. See note Mt.26:28; cp. Eph.1:7; 1 Jn.2:1-2; Heb.9:22.) A man's sins are forgiven and he becomes acceptable to God by believing that Christ's blood was shed for him (1 Jn.1:7).

In him we have redemption through his blood, the forgiveness of sins, in accordance with the riches of God's grace (Eph 1:7)

But if we walk in the light, as he is in the light, we have fellowship with one another, and the blood of Jesus, his Son, purifies us from all sin. (1 John 1:7)

My dear children, I write this to you so that you will not sin. But if anybody does sin, we have one who speaks to the Father in our defense—Jesus Christ, the Righteous One. He is the atoning sacrifice for our sins, and not only for ours but also for the sins of the whole world. (1 John 2:1-2)

Whoever eats my flesh and drinks my blood has eternal life, and I will raise him up at the last day. For my flesh is real food and my blood is real drink. Whoever eats my flesh and drinks my blood remains in me, and I in him. Just as the living Father sent me and I live because of the Father, so the one who feeds on me will live because of me. This is the bread that came down from heaven. Your forefathers ate manna and died, but he who feeds on this bread will live forever." (John 6:54-58)

DEEPER STUDY # 2

(22:19-20) **Lord's Supper—Passover**: note the words "in remembrance of me." By fulfilling the Passover with the shedding of His own blood, Jesus was tying the Lord's Supper to the Passover Feast. In instituting the Lord's Supper, Jesus was showing His disciples that He was, first of all, the great Liberator. A *liberator* differs from a *deliverer*. A deliverer might deliver a person into something as bad or even worse than that which enslaves him, but not a liberator. A liberator sets a person free from whatever bondage grips him. As the disciples partook of the Supper, they were to:

1. Remember how God liberated Israel from Egyptian slavery.
2. Remember how the Lord's blood liberated them from earthly and sinful slavery. The Lord's Supper is to remind the disciples how the blood of the Lamb keeps them safe from the terrible hand of God's judgment.
3. Remember how the blood of Christ makes it possible for Him to return and to liberate them into the eternal presence of God's glory.

4 (22:21-23) **Judas Iscariot**: the great appeals of the Supper. Jesus used the Supper to make three appeals.

1. Jesus used the Supper to appeal to a sinner. Judas had forsaken Jesus. He thought his sin was hid and unknown, but Jesus knew. He had seen all, everything that Judas had done.

2. Jesus used the Supper to warn the sinner. "Woe to that man," Jesus said. The word "woe" means wrath and sorrow, anger and pity. It was a grieving denunciation, a heartrending pronouncement of judgment. Terrible judgment was a sure thing for the sinner Judas, and it broke the heart of God.

Thought 1. Jesus knows the destiny of the sinner, the terrible fate that awaits him. It would be better never to be born than to deny and betray Christ. Note the grace of God in warning the sinner of judgment.

1) The sinner is told in *advance*, before judgment ever comes or is ever pronounced. Judas was told. The sinner can still repent when he *first* hears about judgment. He can still be saved as long as he is living. It is God's grace that warns us of the consequences of our sin, of coming judgment.
2) The sinner is never compelled to repent of his denial or betrayal of Christ. Judas was not forced to turn from his evil; neither is any other sinner. It is God's grace that respects our will and desires. God loves and cares, warns and speaks frankly, but He never forces obedience.

I tell you, no! But unless you repent, you too will all perish." (Luke 13:3, 5)

Repent, then, and turn to God, so that your sins may be wiped out, that times of refreshing may come from the Lord, (Acts 3:19)

Repent of this wickedness and pray to the Lord. Perhaps he will forgive you for having such a thought in your heart. (Acts 8:22)

3. Jesus used the Supper to stir the searching of hearts. The disciples were stirred to ask, "Surely not I?" (Mt.26:22; Mk.14:19). They looked at themselves. They were not accusing one another; rather each one feared lest he be so weak he might fall.

"Watch and pray so that you will not fall into temptation. The spirit is willing, but the body is weak." (Mat 26:41)

So, if you think you are standing firm, be careful that you don't fall! (1 Cor 10:12)

Be on your guard; stand firm in the faith; be men of courage; be strong. (1 Cor 16:13)

Be self-controlled and alert. Your enemy the devil prowls around like a roaring lion looking for someone to devour. (1 Pet 5:8)

	C. The Dispute Over Greatness, 22:24-30 (Mt.20:20-28; Mk.10: 35-45)
1 The disciples argued over position and power	24 Also a dispute arose among them as to which of them was considered to be greatest.
2 The world's attitude about greatness a. To hold authority over people b. To be recognized & honored as a benefactor	25 Jesus said to them, "The kings of the Gentiles lord it over them; and those who exercise authority over them call themselves Benefactors.
3 The Lord's attitude toward greatness a. To act as the youngest b. To act as a servant c. To follow the example of the Lord—to be as He that serveth	26 But you are not to be like that. Instead, the greatest among you should be like the youngest, and the one who rules like the one who serves. 27 For who is greater, the one who is at the table or the one who serves? Is it not the one who is at the table? But I am among you as one who serves.
4 The Lord's encouragement to serve faithfully a. He gives assurance: They have proven themselves b. He makes a covenant 1) They are to inherit a kingdom[DS1] 2) They are to rule	28 You are those who have stood by me in my trials. 29 And I confer on you a kingdom, just as my Father conferred one on me, 30 So that you may eat and drink at my table in my kingdom and sit on thrones, judging the twelve tribes of Israel.

DIVISION X

THE SON OF MAN'S LAST SUPPER: HIS TRAITOR, INSTRUCTIONS, AND WARNINGS, 22:1-38

C. The Dispute Over Greatness, 22:24-30

(22:24-30) **Introduction**: men desire recognition, prestige, position, honor, power, authority. The disciples had such desires. Jesus used their power struggle to teach the world a much needed lesson, a lesson that speaks directly and forcibly to every person.

1. The disciples argued over position and power (v.24).
2. The world's attitude about greatness (v.25).
3. The Lord's attitude about greatness (v.26-27).
4. The Lord's encouragement to serve faithfully (v.28-30).

1 (22:24) **Division—Strife—Position**: the disciples argued. Note three facts.

1. The word "dispute" (philoneikia) means being eager and ready to argue and contend; being alert to strive for one's position. It conveys the idea of giving no ground, of standing up no matter what, of being stubborn, of resisting regardless of circumstances.

2. The disciples were still thinking about an earthly kingdom. They thought Jesus was about to lead an uprising against the Romans and free Palestine, establishing the Messiah's kingdom in Israel. From Israel the Messiah was to rule and reign over the whole earth in behalf of God. (See note, pt.2—Lk.7:21-23. Also see notes—Mt.1:1; DEEPER STUDY # 2—1:18; DEEPER STUDY # 3—3:11; notes—11:1-6; 11:2-3; DEEPER STUDY # 1—11:5; DEEPER STUDY # 2—11:6; DEEPER STUDY # 1—12:16; note—22:42.)

3. The disciples were in the upper room *jockeying* for position. As in most societies, the highest in position sat on the right of the host and the next highest on the left. The highest in position continued to alternate between the right and left until everyone was seated.

Since Jesus was about to set up His kingdom, now was the time to seize the positions of rule and power in His kingdom. Now was the time to assume the seats of honor and authority in His presence. The disciples were trying to assure themselves of key seats and positions in His government. (See outline and notes—-Mt.18:1-4.)

2 (22:25) **Greatness**: the world's attitude about greatness involves two key concepts.

1. There is the concept that greatness is holding authority over people or *lording it over* people: holding position and authority, influence and power, rank and dominion, money and property. Men seek position and wealth for the sake of power. They want to rule or manage people, exercise authority over them, and control their lives.

2. There is the concept of being known and called a benefactor (euergetai), a man who gives and helps others.

Note the word "call." The worldly benefactor wants to be known and called a benefactor, recognized and honored for his help and contribution. He desires to be known as a great man, a man who is generous, thoughtful, concerned, honorable.

> **For whoever exalts himself will be humbled, and whoever humbles himself will be exalted. (Mat 23:12)**
>
> **How can you believe if you accept praise from one another, yet make no effort to obtain the praise that comes from the only God? (John 5:44)**
>
> **He boasts of the cravings of his heart; he blesses the greedy and reviles the LORD. (Psa 10:3)**
>
> **Like clouds and wind without rain is a man who boasts of gifts he does not give. (Prov 25:14)**
>
> **You have trusted in your wickedness and have said, 'No one sees me.' Your wisdom and knowledge mislead you when you say to yourself, 'I am, and there is none besides me.' (Isa 47:10)**
>
> **Though you soar like the eagle and make your nest among the stars, from there I will bring you down," declares the LORD. (Oba 1:4)**

3 (22:26-27) **Greatness**: the Lord's attitude about greatness. The Lord rejected the world's attitude of greatness. True greatness does not seek to hold authority nor to lord it over people; it does not seek position for the sake of authority and power, nor to give and help for the sake of being known and called a benefactor. True greatness is not self-centered and selfish, not worldly-minded.

Note a crucial point: Jesus did not forbid a man from holding a position of greatness or authority. What He was doing was giving instructions to the person who is "greatest among you" (v.26). The Lord's attitude of greatness involves two key concepts.

1. There is the concept of acting as the *youngest*, that is, of taking the last seat, of assuming the lowliest position. In the ancient world, the younger always honored and gave way to the older. Age was looked up to and honored. Jesus was saying that the person who was truly great was the person who took the lowest seat and last place, the person who did not seek the recognition and honor, the credit and esteem, because he held some position or had done some special work or made some unusual gift or given extraordinary help.

> **But when you are invited, take the lowest place, so that when your host comes, he will say to you, 'Friend, move up to a better place.' Then you will be honored in the presence of all your fellow guests. (Luke 14:10)**
>
> **For by the grace given me I say to every one of you: Do not think of yourself more highly than you ought, but rather think of yourself with sober judgment, in accordance with the measure of faith God has given you. (Rom 12:3)**
>
> **Humble yourselves before the Lord, and he will lift you up. (James 4:10)**
>
> **Young men, in the same way be submissive to those who are older. All of you, clothe yourselves with humility toward one another, because, "God opposes the proud but gives grace to the humble." Humble yourselves, therefore, under God's mighty hand, that he may lift you up in due time. (1 Pet 5:5-6)**

2. There is the concept of acting as a servant. The chief person is to serve. The picture Jesus painted is descriptive. The truly great man will serve others just as a table waiter serves the guests at a banquet. The table waiter in Jesus' day was a bond-slave (doulos). The bond-slave was bound every moment of his life, always serving, no matter the hour or call or difficulty (see note, Slave—Ro.1:1).

The truly great person looks for people to help and for ways to help them, whether at work, home, play, or church. He is always seeking those who need a visit, care, attention, company, food, clothing, shelter, money. He seeks for the sake of ministering (cp. Mt.25:34-40).

> **And if anyone gives even a cup of cold water to one of these little ones because he is my disciple, I tell you the truth, he will certainly not lose his reward." (Mat 10:42)**
>
> **Do nothing out of selfish ambition or vain conceit, but in humility consider others better than yourselves. Each of you should look not only to your own interests, but also to the interests of others. (Phil 2:3-4)**

3. There is the concept of following the example of the Lord. The follower is to be like his Lord, yet he is to humble himself and serve and minister to men. Of course, the man who sits at the table is greater than the man who serves. He holds a higher position, but he is not to *act* like it, lording it over the servant. He is to behave like the Lord, serving and ministering to men, even to the servants who are waiting upon him. (See notes—Mk.10:45 for three supreme ways Christ served.)

> **After that, he poured water into a basin and began to wash his disciples' feet, drying them with the towel that was wrapped around him. (John 13:5)**
>
> **Serve wholeheartedly, as if you were serving the Lord, not men, (Eph 6:7)**
>
> **Your attitude should be the same as that of Christ Jesus: Who, being in very nature God, did not consider equality with God something to be grasped, but made himself nothing, taking the very nature of a servant, being made in human likeness. And being found in appearance as a man, he humbled himself and became obedient to death— even death on a cross! (Phil 2:5-8)**

4 (22:28-30) **Faithfulness**: the Lord's encouragement to serve faithfully.

Jesus gave assurance to the disciples who proved themselves. The disciples who *continued* with Jesus, who were faithful, standing by Him and sticking to Him, were given a great promise. The promise was a covenant. Note the word "conferred." The promise was set and fixed in eternity. It could not be revoked nor changed in any form or fashion. The covenant was twofold.

1. The faithful disciple is to be a citizen of the Lord's kingdom (see DEEPER STUDY # 3—Mt.19:23-24). The picture is that of the Marriage Feast of the Lamb. (See note, pt.2—Lk.22:15-18. Also see note—Mt.20:2.)

2. The faithful disciple is to rule (see DEEPER STUDY # 1—Lk.22:30).

DEEPER STUDY # 1

(22:30) **Reward**: Jesus said that the disciples would be rewarded with twelve thrones, each one governing one of the twelve tribes of Israel. When are they to govern? "At the renewal of all things" (Mt.19:28). when the new order of things shall be set up under the rule and reign of Christ. But when is the new order of things to be? There are two possible answers: either the millenial reign of Christ (see DEEPER STUDY # 3—Mt.19:23-24; note—Rev.20:4-6), or the new heavens and earth (Rev.21:1f; cp. 1 Cor.15:23-28).

There are three passages where Christ dealt with the renewal as predicted here.

> **Jesus said to them, "I tell you the truth, at the renewal of all things, when the Son of Man sits on his glorious throne, you who have followed me will also sit on twelve thrones, judging the twelve tribes of Israel. (Mat 19:28)**
>
> **"What is it you want?" he asked. She said, "Grant that one of these two sons of mine may sit at your right and the other at your left in your kingdom."...Jesus said to them, "You will indeed drink from my cup, but to sit at my right or left is not for me to grant. These places belong to those for whom they have been prepared by my Father." (Mat 20:21, 23)**
>
> **You are those who have stood by me in my trials. And I confer on you a kingdom, just as my Father conferred one on me, so that you may eat and drink at my table in**

my kingdom and sit on thrones, judging the twelve tribes of Israel. (Luke 22:28-30)

The fulfillment of this promise seems to be the Messianic kingdom or millenial reign of Christ on earth. This seems to be the way Christ's promise to Israel will be fulfilled.

I will restore your judges as in days of old, your counselors as at the beginning. Afterward you will be called the City of Righteousness, the Faithful City." (Isa 1:26)

Note three things.

1. Some commentators find great difficulty in saying there is ever again to be a distinction between Jew and Gentile, for Christ came to bring peace between all men, breaking down the wall of partition between all. They say that the great weight of Scripture is opposed to there being a distinction between Jew and Gentile again. This interpretation simply says that when Christ returns, that is it: He sets up His *eternal reign and rule forever.* Therefore, the apostles are to rule and reign over the church, spiritual Israel, the true Israel of God (Gal.6:15-16; cp. Ro.2:28-29).

2. Jesus said He will reward the disciples with *a particular honor.* Why? The disciples believed and followed Christ in the embryo stage of Christianity. They adhered to their belief and endured in the face of unbelievable odds.

⇒ Imagine standing before a man who looked like all other men, merely a man, and believing that man to really be the *Son of God.*

⇒ Imagine clinging to and continuing to follow Christ when everyone else turned away from Him (cp. Jn.6:67).

⇒ Imagine following immediately upon the heels of the risen Lord and being instantly responsible for reaching the world. (No wonder God had to plan for His Spirit to infill the disciples and to live within our bodies as He does. See notes—1 Cor.3:16; 6:19-20.)

⇒ Imagine continuing on and on, trying to be obedient and to reach the world for Christ, despite unbelievable odds.

⇒ Imagine confronting and enduring through unbelievable persecution launched from both an immoral government and a fierce religion.

The disciples were not only responsible for more and faced more than most of us will ever know; they were responsible for and faced more than we can ever imagine (cp. 1 Cor.4:9-13; 2 Cor.11:24-28).

3. The disciples were not the only ones to be rewarded. Every true follower of Christ will be greatly rewarded (see notes—Mt.19:29; Lk.16:1-13 for discussion).

Outline	Scripture	Scripture (cont.)	Outline (cont.)
	D. The Denial of Peter Foretold: The Great Warning of Satan's Attack, 22:31-38 (Mt.26:31-35; Mk.14:27-31; Jn.13:36-38)	35 Then Jesus asked them, "When I sent you without purse, bag or sandals, did you lack anything?" "Nothing," they answered.	b. Not forgetting Jesus' resources
		36 He said to them, "But now if you have a purse, take	c. Knowing difficult days lie ahead
1 The warning: Satan's desire is to sift—separate from God	31 "Simon, Simon, Satan has asked to sift you as wheat.	it, and also a bag; and if you don't have a sword, sell your cloak and buy one.	1) Friends will forsake 2) Enemies will be fierce
2 The answer to Satan's attack a. Jesus' interceding b. Turning back c. Helping others	32 But I have prayed for you, Simon, that your faith may not fail. And when you have turned back, strengthen your brothers."	37 It is written: 'And he was numbered with the transgressors'; and I tell you that this must be fulfilled in me. Yes, what is written	d. Knowing Jesus is the Suffering Servant 1) Prophecy refers to Him (Is.53) 2) He is counted as a sinner
3 The preventions against Satan's attack	33 But he replied, "Lord, I am ready to go with you to prison and to death."	about me is reaching its fulfillment."	3) Salvation will be ful filled
a. Knowing the difference between carnal & spiritual commitment	34 Jesus answered, "I tell you, Peter, before the rooster crows today, you will deny three times that you know me."	38 The disciples said, "See, Lord, here are two swords." "That is enough," he replied.	**4 Conclusion: The disciples still do not understand—still think in terms of earthly Messiah**

DIVISION X

THE SON OF MAN'S LAST SUPPER: HIS TRAITOR, INSTRUCTIONS, AND WARNINGS, 22:1-38

D. The Denial of Peter Foretold: The Great Warning of Satan's Attack, 22:31-38

(22:31-38) **Introduction**: Satan attacks God's people. Knowing and understanding this fact helps the believer tremendously. It helps him...

- to recognize and stand against the attacks.
- to recover himself when caving in to the attacks.
- to strengthen others in their stand against the attacks.

Jesus knew the attack which was about to be launched against the disciples. This passage shows how He prepared His disciples. It is a strong warning that Satan does attack the believer.

1. The warning: Satan's desire is to sift the believer, to separate him from God (v.31).
2. The answer to Satan's attack (v.32).
3. The preventions against Satan's attack (v.33-37).
4. Conclusion: the disciples still do not understand—still think in terms of an earthly Messiah (v.38).

1 (22:31) **Temptation—Satan—Spiritual Struggle**: there is the warning. Satan's desire is to sift the believer, that is, to separate him from God. This verse reveals a great deal about temptation. Note three things.

1. The word "you" is plural in the Greek. Satan desires to tempt all the disciples. Jesus addressed the warning to Peter because he was the leader of the group and because he was to go beyond desertion and actually deny Jesus. Peter needed some very special attention.

2. The word "asked" (exeitesato) means to desire somethin, to beg for something. Jesus pictured Satan as begging permission of God to trip the disciples. It is the same picture that is found in Job (Job 1:6f). The Bible is clear in its teaching: God is supreme; anything that goes on in the universe goes on because God allows it, even temptation. Just why He allows temptation is covered in the next point. The truth to see right now is that...

- Jesus did give a glimpse into the spiritual world.
- Satan begged God to let him test and try the disciples.
- Satan is subject to God and has no right or power to *tempt believers* unless God allows it.
- The Lord's prayer does include the words, "Deliver us from the evil one" (a po tou poneron) (see DEEPER STUDY # 9—Mt.6:13).

3. The word "sift" (siniasai) means to shake, to sift in a sieve in order to separate the good grain from the chaff. The picture is that Satan wished...

- to sift and shake the disciples.
- to test and try them.
- to prove they were not genuine.
- to cut the heart of God by showing they were not genuine.
- to disgrace God by proving their disloyalty.

Satan's primary purpose in temptation is to disgrace and cut the heart of God. He does this by challenging God to remove the *sense* of His presence and His blessings from the believer. Satan feels that the believer will fall and turn from God. He suggests to God that the believer will not stand by faith through trial after trial, not without the evidence of some *physical* or *material* blessing. His suggestion seems to be that the believer loves God not for Himself, not because of what Christ has done for him, but because of what he gets out of God. (Cp. Job 1:6-12.)

The presence of Jesus *was* about to be removed from the disciples. He was to die. And the disciples were thinking in terms of a physical kingdom and material rewards (cp. Lk.22:24-30). They did, of course, fail in the trial. However, we must always remember they did not yet know the full meaning of the cross and resurrection. They were living through the events while we are looking back upon them; we have complete understanding of what took place. Their love and devotion for Jesus ran deep. They did repent, returning and committing their lives fully to Him.

Thought 1. Satan's purpose in temptation is to disgrace and cut the heart of God. This should drive us to stand firm through all temptation, no matter the cost—by faith in the power of the Lord. (See note, Satan—Lk.22:3 for a list of the works of Satan.)

No temptation has seized you except what is common to man. And God is faithful; he will not let you be tempted beyond what you can bear. But when you are tempted, he will also provide a way out so that you can stand up under it. (1 Cor 10:13)

In order that Satan might not outwit us. For we are not unaware of his schemes. (2 Cor 2:11)

But I am afraid that just as Eve was deceived by the serpent's cunning, your minds may somehow be led astray from your sincere and pure devotion to Christ. (2 Cor 11:3)

For our struggle is not against flesh and blood, but against the rulers, against the authorities, against the powers of this dark world and against the spiritual forces of evil in the heavenly realms. Therefore put on the full armor of God, so that when the day of evil comes, you may be able to stand your ground, and after you have done everything, to stand. (Eph 6:12-13)

People who want to get rich fall into temptation and a trap and into many foolish and harmful desires that plunge men into ruin and destruction. (1 Tim 6:9)

But each one is tempted when, by his own evil desire, he is dragged away and enticed. (James 1:14)

Be self-controlled and alert. Your enemy the devil prowls around like a roaring lion looking for someone to devour. (1 Pet 5:8)

2 (22:32) **Repentance—Discipleship**: there is the answer when failing and falling under Satan's attack. Jesus wanted Peter to know three things.

1. Jesus is the believer's Intercessor. He was Peter's advocate before God. He had prayed that Peter's faith would not fail. This means Jesus prayed that Peter would not *permanently fall*, that his faith would not *totally fail and be absolutely ruined*, that he would not make a *final and lasting denial* of Jesus. Peter and the others would stumble and fall, but Jesus prayed that they would...

- not remain down.
- not stay in sin.
- not make a final and lasting rejection.
- not desert forever.

Jesus prayed that they would be kept by the power of God and not be snatched out of God's hand (Jn.10:29; 1 Pt.1:5).

My dear children, I write this to you so that you will not sin. But if anybody does sin, we have one who speaks to the Father in our defense—Jesus Christ, the Righteous One. He is the atoning sacrifice for our sins, and not only for ours but also for the sins of the whole world. (1 John 2:1-2)

Who is he that condemns? Christ Jesus, who died—more than that, who was raised to life—is at the right hand of God and is also interceding for us. (Rom 8:34)

Therefore he is able to save completely those who come to God through him, because he always lives to intercede for them. (Heb 7:25)

2. The believer is to turn back to God after falling. The word "turned" (epistrepho) means to turn around, to turn back to, to turn again. The believer is to repent, turn back to God (see note and DEEPER STUDY # 1, Repentance—Acts 17:29-30).

And he said: "I tell you the truth, unless you change and become like little children, you will never enter the kingdom of heaven. (Mat 18:3)

Repent, then, and turn to God, so that your sins may be wiped out, that times of refreshing may come from the Lord, (Acts 3:19)

The eunuch was reading this passage of Scripture: "He was led like a sheep to the slaughter, and as a lamb before the shearer is silent, so he did not open his mouth. (Acts 8:32)

3. The believer is to strengthen his brothers once he has returned to God. The believer is to take what he has learned from falling and...

- teach others how to find the mercy of God.
- help others who have fallen to return.
- strengthen the faith of others to keep them from falling.

My brothers, if one of you should wander from the truth and someone should bring him back, remember this: Whoever turns a sinner from the error of his way will save him from death and cover over a multitude of sins. (James 5:19-20)

Brothers, if someone is caught in a sin, you who are spiritual should restore him gently. But watch yourself, or you also may be tempted. Carry each other's burdens, and in this way you will fulfill the law of Christ. (Gal 6:1-2)

Accept him whose faith is weak, without passing judgment on disputable matters. (Rom 14:1)

We who are strong ought to bear with the failings of the weak and not to please ourselves. (Rom 15:1)

And we urge you, brothers, warn those who are idle, encourage the timid, help the weak, be patient with everyone. (1 Th 5:14)

Restore to me the joy of your salvation and grant me a willing spirit, to sustain me. Then I will teach transgressors your ways, and sinners will turn back to you. (Psa 51:12-13)

3 (22:33-37) **Commitment—Cross—Flesh—Carnal—Desires—Persecution**: the prevention against Satan's attack is fourfold.

1. Prevention 1: knowing the difference between a carnal and a spiritual commitment. Peter immediately declared his loyalty to Jesus. He did not know the difference be-

tween a carnal and spiritual commitment to God. There are three differences.

a. There is the difference between purposes and desires.
   ⇒ A carnal commitment purposes and desires to have *earthly and material things.*
   ⇒ A spiritual commitment purposes and desires to have *spiritual and heavenly things.*

Peter was committed to Jesus in the establishment of an earthly kingdom. That was what he wanted, and he was willing to follow Jesus to achieve the end—even to the point of dying in combat against the Romans (cp. Jn.13:33, 36-14:3). However, when he saw Jesus arrested and tried and apparently powerless, Peter's personal ambition was being crushed. Therefore, his succumbing to temptation was inevitable—not because of his lack of commitment, but because his *purpose and motive for committing himself was wrong.*

For whoever exalts himself will be humbled, and whoever humbles himself will be exalted. (Mat 23:12)

For by the grace given me I say to every one of you: Do not think of yourself more highly than you ought, but rather think of yourself with sober judgment, in accordance with the measure of faith God has given you. (Rom 12:3)

If anyone thinks he is something when he is nothing, he deceives himself. (Gal 6:3)

So, if you think you are standing firm, be careful that you don't fall! (1 Cor 10:12)

Many seek an audience with a ruler, but it is from the LORD that man gets justice. (Prov 29:26)

b. There is the difference between seeing and being blind to the cross.
   ⇒ A carnal commitment ignores or rejects or spiritualizes the real meaning of the cross.
   ⇒ A spiritual commitment sees the cross and leads a person to crucify his flesh by the cross. (See note and DEEPER STUDY # 1—Lk.9:23. Cp. Ro.6:6; 8:13; Gal.2:20; 5:24; Col.3:5.)

Peter's overconfidence was caused by being blind to the cross. It was Jesus hanging upon the cross that was going to cause Peter to deny Jesus. Jesus had told him all about the cross; but Peter had refused to believe it (see notes—Mt.17:22; 18:1-2). The fact that human flesh was so sinful and so depraved that God would have to crucify it was just too much to grasp (see outline and notes—Mt.26:33-34; Ro.6:6-13; pt.2—Gal.2:19-21; 5:24; 6:14-17. Cp. Ro.6:2; Col.3:3.)

Then he said to them all: "If anyone would come after me, he must deny himself and take up his cross daily and follow me. (Luke 9:23)

For we know that our old self was crucified with him so that the body of sin might be done away with, that we should no longer be slaves to sin— (Rom 6:6)

For if you live according to the sinful nature, you will die; but if by the Spirit you put to death the misdeeds of the body, you will live, (Rom 8:13)

I have been crucified with Christ and I no longer live, but Christ lives in me. The life I live in the body, I live by faith in the Son of God, who loved me and gave himself for me. (Gal 2:20)

Those who belong to Christ Jesus have crucified the sinful nature with its passions and desires. (Gal 5:24)

Put to death, therefore, whatever belongs to your earthly nature: sexual immorality, impurity, lust, evil desires and greed, which is idolatry. (Col 3:5)

c. There is the difference between knowing and not knowing the weakness of the human body. Peter boasted confidence in himself, in his own natural strength. *As with all men*, his natural strength failed. The need for the Lord's strength, the presence of the Holy Spirit to conquer self and evil was the great lesson Peter had to learn. Very simply, he and the others had to learn to trust the strength of Jesus, not their own body, not if they wished to please God and to be acceptable to Him.

Those who live according to the sinful nature have their minds set on what that nature desires; but those who live in accordance with the Spirit have their minds set on what the Spirit desires. The mind of sinful man is death, but the mind controlled by the Spirit is life and peace; the sinful mind is hostile to God. It does not submit to God's law, nor can it do so. Those controlled by the sinful nature cannot please God. (Rom 8:5-8)

The man who thinks he knows something does not yet know as he ought to know. (1 Cor 8:2)

If anyone thinks he is something when he is nothing, he deceives himself. (Gal 6:3)

Do not be wise in your own eyes; fear the LORD and shun evil. (Prov 3:7)

Note: the rooster's crowing was probably mentioned to trigger the warning about the weakness of the flesh in the mind of Peter and the others. For the person who has the privilege of hearing the rooster crow, it is a good trigger to remind him of the weakness of his own flesh and the great need to walk with the Spirit of God. (See note, pt.2—Mt.26:33-35.)

2. Prevention 2: not forgetting Jesus' resources. Jesus reminded His disciples how God had taken care of them when He sent them out to preach (see outline and notes—Lk.9:3-5; 10:4 for the background of this event). God provided everything they needed. One of the preventatives against Satan's attacks is to remember God's glorious provisions.

No temptation has seized you except what is common to man. And God is faithful; he will not let you be tempted beyond what you can bear. But when you are tempted, he will also provide a way out so that you can stand up under it. (1 Cor 10:13)

I am not saying this because I am in

need, for I have learned to be content whatever the circumstances. I know what it is to be in need, and I know what it is to have plenty. I have learned the secret of being content in any and every situation, whether well fed or hungry, whether living in plenty or in want. I can do everything through him who gives me strength. (Phil 4:11-13)

And my God will meet all your needs according to his glorious riches in Christ Jesus. (Phil 4:19)

But seek first his kingdom and his righteousness, and all these things will be given to you as well. (Mat 6:33)

3. Prevention 3: knowing that very difficult days lie ahead. Jesus was warning of the perilous days that lay ahead and the need for the disciples to prepare for those days. He was speaking symbolically—of spiritual warfare and spiritual preparation. Two things were to happen to the followers of the Lord.

a. Their friends were to forsake them. They would have to earn their own livelihood while preaching and ministering. They would need their purses and money. No man would help them nor provide housing or upkeep; no man would free them to preach the gospel or minister. They should, but they would not.

The elders who direct the affairs of the church well are worthy of double honor, especially those whose work is preaching and teaching. For the Scripture says, "Do not muzzle the ox while it is treading out the grain," and "The worker deserves his wages." (1 Tim 5:17-18)

b. Their enemies would be fierce. Jesus was not telling His disciples to arm themselves. He was simply using symbolic language to stress a spiritual truth. The persecution they were to face would be so fierce that they must clothe themselves with courage, the kind of courage...

- that is determined to stand and conquer.
- that considers a weapon more important than clothing.
- that gives up its last possession before surrendering.

4. Prevention 4: knowing that Jesus is the Suffering Servant of God. Jesus said three things.

a. The Scripture included prophecies of Him and they "must be fulfilled in me." He was claiming deity, to be the Messiah, the Son of the living God. He was claiming that the prophecy of the Suffering Servant in Isaiah 53 concerned Him. He was the Suffering Servant of God.

Surely he took up our infirmities and carried our sorrows, yet we considered him stricken by God, smitten by him, and afflicted. But he was pierced for our transgressions, he was crushed for our iniquities; the punishment that brought us peace was upon him, and by his wounds we are healed. (Isa 53:4-5)

b. He was to be reckoned and counted among the transgressors. This means that God was to look at Him and count Him as a sinner just like all other men. He was to become one with man even in sin, yet He was to be without sin. Why? So that He could take the place of sinful men, bearing their sins for them. He was to become the substitute for men in bearing both their sins and the guilt and judgment of their sins (see note—Lk.22:43-44).

Christ redeemed us from the curse of the law by becoming a curse for us, for it is written: "Cursed is everyone who is hung on a tree." (Gal 3:13)

But we see Jesus, who was made a little lower than the angels, now crowned with glory and honor because he suffered death, so that by the grace of God he might taste death for everyone. (Heb 2:9)

So Christ was sacrificed once to take away the sins of many people; and he will appear a second time, not to bear sin, but to bring salvation to those who are waiting for him. (Heb 9:28)

He himself bore our sins in his body on the tree, so that we might die to sins and live for righteousness; by his wounds you have been healed. (1 Pet 2:24)

For Christ died for sins once for all, the righteous for the unrighteous, to bring you to God. He was put to death in the body but made alive by the Spirit, (1 Pet 3:18)

But you know that he appeared so that he might take away our sins. And in him is no sin. (1 John 3:5)

c. The things concerning Him "is reaching its fulfillment" (telos echei): an accomplishment, fulfillment, com-pletion. The Suffering Servant of God would fulfill Isaiah 53, and man's salvation would be finally settled, finished. He was to proclaim upon the cross "It is finished" and then bow His head and give up the ghost.

"My food," said Jesus, "is to do the will of him who sent me and to finish his work. (John 4:34)

I have brought you glory on earth by completing the work you gave me to do. (John 17:4)

When he had received the drink, Jesus said, "It is finished." With that, he bowed his head and gave up his spirit. (John 19:30)

4 (22:38) **Conclusion**: the disciples still did not understand. The warning was not grasped. They still thought in terms of an earthly Messiah, of a Messiah who needed their help in the fight against the evil forces of the world. They still refused to accept the spiritual kingdom of the Messiah. Jesus' words "that is enough" did not mean that two swords were enough, but "enough of this kind of talk."

	XI. THE SON OF MAN'S SUFFERINGS: HIS AGONY, TRIALS, AND CRUCIFIXION, 22:39-23:56 **A. Jesus' Great Agony: Bearing Unbelievable Weight, 22:39-46** (Mt.26:36-46; Mk.14: 32-42; Jn.18:1; cp. Heb.5:7-8; 12:3-4)	41 He withdrew about a stone's throw beyond them, knelt down and prayed, 42 "Father, if you are willing, take this cup from me; yet not my will, but yours be done." 43 An angel from heaven appeared to him and strengthened him. 44 And being in anguish, he prayed more earnestly, and his sweat was like drops of blood falling to the ground.	**3 The weight of His own cup of suffering**[DS1] **4 The awful weight of His intense agony**[DS2] a. Seen in the angel's visit b. Seen in His intense praying c. Seen in His sweat
1 Jesus in the Mount of Olives a. His custom to withdraw there for prayer b. His disciples follow **2 The weight of His disciples' great trial**	39 Jesus went out as usual to the Mount of Olives, and his disciples followed him. 40 On reaching the place, he said to them, "Pray that you will not fall into temptation."	45 When he rose from prayer and went back to the disciples, he found them asleep, exhausted from sorrow. 46 "Why are you sleeping?" he asked them. "Get up and pray so that you will not fall into temptation."	**5 The weight of the disciples' continued weakness**

DIVISION XI

THE SON OF MAN'S SUFFERINGS: HIS AGONY, TRIALS, AND CRUCIFIXION, 22:39-23:56

A. Jesus' Great Agony: Bearing Unbelievable Weight, 22:39-46

(22:39-46) **Introduction**: this passage shows the great weight of suffering Jesus underwent in facing the cross.

1. Jesus in the Mount of Olives (v.39).
2. The weight of His disciples' great trial (v.40).
3. The weight of His own cup of suffering (v.41-42).
4. The awful weight of the intense agony (v.43-44).
5. The weight of the disciples' continued weakness (v.45-46).

1 (22:39) **Prayer—Jesus Christ, Prayer Life of**: Jesus entered the Mount of Olives. His disciples were with Him. The significant thing to note is this: it was His custom to seek time alone with God on the mount when in Jerusalem. During the last week of His life, He was spending every night in prayer (see note 2 and DEEPER STUDY # 1—Lk.21:37).

2 (22:40) **Jesus Christ, Sufferings—Discipleship**: Jesus bore the weight of His disciples' great trial. The greatest trial the disciples were to ever know was at hand, and they did not know it. In just a few hours they were going to fall away. They desperately needed to pray that they "will not fall into temptation" (v.40), that they not be so gripped by temptation and sin that they would be too weak to repent when Jesus arose and confronted them. Jesus knew the enormous temptation that was coming upon these men, and He loved and cared for them, so He was bound to feel the pressure of their trial.

> **For we do not have a high priest who is unable to sympathize with our weaknesses, but we have one who has been tempted in every way, just as we are—yet was without sin. Let us then approach the throne of grace with confidence, so that we may receive mercy and find grace to help us in our time of need. (Heb 4:15-16)**
>
> **For our struggle is not against flesh and blood, but against the rulers, against the authorities, against the powers of this dark world and against the spiritual forces of evil in the heavenly realms. Therefore put on the full armor of God, so that when the day of evil comes, you may be able to stand your ground, and after you have done everything, to stand. (Eph 6:12-13)**
>
> **Therefore, dear friends, since you already know this, be on your guard so that you may not be carried away by the error of lawless men and fall from your secure position. (2 Pet 3:17)**

3 (22:41-42) **Jesus Christ, Sufferings**: Jesus bore the weight of His own cup of suffering. In confronting death Jesus turned to God, crying with *loud cries and tears* (cp. Heb.5:7). Four things are seen in this verse.

1. Jesus got all alone and prostrated Himself before God. Luke says He withdrew "about a stone's throw" from the three disciples. Note two significant points. (1) He needed to be alone with God—He was desperate. (b) He fell on His face—the pressure and weight were unbearable.

2. Jesus prayed, "Father (pater)." It is the address of a child's love and dependency and trust. The child knows that His father will hear and turn to him when he calls "Father." But note also the word, "Father." Jesus was broken and weighted down; He had fallen prostrate upon the ground with His face buried in His hands. In desperation He cried out "Father" (cp. Mt.26:39). Just like a child, He cried out to His Father in brokenness and dependency, knowing that His Father would hear Him and turn to help Him.

3. Jesus asked God to take the cup away from Him. (See DEEPER STUDY # 4, Cup—Mt.26:39. Also see Deeper Study # 1—Mt.27:26-44; cp. Mt.20:19.) The human nature and will of Jesus is clearly seen in this experience. He was as much flesh as any man is; therefore, He begged God to choose another way other than the cup, if possible. The ex-

perience of being *separated from God* upon the cross was too much to bear.

4. The divine nature and will of Jesus is also clearly seen in this experience. Note the Lord's words: "Take this cup from me: yet not my will...." The first act, the first impulse and struggle of His will, had come from His flesh: to escape the cup of separation from God. But immediately, the second act, the second impulse and struggle of His will, came from His Godly nature: not to do as He willed, but as God willed.

Jesus' surrender to do God's perfect will in the Garden of Gethsemane was critical.

⇒ It was in His surrender that He was made perfect and was able to stand before God as the Ideal, Perfect Man.

⇒ It was in His surrender to be the Ideal, Perfect Man that His righteousness was able to stand for every man.

⇒ It was in His surrender to be the Ideal, Perfect Man that He was able to bear the cup of God's wrath against sin *for every man.*

⇒ It was in His surrender to be the Ideal, Perfect Man that His sacrifice and sufferings were able to stand for every man.

> **But we see Jesus, who was made a little lower than the angels, now crowned with glory and honor because he suffered death, so that by the grace of God he might taste death for everyone. In bringing many sons to glory, it was fitting that God, for whom and through whom everything exists, should make the author of their salvation perfect through suffering. (Heb 2:9-10)**
>
> **Although he was a son, he learned obedience from what he suffered and, once made perfect, he became the source of eternal salvation for all who obey him (Heb 5:8-9)**
>
> **God made him who had no sin to be sin for us, so that in him we might become the righteousness of God. (2 Cor 5:21)**

DEEPER STUDY # 1

(22:42) **Cup**: Jesus Christ was not fearing nor shrinking from death itself. This is clearly seen in Jn.10:17-18. Death for a cause is not such a great price to pay. Many men have died for causes fearlessly and willingly, some perhaps even more cruelly than Jesus Himself. Shrinking from betrayal, beatings, humiliation, and death—increased by foreknowledge—is not what was happening to Jesus. As stated, some men have faced such trials courageously, even inviting martyrdom for a cause. The Lord knew He was to die from the very beginning, and He had been preparing His disciples for His death (see DEEPER STUDY # 1—Lk.9:22). It was not human and physical suffering from which Jesus was shrinking. Such an explanation is totally inadequate in explaining Gethsemane. The great cup or trial Jesus was facing was separation from God (see note, pt.1—Mt.26:37-38). He was to be the sacrificial *Lamb of God* who was to take away the sins of the world (Jn.1:29). He was to bear the judgment of God for the sins of the world (see note—Mt.27:46-49; cp. Is.53:10). Jesus Himself had already spoken of the "cup" when referring to His sacrificial death (see DEEPER STUDY # 2—Mt.20:22-23; note—Mk.14:41-42; DEEPER STUDY # 2—Jn.18:11).

Scripture speaks of the cup in several ways.

1. The cup is called "the cup of His wrath" (Is.51:17).

2. The cup is associated with suffering and God's wrath (cp. Ps.11:6; Is.51:17; Lk.22:42).

3. The cup is also associated with salvation. Because Jesus drank the cup of suffering and wrath for us, we can "lift up the cup of salvation and call on the name of the Lord" (Ps.116:13). He bears the judgment of God for the sins of the world (Is.53:10).

4 (22:43-44) **Jesus Christ, Suffering**: Jesus bore the awful weight of intense agony. This is seen in three facts.

1. God had to send an angel to strengthen Jesus. What did the angel do? We are not told, but certainly the angel would have shared how His death...

- was an act that glorified and honored God because it was doing exactly what His Father wanted. It was an act of obedience, of love and adoration for God. It was an offering, the perfect offering to God (see note—Eph.5:2).
- was to result in His own glory and honor and exaltation (Heb.12:2; Ph.2:6-11).
- was the only way man could be saved eternally.

Also, the angel probably did some very practical things. We can imagine the angel's embracing His Lord, just holding Him ever so tightly, perhaps infusing strength into His being. The scene of our Lord's being so weak that He had to be embraced and engulfed in the arms of an angel should break the believer's heart. Perhaps the angel wiped the perspiration and blood and tears off His brow. Whatever the scene, we need to see the awful weight and intensity of our Lord's agony.

2. He prayed "more earnestly," more intensely. The reason is seen in the Greek words for "being in anguish" (genomenos en agonia). The Greek (aorist participle) means Jesus experienced a growing agony. The weight upon Him was not only intense, it grew more and more intense. The pressure and sense of suffering became heavier and heavier. The picture is that of His becoming engrossed and embodied in agony. Thus, He prayed more and more earnestly. His prayer grew and increased in intensity even as His agony intensified.

3. He sweat drops like blood. The words "drops of blood" (thromboi) mean thick clots of blood. Apparently Jesus was under so much pressure the capillary veins right under the skin burst and the blood mingled with sweat and poured through the enlarged pores. What Jesus was experiencing can never be known (see DEEPER STUDY # 2, Jesus Christ, Suffering—Lk.22:43-44).

DEEPER STUDY # 2

(22:43-44) **Jesus Christ, Suffering**: words could never express what Jesus experienced. Words to describe the suffering of Jesus are totally inadequate. Using all the descriptive words in the world would be as inadequate as using a syringe to drain an ocean.

1. There was the *mental and emotional agony*: the weight, pressure, anguish, sorrow, and excessive strain such as no man has ever experienced. He was the Son of God, the Maker of heaven and earth; but *now* pressing in ever so heavily upon His mind and spirit were the images, the thoughts of...

- the *hardness and unbelief* of all men everywhere.
- the *rejection* of His own people, the Jews.

- the *malice* of the world's leaders, both Jew and Gentile, religious and civil.
- the *betrayal* of one of His own, Judas.
- the *desertion* of all His men.
- the *denial* by the leader of His own men, Peter.
- the *injustice and condemnation* of His trial.
- the *ridicule and pain* of being scourged, spit upon, slugged, cursed, mocked, crowned with thorns, nailed to the cross, and killed.
- the *wrath of God* that was soon to be cast upon Him as the Sin-Bearer of the world.
- the *departure of God's Spirit* from Him as He bore the sins of the world.

2. There was the *physical experience of death while being the Son of God.* What was it like for the Son of God to die just as all men die? If just the physical aspect of Jesus' death is considered, His death was still different from all other men.

a. Jesus as the Son of God possessed the very seed of life within His being (see DEEPER STUDY # 1—Jn.17:2-3).

b. Jesus as the Son of God possessed no seed of death (Jn.14:6; 1 Tim.6:16; 1 Jn.1:1-2. Cp. Jn.1:4.) But man does. Man possesses the seed of corruption and death; man's sinful nature knows nothing and expects nothing but death. However, the sinless nature of Jesus knew nothing of sin and death. Therefore, the agony and pain of death was bound to be as different from man's death as white is different from black.

There is another fact to note as well. Man suffers the depth of humiliation in death. No matter how much man struggles to live, he irrevocably wastes and wastes away until he is carried into the grave and dust of the ground. But not Jesus. Again He was sinless, perfect even in His human nature. Imagine the humiliation: the Son of God—Perfect Man, Perfect God—having to die upon this earth! No wonder He "began to be sorrowful and troubled!" (Mt.26:37) No wonder He could say, "My soul is overwhelmed with sorrow, to the point of death" (Mt.14:34). In some mysterious way, God made Jesus to become sin for us (2 Cor.5:21).

3. There was *the spiritual experience of death* while being the Son of Man (see note—Mt.5:17-18; DEEPER STUDY # 3—8:20; DEEPER STUDY # 2—Ro.8:3). There is so much in this fact, yet so little can ever be known.

a. First, what is it like to be without sin? Although being fully man, Jesus was sinless. He lived as all men live facing all the trials and temptations that men face, yet He never sinned. He became the Perfect Man, the Ideal Man—all that God wants man to be. Therefore, He became the Pattern for all men.

For we do not have a high priest who is unable to sympathize with our weaknesses, but we have one who has been tempted in every way, just as we are—yet was without sin. (Heb 4:15; cp. 2 Cor.5:21; 1 Pt.2:22; 1 Jn.3:5)

Although he was a son, he learned obedience from what he suffered (Heb 5:8)

And, once made perfect, he became the source of eternal salvation for all who obey him (Heb 5:9)

b. Second, what is it like to bear all the sins of the world? What is it like to be perfect and sinless, and then *all of a sudden* to have all the sins of the world laid upon Oneself? In some mysterious way, God took all the sins of the world and laid the whole *body of sin* upon Jesus. God made Jesus to become sin for us (2 Cor.5:21). Jesus, as the Ideal Man, became the Ideal Sin-Bearer. He bore all the sins and all that sin causes, all the...

- darkness
- pollution
- filth
- dirt
- poison
- weight
- pressure
- anxiety
- turmoil
- corrosion
- worry
- guilt
- savagery
- conflict
- consumption
- strife
- warring
- torture
- enmity
- disturbance

We all, like sheep, have gone astray, each of us has turned to his own way; and the LORD has laid on him the iniquity of us all. (Isa 53:6)

You see, at just the right time, when we were still powerless, Christ died for the ungodly. (Rom 5:6)

God made him who had no sin to be sin for us, so that in him we might become the righteousness of God. (2 Cor 5:21)

So Christ was sacrificed once to take away the sins of many people; and he will appear a second time, not to bear sin, but to bring salvation to those who are waiting for him. (Heb 9:28)

He himself bore our sins in his body on the tree, so that we might die to sins and live for righteousness; by his wounds you have been healed. (1 Pet 2:24)

c. Third, what is it like to bear all the judgment and condemnation of sin for all men? What is it like to be judged and condemned for *all the sins ever committed*? Jesus suffered for the sins of *the whole world*, suffered *separation* from God. The terrifying mystery of this hellish experience is seen in His cry upon the cross, "My God, My God, why have you forsaken me?" (See notes—Mt.27:26-44; 27:46-49; 1 Pt.2:21-25.)

But he was pierced for our transgressions, he was crushed for our iniquities; the punishment that brought us peace was upon him, and by his wounds we are healed. (Isa 53:5)

Christ redeemed us from the curse of the law by becoming a curse for us, for it is written: "Cursed is everyone who is hung on a tree." (Gal 3:13)

But we see Jesus, who was made a little lower than the angels, now crowned with glory and honor because he suffered death, so that by the grace of God he might taste death for everyone. (Heb 2:9)

For Christ died for sins once for all, the righteous for the unrighteous, to bring you to God. He was put to death in the body but made alive by the Spirit, (1 Pet 3:18)

5 (22:45-46) **Jesus Christ, Suffering**: Jesus bore the weight of the disciples' continued weakness. The disciples were weak, so weak in fact that they were of no help to Jesus as He faced the most severe crises of His life. Jesus had to face the cross knowing the terrible weakness of His own men. Note what happened.

1. Jesus arose from prayer and went to the three who were supposed to be praying with Him. They were asleep. The companionship and spirit of prayer and comfort He had sought were not there. All were asleep. He had been left alone to wrestle with God by Himself.

2. Jesus warned them of temptation. They had failed to pray for Him, but they must not fail to pray for themselves. Jesus said, "Get up and pray." Both were important. *Watchfulness* sees and *praying* prepares. They must watch in order to see temptation coming, and they must pray in order to be prepared when temptation struck.

3. Jesus warned of the flesh and its weakness. They were sleeping because of the emotional strain and distress of the evening. As Luke says, they slept because of "sorrow," that is, sadness (Lk.22:45). The evening had been shocking and taxing. They were weary, fatigued, and preoccupied. Concentration in prayer was difficult. They probably fought to stay awake and to pray for their Lord, but the importance of prayer and of spiritual dependancy upon God in facing trials had not yet been learned. They were making two mistakes common among believers.

   a. They were depending upon their own wisdom and strength instead of God's Spirit to fight whatever battles lay ahead.
   b. They were taking God's deliverance for granted instead of assuring themselves of His deliverance through the testimony of prayer. They believed Christ to be the Messiah; therefore, they believed that God was going to deliver them from the Romans no matter what. As carnal, fleshy men are apt to do, the disciples no doubt thought prayer mattered little. They were just presuming upon God, taking His deliverance for granted. What Jesus said was, "Watch and pray, for only as you watch and pray can you keep from falling when the trial comes."

A point needs to be noted here: watchfulness and prayer bear *testimony* to God. When men watch and pray, they demonstrate that dependency and trust in God are well founded. When God answers the prayers of men, He demonstrates that He loves and delivers those who truly look up to Him. Without watching and praying, God allows the disciples to fall in order to teach that dependency and trust in Him are absolutely essential.

4. They were failing to stay awake to pray, to watch and be watchful in prayer. Their spirits were not alive and alert enough to overcome the flesh. The drowsiness and slumber of the flesh were stronger than the spirit (see note, pt.2—Mt.26:42-44; cp. Eph.6:18).

"Watch and pray so that you will not fall into temptation. The spirit is willing, but the body is weak." (Mat 26:41)

So, if you think you are standing firm, be careful that you don't fall! (1 Cor 10:12)

Devote yourselves to prayer, being watchful and thankful. (Col 4:2)

Be self-controlled and alert. Your enemy the devil prowls around like a roaring lion looking for someone to devour. (1 Pet 5:8)

	B. Jesus' Arrest: Terrible	50 And one of them struck	
	Sins Against Jesus,	the servant of the high priest,	
	22:47-53	cutting off his right ear.	
	(Mt.26:47-56; Mk.14:	51 But Jesus answered, "No	b. Jesus rebuked the
	43-52; Jn.18:3-11)	more of this!" And he	disciples
		touched the man's ear and	
1 Deserting Jesus: The be-	47 While he was still speak-	healed him.	
trayer	ing a crowd came up, and the	52 Then Jesus said to the	**3 Being blind to the Son**
a. A professing disciple	man who was called Judas,	chief priests, the officers of	**of God: The religionists**
b. A leader of sinners	one of the Twelve, was lead-	the temple guard, and the el-	
	ing them. He approached Je-	ders, who had come for him,	
	sus to kiss him,	"Am I leading a rebellion,	
c. A deceptive commitment	48 But Jesus asked him,	that you have come with	
	"Judas, are you betraying the	swords and clubs?	
	Son of Man with a kiss?"	53 Every day I was with you	**4 Joining forces with the**
2 Misunderstanding the	49 When Jesus' followers	in the temple courts, and you	**power of darkness**
Lord's will: The disciples	saw what was going to hap-	did not lay a hand on me. But	
a. The disciples misunder-	pen, they said, "Lord, should	this is your hour—when	
stood & ignored Jesus' will	we strike with our swords?"	darkness reigns."	

DIVISION XI

THE SON OF MAN'S SUFFERINGS: HIS AGONY, TRIALS, AND CRUCIFIXION, 22:39-23:56

B. Jesus' Arrest: Terrible Sins Against Jesus, 22:47-53

(22:47-53) **Introduction**: it took only a few minutes to arrest Jesus. However, in those few minutes was painted a dramatic picture of four terrible sins against the Lord, sins that are repeated by too many in every generation.

1. Deserting Jesus: the betrayer (v.47-48).
2. Misunderstanding and ignoring the Lord's will: the disciples (v.49-51).
3. Being blind to the Son of God: the religionists (v.52).
4. Joining forces with the power of darkness (v.53).

1 (22:47-48) **Unbelief—Desertion—Apostasy—Judas**: deserting the Lord, the sin committed by Judas the betrayer. Three things are seen in Judas' desertion.

1. He was a *professing* disciple, a man who claimed to be a follower of the Lord. In fact, he had actually been with the Lord and His followers for over two years. On this very evening, just a few hours before, he had been eating and fellowshipping with the Lord and the other disciples; but ever so quickly, he had turned away.

2. He was a *leader* of sinners, leading the world in its opposition to Jesus. Note the words "was leading them." As pointed out earlier, he chose the world before Jesus—the world's money, position, and recognition (fame). (See note—Mk.14:10.)

The crowd which Judas led is identified by Matthew and Mark as being arresting officers or temple police from the Sanhedrin. John says they included Roman soldiers. Matthew and Mark say they were armed. The soldiers, of course, had their swords; the elders and other officials of the High Priest had armed themselves with boards and sticks (cp. Mt.26:47).

3. He had a *deceptive* commitment to the Lord. Note what happened. It was dark. How would the temple guards be able to recognize Jesus in the dark and keep Him from slipping away? Judas thought and came up with a plan. He would identify Jesus for them by walking up and greeting Jesus with a kiss. A kiss was a sign of friendship and commitment among people in the East, in particular among friends. Judas felt he could deceive the disciples; they would never suspect his sin.

What Judas planned, he did. The sin was bad, but the deception was worse. Jesus' question was searching: "Judas, are you betraying the Son of man with a kiss?" Note: the question was not a rebuke or reproach. Jesus was forcing Judas to think, to search his deceptive heart. He still wanted to reach Judas, if possible (see note—Mt.26:48-50).

> **Thought 1.** How many profess Christ but do not really know Christ nor live for Christ? How many are deceivers just as Judas was: trying to make others think they are followers of Christ when they are really living *for themselves*? How many began to follow Christ but are now falling back into sin just as Judas did?
>
> **Friend deceives friend, and no one speaks the truth. They have taught their tongues to lie; they weary themselves with sinning. (Jer 9:5)**
>
> **The heart is deceitful above all things and beyond cure. Who can understand it? (Jer 17:9)**
>
> **Then we will no longer be infants, tossed back and forth by the waves, and blown here and there by every wind of teaching and by the cunning and craftiness of men in their deceitful scheming. (Eph 4:14)**
>
> **While evil men and impostors will go from bad to worse, deceiving and being deceived. (2 Tim 3:13)**
>
> **For there are many rebellious people, mere talkers and deceivers, especially those of the circumcision group. (Titus 1:10)**
>
> **See to it, brothers, that none of you has a sinful, unbelieving heart that turns away from the living God. (Heb 3:12)**
>
> **They will be paid back with harm for the harm they have done. Their idea of pleasure is to carouse in broad daylight. They are blots and blemishes, reveling in their pleasures while they feast with you. With eyes full of adultery, they never stop**

sinning; they seduce the unstable; they are experts in greed—an accursed brood! (2 Pet 2:13-14)

Many deceivers, who do not acknowledge Jesus Christ as coming in the flesh, have gone out into the world. Any such person is the deceiver and the antichrist. (2 John 1:7)

2 (22:49-51) **Flesh—Commitment—Carnal**: misunderstanding and ignoring the Lord's will, the sin committed by the disciples. Note two things.

1. The disciples misunderstood the Lord's will and the spiritual nature of His kingdom. They were ready to *war in the body or flesh.* The disciple referred to in v.50 was Peter, and the servant whose ear was cut off was Malchus (Jn.18:10). Jesus restored the ear, miraculously healed it (Lk.22:51).

Peter thought the Messiah's hour had come, that Jesus was now ready to free Israel and establish the throne of David as the dominant nation in the world (see notes—Mt.1:1; DEEPER STUDY # 2—1:18; DEEPER STUDY # 3—3:11; notes—11:1-6; 11:2-3; DEEPER STUDY # 1—11:5; DEEPER STUDY # 2—11:6; DEEPER STUDY # 1—12:16; notes—22:42; Lk.7:21-23). Peter drew his sword (note he had one) and struck, slashing off the ear of Malchus.

2. Jesus rebuked the disciples: their carnal commitment, their warring in the body or flesh.

⇒ He told Peter to put his sword back into its sheath where it belonged (Mt.26:52).

⇒ He healed Malchus' ear (Lk.22:51).

The picture painted by the disciples' behavior is carnal commitment, that is, acting and struggling in the flesh. The disciples took their stand for Jesus *in the flesh.* Therefore they failed, and eventually they deserted Jesus. Acting in the flesh will always result in failing and deserting Christ. The disciples' carnal commitment is seen in four mistakes. Each mistake is too often seen in the life of believers.

1. The disciples misunderstood the Lord's Word. First, they thought Jesus was to establish an earthly kingdom. They thought in terms of the earthly, the physical, the material. Therefore, they *failed to grasp the spiritual and eternal kingdom* proclaimed by Jesus. Second, they never accepted the Lord's Word. Jesus had predicted His death and forewarned the disciples, giving them extensive training for months (see notes—Mt.16:13-20; 16:21-28; 17:1-13; 17:22; 17:24-27). Yet they refused to give up their preconceived ideas to accept what Jesus was saying. Therefore, they did not see the eternal world of the Spirit nor the eternal salvation which Jesus was securing.

2. The disciples did not wait for instructions from Jesus. They acted on their own, took matters into their own hands. The disciples had asked, "Lord, should we strike with our swords?" But Jesus had not yet answered. However, this did not stop them; they went ahead and acted on their own.

Thought 1. How like so many of us! Too often, we act without waiting on the Lord.

3. The disciples did not ask Jesus what to do, not again and again. They did not *persist* until Jesus answered.

"Watch and pray so that you will not fall into temptation. The spirit is willing, but the body is weak." (Mat 26:41)

Be always on the watch, and pray that you may be able to escape all that is about to happen, and that you may be able to stand before the Son of Man." (Luke 21:36)

Look to the LORD and his strength; seek his face always. (1 Chr 16:11)

4. The disciples did not think clearly nor act wisely. Their actions could have led to the failure of God's will. It could have led to the death of many. That is what Jesus was saying: "Violence leads to violence. If you draw the sword, the soldiers will cut you down." Among God's people, the place of the sword is in the sheath, not drawn and slashing at people. God's people are to proclaim love and peace, not war and violence, not carnal and fleshly behavior.

So he said to me, "This is the word of the LORD to Zerubbabel: 'Not by might nor by power, but by my Spirit,' says the LORD Almighty. (Zec 4:6)

Those whom I love I rebuke and discipline. So be earnest, and repent. (Rev 3:19)

But in your hearts set apart Christ as Lord. Always be prepared to give an answer to everyone who asks you to give the reason for the hope that you have. But do this with gentleness and respect, (1 Pet 3:15)

3 (22:52) **Sin—Unbelief—Blindness**: being blind to the Son of God, the sin committed by the religionists. The religionists refused to accept Jesus as the Messiah (see note and DEEPER STUDY # 1—Mk.14:1-2). The question of Jesus was piercing. Why did the world treat Him as a thief? They acted as though He stole from them. He did not preach a message that allowed them to live as they wished; it was as though He took the right to live as they wished away from them. He did not praise them, boost their egos, honor their service and gifts. Rather, He told them they were lacking in discernment and sinful, dying and doomed if they did not repent and begin to live as God said (see note—Mt.26:55-56).

Thought 1. Note a crucial point so often not seen. Jesus had to tell the truth in order for men to be saved. God is love, but His love is not like a grandfather's indulgence that accepts wrongdoing. His love is the father's ache and acceptance of repentance and obedience. *Only through repentance and obedience can a man ever know the love of God* (cp. Jn.14:21, 23-24; 15:10, 14). God does not accept a man who does wrong and lives unrighteously. Jesus had to tell men the truth, for He could not deceive men. If men wanted to be acceptable to God and live in His love, then they had to turn away from sin and come to God, believing that He exists and diligently seeking Him.

And without faith it is impossible to please God, because anyone who comes to him must believe that he exists and that he rewards those who earnestly seek him. (Heb 11:6)

Whoever has my commands and obeys them, he is the one who loves me. He who loves me will be loved by my Father, and I too will love him and show myself to him." (John 14:21)

Jesus replied, "If anyone loves me, he will obey my teaching. My Father will love him, and we will come to him and make our home with him. He who does not love me will not obey my teaching. These words you hear are not my own; they belong to the Father who sent me. (John 14:23-24)

If you obey my commands, you will remain in my love, just as I have obeyed my Father's commands and remain in his love. You are my friends if you do what I command. (John 15:10, 14)

4 (22:53) **Satan**: joining forces with the power of darkness. What Jesus said was alarming: "This is your hour, when darkness reigns." Those who opposed Jesus had joined forces with the power of darkness against Jesus. The power of darkness refers to the forces of evil, the evil one himself, Satan (Eph.6:12; Col.1:13). Note these points about the word "hour."

1. An hour is only a short time. It soon passes. Therefore, the power of darkness and those who oppose the Lord will last but a short time. Their hour will soon pass.

2. The power of darkness is always broken and conquered by light. When light appears, the presence and power of darkness are destroyed. So it is with God's Son, the Light of the world. The power of darkness and those who oppose Christ may have their hour now, but their hour is to end. He, the Light of the world, will arise and dispel the darkness and completely do away with it.

3. An hour soon passes, but then what is left? All the hours of life and of eternity. The power of darkness and those who oppose Christ may have an hour, but that will be all. However He, the Light of the world, will give Light to the world forever.

For our struggle is not against flesh and blood, but against the rulers, against the authorities, against the powers of this dark world and against the spiritual forces of evil in the heavenly realms. (Eph 6:12)

For he has rescued us from the dominion of darkness and brought us into the kingdom of the Son he loves, in whom we have redemption, the forgiveness of sins. (Col 1:13-14)

1 The cause of denial a. "Followed at a distance" b. "Sat down" in the midst of the crowd **2 The denial of pretension: Pretending not to know Jesus** a. The charge: Was with Jesus	**C. Peter's Denial: The Great Tragedy of Denial, 22:54-62** (Mt.26:57, 69-75; Mk.14:53-54, 66-72; Jn.18:15-18, 25-27) 54 Then seizing him, they led him away and took him into the house of the high priest. Peter followed at a distance. 55 But when they had kin- dled a fire in the middle of the courtyard and had sat down together, Peter sat down with them. 56 A servant girl saw him seated there in the firelight. She looked closely at him and said, "This man was with him." 57 But he denied it. "Woman	I don't know him," he said. 58 A little later someone else saw him and said, "You also are one of them." "Man, I am not!" Peter replied. 59 About an hour later an- other asserted, "Certainly this fellow was with him, for he is a Galilean." 60 Peter replied, "Man, I don't know what you're talking about!" Just as he was speaking, the rooster crowed. 61 The Lord turned and looked straight at Peter. Then Peter remembered the word the Lord had spoken to him: "Before the rooster crows to- day, you will disown me three times." 62 And he went outside and wept bitterly.	b. The denial: Pretends not to know Jesus **3 The denial of discipleship: Denying that one is a follower of Jesus** **4 The denial of ignorance: Claiming to know nothing about what is being said** a. The charge: Emphatic—was with Jesus b. The denial: Emphatic—know nothing about Him **5 The answer to denial** a. Remembering the Lord's word b. Getting alone c. Experiencing godly sorrow[DSI]

DIVISION XI

THE SON OF MAN'S SUFFERINGS: HIS AGONY, TRIALS, AND CRUCIFIXION, 22:39-23:56

C. Peter's Denial: The Great Tragedy of Denial, 22:54-62

(22:54-62) **Introduction**: denying Jesus is one of the greatest tragedies in all of life. Yet Jesus is denied often, not only by unbelievers but by believers as well. This passage is a study of denial, the awful tragedy of denying Jesus.

1. The cause of denial (v.54-55).
2. The denial of pretension: pretending not to know Jesus (v.56-57).
3. The denial of discipleship: denying that one is a follower of Jesus (v.58).
4. The denial of ignorance: claiming that one knows nothing about what is being said (v.59-60).
5. The answer to denial (v.61-62).

1 (22:54-55) **Apostasy—Jesus Christ, Denied**: the cause of denial given in these verses is twofold. Peter failed Jesus and failed Him miserably.

1. "Peter followed at a distance." *Following Jesus at a distance* means not walking close to Him, not standing and being identified with Him. A man who follows at a distance is not focusing on Christ. His mind and life are not fixed upon the Lord. His commitment is weak; therefore, he is easily…

- distracted by the world and drawn into its ways.
- stricken with fear—the fear of ridicule, embarrassment, abuse, persecution, being cut off, shunned, ignored, ostracized.

> **For God did not give us a spirit of timidity, but a spirit of power, of love and of self-discipline. So do not be ashamed to testify about our Lord, or ashamed of me his prisoner. But join with me in suffering for the gospel, by the power of God, (2 Tim 1:7-8)**

2. Peter "sat down with them" [the crowd], the crowd which represented the world of rejecters. Very frankly, Peter was failing Jesus miserably. Sitting down among the crowd was the last place he should have been. He, of course, should have never forsaken Jesus. But having fled, he should have been off alone with God in prayer, seeking answers and understanding from God (see notes—Mt.26:51-52; 26:55-56). Or he should have been with the other apostles, leading them to seek the face of God for understanding and direction.

> **"Therefore come out from them and be separate, says the Lord. Touch no unclean thing, and I will receive you." "I will be a Father to you, and you will be my sons and daughters, says the Lord Almighty." (2 Cor 6:17-18)**

2 (22:56-57) **Apostasy—Jesus Christ, Denied**: the denial of pretension—pretending not to know Jesus. When confronted, this denial says, "I have nothing to do with Christ."

Note what happened. A maid "looked closly" at Peter. She stared at him, observed him closely, thinking she had seen him with Jesus. She concluded that Peter was one of the Lord's followers: "This man was with Him." There seems to be no threat or danger in this statement to Peter. At worst it seems that it would have led only to some bantering and ridicule. The rejecters standing around were naturally bantering back and forth about Jesus and His claims, considering Him to have been a fool. Peter had an opportunity, perhaps, to be a witness for Jesus, humbly sharing about the love and enormous care of Jesus for people. Perhaps he could have helped to turn some who were standing there to Jesus, or at least stopped some of the mob's ridiculing. We must always remember that John was somewhere in the palace as well, and as far as we know, he was maintaining his composure and testimony for Jesus.

Peter cracked under his fear. He denied Jesus, pretending he did not know Him or have anything to do with Him.

> **Thought 1.** Weak believers fear the crowd. When in church they readily profess Christ, but out in the world, at work or at school, they fear being known as believers. They pretend not to know Christ.
>
> **But whoever disowns me before men, I will disown him before my Father in heaven. (Mat 10:33)**
>
> **A false witness will not go unpunished, and he who pours out lies will not go free. (Prov 19:5)**
>
> **But in your hearts set apart Christ as Lord. Always be prepared to give an answer to everyone who asks you to give the reason for the hope that you have. But do this with gentleness and respect, (1 Pet 3:15)**

3 (22:58) **Apostasy—Jesus Christ, Denied**: the denial of discipleship—denying that one is a follower of Jesus. When confronted, this denial is more emphatic and vocal, "I am not a disciple, not a follower of Christ."

Note the charge: "Thou are also one of them." The charge was true.

⇒ Peter had been with Jesus. He was an apostle; in fact, he was the leader of the apostles.
⇒ Peter was the disciple who had professed that Jesus was the Christ, the Son of God (Mt.16:16).
⇒ Peter was the disciple who had sworn loyalty to Jesus even if it meant death (Mt.26:33-35).

Peter emphatically denied that he was a disciple, a follower of Jesus: "I am not!" Peter was falling (progressing) more and more into sin. He was denying Jesus because he was not by His side, but *standing among* the Lord's rejecters.

⇒ He was standing among the Lord's rejecters because he had fled the Lord.
⇒ He had fled the Lord because he had acted in the flesh (see note—Lk.22:49-51).
⇒ He had acted in the flesh because he had not accepted the Lord's words for what they said.

> **If anyone is ashamed of me and my words in this adulterous and sinful generation, the Son of Man will be ashamed of him when he comes in his Father's glory with the holy angels." (Mark 8:38)**
>
> **So do not be ashamed to testify about our Lord, or ashamed of me his prisoner. But join with me in suffering for the gospel, by the power of God, (2 Tim 1:8)**
>
> **Be strong and courageous. Do not be afraid or terrified because of them, for the LORD your God goes with you; he will never leave you nor forsake you." (Deu 31:6)**

4 (22:59-60) **Apostasy—Jesus Christ, Denied**: the denial of ignorance—claiming that one knows nothing about what is being said. This is the denial that claims ignorance, "I do not know what you are talking about; I know absolutely nothing about the matter." Matthew and Mark say Peter began to curse and swear, *denying any knowledge whatsoever about Jesus.*

Note: this accuser is sure Peter was a follower of Jesus. The man "was certain," insisted upon the fact. He even identified Peter's nationality, a Galilaean Jew. It was common knowledge that Jesus' disciples were Galilaeans.

Peter's chest was bound to be pounding with emotion and fear. His thoughts were flying, trying to figure how to escape. His emotions just burst forth in cursing and swearing, a forceful denial: "Man, I don't know what you're talking about." Note that this denial occurred about one hour after the last one. Peter's failure was a deteriorating failure.

⇒ At first, he pretended not to know Jesus.
⇒ Then he fell even farther. He emphatically denied being a disciple.
⇒ Now, he claimed total ignorance of all. He cursed and swore that he knew absolutely nothing about Jesus.

This is the point: Peter stayed in the crowd, still stood around the rejecters of Jesus—even after they had led him to deny Jesus twice. He was trying to be *of the world*, one of the crowd, when he should have been off praying and seeking to understand the ways of God.

> **Do not set foot on the path of the wicked or walk in the way of evil men. (Prov 4:14)**
>
> **Therefore, dear friends, since you already know this, be on your guard so that you may not be carried away by the error of lawless men and fall from your secure position. (2 Pet 3:17)**
>
> **They claim to know God, but by their actions they deny him. They are detestable, disobedient and unfit for doing anything good. (Titus 1:16)**
>
> **If we endure, we will also reign with him. If we disown him, he will also disown us; (2 Tim 2:12)**
>
> **Without being frightened in any way by those who oppose you. This is a sign to them that they will be destroyed, but that you will be saved—and that by God. (Phil 1:28)**
>
> **With many other words he warned them; and he pleaded with them, "Save yourselves from this corrupt generation." (Acts 2:40)**

5 (22:60-62) **Repentance—Confession**: three steps were involved in Peter's repentance.

1. Remembering the Lord's words. Apparently while the rooster was crowing, the Lord, standing in the chamber of the palace, turned around and caught the eye of Peter (Lk.22:61). And Peter, eye to eye with the Lord, remembered the words the Lord had spoken to him:

> **"Simon, Simon, Satan has asked to sift you as wheat. But I have prayed for you, Simon, that your faith may not fail. And when you have turned back, strengthen your brothers." (Luke 22:31-32)**

In the midst of all His own pain and suffering, the Lord's look told Peter that His Lord had not forgotten him. The Lord still loved and cared for Him and wanted his loyalty and service. Jesus had prayed for Peter, and the power of that prayer was now moving in Peter's heart and life. Peter now remembered His Lord's word and that word began to take effect.

2. Getting alone. Peter left as fast as he safely could from the porch or courtyard through the gate out into the night to get alone at last with God. He was broken, full of anguish and pain for having failed his Lord: he "wept bitterly."

3. Expressing godly sorrow: repentance (see DEEPER STUDY # 1—2 Cor.7:10).

If we confess our sins, he is faithful and just and will forgive us our sins and purify us from all unrighteousness. (1 John 1:9)

Repent of this wickedness and pray to the Lord. Perhaps he will forgive you for having such a thought in your heart. (Acts 8:22)

And prayed: "O my God, I am too ashamed and disgraced to lift up my face to you, my God, because our sins are higher than our heads and our guilt has reached to the heavens. (Ezra 9:6)

Now make confession to the LORD, the God of your fathers, and do his will. Separate yourselves from the peoples around you and from your foreign wives." (Ezra 10:11)

My guilt has overwhelmed me like a burden too heavy to bear. (Psa 38:4)

For I know my transgressions, and my sin is always before me. (Psa 51:3)

When my heart was grieved and my spirit embittered, (Psa 73:21; cp. John 16:8)

He who conceals his sins does not prosper, but whoever confesses and renounces them finds mercy. (Prov 28:13)

Only acknowledge your guilt— you have rebelled against the LORD your God, you have scattered your favors to foreign gods under every spreading tree, and have not obeyed me,'" declares the LORD. (Jer 3:13)

DEEPER STUDY # 1
(22:62) **Repentance**: see note and DEEPER STUDY # 1—Acts 17:29-30.

	D. Jesus Tried Before the Sanhedrin Court: The Phenomenal Claims of Jesus, 22:63-71 (Mt.26:57-68; 27:1; Mk.14:53-65; 15:1; Jn.18:12-14, 19-24)	of the law, met together, and Jesus was led before them.	
		67 "If you are the Christ, " they said, "tell us." Jesus answered, "If I tell you, you will not believe me, 68 And if I asked you, you would not answer.	**2 Claim 1: He is the Messiah**
1 The attitude of religion & the world toward Jesus' claims a. There is physical & verbal abuse	63 The men who were guarding Jesus began mocking and beating him. 64 They blindfolded him and demanded, "Prophesy! Who hit you?" 65 And they said many other insulting things to him.	69 But from now on, the Son of Man will be seated at the right hand of the mighty God." 70 They all asked, "Are you then the Son of God?" He replied, "You are right in saying I am."	**3 Claim 2: He is the Son of Man, exalted** **4 Claim 3: He is the Son of God**
b. There is formal & legal abuse—a formal trial[DS1]	66 At daybreak the council of the elders of the people, both the chief priests and teachers	71 Then they said, "Why do we need any more testimony? We have heard it from his own lips."	**5 Conclusion: The claims understood, but rejected**

DIVISION XI

THE SON OF MAN'S SUFFERINGS: HIS AGONY, TRIALS, AND CRUCIFIXION, 22:39-23:56

D. Jesus Tried Before the Sanhedrin Court: The Phenomenal Claims of Jesus, 22:63-71

(22:63-71) **Introduction**: this is the first trial of Jesus covered by Luke. The thrust of the trial was the phenomenal claims of Jesus, claims which demand a decision from every man.

1. The attitude of religion and the world toward Jesus' claims (v.63-66).
2. Claim 1: the Messiah (v.67-68).
3. Claim 2: the Son of Man, exalted (v.69).
4. Claim 3: the Son of God (v.70).
5. Conclusion: the claims understood, but rejected (v.71).

1 (22:63-66) **World, Response to Jesus—Persecution, of Jesus Christ—Jesus Christ, Trials of**: the attitude of religion and the world to Jesus' claims. The world and formal religion opposed Jesus. This is clearly seen in the treatment of Jesus during the night while He was being held for trial the next morning.

1. There was (and is today) physical and verbal abuse. They ridiculed and mocked and shamed and beat Him. Why? Because of His claims.

> **Remember the words I spoke to you: 'No servant is greater than his master.' If they persecuted me, they will persecute you also. If they obeyed my teaching, they will obey yours also. (John 15:20. Also refer to Jn.15:20-25.)**

2. There was ridicule of His spiritual power. If He were the Son of God, He should know all things, so they mocked and challenged His power: "Prophesy! who hit you?" But God gives no signs, not to the mocking and obstinate and devilish unbeliever. (See note—Mk.8:12.)

3. There were all kinds of blasphemy and cursing spoken against Him. (How tragic! Yet, how much like men today!)

Note the setting for the formal trial of Jesus. This was a trial by the Sanhedrin, the ruling body of the Jews which included both religious and lay leaders (see DEEPER STUDY # 1, Sanhedrin—Mt.26:59). Jesus stood before them all on trial for His life. Note the words "met together": they gathered, resorted, *flocked together* just as a body of vultures over their prey. There is also the idea of accompanying. The picture is that of the Jewish leaders flocking or herding together around Jesus, of being called to accompany one another to their respective seats, ready to pounce on Jesus. There is no question about the evil of their hearts. They *were* ready to pounce on and eliminate Him.

The court was stacked against Jesus. The leaders, both lay and religious, had already *determined* to reject and oppose Him. He was a threat to both their nation and their personal security and position. They feared the loss of both, so they were set on killing Him. (For a discussion of the reasons for their opposition, see notes—Mt.12:1-8; note and DEEPER STUDY # 1—12:10; note—15:1-20; DEEPER STUDY # 2—15:6-9; DEEPER STUDY # 3—16:12.)

> **Thought 1.** The religionists rejected and opposed Christ for two primary reasons, the same two reasons that men reject and oppose Him today.
> 1) Men are unwilling to deny self, to surrender all they are and have to Christ. They fear the loss of some-thing—some security, money, position, power, or pleasure. They love the world and self more than they are willing to love God.
> 2) Men are unwilling to deny their institutional religion: their religious practices that are *man-made, man-conceived, man-honoring*.

Thought 2. Men do *flock together* to oppose Christ. It is easier to oppose Him in the presence of others.

> **Dear friend, do not imitate what is evil but what is good. Anyone who does what is good is from God. Anyone who does what is evil has not seen God. (3 John 1:11)**
>
> **Anyone, then, who knows the good he ought to do and doesn't do it, sins. (James 4:17)**

DEEPER STUDY # 1
(22:66-71) **Jesus, Trials of**: there were at least six trials.
1. An informal trial during the night before Annas (Jn.18:12-14, 19-23).
2. An informal trial by night before Caiaphas and some Sanhedrin officials to find a charge against Jesus (Mt.26:57-68; Mk.14:53-65; Lk.22:54, 63-65).
3. An early morning formal trial before a quickly assembled Sanhedrin to secure the verdict of the full Sanhedrin and to formulate the charge against Jesus (Mt.27:1; Mk.15:1; Lk.22:66-71).
4. A preliminary questioning by Pilate (Mt.27:2, 11-14; Mk.15:1-5; Lk.23:1-5; Jn.18:28-38).
5. A preliminary questioning by Herod (Lk.23:6-12).
6. The formal Roman trial before Pilate (Mt.27:15-26; Mk.15:6-15; Lk.23:13-25; Jn.18:39-40).

The other events following Jesus' arrest seem to be:
1. Peter's denial (Mt.26:58, 69-75; Mk.14:54, 66-72; Lk.22:54-62; Jn.18:15-18, 25-27).
2. Judas' suicide (Mt.27:3-10; Acts 1:18-19). Both of these events took place between the first and second trial.
3. Jesus crowned with thorns and severely beaten by the Roman soldiers (Mt.27:27-30; Mk.15:16-19; Jn.19:1-3).
4. Simon's carrying Jesus' cross (Mt.27:31-32; Mk.15:20-21; Lk.23:26).
5. Jesus warning the women of the coming judgment upon Jerusalem (Lk.23:27-31). (See note—Mt.26:57; 26:59.)

2 (22:67-68) **Jesus Christ, Claims**: Jesus claimed to be the Messiah. The council did not come right out and accuse Jesus. They wanted Him to incriminate Himself; therefore, they questioned Him: "If you are the Christ [Messiah]... Tell us." But Jesus could not answer, not directly. Note two facts.

1. They did not understand the true Messiahship of God. God's Messiahship is spiritual and eternal, not physical and material (see note—Eph.1:3). Jesus had come to save men spiritually, not materially. Therefore if He told them, they would not believe me; and if He asked them questions which would lead them to the truth, they would not answer. He had done this often (Lk.20:7, 26, 40).

2. Jesus did not deny His Messiahship. The way He answered the council was an affirmation. Note His exact words, "If I tell you, you will not believe." It was as though He said, "I am, but if I tell you, declare it vocally, you will not believe it." (See notes—Mt.1:1; DEEPER STUDY # 2—1:18; note—Lk.19:36-38 cp. Mk.11:1-11 for concepts of Messiah.)

> **The woman said, "I know that Messiah" (called Christ) "is coming. When he comes, he will explain everything to us." Then Jesus declared, "I who speak to you am he." (John 4:25-26)**
>
> **So Jesus said, "When you have lifted up the Son of Man, then you will know that I am the one I claim to be and that I do nothing on my own but speak just what the Father has taught me. The one who sent me is with me; he has not left me alone, for I always do what pleases him." (John 8:28-29)**

3 (22:69) **Jesus Christ, Claims**: Jesus claimed to be the Son of Man who will be exalted. Jesus was really making three claims.

1. That He is the Son of Man (see notes—Lk.4:20-21; Jn.1:51; DEEPER STUDY # 3—Mt.8:20. Cp. Dan.7:13-14.)
2. That He will not remain dead even if they kill Him. He will be raised into God's presence.
3. That He will be exalted to sit on the right hand of the power of God.

> **And who through the Spirit of holiness was declared with power to be the Son of God by his resurrection from the dead: Jesus Christ our Lord. (Rom 1:4)**
>
> **God has raised this Jesus to life, and we are all witnesses of the fact. Exalted to the right hand of God, he has received from the Father the promised Holy Spirit and has poured out what you now see and hear. For David did not ascend to heaven, and yet he said, "'The Lord said to my Lord: "Sit at my right hand until I make your enemies a footstool for your feet."' "Therefore let all Israel be assured of this: God has made this Jesus, whom you crucified, both Lord and Christ." (Acts 2:32-36)**
>
> **And his incomparably great power for us who believe. That power is like the working of his mighty strength, which he exerted in Christ when he raised him from the dead and seated him at his right hand in the heavenly realms, far above all rule and authority, power and dominion, and every title that can be given, not only in the present age but also in the one to come. (Eph 1:19-21)**
>
> **Therefore God exalted him to the highest place and gave him the name that is above every name, that at the name of Jesus every knee should bow, in heaven and on earth and under the earth, and every tongue confess that Jesus Christ is Lord, to the glory of God the Father. (Phil 2:9-11)**

4 (22:70) **Jesus Christ, Claims**: Jesus claimed to be the Son of God. Note several facts.

1. "They all" now questioned Jesus. The picture is that of an outroar, voices reacting to His claim to be the Son of Man, voices bursting forth together shouting: "Are you then the Son of God?"
2. The definite article "the" is important. They were not asking if He were *a* son of God like many men claim. They asked if He was "the Son of God."
3. Jesus unquestionably claimed to be "the Son of God." (See note—Mk.14:62 for more discussion.)

> **Then those who were in the boat worshiped him, saying, "Truly you are the Son of God." (Mat 14:33)**
>
> **The beginning of the gospel about Jesus Christ, the Son of God. (Mark 1:1)**
>
> **I have seen and I testify that this is the Son of God." (John 1:34)**
>
> **"For God so loved the world that he gave his one and only Son, that whoever believes in him shall not perish but have eternal life. For God did not send his Son into the world to condemn the world, but to save the world through him. Whoever believes in him is not condemned, but who**

ever does not believe stands condemned already because he has not believed in the name of God's one and only Son. (John 3:16-18)

Jesus heard that they had thrown him out, and when he found him, he said, "Do you believe in the Son of Man?" "Who is he, sir?" the man asked. "Tell me so that I may believe in him." Jesus said, "You have now seen him; in fact, he is the one speaking with you." (John 9:35-37)

What about the one whom the Father set apart as his very own and sent into the world? Why then do you accuse me of blasphemy because I said, 'I am God's Son'? (John 10:36)

Jesus said to her, "I am the resurrection and the life. He who believes in me will live, even though he dies; and whoever lives and believes in me will never die. Do you believe this?" "Yes, Lord," she told him, "I believe that you are the Christ, the Son of God, who was to come into the world." (John 11:25-27)

How much more severely do you think a man deserves to be punished who has trampled the Son of God under foot, who has treated as an unholy thing the blood of the covenant that sanctified him, and who has insulted the Spirit of grace? (Heb 10:29)

If anyone acknowledges that Jesus is the Son of God, God lives in him and he in God. (1 John 4:15)

5 (22:71) **Jesus Christ, Claims**: the claim of Jesus was understood, but the leaders rejected His claim. Jesus had both accepted and claimed the charge being made against Him. He was…

- The Messiah.
- The Son of God.
- The Son of Man.

They had heard enough. In their obstinate unbelief, they condemned Him to death—condemned the Man who had come to save the world from its terrible plight of sin and death, from its desperate need for health and love and for salvation and life.

Just as the Son of Man did not come to be served, but to serve, and to give his life as a ransom for many." (Mat 20:28)

For the Son of Man came to seek and to save what was lost." (Luke 19:10)

	CHAPTER 23 **E. Jesus' First Trial Before Pilate & Herod: The Shirking of Duty & Personal Concern, 23:1-12** (Mt.27:11-14; Mk.15:1-5; Jn.18:28-38)
1 The Sanhedrin dragged Jesus to Pilate[DS1]	Then the whole assembly rose and led him off to Pilate.
2 The trial before Pilate: Shirking duty a. The charges[DS2] 1) He is a revolutionary 2) He opposes taxes 3) He claims to be a King	2 And they began to accuse him, saying, "We have found this man subverting our nation. He opposes payment of taxes to Caesar and claims to be Christ, a king."
b. The questioning of Pilate & the claim of Jesus	3 So Pilate asked Jesus, "Are you the king of the Jews?" "Yes, it is as you say," Jesus replied.
c. The verdict by Pilate: Jesus was innocent	4 Then Pilate announced to the chief priests and the crowd, "I find no basis for a charge against this man."
d. The bitter protest & enlarged charge	5 But they insisted, "He stirs up the people all over Judea by his teaching. He started in Galilee and has come all the way here."
e. The attempt to escape one's duty	6 On hearing this, Pilate asked if the man was a Galilean. 7 When he learned that Jesus was under Herod's jurisdiction, he sent him to Herod, who was also in Jerusalem at that time.
3 The questioning before Herod: Shirking concern a. He sought the spectacular	8 When Herod saw Jesus, he was greatly pleased, because for a long time he had been wanting to see him. From what he had heard about him, he hoped to see him perform some miracle.
b. He was the only man Jesus never answered	9 He plied him with many questions, but Jesus gave him no answer.
c. He listened to false charges by religionists	10 The chief priests and the teachers of the law were standing there, vehemently accusing him.
d. He did not take the Jews seriously: Joked contemptuously	11 Then Herod and his soldiers ridiculed and mocked him. Dressing him in an elegant robe, they sent him back to Pilate.
4 Conclusion: Pilate & Herod were brought together in their opposition to Jesus	12 That day Herod and Pilate became friends—before this they had been enemies.

DIVISION XI

THE SON OF MAN'S SUFFERINGS: HIS AGONY, TRIALS, AND CRUCIFIXION, 22:39-23:56

E. Jesus' First Trial Before Pilate and Herod: The Shirking of Duty and Personal Concern, 23:1-12

(23:1-12) **Introduction**: this passage is a clear portrait of two men who shirked duty and personal concern.

1. The Sanhedrin dragged Jesus to Pilate (v.1).
2. The trial before Pilate: shirking duty (v.2-7).
3. The questioning before Herod: shirking concern (v.8-11).
4. Conclusion: Pilate and Herod were brought together in their opposition to Jesus (v.12).

1 (23:1) **Religionists**: the Sanhedrin dragged Jesus to Pilate. Feelings ran deep. The depth of their obstinate unbelief is seen in the fact that "the whole assembly rose and led Him off to Pilate." Just picture the scene. All members present (seventy one when a full body was present) marched Him to Pilate. They were so opposed to Him that they wanted the full weight of their position and their comrades standing against Him.

> **Thought 1.** Observe obstinate unbelievers. They try to convince and secure as much support as possible against Christ and His followers. Why? To protect their worldly desires and security, their position and authority and wealth.

DEEPER STUDY # 1
(23:1-7) **Pilate**: see DEEPER STUDY # 1—Lk.23:13.

2 (23:2-7) **Jesus Christ, Trials—Pilate**: the trial before Pilate, a picture of *shirking duty*. Note five points.

1. The political charges against Jesus were three (see DEEPER STUDY # 2—Lk.23:2).

2. The questioning of Pilate and the claim of Jesus. This was one of the charges brought against Jesus, and in the eyes of Rome it would be the most serious. Pilate, somewhat surprised by the charge, scornfully asked Jesus, "Are you the King of the Jews?" Jesus strongly claimed that He was: "Yes, it is as you say." However, as John points out, Jesus clearly stated that His kingdom was not of this world. His kingdom was spiritual (Jn.18:36-37).

> **Thought 1.** Jesus is not a political revolutionary, not a threat to any civil government. He is the King of man's spirit and of heaven, of the spiritual dimension of being, not of earth. He came to rule and reign in the hearts and lives of men, in the realm of the spiritual and eternal, not in the realm of the physical and temporal (see note—Eph.1:3).

3. The verdict of Pilate: Jesus was innocent. Note: this is a public verdict. Pilate actually pronounced Jesus innocent to the leaders and the people. However, as shall be seen and as is the case with so many, he lacked the *inner strength* to stand by his convictions. He gave in to the world, going along with their wish.

4. The bitter protest and enlarged charge. The unbelievers, fitfully aroused, accused Jesus. They were closeminded: obstinate, bitter, spiteful. They said He was guilty of leading a revolution throughout all Israel, from Galilee to Jerusalem.

It should be noted that Jesus' purpose was not to defend Himself nor to escape death. His purpose was to surrender to the *sinful behavior* of men. The *sinful behavior* to which He submitted was…

- the very depth of sin itself.
- the ultimate demonstration of sin.
- the greatest sin that could be committed.

The act of sin to which He subjected Himself was the rejection and killing of the Son of God. Standing there before His accusers, He said nothing, enduring their awful indignities. He endured because He was purposed to die for the sins of men.

Note that Pilate actually declared Jesus innocent four different times (Lk.23:4, 14, 15, 22; cp. Jn.18:38; 19:4, 6).

5. The attempt to escape one's duty (Pilate). Pilate wished to release Jesus, for he knew the Lord was innocent. However, he had to guard against upsetting the leaders of the Jewish nation. He was in a dilemma. When he heard Galilee mentioned, he saw a way out of his dilemma. Herod, who was ruler of Galilee, was in town for the Passover. He could send Jesus over to Herod and let him pass judgment. As a Galilaean, Jesus belonged under the jurisdiction of Herod.

The point to note is this: Pilate lacked the courage to do what was right. He knew Jesus was innocent, yet he sought to *escape his duty* to declare the truth. He made four attempts to shirk his duty. (1) He tried to get the Jews to handle the matter themselves (Lk.18:31). (2) He sent Jesus to Herod (Lk.23:7). (3) He tried to get the Jews to accept Jesus as the prisoner to be released at the Passover (Lk.23:17-19; Mk.15:6). (4) He suggested flogging Jesus and then letting Him go (Lk.23:16).

Thought 1. A man who seeks to escape his duty is an unworthy leader. He is not worthy of the responsibility (position, call, or duty).

He is a double-minded man, unstable in all he does. (James 1:8)

Come near to God and he will come near to you. Wash your hands, you sinners, and purify your hearts, you double-minded. (James 4:8)

"No servant can serve two masters. Either he will hate the one and love the other, or he will be devoted to the one and despise the other. You cannot serve both God and Money." (Luke 16:13)

Their heart is deceitful, and now they must bear their guilt. The LORD will demolish their altars and destroy their sacred stones. (Hosea 10:2)

DEEPER STUDY # 2

(23:2) **Jesus Christ, Charges Against**: three political charges were levelled against Jesus.

1. He was charged with perverting the nation, that is, of treason, of being a revolutionary and committing sedition against Rome. The charge, of course, was false. Jesus was not out to pervert people from an earthly nation; He was out to convert people to a heavenly world, to God and His kingdom which were not of this earth (Jn.19:36).

2. He was charged with disobeying the laws of the nation, in particular for not paying taxes. Of course this charge was also false. Jesus had taught that obedience to earthly government was absolutely essential for the believer. (See outline and notes—Lk.20:19-26.)

3. He was charged with claiming to be King, with being a rival to Caesar. Again, this charge was false.
   a. The very reason the Jewish leaders were not accepting Him (so they claimed) was because He had come in the meekness and love of God, not in the armed might of God, liberating their nation from the Roman conquerors (see DEEPER STUDY # 2—Mt.1:18).
   b. Jesus had actually refused to let the people set Him up as King (Jn.6:15).

3 (23:8-11) **Herod's Hardened Heart**: the questioning before Herod, a picture of shirking personal concern. Herod showed no concern whatsoever for the truth, nor for his own soul. The possibility that the true Messiah might actually be standing before Him never crossed his mind. (See note, pt.3—Lk.3:1. Also see DEEPER STUDY # 1,2, Herod—Mt.14:1-14 for more discussion.)

1. Herod sought only the spectacular. He had heard many things about Jesus, the amazing power and miracles He had manifested. As a ruler, a very special person, Herod wanted and felt he deserved…

- the privilege of some sign
- the privilege of gazing
- the privilege of some spectacle

Jesus' power, of course, was not to be used for the spectacular, not for the purpose of satisfying an unbeliever's curiosity. (See notes—Lk.4:9-12; 11:20 for more discussion.)

2. Herod was the only man Jesus never answered. Herod's own household had been penetrated with the gospel. Chuza, Herod's personal steward (Lk.8:3), and Manaen, Herod's foster brother (Acts 13:1), were believers. The nobleman or court official mentioned in the story shared by Jesus was also probably of Herod's court (Jn.4:46). Apparently, the gospel as lived by these persons had little effect upon Herod. Their sharing was but religious foolishness to him. He treated their reports with disdain, perhaps with some abuse. Jesus, knowing the hopelessness of his unresponsive heart, wasted no time and no words upon him. Jesus said nothing to him at all.

3. Herod listened to false charges by the religionists. He had failed to listen to John the Baptist (Lk.9:7-9) and to the witnesses in his own household. He had heard many things about Christ (v.8), yet he had refused to listen, to truly hear and heed. But now, with Jesus standing before him, he listened to the false charges of those who opposed Jesus.

4. Herod set Jesus at nought, treated Him as unimportant. The word "ridicule" (exouthenesas) means to count as nothing, to make nothing of, to think something is unimportant, to count as zero—therefore, to treat with utter contempt.

Note the contrast in the verse. Herod sat there as King with his soldiers surrounding him, and Jesus stood there beaten and battered in torn, ragged clothes. Herod, judging by appearance, counted the Man who claimed to be the Son of God as nothing. This Man and His claim did not matter, not to Herod.

Thought 1. Many count Christ as unimportant. They think He does not matter—that He can be excluded from life, that He and His claim are meaningless. Such people go about counting their own lives and worldly ways dear unto themselves. (Cp. Lk.9:24; 17:33.)

Whoever tries to keep his life will lose it, and whoever loses his life will preserve it. (Luke 17:33)

"Be careful, or your hearts will be weighed down with dissipation, drunkenness and the anxieties of life, and that day will close on you unexpectedly like a trap. (Luke 21:34)

Whoever believes in the Son has eternal life, but whoever rejects the Son will not see life, for God's wrath remains on him." (John 3:36)

I told you that you would die in your sins; if you do not believe that I am the one I claim to be, you will indeed die in your sins." (John 8:24)

See to it, brothers, that none of you has a sinful, unbelieving heart that turns away from the living God. (Heb 3:12)

4 (23:12) **World, Rejection of Jesus**: Pilate and Herod became friends; the worldly are brought together in their opposition against Christ.

Outline	Scripture	Scripture	Outline
	F. Jesus' Second Trial Before Pilate: The Tragedy of a Compromising Man, 23:13-25 (Mt.27:15-25; Mk.15: 6-15; Jn.18:39-19:16)	19 (Barabbas had been thrown into prison for an insurrection in the city, and for murder.) 20 Wanting to release Jesus, Pilate appealed to them again. 21 But they kept shouting, "Crucify him! Crucify him!"	
1 Pilate tried to protect himself, selfishlyDS1 a. A man who knew the truth	13 Pilate called together the chief priests, the rulers and the people, 14 And said to them, "You brought me this man as one who was inciting the people to rebellion. I have examined him in your presence and have found no basis for your charges against him.	22 For the third time he spoke to them: "Why? What crime has this man committed? I have found in him no grounds for the death penalty. Therefore I will have him punished and then release him."	**3 Pilate gave in to worldly pressure** a. He knew the truth: Jesus was innocent
	15 Neither has Herod, for he sent him back to us; as you can see, he has done nothing to deserve death.	23 But with loud shouts they insistently demanded that he be crucified, and their shouts prevailed.	b. He faced loud voices against Jesus
b. A man who tried to appease out of fear	16 Therefore, I will punish him and then release him."[17]	24 So Pilate decided to grant their demand.	c. He compromised—gave in to the worldly cries
2 Pilate tried to compromise truth & clear evidence	18 With one voice they cried out, "Away with this man! Release Barabbas to us!"	25 He released the man who had been thrown into prison for insurrection and murder, the one they asked for, and surrendered Jesus to their will.	d. He allowed injustice & wrong & sin to be done

DIVISION XI

THE SON OF MAN'S SUFFERINGS: HIS AGONY, TRIALS, AND CRUCIFIXION, 22:39-23:56

F. Jesus' Second Trial Before Pilate: The Tragedy of a Compromising Man, 23:13-25

(23:13-25) **Introduction**: compromising with the world is sin. Compromise always leads to trouble and tragedy. Pilate is the picture of a man whose compromise led to the greatest tragedy in human history.

1. Pilate tried to protect himself, selfishly (v.13-16).
2. He tried to compromise truth and clear evidence (v.17-21).
3. He gave in to worldly pressure (v.22-25).

1 (23:13-16) **Compromise—Appeasement—Injustice**: Pilate tried to protect himself, selfishly. He called the court back into session. A decision had been made; he was now ready to give his verdict.

⇒ He had examined Jesus and found no fault in Him: Jesus was innocent.
⇒ He had sent Jesus to Herod for a verdict, and Herod found Jesus innocent.
⇒ No crime worthy of death had been committed by Jesus. Pilate had decided, therefore, that he would chastise Jesus and release Him.

Note that Pilate was trying to appease the Jews. He knew the truth: Jesus was innocent. Jesus should be released and the Jews' behavior rebuked, but Pilate feared displeasing and inflaming the Jews. He was afraid they might cause trouble for him, reporting him to Rome and causing him to lose his position and rule (see DEEPER STUDY # 1—Lk.23:13). Throughout the whole scene Pilate's primary interest was himself, not truth and justice.

Thought 1. A compromising man is self-centered. He seeks to protect himself even at the expense of the truth and justice. He fears losing…

- position, power, influence
- job security, image, acceptance, friends

> **"'Do not pervert justice; do not show partiality to the poor or favoritism to the great, but judge your neighbor fairly. (Lev 19:15)**
>
> **"How long will you defend the unjust and show partiality to the wicked? Selah (Psa 82:2)**
>
> **And I saw something else under the sun: In the place of judgment—wickedness was there, in the place of justice—wickedness was there. (Eccl 3:16)**
>
> **"So I have caused you to be despised and humiliated before all the people, because you have not followed my ways but have shown partiality in matters of the law." (Mal 2:9)**
>
> **I charge you, in the sight of God and Christ Jesus and the elect angels, to keep these instructions without partiality, and to do nothing out of favoritism. (1 Tim 5:21)**
>
> **This day I call heaven and earth as witnesses against you that I have set be-**

---

[17] *Now he was obliged to release one man to them at the Feast.*

fore you life and death, blessings and curses. Now choose life, so that you and your children may live (Deu 30:19)

DEEPER STUDY # 1
(23:13) **Pilate**: the procurator of Judea. He was directly responsible to the Emperor for the administrative and financial management of the country. A man had to work himself up through the political and military ranks to become a procurator. Pilate was, therefore, an able man, experienced in the affairs of politics and government as well as the military. He held office for ten years which shows that he was highly trusted by the Roman government. However, the Jews despised Pilate, and Pilate despised the Jews for their intense practice of religion. When Pilate became procurator of Judea, he did two things that aroused the people's bitter hatred against him forever. First, on his state visits to Jerusalem, he and his military guard rode their stallions into the city with the Roman standard, an eagle sitting atop a pole. All previous governors had removed the standard because of the Jews' opposition to idols. Second, Pilate launched the construction of a new water supply for Jerusalem. To finance the project, he took the money out of the temple treasury. The Jews never forgot or forgave this act. They bitterly opposed Pilate all through his reign, and he treated them with equal contempt (see DEEPER STUDY # 1—Mk.15:1-15). On several occasions, Jewish leaders threatened to exercise their right to report Pilate to the emperor. This, of course, disturbed Pilate to no end and caused him to become even more bitter and contemptuous toward the Jews.

2 (23:18-21) **Compromise**: Pilate tried to compromise the truth despite clear evidence. He saw the evidence: Jesus was innocent, and the religionists were only envious of Jesus, feeling He was a threat to their security. Pilate wanted to declare Jesus innocent, but he felt he had to satisfy the cries of these religious worldlings as well. Therefore, he conceived a compromise. It was a long time custom for Rome to release a popular prisoner to the Jews at the Passover Feast in order to humor and secure more cooperation from the population. Within the prison was a notorious criminal, Barabbas. Pilate had him brought before the people along with Jesus and shouted out that the people could choose which one was to be released.

Pilate felt sure that by pitting Barabbas against Jesus, the people would choose Jesus, the One who had ministered and helped so many of them. How wrong the man of compromise was. (The world will always cry out against Jesus to get rid of Him.)

The point to note is the moral weakness of Pilate. He knew Jesus was innocent. He knew the Jews sought to kill Jesus because they envied Him. Jesus should have been released immediately, but Pilate attempted a compromise instead of standing up for the truth.

Thought 1. Note a crucial point: when the truth is known, it should be proclaimed, not compromised. Compromise results in three tragedies.
1) Compromise weakens character and testimony.
2) Compromise means that the truth is not being done or lived. A person is agreeing to do something less than what he should be doing.
3) Compromise weakens principle, position, and life.

Thought 2. God accepts no compromise concerning His Son, Jesus Christ. A man either stands for Christ or against Christ. There is no neutral ground. Christ is innocent and sinless; He is the Ideal Man, the Son of God in whom all men are to place their trust.

"He who is not with me is against me, and he who does not gather with me, scatters. (Luke 11:23)

That all may honor the Son just as they honor the Father. He who does not honor the Son does not honor the Father, who sent him. "I tell you the truth, whoever hears my word and believes him who sent me has eternal life and will not be condemned; he has crossed over from death to life. (John 5:23-24)

And this is the testimony: God has given us eternal life, and this life is in his Son. He who has the Son has life; he who does not have the Son of God does not have life. (1 John 5:11-12)

Submit yourselves, then, to God. Resist the devil, and he will flee from you. Come near to God and he will come near to you. Wash your hands, you sinners, and purify your hearts, you double-minded. Grieve, mourn and wail. Change your laughter to mourning and your joy to gloom. Humble yourselves before the Lord, and he will lift you up. (James 4:7-10)

3 (23:22-25) **Worldliness—Compromise**: he gave in to worldly pressure. The scene was dramatic, but tragic. The scene can be simply stated. Pilate...
- knew Jesus was innocent (v.22).
- faced loud voices against Jesus (v.23).
- compromised and gave in to the worldly cries (v.24).
- allowed injustice and wrong and sin to be done (v.25).

The point is this: Pilate, the compromising man, was *morally weak.*
- He was not strong enough to do what he knew was right.
- He lacked the moral strength to stand up for Jesus.
- He was too weak to declare the truth.

Thought 1. The pressure of the world to do evil is great. Indecision and compromise are not the way to face the world: decisive dedication to Christ and separation from the world alone can conquer the world.

Therefore, I urge you, brothers, in view of God's mercy, to offer your bodies as living sacrifices, holy and pleasing to God—this is your spiritual act of worship. Do not conform any longer to the pattern of this world, but be transformed by the renewing of your mind. Then you will be able to test and approve what God's will is—his good, pleasing and perfect will. (Rom 12:1-2)

"Therefore come out from them and be separate, says the Lord. Touch no unclean

> **thing, and I will receive you." "I will be a Father to you, and you will be my sons and daughters, says the Lord Almighty." (2 Cor 6:17-18)**
>
> **Do not love the world or anything in the world. If anyone loves the world, the love of the Father is not in him. For everything in the world—the cravings of sinful man, the lust of his eyes and the boasting of what he has and does—comes not from the Father but from the world. (1 John 2:15-16)**

Thought 2. Most men prefer the company of evil, sinful men to that of the Prince of Life. Note: even worldly religionists choose the world over the Prince of Life.

Thought 3. Note a crucial point. It is when we are indecisive or willing to compromise that the pressure to do evil gets to us. Hesitating and being indecisive will cause us to give in to the pressure of sin.

> **By faith Moses, when he had grown up, refused to be known as the son of Pharaoh's daughter. He chose to be mistreated along with the people of God rather than to enjoy the pleasures of sin for a short time. (Heb 11:24-25)**
>
> **Therefore, dear friends, since you already know this, be on your guard so that you may not be carried away by the error of lawless men and fall from your secure position. (2 Pet 3:17)**

G. Jesus' Crucifixion and Its Events,[DS1] **23:26-49**
(Mt.27:26-56; Mk.15: 16-41; Jn.19:16-37)

26 As they led him away, they seized Simon from Cyrene, who was on his way in from the country, and put the cross on him and made him carry it behind Jesus.
27 A large number of people followed him, including women who mourned and wailed for him.
28 Jesus turned and said to them, "Daughters of Jerusalem, do not weep for me; weep for yourselves and for your children.
29 For the time will come when you will say, 'Blessed are the barren women, the wombs that never bore and the breasts that never nursed!'
30 Then "'they will say to the mountains, "Fall on us!" and to the hills, "Cover us!"'
31 For if men do these things when the tree is green, what will happen when it is dry?"
32 Two other men, both criminals, were also led out with him to be executed.
33 When they came to the place called the Skull, there they crucified him, along with the criminals—one on his right, the other on his left.
34 Jesus said, "Father, forgive them, for they do not know what they are doing." And they divided up his clothes by casting lots.
35 The people stood watching, and the rulers even sneered at him. They said, "He saved others; let him save himself if he is the Christ of God, the Chosen One."
36 The soldiers also came up and mocked him. They offered him wine vinegar
37 And said, "If you are the king of the Jews, save yourself."
38 There was a written notice above him, which read: THIS IS THE KING OF THE JEWS.
39 One of the criminals who hung there hurled insults at him: "Aren't you the Christ? Save yourself and us!"
40 But the other criminal rebuked him. "Don't you fear God," he said, "since you are under the same sentence?
41 We are punished justly, for we are getting what our deeds deserve. But this man has done nothing wrong."
42 Then he said, "Jesus, remember me when you come into your kingdom."
43 Jesus answered him, "I tell you the truth, today you will be with me in paradise."
44 It was now about the sixth hour, and darkness came over the whole land until the ninth hour,
45 For the sun stopped shining. And the curtain of the temple was torn in two.
46 Jesus called out with a loud voice, "Father, into your hands I commit my spirit." When he had said this, he breathed his last.
47 The centurion, seeing what had happened, praised God and said, "Surely this was a righteous man."
48 When all the people who had gathered to witness this sight saw what took place, they beat their breasts and went away.
49 But all those who knew him, including the women who had followed him from Galilee, stood at a distance, watching these things.

1 The man who bore His cross: A picture of conversion

2 The great crowd of mourners: A picture of hearts that feel for Jesus

3 The prediction of Jerusalem's doom: A picture of coming judgment
- a. So terrible, people should weep over
- b. So terrible, people will wish to be childless
- c. So terrible, people will wish to be buried alive
- d. Judgment is inevitable

4 The identification with criminals: Being numbered with sinners

5 The crucifixion: The summit of sin & love
- a. At Mount Calvary
- b. Between two criminals

6 The prayer for His enemies: Forgiveness

7 The gambling for His clothes: Being stripped by greed

8 The mocking: Misunderstanding His salvation
- a. By the people & religionists
  - 1) His claim to save
  - 2) His claim to be Messiah
- b. By the soldiers
  - 1) Offering Him wine[DS2]
  - 2) His claim to be King

9 The inscription on the cross: A misunderstood charge

10 The unrepentant thief: A picture of hardness even in death

11 The repentant thief: A picture of true repentance
- a. Fearing God
- b. Declaring Jesus' righteousness
- c. Asking Jesus for a place in His kingdom

12 The awesome darkness: A symbol of separation & loneliness

13 The torn veil of the temple: A symbol of open access into God's presence

14 The great cry of trust: A picture of glorious triumph

15 The centurion's declaration: Jesus' righteousness—a confession to be made by many

16 The people's grief: A picture of stricken conscience

17 The followers of Jesus: A proof that Jesus lived & served well

DIVISION XI

THE SON OF MAN'S SUFFERINGS: HIS AGONY, TRIALS, AND CRUCIFIXION, 22:39-23:56

G. Jesus' Crucifixion and Its Events, 23:26-49

(23:26-49) **Introduction**: the crucifixion of Jesus Christ is both the most shocking event and the most wonderful event of human history. It is the most shocking event in that it is the creature murdering the Creator. It is the most wonderful event in that it is the Creator saving the creature. (Glance at the outline above for the *seventeen events* of the crucifixion as covered by Luke.)

DEEPER STUDY # 1
(23:26-49) **Crucifixion, The**: see outline, note, and DEEPER STUDY # 1—Mt.27:26-44 for more discussion.

1 (23:26) **Conversion—Simon of Cyrene**: the man who bore His cross, a picture of conversion. Note several things.

1. God's plan or providence. Nothing happens by chance, not to the Christian believer. God oversees the life of His people. Thus, Simon's being pressed into carrying the cross for Jesus was in the plan of God.

2. Simon was apparently a pilgrim coming to celebrate the Passover. He was standing along the roadway watching the armed procession make its way through the streets. Apparently there was some expression of concern and sympathy for Jesus, something within his heart that was touched and that reached out to Jesus. God knew this, and directed the soldiers to enlist his help in carrying the Lord's cross.

3. Simon was "the father of Alexander and Rufus" (Mk.15:21). The comment by Mark is interesting. Evidently they were known believers (cp. Acts 13:1; Ro.16:13). The indication is that Simon or at least his two sons were eventually converted.

Thought 1. The man who takes up the cross of Christ will be converted.

Then he said to them all: "If anyone would come after me, he must deny himself and take up his cross daily and follow me. (Luke 9:23)

2 (23:27) **Godly Sorrow—Sympathy**: there was the great crowd of mourners—a picture of hearts that felt for Jesus. A great crowd of people followed and felt for Jesus, especially women. The word "mourned" (ekoptonto) means to cut, strike, smite, beat. They were cut to the core of their hearts, actually feeling pain for Jesus. The word "wailed" (ethrenoun) means to cry out loud, to mourn, groan. They were crying out, unable to hold back the pain cutting their hearts. Some of the people, of course, had been followers of Jesus for a long time and were feeling the depth of their Lord's sufferings; whereas other onlookers, as in any crowd witnessing severe suffering, felt only a natural tenderness and lament over one suffering so much.

Thought 1. A natural response to the Lord's sufferings is not enough. A person must *understand* why Christ suffered and must feel a *godly sorrow* over Christ's having to bear the sins of the world (see DEEPER STUDY # 1—2 Cor.7:10).

Godly sorrow brings repentance that leads to salvation and leaves no regret, but worldly sorrow brings death. (2 Cor 7:10)

Remember those in prison as if you were their fellow prisoners, and those who are mistreated as if you yourselves were suffering. (Heb 13:3)

3 (23:28-31) **Jerusalem, Prophecy of**: there was the prediction of Jerusalem's doom—a picture of coming judgment. The significant point to note is what was upon Jesus' mind: judgment. The people had rejected God's Messiah and salvation, choosing to go the way of the world, and the way of the world was doom and destruction. The destruction coming would be so terrible, people...

- would weep for themselves.
- would wish to be childless.
- would wish to be buried alive.

Verse 31 is a proverbial saying: if the world (Rome) treats a green tree like this (Him, a tree with its full provision of sap), how will it treat a dry tree like Israel, a tree with little if any provision of sap, a tree of no use, with no life left, ready to be cut down and destroyed?

Thought 1. Jerusalem rejected the invitation of God time and again. However, God was patient and demon-strated His patience for generations, but the rejection and killing of His Son were too great to leave unpunished. As soon as Christianity could get a solid foothold in the world, Jerusalem was to be judged and doomed. (See outline and notes—Lk.20:13-18.)

God is patient with every man. But continued rejection of His Son brings judgment and eternal doom.

"For God so loved the world that he gave his one and only Son, that whoever believes in him shall not perish but have eternal life. For God did not send his Son into the world to condemn the world, but to save the world through him. Whoever believes in him is not condemned, but whoever does not believe stands condemned already because he has not believed in the name of God's one and only Son. (John 3:16-18)

Just as man is destined to die once, and after that to face judgment, (Heb 9:27)

4 (23:32) **Jesus Christ, Identified with Sinners**: there was the identification with criminals—a picture of being numbered with sinners. Why was Jesus crucified with criminals? Scripture does not say, but perhaps this was a day set aside for execution, or perhaps the Jewish leaders pressed Pilate to execute Jesus with other criminals. By this, they hoped to add weight to their position that He was no more than a mere man, an imposter who deserved to die just as other criminals. Whatever the reason, the fact that the Son of God was executed right along with other criminals adds to the shame and reproach He bore. This event had been prophesied just as many others had (Is.53:12).

Thought 1. Christ was counted as a sinner that He might bear the sin of many.

Therefore I will give him a portion among the great, and he will divide the spoils with the strong, because he poured out his life unto death, and was numbered with the transgressors. For he bore the sin of many, and made intercession for the transgressors. (Isa 53:12)

5 (23:33) **Crucifixion, The**: the crucifixion was the summit of sin and love. The crucifixion itself was the most horrible of deaths. There was the pain of the driven spikes forced through the flesh of Jesus' hands and feet or ankles. There was the weight of His body jolting and pulling against the spikes as the cross was lifted and rocked into place. There was the scorching sun and the unquenchable thirst gnawing away at His dry mouth and throat. There was the blood oozing from His scourged back, His thorn crowned brow, His stick beaten head. In addition, just imagine the aggravation of flies, gnats, and other insects. And for Jesus, there was the piercing pain of the spear thrust into His side. On and on the sufferings could be described. There has never been a more cruel form of execution than crucifixion upon a cross.

The crucifixion took place on a hill called *"the Skull"* (in Latin, calvaria). We get the name Calvary from the Latin word. (See note, pt.11—Mt.27:26-38.)

Thought 1. In the simplest of terms, Christ was crucified for our sins in order to bring us to God.

He himself bore our sins in his body on the tree, so that we might die to sins and live for righteousness; by his wounds you have been healed. (1 Pet 2:24)

For Christ died for sins once for all, the righteous for the unrighteous, to bring you to God. He was put to death in the body but made alive by the Spirit, (1 Pet 3:18)

Note that two criminals were crucified with Him. He was dying because of them and because of all other men. Why? Because all men are criminals against God, rebelling against Him and breaking His commandments.

For all have sinned and fall short of the glory of God, (Rom 3:23)

Here is a trustworthy saying that deserves full acceptance: Christ Jesus came into the world to save sinners—of whom I am the worst. (1 Tim 1:15)

For Christ died for sins once for all, the righteous for the unrighteous, to bring you to God. He was put to death in the body but made alive by the Spirit, (1 Pet 3:18)

6 (23:34) **Forgiveness—Salvation**: there was the prayer for His enemies—a picture of love and forgiveness to the end. The picture is of Jesus the Mediator. He had come for this very purpose, to stand as the Mediator between God and sinful man. Therefore upon the cross, He prayed for those who stood below crucifying Him. Note several things.

1. It had been predicted that Christ would pray for transgressors (Is.53:12).
2. He prayed for God to forgive those who were crucifying Him. The very purpose for His coming was to make provision for forgiveness of sins. Because of His death, God would be able to forgive the sins of men, even those who were now crucifying Him.
3. The men crucifying Him did not know what they were doing. They did not know who He was.

None of the rulers of this age understood it, for if they had, they would not have crucified the Lord of glory. (1 Cor 2:8)

Thought 1. The most wonderful truth in all the world is this: God will hold no sin against any man if that man will personally trust His Son. If God forgives the men who killed His only Son, God will forgive any man for any sin—if that man will just ask.

The God of our fathers raised Jesus from the dead—whom you had killed by hanging him on a tree. God exalted him to his own right hand as Prince and Savior that he might give repentance and forgiveness of sins to Israel. (Acts 5:30-31)

Repent of this wickedness and pray to the Lord. Perhaps he will forgive you for having such a thought in your heart. (Acts 8:22)

"Therefore, my brothers, I want you to know that through Jesus the forgiveness of sins is proclaimed to you. Through him everyone who believes is justified from everything you could not be justified from by the law of Moses. (Acts 13:38-39)

In whom we have redemption, the forgiveness of sins. (Col 1:14;cp. Col. 2:13)

7 (23:34) **Mortality—Immortality**: there was the gambling for His clothes—a picture of being stripped by the selfishness, greed, and sin of men. Note two points.

1. The custom seems to have been for the executing soldiers to claim whatever they wished of the clothes of crucified criminals. The soldiers stripped Jesus, dividing His clothes among themselves. However, His coat was valuable: it was seamless, one piece of cloth, woven from top to bottom just as the High Priest's coat or cloak was. The soldiers, therefore, decided to gamble by casting lots for it (Jn.19:23-24). This event was foretold in Ps.22:18.
2. Jesus was stripped by the soldiers, stripped of His mortal clothes. There is symbolism in this act: He allowed all His mortality to be stripped so that He might abolish death and bring life and immortality to light.

But it [God's grace] has now been revealed through the appearing of our Savior, Christ Jesus, who has destroyed death and has brought life and immortality to light through the gospel. (2 Tim 1:10)

8 (23:35-37) **Salvation**: there was the mockery, the misunderstanding of His salvation. Note those who mocked and taunted Him.

1. The people and religionists mocked His claim to be the Savior and Messiah. They totally misunderstood God's Messiahship. Both the people and the religionists should have been above this kind of behavior. In addition, they had every opportunity to believe, for He had not hid Himself or His message of salvation. But being part of a sinful crowd and their own unbelief, they led each other to do shameful things.

...Christ [Messiah] Jesus, who gave himself as a ransom for all men—the testimony given in its proper time. (1 Tim 2:5-6)

Here is a trustworthy saying that deserves full acceptance: Christ Jesus came into the world to save sinners—of whom I am the worst. (1 Tim 1:15)

Thought 1. Leaders, civil and religious, are still men. It is not the position or profession that makes a man, but the heart. A heart of unbelief and enmity, a heart willing to become a participant with the sinful crowd, will stoop to do shameful things, no matter the position or profession.

Look, your house is left to you desolate. (Mat 23:38)

2. The soldiers mocked and taunted Him. In particular they mocked His claim to be King, but they did not understand His claim (Jn.18:36. Cp. Jn.18:33-37; Mt.27:11.)

DEEPER STUDY # 2
(23:36)**Wine**: Jesus was offered drugged wine at the beginning of the crucifixion, but He refused it (Mt.27:34; Mk.15:23). He was also offered "wine" just before His death (Jn.19:29), and here the soldiers use "wine"in some form of mockery with Him.

9 (23:38) **Jesus Christ, King**: there was the inscription on the cross—a misunderstood charge. The sign placed above His head, "The King of the Jews," was intended to mock the Jewish authorities and to reproach His claim. However, God overruled and used the sign to proclaim the truth to the whole world (Lk.23:38). The very charges against Jesus proclaimed His deity and honor.

> **And being found in appearance as a man, he humbled himself and became obedient to death— even death on a cross! Therefore God exalted him to the highest place and gave him the name that is above every name, that at the name of Jesus every knee should bow, in heaven and on earth and under the earth, and every tongue confess that Jesus Christ is Lord, to the glory of God the Father. (Phil 2:8-11)**
>
> **To keep this command without spot or blame until the appearing of our Lord Jesus Christ, which God will bring about in his own time—God, the blessed and only Ruler, the King of kings and Lord of lords, who alone is immortal and who lives in unapproachable light, whom no one has seen or can see. To him be honor and might forever. Amen. (1 Tim 6:14-16)**

10 (23:39) **Unbelief**: there was the unrepentant thief—a picture of hardness even in death. The thieves heard the crowd mock Jesus about being the Messiah, the Savior of the world. Hanging there as criminals, guilty before God and men, they should have been searching to see if there were any chance that Jesus could have been who He claimed. They needed to be saved and forgiven. One criminal showed enormous hardness of heart. He mocked the very thought that Jesus was the Christ.

> **"For God so loved the world that he gave his one and only Son, that whoever believes in him shall not perish but have eternal life. For God did not send his Son into the world to condemn the world, but to save the world through him. Whoever believes in him is not condemned, but whoever does not believe stands condemned already because he has not believed in the name of God's one and only Son. (John 3:16-18)**

11 (23:40-43) **Salvation—Repentance**: there was the repentant thief—a picture of true repentance. The second thief demonstrated the steps to salvation and true repentance.

⇒ He feared God (v.40).
⇒ He declared that Jesus was righteous (v.41).
⇒ He asked for Jesus to remember him (v.42).

Note that Jesus promised him eternal life; the repentant man was to be with Christ in paradise *that very day*. (See DEEPER STUDY # 3, Paradise—Lk.16:23.)

> **"Father, I want those you have given me to be with me where I am, and to see my glory, the glory you have given me because you loved me before the creation of the world. (John 17:24)**
>
> **We are confident, I say, and would prefer to be away from the body and at home with the Lord. (2 Cor 5:8)**
>
> **I am torn between the two: I desire to depart and be with Christ, which is better by far; (Phil 1:23)**
>
> **Whoever serves me must follow me; and where I am, my servant also will be. My Father will honor the one who serves me. (John 12:26)**

12 (23:44) **Judgment—Man, State of**: there was the awesome darkness—a symbol of separation and loneliness. The darkness told man something (see note—Mt.27:45 for detailed discussion).

1. Man was separated from the light.

> **This is the verdict: Light has come into the world, but men loved darkness instead of light because their deeds were evil. Everyone who does evil hates the light, and will not come into the light for fear that his deeds will be exposed. (John 3:19-20)**

2. Man stood all alone. He could not see in the dark, not well. He was, so to speak, standing in the world all alone, responsible for his own behavior; and he must face God someday all alone to give an account for his behavior.

> **Just as man is destined to die once, and after that to face judgment, (Heb 9:27)**

13 (23:45) **Access—Jesus Christ, Blood**: there was the torn veil of the temple—a symbol of open access into the very presence of God. Note four facts.

1. The veil or curtain (curtain) which was torn was the inner veil or curtain (katapetasma), the curtain which separated the Holy of Holies from the Holy Place. There was another veil or curtain, an outer curtain (kalumma), which separated the Holy Place from the outer court of the temple.

The Holy of Holies was the most sacred part of the temple. It was the place where the very presence of God was symbolized as dwelling in a very, very special way. It was closed *forever* to everyone except the High Priest. Even he could enter the Holy of Holies only once a year, on the Day of Atonement (Ex.26:33).

2. At the very hour that Jesus died, the High Priest would be rolling back the outer curtain in order to expose the Holy Place to the people who had gathered to worship in the surrounding court. As he rolled back the outer curtain exposing the Holy Place for worship, both he and the worshippers would stand in amazement. Why? Because they would see the inner veil or curtain rent from the top to the bottom. There they would stand, experiencing and witnessing the Holy of Holies, the very special place where the presence of God Himself was supposed to dwell—-a sight that the people had never seen before.

3. The veil or curtain was torn from top to bottom. This symbolized that it was torn by an act of God Himself. It symbolized God's giving direct access into His presence (Heb.6:19; 9:3-12, 24; 10:19-23). Now, through the body of Christ, any man can enter the presence of God anytime, anyplace.

> **And by that will, we have been made holy through the sacrifice of the body of Jesus Christ once for all. (Heb 10:10)**

4. The torn veil or curtain symbolized that all men could now draw near God by the blood of Christ.

> **But now in Christ Jesus you who once were far away have been brought near through the blood of Christ. For he himself is our peace, who has made the two one and has destroyed the barrier, the dividing wall of hostility, (Eph 2:13-14)**

14 (23:46) **Jesus Christ, Work—Purpose**: there was the great cry of trust—a picture of glorious triumph. What Jesus cried out was one word in the Greek, *Tetelestai*, "It is finished" (Jn.19:30). It was a cry of purpose, a shout of triumph. He was dying for a specific purpose and that purpose was now fulfilled (see note—Mt.27:50 for detailed discussion).

> **I am the gate; whoever enters through me will be saved. He will come in and go out, and find pasture. "I am the good shepherd. The good shepherd lays down his life for the sheep. just as the Father knows me and I know the Father—and I lay down my life for the sheep. The reason my Father loves me is that I lay down my life—only to take it up again. No one takes it from me, but I lay it down of my own accord. I have authority to lay it down and authority to take it up again. This command I received from my Father." (John 10:9, 11, 15, 17-18)**

15 (23:47) **Confession**: there was the centurion's declaration—Jesus' righteousness, a picture of the confession to be made by many.

1. The centurion was bound to be a thoughtful and honest man. He was in charge of the crucifixion, which means he was responsible for overseeing all that took place. As the events unfolded upon the cross, he was stricken more and more with the claim of Jesus and the way in which the events were happening. When Jesus shouted out that His purpose was finished, that His death was the climax of His purpose upon earth, the centurion was convinced. The very fact that Jesus' death was purposeful was the clincher. God quickened to the soldier's heart the glorious truth: "Surely this was a righteous man."

2. The centurion was a Gentile. He symbolized all who were to confess Christ in coming generations.

> **That if you confess with your mouth, "Jesus is Lord," and believe in your heart that God raised him from the dead, you will be saved. For it is with your heart that you believe and are justified, and it is with your mouth that you confess and are saved. (Rom 10:9-10)**

16 (23:48) **Preparation—Conscience**: there was the people's grief—a picture of stricken consciences. The people had come for entertainment, but they went away with saddened, grieving hearts. God, being the Sovereign Lord of the universe, saw to it that they were stricken in conscience. They were being prepared for the preaching to come after Pentecost.

> **How much more, then, will the blood of Christ, who through the eternal Spirit offered himself unblemished to God, cleanse our consciences from acts that lead to death, so that we may serve the living God! (Heb 9:14)**

17 (23:49) **Self-Denial**: there were the followers of Jesus—a proof that Jesus lived and served well. Note that the women were at the cross despite the danger. They were off, some distance away, but they were there nevertheless. They still loved and cared, no matter what. They symbolized that Jesus' life was not in vain.

> **For whoever wants to save his life will lose it, but whoever loses his life for me and for the gospel will save it. (Mark 8:35)**

Outline	Scripture	Scripture	Outline
	H. Jesus' Burial: A Secret Disciple Stirred to Step Forth, 23:50-56 (Mt.27:57-61; Mk.15: 42-47; Jn.19:38-42)	53 Then he took it down, wrapped it in linen cloth and placed it in a tomb cut in the rock, one in which no one had yet been laid.	f. A man who cared deeply for Jesus 1) He took care of Jesus' body
1 The secret believer stirred to step forward for Jesus a. A counselor b. A good & upright man c. A man who had feared to stand up for Jesus sometime before d. A man who looked for the Messiah—for God's Kingom e. A man who was changed by the death of Jesus	50 Now there was a man named Joseph, a member of the Council, a good and upright man, 51 Who had not consented to their decision and action. He came from the Judean town of Arimathea and he was waiting for the kingdom of God. 52 Going to Pilate, he asked for Jesus' body.	54 It was Preparation Day, and the Sabbath was about to begin. 55 The women who had come with Jesus from Galilee followed Joseph and saw the tomb and how his body was laid in it. 56 Then they went home and prepared spices and perfumes. But they rested on the Sabbath in obedience to the commandment.	2) He acted quickly **2 The women stirred to loyalty & affection** a. Showed a fearless loyalty b. Showed deep affection c. Showed an ignorance of the resurrection

DIVISION XI

THE SON OF MAN'S SUFFERINGS: HIS AGONY, TRIALS, AND CRUCIFIXION, 22:39-23:56

H. Jesus' Burial: A Secret Disciple Stirred to Step Forth, 23:50-56

(23:50-56) **Introduction**: a secret believer is a tragedy. In a sense he is the tragedy of tragedies, for he fails to confess Jesus publicly. He ignores the fact of what Jesus said: all persons are lost (Mt.10:32-33). Joseph of Arimathea was such a man: a secret believer until the death of Jesus. But the death of Jesus changed him.

1. The secret believer stirred to step forward for Jesus (v.50-54).
2. The women stirred to loyalty and affection (v.55-56).

1 (23:50-54) **Discipleship, Secret—Profession—Believer—Jesus Christ, Death**: the secret believer, Joseph of Arimathea, was stirred to step forward for Jesus. A revealing description is given about Joseph.

1. He was a member of the council, a senator, a member of the Sanhedrin, the ruling body of Israel. Apparently he was
   - highly educated
   - highly esteemed
   - well liked
   - very responsible
   - capable of leadership

2. He was a "good and upright" man. He was a man...
   - of good quality
   - of high morals
   - of feelings
   - of compassion
   - of justice
   - of decision
   - of truth
   - of law

3. He was a man looking for the Messiah and the Kingdom of God (see notes—Lk.2:25-27; DEEPER STUDY # 3—Mt.19:23-24).

4. He was, however, a man who feared to stand up for Jesus. John says he was "a disciple of Jesus, but secretly because he feared the Jews" (Jn.19:38). Joseph probably had met Jesus and arranged private meetings with Him when the Lord had visited Jerusalem, but he feared making a public profession. His position and prestige were at stake. His peers, the other rulers, opposed Jesus. He believed in Jesus, but out of fear he kept his discipleship a secret. Note: when the vote was taken to put Jesus to death, Joseph did abstain from voting, but he did not stand up for Jesus. He did not participate; he simply remained silent.

Thought 1. How many persons are like Joseph? They are believers and good and upright people; however they fear what their friends and fellow workers will say. They fear the loss of position, prestige, promotion, acceptance, popularity, friends, job, income, livelihood.

> **If anyone is ashamed of me and my words, the Son of Man will be ashamed of him when he comes in his glory and in the glory of the Father and of the holy angels. (Luke 9:26)**
>
> **"I tell you, my friends, do not be afraid of those who kill the body and after that can do no more. But I will show you whom you should fear: Fear him who, after the killing of the body, has power to throw you into hell. Yes, I tell you, fear him. (Luke 12:4-5)**
>
> **For God did not give us a spirit of timidity, but a spirit of power, of love and of self-discipline. (2 Tim 1:7)**
>
> **Fear of man will prove to be a snare, but whoever trusts in the LORD is kept safe. (Prov 29:25)**
>
> **"I, even I, am he who comforts you. Who are you that you fear mortal men, the sons of men, who are but grass, (Isa 51:12)**

5. He was a man changed by the death of Jesus. This is seen in two facts.
   a. Joseph actually went to Pilate and begged for the body of Jesus. This was a tremendous act of courage. The Romans either dumped the bodies of crucified criminals in the trash heaps or left the bodies hanging upon the cross for the vultures and animals to consume. The latter served as an example of criminal punishment to the public. Joseph also braved the threat of Pilate's reaction. Pilate was fed up with the *Jesus matter*. Jesus had proven to be very bothersome to him. He could have reacted severely against Joseph.
   b. Joseph risked the disfavor and discipline of the Sanhedrin. They were the ruling body who had instigated and condemned Jesus, and Joseph was a member of the council. There was no question—he

would face some harsh reaction from some of his fellow Sanhedrin members and from some of his closest friends.

The thing that turned Joseph from being a secret disciple to a bold disciple seems to be the cross, the phenomenal events surrounding the cross (the behavior and words of Jesus, the darkness, the earthquake, the torn veil or curtain and other events). When Joseph witnessed all this, his mind connected the claims of Jesus with the Old Testament prophecies of the Messiah. Joseph saw the prophecies fulfilled in Jesus. He stepped forward braving all risks and took his stand for Jesus. A remarkable courage! A courage stirred by the death of Jesus.

Thought 1. Every secret believer needs to study the cross of Christ. Really seeing the cross will turn any secret believer into a bold witness for Christ.

Thought 2. Joseph courageously asked to take care of the physical body of Christ. Today, the body of Christ is the church. We are to boldly step forward and take care of the church. There are special times of need within the church when special courage is needed to step forward and show care. In those times a fresh look at the cross will be helpful and can be used by God to stir us.

So I made up my mind that I would not make another painful visit to you. (2 Cor 2:1)

because we know that the one who raised the Lord Jesus from the dead will also raise us with Jesus and present us with you in his presence. All this is for your benefit, so that the grace that is reaching more and more people may cause thanksgiving to overflow to the glory of God. (2 Cor 4:14-15)

And he died for all, that those who live should no longer live for themselves but for him who died for them and was raised again. (2 Cor 5:15)

6. He was a man who cared deeply for Jesus. The words and acts of these two verses express care and tenderness, love and affection, as well as courage and boldness. Joseph...

- took the Lord's body down from the cross.
- wrapped the body in linen.
- laid the body in a tomb, a tomb in which no man had ever been laid.
- acted quickly, before the Sabbath began. Jesus died at 3 p.m. Friday afternoon which was the day of preparation for the Sabbath (cp. Mk.15:33-34, 37). Work was forbidden on the Sabbath, so if anything was to be done with Jesus' body, it had to be done immediately. Only three hours remained for work. (See note—Mk.15:42 for more discussion.)

This act alone would leave no doubt about the effect of the cross upon Joseph. The cross changed his life. He was no longer a secret believer; he now demonstrated a public stand for Jesus.

Thought 1. Position, power, wealth, fame—none of these can make us bold for Christ. Only true affection for Christ will make us bold, and only as we see the cross of Christ will affection for Christ be aroused.

Thought 2. Christ identified with men perfectly.

⇒ He lived as a man—but perfectly.
⇒ He died as a man—but perfectly (as the Ideal Man).
⇒ He was buried as a man—but perfectly.

He was assigned a grave with the wicked, and with the rich in his death, though he had done no violence, nor was any deceit in his mouth. (Isa 53:9)

For this reason he had to be made like his brothers in every way, in order that he might become a merciful and faithful high priest in service to God, and that he might make atonement for the sins of the people. (Heb 2:17)

Thought 3. God's own Son possessed nothing when He was on earth; therefore when He died, He had to be buried in a borrowed tomb. Note two things.

⇒ Christ is the Savior of the poorest. He was born in a stable. He had no place of His own to lay His head (Mt.8:20; Lk.9:58). His tomb was a borrowed tomb.
⇒ Yet the rich can serve Him just as Joseph of Arimathaea did.

Jesus replied, "Foxes have holes and birds of the air have nests, but the Son of Man has no place to lay his head." (Luke 9:58)

Sell your possessions and give to the poor. Provide purses for yourselves that will not wear out, a treasure in heaven that will not be exhausted, where no thief comes near and no moth destroys. (Luke 12:33)

In everything I did, I showed you that by this kind of hard work we must help the weak, remembering the words the Lord Jesus himself said: 'It is more blessed to give than to receive.'" (Acts 20:35)

For you know the grace of our Lord Jesus Christ, that though he was rich, yet for your sakes he became poor, so that you through his poverty might become rich. (2 Cor 8:9)

This is how we know what love is: Jesus Christ laid down his life for us. And we ought to lay down our lives for our brothers. (1 John 3:16)

2 (23:55-56) **Jesus Christ, Love for—Eternal Life**: the women believers were stirred to loyalty and affection. Note three facts.

1. The women demonstrated a fearless loyalty despite all danger. At the cross the men forsook Jesus, but not the women (Mt.26:56, 69-75; cp. Mt.27:55-56, 61; Mk. 15:41).

2. The women demonstrated a deep affection for Jesus. They took their own money to buy spices and perfumes to embalm Jesus. This they did because they loved Him (Lk.23:56; cp. Mt.27:61; Mk.16:1).

3. The women did not yet understand the resurrection of Jesus. They were preparing His body to lie and eventually to decay in the tomb. The true meaning of *living forever—the human body being remade, recreated, and becoming incorruptible*—had not yet been grasped by them (Jn.5:24-29; cp. 1 Cor.15:42f. Cp. 1 Cor.15:1-58.)

Thought 1. The testimony of these women should stir men to stand up for Christ. Too often it is the women who take the lead in standing forth for Christ. This should not be the case. Men…

- should be loyal to Christ, no matter how grave the danger.
- should love Christ to such an extent that they give all they *are and have* to Christ.
- should seek to understand and grasp the resurrection of Christ in all its fullness.

So do not be ashamed to testify about our Lord, or ashamed of me his prisoner. But join with me in suffering for the gospel, by the power of God, (2 Tim 1:8)

I am not ashamed of the gospel, because it is the power of God for the salvation of everyone who believes: first for the Jew, then for the Gentile. (Rom 1:16)

	CHAPTER 24 **XII. THE SON OF MAN'S GLORY: HIS RESURRECTION & ASCENSION, 24:1-53** **A. Jesus' Empty Tomb: Its Discovery, 24:1-12** (cp. Mt.28:1-15; Mk.16:1-11; Jn.20:1-18)
1 The first day of the week **2 The first witness of the resurrection**	On the first day of the week, very early in the morning, the women took the spices they had prepared and went to the tomb.
3 The great stone rolled away	2 They found the stone rolled away from the tomb,
4 The body's missing from the tomb	3 But when they entered, they did not find the body of the Lord Jesus.
5 The two angels & their unbelievable message a. Their dazzling clothes	4 While they were wondering about this, suddenly two men in clothes that gleamed like lightning stood beside them.
b. Their question	5 In their fright the women bowed down with their faces to the ground, but the men said to them, "Why do you look for the living among the dead?
c. Their proclamation d. Their reminder of Jesus' prophecy	6 He is not here; he has risen! Remember how he told you, while he was still with you in Galilee: 7 'The Son of Man must be delivered into the hands of sinful men, be crucified and on the third day be raised again.'" 8 Then they remembered his words.
6 The immediate unbelief of the apostles	9 When they came back from the tomb, they told all these things to the Eleven and to all the others.
a. The message of the resurrection is carried by women—initially	10 It was Mary Magdalene, Joanna, Mary the mother of James, and the others with them who told this to the apostles.
b. The message of the resurrection is accepted as nonsense	11 But they did not believe the women, because their words seemed to them like nonsense.
7 The continued unbelief of Peter a. He ran to see—hopefully b. He saw evidence: Linen clothes folded & off to the side c. He wondered	12 Peter, however, got up and ran to the tomb. Bending over, he saw the strips of linen lying by themselves, and he went away, wondering to himself what had happened.

DIVISION XII

THE SON OF MAN'S GLORY: HIS RESURRECTION AND ASCENSION, 24:1-53

A. Jesus' Empty Tomb: Its Discovery, 24:1-12

(24:1-12) **Introduction**: the tomb was empty. Discovering the empty tomb was the greatest discovery in human history. However, the great tragedy is that most people either are not aware that Jesus arose or do not believe that He arose. Every man has to discover the fact for himself. The empty tomb and the risen Lord have to become a personal discovery for every man.

1. The first day of the week (v.1).
2. The first witnesses of the resurrection (v.1).
3. The great stone rolled away (v.2).
4. The body's missing from the tomb (v.3).
5. The two angels and their unbelievable message (v.4-8).
6. The immediate unbelief of the apostles (v.9-11).
7. The continued unbelief of Peter (v.12).

1 (24:1) **Jesus Christ, Resurrection**: the first day of the week, Sunday, was the day upon which Jesus arose, the day after the Jewish Sabbath (Saturday). Note three facts.

1. Luke clearly spells out when Jesus arose: "On the first day of the week, very early in the morning." Jesus arose before dawn, before the sun arose on Sunday morning. This was significant to the early Christian believers, so significant that they broke away from the common day for worship during the week, the Sabbath or Saturday. They began to worship on Sunday, the day of the resurrection of their Lord (cp. Acts 20:7; 1 Cor.16:2).

2. Jesus arose on the first day of the week, on Sunday morning. This means that He had been in the grave for three days just as He had said (Mt.12:40; 16:21; 17:23; 20:19; Mk.9:31; 10:34; Lk.9:22; 18:33; 24:7, 46). His resurrection from the dead was a triumph, a conquest over death. Death reigns no more–its rule has been broken (1 Cor.15:55-56; 2 Cor.1:9-10; 2 Tim.1:10; Heb.2:9, 14-15).

3. Again, Jesus arose on the first day of the week, Sunday morning. He was in the grave on the Sabbath, unable to observe the laws governing the great season of the Passover and the Sabbath. He was dead; therefore, the law and its observances had no authority over Him. This is symbolic of the *identification* believers gain in Christ. When a man believes in Jesus Christ, God identifies the man with Christ, in particular with the death of Christ. God counts the man as having died with Christ. Very simply, *in Christ's death* believers become dead to the law (see notes—Ro.7:4; Mt.5:17-18 for more discussion).

2 (24:1) **Jesus Christ, Resurrection**: the first witnesses of resurrection provide strong evidence of the resurrection.

1. They were actual witnesses of Jesus' *death and burial*. They knew He was dead, and they knew where He had been laid. They had followed along behind the procession to the tomb (Mt.15:40-41, 47; cp. Mt.27:55-56, 61; Lk.23:55-56). There was no question whatsoever in their mind about His being dead and buried.

2. They had purchased spices and had *come to anoint* Jesus' body. Apparently they had bought the spices Saturday evening after 6 p.m. when the Sabbath ended. Note:

they arose "very early in the morning, the first day of the week [Sunday]" to go and embalm Him. Again, they knew He was dead, and they cared; so they wanted to take care of His body just as loved ones care for the bodies of their deceased.

3. They were religionists who *strictly obeyed the law.* They were strict in the observance of the Sabbath. Imagine—their loved one was dead, yet they would not break the Sabbath law even to take care of Him (cp. Lk.23:56). The women were obedient to the commandments of God. They were *moral and truthful* and would never think, much less consider, lying about the death and resurrection of Jesus.

3 (24:2) **Jesus Christ, Resurrection**: there was the great stone rolled away from the entrance (see DEEPER STUDY # 1, Stone—Mt.27:65-66). The rolled away stone perplexed the women (v.4). However, the stone had not been rolled back for the benefit of Jesus, but for the witnesses to the resurrection. When Jesus arose, He was in His resurrection body, the heavenly body of the spiritual dimension; and the spiritual dimension has no physical bounds. But the witnesses needed to enter the tomb and see the truth (see outline and notes—Jn.20:1-10).

4 (24:3) **Jesus Christ, Resurrection**: there was the body's missing from the tomb. The account is simple, yet striking: "when they entered they did not find the body of the Lord Jesus." They saw, contemplated that Jesus was not there (Mk.16:6). They saw the slab upon which He had been laid, and *He was not there.*

> **Being fully persuaded that God had power to do what he had promised. (Rom 4:21)**
>
> **For no matter how many promises God has made, they are "Yes" in Christ. And so through him the "Amen" is spoken by us to the glory of God. (2 Cor 1:20)**
>
> **If we are faithless, he will remain faithful, for he cannot disown himself. (2 Tim 2:13)**
>
> **Through these he has given us his very great and precious promises, so that through them you may participate in the divine nature and escape the corruption in the world caused by evil desires. (2 Pet 1:4)**

5 (24:4-8) **Angels—Jesus Christ, Resurrection**: there were the two angels and their message. Note four significant points about the angels.

1. The angels were radiant, dazzling figures. Their garments shone (Mt.28:3)...

- "like lightning" (visible, quick, startling, striking, frightening, brilliant).
- "white as snow" (pure, glistening).

Note the women feared and fell down, bowing in reverence.

2. The angels asked a pointed question: "Why do you look for the living among the dead?" There was a rebuke in the question. They were seeking to honor a dead Savior, a Savior who was as all other men are, frail and powerless to do anything about life and eternity. Their whole being—their thoughts, feelings, and behavior—were focused upon a dead Savior.

They were living just as the world lives—"foreigners to the covenants of the promise, without hope, and without God in the world" (Eph.2:12).

3. The angels proclaimed the glorious news: "He is not here, but he has risen." Note two points.

a. "He is not here": the women could see and did see the fact. The fact was clearly evident: Jesus was not in the tomb. He had been there, for the women had seen Him put there. They had witnessed His death and burial, but He was no longer in the tomb (see note—Lk.23:55-56).

b. "He has risen." Startling, unbelievable words...

- yet, heaven "declares Him to be living" (Heb.7:8).
- yet, Scripture witnesses that He arose (Ro.1:4; Eph.1:19-20).
- yet, He had foretold that He would arise (Lk.9:22; 13:32; 17:25; 18:31-34).

> **And who through the Spirit of holiness was declared with power to be the Son of God by his resurrection from the dead: Jesus Christ our Lord. (Rom 1:4)**
>
> **And his incomparably great power for us who believe. That power is like the working of his mighty strength, which he exerted in Christ when he raised him from the dead and seated him at his right hand in the heavenly realms, (Eph 1:19-20)**

4. The angels reminded the women that Jesus had foretold His death and resurrection (see outline and notes—Lk.18:31-34). Note the words, "Then they remembered His words." The followers of Jesus had always been confused about the prophecy of His death and resurrection. They *would not* accept his words literally, refusing to take His predictions at face value. They symbolized His statements; therefore, they never understood His death and resurrection (see note—Lk.18:34).

But note what happened now. They knew they had been wrong. Conviction struck them, and they became the very first witnesses to the resurrection.

> **Jesus looked at them and said, "With man this is impossible, but with God all things are possible." (Mat 19:26)**
>
> **For nothing is impossible with God." (Luke 1:37)**
>
> **God, who has called you into fellowship with his Son Jesus Christ our Lord, is faithful. (1 Cor 1:9)**
>
> **If we are faithless, he will remain faithful, for he cannot disown himself. (2 Tim 2:13)**
>
> **Let us hold unswervingly to the hope we profess, for he who promised is faithful. (Heb 10:23)**

6 (24:9-11) **Unbelief—Disciples**: the immediate unbelief of the disciples. The women rushed to the disciples to share the glorious news. But the news "seemed to them as like nonsense (hos leros): idle tales, ridiculous talk, wild imagination. "They did not believe the woman." The Greek word is *disbelieved* (epistoun) and is in the imperfect active tense which means they "*kept on disbelieving,*" kept on putting no trust or confidence in what the women were claiming. They were *gripped* with a skeptical, unbelieving spirit.

Thought 1. The disciples were without excuse. Christ had spent month after month drilling His death and resurrection into His disciples. (See notes—Mt.16:21-28; 17:1-13; 17:22; 17:24-27 for more discussion.)

Later Jesus appeared to the Eleven as they were eating; he rebuked them for their lack of faith and their stubborn refusal to believe those who had seen him after he had risen. (Mark 16:14)

Whoever believes in him is not condemned, but whoever does not believe stands condemned already because he has not believed in the name of God's one and only Son. (John 3:18)

See to it, brothers, that none of you has a sinful, unbelieving heart that turns away from the living God. (Heb 3:12)

Let us, therefore, make every effort to enter that rest, so that no one will fall by following their example of disobedience. (Heb 4:11)

7 (24:12) **Unbelief—Peter**: the continued unbelief of Peter. Peter's heart was still drawn to the Lord despite his enormous failure. Hearing that the body of Jesus was no longer in the tomb, he rushed to the tomb with his thoughts flying, wondering what had happened to the Lord.

Note a crucial point. Peter stooped down and saw the evidence: the linen clothes were lying off to the side by themselves. However, Peter did not grasp the significance of the evidence. John said he had rushed to the tomb with Peter and did believe, based upon the evidence of the linen clothes. He also verifies that Peter did not grasp the significance at this point (see note—Jn.20:1-10 for a discussion of this significant point). Peter just "went away," wondering within himself what had really happened.

Thought 1. It is dangerous not to understand the Lord's Word, not to take His Word at face value. Spiritualizing His words, unless the words are clearly symbolic, often leads to serious unbelief and problems.

Thought 2. A person has to be open to the evidence of the resurrection. The tomb is empty; He is risen—and the honest and seeking man will be convinced by the Spirit of God. What is needed is to do as Peter did: run to the tomb to see what really did happen.

He said to them, "How foolish you are, and how slow of heart to believe all that the prophets have spoken! (Luke 24:25)

He said to his disciples, "Why are you so afraid? Do you still have no faith?" (Mark 4:40)

Whoever believes in the Son has eternal life, but whoever rejects the Son will not see life, for God's wrath remains on him." (John 3:36)

I told you that you would die in your sins; if you do not believe that I am the one I claim to be, you will indeed die in your sins." (John 8:24)

B. Jesus' Appearance to Two Believers on the Road to Emmaus: An Immortal Journey, 24:13-35
(Mk.16:12-13)

1 Scene 1: Taking a lonely but thoughtful walk[DS1]
a. They had heard about the resurrection: "That same day"
b. They thought about & discussed the events
2 Scene 2: Considering three critical questions
a. Jesus drew near, but He was unrevealed
b. Question 1: What are you talking about?
1) A gloomy look
2) Answer: The things that have happened
c. Question 2: What events?
1) Jesus' death
a) He was a great prophet
b) He was crucified
c) He was thought to be the Messiah
2) Jesus' prophecy of three days
3) Jesus' empty tomb & perplexing reports
a) Reports of visions
b) Reports of Jesus' being alive

13 Now that same day two
of them were going to a village called Emmaus, about
seven miles from Jerusalem.
14 They were talking with
each other about everything
that had happened.
15 As they talked and discussed these things with each
other, Jesus himself came up
and walked along with them;
16 But they were kept from
recognizing him.
17 He asked them, "What are
you discussing together as
you walk along?" They stood
still, their faces downcast.
18 One of them, named
Cleopas, asked him, "Are you
only a visitor to Jerusalem
and do not know the things
that have happened there in
these days?"
19 "What things?" he asked.
"About Jesus of Nazareth,"
they replied. "He was a
prophet, powerful in word
and deed before God and all
the people.
20 The chief priests and our
rulers handed him over to be
sentenced to death, and they
crucified him;
21 But we had hoped that he
was the one who was going
to redeem Israel. And what is
more, it is the third day since
all this took place.
22 In addition, some of our
women amazed us. They
went to the tomb early this
morning
23 But didn't find his body.
They came and told us that
they had seen a vision of
angels, who said he was
alive.
24 Then some of our companions went to the tomb and
found it just as the women had
said, but him they did not see."
25 He said to them, "How
foolish you are, and how
slow of heart to believe all
that the prophets have spoken!
26 Did not the Christ have to
suffer these things and then
enter his glory?"
27 And beginning with
Moses and all the Prophets,
he explained to them what
was said in all the Scriptures
concerning himself.
28 As they approached the
village to which they were
going, Jesus acted as if he
were going farther.
29 But they urged him
strongly, "Stay with us, for it
is nearly evening; the day is
almost over." So he went in
to stay with them.
30 When he was at the table
with them, he took bread,
gave thanks, broke it and began to give it to them.
31 Then their eyes were
opened and they recognized
him, and he disappeared from
their sight.
32 They asked each other,
"Were not our hearts burning
within us while he talked
with us on the road and
opened the Scriptures to us?"
33 They got up and returned
at once to Jerusalem. There
they found the Eleven and
those with them, assembled
together
34 And saying, "It is true!
The Lord has risen and has
appeared to Simon."
35 Then the two told what
had happened on the way,
and how Jesus was recognized by them when he broke
the bread.

c) Reports confirmed
d. Question 3: Did not the Prophets predict the Messiah's death & resurrection?
1) A mild rebuke
2) His death & resurrection were necessary
3) He explains the Scripture
3 Scene 3: Experiencing the burning truth—Jesus is risen; He is alive
a. The two sought to hear more: Invited Him to stay with them
1) He accepted the invitation
2) He blessed the food
b. God opened their eyes: They knew the Lord
c. They had experienced conviction: A burning within their hearts
4 Scene 4: Proclaiming the immortal witness
a. The two rushed to the disciples
b. The exciting meeting, the immortal witness: Christ is risen
1) Had been seen by Simon
2) Had been seen by the two from Emmaus

DIVISION XII

THE SON OF MAN'S GLORY: HIS RESURRECTION AND ASCENSION, 24:1-53

B. Jesus' Appearance to Two Believers on the Road to Emmaus: An Immortal Journey, 24:13-35

(24:13-35) **Introduction**: this is one of the most beloved accounts of the resurrection story. It is an account of Jesus' helping two ordinary persons who had lost hope and fallen into the pit of sadness and despair. Their experience was an immortal journey.

1. Scene 1: taking a lonely but thoughtful walk (v.13-14).
2. Scene 2: considering three critical questions (v.15-27).
3. Scene 3: experiencing the burning truth—Jesus is risen; He is alive (v.28-32).
4. Scene 4: proclaiming the immortal witness (v.33-35).

1 (24:13-14) **Hopelessness—Despair—Devastation**: the first scene was that of a lonely walk by two persons—two persons who were sad, despairing, and very thoughtful.

The day is important: it was "that same day" that the women discovered the empty tomb and reported it to the disciples (the resurrection day, Easter Sunday). The news had been received with skepticism, as utter nonsense. These two, Cleopas and his companion, had either been present or else had heard the news from some other source. As they made their way to Emmaus they were sad, gripped by a spirit of despair over the Lord's crucifixion. Their hope that Jesus was the promised Messiah had been devastated, dashed against the rocks of death. But in their despair, their thoughts were rushing wildly about, entangled, wondering about the report of the women concerning the empty tomb and the angels. What did it mean?

The point to note is their emotions and thoughts, their...

- sadness and despair (over the Lord's death).
- devastated hope (He is not the Messiah).
- rushing and entangled thoughts (over the reports of an empty tomb and angels).

Thought 1. The scene is a symbol of the despair that grips so many in life. Their hopes are devastated, hopes for...

- family
- school
- meaning and purpose
- profession
- acceptance

In their sadness and despair, somewhere, they hear reports of the empty tomb and of the living Lord; but they do not know what the reports mean, not personally.

"I loathe my very life; therefore I will give free rein to my complaint and speak out in the bitterness of my soul. (Job 10:1)

My life is consumed by anguish and my years by groaning; my strength fails because of my affliction, and my bones grow weak. (Psa 31:10)

My God. My soul is downcast within me; therefore I will remember you from the land of the Jordan, the heights of Hermon—from Mount Mizar. (Psa 42:6)

I sink in the miry depths, where there is no foothold. I have come into the deep waters; the floods engulf me. (Psa 69:2)

But as for me, my feet had almost slipped; I had nearly lost my foothold. (Psa 73:2)

When I tried to understand all this, it was oppressive to me (Psa 73:16)

By the rivers of Babylon we sat and wept when we remembered Zion. (Psa 137:1)

But Zion said, "The LORD has forsaken me, the Lord has forgotten me." (Isa 49:14)

Do not run until your feet are bare and your throat is dry. But you said, 'It's no use! I love foreign gods, and I must go after them.' (Jer 2:25)

Brothers, we do not want you to be ignorant about those who fall asleep [dead], or to grieve like the rest of men, who have no hope. (1 Th 4:13)

Remember that at that time you were separate from Christ, excluded from citizenship in Israel and foreigners to the covenants of the promise, without hope and without God in the world. (Eph 2:12)

DEEPER STUDY # 1

(24:13) **Emmaus**: the city and location are unknown. It was about seven miles out of Jerusalem, which would take somewhere around two hours to travel by foot.

2 (24:15-27) **Jesus Christ, Death—Misconception—Puzzlement—Questioning—Perplexity**: the second scene was consideration of three questions. Note the exact words as Cleopas and his companion walked along: "As they talked and discussed these things with each other, Jesus himself came up and walked along with them;" (suneporeueto, imperfect tense). The idea is that they were so absorbed in their despair and talk that Jesus *was already* walking along with them when they noticed Him. But note: they did not know Him. His resurrected body differed enough that He was not recognized as Jesus without close observation (see DEEPER STUDY # 1—Jn.21:1). In this particular instance, the Lord "held" (restrained, kept) their eyes from recognizing Him as well. Apparently He wanted them to more freely discuss the events with Him.

1. The first question: What are you talking about; what is it that is causing you to look so sad (skuthropoi)? The Greek word means gloomy, dejected, despondent, sullen, overcast. Jesus could see sadness and despair written all over their faces.

Cleopas was surprised that the stranger did not know. "How could anyone be in Jerusalem and not know why we are sad and despairing?" he asked. Terrible things had happened.

Thought 1. These two were seeking to understand the death and empty tomb of Christ. Christ was the subject of their conversation. They were seeking the truth; therefore, Christ drew near them.

"Ask and it will be given to you; seek and you will find; knock and the door will be opened to you. For everyone who asks receives; he who seeks finds; and to him who knocks, the door will be opened. (Mat 7:7-8)

To the Jews who had believed him, Jesus said, "If you hold to my teaching, you are really my disciples. Then you will know the truth, and the truth will set you free." (John 8:31-32)

2. The second question: "What things? What circumstances could possibly cause such sadness and despair?" (v.19-24). Cleopas answered, covering three subjects.

a. Jesus' death.
   - ⇒ He was a great prophet.
   - ⇒ The rulers crucified him. (Note the whole world is implicated. The Jews delivered Him, and the Gentile Romans condemned and crucified Him.)
   - ⇒ We had trusted (elpizomen, hoped) that He was the Messiah, the One who was to save Israel.

b. Jesus' prophecy of three days. There is significance in the term "the third day." Cleopas was sharing how their *dead Master* had told them...
   - to watch for the third day, for some unusual event.
   - that He had spoken of "rising again on the third day," whatever that meant.

- that they thought the words meant that His triumph would take place on the third day. (See outline and notes—Lk.18:31-34 for more discussion.)

c. Jesus' empty tomb and perplexing reports from certain women, reports...
  - of an empty tomb
  - of a vision of angels
  - of Jesus' being alive
  - that had been confirmed
  - that Jesus was not seen

Thought 1. World events and the terrible things that happen in life often make a person sad and despairing—such things as...

- being misunderstood
- being opposed
- being deserted
- being betrayed
- helplessness
- death
- hopelessness
- divisiveness
- loss
- fear
- injustice

Christ is concerned. He wants to know what it is that causes so much sadness and despair. He wants us to share our problems with Him.

Thought 2. The problem with the two from Emmaus, as it is with so many today, was their *shortsightedness* and *unbelief.*

Thought 3. There is one major reason why men refuse to accept a risen Lord. A risen Lord means that a man must subject himself to the Lord and obey and serve Him.

"Therefore let all Israel be assured of this: God has made this Jesus, whom you crucified, both Lord and Christ." (Acts 2:36)

God exalted him to his own right hand as Prince and Savior that he might give repentance and forgiveness of sins to Israel. We are witnesses of these things, and so is the Holy Spirit, whom God has given to those who obey him." (Acts 5:31-32)

Therefore God exalted him to the highest place and gave him the name that is above every name, (Phil 2:9)

Thought 4. Every man should be engrossed in the death of Christ, but he should also believe and be engrossed in the resurrection of the Lord.

He was delivered over to death for our sins and was raised to life for our justification. (Rom 4:25)

Who is he that condemns? Christ Jesus, who died—more than that, who was raised to life—is at the right hand of God and is also interceding for us. (Rom 8:34)

Therefore he is able to save completely those who come to God through him, because he always lives to intercede for them. (Heb 7:25)

3. The third question: "Did not the prophets predict Messiah's death and resurrection?" (v.25-27). Note several facts.

a. Jesus rebuked the two disciples for being dull and slow to believe. He called them "foolish" (anoetoi), which means that they were dull and slow to believe. More was expected of them; they should have known more than they were indicating. They were without excuse, for their minds and hearts were capable of more. Therefore, Jesus rebuked them for being...
  - *slow to believe.*
  - slow to believe *all* the prophets had spoken.

b. Jesus shared that the death and resurrection of the Messiah was a necessity. The words "did not" (ouchi edei) are strong. They mean there was a constraint, an imperative, a necessity laid upon the Messiah to die and arise. He had no choice. His death and resurrection had been planned and willed by God through all eternity. Therefore, He had to fulfill the will of God, for God had ordained...
  - that the Messiah suffer these things.
  - that the Messiah enter into His glory. God's plan was not defeated. He conquered through the death of His Son, the Messiah.

c. Jesus explained the Scripture to the two disciples, taught them book by book, showing them the things concerning the Messiah in each book. Note the words "all the Scriptures." Prophecies of Christ are found in all the Scripture; therefore, Jesus carried the two disciples through the Scripture in a systematic way, book by book, showing them how God's purpose was fulfilled in the death of the Messiah. The two disciples could now be saved eternally, not just during an earthly reign of an earthly Messiah.

Thought 1. The two disciples were feeling hopeless and perplexed, full of sadness and despair for one very simple reason: unbelief. They had *symbolized* or *spiritualized* the Scripture and the clear predictions which Jesus had given his disciples before His death. Therefore, they could not see *beyond* Jesus' death. They were willing to accept and admire a *dead Savior*, a great prophet who had been martyred, but they had great difficulty in accepting a risen Lord. They would not believe the reports of the women, the glorious news of the living Lord.

But they did not believe the women, because their words seemed to them like nonsense. (Luke 24:11)

Let us, therefore, make every effort to enter that rest, so that no one will fall by following their example of disobedience. (Heb 4:11)

Consider him who endured such opposition from sinful men, so that you will not grow weary and lose heart. (Heb 12:3)

3 (24:28-32) **Conviction—Conversion**: the third scene was experiencing the burning truth—Jesus is risen and alive forevermore. Note three important points.

1. The two disciples *sought* to hear more. They invited Jesus to abide with them. The words "acted as if" do not mean Jesus was play-acting. He never pretends. He would have gone on, for He never enters a life or a home without

a personal invitation. The two were seeking the truth, so they wanted Jesus to enter their home and to share more with them. (How unlike so many today!)

Jesus did enter, and He sat down to have dinner with them. He was also asked to give thanks for the meal.

2. God opened the eyes of the two disciples. They immediately knew the Lord. But note why: they had invited Jesus into their home. If they had let Him pass on, the likelihood is that they would never have known it was the Lord.

3. The two disciples had experienced a burning conviction within their hearts.

a. The Word of God being proclaimed is what had stirred the conviction and the burning.

> **Therefore this is what the LORD God Almighty says: "Because the people have spoken these words, I will make my words in your mouth a fire and these people the wood it consumes. (Jer 5:14)**
>
> **"Is not my word like fire," declares the LORD, "and like a hammer that breaks a rock in pieces? (Jer 23:29)**

b. Their response to the conviction—inviting Christ into their home—led to their coming to know Him personally.

> **Here I am! I stand at the door and knock. If anyone hears my voice and opens the door, I will come in and eat with him, and he with me. (Rev 3:20)**
>
> **God, who has called you into fellowship with his Son Jesus Christ our Lord, is faithful. (1 Cor 1:9)**
>
> **For where two or three come together in my name, there am I with them." (Mat 18:20)**

Thought 1. The two had heard the Scripture explained, and they had heard much. But they had to respond, to invite the Lord into their home before God could open their eyes and bring them to a knowledge of Christ.

4 (24:33-35) **Jesus Christ, Resurrection**: the fourth scene was proclaiming the immortal witness. The scene was dramatic. It was night, but the two rushed back to the apostles. When they arrived, they found the apostles and some other disciples already gathered together.

They were all bursting with excitement. To the shock of the two from Emmaus, the group had the same immortal witness to share: "The Lord has risen and has appeared to Simon." As they listened to Simon's experience, they were bursting at the seams, hardly able to contain themselves, waiting to share their own experience.

Finally, their time came to share their experience and the very same immortal witness: "The Lord is risen indeed."

> **And you also must testify, for you have been with me from the beginning. (John 15:27)**
>
> **You will be his witness to all men of what you have seen and heard. (Acts 22:15)**
>
> **"We are witnesses of everything he did in the country of the Jews and in Jerusalem. They killed him by hanging him on a tree, but God raised him from the dead on the third day and caused him to be seen. (Acts 10:39-40)**

	C. Jesus' Appearance to the Disciples: The Great Statements of the Christian Faith, 24:36-49 (Mk.16:14; Jn.20:19-23; 20:26-21:25)
1 Statement 1: Jesus is risen a. Jesus' first words: Peace	36 While they were still talking about this, Jesus himself stood among them and said to them, "Peace be with you."
b. Jesus' impact 1) The disciples startled & frightened	37 They were startled and frightened, thinking they saw a ghost.
2) The disciples were troubled & questioning	38 He said to them, "Why are you troubled, and why do doubts rise in your minds?
c. Jesus' proof [DS1] 1) He is flesh & bones 2) He shows them his wounds	39 Look at my hands and my feet. It is I myself! Touch me and see; a ghost does not 40 Have flesh and bones, as you see I have."
3) He talks	41 When he had said this, he showed them his hands and feet. 42 And while they still did not believe it because of joy and amazement, he asked them, "Do you have anything here to eat?" 42 They gave him a piece of broiled fish, 43 And he took it and ate it in their presence.
2 Statement 2: All Scripture must be fulfilled a. The forewarning b. The utter necessity	44 He said to them, "This is what I told you while I was still with you: Everything must be fulfilled that is written about me in the Law of Moses, the Prophets and the Psalms."
c. The spiritual insight needed	45 Then he opened their minds so they could understand the Scriptures.
d. The particular prophecies 1) Christ must suffer & arise	46 He told them, "This is what is written: The Christ will suffer and rise from the dead on the third day,
2) Repentance & forgiveness must be preached	47 And repentance and forgive-ness of sins will be preached in his name to all nations, beginning at Jerusalem. 48 You are witnesses of these things.
3) The Holy Spirit and power must be sent	49 I am going to send you what my Father has promised; but stay in the city until you have been clothed with power from on high."

DIVISION XII

THE SON OF MAN'S GLORY: HIS RESURRECTION AND ASCENSION, 24:1-53

C. Jesus' Appearance to the Disciples: The Great Statements of the Christian Faith, 24:36-49

(24:36-49) **Introduction**: this was the first appearance of Jesus to *all the disciples at once*. He shared the two great statements (explanations) of the Christian faith.

1. Statement 1: Jesus is risen (v.36-43).
2. Statement 2: all Scripture must be fulfilled (v.44-49).

(24:36-49) **Another Outline**: The Great Statements of the Christian Faith.

1. Statement 1: Jesus is risen (v.36-43).
2. Statement 2: All prophetic Scripture must be fulfilled (v.44-46).
   a. The whole Old Testament.
   b. The death and resurrection of Christ.
3. Statement 3: Repentance and forgiveness of sin are imperative (v.47-48).
   a. The place: To all nations.
   b. The witnesses: You—disciples.
4. Statement 4: Power is to come upon you (v.49).
   a. The power is the Holy Spirit
   b. The power is given by staying and tarrying (praying).

1 (24:36-43) **Jesus Christ, Resurrection; Impact of; World Response to**: statement one is that Jesus is risen. The scene took place at night—the night of the very day of the Lord's resurrection. It was a dramatic scene. The Lord had already made at least four appearances. The four appearances named were to…

- Mary Magdalene (Jn.20:14f).
- the women visiting the tomb (Mt.28:1f; Mk.16:1f).
- the two walking to Emmaus (Lk.24:1f).
- Simon Peter (Lk.24:34; 1 Cor.15:5).

The apostles (minus Thomas) and some other disciples had rushed to the known meeting place. The very air was electric. Excitement beat in the chest of every one, and minds were grasping for understanding. Wonder was beginning to overcome sadness and despair, and hope was beginning to stir great anticipation. Reports of appearances were being buzzed about and argued about. Then all of a sudden out of nowhere, into the very midst of all this, "Jesus Himself stood." Note three things:

1. The very first words Jesus spoke to the disciples after His death: "Peace be with you." This was the regular greeting of the Jews of that day, but it had a very special significance now. The disciples needed peace, the peace that only He could give. And He had now risen from the dead to give that peace to them. (See note, Peace—Jn.14:27.)

> **But now in Christ Jesus you who once were far away have been brought near through the blood of Christ. For he himself is our peace, who has made the two one and has destroyed the barrier, the dividing wall of hostility, (Eph 2:13-14)**
>
> **Peace I leave with you; my peace I give you. I do not give to you as the world gives. Do not let your hearts be troubled and do not be afraid. (John 14:27)**

"I have told you these things, so that in me you may have peace. In this world you will have trouble. But take heart! I have overcome the world." (John 16:33)

2. The impact of Christ's resurrection. The disciples interpreted His sudden appearance in their midst just as they had always interpreted His words—spiritually. When He suddenly appeared, the immediate thought flashing across their minds was that a spirit was appearing to them. They were...

- startled, terrified, frightened, and troubled.
- questioning.

Thought 1. Unbelievers respond to the resurrection in five ways.

1) They are startled, terrified, frightened, and troubled by the resurrection. Why? Because it means they must obey and serve Christ. If He is the *living Lord*, then man is His subject.
2) They question the resurrection, the truth of it. The idea that a man could arise from the dead is beyond their acceptance.
3) They ignore the resurrection, pay no attention to it, and count it as being meaningless.
4) They respond to the resurrection, accepting Jesus Christ as their Savior and Lord.
5) They react to the resurrection—react all the way from mild opposition and cursing to the persecution of any who bear witness to the resurrection.

3. The proof of Christ's resurrection, that He had risen bodily. The outline of the Scripture above shows the four things Christ did to prove that it really was He and not a spirit who stood before the disciples (see DEEPER STUDY # 1—Lk.24:39-43 for discussion).

DEEPER STUDY # 1

(24:39-43) **Jesus Christ, Resurrection—Resurrection, Body of**: the risen Christ was not a spirit (v.39); not a vision, a phantom, an hallucination, or any other figment of man's imagination. He was the risen Lord—bodily—not someone else nor some other spirit. His body was none other than that of Jesus, the carpenter from Nazareth. He had physically risen from the dead and His body was real. It differed, yes, but it was His body. It was perfected and no longer subject to the limitations and frailties of the physical universe and its laws; it was now glorified by the power and spoken Word of God (cp. Ro.1:3-4).

How did the Lord's resurrected body differ from His earthly body? Some idea can be gleaned by looking at His resurrected body and the glorified body promised to the believer.

1. The resurrected body of the Lord was His body, but it was radically changed. It had all the appearance of a physical body, but it was not bound by the physical world and its material substance.

a. It was the same body, not some other body. We know this because His resurrected body bore the marks of the nails in His hands and feet (Jn.20:20, 27), and the disciples could recognize Him after close observation.

b. It was a body that could travel and appear anyplace, at will and by thought—a body unhampered by space,time, material, or substance. When He appeared it was suddenly, even behind locked doors (Lk.24:36; Jn.20:19).

c. It was a body that differed enough that it was not clearly recognized at first, not until it was closely observed.

⇒ Mary Magdalene thought He was the gardener (Jn.20:15).
⇒ The two disciples walking toward Emmaus thought He was a traveller (Lk.24:31).
⇒ The disciples who were fishing did not recognize Him standing on the seashore (Jn. 21:4).

However, after close observation, the Lord was recognized in all these instances.

2. The resurrected, glorified body that is promised to the believer gives some additional insight into the kind of body Christ has. One of the most wonderful promises ever made to man is given in the words:

Who, by the power that enables him to bring everything under his control, will transform our lowly bodies so that they will be like his glorious body. (Phil 3:21; cp. Mt.13:43; Ro.8:17; Col.3:4; Rev.22:5)

For those God foreknew he also predestined to be conformed to the likeness of his Son, that he might be the firstborn among many brothers. (Rom 8:29; cp. 1 Cor.15:49; 2 Cor.3:18)

Dear friends, now we are children of God, and what we will be has not yet been made known. But we know that when he appears, we shall be like him, for we shall see him as he is. (1 John 3:2)

The body of the believer will undergo a radical change just as the Lord's body was radically changed. Several changes are promised the believer.

a. The believer shall receive a spiritual body.

It is sown a natural body [soma psuchikon], it is raised a spiritual body. If there is a natural body, there is also a spiritual body. (1 Cor 15:44)

Note: the spiritual body (soma) still retains the qualities of the earthly body (soma). The same Greek word is used for both bodies. The difference lies in that it will not be a natural (soulish) body but will be a spiritual body. What does this mean? In essence, the body will be perfected; no longer subject to pain, tears, death, sorrow, or crying (Rev.14:4).

⇒ It is sown in corruption; it is raised in incrruption.
⇒ It is sown in dishonor; it is raised in glory.
⇒ It is sown in weakness; it is raised in power.
⇒ It is sown a natural body; it is raised a spiritual body.

Note that the body is the same body on earth that it will be in heaven. The body just undergoes a radical change of nature. The believer will be the same person in heaven that he is on earth, differing only in that he is perfected. Also note the strong, emphatic declaration: There is a "natural body", and there is a "spiritual body" (1 Cor. 15:42-44).

b. The believer shall receive a body that is not "flesh and blood." Flesh and blood are corruptible; they age, deteriorate, die and decay.

I declare to you, brothers, that flesh and blood cannot inherit the kingdom of God, nor does the perishable inherit the imperishable. (1 Cor 15:50)

c. The believer shall receive a body that shall be radically changed.

In a flash, in the twinkling of an eye, at the last trumpet. For the trumpet will sound, the dead will be raised imperishable, and we will be changed. For the perishable must clothe itself with the imperishable, and the mortal with immortality. (1 Cor 15:52-53)

d. The believer shall be given a body that will not need reproduction for continuing the (redeemed) human race.

At the resurrection people will neither marry nor be given in marriage; they will be like the angels in heaven. (Mat 22:30)

2 (24:44-49) **Prophecy, Fulfilled—Jesus Christ, Death**: statement two is that all Scripture must be fulfilled. Note four points:

1. The forewarning Jesus had given in His predictions. His death and resurrection—the literal events happening just as He had said they would—should not have been a surprise. He had foretold the events and forewarned His followers. (See outline and notes—Lk.18:31-34.)

Thought 1. Scripture predicts much that is to happen in the future. However...

- some still will not accept and believe.
- some still spiritualize the predictions.

The greatest of all tragedies is that some still do not accept and believe the Lord's death and resurrection despite the irrefutable evidence.

2. The utter necessity that Christ die and arise. The word "must" (dei) means that His death was an imperative, a necessity, a constraint.

I tell you the truth, until heaven and earth disappear, not the smallest letter, not the least stroke of a pen, will by any means disappear from the Law until everything is accomplished. (Mat 5:18)

This man was handed over to you by God's set purpose and foreknowledge; and you, with the help of wicked men, put him to death by nailing him to the cross. But God raised him from the dead, freeing him from the agony of death, because it was impossible for death to keep its hold on him. (Acts 2:23-24)

As his custom was, Paul went into the synagogue, and on three Sabbath days he reasoned with them from the Scriptures, explaining and proving that the Christ had to suffer and rise from the dead. "This Jesus I am proclaiming to you is the Christ," he said. (Acts 17:2-3)

Note that Christ gave the three divisions of the Old Testament: the law, the prophets, and the psalms. The whole Old Testament prophesied of His coming and His salvation.

3. The spiritual insight needed to understand the Scriptures. Christ opened the disciples' eyes so they could understand.

The man without the Spirit does not accept the things that come from the Spirit of God, for they are foolishness to him, and he cannot understand them, because they are spiritually discerned. (1 Cor 2:14; cp. 1 Cor.2:9-14)

4. The particular prophesies were threefold.

a. Christ must suffer and arise (see outline and note—Lk.18:31-34).

b. Repentance and forgiveness must be preached (see notes and DEEPER STUDY # 1—Acts 17:29-30; DEEPER STUDY # 4—Mt.26:28).

c. The Holy Spirit and power must be sent. As the disciples went forth witnessing, they were to be given the *wonderful* promise (the Holy Spirit) and power of the Father. (See outline and notes, Holy Spirit—Jn.14:15-26; 16:7-15 for a discussion of the prophecies concerning the Holy Spirit which Christ had given to the disciples.) Note two points.

1) The believer was to be equipped for witnessing.

⇒ He was to receive the promise of the Father (the Holy Spirit).

⇒ He was to receive power, being clothed (endusesthe) with power.

2) The source of the spirit and power was God.

⇒ Christ was to send the promise.

⇒ The promise was "from the Father." God gave the promise.

⇒ Believers had to stay, that is, wait upon the Lord and pray for the promise.

⇒ The promise was to come from "on high." God Himself was the Source of power for all evangelism.

But you will receive power when the Holy Spirit comes on you; and you will be my witnesses in Jerusalem, and in all Judea and Samaria, and to the ends of the earth." (Acts 1:8)

When he comes, he will convict the world of guilt in regard to sin and righteousness and judgment: (John 16:8)

Now to him who is able to do immeasurably more than all we ask or imagine, according to his power that is at work within us, (Eph 3:20)

	D. Jesus' Last Appearance: The Ascension,[DS1] **24:50-53** (Mk.16:19-20; Acts 1: 9-11)
1 The purpose of the ascension a. To bless	50 When he had led them out to the vicinity of Bethany, he lifted up his hands and blessed them.
b. To provide a witness & give great assurance	51 While he was blessing them, he left them and was taken up into heaven.
2 The disciples' response to the ascension a. Worshipped Him	52 Then they worshiped him and returned to Jerusalem with great joy.
b. Were filled with joy c. Worshipped in the temple—continually	53 And they stayed continually at the temple, praising God.

DIVISION XII

THE SON OF MAN'S GLORY: HIS RESURRECTION AND ASCENSION, 24:1-53

D. Jesus' Last Appearance: The Ascension, 24:50-53

(24:50-53) **Introduction**: Luke closes his gospel with the ascension of Christ and begins Acts with the ascension of Christ (Acts 1:9-11). The ascension closes the Lord's earthly ministry, His mission to save the world. Therefore, the ascension can be said to be the final chapter, the close, the consummation of His journey upon earth. On the other hand, the ascension opens the Lord's heavenly ministry, His mission of intercession for the world and His mission of bearing witness through the lives of believers. Therefore, the ascension can be said to be the first chapter, the opening, the beginning of His journey into heaven as the Risen Lord. In heaven, Jesus Christ is the risen Lord who is the propitiation "for the sins of the whole world" (1 Jn.2:1-2).

1. The purpose of the ascension (v.50-51).
2. The disciples' response to the ascension (v.52-53).

DEEPER STUDY # 1

(24:50-53) **Jesus Christ, Ascension**: the Lord ascended to the right hand of God, that is, to the position of sovereignty and power (cp. Mk.16:19; Lk.22:69; Acts 1:9-11; 2:36; 5:31; Eph.1:20; Ph.2:9-11; Rev.5:12). The ascension assures (proves, confirms) that seven things are absolutely certain.

1. The ascension assures that God *is*, that He is alive and does exist. The fact that Christ was raised up from the dead and "taken up into heaven" (Lk.24:51) proves that God is. Only God could do such a thing (1 Cor.6:14; 2 Cor.4:14; cp. Jn.3:16. Cp. Acts 2:24, 32; 3:15, 26; 4:14; 5:30; 10:40; 13:30, 33-34; 17:31.)

2. The ascension assures that Christ is God's Son. The very fact that God raised up Christ and "was taken [Him] up into heaven" proves that Christ is God's Son (Mk.16:19; Ro.1:3-4; Ph.2:5-11).

3. The ascension assures that heaven is real (Ph.3:20-31).

4. The ascension assures that the gospel is true. When God raised up Christ and received Him into heaven, God validated the message of Christ. What Christ proclaimed and revealed was true: man faces a critical problem, the problem of sin and death and a future of condemnation and separation from God. However, man can be saved by the cross of Christ (Mk.16:16; 1 Pt.2:24).

5. The ascension assures that the Great Commission is the call and mission of believers. Two things show this. First, Christ has ascended into heaven; therefore, He is gone, no longer on earth. If the gospel is to be carried to the ends of the earth, believers have to do it. They are the ones left on earth to do it. Second, it is the risen and ascended Lord who gave the Great Commission. *As the ascended Lord*, He demands that His commission be fulfilled (Mk.16:15; cp. Mt.28:19-20).

6. The ascension assures that power is available to carry out the Great Commission (Mt.28:18; cp. Mk.16:20).

7. The ascension assures that we have a very special Helper in heaven, One who really loves and cares for us. He is One who is sympathetic with "our weaknesses...tempted in every way, just as we are—yet was without sin" (Heb.4:15). Therefore, He is ever ready to forgive and to look after us through all of life.

1 (24:50-51) **Jesus Christ, Ascension**: the purpose of the ascension. Two general purposes are given by Luke (see note, <u>Ascension</u>—Acts 1:9).

1. The first general purpose of the ascension was to bless the disciples. This was His final blessing, and note: it was the last thing He did on earth. His last gesture and act was to bless His disciples. This showed several things.

   a. It showed that He was the High Priest who had the power to make the sin-offering for them and to bless them with the gift of peace with God. (Cp. Aaron, Lev.9:22.)

   > **Then Aaron lifted his hands toward the people and blessed them. And having sacrificed the sin offering, the burnt offering and the fellowship offering, he stepped down. (Lev 9:22)**

   b. It showed that His blessing was the blessing coming from the ascended Lord who was *in heaven* exalted to the right hand of God.

And his incomparably great power for us who believe. That power is like the working of his mighty strength, which he exerted in Christ when he raised him from the dead and seated him at his right hand in the heavenly realms, far above all rule and authority, power and dominion, and every title that can be given, not only in the present age but also in the one to come. (Eph 1:19-21)

Now to him who is able to do immeasurably more than all we ask or imagine, according to his power that is at work within us, (Eph 3:20)

c. It showed that His blessing was forever, without end, even to the end of the world.

And teaching them to obey everything I have commanded you. And surely I am with you always, to the very end of the age." (Mat 28:20)

d. It showed that His blessing was unlimited, from their ascended and *eternal Lord.*

He is before all things, and in him all things hold together. (Col 1:17)

I am the Alpha and the Omega, the First and the Last, the Beginning and the End. (Rev 22:13)

e. It showed that His blessing was upon them as they went forth as His representatives, witnessing for Him.

Therefore go and make disciples of all nations, baptizing them in the name of the Father and of the Son and of the Holy Spirit, and teaching them to obey everything I have commanded you. And surely I am with you always, to the very end of the age." (Mat 28:19-20)

2. The second general purpose of the ascension was to provide a witness and give great assurance (see DEEPER STUDY # 1—Lk.24:50-53).

2 (24:52-53) **Ascension, Results**: the disciples' response to the ascension was threefold.

1. The disciples worshipped Christ. The ascension stirred worship. Why? The disciples now knew beyond question that He was the true Messiah, the Son of God Himself. He had ascended to the right hand of God; therefore, He was due all the homage, adoration, and praise due God.

Philip said, "Lord, show us the Father and that will be enough for us." Jesus answered: "Don't you know me, Philip, even after I have been among you such a long time? Anyone who has seen me has seen the Father. How can you say, 'Show us the Father'? Don't you believe that I am in the Father, and that the Father is in me? The words I say to you are not just my own. Rather, it is the Father, living in me, who is doing his work. Believe me when I say that I am in the Father and the Father is in me; or at least believe on the evidence of the miracles themselves. (John 14:8-11)

And being found in appearance as a man, he humbled himself and became obedient to death— even death on a cross! Therefore God exalted him to the highest place and gave him the name that is above every name, that at the name of Jesus every knee should bow, in heaven and on earth and under the earth, and every tongue confess that Jesus Christ is Lord, to the glory of God the Father. (Phil 2:8-11)

2. The disciples were filled with joy.
   a. They were filled with joy because their Lord was now exalted and privileged to take His rightful place: sit-ting at the right hand of God and being worshipped eternally. They were filled with joy and rejoicing *for Him.*
   b. They were filled with joy because they now knew that His presence would always be with them. When on earth physically, He could only be in one place and with only a few people at a time. But now, since ascending, He could send His Spirit to dwell with believers everywhere (Omnipresent). Nothing would ever again be able to *separate* their Lord from them.

But I tell you the truth: It is for your good that I am going away. Unless I go away, the Counselor will not come to you; but if I go, I will send him to you. (John 16:7)

Who shall separate us from the love of Christ? Shall trouble or hardship or persecution or famine or nakedness or danger or sword? For I am convinced that neither death nor life, neither angels nor demons, neither the present nor the future, nor any powers, neither height nor depth, nor anything else in all creation, will be able to separate us from the love of God that is in Christ Jesus our Lord. (Rom 8:35, 38-39)

3. The disciples were in the temple continually. The temple was the focus of God's presence and worship, and it was the center of teaching, the place where the people were instructed in the Scriptures. The disciples were bound to focus their lives in the temple or church...

- because Christ had taught that the temple was His "Father's house" and "the house of prayer."

"It is written," he said to them, "'My house will be a house of prayer'; but you have made it 'a den of robbers.'" (Luke 19:46)

To those who sold doves he said, "Get these out of here! How dare you turn my Father's house into a market!" (John 2:16)

- because they wished to praise God for sending the Messiah and to bear public testimony of Him.
- because the temple was the chosen place of God to manifest His presence among His people (see note—1 Cor.3:16).

"Go, stand in the temple courts," he said, "and tell the people the full message of this new life." (Acts 5:20)

Let us not give up meeting together, as some are in the habit of doing, but let us encourage one another—and all the more as you see the Day approaching. (Heb 10:25)

THE

OUTLINE & SUBJECT INDEX

REMEMBER: When you look up a subject and turn to the Scripture reference, you have not only the Scripture, you have *an outline and a discussion* (commentary) of the Scripture and subject.

This is one of the *GREAT VALUES* of **The Preacher's Outline & Sermon Bible®**. Once you have all the volumes, you will have not only what all other Bible indexes give you, that is, a list of all the subjects and their Scripture references, *BUT* you will also have...

- An outline of *every* Scripture and subject in the Bible.
- A discussion (commentary) on every Scripture and subject.
- Every subject supported by other Scriptures or cross references.

DISCOVER THE GREAT VALUE for yourself. Quickly glance below to the very first subject of the Index of Luke. It is:

ABASE - ABASED
Caused by. Selfishness & godless independence. 15:14-16

Turn to the reference. Glance at the Scripture and outline of the Scripture, then read the commentary. You will immediately see the *GREAT VALUE* of the *INDEX* of **The Preacher's Outline & Sermon Bible®**.

OUTLINE AND SUBJECT INDEX

INDEX

INDEX

INDEX

INDEX

PURPOSE STATEMENT

LEADERSHIP MINISTRIES WORLDWIDE

exists to equip ministers, teachers, and laymen in their understanding, preaching, and teaching of God's Word by publishing and distributing worldwide *The Preacher's Outline & Sermon Bible*® and related *Outline* Bible materials, to reach & disciple men, women, boys, and girls for Jesus Christ.

•MISSION STATEMENT•

1. To make the Bible so understandable - its truth so clear and plain - that men and women everywhere, whether teacher or student, preacher or hearer, can grasp its Message and receive Jesus Christ as Savior; and...
2. To place the Bible in the hands of all who will preach and teach God's Holy Word, verse by verse, precept by precept, regardless of the individual's ability to purchase it.

The ***Outline*** Bible materials have been given to LMW for printing and especially distribution worldwide at/below cost, by those who remain anonymous. One fact, however, is as true today as it was in the time of Christ:

• The Gospel is free, but the cost of taking it is not •

LMW depends on the generous gifts of Believers with a heart for Him and a love and burden for the lost. They help pay for the printing, translating, and placing ***Outline*** Bible materials in the hands and hearts of those worldwide who will present God's message with clarity, authority and understanding beyond their own.

LMW was incorporated in the state of Tennessee in July 1992 and received IRS 501(c) 3 non-profit status in March 1994. LMW is an international, nondenominational mission organization. All proceeds from USA sales, along with donations from donor partners, go 100% into under-writing our translation and distribution projects of ***Outline*** Bible materials to preachers, church & lay leaders, and Bible students around the world.

9/98

Box 21310 - Chattanooga, TN 37424 • (423) 855-2181 • FAX (423) 855-8616
• E-Mail - outlinebible@compuserve.com — www.outlinebible.org •

Equipping God's Servants Worldwide

1. **PAYMENT PLANS.** Convenient and affordable ways to get/use your FullSet with easy payments.

2. **NEW TESTAMENT.** In 14 volumes. Deluxe version 3-ring binders. Also: SoftBound Set, 3 volume set, and NIV edition. All on 1 CD-ROM disc.

3. **OLD TESTAMENT.** In process; 1 volume releases about every 6-8 months, in sequence.

4. **THE MINISTERS HANDBOOK.** Acclaimed as a "must-have" for every minister or Christian worker. Outlines more than 400 verses into topics like Power, Victory, Encouragement, Security, Restoration, etc. Discount for quantities.

5. **THE TEACHER'S OUTLINE & STUDY BIBLE™.** Verse-by-verse study & teaching; 45 minute lesson or session. Ideal for study, small groups, classes, even home schooling. Each book also offers a STUDENT JOURNAL for study members.

6. **OUTLINE BIBLE CD-ROM.** Includes all current volumes and books; Preacher, Teacher, and Minister Handbook. 1 disc. WORDsearch STEP format. Also 50+ Bible study tools unlockable on same disc.
   FREE Downloads - www.outlinebible.org

7. THE OUTLINE. Quarterly newsletter to all users and owners of *POSB*. Complimentary.

8. **LMW AGENT PLAN.** An exciting way any user sells *OUTLINE* materials & earns a second income.

9. **DISTRIBUTION.** Our ultimate mission is to provide *POSB* volumes & materials to preachers, pastors, national church leaders around the world. This is especially for those unable to purchase at U.S. price. USA sales gain goes 100% to provide volumes at affordable prices within the local economy.

10. **TRANSLATIONS.** Korean, Russian, & Spanish are shipping first volumes — Others in-process: Hindi, Tamil, Telugu, Chinese, French, German, Finnish.

11. **FUNDING PARTNERS.** To cover the cost of all the translations, plus print, publish, and distribute around the world is a multi million dollar project.

    Church-to-Church Partners send ***Outline*** Bible books to their missionaries, overseas church leaders, Bible Institues and seminaries...at special prices.

12. **REFERRALS.** Literally thousands (perhaps even you!) first heard of *POSB* from a friend. Now Referral Credit pays $16.00 for each new person who orders from a customer's Referral.

13. **CURRICULUM & COPYRIGHT.** Permission may be given to copy specific portions of *POSB* for special group situations. Write/FAX for details.

9/98

For Information about any of the above, kindly FAX, E-Mail, Call, or Write

Please PRAY 1 Minute/Day for LMW!

PO Box 21310, Chattanooga, TN 37424 • (423) 855-2181 • FAX (423) 855-8616
• E-Mail - outlinebible@compuserve.com — www.outlinebible.org •

Sharing

With the World!